W9-AWA-429

STATISTICS
DECISIONS AND APPLICATIONS
IN BUSINESS AND ECONOMICS

Second Edition

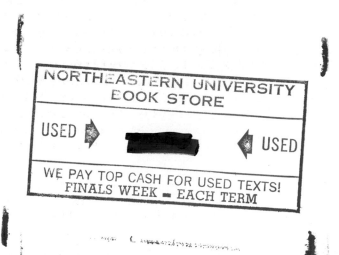

STATISTICS
DECISIONS AND APPLICATIONS IN BUSINESS AND ECONOMICS

Second Edition

MOSHE BEN-HORIM
HAIM LEVY

RANDOM HOUSE   BUSINESS DIVISION   NEW YORK

TO OUR FAMILIES

Second Edition
987654342
Copyright © 1981, 1984 by Random House, Inc.

Library of Congress Cataloging in Publication Data

Ben-Horim, Moshe.
  Statistics, decisions and applications in business
and economics.

  Includes indexes.
  1. Economics—Statistical methods. 2. Commercial
statistics. 3. Statistics. I. Levy, Haim. II. Title.
HB137.B46 1984   330'.028   83-24758.
ISBN 0-394-33587-2

Cover art: Ron Hall
Manufactured in the United States of America by Rand McNally & Co., Taunton, MA.

PREFACE

Statistical theory has barely changed in the past few years, but applications of sophisticated statistical methods in business and economics have rapidly intensified. In part, this trend has become possible because of a dramatic increase in the availability of much improved and affordable computers. Computers have indeed found their way into many of our offices and homes, and they have been effectively applied to perform a multitude of different tasks. All projections show that this trend will continue. Businesses and governments are quickly replacing old decision-making methods that rely on nonquantitative evaluations with new ones based on quantitative analysis of data.

Given the widespread use of quantitative analyses in general and statistical analyses in particular, there is a growing danger of misinterpreting applied statistical analyses and of incorrectly implementing results. In this book we attempt to show how statistical data should be handled and analyzed and how results of analyses should be interpreted and applied. In doing this we tried to maintain a reasonable depth of analysis without recourse to algebra beyond the high-school level.

We have noticed, in teaching statistics in colleges and universities in different parts of the United States and elsewhere, that students often have difficulty grasping relationships between textbook discussions and practical applications. To put it differently, students are eagerly looking for "a formula that will tell us which formula to use." Not unexpectedly, they soon find out that no such formula exists. What they need, instead, is experience. Only experience can tell us which technique to use for each type of analysis—by exposing us to a variety of situations for which statistical analysis is required.

Our belief is that a textbook should attempt to provide this experience by using teaching examples drawn from real life. In pursuit of this idea we have provided a wealth of practical examples and applications, both in the text proper and in the study problems at the end of the chapters. Some of these examples and applications are based on simplified hypothetical data, constructed to demonstrate specific points in a clear and uncomplicated fashion. Others use real data concerning company, industry, economic, or world events, so that students can get the feel of handling some of the practical problems that come up in various fields of business and economics. These examples and applications have been carefully chosen from fields students usually encounter in their business and economics courses. Moreover, we have excluded irrelevant examples from the area of gambling, which involve cards, marbles, urns, and dice; all these have been replaced by relevant business topics such as the following:

- Presentation of business data in annual reports to stockholders
- Analysis of rates of profits obtained in capital market investments
- Inventory management when demand is a random variable
- Choosing among store theft-prevention methods
- Allocation of indirect cost to various company departments
- Measurement of stock risk
- Gains from diversification of investment
- Behavior of interest rates
- Relationship between interest rates and inflation rates
- Extent to which advertising affects sales
- Productivity of a telephone company
- Analysis of banks' cash reserves

and many more.

Problem-solving is probably the best vehicle for studying the material covered in the text. Thus a genuine effort has been made to provide problems that are as good as, or better than, the examples given in the text. Included are problems whose solution requires primarily an intuitive understanding of the material and for which calculations are minimal; problems calling for calculations, for which the student is expected to master the requisite technique; problems straight out of the business and research world (some adjusted a bit to fit the level of the book), and case problems that may well serve as class projects or take-home examinations and provide material for class discussions.

About the Second Edition

The second edition of this book has greatly benefited from comments, suggestions, and corrections from many people. Among the important added features and changes that resulted in this edition are the following:

- Treatment of sampling and sample statistics side by side with population parameters in Chapters 3 and 4
- Presentation of Exploratory Data Analysis (EDA)
- Presentation of Chebyshev's theorem and the Empirical Rule
- Considerable increase in the use of computer printout presentations
- Discussion of the *t* test for matched samples
- Presentation of hypothesis testing in two chapters: Chapter 13 includes hypothesis testing of one population, and Chapter 14 deals with hypothesis testing in comparative studies of two populations.
- Discussion of point estimators and their properties (unbiasedness, consistency, and relative efficiency)
- Inclusion of the test of homogeneity among the chi-square tests
- Revision and rewriting of the regression chapters into three chapters: Chapter 17 presents the technique and theory of simple regression and correlation analysis; Chapter 18 discusses the inferences of simple regression and correlation and presents applications; and Chapter 19 deals with multiple regression analysis, including dummy variables.
- Treatment of dummy variables
- Analysis of residual plots
- Considerable increase in the number of end-of-chapter problems
- New applications
- Addition of case problems to many chapters. Case problems involve more work than end-of-chapter problems and often require the assistance of a computer. Many of the case problems draw on information from the three data sets in Appendix B at the end of the book. The data sets are available on computer cards for use with various statistical packages.
- Thorough updating of examples and problems

Ancillary Materials

For the convenience of instructors, *Statistics: Decisions and Applications in Business and Economics*, Second Edition, is supplemented by a number of ancillary materials. The first is a *Solutions Manual* that provides very detailed solutions to the end-of-chapter problems and case problems. A *Lecture Manual* offers suggestions for alternative course organization and an outline, notes, and teaching objectives for each chapter. It also includes summary tables and explanation of the transparencies. The *Master Transparency Set* includes many of the text's tables and charts and additional material to illustrate concepts discussed in the text. Finally, there is a *Test Item File* containing 765 multiple-choice questions organized on a chapter-by-chapter basis for practice and exams.

Acknowledgments

We wish to acknowledge the assistance of many people who have helped make this book a reality. Among them are:

Benzion Barlev	Azriel Levy
Meir Barnea	Patricia Priola
R. Mark Bisk	Mary Register
Mary S. Broske	Avner Rubin
Gaitona Calais	Pushpalata Shankar
Susanne Freund	Stephen Smith
James Jones	Esther Tuval
Yoram Kroll	Adele Zarmati
Wendy Laidacker	Zeev Zeimer
Zvi Lerman	Dror Zuckerman

We owe special thanks to the academic reviewers, whose suggestions, corrections, and critical evaluation of the manuscript have considerably helped us improve the book:

Hamparsum Bozdogan, University of Virginia
Larry W. Cornwell, Bradley University
Gary Kelley, Texas Tech University
Darlene Lanier, Louisiana State University
Robert B. Miller, University of Wisconsin—Madison
Dan Mohan, West Chester State College
Leonard Presby, William Paterson College
Jacqueline Redder, Virginia Polytechnic Institute
Ernest Scheuer, California State University—Northridge
Stephen A. Straub, Western Illinois University
Dean W. Wichern, University of Wisconsin—Madison
Morty Yalovsky, McGill University

We are particularly grateful to Rinat Bahat, Robert Brooks, and John J. Dinome, Jr., for the excellent and devoted assistance they have given us during the final revision of the book and to Hilda Ben-Nun and Julie Westberry for their very efficient typing of hundreds of manuscript pages. We also wish to acknowledge the secretarial assistance we obtained at the Department of Finance, College of Business Administration, University of Florida; at the School of Business Administration, The Hebrew University; and at the Faculty of Management, McGill University.

Finally, we are greatly indebted to many people at Random House who were associated with this text. Among them are the Executive Editor of the Business Division, Paul Donnelly, whose insights into market trends helped us write a book that responds to the needs of universities today; Project Editors Judith Kromm and Laurel Miller, who did great jobs at different stages of the work; Developmental Editor Anne Mahoney, who assisted us throughout the revision period and was particularly helpful in handling the reviewers' comments and suggestions; and Assistant Editor Lois Refkin, who was in charge of organizing the ancillary materials. We would also like to thank Della Mancuso for her efforts in connection with the production of the book and Casimir Psujek for handling the production of the ancillary material.

CONTENTS

PART 1: DESCRIPTIVE STATISTICS   6

PART 2: PROBABILITY AND DISTRIBUTIONS (DEDUCTION) 128

PART 3:
DECISION-MAKING BASED ON SAMPLES (INDUCTION) 346

PART 4:
REGRESSION AND CORRELATION (INDUCTION CONTINUED)   566

PART 5: OTHER SELECTED TOPICS

706

STATISTICS
DECISIONS AND APPLICATIONS IN BUSINESS AND ECONOMICS

Second Edition

INTRODUCTION

1

CHAPTER ONE OUTLINE

1.1 What Is Statistics All About?

1.2 The Uses of Statistics: A Few Examples

1.3 Statistics in Business and Economics

Key Terms

statistics
descriptive statistics
inferential statistics
induction
decision theory
deduction

Statistics is a vital part of virtually every modern institution and area of study; it is the backbone of both the theory and practice of professional business management; and it is extensively used by governments in planning and applying economic policies. Let us briefly review the meaning of statistics and give examples of its uses.

1.1 What Is Statistics All About?

Statistics is defined as *the collection, organization, presentation, analysis, and interpretation of numerical facts and data.* Statisticians distinguish between **descriptive statistics**, which deals with *the collection, organization, and presentation of data* and to which a relatively short part of this book is devoted, and **inferential statistics**, which deals with *the way we draw general conclusions about the phenomena under consideration, beyond the facts of the observed data.* Most of this book focuses on the way these generalizations are made, how the observed data are used to *evaluate the potential errors* of such generalizations, and how *decision making* is done in the face of uncertainty.

Descriptive statistics is a very important area of statistics, though it is relatively simple and straightforward. The data accumulated by a company and at local, state, and federal levels of government are frequently overwhelming in number, and the task of analyzing many hundreds or thousands of pieces of data might prove very frustrating if the data were unorganized. Therefore, the first step in many statistical analyses is the systematic organization and presentation of the data. When the data are properly summarized in tables or charts, a statistician can determine the type of analysis needed.

Often the speed of data accumulation is so fast that their organization must be handled by computers. Typically the computer will have a built-in program that organizes the data immediately as they are fed in. The organization of the data must allow easy reference, and it should be done in a way that reveals as much of the information inherent in the data as possible. Sometimes, data organization results in a deliberate information loss. For example, suppose an airline company keeps records of its passenger traffic. The data it collects about current passenger traffic might include much more information than it requires for its permanent records. Personal data such as names, addresses, telephone numbers, and so on may be needed for current use but are not normally included in the airline's permanent file. When the personal data are omitted, the firm is still left with enough data to study the profitability of its diverse operations. Exactly which data the company chooses to discard depends on the specific needs of the airline.

When information is needed about a certain body of data, or *population*, it is often impossible to obtain all the data needed. In such cases, a smaller set of data, called a *sample*, is usually gathered. Now, any set of data that is not totally homogeneous can be only approximately represented by a sample. It is the role of statistical inference to *generalize the sample results to the entire set of data* (i.e., the population), a process that is called **induction**. When we use a sample to make inferences about the entire data set of interest, our inferences depend in part on which particular members of the population happen to be included in the sample. Consequently, whatever we may infer about the population is subject to some degree of error, the magnitude of which must be evaluated. This is another function of inferential statistics.

As important as the evaluation of potential errors may be, economists and business managers engaged in decision making frequently must draw clear-cut conclusions and take appropriate action on the basis of sampling results. *Drawing such conclusions and deciding what action to take* is the subject matter of **decision theory**. In real life, we face uncertainty in almost every decision we make. We cannot avoid errors in our decisions, but we should try to minimize them.

No matter how sophisticated statistical analysis becomes, it cannot eliminate decision-making errors. But *properly employed*, statistical tools can minimize the chance for errors. For example, think of a business manager who decides to invest $10 million in developing a new product. If the investment is made without prior study, he or she stands to lose money if there is no demand for the product. It is possible, however, to study the demand by conducting a small survey. The survey will not eliminate the possibility of loss altogether, but the statistical data collected will enable the manager to improve the decision and reduce the chance of loss. Obviously, this type of data collection is not without cost, and the decision maker should weigh this cost against the potential cost of making the wrong decision.

1.2 The Uses of Statistics: A Few Examples

To give you a better feel for the subject of statistics, let us look at a few applications.

1. Descriptive statistics is extensively used by companies in their annual reports to their stockholders. These reports provide a wealth of information about sales, costs, operations, earnings, earnings per share, dividends, dividends per share, and much more. All of the information must be summarized and presented effectively, and most firms use a variety of tables and charts for this purpose.
2. The U.S. Statistical Abstract is another example of a publication that presents huge amounts of data. In this one, the data cover areas such as demography, labor force, production, international trade, prices, and income.
3. Insurance companies make use of statistical **deduction** (*drawing conclusions regarding a certain item from observed phenomena in the population*) in calculating insurance premiums. The premium collected for

life insurance, for example, is based on the probability that the insured will survive the insurance coverage period. This probability is determined from past experience and records of the survival rate of many people at different ages.

4. A company wants to evaluate the effect of advertising on sales. Does it sell more when more money is spent on advertising? And if so, how much more? To answer this question it is possible to take a sample of companies whose advertising expense varies in relation to sales and study the relationship for each company in the sample. On the basis of the sample measurement, the statistician can use statistical inference and derive an estimate of the relationship. Furthermore, statistical inference will enable the statistician to evaluate the potential error to which the estimate is subject. For example, it might be estimated that $1 million of advertising will bring $50 million in additional sales. However, since the estimate is based on a sample it is likely to be in error to some degree. But the use of statistics enables us to determine limits to the error such that we might be able to make a statement like the following: We have 95 percent confidence that $1 million worth of advertising will increase sales anywhere between $45 million and $55 million. This statement gives us an "interval estimate" along with the probability that the true result is included in the interval.

5. Another example of statistical inference and decision making is the comparison of crops from fields that were fertilized with two different fertilizers. The sample of crops can help us make a decision about which of the fertilizers is "better." The difficulty of generalizing from observed crops is that so many factors in addition to the fertilizers determine the size (and quality) of the crop. Weather, irrigation, type of soil, and so on vary from one field to another and from one year to another, making the generalization of which is a "better" fertilizer difficult. Nevertheless, statistical methods can help a great deal in making such generalizations.

6. As another example of statistical inference, consider the labor department's sample of unemployment. Nationwide unemployment rates in the United States must be frequently and accurately determined for proper implementation of fiscal and monetary policies. It would be extremely costly to engage in a direct examination of the country's entire labor force. But if properly chosen, even a relatively small sample can provide highly accurate estimates of the unemployment situation, as well as an assessment of the size of error of the estimate.

7. Statistical inference is widely used for decision making in quality control. Suppose a machine produces certain metal parts that need to be three inches long. Due to mechanical imperfections, the length of the parts varies somewhat, and the quality control people must decide whether deviations from three inches are random and tolerable or whether the deviations are not random and require a machine adjustment. This can be decided on the basis of sample metal parts.

1.3 Statistics in Business and Economics

Statistics make a crucial contribution to business. By glancing through a local newspaper you can verify the fact that a good part of its contents is devoted to descriptive statistics, such as daily price changes in stocks and bonds, company dividends, sports scores, temperatures, prices, and unemployment rates. But the most vital contribution of statistics to business is in providing the tools for meaningful analysis in areas such as business forecasting, credit analysis, quality control, advertising, finance, insurance, management, and many more.

The theory of statistics is the same regardless of the application. Therefore, in principle, tools applied in business and economics are the same as those applied in physical science and other areas. However, unlike physical scientists, business analysts and economists are usually unable to observe data of designed and controlled experiments. As a consequence, we must be constantly aware of the fact that our data are likely to contain errors. When we load our data onto the computer and carry out a certain analysis, the computer responds by doing a mechanical job. The results are meaningful only if the proper data were used, if the proper analysis was employed, and consequently, if there is a good chance that the correct conclusions have been drawn from the analysis. This book attempts to provide the tools for performing proper statistical analyses.

PART 1

DESCRIPTIVE STATISTICS

The area of descriptive statistics deals with alternative methods of presenting statistical data effectively. The presentation of data may be a final goal, or it may be a step toward further analysis.

Chapter 2 discusses the use of tables and charts in the presentation of data. Chapter 3 discusses the concept of data sets, and shows how data are organized in a frequency distribution. In Chapter 4, statistical measures of various data characteristics are developed; these measures are used in statistical analyses.

The applications and examples in Part 1 deal with stock and bond returns, the analysis of cumulative frequency distributions for insurance purposes, the use of charts in financial reporting, and a number of other topics.

HANDLING STATISTICAL DATA: COLLECTION, ORGANIZATION, AND PRESENTATION

Key Terms
statistical data
primary source
secondary source
sampling
editing
mutually exclusive classes
collectively exhaustive classes
tabulation
analytical tables
reference tables
table number
table title
table headnote
table boxhead
table stub
table stub head
table stub body
table cell
table field
table footnotes
table source note
one-way classification table
cross-classified table
percentage table
chart title
chart headnote
chart scale
graph
chart footnote
chart source note
time-series line chart
component-part line chart
horizontal bar chart
vertical bar chart
duo-directional horizontal bar chart
component bar chart
percentage component bar chart
grouped bar chart
pie chart

Statistical data form the foundation of virtually all applied statistical analyses. Since an analysis can be only as good as the data it uses, great care must be taken to ensure that the data are appropriately handled: that the relevant data are collected and screened for errors, and that they are well organized and effectively presented.

A distinction is usually made between *statistical data* and data that are not statistical. **Statistical data** are *facts that bear some sort of measurable relationship to each other* (prices, costs, weights, etc.), whereas data that are not statistical are basically arbitrary (such as item numbers in a sales catalog).

Numerous decisions in business and in government are based on statistical data. As time goes on, the complexity of these decisions is increasing, causing an ever-growing need for statistical data in a variety of areas—finance, marketing, management, accounting, insurance, production, fiscal and monetary economics, quality control, and many more.

We may distinguish the following steps in any statistical study:

1. The collection of relevant data
2. Organization
3. Presentation
4. Analysis
5. Interpretation

This chapter deals with data handling, a subject that includes the first three of these steps: collection, organization, and presentation.

2.1 Data Collection

After a problem has been clearly identified and a decision made to perform a statistical analysis in order to find a solution, relevant data should be collected in preparation for the analysis. The quality of statistical analysis can be no better than the data on which it is based, so the data must be as reliable and as accurate as possible. Therefore we shall always prefer *published* to *unpublished* data. To the extent that reliable published data are available, it is much more economical to use them than to conduct one's own survey. If possible, it is always better to collect published data from their **primary source**—that is, from *the source in which the data were originally published*—than from a **secondary source**, which merely *reproduces the data*.

In addition to published data, there are numerous data files (that is, collections of data) available to the public on computer tapes, particularly in the fields of finance, accounting, and economics. Again, a good search for such tapes should be conducted before one sets out to collect one's own data.

Despite the abundance of published business and economics data, there are many situations in which a special survey must be conducted to obtain the data for a study if it is to be meaningful. One highly efficient method consists of **sampling,** that is, *observing only part of all the existing data*. We discuss sampling in detail in later chapters so further discussion of it is not necessary here. Instead, we will proceed to the next important topic, the organization of statistical data.

2.2 Data Organization

After the data have been collected, they need to be organized. Three procedures must be carried out before data can be presented and analyzed: editing, classification, and tabulation. We shall consider each one of these in turn.

EDITING DATA

Editing involves *a close examination of the statistical data that have been collected.* The purpose of such an examination is to determine whether the data contain errors, to correct any errors that are detected, and to check on any data that appear to be unreliable. Ample editing time should be allowed if the data have been collected via a questionnaire; and editing is of great importance when the data consist of direct observations (the number of defective items found when the quality of a given product is checked, the frequency of busy signals received when a specified number of telephone calls are made, and so on).

When the data consist of records of direct observations, the editing process usually involves looking over the data to determine whether the figures "make sense" and are within a "reasonable range." It is also desirable to find a pattern of internal consistency in the data, if such a pattern exists.

DATA CLASSIFICATION

The best way to classify data depends primarily on the purpose of the study being undertaken and on the nature of the variables involved in it. Given the goal and the variables that will be studied, one can determine the most workable classification method.

Obviously, data may be classified according to a host of variables; the multitude of possibilities makes generalizations about variables very difficult. Nevertheless, for the purpose of classification, we can distinguish among four major types of variables. There are variables related to *time*, such as days, years, age, and so on; variables related to *place*, such as states, cities, and towns; *quantitative* variables such as units sold, cost of production, and payroll deductions; and finally there are *qualitative* variables, such as color, style, and sex.

It is essential that the data be classified into mutually exclusive and collectively exhaustive classes. **Mutually exclusive classes** are *classes that are chosen so that each answer or figure will belong to only one class.* **Collectively exhaustive classes** are *classes that include all the possible answers or the entire range of possible values of the variable of interest.* Suppose, for example, that we wish to classify firms according to number of employees. The classes 0–20 employees, 21–50 employees, 51–100 employees, and 101 or more employees are both mutually exclusive and collectively exhaustive. They are mutually exclusive because at a given point in time, each firm's number of employees can fit into *only one* of these classes. They are also collectively exhaustive because *no firm could have a number of employees that did not fit into any* of the classes.[1]

---

[1] The following is an example of classification that is neither mutually exclusive nor collectively exhaustive: 0–20, 21–50, 50–100. It is not mutually exclusive because if the number of employees is 50, this item of data could be recorded in two classes (21–50 and 50–100) rather than just one. It is also not collectively exhaustive because none of the classes applies to firms with more than 100 employees.

TABULATION

After the data are obtained and the classification system is determined, there remains the task of tabulation as a preparation for the final presentation and analysis. **Tabulation**—*the enumeration and recording of the data in each class for each variable*—can be done either manually or by computer. Manual tabulation is suitable for smaller studies when the data are not too voluminous to handle. When a large volume of data is involved, tabulation by computer may be more efficient. Computer tabulation has the advantages of higher speed and credibility, but these advantages must be contrasted with the relatively high setup and overhead cost of the computer approach.

2.3 Data Presentation: Tables

Statistical data can be presented verbally or by means of tables and charts. Verbal description alone may be sufficient if the data contain very little information. When a large amount of information is to be conveyed, however, verbal description is usually less efficient than a table or a chart.

The construction of a statistical table is determined by the type of data to be presented and the purpose of the presentation. Generally speaking, we distinguish between analytical tables and reference tables. **Analytical tables** are *tables that lead to analytical study.* They must be relatively short so that the reader does not lose sight of the forest among the trees. **Reference tables** *hold more information than analytical tables;* they can be used to verify details. Analytical and reference tables are constructed in basically the same way. The form of a typical cross-classified table is given in Figure 2.1.

PARTS OF THE TABLE

The **table number** is important for *easy reference and citation.* The numbers can be assigned consecutively throughout a report, an article, or a book, or they can contain a chapter number followed by a consecutive subnumber within the chapter. "Table 4.7," for example, refers to Table 7 of Chapter 4.

The **title** provides the reader with *a short statement describing the table's*

Figure 2.1

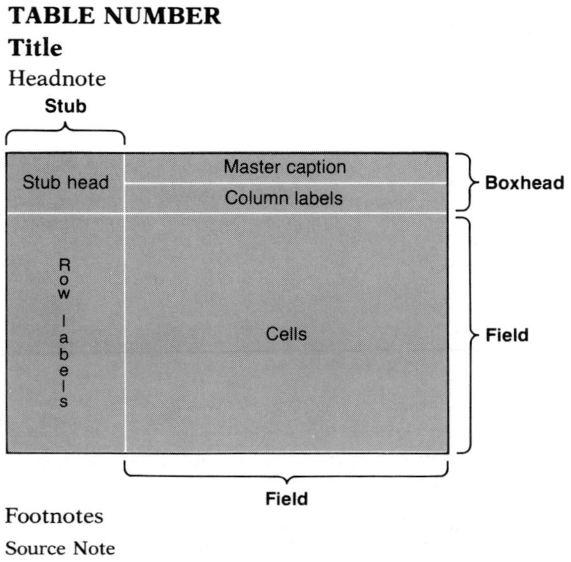

The functional parts of a cross-classified statistical table

contents. It should not be too long, or so short as to omit essential information about the table's contents. The title should answer the following questions: (1) *What* are the data in the table? (2) *Where* do the data apply? (3) *When* do the data apply? (4) *How* are the data classified?

A **headnote** contains *additional information about the table that is not included in the title.* Usually the headnote names the units in which the table's figures are measured: percentages, dollars, or any other unit of measurement.

The **boxhead** contains *the master caption, which states the way the columns are classified, and the column labels.* If the master caption merely repeats information already given in the title, it is usually omitted.

The **stub** contains the **stub head,** stating *the way in which the rows are classified,* and the **body** of the stub, in which *the individual rows are briefly labeled.*

A **cell** is *the intersection of a column and a row;* this is where the individual item of data is inserted.

The **field** of the table is *the total collection of cells.*

Footnotes may be added to *present additional information that is not stated in the title, headnote, captions, or stub.* Footnotes are commonly placed below the stub.

The **source note** provides *an accurate description of the origin of the data presented in the table.* It provides the reader with a way to verify the data or to obtain additional information, and gives the original data collector due recognition. The source note may be omitted only if the source of the data is quite trivial. For example, when data are collected in a survey and then presented in a report, it is not necessary to have a separate source note for each table stating that the source consists of the data collected in the study.

COMMON TYPES OF TABLES

Table 2.1 is probably the simplest of all tables, a **one-way classification table** that presents some data in an organized manner. The rows present specific years, and the field consists of a single column showing the number of shares of American Telephone and Telegraph Company (AT&T) outstanding in each of those years.

Table 2.2 contains more information on AT&T shares than Table 2.1 does. It is a **cross-classified table,** which groups the shares in the years 1977 through 1981 according to type of holder.

TABLE 2.1
Shares Outstanding of American Telephone and Telegraph Company, 1977–81
(in thousands)

December 31 of year	Shares outstanding
1977	647,632
1978	669,549
1979	701,367
1980	741,236
1981	815,108

Source: American Telephone and Telegraph Company, *1981 Statistical Report.*

TABLE 2.2

Shareholders of American Telephone and Telegraph Company, by Type of Holder, 1977–81

(in thousands)

December 31 of year	Type of holder			
	Individuals	*Institutions*	*Brokers*	*Total*
1977	429,565	187,733	30,334	647,632
1978	442,606	195,621	31,322	669,549
1979	465,776	198,384	37,207	701,367
1980	499,794	189,401	52,041	741,236
1981	528,144	214,748	72,216	815,108

Source: American Telephone and Telegraph Company, *1981 Statistical Report.*

In some tables, such as 2.2, a total of the content of the rows is relevant, and in others a total of the content of the columns may be of interest; sometimes, as in Table 2.3, totals are given for both the columns and the rows.

Table 2.3 represents the employees of General Telephone Company of Florida at the end of 1981, by sex and occupation. The sum on the bottom row shows the total of male employees (6,368), the total of female employees (5,686) and the total number of all employees in the company (12,054).

Similarly, the column headed "total" shows the total number of employees in the various occupations. There were 280 officials and managerial assistants, 1,286 professional employees, and so on. The total number of employees, in all the various occupations, is 12,054—obviously the same as the total number of male and female employees.

TABLE 2.3

Employees of General Telephone Company of Florida, by Sex and Occupation, December 31, 1981

Occupation	Male	Female	Total
Officials and managerial assistants	252	28	280
Professional employees	793	493	1,286
Telephone operators	96	1,408	1,504
Construction, installation, and maintenance workers	4,725	560	5,285
Others	502	3,197	3,699
Total	6,368	5,686	12,054

Source: General Telephone Company of Florida, *Annual Report*, 1981.

Percentage tables *show percentages of totals*, either alone or together with the absolute figures. It is essential that the totals of which the percentages are part be clearly identified. Consider, for example, Table 2.3. This table can be presented in two separate percentage tables. One, shown in Table 2.4, presents the percentage of men and women in each occupation. Note that the inclusion of the right-hand "total" column, which demonstrates that the total percentage of men and women in each occupation equals 100 percent, removes all doubt about what the percentages represent: they represent the percentages of men and women employed by the company in any given occupation. The percentages on the bottom row (that is, 52.8 percent for men and 47.2 percent for women) *are not the total, nor are they the simple average of their respective columns.* They are in fact the weighted averages of the

TABLE 2.4

Employees of General Telephone Company of Florida, by Sex and Occupation, December 31, 1981

(percentage)

Occupation	Men	Women	Total
Officials and managerial assistants	90.0%	10.0%	100.00%
Professional employees	61.7	38.3	100.00
Telephone operators	6.4	93.6	100.00
Construction, installation, and maintenance workers	89.4	10.6	100.00
Others	13.6	86.4	100.00
Total	52.8%	47.2%	100.00%

Source: General Telephone Company of Florida, *Annual Report*, 1981. See also Table 2.3.

columns (a concept we shall discuss in Chapter 4); stated more simply, they represent the percentages of men and women in the total number of people employed by the company. Men comprised 52.8 percent and women comprised 47.2 percent of the people employed by General Telephone Company of Florida on December 31, 1981.

Another percentage table—one that reveals different information—can be derived from the data of Table 2.3. If we look at all the male employees first and determine their occupational distribution in percentages, and then do the same thing for the female employees and for all employees, we get Table 2.5. Notice how different the figures in Table 2.5 are from those in Table 2.4. For example, in the first cell on the left on the top line, we have 90.0 percent in Table 2.4 and 3.9 percent in Table 2.5. These two figures represent completely different things. Among all the employees in the occupational category "officials and managers," 90.0 percent were men (and 10.0 percent were women), but among all the men employed by the company, only 3.9 percent were in this particular category, and 96.1 percent (100.0 − 3.9 = 96.1) were in other occupations.

TABLE 2.5

Employees of General Telephone Company of Florida, by Sex and Occupation, December 31, 1981

(percentage)

Occupation	Men	Women	Total
Officials and managerial assistants	3.9%	0.5%	2.3%
Professional employees	12.5	8.7	10.7
Telephone operators	1.5	24.8	12.5
Construction, installation, and maintenance workers	74.2	9.8	43.8
Others	7.9	56.2	30.7
Total	100.0%	100.0%	100.0%

Source: General Telephone Company of Florida *Annual Report*, 1981. See also Table 2.3.

2.4 Data Presentation: Charts and Graphs

Charts and graphs are also frequently used to present data. A pictorial expression of the data often has a greater impact on the reader than a table would have and may help the reader gain a better understanding of the data involved. Like tables, charts and graphs may be used to express the results of analyses. The principal parts of a chart are the **title, headnote, scales, graphs, footnotes,** and **source note.** The title and headnote are presented above the chart, the footnotes and source note below it; all serve the same purpose as those of a table. The horizontal scale, known as the *X*-axis or *X*-scale, is often (though not always) used to classify the data; the vertical scale, known as the *Y*-axis or *Y*-scale, is used to measure the magnitude of the relevant data. Figure 2.2 illustrates the principal parts of a typical chart.

Figure 2.2

The functional parts of a chart

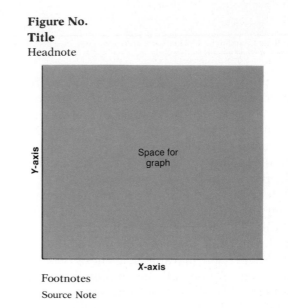

It is difficult—perhaps impossible—to determine the "most appropriate" type of chart or graph for any type of data. It is often very useful to use two or more complementary charts or graphs for illustration, each bringing to the fore a separate fact or set of facts.

LINE CHARTS

As the name indicates, line charts use lines—solid or broken—to represent data. The most common of all line charts is the **time-series line chart,** which simply *exhibits the change in the data over a period of time.* Figure 2.3 is an example of a time-series line chart. Here two graphs are exhibited, representing two series on one chart. One of the graphs represents the value of new issues of common stocks in the United States during 1970–80, and the other represents the value of new issues of bonds. To facilitate reading the graph, grid lines are drawn horizontally and vertically. The grid lines must be drawn in a distinct (and often light) color or shade so that the line graph is easily visible against the chart's background.

One draws a time-series line chart by first placing points on the chart to represent the data and then connecting the points by straight line segments. Let us illustrate this procedure through an example.

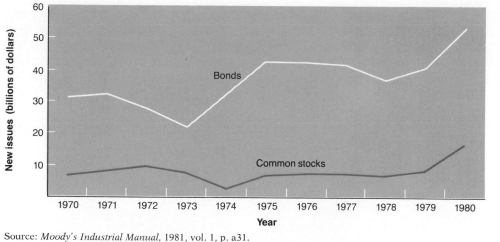

Source: *Moody's Industrial Manual,* 1981, vol. 1, p. a31.

Figure 2.3

New issues of corporate bonds and common stocks, 1970–80

EXAMPLE 2.1

The aggregate of corporate profit before taxes in the United States in the period 1975–81 is shown in Table 2.6. Let us draw a time-series line chart for these data.

TABLE 2.6
Aggregate U.S. Corporate Profits before Taxes, 1975–81
(billions of dollars)

Year	Profits
1975	120.4
1976	155.9
1977	173.9
1978	202.0
1979	255.3
1980	245.5
1981	233.3

Source: *Federal Reserve Bulletin,* various issues.

First, we need to determine the scale for both axes. Our choice of scale depends on the relationship between the size of the chart and the number of data points that need to be represented, and their values. In the case at hand, data for seven years need to be represented on the chart, so the horizontal width available for the chart should be divided into seven equal intervals, each representing one year. The values of the data range from 120.4 to 255.3 (billions of dollars). As the highest value we have is 255.3, we decide to let the vertical axis extend to 260. But we must also consider whether or not the scale should start at zero. If it does, about half of the chart will be unusable, since the lowest value we need to present is 120.4. We therefore use a broken *Y*-axis and present the range from 120 to 260 (billions of dollars) in the available space. In this way we focus only on the *relevant* range of values of the variable of interest. Note the jagged marks near the bottom of the vertical scale in Figure 2.4: they tell the reader that the scale does not start at zero.

Figure 2.4

Aggregate corporate profits in the United States, 1975–81

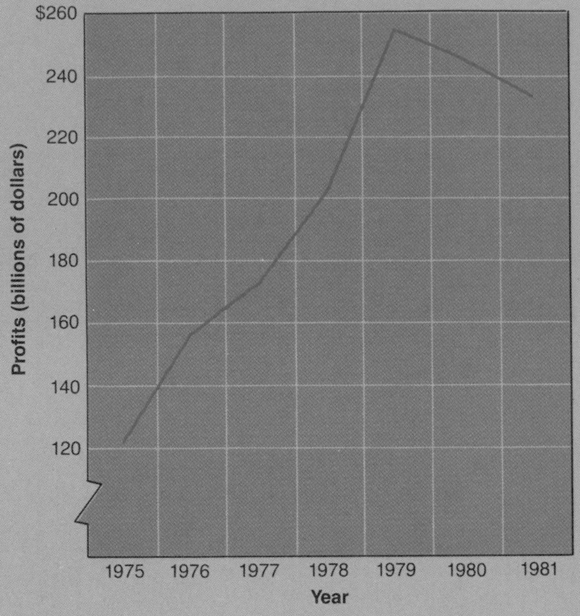

Source: *Federal Reserve Bulletin,* various issues.

Now let us consider another point. Take the first piece of data available: corporate profits in 1975. Clearly, the profits were not generated in full at the beginning of the year or at the end of the year, but gradually throughout the year. Consequently, if we plan to use only one point to represent the 1975 profits, that point is best located over the center of the interval representing the year 1975.

The practice of placing the point over the center of the interval is not followed without exception. Depending on the nature of the variable measured, the point may be placed over the tick mark representing the beginning or the end of the year.

COMPONENT-PART LINE CHARTS

An interesting extension of the line graph is the **component-part line chart**, which is applicable when we want *to show not only the way a given total has changed over time but also the way its components have changed.* Let us simply extend Example 2.1 and look at the components of U.S. corporate profits in the period 1975–81.

EXAMPLE 2.2

Corporate profits are used for three purposes: to pay taxes, to pay dividends to stockholders, and to be retained as "undistributed profit." Table 2.7 shows the profits and their three components for U.S. corporations in the period 1975–81.

TABLE 2.7

Aggregate U.S. Corporate Profits by Components, 1975–81
(billions of dollars)

Year	Taxes	Dividends	Undistributed profits	Total profits
1975	$49.8	$31.9	$38.7	$120.4
1976	64.3	37.9	53.7	155.9
1977	71.8	43.7	58.4	173.9
1978	83.9	49.3	68.8	202.0
1979	87.6	50.1	117.6	255.3
1980	82.3	56.0	107.2	245.5
1981	77.7	63.1	92.5	233.3

Source: *Federal Reserve Bulletin*, various issues.

Figure 2.5 displays the data in a component-part line chart, in which the three components are represented by three layers distinctively shaded and labeled. Note that the amount of each component is represented by the *height of the layer representing that component alone* rather than by the total height from the horizontal axis.

We may use a similar technique when we want to show the components as percentages of the total (Figure 2.6). Again, the percentage of a given component is shown by the height of that component's layer only, rather than by the height measured from the horizontal axis. Figure 2.6 illustrates a very convenient method for representing trends in the *relative* magnitudes of the components and their changes over time. (We cannot, of course, use this method to give information about the trend of the total over the years, as we did in Figure 2.5.)

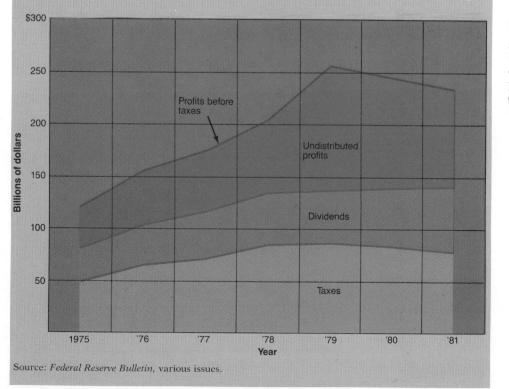

Figure 2.5

Aggregate U.S. corporate profits and components, 1975–81

Source: *Federal Reserve Bulletin*, various issues.

Figure 2.6

Components of U.S. aggregate corporate profits, 1975–81 (percentage)

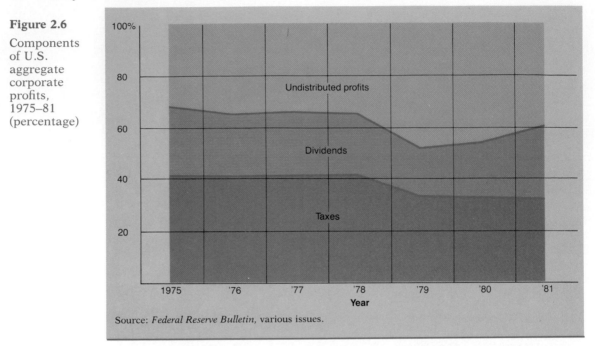

Source: *Federal Reserve Bulletin,* various issues.

BAR CHARTS

Bar charts may be used *to represent data classified by either quantitative or qualitative variables.* An example of a **horizontal bar chart** is given in Figure 2.7, which shows sales of four U.S. auto manufacturers in 1981. The bars are separated for clarity and labeled on the left, in the chart's stub. The bars are organized in order of decreasing length from top to bottom; that is, the longest bar is shown at the top of the chart and the shortest at the bottom. This order may be reversed, of course, so that the shortest bar is at the top and the longest is at the bottom.

Figure 2.7

Sales of U.S. auto manufacturers, 1981 (billions of dollars)

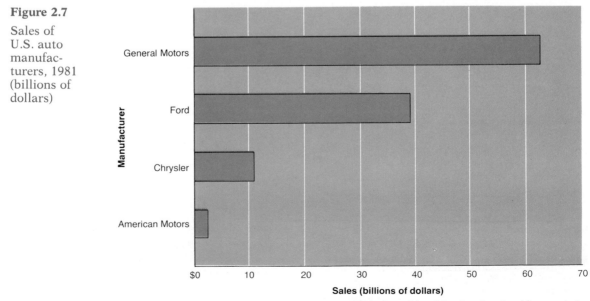

Source: *Value Line Investment Survey,* July 2, 1982. © 1982 by Bernald and Co., Inc. Reprinted by permission of the publisher.

All the bars are of the same width and each company's sales are indicated by the length of its bar. The lengths of the bars are measured against grid lines that run from top to bottom and are marked either at the top or at the bottom of the chart, or both.

The scale showing the value of the variable of interest (sales, in this case) should start at zero to eliminate the possibility of misinterpretation. After all, charts are designed to bring out similarities and differences in data, so great care must be taken to avoid ambiguity.

Sometimes, however, when we start the scale at zero, differences between the bars may be less visible than we would like. In such cases, we may use other devices to clarify the differences. For example, suppose we want to use a bar chart to represent new housing units started for the years 1975–80. These data are represented in Figure 2.8, a **vertical bar chart.** It is *identical to a horizontal bar chart in all respects except that the vertical and horizontal scales have been reversed.* If we want to display the variations in the data more clearly, we may simply *focus directly on the changes in the variable, measured either in absolute amounts or in terms of percentage change.* Figure 2.9 is a **duo-directional horizontal bar chart,** where the percentage changes

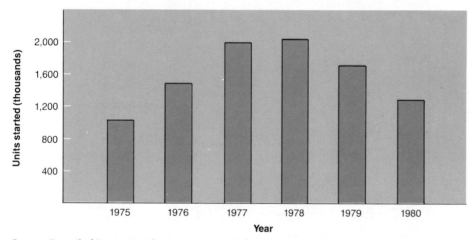

Figure 2.8

New private housing units started, 1975–80

Source: Council of Economic Advisers, *Economic Indicators,* July 1981, p. 19.

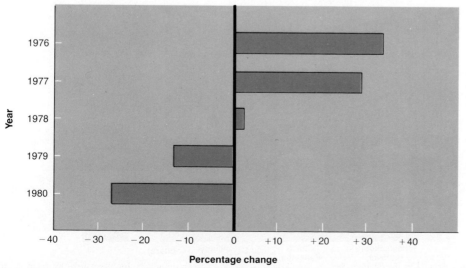

Figure 2.9

Annual percentage change in new private housing units started, 1976–80

Source: Council of Economic Advisers, *Economic Indicators,* July 1981, p. 19.

in new housing units started in the years 1976–80 are plotted. The arrangement of the bars should follow the sequence of time, if relevant, from top to bottom or vice versa. If such order is not relevant and no other dominant criterion for ordering is applicable, the bars should be arranged by length in either decreasing or increasing order.

COMPONENT BAR CHARTS

Like line charts, bar charts may be adapted to *show components of totals.* In Figure 2.10, a **component bar chart,** vertical bars are used to show the deposits in three groups of large commercial banks on December 31, 1981,

Figure 2.10

Deposits in large banks, by location and components, December 31, 1981 (billions of dollars)

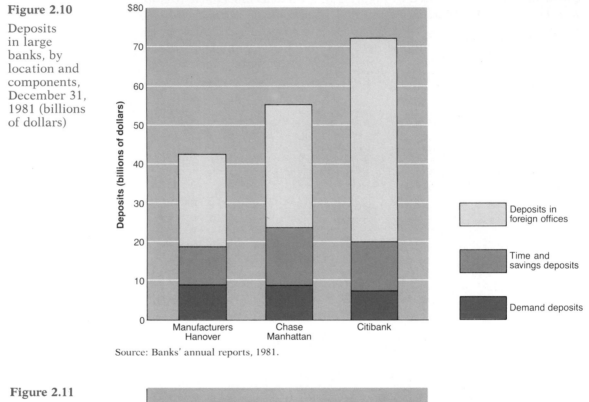

Source: Banks' annual reports, 1981.

Figure 2.11

Percentage distribution of deposits in large banks, by location and component, December 31, 1981

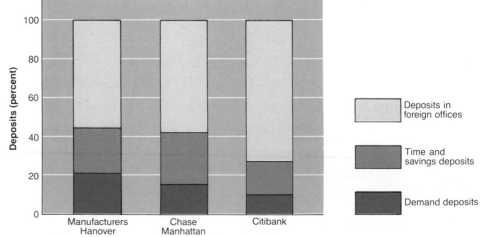

Source: Banks' annual reports, 1981.

broken into three components: demand deposits (that is, deposits in checking accounts), time and savings deposits (deposits not expected to be withdrawn before a specified date and deposits in savings accounts), and deposits in foreign offices. Each component is marked by a distinct shade. When no other particular order is called for, the bars are organized in order of total length.

The limitation of a component bar chart is that the *relative* magnitudes of the components are hard to discern because the totals of the deposits in the three groups of banks are unequal. *When the relative magnitude is of interest,* a **percentage component bar chart** may be drawn, like that in Figure 2.11. Here all three bars have the same length, so that their components may be more readily compared.

GROUPED BAR CHARTS

The **grouped bar chart,** illustrated in Figure 2.12, *provides essentially the same information as the component bar chart, but the components are separated (and grouped).* They are measured from the horizontal axis. The advantage of Figure 2.12 over 2.10 is that it permits the magnitude of each component to be seen more easily. Total deposits, however, may be more readily compared when the data are presented in a component bar chart (Figure 2.10).

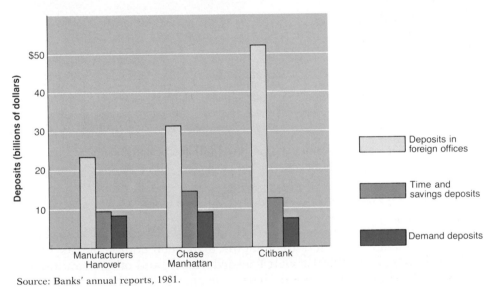

Deposits in foreign offices

Time and savings deposits

Demand deposits

Figure 2.12

Deposits in large banks, by location and component, December 31, 1981 (billions of dollars)

Source: Banks' annual reports, 1981.

PIE CHARTS

The **pie chart** is another pictorial device that may be used to show the proportions of a total represented by its component parts. *The components are expressed as percentages of the whole and are shown as portions of a circle,* like the wedges of a pie. Sometimes the absolute values of the components are also presented. With 360 degrees in the circle, the angle of each component is determined thus:

Angle of component (in degrees) =

$$\text{number of units in component} \cdot \frac{360}{\text{total number of units}}$$

The pie chart should not be subdivided into too many components. Each component should be clearly labeled, with the label preferably positioned horizontally. This type of chart is particularly useful when two related pies are presented side by side. Such is the case in Figure 2.13, showing the U.S. budget for 1981 broken down into receipts and outlays.

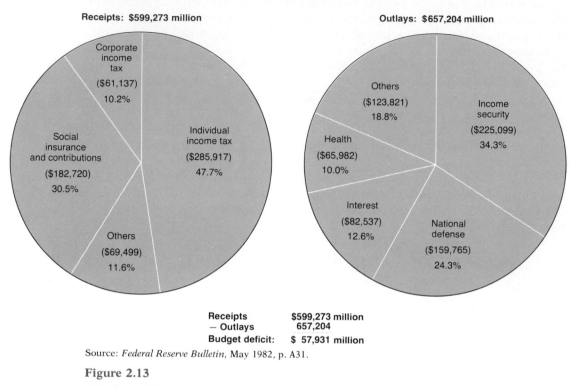

Receipts: $599,273 million

Corporate income tax
($61,137)
10.2%

Individual income tax
($285,917)
47.7%

Social insurance and contributions
($182,720)
30.5%

Others
($69,499)
11.6%

Outlays: $657,204 million

Others
($123,821)
18.8%

Income security
($225,099)
34.3%

Health
($65,982)
10.0%

Interest
($82,537)
12.6%

National defense
($159,765)
24.3%

Receipts	$599,273 million
− Outlays	657,204
Budget deficit:	$ 57,931 million

Source: *Federal Reserve Bulletin,* May 1982, p. A31.

Figure 2.13

U.S. federal budget, 1981: receipts and outlays (millions of dollars)

2.5 Personal Computers and Data Presentation

Data presentation in tables and charts can be easily handled by computers. Advanced personal computers manufactured by such companies as Apple, Tandy (Radio Shack), IBM, Hewlett Packard, Xerox, and others can quickly and efficiently present data in bar charts, pie charts, line charts, and so on.

With today's advanced technology, you can use computers to present data even if you have no knowledge of computer programming. Generally, you simply insert your data, choose the type of graph you want to use, review the chart on the computer's monitor (screen), and if you like it and have a plotter available, you can have a hard copy made. A colorful pie chart, component bar chart, or the like will be graphed by the plotter on a sheet of paper or directly on a transparency.

2.6 A Word of Caution

Graphic presentation can be an attractive, easy-to-understand way to present data so that the reader will grasp the facts at a glance.

You should, however, be aware that it is quite easy to use graphs and charts to give false impressions of what the data represent. Misrepresentation of this kind is common; here we will give one example.

Suppose a soft-drink manufacturer wants to present data to show the sales growth of the company over the last few years. The data, let us assume, are:

Year	Number of bottles sold (in millions)
1979	10
1980	10
1981	12
1982	14
1983	16

The data can be presented in a vertical bar chart. And the bar chart can be set up in several different ways—two of which we show in Figures 2.14*a* and

Figure 2.14

The impact of the horizontal scale choice on a bar chart

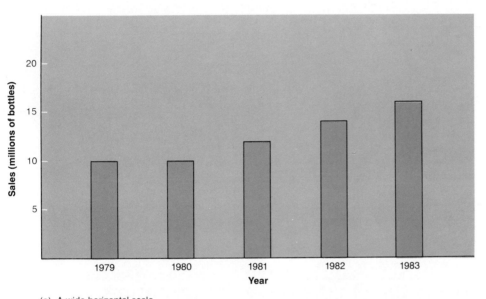

(a) A wide horizontal scale

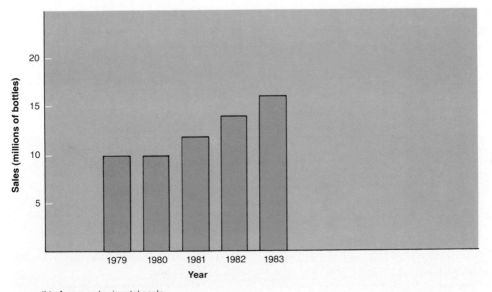

(b) A narrow horizontal scale

2.14*b*. These two charts give quite different impressions of the company sales growth, even though they in fact represent the very same data. The difference between the charts is in the horizontal scale: the chart in Figure 2.14*b* gives the impression of a much faster growth than that in Figure 2.14*a*. The vertical scale likewise can be manipulated. As an example, consider Figure 2.15. In panel *a* the scale is much more condensed than that of panel *b*. As a result, the line in panel *b* looks a lot steeper than that of panel *a*.

It is not possible to say, in either of these instances, which of the panels exhibits a more "correct" presentation; how the data are presented is largely a matter of choice. Nevertheless, it is clear that each presentation makes its own distinct impression on the viewer. You should bear this caution in mind if you are developing a presentation for others to view—and also if you're on the receiving end of a presentation.

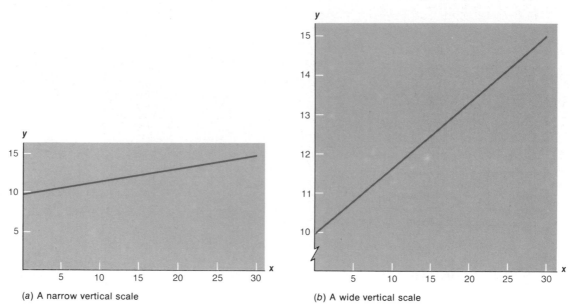

(*a*) A narrow vertical scale

(*b*) A wide vertical scale

Figure 2.15

The impact of the vertical scale choice on a line chart

2.7 APPLICATION:
USING CHARTS FOR FINANCIAL REVIEW

Figure 2.16 is a copy of part of the analysis of American Telephone and Telegraph Company's financial condition and results of operations, as presented in the company's 1981 *Annual Report* to the stockholders. The charts are used to supplement AT&T management's verbal analysis. The figure speaks for itself as it includes a brief explanation of each chart. The charts very effectively present a great deal of data in a limited space.

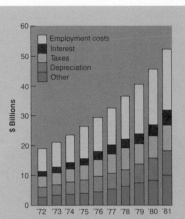

Revenues: Business services provided 52 percent of Bell System operating revenues in 1981, while residence services contributed 41 percent. Together, they accounted for $6.9 billion of the year's $7.4 billion growth in operating revenues.

Expenses: Total expenses in 1981 amounted to $52.3 billion, an increase of 14.5 percent over 1980. Employment costs were $21.4 billion, interest costs $4.4 billion, operating taxes $8.6 billion and depreciation expenses $7.9 billion.

Earnings per share: Despite renewed recession and large depreciation increases not yet fully recovered through repricing, earnings per share were $8.55, up from $8.17 in 1980. The dividend rate was raised to $5.40, the eighth increase in 10 years.

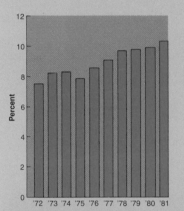

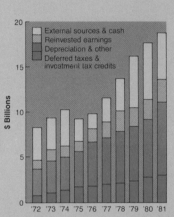

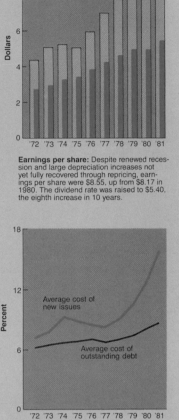

Return on capital: Return on total invested capital increased for the sixth consecutive year, evidencing continued improvements in productivity and the recognition by regulators of higher investor requirements caused by inflation.

Financing: Internal sources provided 73 percent of Bell System capital requirements in 1981, up from 56 percent 10 years ago, reflecting liberalized Federal tax depreciation policies and larger reinvestment of retained earnings.

Cost of debt: Interest costs of Bell System debt issues reached new highs in 1981, although some easing was evident at year's close. Consequently, the average cost of all long and intermediate debt outstanding rose to 8.6 percent by the end of 1981.

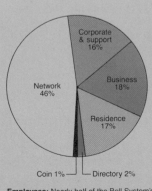

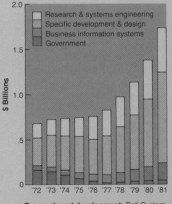

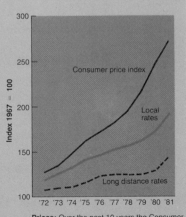

Employees: Nearly half of the Bell System's employees (excluding Western Electric and Bell Laboratories) were involved with the operation of the telecommunications network at the end of 1981, most of them in the Bell operating companies.

Research and development: Bell System R&D expenditures continued to grow substantially in 1981—totaling $1.7 billion, up $350 million over 1980—in recognition of the company's unchanging commitment to technological innovation.

Prices: Over the past 10 years the Consumer Price Index rose about 120 percent. Local and long distance rates increased only 62 and 37 percent, respectively, an achievement made possible by continuing productivity gains and operating efficiencies.

Figure 2.16

Financial charts from American Telephone and Telegraph Company   *(Continued)*

Figure 2.16 (*Continued*)

Financial charts from American Telephone and Telegraph Company

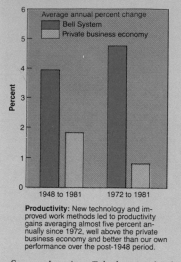

Productivity: New technology and improved work methods led to productivity gains averaging almost five percent annually since 1972, well above the private business economy and better than our own performance over the post-1948 period.

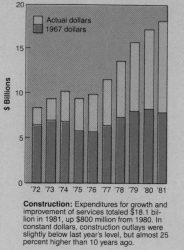

Construction: Expenditures for growth and improvement of services totaled $18.1 billion in 1981, up $800 million from 1980. In constant dollars, construction outlays were slightly below last year's level, but almost 25 percent higher than 10 years ago.

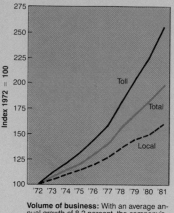

Volume of business: With an average annual growth of 8.2 percent, the company's total volume of business has doubled since 1972, principally because of a nearly three-fold increase in toll calling (long distance, WATS and intercity private line services).

Source: American Telephone and Telegraph Company, *Annual Report*, 1981.

Chapter Summary and Review

A statistical study comprises the following five steps:

1. Data collection
   a. Observing all existing data: a survey; or
   b. Observing part of the existing data: sampling

2. Data organization
   a. Editing the data
   b. Data classification
   c. Tabulation (manual or by computer)

3. Data presentation
   a. Tables (analytical and reference tables)
   b. Charts and graphs (line charts, component-part line charts, bar charts, component bar charts, grouped bar charts, and pie charts)

The next two steps are not covered in Chapter 2 but are dealt with in the rest of the book:

4. Analysis of the data
   a. Estimating parameters
   b. Testing hypotheses regarding various parameters

5. Interpretation of the results and decision making based on the analysis in step 4

Problems

2.1. Explain briefly each of the following:

    (a) Headnote
    (b) Boxhead
    (c) Stub
    (d) Field
    (e) Two-way classification table

2.2. Explain the following concepts:

    (a) Line chart
    (b) Component-part line chart
    (c) Bar chart
    (d) Component bar chart
    (e) Duo-directional bar chart

2.3. What is the advantage of a group bar chart in comparison with a component bar chart? What is the disadvantage?

2.4. Briefly explain the following concepts:

    (a) Primary source of data
    (b) Secondary source of data
    (c) Editing
    (d) Data classification

2.5. When data are classified, the classes must be mutually exclusive and collectively exhaustive. Explain these concepts and their importance.

2.6. Can some data be presented on a bar chart that cannot be presented on a line chart? Explain.

2.7. Table P2.7 provides data on end-of-year mortgage debt outstanding in the United States from 1977 through 1981, classified by type of holder, in millions of dollars.

TABLE P2.7

Type of holder	1977	1978	1979	1980	1981
All holders	$1,019,688	$1,169,412	$1,326,750	$1,451,840	$1,544,797
Major financial institutions	741,544	848,177	938,567	998,386	1,044,037
Federal and related agencies	70,175	81,739	97,084	114,300	126,112
Individuals and others	207,969	239,496	291,099	339,154	374,648

Source: *Federal Reserve Bulletin*, various issues.

    (a) Present the data in two component-part time-series line charts, one with the components measured in absolute values and one with them measured in percentages.
    (b) Present the data in two component bar charts, one with the components measured in absolute values and one with them measured in percentages.

2.8. Table P2.8 provides data on mortgage debt outstanding in the United States at the end of the first quarter of 1981, by type of holder and type of property, in millions of dollars.

TABLE P2.8

All holders		Federal and related agencies	
1 to 4 families	$973,601	1 to 4 families	$ 62,171
Multifamily	139,087	Multifamily	15,117
Commercial	262,140	Commercial	479
Farm	100,115	Farm	38,539
Major financial institutions		**Individuals and others**	
1 to 4 families	669,355	1 to 4 families	242,075
Multifamily	88,186	Multifamily	35,784
Commercial	228,630	Commercial	33,031
Farm	22,094	Farm	39,482

Source: *Federal Reserve Bulletin*, August 1981, p. A39.

(*a*) Organize the data in a two-way classification table.

(*b*) Present the data in two separate tables, in percentages. Explain the information each table provides.

2.9. Table P2.9 provides data concerning consumer installment credit outstanding at the end of June 1981 by type of credit and by holder, in millions of dollars.

TABLE P2.9

Type of credit	Type of holder	Amount outstanding (millions)
Automobile	Commercial banks	$59,192
	Credit unions	21,847
	Finance companies	38,646
Revolving credit	Commercial banks	29,722
	Retailers	23,384
	Gasoline companies	5,364
Mobile home	Commercial banks	10,179
	Finance companies	3,990
	Credit unions	486
	Savings and loans and others	3,069
Other	Commercial banks	44,217
	Finance companies	40,087
	Credit unions	23,353
	Retailers	4,028
	Savings and loans and others	10,895

Source: *Federal Reserve Bulletin*, August 1981, p. A40.

(*a*) Organize the data in a two-way classification table.

(*b*) Organize the data in two separate tables of percentages. Explain the information each of the tables provides.

2.10. (*a*) Suppose a cross-classified table presents data on health spending in the last five years, classified by type of spending (hospitals, physicians, and so on) and by years. Is it possible to separate the table into two tables, one showing the data by type of spending only and one by years only?

(*b*) Had the data originally been presented in two separate single-classification tables as described in part *a*, would it be possible, on the basis of this information alone, to construct a cross-classified table by type of spending and years? Explain.

2.11. Table P2.11 shows full-time school-enrollment rates, in percentages, for male and female populations aged 15–19 and 20–24 in five countries.

TABLE P2.11

	Males				Females				Total			
	1960	*1970*	*1975*	*1980*	*1960*	*1970*	*1975*	*1980*	*1960*	*1970*	*1975*	*1980*
Germany	37 10	52 13	56 13	57 14	32 4	42 8	46 9	47 .9	35 7	47 10	51 11	52 12
U.S.	69 17	75 27	72 24	77 26	59 7	73 13	72 19	77 21	64 12	74 20	72 22	77 24
France	31 8	41 12	49 12	52 14	34 6	50 7	54 7	58 9	32 7	45 10	51 10	55 11
Japan	36 6	65 18	77 20	82 23	43 4	64 7	75 9	80 11	39 5	64 12	76 14	81 17
Sweden	36 18	58 17	58 14	61 14	38 13	54 15	56 15	59 15	37 15	56 16	57 14	60 15

■ 15–19   ■ 20–24

Source: Reprinted from *The OECD Observer*, no. 90 (January 1978), p. 18.

    (*a*) Draw a vertical grouped bar chart indicating the full-time school enrollment for the total population aged 15–19, where for each country, you present a group of four bars, one for each of the years shown.

    (*b*) Do the same as in part *a* for the total population aged 20–24.

2.12. Table P2.12 presents financial data for Allied Stores Corporation for the years 1976–82, in millions of dollars.

TABLE P2.12

Dollars in millions, except per share amounts	*1976*	*1977*	*1978*	*1979*	*1980*	*1981*	*1982*
Sales	$1,797.0	$1,908.1	$2,082.7	$2,210.3	$2,267.7	$2,732.7	$3,215.6
Net earnings	61.4	73.4	81.6	89.2	83.4	88.3	90.7
Per share of common stock							
Earnings—primary	$ 3.33	$ 3.76	$ 4.04	$ 4.36	$ 4.08	$ 4.38	$ 4.41
Earnings—fully diluted	3.07	3.57	3.94	4.31	4.05	4.35	4.33
Dividends paid	0.87½	1.05	1.30	1.55	1.70	1.75	1.80
Equity at year end	26.52	28.99	31.51	34.22	36.89	39.45	41.68
Financial position							
Cash & short-term investments	$ 51.1	$ 80.0	$ 91.3	$ 30.0	$110.2	$ 18.2	$ 13.2
Short-term borrowings	—	—	—	—	—	229.8	33.0
Long-term debt	419.9	430.1	409.1	386.6	458.3	605.0	791.3
Stockholders' equity	503.4	572.3	640.2	702.3	743.1	798.0	867.8

Source: Allied Stores Corporation, *Fact Book*, 1982.

    (*a*) Present the fully diluted earnings per share and the dividend paid per share on a vertical grouped bar chart for the period shown.

    (*b*) Add up the firm's long-term debt and stockholders' equity. The sum of these two components gives the total capitalization. Using a component bar chart, show the two components of the total capitalization over the years.

2.13. Table P2.13 shows the revenues and the net profit of three newspaper publishers for the years 1977–82 (in millions of dollars).

TABLE P2.13

	Revenues			Net profit		
Year	Times Mirror	New York Times	Gannett	Times Mirror	New York Times	Gannett
1977	$1,144	$511	$ 558	$ 96	$26	$ 69
1978	1,428	492	690	142	16	83
1979	1,647	653	1,065	146	36	134
1980	1,869	733	1,215	139	41	152
1981	2,156	845	1,367	150	50	172
1982[a]	2,360	975	1,530	142	64	178

[a]The data for 1982 are estimates.

Source: *Value Line Investment Survey*, June 18, 1982. © 1982 by Arnold Bernald and Co., Inc. Reprinted by permission of the publisher.

(a) Draw the revenues of the three companies on a line chart.

(b) Draw the net profit of the three companies on a line chart.

2.14. Table P2.14 shows the sales of imported cars in the United States by make for the period 1975–80. Present the data in two component-part line charts, one showing the absolute values of the sales, and one showing their percentages of total sales.

TABLE P2.14

	Make (thousands of cars)				
Year	Toyota	Datsun	Honda	Others	Total
1975	278	260	102	924	1,564
1976	347	270	151	723	1,491
1977	493	388	261	922	2,064
1978	442	399	275	877	1,993
1979	508	472	353	986	2,319
1980	582	517	375	916	2,390

Source: *Ward's Automotive Yearbook*, various issues.

2.15. A study of business executives showed that their major fields of study in college had been as shown in Table P2.15 (in percentages). Present the data in a horizontal grouped bar chart (use one group for each of the nine fields of study presented).

TABLE P2.15

Field of study	Undergraduate	Graduate
Humanities	11.0%	0.0%
Business	29.5	46.5
Economics	20.0	7.3
Engineering	21.0	11.0
Physical sciences	6.3	4.4
Social sciences	6.6	0.7
Education	0.9	1.6
Law	3.2	26.5
Other	1.5	2.0
	100.0%	100.0%

Source: Based on Charles G. Burck, "Group Profile of the Fortune 500 Chief Executives," *Fortune*, May 1976.

2.16. Table P2.16 shows the market share of home appliance manufacturers in the United States in the years 1978–83.

TABLE P2.16

Year	Whirlpool	White Consolidated	Maytag	Hoover	Others	Total
1978	33.1%	26.3%	5.2%	11.0%	24.4%	100.0%
1979	31.5	28.0	5.1	10.5	24.9	100.0
1980	29.5	27.1	4.6	10.9	27.9	100.0
1981	31.4	28.0	5.3	9.7	25.6	100.0
1982[a]	31.9	27.3	6.4	9.2	25.2	100.0
1983[a]	30.9	26.6	6.9	8.6	27.0	100.0

[a]Data for 1982 and 1983 are estimates.

Source: Derived from *Value Line Investment Survey*, July 2, 1982.

(a) Present the data in a grouped bar chart.
(b) Present the data in a component bar chart.
(c) Present the data in a component-part line chart.

2.17. In 1979 G. A. Barnett of the Bank of Bermuda published a paper that focused on the average rate of return (that is, the average percentage of profit) obtained by investment in world bond markets in the years 1970–79 and on the risk of those investments (measured by a statistical measure called "standard deviation," which we shall introduce later, in Chapter 4). The average rate of return and the risk of investment in bonds of nine countries are given in Table P2.17.

TABLE P2.17

Country	Average rate of return	Risk
Australia	5.2%	3.4%
United States	7.3	1.5
United Kingdom	7.6	3.8
Canada	7.6	2.1
France	10.0	3.1
Japan	13.3	2.4
Netherlands	13.9	3.1
Switzerland	15.9	3.0
West Germany	16.5	2.9

Source: G. A. Barnett, "The Best Portfolios Are International," *Euromoney*, April 1979.

(a) Present the average rates of return on a horizontal bar chart, with the shortest bar at the top and the longest at the bottom.
(b) Present the risks on a horizontal bar chart, with the shortest bar again at the top and the longest bar at the bottom.
(c) In view of the fact that a high average rate of return and a low risk level are appreciated by investors, was France's performance better than that of the United Kingdom? Why?

2.18. The accountants of Vehicles from A to Z, Inc., have classified last year's operating costs for the firm's three divisions. The classification is shown in Table P2.18.

TABLE P2.18

Costs and expenses (millions of dollars)	Division		
	A	B	C
Raw materials	$120	$70	$80
Wages and salaries	80	80	20
Other operating costs	60	70	40

Present the operating costs data in two separate percentage tables and explain the meaning of each.

2.19. Table P2.19 presents data on commercial banks and savings and loan associations operating in Florida in the years 1970, 1975, and 1980.

TABLE P2.19

Year	Commercial banks			Savings and loan associations		
	Number	*Offices*	*Deposits (millions of dollars)*	*Number*	*Offices*	*Deposits (millions of dollars)*
1970	328	497	$13,985	134	342	$ 8,238
1975	307	742	24,865	123	921	21,536
1980	309	1,500	40,410	130	1,533	44,332

Source: *Florida Statistical Abstracts,* various issues.

(a) Present the data on savings and loan associations on a grouped bar chart in which each group of bars shows the data for a given year.
(b) Present the deposits data of both commercial banks and savings and loan associations in a percent table. Explain the change that has occurred during the period.

2.20 Table P2.20 presents the 1980 personal income in three states by component. Use a component vertical bar chart to present the data.

TABLE P2.20

Source of income (millions of dollars)	State		
	Colorado	*Mississippi*	*New Jersey*
Wages and salaries	$19,027	$ 9,930	$47,047
Proprietors' income	1,970	1,455	3,582
Property income	4,367	1,956	12,114
Other income	3,665	3,285	17,981
Total	$29,029	$16,626	$80,724

Source: Moody's *Municipal & Government Manual 1982,* vol. 2, p. A15.

2.21. Table P2.21 shows the end-of-year value of mutual funds (in billions of dollars) in the years 1975 through 1980.

TABLE P2.21

Year	Money market funds[a] (billions of dollars)	Other mutual funds[b] (billions of dollars)
1975	$ 3.5	$42.2
1976	3.6	50.5
1977	3.8	47.7
1978	10.6	47.5
1979	44.5	52.5
1980	73.0	65.3

[a]These are funds that invest in short-term financial obligations of corporations and governments.
[b]These are funds that invest in stocks.

Source: Reprinted by permission of *The Wiesenberger Investment Companies Service,* 1981 Edition, p. 12 and pp. 40–43. Copyright © 1981, Warren, Gorham & Lamont, Inc., 210 South Street, Boston, Mass. All rights reserved.

Present the data in a component-part line chart in percent and explain the changes that have occurred in these years.

2.22. The values of net plant and equipment of the Aluminum Company of America in the years 1971 through 1980 are shown in Table P2.22.

TABLE P2.22

Year	Net plant and equipment (millions of dollars)
1971	$1,518.5
1972	1,495.4
1973	1,530.2
1974	1,718.2
1975	1,927.0
1976	1,953.4
1977	2,029.6
1978	2,164.6
1979	2,318.9
1980	2,687.3

Source: Aluminum Company of America, *Annual Report*, 1980.

Present the data in a line chart.

2.23. Prepare one pie chart for the assets and one pie chart for the liabilities of the Republic National Bank of New York as of December 31, 1981, given in Table P2.23. Items of less than $100 million should be grouped together under the classification "Other assets" or "Other liabilities." In the assets chart, for the loan category, consider only the loans net of allowance for possible loan losses.

TABLE P2.23

Assets (thousands of dollars)

Cash and demand accounts	$ 169,622
Interest bearing deposits with banks	2,657,402
Precious metals	61,469
Investment securities (approximate market value of $824,652 in 1981 and $912,077 in 1980)	925,451
Federal funds sold and securities purchased under agreements to resell	133,300
Loans (less unearned income of $39,499 in 1981 and $29,123 in 1980)	2,493,836
Allowance for possible loan losses	(45,675)
Loans (net)	2,448,161
Customers' liability under acceptances	530,024
Bank premises and equipment	52,141
Accrued interest receivable	193,535
Other assets	92,393
	$7,263,498

Liabilities and stockholders' equity (thousands of dollars)

Demand deposits in domestic offices	$ 423,199
Time deposits in domestic offices	2,118,013
Deposits in foreign offices	2,772,697
Total deposits	5,313,909
Short-term borrowings	669,848
Acceptances outstanding	539,782
Accrued interest payable	184,146
Other liabilities	38,342
Total liabilities	6,746,027

(Continued)

TABLE P2.23 (Continued)

Stockholders' equity		
Common stock:		
Par value	**$100**	
Shares authorized	**4,500,000**	
Shares outstanding	**3,250,000**	**325,000**
Surplus		**65,000**
Undivided profits		**127,471**
Total stockholders' equity		**517,471**
		$7,263,498

Source: Republic National Bank of New York, *Annual Report*, 1981.

2.24. The percent of market share of a few leading wineries in the United States in 1981 is presented in Table P2.24.

TABLE P2.24

E & J Gallo	25.8%	Wine Group	4.3
United Vintners	9.9	Paul Masson	3.6
Almaden	6.0	Others	45.0
Wine Spectrum	5.4	Total	100.0%

Source: *Business Week*, March 15, 1982, p. 110.

Present the data on a pie chart.

2.25. Tables P2.25*a* and P2.25*b* show 1981 sources of funds and distribution of funds of Grumman Corporation. Present the data in two separate pie charts.

TABLE P2.25*a*
Sources of 1981 funds

Sources	(thousands of dollars)
Net income	$ 20,486
Addition to long-term debt	167,116
Common stock issued	17,574
Other	67,335
Total	$272,511

Source: Grumman Corporation, *Annual Report*, 1981.

TABLE P2.25*b*
Distribution of 1981 funds

Uses	(thousands of dollars)
Reduction of long-term debt	$ 24,820
Expenditure for property plant and equipment	49,691
Cash dividends	19,842
Increase in working capital	154,986
Other	23,172
Total	$272,511

Source: Grumman Corporation, *Annual Report*, 1981.

2.26. Table P2.26 shows the market share of five types of computers in 1975, 1980, and 1985 (estimate). Draw a grouped bar chart of the data, showing five groups of computers with three bars in each group: one for each year.

TABLE P2.26

	Year		
Type of computer	*1975*	*1980*	*1985*[a]
Mainframe computers	83.0%	60.0%	36.0%
Minicomputers	9.5	17.0	21.0
Small business computers	3.5	11.0	13.0
Office word processors	4.0	6.0	10.0
Desktop computers	0.0	6.0	20.0
Total	100.0%	100.0%	100.0%

[a]Data for 1985 are estimates.
Source: *Business Week*, February 15, 1982, pp. 78–79.

2.27. Draw a horizontal bar chart showing the 1981 sales of cigarettes of the twenty top brands, as summarized in Table P2.27.

TABLE P2.27

The Cigarette Business in 1981

The top brands

Rank	*Brand*	*Company*	*Market share (percent)*	*Sales (billions of cigarettes)*	*Percent change in sales vs. 1977*
1	Marlboro	Philip Morris	18.40%	114.9	+ 4.6%
2	Winston	Reynolds	13.20	82.5	+ 1.0
3	Salem	Reynolds	8.70	54.4	+ 0.7
4	Kool	Brown & Williamson	8.45	52.8	− 3.0
5	Camel	Reynolds	4.70	29.4	+10.0
6	Pall Mall	American	4.69	29.3	− 7.3
7	Benson & Hedges	Philip Morris	4.61	28.8	+ 2.7
8	Merit	Philip Morris	4.59	28.4	+ 9.0
9	Vantage	Reynolds	3.75	23.5	− 1.3
10	Kent	Lorillard	2.99	18.7	− 7.5
11	Virginia Slims	Philip Morris	2.50	15.6	+10.1
12	Newport	Lorillard	2.26	14.1	+22.8
13	Carlton	American	2.22	13.9	−11.1
14	Raleigh	Brown & Williamson	1.71	10.7	− 5.3
15	True	Lorillard	1.69	10.0	− 9.2
16	Golden Lights	Lorillard	1.55	9.7	−13.0
17	Viceroy	Brown & Williamson	1.52	9.5	−12.0
18	Tareyton	American	1.48	9.3	−11.4
19	More	Reynolds	1.43	8.9	+27.0
20	Barclay	Brown & Williamson	1.19	7.4	[a]

[a]Brand introduced 1981.
Source: *Business Week*, December 7, 1981, p. 83.

2.28. Table P2.28 shows hypothetical sources and allocations of health-care dollars in a given country for 1982.

TABLE P2.28

Dollars come from (billions of dollars)		*Dollars go to (billions of dollars)*	
Governments	$ 62	Hospital and nursing-home care	$ 76
Direct consumer spending	56	Physicians and other professionals	45
Private insurance	42	Drugs, appliances, and others	31
Philanthropy	2	Construction	5
Total	$162	Research and development	5
		Total	$162

Present the data in two pie charts.

APPENDIX 2A:
Ratio Graphs—The Semilogarithmic Scale

Table 2A.1 presents the U.S. gross national product for a 24-year period in 1972 dollars. The same data are represented by a line chart in Figure 2A.1. Figure 2A.1 clearly shows that with a few exceptions, GNP rose over the period 1958–81 and overall it rose by increasing amounts (dollars) as time went on. For example, the change in GNP between 1958 and 1964, a period

TABLE 2A.1

Gross National Product of the United States, 1958–81

(billions of 1972 dollars)

Year	GNP	Year	GNP
1958	$ 679.5	1970	$1,075.3
1959	720.4	1971	1,122.4
1960	736.8	1972	1,185.9
1961	755.3	1973	1,255.0
1962	799.1	1974	1,248.0
1963	830.9	1975	1,233.9
1964	874.4	1976	1,300.4
1965	925.9	1977	1,371.7
1966	981.0	1978	1,436.9
1967	1,007.7	1979	1,483.0
1968	1,051.8	1980	1,480.7
1969	1,078.8	1981	1,510.3

Source: Council of Economic Advisers, *Economic Indicators,* various issues.

Figure 2A.1

Gross national product of the United States, 1958–81 (billions of 1972 dollars)

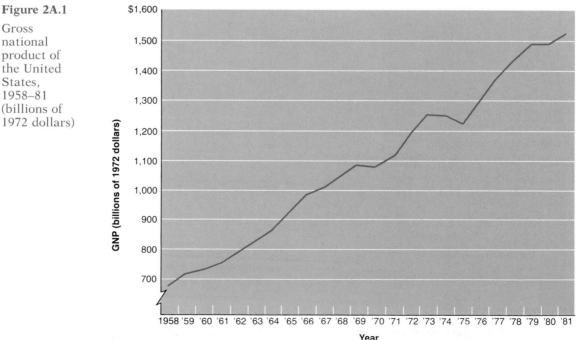

Source: Council of Economic Advisers, *Economic Indicators,* various issues.

of six years, was $194.9 billion, whereas between 1975 and 1981 GNP increased by a greater amount, $276.4 billion. What the graph does not clearly show is that the GNP *percentage change* during the 1975–81 period was less than the *percentage change* during the period 1958–64.[2] When we want to focus on the percentage change in a variable over time, we simply compute the percentage change for every year and present it on a separate graph, such as the one in Figure 2A.2. Figure 2A.2, however, gives no indication of the absolute value of GNP. We can show the absolute value of GNP on a graph in which the *Y*-axis is a logarithmic scale (that is, a scale in which equal intervals represent equal differences in the logarithms of the numbers), as in Figure 2A.3. The graph is called semilogarithmic because only one of the scales is logarithmic, not both. A characteristic of the semilogarithmic chart is that a straight-line graph indicates that the variable exhibits a *constant* percentage change over the years.[3] The steeper the line, the higher the percentage change. There are six typical patterns of ratio graphs, all shown in Figure 2A.4. While the figure is self-explanatory, one must pay attention to the difference between the ratio graph and the ordinary line graph. For example, Figure 2A.4*c* represents a series in which the variable increases at

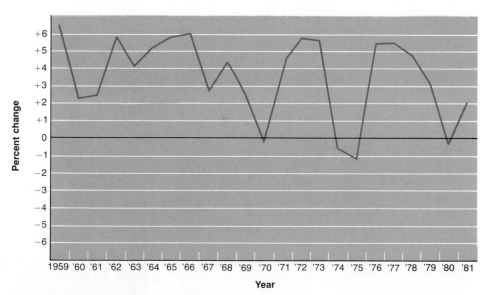

Figure 2A.2

Annual percentage change in U.S. GNP, 1959–81

Source: Derived from Table 2A.1.

[2] In other words, the graph does not reveal that the ratio $GNP_{81}/GNP_{75} = 1{,}510.3/1{,}233.9 = 1.22$ is smaller than the ratio $GNP_{64}/GNP_{58} = 874.4/679.5 = 1.29$.

[3] Let Y_t, Y_{t+1}, and Y_{t+2} be a variable's values at times t, $t + 1$, and $t + 2$, respectively. The values on a logarithmic scale are $\log Y_t$, $\log Y_{t+1}$, and $\log Y_{t+2}$. The slope of the line in the time interval t through $t + 1$ is $\dfrac{\log Y_{t+1} - \log Y_t}{(t + 1) - t} = \log Y_{t+1} - \log Y_t = \log \dfrac{Y_{t+1}}{Y_t}$. Similarly, the slope of the line in the time interval $t + 1$ through $t + 2$ is $\dfrac{\log Y_{t+2} - \log Y_{t+1}}{(t + 2) - (t + 1)} = \log Y_{t+2} - \log Y_{t+1} = \log \dfrac{Y_{t+2}}{Y_{t+1}}$. Constant slope over time means that $\log \dfrac{Y_{t+1}}{Y_t}$ is equal to $\log \dfrac{Y_{t+2}}{Y_{t+1}}$, so that $\dfrac{Y_{t+1}}{Y_t} = \dfrac{Y_{t+2}}{Y_{t+1}}$, but this last relationship implies that the rate of change in Y is equal in the two time intervals. Thus equal slopes on a semilogarithmic scale imply a constant percentage change in the variable Y.

Figure 2A.3

GNP on ratio scale (billions of 1972 dollars)

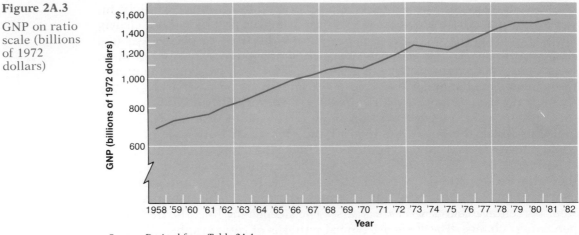

Source: Derived from Table 2A.1.

a decreasing rate. It is possible that the absolute amount of the changes increases from year to year, yet because the base year on which the percentage is calculated changes with each calculation, the percentage is shown as decreasing. This becomes clear from the following hypothetical series:

Year	Level	Absolute change	Percentage change
1981	100	—	—
1982	145	45	45
1983	200	55	38

Figure 2A.4

Typical patterns of ratio graphs

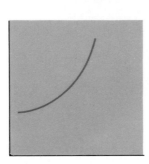

(a) Variables increase at an increasing rate

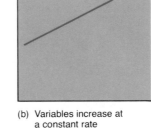

(b) Variables increase at a constant rate

(c) Variables increase at a decreasing rate

(d) Variables decrease at an increasing rate

(e) Variables decrease at a constant rate

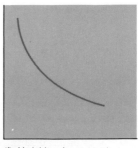

(f) Variables decrease at a decreasing rate

As we emphasized earlier, the semilogarithmic scale is useful when the focus is on the percentage change of variables. A particularly interesting use of the scale is in the comparison of percentage changes of two or more variables over time. Consider Table 2A.2, showing the number of local and long-distance telephone calls placed by the Bell System customers during 1967–81. By looking at the table one cannot easily tell which of the two series, the local or the long-distance calls, grew faster over the years. One has only to glance at Figure 2A.5, however, to see that the graph representing long-distance calls is steeper, and thus to know that long-distance calls had a higher growth rate over the period.

TABLE 2A.2
Local and Long-Distance Telephone Calls Placed by Bell System Customers, 1967–81
(millions)

Year	Local	Long-distance	Total
1967	95,848	5,319	101,167
1968	100,571	5,880	106,451
1969	108,567	6,621	115,188
1970	114,461	7,220	121,681
1971	120,315	7,761	128,076
1972	126,962	8,571	135,533
1973	133,275	9,491	142,766
1974	140,924	10,198	151,122
1975	144,178	10,725	154,903
1976	149,156	11,685	160,841
1977	154,289	12,844	167,133
1978	165,583	14,639	180,222
1979	169,185	16,193	185,378
1980	174,791	17,457	192,248
1981	179,992	18,602	198,594

Source: American Telephone and Telegraph Company, *Statistical Report,* various years.

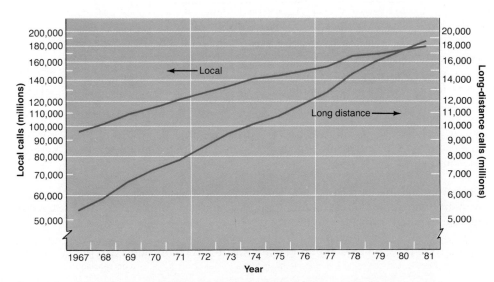

Figure 2A.5

Local and long-distance calls placed by Bell System customers, 1967–81, on a ratio scale (millions of calls)

Source: American Telephone and Telegraph Company, *Statistical Report,* various issues.

APPENDIX PROBLEMS

2A.1. Table P2A.1 shows the number of AT&T's long-distance telephone calls separated into domestic calls and overseas and international calls for the years 1977–81.

TABLE P2A.1

Year	Domestic calls (millions)	Overseas and international calls (millions)
1977	12,591	253
1978	14,330	309
1979	15,821	372
1980	17,007	450
1981	18,072	530

Source: American Telephone and Telegraph Company, *1981 Statistical Report.*

Present the time series data for both types of calls on a chart with a semilogarithmic scale. Compare the slopes of the two graphs. What is your conclusion?

2A.2. Money market funds (MMFs) are investment companies that pool the money of many investors and invest in short-term instruments such as treasury bills and certificates of deposit. Table P2A.2 presents the net worth of money market funds and other mutual funds (which invest in longer-term bonds and in stocks) for the years 1975–82.

TABLE P2A.2

Year	MMFs (billions)	Other mutual funds (billions)
1975	$ 3.5	$42.2
1976	3.6	50.6
1977	3.8	47.7
1978	10.6	47.5
1979	44.5	52.5
1980	73.0	65.3
1981	143.2	71.3
1982	285.4	73.7

Source: Data for the years 1975–80 reprinted from *Wiesenberger Investment Companies Service*, 1981 Edition, pp. 40–43. Copyright © 1981, Warren, Gorham & Lamont, Inc., 210 South Street, Boston, Mass. All rights reserved. The data for 1981 and 1982 are independent estimates.

Present the two series on a chart with a semilogarithmic scale and discuss the meaning of the slopes of the two graphs.

2A.3. Draw the earnings per share (fully diluted) and the dividend paid per share of Allied Stores (Table P2.12) on a semilogarithmic scale. What conclusions can you reach about the growth of the two variables in the last few years?

2A.4. Present the data given in Table P2.22 in a line chart, using a semilogarithmic scale. Was the growth rate in plant and equipment of the Aluminum Company of America steady during the 1975–80 period? Can you tell from the graph?

2A.5. Table P2A.5 presents the price index of building materials in a certain country in the last eight years.

TABLE P2A.5

Year	Index
1	162
2	176
3	187
4	205
5	236
6	274
7	310
8	360

(*a*) Present the index on a semilogarithmic graph.
(*b*) Using the graph, explain the changes in the price index over the period.

FREQUENCY DISTRIBUTIONS

CHAPTER THREE OUTLINE

The segment of statistics dealing with *the collection, organization, and presentation of data,* discussed in Chapter 2, is known as **descriptive statistics.** We shall continue discussing descriptive statistics; at this point, however, we turn to topics that lead directly to statistical analysis.

3.1 Data Sets: Populations and Samples

When we study a given body of data, the need for statistical analysis almost inevitably emerges. But the type of analysis required and the extent and accuracy of the statistical study depend on the characteristics of the data— and, of course, on the goals of the study and the resources available.

Clearly, data vary greatly in type from study to study. Some studies involve a limited amount of data and some involve enormous amounts. Some involve data of nominal measurement, such as income, weight, distance, production, cost, profit; others involve ordinal data (rankings). Still other data are strictly descriptive and qualitative, such as those concerning sex. Yet there are certain similarities in the way we approach all types of data. There is a general terminology, for example, that is used with most types of data; we shall discuss this terminology here.

The first concept we need to discuss is that of the **frame.** Any collection of data relates to some elementary units, and the frame is *the totality of all elementary units.* We use the term **observation** to refer to *an item of information of interest concerning the elementary units in the frame,* and we use the term **population** to refer to *the totality of all the individual observations of interest.* In many cases, we do not find it feasible or economical to study the entire population. In such cases *only a portion of the population is observed, and the data are considered to be a* **sample** *of the population. The data available for a particular study, be it a population or a sample, are referred to as a* **data set.**

To illustrate, consider the annual income of all adult residents of Montana. The list of all of the adult residents of Montana is the frame; the annual income of a Montana resident is an observation; a collection of such observations is a data set. If the data set includes the annual income of some but not all adult residents of Montana, then the data set is a sample. If it includes the annual income of all of them, then it is a population.

Clearly, more than one population can be defined within the same frame, and the frame of interest and the population of interest within it are derived from the goal of the study. In the preceding example, within the frame of Montana residents, we focused on the population of annual incomes of all adult residents. But using the same frame, we can also define the population according to homeownership status: each element (that is, each adult resident) in the frame will be identified as either a homeowner or not. The term "population" thus has a broader meaning in a statistical context than in everyday usage. Ordinarily we use "population" to refer to a group of human beings or a collection of physical objects; in statistical usage, however, the term refers to the data set that is the target of the statistical analysis. Figure 3.1 shows the steps of a statistical analysis.

Figure 3.1

The steps of a statistical analysis

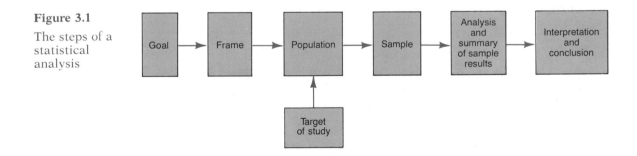

3.2 More About Samples

The population is the ultimate target of the statistical study. But for a variety of reasons, some of which will be listed shortly, it is often not available to us in full, and we have to make do with samples.

A sample is a segment of a population and, as such, is expected to reflect the population, so that by studying the sample we may learn about certain attributes of the total population. To ensure an undistorted picture of the population as a whole, the sample must, with few exceptions, be selected by some *random process*. *A sample selected by a random process* is called a **random sample.** A random sample is constructed in such a way that each population member is given a chance to be selected.[1] Note that not all population members must be given an *equal* chance to be selected; random sample designs that give unequal chances of selection to the population members are discussed in Chapter 11, which deals with sampling and sampling distributions.

WHY SAMPLE?

We explained earlier that a population is the aggregate of all the items having some specified characteristic, a definition that encompasses a wide variety of populations, ranging in size from very small to infinite.

It is obviously impossible to study an infinite population in its entirety, and thus studies of such populations must always rely on samples. Studies concerning finite populations can, at least in principle, be carried out by observing all the members of the population. A *complete enumeration of all the population's members* is called a **census.** But because a census is often either impossible or impractical we frequently use samples to study finite populations as well. Specific reasons for the use of samples are outlined below.

The Cost of Sampling The economic cost of observing a portion of a population is almost invariably less than the cost of observing each and every member of the population. Take, for example, the population of all the parents of high school students in the United States. The planning, data collection, and analysis of a census covering such a population would be extremely expensive. Furthermore, it is inevitable that part of the population would inadvertently be excluded: people move, they go on vacation, they refuse to participate. By contrast, a sample of moderate size involves only a fraction of the cost and can provide satisfactory information concerning the population as a whole.

Accuracy Because a sample involves fewer population members than a census does, each sample observation is normally of better "quality" than each observation in a census. The number of observations involved in a large census often forces the researcher to devote minimal attention to each one. If the study is to be carried out via a sample of interviews, for example, only a handful of interviewers will be needed, and these can be knowledgeable people. If, on the other hand, the study is to be carried out via a census, more interviewers will have to be employed, and some may be less qualified than others. The result with a census is that more observations are provided, but the average quality of the observations is likely to be inferior.

The Time Factor The time factor, an important consideration in every kind of research, is of particular importance in the business world. If we are doing a study designed to find out whether businesses intend to accelerate

---

[1] In the case of an infinite population, the population members are continuously being created by a given process (for example, the human population). In this case it is impossible to give a chance of being selected to population members who have not yet been created or to those who have perished.

or decelerate production next month, we cannot afford to spend two months on our investigation. Likewise, when we are surveying consumers to determine the most appealing design for a given product, we cannot spend a great deal of time on it; otherwise we may find that a competitor has already introduced a similar product that has proved to be successful. Such situations are numerous.

A sample has an advantage over a census in that it can be completed faster. Also, processing the results—the tabulation, typing, coding, punching, and so forth—is a much faster procedure for a sample than it is for a census.

Other Factors   There are other reasons for sampling. In some cases "observing" an item in a population involves the destruction of the item. Worthy of mention here is the well-known anecdote of the joker who struck all his matches in order to test them. To determine the quality or taste of any consumable good, it must be used up, and sampling is obviously needed for this purpose.

Also, some populations are not easily accessible. Such is the case when the population encompasses senior corporate management, high government officials, intensive-care patients, and the like. Reliance on a sample rather than a census is practically mandatory in those cases.

The distinction between "population" and "samples" is very important when conclusions are drawn from observed data. The characteristics of a population can be measured directly. In studying samples, we need the aid of **statistical inference,** which is *the method of studying characteristics of populations and phenomena through the observation of sample data.* Statistical inference is discussed in Part 3 of the book.

3.3 The Frequency Distribution

The methods of analyzing data sets are similar and often identical whether they constitute a sample or a population. In this chapter we present the frequency distributions of data sets and analyze them. Additional ways to summarize quantitative measures of data are discussed in Chapter 4.

The frequency distribution provides a convenient summary of the data by listing all the possible values of the variable and then noting the *frequency* of observations for each value in the data. For example, suppose the data consist of the end-of-period value of amounts of $100 invested in 60 different common stocks. The data are given in Table 3.1, and they should be interpreted in the following way: if we had invested $100 in stock number 1 and waited until the end of the period (say one year), the value of our investment would have been $105. If we had invested $100 in stock number 2, the value at the end of the period would have been $97. Thus our investment would have appreciated in value by $5 in the first case (stock 1) and depreciated by $3 in the second case (stock 2). The data concerning other stocks should be interpreted in a similar way.

While the data values have been assigned sequential numbers for reference (stock 1, stock 2, and so on), we can easily see that the end-of-period values do not appear in any particular order. If we want to see the data presented in order, we can set up a **frequency distribution**—*a summary of the data made by organizing the variable of interest in intervals of increasing value. The intervals in the frequency distribution* are often referred to as **classes.**

TABLE 3.1
End-of-Period Value of $100 Investment in 60 Common Stocks

Stock	Value	Stock	Value	Stock	Value	Stock	Value
1	$105.0	16	$106.4	31	$109.5	46	$ 81.4
2	97.0	17	111.5	32	112.7	47	111.3
3	121.5	18	115.6	33	99.0	48	116.6
4	110.9	19	100.3	34	128.6	49	99.0
5	108.8	20	90.4	35	87.6	50	104.3
6	96.3	21	109.3	36	107.4	51	127.0
7	85.1	22	100.5	37	86.7	52	113.3
8	88.0	23	112.5	38	112.3	53	108.6
9	110.4	24	113.3	39	91.4	54	111.3
10	100.7	25	124.5	40	113.6	55	119.9
11	103.6	26	107.9	41	104.4	56	106.9
12	109.6	27	114.3	42	119.8	57	124.2
13	131.0	28	103.7	43	140.8	58	110.8
14	116.2	29	113.9	44	97.0	59	118.0
15	118.2	30	91.3	45	98.2	60	121.3

SETTING UP A FREQUENCY DISTRIBUTION

To set up a frequency distribution, we first develop a **tally table,** which serves as a *work sheet for preparation of the frequency distribution.* In our tally table, Table 3.2, we show the end-of-period values of the stock in our example organized in classes with a width of $5 each.

To derive the tally table (Table 3.2) from Table 3.1, we simply place a tally mark beside the class to which each observation in Table 3.1 belongs. We then place a check mark beside the observation in the original list of data. In our example, the first observation is $105.0, so the tally mark is placed in class $105.0–under 110.0 (Table 3.2) and a check mark (not shown) is placed beside the first observation in Table 3.1. When the tally table (Table 3.2) is complete, it shows a list of the frequencies (that is, the numbers) of observations beside the classes in which the observations are grouped. And

TABLE 3.2
Tally Table for Stock-Value Data

Class	Tally
$ 80.0–under 85.0	|
85.0–under 90.0	||||
90.0–under 95.0	|||
95.0–under 100.0	⦀⦀ |
100.0–under 105.0	⦀⦀ ||
105.0–under 110.0	⦀⦀ ⦀⦀
110.0–under 115.0	⦀⦀ ⦀⦀ ||||
115.0–under 120.0	⦀⦀ ||
120.0–under 125.0	||||
125.0–under 130.0	||
130.0–under 135.0	|
135.0–under 140.0	
140.0–under 145.0	|

this gives us our frequency distribution: since the number of observations in each class corresponds to the number of tally marks in the class, the frequency distribution may be easily constructed from the tally table by a simple count of the marks in each class. Table 3.3 is the frequency distribution for our example.

TABLE 3.3
Frequency Distribution of
End-of-Period Stock Values

Class	Frequency
$ 80.0–under 85.0	1
85.0–under 90.0	4
90.0–under 95.0	3
95.0–under 100.0	6
100.0–under 105.0	7
105.0–under 110.0	10
110.0–under 115.0	14
115.0–under 120.0	7
120.0–under 125.0	4
125.0–under 130.0	2
130.0–under 135.0	1
135.0–under 140.0	0
140.0–under 145.0	1
Total	60

How does the frequency distribution compare with Table 3.1? Tables 3.1 and 3.3 are two different descriptions of the same data, but Table 3.1 provides more details than Table 3.3, giving the specific end-of-period value of each stock. But while the raw-data table provides more information than does the frequency distribution it does not reveal any systematic pattern in the data. The frequency distribution, although it conceals some details, is appealing to the analyst, since it reveals the general pattern of the data: it presents the data after they have been organized. We easily see, for example, that the most frequent classes in Table 3.3 are the $110.0–under 115.0 and $105.0–under 110.0 classes, and that the frequency tends to decline as we move to outer classes (away from the center) on each side. We also note that the declining frequency with movement away from the center is not without exceptions.

3.4 Graphic Display of Frequency Distributions

THE HISTOGRAM

Graphic display of data is very useful as a means of description, a fact we have already seen in Chapter 2. A large variety of diagrams can be used to present data visually, but the most common type used to represent a frequency distribution is the **histogram,** *a series of bars whose widths indicate class intervals and whose areas indicate corresponding frequencies.* Figure 3.2 is a histogram showing the end-of-period stock-value data of Table 3.3. The frequency in each class is represented by a bar whose width equals that of a class interval and whose height shows the frequency in the class.

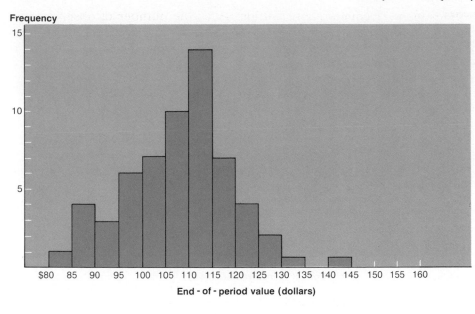

Figure 3.2

Frequency
distribution
of end-of-
period stock
values:
histogram

THE FREQUENCY POLYGON

The **frequency polygon** is an alternative way of displaying the frequency distribution. In Figure 3.3*a* we reproduce the end-of-period value histogram, but this time we add a bold dot to all the midpoints of the top portions of the histogram's bars. Two additional bold dots are placed on the horizontal axis one-half standard width to the left of the lowest class and one-half standard width to the right of the highest class.[2] From this we construct the frequency polygon, shown in Figure 3.3*b*, where the histogram bars have been removed and the bold dots of Figure 3.3*a* are connected with straight line segments. The frequency polygon of 3.3*b* basically represents the same data as the histogram of 3.3*a*, and the choice between them is largely a matter of personal taste. The histogram may look more appealing to some, and the polygon may better suit the tastes of others.

TREATING UNEQUAL CLASS INTERVALS
AND OPEN-ENDED INTERVALS

We sometimes have to present frequency distributions with unequal class intervals, perhaps because we lack full information for some intervals on the specific frequencies that lead to their aggregation or because the data appear very frequently in one section of the distribution and very infrequently in another. When presented in a histogram, the height of the histogram bars in such cases must be adjusted to the width of the interval, so that the *area* of the bars will be proportional to their frequencies.

To see how this is done, consider Table 3.4, which shows the charity donations of a group of 184 individuals as reported on their tax returns. Here we choose the $50 class width to be a "standard width" and adjust the

---

[2] In some frequency distributions not all the class intervals are of the same width (see later discussion): some intervals might be nonstandard in that they are wider than most of the others. This is the reason for the reference to "standard width."

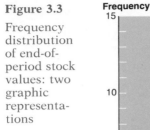

Figure 3.3

Frequency
distribution
of end-of-
period stock
values: two
graphic
representa-
tions

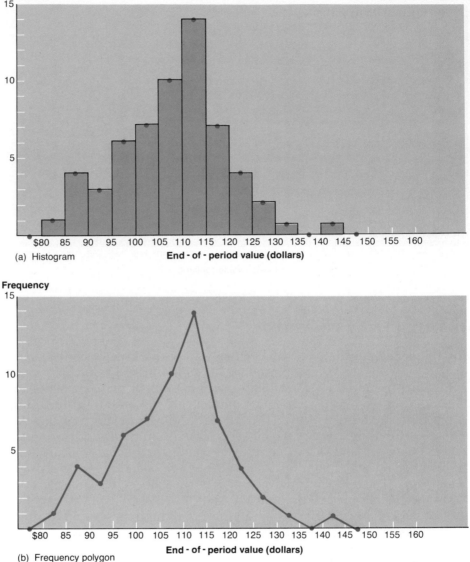

(a) Histogram

(b) Frequency polygon

frequency in nonstandard intervals accordingly.[3] For example, the class "Over 200–400" is 4 times as wide as a standard width (of $50); therefore, a frequency of 40 donors in this interval represents a frequency of 40/4 = 10 donors per $50 interval. Figure 3.4 presents the data of Table 3.4 in a histogram, where the vertical axis measures the frequency per standard width of $50, a method that assures that the area of each bar will be proportional to the frequency it represents.

In some cases, frequency distributions include open-ended class intervals ("Over $500," "Less than 30 percent," etc.). Such intervals have a lower end but no finite upper end or vice versa and therefore cannot be included in histograms or frequency polygons. Their integration into the analysis is accomplished by nongraphical techniques, such as footnotes.

[3] The class intervals in Table 3.4 are defined somewhat differently from those of Table 3.3. We present both classifications because both are commonly used.

TABLE 3.4
Frequency Distribution of Charity Donations

Class (dollars)	Frequency	Number of standard widths in interval[a]	Frequency per standard width
Up to $50	15	1	15
Over 50–100	26	1	26
Over 100–150	34	1	34
Over 150–200	21	1	21
Over 200–400	40	4	10
Over 400–800	48	8	6
Total	184		

[a]A standard interval is $50 wide.

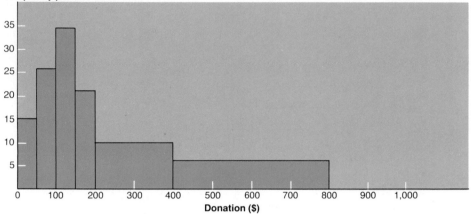

Frequency per $50 width

Donation ($)

Figure 3.4

A histogram of charity donations, with unequal class intervals

3.5 Cumulative Frequency Distribution: "Less Than" and "More Than" Distributions

In Table 3.5 we present two more types of frequency distributions for the data of Table 3.4: the "less than" and the "more than" cumulative distributions. For each starting and ending value of the classes of Table 3.4, the **"less than" cumulative frequency distribution** provides the *total of all the*

TABLE 3.5
"Less Than" and "More Than" Cumulative Frequency Distributions of Charity Donations

Donation	Cumulative frequency distribution	
	"Less than"	"More than"
$ 0	0	184
50	15	169
100	41	143
150	75	109
200	96	88
400	136	48
800	184	0

frequencies of values that are less than or equal to that value, and the **"more than" cumulative frequency distribution** provides the *total of all the frequencies of values that are greater than that value.* To see how many donors have donated money to charity in amounts that are less than or equal to $200, we use the "less than" distribution and find that there were 96 such donors. The "more than" distribution shows, for example, that 143 donors have donated money in amounts greater than $100. The *graph of a cumulative frequency distribution* is called an **ogive.** The "less than" and "more than" ogives for the data in Table 3.5 are shown in Figure 3.5. As we can see, the ogives are obtained by connecting the cumulative values of the starting and ending values of the classes with straight lines. This implies that as an approximation we assume an even distribution of frequency within each interval.

Figure 3.5

"Less than" and "more than" ogives of charity donations

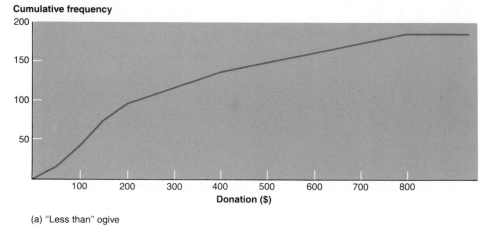

(a) "Less than" ogive

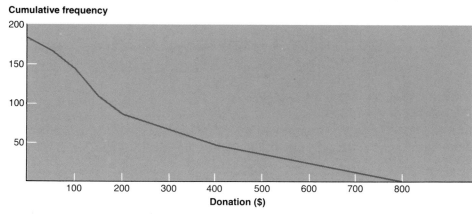

(b) "More than" ogive

3.6 Relative Frequency and Cumulative Relative Frequency Distributions

The frequency distribution shows the *number* of observations in each of the variable's classes. The sum of the frequencies in all the classes equals the total number of observations in the data. If we divide the frequency in each class by the total number of observations, we obtain the *ratio* of the number of observations in the class to the total size of the data set. Let us take an example. Table 3.6 provides the frequency and relative frequency distributions of auto collision damages in city *A* during 1983 according to the amount of damages. We obtain the **relative frequency** column by dividing each of the frequencies in column 2 by the total size of the data set, 380. So the first number in the "relative frequency" column is 56/380 = 0.15, the second number is 128/380 = 0.34, and so on, meaning that 15 percent of the collision damages in city *A* in 1983 were for amounts of up to $1,000, 34 percent were for amounts of over $1,000 and up to $2,000, and so on. The total of the "relative frequency" column is 1.00 (that is, 100 percent), meaning that all of the observations were tabulated.

TABLE 3.6
Frequency and Relative Frequency Distributions of Auto Collision Damages in City *A*, 1983

(1) Damages (dollars)	(2) Frequency	(3) = (2) ÷ 380 Relative frequency
Up to $1,000	56	0.15
Over 1,000–2,000	128	0.34
Over 2,000–3,000	115	0.30
Over 3,000–4,000	81	0.21
Total	380	1.00

The relative frequency distribution is particularly useful for comparing two or more data sets. In Table 3.7, 1983 collision damage data are provided for cities *A* and *B*. Even though both of the frequency distributions are listed side by side over the same categories, it is hard to make a meaningful comparison directly from Table 3.7, because the totals of the data sets differ. When the relative frequencies of both cities are contrasted, however, the differences and similarities become evident. The relative frequency distributions are shown in Table 3.8. A glance at the table shows that in both cities a substantial portion of the damages are for amounts of $2,000 or less and that the proportion of damages declines as amounts rise. A more careful look at Table 3.8 reveals that the major difference between the cities is that the relative frequency of the lower classes is greater in city *B*, while the relative frequency of the higher classes is greater in city *A*. This difference is further emphasized by the "less than" cumulative relative frequency distribution presented in Table 3.9. The "less than" cumulative relative frequency distribution shows the *total* of the relative frequencies up to and

TABLE 3.7
Frequency Distributions of Auto Collision Damages in City *A* and City *B*, 1983

Damages (dollars)	City A	City B
Up to $1,000	56	304
Over 1,000–2,000	128	591
Over 2,000–3,000	115	431
Over 3,000–4,000	81	272
Total	380	1,598

TABLE 3.8
Relative Frequency Distributions of Auto Collision Damages in City *A* and City *B*, 1983

Damages (dollars)	City A	City B
Up to $1,000	0.15	0.19
Over 1,000–2,000	0.34	0.37
Over 2,000–3,000	0.30	0.27
Over 3,000–4,000	0.21	0.17
Total	1.00	1.00

TABLE 3.9
Cumulative Relative Frequency Distribution ("Less Than" Type) of Auto Collision Damages in City *A* and City *B*, 1983

Damages (dollars)	City A	City B
Up to $1,000	0.15	0.19
Up to $2,000	0.49	0.56
Up to $3,000	0.79	0.83
Up to $4,000	1.00	1.00

including a specified value of the variable of interest and is obtained directly from the relative frequency distribution by accumulation.

The cumulative relative frequency distribution is a very useful descriptive measure of the data. It shows, for instance, that in city *A*, 49 percent of all damages in 1983 were of amounts up to $2,000, 79 percent of the damages were of amounts up to $3,000, and so on. A comparison of two or more cumulative relative frequency distributions sometimes proves useful. In our example, for each value on the stub of Table 3.9, the proportion in city *B* is greater than that in city *A*, meaning that for each such value the proportion of damages in city *B* of amounts *less than* that value is greater. For example, 56 percent of the damages were of amounts up to $2,000 in city *B* as compared to only 49 percent in city *A*; 83 percent of the damages were of amounts up to $3,000 in city *B* compared to only 79 percent in city *A*; and so on. We

Figure 3.6

Histograms of relative frequency distributions of auto collision damages in city *A* and city *B*, 1983

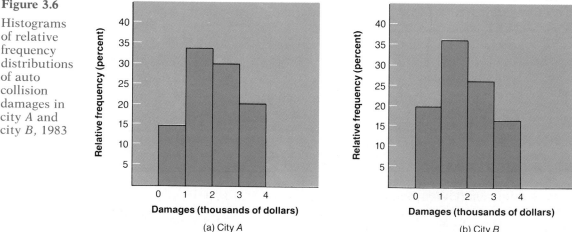

(a) City A

(b) City B

thus see a definite pattern: claims tend to be for lower amounts in city *B* than in city *A*.

Both the relative frequency and the cumulative relative frequency distributions are often presented diagrammatically by a histogram and an ogive, as their respective nonrelative counterparts are. Figure 3.6 shows histograms of the data in Table 3.8, and ogives of the data in Table 3.9 are shown in Figure 3.7.

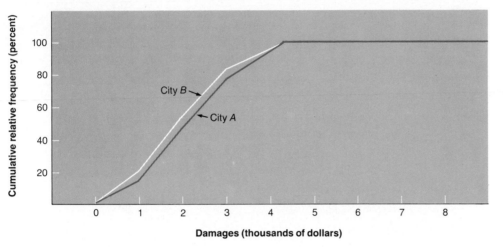

Figure 3.7

Cumulative frequency distributions ("less than" type) of auto collision damages in city *A* and city *B*, 1983

3.7 Determining the Width of Classes in a Frequency Distribution

Up to this point we have assumed that the class limits are given and have focused on deriving and interpreting frequency distributions. Now it is time for us to discuss the way the class width is determined.

There is no formula or rigid rule concerning the determination of class width, but we can offer some valuable guidelines. The key to this problem is the tradeoff between the amount of detail revealed by a large number of classes, on the one hand, and the general pattern of the data revealed by a smaller number of classes, on the other hand. As we reduce the number of classes in a frequency distribution, we eliminate details, and the general pattern of the data becomes clearer. At a given point, however, a further reduction of the number of classes would not only conceal more details but would make it more and more difficult to learn about the overall shape of the distribution. At exactly what level of aggregation this negative tradeoff occurs we cannot say, as the level differs from one case to another. Experience and judgment must be used to determine an optimal breakdown into class intervals. Let us consider an example of a tradeoff.

EXAMPLE 3.1

The weekly orders of a large department store are regularly teletyped to a regional warehouse, where they are processed and from which the merchandise is shipped to the store. Although the store management maintains a carefully planned inventory policy, stockouts are unavoidable because the store carries virtually thousands of items for which the demand varies from day to day. When stockouts occur or when the store's inventory of a given item reaches a low level, a priority order (that is, an emergency order) is teletyped. Such orders are usually sent in the late afternoon or evening, and the merchandise is supposed to reach the store during the following night, to be displayed on the shelf or stored in the storage room the next morning. In Table 3.10, we show the number of hours that elapse between the typing of the priority orders and the arrival of the merchandise in the store on 40 specific working days.

Considering a frequency distribution with half-hour intervals first, we construct a tally table (Table 3.11). From the tally table we derive the frequency distribution (Table 3.12).

Now consider Table 3.13, a more condensed frequency distribution in which one-hour intervals are used.

Finally, suppose we choose only two classes: "Over 4–10" and "Over 10–22." In this case our frequency distribution will be as follows:

Delivery time (hours)	Frequency
Over 4–10	22
Over 10–22	18
Total	40

Figure 3.8 shows the histograms of the frequency distributions obtained by the use of the three alternate classifications. While all three diagrams present the very same data, the differences between them reflect the

TABLE 3.10
Elapsed Time between Sending of Priority Orders and Arrival of Merchandise on 40 Working Days

Day of priority order	Delivery time (hours)	Day of priority order	Delivery time (hours)
1	5.2	21	8.4
2	4.3	22	9.8
3	7.9	23	10.0
4	9.5	24	9.5
5	7.7	25	8.9
6	22.0	26	9.5
7	10.0	27	10.5
8	8.3	28	12.0
9	10.8	29	12.5
10	9.0	30	7.6
11	11.3	31	10.0
12	8.2	32	20.0
13	11.2	33	10.0
14	10.5	34	9.2
15	12.0	35	12.4
16	11.5	36	11.0
17	17.0	37	13.0
18	8.5	38	8.0
19	13.0	39	10.5
20	9.6	40	13.4

TABLE 3.11
Tally Table for Frequency Distribution of Data in Table 3.10

Delivery time (hours)	Tally
Over 4.0– 4.5	|
Over 4.5– 5.0	
Over 5.0– 5.5	|
Over 5.5– 6.0	
Over 6.0– 6.5	
Over 6.5– 7.0	
Over 7.0– 7.5	
Over 7.5– 8.0	||||
Over 8.0– 8.5	||||
Over 8.5– 9.0	||
Over 9.0– 9.5	||||
Over 9.5–10.0	|||| |
Over 10.0–10.5	|||
Over 10.5–11.0	||
Over 11.0–11.5	|||
Over 11.5–12.0	||
Over 12.0–12.5	||
Over 12.5–13.0	||
Over 13.0–22.0	||||

TABLE 3.12
Frequency Distribution Based on Half-Hour Intervals

Delivery time (hours)	Frequency
Over 4.0– 4.5	1
Over 4.5– 5.0	0
Over 5.0– 5.5	1
Over 5.5– 6.0	0
Over 6.0– 6.5	0
Over 6.5– 7.0	0
Over 7.0– 7.5	0
Over 7.5– 8.0	4
Over 8.0– 8.5	4
Over 8.5– 9.0	2
Over 9.0– 9.5	4
Over 9.5–10.0	6
Over 10.0–10.5	3
Over 10.5–11.0	2
Over 11.0–11.5	3
Over 11.5–12.0	2
Over 12.0–12.5	2
Over 12.5–13.0	2
Over 13.0–22.0	4
Total	40

TABLE 3.13
Frequency Distribution Based on One-Hour Intervals

Delivery time (hours)	Frequency
Over 4– 5	1
Over 5– 6	1
Over 6– 7	0
Over 7– 8	4
Over 8– 9	6
Over 9–10	10
Over 10–11	5
Over 11–12	5
Over 12–13	4
Over 13–22	4
Total	40

tradeoff between details and general pattern. Figure 3.8*a* shows the most details, but Figure 3.8*b* aggregates some class intervals and gives a better idea of the structure of the frequency distribution. When the process of aggregation continues, even the general structure of the frequency distribution becomes unclear: in Figure 3.8*c*, where only two classes are presented, so many details have been eliminated that very little information is revealed. The most extreme case happens, of course, when we

Figure 3.8

Histograms
of frequency
distributions
obtained by
use of three
alternate
classifications

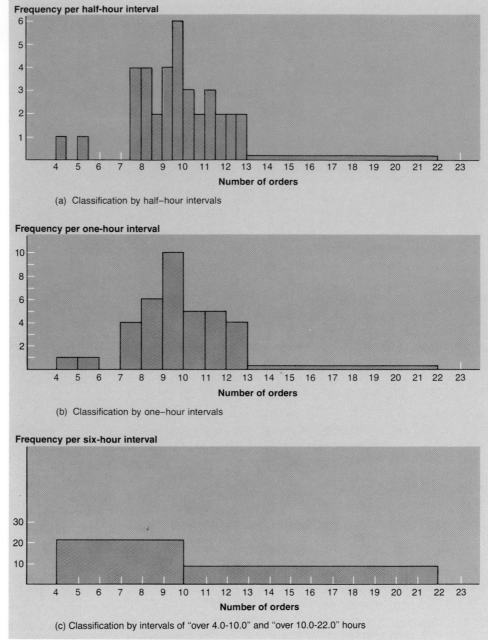

Frequency per half-hour interval

(a) Classification by half–hour intervals

Frequency per one-hour interval

(b) Classification by one–hour intervals

Frequency per six-hour interval

(c) Classification by intervals of "over 4.0-10.0" and "over 10.0-22.0" hours

present all the data in just one class interval. In this case, the histogram contains only one bar, which shows the range of the data and the total number of observations contained in it. Clearly, such a histogram reveals nothing whatsoever about the internal structure of the data; thus its contribution to the data presentation is extremely limited.

Clearly, judgment must be exercised in deciding which interval width to use in presenting a frequency distribution. Whatever the width, however, it is generally *desirable* that the widths of all the classes presented be the same, for ease of reading and interpretation. When class intervals are of unequal widths, misinterpretation can result if the reader overlooks this fact. Nevertheless, although the use of unequal class intervals is undesirable, it is occasionally necessary when one is dealing with data in which the frequency varies greatly from one range to another.

3.8 Using Computers to Construct Frequency Distributions

Computers can be used to construct frequency distributions and to plot histograms of data. In the example shown below, the SAS (Statistical Analysis System developed by SAS Institute) computer package was used to generate a combination of a histogram and a frequency distribution. Data Set 1 (Appendix B, Table B.1) contains data on sales and profits of 100 companies in 1981. For this example we used the sales data. The presentation appears in Figure 3.9, where the histogram is shown vertically. The data were classified into $1,000,000 intervals whose midpoints are shown on the left-hand side of the figure. Accordingly, the first interval ranges from $200,000 to under $1,200,000 with a midpoint at $700,000 (or $700 thousand). The other midpoints were determined in a similar fashion. The frequency in each class is given both by the bar drawn over the midpoint and by the number under the abbreviated frequency title, which shows that the frequency in the first interval is 14, in the second it is 27, and so on. The cumulative frequency, the relative frequency, and the cumulative relative frequency distributions (the last two measured in percentages) are also given. Using the computer program to derive a frequency distribution takes only a few simple commands.

3.9 Exploratory Data Analysis (EDA)

Frequency distributions organize data so that we can study their structure. But at the same time, frequency distributions conceal facts that might be of interest to us. In this section we shall discuss techniques that help uncover such facts.

STEM-AND-LEAF DISPLAYS AND RESIDUAL PLOTS

An assumption we make when we examine a frequency distribution is that the observations are evenly distributed within any interval. This is not always the case: observations might cluster around certain values within the intervals. If we want to reveal possible clustering, we can use the **stem-and-leaf display.** We shall illustrate this technique through examples.

```
                    FREQUENCY HISTOGRAM OF COMPANY SALES


MIDPOINT                                                              CUM.                CUM.
SALES                                                        FREQ     FREQ    PERCENT   PERCENT

   700  |******************************                        14       14     14.00     14.00
  1700  |*******************************************************27       41     27.00     41.00
  2700  |*******************************                       15       56     15.00     56.00
  3700  |**************************                            13       69     13.00     69.00
  4700  |*****************                                      8       77      8.00     77.00
  5700  |**********                                             5       82      5.00     82.00
  6700  |**********                                             5       87      5.00     87.00
  7700  |******                                                 3       90      3.00     90.00
  8700  |                                                       0       90      0.00     90.00
  9700  |****                                                   2       92      2.00     92.00
 10700  |**                                                     1       93      1.00     93.00
 11700  |**                                                     1       94      1.00     94.00
 12700  |                                                       0       94      0.00     94.00
 13700  |**                                                     1       95      1.00     95.00
 14700  |                                                       0       95      0.00     95.00
 15700  |**                                                     1       96      1.00     96.00
 16700  |                                                       0       96      0.00     96.00
 17700  |                                                       0       96      0.00     96.00
 18700  |                                                       0       96      0.00     96.00
 19700  |                                                       0       96      0.00     96.00
 20700  |                                                       0       96      0.00     96.00
 21700  |                                                       0       96      0.00     96.00
 22700  |****                                                   2       98      2.00     98.00
 23700  |                                                       0       98      0.00     98.00
 24700  |                                                       0       98      0.00     98.00
 25700  |                                                       0       98      0.00     98.00
 26700  |                                                       0       98      0.00     98.00
 27700  |                                                       0       98      0.00     98.00
 28700  |                                                       0       98      0.00     98.00
 29700  |                                                       0       98      0.00     98.00
 30700  |                                                       0       98      0.00     98.00
 31700  |                                                       0       98      0.00     98.00
 32700  |                                                       0       98      0.00     98.00
 33700  |                                                       0       98      0.00     98.00
 34700  |                                                       0       98      0.00     98.00
 35700  |                                                       0       98      0.00     98.00
 36700  |                                                       0       98      0.00     98.00
 37700  |                                                       0       98      0.00     98.00
 38700  |**                                                     1       99      1.00     99.00
 39700  |                                                       0       99      0.00     99.00
 40700  |                                                       0       99      0.00     99.00
 41700  |                                                       0       99      0.00     99.00
 42700  |                                                       0       99      0.00     99.00
 43700  |                                                       0       99      0.00     99.00
 44700  |                                                       0       99      0.00     99.00
 45700  |                                                       0       99      0.00     99.00
 46700  |                                                       0       99      0.00     99.00
 47700  |                                                       0       99      0.00     99.00
 48700  |                                                       0       99      0.00     99.00
 49700  |                                                       0       99      0.00     99.00
 50700  |                                                       0       99      0.00     99.00
 51700  |                                                       0       99      0.00     99.00
 52700  |                                                       0       99      0.00     99.00
 53700  |                                                       0       99      0.00     99.00
 54700  |                                                       0       99      0.00     99.00
 55700  |                                                       0       99      0.00     99.00
 56700  |                                                       0       99      0.00     99.00
 57700  |                                                       0       99      0.00     99.00
 58700  |                                                       0       99      0.00     99.00
 59700  |                                                       0       99      0.00     99.00
 60700  |                                                       0       99      0.00     99.00
 61700  |                                                       0       99      0.00     99.00
 62700  |**                                                     1      100      1.00    100.00
 63700  |                                                       0      100      0.00    100.00
 64700  |                                                       0      100      0.00    100.00
        ----+---+---+---+---+---+---+---+---+---+---+---+---+---+
            2   4   6   8   10  12  14  16  18  20  22  24  26
                                 FREQUENCY
```

Source: Data Set 1, Appendix B, Table B.1.

Figure 3.9

SAS computer output showing frequency distribution of company sales

EXAMPLE 3.2

The credit department of a large department store chain regularly receives credit applications. One of the questions asked in the application is the annual income of the applicant. Figure 3.10*a* is a stem-and-leaf display of the incomes (in thousands of dollars) of applicants. The display is organized in the following way: the first digit of the income, "the stem," is placed to the left of the vertical line, and the last digit only, "the leaf," is placed to the right of it. All incomes from $10,000 to $19,000 are recorded on the first stem. Accordingly, the following incomes are displayed on the first stem: $12,000; $15,000; $15,000; $15,000; and $18,000. Other incomes are recorded on their respective stems. The "leaves" on each stem are shown as an **array**, which means that they are *organized in an increasing or decreasing order.* Thus the stem-and-leaf display not only provides information similar to that provided by a frequency distribution, but in addition gives the internal distribution of the data in the intervals. In Figure 3.10*a*, for example, we find a disproportionately large number of incomes ending with 0 and with 5. With 40 incomes in the display and 10 ending digits (0 through 9), we can expect on average a frequency of 4 for each ending digit. However, the display shows 11 incomes ending with the digit 0 and 9 incomes ending with the digit 5. Part *b* of Figure 3.10 supplements part *a*. It is a **residual plot,** which *shows the residual (i.e., the difference) between the actual frequency and the expected frequency for each digit.* The frequency of 0 is 11, which is 7 greater than the 4 expected (11 − 4 = 7). Accordingly, in Figure 3.10*b* the digit 0 is presented with a residual of 7. The actual

Figure 3.10

Stem-and-leaf display and residual plot of credit applicants' income

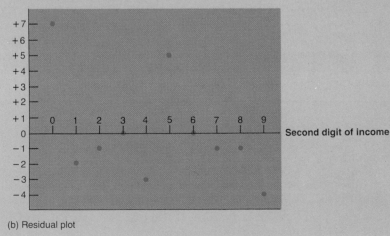

1	2 5 5 5 8
2	0 0 0 0 2 3 5 7
3	0 0 0 1 3 3 4 5 5 8
4	0 0 2 6 6 7 7
5	0 0 1 3 5 6
6	5 5 6 8

(a) Stem-and-leaf display

Residual (thousands of dollars)

(b) Residual plot

frequency of the digit 1 is 2, which is 2 less than the expected frequency. Thus, the residual is -2. The residual plot shows that only the digits 0 and 5 have positive (and large) residuals. It seems very likely that the applicants tend to round off their income (probably upward), and the credit department might decide to examine rounded incomes further in order to obtain more reliable information on these applicants.

EXAMPLE 3.3

The level of impurities in a certain chemical is not allowed to exceed 100 milligrams per liter. The production process is regularly checked by inspectors who measure the level of impurities in the chemical. If the level of impurities is below the allowed level, the chemical is "accepted" and is ready for use. If it is above the allowed level, an inspector must "reject" the chemical and decide to reprocess it. Sixty such measurements are shown in Figure 3.11, which is a stem-and-leaf display of the

Figure 3.11

Stem-and-leaf display of the level of impurities in a chemical (milligrams)

```
 6 | 0  1  2  3  5  8
 7 | 0  1  2  2  3  4  5  7  8  9
 8 | 1  3  4  5  6  6  7  7  8  9  9
 9 | 0  0  1  2  2  6  7  8  8  9  9  9  9  9  9  9  9
10 | 6  8  8
11 | 1  4  5  6  7  8
12 | 1  3  4  5  9
13 | 0  1
```

measurements. For 60 observations we would expect a frequency of about 6 of each digit (0 through 9) among the "leaves." Upon inspection of Figure 3.11 we discover a very high frequency in the fourth stem (90) and a very low frequency in the fifth (100). This indicates a possibility that the inspectors who are in charge of measuring the level of impurities and of deciding the acceptance or rejection of the chemicals tend to accept chemicals whose level of impurities is slightly above the cutoff level of 100 milligrams. The stem-and-leaf display presents information that reinforces this view. Inspection of the stems 90 and 100 shows a high incidence of the digits 8 and 9. It appears that measurements of 100 to 105 were systematically rounded off to 99 or 98 to allow the chemical to be "accepted." This behavior calls for remedial action: the inspectors must become aware of the damage they cause by classifying chemicals as acceptable when they are not.

3.10 APPLICATION:
ANALYSIS OF CUMULATIVE FREQUENCY DISTRIBUTIONS FOR INSURANCE PURPOSES

In its simplest form, life insurance consists of a contractual agreement that works in the following way: the insured person pays the insurance company a certain amount of money every year. This amount is called the premium. If the insured dies during the year, the company pays his or her beneficiaries (usually family members) an amount that has been agreed upon in advance. The higher the amount pledged to the beneficiaries in the event of the death of the insured, the higher the premium. If the insured survives, the insurance company keeps the premium and has no further obligations toward the insured.

Clearly, the insurance premium is related to the probability of the insured's survival. The greater the chance of survival, the lower the premium charged by the insurance company.

All comparative life insurance analyses are based on the premium per $1,000 insurance benefits. For example, if the insured buys a $50,000 life insurance policy (that is, $50,000 will be paid to the beneficiaries at the death of the insured) and the premium is $250 per year, the premium per $1,000 is $5 $\left(= \dfrac{\$250}{\$50,000} \cdot \$1,000 \right)$. From now on, unless we say otherwise, we shall be considering the premium per $1,000 insurance coverage.

Suppose a U.S.-based insurance company is contemplating a plan to expand its operations and offer life insurance to people in Madagascar. As an exploratory step, the company wants to know whether it can offer the insurance in Madagascar at the same premiums it charges in the United States or whether it should charge higher or lower premiums.

The data for the analysis are given in Table 3.14. It shows the frequency of male deaths by age in the United States and Madagascar. Male deaths per 100,000 are given for each country; that is, the data show how many males in each group (of 100,000) die on the average in the first year of life (class 0–1), between their first and fifth years (class 1–5), and so on. Figure 3.12 depicts the ogive of deaths per 100,000 males in the

TABLE 3.14
Death Frequency of Males in U.S. and Madagascar, by Age Group
(per 100,000 males)

	United States		Madagascar	
Age group[a]	Frequency of deaths	Cumulative frequency	Frequency of deaths	Cumulative frequency
0– 1	2,060	2,060	17,584	17,584
1– 5	352	2,412	5,575	23,159
5–10	229	2,641	1,585	24,744
10–15	246	2,887	858	25,602
15–20	772	3,659	1,371	26,973
20–25	1,061	4,720	1,954	28,927
25–30	955	5,675	1,934	30,861
30–35	1,054	6,729	2,093	32,954
35–40	1,411	8,140	2,487	35,441
40–45	2,111	10,251	3,059	38,500
45–50	3,306	13,557	3,830	42,330
50–55	4,789	18,346	4,884	47,214
55–60	7,085	25,431	6,186	53,400
60–65	9,617	35,048	7,682	61,082
65–70	11,828	46,876	9,262	70,344
70–75	13,836	60,712	10,169	80,513
75–80	14,216	74,928	9,377	89,890
80 +	25,072	100,000	10,110	100,000

[a]The class interval 0–1 includes the first birthday; the class interval 1–5 does not include the first birthday but includes the fifth. Other class intervals are defined similarly.

Source: Samuel H. Preston, Nathan Keyfitz, and Robert Schoen, *Causes of Death: Life Tables for National Populations* (New York: Seminar Press, 1972).

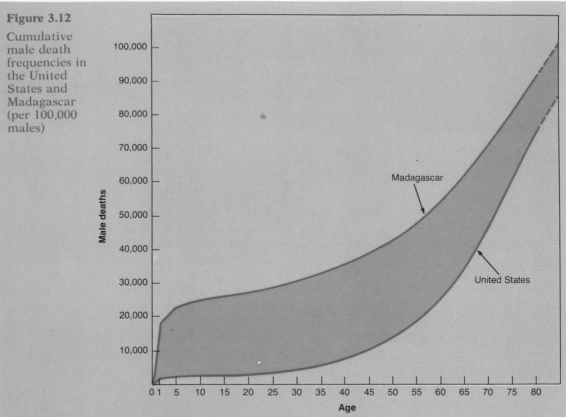

Figure 3.12

Cumulative male death frequencies in the United States and Madagascar (per 100,000 males)

Source: U.S. data from Preston et al., op. cit.

United States and Madagascar. As the figure shows, the ogive of the United States is to the right of the ogive of the male population of Madagascar—a clear indication that males in the United States enjoy greater longevity than those in Madagascar. In every age group we find more male deaths at or prior to that age in Madagascar than in the United States. Consider, for example, the 40-year-olds. For every 100,000 males there are 35,441 deaths of males 40 years old or younger in Madagascar, compared to 8,140 in the United States. This relationship (higher cumulative frequency in Madagascar than in the United States) holds not only for the age of 40 but also for *each and every age we choose to examine.* (Of course, the cumulative frequency in the age interval 80+ is 100,000 in both countries.)

Since the probability of dying at a younger age is greater in Madagascar for any age we choose, the incumbent risk the insurance company takes in Madagascar is greater, and it is obvious that higher premiums must be charged there than in the United States. Using conditional probability (Chapter 5) it is possible to determine how much higher the premiums must be.

Chapter Summary and Review

1. Definitions
   a. Frame: The totality of all the elementary units of interest
   b. Observation: An item of information of interest concerning the elementary units in the frame

    c. Population: The totality of all individual observations of interest in the frame

    d. Sample: A portion of the population

    e. Random sample: Each observation in the population has a known chance to be selected

    f. Array: Quantitative data organized in an increasing or decreasing order

2. Reasons for sampling

    a. Census is impossible with infinite population.

    b. Cost is lower.

    c. Accuracy is increased by concentrating the effort on a smaller number of observations.

    d. Results are obtained quickly.

    e. Other reasons: units are destroyed by observing; populations are not easily accessible.

3. Presentation of the data set: for samples and populations alike

    a. A frequency distribution shows the number of observations in each class interval.

    b. A histogram is a graphic display of a frequency distribution using bars.

    c. A polygon is a graphic display of a frequency distribution using a line graph.

    d. Cumulative frequency distributions

        1. A "less than" cumulative frequency distribution provides the total of all the frequencies of values smaller than or equal to a given value.

        2. A "more than" cumulative frequency distribution provides the total of frequencies of values that are greater than a given value.

    e. Relative frequency distributions provide the ratio of the number of observations in each class to the total number of observations in the data set.

    f. A stem-and-leaf display gives information similar to that of a frequency distribution, but while the latter does not provide a clue about the internal distribution of the frequency within a class interval, the former does.

Problems

3.1. Briefly explain each of the following:

    (*a*) Frame
    (*b*) Population
    (*c*) Sample
    (*d*) Census

3.2. Distinguish between a population and a sample. What determines whether a data set is considered a population or a sample?

3.3. Explain what a tally table is and what its purpose is.

3.4. Briefly explain each of the following:

    (*a*) Frequency distribution
    (*b*) Cumulative frequency distribution
    (*c*) Relative frequency distribution
    (*d*) Cumulative relative frequency distribution

3.5. Distinguish between the frequency polygon and the ogive.

3.6. What are the advantages and disadvantages of having too many class intervals in a frequency distribution? What are the advantages and disadvantages of having too few?

3.7. The following is a list of the Grade Point Averages (GPAs) of 36 students in a class, rounded off to the nearest tenth:

2.0	3.0	2.8
1.5	3.9	1.9
3.3	4.0	3.0
2.0	3.3	2.3
3.6	2.2	1.5
2.8	2.0	2.5
3.3	2.7	2.8
2.9	2.5	2.7
1.9	3.7	2.4
3.2	2.5	4.0
1.4	2.7	1.9
2.6	2.0	2.4

    (*a*) Rearrange the GPAs in ascending order.
    (*b*) Construct a frequency distribution, using an interval width of 0.1. How many class intervals do you have?
    (*c*) Reconstruct the frequency distribution, this time using an interval width of 0.5. How many class intervals do you have?
    (*d*) Reconstruct the frequency distribution one more time, using an interval width of 1.5.
    (*e*) Graph the histograms of the frequency distributions for parts *b*, *c*, and *d*, and discuss the differences among them.

3.8. The following are four different class-interval designations for a frequency distribution of employees' hourly pay in a given company.

(a)	(b)	(c)	(d)
Up to $4.0	$4.0– 7.0	Up to $4.0	Up to $3.99
4.0– 6.0	6.0– 7.0	5.0– 7.0	4.00– 5.99
6.0– 8.0	8.0–11.0	8.0– 10.0	6.00– 7.99
8.0– 10.0	10.0–13.0	11.0 or more	8.00– 9.99
10.0 or more			10.00–11.99
			12.00 or more

Which of the above classifications is appropriate, and what is your specific criticism of each of the other classifications?

3.9. Why is it important to have intervals of equal width in a frequency distribution?

3.10. The rates of return earned by 80 industrial stocks in the past year are presented in a frequency distribution in Table P3.10.

TABLE P3.10

Rate of return (percent)	Frequency
(-20.00)–under (-10.00)	5
(-10.00)–under $\quad 0.00$	15
$\quad 0.00$–under $\quad 10.00$	12
$\quad 10.00$–under $\quad 20.00$	23
$\quad 20.00$–under $\quad 30.00$	18
$\quad 30.00$–under $\quad 40.00$	7
Total	80

(a) Plot the "less than" cumulative relative frequency distribution of the rates of return.
(b) From the graph, determine the rate of return below which 70 percent of the distribution lies.
(c) From the graph, determine the two rates of return between which the center 50 percent of the distribution lies.

3.11. The Center for Management Development conducts conferences, seminars, and courses for top and middle management of business firms. Fifty-one managers have participated in three courses on organizational behavior. Their ages are given in Table P3.11.

TABLE P3.11

Participant	Age	Participant	Age	Participant	Age
1	39	18	53	35	43
2	33	19	40	36	49
3	47	20	40	37	37
4	32	21	42	38	49
5	39	22	35	39	33
6	38	23	50	40	43
7	46	24	33	41	36
8	42	25	57	42	39
9	36	26	38	43	37
10	32	27	43	44	54
11	45	28	37	45	44
12	40	29	40	46	36
13	58	30	34	47	41
14	41	31	43	48	35
15	41	32	39	49	34
16	40	33	35	50	40
17	38	34	59	51	39

(a) Set up a tally table of the participants' ages using age intervals of 3 years, starting at age 30.
(b) Using the tally table, construct a frequency distribution of the ages.
(c) Construct a frequency distribution of the ages using class intervals of 6 years.
(d) Discuss the significance of the interval width. For example, would a class interval of 1 year be appropriate for the case at hand? Explain.

3.12. The loans of a certain bank on December 31, 1980, and on December 31, 1983, by amount, are presented in Table P3.12.

TABLE P3.12

Loan amount (thousands of dollars)	Frequency 12/31/80	Frequency 12/31/83
Under $2,000	900	80
2,000–under 4,000	2,400	1,500
4,000–under 6,000	1,800	1,550
6,000–under 8,000	700	3,400
8,000–under 10,000	150	200
10,000 or more	50	70
Total	6,000	6,800

Derive the relative frequency distribution for December 31, 1980, and for December 31, 1983. Analyze the change that has occurred in the distribution of the loan amounts.

3.13. The management of a food chain has gathered information about the maximum length of time (in days) during which blueberry yogurt stays fresh after it has been brought to the store and put in the freezer. Following are the data gathered for 120 blueberry yogurt cups of three different brands (*A*, *B*, and *C*) as marked:

	Brand A					Brand B				Brand C	
33	33	35	28	32		30	29	28	30	36	35
29	33	32	34	33		29	32	32	32	37	38
34	35	34	33	29		34	26	33	31	34	39
34	31	29	30	33		35	29	30	27	33	35
35	33	34	33	32		30	28	36	29	36	36
32	36	32	31	30		29	35	29	30	36	40
34	34	36	33	32		36	29	31	28	38	37
33	30	32	31	31		28	30	35	31	34	39
35	35	34	32	32		32	28	26	30	37	36
31	33	35	31	32		29	28	26	30	35	38
30	31	36	32	29		25	28	34	27		
				33							

(a) Derive the frequency distribution of yogurt freshness for the brands *A*, *B*, and *C*, as well as for the entire data set combined. When deriving the frequency distribution, do not group the days into intervals. (That is, determine the frequency for 25 days, for 26 days, for 27 days, and so on, without grouping.) Draw histograms of the frequency distributions.

(b) Which of the frequency distributions—the separate ones or the one combining the entire population—is more important for the food chain's management? Explain.

(c) Rework part *a*, but this time derive the *relative* frequency distributions. Are the relative frequency distributions more useful than the frequency distributions for making comparisons? Explain.

3.14. Table P3.14 presents the top 50 managers of pensions by the number of accounts they managed in 1978 and 1979.

TABLE P3.14

1978 rank	1979 rank	Name of manager	Number of accounts 1979	Number of accounts 1978
1	1	Morgan Guaranty Trust	115	119
2	2	Equitable Life	91	89
3	3	Bankers Trust	66	72
4	4	Citibank	51	59
5	5	Harris Trust	47	45
6	6	Prudential Insurance	45	44
10		Wells Fargo Investment Advisors	45	34
6	8	Price (T. Rowe) Associates	41	44
21		Sarofim (Fayez) & Co.	41	26
8	10	Chase Investors Management	39	41
9	11	Putnam Advisory	38	40
11	12	Metropolitan Life Insurance	36	33
13	13	Brown Brothers Harriman	35	32
11		John Hancock	35	33
14	15	Capital Guardian Trust	34	31
30	16	Batterymarch Financial Management	32	20
14		Jennison Associates	32	31
16	18	Scudder, Stevens & Clark	31	30
23	19	Aetna Life & Casualty	29	25
39	20	Delaware Investment Advisers	28	17
18	21	Chemical Bank	27	28
17	22	Endowment Management & Research	26	29
23		Manufacturers Hanover Trust	26	25
19		Mellon Bank	26	27
23		National Bank of Detroit	26	25
27	26	Alliance Capital Management	24	23
21		National Investment Services	24	26
19	28	First National Bank of Chicago	23	27
30		Fischer, Francis, Trees & Watts	23	20
37		State Street Research & Management	23	18
29	31	FMR Investment Management	22	21
23		MacKay-Shields Financial	22	25
30		Rosenberg Capital Management	22	20
30	34	BA Investment Management	21	20
35		Travelers Insurance	21	19
37	36	U.S. Trust	20	18
30	37	American National Bank & Trust	19	20
28		First National Bank of Boston	19	22
39	39	Connecticut General	18	17
35		Thorndike, Doran, Paine & Lewis	18	19
46		Trust Co. of the West	18	14
41	42	Babson (David L.) & Co.	17	16
41		Cleveland Trust	17	16
59		Lord Abbett	17	8
44	45	Eberstadt (F.) & Co.	16	15
50		IDS Advisory	16	12
41	47	Crocker Investment Management	15	16
46		Loomis Sayles	15	14
63	49	BEA Associates	14	7
46		First National Bank in Dallas	14	14

Source: © *Institutional Investor*, April 1979, p. 73.

(a) Derive the frequency distributions of the number of accounts for 1978 and 1979. Use intervals of 10 accounts, starting at 0.

(b) Using the frequency distributions of part *a*, draw the "less than" ogive for each of the two years, and compare the two ogives. What is your conclusion?

3.15. Table P3.15 presents the percentage change in the average prices of stocks in leading countries around the world for periods of 3, 6, 9, and 12 months, ending on April 30, 1982.

TABLE P3.15

	Rank	3 months % change	6 months % change	9 months % change	12 months % change
1	France	9.0%	21.2%	22.2%	1.7%
2	Netherlands	6.9	13.9	2.8	2.6
3	West Germany	3.4	5.4	−3.7	−0.9
4	Switzerland	1.2	3.9	−6.5	−8.0
5	Belgium	0.9	34.2	31.0	15.6
6	Italy	0.3	5.3	−6.0	−25.0
7	Denmark	0.1	5.7	10.2	24.3
8	United Kingdom	−0.1	15.5	4.5	0.5
9	Spain	−1.5	−2.9	−6.4	8.0
10	United States	−3.0	−4.0	−10.7	−11.7
11	Hongkong	−4.8	4.3	−24.8	−10.0
12	Austria	−5.1	−2.6	−9.0	−12.4
13	Australia	−5.4	−6.4	−20.3	−30.6
14	Singapore	−5.7	12.3	−11.7	−20.7
15	Japan	−7.2	−1.2	−10.0	−3.1
16	Sweden	−7.2	−1.3	3.8	31.6
17	Norway	−12.7	−16.0	−15.3	−10.4
18	Canada	−13.3	−16.3	−32.3	−33.3
	The World Index	−3.4	−1.1	−9.6	−9.6

Source: © *Institutional Investor*, June 1982, p. 44.

(a) Derive the frequency distribution for the 3-month and for the 12-month percentage changes, using intervals of 5 percentage points each, starting at −35 percent. (That is, the first interval is −35.0 to −30.1, the second interval is −30.0 to −25.1, the third interval is −25.0 to −20.1, and so on.)

(b) Draw the "less than" ogives for the 3-month and the 12-month data on the same diagram. Can you explain the relationship between the two graphs?

3.16. The dividends paid out as a percentage of net income by 30 manufacturing firms last year were as follows:

Firm	Percentage paid out	Firm	Percentage paid out
1	51.1	16	48.8
2	62.7	17	70.5
3	20.1	18	69.3
4	51.2	19	71.4
5	10.2	20	29.3
6	42.8	21	45.2
7	25.9	22	54.4
8	13.9	23	61.7
9	30.8	24	40.0
10	53.4	25	36.5
11	37.6	26	55.6
12	66.0	27	69.4
13	34.1	28	34.9
14	77.9	29	56.8
15	68.2	30	67.6

(a) Set up a tally table of the data, using intervals of 10.0 percent each and starting at zero.

(b) Write down the frequency distribution of the data, and draw the histogram.

(c) Draw a frequency polygon of the data.

(d) Draw the "less than" and "more than" ogives on one diagram.

(e) Over what percentage dividend payout do the ogives intersect? How many firms have a percentage payout lower than the intersection point, and how many firms have a percentage payout greater than that point? Is this a coincidence? Explain.

3.17. One of the questions on an application for a certain job is the age of the applicant. The classes presented are:

> Up to 24
> 25–28
> 29–32
> 33–36
> 37 or older

(a) In what class does an applicant who is 28 years and 6 months old belong?

(b) What is the interval width of the classes 25–28, 29–32, and 33–36? What are their midpoints?

3.18. Table P3.18 is a list of the 50 largest banks in the world and their deposits and assets in 1981.

TABLE P3.18

Bank	Country	1981 deposits (millions of U.S. dollars)	1981 assets (millions of U.S. dollars)
Bank of America	U.S.	$95,986	$113,092
Banque Nationale de Paris	France	93,018	106,876
Barclays Bank	U.K.	86,812	93,216
Credit Lyonnais	France	84,452	97,924
Credit Agricole	France	80,798	93,838
Deutsche Bank	W. Germany	80,004	85,921
Societe Generale	France	78,154	87,283
National Westminster Bank	U.K.	75,925	82,799
Midland Bank	U.K.	72,175	78,422
Citibank	U.S.	72,040	96,678
Dai-Ichi Kangyo Bank	Japan	67,400	85,430
Royal Bank of Canada	Canada	66,563	72,139
Fuji Bank	Japan	62,730	76,590
Sumitomo Bank	Japan	62,030	79,230
Mitsubishi Bank	Japan	59,030	75,940
Chase Manhattan Bank	U.S.	58,586	73,815
Sanwa Bank	Japan	56,780	68,010
Dresdner Bank	W. Germany	55,574	59,082
Westdeutsche Landesbank	W. Germany	53,849	55,851
Canadian Imperial Bk. of Com.	Canada	50,231	54,363
Industrial Bank of Japan	Japan	49,450	58,020
Lloyds Bank	U.K.	48,391	52,889
Norinchukin Bank	Japan	47,880	57,220
Hongkong & Shanghai Banking	Hongkong	47,500	52,278
Bank of Montreal	Canada	46,658	51,129
Algemene Bank Nederland	Netherlands	44,341	49,600
Mitsui Bank	Japan	44,310	54,030

(Continued)

TABLE P3.18 (*Continued*)

Bank	Country	1981 deposits (millions of U.S. dollars)	1981 assets (millions of U.S. dollars)
Union Bank of Switzerland	Switzerland	44,235	51,886
Banca Nazionale del Lavoro	Italy	43,600	43,600
Swiss Bank Corp.	Switzerland	43,551	48,668
Bank of Tokyo	Japan	43,520	56,120
Commerzbank	W. Germany	43,474	45,404
Tokai Bank	Japan	43,230	52,440
Rabobank Nederland	Netherlands	42,780	44,673
Amsterdam-Rotterdam Bank	Netherlands	42,433	44,197
Manufacturers Hanover Trust	U.S.	42,167	51,603
Bayerische Vereinsbank	W. Germany	41,684	44,294
Long-Term Credit Bank	Japan	41,430	46,200
Hypo-Bank	W. Germany	38,770	40,200
Bayerische Landesbank	W. Germany	38,311	44,743
Mitsubishi Trust & Banking	Japan	38,000	41,350
Morgan Guaranty Trust	U.S.	37,689	50,037
Taiyo Kobe Bank	Japan	37,600	45,060
Credit Suisse	Switzerland	36,473	40,899
Bank of Nova Scotia	Canada	36,392	39,700
Standard Chartered Bank	U.K.	35,066	37,900
Sumitomo Trust & Banking	Japan	33,960	36,830
Banca Commerciale Italiana	Italy	33,800	38,600
Societe Generale de Banque	Belgium	32,786	34,874
Mitsui Trust & Banking	Japan	32,300	36,430

Source: © *Institutional Investor*, July 1982, pp. 188–90.

(*a*) Construct a tally table of the banks' 1981 deposits, using intervals of $10.0 million each and starting at $30.0 million.

(*b*) Using the tally table, derive the frequency distribution of the data.

(*c*) Draw the histogram and the polygon of the frequency distribution obtained in part *b*.

(*d*) Derive the "less than" and the "more than" cumulative frequencies.

(*e*) Draw the "less than" and the "more than" ogives on one chart. What is the deposit amount at which the intersection between the graphs occurs? What proportion of the banks have deposits below the intersection point, and what proportion have deposits above that point? Is this a coincidence? Explain.

3.19. Rework Problem 3.18, but this time do your analysis based on the banks' 1981 assets.

3.20. The diameter of machine parts turned out by a manufacturing process is measured and recorded by inspectors. The parts are acceptable if their diameter is between 0.5985 and 0.6015 inches, and the inspectors are supposed to reject parts which have diameters smaller than 0.5985 inches or greater than 0.6015 inches. A sample of 60 diameters is given below (in inches):

0.6037	0.5973	0.5985	0.6007	0.5994	0.6009
0.5985	0.5985	0.6004	0.5981	0.6011	0.6005
0.6015	0.6015	0.5998	0.6002	0.6015	0.5986
0.5973	0.6029	0.6002	0.6026	0.6010	0.5990
0.5992	0.6001	0.6019	0.6006	0.6005	0.5985
0.6021	0.6001	0.6007	0.6024	0.5989	0.6029
0.5986	0.5985	0.5993	0.5985	0.5991	0.5989
0.6015	0.6010	0.5994	0.6009	0.5996	0.5998
0.5995	0.6022	0.6015	0.6025	0.6008	0.6015
0.6014	0.6028	0.5980	0.5990	0.6038	0.5970

(a) Present the data on a stem-and-leaf display, using the following as stems: 0.597, 0.598, and so on.
(b) Present a residual plot of the data.
(c) What do the presentations in parts *a* and *b* reveal? Explain.

3.21. The retail price of an 8-ounce bottle of skin care lotion in 24 stores is as follows:

$1.69	$1.85	$1.99	$1.92
1.79	1.89	1.87	1.78
1.72	1.77	1.85	1.89
1.75	1.69	1.95	1.89
1.89	1.75	1.69	1.75
1.99	1.94	1.99	1.69

(a) Present the data on a stem-and-leaf display.
(b) Present a residual plot of the data.
(c) What can you say about the product's retail price?

Case Problems

3.1. Table CP3.1 shows the annual rates of return on five types of investments in the years 1926–81. These are rates of profit (or loss) for investors who held their investments for a full year. For example, the rate of return (profit) on common stocks in 1980 was 32.42 percent. In other words, a $100 investment in common stocks in the beginning of 1980 had on average grown to be worth $132.42 at the end of the year.

TABLE CP3.1
Annual Rates of Return on Five Investment Categories, 1926–81
(percent)

	Investment category				
Year	Common stocks	Small stocks	Long-term govt. bonds	Long-term corp. bonds	T. bills
1926	11.62	0.28	7.77	7.37	3.27
1927	37.49	22.10	8.93	7.44	3.12
1928	43.61	39.69	0.10	2.84	3.24
1929	−8.42	−51.36	3.42	3.27	4.75
1930	−24.90	−38.15	4.66	7.98	2.41
1931	−43.34	−49.75	−5.31	−1.85	1.07
1932	−8.19	−5.39	16.84	10.82	0.96
1933	53.99	142.87	−0.08	10.38	0.30
1934	−1.44	24.22	10.02	13.84	0.16
1935	47.67	40.19	4.98	9.61	0.17
1936	33.92	64.80	7.51	6.74	0.18
1937	−35.03	−58.01	0.23	2.75	0.31
1938	31.12	32.80	5.53	6.13	−0.02
1939	−0.41	0.35	5.94	3.97	0.02
1940	−9.78	−5.16	6.09	3.39	0.00
1941	−11.59	−9.00	0.93	2.73	0.06
1942	20.34	44.51	3.22	2.60	0.27
1943	25.90	88.37	2.08	2.83	0.35
1944	19.75	53.72	2.81	4.73	0.33

(*Continued*)

TABLE CP3.1 (*Continued*)
Annual Rates of Return on Five Investment Categories, 1926–81
(percent)

	Investment category				
Year	Common stocks	Small stocks	Long-term govt. bonds	Long-term corp. bonds	T. bills
1945	36.44	73.61	10.73	4.08	0.33
1946	−8.07	−11.63	0.10	1.72	0.35
1947	5.71	0.92	−2.63	−2.34	0.50
1948	5.50	−2.11	3.40	4.14	0.81
1949	18.79	19.75	6.45	3.31	1.10
1950	31.71	38.75	0.06	2.12	1.20
1951	24.02	7.80	−3.94	−2.69	1.49
1952	18.37	3.03	1.16	3.52	1.66
1953	−0.99	−6.49	3.63	3.41	1.82
1954	52.62	60.58	7.19	5.39	0.86
1955	31.56	20.44	−1.30	0.48	1.57
1956	6.56	4.28	−5.59	−6.81	2.46
1957	−10.78	−14.57	7.45	8.71	3.14
1958	43.36	64.89	−6.10	−2.22	1.54
1959	11.95	16.40	−2.26	−0.97	2.95
1960	0.47	−3.29	13.78	9.07	2.66
1961	26.89	32.09	0.97	4.82	2.13
1962	−8.73	−11.90	6.89	7.95	2.73
1963	22.80	23.57	1.21	2.19	3.12
1964	16.48	23.52	3.51	4.77	3.54
1965	12.45	41.75	0.71	−0.46	3.93
1966	−10.06	−7.01	3.65	0.20	4.76
1967	23.98	83.57	−9.19	−4.95	4.21
1968	11.06	35.97	−0.26	2.57	5.21
1969	−8.50	−25.05	−5.08	−8.09	6.58
1970	4.01	−17.43	12.10	18.37	6.53
1971	14.31	16.50	13.23	11.01	4.39
1972	18.98	4.43	5.68	7.26	3.84
1973	−14.66	−30.90	−1.11	1.14	6.93
1974	−26.48	−19.95	4.35	−3.06	8.00
1975	37.20	52.82	9.19	14.64	5.80
1976	23.84	57.38	16.75	18.65	5.08
1977	−7.18	25.38	−0.67	1.71	5.12
1978	6.56	23.46	−1.16	−0.07	7.18
1979	18.44	43.46	−1.22	−4.18	10.38
1980	32.42	39.88	−3.95	−2.62	11.24
1981	−4.91	13.95	1.85	−0.96	14.71

Source: Roger G. Ibbotson and Rex A. Sinquefield, *Stocks, Bonds, Bills, and Inflation: The Past and the Future,* 1982 edition. (Charlottesville, Va.: Financial Analysts Research Foundation, 1982).

(*a*) Present the rate of returns of each of the five types of investments (i.e., common stocks, small stocks, long-term government bonds, long-term corporate bonds, and U.S. Treasury bills) in a frequency distribution, one frequency distribution for each investment type, where the frequency of an interval is measured by the number of years in which the rates of return fall in that interval.

Use the class intervals "(-50) to under (-40)," "(-40) to under (-30)," and so on.

(b) Discuss their similarities and differences.

3.2. (a) Present the sales and profit data of Data Set 1, Appendix B, Table B.1 on one histogram, choosing intervals of $1,000 million width starting at $-$2,000 million.

(b) Present the sales data and the profit data of Data Set 1 in two separate histograms. Use the same class intervals for the sales data as in part a except start at 0 rather than at $-$2,000 million, and use class intervals of $200 million starting at $-$1,200 million for the profit data. Discuss this presentation in comparison with the presentation of part a above. Can you draw a general conclusion?

3.3. The annual rates of return (profit) on 125 mutual funds in the period 1971–80 are presented in Data Set 2, Appendix B, Table B.2. Present the rates of return of the first 10 funds in the "Maximum Capital Gain" category in a histogram. For each fund use the data for the full 10-year period. This way you will have 100 observations: 10 observations for each of the 10 funds. Do the same for the rates of return of the first 5 funds in the "Senior Securities Policy" category. (This category consists of funds that invest primarily in bonds.) In what way are the frequency distributions of the rates of return of the funds in the two categories similar or different?

POPULATION PARAMETERS AND SAMPLE STATISTICS

4

CHAPTER FOUR OUTLINE

Key Terms
parameters
statistics
location measures
dispersion measures
degree of asymmetry
average
mean
arithmetic mean
index
weighted mean
median
percentiles
first quartile
third quartile
fractile
mode
bimodal distribution
skewness
variance
standard deviation
estimator
estimate
unbiasedness
unbiased estimators
biased estimators
Chebyshev's theorem
Empirical Rule
coefficient of variation
interfractile range
interquartile range
range
coefficient of skewness
proportion
geometric mean

While the frequency distribution described in Chapter 3 is an effective tool with which to illustrate data both quantitatively and graphically, additional devices are required for describing data sets easily and clearly. There are two major reasons why such additional devices are needed. First, despite the relative compactness of a frequency distribution, we always welcome further compactness if it can be achieved without significant loss of information. Maximum compactness is particularly appreciated when the problem at hand involves more than one set of data. Second, it is very advantageous from an analytical point of view to be able to separate out and measure *individual characteristics* of the data. The frequency distribution does not separate out individual characteristics.

Thus, we take the additional step of determining certain *quantitative measures of specific characteristics of the data*. These measures are called **parameters** when the data constitute a *population*, and **statistics** when the data constitute a *sample*. The measures we will describe fall into three groups as follows:

1. Location (or central tendency)
2. Dispersion
3. Degree of asymmetry

The advantage of using these measures is that with a separate measure for each characteristic of the data, we can much more conveniently measure and describe differences between data sets as well as variations that occur in a particular data set over time. These variations can then be used to formulate answers to policy questions: the amount by which wages should be allowed to increase in contract negotiations, the degree of additional risk an investment institution should be allowed to undertake, and the like. (The frequency distribution does not directly answer these questions.)

In this chapter, we shall discuss the major **location measures:** the *arithmetic mean*, the *weighted mean*, the *median*, the *mode*, and *percentiles*. The *geometric mean*—also a location parameter—is introduced and contrasted with the arithmetic mean in Appendix 4B. We shall also discuss the major **dispersion measures:** the *variance*, the *standard deviation*, and the *interfractile range*, and touch upon a measure of relative dispersion, the *coefficient of variation*. Then we shall look at a third category of data measures, the **degree of asymmetry,** and discuss *skewness* and *coefficient of skewness*. Finally, we shall consider *proportions*.

4.1 The Arithmetic Mean

The number of years an American young person spends in school before leaving to get a job varies from one person to another and from one population group to another. Consequently, no single number can encompass *all* the information about this variable. This is the case, of course, with any set of data, unless the data are identical to one another. If we say, however, that the *average* number of years Americans spend in school is 12, this figure in itself contains a great deal of information about the subject of interest. In fact, many would argue that among all the *single*-valued measures of quantitative data, the *average* contains the most information.[1] *The* **average** *is also known as the* **mean** *and is denoted by the Greek letter* μ *(pronounced mu) for the population and by* $\overline{X}$ *("X bar") for the sample. It measures the central tendency of the population or the sample; in other words, it measures the data's location.* There are several types of means, and we shall concentrate upon three: the *arithmetic mean*, the *weighted mean*, and the *geometric mean* (discussed in Appendix 4B).

To obtain the **arithmetic mean,** we first *add up the values of all the observations, then divide the sum by the number of data observations.* Let us demonstrate this calculation with an example.

---

[1] Of course, this statement is judgmental and is conceivably open to argument.

EXAMPLE 4.1

Ten marketing courses are currently given at a certain Louisiana college. The numbers of students in these classes are 50, 45, 36, 23, 67, 18, 33, 31, 29, and 42. The mean number of students in a marketing class at the college at the present time is:

$$\frac{50 + 45 + 36 + 23 + 67 + 18 + 33 + 31 + 29 + 42}{10} = \frac{374}{10}$$

$$= 37.4 \text{ students}$$

Following common practice, let us use the letter X to denote the set of data that is given and a subscript to identify each piece of data individually. Thus, the 10 observations of Example 4.1 are respectively denoted $X_1, X_2, X_3, \ldots, X_{10}$, where $X_1 = 50$, $X_2 = 45$, $X_3 = 36$, and so on. The symbols X_1, X_2, X_3, and so on are referred to as "X sub one," "X sub two," "X sub three," or for short, "X one," "X two," "X three."

The subscripts of X constitute a series of consecutive integers known as an **index,** which is traditionally denoted by the letter i.[2] With this notation established, we can say more generally that the ith element of the data is denoted by X_i, where i has the values 1, 2, 3, and so on.

Denoting the number of population observations by N, we may write:

$$\mu = \frac{X_1 + X_2 + X_3 + \cdots + X_N}{N} \tag{4.1}$$

To provide for a more compact expression than Equation 4.1, we introduce an additional mathematical notation: the *summation sign.* To denote summation we use the Greek letter Σ (capital sigma). Specifically, the expression

$$\sum_{i=1}^{N} X_i \tag{4.2}$$

should be read as follows: "sum of X_i, i going from 1 to N." That is to say, the expression stands for the sum of all the X_is, where i runs consecutively from the value $i = 1$ through the value above the summation sign—in this case N. Equation 4.3 should further clarify the notation:

$$\sum_{i=1}^{N} X_i = X_1 + X_2 + X_3 + \cdots + X_N \tag{4.3}$$

When confusion is not likely to arise, we may drop the index and use the shorter expression

$$\Sigma X \tag{4.4}$$

which actually means precisely the same as Expression 4.2, namely, the sum of all the Xs. Using 4.1 and 4.4 and denoting the number of sample obser-

---

[2] When more than one index is required, the letters j and k are also frequently used.

vations by *n*, we may now simply write the equation for obtaining the arithmetic mean of a population and of a sample.

THE POPULATION ARITHMETIC MEAN

$$\mu = \frac{X_1 + X_2 + X_3 + \cdots + X_N}{N} = \frac{\Sigma X}{N} \qquad (4.5)$$

THE SAMPLE ARITHMETIC MEAN

$$\overline{X} = \frac{X_1 + X_2 + X_3 + \cdots + X_n}{n} = \frac{\Sigma X}{n} \qquad (4.6)$$

Here *n* is the number of observations in the sample.

Appendix 4A summarizes the rules of operating with the summation sign, Σ. You would do well to become familiar with it.

CALCULATING THE ARITHMETIC MEAN FROM GROUPED DATA

IGNORE DON'T STUDY Sometimes we need to compute the arithmetic mean without having full information about the values X_i. With only partial information available, the statistician must make the best of the data at hand. A common occurrence is the need to compute the mean from a frequency distribution of the data. In this situation the specific X_i values are unknown, but information is available about the frequencies in the class intervals and about the class interval *midpoints*. Denoting the frequencies by $f_1, f_2, f_3, \ldots$, the class midpoints by X_1, X_2, X_3, and the number of class intervals used by *M*, one calculates the mean from the grouped data in the following way:

POPULATION MEAN CALCULATED FROM GROUPED DATA

$$\mu = \frac{f_1 X_1 + f_2 X_2 + f_3 X_3 + \cdots + f_M X_M}{f_1 + f_2 + f_3 + \cdots + f_M} = \frac{\Sigma f X}{\Sigma f} = \frac{\Sigma f X}{N} \qquad (4.7)$$

SAMPLE MEAN CALCULATED FROM GROUPED DATA

$$\overline{X} = \frac{f_1 X_1 + f_2 X_2 + f_3 X_3 + \cdots + f_M X_M}{f_1 + f_2 + f_3 + \cdots + f_M} = \frac{\Sigma f X}{\Sigma f} = \frac{\Sigma f X}{n} \qquad (4.8)$$

To illustrate the use of Equations 4.7 and 4.8, let us consider an example.

EXAMPLE 4.2

Table 4.1 is a frequency distribution of the "size" of sample accounts receivable of MONEY, Inc. What is the average size of the accounts in the sample?

Consider the first interval of under 20 thousand dollars. There are 80 accounts in this size interval, but we do not have a breakdown of the specific size of any of those accounts. Should we assume that the average size within this interval is $5 thousand? Should we assume $15 thousand? Some other value? When no additional information is available, the most appealing assumption is that the average *within* each interval is equal to the *interval's midpoint*. The midpoint of the first interval is $10 thousand, that of the second interval is $30 thousand, and so on.[3]

TABLE 4.1
Frequency Distribution of Size of Sample Accounts Receivable of MONEY, Inc.

Size of account (thousands of dollars)	Number of accounts
Under 20	80
20–under 40	40
40–under 60	30
60–under 80	30
80–under 180	20
Total	200

Now that we have chosen the interval's midpoint to represent the average in each class, we proceed to calculate the average size:

$$\overline{X} = \frac{(80 \cdot 10) + (40 \cdot 30) + (30 \cdot 50) + (30 \cdot 70) + (20 \cdot 130)}{200}$$

$$= \frac{8{,}200}{200}$$

$$= \$41 \text{ thousand}$$

[3] The midpoint of any interval is simply the average of the two values that bound it. For example, the midpoint of the second interval is $\frac{20+40}{2} = 30$. This rule is not automatically applied to discrete variables, and one should be very careful in locating the intervals' midpoints.

It is often convenient to develop a work sheet to calculate the mean from grouped data, as illustrated in Table 4.2.

Note that the arithmetic mean calculated from grouped data is an *approximation*, since the use of the midpoint for each class interval is only an estimate of the true class-interval average. When the number of classes is large and each class interval is relatively narrow, the approximation is good. If the class intervals are wide and the number of intervals is small, however, the approximation may be quite wide of the mark. In Example 4.2, for instance, the interval 80–under 180 thousand dollars is quite wide. For a midpoint we used $130 thousand, because other information was lacking. If additional information could be obtained to improve the estimate, the average size could be calculated more accurately. Obtaining additional information is essential when we have an open-end class interval. Suppose, for example, the last interval were the open-end interval "80 or more." Such an interval has no midpoint, so the best available information must be used to calculate the average size of the accounts.

TABLE 4.2
Calculating the Mean from Grouped Data

(1) Size of account (thousands of dollars)	(2) Interval midpoint (X)	(3) Frequency (f)	(4) fX
Under 20	10	80	800
20–under 40	30	40	1,200
40–under 60	50	30	1,500
60–under 80	70	30	2,100
80–under 180	130	20	2,600
Total		$\Sigma f = 200$	$\Sigma fX = 8,200$

$$\text{Mean} = \frac{\Sigma fX}{\Sigma f} = \frac{8,200}{200} = 41$$

4.2 The Weighted Mean

IGNORE DONT STUDY

When averaging data, it is often necessary to account for the fact that the data are not all equally important. To give an example, consider a car dealer who sells new and used cars. Suppose the net profit is $800 per new car and $1,200 per used car. Can we say that the mean net profit per car is $(800 + 1,200)/2 = \$1,000$? This will be true only if the new and used cars are equally "important," that is, if the dealer sells an equal number of new and used cars. In any other case, however, the $1,000 (simple) mean will not represent the correct mean net profit per car. If 70 percent of all cars sold by the dealer are new cars and 30 percent are used, the correct mean net profit per car is given by the weighted mean:

$$\text{Weighted mean} = 0.7 \cdot 800 + 0.3 \cdot 1,200 = \$920$$

In general, a weighted mean of the values $X_1, X_2, X_3, \ldots, X_N$ is denoted μ_w for the population and $\overline{X}_w$ for the sample. The formula is given by the equation

FORMULA FOR A WEIGHTED MEAN

$$\text{Weighted mean} = w_1 X_1 + w_2 X_2 + w_3 X_3 + \cdots + w_N X_N = \Sigma w_i X_i \quad \textbf{(4.9)}$$

The w_is are the corresponding weights: the relative frequency of each X_i in the data. By definition, then, the sum of the weights is equal to 1.0:

$$w_1 + w_2 + w_3 + \cdots + w_N = \Sigma w = 1.0$$

Note that the arithmetic mean computed from grouped data is in essence a **weighted mean:** it is *an average of the interval midpoints, where each interval midpoint is weighted proportionally to the frequency of its interval.* To illustrate, notice that the mean of grouped data can be rewritten as follows:

$$\text{Mean} = \frac{f_1X_1 + f_2X_2 + f_3X_3 + \cdots + f_MX_M}{\Sigma f}$$

(4.10)

$$= \frac{f_1}{\Sigma f}X_1 + \frac{f_2}{\Sigma f}X_2 + \frac{f_3}{\Sigma f}X_3 + \cdots + \frac{f_M}{\Sigma f}X_M$$

On the right-hand side of Equation 4.10 we have a weighted mean, where each weight is simply equal to the relative frequency of the interval. When we use Equation 4.10, we find that the mean size of the sample accounts receivable of MONEY, Inc. (Example 4.2) is $41 thousand, as we found before:

$$\overline{X}_w = \left(\frac{80}{200} \cdot 10\right) + \left(\frac{40}{200} \cdot 30\right) + \left(\frac{30}{200} \cdot 50\right)$$

$$+ \left(\frac{30}{200} \cdot 70\right) + \left(\frac{20}{200} \cdot 130\right) = \$41 \text{ thousand}$$

Before continuing, let us look at one more example of the weighted mean.

EXAMPLE 4.3

A firm owns $10 million worth of assets, which were supplied from two sources. The owners of the firm (that is, its shareholders) supplied $6 million, and $4 million was supplied by banks in the form of loans. The $6 million is the *equity capital* of the firm and the $4 million is its *debt capital*. Both the owners and the banks expect some return on their funds. Suppose that the owners require $600,000 a year in return on their money, which amounts to 10 percent on the equity capital, and the banks require $200,000 in return, which amounts to 5 percent on the debt capital. From the point of view of the firm, it is said that the cost of equity capital is 10 percent and the cost of debt capital is 5 percent. Financial theory shows us that the relevant cost of capital for investment decisions is neither the 10 percent cost of equity capital nor the 5 percent of debt capital. Rather, the firm's analysis should focus on the weighted average (or mean) cost of capital. What is the weighted average cost of capital in this example? Since the weight of equity capital in relation to total capital is 6,000,000/10,000,000 = 0.60 and the weight of debt capital is 4,000,000/10,000,000 = 0.40, the weighted average cost of capital is:

Weighted average (or mean) cost of capital
$$= (0.6 \cdot 10\%) + (0.4 \cdot 5\%) = 6\% + 2\% = 8\%$$

4.3 The Median

Although the arithmetic mean is a very useful measure for the location of quantitative data, we need not go through lengthy demonstrations to show that in itself, the mean conveys only a very partial description of the data. To use just one example, consider the annual income of six individuals, *A, B, C, D, E,* and *F,* as shown in Table 4.3. The mean annual income

TABLE 4.3
Annual Income of Six Individuals

Individual	Income
A	$ 6,000
B	7,000
C	5,000
D	6,600
E	7,400
F	190,000
Total	$222,000

is \$222,000/6 = \$37,000, which hardly reflects the annual income of the majority of this group of individuals. The number \$37,000, taken alone, provides no clue to the fact that five of the six individuals involved have incomes below \$7,500.

It is clear that we need additional measures to supplement the information provided by the mean. The next measure we shall discuss is the median.

DEFINITION: THE MEDIAN

The **median** is defined as *the value above and below which lie an equal number of data observations, when the data are arranged in increasing or decreasing order.*

When we rearrange the annual incomes given in Table 4.3 in ascending order we get Table 4.4. The total number of observations in Table 4.4 is even (6), and we can easily identify the two central values as \$6,600 and \$7,000. In fact, any number in the range between \$6,600 and \$7,000 qualifies as the median by our definition, but the midpoint between them is customarily considered to be the median. Thus we identify the median as

$$\text{Median} = (6,600 + 7,000)/2 = \$6,800$$

If the number of data values is odd (rather than even), the median is equal to the central value. For example, if only individuals *A*, *B*, *C*, *D*, and *E* were considered, the median would be \$6,600, since it would be the only value complying with our definition of median:

Individual	Annual income	
C	$5,000	
A	6,000	
D	6,600	← Median
B	7,000	
E	7,400	

The unique merit of the median—a merit not shared by the mean—is that it is not affected by extreme values. Changing the annual income of *F* from \$190,000 all the way down to \$8,000 will leave the median unchanged, whereas the arithmetic mean will be greatly affected. For this reason the mean and the median should be considered as complementing each other, not as substituting for each other: given the mean, the median often provides *additional* information about the data's location and vice versa.

TABLE 4.4
Median Value of Incomes in Table 4.3

	Individual	Annual income
Three data	C	$ 5,000
values below	A	6,000
the median	D	6,600
		← Median income is $6,800
Three data	B	7,000
values above	E	7,400
the median	F	190,000

CALCULATING THE MEDIAN FROM GROUPED DATA

Let us begin our explanation of median calculation from grouped data *[IGNORE DON'T STUDY]* with an example.

EXAMPLE 4.4

The loans outstanding at the Bay Area Bank are classified by size, as shown in Table 4.5. The total number of loans outstanding (N) is 600. The median, therefore, is that amount above which 300 ($= N/2$) of the loans are in smaller amounts and 300 loans are in greater amounts. Looking at the *cumulative* number of loans, we realize that 290 loans are in amounts less than or equal to $10,000, and 390 loans are in amounts less than or equal to $25,000. Thus the median is evidently between $10,000 and $25,000. In other words, the class interval "over $10,000–25,000" is the one containing the median. The specific values of the data within this interval are not known, so exact calculation of the median is not possible. But if we assume that the data are spread evenly throughout the interval containing the median, we can approximate the median by simple interpolation. Since there are 100 loans outstanding within an interval of $15,000 width ("over $10,000–25,000"), the average density in the interval containing the median is one loan per $150 interval: $15,000/100 = $150. Having no other information, we assume that there are 290 loans in amounts up to $10,000; 291 loans in amounts up to $10,150; 292 loans in amounts up to $10,300; 293 loans in amounts up to $10,450; and so on. Starting again at $10,000, we need to add 10 (300 − 290 = 10) more intervals of $150 each to get to the

TABLE 4.5
Frequency Distribution of Bank Loans, by Amount

Amount of loan	Frequency of loans	Cumulative frequency of loans
Up to $5,000	180	180
Over 5,000– 10,000	110	290
Over 10,000– 25,000	100	390
Over 25,000– 50,000	90	480
Over 50,000–100,000	70	550
Over 100,000	50	600
Total	600	

median: $\$10,000 + \dfrac{\$15,000}{100} \cdot 10 = \$11,500$. Thus the median is $\$11,500$, which is the same as $\$10,000 + \dfrac{300 - 290}{100} \cdot \$15,000 = \$11,500$.

Figure 4.1 looks at the median from another viewpoint. Here we display a "less than" ogive. Lacking any data concerning the specific distribution within the various classes, we assume an even and smooth distribution, reflected in the figure by the straight line segments of the ogive. To find the median, we need to find the distance AE, where the

Figure 4.1

Median value of loans in Table 4.5

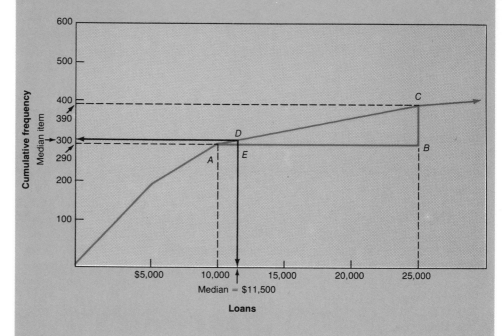

point E is directly underneath D, which in turn is at the same level as the median item: $N/2$ (300 in our example). The following triangles are similar: ABC and AED. From here we get

$$\frac{DE}{CB} = \frac{AE}{AB}$$

or

$$\frac{10}{100} = \frac{AE}{\$15,000}$$

so that

$$AE = \frac{\$15,000}{100} \cdot 10 = \$1,500$$

Adding the $\$1,500$ to the $\$10,000$, which is the lower class limit containing the median, we obtain once again

Median = $10,000 + $1,500 = $11,500

Finally we should note that diagrammatically the median appears at a point exactly under the intersection of the "less than" and "more than" ogives, as Figure 4.2 exhibits. The intersection between the graphs occurs at the loan amount above which 300 (= $N/2$) of the loans are in smaller amounts and 300 are in greater amounts. At this point, the number of "less than" loans ($N/2$) equals the number of "more than" loans. Accordingly, the two ogives must intersect at this point. By definition, the value over which they intersect is the median.

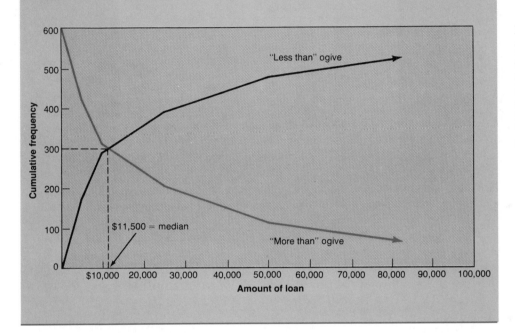

Figure 4.2

The location of the median shown at the intersection of the "less than" and "more than" ogives

Now that we have seen the calculation of the median in an example, let us treat it more generally. To do so we need the following notation:

F Frequency accumulated up to the lower limit of the class containing the median

W The width of the class interval containing the median

f_M The frequency in the class containing the median

L_M The lower limit of the class containing the median

N The total number of data observations[4]

Using this notation, we find the median by the following equation:

[4] If the median of a sample rather than of a population is calculated, the sample size n replaces the population size N in Equation 4.11. Thus the value N in this equation stands for the number of data observations, be it a sample or a population. The same applies to Equation 4.12, which follows.

$$\text{Median} = L_M + \frac{N/2 - F}{f_M} \cdot W \qquad \textbf{(4.11)}$$

It is common to denote the median by M_e.

Equation 4.11 simply represents an interpolation into the class interval containing the median. We assume the observations in this class are spread out evenly over the whole class interval. For Example 4.4, $L_M = \$10,000$, $N/2 = 300$, $F = 290$, $f_M = 100$, and $W = \$15,000$, so again we get

$$\text{Median} = \$10,000 + \frac{300 - 290}{100} \cdot \$15,000 = \$11,500$$

4.4 Percentiles and Fractiles

Just as we would often like to measure the median in order to obtain the value below which 50 percent of the data values are located, so might we also want to find *the values below which some other percentages of the data values are located.* Those values are called **percentiles.** For example, the 10th percentile is that value below which 10 percent of the data values are located. The 25th percentile is that value below which 25 percent of the values are located. The *25th percentile* is also known as the **first quartile** and is denoted Q_1. The *75th percentile*—that value below which 75 percent of the values are located—is also known as the **third quartile** and is denoted Q_3. The median, by this definition, is the 50th percentile.

Instead of referring to a value by the percentage of data values below it, we may choose to refer to it by the *fraction of the data values below the value* and term the value a **fractile** rather than a percentile. Thus the 10th percentile is the 0.10th fractile, the 75th percentile is the 0.75th fractile, and so on (see Figure 4.3).

Figure 4.3

Illustration of percentiles and fractiles

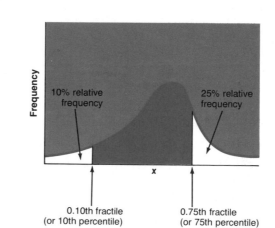

Locating a percentile involves a method similar to that used in locating the median. We denote the *p*th fractile by X_p, so that for $p = 0.10$ we have $X_{0.10}$, which denotes the 10th percentile; for $p = 0.70$ we have $X_{0.70}$, which denotes the 70th percentile; and so on. Thus the location of X_p in grouped data organized in increasing order is given by

$$X_p = L_p + \frac{pN - F}{f_p} \cdot W \qquad\qquad (4.12)$$

where the following notation is used:

F Frequency accumulated up to the lower limit of the class containing the percentile

W The width of the class interval containing the percentile

f_p The frequency in the class containing the percentile

L_p The lower limit of the class containing the percentile

N The total number of data observations

The 41st percentile of the data in Table 4.5 can be found as follows: We first determine $pN = 0.41 \cdot 600 = 246$. Looking at the cumulative frequency distribution of Table 4.5, we find that the 246th observation falls in the interval from over 5,000 to 10,000. Therefore we have $F = 180$; $W = \$5,000$; $f_{0.41} = 110$; and $L_{0.41} = \$5,000$. Substituting in Equation 4.12, we obtain

$$X_{0.41} = \$5,000 + \frac{246 - 180}{110} \cdot \$5,000 = \$8,000$$

We advise you to verify that the 90th percentile (i.e., $X_{0.90}$) of the data in Table 4.5 is equal to (rounded) \$92,857.14.

EXAMPLE 4.5

Suppose the average annual net profits of 280 firms in the past 10 years are given by the frequency distribution in Table 4.6.

TABLE 4.6
Frequency Distribution of Average Annual Net Profits of 280 Firms

Average annual profit	Frequency	Cumulative frequency
Up to $25,000	14	14
Over 25,000– 50,000	30	44
Over 50,000– 75,000	50	94
Over 75,000– 100,000	70	164
Over 100,000– 150,000	57	221
Over 150,000– 200,000	24	245
Over 200,000– 300,000	12	257
Over 300,000– 400,000	13	270
Over 400,000– 500,000	3	273
Over 500,000–1,000,000	3	276
Over 1,000,000	4	280
Total	280	

To find the first quartile, we look at the cumulative frequency to locate the class that contains it. The first quartile in our example is that annual profit below which 70 of the values are located (70 is 25 percent of the 280 firms, so $pN = 0.25 \cdot 280 = 70$). Since 44 firms had profits of up to \$50,000 and 94 firms had profits of up to \$75,000, it is clear that the first quartile is somewhere in the range of over \$50,000–75,000. We further find that $L_{0.25} = \$50,000$; $f_{0.25} = 50$; $W = \$25,000$; and $F = 44$. Substituting these values in Equation 4.12, we find

$$X_{0.25} = \$50,000 + \frac{70 - 44}{50} \cdot \$25,000 = \$63,000$$

In a similar fashion we can locate the 50th percentile (that is, the median), the third quartile, and other percentiles. We urge you to verify that the median is \$91,428.57 and the third quartile is \$140,350.88.

A percentile is useful in determining the location of quantitative data. By using percentiles we can conveniently locate the values of specified percentages of the population or the sample. As we shall soon see, when two or more percentiles are considered simultaneously, they can also serve as measures of dispersion of the data.

4.5 The Mode

Another measure of data location, or central tendency, is the **mode.**

DEFINITION: THE MODE

The **mode** is defined as *the most frequently occurring value in the data.*

When the data are grouped, the *midpoint of the interval with the greatest frequency is considered to be the mode.* For example, the most frequent class in Example 4.5 is "over \$75,000–100,000," since its frequency is 70, which is greater than any of the other class frequencies. The mode, then, is the midpoint of that interval, \$87,500.

A notable advantage of the mode becomes apparent when we deal with categorical data. Here the average and the median are meaningless. Consider the following data on annual sales of cars of various models by a car dealer:

Model	Number of cars sold
Sedan	700
Hatchback	701
Wagon	449
Total	1,850

The mode here is the hatchback, since it was sold more frequently than any other model. Because "model" is a nonquantitative variable, the average and the median are completely irrelevant.

Another case in which the mode is a useful measure of central tendency occurs when the data are quantitative but involve a limited number of discrete values, such as the number of rooms in a house, the number of children in a household, the number of times per year firms pay dividends to their shareholders, and so on. To see the usefulness of the mode for this kind of data, consider Example 4.6.

EXAMPLE 4.6

One thousand households are examined for the number of cars owned by each household, and the following frequency distribution is established:

Number of cars owned by households	Frequency
0	40
1	750
2	180
3	30
Total	1,000

The average number of cars per household is 1.2 cars (verify!), but 1.2 cars per household is somewhat difficult to interpret because *none* of the households owns 1.2 cars. They own 0, 1, 2, or 3 cars. The mode is 1, which simply means that one car is the most frequent number of cars per household. Compared to the mean, this figure is somewhat easier to interpret.

Though the mode has certain advantages, it also has some significant shortcomings. First, it says very little about the data apart from the most frequent value. Consider again the car-dealer example. Although the hatchback is the most frequently sold model, the sedan is sold almost as frequently, yet the mode gives no indication of this fact. Wagons are also sold in great frequency (though materially less than the other two models). This fact, too, is not reflected in the mode. Second, when grouped data are involved, the mode can be artificially changed by rearrangement of the class intervals. Reexamine Example 4.5 and combine the classes "over $25,000–50,000" and "over $50,000–75,000" into one class: "over $25,000–75,000." The frequency in this class will be the sum of the frequencies in the two original classes (30 and 50, respectively). Thus the frequency in the new class interval is 80 (30 + 50 = 80). While the mode was previously considered to be the midpoint of the class "over $75,000–100,000" (that is, $87,500), it will now be redefined as the midpoint of the interval "over $25,000–75,000" (that is, $50,000). A change in the grouping of the data will then significantly affect the mode, though the data remain precisely the same. Only our presentation of the data has changed. Such oversensitivity to grouping is highly undesirable in a population parameter or in a sample statistic.

4.6 Bimodal Distributions

A distribution with more than one mode is referred to as a **bimodal distribution.** Figure 4.4 shows two bimodal distributions. The one in Figure 4.4*a* has two equally frequent modes, while the one in 4.4*b* has two values that occur with significantly greater frequency than neighboring values yet do not occur with the same frequency. Both distributions are considered bimodal. A bimodal distribution is usually heterogeneous in some sense, in-

Figure 4.4

Examples of bimodal distributions

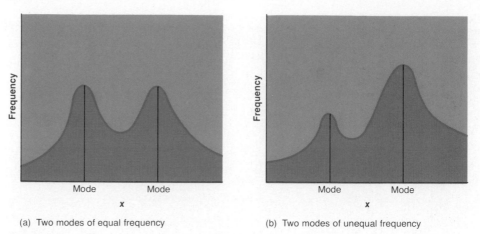

(a) Two modes of equal frequency

(b) Two modes of unequal frequency

dicating that two groups in the population differ from each other in some way. Example 4.7 should clarify this point.

EXAMPLE 4.7

The frequency distribution of the rates of return on 900 stocks and bonds traded on stock exchanges in a given year in the United States is given in Table 4.7.[5] A glance at the table and at Figure 4.5, which graphically displays the distribution, suffices to show that the distribution is bimodal.

TABLE 4.7
Frequency Distribution of Rates of Return on 900 Securities

Rate of return (percent)	Number of securities
Over (−90)–(−50)	8
Over (−50)–(−25)	16
Over (−25)– 0	27
Over 0 – 4	81
Over 4 – 8	220
Over 8 – 12	116
Over 12 – 16	75
Over 16 – 20	100
Over 20 – 24	80
Over 24 – 28	60
Over 28 – 32	45
Over 32 – 36	38
Over 36 – 200	34
Total	900

[5] This is not the place to go into detail about the way rates of return are calculated. Briefly, however, if we invest $100 at the beginning of the year and the *value* of our investment (i.e., the price of the security plus any interest or dividends obtained during the year) rises to $115, the rate of return is 115/100 − 1 = 0.15, or 15 percent. Similarly, if it drops to $88, our rate of return is 88/100 − 1 = −0.12, or a loss of 12 percent on our investment, and so on. Thus, the rate of return is the rate of profit or loss we make on our investment.

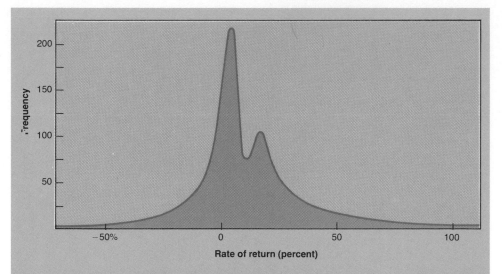

Figure 4.5

Bimodal frequency distribution of rates of return on 900 securities

One of the two modes occurs at the midpoint of the interval "over 4–8 percent," and the other occurs at the midpoint of the interval "over 16–20 percent." Furthermore, the distribution is such that there is a gradual clustering of the data around these two central points as we approach them from the right or the left. This pattern suggests that there is some *economic reason* for the appearance of this distribution. The reason is that there are two *types* of securities making up the group of 900 securities: stocks and bonds. Table 4.8 shows the frequency distribution of the separate rates of return on stocks and bonds.

TABLE 4.8
Frequency Distribution of Rate of Return on 900 Stocks and Bonds

Rate of return (percent)	Number of securities		
	Stocks	*Bonds*	*Total*
Over (−90)–(−50)	8	—	8
Over (−50)–(−25)	16	—	16
Over (−25)– 0	22	5	27
Over 0 – 4	31	50	81
Over 4 – 8	40	180	220
Over 8 – 12	51	65	116
Over 12 – 16	75	—	75
Over 16 – 20	100	—	100
Over 20 – 24	80	—	80
Over 24 – 28	60	—	60
Over 28 – 32	45	—	45
Over 32 – 36	38	—	38
Over 36 – 200	34	—	34
Total	600	300	900

The separate frequency distributions for stocks and bonds are also shown in Figure 4.6. When the two types of securities are considered separately, each of the distributions emerges as a unimodal distribution.

Figure 4.6

Frequency
distributions
of rates of
return on 600
stocks and on
300 bonds
(bimodal
distribution
of Figure 4.5
broken down
into two
unimodal
distributions)

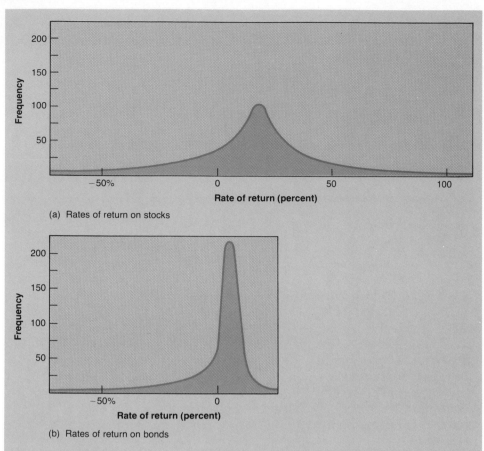

(a) Rates of return on stocks

(b) Rates of return on bonds

When two or more distinct groups of data can be identified, it is generally a good idea to study the groups separately. In that way the characteristics of each group emerge with special clarity.

4.7 Contrasting the Mean, the Median, and the Mode

As we have seen, the analysis of a frequency distribution is significantly more meaningful when the data of interest have a reasonable degree of homogeneity. Assuming a reasonably homogeneous population, let us consider three common shapes of frequency distributions and their respective relationships to the mean, the median, and the mode.

In Figure 4.7 we see mound-shaped (symmetrical), positively skewed, and negatively skewed distributions. (The word **skewness** means *asymmetry*.) The positively skewed distribution has a long right tail and the negatively skewed distribution has a long left tail. The mean, median, and mode of the mound-shaped (symmetrical) distribution coincide at one value. In the skewed distributions, however, the means, medians, and modes occupy separate locations. The mode of the positively skewed distribution (Figure 4.7*b*) is to the left of the median, and the median appears to the left of the mean. The mean appears farthest to the right because observations with extreme values on the right (not countered by extreme values on the left) are incorporated in the calculation of the mean and thus pull the mean value rightward. (Hence

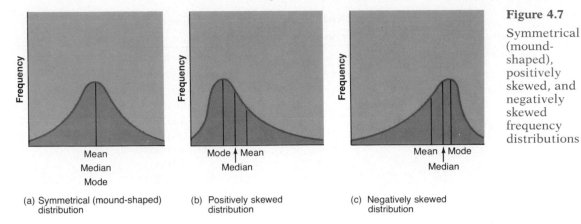

the long tail on the right.) In contrast, these extreme values have no impact on the mode or the median. The order of the measures of the negatively skewed distribution is exactly the opposite: the mode appears to the right of the median, which in turn is to the right of the mean.

We saw earlier that the three location measures—mean, median, and mode—complement one another: each imparts information not given by the other two. Although in most situations we can use all three measures to enlarge our understanding of the data, sometimes one or two of them may be irrelevant. Consider first a garment manufacturer who wants to specialize in the production of pants of only *one size*. The net profit per pair of pants sold is the same for all pairs, regardless of size. A survey of the demand for pants shows the following figures:

Size	Demand (pairs per month)
26	100
28	250
30	300
32	200
34	100

In which size should the manufacturer specialize? The answer must be determined by the mode, that is, size 30. By specializing in this size, the manufacturer will face the greatest demand and therefore will make the greatest profit. The median and arithmetic mean have no significance in this problem.

Now consider a different situation, one in which the median, not the average or the mode, is relevant. Consider a government plan to subsidize housing for large families in neglected urban areas. Suppose the frequencies of the sizes of families considered for the program are as shown in Table 4.9. We want to limit the number of families to that which the available budget can support, using family size as a limiting criterion. The mean (4.97) and the mode (2.0) are not really pertinent. The median (or any other percentile) is much more germane because if we know the median, we can easily determine the number of families entitled to subsidized housing. This figure in turn will have a direct bearing on the size of the program's budget.

Finally, suppose we want to compare the performance of two institutional investors that invest in various stocks. The mean rate of return, rather than

TABLE 4.9
Frequencies of Family Sizes

Size of family	Frequency
2	80,000
3	20,000
4	20,000
5	30,000
6	60,000
7	40,000
8	20,000
9	10,000
10	10,000

the median or the mode, is the relevant measure here, since total performance is affected by the specific rate of return on each stock included in the investment portfolio. Only the mean takes into account the specific values of the rates of return.

We see, then, that although the mean, the median, and the mode are all location measures, sometimes one or two of them may be irrelevant.

4.8 Measures of Data Variability: Variance and Standard Deviation

So far we have developed location measures of central tendency. As important as these measures are, when they stand alone they give only limited information; additional measures are needed to more completely characterize the data. In particular, measures of variability are needed for better representation. There are several variability measures, the most common of which are the variance and the standard deviation.

The **variance** is defined as *the average squared deviation of the data from their arithmetic mean.* A population's variance is commonly denoted by the square of the Greek letter sigma: σ^2. Thus σ is read "sigma" and σ^2 is read "sigma squared." A sample's variance is commonly denoted S^2.

When we calculate a location measure of the data, we follow the same computational procedure regardless of whether the data pertain to a population or to a sample. This is not the case with respect to the variance and the standard deviation. The variance and the standard deviation of sample data are calculated slightly differently from their counterparts in the population. We shall first present the calculation of each of the measures and then explain the difference. The formula for the variance of a population is

---

FORMULA FOR THE VARIANCE OF A POPULATION

$$\sigma^2 = \frac{\Sigma(X - \mu)^2}{N} \tag{4.13}$$

The **standard deviation** is defined as *the (positive) square root of the variance.* The population's standard deviation is denoted by σ. The formula for the standard deviation of a population is

FORMULA FOR THE STANDARD DEVIATION OF A POPULATION

$$\sigma = \sqrt{\frac{\Sigma(X - \mu)^2}{N}} \qquad \qquad (4.14)$$

When we calculate the variance of sample data, the sample mean ($\overline{X}$) replaces the population mean (μ), and the divisor in Equation 4.13 is replaced by the number of sample observations minus 1, namely, $n - 1$. Thus the formula for the sample variance (denoted S^2) is given by

FORMULA FOR THE VARIANCE OF SAMPLE DATA

$$S^2 = \frac{\Sigma(X - \overline{X})^2}{n - 1} \qquad \qquad (4.15)$$

and accordingly, the standard deviation (S) is given by

FORMULA FOR THE STANDARD DEVIATION OF SAMPLE DATA

$$S = \sqrt{\frac{\Sigma(X - \overline{X})^2}{n - 1}} \qquad \qquad (4.16)$$

Let's look at an example that shows how these measures of variability are used.

EXAMPLE 4.8

The following is a list of withdrawals from a savings account during the past year:

Withdrawal number (i)	Withdrawal amount (X)
1	$ 310
2	460
3	350
4	1,060
5	20
6	200

Depending on the purpose of computation, the six withdrawal amounts may be considered either a sample or a population. If the study is an attempt to learn about a larger population of withdrawals of which our data are a sample, sample formulas apply. But if these specific observations are the sole data of interest, then they constitute the population of interest, and population measures apply. Table 4.10 shows the calculations of the variance and standard deviation under the assumption that the withdrawal data constitute a population.

Since the variance is the average squared deviation from the mean, our first step is to determine the population mean, μ. The mean savings withdrawal as shown in Table 4.10 is $400. Once the mean has been

TABLE 4.10

Calculation of the Variance and the Standard Deviation

(1) Withdrawal amount (X)	(2) Deviation from the mean $(X - \mu)$	(3) Squared deviation from the mean $(X - \mu)^2$
$ 310	$ −90	8,100
460	60	3,600
350	−50	2,500
1,060	660	435,600
20	−380	144,400
200	−200	40,000
$\Sigma X = \$2,400$	$\Sigma (X - \mu) = \$0$	$\Sigma(X - \mu)^2 = 634,200$

$$\text{Mean} = \mu = \frac{\Sigma X}{N} = \frac{\$2,400}{6} = \$400$$

$$\text{Variance} = \sigma^2 = \frac{\Sigma(X - \mu)^2}{N} = \frac{634,200}{6} = 105,700$$

$$\text{Standard deviation} = \sigma = \sqrt{\frac{\Sigma(X - \mu)^2}{N}} = \sqrt{105,700} = \$325.12$$

calculated, we continue to develop columns 2 and 3. We obtain column 2 by recording the deviation of each X value from the mean, μ, and column 3 by squaring each term in column 2 individually. We obtain the variance (105,700) by adding the figures in column 3 and dividing the sum (634,200) by the number of observations, 6. We should take note of the fact that columns 1 and 2 are measured in dollars, while column 3 and the variance are measured in dollars squared. Why do we square the $X - \mu$ terms just to obtain magnitudes measured in such unappealing units as dollars squared? The answer lies in the fact that when we measure deviation, we are not interested in the *direction* of a deviation from the mean but rather in its *magnitude*. In more technical terms, this is the problem: the sum of the deviations $X - \mu$ is always equal to zero (see Table 4.10). By squaring the deviations, we find one good way to eliminate the problem: the sum of the squared deviations is never zero, if dispersion exists. To solve the problem of working with dollars squared, we take the square root of the variance and obtain the standard deviation ($325.12), which is measured in dollars.

If we consider the withdrawal data a sample of a larger population, the sample measures are as follows: the sample mean, $\overline{X}$, is

$$\frac{\Sigma X}{n} = \frac{\$2,400}{6} = \$400$$

just as we obtained for the population. The sample variance is given by

$$S^2 = \frac{\Sigma(X - \overline{X})^2}{n-1} = \frac{634,200}{6-1} = 126,840$$

and the standard deviation, S, is

$$S = \sqrt{126,840} = \$356.15$$

By simple algebraic manipulation, we can show that the population variance as given in Equation 4.13 can also be written in the following form, known as the computation formula[6] since it is easier to use when computing the variance.

COMPUTATION FORMULA FOR THE POPULATION VARIANCE

$$\sigma^2 = \frac{1}{N}\Sigma X^2 - \mu^2 \qquad (4.17)$$

The computation formula for the standard deviation is

COMPUTATION FORMULA FOR THE POPULATION STANDARD DEVIATION

$$\sigma = \sqrt{\frac{1}{N}\Sigma X^2 - \mu^2} \qquad (4.18)$$

The calculation of the variance and the standard deviation by use of Equations 4.17 and 4.18 is presented in Table 4.11. This implies, of course, that the data constitute the population of interest.

TABLE 4.11
Variance and Standard Deviation Calculated Using the Computational Formula

(1) Withdrawal amount (X)	(2) X^2
$ 310	96,100
460	211,600
350	122,500
1,060	1,123,600
20	400
200	40,000
$\Sigma X = \$2,400$	$\Sigma X^2 = 1,594,200$

$$\text{Mean} = \mu = \frac{\Sigma X}{N} = \frac{\$2,400}{6} = \$400$$

$$\text{Variance} = \sigma^2 = \frac{1}{N}\Sigma X^2 - \mu^2 = \frac{1}{6}(1,594,200) - 400^2 = 105,700$$

$$\text{Standard deviation} = \sigma = \sqrt{105,700} = \$325.12$$

---

[6] Since $(X - \mu)^2 = X^2 + \mu^2 - 2X\mu$, we also know that $\Sigma(X - \mu)^2 = \Sigma(X^2 + \mu^2 - 2X\mu) = \Sigma X^2 + \Sigma\mu^2 - 2\mu\Sigma X$. Also, since μ is a constant, the expression $\Sigma\mu^2$ is equal to $N\mu^2$. From the definition $\mu = \Sigma X/N$ we know that $\Sigma X = N\mu$, and we therefore get: $\Sigma(X - \mu)^2 = \Sigma X^2 + N\mu^2 - 2\mu N\mu = \Sigma X^2 + N\mu^2 - 2N\mu^2$, or $\Sigma(X - \mu)^2 = \Sigma X^2 - N\mu^2$. Equation 4.17 follows directly, since

$$\sigma^2 = \frac{\Sigma(X - \mu)^2}{N} = \frac{\Sigma X^2 - N\mu^2}{N} = \frac{1}{N}\Sigma X^2 - \mu^2$$

The validity of the computation formula for the sample variance can be shown in a similar way.

The sample variance can also be computed by means of a computation formula, which is as follows:

COMPUTATION FORMULA FOR THE SAMPLE VARIANCE

$$S^2 = \frac{\Sigma X^2 - n\overline{X}^2}{n - 1}$$

(4.19)

The computation formula for the sample standard deviation is

COMPUTATION FORMULA FOR THE SAMPLE STANDARD DEVIATION

$$S = \sqrt{\frac{\Sigma X^2 - n\overline{X}^2}{n - 1}}$$

(4.20)

Again, if the withdrawal data comprise a sample of a larger population of withdrawals whose standard deviation we want to estimate, the estimate can be computed using Equation 4.20:

$$S = \sqrt{\frac{1,594,200 - 6 \cdot 400^2}{6 - 1}} = \$356.15$$

which is the same value as we obtained using Equation 4.16.

CALCULATING VARIANCE AND STANDARD DEVIATION FROM GROUPED DATA

IGNORE DON'T STUDY

In Section 4.1 we explained how the mean can be calculated from grouped data. The basic approach was to assume that all the observations in a class interval have the value of the class midpoint. We can use the same approach to calculate the variance and standard deviation of grouped data. The variance formula applicable to grouped sample data is as follows:[7]

$$S^2 = \frac{\Sigma f(X - \overline{X})^2}{n - 1}$$

(4.21)

The standard deviation is obtained by taking the (positive) square root of the variance. Thus

---

$$S = \sqrt{\frac{\Sigma f(X - \overline{X})^2}{n - 1}}$$

(4.22)

---

[7] If the data constitute a population rather than a sample, replace $\overline{X}$ by μ and $n - 1$ by N in Equations 4.21 and 4.22. The computation formula for the population variance is

$$\sigma^2 = \frac{\Sigma fX^2 - N\mu^2}{N} = \frac{1}{N}\Sigma fX^2 - \mu^2$$

The standard deviation is given by $\sigma = \sqrt{\sigma^2}$.

The equivalent computation formulas, then, are

$$S^2 = \frac{\Sigma f X^2 - n\bar{X}^2}{n - 1} \tag{4.23}$$

$$S = \sqrt{\frac{\Sigma f X^2 - n\bar{X}^2}{n - 1}} \tag{4.24}$$

Example 4.9 shows how to use Equations 4.23 and 4.24.

EXAMPLE 4.9

Suppose we want to calculate the standard deviation of the rate of return of the sample of 300 bonds presented in Example 4.7. Here again are the rates of return for the bonds:

Rate of return (percent)	Frequency
Over (−25)– 0	5
Over 0 – 4	50
Over 4 – 8	180
Over 8 –12	65
Total	300

First we determine the midpoint of each class interval and denote it by X. They are shown in Table 4.12, which is in fact a work sheet for the calculation of the variance. Given the totals of columns 3, 4, and 6, we can easily compute the mean, variance, and standard deviation, as shown at the bottom of the table. For the bond sample we find that $S^2 = 11.89$ (percent squared) and $S = 3.45$ percent. Perform similar calculations for the rate of return on the stocks of Example 4.7, and verify that for the stocks the statistics are: $\bar{X} = 20.33$ percent, $S^2 = 847.94$, and $S = 29.12$ percent.

TABLE 4.12
Calculating Variance and Standard Deviation from Grouped Data

(1) Rate of return (percent)	(2) Class midpoint (X)	(3) Frequency of bonds (f)	(4) fX	(5) X²	(6) fX²
Over (−25)– 0	− 12.5	5	− 62.50	156.25	781.25
Over 0 – 4	2.0	50	100.00	4.00	200.00
Over 4 – 8	6.0	180	1,080.00	36.00	6,480.00
Over 8 –12	10.0	65	650.00	100.00	6,500.00
Total		$\Sigma f = n =$ 300	$\Sigma f X =$ 1,767.50		$\Sigma f X^2 =$ 13,961.25

$$\text{Mean} = \bar{X} = \frac{\Sigma f X}{n} = \frac{1,767.50}{300} = 5.89\%$$

$$\text{Variance} = S^2 = \frac{\Sigma f X^2 - n\bar{X}^2}{n - 1} = \frac{13,961.25 - 300 \cdot 5.89^2}{300 - 1} = 11.89$$

$$\text{Standard deviation} = S = \sqrt{11.89} = 3.45\%$$

By comparing the means and standard deviations of the stock and bond data in our example, we can gain insight into the usefulness of these statistics. Looking at the mean only, we realize that the rate of return on the stocks is materially higher than the rate of return on the bonds (20.33 percent versus 5.89 percent). Given this difference, we might wonder why anyone would invest in bonds when the average rate of return on stocks is so much higher. The standard deviation reveals information that provides the clue to the answer. Although the mean rate of return on the stocks is higher, the variability of the rate of return on the stocks is also substantially higher. Thus investors who are attracted by the high average rate of return on stocks might at the same time be deterred by the variability of that rate. By taking account of both the average and the variance of the rates of return, the investor gets a fuller description of the distributions of the rates of return, and thus of the relative attractiveness of those investments.

We have to this point provided formulas for sample measures (statistics) and population measures (parameters); but we have not explained why we measure the sample variance and the population variance differently. Specifically, we have not yet explained why the divisor in the formula for the sample variance is the sample size minus 1 ($n - 1$), rather than just the sample size. To understand the reason for this, let us mention the concept of an estimator in general. An **estimator** is *a sample statistic used to estimate a population parameter.* An **estimate** is *a specific value of the sample statistic,* computed from a particular sample. For example, the sample mean, $\overline{X}$, is an estimator of the population mean, μ. A specific value of $\overline{X}$ is an estimate of μ. Similarly, the sample variance, S^2, is an estimator of the population variance, σ^2, and a specific value of S^2 is an estimate of σ^2.

The "quality" of estimators is judged by whether or not they have certain properties. A more complete discussion of these properties is given in Chapter 12, but here we shall briefly mention one such property: **unbiasedness.** *Estimators that have the desired property of unbiasedness have a value that will on average equal the quantity they are supposed to estimate;* they are said to be **unbiased estimators.** *Estimators that do not have this property* are said to be **biased estimators.** The mean, $\overline{X}$, of a randomly selected sample is an unbiased estimator of the population mean, μ. This implies that repeated samples will yield $\overline{X}$ values that on average equal the mean, μ, of the population from which they were drawn. Similarly, S^2 is an unbiased estimator of σ^2, whereas if we had used n rather than $n - 1$ for the divisor of S^2, this would not be the case. It does not follow, however, that S is an unbiased estimator of the population standard deviation, σ. The unbiasedness of S^2 is the major justification for using it as a measure of sample variance.

4.9 Chebyshev's Theorem and the Empirical Rule

We have described the mean of a set of data as a location measure and the standard deviation as a dispersion measure of the data. **Chebyshev's theorem** is an important theorem that considers both the mean and the standard deviation of *any* set of data and reveals more about the distribution of the data.

CHEBYSHEV'S THEOREM

For any set of data—population or sample—and any constant k greater than 1, at least the proportion $1 - 1/k^2$ of the data must lie within k standard deviations of the mean.

Setting $k = 2$, for example, we obtain $1 - 1/k^2 = 0.75$. The theorem states that *at least* 75 percent of *any* set of data must lie within 2 standard deviations of the mean. Setting $k = 3$ we get $1 - 1/k^2 = 8/9 = 0.889$, which means that at least 88.9 percent of the data must be within 3 standard deviations of the mean. And setting $k = 1.5$, we find that at least 55.6 percent of the data must lie within 1.5 standard deviations of the mean.

EXAMPLE 4.10

A bottling machine pours tomato ketchup into bottles. The ketchup's mean weight per bottle is 14 ounces, and its standard deviation is 0.04 ounce. At least what percentage of the bottles are filled with between 13.9 and 14.1 ounces?

The range from 13.9 to 14.1 ounces extends 2.5 standard deviations on either side of the mean, 14. This is because the 0.1 ounce interval on either side of the mean is $0.1/0.04 = 2.5$ standard deviations. Thus we set $k = 2.5$ and calculate $1 - 1/k^2 = 1 - 1/2.5^2 = 0.84$. We can state that at least 84 percent of the bottles are filled with between 13.9 and 14.1 ounces of ketchup.

Chebyshev's theorem enhances the interpretation of the standard deviation since it allows us to determine a lower limit to the percentage of the observations within a given number of standard deviations around the mean of the observations. For example, we can state that:

1. At least 75 percent of the observations fall within 2 standard deviations of the mean ($\overline{X} - 2S$ to $\overline{X} + 2S$).
2. At least 8/9 (i.e., about 89 percent) of the observations fall within 3 standard deviations of the mean ($\overline{X} - 3S$ to $\overline{X} + 3S$).

There is a *rule of thumb* called the **Empirical Rule** that applies to mound-shaped distributions such as the one presented in Figure 4.7*a*. It states that:

1. Approximately 68 percent of the observations fall within 1 standard deviation of the mean ($\overline{X} - S$ to $\overline{X} + S$).
2. Approximately 95 percent of the observations fall within 2 standard deviations of the mean ($\overline{X} - 2S$ to $\overline{X} + 2S$).
3. Virtually all the observations fall within 3 standard deviations of the mean ($\overline{X} - 3S$ to $\overline{X} + 3S$).

We should emphasize that while Chebyshev's theorem has a theoretical basis and holds for *all* distributions, the Empirical Rule has no theoretical basis. It has simply been observed that it is approximately right when the distribution is mound-shaped.

4.10 The Coefficient of Variation

The **coefficient of variation,** C, is defined as *the ratio of the standard deviation to the mean.*

THE COEFFICIENT OF VARIATION

$$C = \frac{\text{Standard deviation}}{\text{Mean}} \tag{4.25}$$

The coefficient measures the *relative variability* and is sometimes used to evaluate changes that have occurred in a data set over time or to evaluate differences between data sets. Suppose that the average earnings per share (EPS) of U.S. industrial firms in 1981 was $3.00 and the standard deviation was $0.50. Suppose also that the equivalent figures for 1983 were $4.00 and $0.70, respectively. Clearly, both the average EPS and its standard deviation rose during the period 1981–83, but the coefficient of variation reveals that the variability in EPS across the industrial firms rose faster than the average: the coefficient for 1981 is $C_{81} = 0.5/3 = 0.1667$ and for 1983 it is $C_{83} = 0.7/4 = 0.1750$.

The coefficient of variation is also useful when we compare the variability of two or more distinctive data sets. For example, in a comparison of Japanese workers' income (measured in Japanese yen) with American workers' income, the coefficient of variation can be helpful.

Similarly, when we compare the variability of two or more data sets of widely varying magnitudes, the coefficient of variation can be most appropriate. Let's say we want to compare uniformity of size among people and among ants. Obviously absolute variance of size is greater among people than among ants. This does not mean, however, that people have greater variance of size relative to their own average size. It is quite possible that ants will show greater *relative* variation.

Although the coefficient of variation is appealing as a measure of relative variability, it must be used with care. In many situations, the standard deviation is a more relevant variability measure. Thus differences between data sets should first be analyzed in terms of the mean and the standard deviation separately; then the coefficient of variation may be used as a complementary measure.

4.11 Interfractile Range as a Measure of Dispersion

Although the variance and standard deviation are by far the most popular variability measures, they are by no means the only ones. Let us briefly discuss one more variability measure: the **interfractile range.** The interfractile range is *a single-valued number equal to the range of values between two specified fractiles.* The most common is the **interquartile range,** which is *the range between the first quartile and the third quartile.* Thus the interquartile range contains the middle 50 percent of the data. For example, suppose the first quartile of a set of data is $Q_1 = \$20$ and the third quartile is $Q_3 = \$55$. The interquartile range of these data is $Q_3 - Q_1 = 55 - 20 = \$35$. Figure 4.8 shows the interquartile range. *The interfractile range between the 0th and*

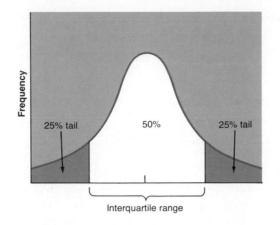

Figure 4.8

The interquartile range

the 1.0th fractile, within which all the data set is concentrated, is known as the **range.** If the lowest value of a set of data is 15 and the highest is 27, the range is $27 - 15 = 12$. The range is a common measure of data variability.

4.12 Measures of Asymmetry

IGNORE DON'T STUDY

Some data characteristics will not be revealed by the variability measures we have been discussing. The degree of asymmetry is an obvious example. We mentioned earlier that sets of data can have symmetrical distributions or they can be negatively or positively skewed. The degree of skewness is an important characteristic of the data for which we need to develop a quantitative measure. One such measure is μ_3, which is the average of cubed deviations from the mean. When applied to a population it is given by

MEASURE OF POPULATION SKEWNESS

$$\mu_3 = \frac{\Sigma(X - \mu)^3}{N} \tag{4.26}$$

When we apply it to a sample, we replace μ with $\overline{X}$ and N with n. If a population is symmetrical, its μ_3 is equal to zero. If a distribution is skewed to the left, μ_3 is negative (and thus it will be said to be negatively skewed); if it is skewed to the right, μ_3 is positive (and it will be said to be positively skewed). For grouped data, the formula is as follows:

MEASURE OF POPULATION SKEWNESS (GROUPED DATA)

$$\mu_3 = \frac{\Sigma f(X - \mu)^3}{N} \tag{4.27}$$

Here again we replace μ with $\overline{X}$ and N with n when the measure is applied to a sample. The value μ_3 is measured in the third power of the units of X. If X is measured in dollars, then μ_3 is measured in cubic dollars. To revert to the original units of X and to obtain a measure that is somewhat more easily interpreted, we often *scale* the skewness by the magnitude σ^3. As a result, we get

THE COEFFICIENT OF SKEWNESS

$$\text{Coefficient of skewness} = \frac{\mu_3}{\sigma^3} \tag{4.28}$$

where μ_3/σ^3 is expressed as a unitless number.

EXAMPLE 4.11

The ages of the population of 2,000 students of the business school of a certain university occur in the frequencies shown in Table 4.13. To calculate the distribution's skewness, we construct Table 4.14.

TABLE 4.13
Frequency Distribution of Ages of Students

Age interval	Frequency
17–under 19	19
19–under 21	708
21–under 23	542
23–under 25	356
25–under 30	260
30–under 35	25
35–under 40	20
40–under 45	33
45–under 50	17
50–under 55	8
55–under 60	12
Total	2,000

TABLE 4.14
Calculation of Parameters: Grouped Data

(1) Age interval	(2) Mid-point (X)	(3) Frequency (f)	(4) fX	(5) X − μ	(6) (X − μ)²	(7) (X − μ)³	(8) f(X − μ)²	(9) f(X − μ)³
17–under 19	18.0	19	342.0	−5.5	30.25	−166.375	574.75	−3,161.12
19–under 21	20.0	708	14,160.0	−3.5	12.25	−42.875	8,673.00	−30,355.50
21–under 23	22.0	542	11,924.0	−1.5	2.25	−3.375	1,219.50	−1,829.25
23–under 25	24.0	356	8,544.0	0.5	0.25	0.125	89.00	44.50
25–under 30	27.5	260	7,150.0	4.0	16.00	64.000	4,160.00	16,640.00
30–under 35	32.5	25	812.5	9.0	81.00	729.000	2,025.00	18,225.00
35–under 40	37.5	20	750.0	14.0	196.00	2,744.000	3,920.00	54,880.00
40–under 45	42.5	33	1,402.5	19.0	361.00	6,859.000	11,913.00	226,347.00
45–under 50	47.5	17	807.5	24.0	576.00	13,824.000	9,792.00	235,008.00
50–under 55	52.5	8	420.0	29.0	841.00	24,389.000	6,728.00	195,112.00
55–under 60	57.5	12	690.0	34.0	1,156.00	39,304.000	13,872.00	471,648.00
Total		$\Sigma f = N = $ 2,000	$\Sigma fX = $ 47,002.5				$\Sigma f(X - \mu)^2 = $ 62,966.25	$\Sigma f(X - \mu)^3 = $ 1,182,558.63

$$\text{Mean} = \mu = \frac{\Sigma fX}{N} = \frac{47,002.5}{2,000} = 23.50$$

$$\text{Variance} = \sigma^2 = \frac{\Sigma f(X - \mu)^2}{N} = \frac{62,966.25}{2,000} = 31.48$$

$$\text{Standard deviation} = \sigma = \sqrt{31.48} = 5.61$$

$$\text{Skewness} = \mu_3 = \frac{\Sigma f(X - \mu)^3}{N} = \frac{1,182,558.63}{2,000} = 591.28$$

$$\text{Coefficient of skewness} = \frac{\mu_3}{\sigma^3} = \frac{591.28}{176.56} = 3.35$$

The positive value of the skewness (either μ_3 or μ_3/σ^3) reflects the fact that some students are substantially older than the bulk of the school's students, whereas no students are substantially younger. The conclusion drawn is that the distribution is not symmetrical, but rather positively skewed (that is, skewed to the right), as the skewness and coefficient of skewness indicate. Note that since σ^3 is always positive, the skewness, μ_3, and the coefficient of skewness, μ_3/σ^3, always have the same sign.

4.13 Proportions

Sometimes our interest focuses on the proportion of data values that have some common characteristic, defined in either quantitative or qualitative terms. The **proportion,** *p,* is given as *the ratio of the number of data values with the specified characteristic to the total number of data values in the data set.* This may be expressed by

FORMULA FOR PROPORTION

$$p = \frac{\text{Number of data values in category}}{\text{Size of population or sample}}$$

We might, for instance, be interested in the proportion of students in Example 4.11 over the age of 30. We obtain the proportion, *p,* by dividing the number of students over 30 (115) by the total number of students in the population (2,000):

$$p = \frac{115}{2,000} = 0.0575 \quad \text{or} \quad 5.75\%$$

Proportion is particularly useful in dealing with qualitative data. For example, when factory products are classified as "nondefective" and "defective," our interest is often in the proportion of defective products produced by the factory.

Chapter Summary and Review

	Sample	Population
1. Mean		
a. Raw data	$\overline{X} = \dfrac{\Sigma X}{n}$	$\mu = \dfrac{\Sigma X}{N}$
b. Grouped data	$\overline{X} = \dfrac{\Sigma fX}{n}$	$\mu = \dfrac{\Sigma fX}{N}$
2. Variance		
a. Raw data	$S^2 = \dfrac{\Sigma(X - \overline{X})^2}{n - 1}$	$\sigma^2 = \dfrac{\Sigma(X - \mu)^2}{N}$

	Sample	Population
1. Computation formula	$S^2 = \dfrac{\Sigma X^2 - n\bar{X}^2}{n-1}$	$\sigma^2 = \dfrac{1}{N}\Sigma X^2 - \mu^2$
b. Grouped data	$S^2 = \dfrac{\Sigma f(X - \bar{X})^2}{n-1}$	$\sigma^2 = \dfrac{\Sigma f(X - \mu)^2}{N}$
1. Computation formula	$S^2 = \dfrac{\Sigma fX^2 - n\bar{X}^2}{n-1}$	$\sigma^2 = \dfrac{1}{N}\Sigma fX^2 - \mu^2$
3. Standard deviation	$S = +\sqrt{S^2}$	$\sigma = +\sqrt{\sigma^2}$
4. Coefficient of variation	$C = S/\bar{X}$	$C = \sigma/\mu$
5. Skewness	$\mu_3 = \dfrac{\Sigma(X - \bar{X})^3}{n}$	$\mu_3 = \dfrac{\Sigma(X - \mu)^3}{N}$

6. For samples and populations

Median: $M_e = L_M + \dfrac{N/2 - F}{f_M} \cdot W$

pth percentile: $X_p = L_p + \dfrac{pN - F}{f_p} \cdot W$

Mode = the most frequently occurring value in the data

Problems

4.1. The arithmetic mean, the median, and the mode are three location measures. They do not measure precisely the same thing. What are the differences among them?

4.2. Demonstrate, using your own numerical example, that the median is not affected by extreme data values.

4.3. Calculate the median of the frequency distribution of Example 4.5. Show that the median is located exactly underneath the intersection of the "less than" and "more than" ogives.

4.4. Calculate the 30th, 40th, 65th, and 85th percentiles of the frequency distribution given in Example 4.5.

4.5. What are the unique characteristics of the mode (those not shared by the other location measures)?

4.6. Multimodal distributions are usually not good subjects for statistical analysis. Why?

4.7. When the mean appears to the left of the median, what is implied with respect to the data's skewness?

4.8. If a variable X is measured in days, what are the units by which its variance is measured? What are the units by which its standard deviation is measured? Explain.

4.9. If a variable X is measured in dollars, what are the units by which skewness, μ_3, is measured? What are the units by which the coefficient of skewness, μ_3/σ^3, is measured? Explain.

4.10. Figure P4.10 depicts electricity production in the United States in 1978 by type of fuel and by region in percentages.

(a) Calculate the mean and variance of the percentage of each of the five energy sources across the 10 regions. Which source of energy exhibits the highest variability?

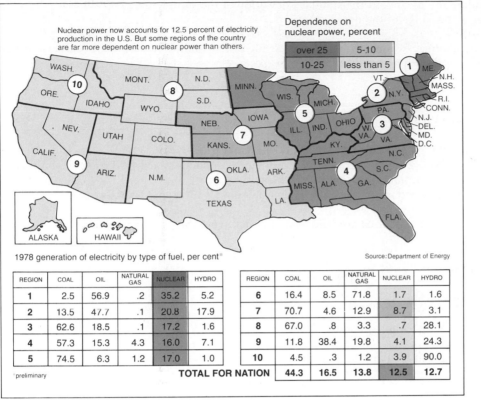

Figure P4.10

U.S. electricity production by type of fuel and region, 1978 (percent)

Nuclear power now accounts for 12.5 percent of electricity production in the U.S. But some regions of the country are far more dependent on nuclear power than others.

Dependence on nuclear power, percent

over 25	5-10
10-25	less than 5

1978 generation of electricity by type of fuel, per cent°

Source: Department of Energy

REGION	COAL	OIL	NATURAL GAS	NUCLEAR	HYDRO
1	2.5	56.9	.2	35.2	5.2
2	13.5	47.7	.1	20.8	17.9
3	62.6	18.5	.1	17.2	1.6
4	57.3	15.3	4.3	16.0	7.1
5	74.5	6.3	1.2	17.0	1.0

REGION	COAL	OIL	NATURAL GAS	NUCLEAR	HYDRO
6	16.4	8.5	71.8	1.7	1.6
7	70.7	4.6	12.9	8.7	3.1
8	67.0	.8	3.3	.7	28.1
9	11.8	38.4	19.8	4.1	24.3
10	4.5	.3	1.2	3.9	90.0
TOTAL FOR NATION	**44.3**	**16.5**	**13.8**	**12.5**	**12.7**

°preliminary

(b) Compare the means you obtained in part *a* with those labeled "total for nation" in Figure P4.10. Are they the same? If not, has the *Newsweek* statistician erred? Explain.

4.11. The following table presents a summary of the lifetimes of a 6,000-tire population of a certain brand (measured in thousands of miles):

Lifetime (thousands of miles)	Number of tires
15.0–under 20.0	600
20.0–under 25.0	1,100
25.0–under 30.0	1,800
30.0–under 35.0	1,200
35.0–under 40.0	700
40.0–under 50.0	600
Total	6,000

(a) Find the median lifetime of this tire population and briefly explain its meaning.
(b) Calculate the average lifetime of the tires. Is the average different from the median? What is implied about the population's skewness?
(c) Calculate the skewness and coefficient of skewness of the distribution.

4.12. The following data represent recent values of earnings per share (in dollars) of nine randomly selected companies listed on the *Fortune* 500 list:

3.25	5.26	2.01
6.12	4.67	0.14
4.06	4.81	5.68

    (*a*) Calculate the mean and the standard deviation of the sample data.

    (*b*) What is the range of the data?

4.13. A candy manufacturer wants to know the shelf life of its candies. A sample of retailers turned up the following shelf lives (in days):

17	2	22	12	25	14
18	7	16	18	16	12
15	10	29	26	13	16

    (*a*) Calculate the mean and the standard deviation of the above sample.

    (*b*) What percentage of the sample data falls within one standard deviation of the mean? Within two standard deviations of the mean?

    (*c*) Are the results of part *b* consistent with Chebyshev's theorem? Explain.

4.14. The following monthly salaries are paid to a sample of 16 public service employees:

$840	$1,050	$1,340	$938	$821	$718	$1,175	$944
$827	$796	$1,197	$698	$754	$1,030	$890	$942

Calculate the following:

    (*a*) The sample mean and standard deviation

    (*b*) The sample range

    (*c*) The first and third quartiles (Q_1 and Q_3) and the interquartile range

    (*d*) The sample median pay

4.15. Table P4.15 gives the recommended retail prices of four products in a sample of four cities.

TABLE P4.15

		City		
Product	*Chicago*	*Miami*	*Houston*	*San Francisco*
A	$ 4.20	$ 4.15	$ 3.95	$ 4.46
B	5.70	4.99	5.29	5.39
C	15.60	15.40	15.99	14.89
D	1.99	1.89	1.65	2.09

    (*a*) Rank the products according to their sample standard deviation.

    (*b*) Rank the products according to their sample coefficient of variation.

    (*c*) Explain the difference between the rankings in parts *a* and *b*.

4.16. The Beta Company sells three kinds of products: 1, 2, and 3. The net profit per item and total number of items sold of each kind are as follows:

Kind of product	*Net profit per item*	*Number of items sold*
1	$ 20	10,000
2	720	5,000
3	1,200	900
		15,900

What is the average net profit per item?

4.17. The production workers of a given firm are ranked *A, B, C,* and *D*. The following table gives the annual salary per worker by rank and the percentage distribution of ranks:

Rank	Annual salary per worker	Workers in rank (percent)
A	$13,000	6.2%
B	12,000	21.8
C	10,500	56.4
D	9,000	15.6
		100.0%

What is the weighted average annual salary of the workers?

4.18. Good and Fast Service Bank, Inc., is providing free checking account service. Since costs have surged in recent months, management has decided that a monthly charge is inevitable and has initiated a study of checking account balances to determine a fair monthly charge. The study shows the following frequency distribution by average monthly balance:

Average monthly balance (dollars)	Frequency
$ 0.00–under 100.00	2,000
100.00–under 200.00	2,500
200.00–under 500.00	10,000
500.00–under 800.00	2,500
800.00–under 1,000.00	1,100
1,000.00–under 5,000.00	1,900
Total	20,000

Calculate the following:

(a) The average monthly balance for the 20,000 sample accounts
(b) The median
(c) The sample variance of the monthly balance
(d) The mode

4.19. The following is a frequency distribution of 200 companies over their last year's earnings:

Net earnings (millions of dollars)	Frequency
$(−4.00)–under 0.00	20
0.00 –under 4.00	50
4.00 –under 8.00	60
8.00 –under 12.00	30
12.00 –under 16.00	40
Total	200

Assume that the data constitute the population of interest and calculate the following:

(a) The mean net earnings
(b) The variance and standard deviation
(c) The coefficient of variation
(d) The 15th percentile
(e) The interquartile range
(f) The mode

4.20. The following monthly salaries are paid to a sample of 20 employees:

$397	$444
480	567
830	457
610	390
642	610
560	480
437	478
425	667
550	565
330	602

(a) Compute the range.
(b) Compute the first and third quartiles and determine the interquartile range.
(c) Compute the sample variance and standard deviation.

4.21. The interest rates charged on a sample of mortgage loans in a certain geographical area are as follows (in percent):

13.2	12.9	13.7	13.7	13.3	12.9	13.1
13.0	13.2	13.3	13.3	13.4	13.0	13.0

(a) Calculate the sample mean and standard deviation.
(b) Calculate the skewness of the sample. Is the sample distribution symmetrical, positively skewed, or negatively skewed?
(c) What is the sample mode?
(d) In what units is the standard deviation of the sample measured? In what units is the variance of the sample measured?

4.22. The hourly earnings of employees of firm ABC and of its subsidiary are presented in Table P4.22.

TABLE P4.22

Hourly earning (in dollars)	Firm ABC	Subsidiary
$ 8.00–under $ 8.50	14	10
8.50–under 9.00	28	17
9.00–under 9.50	47	22
9.50–under 10.00	36	12
10.00–under 10.50	16	5
Total	141	66

(a) Calculate the mean, mode, and median of the hourly earnings of ABC and of its subsidiary.
(b) If you want to compare the location of the hourly earnings in ABC and in its subsidiary, which of the three measures best suits your goal? Explain.

4.23. A population of 400 businesses in a given city had the following profit distribution in the last year:

Profit (thousands of dollars)	Frequency
$(−100)–under (−50)	5
(−50)–under 0	35
0 –under 50	260
50 –under 100	47
100 –under 150	34
150 –under 200	19
Total	400

(*a*) Find the population's average profit.
(*b*) Find the median profit, and show on a chart that the location of the median can be found by the intersection of the "less than" and "more than" ogives.
(*c*) What is the variance of the profit of the above population?
(*d*) Determine the population coefficient of variation.
(*e*) Is the profit distribution skewed? Can you support your answer by calculating the skewness?

4.24. Table P4.24 is a frequency distribution of a population of people who dined in a given restaurant in a period of 90 days.

TABLE P4.24

Number of people	Frequency of days
0– 24	2
25– 49	1
50– 74	10
75– 99	10
100–124	8
125–149	16
150–174	13
175–199	15
200–224	5
225–249	4
250–274	3
275–299	3
Total	90

For the population in Table P4.24, calculate:

(*a*) The mean
(*b*) The median
(*c*) The standard deviation
(*d*) The interquartile range
(*e*) The range between the 10th and 90th percentiles

4.25. The table below presents a sample of monthly rates of return on investment in stocks of two industries for the last five years.

Rate of return (%)	Food company stocks	Oil company stocks
(−5)–under 0	5	5
0 –under 5	5	5
5 –under 10	40	20
10 –under 15	5	20
15 –under 20	5	10
Total	60	60

(*a*) Calculate the mean of the rate of return on the stocks in each of the two industries for the last five years.
(*b*) Calculate the variance of rates of return on each of the two distributions.
(*c*) Can you think of an economic reason that the means and variances of the rates of return on these two industries' stocks might be related to one another, as in this problem?

4.26. A population is examined for its quartiles and median. Suppose the first quartile, Q_1, is 60 and the third quartile, Q_3, is 120. Suppose also the median is 90.

(a) Is it necessarily true that the population is symmetrical? If your answer is positive, explain your reason. If it is negative, give a numerical example to demonstrate your answer.

(b) If $Q_1 = 60$ and $Q_3 = 120$ but the median is 80, is it possible that the skewness $\mu_3 = \dfrac{1}{N} \Sigma(X - \mu)^3$ is equal to zero? Explain and demonstrate numerically.

4.27. Community Savings is a savings bank that makes mortgage loans to community residents. The bank's loan portfolio includes loans made at a variety of interest rates, as follows:

Amount of loans (thousands of dollars)	Interest rates
$ 500	$6\frac{1}{2}\%$
800	7
50	$8\frac{3}{4}$
1,070	$9\frac{3}{4}$

What interest rate does the bank earn on its loan portfolio?

4.28. Marketable securities are securities that can be sold by the original purchaser. The time to maturity is the length of time that must elapse before a security matures. The amount (in millions of dollars) of marketable government bonds with various times to maturity in the years 1980, 1981, and 1982 was as follows:

Year	Up to 1 year	1–5 years	5–10 years	10–20 years	20–30 years
1980	$220,084	$156,244	$38,809	$25,901	$22,679
1981	275,322	188,422	50,851	34,055	32,020
1982	295,476	200,544	52,612	35,822	34,576

Source: *U.S. Treasury Bulletin*, May 1982, p. 30.

For each of the three years (1980, 1981, and 1982), calculate:

(a) The average time to maturity of the bonds held
(b) The standard deviation of the time to maturity
(c) The skewness and coefficient of skewness of the time to maturity

4.29. The following table shows ownership of outstanding U.S. public debt (notes and bonds issued by the federal government and held by the public):

Held by	Amount held in February 1982 (billions of dollars)
Commercial banks	$111.8
Insurance companies	18.7
Mutual savings banks	5.4
Corporations	37.5

Source: *U.S. Treasury Bulletin*, May 1982, p. 59.

What location parameter is appropriate to use in describing the data? Why?

4.30. Scientific Optico, Inc., manufactures a variety of optical tools. One of them is an amateur telescope whose price and cost frequently vary. A sample of prices and production costs per telescope in six recent months follows:

Month	Price	Production cost
1	$49.99	$42.58
2	52.49	45.19
3	50.99	43.37
4	51.29	44.16
5	54.49	48.64
6	57.89	52.17

(*a*) Calculate the mean and standard deviation of the price sample and of the cost sample.

(*b*) Calculate the skewness of the price sample.

(*c*) Calculate the skewness of the cost sample.

(*d*) For each month, subtract the production cost from the price. The difference you obtain is the "variable profit per telescope." Calculate its skewness and compare it with the skewness of the price and the cost. Discuss.

4.31. Moody is a large and well-known financial service that, among other things, rates bonds according to their "quality." The higher the rating, the greater the assurance that interest and principal will be paid and paid on time. Table P4.31 shows the yield (namely, the rate of return) on bonds issued by municipalities and rated Aaa (the highest rating), Aa (the second rating), and A (the third rating) in the last six months of 1981.

TABLE P4.31
Yield on Long-Term Municipal Bonds,
July–December 1981, by Rating and Month

Month	Rating		
	Aaa	Aa	A
July	10.21	10.63	11.04
August	11.10	11.98	12.38
September	11.55	12.60	13.25
October	12.05	12.50	12.84
November	10.98	11.21	12.05
December	11.70	12.16	12.60

Source: Moody's *Municipal & Government Manual*, 1982, vol. 2, p. A11.

Calculate the mean yield for each rating. Rank the means and give an explanation for the way they rank relative to their Moody's rating. Is Moody's rating meaningful? Explain.

4.32. Table P4.32 shows the yearly compensation (salary and other benefits) of financial analysts in a large company.

TABLE P4.32

Compensation (thousands of dollars)	Frequency
$ 0.0–under 10.0	2
10.0–under 20.0	13
20.0–under 30.0	15
30.0–under 40.0	5
40.0–under 50.0	5
50.0–under 60.0	6
60.0–under 70.0	1
70.0–under 80.0	1
Total	48

For this population, calculate:

(a) The mean
(b) The standard deviation
(c) The coefficient of variation
(d) The skewness
(e) The 15th percentile
(f) The median

4.33. Of 11,194 residents of a city, 5,677 do not subscribe to any daily newspaper, 5,049 residents subscribe to one daily newspaper, and 468 subscribe to two daily papers. What is the average number of daily papers per resident to which the city residents subscribe? What is the variance? In what units is the variance measured?

4.34. Suppose frequency distributions of the net profits of some 300 firms are constructed for 1982 and 1983. Suppose the two frequency distributions are exactly the same. Is it possible to determine the mean *change* of net profit of these firms between 1982 and 1983 by comparing the two distributions? Is it possible to determine the variance of the change? The skewness of the change? Explain by means of a numerical example.

4.35. The average household electric bill in a given population is $75 per month. The standard deviation is $15. The average number of household members in the same population is 3.2 and the standard deviation is 0.6. The households exhibit greater variability with respect to which of the two variables? Explain your answer.

4.36. Commercial banks hold some of their deposit liabilities in cash. Consider the following table, which contains information about the percentage of funds held in cash by commercial banks of various sizes.

Total deposits (millions of dollars)	Percent of all banks	Percent of deposits held in cash
$ 0–under 50	20%	10.5%
50–under 100	25	9.9
100–under 150	18	9.0
150–under 200	13	9.1
200–under 250	10	8.0
250–under 300	9	8.2
300–under 350	5	8.0
	100%	

What percentage of all the deposits in the above banks is held in cash?

4.37. Suppose you have determined the individual tax rates of a sample of 63 individual taxpayers. Suppose you compute the sample average and standard deviation and obtain $\overline{X} = 26$ and $S = 5$. Using Chebyshev's theorem, answer the following questions:

(a) At least what percentage of the sample values falls in the range from 17 to 35?
(b) What is the range of values in which we can be sure to find at least 84 percent of the data?

4.38. Consider the following prices for Midwest Corporation's stock at the end of 10 sample trading days:

Day	Price
1	42
2	$42\frac{1}{2}$
3	$41\frac{3}{4}$
4	$41\frac{1}{4}$
5	$40\frac{3}{4}$
6	42
7	42
8	$42\frac{3}{4}$
9	$43\frac{1}{2}$
10	$44\frac{1}{4}$

(a) Calculate the mean, variance, standard deviation, and skewness of the price.

(b) For each day (starting at day 2) calculate the price change from the previous day. Calculate the mean, variance, standard deviation, and skewness of the price changes.

(c) For each day (starting at day 2), calculate the percentage change from the previous day by computing the price change as a percentage of the previous day's price. For example, the price change in day 2 is $42\frac{1}{2} - 42 = \frac{1}{2}$. The percentage change is $\frac{1}{2}/42 = 0.0119$, or 1.19 percent. Calculate the mean, variance, standard deviation, and skewness of the percentage change.

4.39. In 1981 the highest paid U.S. executives were compensated (in salary and other benefits) as shown in Table P4.39.

TABLE P4.39

Company	Executive	Compensation (thousands of dollars)
Schlumberger	Roland Genin	$5,658
Gen. Instrument	Frank G. Hickey	5,261
Metromedia	John W. Kluge	4,231
Schlumberger	Jean Riboud	3,029
United Technologies	Harry J. Gray	2,971
NL Industries	Ray C. Adam	2,904
Cooper Industries	Robert Cizik	2,761
Phibro	David Tendler	2,669
Anheuser-Busch	August A. Busch III	2,617
Union Oil	Fred L. Hartley	2,339
NL Industries	V. R. McLean	2,247
Phibro	Hal H. Beretz	2,221
Rockwell International	Robert Anderson	2,170
General Dynamics	David S. Lewis	2,119

Source: Data from *Business Week*, May 10, 1982, p. 76.

(a) Compute the average compensation of the executives.

(b) What is the median compensation?

(c) What is the standard deviation of the compensation of the executives?

4.40. The use of coupons by consumers was studied by a marketing team of a large firm that was reevaluating its policy on coupon distribution. The distribution of coupon redemption by 650 residents in a one-month period was as shown in Table P4.40.

TABLE P4.40

Number of coupons redeemed in one month	Coupon value				
	5¢	*10¢*	*15¢*	*20¢*	*Total*
0	129	406	473	553	1,561
1	83	18	16	10	127
2	212	118	98	40	468
3	162	96	51	27	336
4	64	12	12	20	108
Total	650	650	650	650	2,600

(a) Determine the average number of coupons redeemed per resident.

(b) What is the total value of the coupons redeemed and what is their average value?

4.41. Table P4.41 presents a frequency distribution of the percentage change of the average stock prices of 32 industries for the week of October 12, 1981.

TABLE P4.41

Percentage change in average stock prices	Frequency of industries
(-8.00)–under (-7.00)	1
(-7.00)–under (-6.00)	0
(-6.00)–under (-5.00)	3
(-5.00)–under (-4.00)	2
(-4.00)–under (-3.00)	2
(-3.00)–under (-2.00)	6
(-2.00)–under (-1.00)	4
(-1.00)–under 0.00	6
0.00 –under 1.00	4
1.00 –under 2.00	1
2.00 –under 3.00	1
3.00 –under 4.00	0
4.00 –under 5.00	1
5.00 –under 6.00	1
Total	32

Source: *Barron's*, October 19, 1981, p. 126. Reprinted by permission of *Barron's*, © Dow Jones & Company, Inc. 1981. All rights reserved.

(a) Calculate the average percentage change in the average stock prices.

(b) Calculate the variance and standard deviation of the percentage change.

(c) Determine the median and mode.

4.42. Thirty-one stores located in various areas around the country were surveyed for the price of a given product. Table P4.42*a* shows the price frequency distribution, and Table P4.42*b* shows the same data with the prices organized in intervals of $2 each.

TABLE P4.42*a*

Price	Frequency
$25.00	1
26.00	3
27.89	4
28.59	2
29.00	3
29.99	3
30.00	3

TABLE P4.42a (Continued)

Price	Frequency
30.99	7
31.00	2
32.90	1
33.00	1
34.00	1
Total	31

TABLE P4.42b

Price interval	Frequency
$25.00–under 27.00	4
27.00–under 29.00	6
29.00–under 31.00	16
31.00–under 33.00	3
33.00–under 35.00	2
Total	31

(a) Denote the price of the product by X and calculate its mean and variance, once using Table P4.42a and once using Table P4.42b.
(b) Explain the difference in the results obtained by using the two tables. Which gives more accurate results? Which is easier to calculate?
(c) Use Table P4.42b to calculate the median and the first and third quartiles.
(d) Compute the skewness and the coefficient of skewness.

4.43. The number of employees of three firms is given below, by age group:

Age	Firm A	Firm B	Firm C
Under 30	550	50	12,222
30–under 40	799	27	10,479
40–under 50	437	32	8,334
50 and over	242	10	6,860

(a) Determine the proportion of employees aged 40 or older in each of the three firms.
(b) What is the proportion of employees aged 40 or older in the three firms combined?
(c) Of all the employees in the three firms, what proportion is younger than 30 and employed by Firm *A*?

Case Problems

4.1. In Case Problem 3.3, you used rates of return of 10 mutual funds in the "Maximum Capital Gain" category and of 5 mutual funds in the "Senior Securities Policy" category. Calculate the mean and the standard deviation of the rates of return in each of the two categories based on the data of these two samples; the rates in each category come from the same population. Compare the means and the standard deviations of the two categories. Does their relationship reinforce the conclusion you reached in Case Problem 3.3? Explain.

4.2. Consider mutual funds numbers 11, 18, 24, 26, and 32 in Data Set 2 Appendix B, Table B.2. Assume you have invested $10,000 in each of the funds in the beginning of 1971 and kept it in the fund through the end of 1980. What was the value of the investment in each fund at the end of 1980? How do your answers compare with the average rate of return of each fund for the period in question? Explain.

4.3. (a) Use the rates of return data of the 19 mutual funds in the "Balanced Funds" category of Data Set 2, Appendix B, Table B.2. (You will have 190 observations in all.) Construct a frequency distribution of the data using class intervals of 5 percent starting at -30 percent. Accordingly, the intervals will be "(-30) to under (-25)," "(-25) to under (-20)," and so on.

(b) Using the frequency distribution, calculate the mean, median, mode, and other descriptive measures of the data. Describe the data verbally using these measures.

(c) Calculate the same measures as in part b, except this time use the raw data, not the frequency distribution. Discuss the differences in the measures as computed by the two methods. Which is more accurate? Which would you normally prefer?

4.4. Use the profit data in Data Set 1, Appendix B, Table B.1. Show that Chebyshev's theorem holds for these data by demonstrating its validity using five alternative values of k of your choice, provided $k > 1$.

4.5. (a) Using the sales data and the profit data in Data Set 1, calculate the following measures for each of the two sets: mean, standard deviation, skewness, median, the first quartile, the third quartile, and the coefficient of variation. What conclusion can you reach from the comparison of these measures of the two distributions? Which distribution has a higher variability? How can you explain the relatively big difference between the mode and the mean of each of the two distributions? What procedure would you suggest to avoid such a big difference?

(b) Suppose the government wants to stimulate the economy by subsidizing 10 percent of the firms with the lowest profit margin. The policy is that "all firms with a profit margin of less than x percent will get a grant." Calculate the value of x. Draw a histogram with class intervals of 4.0, starting at a margin of -14 percent, and determine the class in which x is located.

APPENDIX 4A:
The Summation Operation

Several algebraic rules apply to the summation operation. We shall list here those that are relevant to the material covered in this book.

RULES FOR SUMMATION OPERATIONS

Rule 1: Let X and Y be two variables. Then:

$$\sum_{i=1}^{N} (X_i + Y_i) = \sum_{i=1}^{N} X_i + \sum_{i=1}^{N} Y_i$$

Rule 2: Let a be a constant. Then:

$$\sum_{i=1}^{N} a = \underbrace{a + a + \cdots + a}_{N \ times} = Na$$

Rule 3:

$$\sum_{i=1}^{N} (a + X_i) = \sum_{i=1}^{N} a + \sum_{i=1}^{N} X_i = Na + \sum_{i=1}^{N} X_i$$

Rule 4:

$$\sum_{i=1}^{N} aX_i = a \sum_{i=1}^{N} X_i$$

Rule 5:

$$\sum_{i=1}^{N} X_i^2 = X_1^2 + X_2^2 + \cdots + X_N^2$$

Rule 6:

$$\left(\sum_{i=1}^{N} X_i \right)^2 = \left(X_1 + X_2 + \cdots + X_N \right)^2$$

APPENDIX PROBLEMS

4A.1. Assuming $X_1 = 6.4$, $X_2 = 1.3$, $X_3 = 4.2$, and $X_4 = 5.5$, determine the following values:

(a) $\displaystyle\sum_{i-1}^{4} X_i^2$

(b) $\displaystyle\left(\sum_{i=1}^{4} X_i \right)^2$

(c) $\displaystyle\sum_{i=1}^{4} (a + X_i)$, where $a = 7.0$

4A.2. Assuming $X_1 = 141$, $X_2 = 107$, $X_3 = 96$, $X_4 = 66$, $Y_1 = 43$, $Y_2 = 44$, $Y_3 = 61$, and $Y_4 = 58$, determine the following values:

(a) $\displaystyle\sum_{i=1}^{4} (X_i + Y_i)$

(b) $\displaystyle\sum_{i=1}^{4} 8Y_i$

4A.3. Write each of the following expressions without the summation sign:

(a) $\displaystyle\sum_{i=3}^{6} X_i$ (c) $\displaystyle\sum_{i=1}^{5} (X_i + Y_i)$ (e) $\displaystyle\sum_{i=1}^{5} X_i^2$

(b) $\displaystyle\sum_{i=1}^{4} (X_i - 8)$ (d) $\displaystyle\sum_{i=4}^{6} (X_i - Y_i)$ (f) $\displaystyle\sum_{i=6}^{9} (X_i - 3Y_i^2)$

4A.4. Prove that

(a) $\sum_{i=1}^{N} (X_i - k) = \sum_{i=1}^{N} X_i - Nk$

(b) $\sum_{i=1}^{N} (X_i - \bar{X}) = 0$ when $\bar{X}$ is the mean of the X_is

APPENDIX 4B:
The Geometric Mean

Donna Rogers paid $1,000 in personal income tax two years ago and an additional $3,000 a year ago. The total for the two years was $4,000 and the arithmetic annual average was $4,000/2 = $2,000. Had Rogers paid $2,000 in the first year and an additional $2,000 in the second, her total tax payment for the two years would have been exactly the same: $4,000.

Consider now an investment made by Rogers two years ago. She invested $100, and the value of that investment declined 20 percent in the first year. The value, then, was $80 at the end of the first year. During the second year the value of the investment rose 50 percent—from $80 to $120. The change over the two-year period was an increase of 20 percent in the value of the investment (from $100 to $120). The arithmetic average of the annual per-·centage changes was $(-20\% + 50\%)/2 = 15\%$. Had Rogers earned 15 percent on her investment in the first year and 15 percent again in the second year, *the final value of the investment at the end of the second year would not have been $120*. It would have been $132.25, calculated as follows: the original $100 would have increased in value to $115 at the end of the first year (an increase of 15 percent: $100 · 1.15 = $115) and to $132.25 at the end of the second year (an additional increase of 15 percent: $115 · 1.15 = $132.25).

The second example clearly shows that when percentage changes of a variable's value over time are involved, the arithmetic mean of the percentage changes can be misleading. It should be replaced by the **geometric mean.**

Let the value of the variable at the *beginning* of the first period be denoted by V_0. Let the value at the *end* of the first period be V_1, at the *end* of the second period be V_2, and so on. The rate of change in the variable's value in period i, denoted by R_i, is given as follows:

Period (i)	Rate of change
1	$R_1 = \dfrac{V_1}{V_0} - 1$
2	$R_2 = \dfrac{V_2}{V_1} - 1$
3	$R_3 = \dfrac{V_3}{V_2} - 1$
.	. .
.	. .
.	. .
n	$R_n = \dfrac{V_n}{V_{n-1}} - 1$

The geometric mean of the n periods is given by $\overline{X}_g$:

$$\overline{X}_g = \sqrt[n]{(1 + R_1)(1 + R_2) \cdots (1 + R_n)} - 1$$

$$= \sqrt[n]{\frac{V_1}{V_0} \frac{V_2}{V_1} \cdots \frac{V_{n-1}}{V_{n-2}} \frac{V_n}{V_{n-1}}} - 1 = \sqrt[n]{\frac{V_n}{V_0}} - 1$$

Reconsidering Rogers's investment, we get

Period	Rate of change
1	$R_1 = \dfrac{80}{100} - 1 = -0.2$
2	$R_2 = \dfrac{120}{80} - 1 = 0.5$

so that the geometric mean is

$$\overline{X}_g = \sqrt[2]{(1 - 0.2)(1 + 0.5)} - 1 = \sqrt[2]{1.2} - 1 = 0.095$$

If the investment's value had appreciated 9.5 percent in each of the two years, it would have had a value of $109.50 at the end of the first year ($109.50 = $100 \cdot 1.095) and $119.90 at the end of the second year ($119.90 = $109.5 \cdot 1.095). The deviation from $120 is due to rounding.

If you still have any lingering doubts about the applicability of the geometric mean, you will certainly be convinced after considering another of Rogers's investments. She invested $100 and the value of the investment declined 50 percent (down to $50) in the first year. During the second year the value of the investment rose 100 percent, to $100. All in all, over the two-year period she gained nothing. She started with $100 and still had only $100 after two years. The arithmetic average of the annual percentage change in the value of the investment was $(-50\% + 100\%)/2 = 25\%$. This figure gives the erroneous impression that the value of her investment increased over the two years. The geometric average is as follows:

Period	Rate of change
1	$R_1 = \dfrac{50}{100} - 1 = -0.5$
2	$R_2 = \dfrac{100}{50} - 1 = 1.0$

so that

$$\overline{X}_g = \sqrt[2]{(1 - 0.5)(1 + 1.0)} - 1 = \sqrt[2]{1} - 1 = 0$$

Indeed, where the rate of change of a variable over time is concerned, the geometric mean provides a correct average, whereas the arithmetic mean does not.

APPENDIX PROBLEMS

4B.1. Tom invested $12,000 in the stock market for one year; $6,000 was invested in bonds, on which his rate of return was 6 percent; $3,000 was invested in stock on which his rate of return was −3 percent; and $3,000 was invested in stock on which the rate of return was 15 percent. What was Tom's average rate of return on his investment? Did you use the arithmetic average, the weighted average, or the geometric average? Explain your choice.

4B.2. Tony invested $12,000 in bonds for one year. At the end of the year, his investment was worth 6 percent more: $12,720. He reinvested the money in stock for another year, and his return this time was −3 percent, so his investment at the end of the second year was worth $12,338.40. He then reinvested for another year and his return was 15 percent, so at the end of the third year the investment was worth $14,189.16. What was Tony's average rate of return per year?

4B.3. Would your answer to Problem 4B.2 be any different if the return in the second year were −30 percent (rather than −3 percent) and in the third year 59.357 percent (rather than 15 percent)? Explain.

4B.4. The gross national product (GNP) of Fluctuania has fluctuated over the last few years. The percentage change of GNP over the previous year's level for six recent years is given here. Find the arithmetic mean and the geometric mean of the percentage change. Which is more appropriate?

Year	Percentage change in GNP
1978	−50%
1979	+50
1980	−25
1981	+25
1982	−40
1983	+22

4B.5. Verify your answer to Problem 4B.4 in the following way: assume that Fluctuania's GNP in 1977 was $10 billion, and derive the GNP level for *each* of the years 1978 through 1983, once by applying the actual annual percentage changes as given in Problem 4B.4, once by applying to each year a percentage change equal to the arithmetic mean, and once by applying to each year a percentage change equal to the geometric mean. Of the last two methods, which results in a 1983 GNP level identical to that obtained by applying the actual GNP percentage changes?

4B.6. The arithmetic mean and the geometric mean are two location measures. The geometric mean is not always applicable. When is it applicable?

4B.7. The following are average living costs for a family of four as of December 31 of the last few years:

December 31 of year	0	1	2	3	4
Cost	$15,500	$16,000	$16,450	$17,200	$18,000

(a) Calculate the rate of increase in the cost of living for years 1, 2, 3, and 4.
(b) Calculate the geometric mean annual rate of increase in the cost of living twice, first by using the rates of increase of each of the years and then by using only the cost of living of year 4 and year 0. Explain the relationship between the two.

4B.8. You invested $10,000 in stocks two years ago. The mean rates of return over the two years of investment were as follows:

Arithmetic mean: 40 percent per year
Geometric mean: 38 percent per year

(a) What is the value of your investment now, two years after you made the investment?
(b) What were the rates of return in the last two years? Can you say?

4B.9. Investor *I* invests $500 in stock *A* and $500 in stock *B* for one year. The (arithmetic) average rate of return on the two stocks for the year was zero, so that her investment was worth $1,000 at the end of the year. At that time she sold her investment in *A* and *B* and immediately invested $500 in stock *A* and $500 in stock *B* for another year. The (arithmetic) average rate of return on the two stocks for the second year was also zero. She ended the second year with stocks worth $1,000, a value equal to her initial investment two years earlier, so that her geometric mean rate of return for the two years was zero. Investor *J* followed a different investment strategy during the same two years. He invested $500 in stock *A* and $500 in stock *B* in the beginning of the first year and sold his investment in the stocks after two years, during which he did not buy or sell any of the stock. He realized a geometric average rate of return of 11.80 percent per year.

(a) How do you reconcile the results of *I*'s and *J*'s investments?
(b) Can you determine the rates of return on stocks *A* and *B* in the first and second year? Explain.

PART 2

PROBABILITY AND DISTRIBUTIONS (DEDUCTION)

Chapter 5 introduces and explains basic probability concepts. Chapter 6 deals with the concept and analysis of a random variable. Chapter 7 extends the analysis to the relationship between two random variables. The rest of the chapters in this part of the book concern specific probability distributions, and their applicability to a variety of fields in business and economics. Chapter 8 presents some important discrete distributions; Chapter 9 is devoted to the normal distribution—a distribution that plays a central role in statistical analysis; Chapter 10 deals with additional important continuous distributions.

The applications and examples presented in Part 2 concern the determination of insurance premiums using the conditional probability concept; the relationship between accounting variables; investment diversification and investment risk; budgeting research and development; the need for capital of a company drilling for oil; the "safety first" investment principle; and other topics.

PROBABILITY

5

CHAPTER FIVE OUTLINE

Key Terms
random experiment
basic outcome
sample point
sample space
univariate sample space
bivariate sample space
multivariate sample space
event
simple event
composite event
Venn diagram
intersection
empty event
union
complement
partition
objective probability
subjective probability
addition rule
marginal probabilities
joint probabilities
conditional probability
multiplication rule
Bayes' theorem
independent events
total probability equation
symmetrical sample spaces
permutation
combinations

It is difficult to imagine a world of certainty, in which the outcomes of future processes and phenomena are known in advance. Such a world, if it existed, would doubtless be excruciatingly dull. We are apparently lucky, then, to live in the more exciting world of uncertainty. Paradoxically, however, we are constantly seeking to minimize the uncertainty facing us and to foresee the outcomes of processes subject to chance. We seem to like uncertainty, but would prefer a little less of it than we usually have.

While the total elimination of uncertainty is usually impossible, prudent assessment of the chances involved in uncertain events is important if we are to make "good" decisions. We may have to face uncertainty regarding the *outcomes* of some phenomena, but we are often able to eliminate uncertainty with respect to the *chances* of such outcomes. Thus, if we inquire about the chances, or *probabilities*, of the outcome of a given process, and find that outcome *A* has a 10 percent chance of occurring and outcome *B* has a 90 percent chance, we are better able to assess the process's probable results than we would be if these chances were themselves unknown.

Probability assessment is easy in some simple situations, but it requires careful examination in the complex problems that are typical of the business world. This chapter is devoted to the elementary concepts and rules of probability; these will provide the basis for a better understanding of uncertain processes.

5.1 The Random Experiment and the Sample Space

First, let us consider the concept of the **random experiment**—*any process that has an uncertain outcome or outcomes.* The outcomes of such an experiment will generally differ from one run of the experiment to the next. When we deposit a coin in a coffee machine, we are conducting an experiment. If the machine is properly maintained, there is a good chance we will receive coffee in return, but this is certainly not the only possible outcome. Most of us have had the unfortunate experience of receiving no coffee in return for our coins. If we were lucky, we got our money back; if not, we got neither our coffee nor our money. Similarly, tomorrow's weather may be viewed as a random experiment with a variety of possible outcomes. And predicting a company's profit level for next year is an interesting business example of a random experiment.

POSSIBLE OUTCOMES OF THE RANDOM EXPERIMENT

While our primary objective in this chapter is to determine how *probable* a given outcome or set of outcomes is, we shall first be concerned with all the outcomes that are *possible* as a result of the experiment.

The possible outcomes of some experiments are trivially determined. When we flip a coin, for example, the possible outcomes are simply "heads" and "tails." In many situations, however, the possible outcomes of an experiment are not trivial. They are a function of what we shall call an "outcome." Consider, for example, a change in the price of Stock *A* on the next trading day on the New York Stock Exchange. The number and scope of the possible outcomes of this experiment depend on our choice of definitions. We may choose to differentiate only among the following outcomes: "the price goes up," "the price is unchanged," and "the price goes down." If we desire, however, we may select different classifications for the possible outcomes of the same experiment. Table 5.1 presents three possible classifications; many more classifications of this single experiment's results—in fact, an infinite number—are possible.

TABLE 5.1
Alternative Classifications of an Experiment's Outcome

Alternative A		Alternative B		Alternative C	
Outcome	*Description*	*Outcome*	*Description*	*Outcome*	*Description*
A_1	The stock's price goes up.	B_1	The stock's price goes up.	C_1	The stock's price goes up 3% or more.
A_2	The price does not go up (it declines or stays unchanged).	B_2	The price is unchanged.	C_2	The price goes up by less than 3%.
		B_3	The price goes down.	C_3	The price is unchanged.
				C_4	The price declines by less than 3%.
				C_5	The price declines by 3% or more.

In any random experiment, our choice of classification should depend on the nature and goal of the study in which we are engaged. For that reason we often talk about the *outcomes of interest* of a random experiment. In our Stock Exchange example, under alternative *A* there are only two outcomes of interest. Under alternative *B* there are three, and so on.

BASIC OUTCOMES AND THE SAMPLE SPACE

Each of the possible outcomes of interest in a random experiment is called a **basic outcome.** We note that *one and only one* basic outcome will occur as a result of the experiment. A *basic outcome* is frequently referred to as a **sample point,** and *the set of all possible sample points* of an experiment is known as the **sample space.** We distinguish among *univariate, bivariate,* and *multivariate* sample spaces. A **univariate sample space** is one in which *the sample points are defined by classification of the outcome of one variable,* such as the price change of one stock on a given trading day. A **bivariate sample space** is one in which *the sample points are defined by cross-classification of two variables.* The combination of price changes of two stocks during a given trading day defines a bivariate sample space; so does the price change of a single stock on two particular trading days. A **multivariate sample space** is one in which *the sample points are defined by cross-classification of more than two variables.*

As a simple example of a univariate sample space, consider the classification of people by the brand of toothpaste they most often use. The sample space includes the following sample points:

Colgate
Crest
Close-Up
Ultra Brite
Other

TABLE 5.2
Example of a Bivariate Sample Space: College Students by Seniority and Grade-Point Average (GPA)

GPA	Seniority			
	Freshman	*Sophomore*	*Junior*	*Senior*
0.00–1.99	O_1	O_2	O_3	O_4
2.00–2.99	O_5	O_6	O_7	O_8
3.00–4.00	O_9	O_{10}	O_{11}	O_{12}

In "Other" we include also those people who use no particular toothpaste most often (for example, those who use Colgate half of the time and Crest the other half).

Let us now consider a bivariate sample space. Suppose we have a two-way classification of college students by seniority (freshman, sophomore, junior, senior) and by cumulative grade-point average (GPA). The cross-classification is illustrated in Table 5.2.

Twelve basic outcomes are shown in Table 5.2. For easy reference, we denote each combination of seniority and GPA by the notation $O_1, O_2, \ldots,$ O_{12}. So, for example, O_6 is the notation for a sophomore with a GPA in the range 2.00–2.99.

The twelve basic outcomes shown in Table 5.2 form a sample space, since every student must fit into one (and only one) of the twelve outcomes. Note that some basic outcomes may be redundant, in the sense that no student will have their characteristics. The outcome O_4, for instance, may be redundant in that we expect no senior student to have a cumulative GPA below 2.00.

Finally, let us consider a multivariate sample space—one defined by a cross-classification of more than two variables. Here is a simple example: we may classify U.S. citizens into groups defined by sex, age, occupation, and location of residence.

As we have said, our main interest in this chapter is in the probability of the various outcomes. However, we need to look at combinations of outcomes (that is, events) before we can consider their probability.

5.2 Events

In Section 5.1 we explained how we classify the random experiment's results into what we termed basic outcomes. Quite often we will be interested in questions involving the possibility or the probability of occurrence of results consisting of more than just one basic outcome. To facilitate the handling of problems of this sort, let us consider the concept of event. An **event** is *the result of a random experiment consisting of one or more basic outcomes*. If an event consists of only *one basic outcome*, it is a **simple event;** if it consists of *more than one basic outcome*, it is a **composite event.**

EXAMPLE 5.1

A newsstand operator is selling *Easy Life* magazine, and we want to observe two days of operations. Suppose we define a bivariate sample space in the following way:

Number of magazines sold on second day	Number of magazines sold on first day		
	0–5	*6–10*	*11 or more*
0– 5	O_1	O_2	O_3
6–10	O_4	O_5	O_6
11 or more	O_7	O_8	O_9

Many events involving one or more basic outcomes may be defined over this sample space. Some examples are given in Table 5.3.

TABLE 5.3
Description and Basic Outcomes of Four Events

Event	Description	Basic outcomes of event
A	The number of magazines sold on the first day is less than or equal to 10.	$O_1, O_2, O_4, O_5, O_7, O_8$
B	The number of magazines sold on the second day is greater than or equal to 11.	O_7, O_8, O_9
C	The number of magazines sold on each of the two days does not exceed 5.	O_1. Event C consists of only one basic outcome and thus it is a *simple event*.
D	The number of magazines sold on the first day is greater than or equal to 6 and the number sold on the second day is between 6 and 10 (inclusive).	O_5, O_6

VENN DIAGRAMS

It is often useful to describe events in the sample space on a **Venn diagram** such as the one presented in Figure 5.1, showing the events of Table 5.3. The rectangle itself represents the *sample space,* while the points in it stand for the *basic outcomes.* The sample space is denoted by *U,* which stands for the "universal set," and the basic outcomes of the two-day sale of magazines are represented by nine points within *U.*

We shall frequently use a more schematic Venn diagram, in which the basic outcomes are omitted and only relevant events are plotted in the sample space. Events are described by areas enclosed in circles or other geometrical forms. Figure 5.2, for example, shows events *A* and *D* of Table 5.3 along with all the basic outcomes in the sample space. As we can see, events *A* and *D* overlap, since they have a common basic outcome, O_5.

Figure 5.1

Venn diagram showing nine different sample points

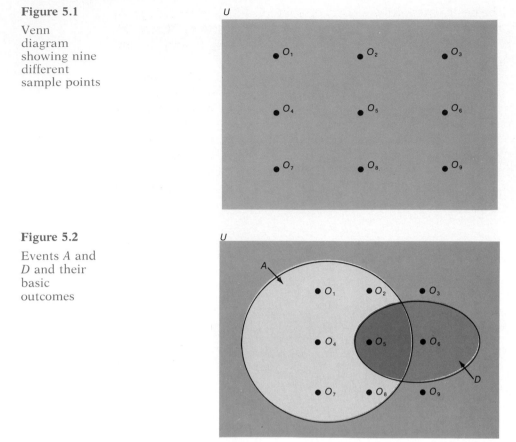

Figure 5.2

Events *A* and *D* and their basic outcomes

In general, we distinguish among the following three possible relationships between two events:

1. The two events have no basic outcomes in common. If this is the case, the events are said to be *mutually exclusive.* Consider, for example, the events "a person is less than 30 years old" and "that person is 30 or older." Since no one person can be both younger than 30 years and (at the same time) 30 years or older, these two events are mutually exclusive. Another example is "driving a Buick" and "driving a Chevy" (same person, same time). Figure 5.3 presents two mutually exclusive events,

Figure 5.3

Two mutually exclusive events

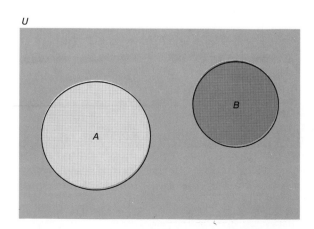

A and *B*. The basic outcomes are not represented by dots in this diagram and will not be presented from here on. The two events in Figure 5.3 do not overlap because, being mutually exclusive, they cannot be observed together.

2. One event entirely overlaps the other. In Figure 5.4 event *A* overlaps the entire event *B*, so that all of the basic outcomes in *B* are in *A* as well; not all the basic outcomes in *A*, however, are in *B*. Notationally we write $B \subset A$, meaning that all of *B* is included in *A*. As an example, suppose that *B* represents all companies in the steel industry that have up to $100 million in net assets and *A* represents all companies in the steel industry with up to $200 million in net assets. Obviously all the companies that belong to *B* also belong to *A*, while companies that belong to *A* are not necessarily included in *B*.

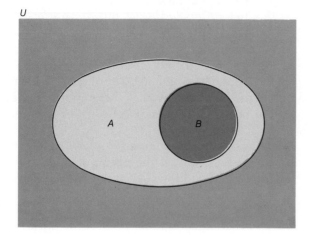

Figure 5.4

One event entirely overlapping another

3. The two events partially overlap one another. Figure 5.5 shows this kind of relationship between events. Here some basic outcomes are common to *A* and *B*, but some basic outcomes in *A* are not in *B*, and others are in *B* but not in *A*. As an example, suppose the experiment involves the random selection of people in Cincinnati for a marketing survey. Suppose *A* is the event "the person selected is a woman" and *B* is the event "the person selected is the parent of at least two children." In this case, *A* and *B* relate to one another as depicted in Figure

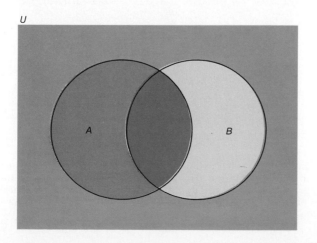

Figure 5.5

Two partially overlapping events

5.5: some of the people are women who are parents of at least two children (and thus belong to both *A* and *B*); some are women who do not have at least two children (and thus belong to *A* but not to *B*); and finally, some are parents of at least two children, but are men (and so they belong to *B* but not to *A*).

Case 3 may be regarded as the general case, with cases 1 and 2 being considered special cases of 3.

PARTS OF THE VENN DIAGRAM

The area in which two (or more) events overlap is called the **intersection** of the events: *A* ∩ *B* (read "*A* intersection *B*," or "*A* and *B*"). In Figure 5.6 the intersection is represented by the darkest region.

An *event that does not include any basic outcome* is an impossible event and is referred to as the **empty event**.[1] The symbol we use for the empty event is ∅. If events *A* and *B* are mutually exclusive, they have no basic outcomes in common, and it follows that in that case we have *A* ∩ *B* = ∅. Suppose Xerox employees' wages range between $6,000 and $100,000 annually. Select an employee and define the following event: "the employee's wage is $150,000 annually." The event is empty, since none of the employees earns more than $100,000 per year.

The *area that encompasses the overlapping as well as the nonoverlapping sections of A and B combined* is called the **union** of events: *A* ∪ *B* (read "*A* union *B*," or "*A* and/or *B*"). The union of *A* and *B* is the entire hatched area in Figure 5.6.

The **complement** of a given event (denoted by a prime next to the event's symbol) is the set of *all basic outcomes that are not included in the event*. If *A* is the event "the train arrived on time," then *A'* is the event "the train did not arrive on time." The complement of *A* ∪ *B* in Figure 5.6, (*A* ∪ *B*)', is represented by the unhatched section of the sample space.

Figure 5.6

Intersection, union, and complement of two events

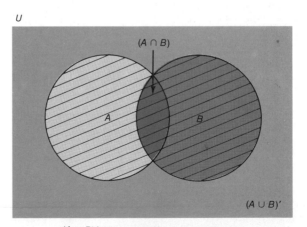

(*A* ∪ *B*) is represented by the hatched area.

[1] The reason an empty event is impossible is that basic outcomes were defined so that one of them must occur as a result of the experiment. Note that the empty event is not really an "event" by our definition: we defined event to be a result of a random experiment consisting of one or more basic outcomes. The term "event" is therefore used as an exception to the general definition.

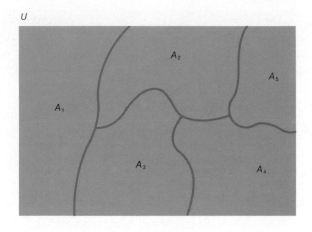

Figure 5.7

Sample space
partitioned
by five
mutually
exclusive
events

Consider Figure 5.7. Here the sample space, U, is *partitioned* by events A_1, A_2, A_3, A_4, and A_5. The events form a **partition** because they are *mutually exclusive* and also *collectively exhaustive* in the sense that their union constitutes the entire sample space. For example, the annual salary of an individual selected at random out of a given population will be in one of the following categories: under \$10,000 (event A_1), \$10,000–under \$20,000 (event A_2), \$20,000–under \$30,000 (event A_3), \$30,000–under \$40,000 (event A_4), \$40,000 or over (event A_5). Obviously events A_1, A_2, A_3, A_4, and A_5 are mutually exclusive and collectively exhaustive. (Note, as a trivial example, that an event and its complement are mutually exclusive and collectively exhaustive.)

Before proceeding, we shall discuss another example and demonstrate the use and the usefulness of the concepts developed so far.

EXAMPLE 5.2

For the purpose of examining the proposed expansion of a major southeastern airport, data on passenger arrivals and departures have been amassed. The daily passenger arrivals and departures are grouped into four classes of interest: 0–1,000, 1,001–5,000, 5,001–10,000, and 10,001 or more. This classification defines a bivariate sample space, as shown in Table 5.4.

TABLE 5.4
Air Traffic, by Arrivals and Departures
(number of passengers)

	Arrivals			
Departures	*0–1,000*	*1,001–5,000*	*5,001– 10,000*	*10,001 or more*
0– 1,000	O_1	O_2	O_3	O_4
1,001– 5,000	O_5	O_6	O_7	O_8
5,001–10,000	O_9	O_{10}	O_{11}	O_{12}
10,001 or more	O_{13}	O_{14}	O_{15}	O_{16}

Let us define several events in the sample space referring to the "results" of a daily operation.

A   There were no more than 1,000 arrivals.
B   There were no more than 10,000 arrivals.
C   There were 1,001–5,000 arrivals.
D   There were 1,001–5,000 departures.
E   There were 10,001 or more departures.
F   There were no more than 1,000 departures.

Table 5.5 identifies the basic outcomes, descriptions, and diagrammatic presentations of some relationships among these events.

TABLE 5.5
Events, Descriptions, and Venn Diagrams of Relationships Among Events

Event	Basic outcomes included	Description	Venn diagram
B'	O_4, O_8, O_{12}, O_{16}	10,001 or more arrivals, regardless of number of departures	
$B \cap F$	O_1, O_2, O_3	0–1,000 departures and up to 10,000 arrivals	
$A \cup F$	$O_1, O_2, O_3, O_4, O_5,$ O_9, O_{13}	0–1,000 arrivals and/or 0–1,000 departures	
$(A \cup F)'$	$O_6, O_7, O_8, O_{10}, O_{11},$ $O_{12}, O_{14}, O_{15}, O_{16}$	1,001 or more arrivals and also 1,001 or more departures	
$A \cap B$	O_1, O_5, O_9, O_{13}	Up to 1,000 arrivals	
$D \cap F$	None	This is an empty event ($\varnothing$). D and F cannot be observed on the same day: they are mutually exclusive	
$A \cap E'$	O_1, O_5, O_9	0–1,000 arrivals and up to 10,000 departures	
$(C \cap D)'$	All basic outcomes except O_6	All arrival and departure combinations except 1,001–5,000 of both	

5.3 The Meaning of Probability

We distinguish between two types of random experiment: one that can be repeated many times under the same circumstances (such as flipping a coin or tossing a die) and one that cannot be repeated many times under the same conditions (such as the process that generates McDonald's profit next year). The outcomes of these two types of experiments lead us to define *two types of probability*. When the experiment can be repeated numerous times under identical conditions, we talk about *objective* probability; when conditions change each time an experiment is repeated, we speak of *subjective* probability. The **objective probability** of an event is its *frequency of occurrence over many repeated experiments*. Examples are the probability that a fetus is a boy or a girl, the probability of a coin flip resulting in "heads," and the like. **Subjective probability** is the probability we assign to the *outcomes of an experiment that cannot be repeated*. The growth of GNP next year is an experiment that can be observed only once, and thus cannot be assigned an objective probability. The importance of subjective probability stems from the fact that it is often an important input into decision making by individuals and groups (such as corporate management). For both objective and subjective probabilities, the following properties and rules hold:

PROPERTY 1

$$0 \le P(A) \le 1$$

The probability of event A is greater than or equal to zero and less than or equal to one.

PROPERTY 2

$$P(U) = 1$$

The probability of the entire sample space, U, is equal to 1. This means that if the experiment takes place, one of the basic outcomes must occur.

PROPERTY 3

When $A \cap B = \varnothing$, $\qquad P(A \cup B) = P(A) + P(B)$

The probability of the union of two *mutually exclusive* events, A and B, is equal to the sum of the probabilities of the individual events. Since A and A' are mutually exclusive events, it follows that the following relationship holds:

$$P(A \cup A') = P(A) + P(A') = P(U) = 1$$

5.4 The Addition Rule

In many situations it becomes necessary to calculate the probability of a combination of events. Venn diagrams help to explain the basic probability rules. First, since the rectangle U represents the entire sample space, its area is equal to 1 (of any desired unit). Second, the areas of all the events in the sample space are proportional to their probability. All events with a 25 percent probability of occurrence take 25 percent of the rectangle's area, and so on. Thus area represents probability in a Venn diagram.

Consider Figure 5.8, in which the union of events A and B (that is, $A \cup B$) is divided into three mutually exclusive subareas:

Area 1: the part of A that is outside of B (i.e., $A \cap B'$)
Area 2: the part of B that is outside of A (i.e., $A' \cap B$)
Area 3: the intersection of A and B (i.e., $A \cap B$)

Figure 5.8

A graphic representation of the addition rule

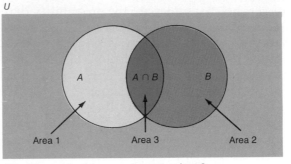

Event A consists of the sum of Area 1 + Area 3.
Event B consists of the sum of Area 2 + Area 3.
It follows that $P(A \cup B) = P(A) + P(B) - P(A \cap B)$.

The following two equations follow directly from our definitions:

$$P(A) = \text{Area } 1 + \text{Area } 3$$

$$P(B) = \text{Area } 2 + \text{Area } 3$$

The probability of the union of A and B [that is, $P(A \cup B)$] is represented by the sum of Areas 1, 2, and 3. We may obtain this probability by adding the probabilities of the two events A and B and subtracting the probability of the intersection. If we add up the probabilities of A and B without subtracting the probability of the intersection, we will be double-counting Area 3, since $P(A) + P(B) = (\text{Area } 1 + \text{Area } 3) + (\text{Area } 2 + \text{Area } 3)$. Thus to get the probability of the union, we have to subtract the probability of the intersection (Area 3), which is expressed by the following:

ADDITION RULE FOR TWO EVENTS

$$P(A \cup B) = P(A) + P(B) - P(A \cap B) \tag{5.1}$$

To learn how to apply the addition rule to more than two events, see Appendix 5A.

EXAMPLE 5.3

Suppose a country music singer is nominated as both Female Vocalist of the Year and Best Entertainer of the Year. Let A be the event "the singer is voted Female Vocalist of the Year," and let B be the event "the singer is voted Best Entertainer of the Year." Suppose also that the following probabilities are assumed: $P(A) = 0.10$; $P(B) = 0.20$; $P(A \cap B) = 0.03$.

What is the probability that the singer will win *at least one* of the two awards—that is, that she will win the first award *and/or* the second? We need to find the probability of the union of the events A and B: $P(A \cup B) = ?$ The answer is given by Equation 5.1:

$$P(A \cup B) = P(A) + P(B) - P(A \cap B) = 0.10 + 0.20 - 0.03 = 0.27$$

For those students still skeptical about the logic behind subtracting the probability of the intersection [that is, $P(A \cap B)$] from the sum of the probabilities of the individual events in order to get the union's probability, here is an additional example that should do the trick.

In rolling a die, let us define the following events: A, the number 1, 2, 4, or 5 appears; B, an even number (that is, 2, 4, or 6) shows up. By these definitions we get $P(A) = \frac{4}{6}$; $P(B) = \frac{3}{6}$. What is the probability of the union of A and B? If we simply add the probabilities of A and B, we get $P(A) + P(B) = \frac{4}{6} + \frac{3}{6} = 1\frac{1}{6}$. But a probability greater than 1 is of course impossible, and we must conclude that $1\frac{1}{6}$ is a wrong answer. The intersection of A and B includes the results 2 and 4, so that $P(A \cap B) = \frac{2}{6}$. The probability of the union of A and B, calculated according to Equation 5.1, is

$$P(A \cup B) = P(A) + P(B) - P(A \cap B) = \frac{4}{6} + \frac{3}{6} - \frac{2}{6} = \frac{5}{6}$$

Indeed, the union includes the five results 1, 2, 4, 5, and 6.

When the events A and B are mutually exclusive, so that $P(A \cap B) = 0$, the addition rule reduces to

$$P(A \cup B) = P(A) + P(B) \qquad \text{when } A \cap B = \varnothing \qquad (5.2)$$

In this case, the generalization of the addition rule to n events follows immediately:

$$P(A_1 \cup A_2 \cup A_3 \cup \cdots \cup A_n) = P(A_1) + P(A_2) + P(A_3) + \cdots + P(A_n) \qquad (5.3)$$

Equation 5.3 applies, of course, only when all n events have no intersection so that they relate to one another as in Figure 5.9.

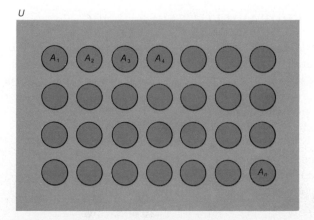

Figure 5.9

Nonintersecting events

5.5 Conditional Probability and the Multiplication Rule

Frequently we are interested in **conditional probability**—*the probability that an event will occur on the condition that some other event has occurred.* Take, for example, the probability that a new novel will become a best seller. Given no information about the novel, we would estimate its chances of becoming a best seller as rather slim. Given additional information regarding the novel, however, we might well reassess our (subjective) estimate of the probability that the novel will become a best seller. For example, if we learn that the author of the novel has already written two best sellers in the past, we undoubtedly would raise our estimate of the probability that the new novel will be a best seller.

Consider another example. Suppose 2 percent of all corporate bonds outstanding today will default in the next year and there exist some financial services that rank the quality of corporate bonds. To simplify matters, suppose a given financial service is using three ranks: *A* for high-quality bonds, *B* for average-quality bonds, and *C* for poor-quality bonds. Let us denote the event "the company will default on its bonds" by *DF*. We might write

$$P(DF) = 0.02$$

If we know the quality of the bond, however, the probability of default may change. Past records may show the following probabilities:

$$P(DF \mid A) = 0.005$$
$$P(DF \mid B) = 0.018$$
$$P(DF \mid C) = 0.045$$

where the probability of the event written to the left of the vertical line is *conditional upon* the occurrence of the event written on its right. For example, $P(DF \mid A)$ (read "the probability of *DF* conditional upon *A*," or "the probability of *DF* given *A*") means the probability of default of bonds graded *A*. If the bond is an *A* bond, the default probability is 0.5 percent; if it is a *B* bond, the probability is 1.8 percent; and if it is a *C* bond, the probability is 4.5 percent. (Note that these conditional probabilities do not add up to $P(DF) = 0.02$. The reason will become clear a little later, when we discuss Bayes' theorem.)

THE JOINT PROBABILITY TABLE

A *joint probability* distribution table will give us further insight into the meaning of conditional probability and help us to develop the relevant equations for calculating it. Consider the breakdown of a company's accounts receivable by balance and age (that is, the length of time the account is outstanding) presented in Table 5.6.

Let us denote four events as follows:

Y   The account is young (i.e., up to 30 days).
O   The account is old (i.e., 31 days or more).
S   The account has a small balance (i.e., up to $500).
L   The account has a large balance (i.e., over $500).

TABLE 5.6
Accounts Receivable, by Age and Balance

		Y	*O*	
		\multicolumn{3}{c}{*Age*}
	Balance	*Up to 30 days*	*31 days or more*	*Total*
S	*Up to $500*	490	110	600
L	*Over $500*	190	10	200
	Total	680	120	800

If we select an account at random, the probabilities of the occurrence of the above events may be simply determined from the *margin* of Table 5.6. For example, to determine the probability of selecting a young account at random, we divide the number of young accounts (680) by the total number of accounts (800); to determine the probability of selecting a small account at random, we divide the number of small accounts (600) by the total number of accounts (800); and so on. The resulting probabilities are:

$$\text{Classification by age}\begin{cases} P(Y) = \dfrac{680}{800} = 0.8500 \\[2ex] P(O) = \dfrac{120}{800} = 0.1500 \end{cases}\Bigg\} \text{add up to 1.0}$$

$$\text{Classification by balance}\begin{cases} P(S) = \dfrac{600}{800} = 0.7500 \\[2ex] P(L) = \dfrac{200}{800} = 0.2500 \end{cases}\Bigg\} \text{add up to 1.0}$$

These are called **marginal probabilities,** since the events (*Y, O, S,* and *L*) are defined in such a way that they *involve classification by one variable only.* For example, the event *L* is defined by the account's balance but not by its age, and so its probability is determined from the *margin* of the table. Such events as *Y ∩ S* and *O ∩ L*, on the other hand, are defined by *two-way classifications*—balance and age—and their probabilities are known as **joint probabilities.** To determine the probability of the event *Y ∩ S*, for example, we find the ratio of the accounts in *Y ∩ S* to the total number of accounts in the sample space. The joint probabilities in our example are as follows:

$$\begin{cases} P(Y \cap S) = \dfrac{490}{800} = 0.6125 \\[2ex] P(Y \cap L) = \dfrac{190}{800} = 0.2375 \\[2ex] P(O \cap S) = \dfrac{110}{800} = 0.1375 \\[2ex] P(O \cap L) = \dfrac{10}{800} = 0.0125 \end{cases}\Bigg\} \text{add up to 1.0}$$

Figure 5.10

Venn
diagram
showing
conditional
probability

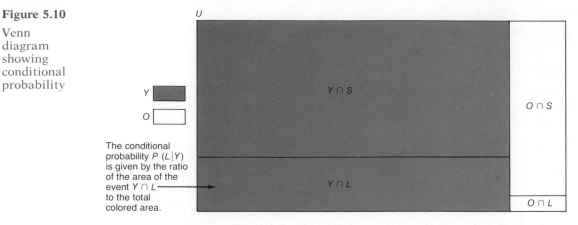

The conditional
probability $P(L|Y)$
is given by the ratio
of the area of the
event $Y \cap L$
to the total
colored area.

Turning now to **conditional probability,** we may ask, for example, what is the probability that the account is "large" *given* that it is "young"? If the account is known to be young, our focus must shift from the entire sample space with its 800 accounts to the more restricted group of 680 young accounts (see Figure 5.10). The conditional probabilities of our example are as follows:

$$\left\{ \begin{array}{l} P(L \mid Y) = \dfrac{190}{680} = 0.2794 \\[3ex] P(S \mid Y) = \dfrac{490}{680} = 0.7206 \end{array} \right\} \text{add up to 1.0}$$

$$\left\{ \begin{array}{l} P(L \mid O) = \dfrac{10}{120} = 0.0833 \\[3ex] P(S \mid O) = \dfrac{110}{120} = 0.9167 \end{array} \right\} \text{add up to 1.0}$$

$$\left\{ \begin{array}{l} P(Y \mid L) = \dfrac{190}{200} = 0.9500 \\[3ex] P(O \mid L) = \dfrac{10}{200} = 0.0500 \end{array} \right\} \text{add up to 1.0}$$

$$\left\{ \begin{array}{l} P(Y \mid S) = \dfrac{490}{600} = 0.8167 \\[3ex] P(O \mid S) = \dfrac{110}{600} = 0.1833 \end{array} \right\} \text{add up to 1.0}$$

Consider another example involving conditional probability.

EXAMPLE 5.4

A given car is produced in two models: Model 1 and Model 2. Each model is produced in two designs: hatchback and wagon. Of all the cars produced, 30 percent are Model 1, and 20 percent are wagons. But 50 percent of Model 1 are wagons. Suppose a car is selected at random.

Let event A be "the car selected is a Model 1" and let B be the event "the car selected is a wagon." The probabilities of A and B are:

$$P(A) = 0.30$$

$$P(B) = 0.20$$

These probabilities are reflected in Figure 5.11 by the relative area of the events in U. They are marginal probabilities. In addition, we know that $P(B \mid A) = 0.50$. This is a conditional probability. Given the condition A, that the car selected is a Model 1, the probability of B rises to 0.50. This probability is presented in Figure 5.11: the intersection of A and B takes 50 percent of the total area of A. Thus if our interest is limited to Area A, there is a 50 percent chance of randomly selecting a wagon.

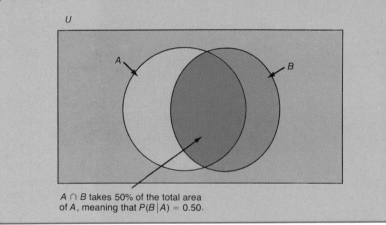

Figure 5.11

Venn diagram showing conditional probability

$A \cap B$ takes 50% of the total area of A, meaning that $P(B \mid A) = 0.50$.

The last example leads us to the first important rule of conditional probability:

$$P(B \mid A) = \frac{P(A \cap B)}{P(A)} \qquad (5.4)$$

where $P(A) \neq 0$.

A similar argument will lead us to the related rule:

$$P(A \mid B) = \frac{P(A \cap B)}{P(B)} \qquad (5.5)$$

where $P(B) \neq 0$.

Let us multiply Equation 5.4 by $P(A)$ and Equation 5.5 by $P(B)$. That yields the following:

MULTIPLICATION RULES FOR CONDITIONAL PROBABILITY

$$P(A \cap B) = P(B \mid A)P(A) \qquad \text{(5.6)}$$

$$P(A \cap B) = P(A \mid B)P(B) \qquad \text{(5.7)}$$

For the application of the multiplication rules to more than two events, see Appendix 5A.

Since the left-hand sides of Equations 5.6 and 5.7 are identical, the right-hand sides of these formulas must be equal to each other as well, so we get

$$P(A \mid B)P(B) = P(B \mid A)P(A) \qquad \text{(5.8)}$$

Dividing both sides of Equation 5.8 by $P(B)$, we derive the following useful formula for conditional probability problems:

BAYES' THEOREM

$$P(A \mid B) = \frac{P(B \mid A)P(A)}{P(B)} \qquad \text{(5.9)}$$

Bayes' theorem is named for the statistician Thomas Bayes. A more detailed version of it is presented later in this chapter.

In Example 5.4, given the probabilities $P(A) = 0.30$, $P(B) = 0.20$, and $P(B \mid A) = 0.50$, we may use Equation 5.9 to find

$$P(A \mid B) = \frac{P(B \mid A)P(A)}{P(B)} = \frac{0.50 \cdot 0.30}{0.20} = 0.75$$

so the probability that a randomly selected car is a Model 1, given that it is a wagon, is 0.75. We urge you to verify Equations 5.6 through 5.9 by using probabilities derived from Table 5.6.

Let us illustrate the usefulness of Equation 5.9 by another example.

EXAMPLE 5.5

An oil company is planning to drill for oil in two locations, field A and field B. Experts estimate the probability of finding oil of acceptable quality to be 20 percent in field A and 25 percent in field B. They also state that if oil of acceptable quality is found in field A, the probability of finding the same in field B is 80 percent (that is, $P(B \mid A) = 0.80$). If oil of acceptable quality is found in field B, what is the probability that such oil will be found in field A?

Let A stand for "oil of acceptable quality is found in field A." Let B stand for "oil of acceptable quality is found in field B."

We may write: $P(A) = 0.20$, $P(B) = 0.25$, $P(B \mid A) = 0.80$. The problem is $P(A \mid B) = ?$ Using Equation 5.9, we get

$$P(A \mid B) = \frac{P(B \mid A)P(A)}{P(B)} = \frac{0.80 \cdot 0.20}{0.25} = \frac{0.16}{0.25} = 0.64$$

Here is another way to approach the problem. While A and B take 20 and 25 percent, respectively, of the entire sample space (see Figure 5.12), they interrelate in such a way that 80 percent of A is overlapped by event B, representing the probability $P(B \mid A) = 0.80$. The area $A \cap B$ is then equal to 0.16 (that is, 80 percent of 0.20). To get $P(A \mid B)$ we find the relative area of $A \cap B$ within the area B, and we get 0.16/0.25 = 0.64.

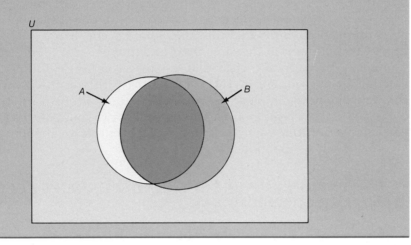

Figure 5.12

Venn diagram: $P(B|A) = 0.80$

5.6 Independent Events

Two events, A and B, are said to be **independent** of one another if and only if the following relationship holds true:

$$P(A \mid B) = P(A) \qquad\qquad \text{(5.10)}$$

In plain English, we say that A and B are independent if and only if the fact that B has occurred does not affect the chance that A will occur. The recovery of patient A, who has had a heart attack in San Francisco, may be regarded as independent of the recovery of patient B in Toronto at the same time; B's recovery or failure to recover has no effect on A's recovery. If, on the other hand, an experimental marketing technique for a new brand of cigarettes is being tried in New York, the results certainly have implications for the probability of success in a different region of the United States. Thus, if SNY stands for the event "success in New York" and SAG stands for "success in Atlanta, Georgia," then $P(SAG \mid SNY) \neq P(SAG)$, and the two events are not independent.

From Equation 5.7 we know that $P(A \cap B) = P(A \mid B)P(B)$. When events A and B are independent, we have $P(A \mid B) = P(A)$. Substituting this result into Equation 5.7 yields $P(A \cap B) = P(A)P(B)$, and thus we summarize the **multiplication rule** as follows:

In general	$P(A \cap B) = P(A \mid B)P(B)$

| If *A* and *B* are independent, the general formula applies but is reduced to | $P(A \cap B) = P(A)P(B)$ | **(5.11)** |

It is interesting to note the relationship between independence and mutual exclusiveness. Specifically, are two mutually exclusive events also independent? (At this point you should be well equipped to answer the question on your own!) The answer is that two mutually exclusive events are necessarily *dependent* on each other. Logically, if the events are mutually exclusive, the occurrence of one of them must *exclude* the occurrence of the other; if the events were independent, the occurrence of one of them *would have no effect* on the probability that the other would occur. If you are in Texas, you cannot be in Illinois at the same time, and thus the two events are mutually exclusive. It is therefore clear that whether you are in Illinois *depends* on whether or not you are in Texas. By contrast, the results of two flips of a coin are independent, since the result of the first flip can in no way affect the result of the second flip. Diagrammatically, two mutually exclusive events have *no intersection*, while two independent events have an intersection with an area given by Equation 5.11.

THE RELATIONSHIP BETWEEN INDEPENDENT EVENTS AND THEIR COMPLEMENTS

Before we turn to the graphic explanation of independence of events, note that if events *A* and *B* are independent, then *A* is also independent of *B'*, *B* is independent of *A'*, and *A'* is independent of *B'*. Let us look once again at Equation 5.5, which is a basic rule of conditional probability that holds for independent as well as dependent events:

$$P(A \mid B) = \frac{P(A \cap B)}{P(B)}$$

This formula holds in general, as we have said, and could be applied to the relationship between *A* and *B'*, *A'* and *B*, *A'* and *B'*. Consider first the relationship between *A* and *B'*:

$$P(A \mid B') = \frac{P(A \cap B')}{P(B')}$$

We know that $P(A \cap B')$ is equal to $P(A) - P(A \cap B)$. This can be verified by a simple Venn diagram showing events *A* and *B*. We also know that $P(B') = 1 - P(B)$; and since it is given that *A* and *B* are independent, it follows that $P(A \cap B) = P(A)P(B)$. Putting all these relationships together, we get

$$P(A \mid B') = \frac{P(A \cap B')}{P(B')} = \frac{P(A) - P(A)P(B)}{1 - P(B)} = \frac{P(A)[1 - P(B)]}{1 - P(B)} = P(A)$$

But if $P(A \mid B') = P(A)$, then *A* and *B'* are independent of one another. Interchanging the roles of A and B, we can similarly show that $P(A' \mid B) = P(A')$, so that A' and B are independent. Finally, we want to show that if A and B are independent, so are A' and B'.

$$P(A' \mid B') = \frac{P(A' \cap B')}{P(B')} = \frac{1 - P(A \cup B)}{1 - P(B)} = \frac{1 - [P(A) + P(B) - P(A \cap B)]}{1 - P(B)}$$

$$= \frac{[1 - P(A)][1 - P(B)]}{1 - P(B)} = 1 - P(A) = P(A')$$

Thus we proved that A' and B' are independent if A and B are independent.

GRAPHIC REPRESENTATION OF INDEPENDENCE AND DEPENDENCE OF EVENTS

Suppose the probabilities of events B_1 and B_2 in Figure 5.13 are 0.60 and 0.40, respectively:

$$P(B_1) = 0.60$$

$$P(B_2) = 0.40$$

Suppose also that event A, which intersects both B_1 and B_2, has a probability of 0.50:

$$P(A) = 0.50$$

As we can see, the bulk of A is concentrated in event B_1. If we have the information that B_1 will occur, then the probability that A will also occur is greater than 0.50: $P(A \mid B_1) > 0.50$. Diagrammatically, the probability $P(A \mid B_1)$ is given by the ratio of the portion of A that overlaps B_1 to the total area of B_1. Similarly, if we have the information that B_2 will occur, then the probability that A will occur is less than 0.50: $P(A \mid B_2) < 0.50$. We can see this in Figure 5.13 by the fact that the colored area in B_2 is less than 50 percent of the total area of B_2. Events A and B_1 are dependent, and so are events A and B_2.

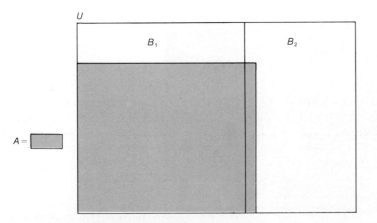

Figure 5.13

Venn diagram: events A and B_1 are dependent; events A and B_2 are dependent

Figure 5.14

Venn
diagram: *A* is
statistically
independent
of B_1 and B_2

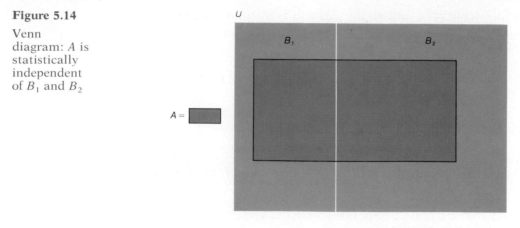

Figure 5.14, by contrast, depicts a situation of statistical independence between *A* and B_1 and between *A* and B_2. The proportion of *A* in B_1 is equal to the proportion of *A* in B_2 (and consequently both are equal to the proportion of *A* in the entire sample space). Any information we may have about the occurrence or nonoccurrence of B_1 (or B_2) does not alter the probability of *A*.

5.7 More on Conditional Probability: Bayes' Theorem

Let us proceed now to discuss a more generalized form of Bayes' theorem. Consider Figure 5.15, in which the sample space is *partitioned* by the events B_1, B_2, B_3, and B_4—in other words, events *B* (that is, B_1, B_2, B_3, and B_4) are mutually exclusive and collectively exhaustive. Event *A* intersects the *B* events. Because events B_1, B_2, B_3, and B_4 are mutually exclusive and thus have no intersection among themselves, event *A* may be expressed as the sum of its intersections with the *B* events:

$$P(A) = P(A \cap B_1) + P(A \cap B_2) + P(A \cap B_3) + P(A \cap B_4) \qquad \text{(5.12)}$$

Figure 5.15

Venn
diagram
demonstrat-
ing Bayes'
theorem

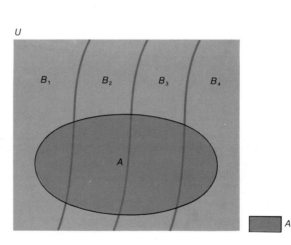

By the multiplication rule (Equations 5.6 and 5.7), we may write

$$P(A \cap B_1) = P(A \mid B_1)P(B_1)$$

$$P(A \cap B_2) = P(A \mid B_2)P(B_2)$$

$$P(A \cap B_3) = P(A \mid B_3)P(B_3)$$

$$P(A \cap B_4) = P(A \mid B_4)P(B_4)$$

(5.13)

and by substituting Equation 5.13 in 5.12, we get the following well-known equation:

TOTAL PROBABILITY EQUATION

$$P(A) = P(A \mid B_1)P(B_1) + P(A \mid B_2)P(B_2) + P(A \mid B_3)P(B_3) + P(A \mid B_4)P(B_4)$$
(5.14)

Sometimes the probabilities on the right-hand side of Equation 5.14 are available, but we need to calculate the probability of one of the B events conditional upon A. Suppose, for example, we want to find $P(B_2 \mid A)$. Using Equation 5.4, we get

$$P(B_2 \mid A) = \frac{P(A \cap B_2)}{P(A)}$$

(5.15)

Given the total probability equation (5.14) and remembering that by the multiplication rule we get $P(A \cap B_2) = P(A \mid B_2)P(B_2)$, we may provide a formula for $P(B_2 \mid A)$ as follows:

$$P(B_2 \mid A) = \frac{P(A \mid B_2)P(B_2)}{P(A \mid B_1)P(B_1) + P(A \mid B_2)P(B_2) + P(A \mid B_3)P(B_3) + P(A \mid B_4)P(B_4)}$$
(5.16)

Equation 5.16 is a generalized form of **Bayes' theorem.**

EXAMPLE 5.6

Delicious Coffee, Inc., produces four types of coffee, each of which is produced in two grades, regular and deluxe. All the coffee is packed in 10-ounce jars. The percentages of each type of coffee produced are as follows:

Type	Percentage
1	20%
2	20
3	10
4	50
Total	100%

The percentage distribution of each type of coffee in regular and deluxe grades is as follows:

Type	Regular	Deluxe	Total
1	80%	20%	100%
2	60	40	100
3	70	30	100
4	95	5	100

One coffee jar is selected at random from the entire production for inspection. Determine the probability that the jar selected contains deluxe coffee. Also, if it is known that the jar contains deluxe coffee, what is the probability that it contains Type 4 coffee?

To obtain the required probabilities let us use the following notation:

T_1 The selected jar contains Type 1 coffee.
T_2 The selected jar contains Type 2 coffee.
T_3 The selected jar contains Type 3 coffee.
T_4 The selected jar contains Type 4 coffee.
D The selected jar contains deluxe coffee.

Our first step is to calculate the probability that the coffee selected is deluxe. Notationally, we are looking for $P(D)$. Using the *total probability formula*, we write

$$P(D) = P(D \mid T_1)P(T_1) + P(D \mid T_2)P(T_2) + P(D \mid T_3)P(T_3) + P(D \mid T_4)P(T_4)$$

Each of the probabilities on the right-hand side is provided in the question. For example, $P(D \mid T_1)$ is the probability that the coffee is deluxe *given* that the selection is made from Type 1 coffee. Since 80 percent of Type 1 is produced in regular grade and 20 percent in deluxe grade, it is obvious that $P(D \mid T_1) = 0.20$. Similarly we determine the rest of the conditional probabilities to be $P(D \mid T_2) = 0.40$, $P(D \mid T_3) = 0.30$, and $P(D \mid T_4) = 0.05$. The distribution of the production by coffee types provides us with the following probabilities: $P(T_1) = 0.20$, $P(T_2) = 0.20$, $P(T_3) = 0.10$, and $P(T_4) = 0.50$. When all these probabilities are substituted in the total probability equation we get

$$P(D) = (0.20 \cdot 0.20) + (0.40 \cdot 0.20) + (0.30 \cdot 0.10) + (0.05 \cdot 0.50)$$

$$= 0.040 + 0.080 + 0.030 + 0.025 = 0.175$$

There is a 17.5 percent chance of obtaining a jar containing deluxe coffee when the selection is made at random. To obtain $P(T_4 \mid D)$ we use the generalized form of Bayes' theorem:

$$P(T_4 \mid D) = \frac{P(D \mid T_4)P(T_4)}{P(D \mid T_1)P(T_1) + P(D \mid T_2)P(T_2) + P(D \mid T_3)P(T_3) + P(D \mid T_4)P(T_4)}$$

The denominator is, by the total probability formula, equal to $P(D)$, which was calculated to equal 0.175. The numerator is the product of $P(D \mid T_4) = 0.05$ and $P(T_4) = 0.50$. We therefore get

$$P(T_4 \mid D) = \frac{P(D \mid T_4)P(T_4)}{P(D)} = \frac{0.05 \cdot 0.50}{0.175} = \frac{0.025}{0.175} = 0.143$$

Thus the probability of selecting Type 4 coffee given that the selection is made from all the deluxe production is 14.3 percent. Figure 5.16 illustrates the situation. The shaded area in the rectangle is 17.5 percent of the total, and of the total shaded area, T_4 accounts for 14.3 percent.

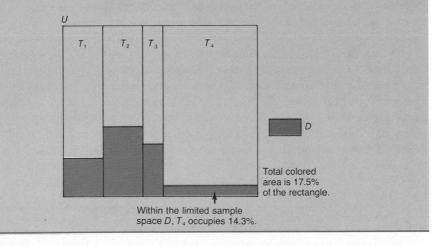

Figure 5.16

Venn diagram showing the conditional probability $P(T_4 \mid D)$

EXAMPLE 5.7

Two types of electric hair blowers are manufactured by Handy Electric Accessories, Inc.: the Handy Blower and the Super Handy Blower. Forty percent of the blowers produced by the company are the Super model. Both models carry a warranty for one year. The company's records show that 3 percent of the Handy Blowers and 1 percent of the Super Handy Blowers are being returned within the warranty period (the first year after purchase) for repair or replacement. When a blower is brought in for repair or replacement, what is the probability that it will be a Super Handy Blower?

Denote the following events:

    HB   The blower is a Handy Blower.
  SHB The blower is a Super Handy Blower.
     R   The blower is being returned within the warranty period.

The information given above may now be easily summarized as follows:

$$P(HB) = 0.60 \qquad P(SHB) = 0.40$$
$$P(R \mid HB) = 0.03 \qquad P(R \mid SHB) = 0.01$$

and the question is $P(SHB \mid R) = ?$ Using the generalized form of Bayes' theorem, we get

$$P(SHB \mid R) = \frac{P(R \mid SHB)P(SHB)}{P(R \mid HB)P(HB) + P(R \mid SHB)P(SHB)}$$

so

$$P(SHB \mid R) = \frac{0.01 \cdot 0.40}{0.03 \cdot 0.60 + 0.01 \cdot 0.40} = \frac{0.004}{0.022} = 0.1818$$

The required probability is thus 18.18 percent.

WHAT IS CONDITIONAL PROBABILITY GOOD FOR?

The primary advantage of conditional probabilities is that they are helpful in decision making. With respect to bonds, for example, the conditional probability of default, given the bond rating of financial services, is valuable information for current and potential bondholders. A few major financial service institutions (Moody's, Standard and Poor's, and others) compile an enormous amount of data in order to keep up with the quality of hundreds of bond issues in the United States so that they can sell this information to institutions and individuals interested in investing in the bond market. Collecting and computing the data costs many millions of dollars every year. This information is bought by investors so that they can improve their bond-trading decisions.

Let us consider one more example of conditional probability. This time we shall focus primarily on the value of knowing the conditional probabilities and the way they can improve our decisions.

EXAMPLE 5.8

A firm is considering drilling an oil well. B_1 is the event that the firm strikes a dry hole and B_2 is the event that oil is found. Let $P(B_1) = 0.90$ and $P(B_2) = 0.10$, as in Figure 5.17. Drilling for oil is very expensive, and the firm can improve its decision (to drill or not to drill) by conducting a seismic test. Let A be the event that the seismic test indicates that there is oil in the field. Suppose $P(A) = 0.35$ and we assume that $P(A \mid B_1) = 0.30$ and $P(A \mid B_2) = 0.80$. In other words, if the field is dry, the probability that the test will suggest that there is oil in the field is 30 percent, but if oil is present, the probability that the test will suggest the presence of oil is 80 percent.

Figure 5.17

Venn diagram showing the conditional probability of striking oil, given the results of a seismic test

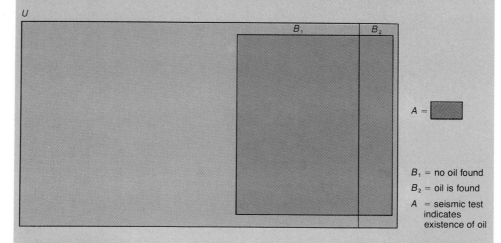

B_1 = no oil found
B_2 = oil is found
A = seismic test indicates existence of oil

The probabilities $P(B_1 \mid A)$ and $P(B_2 \mid A)$ are relevant to the drilling decision because if the seismic test indicates that the field is dry, there will be no drilling. (Otherwise, why bother with the test?) If the test indicates that there is oil in the field, what is the probability of striking oil? If it is high enough, perhaps the test is worth undertaking. If it is not high, it may not be worth spending the money on the seismic test.

In our example we get

$$P(B_1 \mid A) = \frac{P(A \mid B_1)P(B_1)}{P(A \mid B_1)P(B_1) + P(A \mid B_2)P(B_2)}$$

$$= \frac{0.30 \cdot 0.90}{0.30 \cdot 0.90 + 0.80 \cdot 0.10} = \frac{0.270}{0.350} = 0.77$$

and

$$P(B_2 \mid A) = \frac{P(A \mid B_2)P(B_2)}{P(A \mid B_1)P(B_1) + P(A \mid B_2)P(B_2)}$$

$$= \frac{0.80 \cdot 0.10}{0.30 \cdot 0.90 + 0.80 \cdot 0.10} = \frac{0.080}{0.350} = 0.23$$

As we can see, the seismic test could be valuable to the drilling firm. Originally, the probability of finding oil was only 10 percent. After the test, the situation changes. If the test indicates that there is oil in the field, then the probability that oil is indeed present is 23 percent. As we can see, however, there is still a 77 percent chance that the test results will be misleading—that the field is dry when in fact the test indicates there is oil. Deciding whether or not to conduct a seismic test requires additional statistical tools that we do not have at this point. Even at this point, however, our knowledge of probabilities can be useful. Recall that $P(B_1) = 0.90$ and $P(B_2) = 0.10$. But suppose event A is related to events B_1 and B_2 as in Figure 5.18 rather than as in 5.17. What are the probabilities $P(B_1 \mid A)$ and $P(B_2 \mid A)$ now? Event B_1 contains 90 percent of the total area of A, while event B_2 contains 10 percent of A's total area. Thus the information afforded by positive test results (that is, the occurrence of event A) does not change the original probabilities of B_1 and B_2. In short, the test's results are worthless in this case, since $P(B_1 \mid A) = P(B_1)$ and $P(B_2 \mid A) = P(B_2)$. Indeed, as indicated by these equations, B_1 and A are independent, as are B_2 and A. If finding or not finding oil in the field is independent of test results, we shouldn't bother undertaking the costly test.

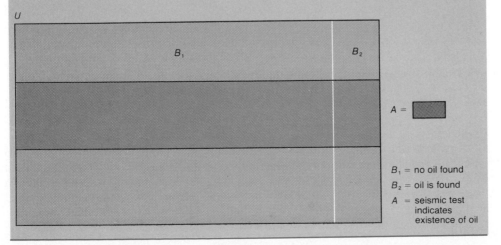

Figure 5.18

Venn diagram showing a case of a worthless seismic test

5.8 Symmetrical Sample Spaces and Counting Techniques

As we saw in Section 5.3, the third property of probability is that if two events are mutually exclusive, the probability of their union is equal to the sum of their probabilities. Since sample points are mutually exclusive by definition and since any event in U is the union of all the sample points included in that event, it follows that the probability of any event is equal to the sum of the probabilities of the sample points included in it. The problem is, however, that the number of basic outcomes in the event is sometimes very large and the probabilities of the basic outcomes themselves are often unknown.

A **symmetrical sample space** is a *set of basic outcomes, all of which have the same probability.* The probability of each sample point in a symmetrical sample space may be fairly easily obtained; therefore, adding up the probabilities of the basic outcomes in order to derive the events' probabilities is a very reasonable thing to do even when the number of basic outcomes involved is very large.

Symmetrical sample spaces are common in gambling, and elsewhere as well. Each of the six possible results (sample points) of rolling a balanced die has the same probability. Each ticket of a lottery is normally given the same chance of being chosen for the big prize as any other ticket. Likewise, quality-control problems involve the random selection of items, so that all items have equal chances of being inspected.

When all the sample points in the sample space have equal probability, the probability of each sample point is equal to $1/n(U)$, where $n(U)$ is the number of sample points in the sample space, U. For example, when we roll a fair die, $n(U)$ is equal to 6 and the probability of any sample point is $1/n(U) = \frac{1}{6}$. The general formula and rule for finding probabilities of sample points in a sample space is

$$P(A) = \frac{n(A)}{n(U)}$$

If an event, A, in a symmetrical sample space contains $n(A)$ sample points $[0 \leq n(A) \leq n(U)]$, it follows that the probability of A is equal to $n(A)/n(U)$.

To illustrate, suppose we want to find the probability of obtaining an odd number (1, 3, or 5) when we roll a fair die. The total number of basic outcomes in the sample space is 6; thus $n(U) = 6$. The number of sample points in the event of interest (let us denote this event by *ODD*) is 3; thus $n(ODD) = 3$. The probability of obtaining an odd number follows immediately:

$$P(ODD) = \frac{n(ODD)}{n(U)} = \frac{3}{6} = \frac{1}{2}$$

Now consider a box containing 30 calculators, 3 of which are defective. If a calculator is selected at random (for inspection, say), the probability that the calculator chosen will be defective (call this event D) is 0.10, since in this case $n(D) = 3$ and $n(U) = 30$, so the probability of D is

$$P(D) = \frac{n(D)}{n(U)} = \frac{3}{30} = 0.10$$

THE ADDITION RULE AND THE MULTIPLICATION RULE FOR COUNTING

In some experiments, the number of sample points in the events is more difficult to determine. In fact, some simple experiments involve symmetrical sample spaces with many millions of sample points, and probability calculations by counting can be carried out only if an efficient technique of counting sample points (in the sample space and in particular events) is available. We turn now to a discussion of some counting rules that, when considered together, provide such a technique.

RULE 1 FOR COUNTING (ADDITION RULE)

If two operations are *mutually exclusive* and if the first operation can be performed in N_1 ways and the second operation can be performed in N_2 ways, then the total operation (that is, either the first *or* the second operation) can be performed in $N_1 + N_2$ ways.

The addition rule applies only in the case of *mutually exclusive* operations, that is, when *only one of the two operations takes place*. As an illustration, suppose one item has to be selected for inspection out of eight items that have been produced today and six items that were produced yesterday. Since only *one* item is to be selected, the two operations (that is, selection from today's production and selection from yesterday's production) are mutually exclusive: if the item chosen is from today's production, no item will be chosen from yesterday's production, and vice versa. Following the first rule, we ascertain that the total number of possible selections is $6 + 8 = 14$. The addition rule can easily be extended to include K different mutually exclusive operations, with $N_1, N_2, \ldots, N_K$ ways in which each can be performed. The total number of ways in which the total operation can be performed is $N_1 + N_2 + \cdots + N_K$.

RULE 2 FOR COUNTING (MULTIPLICATION RULE)

If one operation can be performed in N_1 ways, and if another contingent operation can be performed thereafter in N_2 ways, then the two operations can be performed in $N_1 \cdot N_2$ ways.

Unlike the addition rule, the multiplication rule applies to a situation in which *both* operations will take place (thus the operations are *not* mutually exclusive). Consider, for example, a group made up of five economists and four psychologists. Suppose that one economist and one psychologist have to be selected to work on a given project. The number of possible selections of an economist out of the five available is certainly five, and similarly there are four possible selections of a psychologist. The total number of ways to select the team is $20 = 5 \cdot 4$. Denoting the first economist by E_1, the second by E_2, and so on, and similarly denoting the first psychologist by P_1, the second by P_2, and so on, we list all the 20 possible selections:

$$
\begin{array}{lllll}
E_1, P_1 & E_2, P_1 & E_3, P_1 & E_4, P_1 & E_5, P_1 \\
E_1, P_2 & E_2, P_2 & E_3, P_2 & E_4, P_2 & E_5, P_2 \\
E_1, P_3 & E_2, P_3 & E_3, P_3 & E_4, P_3 & E_5, P_3 \\
E_1, P_4 & E_2, P_4 & E_3, P_4 & E_4, P_4 & E_5, P_4
\end{array}
$$

Figure 5.19

Tree diagram
showing
possible
selection
of one
economist
and one
psychologist

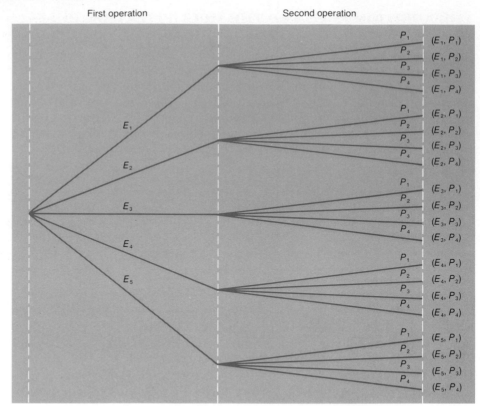

Figure 5.19 provides another way of systematically listing all the possible team selections. The figure features what is known as a "tree diagram"; each selection of the first operation is a "branch" from which extend more "branches," according to the number of possible selections in the second operation.

The multiplication rule of counting can easily be generalized to refer to any number of operations that are not mutually exclusive.

A special case of Rule 2 occurs when the number of ways to perform each of the relevant operations is the same. Consider the letters of the alphabet. Suppose we want to select three letters among *A, B, C, D, E,* and *F.* But suppose also that in the second and/or third selection we may choose to select one or more of the *same* letters that we selected earlier. How many different selections can we make for the first letter? The answer is 6, since there are six letters to choose from. The number of ways in which we can make our second selection also is 6, since repetition is allowed (we often call this selection "selection with replacement," meaning that after the object has been selected it is replaced in the set for possible reselection). Similarly, the number of ways in which we can make our third selection is 6. Thus the total number of ways to select the three letters is $6 \cdot 6 \cdot 6 = 6^3 = 216$.

In general, if we make *K* selections from *n* objects with replacement, n^K *distinct selections are possible.*

PERMUTATIONS

When the number of ways to perform each operation of interest is known, we apply Rule 1 if the operations are mutually exclusive and Rule 2 if they are not. Now how do we determine the number of ways we can perform a given operation? Obviously, it depends on the type of operation we are considering. Let us look at some rules that are helpful in certain situations.

RULE 3 FOR COUNTING (PERMUTATIONS OF *n* OBJECTS)

There are *n*! (read "*n* factorial") different ways to arrange *n* distinct objects, where $n! = n(n - 1)(n - 2) \cdots (3)(2)(1)$ and where $0! = 1$ by definition. *Each arrangement of the objects is called a* **permutation,** and we say that *n*! is the total number of permutations of *n* objects.

Take, for example, the letters *A*, *B*, *C*, and *D*. There are four letters ("objects") in all. To determine the number of possible arrangements, note that we have four ways to select the first letter. Once the first letter has been selected, there are three ways to perform the second operation, namely, selecting the second letter from the remaining three letters. Similarly, there are two ways to select the third letter, and only one way to select the last letter. Of course, no letter can be selected more than once in any arrangement. Using the multiplication rule (Rule 2), we find that the total number of ways to make the selection (that is, to arrange the letters) is

$$4! = 4 \cdot 3 \cdot 2 \cdot 1 = 24$$

Figure 5.20 is a tree diagram showing the 24 possible arrangements of 4 letters. Each arrangement is seen as a branch of the tree. Note that the number *n*! increases very rapidly with *n*. Try to calculate, for example, the number 20! to see how large a number it is.

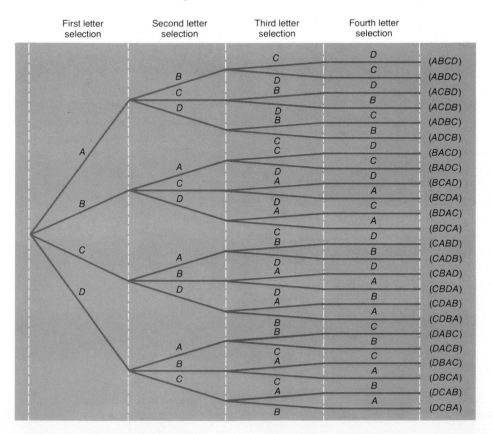

Figure 5.20

Tree diagram: permutations of the letters *A*, *B*, *C*, and *D*

RULE 4 FOR COUNTING (PERMUTATIONS OF *r* OBJECTS TAKEN FROM *n* OBJECTS)

The number of ways in which we can select and arrange *r* objects when the selection is made from a group of *n* objects ($0 \leq r \leq n$) is denoted by P_r^n and is given by the formula:

$$P_r^n = \frac{n!}{(n-r)!}$$

Rule 4 certainly needs explanation. Consider again the four letters *A*, *B*, *C*, and *D*. This time suppose we want to select two letters at a time and arrange them ($n = 4$, $r = 2$). According to Rule 4 we should have $P_2^4 = \frac{4!}{(4-2)!} = \frac{4 \cdot 3 \cdot 2 \cdot 1}{2 \cdot 1} = 12$ different arrangements. The various arrangements are as follows:

Available objects	*A, B, C, D*
Combinations of distinct objects (six combinations)	(*A, B*) (*A, C*) (*A, D*) (*B, C*) (*B, D*) (*C, D*)
Possible permutations (two permutations per each combination)	*A, B* *A, C* *A, D* *B, C* *B, D* *C, D* *B, A* *C, A* *D, A* *C, B* *D, B* *D, C*

To see why we get 12 possible arrangements, note again that there are 4 different ways to make the first selection (we can select the letter *A* or the letter *B* or *C* or *D*). Once the first letter has been selected, the second selection can be made from the remaining three alternatives. Following Rule 2, we multiply the number of possible ways of doing each of these operations and get $4 \cdot 3 = 12$.

Generally, if there are *n* objects and we have to select and arrange two objects, we have *n* ways to make the first selection and $n - 1$ ways to make the second selection. The total number of ways to select and arrange is thus $n(n - 1)$. Similarly, the number of ways to select and arrange three out of *n* objects is $n(n - 1)(n - 2)$. Now, let us take a look at some equations:

$$n(n - 1) = n(n - 1) \left[\frac{(n - 2)(n - 3) \cdots (2)(1)}{(n - 2)(n - 3) \cdots (2)(1)} \right]$$

$$= \frac{n(n - 1)(n - 2)(n - 3) \cdots (2)(1)}{(n - 2)(n - 3) \cdots (2)(1)} \qquad \textbf{(5.17)}$$

$$= \frac{n!}{(n - 2)!}$$

$$n(n - 1)(n - 2) = n(n - 1)(n - 2) \left[\frac{(n - 3)(n - 4) \cdots (2)(1)}{(n - 3)(n - 4) \cdots (2)(1)} \right]$$

$$= \frac{n(n - 1)(n - 2)(n - 3) \cdots (2)(1)}{(n - 3)(n - 4) \cdots (2)(1)} \qquad \textbf{(5.18)}$$

$$= \frac{n!}{(n - 3)!}$$

In general, when we select r objects from n objects, the number of possible arrangements is

$$n(n-1)(n-2)(n-3)\cdots(n-r+1) = \frac{n!}{(n-r)!} \equiv P_r^n \qquad (5.19)$$

Let us illustrate the use of Rule 4 by two examples.

EXAMPLE 5.9

Consider eight candidates eligible to serve on a student government committee at a given university. Assume that three nominees will be selected from the eight candidates, and assume also that their order of selection matters (perhaps because one will serve as committee chairperson and the others as "number 2" and "number 3" people). In how many different ways can this selection be made?

$$P_3^8 = \frac{8!}{(8-3)!} = \frac{8 \cdot 7 \cdot 6 \cdot 5 \cdot 4 \cdot 3 \cdot 2 \cdot 1}{5 \cdot 4 \cdot 3 \cdot 2 \cdot 1} = 8 \cdot 7 \cdot 6 = 336$$

There are 336 different ways of making this selection.

EXAMPLE 5.10

There are 26 letters in the English alphabet. How many 4-letter "words" can be formed from the 26 letters (including the combinations that have no meaning in English) without the repeated use of any letters? Again, by following Rule 4 we get

$$P_4^{26} = \frac{26!}{(26-4)!} = 26 \cdot 25 \cdot 24 \cdot 23 = 358,800$$

COMBINATIONS

The fifth and last rule of counting that we shall consider concerns the number of combinations (rather than permutations) of r objects taken from n objects.

RULE 5 FOR COUNTING (COMBINATIONS OF r OBJECTS TAKEN FROM n OBJECTS)

The number of ways in which we can select different combinations of r objects from a group of n distinct objects ($r \leq n$) is denoted by C_r^n or (more commonly, perhaps) by $\binom{n}{r}$ and is given by the formula

$$\binom{n}{r} = \frac{n!}{(n-r)!r!}$$

Rule 5 deals with **combinations** of r distinct objects taken from n distinct objects. Each combination of r objects can be rearranged in $r!$ permutations, but they will all be counted as just one combination. We can best explain this concept by an example. Below we have listed all possible permutations of three letters taken from among the five letters A, B, C, D, and E. We have arranged the permutations in such a way that each column provides all possible arrangements of the *same* letter combination. In the first column, for instance, we have listed all possible arrangements of the letters A, B, and C, in the second column all the possible arrangements of the letters A, B, and D, and so on.

ABC	ABD	ABE	ACD	ACE	ADE	BCD	BCE	BDE	CDE
ACB	ADB	AEB	ADC	AEC	AED	BDC	BEC	BED	CED
BAC	BAD	BAE	CAD	CAE	DAE	CBD	CBE	DBE	DCE
BCA	BDA	BEA	CDA	CEA	DEA	CDB	CEB	DEB	DEC
CAB	DAB	EAB	DAC	EAC	EAD	DBC	EBC	EBD	ECD
CBA	DBA	EBA	DCA	ECA	EDA	DCB	ECB	EDB	EDC

All of these permutations count as only *one* combination since they consist of the same letters.

In each column there are six different arrangements of letters, but they differ only in the *order* in which the letters are listed, and thus should count as only one combination. This being the case, the number of combinations of r out of n objects must equal P_r^n divided by $r!$, where $r!$ is, of course, the number of possible ways we can arrange r objects. In our example, where $n = 5$ and $r = 3$, we get

$$P_3^5 = \frac{5!}{(5 - 3)!} = \frac{5!}{2!} = 5 \cdot 4 \cdot 3 = 60$$

which is the total number of arrangements listed. For $r!$ we get

$$3! = 3 \cdot 2 \cdot 1 = 6$$

which is the number of possible arrangements we obtain for each group of three letters by merely changing their order. Therefore, the number of *combinations* is

$$\binom{5}{3} = \frac{P_3^5}{3!} = \frac{60}{6} = 10$$

In the general case we find

$$\binom{n}{r} = \frac{P_r^n}{r!} = \frac{\frac{n!}{(n - r)!}}{r!} = \frac{n!}{(n - r)!r!} \tag{5.20}$$

which is the formula provided by Rule 5. It is time to turn to examples.

EXAMPLE 5.11

The First Nebraska Bank is giving out gifts to depositors. Eligible depositors may choose 2 out of 15 gifts. How many possible selections can a depositor make? Obviously, the nature of the problem requires calculation of the number of possible *combinations* of 2 gifts out of the available 15. This is so because the order of selecting the gifts makes no difference here, and therefore we do not wish to count the selection of "gift 1 and gift 2," for example, as a separate selection from "gift 2 and gift 1." Once we recognize the fact that we ought to concern ourselves merely with the number of combinations, we can use Rule 5 to get

$$\binom{15}{2} = \frac{15!}{(15-2)!2!} = \frac{15!}{13!2!} = \frac{15 \cdot 14}{2} = 105$$

Thus there are 105 possible combinations.

EXAMPLE 5.12

Out of four students, a freshman, a sophomore, a junior, and a senior, we are to choose two to do a certain task. What is the probability that the freshman and the senior will be chosen (call this event *A*) if the selection is made at random?

First we should find out how many possible selections of two people out of the four are possible:

$$\binom{4}{2} = \frac{4!}{2!2!} = \frac{4 \cdot 3 \cdot 2 \cdot 1}{(2 \cdot 1) \cdot (2 \cdot 1)} = 6$$

Since the selection of the freshman and the senior is *equally as probable* as any other selection, we get $n(A) = 1$ and $n(U) = 6$, and because the sample space is symmetrical, the probability of *A* is $P(A) = \dfrac{n(A)}{n(U)} = \dfrac{1}{6}$.

EXAMPLE 5.13

Two basketball teams (team *A* and team *B*) are scheduled to play against each other. There are 9 players from whom 5 will be selected to form team *A*, and 12 players from whom 5 will be selected for team *B*. How many different combinations of players (10 in all) can form the teams? To solve this problem we have to use both Rule 5 and Rule 2.

Using Rule 5, we determine the number of possible ways to form each team separately. For team *A* we get

$$\binom{9}{5} = \frac{9!}{4!5!} = \frac{9 \cdot 8 \cdot 7 \cdot 6}{4 \cdot 3 \cdot 2 \cdot 1} = 126$$

For team *B* we get

$$\binom{12}{5} = \frac{12!}{7!5!} = \frac{12 \cdot 11 \cdot 10 \cdot 9 \cdot 8}{5 \cdot 4 \cdot 3 \cdot 2 \cdot 1} = 792$$

Using Rule 2 we get the total number of ways that these two teams can meet each other:

$$\binom{9}{5}\binom{12}{5} = 126 \cdot 792 = 99{,}792$$

EXAMPLE 5.14

Consider a lottery in which three numbers will be drawn at random out of the numbers 1, 2, 3, and 4. A prize of $1,000 will be given to the person who draws the number 123 (one hundred twenty-three) and a prize of $40 will be given to the person who draws any other arrangement of the numbers 1, 2, and 3 (such as 213, 321, and so on).

(a) Determine the probability of getting the $1,000 prize if you have one lottery ticket.
(b) Determine the probability of getting the $40 prize if you have one lottery ticket.

Work the problem under two assumptions:

1. Each of the numbers 1, 2, 3, and 4 can appear only once on the lottery ticket.
2. Each of the numbers 1, 2, 3, and 4 can appear up to three times on a lottery ticket.

Assumption 1 rules out such numbers as 223 and 111, but assumption 2 does not. Consider assumption 1 first. The number 123 (one hundred twenty-three) is one of the possible permutations of three out of four objects. The number of these permutations is

$$P_3^4 = \frac{4!}{(4-3)!} = \frac{4!}{1!} = 4 \cdot 3 \cdot 2 \cdot 1 = 24$$

and so the probability for obtaining the number 123 is

$$P(123) = \frac{1}{P_3^4} = \frac{1}{24}$$

As for the numbers 1, 2, and 3 in any order, here we first have to find the number of combinations of three out of four objects:

$$\binom{4}{3} = \frac{4!}{3!(4-3)!} = \frac{4!}{3!1!} = \frac{4}{1} = 4$$

The four combinations are (1, 2, 3), (1, 2, 4), (1, 3, 4), (2, 3, 4). The combination (1, 2, 3)—which is the one of interest—may come in 3! = 6 different permutations [which are (1, 2, 3), (1, 3, 2), (2, 1, 3), (2, 3, 1), (3, 1, 2), (3, 2, 1)]. One of these permutations will yield the first prize and *any* of the other five will yield the $40 prize. The probability of getting one of those five permutations is

$$P(1, 2, 3) = \frac{5}{P_3^4} = \frac{5}{24}$$

Let us now solve the problem under assumption 2. Here there are $4^3 = 4 \cdot 4 \cdot 4 = 64$ different selections of three out of the four numbers. Only one of them is the number 123, and so

$$P(123) = \frac{1}{4^3} = \frac{1}{64}$$

As for part *b*, there are, again, $3! = 6$ different ways to arrange the numbers 1, 2, and 3, one of which will yield the $1,000 prize and 5 of which will yield the $40 prize. Accordingly, the probability is

$$P(1, 2, 3) = \frac{3! - 1}{4^3} = \frac{5}{64}$$

It is quite easy to find examples that involve more complicated calculations of symmetrical sample spaces than we have considered here. But the rules and types of examples presented above are sufficient for our purpose in this book.

5.9 APPLICATION:
DETERMINING INSURANCE PREMIUMS BY THE USE OF CONDITIONAL PROBABILITIES

Insurance companies make extensive use of probability and conditional probability theory in determining the price (that is, the premium) they charge their policyholders. The computation of these probabilities for life insurance is based on the "life tables" that display the frequency of death per 100,000 in each age group. Customarily, separate tables are compiled for males and females, since a female's chance for survival in each age group is greater than a male's. Table 5.7 is a life table for males in the United States. The table was constructed on the basis of the age distribution of people who had died during a period of several years. It may be interpreted also as anticipated death distribution by age of those who were born in a given year, although there is a continuous trend toward longer life.

How does the insurance company use life tables to determine the required premium for a term life insurance policy? Three major factors affect the desirability to the company of insuring the potential client, and hence the determination of the premium. First, the company may require the potential client to have a physical examination, for if the client is in poor health, his or her conditional probability of death is higher than average, and the company might therefore refuse to insure the applicant. Indeed, most life insurance plans require a physical examination before the issuance of an insurance policy. Once the good health of the potential client has been confirmed by an examination, the premium is determined as a function of the applicant's sex and age. Different premiums are charged for males and females on the basis of their different death fre-

TABLE 5.7
Death Frequencies of Males in the United States, by Age, and Determination of Life Insurance Premiums

(1) Age group[a]	(2) Frequency of death (per 100,000 males)	(3) "More than" cumulative frequency[b] (per 100,000 males)	(4) = (2) ÷ (3) Conditional probability of death	(5) = (4) · $10,000 Required premium for 5 years[c]
0– 1	2,060	100,000	0.0206	$ 206
1– 5	352	97,940	0.0036	36
5–10	229	97,588	0.0023	23
10–15	246	97,359	0.0025	25
15–20	772	97,113	0.0079	79
20–25	1,061	96,341	0.0110	110
25–30	955	95,280	0.0100	100
30–35	1,054	94,325	0.0112	112
35–40	1,411	93,271	0.0151	151
40–45	2,111	91,860	0.0230	230
45–50	3,306	89,749	0.0368	368
50–55	4,789	86,443	0.0554	554
55–60	7,085	81,654	0.0868	868
60–65	9,617	74,569	0.1290	1,290
65–70	11,828	64,952	0.1821	1,821
70–75	13,836	53,124	0.2604	2,604
75–80	14,216	39,288	0.3618	3,618
80+	25,072	25,072	1.0000	10,000

[a]The class interval 0–1 includes the first birthday. The class interval 1–5 does not include the first birthday, but includes the fifth. Other class intervals are defined similarly.
[b]The numbers in column 3 show the frequency of death at ages greater than or equal to the age group.
[c]Except for age groups 0–1 and 80+.
Source: Samuel H. Preston, Nathan Keyfitz, and Robert Schoen, *Causes of Death: Life Tables for Natural Populations* (New York: Seminar Press, 1972).

quencies. Suppose a healthy 50-year-old man is interested in a five-year term life insurance policy in the amount of $10,000; that is to say, a policy under which the insurance company will have to pay $10,000 to his beneficiaries if he dies any time during the next five years.

To determine the premium that the company will charge, we first define the following events:

A   The client will die sometime between the ages of 50 and 55.
B   The client will die sometime after his fiftieth birthday.

Since the client is 50 years old, it is certain that event *B* will occur. Hence the relevant probability for the insurance company is that of death in the age interval 50–55 (event *A*) *given* that event *B* will occur. By Equation 5.5 we know that

$$P(A \mid B) = \frac{P(A \cap B)}{P(B)}$$

The event $A \cap B$ is the intersection of death in the age interval 50–55 and in the (open) interval 50+. The intersection simply means death in the age interval 50–55. The probability of this event is

$$P(A \cap B) = \frac{4,789}{100,000} = 0.04789$$

(see Table 5.7, column 2). The probability of event B is

$$P(B) = \frac{86,443}{100,000} = 0.86443$$

(see Table 5.7, column 3). Hence, the conditional probability that will determine the premium is

$$P(A \mid B) = \frac{P(A \cap B)}{P(B)} = \frac{0.04789}{0.86443} = 0.0554$$

(see Table 5.7, column 4). The required premium should be

$$\text{Premium} = 10,000 \cdot 0.0554 = \$554$$

Figure 5.21 is a Venn diagram showing the conditional probability $P(A \mid B)$. The sample space, U, includes all age groups, event A includes group 50–55, and event B includes groups 50–55, 55–60, 60–65, and so on up to and including 80+. It is clear from the diagram that events A and $A \cap B$ are one and the same. The conditional probability is the ratio of the area of A (darker shade) to the area of B (lighter shade).

A few comments are called for at this juncture. First, the premiums presented in column 5 of Table 5.7 are for a five-year period (except for the intervals 0–1 and 80+). The annual premium is one-fifth of that amount. For example, the $554 for men in the age group 50–55 should be sufficient to cover the policyholder for a five-year period. The annual premium is 554/5 = $110.80. Second, the premiums in the table are for $10,000 coverage. Other coverages require proportional adjustment. An annual premium of $110.80 for $10,000 coverage will be raised to $1,108.00 (= $110.80 · 10) if the coverage is raised from $10,000 to $100,000. Third, insurance companies have administrative costs and other expenses, so the actual premium is higher than that shown.

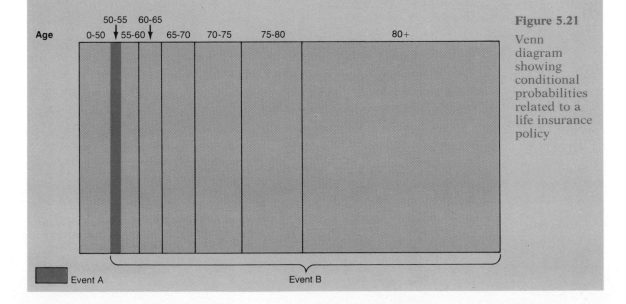

Figure 5.21

Venn diagram showing conditional probabilities related to a life insurance policy

Fourth, although premiums in the table are calculated for all age groups, insurance companies don't usually insure children or people over 65 years of age. Finally, note how the premium rises (disregard premiums for babies) with age as a result of the increase in the conditional probability of death. To see from the Venn diagram how the conditional probability rises with age, consider Figure 5.21 again and imagine sliding event *A* to the right while simultaneously squeezing event *B* so that it always includes only event *A* and the area to its right. When we do so, the proportion of *A* within event *B* (which is the diagrammatic representation of the conditional probability) increases.

Conditional probabilities are also employed in other areas of insurance. Take automobile insurance. The probability of an automobile accident if the insured lives in New York City is far greater than if he or she resides in a rural area of Tennessee. Thus auto insurance premiums in the rural area are significantly lower. The probability of an auto accident changes also as a function of the driver's accident record. Drivers with clean accident records can expect lower premiums than those who have had accidents.

Chapter Summary and Review

1. The addition rule
   a. In general:
   $$P(A \cup B) = P(A) + P(B) - P(A \cap B)$$
   b. If *A* and *B* are mutually exclusive:
   $$P(A \cup B) = P(A) + P(B)$$
   since $P(A \cap B) = 0$
   c. If *A* and *B* are independent:
   $$P(A \cup B) = P(A) + P(B) - P(A)P(B)$$
   since $P(A \cap B) = P(A)P(B)$

2. Conditional probability
   a. In general (assuming $P(A) \neq 0$ and $P(B) \neq 0$):
   $$P(B \mid A) = \frac{P(B \cap A)}{P(A)}$$
   $$P(A \mid B) = \frac{P(A \cap B)}{P(B)}$$
   and
   $$P(A \cap B) = P(B \mid A)P(A)$$
   $$P(A \cap B) = P(A \mid B)P(B)$$
   b. If *A* and *B* are independent:
   $$P(A \mid B) = P(A), \quad P(B \mid A) = P(B), \quad P(A \cap B) = P(A)P(B)$$

3. Counting techniques for symmetrical sample spaces

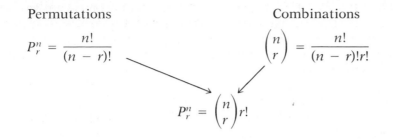

Permutations

$$P_r^n = \frac{n!}{(n-r)!}$$

Combinations

$$\binom{n}{r} = \frac{n!}{(n-r)!r!}$$

$$P_r^n = \binom{n}{r}r!$$

Problems

5.1. Four people will be asked whether they have purchased a new house in the past year. All answers are expected to be either yes or no. The sample space consists of the people's answers. Identify all the sample points in the sample space.

5.2. A newsstand operator has bought 16 magazines. Let *A* be the event "The number of magazines sold is 1, 4, 8, or 16," and let *B* be the event "The number of magazines sold is 0, 2, 4, 6, 8, 10, 12, or 14." Identify these events:

(a) $A \cap B$
(b) $A \cup B$
(c) $(A \cup B)'$
(d) A'

5.3. A car dealer's stock consists of two cars, *a* and *b*. We define the following events:

A Car *a* is sold.
B Car *b* is sold.

Express events *C* through *G* below using events *A* and *B* and their complements.

C Both cars are sold. $A \cup B$
D Neither of the cars is sold.
E At least one car is sold. ——
F Car *a* is sold, but not car *b*.
G One (and only one) car is sold, but which one is not specified.

5.4. You select a firm at random and determine its sales and the percent of total operating cost out of sales. You denote by *A* the event that sales are under \$10 million. You also denote by B_1, B_2, B_3, and B_4 the events that the percent of total operating costs out of sales are: under 50 percent (B_1); 50–under 60 percent (B_2); 60–under 70 percent (B_3); and 70 percent or over (B_4). Describe the following events in words:

(a) $A \cap B_3$
(b) $A' \cap B_4$
(c) $A' \cup B_1$
(d) $A \cup B_2$
(e) $A' \cap B_1$
(f) A'
(g) B_4'
(h) $A' \cap B_1'$

5.5. *A* and *B* are two mutually exclusive events and $P(A) > \frac{1}{2}$. Show that $P(B) < \frac{1}{2}$.

5.6. The probability that a buyer will enter a given furniture store within the next 15 minutes is 0.90. If in the last 14 minutes no buyer has entered the store, is the chance that a buyer will enter the store in the next minute especially high? Explain.

5.7. *A* and *B* are two mutually exclusive events. What is the probability *P*(*A* and *B* are two independent events)? Explain.

5.8. Show that for each pair of events, *A* and *B*, in a sample space, $P(A \cap B) \leq P(A)$ and also $P(A \cap B) \leq P(B)$.

5.9. Mr. Stanford holds corporate bonds of two corporations, *A* and *B*. Consider the following events:

$$AD \quad \text{The price of bond } A \text{ drops.}$$
$$BD \quad \text{The price of bond } B \text{ drops.}$$

(*a*) Describe the events listed below in terms of the bond prices.

$$AD'$$
$$AD \cap BD$$
$$AD' \cap BD$$
$$AD \cup BD$$
$$AD \cup BD'$$

(*b*) Identify each of the events in part *a* on a Venn diagram.
(*c*) Suppose $P(AD) = 0.40$, $P(BD) = 0.50$, and $P(AD \cap BD) = 0.20$. Find $P(AD \cup BD)$ and $P[(AD \cap BD)']$.

5.10. The events *A* and *B* are independent. It is given that $P(A \cap B) = 0.28$ and $P(A' \cap B') = 0.18$. Find $P(A)$ and $P(B)$. (You will need to solve a quadratic equation.)

5.11. Which of the following sets of events are mutually exclusive and collectively exhaustive?

(*a*) Sales will decrease next year.
Sales will increase next year.
Sales will be same next year as this year.
(*b*) Profit will increase next quarter by $100,000 or more.
Profit will increase next quarter by $50,000 or more.
Profit will increase next quarter by less than $50,000.
(*c*) The dollar will get stronger next month compared to the pound sterling.
The dollar will get weaker next month compared to the pound sterling.
(*d*) U.S. imports from Japan will increase next year by more than 5 percent.
U.S. imports from Japan will decrease next year.

5.12. The probability of event *A* is 0.60 and that of *B* is 0.40. Since $P(A) + P(B) = 0.60 + 0.40 = 1.00$, it follows that *A* and *B* have no intersection. Is this statement correct? Explain.

5.13. *C* and *D* are two events and $P(C) = \dfrac{7}{12}$ and $P(D) = \dfrac{3}{4}$. Is it possible that *C* and *D* are mutually exclusive?

5.14. Let *A* and *B* be events in a sample space.

(*a*) Is it possible that $P(A) = \dfrac{1}{4}$, $P(B) = \dfrac{1}{3}$, and $P(A \cup B) = \dfrac{7}{12}$?

(*b*) Is it possible that $P(A) = \dfrac{1}{5}$, $P(B) = \dfrac{2}{7}$, and $P(A \cup B) = \dfrac{1}{2}$?

(*c*) Is it possible that $P(A) = \dfrac{1}{10}$, $P(B) = \dfrac{1}{5}$, and $P(A \cap B) = \dfrac{4}{10}$?

5.15. Let A be the event "The sales of store a were above \$1 million in 1983" and let B be the event "The sales of store b were above \$1 million in 1983." It is given that $P(A) = \frac{1}{2}$, $P(B) = \frac{1}{2}$, and $P(A \mid B) = \frac{3}{4}$.

    (a) Explain the meaning of the following: A', $A \cap B'$.
    (b) Find $P(B \mid A)$.
    (c) Find $P(A \cup B)$.

5.16. The following are probabilities of several events in a given sample space: $P(A) = 0.20$, $P(B) = 0.40$, $P(C) = 0.10$, $P(D) = 0.50$, $P(A \cap B) = 0.08$, $P(A \cap D) = 0.00$, $P(C \cup D) = 0.60$.

    (a) Are A and B mutually exclusive? Are they independent?
    (b) How would you characterize the relationship between A and D?
    (c) How would you characterize the relationship between C and D?
    (d) Give an example of two independent events and of two mutually exclusive events from the business world.

5.17. A manufacturer of a certain personal computer claims that only 10 percent of the computers he sells will need repair in the first year. Assume that this is a correct assessment. If one computer's need of repair is independent of that of another:

    (a) What is the probability that two computers bought from this manufacturer will need repair in the first year after sale?
    (b) What is the probability that only one of the two computers will need repair in the first year?
    (c) What is the probability that neither one of the two computers will need repair in the first year?

5.18. A large pharmaceutical company employs several teams in an effort to find a way to make the production of a certain type of drug economical. Management estimates the probability that a team will be successful within a year at 8 percent. How many teams should management employ if it wants to make the probability of discovering at least one economical process equal to 80 percent? 95 percent? 100 percent? Assume that each team's success is independent of the success of the others.

5.19. A market researcher interviews ten families in order to determine whether they regularly purchase a certain product. The families' purchasing habits are independent. Assuming that the probability of getting a positive answer is 0.40, determine the probability that all ten families will give positive answers, and the probability that all ten families will give negative answers.

5.20. (a) Suppose $P(A) = 0.40$, $P(B) = 0.30$, $P(A \cap B) = 0.10$. Find $P(A \mid B)$ and $P(B \mid A)$.
    (b) Suppose $P(A) = 0.60$, $P(B) = 0.80$, $P(A \mid B) = 0.70$. Find $P(B \mid A)$.
    (c) Suppose $P(A) = 0.20$, $P(B) = 0.60$, $P(A \cup B) = 0.70$. Find $P(B \mid A)$.

5.21. Events A and B are independent. Assume the probabilities $P(A) = 0.40$ and $P(B) = 0.60$, and evaluate the following probabilities:

    (a) $P(A \mid B)$ (d) $P(B')$
    (b) $P(A \cap B)$ (e) $P(A' \cap B')$
    (c) $P(A \cup B)$ (f) $P(A' \cup B')$

5.22. The following probabilities are given:

$$P(A) = 0.50$$
$$P(B) = 0.40$$
$$P(A \mid B) = 0.60$$

Calculate the probability $P(A' \cap B')$.

5.23. A certain salesperson has observed that if she makes an appointment with X, she has a probability of 0.40 of making a sale to X. Furthermore, if she makes a sale to X, there is a probability of 0.60 that she will also make a sale to Y. On the other hand, if she does not make a sale to X, the probability that she will make a sale to Y is 0.10. If she has an appointment with X on a certain day, what is the probability that she will make a sale to Y on that day?

5.24. The following probabilities of events in a sample space are given:

$$P(A \mid B_1) = 0.30 \qquad P(A) = 0.336$$

$$P(A \mid B_2) = 0.40 \qquad P(B_1) = 0.80$$

$$P(A \mid B_3) = 0.50$$

If B_1, B_2, and B_3 are mutually exclusive and collectively exhaustive, what is the probability $P(B_2)$?

5.25. Let A_1, A_2, A_3, and A_4 be mutually exclusive and collectively exhaustive events in a sample space. Assume the following probabilities:

$$P(B) = 0.36 \qquad P(A_1) = 0.30$$

$$P(B \mid A_1) = 0.20 \qquad P(A_2) = 0.20$$

$$P(B \mid A_2) = 0.10 \qquad P(A_3) = 0.40$$

$$P(B \cap A_3) = 0.20$$

(*a*) What is the probability $P(B \cap A_4)$?
(*b*) What is the probability $P(A_4 \mid B)$?

5.26. Show that if A and B are independent, then A' and B' are also independent.

5.27. A and B are two mutually exclusive events. It is given that $P(A) = 0.20$ and $P(B) = 0.40$. Find:

(*a*) $P(A \mid B)$
(*b*) $P(B \mid A)$
(*c*) $P(A \cap B)$
(*d*) $P(A \cup B)$

5.28. The probabilities of events A and B are $P(A) = 0.40$ and $P(B) = 0.50$. What is the probability of the intersection of A and B ($A \cap B$), if it is also known that $P(A \mid B) = 0.20$?

5.29. Define the following events:

    A Firm owns a word processor.
    B_1 Firm's sales are less than \$500,000 a year.
    B_2 Firm's sales are \$500,000 to under \$10 million a year.
    B_3 Firm's sales are \$10 million or more a year.

Assume that:

$$P(A) \ = 0.16 \qquad P(A \mid B_2) = 0.10$$

$$P(B_1) = 0.30 \qquad P(A \mid B_3) = 0.90$$

$$P(B_2) = 0.60$$

(*a*) Find $P(A \cap B_2)$, $P(A \cup B_3)$, and $P(B_3 \mid A)$. Explain what each probability means.
(*b*) Are owning a word processor and the firm's level of sales independent? If so, explain how you reached this conclusion. If not, describe the relationship between them.

5.30. (*a*) In a certain city 20 percent of the households own home video games, and 90 percent own cars. If 10 percent of the households own both home video games and cars, what is the probability that a household selected at random will have a home video game *or* a car?

(*b*) Are home video game ownership and car ownership independent? Explain.

5.31. Events *A* and *B* have the following probabilities:

$$P(A \cap B) = 1/9$$
$$P(A \cap B') = 2/7$$
$$P(A' \cap B) = 1/4$$

(*a*) What is the probability $P(A' \cap B')$?
(*b*) Are *A* and *B* independent?

5.32. The performance of workers is predicted by the results of a certain test. The predicted performance grade is denoted by *PA*, *PB*, *PC*, or *PD*, where *PA* is best and *PD* is worst. The prediction is not perfect, and the actual performance on the job could be better or worse than the prediction. The actual performance is denoted *AA*, *AB*, *AC*, or *AD*, where *AA* means actual performance is the best and *AD* means actual performance is the worst. Suppose the probabilities of the prediction and the actual performance are as shown in Table P5.32.

TABLE P5.32

Actual performance	Prediction				Total
	PA	*PB*	*PC*	*PD*	*Total*
AA	0.10	0.10	0.00	0.00	0.20
AB	0.05	0.20	0.04	0.01	0.30
AC	0.00	0.08	0.20	0.01	0.29
AD	0.00	0.02	0.04	0.15	0.21
Total	0.15	0.40	0.28	0.17	1.00

(*a*) Give the symbolic notation for the probability of each of the following events:

1. The predicted grade is *PC*.
2. The predicted grade is *PB* and the actual performance is *AA*.
3. The actual performance is *AC*, given that the prediction was *PA*.
4. The actual performance is *AB* or *AC*.

(*b*) Explain what each of the following events means:

1. *PC*   2. *PA* ∩ *AB*   3. *AB* ∪ *PA*   4. *PC* | *AB*

(*c*) Determine the probability of each of the events in part *b*.
(*d*) Determine the following probabilities:

1. $P(AA \mid PA)$	5. $P(AA \cap PA)$
2. $P(AB \mid PA)$	6. $P(AA \mid PB)$
3. $P(PB \mid AB)$	7. $P(AD \cap AC)$
4. $P(PB \mid AA)$	8. $P(AC \cup PB)$

5.33. Rework Problem 5.32, but this time use the probabilities in Table P5.33.

TABLE P5.33

Actual performance	Prediction				
	PA	PB	PC	PD	Total
AA	0.00	0.00	0.10	0.10	0.20
AB	0.01	0.04	0.20	0.05	0.30
AC	0.01	0.20	0.08	0.00	0.29
AD	0.15	0.04	0.02	0.00	0.21
Total	0.17	0.28	0.40	0.15	1.00

Suppose the probabilities in Table P5.33 are based on a different test from that on which the probabilities of Table P5.32 are based. Which of the two tests, the one that is the basis for Table P5.32 or the one that is the basis for Table P5.33, would you recommend as a better predictor of job performance? Why?

5.34. Are the events *PB* and *PC* of Table P5.33 independent? Are they mutually exclusive? Explain.

5.35. Two candidates are running for office in a given city. The probability that the first will be elected is 0.70; the probability that the second will be elected is 0.30. If the first is elected, the probability that a new air terminal will be built is 0.60; if the second is elected, the probability is 0.40. What is the probability that a new air terminal will be built?

5.36. Two machines, *m*1 and *m*2, produce 60 percent and 40 percent, respectively, of the total production of Gamma Company. *m*1 produces 3 percent defects and *m*2 produces 4 percent defects. An item is picked at random from the production of the machines.

   (*a*) What is the probability that the item chosen is defective?
   (*b*) If the item chosen is known to be good (not defective), what is the probability that the item selected is a product of *m*1?

5.37. Box *a* holds two 60-watt bulbs, three 75-watt bulbs, and two 100-watt bulbs. Box *b* holds five 60-watt bulbs, one 75-watt bulb, and three 120-watt bulbs. One bulb is picked at random out of one of the two boxes. Given the selection procedure, the probability that the bulb selected is from box *a* is $\frac{1}{3}$, and the probability that the bulb selected is from box *b* is $\frac{2}{3}$.

   (*a*) What is the probability that the bulb selected is a 60-watt bulb?
   (*b*) If it is known that the bulb that was picked is a 60-watt bulb, what is the probability that it was from box *a*?

5.38. Of a given group of people, 40 percent are Republicans, 45 percent are Democrats, and 15 percent are independent. If 50 percent of the Republicans, 20 percent of the Democrats, and 30 percent of the independents are against a certain proposed tax bill, what is the probability that a voter selected at random from the above group is against the bill?

5.39. The probability that a firm will develop new inventions naturally increases as the research and development (R&D) budget increases. A survey of the pharmaceutical industry found that firms that spend less than $2 million annually on R&D have a 20 percent chance of obtaining more than three patents during the next year, whereas firms that spend $2 million or more have a 40 percent chance of obtaining more than three patents during the next year. Eighty percent of the firms in the industry spend less than $2 million on R&D.

   Suppose you randomly select a firm in the pharmaceutical industry, and you find out that it obtained more than three patents during the past year. What is the probability that the firm's annual R&D budget is over $2 million?

5.40. Eighty percent of the students applying for jobs through the placement office of Good College are graduate students, and 20 percent are undergraduates. A graduate student applying through the office has a 60 percent chance of getting a job, while an undergraduate has only a 40 percent chance of being placed in a job.

    (a) What is the probability that a student (randomly selected) who is applying through the office will get a job?

    (b) If it is known that a student has gotten a job, what is the probability that he or she is a graduate student?

5.41. A market research project involves the study of the nutritional value of food and its effect on the demand for food. Two brands of cake mix are being compared. Sixty-five percent of the people surveyed said they pay no attention to nutritional content when they shop for food; 35 percent said they do pay attention. Of the 65 percent who do not consider nutritional content, 50 percent prefer Brand *A* to *B* and 50 percent prefer *B* to *A*. Of the 35 percent who do pay attention to nutritional content, 80 percent prefer brand *A* to *B* and 20 percent prefer *B* to *A*.

    A shopper who intends to buy one of the two brands says she prefers *A* to *B*. What is the probability that she cares about nutritional content?

5.42. Table P5.42 is a cross-classification of a population of 10,000 stockholders by the value of their portfolios and the number of securities in their portfolios.

TABLE P5.42

Value of stock	1–5	6–10	11–15	16+
	Number of securities in portfolio			
Up to $1,999.99	200	100	50	25
$ 2,000.00– 5,999.99	100	400	200	35
$ 6,000.00–10,999.99	50	1,000	200	70
$11,000.00–20,999.99	40	1,500	1,100	100
$21,000 or more	30	3,500	1,000	300

    (a) If one of the 10,000 stockholders is selected at random, what is the probability that he owns 6–10 stocks at a total value of $2,000.00–5,999.99?

    (b) What is the probability that the stockholder selected owns 1–5 stocks?

    (c) If the stockholder selected is known to own stock at a total value of $11,000.00–20,999.99, what is the probability that he owns 16 or more stocks?

    (d) If the stockholder selected is known to own 1–5 stocks, what is the probability that the total value of his holdings is $21,000 or more?

5.43. Table P5.43 shows the frequency distribution of deaths in England and Wales for males and females in various age groups per 100,000 people who were born in a given year.

TABLE P5.43

Age group	Males	Females
0– 1	2,265	1,780
1– 5	340	289
5–10	223	157
10–15	197	122
15–20	474	194
20–25	528	224
25–30	476	288
30–35	567	396
35–40	874	604

(Continued)

TABLE P5.43 (*Continued*)

Age group	Males	Females
40–45	1,414	1,066
45–50	2,413	1,624
50–55	4,061	2,396
55–60	6,746	3,517
60–65	10,240	5,502
65–70	13,456	8,336
70–75	15,611	12,444
75–80	15,875	16,446
80+	24,240	44,615

Source: Samuel H. Preston, Nathan Keyfitz, and Robert Schoen, *Causes of Death: Life Tables for Natural Populations* (New York: Seminar Press, 1972).

Write down the cumulative frequency distributions for males and females. Draw the two ogives in one diagram and explain the conclusion with respect to longevity of males and females in this population.

5.44. The Safety Corporation, an international insurance firm with headquarters in New York, operates in many countries. The firm charges insurance premiums to cover its potential loss plus 30 percent to cover administrative expenses. Table P5.44 shows the frequency of death of males and females in Chile per 100,000 people born in a given year.

TABLE P5.44

Age group	Males	Females
0– 1	11,668	10,313
1– 5	2,493	2,557
5–10	576	527
10–15	438	367
15–20	740	568
20–25	1,197	799
25–30	1,502	1,010
30–35	2,108	1,442
35–40	2,661	1,768
40–45	3,461	1,879
45–50	4,169	2,478
50–55	5,460	3,595
55–60	6,523	4,677
60–65	8,403	6,840
65–70	9,673	8,884
70–75	11,667	11,507
75–80	10,567	12,835
80–85	7,897	11,217
85+	8,797	16,737

Source: Samuel H. Preston, Nathan Keyfitz, and Robert Schoen, *Causes of Death: Life Tables for Natural Populations* (New York: Seminar Press, 1972).

(*a*) Calculate the premium the firm will charge males and females in all age groups in Chile (but ignore people younger than 20).

(*b*) Draw schematic Venn diagrams showing why the premium for females in Chile in the age group 50–55 is higher than in the age group 30–35.

5.45. (*a*) Suppose a 60-year-old American male wants to buy a $100,000 life insurance policy for five years. Using Table 5.7 and assuming that the company does not charge anything above what is needed to cover the risk, what is the insurance premium? Assume that the insurance premium is payable at the beginning of the insurance coverage period.

(*b*) Rework part *a*, this time assuming that the man is 65 years old.

(*c*) Suppose a 60-year-old American man wants to buy a $100,000 life insurance policy for ten years. How much should the insurance company charge? Assume again that the entire premium for the ten years is payable at the beginning of the insurance coverage period.

(*d*) Is the premium determined in part *c* equal to the sum of the premiums determined in parts *a* and *b*? If not, how can the difference be explained? Explain in detail.

5.46. Refer back to Problem 5.45. Would the insurance company make more money by insuring the 60-year-old man for ten years or by insuring him for five years and then renewing for an additional five years?

Hint: Calculate the conditional probability that the man will survive to age 65. His survival, of course, is a necessary condition for a renewal of the insurance policy.

5.47. A committee is to consist of 5 people, to be chosen from a list of 6 Democrats, 4 Republicans, and 2 independents.

(*a*) How many distinctly constituted committees are possible?

(*b*) Assuming an equal chance for each of the 12 candidates to be selected, what is the probability that the committee will have no independents?

(*c*) What is the probability that the committee will consist entirely of Democrats?

5.48. Wendy's offers you eight items to go with your hamburger: ketchup, onions, mustard, pickles, lettuce, tomato, mayonnaise, and relish. Suppose you decide to take three items with your hamburger. How many combinations of items can you choose from? How many combinations of five items can you choose from?

5.49. The employees of Electric Apparatus, Inc., want to elect a committee on which each department will be represented. There are four departments:

> Department *A*   12 employees
> Department *B*   10 employees
> Department *C*   10 employees
> Department *D*   8 employees

(*a*) How many possibilities are there in selecting the committee membership?

(*b*) If the employees decide to disregard the principle of departmental representation, how many possibilities exist?

5.50. A bus company's standby repair crew consists of three electricians and eight mechanics. There are eight repair jobs to be performed, of which two require electrical repair and six require mechanical repair.

(*a*) How many combinations of two electricians can be chosen to perform the jobs?

(*b*) How many combinations of six mechanics can be chosen to perform the jobs?

(*c*) In how many different ways can you assign the electricians and mechanics to their jobs?

5.51 Of 14 tax returns that were filed by residents of a given state, 2 need to be corrected. If only 4 forms will be randomly selected and carefully studied, how many combinations of 4 is it possible to select among the 14 forms with exactly 1 of them needing to be corrected?

5.52. A truck driver has to deliver merchandise from point *A* to points *B*, *C*, *D*, and *E*. How many different routes can he take? Show your solution on a tree diagram and indicate what counting rule you used to get your answer.

5.53. A classroom has 18 available seats.

    (*a*) In how many different ways can a class of 18 students be seated?

    (*b*) If two of the students are absent, in how many ways can the remaining 16 students be seated in the 18 seats?

5.54. A classroom has 20 available seats in one row. In the class there are 20 students, 10 men and 10 women.

    (*a*) In how many different ways can the students be seated if no two men and no two women are supposed to sit next to each other?

    (*b*) Answer part *a* again, this time assuming that one man and one woman are absent (i.e., there are 9 men, 9 women, and 20 seats). Also assume that two students of the same sex are not allowed next to each other even if a vacant seat is between them.

5.55. Answer Problem 5.54 again, this time assuming that all men are to be seated together and all women seated together.

5.56. Thirty-six kinds of ice cream are featured at the Ice Cream Palace. Four friends want to buy one kind of ice cream each.

    (*a*) In how many different arrangements can they buy their ice cream?

    (*b*) If each decides to buy a *different* kind of ice cream, how many arrangements are possible?

5.57. A retail catalog identifies each item by three letters and two digits.

    (*a*) How many items may be assigned a catalog code if the three letters are to appear first? (Assume that no letter or digit may appear more than once in a code.)

    (*b*) How many items may be assigned a catalog code if the letters and digits may appear anywhere in the code? (Make the same assumption as in part *a*.)

APPENDIX 5A:
The Addition and Multiplication Rules for More Than Two Events

The purpose of this appendix is to extend our presentation of the addition and multiplication rules to more than two events. Our primary concern here will be the case involving three events, although equations will be given for the general case of *n* events. Let us begin with the addition rule.

THE ADDITION RULE

Figure 5A.1 shows a sample space in which three events, *A*, *B*, and *C*, intersect one another. The addition rule states that the probability of the union of the three events is given by Equation 5A.1:

$$P(A \cup B \cup C) = P(A) + P(B) + P(C) - P(A \cap B)$$
$$- P(A \cap C) - P(B \cap C) + P(A \cap B \cap C)$$

          (5A.1)

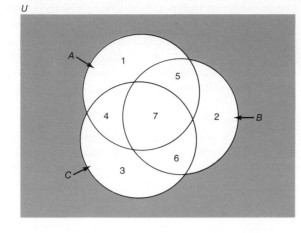

To see why the probability of the union is given by Equation 5A.1, recall that the area *U* is equal to 1.0. Similarly the probability of the union is equal to its corresponding area. In Figure 5A.1, we divided the union's area into seven *mutually exclusive* subareas (designated 1 through 7).

Because the areas are mutually exclusive, it is clear that the probability of the union is equal to the *sum* of the probabilities of areas 1 through 7. It is also clear from the figure that the following is correct:

$$P(A) = 1 + 4 + 5 + 7$$

$$P(B) = 2 + 5 + 6 + 7$$

$$P(C) = 3 + 4 + 6 + 7$$

$$P(A \cap B) = 5 + 7$$

$$P(A \cap C) = 4 + 7$$

$$P(B \cap C) = 6 + 7$$

$$P(A \cap B \cap C) = 7$$

where the numbers on the right-hand side of the equations represent their respective areas.

Substituting the right-hand side of the equations above in Equation 5A.1, we obtain

$$P(A \cup B \cup C) = (1 + 4 + 5 + 7) + (2 + 5 + 6 + 7)$$
$$+ (3 + 4 + 6 + 7) - (5 + 7) - (4 + 7) - (6 + 7) + 7$$
$$= 1 + 2 + 3 + 4 + 5 + 6 + 7$$

This calculation shows that Equation 5A.1 is indeed correct.

For example, consider a publishing group that is planning to introduce three new textbooks written by different authors in three totally different areas. The publishers consider the sale of 10,000 copies of a book a success, and they estimate that the probability of success for each of the three books is 0.60. Denoting the success of the first book by *A*, that of the second book by *B*, and that of the third by *C*, we may write $P(A) = P(B) = P(C) = 0.60$. Since the books are on different subjects and written by different authors, their successes are considered independent of one another. What is the probability that at least one of the three books will succeed? The answer is certainly *not* given by the sum of $P(A)$, $P(B)$, and $P(C)$. The answer can be found by use of Equation 5A.1, but before using this formula we remember that as a result of the independence of the events we have $P(A \cap B) = P(A \cap C) = P(B \cap C) = 0.60 \cdot 0.60 = 0.36$ and $P(A \cap B \cap C) = 0.60 \cdot 0.60 \cdot 0.60 = 0.216$.

Using Equation 5A.1, we obtain

$$P(A \cup B \cup C) = 0.600 + 0.600 + 0.600 - 0.360 - 0.360 - 0.360 + 0.216$$

$$= 0.936$$

Thus there is a 93.6 percent chance that at least one of the three books will be a success.

Now suppose the publishing group is interested in knowing the probability that two of the books will be successful (*a*) if they publish only two and (*b*) if they publish all three books.

If the publishers go ahead with only two books, the probability of two successes is given by the probability of the intersection $P(A \cap B)$, where success for the respective books is denoted by A and B. Recalling that A and B are independent, we get

$$P(A \cap B) = P(A)P(B) = 0.60 \cdot 0.60 = 0.36$$

so there is a 36 percent chance of succeeding with both books.

If all three books are published, the probability of succeeding with (exactly) two books is given by the sum of the areas 4, 5, and 6 in Figure 5A.1. To get this area we add $P(A \cap B) = 5 + 7$, $P(A \cap C) = 4 + 7$, and $P(B \cap C) = 6 + 7$ and subtract $P(A \cap B \cap C) = 7$ three times. This gives us

$$4 + 5 + 6 = P(A \cap B) + P(A \cap C) + P(B \cap C) - 3P(A \cap B \cap C)$$

$$= 0.36 + 0.36 + 0.36 - 3(0.216)$$

$$= 0.432$$

or 43.2 percent. Note the increase of the probability of two successes from 36 percent to 43.2 percent with the publication of the third book. This increase, however, is not the only benefit to the publishing group. They also benefit from the fact that if three books are published, there is a 21.6 percent chance of three successes, compared with zero chance if only two books are published. We leave it to you to find the change in the probability of succeeding with exactly one book when two and then three books are published.

The generalization of the addition rule to n events (call them A_1, A_2, . . ., A_n) is as follows:

$$P(A_1 \cup A_2 \cup \cdots \cup A_n) = [P(A_1) + P(A_2) + \cdots + P(A_n)]$$

$$- \left[\begin{array}{l} \text{the sum of the probabilities of all the} \\ \text{intersections of two events} \end{array} \right]$$

$$+ \left[\begin{array}{l} \text{the sum of the probabilities of all the} \\ \text{intersections of three events} \end{array} \right]$$

$$- \begin{bmatrix} \text{the sum of the probabilities of all the} \\ \text{intersections of four events} \end{bmatrix}$$

$$+ \cdots$$

where the sign in front of each set of brackets is the opposite of the sign of the preceding set.

THE MULTIPLICATION RULE

The multiplication rule for two events is given in the text by Equation 5.7:

$$P(A \cap B) = P(A \mid B)P(B)$$

Suppose that in place of event B in Equation 5.7 we substitute the intersection of B and another event, C. Then we get

$$P[A \cap (B \cap C)] = P[A \mid (B \cap C)]P(B \cap C) \qquad \text{(5A.2)}$$

Using Equation 5.7 for $P(B \cap C)$ we get

$$P(B \cap C) = P(B \mid C)P(C)$$

Noting that $P[A \cap (B \cap C)] = P(A \cap B \cap C)$ and substituting the right-hand side of the last equation in Equation 5A.2, we get

---

MULTIPLICATION RULE FOR THREE EVENTS

$$P(A \cap B \cap C) = P[A \mid (B \cap C)]P(B \mid C)P(C) \qquad \text{(5A.3)}$$

Suppose that the publishers we spoke of earlier are considering publishing three books by the *same* author. Consider one of the books. Let the success of this book be denoted by C, and suppose that the publishers assume $P(C) = 0.60$. With respect to the second book, the publishers estimate that if C occurs, the probability that the second book will succeed (event B) is 0.80. That is to say,

$$P(B \mid C) = 0.80$$

Finally, the publishers estimate that if both B and C occur, the probability that the remaining book will be a success (event A) is 0.85. This means that

$$P[A \mid (B \cap C)] = 0.85$$

The probability that all three books will be successful is, by Equation 5A.3,

$$P(A \cap B \cap C) = 0.85 \cdot 0.80 \cdot 0.60 = 0.408$$

or 40.8 percent.

APPENDIX PROBLEMS

5A.1. A business firm is examining three investment proposals: *a*, *b*, and *c*. Let us define the following events:

> A   Proposal *a* is profitable.
> B   Proposal *b* is profitable.
> C   Proposal *c* is profitable.

Using the definitions of *A*, *B*, and *C* and relationships between events (intersection, union, and so on), express the following: "At most, two proposals are profitable."

5A.2. Consider three events, *A*, *B*, and *C*. It is given that

$$P(A) = P(B) = P(C)$$
$$P(A \cap B' \cap C') = P(A' \cap B \cap C') = P(A' \cap B' \cap C)$$
$$P(A \cap B) = P(A \cap C)$$

Prove that $P(A \cap C) = P(B \cap C)$.

5A.3. A salesperson has three products in stock that depreciate within one day. Assume that the probability that he will sell any one of them is $\frac{1}{4}$. Thus if selling the first product is denoted by *A*, selling the second product by *B*, and selling the third by *C*, then $P(A) = P(B) = P(C) = \frac{1}{4}$. The probability that he will sell any two of them is $\frac{1}{6}$, and the probability that he will sell all three of them is $\frac{1}{12}$. What is the probability that the salesperson will not sell any of the three products?

5A.4. A person owns three securities listed on the New York Stock Exchange. The probability that the price of any of the three securities will go up the next day is $\frac{1}{5}$. The probability that the prices of all three will go up is $\frac{1}{16}$, and the probability that the price of none of them will go up is $\frac{5}{8}$. What is the probability that the price of at least two of the three securities will go up?

RANDOM VARIABLES, PROBABILITY DISTRIBUTIONS, AND DISTRIBUTION MOMENTS

6

Key Terms
random variable
discrete random variable
continuous random variable
probability distribution
probability function
probability mass function
probability density function
cumulative distribution function
uniform distribution
expected value (mean)
variance
standard deviation
Chebyshev's theorem
Empirical Rule
standardized random variable
skewness
coefficient of skewness
kurtosis

6.1 Random Variables and Probability Distributions

Our interest in a random experiment is often diverted from the events that take place in the sample space to a variable (or variables) whose numerical value is determined by the result of the random experiment. Such a variable, the value of which is determined by *chance*, is called a *random variable*. Formally, we define it thus:

DEFINITION: RANDOM VARIABLE

A **random variable** is *a variable whose numerical value is determined by the outcome of a random experiment.*

A random variable may be either *discrete* or *continuous*. A **discrete random variable** may *take its value from some finite number or from a countable infinite number of possible outcomes.* For example, if a random variable can take on only one of the values 0, 1, 2, 3, or 4, the random variable is discrete. As

185

another example, if 100 products are examined, the number of products that will be found to be of unacceptable quality is a discrete random variable. It can take on any integer number in the range from 0 to 100. A **continuous random variable** may *assume any numerical value on a continuous scale within a given interval and thus has an infinite number of possible outcomes.* The interval within which the values of the variable may lie is called the *range.* It may be narrow or as wide as the entire range of real numbers: $-\infty$ to ∞. Such variables as weight, speed, volume, distance, and time are continuous. Regardless of the width of the interval, a continuous random variable assumes only one of the infinite number of possible values, and so the probability that such a variable will have a particular value is practically zero. For example, the probability that the weight of the coffee in any "10-ounce" coffee jar is precisely equal to 10 ounces is practically zero, as we can be quite sure that there is some deviation between the actual coffee weight and the weight stated on the label. The deviation could be as tiny as one-thousandth of an ounce or one-millionth of an ounce, but some deviation is sure to exist.

An analysis of a random variable usually requires that we know the probability that the variable will take on certain values. We therefore define the **probability distribution,** or the **probability function.** The probability distribution of a discrete random variable is described by a **probability mass function** because the probability is "massed" at certain discrete values of the random variable. The probability distribution of a continuous random variable is described by a **probability density function** because it shows how "dense" an interval is, with the probability that the variable will take on a value in the interval. For brevity, we often refer to these functions as "mass function" or "density function" and use "probability distribution" to refer to either one.

DEFINITION: PROBABILITY DISTRIBUTION OF A DISCRETE RANDOM VARIABLE

A **probability distribution** of a discrete random variable is *a systematic listing of all the possible values a discrete random variable can take on, along with their respective probabilities.*

We will define the probability density function later. For now, let us consider examples of discrete random variables and their probability distributions.

EXAMPLE 6.1

Two research teams of a pharmaceutical firm are trying independently to develop totally different types of drugs. The probability of each team's success is 0.40. If the first team succeeds, the anticipated annual sales of the drug it develops are estimated at $400,000. If the second team succeeds, the annual sales of its drug are expected to reach $600,000. For convenience, let us define the two events:

  A The first team succeeds in developing its drug.
  B The second team succeeds in developing its drug.

There are four possible basic outcomes in the sample space: $A \cap B$, $A' \cap B$, $A \cap B'$, $A' \cap B'$. From the data we know that $P(A) = P(B) =$

0.40, and therefore $P(A') = P(B') = 0.60$. Since events A and B are independent, it follows that A' and B, A and B', and A' and B' are also independent pairs of events (see Chapter 5, Section 5.6), so the probabilities of their intersections are as follows:

$$P(A \cap B) = P(A)P(B) \quad = 0.4 \cdot 0.4 = 0.16$$

$$P(A' \cap B) = P(A')P(B) \quad = 0.6 \cdot 0.4 = 0.24$$

$$P(A \cap B') = P(A)P(B') \quad = 0.4 \cdot 0.6 = 0.24$$

$$P(A' \cap B') = P(A')P(B') = 0.6 \cdot 0.6 = \underline{0.36}$$
$$1.00$$

Each of the four basic outcomes in the sample space is associated with estimated drug sales, and the value of these sales is the random variable in which we are interested. For example, event $A \cap B$ means that both teams are successful; in this event, drug sales are estimated to be $400,000 + $600,000 = $1,000,000. Similarly, event $A' \cap B$ means that the second team is successful and the first team is not. The drug sales associated with this event are $0 + $600,000 = $600,000. Table 6.1 lists the four possible events along with their probabilities and their respective drug sales.

TABLE 6.1
Probabilities of Four Events and Associated Sales

Event	Probability	Drug sales
$A \cap B$	0.16	$1,000,000
$A' \cap B$	0.24	600,000
$A \cap B'$	0.24	400,000
$A' \cap B'$	0.36	0
	1.00	

As we have mentioned, in many instances our principal interest is not directed specifically toward the events that take place in the sample space, but rather toward their implications for other numerical variables whose values are determined by these events. In our example, management will probably be concerned about the probability distribution of the sales that will be generated by the new drugs. We then simply use X to represent the sales of the new drugs. The random variable X has the following (discrete) probability distribution:

x	$P(x)$
$ 0	0.36
400,000	0.24
600,000	0.24
1,000,000	0.16
	1.00

Note the distinction between X and x. While X represents the random variable, x is a specific value assumed by X. Since all possible values of the random variable X must be listed in a probability distribution, the sum of all the probabilities must always equal 1.00.

Diagrammatically, the probability distribution of X is presented in Figure 6.1. The probability of every possible value of X is represented by a bar with a height equal to the probability of the occurrence of that value.

Figure 6.1

Probability distribution of random variable X

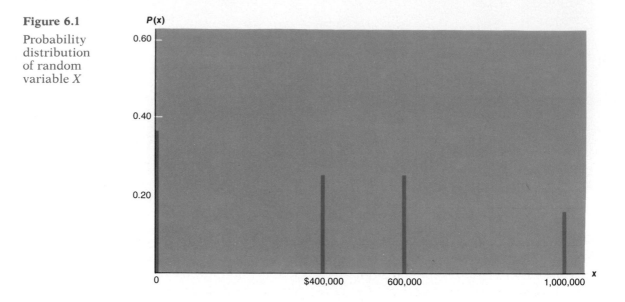

THE CUMULATIVE DISTRIBUTION FUNCTION

An interesting function to consider for some types of statistical analyses is the **cumulative distribution function.** Denoting the cumulative distribution function by $F(x)$, we define the function in the following way:

$$F(x) = P(X \leq x) \tag{6.1}$$

This definition holds for both discrete and continuous random variables. For any value of X, such as x, the cumulative function gives us the probability that X will be less than or equal to x. For our two drug teams, the probability that X will be less than or equal to \$200,000, say, is 0.36, the probability that X will be less than or equal to \$600,000 is 0.84, and so on. Systematically, we may write the cumulative distribution function as follows:

$$F(x) = \begin{cases} 0.00 & x < 0 \\ 0.36 & \$0 \leq x < \$400,000 \\ 0.60 & \$400,000 \leq x < \$600,000 \\ 0.84 & \$600,000 \leq x < \$1,000,000 \\ 1.00 & \$1,000,000 \leq x \end{cases}$$

The range of x is listed on the right and the respective value of $F(x)$ is listed on the left. Note that the function $F(x)$ must be defined over the entire range $(-\infty, \infty)$, and so the intervals listed on the right should cover all of this range in a systematic order ranging from the lowest to the highest values of X. Diagrammatically, as depicted in Figure 6.2, the function looks fairly simple. The function starts at zero on the left and rises to 1 on the right.

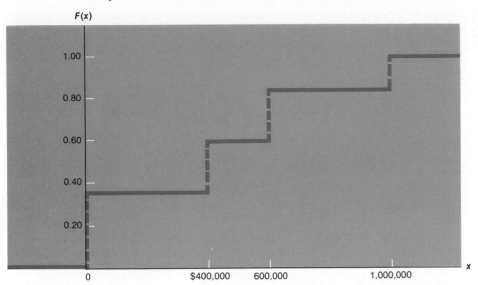

Figure 6.2

Cumulative distribution function of X, *F(x)*

The cumulative function $F(x)$ provides us with an answer to the question "What is the probability that X will be *less than or equal to* some value x?" Because the probability distribution of our example is discrete, the cumulative function is a "step function." At each such step, the cumulative probability is read off the top of the vertical line. In Figure 6.2, the probability $F(\$400,000)$, for example, is 0.60, not 0.36.

Before turning to examples of continuous random variables, let us consider one more example of a discrete variable.

EXAMPLE 6.2

The revenues of a certain state are based heavily on sales tax. When the economy is booming, more sales are made and the amount of money collected in taxes increases; when the economy is in a recession, the amount decreases. This has direct implications for the state's budget and its ability to financially support its hospitals, schools, highway system, and allocations to numerous public programs. A state economist predicts the following probability distribution of tax collections:

Economic activity	Probability for this activity $P(x)$	Sales tax collection (x) (billions of dollars)
Recession	0.10	$14.0
Less than average	0.15	15.5
Average	0.25	17.0
Better than average	0.40	18.5
Boom	0.10	20.0

Note that conventionally we list the lowest values of a random variable first and its highest values last. Therefore, the economic activities are listed starting with the activity that results in the lowest sales tax collection and ending with the activity that results in the highest collection.

Constructing the cumulative probability distribution, we get

$$F(x) = \begin{cases} 0.00 & x < 14.0 \\ 0.10 & 14.0 \le x < 15.5 \\ 0.25 & 15.5 \le x < 17.0 \\ 0.50 & 17.0 \le x < 18.5 \\ 0.90 & 18.5 \le x < 20.0 \\ 1.00 & 20.0 \le x \end{cases}$$

The probability distribution of the sales tax collection is shown in Figure 6.3*a*. The cumulative probability distribution is presented graphically in Figure 6.3*b*. It shows the probability of having at least a specific tax collection. For example, it shows that there is a 90 percent chance that the tax collection will be less than or equal to any amount in the range from $18.5 billion to under $20 billion. The probability that the tax collection will be less than or equal to, say, $19.2 billion is 0.90, because 19.2 falls in the range from 18.5 to under 20.0.

Figure 6.3

Probability distribution and cumulative distribution of sales tax collection, *X*

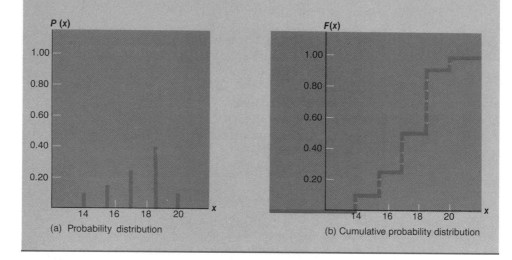

(a) Probability distribution

(b) Cumulative probability distribution

CONTINUOUS RANDOM VARIABLES

Let us now discuss continuous random variables. Consider the amount of fluid poured into soda bottles by a bottling machine. The machine is adjusted to fill each bottle with 64 ounces of soda, but in fact there are slight deviations from one bottle to another. Past records show that the amount of soda per bottle varies within the range of 63 to 65 ounces, although most bottles contain $63\frac{1}{2}$ to $64\frac{1}{2}$ ounces. The amount of soda in the next bottle filled by the machine is a continuous random variable whose probability distribution is given by a density function.

DEFINITION: PROBABILITY DENSITY FUNCTION

A probability density function of a continuous random variable *X* is a curve denoted $f(x)$, and $f(x)$ is always nonnegative: $f(x) \ge 0$. The area under the curve and above the *X*-axis over any interval is equal to the probability that *X* will take on a value in that interval.

The nonnegativity of $f(x)$ stems from the fact that the area under the curve and above the *X*-axis represents probability, which is always nonnegative. The density function of the soda weight is depicted in Figure 6.4. It is important to note that the height of the function does *not* indicate the probability, as it does in the case of a discrete random variable. The probability is read off the graph in a different way, as we shall soon see.

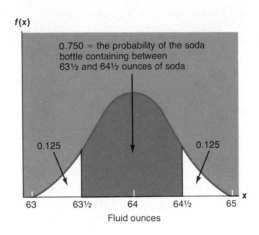

f(x)

0.750 = the probability of the soda bottle containing between 63½ and 64½ ounces of soda

0.125   0.125

63   63½   64   64½   65   X

Fluid ounces

Figure 6.4

Density function of the continuous soda weight, *X*

A property of all density functions is that the area under the curve over the entire range of the variable is equal to 1 (measured in any desired units). This is analogous to the equivalent property of discrete random variables, whose probabilities always total 1. Thus the area under the mound-shaped curve in Figure 6.4 is equal to 1. The probability that the random variable will obtain values within any interval is represented diagrammatically by the area under the density function over that interval. For example, the probability that the amount of soda in any given bottle will be somewhere between $63\frac{1}{2}$ and $64\frac{1}{2}$ ounces is shown in Figure 6.4 by the dark area in the center. If it is equal to 0.75, then there is a 75 percent chance that the next bottle filled will contain between $63\frac{1}{2}$ and $64\frac{1}{2}$ ounces of soda. Twelve and a half percent of the bottles are filled with less than $63\frac{1}{2}$ ounces of soda, and the remaining $12\frac{1}{2}$ percent are filled with more than $64\frac{1}{2}$ ounces; thus the two white tails of the density function are equal to 0.125 each. We noted earlier that the probability of any single value of a continuous random variable is equal to zero. Diagrammatically, over a single value (say, $63\frac{3}{4}$ ounces), we can draw only a vertical line, but the *area* of a line is zero, and therefore so is the probability of that value.

The cumulative probability function of the soda weight is shown in Figure 6.5. Note the relationship between the density function and the cumulative probability function. Accumulating from left to right, the accumulated area at $63\frac{1}{2}$ ounces is 0.125 (Figure 6.4), which is the *level* of the cumulative graph. The density is symmetrical around 64 ounces, so at 64 ounces the cumulative function reaches 0.50 and at $64\frac{1}{2}$ ounces the accumulation is 0.875, corresponding to a right tail of 0.125 under the density curve.

Figure 6.5

Cumulative distribution of the continuous soda weight, *X*

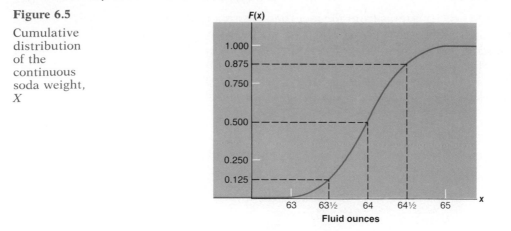

THE UNIFORM DISTRIBUTION

To clarify further the concept of a density function, let us now focus on a simple but common one: the **uniform distribution.**

Assume that the variable *X* can take on any value in the range from 10 to 20 and that the probability that the variable will assume a value within any interval in this range is the same as the probability that it will assume a value in any other interval of the same width in that range. For example, the probability that *X* will assume a value in the range from 11 to 13 is the same as the probability that it will assume a value in the range from 15 to 17 (since both intervals have the same width). If the above conditions hold, then *X* is uniformly distributed and the area under the density function is a rectangle of the type shown in Figure 6.6. The rectangle's area is equal to 1, meaning that *X* is sure to take on a value in the range from 10 to 20. Formally we have $P(10 \leq X \leq 20) = 1$.

Since the width of the range is 10 units ($20 - 10 = 10$), the height of the density function must be $\frac{1}{10}$, so as to make the rectangle's area equal to 1 ($10 \cdot \frac{1}{10} = 1$). With this in mind, we can easily determine probabilities under the uniform probability distribution. To illustrate, let us find the probability that *X* will assume a value between 14 and 18. This probability is graphically

Figure 6.6

Density function of a uniformly distributed random variable

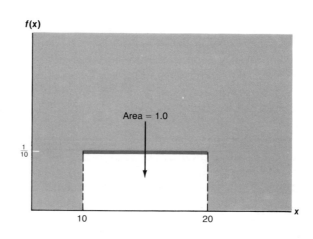

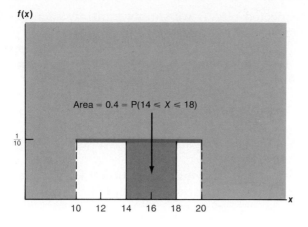

Figure 6.7

Uniformly distributed random variable X, showing the probability that X will assume a value between 14 and 18

shown by the darkest area in Figure 6.7, which is equal to the width, 4 (= 18 − 14), times the height, $\frac{1}{10}$, or $4 \cdot \frac{1}{10} = 0.40$. So we conclude that the probability is 0.40. Note that 0.40 is the ratio of the darkest area in Figure 6.7 to the total area in the range (10–20), since the latter is equal to 1.

Another method that can be used to find probabilities of continuous random variables involves integration. To avoid unnecessary complications, we present this approach in Appendix 6A.

It seems in order to note at this point that we occasionally treat some discrete random variables as continuous and vice versa. For example, variables measured in dollars—profit, net return on investment, a firm's operating costs, and the like—are theoretically discrete because in any finite range the possible outcomes are determined by the number of cents within the interval (the cent being the smallest monetary unit). Because of the large number of possible values that the variable may assume, however, it is often regarded as continuous. On the other hand, a variable such as age, which is basically continuous, is often broken down into age intervals and treated as a discrete variable.

6.2 Expected Values of Random Variables

Now that we have become familiar with the concept of a probability distribution for a random variable, we can go on to consider its expected value. In many situations we may be interested in the value of the variable "on the average."

Let us consider a game in which the prizes are $0, $10, and $20, and the probabilities are 0.50, 0.25, and 0.25, respectively. This information is summarized in the following probability distribution for the prize X:

Prize (x)	P(x)
$ 0	0.50
10	0.25
20	0.25

To find the "expected prize," we simply multiply each possible prize by its corresponding probability and total the products. This procedure gives us the weighted average value of the prize in which the probabilities are used as weights. Denoting the *expected value* of X (or the *mean of X*) by E(X), we may simply write

$$E(X) = \$0(0.50) + \$10(0.25) + \$20(0.25) = \$0.00 + \$2.50 + \$5.00 = \$7.50$$

We can expect to win $7.50 per game, on the average, if the game is repeated many times.

Another convenient and conventional notation for the mean of a random variable is μ, which we used earlier for a population mean. So, turning to the formal definition, we can state

---

THE EXPECTED VALUE OF A DISCRETE RANDOM VARIABLE

The **expected value**, or **mean (μ)**, of a discrete random variable is the *sum of the products of all possible values of the random variable and their corresponding probabilities.* The expected value of a discrete random variable can be expressed as follows:

$$\mu \equiv E(X) = \Sigma x P(x) \tag{6.2}$$

Again, x refers to each value that X assumes. The formula for the expected value of a continuous random variable involves integration; it is presented in Appendix 6A.

Let us further illustrate the calculation of the mean of a random variable with several examples.

EXAMPLE 6.3

One of the people questioned in a survey on consumers' anticipation of next year's rate of inflation (X) has given the following probability distribution:

x (percent)	P(x)
4	0.05
5	0.06
6	0.20
7	0.30
8	0.25
9	0.10
10	0.04
	1.00

This consumer, then, believes that there is a 5 percent chance that next year's inflation rate will be 4 percent, a 6 percent chance that next year's inflation rate will be 5 percent, a 20 percent chance that the rate will be 6 percent, and so on. The mean rate anticipated by this individual is

7.1 percent, calculated as follows:

$$\mu \equiv E(X) = \Sigma x P(x)$$

$$\mu \equiv 4(0.05) + 5(0.06) + 6(0.20) + 7(0.30) + 8(0.25)$$
$$+ 9(0.10) + 10(0.04)$$
$$= 0.20 + 0.30 + 1.20 + 2.10 + 2.00 + 0.90 + 0.40$$
$$= 7.10$$

Thus the one value that best represents this individual's anticipation of next year's inflation rate is 7.1 percent.

EXAMPLE 6.4

A stockholder who has $10,000 worth of stock in a given company is unsure about the amount of cash dividends the firm will decide to distribute. Her expectations are probabilistic: she assumes a 25 percent chance that her dividends will amount to $500, a 50 percent chance that they will amount to $700, and a 25 percent chance that they will amount to $1,000. The expected value of the dividends she anticipates is equal to the sum of the products of the dividends and their respective probabilities, so that

$$E(X) = \$500(0.25) + \$700(0.50) + \$1,000(0.25)$$
$$= \$125 + \$350 + \$250$$
$$= \$725$$

EXAMPLE 6.5

The number of children (X) per married couple in Massachusetts, ten years after marriage, was determined from a frequency distribution to be as follows:

x	$P(x)$
0	0.20
1	0.26
2	0.21
3	0.15
4	0.12
5	0.04
6	0.02
	1.00

If we select a couple at random, there is a 20 percent chance that they have no children, a 26 percent chance that they have one child, and so on. The expected value of X is

$$E(X) = 0(0.20) + 1(0.26) + 2(0.21) + 3(0.15) + 4(0.12)$$
$$+ 5(0.04) + 6(0.02)$$
$$= 0.00 + 0.26 + 0.42 + 0.45 + 0.48 + 0.20 + 0.12$$
$$= 1.93$$

Thus the expected number of children is 1.93 per married couple. Needless to say, no one has 1.93 children, but the expected number of children per 100 married couples is $1.93 \times 100 = 193$ children.

6.3 The Variance and the Standard Deviation of a Random Variable

The mean of a probability distribution is a very useful and informative piece of data, but we are often interested also in other measures of a distribution. The *variance* and the *standard deviation* are measures of the dispersion of a random variable around its mean. While it is interesting to know that the expected number of children of a randomly selected couple in Massachusetts after ten years of marriage is 1.93, this figure does not reflect the degree to which the couples differ from one another with respect to the number of children they have. The variance and standard deviation reflect this degree of diversity.

Technically, the **variance** is the *expected value of the squared deviation of a random variable from its mean*. A general formula for the variance, which applies to both discrete and continuous variables, is

$$\sigma^2 \equiv V(X) = E(X - \mu)^2 \tag{6.3}$$

The symbol σ^2 (sigma squared) is the common notation for the variance, but we will also refer to it by the notation $V(X)$. Equation 6.3 applies to both discrete and continuous variables. The variance of a discrete variable can be computed by using the following formula:

$$\sigma^2 = \Sigma(x - \mu)^2 P(x) \tag{6.4}$$

A computation formula for the variance of a continuous variable is given in Appendix 6A.

To illustrate the calculation of the variance of a discrete variable, we offer the following example.

EXAMPLE 6.6

To determine how frequently a cigarette machine should be restocked, the average as well as the dispersion of the number of cigarette packs bought (X) has to be determined. Suppose the probability distribution of *X* is as follows:

x	*P(x)*
10	0.10
11	0.15
12	0.25
13	0.25
14	0.20
15	0.05
	1.00

We first calculate the mean number of cigarette packs bought:

$$\mu = 10(0.10) + 11(0.15) + 12(0.25) + 13(0.25) + 14(0.20) + 15(0.05)$$

$$= 1.00 + 1.65 + 3.00 + 3.25 + 2.80 + 0.75$$

$$= 12.45$$

The variance may now be easily calculated by means of Equation 6.4:

$$V(X) = \Sigma(x - \mu)^2 P(x)$$

$$\sigma^2 = (10.00 - 12.45)^2 \cdot 0.10 + (11.00 - 12.45)^2 \cdot 0.15$$

$$+ (12.00 - 12.45)^2 \cdot 0.25 + (13.00 - 12.45)^2 \cdot 0.25$$

$$+ (14.00 - 12.45)^2 \cdot 0.20 + (15.00 - 12.45)^2 \cdot 0.05$$

$$= 0.600 + 0.315 + 0.051 + 0.076 + 0.481 + 0.325$$

$$= 1.848$$

The **standard deviation,** which we denote by σ (sigma), is also a measure of the dispersion of a probability distribution and is simply equal to *the positive square root of the variance.*[1] In our last example we get $\sigma = \sqrt{1.848} = 1.359$. While the mean number of cigarette packs bought is 12.45, there is a standard deviation of 1.359 packs around that mean.

---

[1] Just as in the case of a population or sample variance, we note here that the standard deviation is expressed in more easily interpreted units than those of the variance. To illustrate, consider the following distribution of *X:*

x	*P(x)*
$10	$\frac{1}{2}$
20	$\frac{1}{2}$
$\mu = \$15$	

$$\sigma^2 = (10 - 15)^2 \cdot 0.50 + (20 - 15)^2 \cdot 0.50 = 25 \cdot 0.50 + 25 \cdot 0.50 = 25$$

The variance is equal to 25 "squared dollars." When we take the standard deviation we get $\sigma = \sqrt{25} = \$5$. Thus the standard deviation is easier to interpret intuitively, since it is expressed in the same units as the data.

A COMPUTATION FORMULA FOR THE VARIANCE

Equation 6.3 may be simplified in the following way:

$$\sigma^2 = E(X - \mu)^2 = E(X^2 + \mu^2 - 2X\mu) = E(X^2) + E(\mu^2) - E(2X\mu)$$

Since μ is a constant, we get[2]

$$\sigma^2 = E(X^2) + \mu^2 - 2\mu E(X) = E(X^2) + \mu^2 - 2\mu^2 = E(X^2) - \mu^2$$

We therefore conclude that

$$\sigma^2 = E(X^2) - \mu^2 \qquad \textbf{(6.5)}$$

where $E(X^2)$ is simply the expected value of the variable X^2. We should note that Equation 6.5 applies to both discrete and continuous random variables. To find the variance in Example 6.6 using Equation 6.5, we first calculate $E(X^2)$ as follows:

$$E(X^2) = 10^2(0.10) + 11^2(0.15) + 12^2(0.25) + 13^2(0.25)$$
$$+ 14^2(0.20) + 15^2(0.05)$$
$$= 156.85$$

so that by Equation 6.5 we get

$$\sigma^2 = 156.85 - (12.45)^2 = 156.85 - 155.00 = 1.850$$

and $\sigma = \sqrt{1.850} = 1.360$: we obtained the same results earlier when we used Equation 6.4. (The deviation here is due to rounding.)

6.4 Chebyshev's Theorem and the Empirical Rule

In Chapter 4 we employed **Chebyshev's theorem** and the so-called **Empirical Rule** to calculate the percentage of data observations that fall in a range of k standard deviations around the mean. Similar rules apply to random variables, and they enhance the importance of the standard deviation as a measure of variability.

CHEBYSHEV'S THEOREM

The probability that a random variable with mean μ and standard deviation σ will take a value within k standard deviations (for $k \geq 1$) of its mean is *at least* $1 - 1/k^2$. Said differently, the probability of outcomes beyond k standard deviations from μ is *at most* $1/k^2$. Formally:

$$P(|X - \mu| > k\sigma) \leq \frac{1}{k^2} \qquad \textbf{(6.6)}$$

---

[2] See the discussion in Section 6.5.

EXAMPLE 6.7

A random variable has a mean of $300 and a standard deviation of $5. What is the probability that the random variable will take on a value in the range between $290 to $310? Since the range from $290 to $310 covers two standard deviations on each side of the mean, $300, we set $k = 2$ and find that, by Chebyshev's theorem, the probability is at least $1 - 1/k^2 = 1 - 1/2^2 = 3/4 = 0.75$.

How will the probability change if we set $\sigma = \$2.5$ instead of $\sigma = \$5$? In this case the range from $290 to $310 covers four standard deviations from the mean on each side. Accordingly, we have $k = 4$ and $1 - 1/k^2 = 1 - 1/4^2 = 15/16 = 0.9375$, meaning that there is at least a 93.75 percent chance that the random variable will take on a value in the range from $290 to $310.

EXAMPLE 6.8

The number of employee work hours per month in Bone's Department Store is a random variable with a mean of 10,000 hours and a standard deviation, σ, of 100 hours. What does Chebyshev's theorem tell us about the probability that the work hours in a randomly selected month will fall between 9,800 and 10,200? This range covers two standard deviations on each side of the mean, hence the probability that the number of work hours will fall within the range is *at least*

$$1 - \frac{1}{k^2} = 1 - \frac{1}{2^2} = 1 - \frac{1}{4} = 0.75$$

What is the range of work hours such that the probability that a month's work hours will fall within this range is at least 0.99? To solve this problem, we set: $1 - 1/k^2 = 0.99$. Solving this equation, we obtain

$$\frac{1}{k^2} = 0.01$$

and

$$k = 10$$

Hence, the upper value of the range is $10,000 + 10 \cdot 100 = 11,000$ hours, and the lower value of the range is $10,000 - 10 \cdot 100 = 9,000$ hours.

Clearly, if the probability distribution is known, a more precise probability can be calculated. However, when the probability distribution is unknown, Chebyshev's theorem can often provide a good clue to the probability of events of the random variable of interest.

The importance of Chebyshev's theorem derives from the fact that it is based on statistical theory and that it holds for all discrete and continuous distributions regardless of their shape. A weakness of the theorem is that for small values of k, the theorem tells us very little about the distribution. For example, choosing $k = 1$, we get $1 - 1/k^2 = 0$, which means that the probability that a random variable will take on a value within one standard deviation from the mean is at least zero. This statement does not tell us much about the distribution. The Empirical Rule is a rule of thumb that applies only to discrete and continuous random variables whose probability distribution is mound-shaped (similar to the one described in Figure 6.4).

THE EMPIRICAL RULE

A rule of thumb for a mound-shaped probability distribution (discrete or continuous) is as follows:

1. There is a probability of *approximately* 0.68 that the random variable will take on a value within one standard deviation from the mean ($\mu - \sigma$ to $\mu + \sigma$).
2. There is a probability of *approximately* 0.95 that the random variable will take on a value within two standard deviations from the mean ($\mu - 2\sigma$ to $\mu + 2\sigma$).
3. The probability that the random variable will take on a value within three standard deviations from the mean ($\mu - 3\sigma$ to $\mu + 3\sigma$) is *approximately* 1.0.

6.5 Linear Transformation of a Random Variable

It often becomes necessary to find the expected value and the variance of a transformed random variable. Assume, for example, that the net return on a $100 investment (after one year, say) is the random variable X, whose probability distribution (rather simplified, of course) is given below.[3]

x	$P(x)$
−$10	1/8
5	1/8
12	1/2
15	1/8
22	1/8

Thus the expected net return on the $100 investment is

$$E(X) = (-\$10) \cdot \frac{1}{8} + \$5 \cdot \frac{1}{8} + \$12 \cdot \frac{1}{2} + \$15 \cdot \frac{1}{8} + \$22 \cdot \frac{1}{8} = \frac{\$80}{8} = \$10$$

Given that $10 represents the expected return on the $100 investment, we might be interested in finding the expected return on an $850 investment. It can easily be shown that the expected value of the return on the investment is $85, which equals 8.5 times the return on $100. This example may be generalized. If $E(X) = \mu$ and b is a constant,[4] then

---

[3] A net return of −$10 means that only $90 was returned on the $100 investment, and thus there was a net loss of $10. Similarly, a net return of $22 means that $122 was returned on the $100 investment.

[4] In the case of a discrete random variable, we can easily show that Equation 6.7 follows from the simple rules of summation: $E(bX) = \Sigma(bx)P(x) = b\Sigma xP(x) = bE(X)$. The treatment of a continuous random variable is presented in Appendix 6A.

The expected value of the multiple of a random variable is equal to the multiple of the expected value.

$$E(bX) = b\mu \tag{6.7}$$

It can also be shown that for a constant a, the following rule applies:[5]

$$E(a + X) = a + \mu \tag{6.8}$$

Combining the results of Equations 6.7 and 6.8, we get

$$E(a + bX) = a + b\mu \tag{6.9}$$

If, for instance, there is a $3 fixed transaction cost involved in an investment (so that this cost is not a function of the amount invested) and $850 is invested in the stock, the expected net return after the transaction cost may be calculated in the following way (by Equation 6.9):

$$E(-3 + 8.5X) = -3 + 8.5E(X) = -3 + (8.5 \cdot 10) = \$82$$

While the expected return before the transaction cost is $85, because of the $3 transaction cost (independent of volume) the expected net return is $85 − $3 = $82, as we found when we used Equation 6.9.

Adding a constant (either positive or negative) to a random variable has an effect on the expected value of a variable, as shown by Equations 6.8 and 6.9, but there is no such effect on the variance. Consider a group of students standing barefoot on the floor of a gym. Let their heights be the variable under consideration. The average height and variance of height for the group may be easily calculated. Now suppose each of the students is given identical pairs of sneakers to wear. The height of each student measured from the floor to the top of his or her head is now greater by, say, one inch. Since all the sneakers are identical by assumption, each student is now one inch taller. What happens to the average height? It increases one inch. What happens to the variance? Nothing! It remains unchanged since all heights relate to *one another* and to the *average height* in the same way as they did originally. We thus conclude[6]

$$V(a + X) = V(X) = \sigma^2 \tag{6.10}$$

---

[5] In the case of a discrete random variable, Equation 6.8 follows directly from the simple rules of summation, as follows:

$$E(a + X) = \Sigma(a + x)P(x) = \Sigma aP(x) + \Sigma xP(x) = a\Sigma P(x) + \Sigma xP(x)$$

Equation 6.8 follows directly, since $\Sigma P(x) = 1$ and $\Sigma xP(x) = \mu$. A similar proof holds for the continuous random variable, as shown in Appendix 6A.

[6] The proof is rather simple. From Equation 6.3 we know that $\sigma^2 = E(X - \mu)^2$. The mean of the variable $a + X$ is equal to $a + \mu$, as indicated by Equation 6.8. The variance of $a + X$ is

$$\sigma_{a+X}^2 = E[(a + X) - (a + \mu)]^2 = E[a + X - a - \mu]^2 = E(X - \mu)^2 = \sigma_X^2$$

When we multiply a variable by a constant, the variance of the product is[7]

$$V(bX) = b^2\sigma^2 \tag{6.11}$$

Combining Equations 6.10 and 6.11, we obtain

$$V(a + bX) = b^2\sigma^2 \tag{6.12}$$

and the standard deviation of $(a + bX)$ is

$$SD(a + bX) = \sqrt{b^2\sigma^2} = |b|\sigma \tag{6.13}$$

where $|b|$ is the absolute value of b.

An interesting application of the linear transformation formulas occurs when we subtract the mean of a random variable from the variable itself and then divide the difference by the standard deviation of the variable. Let μ and σ be the mean and the standard deviation, respectively, of the variable X. The variable $(X - \mu)/\sigma$ is called a **standardized random variable,** and we can show that its mean is equal to 0 and its standard deviation is equal to 1. To see this, simply recall that μ and σ are constants for any given random variable. Accordingly

$$E\left(\frac{X - \mu}{\sigma}\right) = \frac{1}{\sigma} E(X - \mu) = \left(\frac{1}{\sigma}\right)(\mu - \mu) = 0 \tag{6.14}$$

and

$$V\left(\frac{X - \mu}{\sigma}\right) = \frac{1}{\sigma^2} V(X - \mu) = \frac{1}{\sigma^2} V(X) = \frac{\sigma^2}{\sigma^2} = 1 \tag{6.15}$$

and the standard deviation of the standardized variable is

$$SD\left(\frac{X - \mu}{\sigma}\right) = 1 \tag{6.16}$$

6.6 Skewness and Kurtosis

The mean and the variance of a probability distribution are important parameters reflecting location and dispersion. While they give us considerable information about the distribution, often there are additional characteristics of interest to us which are exhibited neither in the mean nor in the variance. The degree of asymmetry, for instance, is not reflected in these parameters.

---

[7] To derive Equation 6.11, we again go back to Equation 6.3:

$$\sigma_{bX}^2 = E[(bX) - E(bX)]^2 = E\{b[X - E(X)]\}^2$$
$$= E\{b^2[X - E(X)]^2\} = b^2E(X - \mu)^2$$
$$= b^2\sigma_X^2$$

SKEWNESS

The third moment[8] of a distribution about its mean—the *third central moment*, called **skewness**—*measures the degree of asymmetry of the function.* Skewness (μ_3) is defined as follows:

FORMULA: SKEWNESS

$$\mu_3 = E(X - \mu)^3 \qquad (6.17)$$

To see the importance of skewness and its meaning, take a look at Figure 6.8. Here three continuous probability distributions are drawn with the same mean and variance but different skewnesses. The distribution drawn in part *a* is positively skewed ($\mu_3 > 0$), the one in part *b* is symmetrical so that its skewness is equal to zero ($\mu_3 = 0$), and the one in part *c* is negatively skewed ($\mu_3 < 0$).

It is impossible to discriminate among these three distributions in terms of their means and variances. The distributions are not the same, however, and so the information augmented by μ_3 is often relevant and sometimes vital for the analysis of the random variables' behavior. Take Mr. Young Fearful, for example, a young college graduate in business administration who has $30,000 available for investment in a new business. Mr. Fearful considers three potential investment alternatives and soon realizes that profits in the "real world" can never be known in advance. His collection of information indicates, though, that the profit probability distributions of his three alternatives follow the three patterns presented in Figure 6.8. To avoid the risk of severe loss, on the one hand, and to maintain at least some chance of extremely high profits, on the other, he chooses the investment whose profit probability distribution is positively skewed. Note that information dealing only with the mean and the variance would not suffice to inform Mr. Fearful as to which of the probability distributions leaves him more vulnerable to severe losses.

Most people, whether fearful or not, would probably agree with Mr. Fearful's choice. This, however, does not imply that in general, positive skewness is a desirable feature for a probability distribution. If, for example, the curves in Figure 6.8 are thought of as alternative cost distributions, most people would undoubtedly prefer the negatively skewed distribution, so as to avoid the chance of incurring very high costs. Thus, the attractiveness of positive or negative skewness depends on the type of variable under consideration; but in all cases, as we can see, skewness reveals information about the distribution not revealed by the mean or the variance.

Skewness, as defined in Equation 6.17, is difficult to interpret numerically. An index that is often easier to handle is the **coefficient of skewness,** which is expressed thus:

---

[8] In general, we define the *n*th moment of a variable as the expected value of the *n*th power of the variable: $E(X^n)$. Accordingly, the first moment of a variable is its mean: $E(X^1) = E(X) = \mu$. The *n*th moment of a random variable about an arbitrary point a is given by $E(X - a)^n$. The *n*th *central moment* of a random variable is defined in the following way: $\mu_n = E(X - \mu)^n$. A moment is called *central* only if it is taken about the mean. From these definitions it is clear that the first central moment of a variable is equal to zero: $E(X - \mu) = 0$; and the second central moment is the variance: $E(X - \mu)^2 \equiv V(X)$. The skewness and kurtosis (discussed in this section) are the third and fourth central moments, respectively.

Figure 6.8

Continuous probability distributions with the same mean and variance, but different skewnesses

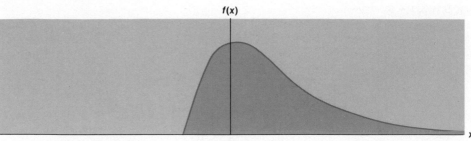

f(x)

(a) Positively skewed distribution

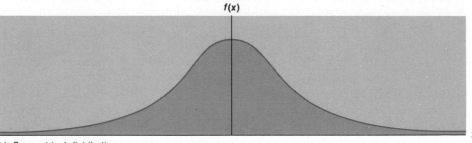

f(x)

(b) Symmetrical distribution

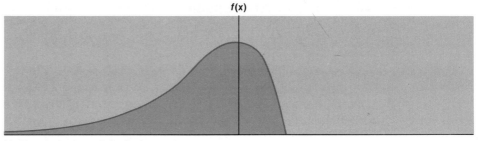

f(x)

(c) Negatively skewed distribution

FORMULA: THE COEFFICIENT OF SKEWNESS

$$\text{Coefficient of skewness} = \frac{E(X - \mu)^3}{\sigma^3} = \frac{\mu_3}{\sigma^3} \qquad (6.18)$$

Whereas skewness is measured in cubic units (such as cubic dollars), the coefficient of skewness is a unitless number.

Let us turn now to an example that will illustrate the calculation of skewness and the coefficient of skewness. Our example involves a distribution famous for its high positive skewness: the distribution of lottery prizes.

EXAMPLE 6.9

One hundred thousand tickets are issued weekly under a state lottery program. The tickets are offered to the general public for $3 each. The following is a list of prizes given in the lottery:

Number of prizes	Amount of each prize
1	$10,000
2	5,000
500	100
10,000	3
89,497	0

Find the expected value as well as the standard deviation and skewness of the prize distribution. Also, find the expected loss involved for a single lottery ticket.

The solution is straightforward. We start by calculating the expected prize $E(X)$:[9]

$$E(X) = 0.00001(10,000) + 0.00002(5,000)$$
$$+ 0.005(100) + 0.1(3) + 0.89497(0)$$
$$= \$1$$

The expected value of the prize is $1; therefore, the expected loss is $3.00 − $1.00 = $2.00, since the tickets are sold for $3. The variance is calculated as follows:

$$\sigma^2 \equiv V(X) = 0.00001(10,000 - 1)^2 + 0.00002(5,000 - 1)^2$$
$$+ 0.005(100 - 1)^2 + 0.1(3 - 1)^2 + 0.89497(0 - 1)^2$$
$$= 1,549.90 \text{ (squared dollars)}$$

and the standard deviation is

$$\sigma = \sqrt{1,549.90} = \$39.37$$

Let us now calculate the skewness of the distribution:

$$\mu_3 = 0.00001(10,000 - 1)^3 + 0.00002(5,000 - 1)^3 + 0.005(100 - 1)^3$$
$$+ 0.1(3 - 1)^3 + 0.89497(0 - 1)^3$$
$$= 12,500,352 \text{ (cubic dollars)}$$

To get the coefficient of skewness we divide by σ^3:

$$\text{Coefficient of skewness} = \frac{\mu_3}{\sigma^3} = \frac{12,500,352}{(39.37)^3} = 204.85$$

Both μ_3 and the coefficient of skewness indicate a strong positive skewness of the prize distribution.

[9] Since there are 100,000 tickets outstanding weekly, the probability of getting the first prize is 1/100,000 = 0.00001, the probability of getting the second prize is 2/100,000 = 0.00002, and so on.

While a knowledge of all or many of the distribution's moments—such as σ^2, μ_3, $\mu_4 = E(X - \mu)^4$, and so on—is sometimes interesting for theoretical problems in statistics, for practical purposes a moment may be relevant only as long as it reveals information that can be intuitively understood. In general, the higher the order of a moment,[10] the less vital its informational content, and the less useful it is in elementary applications of statistics. It is more difficult to understand the fourth moment—or, as it is called, *kurtosis*—than it is to understand the skewness. It is perhaps impossible to give any intuitive explanation of the fifth moment [i.e., $\mu_5 = E(X - \mu)^5$] or of any moment of higher order. Let us, then, just briefly describe kurtosis.

KURTOSIS

The *fourth central moment* of a probability distribution, called **kurtosis,** is given by the following formula:

FORMULA: KURTOSIS

$$\mu_4 = E(X - \mu)^4 \qquad\qquad \textbf{(6.19)}$$

Kurtosis is a measure of the degree of *peakedness* of the distribution.

Figure 6.9 presents two sets of two distributions each. The two distributions in each set are equal with respect to the first three moments. They differ, however, in their kurtosis. To illustrate numerically, consider the distribution of X and Y:

Figure 6.9

Two pairs of distributions of equal mean, variance, and skewness, but unequal kurtosis

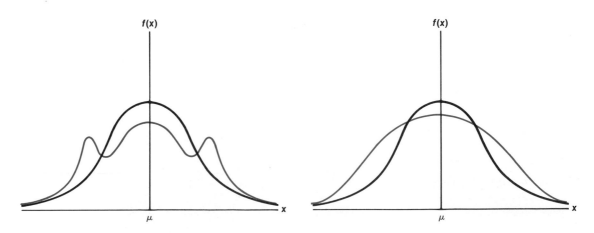

---

[10] The central moment $\mu_n = E(X - \mu)^n$ is said to be of order n. The greater n is, the higher the order of the moment.

x	$P(x)$	y	$P(y)$
-4	0.10	-4	0.05
-2	0.20	-2	0.40
0	0.40	0	0.10
2	0.20	2	0.40
4	0.10	4	0.05

$$\mu = 0 \qquad\qquad \mu = 0$$
$$\sigma^2 = 4.8 \qquad\qquad \sigma^2 = 4.8$$
$$\mu_3 = 0 \qquad\qquad \mu_3 = 0$$
$$\mu_4 = 57.6 \qquad\qquad \mu_4 = 38.4$$

These functions are shown in Figure 6.10. Being symmetrical around zero, they both have mean and skewness equal to zero. The variance can be shown to equal 4.8 for X as well as for Y. They differ, however, in their peakedness. Let us calculate their kurtosis. For X we get

$$\mu_4^X = (-4 - 0)^4 \cdot 0.10 + (-2 - 0)^4 \cdot 0.20 + (0 - 0)^4 \cdot 0.40$$
$$+ (2 - 0)^4 \cdot 0.20 + (4 - 0)^4 \cdot 0.10$$
$$= 256 \cdot 0.10 + 16 \cdot 0.20 + 0 \cdot 0.40 + 16 \cdot 0.20 + 256 \cdot 0.10$$
$$= 25.6 + 3.2 + 0 + 3.2 + 25.6$$
$$= 57.6$$

For Y we get

$$\mu_4^Y = (-4 - 0)^4 \cdot 0.05 + (-2 - 0)^4 \cdot 0.40 + (0 - 0)^4 \cdot 0.10$$
$$+ (2 - 0)^4 \cdot 0.40 + (4 - 0)^4 \cdot 0.05$$
$$= 256 \cdot 0.05 + 16 \cdot 0.40 + 0 \cdot 0.10 + 16 \cdot 0.40 + 256 \cdot 0.05$$
$$= 12.8 + 6.4 + 0 + 6.4 + 12.8$$
$$= 38.4$$

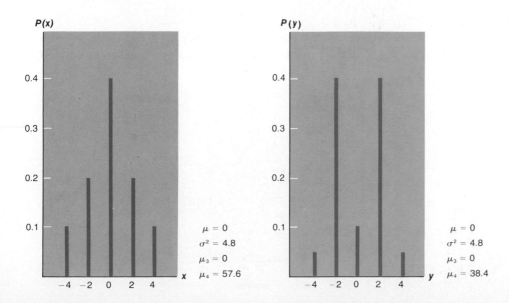

Figure 6.10

Two discrete distributions with equal mean, variance, and skewness, but different kurtosis

To conclude our discussion of third and fourth distribution moments, we note that once a probability distribution is specified, there is no difficulty involved in calculating its moments. The information entailed in moments of high orders is quite limited. If you are still not fully convinced, we suggest the following exercise. Try to draw a probability distribution with the following moments: $\mu = 0$, $\sigma^2 = 8$, $\mu_3 = 4$, $\mu_4 = 80$, and let the higher moments be unrestricted so that when you are searching for your distribution you can disregard them. You will soon realize that it will take you only seconds to find a distribution with $\mu = 0$, minutes to find a distribution with $\sigma^2 = 8$, and a considerably longer time to find a distribution that will also comply with the third and fourth moments' values.

6.7 The Relationship Between a Population's Frequency Distribution and the Probability Distribution of a Random Variable

In Chapters 3 and 4 we presented the concept of a population, its frequency distribution, and its parameters. In this chapter we have discussed the notion of a random variable, its probability distribution, and its parameters. There is a delicate distinction between these two formulations (populations and random variables), and it is to the clarification of this distinction that this section is devoted.

Suppose a small town of 100 adult residents has the following annual income frequency distribution:

Income (X)	Frequency (f)	Relative frequency f/100
$ 5,000	10	0.10
12,000	60	0.60
15,000	30	0.30
$\Sigma f = N = 100$		$\Sigma \dfrac{f}{N} = 1.00$

Figure 6.11 shows the relative frequency distribution of the town's income. The above data show that 10 percent of the town's population earn $5,000

Figure 6.11

Relative frequency distribution of town income

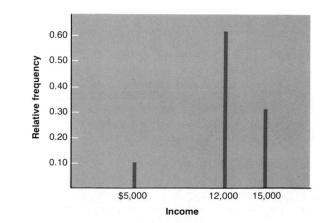

annually, 60 percent earn $12,000, and 30 percent earn $15,000. *These are descriptive data.* Now suppose we would like to select *one person at random* out of the town's population. The income of that person, before selection, is a random variable. There is a 10 percent chance that his income is $5,000, a 60 percent chance that it is $12,000, and a 30 percent chance that it is $15,000. The probability distribution of the random variable does not differ in any way from the relative frequency distribution shown in Figure 6.11. We only need to replace the words "relative frequency" by "probability" to obtain a probability distribution. Thus, the sole difference between the frequency distribution and the probability distribution is in the differing interpretations given to them. When dealing with the population, we can state with *full certainty* that 10 percent of the population have incomes of $5,000; 60 percent have incomes of $12,000; and so on. There is no such certainty with respect to the random variable, since the relative frequencies are interpreted here as the probability of occurrence of *uncertain* outcomes. We should note that the mean income computed from the frequency distribution ($12,200, as you can verify) is equal to the expected income of the random variable. This is similarly true with respect to other parameters, such as the variance and the skewness, but the same distinction between a population's frequency and a random variable's probability is carried over to them as well.

Consider a newly formed firm whose management is trying to forecast its sales for the coming year. Past data are not available, and sales cannot be known with certainty in advance. Unlike the situation in the previous example, it is clear that next year's sales is a random variable, and no parallel population exists whose relative frequency is equal to the probability distribution of the random variable. The probability distribution of this random variable is subjective and has nothing to do with any population's frequency distribution.

Chapter Summary and Review

	Random variable X	Transformation of X: $Y = a + bX$
1. Expected value[11]	$\mu_X = E(X) = \Sigma x\, P(x)$	$\mu_Y = E(Y) = a + b\mu_X$
2. Variance[11]	$\sigma_X^2 \equiv V(X) = E(X - \mu_X)^2 = \Sigma(x - \mu_X)^2 P(x)$	$\sigma_Y^2 \equiv V(Y) = b^2\sigma_X^2$
3. Standard deviation	$\sigma_X \equiv SD(X) = \sqrt{\sigma_X^2}$	$\sigma_Y \equiv SD(Y) = |b|\sigma_X$
4. Skewness[11]	$\mu_3^X = E(X - \mu_X)^3 = \Sigma(x - \mu_X)^3\, P(x)$	$\mu_3^Y = b^3\mu_3^X$
5. Kurtosis[11]	$\mu_4^X = E(X - \mu_X)^4 = \Sigma(x - \mu_X)^4\, P(x)$	$\mu_4^Y = b^4\mu_4^X$
6. nth central moment ($n \geq 2$)	$\mu_n^X = E(X - \mu_X)^n = \Sigma(x - \mu_X)^n\, P(x)$	$\mu_n^Y = b^n\mu_n^X$

[11] The right-hand side of the equation, which includes a summation sign, applies only to discrete random variables. The expected value of a continuous random variable is given by $\mu = \int x f(x) dx$, and the nth central moment ($n \geq 2$) of a continuous variable is given by $\mu_n = \int (x - \mu)^n f(x) dx$. For details see Appendix 6A.

Measurement Units of the Various Measures

μ Expected value—units (e.g., dollars)

σ^2 Variance—units squared (e.g., dollars squared)

σ Standard deviation—units (e.g., dollars)

$\dfrac{\sigma}{\mu}$ Coefficient of variation— $\dfrac{\text{units}}{\text{units}}$ = a unitless number

μ_3 Skewness—cubed units (e.g., cubed dollars)

$\dfrac{\mu_3}{\sigma^3}$ Coefficient of skewness— $\dfrac{\text{cubed units}}{\text{cubed units}}$ = a unitless number

μ_4 Units raised to the 4th power

μ_n Units raised to the nth power

Problems

6.1. In a football game between Team A and Team B, the probability concerning the game's outcome is as follows:

Event	Probability
Team A will win	0.60
Team A will not win	0.40
	1.00

    (*a*) Have we defined a random variable above?
    (*b*) If not, define one related to the game, and write down its probability distribution.

6.2. Is the cumulative probability distribution of a discrete random variable discrete or continuous? Why?

6.3. Over each of the sample spaces of the following random experiments, define two random variables:

    (*a*) A coin is flipped once, and a head or a tail is observed.
    (*b*) Two coins are flipped, and heads and tails are observed.
    (*c*) Next Tuesday's weather.

6.4. Classify the following random variables as discrete or continuous:

    (*a*) The number of children present in a classroom at a given time
    (*b*) The daily volume of gasoline sold at a given gas station
    (*c*) Tomorrow's temperature
    (*d*) The daily number of customers coming into a furniture store

6.5. The probability distribution of X, the length of stay of a hotel guest (measured in days), is as follows:

x	1	2	3	4
$P(x)$	0.40	0.25	0.20	0.15

(a) Calculate and explain the meaning of each of the following probabilities: $P(X = 2)$, $P(X \leq 3)$, $P(X > 1)$, $P(1 < X \leq 4)$.

(b) Write down the cumulative probability distribution of X.

(c) Present the probability distribution and the cumulative distribution on two separate charts.

6.6. The owner of a gas station has offered to let a rent-a-car company use his facilities to rent cars to customers. Each time a car is rented through the gas station, the gas station owner will get $3 from the rent-a-car company. It will cost the gas station $60 per day to provide the service. The number of daily cars rented through the gas station is a random variable as follows:

x	10	20	30	40
$P(x)$	0.15	0.25	0.45	0.15

(a) What is the probability that the rental income will exceed the cost on a certain day?

(b) What is the expected value of the number of rentals per day?

(c) What is the expected value of the gas station profit from the rentals?

6.7. The following is a cumulative probability distribution of the random variable X:

$$F(x) = \begin{cases} 0.00 & x < \$100 \\ 0.15 & \$100 \leq x < \$150 \\ 0.45 & \$150 \leq x < \$300 \\ 0.80 & \$300 \leq x < \$500 \\ 1.00 & \$500 \leq x \end{cases}$$

Write down X's probability distribution.

6.8. Meat orders are placed periodically by a large meat store. The delivery period (that is, the time that elapses between the placement of the order and the delivery of the meat) is a random variable, X (measured in days), with the following probability distribution:

$$P(X = x) = \begin{cases} \dfrac{1}{10} \cdot (7 - x) & x = 3, 4, 5, 6 \\ 0 & \text{otherwise} \end{cases}$$

(a) Is the probability distribution discrete or continuous?

(b) Graph the probability distribution.

(c) Write down and graph the cumulative distribution function.

6.9. Consider the following distributions of X_1, X_2, and X_3:

x_1	$P(x_1)$	x_2	$P(x_2)$	x_3	$P(x_3)$
0	$\frac{1}{4}$	0	$\frac{3}{8}$	0	$\frac{1}{2}$
10	$\frac{1}{4}$	10	$\frac{1}{8}$	30	$\frac{1}{2}$
20	$\frac{1}{4}$	20	$\frac{1}{8}$		
30	$\frac{1}{4}$	30	$\frac{3}{8}$		

(a) Find the means of X_1, X_2, and X_3.

(b) Determine *without any calculations* which of the distributions has the greatest variance. Explain how you reached your decision.

(c) Verify your answer to part b by calculating the variances.

6.10. Calculate the mean, variance, skewness, and kurtosis of the following distributions:

x_1	$P(x_1)$	x_2	$P(x_2)$
10	$\frac{1}{4}$	0	$\frac{1}{8}$
20	$\frac{1}{4}$	20	$\frac{1}{4}$
30	$\frac{1}{4}$	30	$\frac{1}{4}$
40	$\frac{1}{4}$	50	$\frac{3}{8}$

6.11. Hetty and Taily play the following game: Hetty starts off with one cent and Taily with two cents. Hetty and Taily *simultaneously* flip one coin each. If both coins fall on the same side, Taily gives Hetty one cent. If the coins fall on different sides, Hetty gives Taily one cent. The game continues until either Hetty or Taily has all three coins.

    (*a*) Write down the probability distribution of X, where X is the number of flips required to end the game.

    (*b*) Write down the cumulative probability distribution of X.

6.12. Compute the mean, variance, standard deviation, skewness, and kurtosis of the variables $X_1, X_2, X_3, X_4,$ and X_5, whose probability distributions are given below:

x_1	$P(x_1)$	x_2	$P(x_2)$	x_3	$P(x_3)$
10	$\frac{1}{2}$	10	$\frac{3}{4}$	10	$\frac{9}{10}$
20	$\frac{1}{2}$	20	$\frac{1}{4}$	20	$\frac{1}{10}$

x_4	$P(x_4)$	x_5	$P(x_5)$
10	$\frac{1}{4}$	10	$\frac{1}{10}$
20	$\frac{3}{4}$	20	$\frac{9}{10}$

6.13. Compute the mean, variance, standard deviation, skewness, and kurtosis of the variables $X_1, X_2,$ and X_3 whose probability distributions are given below:

x_1	$P(x_1)$	x_2	$P(x_2)$	x_3	$P(x_3)$
100	$\frac{1}{2}$	90	$\frac{1}{2}$	70	$\frac{1}{2}$
120	$\frac{1}{2}$	130	$\frac{1}{2}$	150	$\frac{1}{2}$

6.14. A painting service is bidding for a contract on which it hopes to make a profit of $40,000. The cost of preparing the bid and submitting it is $3,000, and the probability that the company will get the contract is 0.50. What is the expected profit, its standard deviation, and its skewness?

6.15. Illinois Chemicals, Inc., produces a certain quantity of a given chemical every day. The quantity produced is a random variable (X) having a uniform distribution in the range from 16 to 19 pounds.

    (*a*) Write down and draw the density function of X.

    (*b*) Write down and draw the cumulative probability distribution.

    (*c*) Calculate the probability that production on a certain day will be between 17 and 17.5 pounds.

6.16. The random variable X has a uniform distribution in the range from -7 to 53. Calculate the following:

(a) The 10th percentile of the distribution
(b) The median
(c) The 80th percentile

6.17. The random variable X is symmetrical around 10. The value $E(X^2)$ is equal to 200. Calculate the variance and standard deviation of X.

6.18. The random variable X is symmetrical around 10. Can you say what the lowest possible value of $E(X^2)$ must be?
Hint: Assume $E(X^2) = 2$ and calculate the variance using the computational formula.

6.19. Determine whether the following can be probability distributions:

(a) $P(x) = \dfrac{1}{2}$ for $x = 1, 2$

(b) $P(x) = \dfrac{1}{3}$ for $x = 0, 1, 2, 3$

(c) $P(x) = \dfrac{x}{5}$ for $x = 0, 2, 3$

(d) $P(x) = \dfrac{x - 5}{10}$ for $x = 0, 5, 10, 15$

(e) $P(x) = \dfrac{x^2}{10}$ for $x = -1, 0, 3$

6.20. The German state lottery is often advertised in American magazines. An ad appearing in the January 8, 1979 issue of *Business Week* is an example. According to the ad, a ticket costs 618 German marks (DM). While the actual lottery is a bit more involved, we will assume that there are 106,643 prizes, as shown in Table P6.20. Find the expected value of the prize, assuming that you bought one ticket, and compare it to the ticket's price. Also calculate the standard deviation and the coefficient of skewness of the prize. Note that 300,000 tickets were sold altogether, each having an equal chance of winning.

TABLE P6.20

Number of prizes	Amount (DM)
193,357	0
6,000	200
6,600	300
7,800	400
8,730	500
73,260	600
390	700
420	800
2,850	1,000
150	2,000
120	3,000
135	5,000
96	10,000
24	25,000
12	50,000
35	100,000
21	1,000,000
Total 300,000	

6.21. According to Problem 6.20, what would be your expected profit (or loss) if you had joined with a friend, bought two tickets, and plan to share the cost and all prospective prizes equally?

6.22. Write down the probability distribution of a discrete random variable of your choice. Make sure the function has the following parameters: $\mu = 70$, $\sigma = 25$, $\mu_3 = 0$. Calculate the distribution's kurtosis.

6.23. The number of buyers, X, of a certain product from a given salesperson has the following probability distribution:

x	0	1	2	3	4	5	6
$P(x)$	0.15	0.16	0.20	0.18	0.15	0.10	0.06

(a) Calculate the following probabilities: $P(X \leq 4)$, $P(2 \leq X < 6)$, $P(X > 2)$, $P(X \leq 3)$.
(b) Calculate the expected value and the standard deviation of X.
(c) Verify that Chebyshev's theorem holds for X, given the values $k = 1.1, 1.3, 1.5,$ and 1.6.

6.24. Using Chebyshev's theorem, we can find a lower bound for the probability that a random variable will take on a value in the range within k standard deviations from its mean. What is the lower bound of the probability for the following ranges:

(a) 1.6 standard deviations from the mean
(b) 1.2 standard deviations from the mean
(c) 2 standard deviations from the mean
(d) 3 standard deviations from the mean

6.25. The number of "Big Macs" sold by McDonald's restaurant between 7 P.M. and 9 P.M. is a random variable with mean $\mu = 100$ and standard deviation $\sigma = 5$. Use Chebyshev's theorem to determine the probability that the number of "Big Macs" sold will be between 80 and 120. What is the probability that sales will be between 60 and 120 "Big Macs"?

6.26. (a) The number of newspapers bought at a given stand is a random variable whose mean and standard deviation are 150 and 5, respectively. Using Chebyshev's theorem, we determine that the probability for daily newspaper sales of between x_1 and x_2 newspapers is at least 75 percent. Determine the values of x_1 and x_2.
(b) Suppose that each newspaper costs 25 cents. Consider the daily revenue (in dollars) rather than the number of newspapers sold. Calculate the mean and standard deviation of the new random variable and answer part a again, this time for the daily revenue.

6.27. Suppose you are offered two alternative bets:

1. A random variable is drawn from an unknown distribution whose mean $\mu = 0$ and $\sigma = 1$. If the random variable falls within the range $(-1, 1)$, you get a prize of $1,000. Otherwise, you get nothing.
2. A random variable is drawn from an unknown distribution whose mean is $\mu = 100$ and standard deviation is $\sigma = 10$. If the random variable falls within the range $(70, 130)$, you get $1,000. Otherwise, you get nothing.

Assume that you are offered a chance to play, free of charge, only one of these lotteries. Which one would you choose? Explain.

6.28. Using Chebyshev's theorem we can state that the probability that a random variable will fall outside of the range within k standard deviations of its mean is at most 17.3611 percent. What is the value of k?

6.29. The random variable X has a uniform probability distribution in the range from $-\$5$ to $\$25$.

(a) Calculate the following probabilities:

    1. $P(X \le \$0)$
    2. $P(-\$3 \le X \le \$4)$
    3. $P(X \ge -\$1)$
    4. $P(X = \$12)$

(b) What is the probability that the random variable X will take on a value that deviates from its mean by more than $10?

6.30. The lifetime of a battery is a random variable having a uniform distribution over the range from 500 to 600 hours.

    (a) Write down the density function $f(x)$ and the cumulative distribution $F(x)$.
    (b) Apply $F(x)$ to calculate the probability that an inspection of a random battery will reveal a lifetime of between 550–575 hours.

6.31. The probability distribution of the random variable X is as follows:

x	$P(x)$
20	0.10
40	0.20
60	0.40
80	0.20
100	0.10

    (a) For each value x calculate the standardized value $(x - \mu)/\sigma$.
    (b) Show that the expected value of the standardized variable is equal to zero and that its standard deviation is equal to 1.

6.32. A portfolio of assets owned by a family yields the following random income X (in thousands of dollars):

x	$P(x)$
$100	1/4
200	1/2
400	1/4

    (a) Calculate the mean and the variance of X.
    (b) Assume now that X is to be divided equally among 10 members of the family. Calculate the expected value and the variance of income to each member of the family. Do your calculation twice: one time by direct calculation and one time by applying the linear transformation formulas.

6.33. The following is a company's anticipated sales distribution:

x	$P(x)$
$20,000	0.20
25,000	0.20
30,000	0.20
35,000	0.20
40,000	0.20
	1.00

(a) Find the expected value of the sales and the variance of sales.

(b) Find the expected value and variance of sales when the latter is expressed in thousands of dollars.

(c) If there is a fixed cost of $15,000 and a variable cost of $.50 per unit, what are the expected value and variance of the profit? Assume that the company sells each unit of production for $1.

   Hint: If the price of the product is denoted as P, the variable cost per unit as C, the number of units sold as X, fixed cost as F, and profit as π, π is given by

$$\pi = (P - C)X - F$$

6.34. The Alpha Company employs salespersons to market its products. Each salesperson is paid $120 a week plus 15 percent commission on the sales he or she makes. The number of items a salesperson sells in one week is a random variable whose probability distribution is the same for all salespersons and is as follows:

x	$P(x)$
10	0.15
11	0.15
12	0.40
13	0.15
14	0.15
	1.00

The price of each item sold is $100.

(a) Find the expected weekly income of one salesperson.

(b) Find the standard deviation of the weekly income of one salesperson.

(c) Answer parts a and b again, this time assuming that the weekly fixed income has risen from $120 to $150.

(d) What are the answers to a and b if the weekly income is $200 plus 20 percent commission?

6.35. A medical insurance plan for individuals that covers the expenses of visits to the doctor is based on an insurance premium of $120 per year. Suppose each visit of the insured to a doctor costs $25, of which 20 percent is paid by the insured and 80 percent by the insurance company. Also assume that each policy contains a $50 deductible clause, so that the first two visits to a doctor are not covered by the plan. Suppose the probability distribution describing the chances that an individual will visit a doctor a given number of times per year is as shown in Table P6.35. Find the company's expected income (i.e., $120 minus the expected payments to cover the cost of doctor visits) from one policy and its variance.

TABLE P6.35

Number of doctor visits	Probability
0	0.10
1	0.30
2	0.20
3	0.08
4	0.07
5	0.06
6	0.05
7	0.04
8	0.04
9	0.04
10	0.02
	1.00

6.36. The ABC Company supplies a given item to the DEF Company. According to the contract between the companies, ABC will supply exactly 10,000 items at a price of $100 each. The production cost of the items consists of $200,000 in fixed costs plus additional variable costs in the amount of $C per item, where C is a random variable having the following probability distribution:

c	P(c)
$6	0.30
7	0.40
8	0.20
9	0.10
	1.00

(a) Calculate the skewness of the variable cost per unit, C.

(b) Calculate the skewness of total variable costs (i.e., variable cost per unit times the number of units produced).

(c) ABC's net profit is equal to the revenues less variable costs and less fixed costs. Find the skewness and coefficient of skewness of the net profit. Ignore taxes. What is the relationship between the skewness of C and the skewness of the net profit?

Hint: Avoid unnecessary calculations and use the fact that the net profit is a linear transformation of the variable cost per unit, C.

6.37. "If X is a random variable whose skewness is $\mu_3 = 0$, then the skewness of the random variable $-X$ is necessarily also zero." Appraise this statement.

6.38. Suppose the return on a $100 investment is a random variable X that has the following distribution:

x	P(x)
80	1/2
250	1/2

(a) Calculate the mean, the variance, and the skewness of the return X.

(b) Define a new random variable $Y = X - I$, where I is the $100 investment and Y is the *net* income. Calculate the mean, standard deviation, and skewness of Y.

APPENDIX 6A:
Treating Continuous Random Variables with Calculus

All density functions are such that the area under the curve over the entire range of the variable is equal to 1 (measured in any desired units). The probability that a random variable will assume values within a given interval is equal to the area under the curve over the designated interval divided by the total area under the curve. Since the total area under the curve is equal to 1, the probability is simply equal to the area under the curve over the interval. Since the area under the curve represents probability and since probability is always nonnegative, it is clear that $f(x) \geq 0$ for every density function. Furthermore, since the total area under the curve is equal to 1, it follows that $\int_{-\infty}^{\infty} f(x)dx = 1$. Let A denote the probability that a random variable, X, will assume a value in the interval (a, b). The probability is represented in Figure 6A.1 by the darkest area.

Figure 6A.1

Continuously distributed random variable X, showing the probability that X will assume a value between a and b

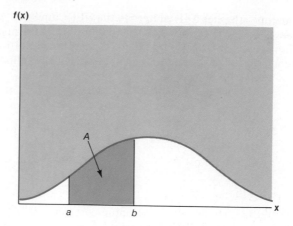

By the rules of calculus we know that the area under the curve over a given interval is given by the integral of the function that describes that curve:

$$P(A) = P(a \leq X \leq b) = \int_a^b f(x)dx \tag{6A.1}$$

In principle, the probability of every event may be calculated by integration, but in practice, because of complicated density functions, such calculations may be cumbersome. We leave the more cumbersome functions for more advanced texts and use simple, straightforward distributions to illustrate the role of integration in calculating probabilities.

Let us start with the uniform distribution. Figure 6A.2 is a reproduction of Figure 6.7. The figure shows the uniform density function of a random variable, X. The function is as follows:

$$f(x) = \begin{cases} \frac{1}{10} & 10 \leq x \leq 20 \\ 0 & \text{otherwise} \end{cases}$$

For all values of X between 10 and 20 the density function is equal to $\frac{1}{10}$; for values of X outside that range, $f(x) = 0$. Therefore, the basic requirement

Figure 6A.2

Uniformly distributed random variable X, showing the probability that X will assume a value between 14 and 18

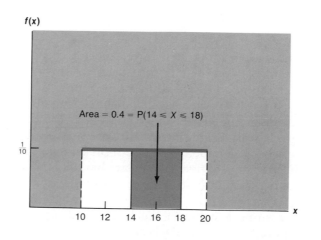

for a density function—that $f(x) \geq 0$ for all x—holds. To find the probability of X falling between 14 and 18 we integrate the density function:

$$P(14 \leq X \leq 18) = \int_{14}^{18} \frac{1}{10}\, dx = \frac{x}{10} \bigg]_{14}^{18} = \frac{18}{10} - \frac{14}{10} = \frac{4}{10} = 0.40$$

Note that for a continuous variable the following probabilities are equal:

$$P(a \leq X \leq b) = P(a < X \leq b) = P(a \leq X < b) = P(a < X < b)$$

Consider any uniform random variable that may assume values in the range (α, β). The range's width is $(\beta - \alpha)$, so the height of the density function must be equal to $1/(\beta - \alpha)$ to ensure that the total area under the function will just equal 1 (see Figure 6A.3). The probability that X will assume a value less than α is zero. The probability that X will assume a value less than or equal to β is 1. The probability that X will assume a value smaller than some x, where x is somewhere between α and β, is as follows:

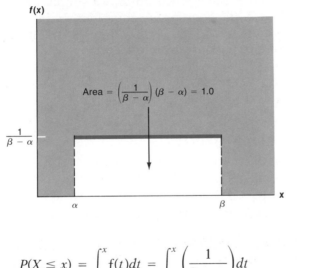

Figure 6A.3

Uniform density function over the interval (α, β)

$$P(X \leq x) = \int_{\alpha}^{x} f(t)\,dt = \int_{\alpha}^{x} \left(\frac{1}{\beta - \alpha} \right) dt$$

$$= \frac{t}{\beta - \alpha} \bigg]_{\alpha}^{x} = \frac{x}{\beta - \alpha} - \frac{\alpha}{\beta - \alpha} \qquad \textbf{(6A.2)}$$

$$= \frac{x - \alpha}{\beta - \alpha}$$

Thus the uniform cumulative probability function may be written systematically as in Equation 6A.3 and presented diagrammatically as shown in Figure 6A.4.

$$F(x) = \begin{cases} 0 & x < \alpha \\[2mm] \dfrac{x - \alpha}{\beta - \alpha} & \alpha \leq x \leq \beta \\[2mm] 1 & \beta < x \end{cases} \qquad \textbf{(6A.3)}$$

Figure 6A.4

Uniform cumulative probability function

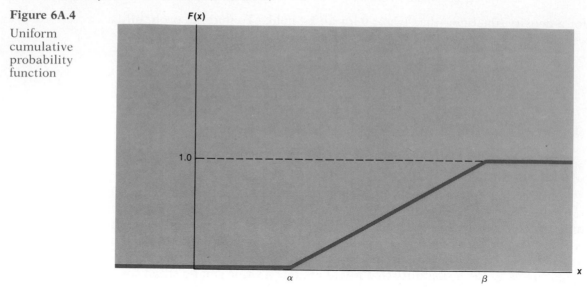

The moments of continuous variables can be calculated in much the same way as those of discrete random variables: we simply apply integration instead of summation in the appropriate equations. In fact, integration is the equivalent of summation for continuous variables. The mean, variance, and skewness of a discrete random variable, X, are

$$\mu = \Sigma x P(x)$$
$$\sigma^2 = \Sigma (x - \mu)^2 P(x) = \Sigma x^2 P(x) - \mu^2 \qquad \textbf{(6A.4)}$$
$$\mu_3 = \Sigma (x - \mu)^3 P(x)$$

If X is continuous, the respective equations are

$$\mu = \int x f(x) dx$$
$$\sigma^2 = \int (x - \mu)^2 f(x) dx = \int x^2 f(x) dx - \mu^2 \qquad \textbf{(6A.5)}$$
$$\mu_3 = \int (x - \mu)^3 f(x) dx$$

where the integrals go from $-\infty$ to $+\infty$.

The nth central moment is defined as follows:

$$\mu_n = \int (x - \mu)^n f(x) dx \qquad \textbf{(6A.6)}$$

Consider again the following uniform probability distribution:

$$f(x) = \begin{cases} \dfrac{1}{\beta - \alpha} & \alpha \leq x \leq \beta \\ 0 & \text{otherwise} \end{cases}$$

The mean and variance are calculated as follows:

$$\mu = \int_\alpha^\beta x f(x) dx = \int_\alpha^\beta \frac{x}{\beta - \alpha} dx = \frac{1}{\beta - \alpha} \int_\alpha^\beta x \, dx = \frac{1}{\beta - \alpha} \cdot \frac{x^2}{2} \Big]_\alpha^\beta$$

$$= \frac{\beta^2 - \alpha^2}{2(\beta - \alpha)} = \frac{(\beta - \alpha)(\alpha + \beta)}{2(\beta - \alpha)} = \frac{\alpha + \beta}{2}$$

$$E(X^2) = \int_\alpha^\beta x^2 f(x) \, dx = \int_\alpha^\beta \frac{x^2}{\beta - \alpha} dx = \frac{1}{\beta - \alpha} \int_\alpha^\beta x^2 dx = \frac{1}{\beta - \alpha} \cdot \frac{x^3}{3} \Big]_\alpha^\beta$$

$$= \frac{\beta^3 - \alpha^3}{3(\beta - \alpha)} = \frac{(\beta - \alpha)(\beta^2 + \alpha\beta + \alpha^2)}{3(\beta - \alpha)} = \frac{\beta^2 + \alpha\beta + \alpha^2}{3}$$

$$\sigma^2 = E(X^2) - \mu^2 = \frac{\beta^2 + \alpha\beta + \alpha^2}{3} - \left(\frac{\alpha + \beta}{2}\right)^2$$

$$= \frac{4\beta^2 + 4\alpha\beta + 4\alpha^2 - 3\beta^2 - 6\alpha\beta - 3\alpha^2}{12} = \frac{(\beta - \alpha)^2}{12}$$

Let us look at one more example of a continuous random variable. Consider the density function of Figure 6A.5:

$$f(x) = \begin{cases} 0.06x - 5.95 & 100 \leq x \leq 105 \\ 0 & \text{otherwise} \end{cases}$$

For every value of x between 100 and 105 we get $f(x) > 0$, and for every x value outside of this range we have $f(x) = 0$. Therefore, for every x we have $f(x) \geq 0$. Furthermore, the area under the curve equals 1:

$$\int_{100}^{105} (0.06x - 5.95) \, dx = \frac{0.06x^2}{2} \Big]_{100}^{105} - 5.95 \, x \Big]_{100}^{105} = 1$$

Figure 6A.5

The density function $f(x)$

This verifies that $f(x)$ is a density function. Let us calculate the expected value and variance of X:

$$E(X) = \int_{100}^{105} xf(x)\,dx = \int_{100}^{105} x(0.06x - 5.95)dx$$

$$= \frac{0.06x^3}{3}\Big]_{100}^{105} - \frac{5.95\,x^2}{2}\Big]_{100}^{105}$$

$$= 3{,}152.50 - 3{,}049.375 = 103.125$$

Next let us calculate $E(X^2)$:

$$E(X^2) = \int_{100}^{105} x^2(0.06x - 5.95)\,dx = \frac{0.06x^4}{4}\Big]_{100}^{105} - \frac{5.95x^3}{3}\Big]_{100}^{105}$$

$$= 323{,}259.375 - 312{,}622.9168 = 10{,}636.4582$$

From this result we obtain:

$$V(X) = E(X^2) - \mu^2 = 10{,}636.4582 - 103.125^2 = 1.692575$$

To find a probability such as $P(102 \le X \le 104.5)$, we calculate:

$$P(102 \le X \le 104.5) = \int_{102}^{104.5} f(x)dx = \int_{102}^{104.5} (0.06x - 5.95)\,dx$$

$$= \frac{0.06x^2}{2}\Big]_{102}^{104.5} - 5.95x\Big]_{102}^{104.5} = 0.6125$$

APPENDIX SUMMARY AND REVIEW

The following hold for every continuous density function:

1. $f(x) \ge 0$ for all x
2. $\int f(x)dx = 1$
3. $P(a \le X \le b) = \int_a^b f(x)dx$

The following hold for every continuous random variable:

1. The first moment (mean):

$$\mu = \int xf(x)\,dx$$

2. The second central moment (variance):

$$\sigma^2 = \int (x - \mu)^2 f(x)\,dx = \int x^2 f(x)dx - \mu^2$$

3. The third central moment (skewness):

$$\mu_3 = \int(x - \mu)^3 f(x)\, dx$$

4. The nth central moment:

$$\mu_n = \int(x - \mu)^n f(x)\, dx$$

APPENDIX PROBLEMS

6A.1. A continuous random variable, X, has a density function such that $f(x) > 0$ in the range $5 \leq x \leq 10$ and $f(x) = 0$ in every other range. Write out—in general terms, using an integral expression—the following probabilities: $P(X \leq 5)$, $P(X \leq 10)$, $P(5 \leq X \leq 8)$, $P(5 < X < \infty)$, $P(5 < X \leq 8)$, and $P(X > 10)$.

6A.2. The lengths of harvested sugar canes have the following density function (X is measured in inches):

$$f(x) = \begin{cases} \frac{1}{20} & 10 \leq x \leq 30 \\ 0 & \text{otherwise} \end{cases}$$

    (*a*) Write down the cumulative distribution function.
    (*b*) One cane is selected at random. What is the probability that its length is precisely 18 inches? What is the probability that its length (x) is in the range $10 < x < 20$?

6A.3. Calculate the mean and standard deviation of the length of the sugar canes (Problem 6A.2). Can you tell, without calculating, the skewness of X? Explain.

6A.4. The random variable X has a uniform distribution with parameters $\alpha = 0$ and $\beta = 10$. The random variable Y is defined as follows: $Y = 5X$.

    (*a*) Write the density functions and the cumulative distribution functions of X and Y.
    (*b*) Draw the functions on charts.
    (*c*) Calculate the means of X and Y. What is the relationship between the means?
    (*d*) Calculate the variances of X and Y. What is the relationship between them?

6A.5. Suppose the before-tax earnings (X) of a firm is a uniformly distributed random variable with parameters α and β (assume $\alpha > 0$ and $\beta > 0$). Assume that the tax rate imposed on the firm is $T = 0.46$, or 46 percent. The after-tax earnings are given by $(1 - T)X$. Write down the density function of the after-tax earnings.

6A.6. The density function of variable X is given by:

$$f(x) = \begin{cases} 0.2 + 0.04x & -5 \leq x \leq 0 \\ 0.2 - 0.04x & 0 \leq x \leq 5 \\ 0 & \text{otherwise} \end{cases}$$

    (*a*) Draw the density function.
    (*b*) Show that $\int_{-\infty}^{\infty} f(x)\, dx = 1$.
    (*c*) Find $P(-3 \leq X \leq 0)$.
    (*d*) Find $P(1 \leq X \leq 4)$.

    (e) Calculate the expected value of X.

    (f) Calculate the variance of X.

6A.7. The following is the density function of X:

$$f(x) = \begin{cases} 0.04 - 0.0001x & 250 \leq x \leq 350 \\ 0 & \text{otherwise} \end{cases}$$

    (a) Draw the density function.

    (b) Show that $\int_{-\infty}^{\infty} f(x)\, dx = 1$.

    (c) Find $P(250 \leq X \leq 320)$.

    (d) Calculate the expected value of X.

    (e) Calculate the variance of X.

    (f) Write the cumulative probability function of X.

THE RELATIONSHIP BETWEEN TWO RANDOM VARIABLES

Key Terms
joint probability distribution
marginal probability
conditional probability
covariance
coefficient of correlation

7.1 The Joint Probability Distribution

In Chapter 6 we focused on the probability distribution of one random variable. Quite often in statistical analysis we deal with more than one variable. When two or more random variables are of interest, we may want to learn about their *combined outcomes*. For example, we may want to know the probability of facing a given combination of input and output prices, the probability of facing a given combination of revenues and expenses, the probability that temperatures will fall within a given range in the next two or more days, the combined effect of an advertising campaign in two states, the changes in two securities' prices in the next year, and the like. We approach such situations by looking at a **joint probability distribution,** which specifies the *probability of each possible outcome combination of the variables considered.* Back in Chapter 5 we discussed the joint probability, marginal probability, and conditional probability of events. The discussion in this section will follow very similar lines, the major difference being that here we will concern ourselves with the distribution of random variables rather than with the probabilities of events. We shall illustrate the joint probability distribution concept using an example.

EXAMPLE 7.1

Subfreezing temperatures can cause severe damage to citrus crops. A citrus grower who has orange groves in both Florida and California estimates that temperatures in the range 24–32°F in either location (we shall call this range of temperatures "freeze") will cause $100,000 in crop damage, and temperatures under 24°F in either location (we shall call this range of temperatures "hard freeze") will cause $400,000 in crop damage. Suppose the probability that temperatures will drop into these ranges next winter in either Florida or California is as follows:

Temperature range	Freeze damage (thousands of dollars)	Probability
Hard freeze	$400	0.02
Freeze	100	0.08
Normal	0	0.90

The possibility of future damage is taken into consideration when citrus prices are determined: because of the risk of future freeze damage, the grower sets his prices at levels that will compensate him for anticipated losses. Let us assume that in determining his citrus prices, the grower considers the probability of freeze damage in both Florida and California. Denoting damage in Florida by X_1 and damage in California by X_2 and assuming (for the sake of the example only) that the temperatures in the two locations are independent, we can construct the *joint probability distribution* for X_1 and X_2 as given in Table 7.1.

TABLE 7.1
The Joint Distribution of X_1 and X_2

x_2	x_1 $400	$100	$0	Marginal probability of X_2
$400	0.0004	0.0016	0.0180	0.02
$100	0.0016	0.0064	0.0720	0.08
$ 0	0.0180	0.0720	0.8100	0.90
Marginal probability of X_1	0.02	0.08	0.90	1.00

The table systematically lists the probabilities for all possible combinations of X_1 and X_2. These probabilities—namely, $P(X_1 = x_1, X_2 = x_2)$—are denoted by $P(x_1, x_2)$. For example, the probability that no damage in Florida (i.e., $X_1 = 0$) will coincide with damages of $100,000 in California (i.e., $X_2 = 100$) is $P(X_1 = 0, X_2 = 100) = 0.90 \cdot 0.08 = 0.0720$. Similarly, $P(X_1 = 400, X_2 = 400) = 0.02 \cdot 0.02 = 0.0004$, and so on.

Note that the sum of all the joint probabilities must equal 1, meaning that one of the combinations must be observed. This is only logical, of course, since the joint probability is by definition a systematic listing of the probabilities of *all* the possible combinations of X_1 and X_2, where no two combinations may overlap.

To generalize our conclusions from Example 7.1, we note again that the joint probability of X_1 and X_2 is denoted by $P(x_1, x_2)$ and the sum of all these probabilities is equal to 1:

$$\sum_{x_1} \sum_{x_2} P(x_1, x_2) = 1.0 \tag{7.1}$$

Similarly, we should extend our definition of the probability of events in a bivariate sample space (Chapter 5) to identify the marginal probability and the conditional probability for the case of two random variables. The **marginal probability** of X_1, $P(x_1)$, is given by the following equation:

$$P(x_1) = \sum_{x_2} P(x_1, x_2) \tag{7.2}$$

Similarly, the marginal probability of X_2, $P(x_2)$, is given by the equation

$$P(x_2) = \sum_{x_1} P(x_1, x_2) \tag{7.3}$$

In short, the marginal probability of the variable X_1 is its probability distribution disregarding the various values undertaken by X_2, and the marginal probability of X_2 is its probability distribution disregarding the various values undertaken by X_1.

To illustrate by referring back to Example 7.1, we can find the probability $P(X_1 = 100)$ by simply summing the probabilities in the column $X_1 = 100$ for all the possible values of X_2:

$$P(X_1 = 100) = \sum_{x_2} P(100, x_2) = 0.0016 + 0.0064 + 0.0720 = 0.0800$$

In a similar manner, we obtain the probability $P(X_2 = 0)$ by summing the probabilities under $X_2 = 0$ for all the possible values of X_1:

$$P(X_2 = 0) = \sum_{x_1} P(x_1, 0) = 0.0180 + 0.0720 + 0.8100 = 0.9000$$

The marginal probabilities are displayed in the *margins* of the joint probability distribution table (Table 7.1), but this, of course, does not indicate that marginal probabilities are at all "marginal" in their importance.

In Table 7.1 each joint probability is equal to the product of its components' respective marginal probabilities because, by assumption, X_1 and X_2 are *independent*. Thus the joint probability $P(X_1 = 100, X_2 = 0) = 0.0720$ is equal to the product of the marginal probabilities $P(X_1 = 100) = 0.08$ and $P(X_2 = 0) = 0.90$. Indeed, $0.08 \cdot 0.90 = 0.0720$. Random variables are independent only in special cases; thus we may generalize as follows:

$$P(x_1, x_2) = P(x_1)P(x_2) \quad \text{if } X_1 \text{ and } X_2 \text{ are independent} \tag{7.4}$$

$$P(x_1, x_2) \neq P(x_1)P(x_2) \quad \text{if } X_1 \text{ and } X_2 \text{ are not independent}$$

The **conditional probability** of X_1 given some value for X_2 is equal to the joint probability of X_1 and X_2 divided by the marginal probability of X_2, as noted in the following formula:

$$P(x_1 \mid x_2) = \frac{P(x_1, x_2)}{P(x_2)} \tag{7.5}$$

The conditional probability of X_2 given the value of X_1 is similarly defined:

$$P(x_2 \mid x_1) = \frac{P(x_1, x_2)}{P(x_1)} \tag{7.6}$$

Note that Equations 7.5 and 7.6 are merely conversions of the familiar conditional probability equations for events A and B:

$$P(A \mid B) = \frac{P(A \cap B)}{P(B)}$$

and

$$P(B \mid A) = \frac{P(A \cap B)}{P(A)}$$

To illustrate, we use Table 7.1 again:

$$P(X_1 = 0 \mid X_2 = 100) = \frac{P(X_1 = 0, X_2 = 100)}{P(X_2 = 100)} = \frac{0.072}{0.080} = 0.90$$

X_1 and X_2 in Example 7.1 are independent, so we get $P(X_1 = 0 \mid X_2 = 100) = P(X_1 = 0) = 0.90$. Again this result is not typical, and we generalize as follows:

$$\begin{aligned} P(x_1 \mid x_2) = P(x_1) &\qquad \text{if } X_1 \text{ and } X_2 \text{ are independent} \\ P(x_1 \mid x_2) \neq P(x_1) &\qquad \text{if } X_1 \text{ and } X_2 \text{ are not independent} \end{aligned} \tag{7.7}$$

Table 7.4 in the next section is an example of a joint probability distribution in which the variables are not independent. That table can be used to verify Equations 7.4 and 7.7.

7.2 The Covariance and the Correlation Coefficient

A joint probability distribution contains a great deal of information but is often cumbersome to handle. Just as in the case of a probability distribution of one variable, where we use parameters to measure characteristics of that variable, in this case we want to obtain simple measures both of the relationship between variables and of the linear combinations of two (or more) random variables. Suppose, for example, that the citrus grower in Example 7.1 is concerned with the total potential loss from Florida and California. The relevant variable here is X, which equals the sum of X_1 and X_2:

$$X = X_1 + X_2$$

From the joint distribution given in Table 7.1 we can derive the probability distribution of X. We derive X's probability distribution by sorting out all the possible combinations of X_1 and X_2 with corresponding probability data, setting the sum of their values equal to X, and grouping identical values. Table 7.2 provides the details.

TABLE 7.2
Derivation of the Probability Distribution of X

Possible combination		Probability of		Rearranged	Rearranged
x_1	x_2	combination	$x = x_1 + x_2$	x	probability
0	0	0.8100	0 ⟶ 0		0.8100
0	100	0.0720	100 ⟶ 100		0.1440
0	400	0.0180	400		
100	0	0.0720	100 ⟶ 200		0.0064
100	100	0.0064	200		
100	400	0.0016	500 ⟶ 400		0.0360
400	0	0.0180	400 ⟶ 500		0.0032
400	100	0.0016	500		
400	400	0.0004	800 ⟶ 800		0.0004
					1.0000

After a systematic summary of the data, we derive the probability distribution of *X* shown in Table 7.3.

Given Table 7.3, it is a simple matter to obtain the mean and the variance of *X*'s distribution (these parameters are important, because decision making concerning the variable *X* may very well hinge on their values). It is often advantageous to be able to determine the mean and variance of *X* without having the benefit of full information concerning its probability distribution. It is possible to do so, but first we need to learn about the covariance and the coefficient of correlation between two random variables.

The **covariance** is a *statistical measure of the linear mutual variability of two random variables*. Its sign reflects the direction of the mutual variability: if the variables tend to move in the same direction, the covariance is positive; if the variables tend to move in opposite directions, the covariance is negative. Specifically, the covariance between two random variables *X* and *Y* [denoted by $COV(X, Y)$ or $\sigma_{X,Y}$] is defined as follows:

$$COV(X, Y) \equiv \sigma_{X,Y} = E[(X - \mu_X)(Y - \mu_Y)] \qquad (7.8)$$

μ_X and μ_Y are the means of *X* and *Y*, respectively. For discrete variables, Equation 7.8 may be written as follows:

$$\sigma_{X,Y} = \sum_x \sum_y (x - \mu_X)(y - \mu_Y)P(x, y) \qquad (7.9)$$

TABLE 7.3
The Probability Distribution of $X = X_1 + X_2$

x (thousands of $)	$P(x)$
0	0.8100
100	0.1440
200	0.0064
400	0.0360
500	0.0032
800	0.0004
	1.0000

Equation 7.8 may be written yet another way, one that is more suitable for computations:[1]

$$COV(X, Y) \equiv \sigma_{X,Y} = E(XY) - \mu_X \mu_Y \qquad (7.10)$$

Let us now turn to an example showing what covariance is and how to calculate it.

EXAMPLE 7.2

A representative of Be-on-the-Safe-Side Insurance Company is scheduled to meet with two people to discuss with each the sale of two different insurance policies: life insurance and health insurance. Let the number of life insurance policies sold be denoted by X and let the number of health insurance policies sold be denoted by Y. Suppose the joint probability of X and Y is as shown in Table 7.4.

TABLE 7.4
The Joint Probability Distribution of X and Y

		x		Marginal probability of Y
y	0	1	2	
0	0.26	0.06	0.09	0.41
1	0.07	0.12	0.21	0.40
2	0.04	0.10	0.05	0.19
Marginal probability of X	0.37	0.28	0.35	1.00

Examining the marginal probabilities of X and Y, we first find their expected values:

$$E(X) = 0 \cdot 0.37 + 1 \cdot 0.28 + 2 \cdot 0.35 = 0.98$$

$$E(Y) = 0 \cdot 0.41 + 1 \cdot 0.40 + 2 \cdot 0.19 = 0.78$$

We can proceed to construct Table 7.5, in which we calculate the covariance between X and Y by means of Equation 7.9. Note that while the positive sign of $\sigma_{X,Y}$ indicates that X and Y do tend to move in the same direction—in other words, when more life insurance policies are sold, there is a tendency to sell more health insurance policies as well—the covariance does not tell us the *strength* of this tendency. Before we develop a measure that will show us the *strength* as well as the *direction* of the relationship, let us recalculate the covariance, this time using Equation 7.10. First we turn to Table 7.6, in which we calculate the expected value of the product XY.

[1] A simple proof confirms the equality of Equations 7.8 and 7.10:

$$\sigma_{X,Y} = E[(X - \mu_X)(Y - \mu_Y)] = E(XY - Y\mu_X - X\mu_Y + \mu_X\mu_Y)$$

$$= E(XY) - \mu_X E(Y) - \mu_Y E(X) + \mu_X\mu_Y$$

$$= E(XY) - \mu_X\mu_Y - \mu_Y\mu_X + \mu_X\mu_Y = E(XY) - \mu_X\mu_Y$$

TABLE 7.5
Work Sheet for Calculation of Covariance

(1) x	(2) y	(3) P(x, y)	(4) (x − μ_X)	(5) (y − μ_Y)	(6) (x − μ_X)(y − μ_Y)	(7) = (3) · (6) P(x, y) · (x − μ_X)(y − μ_Y)
0	0	0.26	−0.98	−0.78	0.7644	0.1987
0	1	0.07	−0.98	0.22	−0.2156	−0.0151
0	2	0.04	−0.98	1.22	−1.1956	−0.0478
1	0	0.06	0.02	−0.78	−0.0156	−0.0009
1	1	0.12	0.02	0.22	0.0044	0.0005
1	2	0.10	0.02	1.22	0.0244	0.0024
2	0	0.09	1.02	−0.78	−0.7956	−0.0716
2	1	0.21	1.02	0.22	0.2244	0.0471
2	2	0.05	1.02	1.22	1.2444	0.0622
		1.00			Total $\sigma_{X,Y}$ =	0.1755

TABLE 7.6
Work Sheet for Calculation of $E(XY)$

(1) x	(2) y	(3) P(x, y)	(4) xy	(5) = (3) · (4) P(x, y) · (xy)
0	0	0.26	0	0.00
0	1	0.07	0	0.00
0	2	0.04	0	0.00
1	0	0.06	0	0.00
1	1	0.12	1	0.12
1	2	0.10	2	0.20
2	0	0.09	0	0.00
2	1	0.21	2	0.42
2	2	0.05	4	0.20
		1.00		Total = $E(XY)$ = 0.94

Recalling that $\mu_X = 0.98$ and $\mu_Y = 0.78$, we apply Equation 7.10 and find that

$$\sigma_{X,Y} = E(XY) - \mu_X \mu_Y = 0.94 - 0.98 \cdot 0.78 = 0.1756$$

the same value we obtained when we used Equation 7.9. (The slight deviation is due to rounding.) Note the advantage of Equation 7.10: the values of X and Y in our example are integers. Therefore, the products XY also are integers, so calculations are relatively easy. In contrast, with Equation 7.9 we have the expressions $(x - \mu_X)$ and $(y - \mu_Y)$, which are often not integers even when x and y are. This makes the calculation by Equation 7.9 much more cumbersome.

As we mentioned earlier, the covariance shows the direction of the relationship between variables. Positive covariance reflects the tendency of the variables to move together: when one increases (decreases), the other tends to increase (decrease) as well. We say that these variables have a *direct* relationship. Zero covariance indicates that the variables have no tendency to move in the same direction. In this case we say that the variables are *uncorrelated*. If two variables are independent, their covariance equals zero. Negative correlation reflects the tendency of variables to move in opposite directions: when one increases (decreases), the other tends to decrease (increase). This kind of relationship is said to be an *inverse* relationship.

Apart from the direction of the relationship between variables, we may want to measure its strength. We can easily do so by *scaling* the covariance to obtain the coefficient of correlation.

The **coefficient of correlation,** denoted by the Greek letter ρ (rho), is equal to *the covariance divided by the product of the variables' standard deviations*. Denoting the standard deviation of X and Y by σ_X and σ_Y, we can express the covariance as the product of ρ, σ_X, and σ_Y:

$$\rho = \frac{\sigma_{X,Y}}{\sigma_X \sigma_Y} \tag{7.11}$$

and

$$\sigma_{X,Y} = \rho \sigma_X \sigma_Y \tag{7.12}$$

It can be shown that ρ is always less than or equal to 1.0 and greater than or equal to -1.0:

$$-1 \le \rho \le 1 \tag{7.13}$$

If $\rho = +1.0$, X and Y are said to be *perfectly positively correlated*. If $\rho = 0$, X and Y are *uncorrelated*. If two variables are independent, their correlation coefficient equals zero. If $\rho = -1.0$, X and Y are said to be *perfectly negatively correlated*. The closer ρ is to either $+1.0$ or -1.0, the stronger the relationship between the variables. The closer it is to zero, the weaker their relationship. Figure 7.1 illustrates a few possible relationships between X and Y.

Figure 7.1

Alternative relations between two variables and the respective coefficients of correlation

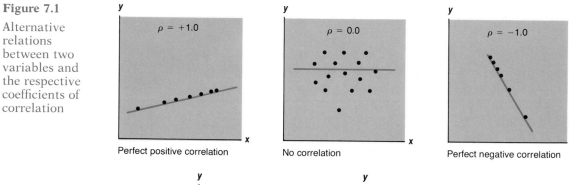

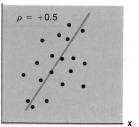

Calculating the correlation coefficient between X and Y in Example 7.2, we find

$$\sigma_X^2 = 0.37\ (0 - 0.98)^2 + 0.28\ (1 - 0.98)^2 + 0.35\ (2 - 0.98)^2$$

$$= 0.37 \cdot 0.9604 + 0.28 \cdot 0.0004 + 0.35 \cdot 1.0404 = 0.7196$$

and

$$\sigma_X = \sqrt{0.7196} = 0.8483$$

In addition

$$\sigma_Y^2 = 0.41\ (0 - 0.78)^2 + 0.40\ (1 - 0.78)^2 + 0.19\ (2 - 0.78)^2$$

$$= 0.41 \cdot 0.6084 + 0.40 \cdot 0.0484 + 0.19 \cdot 1.4884 = 0.5516$$

and

$$\sigma_Y = \sqrt{0.5516} = 0.7427$$

Recalling that $\sigma_{X,Y} = 0.1756$ and using Equation 7.11, we obtain

$$\rho = \frac{\sigma_{X,Y}}{\sigma_X \sigma_Y} = \frac{0.1756}{0.8483 \cdot 0.7427} = 0.2787$$

This means that the relationship between X and Y is direct but not strong.

7.3 The Sample Covariance and Correlation Coefficient

The population covariance and correlation coefficient are often unknown and need to be replaced by their corresponding measures in the sample: the sample covariance and sample correlation coefficient. The *unbiased* estimator of $\sigma_{X,Y}$ is $S_{X,Y}$, and it is given by

$$S_{X,Y} = \frac{1}{n-1} \Sigma(X - \overline{X})(Y - \overline{Y}) = \frac{1}{n-1}\ (\Sigma XY - n\overline{X}\overline{Y}) \qquad \textbf{(7.14)}$$

The sample correlation coefficient, r, is given by

$$r = \frac{S_{X,Y}}{S_X S_Y} \qquad \textbf{(7.15)}$$

where S_X and S_Y are simply the unbiased estimators of the standard deviations of X and Y, respectively. It can be shown that r is also given by Equation 7.16, which is a more direct computational formula than Equation 7.15.

$$r = \frac{\Sigma XY - n\overline{X}\overline{Y}}{\sqrt{\Sigma X^2 - n\overline{X}^2}\ \sqrt{\Sigma Y^2 - n\overline{Y}^2}} \qquad \textbf{(7.16)}$$

Many business calculators can give you the value of *r* at the push of a button, once the data have been loaded into them.

EXAMPLE 7.3

A large hotel in the Northeast has pursued an aggressive advertising campaign to attract tourists. In an attempt to make a cost-benefit analysis of the campaign, the hotel asks its guests how they heard of the hotel and what made them choose it over others. This information can be used to determine if the advertising expense has been worthwhile and if it should be continued. Part of the information collected in the eight years since the campaign began is shown in Table 7.7, columns 1, 2, and 3. Column 1 identifies the year, column 2 shows the advertising expense (X) in each year (in thousands of dollars), and column 3 shows the estimated extra profit, net of all expenses except advertising, attributed directly to the campaign (Y). Table 7.7 is also a work sheet for calculating the covariance and correlation coefficient between the advertising expense and the extra profit. From the table, we see that $\Sigma(X - \bar{X})(Y - \bar{Y}) = 6{,}300$, and by employing Equation 7.14, we find the sample covariance:

$$S_{X,Y} = \frac{\Sigma(X - \bar{X})(Y - \bar{Y})}{n - 1} = \frac{6{,}300}{8 - 1} = 900$$

To find the sample coefficient of correlation we first compute the standard deviations of X and Y:

$$S_X = \sqrt{\frac{\Sigma(X - \bar{X})^2}{n - 1}} = \sqrt{\frac{4{,}410}{8 - 1}} = 25.0998$$

$$S_Y = \sqrt{\frac{\Sigma(Y - \bar{Y})^2}{n - 1}} = \sqrt{\frac{22{,}158}{8 - 1}} = 56.2621$$

TABLE 7.7
A Work Sheet for Calculating the Covariance and Correlation Between Advertising Expense and Net Extra Profit
(thousands of dollars)

(1) Year	(2) Advertising expense X	(3) Net extra profit Y	(4) $(X - \bar{X})$	(5) $(Y - \bar{Y})$	(6) $(X - \bar{X})^2$	(7) $(Y - \bar{Y})^2$	(8) $(X - \bar{X})(Y - \bar{Y})$
1	$ 60	$111	−3	21	9	441	−63
2	75	18	12	−72	144	5,184	−864
3	30	63	−33	−27	1,089	729	891
4	102	144	39	54	1,521	2,916	2,106
5	69	108	6	18	36	324	108
6	84	162	21	72	441	5,184	1,512
7	30	6	−33	−84	1,089	7,056	2,772
8	54	108	−9	18	81	324	−162
Total	$504	$720	0	0	4,410	22,158	6,300

$\bar{X} = 63 \quad \bar{Y} = 90$

The sample correlation coefficient is given by Equation 7.15:

$$r = \frac{S_{X,Y}}{S_X S_Y} = \frac{900}{25.0998 \cdot 56.2621} = 0.6373$$

The sample correlation coefficient is positive, showing a direct relationship between X and Y. This means that, at least as we can judge from the sample data, the net extra profit tends to increase as advertising increases. The value of the sample correlation coefficient, 0.6373, shows that it is quite a bit greater than zero, but at the same time, it is also far from perfect. We have calculated the sample correlation coefficient by using Equation 7.15. We encourage you to recalculate its value, using Equation 7.16.

7.4 Effects of a Linear Transformation of Two Random Variables on Their Covariance and Correlation

In Chapter 6 we determined the effect of a linear transformation of a random variable on its mean and variance. Here we shall examine the effect of a linear transformation of random variables on their covariance and correlation coefficient. The results obtained in this section will then be used in Sections 7.6 and 7.7, where we discuss interesting applications.

Let $X_1 = a + bX$ and $Y_1 = c + dY$, where a, b, c, and d are constants. Let us derive an expression for $COV(X_1, Y_1)$ in terms of $\sigma_{X,Y}$ and the constants a, b, c, and d. First, we recall (from Chapter 6) that

$$\mu_{X_1} = E(a + bX) = a + b\mu_X$$

and

$$\mu_{Y_1} = E(c + dY) = c + d\mu_Y$$

Using the covariance definition (Equation 7.10), we write

$$COV(X_1, Y_1) = E(X_1 Y_1) - \mu_{X_1}\mu_{Y_1}$$

$$= E[(a + bX)(c + dY)] - (a + b\mu_X)(c + d\mu_Y)$$

$$= E(ac + bcX + adY + bdXY)$$

$$\quad - (ac + bc\mu_X + ad\mu_Y + bd\mu_X\mu_Y)$$

$$= ac + bc\mu_X + ad\mu_Y + bdE(XY)$$

$$\quad - ac - bc\mu_X - ad\mu_Y - bd\mu_X\mu_Y$$

$$= bdE(XY) - bd\mu_X\mu_Y = bd[E(XY) - \mu_X\mu_Y] = bd\sigma_{X,Y}$$

This may be shortened to the following:

$$COV(X_1, Y_1) = COV[(a + bX), (c + dY)] = bd\sigma_{X,Y} \tag{7.17}$$

In particular, let us note that

$$COV[(bX), (dY)] = bd\sigma_{X,Y} \tag{7.18}$$

Given the effect of a linear transformation on the covariance and recalling from Chapter 6 the effect on the standard deviation

$$\sigma_{X_1} \equiv \sigma_{(a+bX)} = |b|\sigma_X$$

$$\sigma_{Y_1} \equiv \sigma_{(c+dY)} = |d|\sigma_Y$$

we can use Equation 7.11 to get

$$\rho_{X_1,Y_1} = \frac{\sigma_{X_1,Y_1}}{\sigma_{X_1}\sigma_{Y_1}} = \frac{bd\sigma_{X,Y}}{(|b|\sigma_X)\cdot(|d|\sigma_Y)} = \frac{bd}{|b|\,|d|}\cdot\frac{\sigma_{X,Y}}{\sigma_X\sigma_Y} = \begin{cases} +\,\rho_{X,Y} & \text{if } bd > 0 \\ -\,\rho_{X,Y} & \text{if } bd < 0 \end{cases} \tag{7.19}$$

Equation 7.19 shows that a linear transformation of the variables could affect their correlation. If $bd > 0$, then $\rho_{X_1,Y_1} = \rho_{X,Y}$, and if $bd < 0$, then $\rho_{X_1,Y_1} = -\rho_{X,Y}$. Note that if only one variable is being linearly transformed, we can still use Equations 7.17, 7.18, and 7.19 to determine the effect on the covariance and the correlation. For example, to get the covariance between $X_1 = a + bX$ and Y, we use Equation 7.17, where $c = 0$ and $d = 1$, and we get $\sigma_{X_1,Y} = b\sigma_{X,Y}$.

Linear transformation of variables affects sample measures in much the same way as it affects population parameters. To be more specific, let

$$X_1 = a + bX$$

and

$$Y_1 = c + dY$$

so that

$$\overline{X}_1 = \frac{1}{n}\Sigma(a + bX) = \frac{1}{n}na + \frac{1}{n}b\Sigma X = a + b\overline{X}$$

and

$$\overline{Y}_1 = \frac{1}{n}\Sigma(c + dY) = \frac{1}{n}nc + \frac{1}{n}d\Sigma Y = c + d\overline{Y}$$

For the sample covariance we obtain

$$S_{X_1,Y_1} = \frac{1}{n-1}\Sigma(X_1 - \overline{X}_1)(Y_1 - \overline{Y}_1)$$

$$= \frac{1}{n-1}\Sigma[a + bX - (a + b\overline{X})][c + dY - (c + d\overline{Y})] \tag{7.20}$$

$$= \frac{1}{n-1} \Sigma b(X - \overline{X}) \, d(Y - \overline{Y}) = bd \, \frac{1}{n-1} \Sigma (X - \overline{X})(Y - \overline{Y})$$

$$= bd S_{X,Y}$$

Similarly, the sample standard deviations of X and X_1 and of Y and Y_1 are related as follows:

$$S_{X_1} = |b| \, S_X$$

and

$$S_{Y_1} = |d| \, S_Y$$

Hence the sample correlation of X_1 and Y_1 is given by

$$r_{X_1,Y_1} = \frac{S_{X_1,Y_1}}{S_{X_1} \, S_{Y_1}} = \frac{bd \, S_{X,Y}}{(|b|S_X)(|d|S_Y)} = \frac{bd}{|b| \, |d|} \, r_{X,Y} = \begin{cases} +r_{X,Y} & \text{if } bd > 0 \\ -r_{X,Y} & \text{if } bd < 0 \end{cases} \quad \textbf{(7.21)}$$

7.5 The Sum of Two Random Variables

We frequently want to calculate the mean and variance of the sum of two random variables. For example, we might want to calculate the mean and the variance of the *total* freeze loss in Florida and California (Example 7.1) or of the *total* number of insurance policies, life and health, that will be sold (Example 7.2) or the like. One way we can go about the task is to derive explicitly the distribution of the sum from the joint distribution of the variables, as was explained in Section 7.2. But if we are interested in obtaining the mean and the variance of the distribution of the sum, we can derive them more directly as functions of the means and variances of the individual variables and their covariance.

Let Z be the sum of two random variables, X and Y:

$$Z = X + Y \quad \textbf{(7.22)}$$

The expected value of Z is

$$\mu_Z \equiv E(Z) = E(X + Y) = E(X) + E(Y) \equiv \mu_X + \mu_Y \quad \textbf{(7.23)}$$

and the variance of Z is (by definition)

$$\sigma_Z^2 \equiv V(Z) = E(Z - \mu_Z)^2 \quad \textbf{(7.24)}$$

Using Equations 7.22 and 7.23, we may write

$$\sigma_Z^2 = E[(X + Y) - (\mu_X + \mu_Y)]^2 = E[(X - \mu_X) + (Y - \mu_Y)]^2$$

$$= E[(X - \mu_X)^2 + (Y - \mu_Y)^2 + 2(X - \mu_X)(Y - \mu_Y)]$$

$$= E(X - \mu_X)^2 + E(Y - \mu_Y)^2 + 2E[(X - \mu_X)(Y - \mu_Y)] \quad \textbf{(7.25)}$$

$$= \sigma_X^2 + \sigma_Y^2 + 2\sigma_{X,Y}$$

Using an expansion similar to Equation 7.25, we can show that the following equation holds:

$$V[(a + bX) + (c + dY)] = b^2\sigma_X^2 + d^2\sigma_Y^2 + 2bd\sigma_{X,Y} \tag{7.26}$$

In particular, if $a = c = 0$, $b = 1$, and $d = -1$, we get

$$V(X - Y) = \sigma_X^2 + \sigma_Y^2 - 2\sigma_{X,Y} \tag{7.27}$$

and if $a = c = 0$ while b and d are any unspecified constants, we get

$$V(bX + dY) = b^2\sigma_X^2 + d^2\sigma_Y^2 + 2bd\sigma_{X,Y} \tag{7.28}$$

Similarly, the sample variance of $[(a + bX) + (c + dY)]$ is given by

$$b^2S_X^2 + d^2S_Y^2 + 2bdS_{X,Y} \tag{7.29}$$

Let us proceed with some interesting applications of these equations.

7.6 APPLICATION 1:
TRANSFORMATION OF ACCOUNTING VARIABLES—REVENUES, BEFORE-TAX PROFIT, AND AFTER-TAX PROFIT

We have considered the expected value and the variance of a sum of random variables and the impact of a linear transformation on various parameters of the distribution. In this section we show how all this knowledge can be used in connection with a practical business issue: the relationship between revenues and expenses in certain types of company operations and the impact of such a relationship on net profit fluctuations.

Table 7.8 presents actual data for the American Telephone and Telegraph Company

TABLE 7.8
AT&T Operating Revenues, Operating Expenses, Net Income before Tax, Tax, and Net Income after Tax, 1972–81
(in billions of dollars)

(1) Year	(2) Total operating revenues X	(3) Total operating expenses Y	(4) Net income before tax $Z = X - Y$	(5) Tax at average rate $TZ = 48\% \, Z$	(6) Net income after tax $Z_T = (1 - T)Z$
1972	$ 20.9	$ 13.5	$ 7.4	$ 3.55	$ 3.85
1973	23.5	15.0	8.5	4.08	4.42
1974	26.2	16.7	9.5	4.56	4.94
1975	28.9	18.8	10.1	4.85	5.25
1976	32.8	21.0	11.8	5.66	6.14
1977	36.4	23.5	12.9	6.19	6.71
1978	41.0	26.5	14.5	6.96	7.54
1979	45.4	30.2	15.2	7.30	7.90
1980	50.9	34.3	16.6	7.97	8.63
1981	58.2	39.3	18.9	9.07	9.83
Total	$364.2	$238.8	$125.4	$60.19	$65.21

Source: Columns 2 and 3, AT&T annual reports.

(AT&T). It displays AT&T's revenues, operating expenses, net income before tax, taxes, and net income after tax for the 10 years 1972–81. Denoting operating revenue by X, operating expense by Y, net income before tax by Z, tax rate (assumed constant) by T, and net income after tax by Z_T, we may write

$$Z = X - Y$$

$$Z_T = (1 - T)Z$$

The mean and variance of Z_T can be calculated in two alternative ways: by operating directly on the variable Z_T or by operating on X and Y and using our knowledge of their relationship. Table 7.9 is a work sheet for calculating the means and variances of X and Y as well as their correlation. The measures themselves are calculated at the bottom of the table.

TABLE 7.9
A Work Sheet for Calculating $\overline{X}$, $\overline{Y}$, S_X^2, S_Y^2, $S_{X,Y}$, and r

Year	X	Y	$X - \overline{X}$	$(X - \overline{X})^2$	$(Y - \overline{Y})$	$(Y - \overline{Y})^2$	$(X - \overline{X})(Y - \overline{Y})$
1972	20.9	13.5	−15.52	240.87	−10.38	107.74	161.10
1973	23.5	15.0	−12.92	166.93	−8.88	78.85	114.73
1974	26.2	16.7	−10.22	104.45	−7.18	51.55	73.38
1975	28.9	18.8	−7.52	56.55	−5.08	25.81	38.20
1976	32.8	21.0	−3.62	13.10	−2.88	8.29	10.43
1977	36.4	23.5	−0.02	0.00	−0.38	0.14	0.01
1978	41.0	26.5	4.58	20.98	2.62	6.86	12.00
1979	45.4	30.2	8.98	80.64	6.32	39.94	56.75
1980	50.9	34.3	14.48	209.67	10.42	108.58	150.88
1981	58.2	39.3	21.78	474.37	15.42	237.78	335.85
Total	364.2	238.8	0.00	1,367.56	0.00	665.54	953.33

$$\overline{X} = \frac{\Sigma X}{n} = \frac{364.2}{10} = 36.42 \qquad \overline{Y} = \frac{\Sigma Y}{n} = \frac{238.8}{10} = 23.88$$

$$S_X^2 = \frac{\Sigma(X - \overline{X})^2}{n - 1} = \frac{1,367.56}{9} = 151.95$$

$$S_Y^2 = \frac{\Sigma(Y - \overline{Y})^2}{n - 1} = \frac{665.54}{9} = 73.95$$

$$S_{X,Y} = \frac{\Sigma(X - \overline{X})(Y - \overline{Y})}{n - 1} = \frac{953.33}{9} = 105.93$$

$$r = \frac{S_{X,Y}}{S_X S_Y} = \frac{105.93}{(\sqrt{151.95})(\sqrt{73.95})} = 0.9993$$

Let us calculate $S_{Z_T}^2$ first by making use of the relationships between Z and Z_T, then by direct calculation. Since operating profit, Z, is equal to total operating revenues minus total operating expenses, we write

$$Z = X - Y$$

From here

$$\overline{Z} = \overline{X} - \overline{Y} = 36.42 - 23.88 = 12.54$$

Assuming a tax rate of 48 percent, the after-tax profit is $Z_T = (1 - T) Z = (1 - 0.48) Z = 0.52Z$. Since $1 - T = 0.52$, a constant by our assumption, we may write

$$\bar{Z}_T = (1 - T) \bar{Z} = 0.52 \cdot 12.54 = 6.52$$

For the sample variance of Z, we use Equation 7.29 (setting $b = 1$ and $d = -1$) and get

$$S_Z^2 = S_X^2 + S_Y^2 - 2 S_{X,Y}$$

$$= 151.95 + 73.95 - 2 \cdot 105.93 = 14.04$$

For $S_{Z_T}^2$ we obtain

$$S_{Z_T}^2 = (1 - T)^2 S_Z^2 = 0.52^2 \cdot 14.04 = 3.80$$

We can also calculate $S_{Z_T}^2$ directly. A work sheet for this calculation is provided in Table 7.10. For S_Z^2 we get

$$S_Z^2 = \frac{\Sigma(Z - \bar{Z})^2}{n - 1} = \frac{126.46}{10 - 1} = 14.05$$

and for $S_{Z_T}^2$ we get

$$S_{Z_T}^2 = \frac{\Sigma(Z_T - \bar{Z}_T)^2}{n - 1} = \frac{34.18}{10 - 1} = 3.80$$

These are the same values as obtained earlier (with the exception of rounding errors), and we note again that we have

$$3.80 = 0.52^2 \cdot 14.05$$

TABLE 7.10
A Work Sheet for Calculating S_Z^2 and $S_{Z_T}^2$

Year	Z	$Z - \bar{Z}$	$(Z - \bar{Z})^2$	Z_T	$Z_T - \bar{Z}_T$	$(Z_T - \bar{Z}_T)^2$
1972	7.4	−5.14	26.42	3.85	−2.67	7.13
1973	8.5	−4.04	16.32	4.42	−2.10	4.41
1974	9.5	−3.04	9.24	4.94	−1.58	2.50
1975	10.1	−2.44	5.95	5.25	−1.27	1.61
1976	11.8	−0.74	0.55	6.14	−0.38	0.14
1977	12.9	0.36	0.13	6.71	0.19	0.04
1978	14.5	1.96	3.84	7.54	1.02	1.04
1979	15.2	2.66	7.08	7.90	1.38	1.90
1980	16.6	4.06	16.48	8.63	2.11	4.45
1981	18.9	6.36	40.45	9.83	3.31	10.96
Total	125.4	0.00	126.46	65.21	0.01[a]	34.18

$$\bar{Z} = \frac{125.4}{10} = 12.54 \qquad \bar{Z}_T = \frac{65.21}{10} = 6.52$$

$$S_Z^2 = \frac{126.46}{10 - 1} = 14.05 \qquad S_{Z_T}^2 = \frac{34.18}{10 - 1} = 3.80$$

[a]The deviation from zero is due to rounding.

From the point of view of corporate planning, it is advantageous to minimize profit fluctuations (that is, variance) as much as possible. As we saw, the correlation coefficient between AT&T's revenues and expenses is very close to 1.0. Thus, when revenues go up, expenses go up as well, and when revenues go down, expenses also show a strong tendency to decline. To see what this relationship does to the variance of AT&T's profits, suppose the correlation between revenues and expenses were lower. If it were equal to zero ($r = 0$), the variance of the profit before tax, Z, would have been (recall that $S_{X,Y} = rS_XS_Y$):

$$S_Z^2 = S_X^2 + S_Y^2 - 2rS_XS_Y = 151.95 + 73.95 - 2 \cdot 0 \cdot \sqrt{151.95} \cdot \sqrt{73.95} = 225.90$$

compared to only 14.05 when $r = 0.9993$. Now suppose revenues and expenses tended to move in opposite directions, so that when revenues go up, expenses tend to go down, and vice versa. In the most extreme case, the correlation is $r = -1.0$; the variance is

$$S_Z^2 = S_X^2 + S_Y^2 - 2rS_XS_Y = 151.95 + 73.95 - 2 \cdot (-1) \cdot \sqrt{151.95} \cdot \sqrt{73.95} = 437.91$$

Thus, AT&T's profit would be substantially less stable (that is, fluctuating over the years) if indeed there were a negative relationship between revenues and expenses. The explanation for the high profit variance in the case of negative correlation is straightforward: negative correlation means that when gross revenues go up, expenses go down—a combination that results in a very high profit. On the other hand, when revenues are low, expenses are high—a combination that results in a very low profit (or loss). In contrast, if revenues and expenses are moving together, the profit tends to be stable over time.

Figures 7.2 and 7.3 show hypothetical relationships between the two variables X and Y. Each of the variables fluctuates upward and downward over time. In Figure 7.2 we

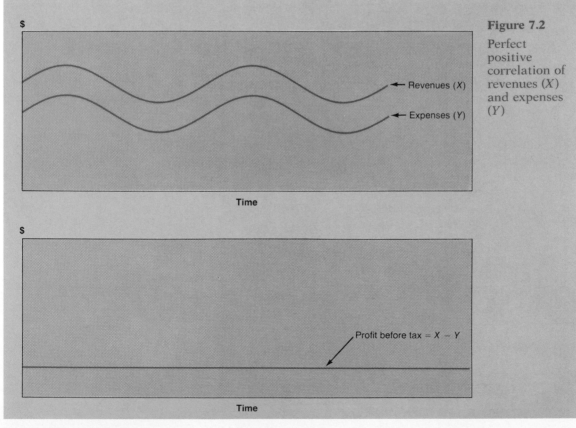

Figure 7.2

Perfect positive correlation of revenues (X) and expenses (Y)

Figure 7.3

Perfect negative correlation of revenues (X) and expenses (Y)

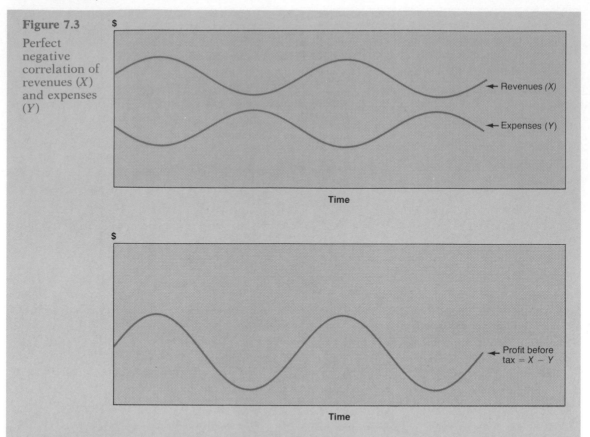

assume that X and Y have a perfect positive correlation, so that their fluctuations move together. In Figure 7.3, however, the variables move in opposite directions, meaning that they have a perfect negative correlation. The variable $X - Y$ is perfectly stable over time in Figure 7.2, where the correlation is perfectly positive. In Figure 7.3, on the other hand, the variable $X - Y$ fluctuates considerably. These results sit well with the calculations we presented for AT&T.

The implication of all this is that business managers should strive to bring about as high a correlation between revenues and expenses as is practicable. Managers can do so by monitoring wage contracts, contracts with other major material suppliers, and pricing policy.

7.7 APPLICATION 2:
INVESTMENT DIVERSIFICATION

If you want to reduce your investment risk, don't put all your eggs in one basket. This common-sense rule has been known for centuries. It was not until the early 1950s, however, that Harry Markowitz formally proved that investment diversification may reduce the variability of its return for any given level of expected return.[2] Let us consider how this reduction in the diversity of return comes about.

Consider two common stocks, Stock 1 and Stock 2. Suppose we want to invest a given amount of money in one of these stocks or to split our investment between the two. Since stock prices and dividends are not known in advance, we regard the *rate of return* on both Stock 1 and Stock 2 as random variables. The rate of return is the rate of profit made on a stock. For example, if we invest $100 and the market value of our investment rises to $110, our rate of return is

$$\frac{110}{100} - 1.0 = 1.1 - 1.0 = 0.10, \text{ or } 10\%$$

If we invest $250 and the market value of our investment declines to $220, our rate of return is

$$\frac{220}{250} - 1.0 = 0.88 - 1.00 = -0.12, \text{ or } -12\%$$

In general, the rate of return is the profit or loss expressed as a percentage of our original investment. Denoting the rate of return on Stock 1 by R_1 and on Stock 2 by R_2, we must choose the (unknown) return R_1, the (unknown) return R_2, or the (unknown) return from a combination of R_1 and R_2. Ignoring the way we make the *choice* between these alternatives, let's examine the statistical characteristics of our investment alternatives. We denote the means and variances of R_1 and R_2 by μ_1, μ_2, σ_1^2, and σ_2^2, respectively:

$$E(R_1) \equiv \mu_1 \qquad E(R_2) \equiv \mu_2$$

$$V(R_1) \equiv \sigma_1^2 \qquad V(R_2) \equiv \sigma_2^2$$

Let us also denote the covariance between R_1 and R_2 by $\sigma_{1,2}$ and their correlation coefficient by ρ. We then have

$$\rho = \frac{\sigma_{1,2}}{\sigma_1 \sigma_2} \tag{7.30}$$

and it follows that

$$\sigma_{1,2} = \rho \sigma_1 \sigma_2 \tag{7.31}$$

Now suppose we invest a portion of our funds in Stock 1 and the rest in Stock 2. Denote the proportion of our investment allocated to Stock 1 by P_1 and the proportion allocated to Stock 2 by P_2. Assuming that the entire investment is split between Stock 1 and Stock 2, we have $P_1 + P_2 = 1$. The return, R_P, on our entire investment portfolio is

$$R_P = P_1 R_1 + P_2 R_2$$

If we invest $100, allocating $60 to Stock 1 and $40 to Stock 2, our return, R_P, will be $R_P = 0.6R_1 + 0.4R_2$. If R_1 turns out to be 0.20 (that is, 20 percent) and R_2 turns out to be -0.10 (that is, a loss of 10 percent), the rate of return on the entire investment

[2] H. W. Markowitz, "Portfolio Selection," *Journal of Finance*, 6 (March 1952), and *Portfolio Selection* (New York: Wiley, 1959).

portfolio, R_P, will be $R_P = 0.60 \cdot 0.20 + 0.40 \cdot -0.10 = 0.12 - 0.04 = 0.08$, or 8 percent. This is so because the \$60 invested in Stock 1 yields a 20 percent return equal to \$12 and the \$40 invested in Stock 2 yields a negative 10 percent return equal to a loss of \$4. Our total return, therefore, is \$12 − \$4 = \$8, which is equal to 8 percent on the \$100 invested.

We are now ready to apply some of our earlier results to the investment diversification example. Examining the expected value and the variance of R_P, we find[3]

$$\mu_P = P_1\mu_1 + P_2\mu_2 \tag{7.32}$$

$$\sigma_P^2 = P_1^2\sigma_1^2 + P_2^2\sigma_2^2 + 2P_1P_2\sigma_{1,2} \tag{7.33}$$

Using Equation 7.31, we may write

$$\sigma_P^2 = P_1^2\sigma_1^2 + P_2^2\sigma_2^2 + 2P_1P_2\rho\sigma_1\sigma_2 \tag{7.34}$$

When R_1 and R_2 are either perfectly correlated or uncorrelated, Equation 7.34 takes on the following specific forms:

$$
\begin{aligned}
\text{If } \rho = +1.0 \quad & \sigma_P^2 = P_1^2\sigma_1^2 + P_2^2\sigma_2^2 + 2P_1P_2\sigma_1\sigma_2 = (P_1\sigma_1 + P_2\sigma_2)^2 \\
& \sigma_P = P_1\sigma_1 + P_2\sigma_2 \\
\text{If } \rho = 0 \quad & \sigma_P^2 = P_1^2\sigma_1^2 + P_2^2\sigma_2^2 \\
& \sigma_P = \sqrt{P_1^2\sigma_1^2 + P_2^2\sigma_2^2} \\
\text{If } \rho = -1.0 \quad & \sigma_P^2 = P_1^2\sigma_1^2 + P_2^2\sigma_2^2 - 2P_1P_2\sigma_1\sigma_2 = (P_1\sigma_1 - P_2\sigma_2)^2 \\
& \sigma_P = \sqrt{(P_1\sigma_1 - P_2\sigma_2)^2} = |P_1\sigma_1 - P_2\sigma_2|
\end{aligned}
\tag{7.35}
$$

Of course, Equation 7.34 is general and includes all the cases listed in 7.35 as special cases.

Let us illustrate the implications of Equations 7.32–7.35 for portfolio characteristics. For purposes of illustration, assume the following parameters:

$$\mu_1 = 0.20 \qquad \mu_2 = 0.10$$

$$\sigma_1 = 0.26 \qquad \sigma_2 = 0.16$$

$$\rho = +1.0$$

Considering a portfolio consisting of 50 percent investment in Stock 1 and 50 percent in Stock 2, we obtain, by Equations 7.32, 7.34, and 7.35

$$\mu_P = 0.5 \cdot 0.20 + 0.5 \cdot 0.10 = 0.10 + 0.05 = 0.15$$

$$\sigma_P = 0.5 \cdot 0.26 + 0.5 \cdot 0.16 = 0.13 + 0.08 = 0.21$$

---

[3] By the equations developed earlier, we get

$$\mu_P \equiv E(R_P) = E(P_1R_1 + P_2R_2) = P_1E(R_1) + P_2E(R_2) = P_1\mu_1 + P_2\mu_2$$

$$\sigma_P^2 \equiv V(R_P) = V(P_1R_1 + P_2R_2) = P_1^2\sigma_1^2 + P_2^2\sigma_2^2 + 2P_1P_2\rho\sigma_1\sigma_2$$

(see Equation 7.28 where $b = P_1$ and $d = P_2$).

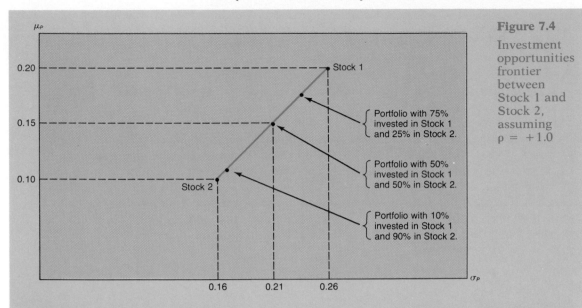

As one can easily verify, the combination of $\mu_P = 0.15$ and $\sigma_P = 0.21$ plots exactly in the middle of the chord that combines the expected return and standard deviation combinations of Stock 1 and Stock 2 in Figure 7.4.

What if we change our investment proportions? For example, what if we invest 75 percent of our funds in Stock 1 and only 25 percent in Stock 2? We can easily show that in this case, our portfolio's (μ, σ) combination will move closer to Stock 1 (Figure 7.4) along the chord combining Stock 1 and Stock 2:

$$\mu_P = 0.75 \cdot 0.20 + 0.25 \cdot 0.10 = 0.150 + 0.025 = 0.175$$

$$\sigma_P = 0.75 \cdot 0.26 + 0.25 \cdot 0.16 = 0.195 + 0.040 = 0.235$$

In general, the higher the proportion invested in Stock 1, the closer the (μ, σ) characteristics of the portfolio to that of Stock 1, and conversely for Stock 2.

Consider Equation 7.34, and recall that $-1.0 \leq \rho \leq +1.0$. Since P_1, P_2, σ_1, and σ_2 are all positive magnitudes, it is clear that σ_P reaches its maximum (for given P_1 and P_2) when $\rho = +1.0$. Suppose we change our assumptions regarding the correlation coefficient between the returns of Stock 1 and Stock 2. Such a change will have *no impact* on μ_P (since μ_P is not a function of ρ), but will have an impact on σ_P. Assuming, for example, an even split between Stock 1 and Stock 2 (i.e., $P_1 = P_2 = 0.5$) and letting $\rho = 0$, we find through applying Equations 7.32 and 7.35 that

$$\mu_P = 0.5 \cdot 0.20 + 0.5 \cdot 0.10 = 0.10 + 0.05 = 0.15$$

$$\sigma_P^2 = 0.5^2 \cdot 0.26^2 + 0.5^2 \cdot 0.16^2$$

$$= 0.25 \cdot 0.0676 + 0.25 \cdot 0.0256$$

$$= 0.0169 + 0.0064 = 0.0233$$

For σ_P we obtain

$$\sigma_P = \sqrt{0.0233} = 0.1526$$

which is *less than* the σ_P value obtained under the assumption that $\rho = +1.0$.

It can easily be shown that simply by varying our investment proportions in Stock 1 and Stock 2 we can construct portfolios with any desired (μ, σ) combination along the "investment opportunities frontier" shown in Figure 7.5.

Table 7.11 presents the portfolio expected rate of return and standard deviation for various investment proportions in Stock 1 and Stock 2, assuming five alternative values for ρ. The data are presented graphically in Figure 7.6. For a given correlation coefficient, we could, as explained earlier, move along the relevant "investment opportunities frontier" by varying the investment proportions. Without involving ourselves in the question of how an investor is to select the optimal investment allocation between Stock 1 and Stock 2, we can easily understand the motive for investment diversification: to construct a portfolio with relatively low risk (as measured by σ_P) in relation to the expected return. In the extreme case, where $\rho = -1.0$, it is possible to construct a riskless portfolio out of two risky securities. In our example, if we set

$$P_1 = \frac{0.16}{0.16 + 0.26} = \frac{0.16}{0.42}$$

and

$$P_2 = \frac{0.26}{0.16 + 0.26} = \frac{0.26}{0.42}$$

we get

$$\sigma_P = \left| \frac{0.16}{0.42} \cdot 0.26 - \frac{0.26}{0.42} \cdot 0.16 \right| = 0$$

Figure 7.5

Investment opportunities frontier between Stock 1 and Stock 2, assuming $\rho = 0.0$

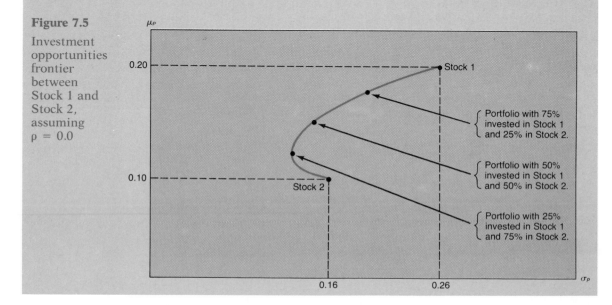

TABLE 7.11
Portfolio Expected Rate of Return and Standard Deviation Given Five Alternative Values of ρ

Portfolio number	P_1	P_2	$\mu_P = P_1\mu_1 + P_2\mu_2$	$\sigma_P = \sqrt{P_1^2\sigma_1^2 + P_2^2\sigma_2^2 + 2P_1P_2\rho\sigma_1\sigma_2}$				
				$\rho = +1.0$	$\rho = +0.5$	$\rho = 0.0$	$\rho = -0.5$	$\rho = -1.0$
1	1.00	0.00	0.200	0.260	0.260	0.260	0.260	0.260
2	0.75	0.25	0.175	0.235	0.218	0.199	0.178	0.155
3	0.50	0.50	0.150	0.210	0.184	0.153	0.114	0.050
4	0.25	0.75	0.125	0.185	0.163	0.136	0.104	0.055
5	0.00	1.00	0.100	0.160	0.160	0.160	0.160	0.160

We leave discussion of the selection of the "best" portfolio, as well as the generalization to the multisecurity case, to textbooks in finance.

Now let us evaluate the possible gains from portfolio diversification in the case of two actual stocks: Republic Steel (RS) and General Food (GF). Table 7.12 provides the rates of return on these two stocks in the years 1971–80. The table is also a work sheet for calculating the sample means, standard deviations, and correlation coefficient. The following estimates have been obtained (rounded):

	Mean (%)	Standard deviation (%)
RS(R_1)	17.0	27.5
GF(R_2)	15.2	36.6
	$r = 0.0397$	

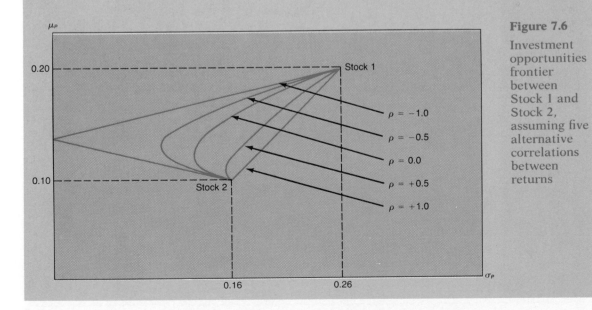

Figure 7.6

Investment opportunities frontier between Stock 1 and Stock 2, assuming five alternative correlations between returns

TABLE 7.12
A Work Sheet for Calculating Sample Measures of the Rates of Return of Republic Steel (RS) and General Food (GF)

(1) Year	(2) Rate of return on RS (R_1)	(3) Rate of return on GF (R_2)	(4) $R_1 - \overline{R}_1$	(5) $R_2 - \overline{R}_2$	(6) $(R_1 - \overline{R}_1)^2$	(7) $(R_2 - \overline{R}_2)^2$	(8) $(R_1 - \overline{R}_1)(R_2 - \overline{R}_2)$
1971	22.5	−23.7	5.5	−38.9	30.25	1,513.21	−213.95
1972	9.3	8.6	−7.7	−6.6	59.29	43.56	50.82
1973	−18.6	4.3	−35.6	−10.9	1,267.36	118.81	388.04
1974	48.1	−52.2	31.1	−67.4	967.21	4,542.76	−2,096.14
1975	44.4	62.4	27.4	47.2	750.76	2,227.84	1,293.28
1976	56.0	61.4	39.0	46.2	1,521.00	2,134.44	1,801.80
1977	−20.1	9.8	−37.1	−5.4	1,376.41	29.16	200.34
1978	−11.0	52.6	−28.0	37.4	784.00	1,398.76	−1,047.20
1979	17.1	17.1	0.1	1.9	0.01	3.61	0.19
1980	22.3	11.7	5.3	−3.5	28.09	12.25	−18.55
Total	170.0	152.0	0.0	0.0	6,784.38	12,024.40	358.63

$$\overline{R}_1 = \frac{\Sigma R_1}{n} = \frac{170.0}{10} = 17.0 \qquad \overline{R}_2 = \frac{\Sigma R_2}{n} = \frac{152.0}{10} = 15.2$$

$$S_{R_1}^2 = \frac{\Sigma(R_1 - \overline{R}_1)^2}{n - 1} = \frac{6,784.38}{9} = 753.8200 \qquad S_{R_1} = 27.4558$$

$$S_{R_2}^2 = \frac{\Sigma(R_2 - \overline{R}_2)^2}{n - 1} = \frac{12,024.40}{9} = 1,336.0444 \qquad S_{R_2} = 36.5519$$

$$S_{R_1,R_2} = \frac{\Sigma(R_1 - \overline{R}_1)(R_2 - \overline{R}_2)}{n - 1} = \frac{358.63}{9} = 39.8478$$

$$r = \frac{S_{R_1,R_2}}{S_{R_1} S_{R_2}} = \frac{39.8478}{27.4558 \cdot 36.5519} = 0.0397$$

TABLE 7.13
Portfolio Mean and Standard Deviation for Alternative Investment Proportions

(1) Portfolio	(2) P_1	(3) P_2	(4) $\overline{R}_P = P_1\overline{R}_1 + P_2\overline{R}_2$	(5) $S_P = \sqrt{P_1^2 S_1^2 + P_2^2 S_2^2 + 2P_1P_2 r S_1 S_2}$
1	0.0	1.0	15.20	36.55
2	0.1	0.9	15.38	33.12
3	0.2	0.8	15.56	29.97
4	0.3	0.7	15.74	27.19
5	0.4	0.6	15.92	24.91
6	0.5	0.5	16.10	23.29
7	0.6	0.4	16.28	22.46
8	0.7	0.3	16.46	22.50
9	0.8	0.2	16.64	23.42
10	0.9	0.1	16.82	25.12
11	1.0	0.0	17.00	27.46

Applying the portfolio mean and standard deviation formulas to the sample measures, we have

$$\text{Mean return} \equiv \overline{R}_P = P_1 \overline{R}_1 + P_2 \overline{R}_2$$

$$\text{Standard deviation of return} \equiv S_P = \sqrt{P_1^2 S_1^2 + P_2^2 S_2^2 + 2 P_1 P_2 \, r \, S_1 \, S_2}$$

Table 7.13 shows the sample mean and standard deviation obtained when alternative values of P_1 and P_2 are assumed for the portfolio. Figure 7.7 presents the frontier and shows that a diversification between the two stocks could reduce the portfolio standard deviation considerably. For example, investing 60 percent of the investable funds in RS and 40 percent in GF reduces the portfolio standard deviation to 22.49 percent.

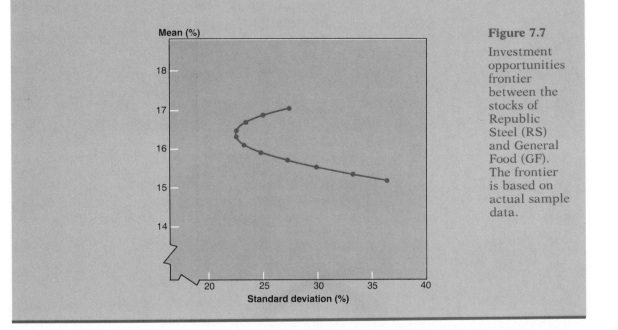

Figure 7.7

Investment opportunities frontier between the stocks of Republic Steel (RS) and General Food (GF). The frontier is based on actual sample data.

Chapter Summary and Review

1. The joint probability distribution of X_1 and X_2 is given by

$$P(x_1, x_2) = P(X_1 = x_1, X_2 = x_2)$$

2. The marginal probabilities of X_1 and X_2 are given by

$$P(x_1) = \sum_{x_2} P(x_1, x_2)$$

$$P(x_2) = \sum_{x_1} P(x_1, x_2)$$

3. The conditional distributions are given by

$$P(x_1 \mid x_2) = \frac{P(x_1, x_2)}{P(x_2)}$$

$$P(x_2 \mid x_1) = \frac{P(x_1, x_2)}{P(x_1)}$$

4. The covariance between two variables, X and Y, is defined as

$$COV(X, Y) \equiv \sigma_{X,Y} = E[(X - \mu_X)(Y - \mu_Y)] = E(XY) - \mu_X \mu_Y$$

The sample estimator of the covariance is

$$S_{X,Y} = \frac{1}{n-1} \sum (X - \bar{X})(Y - \bar{Y}) = \frac{1}{n-1} (\Sigma XY - n\bar{X}\bar{Y})$$

5. The correlation between X and Y is defined as

$$\rho = \frac{\sigma_{X,Y}}{\sigma_X \sigma_Y}$$

and it is always true that

$$-1 \le \rho \le 1$$

The sample estimator of the correlation coefficient is

$$r = \frac{S_{X,Y}}{S_X S_Y}$$

6. The mean and variance of the sum of two random variables are

$$E(X + Y) = \mu_X + \mu_Y$$

and

$$V(X + Y) = \sigma_X^2 + \sigma_Y^2 + 2\sigma_{X,Y}$$

7. Linear transformation rules
   Define $X_1 = a + bX$ and $Y_1 = c + dY$. Then
   a. $\sigma_{X_1, Y_1} = bd\, \sigma_{X,Y}$
   b. $\rho_{X_1, Y_1} = \rho_{X,Y}$ if b and d have the same sign, and $\rho_{X_1, Y_1} = -\rho_{X,Y}$ if b and d have different signs.
   c. $V(X_1 + Y_1) = b^2 V(X) + d^2 V(Y) + 2bd\,\sigma_{X,Y}$

8. For two stocks with returns R_1 and R_2, we have
   a. Portfolio return: $R_P = P_1 R_1 + P_2 R_2$, where P_i is the investment proportion in stock i
   b. Portfolio mean return: $\mu_P = P_1 \mu_1 + P_2 \mu_2$
   c. Portfolio variance: $\sigma_P^2 = P_1^2 \sigma_1^2 + P_2^2 \sigma_2^2 + 2P_1 P_2 \rho \sigma_1 \sigma_2$

Problems

7.1. (*a*) The following is a joint probability distribution of two random variables, X_1 and X_2:

	x_1		
x_2	20	40	60
5	$\frac{1}{3}$	0	0
10	0	$\frac{1}{3}$	0
15	0	0	$\frac{1}{3}$

Write down the marginal probability distributions of X_1 and X_2 and find their correlation coefficient.

(*b*) Do the calculations specified in part *a* again, this time for the variables Y_1 and Y_2, whose joint probability distribution is

	y_1		
y_2	20	40	60
5	0	0	$\frac{1}{3}$
10	0	$\frac{1}{3}$	0
15	$\frac{1}{3}$	0	0

(*c*) Do the calculations one more time, this time for the variables Z_1 and Z_2, whose joint probability distribution is

	z_1		
z_2	20	40	60
5	$\frac{1}{9}$	$\frac{1}{9}$	$\frac{1}{9}$
10	$\frac{1}{9}$	$\frac{1}{9}$	$\frac{1}{9}$
15	$\frac{1}{9}$	$\frac{1}{9}$	$\frac{1}{9}$

7.2. The random variables X and Y are independent of one another and have the following probability distributions:

$$P(x) = \begin{cases} \frac{1}{6} & x = 0, 1, 2, 3, 4, 5 \\ 0 & \text{otherwise} \end{cases}$$

$$P(y) = \begin{cases} \frac{1}{3} & y = 6, 7, 8 \\ 0 & \text{otherwise} \end{cases}$$

(*a*) Write down the joint probability $P(x, y)$.

(*b*) Find the probabilities

$$P(X = 0 \mid Y = 6)$$
$$P(X = 1 \mid Y = 7)$$
$$P(Y = 6 \mid X = 2)$$
$$P(Y = 5 \mid X = 3)$$

7.3. The random variables X and Y are independent and have the following probability distributions:

$$P(x) = \begin{cases} \frac{1}{4} & x = 10, 11, 12, 13 \\ 0 & \text{otherwise} \end{cases}$$

$$P(y) = \begin{cases} \frac{1}{4} & y = 20, 30, 40, 50 \\ 0 & \text{otherwise} \end{cases}$$

(a) Write down the joint probability distribution $P(x, y)$.

(b) Suppose now that X and Y are not independent. Rather, the following conditional probabilities are given:

$$P(Y = 20 \mid X = 10) = 1$$
$$P(Y = 30 \mid X = 11) = 1$$
$$P(Y = 40 \mid X = 12) = 1$$
$$P(Y = 50 \mid X = 13) = 1$$

Write down the joint probability distribution of X and Y and find the correlation coefficient of the two variables.

7.4. Let X be uniformly distributed over the range from 30 to 70 and let Y be uniformly distributed from 40 to 60. Assume that X and Y are independent. Derive the probability of X and the probability of Y over the following intervals:

$$30 \text{ to } 40$$
$$40 \text{ to } 50$$
$$50 \text{ to } 60$$
$$60 \text{ to } 70$$

(a) Tabulate your results to show the joint probability distribution of X and Y by the above intervals.

(b) Derive the following *conditional* distribution (using the above intervals):

$$P(X \mid 40 \le Y \le 50)$$

(c) Derive the following *conditional* distribution (using the above intervals):

$$P(Y \mid 60 \le X \le 70)$$

(d) Draw a conclusion about the shape of the *conditional* distributions $P(x \mid y)$ and $P(y \mid x)$ when x and y are two *independent* uniform variables.

7.5. The joint probability distribution of X_1 and X_2 is given by

x_2	x_1		
	1	*2*	*3*
2	0.05	0.15	0.05
4	0.10	0.25	0.15
6	0.10	0.15	0.00

(a) Calculate the marginal probability distributions $P(x_1)$ and $P(x_2)$.

(b) Calculate the following conditional probabilities:

$$P(X_1 = 1 \mid X_2 = 2)$$
$$P(X_1 = 2 \mid X_2 = 6)$$
$$P(X_2 = 6 \mid X_1 = 3)$$

(c) Check whether X_1 and X_2 are independent.

7.6. The random variables X_1 and X_2 have the following probability distributions:

x_1	$P(x_1)$	x_2	$P(x_2)$
0	1/2	2	1/2
1	1/2	4	1/2

Given that $COV(X_1, X_2) = 10$, calculate the value $E(X_1 X_2)$.

7.7. Table P7.7a shows the joint probability of the (average) price of 100 percent cotton clothing (X_1) and the (average) price of raw cotton (X_2). Table P7.7b shows the joint probability of the price of a certain model car (Y_1) and the (average) price of gasoline (Y_2).

TABLE P7.7a

X_2 *(dollars per pound)*	X_1 *(dollars per unit)*		
	100	*150*	*200*
5	0.20	0.01	0.01
10	0.01	0.30	0.01
15	0.01	0.05	0.40

TABLE P7.7b

Y_2 *(dollars per gallon)*	Y_1 *(dollars per car)*		
	6,000	*7,000*	*8,000*
1.0	0.01	0.05	0.30
1.2	0.01	0.20	0.01
1.4	0.40	0.01	0.01

Calculate the covariances $COV(X_1, X_2)$ and $COV(Y_1, Y_2)$, and find the correlations ρ_{X_1, X_2} and ρ_{Y_1, Y_2}. What is your interpretation of their values? Explain.

7.8. (a) Calculate the covariance between the random variables Y and X where it is given that Y can take on only two values (2 and 4) with equal probability, while X can take on only one value, 4, with probability 1.

(b) Now make the transformation

$$Y_1 = a + bY$$
$$X_1 = c + dX$$

Is it necessarily true that $COV(X_1, Y_1) = 0$? Prove your answer.

7.9. The correlation between two random variables X and Y is $\rho = -0.75$. It is given that $X = 1, 2,$ or 3 with equal probability of $\frac{1}{3}$ and $Y = -1, -2,$ or -3 with equal probability of $\frac{1}{3}$. Calculate the value $COV(X, Y)$.

7.10. It is given that $\rho_{X,Y} = \sigma_{X,Y}$. Prove that $\sigma_X = 1/\sigma_Y$.

7.11. The joint distribution of daily checking account deposits (D) and withdrawals (W) in a given branch of the Save for Tomorrow Bank is as follows (in thousands of dollars):

		d	
w	*400*	*600*	*800*
400	0.12	0.15	0.18
600	0.10	0.05	0.08
800	0.16	0.07	0.09

What are the covariance and the correlation coefficient of the deposits and withdrawals?

7.12. The joint grade distribution anticipated by a business administration major for tests in calculus and in business statistics is as follows:

Grade in statistics (*y*)	Grade in calculus (*x*)		
	(*C*) 2	(*B*) 3	(*A*) 4
(*C*) 2	0.03	0.05	0.08
(*B*) 3	0.07	0.10	0.08
(*A*) 4	0.09	0.20	0.30

Using the numerical scale for grades and denoting the grade in calculus by X and that in statistics by Y, give the marginal probability distribution of X and the marginal distribution of Y. Determine whether or not X and Y are independent random variables.

7.13. Compute the covariance and the correlation coefficient of X and Y in Problem 7.12. Interpret the meaning of these parameters.

7.14. Let X_1 and X_2 be two random variables with identical probability distributions as given below:

x_1	$P(x_1)$	x_2	$P(x_2)$
20	0.25	20	0.25
22	0.25	22	0.25
24	0.25	24	0.25
26	0.25	26	0.25
	1.00		1.00

(*a*) Write down a joint probability distribution of X_1 and X_2 such that their covariance will be equal to zero.
(*b*) Do the same as in part *a*, but this time make the covariance positive.
(*c*) Repeat part *a* once more, this time making the covariance of X_1 and X_2 negative.

7.15. An international textile firm operates in two countries, Japan and the United States. The net profits (in millions of dollars) from the two countries have the following joint probability distribution:

Japan	United States		
	−2	*+2*	*+8*
− 2	0.20	0.12	0.05
+ 4	0.08	0.20	0.10
+ 12	0.08	0.07	0.10

(a) Find the expected net profit from each country separately and from both of them combined.

(b) Find the standard deviation of the net profit from each country separately.

(c) Find the covariance and the coefficient of correlation of the net income from the two countries.

(d) What is the standard deviation of the total net income (that is, from both countries together)?

(e) Suppose the joint probability distribution of the net income from both countries were as follows:

	United States		
Japan	− 2	+ 2	+ 8
− 2	0.10	0.12	0.15
+ 4	0.08	0.20	0.10
+ 12	0.18	0.07	0.00

Would the expected total net profit and its standard deviation be any different from what you found in parts *a* and *d* above? Explain *without* performing the calculation again.

7.16. Returning now to Problem 6.34 in Chapter 6, recall that a salesperson's income is $120 plus 15 percent commission on the sales he or she makes throughout the week. Each item is sold for $100, and the probability distribution of the number of items sold in a week is

x	$P(x)$
10	0.15
11	0.15
12	0.40
13	0.15
14	0.15
	1.00

Assume that sales in two consecutive weeks are independent.

(a) What is the probability that a given salesperson will make $285 or less in each of two consecutive weeks?

(b) What is the probability that the salesperson will make $300 or less in one week and more than $300 the following week?

(c) Write down the probability distribution and the cumulative probability distribution of a salesperson's total income in two consecutive weeks.

7.17. Tell whether the correlation between the following pairs of variables is likely to be positive, zero, or negative. Explain.

(a) Changes in the prices of real estate in New York and Chicago over the years

(b) Personal income and number of telephone extensions in various households

(c) Number of family members and number of rooms in the family's dwelling

(d) Number of family members and number of *rooms per person* in the family's dwelling

(e) The numbers that fall uppermost on two balanced dice tossed simultaneously

7.18. Let X and Y be two independent random variables with the following probability distributions:

$$P(x) = \begin{cases} \frac{1}{4} & x = 1, 2, 3, 4 \\ 0 & \text{otherwise} \end{cases}$$

$$P(y) = \begin{cases} \frac{1}{2} & y = 5, 6 \\ 0 & \text{otherwise} \end{cases}$$

Define a random variable Z such that

$$Z = X + Y$$

Calculate and draw the probability distribution of Z.

7.19. Let X and Y be two independent random variables with the following probability distributions:

$$P(x) = \begin{cases} \frac{1}{3} & x = 0, 1, 2 \\ 0 & \text{otherwise} \end{cases}$$

$$P(y) = \begin{cases} \frac{1}{2} & y = 6, 7 \\ 0 & \text{otherwise} \end{cases}$$

Define a random variable Z such that

$$Z = X + 2Y$$

(a) Write down and draw the probability distribution of Z.
(b) Find $P(2 \leq Z \leq 8)$ and $P(12 < Z \leq 15)$.

7.20. The following is the joint probability distribution of X and Y:

		x	
y	*100*	*200*	*300*
50	0.05	0.05	0.20
100	0.05	0.30	0.05
150	0.20	0.05	0.05

(a) Can you say whether the covariance of X and Y is positive, zero, or negative without any calculations? Explain.
(b) Calculate the covariance of X and Y.
(c) Calculate the correlation coefficient of X and Y.

7.21. Calculate the covariance between the variable X and itself:

x	$P(x)$
1	$\frac{1}{16}$
2	$\frac{6}{16}$
3	$\frac{6}{16}$
4	$\frac{3}{16}$

What is the relationship between this covariance and the variance of X? Explain.

7.22. Mutual funds are financial institutions that invest large amounts of money in bonds and stocks. The collection of the bonds and stocks of a mutual fund is its portfolio. The mean rates of return of eight mutual fund portfolios and their standard deviations are shown in Table P7.22.

TABLE P7.22

Mutual fund	Mean rate of return on portfolio (percent)	Standard deviation of portfolio (percent)
1	10	12
2	20	18
3	15	15
4	12	14
5	8	10
6	22	20
7	18	20
8	10	20

(a) Mark the combination of mean rate of return and standard deviation of the rate of return on a diagram. Do it in such a way that each portfolio will be represented as a point on a diagram showing the mean rate of return on the vertical axis and the standard deviation on the horizontal axis. You will have eight points altogether.

(b) Calculate the correlation coefficient between the mean rate of return and the standard deviation. Assume a probability of $\frac{1}{8}$ for each combination of mean rate of return and standard deviation.

(c) Can you tell the sign of the correlation coefficient from the diagram? Explain.

7.23. The profit of a firm is equal to revenues minus costs. The firm has contracted for all of the supplies it will need during the coming year, and a strike is ruled out since the firm has contracted with the workers as well. The firm produces and sells two products. The price of the first, product 1, is \$10 per unit, and the price of the second, product 2, is \$20 per unit. Next year's demand for both products is uncertain; the probability distributions of various numbers of units, Q, are as follows:

q_1	$P(q_1)$	q_2	$P(q_2)$
4,000	$\frac{1}{4}$	1,000	$\frac{1}{2}$
5,000	$\frac{1}{4}$	2,000	$\frac{1}{2}$
6,000	$\frac{1}{4}$		
7,000	$\frac{1}{4}$		

Suppose the firm has produced 7,000 units of product 1 and 2,000 units of product 2 at a total cost of \$70,000.

Find the expected value and standard deviation of the profit under the following alternative assumptions:

(a) The correlation between Q_1 and Q_2 is equal to -0.6.
(b) The correlation between Q_1 and Q_2 is equal to 0.
(c) The correlation between Q_1 and Q_2 is equal to $+0.6$.

7.24. The profit of a firm is equal to revenues minus costs. The firm has contracted to supply 10,000 units of production at \$100 per unit. To produce the items the firm needs to use 500 units of one input (call it input 1) and 1,000 units of another input (call it input 2). The prices of input 1 (X_1) and of input 2 (X_2) are random variables with the following probability distributions:

x_1	$P(x_1)$	x_2	$P(x_2)$
1,000	$\frac{1}{2}$	18	$\frac{1}{2}$
1,200	$\frac{1}{2}$	22	$\frac{1}{2}$

Find the expected value of the profit and its standard deviation under the following assumptions:

(*a*) The correlation between X_1 and X_2 is equal to -0.6.
(*b*) The correlation between X_1 and X_2 is equal to 0.
(*c*) The correlation between X_1 and X_2 is equal to $+0.6$.

7.25. The mean rate of return and standard deviation of Stocks 1 and 2 are given below:

	Stock 1	*Stock 2*
Mean	10%	20%
Standard deviation	20%	30%

Given that the correlation is $\rho = -1$, find the investment proportions in Stock 1 and Stock 2 that yield a zero variance on the investment portfolio.

7.26. Ms. Johns invests $1,000 in two stocks, *A* and *B*. Their rates of return (profit expressed in percent) are given by the following probability distributions:

Stock A		*Stock B*	
Return	*Probability*	*Return*	*Probability*
-10%	$\frac{1}{3}$	-10%	$\frac{1}{2}$
0	$\frac{1}{3}$	50	$\frac{1}{2}$
$+40$	$\frac{1}{3}$		

(*a*) Assume that the rates of return from the two stocks are independent. Calculate the mean and standard deviation on a portfolio that consists of the following alternative investment proportions:

Proportion in A	*Proportion in B*
0.0	1.0
0.1	0.9
0.3	0.7
0.5	0.5
0.9	0.1
1.0	0.0

Draw the frontier showing the tradeoff between expected rate of return and standard deviation.

(*b*) Repeat part *a*, assuming first that $\rho = -1$ and then that $\rho = +1$.

7.27. Let X_1 and X_2 be the number of units sold on two successive days. Let X_1 and X_2 be *statistically independent,* and let the probability distribution of X_1 be

x_1	$P(x_1)$
20	0.4
23	0.5
26	0.1

Let the probability distribution of X_2 be identical to that of X_1 and let the sales price be $4 per unit.

  (*a*) Find the expected value of X_1 and X_2.
  (*b*) Find the standard deviation of X_1 and X_2.
  (*c*) Let $Z = 4(X_1 + X_2)$. What does Z represent?
  (*d*) What are the expected value and standard deviation of Z?

7.28. The mean rate of return on Stock A is 10 percent and on Stock B 20 percent. The standard deviation of the rate of return is 8 percent on Stock A and 24 percent on Stock B. Suppose the correlation coefficient of the returns on A and B is $+0.40$. What is the standard deviation of the return on portfolio P, which is composed of Stocks A and B only and whose expected rate of return is 16 percent?

7.29. The mean rate of return and standard deviation of Stocks 1 and 2 are given below:

	Stock 1	*Stock 2*
Mean	12%	20%
Standard deviation	10	28

  (*a*) Assume that the correlation coefficient between the rates of return is equal to -1.0, and find the mean rate of return and standard deviation of the following portfolios:

     1. 0 percent in Stock 1 and 100 percent in Stock 2.
     2. 25 percent in Stock 1 and 75 percent in Stock 2.
     3. 50 percent in Stock 1 and 50 percent in Stock 2.
     4. 75 percent in Stock 1 and 25 percent in Stock 2.
     5. 100 percent in Stock 1 and 0 percent in Stock 2.

  (*b*) Rework part *a* four more times, assuming that the correlation coefficient is alternatively $-0.5, 0, +0.5,$ and $+1.0$.

7.30. In Problem 3.18 you constructed a frequency distribution of the 50 largest banks in the world by their deposits. The frequency distribution was in intervals of $10 million, starting at $30 million. In Problem 3.19 you constructed a frequency distribution of the same banks by their assets.

  (*a*) Construct a two-way classification frequency table of the banks by their deposits and by their assets, using the same class intervals as in Problems 3.18 and 3.19.
  (*b*) From the table you set up for part *a*, derive the joint probability table that will show the probability that a bank picked at random among the 50 largest will belong to any of the table's cells.
  (*c*) Use the joint probability table to calculate the covariance and the correlation coefficient of the two variables. The values of the variables corresponding to each cell are the midpoints of the respective classes.

7.31. Mr. Jackson owns a $100,000 house and has just bought a lottery ticket. There is a probability of 1 percent that a fire will cause heavy damage to the house, reducing its value to $20,000. There is a 3 percent probability that a less severe fire will strike the house, reducing its value to $80,000. Otherwise the value of the house will stay at $100,000. The lottery ticket gives Mr. Jackson a 1 percent chance to win $300,000, a 5 percent chance to win $100,000, and a 94 percent chance of winning nothing. Denote the value of the house by X_1 and the value of the lottery prize by X_2 and answer the following questions:

  (*a*) Do you think that X_1 and X_2 are independent random variables? Explain.
  (*b*) Write down the joint probability distribution of X_1 and X_2.
  (*c*) Let $X = X_1 + X_2$. What is the meaning of X? Write down the probability distribution of X.

(d) Calculate the expected value and variance of X and explain their meaning.

(e) Suppose Mr. Jackson insures his house. He pays a \$1,000 premium to the insurance company, which is obligated to compensate him fully for damages to his house in case of fire. Write down the probability distribution of the insured value of the house plus the lottery prize.

(f) Mr. Jackson's insurance company received his \$1,000 premium and may have to pay for damages. What is the expected value of the net amount the firm will receive from Mr. Jackson? What is the variance of this amount?

7.32. An insurance company has insured two houses against fire. The value of each house is \$100,000. For each of these houses there is a probability of 1 percent that a fire will strike, reducing the house's value to \$10,000. There is a 2 percent probability of a less severe fire that would reduce the house's value to \$70,000.

The joint probability distribution of the value of the two houses is as follows:

Value of second house, x_2	Value of first house, x_1		
	\$10,000	*\$70,000*	*\$100,000*
\$ 10,000	0.005	0.010	0.005
70,000	0.005	0.010	0.005
100,000	0.000	0.000	0.960

(a) Are X_1 and X_2 independent random variables? If not, do you think the two houses are located in the same or nearby neighborhoods? Explain.

(b) In case of fire, the insurance company guarantees the owner of each house at least \$95,000, no matter how bad the fire damages are. Obviously, if no fire strikes, the insurance company does not pay the homeowners anything. Suppose the insurance company charges a \$2,000 insurance premium per house. Write down the probability distribution of the insurance firm's net income from both houses, and calculate its mean and variance.

(c) Repeat part b, assuming that X_1 and X_2 are independent. Contrast and explain your answers for parts b and c.

7.33. Table P7.33 provides the annual rates of return on the stocks of IBM and Xerox for the years 1972–81.

TABLE P7.33

Year	Rates of return	
	IBM	*Xerox*
1972	19.8	21.1
1973	− 17.2	− 22.1
1974	− 57.5	− 30.0
1975	0.4	37.7
1976	17.2	28.3
1977	− 17.6	1.8
1978	18.5	13.9
1979	21.4	− 9.5
1980	1.2	11.3
1981	− 28.1	− 11.1

(a) Calculate the sample means and standard deviations of the rates of return.

(b) Calculate the correlation coefficient between the rates of return of the two stocks.

(c) Suppose you construct an investment portfolio by investing a proportion (P) in IBM stock and a proportion ($1 - P$) in Xerox stock. Calculate the mean and standard deviation of the portfolio for the values $P = 0.0, 0.1, 0.2, 0.3, \ldots, 0.9, 1.0$.

(d) Draw the investment opportunities frontier based on your calculations in part c.

Case Problems

7.1. (*a*) Using the rates of return data of Data Set 2, Appendix B, Table B.2, estimate the correlation coefficient between the rates of return of "44 Wall Street Fund" (fund number 10) and "International Investors" (fund number 116). Calculate a few points on the investment opportunities frontier of the two funds in the mean-standard deviation plane, and present the frontier graphically. Evaluate the gains from diversification between the two mutual funds.

(*b*) Inspect the rates of return on mutual funds in Data Set 2. If you want to diversify your investment between two mutual funds that will be chosen at random, do you stand to gain a lot from such a diversification? Explain. Answer this question without performing any calculations and distinguish between two mutual funds that are chosen from the same category and two mutual funds that are chosen from different categories.

7.2. (*a*) Take the first two mutual funds out of those listed in the "Maximum Capital Gains" section in Data Set 2, Appendix B, Table B.2. Draw the investment opportunities frontier between the two funds.

(*b*) Draw the investment opportunities frontier between the first fund you selected in part *a* and "International Investors" (fund number 116).

(*c*) Explain the difference between the shapes of the two frontiers (the one from part *a* and the one from part *b*). What does it imply about gains from diversification?

7.3. (*a*) Firms 50 through 75 in Data Set 1, Appendix B, Table B.1, belong to the chemicals industry. Use the data of these firms to study the relationship of profitability and the size of the firm.

(*b*) Repeat part *a* using data of the aerospace industry (firms 1 through 10).

IMPORTANT DISCRETE DISTRIBUTIONS

Key Terms
Bernoulli process
binomial probability distribution
geometric probability distribution
Poisson probability distribution
hypergeometric probability distribution
finite population correction

Some probability distributions (discrete and continuous) are more common than others, and hence deserve special attention. In this chapter we focus on four important discrete probability distributions: the binomial, the geometric, the Poisson, and the hypergeometric probability distributions. All of these distributions have both theoretical and practical applications. We shall begin by describing the Bernoulli process and in doing so lay the foundation for the introduction of binomial and geometric distributions.

In Chapters 9 and 10 we shall discuss several important continuous distributions.

8.1 The Bernoulli Process

Many business-related processes consist of a number (great or small) of repetitive independent trials: making a series of telephone calls, responding to signals requiring immediate attention (such as a firefighter's response to fire alarms), periodically examining the quality of items produced by a given machine, and so on. These series of trials can each be represented as a **Bernoulli process** (named after Jakob Bernoulli, a seventeenth-century Swiss mathematician). A Bernoulli process has three characteristics:

1. It consists of repetitive and statistically *independent* trials; the outcome of one trial does not affect the outcome of other trials.
2. Each trial in the process must result in one of two mutually exclusive possible outcomes. Traditionally, one of the outcomes is called "success" and the other "failure," although they may involve no accomplishments or disappointments of any kind. It follows that P("success") $= 1 - P$("failure").
3. The probability of "success" in one trial is the same as in any other trial. Accordingly, the probability of "failure" in a trial is also the same as in any other trial.

As an example of a Bernoulli process, consider "making a series of telephone calls, independent of one another." One trial in this process is "making a telephone call." The result of this trial may be described in a variety of pairs of mutually exclusive events such as "reached a wrong number" versus "reached the correct number" or "operator's assistance was required" versus "operator's assistance was not required," and so on. Suppose we are interested in just one aspect of the result: whether or not the call was long-distance. In this case, we may describe the trial as a *dichotomy* (that is, as having two and only two possible outcomes) because the outcome must be that the call either was or was not long-distance. No other outcomes are possible according to this classification: the two outcomes are mutually exclusive and collectively exhaustive.

Given that the telephone calls are picked at random, the process is classified as a Bernoulli process because:

1. The calls consist of repetitive occurrences and they are independent of one another.
2. They each have only two possible outcomes, which are mutually exclusive.
3. The probability of "success" is the same for all trials ("success" being either "the call is a long-distance call" or "the call is not a long-distance call," however we would like to define it).

Another example of the Bernoulli process is firefighters' responsiveness to a fire alarm. It could be thought of as a process in which each response is considered to be one trial with two possible outcomes. We may want to consider the following pair of outcomes: "at most one fire engine responded" versus "more than one fire engine responded." Alternatively, we might consider "the alarm was false" versus "the alarm was not false," and so on. The classification depends on the goal of our analysis.

The letter p is customarily used to denote the probability of success for any given trial ($0 \le p \le 1$). The probability of "failure" is denoted by q ($0 \le q \le 1$) and is computed as follows:

$$q = 1 - p \tag{8.1}$$

From a statistical point of view, there are two interesting random variables related to the Bernoulli process. The first is *the number of successes that occur when the process consists of a predetermined number of trials.* The probability distribution of this random variable is called the **binomial probability dis-**

tribution. The second is *the number of trials that it takes to obtain the first success.* The probability distribution here is known as the **geometric probability distribution.** We begin with a discussion of the binomial probability distribution.

8.2 The Binomial Probability Distribution

Suppose *n* trials of a Bernoulli process are observed. The number of successes that occur in the process is a random variable whose probability distribution is known as a *binomial probability distribution.* Denoting the random variable by *X*, we write

$$X \sim B(n, p)$$

where the symbol ~ stands for "is distributed" and *B* stands for "binomially."

Thus, $X \sim B(n, p)$ is read, "The random variable *X* is distributed binomially with the parameters *n* and *p*."

If *x* denotes a specific value of the variable *X*, our immediate interest is in determining the probability that *X* will take on that value—that is, in determining $P(X = x)$.

Let us derive the probability distribution by means of an example.

EXAMPLE 8.1

Twenty percent of all clothing items ordered from a mail-order firm are returned within a week of receipt. Suppose six orders are received and we want to determine the probability distribution of the number of returns.

The number of returns is a binomial random variable since all of the following hold true:

1. The experiment consists of six *independent* trials.
2. There are *only two possible outcomes* of interest for each trial: the order will either be returned or not.
3. The probability that a given order will be returned is *the same* as for any other order.

In this example, $n = 6$ and $p = 0.2$. It follows that $q = 1 - p = 1 - 0.2 = 0.8$. Using compact statistical notation, we write $X \sim B(6, 0.2)$. The possible values that *X* can take on are 0, 1, 2, 3, 4, 5, and 6. Let us determine the probability of each of these outcomes. First, consider the probability that there will be no returns—that is, $P(X = 0)$. The probability that the *first order* will not be returned is equal to 0.80. The probability that the *second order* will not be returned is also 0.80. Since we assume that the returns of the first and the second orders are independent, it follows that the probability of the intersection of the two events (that is, that *neither* order will be returned) is equal to the product of the probability of the two events: $0.80 \cdot 0.80 = 0.64$. By the same token, the probability that none of the six orders will be returned is equal to

$$0.80 \cdot 0.80 \cdot 0.80 \cdot 0.80 \cdot 0.80 \cdot 0.80 = 0.80^6 = 0.26214$$

or

$$P(X = 0) = q^n = 0.80^6 = 0.26214$$

Now let us generalize the results of this example and proceed to derive the binomial probability distribution. Suppose we denote a success in a given trial by S and a failure by F. The event that all six trials will result in failures may be described as

$$\{F, F, F, F, F, F\}$$

This is the only event that will make X equal to zero, and as we have seen, $P(X = 0) = q^n = 0.26214$. There are six distinguishable events that will make X equal to 1:

$$\{S, F, F, F, F, F\}$$
$$\{F, S, F, F, F, F\}$$
$$\{F, F, S, F, F, F\}$$
$$\{F, F, F, S, F, F\}$$
$$\{F, F, F, F, S, F\}$$
$$\{F, F, F, F, F, S\}$$

The location of the letter S in each pair of braces signals the sequential trial in which the success has occurred. For example, the first series describes a success in the first trial followed by five failures; the second series describes a failure in the first trial, success in the second, and failure in all the four succeeding trials; and so on.

The number of events that make $X = 1$ is $\binom{6}{1}$, since there are $\binom{6}{1}$ possible combinations of one S and five Fs. Recalling from Section 5.8 that $\binom{n}{r} = \dfrac{n!}{(n - r)!r!}$, we get $\binom{6}{1} = \dfrac{6!}{5!\,1!} = 6$. Each of the six events has a probability of $(0.80)^5(0.20) = 0.065536$, since each involves one success with a probability of 0.20 and five failures with a probability of 0.80 each. Accordingly, the probability of $X = 1$ is 6 times 0.065536, or

$$P(X = 1) = 6 \cdot 0.065536 = 0.39322$$

To find the probability that X equals 2, we first find the number of possible combinations of two successes in six trials. There are $\binom{6}{2} = \dfrac{6!}{4!\,2!} = \dfrac{6 \cdot 5}{2} = 15$ such combinations:

$$\{S, S, F, F, F, F\} \qquad \{F, S, F, F, F, S\}$$
$$\{S, F, S, F, F, F\} \qquad \{F, F, S, S, F, F\}$$
$$\{S, F, F, S, F, F\} \qquad \{F, F, S, F, S, F\}$$
$$\{S, F, F, F, S, F\} \qquad \{F, F, S, F, F, S\}$$

$\{S, F, F, F, F, S\}$ $\{F, F, F, S, S, F\}$

$\{F, S, S, F, F, F\}$ $\{F, F, F, S, F, S\}$

$\{F, S, F, S, F, F\}$ $\{F, F, F, F, S, S\}$

$\{F, S, F, F, S, F\}$

Each of the above combinations has a probability of $(0.20)^2(0.80)^4 = 0.016384$ of occurrence, so that the probability for X to equal 2 is

$$P(X = 2) = \binom{6}{2} (0.20)^2(0.80)^4 = 15 \cdot 0.016384 = 0.24576$$

We now generalize as follows:

THE PROBABILITY DISTRIBUTION OF A BINOMIAL RANDOM VARIABLE

$$P(X = x) = \binom{n}{x} p^x q^{n-x} \tag{8.2}$$

Using Equation 8.2, we get the following probability distribution and cumulative distribution of X:

x	$P(x)$	$\Sigma P(x)$
0	0.26214	0.26214
1	0.39322	0.65536
2	0.24576	0.90112
3	0.08192	0.98304
4	0.01536	0.99840
5	0.00154	0.99994
6	0.00006	1.00000
	1.00000	

Both functions are shown in Figure 8.1.

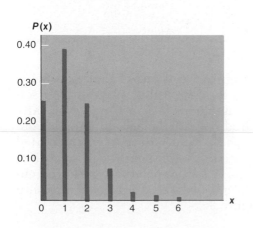

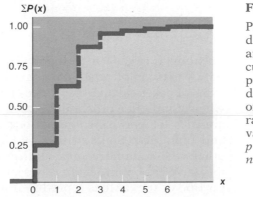

Figure 8.1

Probability distribution and cumulative probability distribution of a binomial random variable with $p = 0.2$ and $n = 6$

Let us look at another example involving the binomial distribution.

EXAMPLE 8.2

A test consisting of 20 true–false questions is taken by a student who is *totally unprepared* and therefore decides to make purely random choices between the true and false answers. The number of correct answers the student will give is a binomial random variable with $n = 20$ as the number of trials and $p = 0.5$ as the probability of success:

$$X \sim B(20, 0.5)$$

Suppose we want to calculate the probability that the student will give exactly 5 correct answers. We follow Equation 8.2 and get

$$P(X = 5) = \binom{20}{5}\left(\frac{1}{2}\right)^5\left(\frac{1}{2}\right)^{15} = 15{,}504 \cdot 0.03125 \cdot 0.00003052 = 0.0148$$

Suppose now that at least 8 correct answers are required to pass the test. The probability that the student will pass is

$$P(X \geq 8) = 1 - P(X \leq 7)$$
$$= 1 - [P(X = 0) + P(X = 1) + \cdots + P(X = 7)]$$

where each probability within the brackets may be separately calculated by means of Equation 8.2. Calculations show that

$$P(X = 0) + P(X = 1) + \cdots + P(X = 7) = 0.1316$$

so that

$$P(X \geq 8) = 1 - 0.1316 = 0.8684$$

Do not rejoice over this result; most professors will pass their students only if they answer at least 14 of 20 questions correctly. If you calculate, you will find out that the probability for this event is only 0.0577, or 5.77 percent, if the student is guessing.

Although calculating binomial probabilities by means of Equation 8.2 is not overly complicated, particularly with the increasing availability of scientific pocket calculators, it does become a tedious task at times, especially when cumulative probabilities are required. To ease the task, binomial probabilities for various combinations of n and p values have been calculated and tabulated. Some of these tables provide the probability distribution, others the cumulative probabilities. Table A.1 in Appendix A gives the cumulative probabilities for a variety of n and p values. For convenience, a portion of the table is reproduced in Figure 8.2.

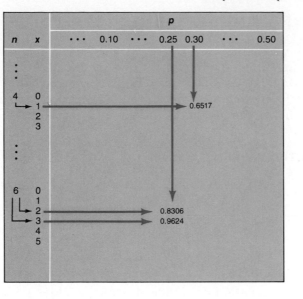

Figure 8.2

A schematic
description of
the binomial
cumulative
probability
distribution
table

To find a cumulative probability, we locate the n and p values in the left-hand column and the top row, respectively. In the second column from the left are the values of x. Figure 8.2 shows, for example, that the cumulative value for $p = 0.25$, $n = 6$, and $x = 3$ is 0.9624.

Figure 8.2 warrants a few additional comments. First, it shows only selected values of n and p. For values not shown in the table, we need either to perform calculations or to use more detailed tables. If approximation suffices, we can interpolate. Second, the values of p presented in the binomial table are less than or equal to 0.50. For values greater than 0.50 use $1 - p$ and find the probability $1 - P(X \le n - x - 1)$ instead. For example, suppose we want to find the probability $P(X \le 2)$, assuming that $n = 4$ and $p = 0.70$. Since $p > 0.50$, we first use the table to find $P(X \le 4 - 2 - 1) = P(X \le 1)$, using $p = 1 - 0.70 = 0.30$. This probability equals 0.6517, and we then compute $P(X \le 2)$ for $n = 4$ and $p = 0.70$ to equal $1 - 0.6517 = 0.3483$. In other words we make use of the following relationship:

$$P(\text{number of ``successes''} \le x)$$

$$= 1 - P(\text{number of ``successes''} \ge n - x)$$

$$= 1 - P(\text{number of ``failures''} \le n - x - 1)$$

Finally, the (noncumulative) probability for any listed value of n, p, and x is obtained by subtracting the cumulative probability of the value $x - 1$ from that of x. For example, to find the probability $P(X = 3)$, assuming that $n = 6$ and $p = 0.25$, we subtract $P(X \le 2) = 0.8306$ from $P(X \le 3) = 0.9624$, where the last two numbers are read off the table, and we get

$$P(X = 3) = P(X \le 3) - P(X \le 2) = 0.9624 - 0.8306 = 0.1318$$

8.3 Properties of the Binomial Distribution

In this section we shall discuss the mean, the variance, and the skewness of a binomial distribution. If a binomial experiment consists of 100 trials, each of which has 0.15 probability of success, the expected number of successes is $0.15 \cdot 100 = 15$. In general, if the probability of success is p and the number of trials is n, the expected value of the binomial variable is np.[1] In short:

THE EXPECTED VALUE OF A BINOMIAL VARIABLE

If

$$X \sim B(n, p)$$

then

$$E(X) = np \qquad (8.3)$$

To see that the equation does indeed work, consider a binomial random variable with $n = 3$ and $p = 0.3$:

$$X \sim B(3, 0.3)$$

The probability distribution of X is given by Equation 8.2 and is calculated as follows:

x	$P(x)$
0	$\binom{3}{0}(0.3^0)(0.7^3) = 0.343$
1	$\binom{3}{1}(0.3^1)(0.7^2) = 0.441$
2	$\binom{3}{2}(0.3^2)(0.7^1) = 0.189$
3	$\binom{3}{3}(0.3^3)(0.7^0) = 0.027$
	$\overline{1.000}$

Computing the expected value of X from the above probability distribution, we obtain

$$E(X) = 0 \cdot 0.343 + 1 \cdot 0.441 + 2 \cdot 0.189 + 3 \cdot 0.027 = 0.900$$

which is the same value we obtain when we use Equation 8.3, since $np = 3 \cdot 0.3 = 0.900$.

The variance of a binomial random variable is given by npq (for proof see Appendix 8A):

THE VARIANCE OF A BINOMIAL RANDOM VARIABLE

$$V(X) = npq \qquad (8.4)$$

---

[1] A proof is provided in Appendix 8A.

As always, the standard deviation is obtained by taking the square root of the variance:

THE STANDARD DEVIATION OF A BINOMIAL RANDOM VARIABLE

$$SD(X) = \sqrt{npq} \qquad (8.5)$$

Our next step is to see whether Equation 8.5 "makes sense." We know that when $p = 0$ or $q = 0$, the variance is also equal to zero, since if $p = 0$, we know in advance that *all* trials, without exception, will result in "failure." Therefore there is no room for any variability. Similarly, if $q = 0$, *all* trials must result in "success," and hence again there is no variance in the outcomes. For any other values of p, the variance, as given in Equation 8.4, is not equal to zero, and as a result the outcome of one trial can differ from that of the next. In other words, the outcomes have a certain degree of variability. It can be shown that the variance reaches its maximum when $p = q = \frac{1}{2}$.

Graphically, the relationship between the value of p and the standard deviation of X (for a given value of n) is shown in Figure 8.3.

Obviously, we can compute the variance of a binomial random variable directly by Equation 6.3 or 6.5. Using Equation 6.5 for the variance of $X \sim B(3, 0.3)$, we proceed as follows:

x	x^2	$P(x)$
0	0	0.343
1	1	0.441
2	4	0.189
3	9	0.027
		1.000

$$E(X^2) = \Sigma x^2 P(x)$$

$$= 0 \cdot 0.343 + 1 \cdot 0.441 + 4 \cdot 0.189 + 9 \cdot 0.027$$

$$= 0.000 + 0.441 + 0.756 + 0.243$$

$$= 1.440$$

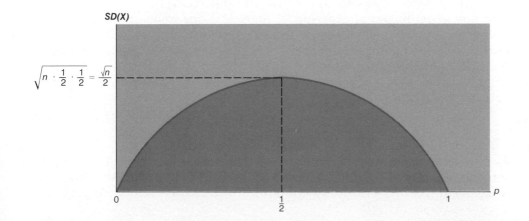

Figure 8.3

The relationship between the value of p and the standard deviation of X when $X \sim B(n, p)$

Thus $V(X) = E(X^2) - \mu^2 = 1.44 - 0.90^2 = 1.44 - 0.81 = 0.63$. Indeed, by Equation 8.4 we obtain $V(X) = npq = 3 \cdot 0.3 \cdot 0.7 = 0.63$.

To summarize:

If

$$X \sim B(n, p)$$

then

$$E(X) = np$$
$$V(X) = npq$$
$$SD(X) = \sqrt{npq}$$

In Appendix 8A we develop an expression for the skewness of a binomial random variable. There it is shown that a binomial distribution is symmetrical when $p = q = \frac{1}{2}$ and asymmetrical in all other cases. For any given value of p not equal to $\frac{1}{2}$, however, the greater the value of n, the less the skewness of the distribution. This important property of the binomial distribution is shown in Figure 8.4 for three values of p. Note that for all combinations of n and p such that the two conditions $np \geq 5$ and $nq \geq 5$ are met, the distribution is not only close to symmetrical but also bell-shaped, and it resembles the shape of a normal distribution (see Chapter 9). This fact will aid us substantially in approximating binomial probabilities once we have concluded our discussion of the normal distribution.

8.4 The Number of Successes in a Binomial Experiment Expressed in Terms of Proportions

A binomial variable measures the *number* of trials resulting in success in a Bernoulli process spanning n independent trials. Often, however, it is convenient to express the result in terms of the *proportion* of trials resulting in success. We can easily do so by dividing the number of successes in the experiment (X) by the number of trials (n). Thus, the variable X/n measures the proportion of trials resulting in success. For example, if 20 trials resulted in 8 successes, the experiment's result could be expressed as "8 successes" or as "40 percent successes" ($\frac{8}{20} = 0.40$, or 40 percent).

In any given binomial experiment, there is a one-to-one relationship between the value X and the value X/n. Consequently, the probability distribution of X/n is identical to that of X and is given by substituting the value X/n in Equation 8.2. Accordingly

---

$$P\left(\frac{X}{n} = \frac{x}{n}\right) = \binom{n}{x} p^x q^{n-x} \tag{8.6}$$

As an example, consider $X \sim B(10, 0.6)$. The probability that $X = 4$ is the same as the probability that $X/n = 4/10 = 0.4$, since both result from the same event (that is, 4 successes out of the 10 trials). Therefore we get

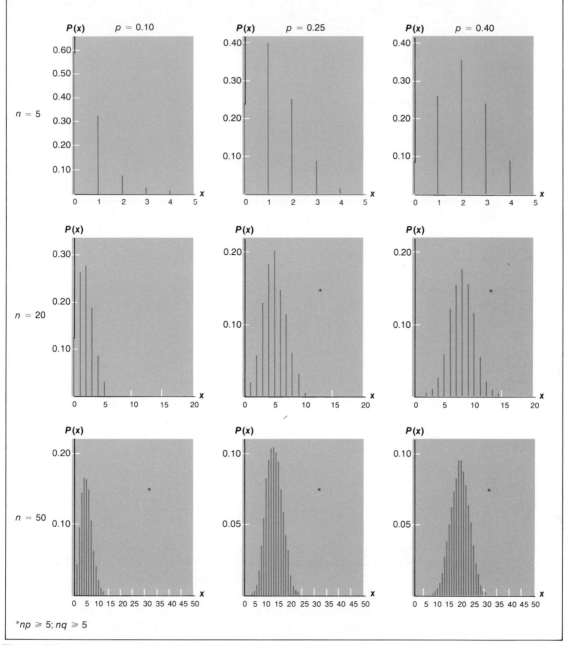

Figure 8.4

The shape of the binomial distribution for various combinations of *n* and *p*

$$P(X = 4) = P\left(\frac{X}{n} = 0.4\right) = \binom{10}{4}(0.6^4)(0.4^6) = 0.1115$$

We can calculate the mean and variance of the variable X/n by implementing previously derived equations. Using the equations applicable to transformed variables (see Chapter 6)—that is, $E(bX) = b\mu$ and $V(bX) = b^2V(X)$—we stipulate $b = 1/n$ and find that

$$E\left(\frac{X}{n}\right) = E\left(\frac{1}{n} \cdot X\right) = \frac{1}{n} \cdot np = p$$

$$V\left(\frac{X}{n}\right) = V\left(\frac{1}{n} \cdot X\right) = \frac{1}{n^2} \cdot V(X) = \frac{1}{n^2} \cdot npq = \frac{pq}{n}$$

We may summarize as follows:

If

$$X \sim B(n, p)$$

then, for the proportion X/n, we have

$$E\left(\frac{X}{n}\right) = p$$

$$V\left(\frac{X}{n}\right) = \frac{pq}{n} \tag{8.7}$$

$$SD\left(\frac{X}{n}\right) = \sqrt{\frac{pq}{n}}$$

Here again, we notice that the variance of X/n equals zero when either $p = 0$ or $q = 0$ and reaches its maximum when $p = q = \frac{1}{2}$.

It is interesting to note that even when p is not equal to 0 or 1, the variance of the proportion approaches zero as the number of trials, n, increases.

8.5 The Geometric Probability Distribution

Suppose we observe a Bernoulli process and instead of counting the number of successes for a predetermined number of trials, as we do in the case of a binomial distribution, we focus on the number of trials it takes to get the first success. This random variable can take on the integer values 1, 2, 3, 4, 5, . . ., and so on. Its distribution is known as the *geometric distribution*. This probability distribution can be calculated without difficulty. Let us denote the random variable by X. For X to equal 1 there must be a success in the first trial. The probability for that is obviously equal to p by definition. For X to equal 2 there must be a failure in the first trial and a success in the second. The probability of obtaining a failure in the first trial is q by definition, and the probability of obtaining a success in the second is once again p. Because the two events are independent, the combination of a failure followed by a success has the probability of qp. Similarly, for X to equal 3 there must be two failures followed by a success, and the probability for that is $qqp = q^2p$.

Generally for X to equal x, there must be $x - 1$ failures followed by one success, and the probability for that is

THE GEOMETRIC PROBABILITY DISTRIBUTION

$$P(X = x) = q^{x-1}p \qquad x = 1, 2, 3, \ldots \qquad (8.8)$$

This geometric probability distribution is summarized in Table 8.1. Two examples are presented graphically in Figure 8.5: in one of them we assumed $p = \frac{1}{2}$ and in the other $p = \frac{1}{4}$.

TABLE 8.1
A Description of the Geometric Probability Distribution

Value of geometric random variable X	Description of experiments' results	Probability[a]
1	S	p
2	F, S	qp
3	F, F, S	q^2p
4	F, F, F, S	q^3p
.	.	.
.	.	.
.	.	.
x	$\underbrace{F, F, F, F, \ldots, F,}_{(x-1)\ \text{times}} S$	$q^{(x-1)}p$
.	.	.
.	.	.
.	.	.

[a]Note that the sum of the probabilities will equal 1: $p + qp + q^2p + q^3p + \cdots = p(1 + q + q^2 + q^3 + \cdots)$ where in the parentheses we have an infinite geometric progression whose sum is $1/(1-q)$. Since $p = 1 - q$ we obtain:

$$p(1 + q + q^2 + q^3 + \cdots) = p \cdot \frac{1}{1 - q} = p \cdot \frac{1}{p} = 1$$

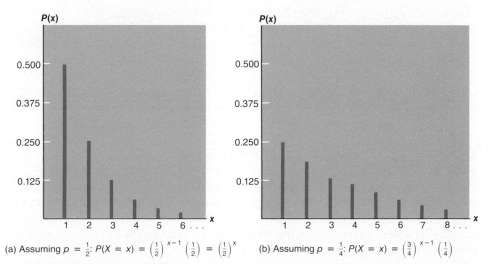

(a) Assuming $p = \frac{1}{2}$: $P(X = x) = \left(\frac{1}{2}\right)^{x-1}\left(\frac{1}{2}\right) = \left(\frac{1}{2}\right)^x$ (b) Assuming $p = \frac{1}{4}$: $P(X = x) = \left(\frac{3}{4}\right)^{x-1}\left(\frac{1}{4}\right)$

Figure 8.5

The geometric probability distribution

It can be shown that the expected value of the geometric variable is $\frac{1}{p}$ and the variance equals $\frac{1}{p}\left(\frac{1}{p} - 1\right)$.

If X has a geometric distribution with parameter p, then

$$E(X) = \frac{1}{p}$$

$$V(X) = \frac{1}{p}\left(\frac{1}{p} - 1\right) \tag{8.9}$$

$$SD(X) = \sqrt{\left(\frac{1}{p}\right)\left(\frac{1}{p} - 1\right)}$$

EXAMPLE 8.3

Robert Scientific, Inc., has a 24-hour toll-free telephone number for customers to call in their orders. The rate of incoming calls from 8 P.M. to midnight is 0.2 per minute. What is the probability that the next incoming call will occur in the fifth minute starting from now?

For this event to happen we need to observe four "failures" (i.e., four minutes with no incoming calls) followed by a "success." The probability of this occurrence is given by the geometric distribution

$$P(X = 5) = q^4 p = 0.8^4 \cdot 0.2 = 0.08192$$

If we want to find the expected value and variance of the number of minutes it takes until the first call occurs, we compute

$$E(X) = \frac{1}{p} = \frac{1}{0.2} = 5 \text{ minutes}$$

$$V(X) = \frac{1}{p}\left(\frac{1}{p} - 1\right) = \frac{1}{0.2}\left(\frac{1}{0.2} - 1\right) = 5(5 - 1) = 20$$

and the standard deviation is equal to

$$SD(X) = \sqrt{20} = 4.472 \text{ minutes}$$

8.6 The Poisson Probability Distribution

The **Poisson probability distribution** is usually applied in the case of *discrete* independent "successes" occurring on a *continuous* scale. In particular, it is employed when "successes" occur within specified units of time, space, or volume—those dimensions being measured, of course, on a continuous scale. The Poisson probability distribution is applicable to examples of car arrivals at toll booths in a unit of time, calls within a telephone exchange in a unit of time, the number of flaws in a piece of fabric of unit size or in an item of glassware, and so on. Its formula is given by the following:

POISSON PROBABILITY DISTRIBUTION

$$P(X = x) = \frac{\lambda^x e^{-\lambda}}{x!} \qquad x = 0, 1, 2, 3, \ldots \tag{8.10}$$

where λ is the only parameter of the Poisson probability distribution and is equal to the average number of "successes" in the relevant unit of time, space, or volume, and e, the base of natural logarithms, is a constant approximately equal to 2.71828.

Consider, for example, the number of car arrivals at a given toll booth. If there are 180 arrivals per hour ("on the average"), then the average number of arrivals per minute is given by the ratio 180/60 = 3. If we want to find the probability that 5 cars will arrive within a certain minute, we set $\lambda = 3$ and solve

$$P(X = 5) = \frac{3^5 \cdot 2.71828^{-3}}{5!} = \frac{243 \cdot 0.049787}{120} = 0.1008$$

Similarly, if we want to find the probability that the number of arrivals in a given minute will equal exactly 10, we calculate

$$P(X = 10) = \frac{3^{10} \cdot 2.71828^{-3}}{10!} = \frac{59,049 \cdot 0.049787}{3,628,800} = 0.00081$$

For your convenience, a table for e^x and e^{-x} is furnished in Table A.3 in Appendix A at the back of this book, though most scientific pocket calculators nowadays can generate these numbers at the push of a button.

A cumulative Poisson distribution table is provided in Appendix A, Table A.2. A portion of it is presented schematically in Figure 8.6. It shows that

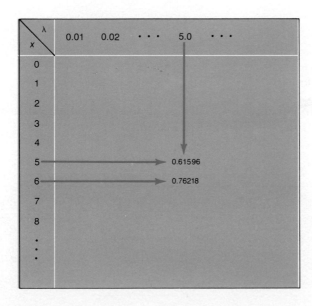

Figure 8.6

A schematic description of the Poisson cumulative distribution table

when $\lambda = 5.0$ the cumulative probability $P(X \leq 6)$ for a Poisson distribution is equal to 0.76218. Other values may be easily found in Table A.2 in a similar fashion. To find the noncumulative probability, we use the relationship

$$P(X = x) = P(X \leq x) - P(X \leq x - 1)$$

as we did for the binomial distribution. For example, assuming again that $\lambda = 5$ and examining $P(X = 6)$, we calculate as follows:

$$P(X = 6) = P(X \leq 6) - P(X \leq 5) = 0.76218 - 0.61596 = 0.14622$$

Two examples of the Poisson probability distribution are presented graphically in Figure 8.7: in one we assumed $\lambda = 2$ and in the other, $\lambda = 5$.

Figure 8.7

The Poisson probability distribution

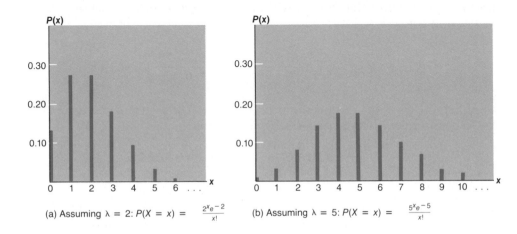

(a) Assuming $\lambda = 2$: $P(X = x) = \dfrac{2^x e^{-2}}{x!}$ (b) Assuming $\lambda = 5$: $P(X = x) = \dfrac{5^x e^{-5}}{x!}$

It can be shown (see Appendix 8B) that the mean of a Poisson distribution is equal to λ and so is the variance:

If X has a Poisson probability distribution with the parameter λ, then

$$E(X) = \lambda$$
$$V(X) = \lambda \tag{8.11}$$
$$SD(X) = \sqrt{\lambda}$$

The following examples illustrate the use of the Poisson distribution. Another illustration is the subject of Section 8.11.

EXAMPLE 8.4

The average occurrence of flaws in a fabric is one every 5 square yards. If 10 square yards are examined, what is the probability that at least two flaws will be found?

Since the "average occurrence" is given per 5 square yards, we first compute the average occurrence per 10 square yards and obtain $10/5 = 2$. Thus there are "on average" 2 flaws in 10 square yards of the fabric, and we set $\lambda = 2$. We now note that $P(X \geq 2) = 1 - P(X < 2) = 1 - P(X \leq 1)$. Using the Poisson probability distribution formula, we compute

$$P(X = 0) = \frac{2^0 \, e^{-2}}{0!} = 0.13534$$

$$P(X = 1) = \frac{2^1 e^{-2}}{1!} = 0.27067$$

and the answer is

$$P(X \geq 2) = 1 - [P(X = 0) + P(X = 1)]$$
$$= 1 - (0.13534 + 0.27067)$$
$$= 0.59399$$

EXAMPLE 8.5

The rate of arrival of customers at a drive-through bank is 1 per minute. The manager wants to decide how many tellers should be serving these customers. He wants to know the probability that more than 10, 12, or 15 customers will arrive during any 10-minute period.

Since he is interested in a 10-minute period, we set $\lambda = 10$, which is the average number of customers arriving in a period of 10 minutes. Using Appendix Table A.2 with $\lambda = 10$, we compute:

$$P(X > 10) = 1 - P(X \leq 10) = 1 - 0.58304 = 0.41696$$
$$P(X > 12) = 1 - P(X \leq 12) = 1 - 0.79156 = 0.20844$$
$$P(X > 15) = 1 - P(X \leq 15) = 1 - 0.95126 = 0.04874$$

8.7 The Poisson Approximation to the Binomial

Calculating binomial probabilities becomes tedious at times. Although tables are available, they are sometimes not handy or not sufficiently detailed, and many problems do not justify the use of a computer, particularly if the number of probabilities we need to calculate is small. In these cases, it is often useful to approximate a binomial probability. We will discuss two approximations, one reached by using the normal distribution and one reached by using the Poisson distribution. The normal approximation to the binomial distribution will be discussed in the next chapter after the normal distribution has been introduced and explained. Here we want to discuss the way the Poisson distribution can be used to approximate binomial probabilities.

When the number of trials in a binomial distribution, n, is large and the probability of success is small, we can set $\lambda = np$ and use the Poisson distribution to approximate the binomial. The larger the number of trials and the smaller the probability of success, the better the approximation. The following example demonstrates the procedure.

EXAMPLE 8.6

Electric bills in a given residential area are based on actual readings of electric meters by Southern Electric Company employees. On average, 1 percent of the bills are incorrect. If 800 bills are being processed, what is the probability that 6 bills are in error? Using the binomial formula, we compute

$$P(X = 6) = \binom{800}{6}(0.01^6)(0.99^{794}) = 0.12229$$

However, the computation of the binomial probability with a large n and small p is tedious. Even with an advanced pocket calculator, you might encounter problems working out the above probability. With the Poisson probability distribution, we can easily approximate it. We first find the expected number of errors in 800 bills:

$$E(X) = np = 800 \cdot 0.01 = 8$$

Setting $\lambda = np = 8$, we solve

$$P(X = 6) = \frac{8^6 e^{-8}}{6!} = 0.12214$$

which is a very good approximation to the probability obtained using the binomial formula.

A rule of thumb for precision to at least two decimal places is that the Poisson is a good approximation to the binomial if $n/p > 500$. Even when the ratio n/p is smaller, the approximation may still be quite reasonable. Taking, for example, $n = 20$ and $p = 0.10$ so that $n/p = 200$ we obtain the approximation shown in Table 8.2, which for many purposes is quite good. When the approximation of the Poisson distribution is not satisfactory, the normal distribution (see Chapter 9) might provide a good approximation.

TABLE 8.2
The Poisson Approximation to the Binomial
($n = 20$; $p = 0.10$)

x	*Probability by binomial distribution*	*Probability by Poisson approximation*[a]
0	0.1216	0.1353
1	0.2702	0.2707
2	0.2852	0.2707
3	0.1901	0.1804
4	0.0898	0.0902
5	0.0319	0.0361
6	0.0089	0.0120
.	.	.
.	.	.
.	.	.

[a] $\lambda = np = 20 \cdot 0.10 = 2$

8.8 The Hypergeometric Probability Distribution

Consider a finite population consisting of N objects separable into two distinguishable groups, with n objects in one group (call it "Group 1") and $N - n$ objects in the other (call it "Group 2"). Suppose x objects ($0 \leq x \leq N$) are selected at random and without replacement from the N objects in such a way that each object has the same probability of being selected. Let a selection from Group 1 be called a "success" and a selection from Group 2 be called a "failure"; then the hypergeometric random variable is the number of "successes" in the experiment. The **hypergeometric probability distribution** provides the formula needed to find the probability that exactly x_n out of x objects will be "successes" and $x - x_n$ out of x will be "failures." That formula is

---

HYPERGEOMETRIC PROBABILITY DISTRIBUTION

$$P(X_n = x_n) = \frac{\binom{n}{x_n}\binom{N - n}{x - x_n}}{\binom{N}{x}} \qquad x_n = 0, 1, 2, \ldots, \min(x, n) \quad \textbf{(8.12)}$$

Note: If $x - (N - n) > 0$, the minimum value of x_n is $x - (N - n)$, not 0.

In the numerator we have the total number of combinations of x_n objects out of n and $(x - x_n)$ objects out of the remaining $N - n$. In the denominator we have the total number of combinations of x objects out of N. Since each selection has the same chance of being made, the probability of each selection is given as the ratio of the two. Whereas the trials of the binomial distribution are independent and the probability for success is unchanged from one trial to another, this is not the case in the hypergeometric distribution. To clarify, consider a shipment of 15 cameras, of which 4 are defective. The probability of choosing a defective camera in the first trial is obviously 4/15. The probability of choosing a defective camera in the second trial is either 3/14 (a defective camera having been selected in the first trial) or 4/14 (a good camera having been selected in the first trial). Here the result of the second trial is *not independent* of the result of the first trial, and furthermore, the probability of success is not the same in both trials. It would therefore be inappropriate to use the binomial distribution to calculate the probability of events in this experiment. The hypergeometric distribution is called for. Here the number of items in the population (N) is equal to 15, with 4 belonging to one subpopulation group (n) and 11 belonging to another ($N - n$). To find the probability of getting exactly 2 defective cameras when a total of 6 are examined, we specify $x = 6$, $x_n = 2$, $x - x_n = 4$, and $N = 15$, and substitute these figures in Equation 8.12:

$$P(X_n = 2) = \frac{\binom{4}{2}\binom{11}{4}}{\binom{15}{6}} = \frac{\dfrac{4!}{2!2!} \cdot \dfrac{11!}{7!4!}}{\dfrac{15!}{9!6!}} = \frac{6 \cdot 330}{5,005} = \frac{1,980}{5,005} = 0.3956$$

Similarly, the probability that 5 cameras will be examined and none will be defective is as follows:

$$P(X_n = 0) = \frac{\binom{4}{0}\binom{11}{5}}{\binom{15}{5}} = \frac{\frac{4!}{4!0!} \cdot \frac{11!}{6!5!}}{\frac{15!}{10!5!}}$$

$$= \frac{1 \cdot 462}{3{,}003} = \frac{462}{3{,}003} = 0.1538$$

The hypergeometric probability distribution is applicable to finite populations when the sampling is done without replacement. When the sampling involves replacement, the distribution is binomial, as it would be in the above example if the cameras were replaced for possible reselection. If they were, then the probabilities for success and failure would be 4/15 and 11/15, respectively, and the trials would be independent of one another. The probability of choosing 2 defective cameras in this case is given by

$$P(X_n = x_n) = \binom{x}{x_n} \left(\frac{n}{N}\right)^{x_n} \left(\frac{N-n}{N}\right)^{x-x_n}$$

which translates to

$$P(X_n = 2) = \binom{6}{2} \left(\frac{4}{15}\right)^2 \left(\frac{11}{15}\right)^4 = 0.3085$$

compared to the 0.3956 probability we calculated using the hypergeometric distribution. A better approximation of the hypergeometric by the binomial distribution is achieved when the population is large. To see this, consider a shipment of 20,000 ballpoint pens, of which 500 do not meet some quality standards and are thus called "defective." If a random sample of 20 ballpoint pens is selected for quality determination, the binomial distribution may be used to calculate the probability of getting a certain number of defective pens. This is possible because pen qualities are assumed to be independent of one another and each trial has only two possible outcomes ("the pen is defective" and "the pen is not defective"). The third requirement of the binomial distribution, namely, that the probability of success is the same for all trials, is not strictly met, but the change of the probability from one trial to another is so small that it may be safely ignored. In the first trial, for example, the probability of obtaining a defective pen is 500/20,000. In the second trial, the probability is either 499/19,999 (a defective pen having been chosen in the first trial) or 500/19,999 (a good pen having been chosen in the first trial). The probability of choosing a defective pen in the second trial is for all practical purposes the same as the probability in the first trial.

To get a feeling for how well the binomial distribution approximates the hypergeometric distribution, let us choose a finite population of 80, of which 20 are "successes" and 60 are "failures." We select 8 objects at random without replacement. Notationally, $N = 80$, $n = 20$, and $x = 8$. The hypergeometric probability is given by

$$P(X_n = x_n) = \frac{\binom{20}{x_n}\binom{60}{8 - x_n}}{\binom{80}{8}}$$

If we use the binomial distribution regardless of the fact that the selection is without replacement, then the probabilities obtained will be only an approximation, given by

$$P(X_n = x_n) = \binom{8}{x_n}\left(\frac{1}{4}\right)^{x_n}\left(\frac{3}{4}\right)^{8 - x_n}$$

where 1/4 is the probability of "success": 20/80 = 1/4. Table 8.3 compares the probabilities obtained with the hypergeometric distribution and the binomial approximation for this example. We can see that the approximation is "reasonably" good.

It can be shown that the mean and variance of the hypergeometric distribution are as follows:

$$E(X_n) = x\frac{n}{N}$$

and

(8.13)

$$V(X_n) = \frac{N - x}{N - 1}\left[x\left(\frac{n}{N}\right)\left(1 - \frac{n}{N}\right)\right]$$

The ratio n/N represents the proportion of "successes" in the entire population, which is the same as the probability for success in a trial in which the selection was done with replacement. Furthermore, x is the number of

TABLE 8.3
The Binomial Approximation to the Hypergeometric Distribution

x_n	Hypergeometric probability[a]	Binomial approximation[b]
0	0.0883	0.1001
1	0.2665	0.2670
2	0.3281	0.3115
3	0.2148	0.2076
4	0.0815	0.0865
5	0.0183	0.0231
6	0.0024	0.0038
7	0.0002	0.0004
8	0.000004	0.00002
Total	≈1.0000	≈1.0000

[a] $P(X_n = x_n) = \dfrac{\binom{20}{x_n}\binom{60}{8 - x_n}}{\binom{80}{8}}$

[b] $P(X_n = x_n) = \binom{8}{x_n}\left(\frac{1}{4}\right)^{x_n}\left(\frac{3}{4}\right)^{8 - x_n}$

trials in the experiment, and the product $x \dfrac{n}{N}$ corresponds to the np of the binomial distribution. The variance formula also corresponds to the variance of the binomial distribution in a similar way: $x\left(\dfrac{n}{N}\right)\left(1 - \dfrac{n}{N}\right)$ corresponds to npq for the binomial variable. The hypergeometric variance, however, includes a **finite population correction,** $\dfrac{N - x}{N - 1}$, which accounts for the fact that the selection is done out of a finite population without replacement. When the population consists of $N = 15$ cameras, of which $n = 4$ are defective, and we select $x = 6$, the expected value, variance, and standard deviation of the number of defective cameras we will choose is

$$E(X_n) = 6 \cdot \frac{4}{15} = 1.6$$

$$V(X_n) = \frac{15 - 6}{15 - 1}\left[6 \cdot \left(\frac{4}{15}\right) \cdot \left(1 - \frac{4}{15}\right)\right] = 0.7543$$

$$SD(X_n) = \sqrt{0.7543} = 0.8685$$

8.9 APPLICATION 1:
BUDGETING RESEARCH AND DEVELOPMENT (THE BINOMIAL DISTRIBUTION)

Almost every large company invests a significant amount of money in the development of new products and production processes. For example, General Motors spent $2.25 billion on research and development (R&D) in 1981, and in the same year the Ford Motor Company spent $1.72 billion, AT&T spent $1.69 billion, and IBM spent $1.61 billion. Some companies spent more than 10 percent of sales on R&D. A comprehensive list of R&D expenditures by U.S. companies is published in *Business Week* once a year, around June or July. Governments also allocate sizable budgets for this purpose when new products are considered important for reasons of public health, safety, or well-being.

In the late 1950s, a strategy known as the "parallel-path strategy" was developed by the RAND Corporation, one of America's think tanks. Richard Nelson provided a framework in which the costs and benefits of the parallel-path strategy can be studied analytically.[2] The problem dealt with is the development of a project at minimum cost.

Suppose n teams are working independently of one another in attempts to develop new products. Suppose further that each team needs a $5 million annual budget and has a 10 percent chance of succeeding. Clearly, the more teams employed, the greater the chance that at least one of them will succeed in developing a new product. It is also clear, however, that the larger the number of teams, the bigger the budget. The correct determination of the number of teams that should work on a project depends on a clear presentation of the appropriate data. Let us start by posing the following question: How

[2] Richard Nelson, "Uncertainty, Learning, and the Economics of Parallel Research and Development Effort," *Review of Economics and Statistics*, November 1961.

much should the firm spend on R&D if it wants to achieve a 95 percent chance of discovering at least one new product?

Since the teams are assumed to be working independently, the binomial distribution can be used. The probability of at least one discovery is

$$P(X \geq 1) = 1 - P(X = 0) = 1 - \binom{n}{0} p^0 q^{(n-0)} = 1 - q^n$$

where X is the number of discoveries and n is the number of teams working on the discovery of new products.

Recalling that the probability of success, p, is equal to 0.10 and that the probability of failure, q, is equal to $1 - 0.10 = 0.90$, we get

$$P(X \geq 1) = 1 - q^n = 1 - 0.90^n$$

It is obvious that if the firm wants to ensure at least one discovery, it must employ an infinite number of teams, since as n approaches infinity, the probability $P(X \geq 1)$ approaches 1.0. An infinite number of teams calls for an infinite budget. In other words, no matter how large the budget, success is never certain. A realistic budget, implying a finite number of teams, always entails the risk that no discovery will be made. If the firm will be satisfied with a 95 percent chance of at least one discovery, however, the number of teams required can be financed within a budget that is wholly feasible. In this case we have

$$P(X \geq 1) = 1 - 0.90^n \geq 0.95$$

or

$$0.90^n \leq 0.05$$

It can be shown that the minimum value of n that solves the above inequality is 29.[3] Since each team needs a \$5 million budget, that total budget must be at least $5 \cdot 29 = $ \$145 million in order to achieve a 95 percent chance of getting at least one discovery.

Table 8.4 shows the number of teams and corresponding budgets required for R&D, assuming different specified probabilities of at least one discovery. Figure 8.8 shows the same data diagrammatically. Given Table 8.4 and Figure 8.8, policy makers can

---

[3] One way to solve for n is to take the logarithm on both sides of the inequality

$$0.90^n \leq 0.05$$

so that

$$n \log 0.90 \leq \log 0.05$$

It follows that

$$n \geq \frac{\log 0.05}{\log 0.90} = \frac{-1.30103}{-0.04576} = 28.43$$

or $n = 29$. Note that we change the inequality direction because log 0.90 is negative. Another way of solving for n is by trial and error.

TABLE 8.4
Number of R&D Teams and Total Budget Required for Alternative Specified Probabilities of at Least One Discovery when $p = 0.10$

Required probability for at least one discovery	Number of teams	Budget per team (millions of dollars)	Total R&D budget (millions of dollars)
0.50	7	$5	$ 35
0.60	9	5	45
0.70	12	5	60
0.80	16	5	80
0.90	22	5	110
0.95	29	5	145
0.99	44	5	220
1.00	∞	5	∞

clearly see how the probability of at least one discovery is directly related to budget size. They will base their R&D budget on both the importance they assign to the achievement of at least one discovery and the availability of funds.

Huge budgets are allocated annually for cancer research. The history of cancer research is very similar to the case we outlined above, but here, unfortunately, the success probability is particularly small. As a result, the budget rises sharply with the slightest increase in probability for at least one discovery. As an illustration, suppose that the cancer research case is characterized by a probability $p = 0.0001$ and each team's budget is $2 million. To get a rather moderate 50 percent chance for at least one breakthrough in cancer research, we need n teams such that

$$P(X \geq 1) = 1 - 0.9999^n \geq 0.50$$

or

$$0.9999^n \leq 0.50$$

which means that n has to be 6,932 and the budget must be $2 \cdot 6{,}932 = \$13{,}864$

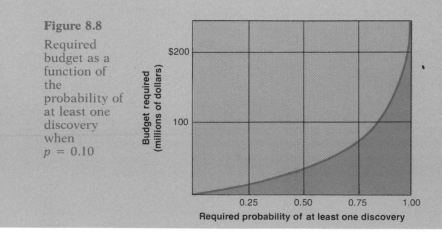

Figure 8.8

Required budget as a function of the probability of at least one discovery when $p = 0.10$

million, or $13.864 billion.[4] This staggering sum of money can be budgeted only over a span of several years, a fact that helps to explain the absence of a major breakthrough to date in cancer research. Since the success probability of each team is so small ($p = 0.0001$) and the number of trials (that is, teams) is so large, the Poisson probability distribution approximates the binomial very well.

We saw that 6,932 teams require a huge budget. Suppose the real budget allows for the employment of only 1,000 teams. Stipulating $\lambda = np = 1,000 \cdot 0.0001 = 0.10$, we find from Table A.2 in Appendix A that there is a 0.90484 probability of zero breakthroughs under these conditions.

Sadly, the probability of at least one breakthrough would therefore be a scant $1 - 0.90484 = 0.09516$.

[4] To get 6,932 we solve

$$0.9999^n \leq 0.50$$

$$n \log 0.9999 \leq \log 0.50$$

$$n \geq \frac{\log 0.50}{\log 0.9999} = \frac{-0.30102999}{-0.00004343} = 6,931.4$$

and n should be at least 6,932.

8.10 APPLICATION 2:
OIL DRILLING AND THE NEED FOR CAPITAL (THE GEOMETRIC DISTRIBUTION)

Drilling an oil field is a very risky venture from a financial standpoint. It is true that there are some areas of the Middle East where you can't build a sand castle without striking black gold, but in most regions of the world oil remains a scarce and precious commodity. The financial risk entailed in drilling for oil stems from the ever-present possibility of striking a dry hole.

Drilling is expensive, and a series of consecutive dry holes could lead to bankruptcy. Consequently, a responsible firm must take account of the probability of striking a series of dry holes in order to take the appropriate preparatory steps.

Suppose that drilling a well costs $10 million. If a well is found to be dry, the company loses $10 million. If the firm strikes oil, however, the net profit is $100 million. Suppose further that the probability of striking oil in each potential oil field is 0.2.

One interesting question that arises is how much initial capital a starting company should have in order to avoid bankruptcy by a given probability. The concern here is with the chance of striking a given number of consecutive dry holes: if the budget for drilling is exhausted before oil is found, bankruptcy occurs. The geometric probability distribution is applicable. Denoting a dry hole by D and a wet hole (wet with oil, not water) by W, the event of striking $n - 1$ dry holes followed by 1 wet hole is symbolically expressed in the following way:

$$\underbrace{D, D, D, \ldots, D}_{(n-1) \text{ times}}, W$$

The probability of such a sequence is

$$0.80^{n-1} \cdot 0.20$$

Table 8.5 shows the budget required to finance a sequence of dry holes.

TABLE 8.5
Budget Required to Avoid Bankruptcy in the Face of Various Numbers of Dry Holes When
$p = 0.20$

(1) Number of trial at which first wet hole is found (n)	(2) = (1) − 1 Number of dry holes (n − 1)	(3) = $0.80^{(n-1)} \cdot 0.20$ Probability of striking this many dry holes	(4) Cumulative probability	(5) = (1) · $10 Required budget (millions of dollars)
1	0	0.20000	0.20000	$ 10
2	1	0.16000	0.36000	20
3	2	0.12800	0.48800	30
4	3	0.10240	0.59040	40
5	4	0.08192	0.67232	50
6	5	0.06554	0.73786	60
7	6	0.05243	0.79029	70
8	7	0.04194	0.83223	80
9	8	0.03355	0.86578	90
10	9	0.02684	0.89262	100
11	10	0.02147	0.91409	110
.	.	.	.	.
.	.	.	.	.
.	.	.	.	.

The table shows the relationship between the available budget and the probability of avoiding bankruptcy. For example, if a budget of $50 million is available, the company can withstand up to four dry holes, and the probability that oil will be found in one of the first five holes is 0.67232.

From Table 8.5 and Figure 8.9 we can see that the higher we want the probability of avoiding bankruptcy to be, the higher the initial budget requirement. For example, a $70 million budget is required in order to render the firm solvent in the face of six consecutive dry wells and the construction of a seventh. The probability that the number of dry wells the firm encounters will be less than or equal to 6 is 0.79029. Similarly, a $100 million budget gives the firm the opportunity to weather nine dry holes and

Figure 8.9

Cumulative probability of striking various numbers of consecutive dry holes and the budget required to avoid bankruptcy for alternative values of p

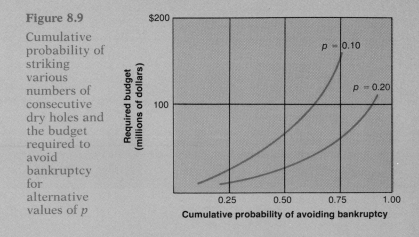

start the tenth. There is a 0.89262 probability that the number of dry holes the firm will strike will be less than or equal to 9.

In Figure 8.9, curves demonstrate the relationship between the budget and the probability of avoiding bankruptcy for $p = 0.10$ and for $p = 0.20$. As expected, the curves show that the required budget for each cumulative probability of avoiding bankruptcy is higher for $p = 0.10$ than it is for $p = 0.20$.

8.11 APPLICATION 3:
MANAGING THE INVENTORY OF DATA PROCESSING, INC. (THE POISSON DISTRIBUTION)*

Industrial companies, wholesalers, and retailers have large inventories, and they devote a great deal of effort to their proper management. In fact, inventory management can make a big difference to the overall profitability of a company. If inventories are too high, the company will have to pay for such items as storage, insurance, and financing of the excess inventories. On the other hand, if inventories are too low, the company runs a high risk of stockouts (i.e., running out of stock). One possible management objective is to keep inventories at the lowest possible level without allowing stockouts more than a specified percent of the time. For example, consider the case of Data Processing, Inc., a company that sells (among other things) a well-known brand of personal computers. The manager, who recently received her MBA degree in management and marketing, knows that it takes 10 days to receive an order (i.e., the delivery period is 10 days), and she will not tolerate more than a 5 percent chance of running out of stock. She also found that the usage of inventory follows a Poisson distribution[5] with an average usage rate of 6 units per 10 days. In other words, on average, 6 units are used in a 10-day period, so $\lambda = 6$. The probability of selling X units during a delivery period (10 days) is given by

$$P(X = x) = \frac{\lambda^x e^{-\lambda}}{x!} = \frac{6^x e^{-6}}{x!}$$

So, for example, the probability of selling 5 units during the delivery period is

$$P(X = 5) = \frac{6^5 e^{-6}}{5!} = 0.16062$$

and the probability of selling up to 5 units during the delivery period is

$$P(X \leq 5) = 0.44568$$

as can be determined directly from Table A.2 in Appendix A, using $x = 5$ and $\lambda = 6$.

* This application draws heavily on Nyles V. Reinfeld, "Inventory Control," in *The Encyclopedia of Management*, ed. Carl Hayel (New York: Van Nostrand Reinhold Company, 1982), pp. 930–939. Nyles V. Reinfeld is the director of National Institute of Management, Inc., Bath, Ohio.

[5] Studies begun in 1923 at the Bell Telephone Laboratory under the direction of R. H. Wilson show that inventory usage tends to follow the Poisson distribution. In a later chapter we will describe a statistical test by which we can accept or reject a hypothesis that a certain observed variable follows a known probability distribution.

If the manager were to wait until there were only 5 units of inventory left in stock before placing a new order, there would be a probability of 55.432 percent ($1 - 0.44568 = 0.55432$) that while the new order is on the way the usage of the inventory would exceed the available 5 units and a stockout would occur. In other words, the probability of stockout is the probability that the number of units needed during the delivery period exceeds the number of units available at the point of reordering:

$$\text{Probability of stockout} = P(X > 5) = 1 - P(X \le 5) = 55.432\%$$

Using Table A.2 in Appendix A, we can easily determine the probability of stockouts for various available units of inventory.

Continuing our assumption that the average usage in a 10-day period is $\lambda = 6$, we can see from the table that if the reorder of inventory takes place when 9 units of inventory are available, the probability of a stockout is

$$\text{Probability of stockout} = P(X > 9) = 1 - P(X \le 9) = 1 - 0.91608 = 8.392\%$$

and if the manager reorders when 10 units of inventory are still available, the probability is

$$\text{Probability of stockout} = P(X > 10) = 1 - P(X \le 10) = 1 - 0.95738 = 4.262\%$$

Given Data Processing's policy of keeping inventories at the lowest possible level without allowing more than a 5 percent chance of a stockout, the manager should place a new order when the inventory is down to 10 units. Thus the reorder point is 10 units of inventory.

Table 8.6 shows the reorder point for alternative average usage values, λ, and the probability of running out of stock. The table shows that if management wanted to allow only a 4 percent chance of a stockout and $\lambda = 6$, the reorder point would be 11 units. If $\lambda = 10$ and the allowed chance of a stockout is 1 percent, the reorder point is 18 units, and so forth. Table 8.6 shows the reorder points for a limited number of combinations of λ and stockout probabilities, but more detailed tables can very easily be derived.

TABLE 8.6
Inventory Reorder Points
(days)

Average usage per delivery time (λ)	Probability of running out of stock (percentages)												
	20	18	15	12	10	9	8	7	6	5	4	3	2	1
1	2	2	2	2	2	2	3	3	3	3	3	3	3	4
2	3	3	3	4	4	4	4	4	4	5	5	5	5	6
3	4	5	5	5	5	5	6	6	6	6	6	7	7	8
4	6	6	6	6	7	7	7	7	7	8	8	8	9	9
5	7	7	7	8	8	8	8	8	9	9	9	10	10	11
6	8	8	9	9	9	9	10	10	10	10	11	11	12	12
7	9	9	10	10	10	11	11	11	11	12	12	12	13	14
8	10	11	11	11	12	12	12	12	13	13	13	14	14	15
9	11	12	12	13	13	13	13	14	14	14	15	15	16	17
10	13	13	13	14	14	14	15	15	15	15	16	16	17	18

Chapter Summary and Review

Variable	Probability distribution	Values the variable can take on	Mean	Variance
1. Binomial	$P(X = x) = \binom{n}{x} p^x q^{n-x}$	$x = 0, 1, 2, \ldots, n$	np	npq
2. Proportion of "successes" in a binomial experiment	$P\left(\dfrac{X}{n} = \dfrac{x}{n}\right) = \binom{n}{x} p^x q^{n-x}$	$0 \leq \dfrac{x}{n} \leq 1$	p	$\dfrac{pq}{n}$
3. Geometric	$P(X = x) = q^{x-1} p$	$x = 1, 2, 3, \ldots$	$\dfrac{1}{p}$	$\dfrac{1}{p}\left(\dfrac{1}{p} - 1\right)$
4. Poisson	$P(X = x) = \dfrac{\lambda^x e^{-\lambda}}{x!}$	$x = 0, 1, 2, 3, \ldots$	λ	λ
5. Hypergeometric	$P(X_n = x_n) = \dfrac{\binom{n}{x_n}\binom{N-n}{x-x_n}}{\binom{N}{x}}$	$\begin{array}{l} x_n = 0, 1, 2, \ldots, \\ \min(x, n)^* \end{array}$	$x\dfrac{n}{N}$	$\dfrac{N-x}{N-1}\left[x\left(\dfrac{n}{N}\right)\left(1 - \dfrac{n}{N}\right)\right]$

*Note: If $x - (N - n) > 0$, then the minimum value of x_n is $x - (N - n)$.

Problems

8.1. Give an example of a Bernoulli process. Explain why it is a Bernoulli process, and define two random variables related to this process, one that has a binomial probability distribution and one that has a geometric probability distribution.

8.2. Let X be a random variable with a binomial probability distribution. Let the parameters of X be $n = 6$ and $p = 0.3$. What are the following probabilities?

$$P(X = 0) \qquad P(2 \leq X \leq 6)$$
$$P(X = 2) \qquad P(2 < X < 6)$$
$$P(X = 6)$$

8.3. Forty percent of the adults making at least \$20,000 per year own stocks. Five people are randomly selected out of this population.

    (a) Find the probability that they include 0, 1, 2, 3, 4, or 5 people who own stock.
    (b) Draw the probability distribution obtained in part *a*.

8.4. Experience shows that 25 percent of all families who get Sears mail-order catalogs place at least one order. Calculate the probability that out of 10 randomly selected families who receive the catalog only one will place an order.

8.5. Suppose an admission test for a certain university is designed so that the probability of passing it is 60 percent. Find the probability that among 20 candidates who take the test:

    (*a*) No one will pass.
    (*b*) All will pass.
    (*c*) More than 10 will pass.

8.6. A test consists of 20 true–false questions. If a student decides to answer the questions by a random selection process, what is the student's probability of giving more than 8 correct answers?

8.7. Exxon Corporation is interviewing candidates for a new job. The firm needs three persons for the new job and designs a written test so that the probability of passing it is equal to 0.60. Determine the probability that exactly three applicants will pass the test if there are

    (*a*) 3 applicants
    (*b*) 5 applicants
    (*c*) 10 applicants

8.8. An oil company has an option to drill oil fields in Texas and in California. For every hole that is drilled, the probability of hitting a wet hole in California is 0.05; in Texas it is 0.10. Assume that the drilling trials are independent of one another.

    (*a*) Calculate the probability that the first wet hole in California will be drilled on the 10th trial.
    (*b*) Calculate the probability that the first wet hole in Texas will be drilled on the 10th trial.
    (*c*) Drilling in Texas costs $150,000 per hole, and in California it costs only $100,000. The oil company has a budget of $600,000. Where would you advise the firm to drill in order to minimize the probability that the entire budget will be gone before the first wet hole has been discovered?

8.9. Suppose that the probability of success in a Bernoulli process is $p = 0.20$ and the probability of failure is $q = 1 - p = 0.80$. Which of the following events has a greater probability?

    (*a*) The occurrence of 9 successes out of 10 trials.
    (*b*) The occurrence of the first success on the 10th trial.

8.10. Five percent of the products made by a certain machine are defective.

    (*a*) If a sample of eight items is taken, what is the probability that exactly three of them are defective?
    (*b*) If a sample of eight items is taken, what is the probability that the first three items selected will be defective and all the rest will be good?

8.11. A clothing store permits garments to be returned within 10 days of purchase. The store's experience shows a 15 percent chance of return. If 15 garments are sold to 15 (independent) individuals, what is the probability that not more than 20 percent of the garments will be returned? What is the probability that at least 40 percent of the garments will be returned?

8.12. Stock market investors have become increasingly interested in the option market in recent years. An option is a security granting its owner the option to buy a specified stock at a specified price during a specified period of time. For example, suppose the owner of a Boeing option has the option to buy Boeing stock at $80 a share during the period from January through August. The stock's price at the beginning of this period is $74½. Obviously, if the stock's price should rise above $80, the holder of the option would be in a position to make a profit by exercising the option. Suppose there is a probability of ⅛ that the price of Boeing stock would go above $80 in any of the ensuing months, and the price during each month is independent of the price during the other months.

(a) What is the probability that the stock price will remain at $80 or below in all of the eight months from January through August?

(b) What is the probability that there will be exactly two months when the price would rise above $80?

(c) What is the probability that six months will pass before the price rises above $80?

8.13. A casino offers you the following game: you spin a roulette wheel that has an equal probability of stopping on the numbers 1, 2, 3, . . . , 10. If it stops on 10 after the first spin, you get $1,000 and the game is over. Otherwise you spin again. If it stops on 10 after the second spin, you get $2,000 and the game ends. Otherwise you spin again. In general, when the wheel stops on 10 the game is over and the prize is equal to $1,000 · 2^{x-1} where x is the number of spins it takes the wheel to stop on 10 for the first time. If you spin five times and it never stops on 10, the game is over and you do not get a prize.

(a) Calculate the probability that the wheel will stop on 10 for the first time on spin number four.

(b) Calculate the probability that you will win no prize in this game.

(c) Calculate the expected value of the prize.

(d) Suppose it costs $3,000 to play the game. What is the casino's expected gain from each game that is played?

8.14. A new apartment complex consists of 20 apartments, each rented for one year. There is a 20 percent chance that any 1 apartment rented for a year will be vacated before the end of the year.

(a) What is the expected number of apartments that will become vacant before the end of the year? What is the variance?

(b) What is the probability that more than 4 apartments will be vacated before the end of the year?

8.15. Find the mean and variance of a binomial random variable whose n equals 18 and whose p equals 0.10.

8.16. Find the parameters n and p of a binomial probability distribution for which the mean is 8 and the variance is 1.6.

8.17. A multiple-choice test consists of six questions with four possible answers to each. Only one of the four answers is correct. Suppose a student who is totally unprepared for the test selects his answers at random.

(a) What is the probability that he will score a grade of 50 (out of 100) if each question has an equal weight?

(b) Rework part *a*, assuming that the test consists of 10 equally weighted questions.

(c) Suppose that a student must answer at least 50 percent of the questions correctly in order to pass the test. How many questions do we need to include in the test if we want to make the probability of passing the exam by mere chance equal to 5 percent or less? (Assume that the number of multiple-choice questions in the test is even and use the binomial table to find your answer.)

8.18. The probability that a tornado will strike a given area during a given year is 0.04. What is the probability that at least one tornado will strike in a period of 30 years? Solve the problem once using the binomial formula and once using the Poisson formula.

8.19. Let X have a binomial probability distribution with $n = 100$ and $p = 0.02$. Use the Poisson approximation to determine $P(1 < X \leq 3)$, $P(1 \leq X \leq 3)$, $P(1 \leq X < 3)$, and $P(1 < X < 3)$.

8.20. Out of 20,000 items 1,000 are defective. A sample of 100 is taken without replacement and 4 of them are found to be defective. Using the Poisson probability distribution, determine the *approximate* probability of this sample result, and explain why the probability you have calculated is approximate rather than precise.

8.21. The proportion of defective items produced by a company is 0.04. Batches of 100 items are shipped out. The cost incurred by the company as a result of defective items is as follows:

Number of defective items per batch	Cost incurred
0	$ 0.00
1	3.00
2	6.00
3	9.00
4 or more	12.00

Use the Poisson approximation in this problem.

  (*a*) What is the probability that 4 or more defective items will be contained in a given batch?
  (*b*) Compute the probability that a given batch will contain exactly 1 defective item.
  (*c*) Compute the expected loss per batch of 1,000 items due to defective items.
  (*d*) Compute the probability that 2 randomly selected batches out of 100 batches will both be free of defective items.

8.22. A bank grants loans to firms only if their financial position is thought to be satisfactory. The probability that a firm will be unable to repay its loan after having been found to be solvent is 0.001. Three thousand firms have received loans.

  (*a*) What is the probability that exactly 4 firms will be unable to repay their loans?
  (*b*) What is the probability that more than 2 firms will be unable to repay their loans?

8.23. A utility company's records show that the time that elapses from the moment customers receive their utility bills until they actually make the payment is exponentially distributed with a mean of 12 days. What is the probability that a customer will pay a bill within 10 days of receiving it?

8.24. An insurance company receives $\lambda = 10$ claims per day, on average.

  (*a*) What is the probability that it will receive 5 claims on a given day?
  (*b*) What is the probability that it will receive no more than 8 claims on a given day?

8.25. The average number of accidents on a given hazardous road is 0.5 per day. Calculate the following probabilities:

  (*a*) No accidents on a given day
  (*b*) 3 accidents on a given day
  (*c*) At least 1 accident on a given day

8.26. Half of the employees in Luta City earn $25,000 or more a year, and half earn less than $25,000 a year. A random sample of 100 people is taken. Determine the approximate probability that the sample proportion of the people earning $25,000 or more a year falls between

  (*a*) 0.49 and 0.51
  (*b*) 0.48 and 0.52

Solve this problem by using Chebyshev's theorem.

8.27. According to Chebyshev's theorem, the interval from $\mu - 2\sigma$ to $\mu + 2\sigma$ includes at least 3/4 of the probability in a distribution of a random variable (recall that in this case $k = 2$ and $1 - 1/k^2 = 3/4$). Verify this rule for the following binomial variables:

    (a) $n = 6, p = 0.2$
    (b) $n = 4, p = 0.05$

8.28. According to the so-called Empirical Rule, mound-shaped distributions have about 68 percent of the probability in the range from $\mu - \sigma$ to $\mu + \sigma$. Verify this rule of thumb for the following binomial variables:

    (a) $n = 16, p = \frac{1}{2}$
    (b) $n = 30, p = 0.4$

8.29. Verify Chebyshev's theorem with $k = 1.5$ for the Poisson distribution for which $\lambda = 4$. Recall that the mean of the distribution is 4 and so is the variance. Also recall that according to the theorem, at least 5/9 of the distribution should be in the range from $\mu - 1.5\sigma$ to $\mu + 1.5\sigma$, since $1 - 1/k^2 = 1 - 1/1.5^2 = 5/9$.

8.30. Calculate the expected value and the variance of a random variable X whose distribution follows the Poisson distribution with the parameter λ.

$$P(X = x) = \frac{e^{-\lambda}\lambda^x}{x!} \qquad \text{for } x = 0, 1, 2, \ldots$$

8.31. Show that the probabilities of the geometric distribution add up to 1. In other words, given that

$$P(x) = pq^{x-1} \qquad \text{for } x = 1, 2, \ldots$$

show that

$$\sum_{x=1}^{\infty} P(x) = 1$$

8.32. Show that the probabilities of the Poisson distribution add up to 1. In other words, given that

$$P(x) = \frac{e^{-\lambda}\lambda^x}{x!}$$

show that

$$\sum_{x=0}^{\infty} P(x) = 1$$

Hint:

$$e = 1 + \frac{1}{1!} + \frac{1}{2!} + \frac{1}{3!} + \cdots$$

and

$$e^{\lambda} = 1 + \frac{\lambda}{1!} + \frac{\lambda^2}{2!} + \frac{\lambda^3}{3!} + \cdots$$

8.33. A 40-page monograph in three parts was typed by three typists. The first part of the manuscript, containing 12 pages, was typed by Marie; the second part, 20 pages long, was typed by Linda; and the last part, 8 pages long, was typed by Robert. Three of the manuscript pages are picked at random.

(*a*) What is the probability that they are the *first* 3 pages typed by Marie?
(*b*) What is the probability that all 3 pages were typed by Robert?
(*c*) What is the probability that of the 3 pages selected, one was typed by Marie, one by Linda, and one by Robert?

8.34. A random sample of 10 is taken from a lot of 50 items.

(*a*) What is the probability of getting 2 or more defective items if the lot contains 10 percent defective items?
(*b*) What is the probability of getting exactly 1 defective item if the lot contains 20 percent defective items?
(*c*) Suppose the sample of 10 is drawn from a lot of 50,000 items. Would you use the binomial distribution to calculate the probabilities of parts *a* and *b*? Explain.

8.35. Out of 10 cars that park in a certain garage in the city, 6 are in bad mechanical condition. The police department randomly picked 6 cars from those in the garage for inspection. What is the probability that the sample includes at least 4 cars in bad mechanical condition?

8.36. Verify Chebyshev's theorem with $k = 2.1$ for the geometric distribution for which $p = 0.2$. Recall that the mean and variance of the geometric distribution are $E(X) = \dfrac{1}{p}$, $V(X) = \dfrac{1}{p}\left(\dfrac{1}{p} - 1\right)$.

8.37. Verify Chebyshev's theorem with $k = 1.8$ for the hypergeometric distribution with the following parameters: $N = 12, n = 4, x = 4$.

8.38. Assume the following parameters of the hypergeometric distribution: $N = 12, n = 6, x = 4$. Calculate the probability of $x_n = 0, 1, 2, 3, 4$.

(*a*) Is the distribution symmetrical? Why?
(*b*) Can you specify the condition under which the distribution is symmetrical?
(*c*) Does your condition hold also when x is odd, rather than even?

8.39. A bookstore has 14 copies of a certain book and 6 of these have missing pages. A librarian wants to purchase 5 copies of the book and selects them at random.

(*a*) What is the probability that none of the 5 books will have missing pages?
(*b*) What is the probability that among the 5 books the number of books with missing pages is greater than 2?
(*c*) What are the expected value and standard deviation of the number of books with missing pages that the librarian will buy?

Case Problems

8.1. Data Set 2, Appendix B, Table B.2, provides a 10-year record of rates of return of mutual funds. Assume that the probability that a mutual fund will have a nonpositive rate of return in a given year is independent across years and is equal to 0.50.

(*a*) What is the probability that a mutual fund will have four nonpositive rates of return in a period of 10 years, as happened in the case of Phoenix-Chase Growth Fund Series (fund number 19)?
(*b*) What is the probability that a mutual fund will have four nonpositive rates of return in a period of 10 years *in the same order* as happened in the case of Phoenix-Chase Growth Fund Series?

(c) What is the probability that in a period of 10 years, the first nonnegative rate of return will occur in the fifth year (as in General Securities, fund number 51)? What is the probability that the first nonnegative rate of return will occur in the first year (as in the case of Dodge & Cox Stock Fund, fund number 47)?

8.2. Suppose you have $10,000 that you want to invest in mutual funds, and you decide to diversify your investment in five funds, investing $2,000 in each. You choose the funds at random out of the list of funds in Data Set 2, Appendix B, Table B.2, without replacement.

(a) What is the probability that two of the funds you select will be from the "Maximum Capital Gains" section and three of them will be from any other section?

(b) What is the probability that all five of them will be from the "Maximum Capital Gains" section?

8.3. For the last several years Joe Granville, a well-known financial analyst, has been forecasting the direction of the Dow-Jones Industrials (DJI) stock index without the usual double talk; in his *Granville Market Letter*, sent to his subscribers, he unambiguously advises them when to buy and when to sell. Granville's view is that the stock market is like a tide and the stocks are the boats carried by the tide. In his view, when the market is moving upward, nearly all the stocks are moving upward and when the market is moving downward, nearly all the stocks are moving downward. He claims that he can forecast the ups and downs of the "boats," and hence he advises his subscribers to buy the stocks before the "up" moves and to sell before the "down" moves. If the forecast is accurate, this process should yield high profit.

Consider two examples of Granville's service power:

(a) On Monday, April 21, 1980, he sent an early warning telegraph to his subscribers telling them that he was changing his earlier recommendation and suggesting to buy stocks. An influx of buying orders came the day after, and the DJI index jumped up nearly 30 points.

(b) On January 6, 1981, Granville's recommendation to his subscribers was to sell everything. The market opened with a sharp downturn. The DJI index fell by nearly 24 points on a record volume of about 93 million shares.

Some people consider Joe Granville to be one of the most powerful people in the world because he is able to influence the trend of the stock market by advising to buy or to sell.

The question, of course, is whether Granville can indeed forecast the market trend. In order to test Granville's forecasting power, Baesel, Shows, and Thorp (BST)[6] have collected data on 719 trading days and applied the hypergeometric distribution. During the 719 days, there were 372 "up" days, of which Granville had predicted 254. BST used

[6] J. Baesel, G. Shows, and E. Thorp, "Can Joe Granville Time the Market?" *Journal of Portfolio Management*, Spring 1982.

the hypergeometric to calculate the probability that Granville's performance was just a lucky guess. In order to calculate this probability, the *Granville Market Letter* recommendations in the period from December 4, 1978 through November 5, 1981 were examined; Granville's forecasted "up" days are summarized in Table CP8.3.

TABLE CP8.3
"Ups" and "Downs" in the DJI Index and Granville's Forecast

	Number of trading days	Actual price change	
		"Up" days	"Down" days
DJI index	719 (100.0%)	372 (51.7%)	347 (48.3%)
Granville's "up" days forecast	446 (100.0%)	254 (57%)	192 (43.0%)

Out of the 719 sample trading days, 372 were "up" days and 347 were "down" days. During this period Granville forecasted 446 "up" days, and 254 of them were actually "ups" and 192 were "downs." Thus, BST concluded that in 57 percent of the cases he was correct in his prediction while the chance of being correct by randomly selecting a particular "up" day was only 51.7 percent. Accordingly, they concluded that Granville was clearly doing better than mere chance.

BST then tested whether Granville's performance was *significantly* different from the results of a chance selection. They applied the hypergeometric probability distribution, claiming that the probability of selecting x "up" days in a forecast under the conditions of Table CP8.3 is

$$P(X = x) = \frac{\binom{372}{x}\binom{347}{446-x}}{\binom{719}{446}}$$

The probability of predicting exactly 254 "up" days is

$$P(X = 254) = \frac{\binom{372}{254}\binom{347}{192}}{\binom{719}{446}}$$

This probability is very small, and because of the large numbers involved, calculating it without the aid of a computer is impractical. Calculations show that the probability of making a forecast *at least* as good as Granville's under the market conditions described in Table CP8.3 is

$$P(X \geq 254) = P(X = 254) + P(X = 255) + \cdots + P(X = 372)$$

$$= 0.000231$$

or 0.0231 percent. In short BST concluded that if Granville did not have a forecasting power he would have only a 2 in 10,000 chance (i.e., about 0.02 percent) of making such a prediction. Thus there is virtually no question that he has an ability to predict market trends.

Do you agree with the application of the hypergeometric distribution for calculating the probability that indicates Granville's forecasting power? If the application of the hypergeometric distribution is appropriate in your opinion, defend it. If it is inappropriate, explain in detail why it is inappropriate and suggest another probability distribution that is suitable for this specific case. Your discussion should be supported by a numerical example. To make the numbers manageable, assume the following hypothetical scenario: 12 days were observed, of which 6 were "up" days and 6 were "down" days. Assume that the forecast was for 7 "up" days, of which 5 were actually "up" days.

APPENDIX 8A:
The Parameters of the Binomial Probability Distribution

In this appendix we shall prove that the mean, variance, and skewness of a binomial random variable are equal to np, npq, and $npq(q - p)$, respectively.

Let $X \sim B(n, p)$. X may be thought of as the sum of $X_1, X_2, X_3, \ldots, X_n$, where each of the X_i variables is the number of "successes" in the ith trial. Thus each X_i has a probability of p to equal 1 and a probability of q to equal 0. It follows that

$$E(X_i) = p \cdot 1 + q \cdot 0 = p$$

Equation 8.3 follows, since

$$E(X) = E(X_1 + X_2 + X_3 + \cdots + X_n)$$

$$= E(X_1) + E(X_2) + E(X_3) + \cdots + E(X_n)$$

$$= \underbrace{p + p + p + \cdots + p}_{n \text{ times}} = np$$

Since the X_i variables are statistically independent of one another, the variance of their sum is equal to the sum of their variances. For X_i we get

x_i	$x_i - \bar{x}_i$	$(x_i - \bar{x}_i)^2$	$P(x_i)$	$(x_i - \bar{x}_i)^2 P(x_i)$
0	$-p$	p^2	q	$p^2 q$
1	$1 - p = q$	q^2	p	$q^2 p$
				$V(X_i) = p^2 q + q^2 p$

The variance of X_i may be rewritten $V(X_i) = pq(p + q)$, and since $p + q = 1$, we get $V(X_i) = pq$. Finally, recalling that the trials are independent of one another

$$V(X) = V\left(\sum_{i=1}^{n} X_i\right) = \sum_{i=1}^{n} V(X_i) = \sum_{i=1}^{n} pq = npq$$

To determine the skewness we again consider x_i first: ·

x_i	$x_i - \bar{x}_i$	$(x_i - \bar{x}_i)^3$	$P(x_i)$	$(x_i - \bar{x}_i)^3 P(x_i)$
0	$-p$	$-p^3$	q	$-p^3 q$
1	$1 - p = q$	$+q^3$	p	$q^3 p$
				Skewness $= -p^3 q + q^3 p$

After rearranging, we get

$$\text{Skewness} = pq(q^2 - p^2) = pq(q + p)(q - p) = pq(q - p)$$

For X we get

$$\text{Skewness} = npq(q - p)$$

It is clear that the distribution is negatively skewed if $p > q$, symmetrical if $p = q$, and positively skewed if $p < q$.

APPENDIX 8B:
The Mean and Variance of the Poisson Distribution

The expected value of the Poisson distribution is given by

$$E(X) = \sum_{x=0}^{\infty} x \frac{\lambda^x e^{-\lambda}}{x!} \tag{8B.1}$$

Since the first term (with $x = 0$) is equal to zero, the expected value can be rewritten as

$$E(X) = \sum_{x=1}^{\infty} x \frac{\lambda^x e^{-\lambda}}{x!} = \lambda \sum_{x=1}^{\infty} \frac{\lambda^{x-1} e^{-\lambda}}{(x - 1)!} \tag{8B.2}$$

Substituting $z = x - 1$, we get

$$\sum_{x=1}^{\infty} \frac{\lambda^{x-1} e^{-\lambda}}{(x - 1)!} = \sum_{z=0}^{\infty} \frac{\lambda^z e^{-\lambda}}{z!} \tag{8B.3}$$

The right-hand side of Equation 8B.3 is simply the sum of the probabilities of a Poisson random variable, and therefore it is equal to 1. Using this result in Equation 8B.2, we obtain

$$E(X) = \lambda \sum_{z=0}^{\infty} \frac{\lambda^z e^{-\lambda}}{z!} = \lambda \tag{8B.4}$$

or

$$E(X) = \lambda \tag{8B.5}$$

To calculate the variance, we first examine $E(X^2)$:

$$E(X^2) = \sum_{x=0}^{\infty} x^2 \frac{\lambda^x e^{-\lambda}}{x!} \qquad \text{(8B.6)}$$

Substituting $x^2 = x(x - 1) + x$, we obtain

$$E(X^2) = \sum_{x=0}^{\infty} [x(x - 1) + x] \frac{\lambda^x e^{-\lambda}}{x!} = \sum_{x=0}^{\infty} x(x - 1) \frac{\lambda^x e^{-\lambda}}{x!} + \sum_{x=0}^{\infty} x \frac{\lambda^x e^{-\lambda}}{x!} \qquad \text{(8B.7)}$$

and thus

$$E(X^2) = \sum_{x=0}^{\infty} x(x - 1) \frac{\lambda^x e^{-\lambda}}{x!} + \lambda \qquad \text{(8B.8)}$$

Now for $x = 0$ and for $x = 1$, the first term on the right-hand side of Equation 8B.8 vanishes, so we can start the summation from $x = 2$. Substituting $z = x - 2$, we obtain

$$E(X^2) = \lambda^2 \sum_{x=2}^{\infty} \frac{\lambda^{x-2} e^{-\lambda}}{(x - 2)!} + \lambda = \lambda^2 \sum_{z=0}^{\infty} \frac{\lambda^z e^{-\lambda}}{z!} + \lambda = \lambda^2 + \lambda \qquad \text{(8B.9)}$$

Finally

$$V(X) = E(X^2) - \mu^2 = \lambda^2 + \lambda - \lambda^2 = \lambda$$

or

$$V(X) = \lambda \qquad \text{(8B.10)}$$

THE NORMAL DISTRIBUTION

CHAPTER NINE OUTLINE

Key Terms
normal distribution
standard normal distribution
fractile
percentile

9.1 Introduction

One of the most popular probability distributions is the continuous, bell-shaped **normal distribution**, an example of which is shown in Figure 9.1*a*. The random variable X is measured along the horizontal axis, while the vertical axis specifies corresponding values of the density function. The cumulative distribution is shown in Figure 9.1*b*.

The normal distribution is symmetrical about the mean (μ), the distribution's mean in this case being identical with its median and mode. The shapes of the normal and cumulative distributions shown in Figure 9.1*a* and 9.1*b* indicate that X's value is more likely to fall close to the mean of the distribution than farther to the left or right, since X is more densely distributed in the immediate vicinity of μ than at either side. The variable can, however, take on any real value in the range $-\infty$ to $+\infty$: although the distribution's tails approach the horizontal axis as X deviates from μ to either side, they never quite touch it.

Many random variables in business and economics have probability distributions that can be fairly well approximated by a normal distribution. Examples are the rate of return on stocks, the time it takes to perform a given task, and the length of pieces of fabric cut out by a machine. As we shall see later, even discrete random variables often have probability distributions that can be approximated by the normal distribution.

Figure 9.1 depicts one particular normal distribution. There is an infinite number of other normal distributions, differing from each other in mean, standard deviation, or both. Thus, the normal distribution is specified by its mean and standard deviation, and we often use the expression $X \sim N(\mu, \sigma)$, which is read "X is distributed normally with mean μ and standard deviation

The normal
distribution

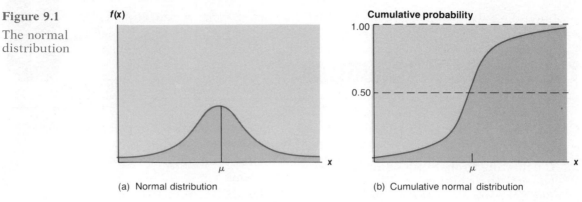

(a) Normal distribution

(b) Cumulative normal distribution

σ." Figure 9.2*a* shows two normal distributions having the same standard
deviation but different means; Figure 9.2*b* shows two normal distributions
with the same mean but different standard deviations; and Figure 9.2*c* shows
two normal distributions that differ in both mean and standard deviation.

The fact that the normal distribution is specified by its mean and standard
deviation means that once we know μ and σ, the entire probability distribution is described.

9.2 Calculating Probabilities Involving a Normal Distribution

To be able to handle problems involving the normal distribution, we must
be able to calculate the probability of events concerning the distribution. In
this section we shall discuss the method of calculation in detail.

It is important to remember that just as in the case of any other density
function, the area under the normal curve is equal to 1. Since the normal
curve is symmetrical about μ, it follows that the areas to the right and left
of μ are equal to each other, and thus each is equal to 0.5.

Figure 9.2

Normal distributions with different means and standard deviations

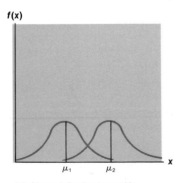

(a) Normal distributions with
the same standard deviation
but different means

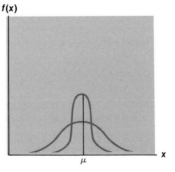

(b) Normal distributions
with same mean but
different standard deviations

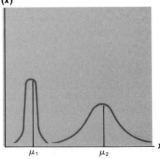

(c) Normal distributions
with different means
and standard deviations

Suppose we want to find the probability of a normal random variable, X, whose probability distribution is represented in Figure 9.3 and whose value is in the range from x_1 to x_2. To do this we need to take the integral of the density function over the range from x_1 to x_2. However, the normal distribution density function is rather cumbersome for integration,[1] so we would like to find a better way of handling the problem.

Imagine that some kind soul graciously calculated the area under a normal curve over all the possible intervals of X and presented the calculations to us in a table. We could then use the table and avoid the need for integration. There is one difficulty with this approach, however. Since there is an infinite number of normal distributions (differing in their μ and σ combinations), we would actually need an infinite number of normal distribution tables— one per distribution—for this method to be feasible. Obviously this method is impractical; we need a more efficient way to solve our problem.

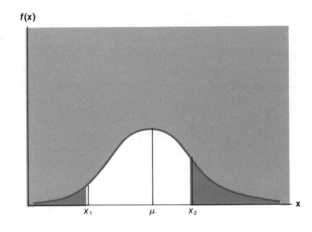

Figure 9.3

The probability under a normal distribution over the range from x_1 to x_2

THE STANDARD NORMAL DISTRIBUTION

Normal distributions, although they differ from one another, belong to the same family of distributions and thus have common characteristics—a fact we can exploit to our benefit. The calculations needed are rather simple and may be easily illustrated with the help of Figure 9.4. Here two normal distributions are presented, one that we call the **"standard" normal distribution** (its mean is zero, its standard deviation equals 1, and the value of any given point on the distribution is denoted by Z) and another selected arbitrarily (its mean is μ, its standard deviation is σ, and the value of any given point on the distribution is denoted by X). Comparing the two distributions, we find that the areas to the right and left of any X value under the normal distribution of X are equal to the areas to the right and left of the corresponding Z value under the standard normal distribution; "corresponding" here means that the X value and the Z value are situated at the same distance from their respective means *where distance is measured by units of standard deviations*. Thus, the area under the "standard" curve over the interval from 0 to 1 is equal to the area of the other normal curve over the interval from μ to $\mu + \sigma$. Similarly, the area under the standard curve over the interval

---

[1] The normal curve is given by the following: $f(x) = \dfrac{1}{\sigma\sqrt{2\pi}} \cdot e^{-\frac{1}{2}[(x-\mu)/\sigma]^2}$. For details see Appendix 9A.

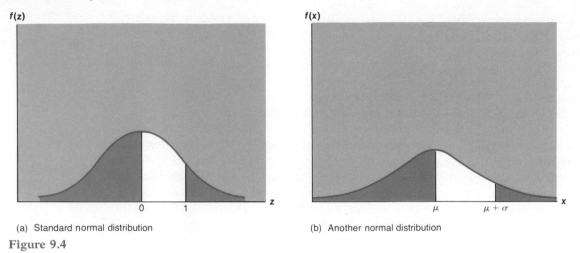

(a) Standard normal distribution

(b) Another normal distribution

Figure 9.4

The "standard" normal distribution and another normal distribution and their relationship

from 0 to 2 is equal to the area of the other curve over the interval from μ to $\mu + 2\sigma$, and so on. A simple method of evaluating areas under a normal curve now becomes possible. Suppose we document in a table the areas over alternative intervals for the "standard" distribution. Facing a problem concerning the area (probability) under some other normal distribution, we could then easily find the "corresponding" area under the standard distribution and derive the desired probability from the table.

To illustrate, suppose X is a random variable having a normal distribution with a mean of 500 and a standard deviation of 50, or $X \sim N(500, 50)$. And suppose we want to find the probability that a certain variable will assume a value in the interval from 500 to 575, or in symbolic notation, $P(500 \le X \le 575) = ?$ We realize that the value 500 is the mean of the distribution and thus corresponds to the value 0 of the standard normal distribution. The value 575 is 1.5 standard deviations (of 50 units each) to the right of 500 and therefore corresponds to the value $Z = 1.5$, so $P(500 \le X \le 575) = P(0 \le Z \le 1.5)$. As probabilities for any normal distribution can be calculated by means of the standard normal distribution, probability tables for Z variables alone are clearly sufficient.

In order to make efficient use of the standard distribution in calculating probabilities under any normal curve, we need to make two clarifications. First, we need to learn how to use the normal distribution table, so that once a question is formulated in terms of the variable Z, we know how to find the desired probability. Second, we need to find a fast computational method to enable us to switch from any value on the X scale to its corresponding value on the Z scale. Both of these procedures will now be discussed.

USING THE NORMAL DISTRIBUTION TABLE

We find probabilities concerning the standard normal variable Z by using the normal distribution table inside the back cover of this text. The table lists the areas accumulated under the normal curve, from the value zero up to a variety of Z values. For example, to find the area (probability) under the standard normal curve over the interval from 0 to 2, we go down the far left-hand column of the table (the column headed "Z") until we get to the value

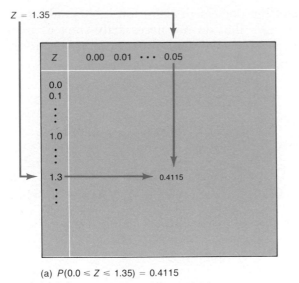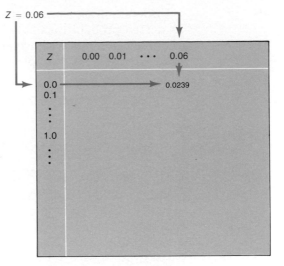

(a) $P(0.0 \leq Z \leq 1.35) = 0.4115$ (b) $P(0.0 \leq Z \leq 0.06) = 0.0239$

Figure 9.5

Using the normal distribution table

2.0. Moving one column to the right, we see the number 0.4772, which is the area under the standard normal curve over the desired range from 0 to 2. We thus conclude that

$$P(0 \leq Z \leq 2) = 0.4772$$

Suppose we now want to find the area over the interval that starts at 0 and ends at 1.35. We go down the left-hand column once again, but this time we go down to the value 1.3. To find the second decimal digit, we move to the right until we reach the column headed 0.05. The number we have located states the proper area: 0.4115. Figure 9.5*a* shows the location of the number 0.4115 in the table. Figure 9.5*b* shows how to find the area accumulated under the normal curve over the interval from 0.00 to 0.06.

Figure 9.6 demonstrates that a standard normal distribution's *Z score is measured along the horizontal axis and its probability is given by the area under the probability function and over the horizontal domain.*

Figure 9.6

Graphic presentation of probabilities under the "standard" normal distribution

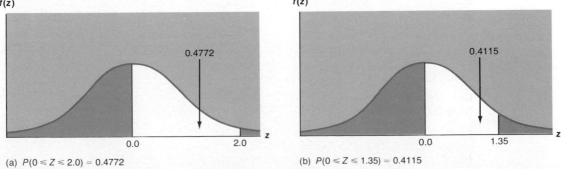

(a) $P(0 \leq Z \leq 2.0) = 0.4772$ (b) $P(0 \leq Z \leq 1.35) = 0.4115$

Understanding the structure of the normal distribution table enables us to derive probabilities over intervals that do not necessarily start at zero and over intervals with negative Z values. We shall illustrate the procedures used with several examples.

EXAMPLE 9.1

$$P(1.00 \leq Z \leq 2.15) = P(0.00 \leq Z \leq 2.15) - P(0.00 \leq Z \leq 1.00)$$

$$= 0.4842 - 0.3413$$

$$= 0.1429$$

This procedure becomes clear once we take a look at Figure 9.7. The light-colored area in Figure 9.7 is equal to the difference between the areas over the intervals from 0.00 to 2.15 and from 0.00 to 1.00. The probabilities 0.4842 and 0.3413 are taken directly from the normal distribution table.

Figure 9.7

Showing the probability $P(1.00 \leq Z \leq 2.15)$

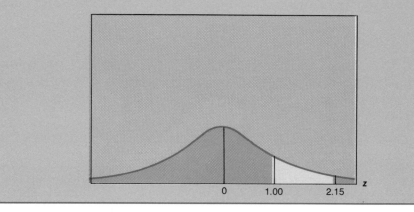

EXAMPLE 9.2

$$P(-1.60 \leq Z \leq 0.00) = P(0.00 \leq Z \leq 1.60)$$

$$= 0.4452$$

Here we simply take advantage of a well-known property of the standard normal distribution: it is symmetrical around zero. The area from -1.60 to 0.00 in Figure 9.8 is equal to the area over the symmetrical interval in the positive range.

Figure 9.8

Showing the probability $P(-1.60 \leq Z \leq 0.00)$

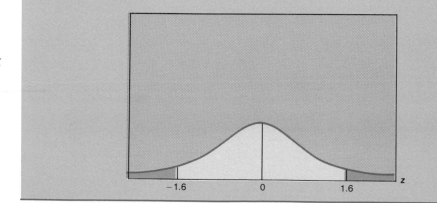

EXAMPLE 9.3

$$P(-0.93 \leq Z \leq -0.04) = P(0.04 \leq Z \leq 0.93)$$

$$= 0.3238 - 0.0160$$

$$= 0.3078$$

Once again we take advantage of the symmetry around zero. Then we use the procedure of Example 9.1 again (see Figure 9.9).

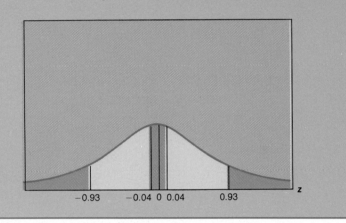

Figure 9.9

Showing the probability $P(-0.93 \leq Z \leq -0.04)$

EXAMPLE 9.4

$$P(Z \geq 0.85) = 0.5000 - P(0 \leq Z \leq 0.85)$$

$$= 0.5000 - 0.3023$$

$$= 0.1977$$

The total area to the right of zero in Figure 9.10 is 0.5, and thus the area to the right of $Z = 0.85$ is the complement (to 0.5) of the area over the range from 0.00 to 0.85.

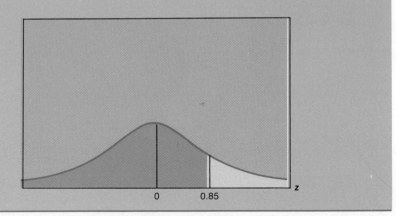

Figure 9.10

Showing the probability $P(Z \geq 0.85)$

EXAMPLE 9.5

$$P(-1.40 \leq Z \leq 2.50) = P(-1.40 \leq Z \leq 0.00) + P(0.00 \leq Z \leq 2.50)$$

$$= P(0.00 \leq Z \leq 1.40) + P(0.00 \leq Z \leq 2.50)$$

$$= 0.4192 + 0.4938$$

$$= 0.9130$$

Figure 9.11 makes it quite clear that the area over the range from -1.40 to 2.50 is equal to the sum of the areas over the intervals from -1.40 to 0.00 and from 0.00 to 2.50. The area over the interval from -1.40 to 0.00 is equal to that over the corresponding positive interval (0.00 to 1.40), which is given in the table.

Figure 9.11

Showing the probability $P(-1.40 \leq Z \leq 2.50)$

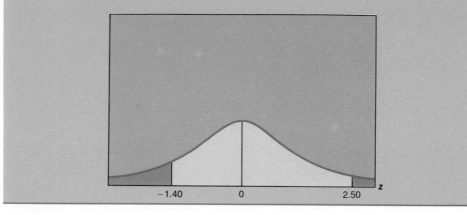

EXAMPLE 9.6

$$P(Z \leq -1.00) = P(Z \geq 1.00)$$

$$= 0.5000 - P(0.00 \leq Z \leq 1.00)$$

$$= 0.5000 - 0.3413$$

$$= 0.1587$$

We first realize that the area to the left of -1.0 in Figure 9.12 is equal to the area to the right of 1.0, and then we obtain the required probabilities from the table.

Figure 9.12

Showing the probability $P(Z \leq -1.00)$

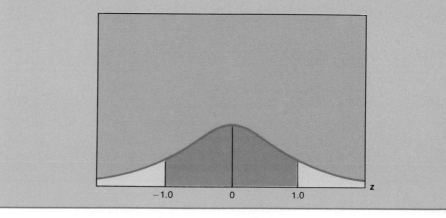

At this point we urge you to use the normal distribution table inside the back cover of the book to verify the following probabilities:

$$P(0.00 \le Z \le 1.24) = 0.3925$$
$$P(-2.00 \le Z \le -0.55) = 0.2684$$
$$P(Z \le -1.44) = 0.0749$$
$$P(-0.56 \le Z \le 0.56) = 0.4246$$
$$P(Z \le 1.67) = 0.9525$$
$$P(Z \le 0) = 0.5000$$
$$P(2.06 \le Z \le 3.06) = 0.0186$$
$$P(-1.00 \le Z \le 2.00) = 0.8185$$
$$P(-1.00 \le Z \le 0.50) = 0.5328$$
$$P(Z \le -1.50) = 0.0668$$

TRANSFORMING X VALUES INTO Z VALUES AND VICE VERSA

We now take another step toward the calculation of probabilities for any normal variable. Note that when we perform a linear transformation on a normal random variable, the transformed variable is also normally distributed. Therefore, a standardized normal variable has a standard normal distribution. Accordingly, when we take a normal variable, X, subtract its mean, and then divide by the standard deviation, we get a standard normal variable.

If

$$X \sim N(\mu, \sigma)$$

then[2]

$$\left(\frac{X - \mu}{\sigma}\right) \sim N(0, 1) \tag{9.1}$$

Thus we may write

$$Z = \frac{X - \mu}{\sigma} \tag{9.2}$$

[2] In Chapter 6, when we discussed linear transformation of random variables we saw that

$$E\left(\frac{X - \mu}{\sigma}\right) = \frac{1}{\sigma} E(X - \mu) = \frac{1}{\sigma}(\mu - \mu) = 0$$

and

$$V\left(\frac{X - \mu}{\sigma}\right) = \frac{1}{\sigma^2} V(X - \mu) = \frac{1}{\sigma^2} V(X) = \frac{\sigma^2}{\sigma^2} = 1$$

Since a standardized normal variable is normally distributed, we may write

$$\left(\frac{X - \mu}{\sigma}\right) \sim N(0, 1)$$

It follows that

$$X = \mu + \sigma Z \tag{9.3}$$

As Equation 9.2 can be used to find a Z value, given a specific value of X, so can Equation 9.3 be used to find an X value, given a specific value of Z. Given a problem concerning the probability of X, such as $P(X \le x)$, where x is any real number, we convert X into a Z variable by subtracting μ and then dividing by the standard deviation, σ:

$$P(X \le x) = P\left(\frac{X - \mu}{\sigma} \le \frac{x - \mu}{\sigma}\right) = P\left(Z \le \frac{x - \mu}{\sigma}\right) \tag{9.4}$$

The last probability on the right may be determined directly from the normal distribution table inside the back cover of the book.

To see in detail why Equation 9.4 is correct, consider the following:

If

$$X \le x$$

then

$$X - \mu \le x - \mu$$

and

$$\frac{X - \mu}{\sigma} \le \frac{x - \mu}{\sigma} \quad \text{(recall that } \sigma > 0\text{)}$$

From this we see that the probability that $X \le x$ is equal to the probability that $\dfrac{X - \mu}{\sigma} \le \dfrac{x - \mu}{\sigma}$, meaning that Equation 9.4 holds.

EXAMPLE 9.7

A machine pours soda into bottles. Suppose experience has shown that the weight of the soda poured is normally distributed and assume that the amount of soda by weight that is poured into each bottle is a normal random variable with a mean of 64 ounces and a standard deviation of 1.5 ounces. What is the probability that the amount of soda that the machine will pour into the next bottle will be more than 65 ounces? Following Equation 9.4, we write[3]

$$P(X \ge 65.0) = P\left(\frac{X - 64.0}{1.5} \ge \frac{65.0 - 64.0}{1.5}\right) = P(Z > 0.67) = 0.2514$$

To find the probability that the amount of soda will be less than 62.5 ounces, we calculate as follows:

$$P(X \le 62.5) = P\left(\frac{X - 64.0}{1.5} \le \frac{62.5 - 64.0}{1.5}\right) = P(Z \le -1.0) = 0.1587$$

[3] Note that for a continuous distribution the probabilities $P(X > 65)$ and $P(X \ge 65)$ are equal.

EXAMPLE 9.8

Continuing Example 9.7, we may ask, "What is the probability that the amount of soda in the next bottle will differ from the mean of 64 by at least 2 ounces?"

For this to happen, the bottle has to contain either less than 62 ounces or more than 66 ounces. In other words, we are asking $P(X \leq 62) + P(X \geq 66) = ?$ Once again we want to convert the problem into one dealing with the variable Z, and we proceed as follows:

$$P(X \leq 62) = P\left(\frac{X - 64.0}{1.5} \leq \frac{62.0 - 64.0}{1.5}\right) = P(Z \leq -1.33) = 0.0918$$

$$P(X \geq 66) = P\left(\frac{X - 64.0}{1.5} \geq \frac{66.0 - 64.0}{1.5}\right) = P(Z \geq 1.33) = 0.0918$$

Therefore

$$P(X \leq 62) + P(X \geq 66) = 0.0918 + 0.0918 = 0.1836$$

Let us recall for a moment the Empirical Rule, which is a rule of thumb for the dispersion of mound-shaped distributions around their mean. According to the rule, about 68 percent of the distribution should be in the range from $\mu - \sigma$ to $\mu + \sigma$, about 95 percent should be in the range from $\mu - 2\sigma$ to $\mu + 2\sigma$, and almost 100 percent of the distribution should be in the range from $\mu - 3\sigma$ to $\mu + 3\sigma$. The exact probabilities under the normal curve are 68.26 percent, 95.44 percent, and 99.73 percent, respectively. This, of course, is very close to what the Empirical Rule predicts.

FINDING FRACTILES UNDER THE NORMAL DISTRIBUTION

It is sometimes necessary to find fractiles under the normal distribution. For a random variable X, a **fractile** is *a value of X, such that the probability of X assuming values less than or equal to it, is a specified fraction.* (When the fractile is *expressed as a percentage*, it is called a **percentile**.) As an example, the 0.50 fractile, or the 50th percentile, of any normal distribution is its mean, μ.

When we have to find a certain fractile for a given normal distribution, we first find the fractile for the standard normal distribution in the standard

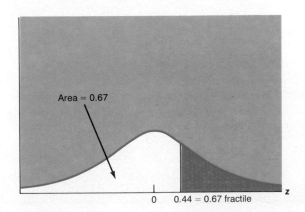

Figure 9.13

The 0.67 fractile on the standard normal distribution

normal distribution table. For example, the 0.67 fractile is that z value up to which the accumulated area is equal to 0.67 (accumulation going from left to right). The table shows that $z = 0.44$ is the 0.67 fractile (see Figure 9.13).

Once the fractile on the standard normal distribution has been determined, we use Equation 9.3 to derive the fractile for the distribution of X. We shall demonstrate this procedure with examples.

EXAMPLE 9.9

The inventory manager of a large firm estimates that the period of time (measured in days) that passes between the ordering of a given item and its actual receipt with regular delivery service (that is, not on an emergency delivery basis) is a random variable having a normal distribution, with a mean of six working days and a standard deviation of two working days. Find the 75th percentile of the distribution.

Our first step is to find the 75th percentile on the Z scale. The standard normal distribution table shows that the area over the range from 0.000 to 0.675 is approximately 0.25, but since there is an area equal to 0.50 over the negative range, the total area in the range from $-\infty$ to 0.675 is equal to 0.75. It follows that 0.675 is the 75th percentile on the Z scale. Using Equation 9.3, we get

$$x = \mu + z\sigma = 6.0 + (0.675 \cdot 2) = 6.0 + 1.35 = 7.35 \text{ days}$$

This means that 75 percent of the time, the delivery period is 7.35 days or less.

EXAMPLE 9.10

Find the 20th percentile of the distribution in Example 9.9. We again refer first to the standard distribution. Since it is symmetrical around zero, it follows that the 20th percentile must equal the negative magnitude of the 80th percentile. A glance at the Z table will reveal that the 80th percentile is equal to 0.84, and it follows that the 20th percentile equals -0.84. Equation 9.3 yields

$$x = \mu + z\sigma = 6 + (-0.84 \cdot 2) = 6 - 1.68 = 4.32 \text{ days}$$

EXAMPLE 9.11

Mrs. Joannie Yost has to be at work at 9 A.M. Commuting time is a random variable having a normal distribution, with a mean of 40 minutes and standard deviation of 10 minutes. If she wants to make sure she is not late for work more than 3 percent of the time, at what time does she have to leave home in the morning?

We first have to find the 97th percentile of the Z distribution. From the normal distribution table we find that this value is equal to 1.88. On the relevant (time) distribution, therefore, the 97th percentile is

$$x = \mu + \sigma z = 40 + (10 \cdot 1.88) = 40 + 18.8 \approx 59 \text{ minutes}$$

and so she must leave home at 8:01 in the morning.

9.3 The Normal Approximation to the Binomial Distribution

The binomial distribution was discussed in Chapter 8, and one method for its approximation (the Poisson distribution) has been discussed as well. In this section we present an approximation procedure that is useful particularly for approximating the cumulative binomial distribution over a given interval. Here we use the normal probability distribution to approximate the binomial probability distribution.

The idea is quite simple and the procedure for implementing it is straightforward. When we discussed the binomial distribution we noted that in all those cases where $np \geq 5$ and $nq \geq 5$, the general shape of the binomial distribution resembles the normal distribution shape. Since the mean and the standard deviation of the binomial distribution are np and $\sqrt{npq}$, respectively, we may write

If

$$X \sim B(n, p)$$

$$np \geq 5$$

$$nq \geq 5$$

then

$$X \simeq N(np, \sqrt{npq})$$

where $\simeq$ means "is approximately distributed." Furthermore, we can standardize the variable X to get the following equation:

$$Z = \frac{X - np}{\sqrt{npq}} \simeq N(0, 1) \qquad (9.5)$$

Before proceeding, let us illustrate the preceding argument with the help of a diagram. Let X be a binomial variable with 15 trials and a probability of success equal to 0.4, or in short, $X \sim B(15, 0.4)$. We first check on np and nq. In the case at hand, we find that $np = 15 \cdot 0.4 = 6$, which indeed is greater than 5, and $nq = 15 \cdot 0.6 = 9$, which is also greater than 5. In Figure 9.14 we plot the binomial probability distribution (omitting the tails) as a histogram, along with the normal density function.

The probability of each possible outcome is represented by the *area of the bar centered above it*. The width of each bar is equal to 1, so the area of the bar is equal to its height. For example, the probability that $X = 4$ is given in the diagram by the area of the bar centered on the value 4 (thus ranging from 3.5 to 4.5). The normal distribution that has been superimposed on the histogram has a mean of 6 ($= np$) and a standard deviation of 1.9 ($= \sqrt{npq}$). The area of the darkest box in Figure 9.14, which represents the exact probability that X will equal 4, *is fairly well approximated by the area under the normal curve over the range from 3.5 to 4.5*. Thus we write

$$P_B(X = 4) \approx P_N(3.5 \leq X \leq 4.5)$$

Figure 9.14

Binomial
probability
distribution,
plotted as a
histogram, on
the
background
of a normal
distribution

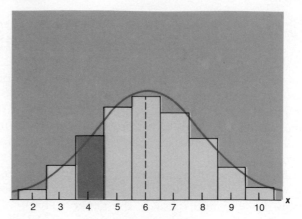

where the subscript B means "calculated by the binomial distribution" and the subscript N means "calculated by the normal distribution." In summary, we conclude that when we work under the assumption of a binomial distribution, the probability that X will equal 4 is approximately equal to the probability derived under the assumption of a normal distribution that X will take on values in the interval from 3.5 to 4.5. Since we also know that $X \simeq N(6, 1.9)$, we can proceed as follows:

$$P_B(X = 4) \approx P_N(3.5 \leq X \leq 4.5)$$

$$= P_N\left(\frac{3.5 - 6.0}{1.9} \leq \frac{X - 6.0}{1.9} \leq \frac{4.5 - 6.0}{1.9}\right)$$

$$= P_N(-1.32 \leq Z \leq -0.79)$$

$$= 0.1214 \qquad .$$

Assuming a binomial distribution, we find that

$$P(X = 4) = \binom{15}{4}(0.4^4)(0.6^{11}) = 1{,}365 \cdot 0.0256 \cdot 0.003628 = 0.1268$$

Indeed, the approximation is good. To find the probability that X will fall within the interval from 3 to 8 by means of the binomial distribution, we would have to go through very extensive calculations, since

$$P(3 \leq X \leq 8) = P(X = 3) + P(X = 4) + \cdots + P(X = 8)$$

and each term to the right of the equals sign has to be calculated by the binomial distribution equation. When we use the normal approximation procedure, however, the calculation is much easier. Figure 9.15 shows that the total area of the histogram bars centered over the values 3 through 8 is fairly well approximated by the normal curve over the range from 2.5 to 8.5, so we may write

$$P_B(3 \leq X \leq 8) \approx P_N(2.5 \leq X \leq 8.5)$$

$$= P_N\left(\frac{2.5 - 6.0}{1.9} \leq \frac{X - 6.0}{1.9} \leq \frac{8.5 - 6.0}{1.9}\right)$$

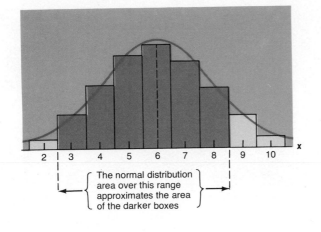

Figure 9.15

Binomial probability distribution, plotted as a histogram: the area of the six bars is approximated by the area under the normal curve over the interval from 2.5 to 8.5

$$= P_N(-1.84 \leq Z \leq 1.32)$$

$$= 0.8737$$

To calculate the probability $P(X > 4)$ we must first recognize that $P_B(X > 4) = P_B(X \geq 5)$. Therefore, the approximation works as follows:

$$P_B(X > 4) = P_B(X \geq 5) \approx P_N(X \geq 4.5)$$

$$= P\left(Z \geq \frac{4.5 - 6}{1.9}\right)$$

$$= P(Z \geq -0.789)$$

$$= 0.7849$$

Another example may be helpful.

EXAMPLE 9.12

If 10 percent of all business executives fill out a given marketing survey questionnaire, what is the probability of getting at least 15 questionnaires back out of 200 distributed to executives? What is the probability that between 23 and 33 (inclusive) questionnaires will be filled out?

Assuming that the decision to fill out the questionnaire is made independently by each executive, the number of questionnaires that will be filled out is a binomial random variable: $X \sim B(200, 0.1)$. Our first problem is $P(X \geq 15) = ?$ If we use the normal approximation, the solution comes rather easily. We first calculate the mean and the standard deviation of the variable:

$$E(X) = np = 200 \cdot 0.1 = 20$$

$$SD(X) = \sqrt{npq} = \sqrt{200 \cdot 0.1 \cdot 0.9} = \sqrt{18} = 4.24$$

Now

$$P_B(X \geq 15) \approx P_N(X \geq 14.50)$$

$$= P\left(\frac{X - 20.00}{4.24} \geq \frac{14.50 - 20.00}{4.24}\right)$$

$$= P(Z \geq -1.30)$$

$$= 0.9032$$

Next, to find the probability that between 23 and 33 questionnaires will be filled out, we compute

$$P_B(23 \leq X \leq 33) \approx P_N(22.5 \leq X \leq 33.5)$$

$$= P\left(\frac{22.50 - 20.00}{4.24} \leq \frac{X - 20.00}{4.24} \leq \frac{33.50 - 20.00}{4.24}\right)$$

$$= P(0.59 \leq Z \leq 3.18)$$

$$= 0.2769$$

9.4 APPLICATION:
THE "SAFETY-FIRST" PRINCIPLE AND INVESTMENT DECISIONS

Aside from the fact that we haven't the talent for it, most of us would reject Evel Knievel's glamorous way of once making a living primarily because of the high probability of what we might term disastrous consequences. A similar attitude is exhibited by firms in their investment decisions. They normally search for ways to increase their profits, but they tend to reject investment projects that are overly risky. The drive for survival will cause the firm to reject risky projects even at the price of foregoing a potentially high profit. This fact has been recognized by notable economists. In 1952, A. D. Roy wrote:

> Decisions taken in practice are less concerned with whether a little more of this or of that will yield the largest net increase in satisfaction than with avoiding known rocks of uncertain positions or with deploying forces so that, if there is an ambush around the next corner, total disaster is avoided.

He added:

> For large numbers of people some such idea of a *disaster* exists, and the principle of Safety First asserts that it is reasonable and probable in practice, that an individual will seek to reduce as far as is possible the chance of such a catastrophe occurring.[4]

Herbert A. Simon, the 1978 Nobel Prize winner in economics, who analyzed the objectives of the business firm, wrote that "the objectives of the entrepreneur are closely related to the *survival* of the organization." He also wrote, "If these two sets of contracts are sufficiently advantageous, the entrepreneur makes a profit and, what is perhaps more important for our purpose, the *organization remains in existence*."[5]

[4] A. D. Roy, "Safety First and the Holding of Assets," *Econometrica*, July 1952.
[5] Herbert A. Simon, *Administrative Behavior*, 2nd ed. (New York: Macmillan, 1959).

Richard M. Cyert and James G. March claim that an alternative goal to profit maximization is to "maximize the security level of the organization (i.e., the probability that the organization will survive over indefinite future)."[6]

Consider now three potential investment projects whose returns are denoted by X_1, X_2, and X_3, of which the firm needs to select only one. According to the safety-first rule, the firm will choose the investment that minimizes the probability of receiving income below D, the disaster level. Any income below D means a company catastrophe that may lead to the replacement of current management or to bankruptcy. In short, according to the safety-first rule, the focus is on the probabilities

$$P(X_1 < D)$$

$$P(X_2 < D)$$

$$P(X_3 < D)$$

Note that the value D is determined by the firm's management and varies from one firm to another. For some firms D could equal zero; for others it could be some positive value. For example, if the firm has some debt, D is likely to be positive: unless enough money is generated from the investment, the firm may be unable to pay its debt and may be forced into bankruptcy. At any rate, earnings that do not suffice to cover the interest will cause the stockholders to consider the investment a failure. Suppose the returns X_1, X_2, and X_3 (measured in millions of dollars) are normally distributed as follows:

$$X_1 \sim N(10.0, 10.0)$$

$$X_2 \sim N(8.0, 5.0)$$

$$X_3 \sim N(7.0, 4.2)$$

Of the three investments, we expect the highest profit from X_1 ($10 million), but X_1 is also the riskiest ($10 million standard deviation). The lowest profit is expected from X_3 ($7 million), but its risk as measured by the standard deviation is the lowest ($4.2 million). Investment X_2 is in between, with respect to both expected value and standard deviation. Denoting the respective means and standard deviations by μ_1, μ_2, μ_3, σ_1, σ_2, and σ_3, we have

$$\mu_1 > \mu_2 > \mu_3$$

$$\sigma_1 > \sigma_2 > \sigma_3$$

Suppose that if the income generated from the chosen project is less than $3 million, the firm will face disaster. In that case, $D = 3$, and by the safety-first rule, the investment with the lowest probability $P(X < D)$ should be chosen. Recalling our assumption that X_1, X_2, and X_3 are normally distributed, we get

$$P(X_1 < D) = P(X_1 < 3) = P\left(\frac{X_1 - 10}{10} < \frac{3 - 10}{10}\right) = P(Z < -0.70) = 0.2420$$

$$P(X_2 < D) = P(X_2 < 3) = P\left(\frac{X_2 - 8}{5} < \frac{3 - 8}{5}\right) = P(Z < -1.00) = 0.1587$$

$$P(X_3 < D) = P(X_3 < 3) = P\left(\frac{X_3 - 7}{4.2} < \frac{3 - 7}{4.2}\right) = P(Z < -0.95) = 0.1711$$

[6] Richard M. Cyert and James G. March, *Behavioral Theory of the Firm* (Englewood Cliffs, N.J.: Prentice-Hall, 1963).

Thus the second project, which has the smallest probability of disaster, should be selected.

BAUMOL'S "EXPECTED GAIN-CONFIDENCE LIMIT" CRITERION

Although the safety-first criterion is an important rule for investment decisions, we must note that it gives consideration exclusively to the *safety* of investment. William J. Baumol suggested a similar rule that puts more weight on the project's profitability.[7] Baumol asserts that investment in one project whose return is X_1 is better than another whose return is X_2 if the following *two* conditions are met:

$$\mu_1 > \mu_2$$

$$L_1 > L_2$$

where

$$L_1 \equiv \mu_1 - k\sigma_1$$

$$L_2 \equiv \mu_2 - k\sigma_2$$

μ_1 and σ_1 are the expected return and standard deviation of X_1, and μ_2 and σ_2 are the corresponding parameters of X_2. The constant k is determined by the firm. The criterion, then, asserts that X_1 is better than X_2 if $\mu_1 > \mu_2$ *and* $L_1 > L_2$. Specifying $k = 2$, for example, and reexamining our three previous investment projects, X_1, X_2, and X_3, we now compute

$$L_1 = \mu_1 - 2\sigma_1 = 10.0 - 2 \cdot 10.0 = -10.0$$

$$L_2 = \mu_2 - 2\sigma_2 = 8.0 - 2 \cdot 5.0 = -2.0$$

$$L_3 = \mu_3 - 2\sigma_3 = 7.0 - 2 \cdot 4.2 = -1.4$$

Comparing X_1 to X_2, we get

$$\mu_1 = 10 > 8 = \mu_2$$

and

$$L_1 = -10 < -2 = L_2$$

so it is not clear which of the two is better. Comparing X_1 to X_3, we find that

$$\mu_1 = 10 > 7 = \mu_3$$

$$L_1 = -10 < -1.4 = L_3$$

Again it is not clear which of the two is a better investment. Finally we compare X_2 and X_3 and see that

$$\mu_2 = 8 > 7 = \mu_3$$

$$L_2 = -2.0 < -1.4 = L_3$$

so that none of them can be said to be definitely better than the others.

[7] William J. Baumol, "An Expected Gain-Confidence Limit Criterion for Portfolio Selection," *Management Science*, October 1963.

While the second project is the best of the three according to the safety-first criterion, the expected gain-confidence limit criterion could not, in this particular example, single out any of the three as the best investment project. Selection among the three in this case is left to management or to the financial analyst, who will apply more sophisticated investment analysis.

Chapter Summary and Review

Distribution	Density function	Mean	Standard deviation	Skewness
1. Normal	$f(x) = \dfrac{1}{\sigma\sqrt{2\pi}} \cdot e^{-\frac{1}{2}[(x - \mu)/\sigma]^2}$	μ	σ	0
2. Standard normal	$f(z) = \dfrac{1}{\sqrt{2\pi}} \cdot e^{-\frac{1}{2}z^2}$	0	1	0

Rules for Calculating Probabilities of Normal Variables (assume $a < b$)

1. $P(a \leq X \leq b) = P\left(\dfrac{a - \mu}{\sigma} \leq \dfrac{X - \mu}{\sigma} \leq \dfrac{b - \mu}{\sigma}\right) = P\left(\dfrac{a - \mu}{\sigma} \leq Z \leq \dfrac{b - \mu}{\sigma}\right)$

2. $P(Z \leq -a) = 1 - P(Z \leq a)$

3. $P(a \leq Z \leq b) = P(Z \leq b) - P(Z \leq a)$

4. $P(Z \geq a) = 1 - P(Z \leq a)$

Problems

9.1. Calculate the following probabilities concerning the standard normal distribution.

(a) $P(Z \geq 0.50)$
(b) $P(Z \leq 2.30)$
(c) $P(Z \geq -1.50)$
(d) $P(0.60 \leq Z \leq 0.65)$

(e) $P(Z \leq -1.10)$
(f) $P(Z \leq -2.50)$
(g) $P(Z \geq -4.00)$

9.2. If a random variable has a standard normal distribution, find the probability that it will take on a value

(a) Greater than 1
(b) Smaller than 1
(c) Greater than -0.50
(d) Smaller than 1.645
(e) Between 0.95 and 1.05

9.3. Calculate the following probabilities for X, where X is normally distributed with a mean of 120 and standard deviation of 20.

(a) $P(X \geq 140)$
(b) $P(X \leq 105)$
(c) $P(X \leq 145)$
(d) $P(107 \leq X \leq 128)$

(e) $P(X \leq 80)$
(f) $P(122 \leq X \leq 130)$
(g) $P(100 \leq X \leq 115)$

9.4. Find the value z_α, such that the area under the standard normal curve to the right of z_α is equal to α. Assume the following values of α:

    (*a*) 0.05
    (*b*) 0.10
    (*c*) 0.50

9.5. The variable X is normally distributed with a mean of 70 and standard deviation of 8. Find

    (*a*) The 50th percentile
    (*b*) The 20th percentile
    (*c*) The 90th percentile

9.6. The annual income of high school graduates in their first year at work is normally distributed, with a mean of $6,000 and standard deviation of $800. One youth is picked at random from this population. Find the probabilities that the youth's income

    (*a*) Is less than $5,000
    (*b*) Exceeds $7,500
    (*c*) Is less than $7,000
    (*d*) Is between $5,500 and $5,900
    (*e*) Is between $5,400 and $8,600

9.7. If the bottom 5 percent of wage earners in the population referred to in Problem 9.6 is to receive a pay raise, what is the income level below which a youth will receive a pay raise?

9.8. Suppose $X \sim N(10, 1)$ and $Y \sim N(8, \frac{1}{2})$. Which of the following events has a greater probability? Show your calculations.

    (*a*) X will be greater than 12.
    (*b*) Y will be smaller than 6.5.

9.9. A normal distribution has a mean $\mu = 10$. It is given that 5 percent of the area under the curve is to the right of the value 11.645. Calculate

    (*a*) The area to the left of 8.0
    (*b*) The area to the right of 10.5
    (*c*) The area to the right of 10.0

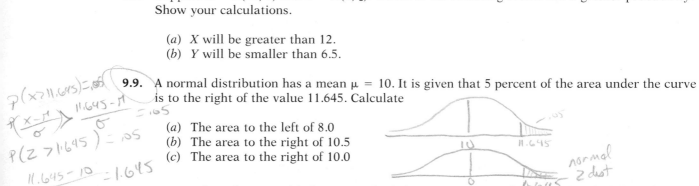

9.10. A normal random variable has a standard deviation $\sigma = 10$. If there is a probability of 0.8888 that the random variable will take on a value less than 100, what is the probability that it will take on a value greater than 110?

9.11. The weight of oranges received from a given orange grove is normally distributed with a mean $\mu = 6$ ounces per orange and a standard deviation $\sigma = 2$ ounces per orange.

    (*a*) What percentage of these oranges weigh more than 7 ounces?
    (*b*) Suppose only oranges that weigh at least 6.5 ounces can be graded "fancy." What percentage of the oranges meet this standard?

9.12. If 20 percent of all families own at least two cars, what is the probability of finding 250 or more families who own at least two cars in a random sample of 1,000 families?

9.13. The random variable X is distributed normally with an unknown mean and a standard deviation of 20. Find the mean if $P(X \le 60) = 0.05$.

9.14. The random variable X is distributed normally with an unknown standard deviation and a mean of 100. Find the standard deviation if $P(X \geq 110) = 0.16$.

9.15. Fly-South Airlines flies several times a week from New York City to Montevideo. All flights are scheduled to leave New York at 10 A.M. The flight's duration is a random variable with a normal distribution, a mean of 10 hours, and a standard deviation of a half-hour. Assume that a given plane leaves New York exactly on time.

   (a) What is the probability that the plane will arrive at Montevideo *after* 8:30 P.M. New York time?
   (b) What is the probability that the arrival time will be between 7:45 P.M. and 8:30 P.M. New York time?
   (c) Does the assumption that the flight's duration is normally distributed sound reasonable to you? Explain.

9.16. Mr. Investor has $1,000 that he wishes to invest in common stock. His broker recommends two stocks, A and B. Both have a normal distribution of returns, as follows:

$$X_A \sim N(1,100; 40)$$

$$X_B \sim N(1,140; 50)$$

Mr. Investor wants to select only *one* stock of the two. Obviously, Stock B has a higher expected return ($1,140 versus $1,100 for Stock A). Stock B, however, is more risky in the sense that the standard deviation of B's return is greater than that of A ($50 versus $40). Mr. Investor wants to choose the stock that has the smaller probability of returning less than $1,000. Which stock should Mr. Investor choose?

9.17. An investor has to choose between two investments whose returns are X_1 and X_2. It is known that

$$X_1 \sim N(8\%, 10\%)$$

$$X_2 \sim N(7\%, 9\%)$$

The investor wants to minimize the probability of earning less than 5 percent. Which of these two investments should she select?

9.18. Mr. and Mrs. Harris want to get a mortgage on a house they are buying. The bank offers them two alternative financing schemes:

   1. To pay a flat 12 percent interest on the mortgage
   2. To pay a variable rate that will go up or down according to market conditions

They think that under the second alternative the expected value of the rate is 10.3 percent and its standard deviation is 0.8. They will take the second alternative only if the probability that they will pay less than 12 percent is at least twice as great as the probability that they will have to pay more than 12 percent. Which alternative should they choose? Show your calculations. Assume that the variable interest rate is normally distributed.

9.19. Mr. and Mrs. Douglas are buying a home. They went to two banks to inquire about a mortgage. Both banks have offered them a variable rate of interest that will vary according to market conditions. The terms of the two offers they received were different, and they estimated as follows:

   1. The expected value and standard deviation of the interest rate they will have to pay if they accept the offer of Bank A are 12.4 and 2.6, respectively.

2. The expected value and standard deviation of the interest rate they will have to pay if they accept the offer of Bank *B* are 13.0 and 1.8, respectively.

They decide to choose the offer under which the probability that the rate of interest will go over 14.6 percent is lower. Which offer should they accept?

9.20. Mr. Ritchy is not a professional photographer, and 10 percent of the pictures he takes are of unsatisfactory quality. If he takes 36 pictures, what is the probability that between 2 and 6 of them (inclusive) are of unsatisfactory quality? Use the normal approximation to the binomial distribution in solving this problem.

9.21. A department store is considering a direct-mail advertising campaign. For simplicity, assume that each person who shops at the store brings a profit of $4 before considering the cost of advertising. If printing and mailing the ads costs the store $720 and 10,000 ads are mailed out, what is the probability that the advertising campaign will be profitable to the store? Assume that 2 percent of the people who receive the ad go shopping at the store. Use the normal approximation to the binomial distribution to solve this problem.

9.22. If 20 percent of all the clothing purchased at a given department store is returned to the store within 7 days of purchase, what is the probability that of 160 articles of clothing sold on a given day, between 25 and 35 (inclusive) will be returned within 7 days?

9.23. The XYZ company extends credit to new customers only if they pass the company's test for reliability. However, 3 percent of new customers who pass the test are found to be unreliable (that is, they pay late or not at all). If 500 new customers are approved for credit after the reliability test, what is the probability that between 10 and 20 (inclusive) customers are unreliable?

9.24. (*a*) Find the probability that $Z \geq 1.96$, where Z is the standard normal random variable.
(*b*) Find the probability that $Z^2 \geq 3.84$. Note that $1.96^2 = 3.84$.

Keep the answers in mind when you read about the chi-square distribution in Chapter 10.

9.25. Assume that $X \sim N(\mu, \sigma)$ where $\mu = 0$ and $\sigma = 1$.

(*a*) Calculate the probability of outcomes within k standard deviations from the mean, assuming alternatively that $k = 1.5, 2, 3,$ and 4.
(*b*) Suppose $\mu = 0$ and $\sigma = 1$, but the probability distribution is unknown. Use Chebyshev's theorem (Chapter 6) to calculate the probability of part *a* above. Compare the results of parts *a* and *b*. What can you conclude from this comparison?
(*c*) Employ the Empirical Rule (Chapter 6) to predict the probability of outcomes within 1, 2, and 3 standard deviations from the mean. Compare your answers to the actual probabilities under the normal curve. Is the Empirical Rule useful for populations whose distributions are normal? Explain.

APPENDIX 9A:
Properties of the Normal Distribution

The normal density function is given mathematically by

$$f(x) = \frac{1}{\sigma\sqrt{2\pi}} \cdot e^{-\frac{1}{2}[(x-\mu)/\sigma]^2} \qquad \begin{matrix} -\infty < \mu < \infty \\ \sigma > 0 \\ -\infty < x < \infty \end{matrix}$$

where π is the ratio of the circumference to the diameter of a circle and is approximately equal to 3.1416, and e is the limit of $\left(1 + \dfrac{1}{n}\right)^n$ for n approaching infinity and is approximately equal to 2.7183.

Since π and e are constants, the function has only two parameters: μ and σ. Note the following properties of the function:

1. Since there is a negative sign to the power of e, the smaller the value $\dfrac{1}{2}\left(\dfrac{x - \mu}{\sigma}\right)^2$, the greater $f(x)$. Indeed, for $x = \mu$, this term reaches its lowest value, zero, and therefore $f(x)$ obtains its maximum. Thus, $x = \mu$ is the mode of the normal distribution.

2. Since the term $\dfrac{x - \mu}{\sigma}$ is squared, we get the same value for $f(x)$ whether x is m units below μ or m units above μ. Take $m = 5$, for example, and assume $\mu = 10$ and $\sigma = 1$. Both $x = 15$ and $x = 5$ give us the same value of $f(x)$, as shown below:

$$\text{For } x = 15 \quad \left(\frac{x - \mu}{\sigma}\right)^2 = \left(\frac{15 - 10}{1}\right)^2 = 25$$

$$\text{For } x = 5 \quad \left(\frac{x - \mu}{\sigma}\right)^2 = \left(\frac{5 - 10}{1}\right)^2 = 25$$

Thus, $f(x)$ is symmetrical around μ.

3. Since the distribution $f(x)$ is symmetrical, the mode $x = \mu$ is also the mean and the median of the distribution.

4. For a given σ, the higher the mean (μ) of the function, the more the central location parameters (mean, mode, median) shift to the right, and so does the entire distribution.

5. Analyzing the effects of changes in σ (for a given μ) is a little more complicated; σ appears in $f(x)$ both in the denominator (that is, in the term $\dfrac{1}{\sigma\sqrt{2\pi}}$) and in the power of e.

When σ rises, the first term decreases. On the other hand, since $e^{-\frac{1}{2}[(x - \mu)/\sigma]^2}$ may be written as $1/e^{\frac{1}{2}[(x - \mu)/\sigma]^2}$, it is clear that when σ increases, this last term increases as well. Thus, unlike the increase in μ, an increase in σ leads to two conflicting factors, and we cannot unambiguously determine if $f(x)$ increases or decreases. We can assert, however, that for values relatively close to μ, the importance of a change in σ on the term $e^{-\frac{1}{2}[(x - \mu)/\sigma]^2}$ is small, and therefore the change in the first term dominates: $f(x)$ will decrease. Thus, for example, in the extreme case, where $x = \mu$, the importance of a change in σ on the second term is zero and only the change in the first term has an impact. Therefore, when $x = \mu$, an increase in σ causes a decrease in $f(x)$. For values of x far below or above μ, the opposite holds: an increase in σ brings an increase in $f(x)$. Comparing two normal distributions with the same mean and different standard deviations, we find a relationship like that shown in Figure 9A.1.

Figure 9A.1

Comparing
two normal
distributions
with equal
means and
unequal
standard
deviations

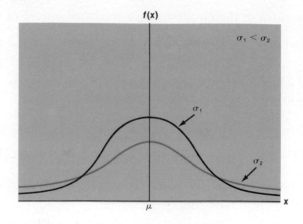

6. The probability that the random variable will be greater than some value, a, or that it will fall between two values, a and b, is simply the related area under the curve $f(x)$. We calculate this area by taking the integral of $f(x)$. Let us consider a few examples:

   (a) The probability that X will be smaller than value a is given by

$$F(a) = P(X \leq a) = \int_{-\infty}^{a} f(x)\, dx$$

   (b) The probability that X falls between some two values, a and b $(b > a)$, is

$$P(a \leq X \leq b) = \int_{a}^{b} f(x)\, dx$$

   This can be written also as $F(b) - F(a)$.

   (c) The probability that X will be greater than some value a is

$$P(X > a) = \int_{a}^{\infty} f(x)\, dx = 1 - \int_{-\infty}^{a} f(x)\, dx = 1 - F(a)$$

   (d) The probability that X will be less than or equal to some value $-a$ is

$$P(X \leq -a) = \int_{-\infty}^{-a} f(x)\, dx = \int_{a}^{\infty} f(x)\, dx = 1 - F(a)$$

   (e) By the definition of probability

$$\int_{-\infty}^{\infty} f(x)\, dx = 1$$

7. Calculating the integral of $f(x)$ is not a simple task. Of course, one could calculate it for an individual pair of μ and σ and prepare the appropriate table of probabilities. But this still would not suffice, since for

each pair of μ and σ we would need a separate table: an infinite number of tables to cover every possibility.

To relieve us of the need to embark on this impossible task, there is a table that, along with a simple transformation, provides the information required to calculate all such probabilities. This table is the normal distribution table with mean equal to zero ($\mu = 0$) and standard deviation equal to 1 ($\sigma = 1$). To illustrate, suppose that we have a normal distribution with $\mu = 10$ and $\sigma = 5$ and we want to calculate the probability that $X \leq 15$. Thus we are looking for the probability $P(X \leq 15)$. But the following events are identical:

Event A $X \leq 15$

Event B $X - 10 \leq 15 - 10$

Event C $\dfrac{X - 10}{5} \leq \dfrac{15 - 10}{5}$

When event A holds, event B holds, and vice versa. Whenever A occurs, C occurs, and vice versa. Thus, events A, B, and C are identical and therefore have the same probabilities: $P(A) = P(B) = P(C)$. However,

$P(C) = P\left[\left(\dfrac{X - \mu}{\sigma} \right) \leq \left(\dfrac{15 - 10}{5} \right) \right]$, or $P(Z \leq 1)$. Thus, concerning our-

selves with the original distribution with $\mu = 10$ and $\sigma = 5$, we turn our attention to the standardized normal distribution, Z, and ponder the probability that $Z \leq 1$. Since we can calculate any probability by shifting to the Z distribution, one table is sufficient for all normal distributions. Note that the expected value of Z is given by $E(Z) =$

$E\left(\dfrac{X - \mu}{\sigma} \right) = \dfrac{1}{\sigma} E(X - \mu) = \dfrac{1}{\sigma}[E(X) - \mu]$, but since $E(X) = \mu$, we get

$E(Z) = 0$.

The variance of Z is calculated as follows:

$$V(Z) = V\left(\dfrac{X - \mu}{\sigma} \right) = \dfrac{1}{\sigma^2} V(X - \mu)$$

$$= \dfrac{1}{\sigma^2} V(X) = \dfrac{\sigma^2}{\sigma^2} = 1$$

Recall that $V(X - \mu) = V(X)$ since μ is a constant.

Thus, the parameters of the distribution of Z are $\mu = 0$ and $\sigma = 1$.

OTHER CONTINUOUS DISTRIBUTIONS

A general discussion of continuous probability distributions has already been provided in Chapter 6. In addition, two important continuous distributions have been analyzed in detail: the uniform distribution (Chapter 6) and the normal distribution (Chapter 9). In this chapter we introduce four additional important continuous probability distributions: the exponential distribution, the chi-square distribution, the Student *t* distribution, and the *F* distribution. Our discussion will include descriptions of these distributions, their major properties, the use of their respective tables, and a brief discussion of the interrelationships among the normal, chi-square, Student *t*, and *F* distributions.

10.1 The Exponential Distribution

The Poisson probability distribution, which was introduced in Chapter 8, provides the probability of obtaining a given number of "successes" in a continuous dimension, such as time or space. The closely related **exponential distribution** is the *interval of time or space it takes to get the first "success."* For example, if the number of traffic accidents in an interval of time follows the Poisson distribution, then the length of time from one accident to another follows the exponential distribution.

The exponential distribution is extremely useful in business statistics: it applies to the length of time that must pass before the first incoming telephone call, the length of time it takes until the first customer enters a store, the length of time before a public phone is used, the length of time one must wait for a cab in a given location, or the distance to the next defect when a bolt of cloth has an average of λ defects per yard.

Denoting the mean rate at which events occur over time or space by λ and the time duration or distance to the first "success" by t, we can write the following:

THE EXPONENTIAL DENSITY FUNCTION

$$f(t) = \begin{cases} 0 & \text{for } t < 0 \\ \lambda e^{-\lambda t} & \text{for } t \geq 0 \end{cases} \qquad \textbf{(10.1)}$$

where e is the previously mentioned mathematical constant that equals approximately 2.7183 and λ is the parameter of the distribution: $\lambda > 0$.

The "less than" form of the cumulative probability distribution function is given by the following:

$$P(T \leq t) = \begin{cases} 0 & \text{for } t < 0 \\ 1 - e^{-\lambda t} & \text{for } t \geq 0 \end{cases} \qquad \textbf{(10.2)}$$

where T is the random variable of which t is a specific value.

The "greater than" form of the cumulative distribution is as follows: for values $t \leq 0$ we have $P(T \leq t) = 0$, which means that $P(T > t) = 1 - 0 = 1$. For values $t \geq 0$ we have $P(T \leq t) = 1 - e^{-\lambda t}$, which means that $P(T > t) = 1 - (1 - e^{-\lambda t}) = e^{-\lambda t}$. We therefore summarize:

$$P(T > t) = \begin{cases} 1 & \text{for } t < 0 \\ e^{-\lambda t} & \text{for } t \geq 0 \end{cases} \qquad \textbf{(10.3)}$$

Figure 10.1 represents two exponential density functions, for which λ equals 2 and $\frac{1}{2}$ alternatively, and Figures 10.2*a* and 10.2*b* represent the corresponding "less than" and "greater than" cumulative probability functions for the respective alternative values of λ. From Figures 10.1 and 10.2 we see that the densest area of the distribution is in the vicinity of $t = 0$ and it gets less dense as t gets larger.

Figure 10.1

Two exponential density functions specified by two alternative values of λ

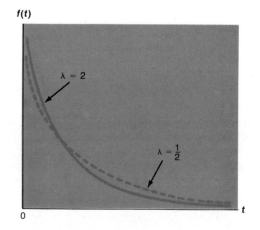

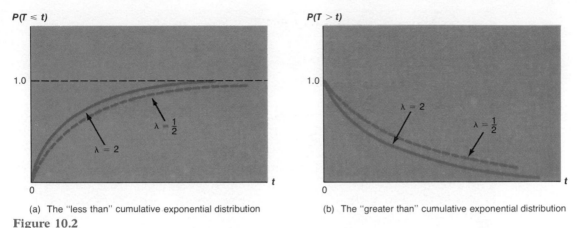

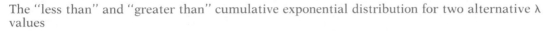

(a) The "less than" cumulative exponential distribution   (b) The "greater than" cumulative exponential distribution

Figure 10.2

The "less than" and "greater than" cumulative exponential distribution for two alternative λ values

Note that there is a relationship between the exponential and the Poisson distributions, despite the fact that one is continuous and the other is discrete. The relationship is analogous to the relationship between the geometric and the binomial distributions. In the case of the binomial distribution, we conduct an experiment that consists of a given number of trials and measure the number of successes. The geometric distribution measures the number of trials that are required before the first success occurs. Similarly, the Poisson distribution measures the number of successes in a given time, space, or volume unit, while the exponential distribution measures the time, space, or volume up to the first success. It can be shown that the mean and the variance of T are

$$E(T) = \frac{1}{\lambda}$$

$$V(T) = \frac{1}{\lambda^2}$$

(10.4)

Let us examine the use of the exponential distribution in a few examples.

EXAMPLE 10.1

Suppose telephone calls are arriving at a rate of 4 per minute (that is, *on the average* four calls arrive per minute). If we assume that the calls are independent of each other, then the time intervals between calls follow the exponential distribution. What is the probability that the next call will arrive within $\frac{1}{2}$ minute? within $1\frac{1}{2}$ minutes?

Following Equation 10.2 and specifying $\lambda = 4$, we get

$$P(T \leq 0.50) = 1 - e^{-4(0.50)} = 1 - e^{-2}$$

Table A.3 in Appendix A at the end of the book indicates that $e^{-2} = 0.135$, a value you can easily obtain on almost any scientific calculator. Therefore

$$P(T \le 0.50) = 1 - 0.135 = 0.865$$

Similarly, for $t = 1.5$ we get

$$P(T \le 1.5) = 1 - e^{-4(1.5)} = 1 - e^{-6} = 1 - 0.00248 = 0.99752$$

Thus, there is a probability of 86.50 percent that the first call will arrive within $\frac{1}{2}$ minute and about 99.75 percent that the first call will arrive within $1\frac{1}{2}$ minutes.

To see the relationship between the exponential and the Poisson distributions, let us find the probability that the first call will not arrive within the next $\frac{1}{2}$ minute. Using the exponential distribution we calculate

$$P(T > 0.50) = e^{-\lambda t} = e^{-4(0.50)} = e^{-2} = 0.135$$

We can also calculate this probability by using the Poisson distribution, requiring that the number of calls arriving in the first $\frac{1}{2}$ minute is zero. Since the average rate of calls is 2 per $\frac{1}{2}$ minute, we set

$$P(X = 0) = \frac{2^0 e^{-2}}{0!} = e^{-2} = 0.135$$

which is, of course, the same result as we obtained using the exponential distribution.

EXAMPLE 10.2

On September 23, 1976, a failure in the sound system occurred during the first televised debate between former president Gerald Ford and presidential candidate Jimmy Carter. The failure, which lasted for about a half hour, interrupted the debate for the approximately 90 million viewers. Suppose the sound-system time distribution up to the next failure is exponential, with an average failure rate of 1 in 10 hours.

(a) What is the probability that a system will fail during a 3-hour event?
(b) Suppose that a backup system with the same time distribution between failures automatically takes over in case of a failure and that this backup system is totally independent of the first system. If a half-hour-long failure occurs in the first system, what is the probability that during this failure the backup system will also fail?

Let us first solve part *a*. The "less than" cumulative function is $P(T \le t) = 1 - e^{-\lambda t}$. In our case, the average number of failures in an hour is $\frac{1}{10}$, so we get $\lambda = \frac{1}{10}$. Since the event is expected to last 3 hours, the probability of a failure during the event is

$$P(T \le 3) = 1 - e^{-(1/10) \cdot 3} = 1 - e^{-0.30} = 1 - 0.7408 = 0.2592$$

Note that the unit of time for which λ is defined is of no consequence to the final solution. We could just as easily solve the problem by using minutes rather than hours. We would simply express λ as the average number of failures per minute and get $\lambda = \dfrac{1}{10 \cdot 60} = \dfrac{1}{600}$. There are 180 minutes in three hours, so

$$P(T \le 180) = 1 - e^{-(1/600) \cdot 180} = 1 - e^{-0.30} = 0.2592$$

which is identical to our earlier result.

To solve part *b*, we assume a half-hour-long failure of the first system and a backup system with the same time-between-failures distribution. The probability of a failure of the backup system during a half-hour period is therefore

$$P(T \le 0.50) = 1 - e^{-(1/10) \cdot 0.50} = 1 - e^{-0.05} = 1 - 0.9512 = 0.0488$$

We can further calculate the probability that both systems will fail: $0.2592 \cdot 0.0488 = 0.01265$, where this probability *assumes* that the failure of the first system will last a half hour and that the backup system is totally independent of the main system.

EXAMPLE 10.3

A large new factory is contemplating a contingency plan for coping with potential power failures. It is estimated that a power failure causes $50,000 in damages. The factory is open 120 hours per week and power failures occur at an average rate of $\lambda = 0.003$ per hour. The purchase of a backup generator at a cost of $25,000 is considered. Should the generator be purchased?

Let us first find the probability of having a power failure in a given week:

$$P(T \le 120) = 1 - e^{-0.003 \cdot 120} = 1 - e^{-0.36} = 1 - 0.698 = 0.302$$

The expected damage in one week due to power failure is $50,000 \cdot 0.302 = \$15,100$. This amount is less than the cost of the generator, but when a longer period than one week is considered, we may find that the generator is well worth its purchase price. Take a four-week period (480 hours), for example. The failure probability is

$$P(T \le 480) = 1 - e^{-0.003 \cdot 480} = 1 - e^{-1.44} = 1 - 0.237 = 0.763$$

Even if we do not consider the possibility of more than one failure in any one week, the expected damage is $50,000 \cdot 0.763 = \$38,150$, a sum that justifies the purchase of the generator. Buying the generator is particularly wise under these conditions, since operating cost is negligible and it can be expected to remain in working order far beyond the first four weeks.

10.2 The Chi-Square Distribution

An important continuous probability distribution with wide applications is the chi-square distribution. Given a normally distributed random variable $X \sim N(\mu, \sigma)$, the *probability distribution of the squared deviation of the variable from its mean* can be analyzed by the **chi-square distribution**. Also, the sum of the squared deviations of each of a number of independent normal variables from their respective means can be analyzed by the chi-square distribution. The details of the actual use of the chi-square distribution are described in Chapters 12, 13, and 15.

The particular shape of the chi-square function, like that of the exponential probability function, depends on one parameter alone. The parameter that specifies the chi-square distribution is known as the **degrees of freedom** of the distribution (often denoted *df*), and it represents the number of random variables inherent within the chi-square variable.[1] A chi-square variable with n degrees of freedom is denoted by $\chi^{2(n)}$. As the chi-square variable is a squared magnitude or the sum of squared magnitudes, it can assume only positive values, and thus it is located over the positive range of real numbers. The distribution is unimodal and skewed to the right. Figure 10.3 depicts some chi-square distributions. As we can see, the higher the number of degrees of freedom, the farther the probability distribution stretches toward the right.

A notation we will use in many applications is the $\chi^{2(n)}$ symbol with a subscript α (that is, $\chi^{2(n)}_{\alpha}$), which indicates the $\chi^{2(n)}$ value (or score) that bounds a right-tail area equal to α. For example, $\chi^{2(10)}_{0.05}$ is the value that bounds a 5 percent right-hand tail under the $\chi^{2(10)}$ distribution. Since the total area under any chi-square distribution is equal to 1, it follows that the area under the curve to the left of $\chi^{2(n)}_{\alpha}$ must equal $1 - \alpha$. Figure 10.4 illustrates the location

Figure 10.3

Some chi-square density functions

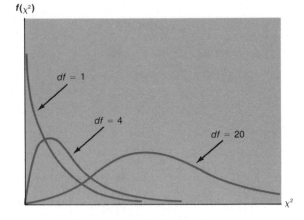

$f(\chi^2)$

$df = 1$

$df = 4$

$df = 20$

χ^2

---

[1] If Z is a standard normal variable, then Z^2 has a chi-square distribution with *one* degree of freedom. If Z_1 and Z_2 are two *independent* standard normal variables, then the variable $Z_1^2 + Z_2^2$ has a chi-square distribution with two degrees of freedom. Denoting a chi-square variable with n degrees of freedom by $\chi^{2(n)}$, we may write

$$\chi^{2(n)} = Z_1^2 + Z_2^2 + \cdots + Z_n^2 = \sum_{i=1}^{n} Z_i^2$$

where all the Z variables are *independent* standard normal variables.

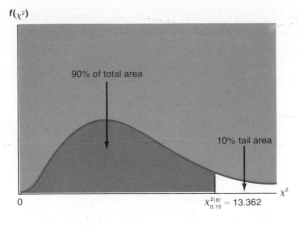

Figure 10.4

A chi-square distribution: the location of $\chi^{2(8)}_{0.10}$

of the chi-square score $\chi^{2(8)}_{0.10}$. It equals 13.362, and on the $\chi^{2(8)}$ distribution, it bounds a 10 percent right-tail area.

USING THE CHI-SQUARE TABLE

Since the chi-square distribution is a function of its degrees of freedom, it is impractical to provide a separate table comparable to the normal distribution table for each chi-square distribution. Instead, a limited number of more frequently used chi-square scores are provided for each distribution. The chi-square table is presented in Table A.4, Appendix A, and a schematic description of it is provided in Figure 10.5. When we want to find a given chi-square score, we first go down the left-hand column (headed df, for "degrees of freedom") to the desired degrees of freedom and then move across the table horizontally to the right until we reach the column denoting the desired right-tail area. For example, if we are looking for the chi-square score that leaves a right-tail area of 10 percent under the $\chi^{2(15)}$ distribution, we go down the left-hand column to "15" (see Figure 10.5), then cross to the right column headed "0.10." The number indicated in the table, 22.307, is the chi-square score that bounds a right tail of 10 percent under $\chi^{2(15)}$. To find a chi-

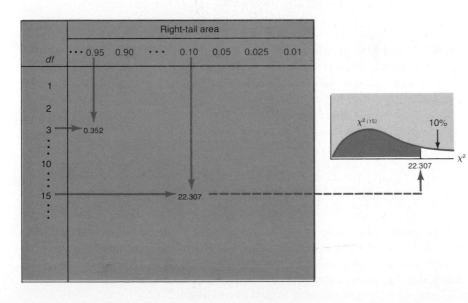

Figure 10.5

Chi-square distribution table

square score that bounds a given left-tail area, we follow across the table to the column denoting the complement (to 1) of that area. For example, to find the $\chi^{2(3)}$ score that bounds a 5 percent *left-tail* area, we go down the left-hand column to the appropriate degrees-of-freedom row and then move to the right to the column headed "0.95" (since 0.95 is the complement of 0.05 for 1.0, and a left-tail area of 5 percent is complemented by an area of 95 percent on the right). In the case at hand, the chi-square score is equal to 0.352, as illustrated in Figure 10.5. We urge you to verify the following values:

$$\chi^{2(8)}_{0.01} = 20.090$$

$$\chi^{2(12)}_{0.05} = 21.026$$

$$\chi^{2(30)}_{0.10} = 40.256$$

$$\chi^{2(20)}_{0.95} = 10.851$$

$$\chi^{2(20)}_{0.05} = 31.410$$

$$\chi^{2(3)}_{0.95} = 0.352$$

It can be shown that the expected value of a chi-square variable with n degrees of freedom is equal to n, and its variance is equal to $2n$:

$$E[\chi^{2(n)}] = n$$

$$V[\chi^{2(n)}] = 2n$$

(10.5)

As we can see, the mean and variance as well as the entire shape of the distribution are completely specified by the parameter n—the number of degrees of freedom.

APPLICATIONS OF THE CHI-SQUARE DISTRIBUTION

The chi-square distribution is applied in a variety of statistical analyses. In this book it will be used for the following:

1. To study the variance of random samples. When a random variable follows a normal distribution and a random sample is drawn out of that distribution, then the chi-square probability distribution can be used to analyze the variance of the sample. For example, assume that a certain variable, X (such as the sales tax collected daily in a given state), is normally distributed. Now, if we draw a random sample of n independent days, the sample variance is

$$S^2 = \frac{\sum_{i=1}^{n} (X_i - \bar{X})^2}{n - 1} = \frac{1}{n - 1} \sum_{i=1}^{n} (X_i - \bar{X})^2$$

On the right-hand side of this equation the constant $1/(n - 1)$ multiplies n squared deviations. It can be shown that only $n - 1$ of these deviations are independent of one another. Therefore S^2 can be analyzed using the chi-square distribution with $(n - 1)$ degrees of freedom. We will see an example of such analysis in Chapter 12.

2. To infer, based on sample data, whether or not two random variables are independent of one another. This "test of independence" is presented in Chapter 15.
3. To infer, based on sample data, whether or not two or more populations are homogeneous with respect to a certain variable. For example, we can use the chi-square distribution to examine whether the political affiliation of voters seems to vary (i.e., not to be homogeneous) across different regions of the country or whether their affiliations seem to be the same (i.e., to be homogeneous). This "test of homogeneity" is presented in Chapter 15.
4. To infer, based on sample data, whether a given variable follows a known distribution (such as the normal distribution, the Poisson distribution, etc.). This test is known as the "goodness-of-fit" test and is presented in Chapter 15.

10.3 The Student t Distribution

Another important probability distribution is the **Student t distribution** (or simply, the t distribution). This distribution was introduced in 1908 by W. S. Gosset, who used "Student" as a pseudonym. The t distribution is similar in its general shape to the standard normal distribution. Like the standard normal distribution, the t distribution is bell-shaped, with its mean, median, and mode coinciding at zero. The difference between the two, as illustrated in Figure 10.6, is that the t distribution is more dispersed and thus has thicker tails. While there is only one standard normal distribution, there is a whole family of t distributions, distinguishable by a parameter called the *degrees of freedom* (just as in the case of the chi-square distribution), which reflects the number of independent random variables inherent in the t variable.[2] A t distribution with 1 degree of freedom (denoted by $t^{(1)}$) is somewhat different from a t distribution with 2, 5, or 10 degrees of freedom. Figure 10.6 shows two t distributions, one with 5 degrees of freedom ($t^{(5)}$) and the other with 30 degrees of freedom ($t^{(30)}$). While the shape of the

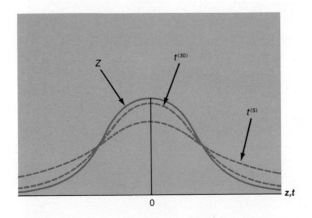

Figure 10.6

The t density function compared with the normal curve

---

[2] The t distribution is constructed as a ratio of a standard normal variable, Z, to the square root of an independent chi-square variable divided by its degrees of freedom. Denoting the chi-square variable by $\chi^{2(n)}$ and assuming that $\chi^{2(n)}$ and Z are independent, the random variable $Z/\sqrt{\chi^{2(n)}/n}$ has a t distribution with n degrees of freedom.

$t^{(5)}$ distribution differs considerably from that of the standard normal distribution, the $t^{(30)}$ distribution is in fact very much like the standard normal distribution. As the number of degrees of freedom increases beyond 30, the t distribution resembles even more closely the shape of the standard normal distribution.

Since the t distribution (like the chi-square distribution) is a function of the number of degrees of freedom, only a limited number of the more frequently used critical t scores are presented in the t distribution table inside the back cover of the book. We shall use the notation $t_\alpha^{(n)}$ to denote that t score that bounds a right-tail area equal to α under the $t^{(n)}$ distribution. It follows directly that $t_{\alpha/2}^{(n)}$ is that t score that bounds a right tail equal to $\alpha/2$ on the $t^{(n)}$ distribution. Figure 10.7 helps clarify the notation $t_\alpha^{(n)}$: the t score 2.110, which is $t_{0.025}^{(17)}$, bounds a right-tail area of 2.5 percent under the $t^{(17)}$ distribution. Figure 10.8 describes the way we find $t_\alpha^{(n)}$ in the t distribution table: the value $t_{0.025}^{(17)}$, for example, may be found at the intersection of 17 df (degrees of freedom) in the left-hand column of the table and the 0.025 value at the top of the table.

As additional examples, let us find $t_\alpha^{(8)}$, $t_{\alpha/2}^{(8)}$, and $t_\alpha^{(\infty)}$, assuming that $\alpha = 0.05$. Since $\alpha = 0.05$, obviously $\alpha/2 = 0.025$. Focusing on $t^{(8)}$ first, we find that $t_{0.05}^{(8)} = 1.860$, as indicated in the table at the intersection of 8 df

Figure 10.7

A t distribution ($t^{(17)}$) showing the value $t_{0.025}^{(17)}$

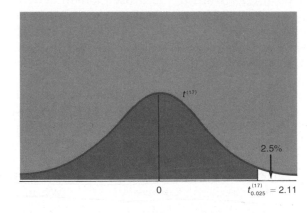

Figure 10.8

The t-distribution table

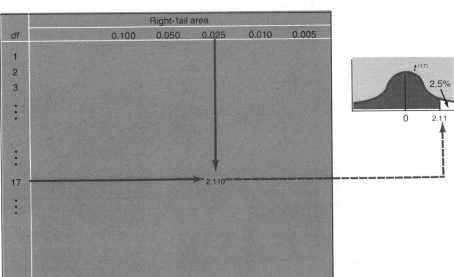

and 0.050, and similarly we find that $t^{(8)}_{0.025} = 2.306$. We find that $t^{(\infty)}_{0.05}$ is equal to 1.645, a number we are well acquainted with from the normal distribution table. More specifically, we realize that $t^{(\infty)}_{0.05} = z_{0.05}$, and in general, for any given α we get $t^{(\infty)}_{\alpha} = z_{\alpha}$. When the number of degrees of freedom approaches infinity, the t distribution approaches the standard normal distribution, and as a result, all the individual t scores approach their respective scores on the standard normal distribution. We urge you to practice by verifying the following values:

$$t^{(10)}_{0.05} = 1.812 \qquad t^{(27)}_{0.025} = 2.052$$

$$t^{(15)}_{0.10} = 1.341 \qquad t^{(30)}_{0.10} = 1.310$$

$$t^{(1)}_{0.005} = 63.657 \qquad t^{(6)}_{0.010} = 3.143$$

Since the t distribution is a symmetrical distribution around zero, the expected value of $T^{(n)}$ (a random variable having the distribution $t^{(n)}$) is equal to zero. Its variance can be shown to equal $n/(n-2)$ for $n > 2$:

$$E[T^{(n)}] = 0 \qquad \text{for } n > 1 \tag{10.6}$$

$$V[T^{(n)}] = \frac{n}{(n-2)} \qquad \text{for } n > 2$$

The t distribution possesses no mean when $n = 1$ and no variance when $n \leq 2$.

APPLICATIONS OF THE t DISTRIBUTION

The t distribution has very important applications. The applications presented in this book are concentrated in three areas, as follows:

1. To make inferences, based on sample data, about the mean of a population when the variance is unknown. The t distribution is applicable if the population of interest is normally distributed.
2. To make inferences, based on sample data, about the means of two populations. For example, is the average productivity of workers in two separate assembly lines the same? Is the average achievement of public school students equal to that of private school students? Under certain conditions, the answers to these and similar questions can be inferred by using the t distribution.
3. To analyze the results of regression analysis. Virtually all computer regression packages print out—as standard procedure—the appropriate values of the t distribution that show whether the regression results are meaningful and in what way. A detailed explanation must await the presentation of regression analysis in Chapter 18.

10.4 The *F* Distribution

The **F distribution** is located over *the range of positive real numbers*. It is a unimodal and positively skewed distribution, as illustrated in Figure 10.9. The F distribution has two parameters, n_1 and n_2, which are degrees of

Figure 10.9

An *F* distribution: $F^{(4,10)}$ and the location of the value $F_{0.05}^{(4,10)}$

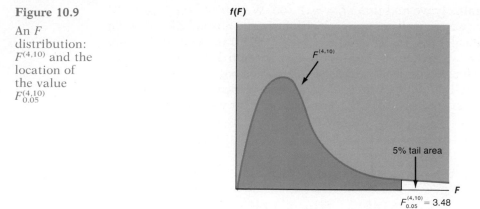

f(F)

$F^{(4,10)}$

5% tail area

F

$F_{0.05}^{(4,10)} = 3.48$

freedom whose meaning is briefly described as follows: if two independent chi-square variables have n_1 and n_2 degrees of freedom respectively, then the ratio $\dfrac{[\chi^{2(n_1)}/n_1]}{[\chi^{2(n_2)}/n_2]}$ has an *F* distribution with degrees of freedom n_1 and n_2, or

$$\frac{\dfrac{\chi^{2(n_1)}}{n_1}}{\dfrac{\chi^{2(n_2)}}{n_2}} \sim F^{(n_1, n_2)} \tag{10.7}$$

The function's exact shape depends solely on the values of the parameters n_1 and n_2. In Figure 10.9 the parameters shown are 4 and 10, and $F_{0.05}^{(4,10)} = 3.48$ is the *F* score that bounds a 5 percent right-tail area.

Let us turn to a description of the *F* distribution table. Three *F* distribution tables are given in this book: one for the upper 5 percent tail, one for the 2.5 percent tail, and one for the 1 percent tail. Consider, for example, the 5 percent table. The table (schematically reproduced in Figure 10.10) gives us

Figure 10.10

The *F* distribution table: upper 5 percent tail

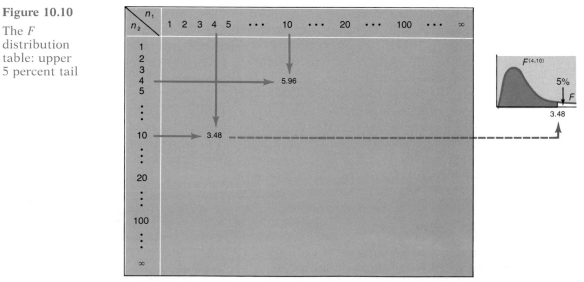

the F scores that bound right-tail areas of 5 percent for various combinations of n_1 and n_2. Be careful not to mistake n_1 for n_2. As Figure 10.10 shows, $F_{0.05}^{(4,10)} = 3.48$ is not the same as $F_{0.05}^{(10,4)} = 5.96$. Note that the degrees of freedom listed first are those of the numerator (Equation 10.7), and the degrees of freedom listed second are those of the denominator.

Although only right-hand side tail areas will be needed for the F test that will be presented in later chapters, we should note that the left-hand side values (i.e., percentiles below 50 percent) can be found using the following relationship:

$$F_\alpha^{(n_1,n_2)} = \frac{1}{F_{1-\alpha}^{(n_2,n_1)}} \tag{10.8}$$

Note the reversal of the degrees of freedom in Equation 10.8. An example of using this relationship is as follows. To determine $F_{0.975}^{(6,15)}$ we first find $F_{0.025}^{(15,6)} = 5.27$ in Appendix A, Table A.5b. We then compute:

$$F_{0.975}^{(6,15)} = \frac{1}{F_{0.025}^{(15,6)}} = \frac{1}{5.27} = 0.190$$

The value 0.190 bounds a 2.5 percent left-hand-side tail on the $F^{(6,15)}$ distribution, while the value $F_{0.025}^{(6,15)} = 3.41$ bounds a 2.5 percent right-hand-side tail. We urge you to verify the following values:

$$F_{0.05}^{(4,7)} = 4.12 \qquad F_{0.95}^{(1,4)} = 0.00445$$

$$F_{0.05}^{(7,9)} = 3.29 \qquad F_{0.95}^{(5,8)} = 0.207$$

$$F_{0.025}^{(20,28)} = 2.23 \qquad F_{0.975}^{(10,20)} = 0.292$$

$$F_{0.025}^{(12,12)} = 3.28 \qquad F_{0.990}^{(3,3)} = 0.034$$

In conclusion, we note that the expected value of $F^{(n_1,n_2)}$ is equal to $\frac{n_2}{n_2 - 2}$ for $n_2 > 2$ and its variance is equal to $\frac{2n_2^2(n_1 + n_2 - 2)}{n_1(n_2 - 2)^2(n_2 - 4)}$ for $n_2 > 4$. The F distribution has no mean when $n_2 \le 2$ and no variance when $n_2 \le 4$.

APPLICATIONS OF THE F DISTRIBUTION

The F distribution, like the other distributions presented in this chapter, plays a central role in statistics. This book presents the following applications of the F distribution:

1. To infer, based on sample data, whether the variances of two populations are the same. This will be discussed in Chapter 14.
2. To infer, based on sample data, whether the means of three or more populations are equal to one another. This is done via an analysis of variance, which is presented in Chapter 16.

Chapter Summary and Review

Random variable	Density or relationship to other variables	Parameters	Uses
1. Exponential	Density: $$f(t) = \begin{cases} 0 & t < 0 \\ \lambda e^{-\lambda t} & t \geq 0 \end{cases}$$	λ	1. Determining first "success" in an interval of time, space, or volume
2. χ^2	Relationship to Z: $$\sum_{i=1}^{n} Z_i^2 \sim \chi^{2(n)}$$	n (df)	1. Study of variance 2. Test of independence 3. Test of homogeneity 4. Test of goodness of fit
3. t	Relationship to Z: $$t^{(n)} = \frac{Z}{\sqrt{\chi^{2(n)}/n}}$$	n (df)	1. Estimating the mean when σ is unknown 2. Estimating difference between two means 3. Analyzing regression results
4. F	Relationship to χ^2: $$\frac{\dfrac{\chi^{2(n_1)}}{n_1}}{\dfrac{\chi^{2(n_2)}}{n_2}} \sim F^{(n_1, n_2)}$$	n_1, n_2 (df)	1. Comparing the variances of two populations 2. Analysis of variance

Problems

10.1. Find the probability that an exponentially distributed random variable with mean $1/\lambda = 10$ will take on values as follows:

    (*a*) Between 0 and 5
    (*b*) Less than 4
    (*c*) Greater than 8

10.2. The lifetime of an electric bulb is an exponentially distributed random variable with a standard deviation of 200 hours. What is the probability that such a bulb will last

    (*a*) At least 10 hours
    (*b*) At most 50 hours
    (*c*) Between 10 and 20 hours

10.3. The time you wait in a bank until you are served by a teller is exponentially distributed with mean $1/\lambda = 10$ minutes. Calculate the probability that you will have to wait between 5 and 15 minutes.

10.4. Suppose that T_1 and T_2 are random variables, both having exponential distributions. Furthermore, it is given that

$$\sigma_{T_1}^2 = 100$$

and

$$\sigma_{T_2}^2 = 81$$

Which of the following two events has a higher probability:

1. $T_1 \geq 20$
2. $T_2 \leq 15$

10.5. There are two exponentially distributed variables T_1 and T_2 with parameters λ_1 and λ_2, respectively, where λ_1 is greater than λ_2. Prove that for every value t, the cumulative distribution of T_1 is above the cumulative distribution of T_2.

10.6. Flaws in a certain kind of fabric occur randomly with a mean of one flaw per 80 square feet. What is the probability that a piece of fabric measuring 40 feet by 3 feet will have at least one flaw? Use the exponential probability distribution, then calculate again using the Poisson probability distribution.

10.7. (a) The time period (in hours) between notification of an out-of-order telephone and the time the phone company puts the telephone back into service is distributed in the form of an exponential probability distribution, with the parameter $\lambda = 0.12$. What is the probability that the time period will be less than 8 hours? Less than 12 hours? More than 24 hours?
  (b) Suppose your telephone was knocked out of service when a tornado struck the city. Would the exponential probability distribution with $\lambda = 0.12$ be applicable for the time period that will pass before the telephone will be in working order again? Explain.

10.8. The length of time required to service a person at a given motor-vehicle license bureau is exponentially distributed with a mean of 5.0 minutes.

  (a) What percentage of people are served within 1 minute? 2 minutes? 5 minutes?
  (b) Graph the cumulative probability distribution of the service time.
  (c) From the graph, determine the length of time t_0, such that the probability that the service time will take more than t_0 minutes is 0.60.

10.9. If the median of an exponential probability distribution is 3, what is the parameter λ?

10.10. The following are descriptions of random variables that have either a Poisson or an exponential distribution. Which do you think has a Poisson distribution and which is exponentially distributed?

  (a) The number of flaws in a piece of cloth.
  (b) The distance, on a piece of cloth, from one flaw to the next.
  (c) The number of car accidents occurring in one week at a given location.
  (d) The length of time from one car accident to another at a given location.

10.11. Let T be a random variable distributed exponentially with $\lambda = 4$: $f(t) = \lambda e^{-\lambda t}$. Find the following probabilities:

  (a) $P(T \leq 2)$
  (b) $P(T \leq 4)$
  (c) $P(3 \leq T \leq 5)$
  (d) $P(T \geq 3)$

10.12. At an outpatient clinic for blood tests, the rate of arrivals is 20 per hour.

  (*a*) What is the probability that it will be more than 5 minutes before the next patient arrives?
  (*b*) What is the probability that it will be less than 10 minutes before the next patient arrives?
  (*c*) What is the average length of time between one arrival and the next?

10.13. Find the following values of the chi-square variable:

  (*a*) $\chi^{2(9)}_{0.05}$
  (*b*) $\chi^{2(30)}_{0.10}$
  (*c*) $\chi^{2(1)}_{0.05}$

10.14. Find the following probabilities concerning the chi-square distribution:

  (*a*) $P[\chi^{2(1)} \leq 3.841]$
  (*b*) $P[\chi^{2(2)} \leq 9.210]$
  (*c*) $P[\chi^{2(20)} \geq 37.566]$

10.15. A random variable has a chi-square distribution and its variance is equal to 2. What is the variable's number of degrees of freedom and what is the probability that the variable will be greater than 3.841?

10.16. A random variable has a chi-square distribution with 10 degrees of freedom. What is the probability that the random variable will fall between 3.940 and 18.307?

10.17. A random variable has a chi-square distribution with n degrees of freedom. Consider the probability $P(\chi^{2(n)} \geq 10)$. Is it true that the greater the number of degrees of freedom, n, the greater the probability? Explain.

10.18. Find the following values of the t variable:

  (*a*) $t^{(1)}_{0.05}$
  (*b*) $t^{(10)}_{0.025}$
  (*c*) $t^{(30)}_{0.005}$

10.19. Find the following probabilities for the t distribution:

  (*a*) $P[0 \leq t^{(1)} \leq 12.706]$
  (*b*) $P[-1.476 \leq t^{(5)} \leq 2.571]$
  (*c*) $P[-1.303 \leq t^{(40)} \leq 1.303]$
  (*d*) $P[-1.96 \leq t^{(\infty)} \leq 1.96]$

10.20. Consider the random variable $F^{(5,10)}$. The probability that it will be greater than 4.5 is

  (*a*) Between 1 percent and 2.5 percent
  (*b*) Between 2.5 percent and 5 percent

Which of the above is the correct answer?

10.21. State which of the following probabilities is greater:

  (*a*) $P(F^{(5,10)} > 3.33)$
  (*b*) $P(F^{(10,5)} > 3.33)$

Explain.

10.22. According to Chebyshev's theorem, the probability that a random variable will take on a value in the range of 1.4 standard deviations around the mean is at least $1 - 1/1.4^2 = 24/49$. Prove that the theorem holds with $k = 1.4$ for an exponentially distributed variable with $\lambda = 4$.

10.23. (*a*) Show that Chebyshev's theorem with $k = 2$ holds for the chi-square distribution with $n = 6$ degrees of freedom. Recall that according to the theorem, the probability that a random variable will fall within two standard deviations of the mean is at least $1 - 1/k^2 = 1 - 1/4 = 3/4$.

(*b*) According to the Empirical Rule, about 95 percent of the probability of a mound-shaped distribution falls in the range from $\mu - 2\sigma$ to $\mu + 2\sigma$. Use the chi-square table (Appendix A, Table A.4) to *approximate* the probability that a chi-square distribution with six degrees of freedom falls within this range.

(*c*) Repeat part *b* for chi-square distributions with 1 degree of freedom, 20 degrees of freedom, and 30 degrees of freedom.

10.24. The Empirical Rule is a rule of thumb for mound-shaped distributions. According to the rule, approximately 95 percent of a distribution falls between $\mu - 2\sigma$ and $\mu + 2\sigma$, and about 100 percent falls between $\mu - 3\sigma$ and $\mu + 3\sigma$. Determine whether the rule holds for the following distributions:

(*a*) $t^{(5)}$

(*b*) $t^{(30)}$

(*c*) $F^{(8,12)}$

(*d*) $F^{(40,60)}$

PART 3

DECISION-MAKING BASED ON SAMPLES (INDUCTION)

Up to now, we have discussed the presentation of statistical data, calculation of statistical measures, and deduction from population structure to probabilities involving individual observations. We have also seen that statistical measures such as the sample mean and sample variance are used to make inferences about their counterparts in the population. Most of the remainder of this book is devoted to furthering our knowledge of induction: using statistical inference to learn about the structure and characteristics of a population by looking at only a part of that population—i.e., a sample. Chapter 11 discusses sampling and sampling distributions in general, Chapter 12 deals with point and interval estimation, and Chapters 13 through 16 deal with various tests of hypotheses.

SAMPLING AND SAMPLING DISTRIBUTIONS

Key Terms
statistical inference
sample
random sample
nonsampling errors
measurement error
sampling errors
statistic
convenience sample
judgment sample
probability sample
simple random sample
strata
stratified random sample
cluster
cluster random sample
sampling distribution
standard error
finite population correction factor
central limit theorem

11.1 Introduction and Review

Sampling is the core of wide areas in statistics, and in recognition of that fact we shall devote most of the remainder of this book to **statistical inference,** those methods by which the characteristics of populations and phenomena are studied through the observation of sample data. In this chapter we shall review and expand our earlier discussion of samples (Chapters 3 and 4) and the reasons for sampling. We shall also discuss the errors associated with samples and describe alternative sampling designs.

A **sample** is a *segment of a population* and, as such, is expected to reflect the population, so that by studying the sample we can characterize the total population. To ensure an undistorted picture of the population as a whole, the sample must, with few exceptions, be selected by some *random process.* *A sample selected by a random process* is called a **random sample**. A random sample is constructed in such a way that each population member has a chance to be selected.[1] Note that not all population members must be given

---

[1] In the case of an infinite population, the population members are continuously being created by a given process (for example, the human population). In this case it is impossible to give population members who have not yet been created or those who have perished a chance of being selected.

an *equal* chance to be selected; various random sample designs exist that give unequal chances of selection to the population members. A few such sample designs will be discussed later in the chapter.

There are a number of reasons that the study of samples is often preferred over a study of the entire population. They include cost, accuracy, time, and other considerations:

1. *Cost of sampling.* Since the sample is, by definition, smaller than the entire population and in many cases considerably smaller, observing a sample often costs only a fraction of what it would cost to observe a whole population.

2. *Accuracy.* A sample involves fewer data than does the entire population. Accordingly, more attention is usually given to any individual observation in a sample than in a census. Few as they might be, the sample observations are usually of higher quality because they are better screened for errors in measurements and for duplications, misclassifications, and so on.

3. *The time factor.* A sample has an advantage over a census in that it can be completed more quickly. This is true both for the collection of the data and for the processing of the results. Both can be completed faster when a smaller number of observations is involved. The time factor has a particular significance in business, where competitiveness often requires that data be obtained and analyzed very quickly.

4. *Other reasons for sampling.* Among other reasons for sampling, we should mention (as we did in Chapter 3) the difficulty we often encounter in identifying and reaching the population, the destruction of the data as they are being observed (sampling the taste of wine, for example), and the fact that some populations are not easily accessible.

11.2 Errors Associated with Samples

Since a sample is by definition a portion of the population, it is not generally capable of providing a full and flawless reflection of the population as a whole. There will be certain discrepancies between the population and the sample. We distinguish two major sources of such discrepancies: nonsampling errors and sampling errors.

NONSAMPLING ERRORS

Nonsampling errors are *errors that result either from improper selection of sample observations or from erroneous information obtained from the observations.* Let us look at each of these in turn.

Improper Selection   *Improper selection* of sample observations occurs when a given section of the population has an unduly low or unduly high chance of being selected for the sample. Consider a random sample selected for the purpose of discovering the proportion of people in a developing country who have telephones in their homes. It would surely be absurd to perform the study through telephone interviews. Similarly, we would not go to a church in order to find out the proportion of people who believe in God. Although these are extreme examples, they make an important point. Far too often, samples are selected without careful preparation to ensure full and balanced coverage of the entire population under consideration. To consider a more realistic example, suppose a sample is being selected with the goal of uncovering some common characteristics of investors in common stocks. It will be necessary to get the consent of the stockholders before answers to such questions can be obtained. Yet it is possible that heavy investors may be reluctant to discuss the very matters that are of interest to the researcher. If such is the case, people who own large amounts of common stocks may have an unduly low representation in the sample results and people with small holdings may have an unduly high representation. How are such difficulties overcome? There are various methods for dealing with them, including the *stratified sample* (which will be discussed later in this chapter).

Erroneous Information   *Erroneous information*, including *misunderstandings, approximations, and incorrect observations*, is often referred to as **measurement error**. Consider a sample of TV viewers who are asked how many hours per week they spend watching TV. Approximation is probably the best people can do in response to such a question. Likewise, when a sample requires people's opinions, there is always the risk of some misunderstanding and differences of interpretation. If the interview involves intimate questions that upset the interviewee in any way—questions about the subject's age, health, sex life, immoral or unethical activities, and the like—wrong information may be given. And sometimes, as when we measure people's height, the distance between two points, and so on, simple inaccuracies creep in.

STATISTICS AND SAMPLING ERRORS

A **statistic** is a *summary measure of the sample data*. Since sample data depend on the specific observations that happen to be in the sample, it is clear that a statistic is a random variable. A statistic is usually used for estimation: when we want to base our estimate of a population parameter on sample data, we compute the parameter's corresponding value in the sample and use it as an estimate of the parameter. The simplest example is the use of sample data to estimate the population mean. The mean lifetime of light bulbs in a sample is the counterpart of the mean lifetime for the entire population of light bulbs out of which the sample has been selected, and thus serves as an estimator of the population's mean. Whereas the population mean is a fixed value, the sample mean is a statistic and its value is random (provided the sample observations were selected at random). A "hat" over a parameter is a common notation used to indicate an estimator. Thus if μ denotes the population mean, $\hat{\mu}$ denotes its sample counterpart. Similarly, if σ denotes the standard deviation, $\hat{\sigma}$ denotes its counterpart (which is a statistic) in the sample. Some of the more common parameters, such as μ and σ, have additional notation for their sample counterparts. While μ and σ denote the population mean and standard deviation respectively, $\overline{X}$ and S (in addition to $\hat{\mu}$ and $\hat{\sigma}$) are commonly used for the average and standard deviation of the sample data, as we saw in earlier chapters.

Sampling errors are *errors that result from the chance selection of the sampling units*. They occur when a portion, rather than the entire population, is observed. The larger the sample size, the smaller the magnitude of sampling errors expected; when a census is taken, no sampling errors should occur.

11.3 Balancing Sampling Costs Against Error Costs

We mentioned earlier the costs of sampling, which are incurred in the planning and gathering of the data as well as in the analysis of results. In most cases it is possible to identify two cost components: fixed and variable costs. Our concern here is with the variable cost, which increases directly with the size of the sample. (Whether or not the fixed cost can be identified is not essential to our discussion.) The important thing for us to remember is that almost without exception, the cost of sampling rises with the sample size. On the other hand, increasing the sample size helps us to reduce sampling errors. Recall that as the number of observations increases, sampling errors decrease and the picture of the population reflected by the sample emerges with increasing fidelity.

HOW LARGE SHOULD A SAMPLE BE?

We will not attempt to provide an analytical solution to the optimal sample size. Instead, we will outline the important factors that ultimately determine it.

First, the sample size may be determined by factors other than cost: accessibility and time. We will not discuss these matters here because these factors vary considerably according to circumstance and are by nature unique to the specific situation. Suffice it to say that when time or accessibility is rigidly limited, the sample size is to a large extent fixed by these constraints.

If we assume that time is available and the population is accessible, we must then consider the cost factor. Sampling errors can be, and normally are, costly. Depending on the issue at hand, the cost may be pecuniary or nonpecuniary. Some costs may be measured in unhappiness, pain, illness, or even death. We shall assume, however, that such costs can eventually be expressed and evaluated in dollar amounts.

When the sample size increases, the two contrasting cost considerations (that is, the cost of sampling and the potential cost of sampling errors) are affected in two opposite ways: the actual cost of sampling increases while the potential cost resulting from sample errors decreases. Although the manner in which the cost components vary with sample size is specific to the problem at hand, this relationship generally holds. Table 11.1 presents a hypothetical example in which the known cost of sampling and the expected cost of sampling errors are given for selected levels of sample size. The two cost components conform to the relationship described above: the cost of sampling increases and the expected cost of sampling errors decreases with sample size. In this example, the cost of sampling is assumed to be $500 plus $2 for each observation. The expected cost of sampling errors is assumed to be related to the sample size (n) in the following way: cost $= 10,000 \cdot n^{-1.1}$. In addition to the two cost components, the table presents the total cost, which is simply their sum. As we can easily see, the total cost does not move in only one direction as the sample size grows. Rather, the total cost first declines to a minimum, then rises. The relationship between the sample size and the various cost functions is shown in Figure 11.1. Although the specific cost functions assumed are unique to our example, the general relationships to sample size are typical of most situations. If cost functions are specified, it is relatively simple to derive the sample size that minimizes total cost.

TABLE 11.1
Costs Associated with Sampling in Relation to Sample Size:
A Hypothetical Example

Sample size	Cost of sampling	Expected cost of sampling errors[a]	Total cost
10	$520	$794	$1,314
20	540	371	911
30	560	237	797
40	580	173	753
50	600	135	735
60	620	111	731
70	640	93	733
80	660	81	741
90	680	71	751
100	700	63	763

[a]The table presents the sample size in intervals of 10 observations. Obviously, a more refined schedule would show optimal sample size in the neighborhood of (but not necessarily exactly at) 60 observations.

The mere act of specifying the cost function is not necessarily trivial or costless. If we need to draw a sample in the first place, it is because we lack information about the population. If the population variance is unknown, it is difficult to evaluate potential sampling errors and their cost. A possible way around this problem is to take a relatively small sample (often called a "pilot sample") and use it to obtain an estimate of the population variance and the potential sampling errors. The procedure described above may then be employed. When the cost function is not specified for some reason, we may use an alternative approach to determine a desirable sample size. We specify a maximum tolerable error in estimation and then determine the sample size for which the probability of making an error that will be greater than the one specified does not exceed a given value (say 1 percent). We shall discuss this approach further in Chapter 12.

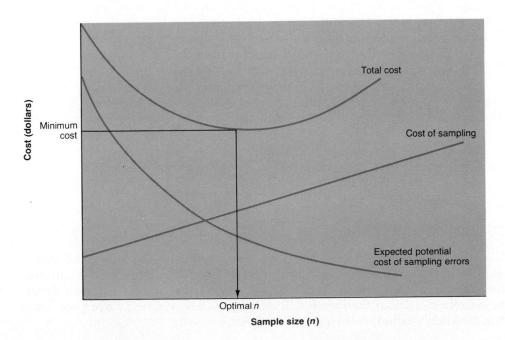

Figure 11.1

A typical relationship between sample size and cost components

11.4 Types of Samples

Samples are distinguished by the processes used to select them. We speak of convenience samples, judgment samples, and random samples.

CONVENIENCE SAMPLES

A **convenience sample** is one that is selected primarily on the basis of sampling convenience.

Suppose we want to study some behavioral aspects of tourists in the United States (such as dining, lodging, or recreational activities). If we select our sample from those who stay at a nearby hotel, we are using a convenience sample. Similarly, if we try to study new trends of institutional behavior in the capital markets by gathering data from the nearest brokerage house, the sample obtained is a convenience sample.

Convenience is always an appealing feature, but it is clear that a convenience sample is less representative of the whole population than one that is selected in a more diversified manner. When we approach the tourists in a particular hotel, we are dealing with a very specific segment of the tourist community. Depending on the type of hotel selected, we may be dealing with high-income or low-income tourists. The mere fact that the tourists are staying in that particular hotel could reflect some characteristic that they share with each other but not with the entire population of tourists in the United States.

Sometimes the group to which we have convenient access constitutes a very large portion of the population. Suppose we want data on the rates of return on common stocks. There are virtually hundreds of companies whose common stock is traded in the capital markets. Amazingly large amounts of data based on the rates of return of about 900 common stocks are compiled by the Center for Research on Securities Prices (CRSP) at the University of Chicago. The data are available on computer tapes known as "CRSP tapes." Although hundreds of common stocks are not represented on the CRSP tapes (such as those traded in the over-the-counter market), most recent studies of common stock returns have used samples from the CRSP tapes. In a sense, such samples are convenience samples. Because the data on the tapes pertain to a substantial part of the population, however, and because data on the returns on all the common stocks not represented on the tapes would be expensive to collect, there is a general tendency to make do with the convenience sample. From a statistical point of view, however, there is always the danger that the convenience sample may be less representative of the total population than a sample selected systematically from all the population's segments would be.

JUDGMENT SAMPLES

A **judgment sample** is one that is selected primarily on the basis of judgment. The primary reason we might want to base our selection of a sample on judgment—rather than on chance—is that we believe such a sample to be more reflective of the population characteristics. We may have good reason for such a belief if the sample size is very small.

For example, if we need a sample of public-school students and our re-sources enable us to sample only two schools, we may be wise to use judgment in the selection of the schools. If we leave the selection of those schools to chance alone, we may select schools that are atypical in some respect. Of course, if the sample size is even moderately large, random selection will prove more advantageous than judgment.

The main problem with judgment samples is that since the observations are not selected at random, there is no way we can estimate sampling errors.

PROBABILITY SAMPLES

Probability samples are selected in such a way that the *probability* that each element in the population will be selected is known in advance. Such samples are obtained following various designs. The most common design is the simple random sample; other well-known designs are the stratified random sample and the cluster random sample.

The Simple Random Sample and the Use of the Random Numbers Table   The convenience and judgment samples have their advantages, but their main deficiency is that they do not enable us to assess sampling errors. Probability samples, on the other hand, allow us to assess the sampling errors involved. Statistical theory is thus more relevant and applicable to these types of samples.

A **simple random sample** is one that is selected in such a way that it *assures equal probability of selection to all samples of the same size*. For example, if the population is of size 4 and consists of the letters *A*, *B*, *C*, and *D*, and if the sample is to be of size 3, then the following samples—all the possible samples of size 3—must be guaranteed equal probability of selection (that is, $\frac{1}{4}$):

$$A, B, C$$
$$A, B, D$$
$$A, C, D$$
$$B, C, D$$

If the sample is to consist of two letters, then the following samples should be guaranteed equal probability (that is, $\frac{1}{6}$):

A, B	*B, C*
A, C	*B, D*
A, D	*C, D*

Similarly, if the sample is of size 1, each of the elements *A*, *B*, *C*, and *D* should have a $\frac{1}{4}$ probability of being selected.

This definition of simple random selection applies to a finite population only. When the population is infinite, we must interpret the simple random selection in a somewhat different way. A correct procedure for selecting a random sample is to assign a serial number to each of the population elements and to select the sample by drawing a prespecified number of serial numbers at random. A good way of selecting serial numbers at random is to use the random numbers table (see Appendix A, Table A.13). Suppose 150 observations are to be picked from 2,500 population elements, all of which have been assigned serial numbers ranging from 0001 to 2500. Our first step is to enter the table at a page selected blindly, in a totally haphazard way—

literally closing the eyes while making the page selection. A number on the page should be selected fortuitously in a similar fashion. The number selected is the starting number. Note that a four-digit number must be read in our example. After the starting number has been selected, we read additional four-digit numbers by moving horizontally or vertically on the page, selecting other pages at random as the need arises. If a number is in the range 0001 through 2500, it is recorded. If it is out of this range, the number is not recorded and we continue reading other numbers. When 150 numbers are recorded, the process is discontinued. The sample is constructed so as to consist of the 150 elements whose serial numbers have been selected.

A distinction must be made here between simple *random* sampling and *haphazard* sampling. In simple random sampling we take positive action to make sure that each element in the population is given an equal probability of selection. In haphazard selection, no such action is taken. Investigating public opinion on the women's liberation movement through telephone interviews conducted on weekday mornings is haphazard and is likely to include an unduly large proportion of housewives and other people who are not employed outside the home. A simple random sample must ensure that each member of the population has the same probability of selection.

The Stratified Random Sample It is often possible to identify distinguishable **strata** (i.e., *homogeneous groups*) within the population under consideration. For various reasons it might be more efficient and thus desirable to *give unequal emphasis in the sample to the various population strata*—that is, to take a **stratified random sample**.

One such reason might be a lack of homogeneity among the population strata. Suppose we have a list of 1,000 commercial banks in a given population and we want to select 50 of them for a sample. The 1,000 banks naturally vary in size. Although large banks may make up only a small percentage of the population, we may wish to give them a greater probability of being selected, because if more large banks are chosen, we will obtain better coverage of the total deposits. We could define two strata: (1) "large" banks (those with $100 million or more in deposits) and (2) all the others. If only 30 of the 1,000 banks are defined as large, we may decide to allocate our sample in such a way that 20 banks will be selected among the large banks and the rest will be selected among the others. So, although only 3 percent of the banks in the population are large (30 out of 1,000), the large banks will make up 40 percent (20 out of 50) of the observations in the sample. This procedure of sample selection will better meet our need to obtain even coverage of the deposits in the 1,000 banks.

There are other reasons that unproportional representation of population strata might lead to greater efficiency. Consider a population with two distinguishable strata that have unequal variances. It is often advantageous to obtain a greater proportion of sample observations from the more diverse group of the population than from the less diverse group. Needless to say, the same principle also applies when the population consists of more than two groups.

Stratified sampling may also be used when the costs of error are unequal in two or more population segments. Take, for instance, a sample designed to study patients who are being treated for a given illness by two different methods, *A* and *B*. Suppose treatment *A* has more unpleasant side effects than treatment *B*. We may want to obtain a more precise estimate of the effectiveness of treatment *A* (and thus obtain a greater proportion of cases treated by method *A* in the sample) to determine whether the treatment is worth the unpleasant side effects it produces.

Stratified sampling is primarily important if the overall sample size is small. If only a small number of observations is taken and if distinguishable groups in the population exist, it is quite possible that not all of them will be well represented in a random sample. For example, suppose an infinite population is composed of two strata: group 1, consisting of 80 percent of the population, and group 2, consisting of 20 percent. If only five observations are taken at random, there is a 32.77 percent chance that they will all be from group 1 and no representative of group 2 will be selected; denoting the probability of a random selection from group 2 by *p*, we get $p = 0.20$ and $q = 0.80$. By the binomial formula we find $P(X = 0) = \binom{5}{0}(0.20)^0(0.80)^5$

$= 1 \cdot 1 \cdot 0.32768 = 0.32768$, which is approximately 32.77 percent. Such a sample is unrepresentative of group 2, and it is desirable to take steps in advance to ensure the selection of members of group 2. Of course, as the sample size increases, simple rules of probability are likely to bring about a more even and well-balanced representation of all the population's groups in a simple random sample, and no special steps will need to be taken to ensure balanced representation.

The Cluster Random Sample A population stratum is one that is homogeneous with respect to the characteristic with which we are concerned. Sometimes we define *groups within homogeneous population strata on the basis of their accessibility*. We refer to such groups as **clusters. Cluster random samples** are used almost exclusively when groups are defined by geographical location. A personal interview with 100 people across the country could require 100 trips to various locations. To minimize our costs, we might decide to divide the country into states, counties, or cities, and choose—by a simple random process—a limited number of such geographical areas. We might, for example, choose 5 cities and hold our personal interviews there, thus making only 5 trips instead of 100. Cluster samples result in greater sampling errors than do simple random samples (which yield the smallest sampling errors), because people from one cluster may be more similar to one another than they are to people in other locations. But the money we save by focusing on a limited number of clusters can be used to increase the sample size and offset at least part of the otherwise relatively large sampling errors. Sometimes the savings effected by use of a cluster sample rather than a random sample may be substantial.

11.5 Sampling Distributions

As noted earlier (see Section 11.2), a statistic is a summary measure of sample data. Before the sample is taken, the statistic is a random variable rather than a fixed value. Accordingly, each statistic is characterized by a probability distribution that shows the functional relationship between each possible value and the probability (or density) that the sample statistic will assume that value. *The probability distribution of a statistic* is called a **sampling distribution**. We already know that the main objective of drawing samples is estimating population parameters. But only by mere chance would we obtain a sample estimate that equals the population parameter whose value we are estimating: in general, there will be a deviation between the sample estimate and the population parameter of interest. Knowing the sampling distribution of our statistic allows us to calculate the probability of such potential deviations. This is what makes sampling distributions a focus of interest when it comes to sampling and estimation.

In the next chapter, we shall discuss certain properties that are derived in a sampling distribution of a statistic. For now, however, we want to concentrate on one particular statistic, the sample mean $\overline{X}$, and explain the meaning of its sampling distribution and how it changes with the sample size. You should bear in mind that the discussion refers to the sample mean, which is a statistic of major importance and also serves as an example of sampling distributions of other statistics as well, even though those might have different properties.

THE SAMPLING DISTRIBUTION OF $\overline{X}$

Intuitively we know that the greater the sample size (that is, the larger the number of observations taken), the closer the estimated mean tends to be to the true mean of the entire population. By averaging the heights of 20 U.S. citizens, we more accurately portray the mean U.S. citizen's height than if we merely average the heights of 5 of them. Likewise, the mean height of 100 citizens will probably be even closer to the "true" mean height (the mean height of *all* U.S. citizens).

This point is very crucial to a good understanding of sampling and estimation, and it deserves a detailed illustration. Suppose that the store manager of the Gorgeous Lamps Company is analyzing the frequency of his inventory orders. One of his objectives is to estimate the mean delivery period (that is, the average number of days it takes from the time an order is placed until the merchandise is actually delivered to the store). Let us assume that the delivery period—which is a random variable—has the probability distribution shown in Table 11.2. The mean delivery period is 10 days:

$$E(X) = 4 \cdot 0.01 + 5 \cdot 0.02 + 6 \cdot 0.05 + \cdots + 14 \cdot 0.05 + 15 \cdot 0.02$$
$$+ 16 \cdot 0.01$$
$$= 10.00$$

Looking at the probability distribution in Table 11.2, we would expect to find, on the average, a delivery period of 4 days occurring once in 100 times, a delivery period of 5 days twice in 100 times, a period of 6 days 5 times in 100, and so on.

Suppose the probability distribution is not known to the manager, perhaps because no records were kept in the past. If he wants to estimate the mean, he will have to take a sample of delivery periods, whose mean, $\overline{X}$, will serve as a proxy to (estimate of) the population mean, μ. How good the proxy will be depends on the number of observations taken. If only one observation is taken—in other words, if only one delivery period is observed and used as an estimate—then the likelihood is fairly good that the estimated delivery period will differ substantially from the true mean delivery period. For example, out of 100 delivery periods, 56 (on the average) are either less than or equal to 8 days or greater than or equal to 12 days—in other words, there

TABLE 11.2
Probability Distribution of Delivery Periods

Delivery period, X (in days)	Probability
4	0.01
5	0.02
6	0.05
7	0.08
8	0.12
9	0.14
10	0.16
11	0.14
12	0.12
13	0.08
14	0.05
15	0.02
16	0.01
	1.00

are 56 periods in 100 that deviate from the mean of the distribution by 2 or more days. Similarly, 84 periods in 100 (on the average) are either less than or equal to 9 days or greater than or equal to 11 days—in other words, 84 periods in 100 deviate from the mean by 1 or more days. Thus, by taking a sample of only one observation, the manager faces the likelihood of coming up with an inaccurate estimate. If, however, he bases the estimate on the mean of, say, 5 observations, *the probability that the sample mean will miss the true mean by 2 or more days is far below 56 percent, and the probability that it will miss the true mean by one or more days is far below 84 percent. This is the major reason that more than one observation is generally needed to estimate population parameters.* Technically, we state that the variance of the mean of n observations is smaller than the variance of one observation. The above discussion implies that the sampling distribution of $\overline{X}$ becomes more condensed about the true mean as the sample size increases.

To illustrate our argument, we can take a close look at the means of samples of various sizes. We begin by constructing Table 11.3, in which 100 delivery periods are listed in frequencies implied by the probability distribution. The number 4 appears once, the number 5 appears twice, the number 6 appears five times, and so on, according to their probability of occurrence.

TABLE 11.3
One Hundred Delivery Periods Implied "on the Average" by the Probability Distribution of X

4	7	8	9	9	10	11	11	12	13
5	7	8	9	9	10	11	11	12	13
5	7	8	9	10	10	11	12	12	14
6	7	8	9	10	10	11	12	12	14
6	7	8	9	10	10	11	12	13	14
6	7	8	9	10	10	11	12	13	14
6	8	8	9	10	10	11	12	13	14
6	8	8	9	10	10	11	12	13	15
7	8	9	9	10	11	11	12	13	15
7	8	9	9	10	11	11	12	13	16

After assigning a serial number to each of the numbers in Table 11.3, we draw random samples of various sizes out of the table, using the random numbers table (see Appendix A, Table A.13). Note that any of the numbers in Table 11.3 can be selected more than once, depending on the number of times its serial number appears in the random numbers table. This sampling with replacement procedure guarantees that the samples are chosen by a random selection process out of the specified probability distribution.

First we select 20 samples of one observation each. These samples are listed in Table 11.4, and as we can see, if only one observation were to be used as an estimate for the mean, our error might be large: quite a few of the observations listed in Table 11.4 vary substantially from the true mean, 10. In Table 11.5, 20 random samples of 5 observations each and their respective means are listed. An examination of the sample means shows, for example, that *not even one sample mean deviates from 10 by two or more days*. (Contrast the observations in Table 11.4: a relatively large percentage of these *individual* observations deviate from 10 by two or more days.) When we take *sample means*, large deviations from the true mean are possible, but they are far less probable than when we take individual observations. The greater the sample size, the greater the tendency of the sample mean to cluster around the true mean of the distribution, and the rarer large deviations become. Table 11.6 presents a set of 20 randomly selected samples of 12 observations each. We obtained these observations by choosing them from Table 11.3, using the random numbers table (Appendix A, Table A.13). Here, as expected, the means of the various samples cluster even more closely around the true mean. Only 4 of the sample means in Table 11.6 deviate by 1 or more days from the distribution mean, compared to 9 for samples of size 5 (Table 11.5) and 17 for samples of size 1 (Table 11.4). This tendency of the sample means to cluster more closely around the distribution mean as the sample size increases is seen also in Figure 11.2, in which the means of the samples of Tables 11.4, 11.5, and 11.6 are presented together.

TABLE 11.4
Twenty Randomly Selected Samples of One Observation Each

12	12	6	9	7	14	7	10	8	10
11	14	12	10	11	5	12	13	9	7

TABLE 11.5
Twenty Randomly Selected Samples of Five Observations Each and Their Means

1	*2*	*3*	*4*	*5*	*6*	*7*	*8*	*9*	*10*
14.0	11.0	9.0	8.0	11.0	10.0	10.0	10.0	14.0	10.0
10.0	7.0	13.0	9.0	9.0	8.0	7.0	10.0	7.0	9.0
9.0	9.0	9.0	9.0	11.0	10.0	9.0	10.0	10.0	10.0
10.0	6.0	11.0	8.0	7.0	8.0	11.0	6.0	10.0	7.0
12.0	12.0	8.0	7.0	10.0	12.0	7.0	13.0	8.0	14.0
$\overline{X}_1 = 11.0$	$\overline{X}_2 = 9.0$	$\overline{X}_3 = 10.0$	$\overline{X}_4 = 8.2$	$\overline{X}_5 = 9.6$	$\overline{X}_6 = 9.6$	$\overline{X}_7 = 8.8$	$\overline{X}_8 = 9.8$	$\overline{X}_9 = 9.8$	$\overline{X}_{10} = 10.0$

11	*12*	*13*	*14*	*15*	*16*	*17*	*18*	*19*	*20*
9.0	14.0	10.0	10.0	11.0	7.0	12.0	12.0	9.0	8.0
7.0	5.0	9.0	9.0	11.0	11.0	14.0	11.0	8.0	9.0
7.0	13.0	11.0	9.0	6.0	11.0	10.0	12.0	10.0	13.0
12.0	15.0	11.0	13.0	11.0	8.0	8.0	9.0	9.0	10.0
9.0	11.0	8.0	10.0	7.0	12.0	12.0	8.0	5.0	15.0
$\overline{X}_{11} = 8.8$	$\overline{X}_{12} = 11.6$	$\overline{X}_{13} = 9.8$	$\overline{X}_{14} = 10.2$	$\overline{X}_{15} = 9.2$	$\overline{X}_{16} = 9.8$	$\overline{X}_{17} = 11.2$	$\overline{X}_{18} = 10.4$	$\overline{X}_{19} = 8.2$	$\overline{X}_{20} = 11.0$

TABLE 11.6
Twenty Randomly Selected Samples of 12 Observations Each and Their Means

1	2	3	4	5	6	7	8	9	10
14.0	6.0	11.0	8.0	10.0	9.0	9.0	11.0	14.0	9.0
8.0	14.0	10.0	10.0	13.0	8.0	10.0	11.0	10.0	11.0
11.0	6.0	12.0	14.0	10.0	10.0	14.0	10.0	9.0	8.0
9.0	15.0	10.0	12.0	12.0	4.0	9.0	11.0	10.0	8.0
7.0	8.0	11.0	12.0	8.0	8.0	13.0	9.0	12.0	9.0
9.0	14.0	7.0	10.0	12.0	7.0	14.0	9.0	11.0	9.0
10.0	16.0	12.0	15.0	7.0	11.0	15.0	12.0	7.0	8.0
13.0	11.0	10.0	13.0	11.0	8.0	14.0	11.0	9.0	7.0
10.0	12.0	10.0	8.0	10.0	12.0	9.0	5.0	6.0	15.0
14.0	8.0	14.0	10.0	7.0	8.0	11.0	8.0	12.0	9.0
7.0	10.0	11.0	8.0	14.0	11.0	11.0	13.0	9.0	13.0
9.0	11.0	8.0	10.0	6.0	11.0	11.0	9.0	13.0	10.0
$\overline{X}_1 = 10.1$	$\overline{X}_2 = 10.9$	$\overline{X}_3 = 10.5$	$\overline{X}_4 = 10.8$	$\overline{X}_5 = 10.0$	$\overline{X}_6 = 8.9$	$\overline{X}_7 = 11.7$	$\overline{X}_8 = 9.9$	$\overline{X}_9 = 10.2$	$\overline{X}_{10} = 9.7$

11	12	13	14	15	16	17	18	19	20
11.0	9.0	9.0	9.0	8.0	9.0	10.0	11.0	8.0	9.0
9.0	11.0	10.0	6.0	10.0	7.0	10.0	10.0	11.0	8.0
11.0	7.0	7.0	14.0	13.0	7.0	11.0	14.0	6.0	8.0
7.0	10.0	14.0	11.0	13.0	12.0	12.0	12.0	10.0	11.0
9.0	10.0	6.0	8.0	13.0	9.0	5.0	11.0	12.0	12.0
10.0	10.0	11.0	12.0	8.0	14.0	4.0	9.0	11.0	14.0
8.0	6.0	11.0	8.0	12.0	7.0	10.0	5.0	5.0	4.0
10.0	15.0	6.0	9.0	10.0	13.0	12.0	9.0	9.0	14.0
8.0	14.0	11.0	7.0	12.0	15.0	7.0	9.0	10.0	13.0
12.0	7.0	11.0	11.0	12.0	11.0	8.0	11.0	11.0	8.0
10.0	10.0	9.0	9.0	9.0	10.0	8.0	10.0	8.0	12.0
7.0	10.0	13.0	8.0	11.0	9.0	10.0	10.0	5.0	8.0
$\overline{X}_{11} = 9.3$	$\overline{X}_{12} = 9.9$	$\overline{X}_{13} = 9.8$	$\overline{X}_{14} = 9.3$	$\overline{X}_{15} = 10.9$	$\overline{X}_{16} = 10.2$	$\overline{X}_{17} = 8.9$	$\overline{X}_{18} = 10.1$	$\overline{X}_{19} = 8.8$	$\overline{X}_{20} = 10.1$

It is extremely important to realize that *in most sampling situations, only one sample is taken*. However, from the tendency of sample means to cluster more closely around the distribution mean as the sample size increases, it follows that *the larger the sample size, the greater the probability that the mean of the one sample taken will be closer to the distribution mean.*

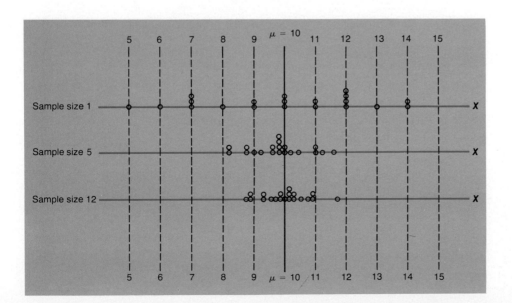

Figure 11.2

The dispersion of means of samples of various sizes taken from the distribution of delivery periods

THE VARIANCE AND STANDARD ERROR
OF THE SAMPLE MEAN, $\overline{X}$

If the nature of the distribution of $\overline{X}$ is understood, the mathematics should be straightforward. We have already explained that $\overline{X}$ is a random variable. The delivery-period example illustrated another important characteristic of $\overline{X}$: the average of many sample means tends toward the mean of the distribution, or $E(\overline{X}) = \mu$. Let us see how we can get this result by using simple equations involving random variables.

Since, by definition

$$\overline{X} = \frac{\Sigma X}{n} = \frac{X_1 + X_2 + \cdots + X_n}{n}$$

we may write

$$E(\overline{X}) = E\left(\frac{X_1 + X_2 + \cdots + X_n}{n}\right) = E\left[\frac{1}{n}(X_1 + X_2 + \cdots + X_n)\right]$$

$$= \frac{1}{n}E(X_1 + X_2 + \cdots + X_n) = \frac{1}{n}[E(X_1) + E(X_2) + \cdots + E(X_n)]$$

Since $X_1, X_2, \ldots, X_n$ are all taken from the same population, they all have the same mean, μ:

$$E(X_1) = E(X_2) = \cdots = E(X_n) = \mu$$

so that

$$E(\overline{X}) = \frac{1}{n}\underbrace{[\mu + \mu + \cdots + \mu]}_{n \text{ times}} = \frac{1}{n} \cdot n\mu = \mu$$

In brief, we may write

$$E(\overline{X}) \equiv \mu_{\overline{X}} = \mu \tag{11.1}$$

where $\mu_{\overline{X}}$ denotes the expected value, or the mean, of $\overline{X}$.

We have shown that the variability of $\overline{X}$ decreases with the sample size. Now let us take a closer look at it by examining the variance of $\overline{X}$. Denoting the variance of $\overline{X}$ by $\sigma_{\overline{X}}^2$, we write

$$V(\overline{X}) \equiv \sigma_{\overline{X}}^2 = V\left(\frac{\Sigma X}{n}\right) = V\left(\frac{X_1 + X_2 + \cdots + X_n}{n}\right)$$

$$= V\left[\frac{1}{n}(X_1 + X_2 + \cdots + X_n)\right] \tag{11.2}$$

$$= \frac{1}{n^2}V(X_1 + X_2 + \cdots + X_n)$$

Assuming that $X_1, X_2, \ldots, X_n$ are independent observations, we get

$$V(X_1 + X_2 + \cdots + X_n) = V(X_1) + V(X_2) + \cdots + V(X_n)$$

and since the variances of all the X_is are equal to one another (different observations of the same distribution) and are denoted by σ^2, we get

$$V(X_1) + V(X_2) + \cdots + V(X_n) = \underbrace{\sigma^2 + \sigma^2 + \cdots + \sigma^2}_{n \text{ times}} = n\sigma^2 \qquad (11.3)$$

Substituting Equation 11.3 into Equation 11.2 yields

$$\sigma_{\overline{X}}^2 = \frac{1}{n^2} n\sigma^2 = \frac{\sigma^2}{n} \qquad (11.4)$$

As a direct result, we find

$$\sigma_{\overline{X}} = \sqrt{\frac{\sigma^2}{n}} = \frac{\sigma}{\sqrt{n}} \qquad (11.5)$$

where $\sigma_{\overline{X}}$ stands for "**standard error** of $\overline{X}$," which is *simply the standard deviation* of $\overline{X}$.

$$\sigma_{\overline{X}}^2 = \frac{\sigma^2}{n}$$

$$ \qquad (11.6)$$

$$\sigma_{\overline{X}} = \frac{\sigma}{\sqrt{n}}$$

THE SAMPLING DISTRIBUTION OF $\overline{X}$ WHEN THE POPULATION IS FINITE

We have seen that the standard error of $\overline{X}$ is given by the expression $\sigma_{\overline{X}} = \sigma/\sqrt{n}$. The estimated standard error is given by $S_{\overline{X}} = S/\sqrt{n}$ where S is the sample standard deviation:

$$S = \sqrt{\frac{\Sigma(X - \overline{X})^2}{n - 1}}$$

These expressions are correct for infinite populations or for finite populations when sampling is done with replacement. When the population is finite and sampling is done without replacement, the above expressions overstate the standard error of $\overline{X}$. To illustrate, suppose the population consists of the annual income of 36 students in a statistics class. Since the population is *defined* as the income of those 36 students, it is clear that if all 36 students have been sampled, the sample mean, $\overline{X}$, will *precisely* equal the population mean. This does not mean that there is no variability in the income of the 36 students but only that the population mean has been estimated with full precision. For example, if $\sigma = \$600$, the expression $\sigma_{\overline{X}} = \sigma/\sqrt{n}$ incorrectly indicates that the standard deviation of $\overline{X}$ for $n = 36$ is $\sigma_{\overline{X}} = 600/\sqrt{36} = \$100$. However, since the 36 students are *defined* as the population, it is clear that the mean of the 36 incomes is *precisely* the mean of the population and no standard error is involved: $\overline{X}$ is identical to μ.

Indeed, $\sigma/\sqrt{n}$ should be multiplied by a **finite population correction factor**, $\sqrt{\dfrac{N - n}{N - 1}}$, when sampling without replacement from finite populations, where N is the population size and n is the sample size. More specifically, for a finite population and sampling without replacement, the standard error of $\overline{X}$ is given by the equation

$$\sigma_{\overline{X}} = \frac{\sigma}{\sqrt{n}} \sqrt{\frac{N - n}{N - 1}} \tag{11.7}$$

Its estimator, the sample standard deviation, is given by the equation

$$S_{\overline{X}} = \frac{S}{\sqrt{n}} \sqrt{\frac{N - n}{N - 1}} \tag{11.8}$$

Clearly, when $N = n$, we get $\sigma_{\overline{X}} = S_{\overline{X}} = 0$ as in the above example. Accordingly, if we include all 36 students in our sample, the estimator $\overline{X}$ has zero variance. On the other hand, if N is very large compared to n, the term $\sqrt{\dfrac{N - n}{N - 1}}$ is very close to 1, and $\sigma/\sqrt{n}$ and $S/\sqrt{n}$ are good proxies for $\sigma_{\overline{X}}$ and $S_{\overline{X}}$, respectively. For example, suppose $N = 11{,}000$, $n = 1{,}000$, and $\sigma = 100$. Disregarding the correction factor, we get

$$\sigma_{\overline{X}} = \frac{\sigma}{\sqrt{n}} = \frac{100}{\sqrt{1{,}000}} = \frac{100}{31.6} = \$3.16$$

After correcting for the finite population, we obtain

$$\sigma_{\overline{X}} = \frac{\sigma}{\sqrt{n}} \sqrt{\frac{N - n}{N - 1}} = \frac{100}{\sqrt{1{,}000}} \sqrt{\frac{11{,}000 - 1{,}000}{11{,}000 - 1}}$$

$$= 3.16 \sqrt{\frac{10{,}000}{10{,}999}} = 3.16\sqrt{0.909}$$

$$= \$3.01$$

As a rule of thumb, if $n/N \leq 0.05$, the correction factor is relatively close to 1 and can be ignored.

THE SAMPLING DISTRIBUTION OF $\overline{X}$ WHEN X IS NORMALLY DISTRIBUTED

Our main concern in the remainder of this chapter is the distribution of $\overline{X}$ when the random variable X is normally distributed. The main rule to remember here is that when X is normally distributed, then $\overline{X}$ is also normally distributed with the same mean, μ. Using statistical notation, if

$$X \sim N(\mu, \sigma)$$

then

$$\overline{X} \sim N(\mu, \sigma_{\overline{X}}) \tag{11.9}$$

and $\sigma_{\overline{X}}$ is equal to $\sigma/\sqrt{n}$ if the population is infinite (or if it is finite and the sampling is done with replacement[2]) and to $\dfrac{\sigma}{\sqrt{n}}\sqrt{\dfrac{N-n}{N-1}}$ if the population is finite and the sampling is done without replacement. Unless otherwise indicated, we shall assume $\sigma_{\overline{X}} = \sigma/\sqrt{n}$.

When we discussed the normal distribution we agreed that if

$$X \sim N(\mu, \sigma)$$

then

$$\frac{X - \mu}{\sigma} \sim N(0, 1)$$

Thus, by subtracting the mean from a normally distributed random variable and dividing the difference by the standard deviation of the distribution, we obtain the variable Z, which measures deviations from the mean in units of standard deviation:

$$Z = \frac{X - \mu}{\sigma}$$

and

$$X = \mu + \sigma Z$$

Similar relationships exist in the distribution of $\overline{X}$, so that Z is obtained when we subtract the mean of $\overline{X}$ (that is, μ) and divide by the standard error of $\overline{X}$ (that is, $\sigma_{\overline{X}}$).

If

$$\overline{X} \sim N(\mu, \sigma_{\overline{X}})$$

then

$$\frac{\overline{X} - \mu}{\sigma_{\overline{X}}} \sim N(0, 1) \tag{11.10}$$

---

[2] Sampling "with replacement" or "with repetition" allows one to draw as many observations as required from a finite population. It makes the population equivalent to one in which each observation in the finite set has an infinite number of duplicates.

or

$$Z = \frac{\overline{X} - \mu}{\sigma_{\overline{X}}}$$

and

$$\overline{X} = \mu + \sigma_{\overline{X}}Z$$

Example 11.1 is an application of the relationships just established.

EXAMPLE 11.1

Suppose the daily revenue of a laundromat chain is normally distributed with a mean of $20,000 and a standard deviation of $4,000. Find the probability that the average daily revenue for 25 days will be between $19,000 and $21,000.

Our approach is to convert the question from one concerning the probability of $\overline{X}$, for which $\mu_{\overline{X}} = 20$ (thousand dollars) and $\sigma_{\overline{X}} = 4/\sqrt{25}$, to one concerning the corresponding distribution of Z. We proceed as follows:

$$P(19 \leq \overline{X} \leq 21) = P\left(\frac{19 - 20}{4/\sqrt{25}} \leq \frac{\overline{X} - 20}{4/\sqrt{25}} \leq \frac{21 - 20}{4/\sqrt{25}}\right)$$

$$= P\left(\frac{-1.0}{0.8} \leq Z \leq \frac{1.0}{0.8}\right) = P(-1.25 \leq Z \leq 1.25)$$

$$= 0.7888$$

Any other problem concerning the probability of $\overline{X}$ may be tackled in a similar way. For example, to find the probability that the average daily revenue for 36 days will exceed $20,400, we calculate

$$P(\overline{X} \geq 20.4) = P\left(\frac{\overline{X} - 20}{4/\sqrt{36}} \geq \frac{20.4 - 20.0}{4/\sqrt{36}}\right) = P\left(Z \geq \frac{0.40}{4/6}\right)$$

$$= P(Z \geq 0.6)$$

$$= 0.2743$$

To calculate the probability that the average revenue for 64 days will be less than $19,100, we proceed as follows:

$$P(\overline{X} \leq 19.1) = P\left(\frac{\overline{X} - 20}{4/\sqrt{64}} \leq \frac{19.1 - 20.0}{4/\sqrt{64}}\right) = P\left(Z \leq \frac{-0.9}{0.5}\right)$$

$$= P(Z \leq -1.8)$$

$$= 0.0359$$

We have shown that the variance of the sampling distribution of $\overline{X}$ decreases as the sample size increases. We have also illustrated how the probability of various events concerning $\overline{X}$ can be calculated if the sampling distribution is normal. But you may wonder at this point whether the applicability of the approach presented in this section is hampered by the fact that it hinges on the assumption of a normal distribution. In the following section we shall present the well-known central limit theorem, which will show that the assumption of distribution normality is not always vital.

11.6 The Central Lim

Let X be a random variable having *any distribution at all* with mean μ and standard deviation σ, and let $\overline{X}$ be the mean of a random sample taken from this distribution. We then have the following theorem:

CENTRAL LIMIT THEOREM

The probability distribution of $\dfrac{\overline{X} - \mu}{\sigma/\sqrt{n}}$ will approach that of a standard normal distribution as the number of observations, n, increases.

The **central limit theorem** has far-reaching implications. After all, when we are conducting a study on the time needed to transport merchandise from warehouses to department stores, or when we are studying late flight arrivals and departures, the profit distribution across firms in a given industry, the distribution of hourly earnings in a given occupation, the effect of counter-display position on the marketing of a product, or similar phenomena, we generally do not know whether the variables under study are normally distributed. But we do know from the central limit theorem that the *mean* of a sample of observations approximates a normal distribution— provided that the observations are independent of one another and the number of observations is large. The larger the sample size, other things being equal, the closer the distribution to normal. Twenty-five independent observations will generally produce a mean with a distribution pretty close to normal.[3]

Consider Figure 11.3. Here we present several distributions that differ from the normal and examine the distribution of their sample means. Three columns of diagrams are shown. Each column presents a different distribution. The left column, for example, shows the distribution of sample means of various sizes taken from a uniform distribution. The right column shows the same for a U-shaped distribution, and yet another distribution is presented in the center column. The mean of 2 observations taken independently from the uniform distribution has a triangular sampling distribution, while the mean of 10 observations has a sampling distribution similar to the normal. With a sample of 25 observations, the sampling distribution of the mean is close to normal in all three cases, even though the original distributions (shown in the top line of diagrams in Figure 11.3) vary considerably from the normal. As the sample size increases (other things held constant), the distributions of the means tend to be more and more like the normal distribution.

---

[3] Note that the normal approximation of the binomial distribution, presented in Chapter 9, makes use of the fact that a sample mean tends to be normally distributed when the observations are independent.

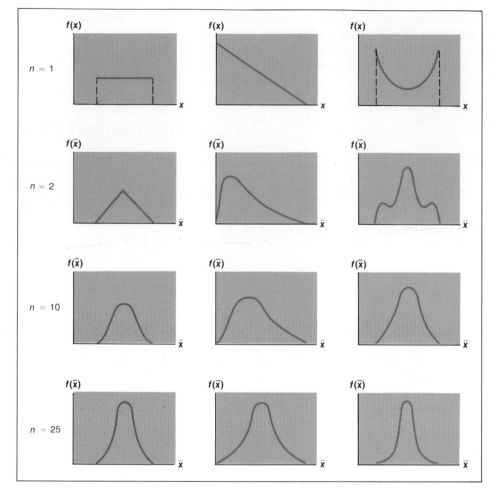

In this chapter we have concentrated on the sampling distribution of $\overline{X}$, assuming that the sample is random and drawn from a normal distribution or, alternatively, that the sample is random and large enough, making the sampling distribution of $\overline{X}$ approximately normal. There are other statistics of interest to us whose sampling distributions are not normal. An example is the estimator of the variance, $S^2 = \dfrac{\Sigma(X - \overline{X})^2}{n - 1}$, which is not normally distributed even if the distribution of X is normal. We shall consider the sampling distributions of some of these statistics in later chapters.

Chapter Summary and Review

1. The main reasons for sampling
   a. Cost saving
   b. Accuracy in measurement
   c. Time factor (can be completed quickly)
   d. Others (e.g., destruction of the unit while sampled)

2. Errors associated with samples
   a. Nonsampling errors (improper selection, erroneous information, etc.)
   b. Sampling errors

3. Statistic vs. parameter
   a. A parameter is a summary value of the population.
   b. A statistic is a corresponding summary value in the sample.
   c. A statistic is a random variable; a parameter is not.

4. Factors that determine the sample size
   a. Sampling cost per unit
   b. The cost involved with the sampling error

5. Types of samples
   a. Convenience samples
   b. Judgment samples
   c. Probability samples (simple random sample, stratified random sample, and cluster random sample)

6. Sampling distribution
   A sampling distribution is a probability distribution of a sample statistic.

7. The expected value and variance of the sample mean, $\overline{X}$
   a. The expected value: $E(\overline{X}) \equiv \mu_{\overline{X}} = \mu$ for infinite and finite populations alike.
   b. The variance:
      1. For an infinite population or sampling with replacement from a finite population:
      $$V(\overline{X}) \equiv \sigma_{\overline{X}}^2 = \frac{\sigma^2}{n}$$
      2. For sampling without replacement from a finite population:
      $$V(\overline{X}) \equiv \sigma_{\overline{X}}^2 = \frac{\sigma^2}{n}\left(\frac{N-n}{N-1}\right) \quad \text{and} \quad \sigma_{\overline{X}} = \frac{\sigma}{\sqrt{n}}\sqrt{\frac{N-n}{N-1}}$$

8. a. If $X \sim N(\mu, \sigma)$, then $\overline{X} \sim N(\mu, \sigma_{\overline{X}})$ where $\sigma_{\overline{X}}$ is defined as in number 7.
   b. The central limit theorem states that if observations are independent and the sample is random and large (over 25 observations), then the following holds approximately: $\overline{X} \sim N(\mu, \sigma_{\overline{X}})$, even if the sample is drawn from a distribution that is not normal.

Problems

11.1. Why do we use samples rather than censuses in many studies of populations?

11.2. Distinguish between sampling errors and nonsampling errors.

11.3. Explain what a sampling distribution is.

11.4. List and briefly explain the major types of samples, indicating in each case whether it is a probability sample and under what circumstances it is most appropriately used.

11.5. Suppose the cost of sampling is $10 per observation. What is the optimal sample size if the population's variance is zero? Explain.

11.6. Discuss the following statement: "If $\overline{X}$ is the mean of n observations drawn from a given population and $P(X \geq 100) = 0.30$, then $P(\overline{X} \geq 100) = 0.30$ also."

11.7. A simple random sample of 5 insurance firms is drawn out of a population of 100 firms. What is the probability that a given sample will be selected?

11.8. How many simple random samples of size n can be drawn from a finite population of size N? Apply your formula to the following specific cases:

(a) $N = 10, n = 2$
(b) $N = 100, n = 2$

11.9. Suppose you want to select three of the following five firms for a study: General Motors, Ford, Coca-Cola, Pepsi Cola, and IBM. List all possible choices. What is the probability that IBM will be in the sample? What is the probability that both automotive firms (General Motors and Ford) will be in the sample?

11.10. A simple random sample of firms is drawn from a finite population. The population size is N and the sample size is n. Suppose that TWA is included in this population.

(a) How many samples of size n can be formed?
(b) How many of these would include TWA?
(c) What is the probability that the sample will include TWA?

11.11. Suppose there are 1,000 companies in the electronics industry and 10 of them make up 90 percent of the total assets of this industry. A sample of $n = 10$ firms is planned for a study of the structure of assets of the firms in the industry. What kind of random sample would you advise? Explain.

11.12. A given population is divided into two distinguishable strata of equal size. It is given that $\sigma_1 = \$10$ and $\sigma_2 = \$1,000$, where σ stands for the standard deviation of the random variables of interest in the respective strata. To which stratum will you allocate a larger number of observations if you want to minimize the sampling errors given a certain number of observations? Why?

11.13. A research study of consumption habits is taking place in a given country in Africa. A sample of size $n = 10,000$ families will be surveyed. The population is scattered in many villages across a vast geographical area. What type of sample would you recommend for the study?

11.14. X is a random variable distributed as follows: $X \sim N(150, 25)$. A sample of 25 observations is taken. What is the probability that the sample's mean is greater than 140 but less than 147.5?

11.15. X is a random variable distributed as follows: $X \sim N(200, 20)$. A sample is drawn from an infinite population, and the following probability concerning the sample mean holds:

$$P(\overline{X} \geq 203.92) = 0.025$$

What is the sample size?

11.16. The 1981 sales and profits of 45 firms in the chemicals industry is given in Table P11.16 (in millions of dollars). Assume that the 45 firms constitute the entire industry (i.e., the population). Suppose now that the population's mean sales is not known and that you are trying to estimate it by taking random samples of various sizes.

(a) Using the random digit table (Appendix A, Table A.13) for the selection, choose samples of sizes 5, 10, 20, 40, and 45.
(b) Compare your estimate with the population mean. What is the relationship between the sample size and the deviation of the sample mean from the population mean? Explain.

11.17. "If $X \sim N(\mu, \sigma)$ and the population is infinite, then the average of a sample of n independent observations, $\overline{X}$, is given by $\overline{X} \sim N\left(\mu, \dfrac{\sigma}{\sqrt{n}}\right)$." Show graphically the relationship between the distributions of X and $\overline{X}$.

11.18. Suppose $X \sim N(\mu, \sigma)$, where $\mu = 0$ and $\sigma = 9$. Calculate the probability $P(\overline{X} \leq 3)$ if $\overline{X}$ is the average of a sample of size n and n is alternatively equal to 9, 64, 81, and 100.

11.19. Repeat Problem 11.18, but this time calculate the probability $P(-3 \leq \overline{X} \leq 3)$.

TABLE P11.16

Company	Sales	Profits
Air Products & Chemicals	1,570	126
Akzona	1,188	12
Allied	6,407	348
American Cyanamid	3,649	197
Betz Laboratories	253	29
Celanese	3,752	144
Church & Dwight	127	6
Crompton & Knowles	243	9
Detrex Chemical Industries	79	4
Dexter	523	26
Diamond Shamrock	3,376	230
Dow Chemical	11,873	564
Du Pont	22,810	1,081
Essex Chemical	173	8
Ethyl	1,757	91
Ferro	702	26
Fuller (H.B.)	329	14
Grace (W.R.)	6,521	361
Great Lakes Chemical	150	18
Hercules	2,718	136
Hunt (Philip A.) Chemical	112	4
Intl. Minerals & Chemical	1,985	154
Koppers	2,019	52
Lawter International	88	10
Loctite	214	10
Lubrizol	878	92
MacDermid	61	4
Mississippi Chemical	392	2
Monsanto	6,948	445
Morton-Norwich Products	958	53
Nalco Chemical	667	81
Olin	2,001	93
Pennwalt	1,056	37
Petrolite	297	28
Products Research & Chemical	55	3
Quaker Chemical	107	8
Reichhold Chemicals	950	17
Rohm & Haas	1,885	93
SCM	1,938	57
Stauffer Chemical	1,726	150
Stepan Chemical	205	7
Sun Chemical	599	35
Thiokol	721	37
Union Carbide	10,168	649
Witco Chemical	1,292	39

Source: *Business Week*, July 5, 1982, pp. 58–59.

POINT ESTIMATION AND CONFIDENCE INTERVALS FOR ONE POPULATION

The major objective of sampling, as noted in Chapter 11, is to acquire information about a population. More precisely, we take samples in order to obtain estimates of important parameters (such as the mean and the standard deviation) of populations. In this chapter we shall discuss the topic of estimation more rigorously, focusing specifically on point estimation and interval estimation of important parameters. In order to get a feel for the difference between the two types of estimation, consider the following statements concerning the estimation of the mean height of adults in a given population:

1. The sample mean is equal to 5'7"; thus 5'7" is our estimate of the mean height in the population considered.
2. The sample shows that we should have 95 percent confidence that the interval from 5'5" to 5'9" contains the true mean population height.

Statement 1 provides us with a **point estimate**, whereas statement 2 gives an **interval estimate**. In statement 1, only one value is given as the estimated mean height; thus the term "point estimate." Statement 2 is a probabilistic one concerning the chance that a given interval includes the true mean of the population.

We shall begin the chapter by discussing point estimators and their properties. Then we shall discuss confidence intervals.

12.1 Point Estimators and Their Properties

The use of a sample statistic to determine a single value to use as an estimate of a population parameter, such as a population mean or a population proportion, is called *point estimation*. We saw in Chapter 11 that statisticians distinguish between the value of a statistic before the sample has been taken and after it has been taken. Prior to sampling, the statistic is *a random variable whose value is unknown*, and it is called an **estimator**. An **estimate** is a *specific value of an estimator computed from the sample data after the sample has been observed*. It follows that point estimators are in fact statistics whose probability distributions are sampling distributions, a concept we explained in detail in the previous chapter.

When we want to estimate a certain population parameter, we usually have the choice of a number of alternative estimators. Therefore it is important for us to know the properties of estimators and to determine which of the alternative estimators has "better" properties. For example, if we want to estimate a population mean, there are a large number of alternative estimators we can use. Examples are

1. The sample mean
2. The sample median
3. The midpoint between the lowest and highest values of the sample observations

By studying the properties of alternative estimators, we can choose the one that best suits our needs. In this particular example it can be shown that the sample mean has the "best" properties, compared to other estimators.[1] Therefore we prefer the sample mean over other estimators when we estimate the mean of a population. Let us discuss some properties of estimators.

UNBIASEDNESS

An estimator is **unbiased** if the mean of its sampling distribution is equal to the parameter of the population that it estimates. Conversely, if the mean of its sampling distribution is not equal to the population parameter that it estimates, the estimator is said to be **biased**. Denoting the population parameter of interest by θ and the estimator by $\hat{\theta}$, we say that $\hat{\theta}$ is an unbiased estimator of θ if

$$E(\hat{\theta}) = \theta$$

and $\hat{\theta}$ is a biased estimator of θ if

$$E(\hat{\theta}) \neq \theta$$

Figure 12.1 shows the sampling distribution of two estimators, $\hat{\theta}_1$ and $\hat{\theta}_2$, of a population parameter, θ. The mean of the sampling distribution of $\hat{\theta}_1$ equals the population parameter θ, implying that $\hat{\theta}_1$ is an unbiased estimator of θ, and the mean of the sampling distribution of $\hat{\theta}_2$ is not equal to θ, implying that $\hat{\theta}_2$ is a biased estimator of θ. Of course, it is desirable that an estimator be unbiased.

---

[1] This statement is correct for most, though not all, populations.

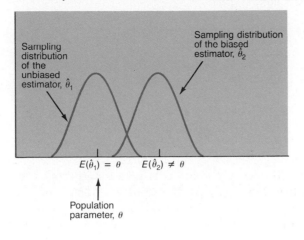

Figure 12.1

The sampling distribution of an unbiased estimator, $\hat{\theta}_1$, and of a biased estimator, $\hat{\theta}_2$

Examples of unbiased estimators are

1. The sample mean as an estimator of a population mean
2. The sample variance $\dfrac{\Sigma(X - \overline{X})^2}{n - 1}$ as an estimator of a population variance
3. The sample median as an estimator of a population mean when the population is unimodal and symmetrical

Examples of biased estimators are

1. The sample median as an estimator of a population mean when the population is skewed. Recall that when a population is skewed, the mean and median do not coincide.
2. The sample variance $\dfrac{\Sigma(X - \overline{X})^2}{n}$ as an estimator of a population variance
3. The sample median as an estimator of a population median

Figures 12.2, 12.3, and 12.4, which were generated on a computer, allow us to take a closer look at the meaning of unbiased and biased estimators. They are all based on random samples of sales data from 100 firms. The data are given in Data Set 1, Appendix B, Table B.1, and are considered to be the population of interest. Let us examine Figure 12.2, which was constructed in the following way: out of the population of 100 sales observations, 1 observation was drawn at random and its value was recorded. Then it was replaced in the data set for possible reselection. A second observation was drawn, recorded, and replaced. The process was repeated a total of 5 times. The first 5 observations drawn in this fashion constituted the first sample. Their mean was calculated to be 2,798.80 thousand dollars, or $2,798,800. This value was recorded in Figure 12.2 and denoted by the letter *A* on the extreme left, where the number of samples (horizontal axis) is equal to 1. Next, *2 other samples* of 5 observations each were drawn with replacement. These 2 samples were independent of one another and also independent of the first sample. The means of the second and third samples were calculated, and the average of those was calculated to equal 5,227.30 thousand dollars. This value was also recorded in Figure 12.2 and denoted by the letter *A*, although in this case the number of samples equals 2 on the horizontal axis.

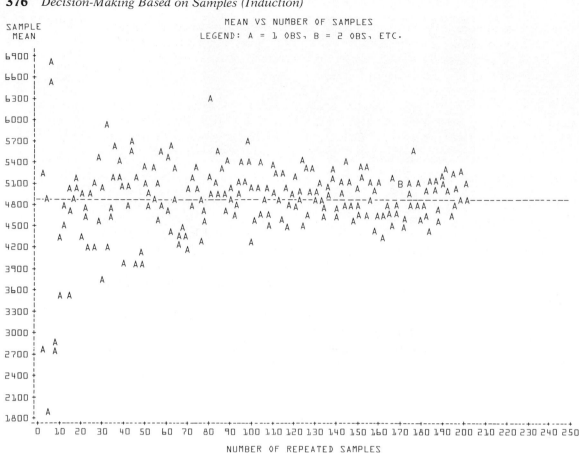

Figure 12.2

The average of sample means in repeated samples

Then 3 independent samples were drawn at random and the process continued until the number of samples drawn at the last step was 200. Each of the samples consisted of 5 observations: the horizontal axis does not represent the sample size (which was fixed throughout the procedure at 5 observations); it represents the number of samples whose means were averaged. The average of the last 200 samples (of 5 observations each) was 4,883.64 thousand dollars.

The mean of the entire 100-firm population is 4,910.04 thousand dollars and is shown by a dashed horizontal line in Figure 12.2. A number of interesting points are clearly manifested in the figure. They are:

1. The average of a small number of sample means (see the left-hand side of Figure 12.2) fluctuates considerably more than does the average of a large number of sample means. As we move to the right of the figure and increase the number of samples whose means are averaged, the averages tend to bunch more closely together.

2. The bunching occurs right around the population mean. This is a result of the fact that *the sample mean is an unbiased estimator of the population mean*. This is in fact what is meant when an estimator is said to be unbiased. It means that in repeated independent samples the average of the measure of interest (which, in our case, is $\overline{X}$) approaches the population parameter of interest (μ, in this case).

3. The various sample means in Figure 12.2 are scattered around the population mean in no particular order (other than their convergence toward μ as the number of samples grows). This is the result of the randomness of the selected sample data.

Figure 12.3 shows the scatter of the averages of sample variances, for the sample firms and sampling procedures represented in Figure 12.2. The variance of each group of 5 sample observations was calculated, and those sample variances were averaged for as many samples as were repeated. The measure of sample variance used is the *unbiased* estimator, $\dfrac{\Sigma(X - \overline{X})^2}{n - 1}$. This estimator is denoted *VAR1* in Figure 12.3. On the left-hand side of Figure 12.3, the average of a small number of sample variances (*VAR1*) is represented. As we move to the right, the average of larger and larger numbers of repeated samples (of 5 observations each) are represented. On the extreme right, the average of 200 repeated sample variance measures is represented. The population variance is 61,174,790 (measured in squared thousands of dollars), and we can see how the unbiased sample variance tends to bunch around the population variance as the number of samples increases, in much the same way the sample means do in Figure 12.2.

An interesting deviation from this pattern is shown in Figure 12.4, where the *biased* estimator of the variance, $\dfrac{\Sigma(X - \overline{X})^2}{n}$, was computed for each of

Figure 12.3

The average of unbiased estimator of the variance in repeated samples

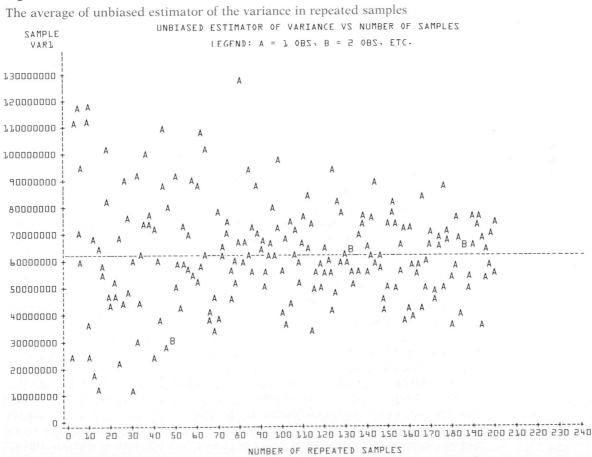

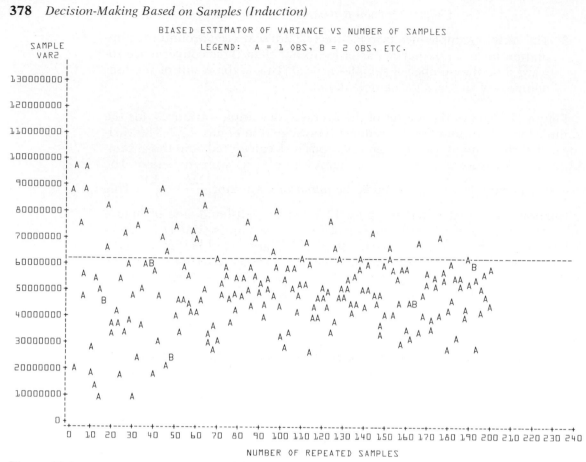

Figure 12.4

The average of biased estimator of the variance in repeated samples

the samples and presented in a similar fashion to the measures of Figures 12.2 and 12.3. The measure $\dfrac{\Sigma(X - \overline{X})^2}{n}$ is denoted *VAR2* in Figure 12.4. The tendency of the average of many sample variances to bunch together is again evident, but this time it does not occur around the population variance (the dashed line) because the measure used is a biased estimator of the population variance. Since each sample variance has as a divisor $n = 5$, rather than $n - 1 = 4$, the variances are smaller than their unbiased equivalents and the estimator *VAR2* is **downward biased**. In other words, in repeated samples, the average of *VAR2* tends to converge around a smaller value than the population variance. This is why most of the points in Figure 12.4 fall below the dashed line, which represents the population variance. **Upward biased** estimators give estimates that, on average, are greater than the population parameter they are supposed to estimate.

CONSISTENCY

A **consistent** estimator is one that has a higher probability of being close to the population parameter of interest, θ, as the sample size increases. An example of a consistent estimator is the sample mean, $\overline{X}$. We saw in the previous chapter that the standard error of $\overline{X}$, namely, the standard deviation of the sampling distribution of $\overline{X}$, is equal to $\sigma/\sqrt{n}$ where σ is the population

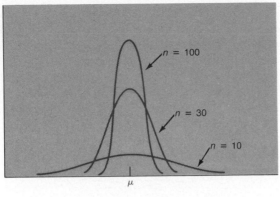

Figure 12.5

The sample mean, $\overline{X}$, is a consistent estimator of μ

standard deviation. As the sample size, n, increases, the standard error of $\overline{X}$ gets smaller. Since $\overline{X}$ is also an unbiased estimator, the sampling distribution of $\overline{X}$ becomes more condensed around the population mean when the sample size becomes larger.[2] This is shown in Figure 12.5.

RELATIVE EFFICIENCY

Consider two unbiased estimators, $\hat{\theta}_1$ and $\hat{\theta}_2$. Let the standard error of $\hat{\theta}_1$ for a given sample size be denoted by σ_1 and the standard error of $\hat{\theta}_2$ for the same sample size be denoted by σ_2. Then

$$\text{The \textbf{efficiency} of } \hat{\theta}_1 \text{ relative to } \hat{\theta}_2 = \frac{\sigma_1^2}{\sigma_2^2} \qquad \textbf{(12.1)}$$

If $\hat{\theta}_1$ is more efficient relative to $\hat{\theta}_2$, then the ratio in Equation 12.1 is less than 1.0. Simply stated, if the standard error of $\hat{\theta}_1$ is smaller than that of $\hat{\theta}_2$ for the same sample size, then $\hat{\theta}_1$ is more efficient. This situation is illustrated in Figure 12.6.

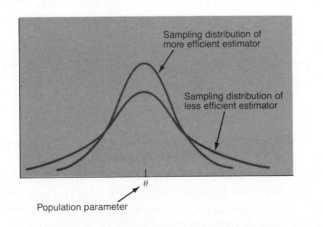

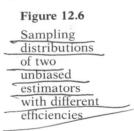

Figure 12.6

Sampling distributions of two unbiased estimators with different efficiencies

---

[2] The sample mean is both an unbiased and a consistent estimator of the population mean, μ. However, even a biased estimator can be consistent. As an example, consider the statistic $\overline{X} - (1/n)$ as an estimator for the mean μ. Since $E(\overline{X}) = \mu$, it is clear that $E[\overline{X} - (1/n)] = \mu - (1/n)$, which means that the estimator is biased. Nevertheless, since the size of the bias, $1/n$, decreases as the sample size increases and since the standard error of the sampling distribution diminishes with the sample size, it is clear that the estimator $\overline{X} - (1/n)$ is consistent, although biased.

Two unbiased estimators with different efficiencies are the mean and the median of samples drawn from a unimodal symmetrical distribution. For any sample size greater than 2, the median has a larger standard error compared to the mean, indicating that for such populations the sample mean is a more efficient estimator of the population mean than the median. It can be shown that the variance of the sample median of a normal distribution is equal to $\pi\sigma^2/2n$, where π is approximately equal to 3.142, the population variance is σ^2, and n is the sample size. Since the variance of a sample mean is equal to σ^2/n, the ratio of the variances is

$$\frac{\sigma^2_{\text{median}}}{\sigma^2_{\text{mean}}} = \frac{\pi\sigma^2/2n}{\sigma^2/n} = \frac{\pi}{2} = 1.57$$

Thus the sample mean is a more efficient estimator of μ than the sample median. In fact, it can be shown that the mean is the most efficient estimator of μ when the population is normally distributed: of all unbiased estimators of μ, the sample mean has the smallest standard error.

The concept of relative efficiency can be extended to include biased estimators as well, by comparing the estimators' *mean square errors* instead of their variances. Whereas an estimator's variance is a measure of the dispersion of the sampling distribution around the estimator's expected value, the mean square error is a measure of dispersion around the true population parameter. Denoting the mean square error by *MSE*, we may write

$$MSE(\hat{\theta}) = E(\hat{\theta} - \theta)^2 \tag{12.2}$$

The variance of the sampling distribution of $\hat{\theta}$ is given by

$$\sigma^2_{\hat{\theta}} = E[\hat{\theta} - E(\hat{\theta})]^2 \tag{12.3}$$

If the estimator is unbiased, then $E(\hat{\theta}) = \theta$, and the mean square error is equal to the variance of the sampling distribution. But if the estimator is biased, the mean squared error is greater than the variance of the sampling distribution. For example, in Figure 12.1, the expected variability of $\hat{\theta}_2$ around the true parameter, θ, is greater than around $E(\hat{\theta}_2)$, which is at the center of the distribution.

A point estimate does not give us a feel for the magnitude of the error attributable to sampling errors. Interval estimates help us evaluate the magnitude of such potential errors.

12.2 Interval Estimation of a Population Mean

We shall illustrate the concept of interval estimation by concentrating first on interval estimation of the mean, assuming that the sampling distribution of $\overline{X}$ is normal or approximately so. For this procedure the sample size must be large and the central limit theorem holds, or alternatively, the population of interest must be normally distributed.

Let us denote the fractile $1 - \alpha$ on the standard normal distribution ($\alpha < 0.50$) by z_α. For example, if $\alpha = 0.10$, then $z_{0.10}$ is the 0.90 fractile of the distribution, as shown in Figure 12.7. The standard normal table shows that this value equals 1.282, and it bounds a right-hand tail equal to α (0.10 in this example).

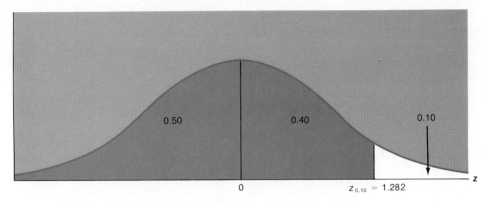

Figure 12.7

The location of $z_{0.10}$ on the standard normal scale

In general, z_α is that Z score which bounds a right tail equal to α, and it follows that $z_{\alpha/2}$ is that Z score which bounds a right tail equal to $\alpha/2$, as shown in Figure 12.8.

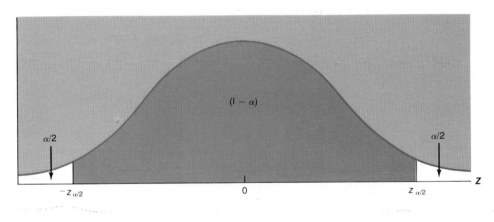

Figure 12.8

The area between $-z_{\alpha/2}$ and $z_{\alpha/2}$ and in the two tails of the standard normal distribution

EXAMPLE 12.1

Suppose we want to find z_α and $z_{\alpha/2}$ where α is equal to 0.02. Since α is equal to 0.02, z_α is that Z score which bounds a 2 percent right tail under the standard normal distribution ($z_{0.02}$). To locate this Z score, we need to find that score up to which there is an accumulated area of 0.48, starting from $z = 0$. The normal distribution table specifies this value to be approximately 2.054. Since $\alpha = 0.02$, $\alpha/2$ must equal 0.01, and $z_{\alpha/2}$ is that Z score up to which there is an accumulated area of 0.49 (starting at $z = 0$). The normal distribution table assigns a value of approximately 2.326 to this Z score (see Figure 12.9).

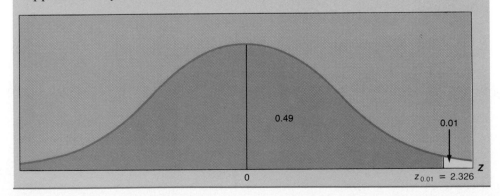

Figure 12.9

The location of $z_{\alpha/2} = z_{0.01}$ on the standard normal scale ($\alpha = 0.02$)

Notice that if z_α bounds a right tail of α, the negative value $-z_\alpha$ is the one that bounds a left tail equal to α. Similarly, the area to the left of $-z_{\alpha/2}$ is equal to $\alpha/2$. Figure 12.8 shows a standard normal distribution with both $z_{\alpha/2}$ and $-z_{\alpha/2}$ plotted along the horizontal axis. It is clear from the graph and from our earlier definitions that the sum of the right-tail area ($\alpha/2$) and the left-tail area ($\alpha/2$ as well) is equal to α, implying that the area between $-z_{\alpha/2}$ and $z_{\alpha/2}$ equals $1 - \alpha$. Note that $\alpha/2 + \alpha/2 + (1 - \alpha) = 1$, the entire area under the density function.

Since the area over the range from $-z_{\alpha/2}$ to $z_{\alpha/2}$ is equal to $1 - \alpha$ and since the area under the curve represents probability, we may write, as a direct conclusion

$$P(-z_{\alpha/2} \le Z \le z_{\alpha/2}) = 1 - \alpha \tag{12.4}$$

and since $\dfrac{\overline{X} - \mu}{\sigma_{\overline{X}}} = Z$, as we saw in Chapter 11 (Equation 11.10), we may write

$$P\left(-z_{\alpha/2} \le \frac{\overline{X} - \mu}{\sigma_{\overline{X}}} \le z_{\alpha/2}\right) = 1 - \alpha \tag{12.5}$$

Multiplying within the parentheses by $\sigma_{\overline{X}}$ yields

$$P\left(-\sigma_{\overline{X}} \cdot z_{\alpha/2} \le \overline{X} - \mu \le \sigma_{\overline{X}} \cdot z_{\alpha/2}\right) = 1 - \alpha \tag{12.6}$$

and adding the constant μ to each term in the parentheses gives

$$P(\mu - \sigma_{\overline{X}} \cdot z_{\alpha/2} \le \overline{X} \le \mu + \sigma_{\overline{X}} \cdot z_{\alpha/2}) = 1 - \alpha \tag{12.7}$$

Note that Equation 12.7 holds for infinite as well as finite populations, where for infinite populations, $\sigma_{\overline{X}} = \dfrac{\sigma}{\sqrt{n}}$ and, for finite populations, $\sigma_{\overline{X}} = \dfrac{\sigma}{\sqrt{n}} \sqrt{\dfrac{N - n}{N - 1}}$. Finally, if we denote

$$e = \sigma_{\overline{X}} \cdot z_{\alpha/2} \tag{12.8}$$

where e stands for "error," we can derive from Equation 12.7 the following expression:

$$P(\mu - e \le \overline{X} \le \mu + e) = 1 - \alpha \tag{12.9}$$

Equations 12.7 and 12.9 may be interpreted to mean that if the sample mean is normally distributed, the probability is $1 - \alpha$ that it will be within the range from $\mu - e$ to $\mu + e$ and thus will not miss the population mean, μ, by more than e—the **tolerable error**. Consequently, there is a probability α—called the **risk probability**—that $\overline{X}$ will miss the mean by more than the tolerable error, e. Figure 12.10 helps clarify this point.

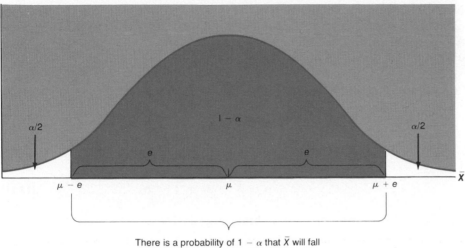

Figure 12.10

The relationship between the risk probability, α, and the tolerable error, *e*

There is a probability of $1 - \alpha$ that $\bar{X}$ will fall within this range and will miss μ by no more than *e*. There is a risk probability equal to α that $\bar{X}$ will miss by more than *e*.

EXAMPLE 12.2

Suppose we plan to draw a random sample to determine the average amount invested in common stock by individuals in the age group 18–23 in the United States. For the sake of simplicity, assume a normal distribution and that the standard deviation of the investment in common stock is known to equal $100. If 81 individuals will be surveyed, determine a symmetrical interval around the true mean common stock investment within which the sample mean is expected with 90 percent probability.

When we use Equation 12.8, the solution to the problem becomes a simple matter indeed. The data given in the problem are

$$\sigma = 100$$

$$n = 81$$

$$1 - \alpha = 0.90$$

It follows that $\alpha = 0.10$ and $\alpha/2 = 0.05$, and from the normal distribution table (inside the back cover of this book), we get $z_{0.05} = 1.645$. Substituting in Equation 12.8 yields

$$e = \frac{100}{\sqrt{81}} \cdot 1.645 = 18.28$$

and we conclude that

$$P(\mu - 18.28 \leq \bar{X} \leq \mu + 18.28) = 0.90$$

Thus, although we do not know the value of the population mean, μ, there is a 90 percent probability that the sample mean will fall within the range from $\mu - 18.28$ to $\mu + 18.28$, *so we have 90 percent confidence that the population mean is not being missed by more than $18.28.*

Note that while the total width of the interval from $\mu - e$ to $\mu + e$ is equal to $2e$ (see Figure 12.10), the half-interval width, e, is often of more concern.

An equation similar (but not identical) to 12.7 may be developed to provide the following:[3]

CONFIDENCE INTERVAL FOR A POPULATION'S MEAN

$$P(\overline{X} - \sigma_{\overline{X}} \cdot z_{\alpha/2} \leq \mu \leq \overline{X} + \sigma_{\overline{X}} \cdot z_{\alpha/2}) = 1 - \alpha \qquad (12.10)$$

Or, using $e = \sigma_{\overline{X}} \cdot z_{\alpha/2}$

$$P(\overline{X} - e \leq \mu \leq \overline{X} + e) = 1 - \alpha \qquad (12.11)$$

which holds for infinite as well as finite populations.

Figure 12.11

Interval estimation

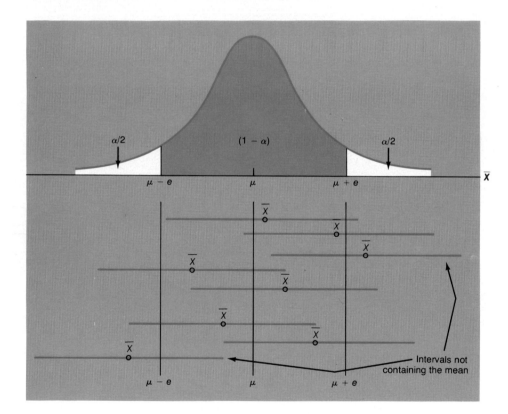

[3] Consider Equation 12.6 once again:

$$P\left(-\sigma_{\overline{X}} \cdot z_{\alpha/2} \leq \overline{X} - \mu \leq \sigma_{\overline{X}} \cdot z_{\alpha/2}\right) = 1 - \alpha$$

Multiplying within the parentheses by -1 (thereby changing the direction of the inequality signs) gives

$$P\left(\sigma_{\overline{X}} \cdot z_{\alpha/2} \geq -\overline{X} + \mu \geq -\sigma_{\overline{X}} \cdot z_{\alpha/2}\right) = 1 - \alpha$$

Adding $\overline{X}$ to each term within the parentheses gives

$$P\left(\overline{X} + \sigma_{\overline{X}} \cdot z_{\alpha/2} \geq \mu \geq \overline{X} - \sigma_{\overline{X}} \cdot z_{\alpha/2}\right) = 1 - \alpha$$

Finally, reversing the terms within the parentheses yields Equation 12.10.

Equations 12.10 and 12.11 determine a *symmetrical interval around the sample mean* $\overline{X}$ and assert that the probability that the interval established includes the true mean of the distribution (μ) is equal to $1 - \alpha$. The interval established, from $\overline{X} - e$ to $\overline{X} + e$, is called the **confidence interval**, and $1 - \alpha$ is known as the **confidence level**. The quantity α, as we have seen, is often termed the *risk probability*.

It must be understood that the confidence interval may not actually contain the mean. The interval is centered on $\overline{X}$, whose value varies from one sample to another. Thus, the interval ends are random variables, and when $\overline{X}$ differs considerably from μ, the interval may very well not contain the mean. In Figure 12.11, where a few confidence intervals are shown, all but two contain the value μ. In general, $100(1 - \alpha)$ percent of all intervals of size n formed are expected to contain μ.

EXAMPLE 12.3

Florida Paper, Inc., has agreed to buy paper for recycling from the Central Florida Waste Collection Company (CFWCC). Under the agreement, CFWCC will supply the waste paper in packages of 300 pounds each, for which Florida Paper will pay by the package. To speed up waste packing, CFWCC is packaging 300 pounds by *approximation*. Florida Paper does not object to this procedure as long as it gets 300 pounds per package *on the average*. CFWCC has an interest not to exceed 300 pounds per package, because it is not being paid for more, and not to go under 300 pounds, because Florida Paper might terminate the agreement if it does. To estimate the mean weight of waste paper in a package, CFWCC weighed 75 randomly selected packages and found that the mean weight was 290 pounds. Assuming that the standard deviation of weight in the packages is 15 pounds, let us determine whether we can indeed assume that there are 300 pounds per package in the population.

Let us first identify the values given above. The sample mean is 290 pounds, so $\overline{X} = 290$. The number of observations taken is 75, so $n = 75$. The population's standard deviation, σ, is assumed to equal 15 pounds. To summarize:

$$\overline{X} = 290$$

$$\sigma = 15$$

$$n = 75$$

The point estimate produced by the sample ($\overline{X} = 290$) is less than the agreed upon mean weight of waste paper per package. We know, however, that the sample mean almost always differs from the population mean. Suppose we want to construct a confidence interval with a 99 percent confidence level. According to the central limit theorem, the distribution of $\overline{X}$ is approximately normal, so we let $1 - \alpha$ equal 0.99, which implies that $\alpha = 0.01$, $\alpha/2 = 0.005$, and $z_{\alpha/2} = 2.575$. Substituting our data in Equation 12.10 yields

$$P\left(290 - \frac{15}{\sqrt{75}} \cdot 2.575 \leq \mu \leq 290 + \frac{15}{\sqrt{75}} \cdot 2.575\right) = 0.99$$

$$P(290 - 4.46 \leq \mu \leq 290 + 4.46) = 0.99$$

or

$$P(285.54 \leq \mu \leq 294.46) = 0.99$$

The confidence interval is thus 285.54 to 294.46, indicating 99 percent confidence that the interval from 285.54 to 294.46 covers the mean weight per package. It also indicates that there is only a 1 percent chance that the true mean weight per package (μ) is not covered by this interval. It is quite likely, then, that the mean weight per package is less than 300 pounds.

Tests of a similar nature are dealt with more directly in Chapter 13. The methodology there is somewhat different, but the essence of the problem is the same.

12.3 Factors Determining the Width of a Confidence Interval

It is important to note here that e is determined by three factors: the standard deviation of the population, σ; the sample size, n; and the risk probability, α. Let us examine the effect of each of these factors on the width of the interval around μ.

The Effect of a Change in Standard Deviation Suppose that in Example 12.2, we assume $\sigma = \$150$ rather than $\$100$. This increase of 50 percent in σ will cause a 50 percent increase in e. Using $\sigma = 150$, we get $e = (150/\sqrt{81}) \cdot 1.645 = 27.42$, which is exactly 50 percent greater than 18.28. Thus the interval is wider for the same α.

The Effect of a Change in $1 - \alpha$ Since the value of Z is not a linear function of α or $1 - \alpha$, we cannot generally determine the exact magnitude of the effect of a change in $1 - \alpha$ on e. We can, however, generally state the direction of the change: an increase in $1 - \alpha$ causes a widening of the interval (in other words, an increase in e), and a decrease in $1 - \alpha$ causes a narrowing of the interval (a decrease in e). If $1 - \alpha$ increases from 0.90 to 0.95, we get

$$1 - \alpha = 0.95 \qquad \alpha = 0.05 \qquad \frac{\alpha}{2} = 0.025 \qquad z_{\alpha/2} = 1.96$$

Thus $e = (100/\sqrt{81}) \cdot 1.96 = 21.78$, which is greater than 18.28.

The Effect of a Change in Sample Size Returning to the original data for Example 12.2, suppose we now increase the sample size from 81 to 324 (a fourfold increase: $81 \cdot 4 = 324$). We see that e decreases by a factor of 2 (which is equal to the square root of 4, since there is a square-root operator on n):

$$e = \frac{100}{\sqrt{324}} \cdot 1.645 = 9.14$$

Indeed, 9.14 is half of the original value of e, 18.28. Thus the interval is narrower for the same α.

RELATIONSHIPS AMONG THE FACTORS DETERMINING *e*

Now let us take a close look at the usefulness of Equation 12.10.

Determining the Sample Size   Consider a real-estate firm that is interested in building an apartment complex in a given location. Profitability calculations are crucially dependent on precise estimates of rent paid for apartments of similar size and quality in that location. To determine the existing mean rent paid for two-bedroom apartments, the company is using an estimated figure based on rents paid for similar apartments in the area. If we know that the standard deviation of the rent is $40, how many observations have to be taken so that we will have a 99 percent probability that the average of *all* the rents (for similar apartments) in the area is not missed by more than $5? Assume that the market is very large and that the population can be considered infinite.

This problem may be easily solved if we make use of Equations 12.8 and 12.11. Since we are maintaining a 99 percent probability that the mean is not missed by more than $5, we know that $1 - \alpha$ should equal 0.99 and *e* should equal 5 (dollars). Note that since $1 - \alpha = 0.99$, α must equal 0.01, which implies that $\alpha/2 = 0.005$ and (by the normal distribution table) $z_{\alpha/2} = 2.575$. We can now proceed directly to the solution. In the case of an infinite population we have

$$e = \frac{\sigma}{\sqrt{n}} z_{\alpha/2}$$

Multiplying both sides by $\sqrt{n}$ gives

$$\sqrt{n} \cdot e = \sigma z_{\alpha/2} \qquad \textbf{(12.12)}$$

Dividing by *e* yields

$$\sqrt{n} = \frac{\sigma z_{\alpha/2}}{e} \qquad \textbf{(12.13)}$$

Finally, after squaring both sides of Equation 12.13, we get

$$n = \frac{\sigma^2 z_{\alpha/2}^2}{e^2} \qquad \textbf{(12.14)}$$

We substitute $\sigma = 40$, $z_{\alpha/2} = 2.575$, and $e = 5$ in Equation 12.14 and get

$$n = \frac{40^2 \cdot 2.575^2}{5^2} = \frac{1,600 \cdot 6.6306}{25} = 424.36$$

Since *n* must be an integer, the smallest sample size that will guarantee at least 99 percent confidence that the sample mean does not miss the population mean by more than $5 is 425.[4] Figure 12.12 illustrates the solution.

---

[4] Note that we should round off fractions in an upward direction even when the first decimal digit is less than 5.

Figure 12.12
The change in risk probability, α, with a change in sample size, *n*

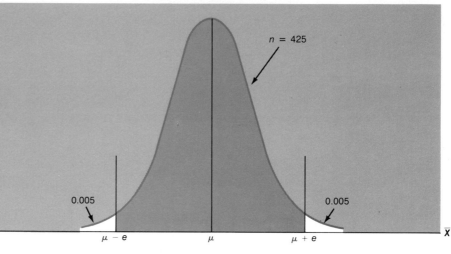

The risk probability is represented by the white tails.

The assumption that σ is known determines the degree of dispersion of the distribution of rents. The assumption that $1 - \alpha = 0.99$ determines a tail of 0.005 percent on each side of the distribution and the predetermined value of *e* (5) fixes an interval around the population mean, μ. The probability distribution of $\overline{X}$ becomes less and less dispersed as the sample size increases. Our problem was to determine the smallest sample size that will force at least 99 percent of the $\overline{X}$ distribution area into the interval from $\mu - e$ to $\mu + e$.

Determining the Probability that the Sample Mean Will Fall Within a Given Interval of Error Let us turn now to a different type of situation. Suppose the number of observations to be taken is fixed (perhaps because of a budget constraint or time limitation). In this kind of situation we can either solve for e when $1 - \alpha$ is given or solve for $1 - \alpha$ when e is given. Suppose a consumer protection organization is concerned with the mean difference between estimates given on car repairs and the actual bills. To evaluate the mean discrepancy, 100 discrepancies are observed. If the standard deviation of the discrepancies is $15, what is the probability that the mean discrepancy as estimated from the sample does not deviate from the true mean discrepancy by more than $3? Assume a normal distribution. Given $\sigma = 15$, $n = 100$, and $e = 3$, we simply have to determine the area under the normal curve (having a standard deviation of $\sigma_{\bar{x}} = 15/\sqrt{100} = 1.5$) over the interval from $\mu - 3$ to $\mu + 3$. The solution may easily be derived if we use Equation 12.8 again. Remember that with an infinite population Equation 12.8 is $e = (\sigma/\sqrt{n}) z_{\alpha/2}$. Multiplying both sides by $\sqrt{n}/\sigma$ gives us

$$z_{\alpha/2} = \frac{e\sqrt{n}}{\sigma} \qquad (12.15)$$

In this case we get

$$z_{\alpha/2} = \frac{3 \cdot \sqrt{100}}{15} = \frac{30}{15} - 2$$

From the normal distribution table (inside the back cover of this text) we find that the accumulated area under the standard normal distribution over the range from 0 to 2 is equal to 0.4772, so the tail to the right of 2 must be equal to 0.0228 (= 0.5 − 0.4772). If the tail to the right of $z_{\alpha/2}$ is equal to 0.0228, then, by definition, we get $\alpha/2 = 0.0228$, implying that $\alpha = 0.0456$ and that $1 - \alpha = 0.9544$. Thus we have a probability of 95.44 percent that the sample mean will not deviate from the population mean by more than $3.

Determining the Value of e, Given the Risk Probability and the Sample Size If the number of observations taken in a sample is, say, 64, what is the maximum error we can get with a 90 percent probability?

Here we apply Equation 12.8 directly:

$$e = \frac{\sigma}{\sqrt{n}} z_{\alpha/2} = \frac{15}{\sqrt{64}} \cdot 1.645 = 3.084$$

This means that there is a 90 percent chance that our estimate will not miss the true mean by more than $3.084.

THE TRADEOFF BETWEEN CONFIDENCE LEVEL AND INTERVAL WIDTH

In a textbook problem the confidence level is often indicated, so we are relieved of the need to determine it. In real life, however, a researcher has to determine the confidence level before the confidence interval may be established. While a high confidence level is desirable, there is a tradeoff between the confidence level and the confidence interval width. For any given sample size, the higher the confidence level, the wider the interval derived.

Suppose a restaurant manager wants to know how many waiters to employ and how much food to prepare for dinner. By constructing confidence intervals, she might find that there is a confidence level of 0.80 that the mean number of people who come to dine is between 90 and 110, a confidence level of 0.90 that the mean number of people who come to dine is between 80 and 120, and a confidence level of 0.99 that, on the average, between 50 and 150 people dine in the restaurant. There is a tradeoff, then, between precision in terms of the confidence level and accuracy in terms of the interval width within which the population mean is believed to lie.

Choosing a very high level of confidence is likely to make the interval too wide to be meaningful. The interval of from 50 to 150 diners is probably too broad to enable the restaurant's management to make any kind of decision. An interval such as 90 to 110 people is more specific and of greater assistance to management. There is, however, a good chance (20 percent) that the interval 90 to 110 does not really cover the true mean of the population. Hence a tradeoff between a high probability statement and a wider interval exists, as long as the sample size is held constant.

In most cases a confidence level between 0.90 and 0.99 is chosen, and the decision of which level to choose within that range depends on the type of question under consideration. At all times, however, the tradeoff between precision in the confidence level and accuracy in the width of the interval should be kept in mind.

This tradeoff may be illustrated diagrammatically as well. Figure 12.13

Figure 12.13

Tradeoff between confidence level and interval width

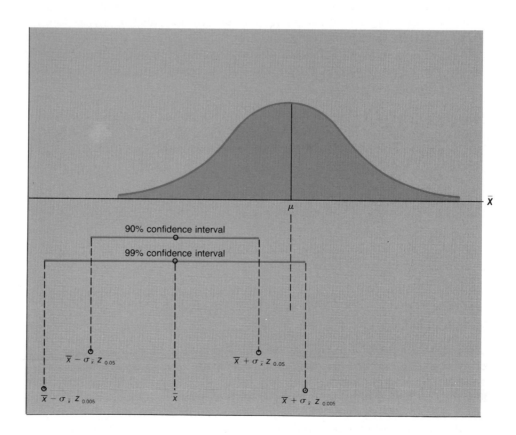

shows a given normal distribution that *cannot be observed by the researcher*; its mean is to be estimated by a confidence interval. Figure 12.13 also shows a hypothetical sample mean around which two confidence intervals are constructed, one with a 90 percent confidence level and an alternative one with a 99 percent confidence level. While the interval with the 90 percent confidence level (the narrower interval) misses μ in this example, the 99 percent interval is wide enough to cover μ. The wider the interval constructed, the greater the chance that it will include the true mean—but the less meaningful its implications will be.

12.4 Constructing a Confidence Interval for μ When σ Is Unknown

The extensive use we have made of the normal distribution is well justified. Many variables in business and economics have normal or close-to-normal distributions. Furthermore, we have pointed out that even in those cases in which the population distribution differs from the normal, the sample mean is approximately normally distributed as long as we have a sufficient number of independent observations in the sample (the central limit theorem). We have been assuming, however, that while the population mean, μ, is unknown and has to be estimated, the population standard deviation σ, is known and may be used to provide an interval estimate for the population mean. We shall now assume instead that σ is unknown and attempt to establish a confidence interval for μ. Here, instead of using Z scores, of the standard normal distribution, we use the t distribution, which we discussed in Chapter 10.

Recalling our definition of z_α as that Z score which bounds a right tail equal to α on the standard normal distribution, we shall use similar notation to denote scores of the t distribution in the following fashion: $t_\alpha^{(n)}$ *will denote that t score which bounds a right tail equal to α on the $t^{(n)}$ distribution*. It also follows directly that $t_{\alpha/2}^{(n)}$ is that t score which bounds a right tail equal to $\alpha/2$ on the $t^{(n)}$ distribution. Consider the example given in Figure 12.14: the value $t_{0.025}^{(17)}$ is the $t^{(17)}$ score that bounds a 2.5 percent right tail. The t distribution table (inside the back cover of this book) assigns the number 2.110 to this score.

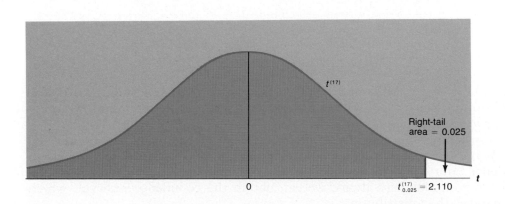

Figure 12.14

The location of the $t_{0.025}^{(17)}$ score

EXAMPLE 12.4

Determine the $t_\alpha^{(8)}$, $t_{\alpha/2}^{(8)}$, and $t_\alpha^{(\infty)}$ scores if $\alpha = 0.05$.

Since $\alpha = 0.05$, it is clear that $\alpha/2 = 0.025$. Focusing on the $t^{(8)}$ distribution first, we locate $t_{0.05}^{(8)} = 1.860$ in the t distribution table at the intersection of 8 degrees of freedom and $t_{0.050}$; similarly we determine that $t_{0.025}^{(8)} = 2.306$. As for $t_{0.05}^{(\infty)}$, we discover that this t score is equal to 1.645, a figure with which we are well acquainted from the normal distribution table. More specifically, we realize that $t_{0.05}^{(\infty)} = z_{0.05}$, and that, in general, for any α we get $t_\alpha^{(\infty)} = z_\alpha$. When the number of degrees of freedom approaches infinity, the t distribution approaches the standard normal distribution, as shown in Chapter 10. As a result, all the t scores approach their respective scores on the standard normal distribution.

When the standard deviation of the population is unknown and we need to provide an interval estimate for the mean of the distribution, it is necessary to substitute the estimated standard deviation for the true standard deviation. Thus, instead of using the statistic $\dfrac{\overline{X} - \mu}{\sigma_{\overline{X}}}$, we must use $\dfrac{\overline{X} - \mu}{S_{\overline{X}}}$, where $S_{\overline{X}}$ is the estimator of $\sigma_{\overline{X}}$:

$$S_{\overline{X}} = \frac{S}{\sqrt{n}} \tag{12.16a}$$

for an infinite or a finite population with replacement population and

$$S_{\overline{X}} = \frac{S}{\sqrt{n}} \sqrt{\frac{N - n}{N - 1}} \tag{12.16b}$$

for a finite population (and sampling without replacement). S is the familiar standard deviation of X:

$$S = \sqrt{\frac{\Sigma(X - \overline{X})^2}{n - 1}} = \sqrt{\frac{\Sigma X^2 - n\overline{X}^2}{n - 1}}$$

Whereas $\dfrac{\overline{X} - \mu}{\sigma_{\overline{X}}}$ has a standard normal distribution, $\dfrac{\overline{X} - \mu}{S_{\overline{X}}}$ has a t distribution with $(n - 1)$ degrees of freedom. Thus

$$\frac{\overline{X} - \mu}{S_{\overline{X}}} \sim t^{(n-1)} \tag{12.17}$$

Note that when the sample involves more than 30 observations, the t distribution in Equation 12.17 has at least 30 degrees of freedom and it closely approximates the normal distribution.

Earlier we saw how a confidence interval for the mean can be derived when σ is known. Using a similar approach, it is possible to derive a confidence interval for the mean when the standard deviation is unknown. Following similar derivations, we can obtain the confidence interval, which involves the t distribution:

$$P\left(\overline{X} - S_{\overline{X}} \cdot t_{\alpha/2}^{(n-1)} \leq \mu \leq \overline{X} + S_{\overline{X}} \cdot t_{\alpha/2}^{(n-1)}\right) = 1 - \alpha \qquad (12.18)$$

Equation 12.18 implies that when the standard deviation is unknown, a confidence interval with a confidence level of $(1 - \alpha)$ is

$$\overline{X} - S_{\overline{X}} \cdot t_{\alpha/2}^{(n-1)} \leq \mu \leq \overline{X} + S_{\overline{X}} \cdot t_{\alpha/2}^{(n-1)} \qquad (12.19)$$

EXAMPLE 12.5

The Consumer Protection Agency of Wyoming advocates truth in advertising and in labeling. As part of its regular activities, the agency conducts market surveys involving estimation by samples of products' weight. One of the products sampled consists of bags of charcoal briquettes advertised to contain 5 pounds of briquettes. A sample of 16 bags had the following weights (in pounds): 4.8, 4.7, 5.0, 5.2, 4.7, 4.9, 5.0, 5.0, 4.6, 4.7, 5.0, 5.1, 4.7, 4.5, 4.9, 4.9.

The Consumer Protection Agency needs to estimate and derive from these data the confidence interval for the mean weight of the bags of charcoal briquettes at a confidence level of 95 percent.

The point estimate may simply be obtained by averaging the 16 weights to obtain

$$\Sigma X = 4.8 + 4.7 + 5.0 + 5.2 + \cdots + 4.9 = 77.7$$

$$\overline{X} = \frac{77.7}{16} = 4.856 \text{ pounds}$$

To obtain an interval estimate for the mean, we first calculate the sample standard deviation, S:

$$\Sigma X^2 = 4.8^2 + 4.7^2 + 5.0^2 + 5.2^2 + \cdots + 4.9^2 = 377.89$$

$$n\overline{X}^2 = 16 \cdot 4.856^2 = 16 \cdot 23.581 = 377.29$$

$$S = \sqrt{\frac{377.89 - 377.29}{16 - 1}} = \sqrt{\frac{0.60}{15}} = \sqrt{0.04} = 0.20$$

Since $\dfrac{\overline{X} - \mu}{S/\sqrt{n}} \sim t^{(15)}$ and since $\alpha/2 = 0.025$, the t value to be used here is $t_{0.025}^{(15)} = 2.131$. Using Equation 12.19, we determine that the confidence interval is

$$4.856 - \frac{0.20}{\sqrt{16}} \cdot 2.131 < \mu < 4.856 + \frac{0.20}{\sqrt{16}} \cdot 2.131$$

or

$$4.749 < \mu < 4.963$$

The interval obtained implies that there is a 95 percent chance that the range between 4.749 and 4.963 includes the true mean weight and thus that there is at most 5 percent confidence that the mean weight is really 5 pounds.

The confidence interval constructed when the standard deviation of the population is unknown is wider (other things being equal) than that constructed when it is known. If we definitely knew that $\sigma = 0.20$ (Example 12.5), the interval would have been

$$\overline{X} - \frac{\sigma}{\sqrt{n}} z_{\alpha/2} < \mu < \overline{X} + \frac{\sigma}{\sqrt{n}} z_{\alpha/2}$$

which for our example is

$$4.856 - \frac{0.20}{\sqrt{16}} \cdot 1.96 < \mu < 4.856 + \frac{0.20}{\sqrt{16}} \cdot 1.96$$

or

$$4.758 < \mu < 4.954$$

Indeed, this interval is narrower than the interval between 4.749 and 4.963, which we obtained for the unknown σ. The wider interval reflects the uncertainty concerning the value of σ: if σ is estimated, we need to allow a wider range to be sure that the unknown μ will fall within it.

12.5 Point Estimate and Confidence Interval for a Proportion

Just as when we estimated the mean of a distribution, when we want to estimate a population's proportion using a random sample, our result is subject to sampling error. To describe the sample results more meaningfully, we must provide both point and interval estimates for the proportion.

In Chapter 8 we expressed the number of successes in a binomial experiment in terms of the proportion of the trials resulting in success by simply dividing the number of successes (X) by the total number of trials (n) to get X/n. We denote X/n by $\overline{p}$ and recall that

$$E(\overline{p}) = p$$

$$\sigma_{\overline{p}}^2 = \frac{pq}{n} \tag{12.20}$$

$$\sigma_{\overline{p}} = \sqrt{\frac{pq}{n}}$$

Our point estimate for the true population proportion is the statistic $\overline{p} = X/n$. To obtain an interval estimate, we recall that X and therefore X/n have approximately normal distributions (provided that $np \geq 5$ and $nq \geq 5$). When the normal approximation applies, we may write

$$\overline{p} \sim N\left(p, \sqrt{\frac{pq}{n}}\right) \tag{12.21}$$

so that

$$\frac{\overline{p} - p}{\sqrt{\dfrac{pq}{n}}} \sim N(0, 1) \qquad \textbf{(12.22)}$$

However, since the standard deviation is equal to $\sqrt{\dfrac{pq}{n}}$ and p is unknown (if it were known, we would not have needed the estimation to begin with), we shall use the estimated standard error $S_{\overline{p}} = \sqrt{\dfrac{\overline{p}(1 - \overline{p})}{n}}$ and obtain

$$\frac{\overline{p} - p}{S_{\overline{p}}} \simeq N(0, 1) \qquad \textbf{(12.23)}$$

Following an approach similar to the one we used to derive a confidence interval for the mean, we can construct a confidence interval for the true proportion and obtain the following:

$$P(\overline{p} - S_{\overline{p}} \cdot z_{\alpha/2} \leq p \leq \overline{p} + S_{\overline{p}} \cdot z_{\alpha/2}) = 1 - \alpha \qquad \textbf{(12.24)}$$

Note that the widest interval is obtained when $\overline{p} = \frac{1}{2}$ (other things being held constant).

EXAMPLE 12.6

A new program for a youth club is planned in a small city. To determine whether or not the program will get the city government's support, it is necessary to estimate the proportion of young people who plan to use the club's facilities. A survey of 100 randomly selected young people has shown that 22 will use the facilities if they become available.

To obtain a point estimate of the proportion of young people who plan to use the facilities, we merely divide the number of successes (22) by the total number of trials (100) to get $X/n = 22/100 = 0.22$. We then estimate the standard error $S_{\overline{p}}$:

$$S_{\overline{p}} = \sqrt{\frac{\overline{p}(1 - \overline{p})}{n}} = \sqrt{\frac{0.22 \cdot 0.78}{100}} = 0.0414$$

To construct the confidence interval for the true proportion with a confidence level of 99 percent, we apply Equation 12.24:

$$P(0.22 - 0.0414 \cdot 2.575 \leq p \leq 0.22 + 0.0414 \cdot 2.575)$$

$$= P(0.1134 \leq p \leq 0.3266)$$

$$= 0.99$$

The sample indicates that there is a 99 percent chance that the interval between 11.34 and 32.66 percent contains the true population proportion.

12.6 Point Estimate and Confidence Interval for the Variance

In Chapter 4 we presented the measure $S^2 = \dfrac{\Sigma(X - \overline{X})^2}{n - 1}$. In Section 12.1 we explained that S^2 is an unbiased estimator of the population variance, σ^2.

Statistical theory shows that when the population of interest is normally distributed, the sum of squared deviations divided by the population variance has a chi-square distribution with $(n - 1)$ degrees of freedom:

$$\frac{\Sigma(X - \overline{X})^2}{\sigma^2} \sim \chi^2_{(n-1)} \qquad\qquad (12.25)$$

or

$$\frac{(n - 1)S^2}{\sigma^2} \sim \chi^2_{(n-1)} \qquad\qquad (12.26)$$

We can use Equation 12.26 to construct a confidence interval for the population variance:

$$P\left(\chi^2_{1-\alpha/2 (n-1)} \leq \frac{(n - 1)S^2}{\sigma^2} \leq \chi^2_{\alpha/2 (n-1)} \right) = 1 - \alpha$$

By taking reciprocals in the parentheses and reversing the inequalities we obtain

$$P\left(\frac{1}{\chi^2_{\alpha/2 (n-1)}} \leq \frac{\sigma^2}{(n - 1)S^2} \leq \frac{1}{\chi^2_{1-\alpha/2 (n-1)}} \right) = 1 - \alpha$$

Finally, after multiplying by $(n - 1)S^2$ we derive the confidence interval

$$P\left(\frac{(n - 1)S^2}{\chi^2_{\alpha/2 (n-1)}} \leq \sigma^2 \leq \frac{(n - 1)S^2}{\chi^2_{1-\alpha/2 (n-1)}} \right) = 1 - \alpha \qquad\qquad (12.27)$$

EXAMPLE 12.7

The risk of a stock investment is often measured by the variance of the rate of return (i.e., the rate of profit) on the money invested. A sample of 26 annual rates of return was taken. The sample estimate of S was 15 percent ($S^2 = 15^2 = 225$). Find a 95 percent confidence interval for the population variance.

To find a 95 percent confidence interval for the population variance σ^2, assuming that the rates of return are normally distributed, we first use the chi-square table (Appendix A, Table A.4) to find

$$\chi^2_{0.975 (25)} = 13.120 \quad \text{and} \quad \chi^2_{0.025 (25)} = 40.646$$

The lower limit of the confidence interval is

$$\frac{(n-1)S^2}{\chi^{2(n-1)}_{\alpha/2}} = \frac{(26-1) \cdot 225}{40.646} = 138.39$$

and the upper limit is

$$\frac{(n-1)S^2}{\chi^{2(n-1)}_{1-\alpha/2}} = \frac{(26-1) \cdot 225}{13.120} = 428.73$$

So the confidence interval is

$$138.39 \le \sigma^2 \le 428.73$$

This implies that we should have 95 percent confidence that the variance is covered by the interval from 138.39 to 428.73. It also implies that our confidence interval for the standard deviation of the rate of return ranges from $\sqrt{138.39} = 11.76$ percent to $\sqrt{428.73} = 20.71$ percent.

12.7 APPLICATION 1:
THE ELECTION PROBLEM

Every presidential election campaign is accompanied by a flood of forecasts assessing each candidate's chances of winning. The forecasts are based on polls that estimate the proportion of voters who are expected to vote for each candidate on election day. The sampling is carried out on a state-by-state basis, with a separate estimate derived for each state. Depending on the poll results in each state, the candidates must decide whether to increase their campaign efforts in the state or to concede it to their rival and concentrate their efforts on campaigns in other states.

Suppose that one week before the election, a sample of 900 voters in New York reveals that 400 would vote for the Democrat and 500 would vote for the Republican. Should the Democratic candidate concede New York State? Could the Democrat still win New York's electoral seats?

The point estimate of the proportion of Democratic votes in New York is $\bar{p} = X/n = 400/900 = 0.444$. If 4/9 of the voters do vote for the Democratic candidate and 5/9 of them vote for the Republican, the Democrat will lose the New York State electors. In view of the poll's results, however, is it possible that the Democrat may get 51 percent of the votes in New York? By constructing a 0.95 confidence interval for the true proportion, p, we see that there is a 95 percent chance that the true proportion is covered by the interval between 41.2 and 47.6 percent—an interval that does *not* cover the value of 0.51.

$$P(\bar{p} - S_{\bar{p}} \cdot z_{\alpha/2} \le p \le \bar{p} + S_{\bar{p}} \cdot z_{\alpha/2}) = 1 - \alpha$$

$$P\left[\bar{p} - \sqrt{\frac{\bar{p}(1-\bar{p})}{n}} \cdot z_{\alpha/2} \le p \le \bar{p} + \sqrt{\frac{\bar{p}(1-\bar{p})}{n}} \cdot z_{\alpha/2}\right] = 1 - \alpha$$

Using $\alpha = 0.05$, $\bar{p} = 0.444$, and $n = 900$, we get

$$P\left(0.444 - \sqrt{\frac{0.444 \cdot 0.556}{900}} \cdot 1.96 \leq p \leq 0.444 + \sqrt{\frac{0.444 \cdot 0.556}{900}} \cdot 1.96\right) = 0.95$$

$$P(0.412 \leq p \leq 0.476) = 0.95$$

Note that we should not be too concerned by the fact that the standard deviation of $\bar{p}$ used to construct the above confidence interval is itself an estimate. Taking the largest possible value of the standard deviation (which is obtained when $p = 0.5$), we get

$$\sigma_{\bar{p}} = \sqrt{\frac{0.5 \cdot 0.5}{900}} = 0.01667$$

Thus the confidence interval becomes

$$0.444 - 0.01667 \cdot 1.96 < p < 0.444 + 0.01667 \cdot 1.96$$

or

$$0.411 < p < 0.477$$

—an interval very close to that obtained above. This interval does not include the value 0.51 either. Should the Democratic candidate stop campaigning in New York and concentrate on other states? No, because a week still remains before election day and New York is a large state with a large number of electors. Our advice would be to campaign heavily in New York, since a gain of about 5 percent of the voters would give the Democrat a reasonable chance of winning the state.

Now assume that out of a sample of 2,500 voters in Kentucky only 500—20 percent—support the Republican candidate. Should the Republican keep on campaigning in Kentucky or focus on other states?

A 95 percent confidence interval at the highest possible value of the standard deviation of $\bar{p}$ is

$$0.20 - \sqrt{\frac{0.5 \cdot 0.5}{2,500}} \cdot 1.96 < p < 0.20 + \sqrt{\frac{0.5 \cdot 0.5}{2,500}} \cdot 1.96$$

$$0.20 - 0.0196 < p < 0.20 + 0.0196$$

or

$$0.1804 < p < 0.2196$$

If we used $\bar{p} = 0.20$ instead of 0.50 for the standard deviation, we would have gotten an even narrower range; thus it is clear that the true p is most probably substantially below 51 percent. Our advice to the Republican would be to concentrate on states other than Kentucky.

12.8 APPLICATION 2:
QUALITY CONTROL

Before the 1930s, American firms were relatively small and quality control had not been instituted. Then the concept of quality control was developed, thanks mainly to Walter A. Shewhart of Bell Telephone Laboratories. Modern industry is characterized by mass production, and quality control departments exist in many industrial firms. Today consumers are so conscious of the quality and safety of the products they buy that a defective or unsafe product may greatly hurt a firm's reputation. Therefore businesses are concerned about keeping their products at a specified level of quality.

Take a bottling company. Soft-drink bottles are filled by automatic machines that are set to seal the bottles with an interior pressure of 2 atmospheres. The pressure may vary from one bottle to another, however, owing to improper setting of the filling machine or other reasons. A pressure greater than 2.5 atmospheres may cause an explosion; in fact, many soft-drink buyers have been injured by such explosions. One way to avoid explosions is to decrease the pressure all the way down to, say, 1 atmosphere. At such low pressure, however, the soft drink loses its taste and value.

The quality control process that's important here is a checking procedure through which management tries to eliminate systematic changes in the degree of pressure. If such a systematic change occurs, production should be stopped while the machine is adjusted. Because the pressure in the bottles is a random variable, when should we stop the machine? Suppose that the quality control department takes a sample of 10 bottles every hour and the average pressure, $\overline{X}$, is measured. Past experience shows that

$$\overline{X} \sim N(\mu, \sigma_{\overline{X}})$$

where $\mu = 2$ and $\sigma_{\overline{X}} = 0.15$.

The quality control department establishes an upper control limit (*UCL*) and lower control limit (*LCL*) such that the probability that the average pressure of 10 bottles ($\overline{X}$) will be greater than *UCL* is one-half of 1 percent (that is, 0.005) and the probability that $\overline{X}$ will be lower than *LCL* is also 0.005. To determine *UCL* we write

$$P(\overline{X} > UCL) = P\left(\frac{\overline{X} - \mu}{\sigma_{\overline{X}}} > \frac{UCL - \mu}{\sigma_{\overline{X}}}\right) = P\left(Z > \frac{UCL - \mu}{\sigma_{\overline{X}}}\right)$$

$$= P\left(Z > \frac{UCL - 2}{0.15}\right)$$

$$= 0.005$$

From the normal distribution table (inside the back cover of the book) we find that the value above which there is a 0.005 right-tail area is 2.575, so

$$\frac{UCL - 2}{0.15} = 2.575$$

and it follows that

$$UCL = 2 + 0.15 \cdot 2.575 = 2.386 \text{ atmospheres}$$

Similarly, *LCL* is determined as follows:

$$P(\overline{X} < LCL) = P\left(\frac{\overline{X} - \mu}{\sigma_{\overline{X}}} < \frac{LCL - \mu}{\sigma_{\overline{X}}}\right) = P\left(Z < \frac{LCL - 2}{0.15}\right) = 0.005$$

Therefore

$$\frac{LCL - 2}{0.15} = -2.575$$

and

$$LCL = 2 - 0.15 \cdot 2.575 = 1.614 \text{ atmospheres}$$

Figure 12.15 is a quality control chart showing the *UCL* and *LCL*. The average pressure of 10 bottles as measured every hour is plotted on the chart. As long as the points representing $\overline{X}$ are between the *UCL* and the *LCL*, production continues. Such results as those seen in Figure 12.16, however, show very clearly that since 10 A.M. the machine has shown a tendency to move out of adjustment and since 3 P.M. the averages have been out of the acceptable limits. The bottles produced from 3 P.M. on are of unacceptable quality. The machine should be stopped and adjusted.

More sophisticated quality control methods exist, of course, but many of them are based on the confidence-interval approach.

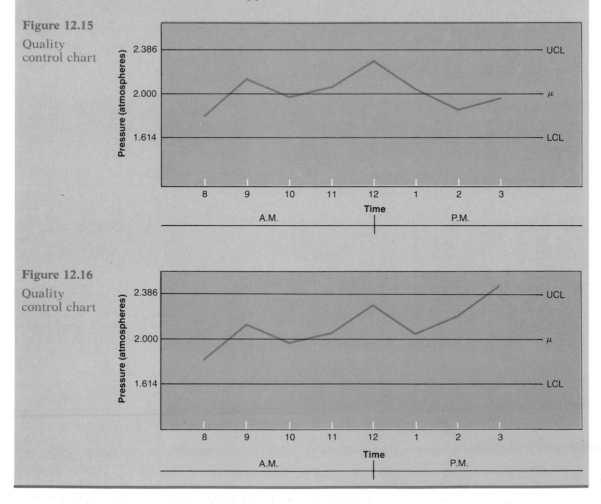

Figure 12.15
Quality control chart

Figure 12.16
Quality control chart

Chapter Summary and Review

1. Point estimation
   Point estimation is the use of a sample statistic to determine a single value as an estimate of a population parameter.
   a. Unbiasedness: An estimator is unbiased if the mean of its sampling distribution is equal to the population parameter of interest.
   b. Consistency: A consistent estimator is one which has a higher probability of being close to the population parameter of interest as the sample size increases.
   c. Relative efficiency: If two estimators are unbiased, the one having the smaller standard error is the more efficient of the two.

2. Confidence interval for the mean (the sampling distribution is normal)
   a. If σ is known:

   $$P(\overline{X} - \sigma_{\overline{X}} \cdot z_{\alpha/2} \leq \mu \leq \overline{X} + \sigma_{\overline{X}} \cdot z_{\alpha/2}) = 1 - \alpha$$

   b. If σ is unknown:

   $$P(\overline{X} - S_{\overline{X}} \cdot t_{\alpha/2}^{(n-1)} \leq \mu \leq \overline{X} + S_{\overline{X}} \cdot t_{\alpha/2}^{(n-1)}) = 1 - \alpha$$

3. Definition
   a. Confidence interval: $\overline{X} - e, \overline{X} + e$
   b. Confidence level: $1 - \alpha$
   c. Risk probability: α
   d. Tolerable error: e

4. Confidence interval for a proportion
   a. $P(\overline{p} - S_{\overline{p}} \cdot z_{\alpha/2} \leq p \leq \overline{p} + S_{\overline{p}} \cdot z_{\alpha/2}) = 1 - \alpha$

   where

   $$S_{\overline{p}} = \sqrt{\frac{\overline{p}(1 - \overline{p})}{n}}$$

   b. For conservative interval use $\overline{p} = \frac{1}{2}$

5. Confidence interval for the variance

   $$P\left(\frac{(n - 1)S^2}{\chi_{\alpha/2}^{2(n-1)}} \leq \sigma^2 \leq \frac{(n - 1)S^2}{\chi_{1-\alpha/2}^{2(n-1)}}\right) = 1 - \alpha$$

   where $S^2 = \Sigma(X - \overline{X})^2/(n - 1)$.

Problems

12.1. A random sample of five observations is randomly drawn out of a population of size $N = 100$. The observations are 5, 6, 4, 0, and -3.

   (a) Calculate a point estimate of the mean and of the standard deviation, σ.
   (b) Calculate the estimate of $\sigma_{\overline{X}}$ twice: first under the assumption that the sampling is done with replacement and then under the assumption that it is done without replacement.

12.2. Let $\overline{X}$ be a sample mean. Suppose you use the estimator $\frac{3}{2}\overline{X}$ to estimate the population mean, μ. Is this a biased or unbiased estimator of μ? If it is biased, state the size of the bias in percent of μ.

12.3. Suppose you use the statistic $\dfrac{\Sigma(X - \overline{X})^2}{n - 2}$ to estimate the population variance, σ^2. Is this an upward-biased or a downward-biased estimator? Explain and illustrate with a numerical example.

 12.4. The daily return per \$100 investment in a given stock is a random variable whose distribution is normal. The following is a random sample of five daily returns on the stock:

Day	Return
1	−0.2
2	0.1
3	0.1
4	−0.6
5	−0.9

(*a*) Construct a 95 percent confidence interval for the mean daily rate of return on the stock, assuming that the variance is 0.1.

(*b*) Rework part *a*, this time assuming that the variance is unknown.

12.5. The amount of oil piped into a barrel by Quality Oil Corporation is a random variable normally distributed with a known standard deviation of 3 gallons. Thirty-six barrels are randomly and independently selected, and the average number of gallons in a barrel is found to be 102.

(*a*) What is the probability that the 102-gallon average of the sample is within 2 gallons of the actual population mean?

(*b*) Construct a confidence interval around the mean of the above population (using a 99 percent confidence level).

12.6. A health insurance company is conducting periodic surveys on the cost of health services in order to update its health insurance premiums. Suppose you head a research team whose responsibility is to estimate the cost of hospitalization (excluding the cost of special services) per day in California. If the standard deviation of the cost of hospitalization per day is \$40, how many observations will you need in order to determine the cost with only a 2 percent probability of making an error in excess of \$4?

12.7. Referring to Problem 12.6, imagine that as a result of a recent recession, your office is subject to serious budget cuts, and consequently you can sample only 25 observations. The sample shows that the daily hospitalization cost is \$170 (on the average) and that the standard deviation is \$30. Determine a 99 percent confidence interval for the mean hospitalization cost, and briefly explain the meaning of the interval.

12.8. The number of dollars collected in tolls per day (Monday through Friday) on a given bridge is a random variable with a known standard deviation of \$4,000. A sample of 16 observations is taken to estimate the mean toll collection. What is the probability that the estimate will be off by more than \$2,570 from the true mean collection?

12.9. The number of miles per gallon obtained by a given type of car is a random variable normally distributed with a mean of 20 miles and a standard deviation of 1 mile. Four such cars are randomly selected and the average miles per gallon are measured. Find the probability that the sample mean is between 20.5 and 21.0 miles.

12.10. The gas consumption of a given model car is normally distributed with a mean of 10 miles per gallon and a standard deviation of 2 miles per gallon, that is, $X \sim N(10, 2)$. A sample of nine cars of this model has been taken. They were all driven the same distance and under the same conditions. Calculate the probability $P(9 \leq \overline{X} \leq 11)$, where $\overline{X}$ is the sample mean.

12.11. The daily revenue of a department store chain is normally distributed with a mean of $50,000 and a standard deviation of $3,000. Find the probability that the average daily revenue over 36 days will be smaller than $51,000.

12.12. A random sample of size $n = 81$ days is taken with the purpose of determining the mean daily waste disposal of an industrial firm. What is the maximum size of the tolerable error, e, if the standard deviation is $\sigma = 4$ tons? Use $\alpha = 0.05$ and assume that the variable is normally distributed. How would your answer change if the sample size were $n = 2,500$?

12.13. A bank executive wants to estimate the average number of daily customers. He wants to have 99 percent confidence that the error will not exceed 5. It is known that the daily number of customers is normally distributed with a standard deviation of 100. How many days should be sampled?

12.14. A random sample of 100 observations reveals that $\overline{X} = 96$. Knowing that $\sigma = 10$ and that the distribution is normal, calculate a 0.95 confidence interval for the population mean.

12.15. The monthly incomes of a random sample of five students are $300, $400, $200, $700, $1,000. Assuming that the income is normally distributed, find the 0.99 confidence interval for the mean income of the student population.

12.16. Suppose you wanted to construct a confidence interval for a mean of a normal distribution with an unknown variance. If Z values were used, would the confidence interval be narrower or wider than that obtained by use of t values? Does your answer depend on the sample size? Explain.

12.17. To determine the optimal number of items a company should hold in inventory, it is necessary to estimate the average weekly sales of that particular item. A random sample is taken, and the number of items sold per week is as follows: 64, 57, 49, 81, 76, 70, 59. Assume that the number of items sold is normally distributed. Give a point estimate and an interval estimate for the mean number of items sold per week, assuming a 95 percent confidence level. Explain the meaning of your interval estimate.

12.18. For scheduling purposes, a bus company wants to estimate the average time it takes a bus to get from City *A* to City *B*. A sample of 25 trips is taken and the average time is found to be 80 minutes. The standard deviation in the sample is 10 minutes.

    (*a*) Give an interval estimate for the mean trip duration at a confidence level of 90 percent.
    (*b*) Explain the meaning of the interval constructed in part *a*.
    (*c*) Suppose the bus company wants to estimate the mean trip duration with a maximum error of 2 minutes and a 0.05 risk of exceeding this error. What sample size is required if we assume that σ is known and equal to 10?

12.19. The proportion of a certain brand of tires that will become flat within the first 1,000 miles is to be estimated by a sample. To assure randomness and independence, each tire examined is mounted on a different kind of car. One hundred tires are examined and 5 of them become flat within the first 1,000 miles.

    (*a*) Construct an interval estimate for the true proportion at a 99 percent confidence level.
    (*b*) What is the sample size required to determine the proportion in such a way that the probability of making an error in excess of 0.01 is 0.05?

12.20. A sample of 14 out of 48 firms in a given industry is observed. The sample shows that 6 firms use a given technology known as Technology A. Give a 95 percent interval estimate for the proportion of firms using Technology A in the industry. If all 48 firms are observed, what is the standard deviation of the estimated proportion? Explain.

12.21. A firm is considering producing and promoting a new product. It is estimated that the product will be profitable if at least 5 percent of the population buy it within the first year of its introduction. A survey of 200 people has shown that 6 would buy the product.

(a) Estimate the proportion of buyers in the population.
(b) Construct a 99 percent confidence interval for the proportion of buyers in the population.
(c) If the true proportion of buyers is exactly 0.05 (i.e., 5 percent), what is the probability that 200 observations selected at random will include 6 or fewer buyers?
(d) If the true proportion of buyers is exactly 0.05, what is the probability that 10,000 observations selected at random will include 300 or fewer buyers?
(e) Suppose the true proportion of buyers is exactly 0.05. What is the sample size required so that the probability of missing the true proportion by more than 0.005 will not exceed 5 percent?

12.22. One month before the election of a new U.S. president, a survey of 10,000 randomly selected voters in a certain state showed that 4,500 favored the Democratic candidate.

(a) Estimate the proportion of voters favoring the Democratic candidate in this state.
(b) Give a 95 percent confidence interval for the above proportion.
(c) Rework parts *a* and *b*, this time assuming that the sample size was 100, of whom 45 favored the Democratic candidate.

12.23. "Constructing a confidence interval for a proportion, p, is somewhat problematic. The problem is that if p is unknown, the standard deviation is also unknown and it is impossible to construct the interval. On the other hand, we can always be conservative and estimate the standard deviation by using $p = \frac{1}{2}$." Evaluate this statement.

12.24. Suppose that when estimating a proportion, p, we want to make sure we have a 95 percent chance that the true proportion will not be missed by more than 0.01. How many observations are needed to achieve this result?

12.25. CLC Motor Corporation has introduced a new car. A sample of 10 cars examined for their miles-per-gallon performance has shown the following results:

Car	Miles per gallon
1	20
2	28
3	27
4	29
5	30
6	32
7	25
8	24
9	30
10	35

(a) Estimate the mean miles per gallon of the new car.
(b) Construct a 95 percent confidence interval for the mean miles per gallon on the assumption that σ is known and equals 2.0.
(c) Suppose we want to construct a confidence interval for the mean miles per gallon such

that its width will be only 50 percent of the width obtained in part *b*. If the sample size is not increased, what is the confidence level of the confidence interval so constructed?

(*d*) Suppose we want to construct a confidence interval for the mean miles per gallon such that its width will be 50 percent of the width of the interval obtained in part *b* and still maintain a 95 percent confidence level. What is the sample size needed?

12.26. When a 95 percent confidence interval for the mean of an infinite population is constructed, is it true that the interval constructed is *necessarily* wider when σ is unknown than when it is known? Explain.

12.27. (*a*) Assume that the actual expenditure on drugs per household of three in a given location is normally distributed, and its average has to be estimated with an accuracy of $2 and 95 percent probability (i.e., there should be 95 percent probability that the estimated mean is not off by more than $2 from the true mean of the distribution). If the standard deviation of drug expenditures is $14 and each observation costs $3 to make, determine the budget for the sample.

(*b*) If the sample size is 64 observations, what is the probability that the error will not exceed $3?

12.28. You want to estimate the mean of a population. The cost of sampling is $1 per observation. The expected cost of sampling errors is related to the sample size, *n*, in the following way:

$$\text{Expected cost of sampling} = \frac{10{,}976}{n^2}$$

What sample size will you choose if your goal is to minimize total costs? (Hint: Try the range $20 \le n \le 30$).

12.29. Table P12.29 provides data on long-term debt as a percentage of total invested capital in 1981 for 12 paper manufacturers. Assume that the 12 firms represent a sample taken from a very large population of firms.

TABLE P12.29

Bemis	32.4%
Boise Cascade	37.9
Champion International	34.5
Chesapeake Corp. of Virginia	29.3
Consolidated Papers	7.9
Crown Zellerbach	33.2
Diamond International	20.2
Federal Paper Board	59.5
Fort Howard Paper	11.3
Georgia-Pacific	33.5
Great Northern Nekoosa	26.7
Hammermill Paper	35.9

Source: *Business Week*, March 1, 1982, p. 73.

(*a*) Give the point estimate of the long-term debt as a percentage of the invested capital in the industry.

(*b*) Give a 95 percent confidence interval for your estimate, assuming that σ is known to be 10.

(*c*) Again give a 95 percent confidence interval for your estimate, this time assuming that σ is unknown.

12.30. Many businesses invest part of their profit in research and development (R&D). The R&D of a sample of 10 firms is shown in Table P12.30.

TABLE P12.30

Firm	R&D as a percentage of sales
1	2%
2	0
3	6
4	3
5	4
6	2
7	6
8	8
9	7
10	4

(a) Calculate unbiased estimates of the mean and variance of the R&D spending, based on the above sample.
(b) Construct a 95 percent confidence interval for the variance.
(c) What assumptions are needed for the confidence interval for the variance to be valid?

12.31. Suppose the sample variances of two different samples are

$$S_1^2 = S_2^2 = 100$$

You want to construct a 95 percent confidence interval for the variance of the first population, σ_1^2, based on S_1^2, and for the variance of the second population, σ_2^2, based on S_2^2. Suppose the number of observations was 11 in the first sample and 31 in the second. Which confidence interval is wider? Explain.

12.32. A survey of 100 randomly selected voters in Chicago reveals that 40 of them intend to vote Democratic in an upcoming election for president.

(a) Estimate the proportion of voters who will vote Democratic in Chicago in the next election.
(b) Find the 0.99 confidence interval for the proportion of voters in Chicago who will vote for the Democratic candidate.

12.33. A random sample of 10 days reveals the following daily output of a given machine (in units): 5, 6, 7, 8, 9, 4, 3, 9, 9, and 10.

(a) Find a point estimate of the variance of the daily units produced.
(b) Assuming that production is normally distributed, calculate the 0.95 confidence interval for the variance.

12.34. Suppose that the number of defects in a fabric per 50 square yards is normally distributed with a mean of 2 and a standard deviation of 0.4. The quality control department takes a daily sample of 100 units, consisting of fabric pieces of 50 square yards each.

(a) Calculate the upper control limit (*UCL*) given that the probability that $\overline{X} \geq UCL$ is 5 percent.
(b) Suppose that in a daily sample the quality control department finds an average of 4 defects. Should the machine be stopped?

Case Problems

12.1. (Extensive computer work needed) The meaning of biased and unbiased estimators was demonstrated in this chapter by drawing random samples with replacement from the sales data in Data Set 1, Appendix B, Table B.1. Three estimators were considered: the mean, the variance estimator $\dfrac{\Sigma(X - \bar{X})^2}{n - 1}$, and the variance estimator $\dfrac{\Sigma(X - \bar{X})^2}{n}$. Repeat this demonstration using the profit margin data from Data Set 1.

12.2. Assume that the profit margin data that appear in Data Set 1 constitute a sample taken from a normal population whose mean, μ, and variance, σ^2, are unknown.

(*a*) Find the point estimate for the mean, μ.
(*b*) Find the 95 percent confidence interval for the population mean profit margin.
(*c*) How would you change your answer to part *b* if σ were known and equaled 4 percent?
(*d*) Estimate the proportion of companies in the population with profit margins below 5 percent.
(*e*) Find a 95 percent confidence interval for the population proportion of part *d*.

12.3. Data Set 2, Appendix B, Table B.2, consists of the annual rates of return (for 1971–1980) of eight groups of mutual funds. Consider this period to be a random sample of an infinite population of rates of return, past, present, and future. Estimate the mean rate of return of each group (you will construct eight intervals), treating each group as a separate population, and construct 95 percent confidence intervals for the mean of each group of funds. What can you say about the relationships between the means and standard deviations of the eight groups of data? Do you see any pattern among them? Explain.

12.4. The 1981 profit margin data for 100 firms are listed in Data Set 1, Appendix B, Table B.1. Consider these data to be the population of interest and assume that the population is normally distributed.

(*a*) Calculate the population mean.
(*b*) Draw a random sample of five observations out of the population (use the random digits table in Appendix A, Table A.13) and give a point estimate and a 95 percent confidence interval for the population mean.
(*c*) Repeat part *b* three more times, using sample sizes of 30, 80, and 100 firms. Note that in the last case you observe the entire population. Explain your results.

12.5. For each of the eight groups of mutual funds in Data Set 2, Appendix B, Table B.2, estimate the proportion of annual rates of return that are 10 percent or over, treating the data as a sample of the infinite population of past, present, and future rates of return. If you wanted to choose one of the eight groups for investment, based solely on the above estimate, which of these groups would you select? Is this estimate a "good" criterion for selecting the group of mutual funds for your investments? Explain.

HYPOTHESIS TESTING: ONE POPULATION

CHAPTER THIRTEEN OUTLINE

Key Terms
decision rule
null hypothesis
alternative hypothesis
Type I error
Type II error
critical value
acceptance region
rejection region
test statistic
significance level
upper-tail test
lower-tail test
simple hypothesis
composite hypothesis
power of a test
power function

Chapter 12 dealt with estimation of population parameters. In this and the coming chapters we shall show more directly how sampling may be used as a guide in decision-making processes. In fact, we often rely heavily on sample data in decision making. Public opinion polls may help a presidential candidate to decide whether to keep running or drop out of a primary race. A market survey may help a firm to estimate consumer interest in a given product and thus to determine whether or not funds should be allocated to research and development of that product. A sample of items produced by a machine may determine whether the machine should be stopped for adjustment or allowed to keep running. Sample results may be used as either the sole determinant of a decision or as a major input in the decision-making process.

In this chapter we deal with hypothesis testing for one population. In Chapter 14 we shall consider tests comparing two populations.

13.1 Basic Hypothesis-Testing Concepts: An Example Involving A Discrete Distribution

We shall now develop a systematic method of decision making based on sample results. We shall begin by introducing a simple example that makes no assumptions with regard to the shape of the probability distribution of the random variable. Our example will clearly illustrate the main idea and procedures involved in hypothesis testing.

A large hospital is using a given medicine that is effective for 50 percent of the patients treated with it. The hospital's doctors are greatly concerned about the fact that 50 percent of patients are not helped by it. The cost of the medicine is $100 a dose, and one dose is enough to treat a patient. After years of laboratory research, Merca Company has announced the discovery of a superior medicine. Merca claims that the new medicine is effective for 70 percent of the patients treated. One dose of the new medicine is enough to treat a patient, but the cost per dose is $1,100. Suppose we must decide on behalf of the hospital whether or not to buy the Merca product. Our first logical step will be to find out whether the new medicine really constitutes a significant improvement over the old one. In other words, we must look for evidence to support or reject Merca's claim.

The hospital's management decides to buy eight doses of the new medicine and try it on eight patients. Denoting the number of patients *cured* by the new medicine by X, we realize that the "experiment" may result in the following values of X: 0, 1, 2, 3, 4, 5, 6, 7, or 8. It is important to realize that Merca's claim refers to the *probability* of curing a patient, and in any experiment involving a finite number of patients, X can take on any of the values 0, 1, 2, 3, 4, 5, 6, 7, and 8 *even if Merca's claim is correct*. In order to make a decision, we must have a **decision rule** that will prudently take into consideration the probabilistic nature of the problem.

ESTABLISHING THE DECISION RULE

The first step in any decision-making process of hypothesis testing is the division of the sample space into two mutually exclusive and collectively exhaustive sets in such a way that any of the experiment's results will lead to a clear decision. For example, suppose we decide that if $X = 7$ or $X = 8$, there is a high enough percentage of successes to support Merca's claim and to warrant the adoption of the new medicine, but if $X = 0, 1, 2, 3, 4, 5,$ or 6, the frequency of successes is not high enough to support Merca's claim and to warrant the adoption of the new medicine. Obviously, the sets A ($X = 7, 8$) and B ($X = 0, 1, 2, 3, 4, 5, 6$) are mutually exclusive since $A \cap B = \emptyset$, and they are collectively exhaustive since $A \cup B$ contains the entire set of possibilities. The decision rule, then, is to accept Merca's claim if the experiment's result is in set A and reject it if the result is in set B.

THE NULL HYPOTHESIS AND THE ALTERNATIVE HYPOTHESIS

Hypothesis-testing procedures are generally conservative. In our example, the conservatism is built into the test, since the old medicine will be used unless the new one is proved to be better: we "disbelieve" the new medicine's claim unless we can substantiate improvement. We formulate two distinct hypotheses, which are called the *null hypothesis* and the *alternative hypothesis*, and take an initial stand favoring the null hypothesis.

The **null hypothesis**, denoted by H_0, states that the new medicine does not increase the proportion of patients cured. Formally we write

$$H_0: \quad p = 0.50$$

where p stands for the proportion of patients cured.

The **alternative hypothesis**, denoted by H_1, states that the new medicine increases the proportion of patients cured. In our example the alternative is rather specific: the proportion of patients cured must be equal to 70 percent. Formally we write

$$H_1: \quad p = 0.70$$

Recall that our decision rule divides the possible outcomes of the experiment into two mutually exclusive and collectively exhaustive sets:

Accept H_0 if $X = 0, 1, 2, 3, 4, 5, 6$.

Reject H_0 if $X = 7, 8$.

ERRORS IN HYPOTHESIS TESTING: TYPE I AND TYPE II

Because of the probabilistic nature of the experiment's results, our acceptance or rejection of H_0 may be either "correct" or "erroneous." The possibility (and the probability) of errors in the decision-making process is at the core of hypothesis testing.

What kinds of errors can we commit? First, it is possible that, in truth, the new medicine is no better than the old one, that on the average it really cures no more than 50 percent of patients treated; in other words, that $p = 0.50$ and H_0 is really correct. In the experiment conducted by the hospital we may by chance get the result $X = 7$ or $X = 8$, and thus, following the decision rule, we may decide to adopt the new medicine even though it is no better than the old. This type of error—namely, accepting H_1 when in fact H_0 is correct—is known as a **Type I error**. The probability of committing a Type I error can be easily calculated by the binomial distribution equation:[1]

$$P\{X = 7, 8\} = P(X = 7) + P(X = 8)$$

$$= \binom{8}{7}(0.5)^7(0.5)^1 + \binom{8}{8}(0.5)^8(0.5)^0 = 0.035$$

or

$$P\{X = 7, 8\} = 3.5\%$$

[1] In earlier chapters we used a lower-case letter to denote specific values assumed by a random variable. We feel that a distinction between upper-case and lower-case letters in this and the following chapters would make the notation cumbersome. Thus, only upper-case letters will be used.

The reason we use 0.5 as the success probability in this binomial experiment is that we assumed that the probability is *in truth* equal to 0.50.

At this point, have we considered all possible errors? Not really. We still have to consider the possibility of deciding against adoption of the new medicine when it does provide an improvement and cures, on the average, 70 percent of patients, as the Merca Company claims. The error of accepting H_0 when in fact H_1 is correct is known as **Type II error**. This error can occur in our example if in fact $p = 0.70$ when the experiment provides results with X equal to one of the values 0, 1, 2, 3, 4, 5, 6. This probability is equal to 74 percent:

$$P\{0 \leq X \leq 6\} = \sum_{X=0}^{6} \binom{8}{X}(0.70)^X(0.30)^{8-X} = 0.74$$

or

$$P\{0 \leq X \leq 6\} = 74\%$$

Note that the probability of success used here is 0.70 because it is assumed that this is *in truth* the probability of curing a patient.

Given the two possible errors and their respective probabilities, can we consider this statistical test a good one? Almost everyone is sure to agree that the 74 percent chance of committing the second type of error is much too high. Such a high probability gives very little chance for the new medicine to prove itself, since even if the new medicine is an improvement, under the procedure we have adopted there is a 74 percent chance that its merits will not be recognized.

This high probability of 74 percent for a Type II error is such an absurdity that Merca's management would be better off if the hospital's administrator made the decision by flipping a coin rather than by carrying out the experiment. That way the new medicine would have a 50 percent chance of being adopted, whereas under the procedure we have described, the chance would be only 26 percent ($1.00 - 0.74 = 0.26$).

One possible way to give the new medicine a better chance is to modify the decision rule. Suppose we establish the following decision rule:

Accept H_0 if $X = 0, 1, 2, 3, 4, 5$.

Reject H_0 if $X = 6, 7, 8$.

Under this decision rule, the probability of a Type II error—that of deciding against the new medicine if it is actually superior—drops from 74 percent to 45 percent:

$$P\{X = 0, 1, 2, 3, 4, 5\} = \sum_{X=0}^{5} \binom{8}{X}(0.7)^X(0.3)^{8-X} = 0.45$$

At the same time, however, the probability of the Type I error—that of deciding to adopt the new medicine when in truth it does not provide any improvement over the old—increases to 14 percent, up from 3.5 percent under the previous decision rule:

$$P\{X = 6, 7, 8\} = \sum_{X=6}^{8} \binom{8}{X}(0.5)^X(0.5)^{8-X} = 0.14$$

We thus conclude that *by changing the decision rule, we can decrease the probability of committing one type of error only at the expense of increasing the probability of committing the other.*

The Effect of Sample Size on Type I and Type II Errors   Fortunately, there is a way to decrease the probability of both types of errors simultaneously: by *increasing the sample size.* Suppose we try the new medicine on 60 (rather than just 8) patients. Suppose also that we adopt the following decision rule:

Accept H_0 if $X = 0, 1, 2, 3, \ldots, 36, 37$.

Reject H_0 if $X = 38, 39, 40, \ldots, 59, 60$.

In this case, the probability of favoring the new medicine when it is really no better than the old one (and thus committing a Type I error) is

$$P\{38 \leq X \leq 60\} = \sum_{X=38}^{60} \binom{60}{X}(0.5)^X(0.5)^{60-X} = 0.026$$

or 2.6 percent. The probability of committing the Type II error (that is, rejecting the new medicine even though it is better than the old) is

$$P\{0 \leq X \leq 37\} = \sum_{X=0}^{37} \binom{60}{X}(0.70)^X(0.30)^{60-X} = 0.102$$

or 10 percent.

It is evident, then, that by increasing the sample size we may decrease the probabilities of both errors. Yet, while this analysis may lead to the conclusion that the larger the sample size, the lower the error probabilities, we should not forget that the sample size is often limited because of cost, time, and other factors. The hospital must consider three types of cost involved in the statistical test:

1. If the new medicine is *accepted* when in truth it is no better than the old, there will be $1,000 extra cost per patient with no extra benefit. The loss will continue until the hospital realizes that the new medicine is indeed no improvement over the old.
2. If the new medicine is *rejected* when in truth it is better than the old, there will be a social cost (more sick people who can in fact be cured) as well as an economic cost, since the hospital may lose patients to other hospitals that are using the new medicine.
3. Each sample observation has its cost. In our case, this cost amounts to $1,000.

To conclude our example, let us touch upon one more point. Suppose Merca claims that the new medicine is 100 percent effective. What would be our decision rule in this case, and how would the error probabilities be affected? The decision rule becomes rather simple: we shall accept Merca's claim only if all patients treated are cured by the new medicine and reject it if one or more patients are not cured. In such a situation, the probability of committing the Type II error (rejecting the new medicine when it really cures 100 percent of patients) is equal to zero. Nevertheless, the probability of the Type I error (accepting the new medicine when in truth it is no better than the old) is greater than zero. It will depend on the number of patients treated in the experiment, since occasionally all patients in the sample would also recover with the old medicine.

13.2 Testing Hypotheses About the Mean of a Distribution

Now that we have been exposed to the basic concepts and tradeoffs involved in hypothesis testing, we shall discuss some specific hypothesis-testing procedures. Here, we shall look at some examples involving continuous probability distributions. We shall assume that the *mean* of the sample is normally distributed; although this is not really the case under all circumstances, the central limit theorem suggests that the assumption is acceptable in a wide range of situations. (When the assumption of normality cannot be accepted, we should use nonparametric hypothesis-testing procedures, some of which are detailed in Chapter 22.)

First, let us consider the following situation. The management of a movie house is searching for ways to boost profits, which have been declining lately as a result of soaring costs. In the past the management has shown only movies rated *G* ("suitable for general audiences"). The average weekly revenue has been $3,000. It has now been suggested that movies rated *PG* and *R* ("parental guidance suggested" and "restricted") be shown. The theater management has decided to have a 16-week trial period during which *PG*- and *R*-rated movies are to be run, and to permit these movies to continue after the trial period only if mean weekly revenue increases significantly.

We shall simplify matters here by dichotomizing the possible results of the trial period. We assume that management believes that expected weekly revenue will either stay at $3,000 or rise to $3,250 (any other values being ruled out at this stage for the sake of simplicity). We shall assume further that management has agreed not to change the existing *G* policy unless *significant* evidence exists that the new average weekly revenue is $3,250. We shall also assume that weekly revenues are normally distributed with a standard deviation equal to $400. Note that this assumption implies that the mean revenue for the 16-week trial period is normally distributed with a standard error of $400/\sqrt{16} = \$100$.

Insight into the possible events during the trial period and into the decision reached on the basis of the trial may be gained from Figure 13.1. Here the sampling distribution of the mean weekly revenue in the trial period is graphed in two ways: the first, headed H_0 (the null hypothesis), assumes that the mean weekly revenue is $3,000, and the second, headed H_1 (the alternative or alternate hypothesis), assumes that the mean weekly revenue is $3,250. In both cases, the standard error of the sampling distribution is $400/\sqrt{16} = \$100$. Notationally, we state the null and the alternative hypotheses as

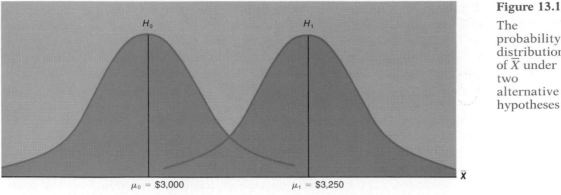

Figure 13.1

The probability distribution of $\overline{X}$ under two alternative hypotheses

$$H_0: \quad \mu = \mu_0 = \$3,000$$

$$H_1: \quad \mu = \mu_1 = \$3,250$$

Obviously, the actual 16-week average revenue for the trial period ($\overline{X}$) is not likely to equal exactly \$3,000 or precisely \$3,250. After the trial period is over and $\overline{X}$ is calculated, management may conclude either that the null hypothesis (H_0) is more likely to be correct *or* that the alternative (H_1) is more likely to be correct. Clearly if $\overline{X}$ is in the neighborhood of \$3,000, H_0 will seem to be more likely, so that if \$2,990 or \$3,015 is the average revenue of the 16-week period, it will be reasonable to accept H_0 and reject H_1—to conclude that \$3,000 is still the weekly average revenue and that no significant evidence exists of an increase in average weekly revenue as a result of the policy change. But if the 16-week trial period produces a mean in the neighborhood of \$3,250, such as \$3,230, \$3,246, or \$3,270, management will have good reason to accept H_1 and reject H_0—to conclude that significant evidence exists of an increase from \$3,000 to \$3,250 weekly revenue as a result of the new policy. The question, of course, is which hypothesis the management should accept if the sample mean (the weekly mean in the trial period) falls somewhere between \$3,000 and \$3,250—around \$3,125, say.

THE ACCEPTANCE AND REJECTION REGIONS

In order to choose between the two alternatives efficiently and objectively, we need to establish a cutoff point for $\overline{X}$. (Recall that in the previous example we also had to choose the cutoff point that represented the minimum number of patients cured by the new medicine.) Suppose we select \$3,125, the midpoint between \$3,000 and \$3,250, as a cutoff point. This selection implies the following decision rule:

Accept H_0 if the sample mean, $\overline{X}$, is less than or equal to \$3,125.

Reject H_0 if $\overline{X}$ is greater than \$3,125.

While we have selected the midpoint between the two means to serve as the cutoff point for decision making in this case, the midpoint, in general, is not a good cutoff point, for two reasons:

1. Only in a limited number of cases is the distribution's mean under the alternative hypothesis, H_1, so well defined as in our (admittedly simplified) example. When the mean under H_1 is not numerically specified, no midpoint exists, and a different approach to the determination of the cutoff point must be found.

2. The midpoint in our example, $3,125, is 1.25 standard errors (of $100 each) to the right of $3,000. The tail area of H_0 to the right of $3,125 is the same as the tail area of the Z distribution to the right of $Z = 1.25$ and is equal to 0.1056. The probability of rejecting the null hypothesis when in fact it is correct (that is, committing a Type I error) is thus equal in our case to 10.56 percent, which, in the opinion of the management, may be either too high or too low. Depending on the management's attitude toward the proposed policy change, the probability may be set at a different level, say 5 percent. In such a case we merely have to set *the cutoff point*—or, as it is often called, the **critical value**—at the point that bounds a 5 percent right tail under the distribution, assuming H_0 is correct.

Recalling that $Z_{0.05} = 1.645$ bounds a 5 percent right tail under the standard normal distribution, we can easily get the critical value:

$$\overline{X}^* = \mu_0 + Z_{0.05}\sigma_{\overline{X}} = \mu_0 + Z_{0.05}\frac{\sigma}{\sqrt{n}} \qquad \textbf{(13.1)}$$

$\overline{X}^*$ is the critical value and μ_0 is the distribution mean, assuming H_0 is correct. In our case we have

$$\overline{X}^* = 3,000 + 1.645 \cdot \frac{400}{\sqrt{16}} = 3,000 + 164.5 = \$3,164.5$$

Figure 13.2 clearly illustrates the location of $\overline{X}^*$: it bounds a 5 percent right tail of the H_0 distribution. The importance of the critical value is that it leads to a decision rule by defining the **acceptance region** (of the null hypothesis) and the **rejection region** (of the null hypothesis). If the sample

Figure 13.2

The location of the critical value, the acceptance region, and the rejection region

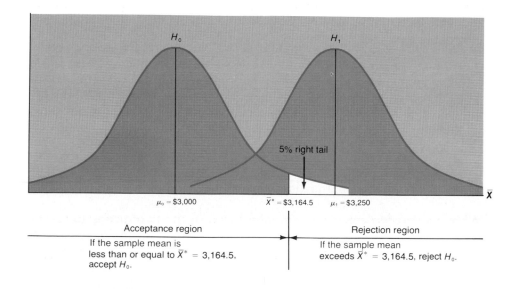

H_0 H_1

5% right tail

$\mu_0 = \$3,000$ $\overline{X}^* = \$3,164.5$ $\mu_1 = \$3,250$ $\overline{X}$

Acceptance region   Rejection region

If the sample mean is less than or equal to $\overline{X}^* = 3,164.5$, accept H_0.

If the sample mean exceeds $\overline{X}^* = 3,164.5$, reject H_0.

mean, $\overline{X}$, does not exceed \$3,164.5—that is, if the mean revenue for the 16-week trial period is less than or equal to \$3,164.5—the null hypothesis should be accepted. If the sample mean exceeds \$3,164.5, however, the null hypothesis should be rejected.

USING A TEST STATISTIC HAVING A STANDARD NORMAL DISTRIBUTION

As you recall, we have defined a statistic as a function of the observations in the sample. A **test statistic** is *a statistic used as a vehicle to test hypotheses*.

Thus far we have been using $\overline{X}$ as our test statistic. Before proceeding, let us suggest a different (though similar) procedure to test the hypothesis under consideration. Instead of using $\overline{X}$ as our test statistic, we shall use $Z = \dfrac{\overline{X} - \mu_0}{\sigma/\sqrt{n}}$, which has a standard normal distribution. Let us set the critical value Z^* at $Z_{0.05}$, so that all Z values less than or equal to $Z_{0.05} = 1.645$ are in the acceptance region and all Z values that are greater than $Z_{0.05}$ are in the rejection region. Now suppose the sample mean is equal to \$3,140. The respective test statistic value is

$$Z = \frac{\overline{X} - \mu_0}{\sigma/\sqrt{n}} = \frac{3,140 - 3,000}{400/\sqrt{16}} = 1.40$$

Since 1.40 is in the acceptance region, we conclude that there is no significant evidence that merits rejection of the null hypothesis, which claims that the new policy will keep the mean revenue at \$3,000 per week. If the value of the test statistic had exceeded 1.645, the null hypothesis should have been rejected. Obviously, both approaches (the one using $\overline{X}$ and the one using Z) *lead to the same acceptance or rejection decision*, and the approach we choose to use is largely a matter of taste.

The acceptance or rejection of the null hypothesis depends, among other things, on the exact location of $\overline{X}^*$, the critical value, in relation to μ_0. The location of $\overline{X}^*$, in turn, is a function of the probability we set for rejecting the null hypothesis when in fact it is correct. This probability is equal to 5 percent in our example and is represented by the tail of the null hypothesis distribution over the rejection region (see Figure 13.3). In general, we shall

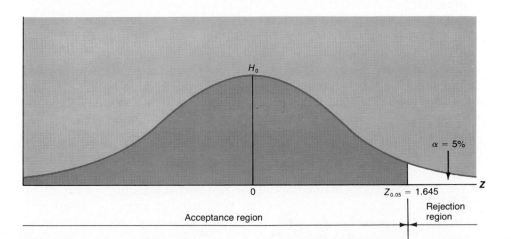

Figure 13.3

The acceptance and rejection regions and the test significance level, α, when the test statistic is $Z = \dfrac{\overline{X} - \mu_0}{\sigma/\sqrt{n}}$ and $\alpha = 0.05$

denote this probability by α and call it the test's **significance level**. The significance level of the test, denoted by α, is *the probability of rejecting the null hypothesis when it is in truth correct* (and should be accepted). It equals the probability of committing a Type I error.

UPPER-TAIL AND LOWER-TAIL TESTS

There is one thing you should note at this point. In our example, we positioned the rejection region to the right of the null hypothesis mean (see Figure 13.2) because the alternative mean, μ_1, is *greater* than the null hypothesis mean, μ_0. This type of test is known as an **upper-tail test**. In the case in which $\mu_1 < \mu_0$, the test is known as a **lower-tail test,** and the rejection region is located to the left of μ_0, as the following example illustrates.

A greeting-card printer has been told of the availability of a new machine that will produce the same output (from the point of view of both quality and quantity) as the machine that is currently in use, but the new machine reportedly will bring savings in operating costs because it can be adjusted more easily when card design is changed, it has a lower breakdown rate, and so on. The existing machine costs an average of $100 a week to operate. Assume that operating cost is normally distributed with a weekly standard deviation of $25 for both machines and that a sample of 9 weeks has shown an average operating cost of $75 per week for the new machine. Set $\alpha = 0.01$ and test the following hypotheses:

$$H_0: \mu = \mu_0 = 100$$

$$H_1: \mu = \mu_1 < 100$$

The null hypothesis may also be written in the following way:

$$H_0: \quad \mu = \mu_0 \geq 100$$

The testing procedure in this case is precisely the same as when H_0 is $\mu = 100$.

This example differs from our earlier example in two ways:

1. The alternative hypothesis assumes that μ_1 is *less than* μ_0.
2. No specific value is assumed for μ_1, and H_1 indicates only that it is less than 100.

Let us use $Z = \dfrac{\overline{X} - \mu_0}{\sigma/\sqrt{n}}$ as our test statistic. Since $\alpha = 0.01$ and since the alternative hypothesis suggests that μ_1 is *less than* μ_0, we set the critical value at $-Z_{0.01}$, since this Z score bounds a lower-tail area equal to 1 percent (see Figure 13.4). The acceptance region includes all the Z values that are greater than $-Z_{0.01} = -2.326$. Our decision rule is as follows:

Accept H_0 if the test statistic appears within the acceptance region.

Reject H_0 if the test statistic appears within the rejection region.

All we have to do now is to compute the test statistic value:

$$Z = \frac{\overline{X} - \mu_0}{\sigma/\sqrt{n}} = \frac{75 - 100}{25/\sqrt{9}} = \frac{-25}{25/3} = -3$$

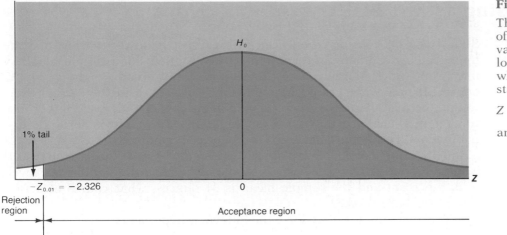

Figure 13.4

The location of the critical value in a lower-tail test when the test statistic is

$$Z = \frac{\overline{X} - \mu_0}{\sigma/\sqrt{n}}$$

and $\alpha = 0.01$

A glance at Figure 13.4 will reveal that -3 is in the rejection region, so we reject the null hypothesis and conclude that statistically significant evidence exists showing that the operating cost of the new machine is less than $100. This conclusion is subject to a possible error, but the chance that such an error has been committed is less than 1 percent.

The same problem may be solved with $\overline{X}$ as the test statistic (see Figure 13.5). We first determine the critical value ($\overline{X}^*$) as follows:

$$\overline{X}^* = \mu_0 + (-Z_{0.01})\frac{\sigma}{\sqrt{n}} = 100 + (-2.326) \cdot \frac{25}{\sqrt{9}}$$

$$= 100 - 19.38 = 80.62$$

Our decision rule is

Accept H_0 if $\overline{X} \geq 80.62$.

Reject H_0 if $\overline{X} < 80.62$.

Since $\overline{X} = 75$ and it is in the rejection region, we reject the null hypothesis and reach the same conclusion as before.

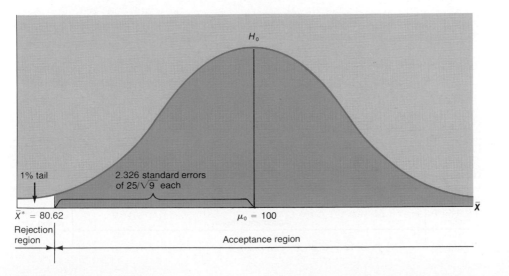

Figure 13.5

The location of the critical value in a lower-tail test when the test statistic is $\overline{X}$ and $\alpha = 0.01$

13.3 Using a Two-Tailed Test on the Mean

So far we have considered only one-tailed tests: the lower-tail test and the upper-tail test. Sometimes the test may be two-tailed. For example, a bakery may want to test the hypothesis that its loaves of bread weigh exactly 32 ounces. It may want to take corrective measures both in the case of over-weight (because of unnecessary cost) and in the case of underweight (because this might alienate customers). Suppose the loaves' weight is normally distributed with a standard deviation of 2 ounces. Periodically the bakery takes a random sample of 20 loaves and decides (on the basis of the sample result) whether or not corrective measures should be taken. If the significance level, α, is 5 percent and the sample mean is 31 ounces, what course of action should the bakery take?

In this two-tailed test we have the following hypotheses:

$$H_0: \quad \mu = \mu_0 = 32$$

$$H_1: \quad \mu \neq 32$$

Since a significant deviation above or below 32 ounces would be consistent with the alternative hypothesis, the rejection region should be split between the two tails of the distribution. Thus we allocate the probability α equally to both tails of the Z distribution and determine two critical values, $-Z_{0.025} = -1.96$ and $Z_{0.025} = 1.96$, as illustrated in Figure 13.6, where the test statistic is $Z = \dfrac{\bar{X} - \mu_0}{\sigma/\sqrt{n}}$. If the value of the test statistic falls between the two critical values (that is, in the acceptance region), H_0 is accepted; otherwise it is rejected. In our case we have

$$Z = \frac{\bar{X} - \mu_0}{\sigma/\sqrt{n}} = \frac{31 - 32}{2/\sqrt{20}} = \frac{-1}{2/4.472} = -2.236$$

This value, -2.236, is well outside the acceptance region. Thus the null hypothesis is rejected: corrective measures should be undertaken.

Figure 13.6

The location of the critical values in a two-tailed test when the test statistic is

$Z = \dfrac{\bar{X} - \mu_0}{\sigma/\sqrt{n}}$

and $\alpha = 0.05$

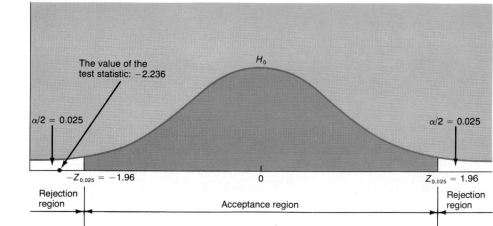

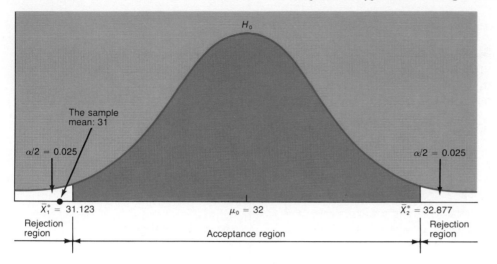

Figure 13.7

The location of the critical values in a two-tailed test when the test statistic is $\overline{X}$ and $\alpha = 0.05$

As before, we may decide instead to use $\overline{X}$ as the test statistic and determine two critical values, $\overline{X}_1^*$ and $\overline{X}_2^*$ (see Figure 13.7), as follows:

$$\overline{X}_1^* = \mu_0 + (-Z_{0.025})\frac{\sigma}{\sqrt{n}} = 32 - 1.96 \cdot \frac{2}{\sqrt{20}} = 32 - 0.877 = 31.123$$

$$\overline{X}_2^* = \mu_0 + Z_{0.025}\frac{\sigma}{\sqrt{n}} = 32 + 1.96 \cdot \frac{2}{\sqrt{20}} = 32 + 0.877 = 32.877$$

Since 31, the sample mean, is outside the acceptance region—the interval between 31.123 and 32.877—we reject the null hypothesis and advise taking corrective measures.

We want to emphasize once again that the decision concerning the acceptance or rejection of the null hypothesis is reached whether $\overline{X}$ or $Z = \frac{\overline{X} - \mu_0}{\sigma/\sqrt{n}}$ is chosen as the test statistic. It should also be clear that *using one test statistic is sufficient to draw the proper conclusion.* We have presented the procedures involving $\overline{X}$ and $Z = \frac{\overline{X} - \mu_0}{\sigma/\sqrt{n}}$ side by side only for the purpose of providing further insight.

Note the similarity between the two-tailed test and the confidence interval. If a confidence interval is constructed around $\overline{X}$ at a confidence level $(1 - \alpha)$ and μ_0 is included in it, then a two-tailed test of hypotheses with a significance level α will lead to the acceptance of H_0. If the confidence interval does not cover the value μ_0, however, the corresponding test will require the rejection of H_0. In the previous example, we rejected H_0 because the sample mean ($\overline{X} = 31$) was outside the acceptance region (from 31.123 to 32.877). At the same time, a 95 percent confidence interval is $\overline{X} \pm Z_{\alpha/2}\frac{\sigma}{\sqrt{n}} = 31 \pm 1.96 \cdot \frac{2}{\sqrt{20}} = 31 \pm 0.877$, or the interval from 30.123 to 31.877. This interval does not cover $\mu_0 = 32$, and H_0 is rejected.

We can summarize the hypothesis-testing procedures for upper-tail, lower-tail, and two-tailed tests as follows:

PROCEDURE FOR UPPER-TAIL TEST

Step 1: Clearly identify the null and alternative hypotheses:

$$H_0: \quad \mu \leq \mu_0$$

$$H_1: \quad \mu > \mu_0$$

Step 2: Determine the significance level, α, that will be suitable for the test.

Step 3: Choose your test statistic, Z or $\overline{X}$, and proceed accordingly. Determine the critical value and the decision rule.

If $Z = \dfrac{\overline{X} - \mu_0}{\sigma/\sqrt{n}}$ is the test statistic	If $\overline{X}$ is the test statistic
the critical value is	the critical value is
$$Z_\alpha$$	$$\overline{X}^* = \mu_0 + Z_\alpha \cdot \frac{\sigma}{\sqrt{n}}$$
and the decision rule is	and the decision rule is
Accept H_0 if $Z \leq Z_\alpha$. Reject H_0 if $Z > Z_\alpha$.	Accept H_0 if $\overline{X} \leq \overline{X}^*$. Reject H_0 if $\overline{X} > \overline{X}^*$.

Step 4: Calculate the value of the test statistic using the sample data.

Step 5: Apply the decision rule established in step 3, and accept or reject H_0 accordingly.

PROCEDURE FOR LOWER-TAIL TEST

Step 1: Clearly identify the null and alternative hypotheses:

$$H_0: \quad \mu \geq \mu_0$$

$$H_1: \quad \mu < \mu_0$$

Step 2: Determine the significance level, α, that will be suitable for the test.

Step 3: Choose your test statistic, Z or $\overline{X}$, and proceed accordingly. Determine the critical value and the decision rule.

If $Z = \dfrac{\overline{X} - \mu_0}{\sigma/\sqrt{n}}$ is the test statistic	If $\overline{X}$ is the test statistic
the critical value is	the critical value is
$$-Z_\alpha$$	$$\overline{X}^* = \mu_0 - Z_\alpha \cdot \frac{\sigma}{\sqrt{n}}$$
and the decision rule is	and the decision rule is
Accept H_0 if $Z \geq -Z_\alpha$. Reject H_0 if $Z < -Z_\alpha$.	Accept H_0 if $\overline{X} \geq \overline{X}^*$. Reject H_0 if $\overline{X} < \overline{X}^*$.

Step 4: Calculate the value of the test statistic using the sample data.

Step 5: Apply the decision rule established in step 3, and accept or reject H_0 accordingly.

PROCEDURE FOR TWO-TAILED TEST

Step 1: Clearly identify the null and alternative hypotheses:

$$H_0: \quad \mu = \mu_0$$

$$H_1: \quad \mu \neq \mu_0$$

Step 2: Determine the significance level, α, that will be suitable for the test.

Step 3: Choose your test statistic, Z or $\overline{X}$, and proceed accordingly. Determine the two critical values and the decision rule.

If $Z = \dfrac{\overline{X} - \mu_0}{\sigma/\sqrt{n}}$ is the test statistic	If $\overline{X}$ is the test statistic
the critical values are	the critical values are
$$-Z_{\alpha/2}$$	$$\overline{X}_1^* = \mu_0 - Z_{\alpha/2} \cdot \frac{\sigma}{\sqrt{n}}$$
$$Z_{\alpha/2},$$	$$\overline{X}_2^* = \mu_0 + Z_{\alpha/2} \cdot \frac{\sigma}{\sqrt{n}}$$
and the decision rule is	and the decision rule is
Accept H_0 if $-Z_{\alpha/2} \leq Z \leq Z_{\alpha/2}$.	Accept H_0 if $\overline{X}_1^* \leq \overline{X} \leq \overline{X}_2^*$.
Reject H_0 if $Z < -Z_{\alpha/2}$ or if $Z > Z_{\alpha/2}$.	Reject H_0 if $\overline{X} < \overline{X}_1^*$ or if $\overline{X} > \overline{X}_2^*$.

Step 4: Calculate the value of the test statistic using the sample data.

Step 5: Apply the decision rule established in step 3, and accept or reject H_0 accordingly.

13.4 Type I Error, Type II Error, and the Power of the Test

In the example given in Section 13.1, we indicated the possibility of committing an error by accepting a hypothesis that is not correct. Here we shall consider the probabilities of error in testing hypotheses concerning the mean of a distribution, assuming $\overline{X}$ is normally distributed, as in Section 13.2.

The decision rule illustrated in Section 13.2 may lead to either correct or incorrect decisions (inferences). If H_0 is right and it is accepted, a correct decision has been made; if H_0 is wrong and it is rejected, again a correct decision has been made. Because of sampling errors, however, the test statistic may appear in the rejection region even though H_0 may be correct, leading us to (incorrectly) reject H_0 (Type I error). It is also possible that H_1 is correct, but the test statistic appears in the acceptance region, so we (incorrectly) accept H_0 (Type II error). These four possibilities are summarized in the following table:

POSSIBLE DECISIONS IN HYPOTHESIS TESTING

	True situation	
Decision	H_0 is correct	H_1 is correct
Accept H_0	Correct decision	Incorrect decision (Type II error)
Reject H_0	Incorrect decision (Type I error)	Correct decision

Thus our decision is subject to two possible errors. A Type I error occurs when H_0 is correct but sampling errors lead us to reject it. A Type II error occurs when H_1 is correct but we reject it in favor of H_0, again because of sampling errors. Note that neither *ex ante* (that is, before the sample is selected) nor *ex post* (that is, after the sample data become available) is it possible to determine whether an error of either type has been committed. In order to make a prudent decision on the basis of the sample data, we must be aware of the *probability* of committing each type of error. The probabilities can be understood with the help of Figure 13.8.

Consider first the probability of committing a Type I error. By definition, this error occurs when $\overline{X}$ falls somewhere within the rejection region when H_0 is in fact the correct hypothesis. This probability is represented in Figure 13.8 by that part of the right-tail area of the H_0 distribution which lies in the rejection region. Recall that this tail was set equal to α (the chosen significance level of the test) by positioning $\overline{X}^*$ where it leaves a tail area equal to α. We conclude, then, that the significance level of a test, α, is also the probability of committing a Type I error.

The probability of committing a Type II error is represented in Figure 13.8 by that part of the tail of the H_1 distribution which extends into the acceptance region. This probability, denoted by β, is defined as follows:

$$\beta = P(\text{committing Type II error})$$
$$= P(\text{test statistic appears in the} \tag{13.2}$$
$$\text{acceptance region when } H_1 \text{ is correct})$$

Figure 13.8

The probabilities of Type I and Type II errors: the upper-tail test case

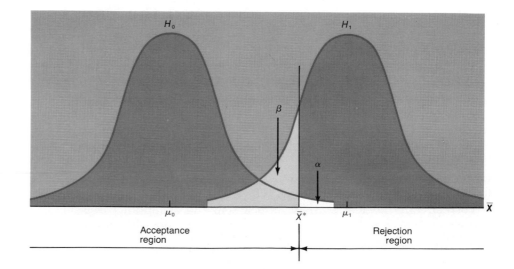

In other words, the probability of a Type II error (β) is equal to the probability that the test statistic will fall within the acceptance region *when H_1 is correct*. We shall often write the probability on the right-hand side of Equation 13.2 in a slightly more compact form:

$$\beta = P_{H_1}(\text{test statistic shows in the acceptance region}) \qquad \textbf{(13.3)}$$

The subscript H_1 in Equation 13.3 means that the probability is conditional upon the correctness of H_1.

CALCULATING THE PROBABILITY OF A TYPE II ERROR

When H_1 is a **simple hypothesis**—that is, *its parameter μ_1 has a single specific value* (for example, H_1: $\mu = 10$)—β is also a single probability value. Frequently, however, the alternative hypothesis is a **composite hypothesis** rather than a simple hypothesis—that is, *its parameter has a value within a given range of values* (for example, H_1: $\mu > 10$). In such cases, the probability of a Type II error is specified as a function rather than a single value. This function is discussed in Appendix 13A. Let us consider here the calculation of β in the case of a simple alternative hypothesis.

When the alternative hypothesis is simple, we test H_0: $\mu = \mu_0$ against H_1: $\mu = \mu_1$; the test is a lower-tail test if $\mu_1 < \mu_0$ and an upper-tail test if $\mu_1 > \mu_0$. In an upper-tail test (like the one described in Figure 13.8), the acceptance region is to the left of $\overline{X}^*$. In this case we proceed in the following manner:

$$\beta = P_{H_1}(\overline{X} \text{ shows in the acceptance region}) = P_{H_1}(\overline{X} \le \overline{X}^*) \qquad \textbf{(13.4)}$$

To find the probability in Equation 13.4, which is conditional upon the correctness of H_1, we must transform $\overline{X}$ into a Z variable. Assuming that μ_1 is the true mean and that σ is known, we can transform $\overline{X}$ into Z by subtracting μ_1 and dividing by $\sigma/\sqrt{n}$:

$$Z = \frac{\overline{X} - \mu_1}{\sigma/\sqrt{n}} \qquad \textbf{(13.5)}$$

Substituting Equation 13.5 in Equation 13.4 and performing a similar transformation on $\overline{X}^*$, we obtain

$$\beta = P_{H_1}(\overline{X} \le \overline{X}^*) = P_{H_1}\left(\frac{\overline{X} - \mu_1}{\sigma/\sqrt{n}} \le \frac{\overline{X}^* - \mu_1}{\sigma/\sqrt{n}}\right) = P\left(Z \le \frac{\overline{X}^* - \mu_1}{\sigma/\sqrt{n}}\right) \qquad \textbf{(13.6)}$$

In the case of a lower tail, after performing similar derivations, we get

$$\beta = P_{H_1}(\overline{X} \ge \overline{X}^*) = P\left(Z \ge \frac{\overline{X}^* - \mu_1}{\sigma/\sqrt{n}}\right) \qquad \textbf{(13.7)}$$

To summarize, the probability of a Type II error when H_1 is a simple hypothesis is as follows:

PROBABILITY OF A TYPE II ERROR FOR LOWER-TAIL ALTERNATIVE

$$(\mu_0 > \mu_1) \qquad \textbf{(13.8L)}$$

$$\beta = P\left(Z \ge \frac{\overline{X}^* - \mu_1}{\sigma/\sqrt{n}}\right)$$

PROBABILITY OF A TYPE II ERROR FOR UPPER-TAIL ALTERNATIVE

$$(\mu_0 < \mu_1)$$

$$\beta = P\left(Z \le \frac{\overline{X}^* - \mu_1}{\sigma/\sqrt{n}}\right)$$

(13.8U)

The **power of a test** is the probability of accepting H_1 when H_1 is correct. This probability is equal to $1 - \beta$. Obviously, other things being equal, the greater the power of the test, the better the test.

EXAMPLE 13.1

To test H_0: $\mu = \mu_0 = 130$ against H_1: $\mu = \mu_1 = 125$, a sample of 64 observations is used. Assume that σ is equal to 25 and that the level of significance used is $\alpha = 0.05$. Determine the probability of committing a Type II error and the power of the test.

Following the procedure for determining $\overline{X}^*$ in the case of a lower-tail test such as the one at hand, we write

$$\overline{X}^* = \mu_0 - Z_\alpha \frac{\sigma}{\sqrt{n}} = 130 - 1.645 \cdot \frac{25}{\sqrt{64}} = 130 - 5.14 = 124.86$$

Once $\overline{X}^*$ is known, we can calculate β by using Equation 13.8L:

$$\beta = P\left(Z \ge \frac{124.86 - 125.00}{25/\sqrt{64}}\right) = P(Z \ge -0.04) = 0.5160$$

The power of this test is equal to $1 - \beta = 1 - 0.5160 = 0.4840$, indicating that there is only a 48.4 percent chance that if H_1 is correct it will be accepted.

To illustrate the procedure for an upper-tail test, let us change only one parameter in the previous set of numbers. Let us change H_1: $\mu = 125$ to H_1: $\mu = 137$. We first find the critical value:

$$\overline{X}^* = \mu_0 + Z_\alpha \frac{\sigma}{\sqrt{n}} = 130 + 1.645 \cdot \frac{25}{\sqrt{64}} = 135.14$$

We now use Equation 13.8U for the upper-tail test:

$$\beta = P\left(Z \le \frac{135.14 - 137}{25/\sqrt{64}}\right) = P(Z \le -0.60) = 0.2743$$

The power of this test is equal to $1 - \beta = 1 - 0.2743 = 0.7257$.

13.5 The Tradeoff Between α and β

Since both α and β are probabilities of committing errors in hypothesis testing, we are naturally interested in ways to minimize them. In our introductory example (Section 13.1) we discussed the tradeoff between α and β. We shall now discuss that same tradeoff in testing hypotheses of the mean when normal distributions are assumed. We shall show that for any given

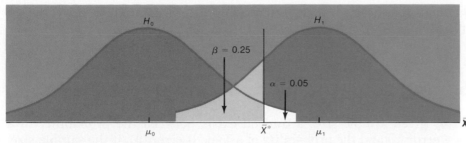

(a) The significance level (α) is set to equal 5%, and β is equal to 25%.

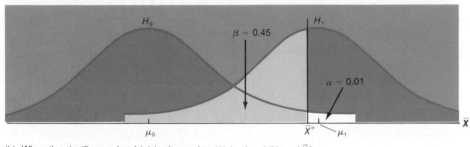

(b) When the significance level (α) is changed to 1% by the shifting of $\overline{X}^*$ to the right, β increases from 25% to 45%.

Figure 13.9

The tradeoff between α and β: the upper-tail case

sample size, there is a tradeoff between α and β, so that when α is lowered, β increases, and vice versa. Figure 13.9 helps to clarify the type of tradeoff that exists between α and β. In Figure 13.9a, α is equal to 5 percent and the resulting probability of a Type II error is 25 percent. In Figure 13.9b, α is 1 percent. We make α equal to 1 percent by shifting $\overline{X}^*$ to the right of its position in 13.9a. While this shift lowers α, it simultaneously increases β from 25 percent to 45 percent. The same sort of tradeoff, of course, exists in the case of a lower-tail test, as illustrated in Figure 13.10. While it is more

Figure 13.10

The tradeoff between α and β: the lower-tail case

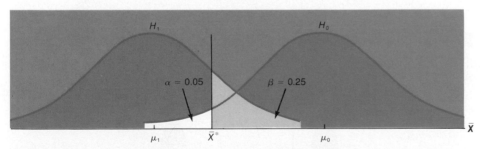

(a) The significance level (α) is set to equal 5%, and β is equal to 25%.

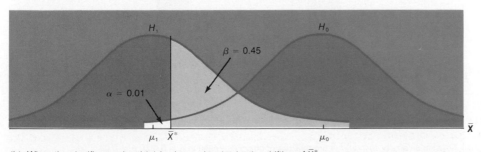

(b) When the significance level (α) is changed to 1% by the shifting of $\overline{X}^*$ to the left, β increases from 25% to 45%.

difficult to see the tradeoff between α and β in a diagram of a two-tailed test, it does exist in this case as well.

13.6 The Relationship Among α, β, and *n*

For any given sample size, a tradeoff exists between the probability of a Type I error (α) and the probability of a Type II error (β). If the sample size, *n*, is allowed to increase, however, it is possible for both α and β to decrease simultaneously, as we saw in Section 13.1. Figure 13.11 shows the effect of increased sample size on both α and β in the case of a lower-tail test, assuming $\overline{X}$ to be normally distributed.

In Figure 13.11*a*, the distributions are rather dispersed, giving rise to the following error probabilities: α = 0.05, β = 0.38. When the sample size increases (from *n* to some greater value, *n'*), the distributions become more condensed around the (true) mean. If we hold $\overline{X}^*$ in Figure 13.11*b* in the same position as in 13.11*a*, both α and β will decrease. In the case illustrated, α is decreased to 0.005 and β to 0.08. The effect of increasing the sample size is positive: it decreases the probability of both Type I and Type II errors,

Figure 13.11

The effect of sample size on α and β

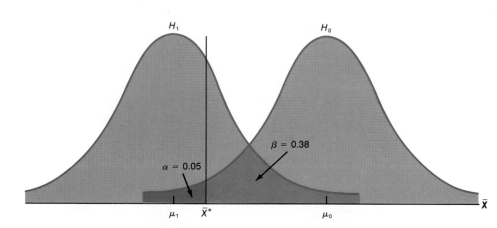

(a) For sample size *n*, the probabilities of error are α = 0.05, β = 0.38.

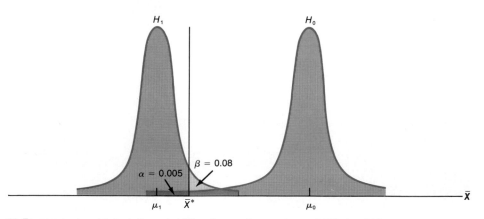

(b) For sample size *n'* (*n'>n*), the probabilities of errors decrease to α = 0.005, β = 0.08.

and it increases the power of the test $(1 - \beta)$. The only problems we run into when the sample size is increased are related to availability of observations and cost of sampling (see Section 13.1). The question of deriving optimal sample size when you consider possible losses resulting from acceptance of the wrong hypothesis, as well as from the cost of sampling, is left for more advanced texts in decision making.

EXAMPLE 13.2

Let X be the number of cars served per day at a certain gas station. Let μ be the mean of X, and consider testing H_0: $\mu = \mu_0 = 300$ against H_1: $\mu = \mu_1 = 310$. Assume that the standard deviation of X is equal to 30. At first, let us suppose that the significance level (and thus also the probability of committing a Type I error) is equal to 5 percent: $\alpha = 0.05$. Determine the probability of committing a Type II error under two alternative assumptions regarding sample size: (a) $n = 36$, (b) $n = 144$.

Assuming $n = 36$ first, we determine the critical value, $\overline{X}^*$, as follows:

$$\overline{X}^* = \mu_0 + Z_\alpha \frac{\sigma}{\sqrt{n}} = 300 + 1.645 \cdot \frac{30}{\sqrt{36}} = 308.23$$

Given this critical value, the probability of committing a Type II error is easily calculated:

$$P(\text{Type II error}) \equiv \beta = P_{H_1}(\overline{X} \leq 308.23)$$

$$= P\left(\frac{\overline{X} - 310}{30/\sqrt{36}} \leq \frac{308.23 - 310}{30/\sqrt{36}}\right)$$

$$= P(Z \leq -0.35) = 0.3632$$

Assuming now that $n = 144$, $\overline{X}^*$ is

$$\overline{X}^* = \mu_0 + Z_\alpha \frac{\sigma}{\sqrt{n}} = 300 + 1.645 \cdot \frac{30}{\sqrt{144}} = 304.11$$

The probability of committing a Type II error under this assumption is

$$\beta = P\left(\frac{\overline{X} - 310}{30/\sqrt{144}} \leq \frac{304.11 - 310}{30/\sqrt{144}}\right) = P(Z \leq -2.36) = 0.0091$$

Although in this example we saw only that β decreased as a result of an increase in sample size, it is quite possible to demonstrate a simultaneous reduction in both α and β. With a sample of 144 observations, we can decrease α from 5 percent to 1 percent and get a new critical value:

$$\overline{X}^* = \mu_0 + Z_\alpha \frac{\sigma}{\sqrt{n}} = 300 + \frac{30}{\sqrt{144}} \cdot 2.326 = 305.82$$

Thus the probability of a Type I error is reduced from 5 percent to 1 percent, and as we can see, the Type II error probability also decreases from its original 36.32 percent all the way to 4.75 percent:

$$\beta = P\left(\frac{\overline{X} - 310}{30/\sqrt{144}} \leq \frac{305.82 - 310.0}{30/\sqrt{144}}\right) = P(Z \leq -1.67) = 0.0475$$

13.7 Testing Hypotheses About the Mean of a Distribution When the Standard Deviation Is Unknown

The statistic used earlier in this chapter to test hypotheses about the mean of a distribution was $\dfrac{\overline{X} - \mu_0}{\sigma/\sqrt{n}}$. This test statistic can be used if σ is known. If σ is unknown, however, we substitute S for σ in the test statistic to get $T = \dfrac{\overline{X} - \mu_0}{S/\sqrt{n}}$, where the S statistic is the sample standard deviation:

$$S = \sqrt{\frac{\Sigma(X - \overline{X})^2}{n - 1}} = \sqrt{\frac{\Sigma X^2 - n\overline{X}^2}{n - 1}}$$

The test statistic T has a t distribution with $(n - 1)$ degrees of freedom, provided the sample is drawn from a normal distribution. When the sample is large, T is approximately distributed according to $t^{(n-1)}$ even if the sample is drawn from a distribution other than normal. The prescribed steps for testing the population mean when σ is unknown can be summarized as follows:

PROCEDURE FOR TESTING HYPOTHESES ABOUT THE MEAN WHEN THE STANDARD DEVIATION IS UNKNOWN

Step 1: Clearly identify the null and alternative hypotheses.

Step 2: Determine the significance level, α, that will be suitable for the test.

Step 3: Determine the critical value(s) and the decision rule. Step 3 varies slightly from one test to another, depending on whether we are dealing with an upper-tail, lower-tail, or two-tailed test.

    (*a*) For a lower-tail test, the critical value is $-t_\alpha^{(n-1)}$. Accept H_0 if the test statistic is greater than the critical value; otherwise reject.

    (*b*) For an upper-tail test, the critical value is $t_\alpha^{(n-1)}$. Accept H_0 if the test statistic is less than the critical value; otherwise reject.

    (*c*) For a two-tailed test, the critical values are $-t_{\alpha/2}^{(n-1)}$ and $t_{\alpha/2}^{(n-1)}$. Accept H_0 if the test statistic is between the two values; otherwise reject.

Step 4: Calculate the value of the test statistic by using the sample data: $T = \dfrac{\overline{X} - \mu_0}{S/\sqrt{n}}$.

Step 5: Apply the decision rule established in step 3 and accept or reject H_0 accordingly.

EXAMPLE 13.3

The watches produced by Exact Time, Inc., are said to tell the correct time to within 5 seconds per month, on the average. A random sample of nine watches is observed for a month. The time discrepancies in seconds are as follows: 2, 7, 6, 1, 10, 10, 7, 5, and 5. Assuming that the time discrepancies are normally distributed, would you accept or reject the company's claim? Assume a significance level of 5 percent.

Following the steps established for testing hypotheses concerning the distribution's mean when σ is unknown, we first identify the hypotheses involved:

$$H_0: \quad \mu \leq 5$$

$$H_1: \quad \mu > 5$$

The significance level is 5 percent, so $\alpha = 0.05$. Since σ is unknown and nine observations are available, our test statistic has a t distribution with 8 ($= n - 1$) degrees of freedom. Furthermore, since we are dealing with an upper-tail test, the critical value is $t_{0.05}^{(8)} = 1.86$. Our decision rule will therefore be:

$$\text{Accept } H_0 \text{ if } T = \frac{\overline{X} - \mu_0}{S/\sqrt{n}} \leq 1.86 \text{ and reject } H_0 \text{ if } T > 1.86.$$

Our next step is to calculate the value of the test statistic. This is done in Table 13.1.

TABLE 13.1
Calculating the Value of the Test Statistic

i	X	X^2	*Calculation of test statistic, T*
1	2	4	
2	7	49	$\overline{X} = \dfrac{\Sigma X}{n} = \dfrac{53}{9} = 5.889$
3	6	36	
4	1	1	
5	10	100	$S = \sqrt{\dfrac{\Sigma X^2 - n\overline{X}^2}{n - 1}} = \sqrt{\dfrac{389 - 9 \cdot 5.889^2}{9 - 1}} = \sqrt{9.61} = 3.100$
6	10	100	
7	7	49	
8	5	25	$T = \dfrac{\overline{X} - \mu_0}{S/\sqrt{n}} = \dfrac{5.889 - 5.000}{3.100/\sqrt{9}} = \dfrac{0.889}{1.033} = 0.861$
9	5	25	
	$\Sigma X =$ 53	$\Sigma X^2 =$ 389	

The last step is to determine whether the value of the test statistic falls within the acceptance or rejection region and to make our decision accordingly. Following the decision rule established for this problem, we cannot reject H_0, since 0.861 (the value of the test statistic) is less than 1.86 (the critical value). We thus conclude that while the sample shows a mean time discrepancy greater than 5 seconds, it is not significantly greater than 5, and the null hypothesis cannot be rejected.

We have already mentioned several times that as the number of degrees of freedom increases, the t distribution's shape approaches that of the standard normal distribution. The t table inside the back cover of the book shows that when the degrees of freedom are very large (i.e., when they approach infinity) the t values are equal to the respective z values. For degrees of freedom greater than 30, the table is not always detailed enough, but we can either approximate or use the corresponding z values.

13.8 Testing Hypotheses About a Proportion

In this section we discuss the testing of hypotheses concerning a proportion. The example given in Section 13.1 also concerns a proportion and uses the binomial probability distribution, but here we shall be using the normal approximation to the binomial distribution.

In principle, all tests of hypotheses are alike in rationale and procedure. They differ only in the test statistic that is used, and in its distribution. Let us, then, consider the test statistic for the testing of a proportion.

In our discussion of the binomial distribution in Chapter 8, we noted that the number of successes of a binomial experiment (X) may also be expressed as a proportion of successes if we just divide X by the number of trials in the experiment (n). Thus $\bar{p} \equiv X/n$ is the sample proportion of successes, which serves as a statistic for estimating the distribution's probability of success (p), as discussed in Chapter 12. We also recall that $E(\bar{p}) = p$, that the standard deviation of $\bar{p}$ is $\sigma_{\bar{p}} = \sqrt{pq/n}$, and that if both np and nq are greater than or equal to 5, the sampling distribution of $\bar{p}$ is approximately normal. We shall assume throughout this section that np and nq meet this requirement.

Suppose the distribution's probability of success is unknown, and we want to test hypotheses concerning its value. The null hypothesis takes the form

$$H_0: \quad p = p_0$$

The alternative hypothesis may take one of three familiar forms:

$$H_1: \quad p = p_1 < p_0 \qquad \text{(lower-tail test)}$$

or

$$H_1: \quad p = p_1 > p_0 \qquad \text{(upper-tail test)}$$

or

$$H_1: \quad p = p_1 \neq p_0 \qquad \text{(two-tailed test)}$$

In testing any of these forms, we can proceed along one of two avenues: we may use either $\bar{p}$ or $P = \dfrac{\bar{p} - p_0}{\sigma_{\bar{p}}}$ as our test statistic. If we use $\bar{p}$ as our test statistic, the critical values (p^*) and the decision rules are

LOWER-TAIL TEST

$$p^* = p_0 - Z_\alpha\, \sigma_{\bar{p}}$$

Accept H_0 if $\bar{p} \geq p^*$; otherwise reject H_0.

UPPER-TAIL TEST

$$p^* = p_0 + Z_\alpha\, \sigma_{\bar{p}}$$

Accept H_0 if $\bar{p} \leq p^*$; otherwise reject H_0.

TWO-TAILED TEST

$$p_1^* = p_0 - Z_{\alpha/2}\, \sigma_{\bar{p}}$$

$$p_2^* = p_0 + Z_{\alpha/2}\, \sigma_{\bar{p}}$$

Accept H_0 if $p_1^* \leq \bar{p} \leq p_2^*$; otherwise reject H_0.

Note that in all three cases we obtain the value of $\sigma_{\bar{p}}$ by assuming that H_0 is correct and using the formula $\sigma_{\bar{p}} = \sqrt{\dfrac{p_0 q_0}{n}}$, where $q_0 = (1 - p_0)$.

EXAMPLE 13.4

The annexation to a city of an unincorporated area is on the ballot in an upcoming election. Voters may vote either for or against the annexation. A local newspaper is predicting that 60 percent of the votes will favor annexation and 40 percent will oppose it. A random sample of 100 people reveals that 58 are for annexation and 42 are against. Would you accept the newspaper's prediction at a 1 percent significance level? The hypotheses to be tested are

$$H_0: \quad p = 0.60$$

$$H_1: \quad p \neq 0.60$$

First we must choose the test statistic. Although only one statistic is necessary to reach a decision, we shall work out the problem with both $\bar{p}$ and $P = \dfrac{\bar{p} - p_0}{\sigma_{\bar{p}}}$ as test statistics. Note that $\sigma_{\bar{p}} = \sqrt{\dfrac{pq}{n}}$; assuming that H_0 is correct, we get

$$\sigma_{\bar{p}} = \sqrt{\frac{0.6 \cdot 0.4}{100}} = \sqrt{0.0024} = 0.049$$

The derivation of the critical values and the decision rules are shown in Table 13.2.

TABLE 13.2
Critical Values and Decision Rules for Two Alternative Test Statistics

Test statistic: $\bar{p}$	*Test statistic: $P = \dfrac{\bar{p} - p_0}{\sigma_{\bar{p}}}$*
Critical values:	Critical values:
$p_1^* = p_0 - Z_{\alpha/2}\,\sigma_{\bar{p}}$	$Z_1^* = -Z_{\alpha/2} = -2.575$
$\quad = 0.6 - 2.575 \cdot 0.049 = 0.474$	$Z_2^* = Z_{\alpha/2} = 2.575$
$p_2^* = p_0 + Z_{\alpha/2}\,\sigma_{\bar{p}}$	
$\quad = 0.6 + 2.575 \cdot 0.049 = 0.726$	
Accept H_0 if $\bar{p}$ falls between 0.474 and 0.726; otherwise reject H_0.	Accept H_0 if P falls between -2.575 and 2.575; otherwise reject H_0.

In our example we have $\bar{p} = \dfrac{58}{100} = 0.58$. Thus $\bar{p}$ falls in the acceptance region and H_0 is not rejected. The same conclusion is reached, of course, if we use the test statistic $P = \dfrac{\bar{p} - p_0}{\sigma_{\bar{p}}}$:

$$P = \frac{\bar{p} - p_0}{\sigma_{\bar{p}}} = \frac{0.58 - 0.60}{0.049} = -0.408$$

Again we do not reject H_0 and conclude that there is not enough evidence to reject the newspaper's prediction.

13.9 Testing Hypotheses About a Variance

Just as we may be interested in testing hypotheses concerning the mean of a distribution, we may also be interested in testing hypotheses concerning the distribution's variance. The null hypothesis takes the form

$$H_0: \quad \sigma^2 = \sigma_0^2$$

and once again the alternative may be one of the following:

$$H_1: \quad \sigma^2 < \sigma_0^2 \quad \text{(lower-tail test)}$$

or

$$H_1: \quad \sigma^2 > \sigma_0^2 \quad \text{(upper-tail test)}$$

or

$$H_1: \quad \sigma^2 \neq \sigma_0^2 \quad \text{(two-tailed test)}$$

The test statistic, which we shall call CS (for "chi square"), is

$$CS = \frac{\Sigma(X_i - \overline{X})^2}{\sigma_0^2} = \frac{(n-1)S^2}{\sigma_0^2} \qquad (13.9)$$

The sample variance S^2 is given by $S^2 = \frac{\Sigma(X_i - \overline{X})^2}{n-1}$, and it follows directly that $\Sigma(X_i - \overline{X})^2 = (n-1)S^2$.

As explained in Chapter 10, if the population from which X is drawn has a normal distribution, then the statistic CS has a χ^2 distribution with $(n-1)$ degrees of freedom:

$$CS = \frac{(n-1)S^2}{\sigma_0^2} \sim \chi^2_{(n-1)} \qquad (13.10)$$

The acceptance and rejection regions will be determined by the number of degrees of freedom of the chi-square distribution of CS, by the particular α chosen for the test, and by the type of alternative hypothesis considered (lower-tail, upper-tail, or two-tailed alternative). We shall illustrate the procedure with an example concerning a two-tailed alternative.

EXAMPLE 13.5

A well-known model for corporate cash management implies that the amount of cash a firm should hold is a function of several variables, among them the daily variance of net cash balances. Thus, if a firm receives \$50,000 in payments and pays out \$55,000 on a given day, the net cash flow for the day is $-\$5,000$, and if receipts are \$30,000 and payments are \$10,000 on the next day, the net cash flow for the day is \$20,000, and so forth. It is the variance of the daily net cash flow that is relevant to cash management, according to this model.

The variance of the net daily cash flow of a certain firm in the past was 400,000 (dollars squared). The firm has undergone a substantial change recently, and the corporate manager wants to test the following hypotheses regarding the current variance of the daily net cash flow (where figures are in thousands of dollars squared):

$$H_0: \quad \sigma^2 = 400$$

$$H_1: \quad \sigma^2 \neq 400$$

The manager feels that past data are not particularly relevant and decides to estimate the daily net cash-flow variance by using data from the next 20 days. The 20-day period provides the net cash-flow series shown in Table 13.3.

TABLE 13.3
Net Cash Flow on 20 Consecutive Days
(thousands of dollars)

i	X_i	i	X_i
1	−5	11	31
2	−6	12	−4
3	8	13	15
4	20	14	17
5	25	15	2
6	2	16	8
7	0	17	21
8	−3	18	13
9	11	19	1
10	13	20	22

We first establish a significance level for the test, say, $\alpha = 0.05$. Now we determine that the statistic we shall use is

$$CS = \frac{(n-1)S^2}{\sigma_0^2}$$

and its distribution is $\chi^{2(n-1)} = \chi^{2(19)}$. As a result we determine the critical values from the chi-square distribution table (Appendix A, Table A.4):

$$CS_1^* = \chi^{2(19)}_{0.975} = 8.907$$

$$CS_2^* = \chi^{2(19)}_{0.025} = 32.852$$

These values determine the acceptance and rejection regions, so we shall accept H_0 if the test statistic falls between 8.907 and 32.852, and reject H_0 if it falls outside this range (see Figure 13.12).

Figure 13.12

Critical values and acceptance and rejection regions for the chi-square test when $\alpha = 0.05$

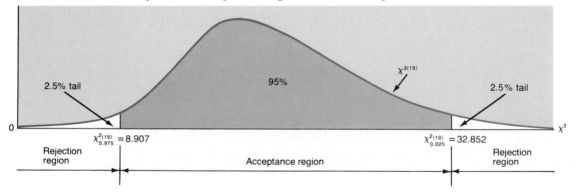

We now calculate the value of the test statistic:

$$\Sigma X = 191$$

$$\overline{X} = \frac{191}{20} = 9.55$$

$$\Sigma X^2 = 4,107$$

$$n = 20$$

For S^2 we calculate

$$S^2 = \frac{\Sigma X^2 - n\overline{X}^2}{n - 1} = \frac{4,107 - 20 \cdot 9.55^2}{19}$$

$$= \frac{4,107 - 1,824.05}{19} = 120.16$$

Next, for the test statistic, we compute

$$CS = \frac{(n - 1)S^2}{\sigma_0^2} = \frac{19 \cdot 120.16}{400} = 5.71$$

and therefore, applying our decision rule, we decide to reject the null hypothesis. In light of the sample results, it seems very unlikely that the variance of the daily net cash flow is equal to 400.

13.10 Limitations

In this chapter we have presented the basic concepts of classical hypothesis-testing procedures along with a discussion of specific types of hypotheses and the ways they should be tested. We have indicated several times that some procedures are based on the *assumption* that the observations in our samples are drawn from normal distributions. The central limit theorem allows us to apply those procedures when the sample sizes are large and the observations are independent, even if the original distributions are not normal.

We should keep in mind, however, that when these assumptions do not hold and when the central limit theorem does not justify the use of the procedures described in this chapter, we should take extra care in interpreting the test results and consider using other statistical methods, such as nonparametric methods, which we discuss in Chapter 22. Much too often statistical methods are used without first ascertaining that the tests and procedures used are applicable. We urge you to bear these limitations in mind.

Chapter Summary and Review

Test of One Mean

Hypotheses	Test statistic	Decision rule
Standard deviation is known:		
(a) $H_0: \mu \leq \mu_0$ $H_1: \mu > \mu_0$	$Z = \dfrac{\overline{X} - \mu_0}{\sigma/\sqrt{n}}$	Reject H_0 if test statistic is greater than Z_α.
(b) $H_0: \mu \geq \mu_0$ $H_1: \mu < \mu_0$	Z	Reject H_0 if test statistic is smaller than $-Z_\alpha$.
(c) $H_0: \mu = \mu_0$ $H_1: \mu \neq \mu_0$	Z	Reject H_0 if test statistic is either greater than $Z_{\alpha/2}$ or smaller than $-Z_{\alpha/2}$.
Standard deviation is unknown:		
(a) $H_0: \mu \leq \mu_0$ $H_1: \mu > \mu_0$	$T = \dfrac{\overline{X} - \mu_0}{S/\sqrt{n}}$	Reject H_0 if test statistic is greater than $t_\alpha^{(n-1)}$.
(b) $H_0: \mu \geq \mu_0$ $H_1: \mu < \mu_0$	T	Reject H_0 if test statistic is smaller than $-t_\alpha^{(n-1)}$.
(c) $H_0: \mu = \mu_0$ $H_1: \mu \neq \mu_0$	T	Reject H_0 if test statistic is either greater than $t_{\alpha/2}^{(n-1)}$ or smaller than $-t_{\alpha/2}^{(n-1)}$.

Test of One Proportion

Hypotheses	Test statistic	Decision rule
(a) $H_0: p \leq p_0$ $H_1: p > p_0$	$P = \dfrac{\overline{p} - p_0}{\sqrt{\dfrac{p_0 q_0}{n}}}$	Reject H_0 if test statistic is greater than Z_α.
(b) $H_0: p \geq p_0$ $H_1: p < p_0$	P	Reject H_0 if test statistic is smaller than $-Z_\alpha$.
(c) $H_0: p = p_0$ $H_1: p \neq p_0$	P	Reject H_0 if test statistic is either greater than $Z_{\alpha/2}$ or smaller than $-Z_{\alpha/2}$.

Explanation: $\overline{p}$ is equal to the number of "successes" in the binomial distribution divided by the number of trials; that is, $\overline{p} = X/n$. Note also that $q_0 = 1 - p_0$.

Assumption: These normal approximations are valid only if np_0 and nq_0 are greater than 5. If they are not, use the binomial distribution.

Test of Single Variance

Hypotheses	Test statistic	Decision rule
(a) $H_0: \sigma^2 = \sigma_0^2$ $H_1: \sigma^2 > \sigma_0^2$	$CS = \dfrac{(n-1)S^2}{\sigma_0^2}$	Reject H_0 if CS is greater than $\chi_\alpha^{2(n-1)}$.
(b) $H_0: \sigma^2 = \sigma_0^2$ $H_1: \sigma^2 < \sigma_0^2$	CS	Reject H_0 if CS is smaller than $\chi_{1-\alpha}^{2(n-1)}$.
(c) $H_0: \sigma^2 = \sigma_0^2$ $H_1: \sigma^2 \neq \sigma_0^1$	CS	Reject H_0 if CS is either greater than $\chi_{1-\alpha/2}^{2(n-1)}$ or smaller than $\chi_{\alpha/2}^{2(n-1)}$.

Assumption: The observations are drawn from a normal distribution.

Problems

13.1. Explain the following terms:

    (*a*) Acceptance region
    (*b*) Rejection region
    (*c*) Significance level
    (*d*) Type I error
    (*e*) Type II error

13.2. Use a graphic presentation to explain and evaluate the following statements:

    (*a*) "The probability of committing a Type I error is always smaller than that of committing a Type II error."
    (*b*) "It is absolutely impossible to have a statistical test and choose between hypotheses without running the risk of committing either a Type I or a Type II error."
    (*c*) "No matter what the alternative hypothesis, a two-tailed test is always better than a one-tailed test."
    (*d*) "When testing hypotheses, we should pay very little attention to the power of the test. Rather, we should concentrate on minimizing the probability of committing a Type II error for a given level of significance."

13.3. Evaluate and graphically explain the following statement: "When H_0: $\mu = \mu_0$ is tested against H_1: $\mu > \mu_0$, the power of the test is never smaller than the significance level, α."

13.4. "If the hypothesis H_0: $\mu = \mu_0$ is rejected in a one-tail test at a certain level of significance, then it will certainly be rejected against a two-tail alternative with the same significance level." Do you agree? Explain.

13.5. "When one decides to reject one hypothesis and accept another, at least one type of error must be committed." Do you agree? Explain.

13.6. "While we do not know ahead of time if an error will be committed, it becomes apparent after the decision has been made whether an error has been committed or not." Do you agree? Explain.

13.7. Suppose we test the hypothesis H_0: $\mu = 10$ against H_1: $\mu > 10$. If $n = 10$, $\overline{X} = 10.1$, and $S = 0$, what is the lowest significance level under which H_0 would be rejected?

13.8. The weekly income of the residents of the city of Buka is normally distributed: $X \sim N(\mu, \sigma)$, where σ is known to equal 10. A sample of 100 residents is chosen (i.e., $n = 100$) and their income is measured. Suppose we test the hypothesis

$$H_0: \mu = \$200.00$$

against

$$H_1: \mu = \$202.00$$

    (*a*) If the significance level $\alpha = 0.05$ is used to test the above hypothesis, what is the critical value $\overline{X}^*$ such that if the observed sample mean, $\overline{X}$, is greater than $\overline{X}^*$, H_0 will be rejected?
    (*b*) Calculate the probability of committing a Type II error. Are you satisfied with this test? What is the probability of accepting H_1 when indeed $\mu = \$202.00$?
    (*c*) Suppose that in order to avoid such a high probability of a Type II error, we decide to increase α. What will α be if the test is adjusted so that $\beta = 0.20$?

(*d*) As we have seen, the initial level of the probability of a Type II error is very high. Reducing this error involves an increase in the probability of a Type I error. Suppose now that you want neither a Type I error nor a Type II error to have a probability exceeding 5 percent. What is the minimum sample size, *n*, that will achieve this goal?

(*e*) Illustrate your answers to parts *a*, *b*, *c*, and *d* on a chart.

13.9. A toy manufacturer is considering the purchase of a new machine to replace an old one. The old machine produces on average 10 units of a given toy per hour. A random sample of 16 hours of production has been examined. The sample mean was 11 units per hour. Test the hypothesis that the mean production of the new machine is greater than 10 units per hour. Assume that the distribution of units produced is normal (for all practical purposes) and its standard deviation is 2 units. Use a significance level of 5 percent.

13.10. The mean life of a certain light bulb is 1,000 hours and its standard deviation is 100 hours. A new brand of bulb has been introduced to the market. A sample of 100 bulbs of the new brand reveals a sample mean of 1,050 hours. Use a 1 percent significance level to test the hypothesis that the mean life of the new brand of bulbs is different from 1,000 hours.

13.11. A realtor claims that the mean number of visitors in a given shopping mall is $\mu = 5,000$ per day. A businessperson who is considering renting a shop in the mall conducted a random survey over 4 days and found that the numbers of shoppers were 4,500; 5,000; 5,100; and 5,200. Assuming that the daily number of shoppers is normally distributed with a standard deviation of 100 and that the above sample is random, use a 5 percent significance level to test the null hypothesis that $\mu = 5,000$ against the alternative hypothesis that $\mu < 5,000$.

13.12. In testing H_0: $\mu = \mu_0 = 150$ against the alternative H_1: $\mu = \mu_1 = 130$, a sample of one observation is used. Assume a normal distribution and that $\sigma = 36$. What is the probability of committing a Type II error and what is the power of the test if the significance level of the test is 5 percent?

13.13. The monthly output of a plywood manufacturer was measured in eight randomly selected months. The results obtained (in tons) are 110, 120, 100, 102, 130, 140, 150, and 140. Test the hypothesis that the mean monthly output of the plant is 140 tons against the alternative hypothesis that the mean monthly output is 120 tons. Assume that output is a random variable, *X*, with a normal distribution, and choose a significance level $\alpha = 0.05$.

13.14. The price-earnings ratio, *P/E*, measures the number of times greater than the earnings per share, *E*, a share's price, *P*, is. Table P13.14 presents the price-earnings ratio for firms in two industries. Assume that the companies shown are randomly selected from infinitely large industries (of course, this is only an approximation), and test the hypothesis:

$$H_0: \mu = 9.0$$

against

$$H_1: \mu < 9.0$$

where μ is the mean price-earnings ratio in the container industry. Use the significance level $\alpha = 0.05$, and assume that σ is known to equal 2.0.

TABLE P13.14

Firm	Price-earnings ratio
Container manufacturers	
American Can	7
Anchor Hocking	6
Ball	6
Brockway Glass	7
Continental Group	4
Crown Cork & Seal	6
Dorsey	6
Kerr Glass Mfg.	5
Maryland Cup (3)	7
National Can	9
Owens-Illinois	5
Stone Container	6
Drug companies	
Abbott Laboratories	14
American Home Products	12
American Hospital Supply	14
Baxter Travenol Laboratories	17
Becton, Dickinson (3)	13
Johnson & Johnson	15
Lilly (Eli)	12
Mallinckrodt	15
Merck	16
Pfizer	16
Richardson-Vicks (6)	8
Robins (A. H.)	7
Schering-Plough	9
Searle (G. D.)	12
SmithKline	12
Sterling Drug	12
Syntex (5)	11
Upjohn	10

Data from *Business Week*, March 15, 1982, p. 80.

13.15. A fast-food chain opened an outlet in a small town one year ago. The standard deviation of the outlet's daily sales is $810. The management of the chain is not fully satisfied with the volume of business and has decided to close the outlet, unless the mean daily sales increases to more than $2,000. A sample of nine days was observed and sales were as follows:

Day:	1	2	3	4	5	6	7	8	9
Sales:	$2,000	1,000	3,000	2,000	1,500	1,800	1,900	2,000	1,900

Denote the mean daily sales by μ, use $\alpha = 0.10$, and test

$$H_0: \quad \mu = \$2,000$$

$$H_1: \quad \mu < \$2,000$$

Should the outlet be closed?

13.16. Repeat Problem 13.15 assuming that the population standard deviation is unknown.

13.17. You test the null hypothesis H_0: $\mu = \mu_0$ against H_1: $\mu < \mu_0$ and you reject H_0. Is it possible that using the same sample data and the same α, you would accept H_0 if the alternative hypothesis were H_1: $\mu \neq \mu_0$ rather than H_1: $\mu < \mu_0$? Explain.

13.18. In testing hypotheses about a population mean (standard deviation is known to equal $10), you obtain the sample statistic $Z = 1.7$. What must have been the value of the sample mean if we know that $\mu_0 = 100$ and the sample size, n, was also 100? Explain.

13.19. Mail delivery time (in days) is examined. The null hypothesis is H_0: $\mu = 3$ days and the alternative hypothesis is H_1: $\mu > 3$ days. The sample observations are $X_1 = 2, X_2 = 4, X_3 = 5$, $X_4 = 1, X_5 = 4$, and $X_6 = 6$. It was decided to reject the null hypothesis. What is the minimum value that could have been used for α in the test?

13.20. A company is contemplating a switch from manual to automatic handling of a certain product. Before making a decision, the company wants to determine the mean length of time it takes employees to complete the job manually. A sample of 20 random observations showed that $\overline{X} = 1.4$ and $\Sigma(X - \overline{X})^2 = 10$.

The following hypotheses are tested:

$$H_0: \quad \mu = 1 \text{ hour}$$

$$H_1: \quad \mu > 1 \text{ hour}$$

If H_0 is rejected, the new machine will be purchased. Using $\alpha = 0.01$, what should the company do, based on the sample results? Assume that the time it takes to complete the job is normally distributed.

13.21. Consider testing H_0: $\mu = \mu_0 = 100$ against H_1: $\mu = \mu_1 = 102$. Assume a normal distribution, a standard deviation of 10, and a significance level of 5 percent. Calculate the probability of a Type II error and the power of the test for the following alternative sample sizes:

    (*a*) $n = 36$
    (*b*) $n = 10,000$

13.22. The score on a given test is a random variable whose mean for the general student population is 6. A group of nine students has been randomly selected from the general student population to take a special preparatory course before taking the test. Their test scores were as follows: 4, 6, 5, 10; 7, 7, 8, 8, and 8. Assuming a normal distribution of the scores and a significance level of 1 percent, test the hypothesis that taking the preparatory course significantly increases the mean score.

13.23. During wage negotiations, the management of a large textile manufacturer advanced the claim that 50 percent of the workers in the industry earn more than $15,000 a year. The union claims that this estimate is wrong and that the correct proportion is 30 percent.

A random sample of 100 workers in the industry was taken. The sample showed that 40 percent of the workers earned less than $15,000.

    (*a*)   Test the null hypothesis under which the correct proportion is $p = 0.50$ against H_1: $p = 0.30$. Use $\alpha = 0.05$.
    (*b*)   Calculate the power of the test.

13.24. A Las Vegas casino offers the following game. You roll a die and if an even number shows up you win a prize; otherwise, you don't. Suppose you want to determine if the die is balanced and gives you a 50 percent chance to come up with an even number. You roll the die 20 times and an even number comes up in 5 out of the 20 times.

(a) Use $\alpha = 0.05$ and test the hypothesis that the chance of getting an even number is 50 percent.

(b) Denote the probability of an odd number showing by p, and test H_0: $p = p_0 = 0.50$ against H_1: $p = p_1 = 0.70$. Calculate the power of the test.

13.25. It is claimed that 40 percent of all families who own a house in California have an annual income of \$40,000 or more. A random sample of 1,000 families who own houses in California reveals that 450 have an income of \$40,000 or more. Test the null hypothesis H_0: $p = 0.40$ against the alternative hypothesis H_1: $p \neq 0.40$. Use a 5 percent significance level.

13.26. In planning a new airline route, management assumed that the variance of monthly passenger traffic would be 30 (squared thousands of passengers). The numbers of monthly passengers (in thousands) during the first 15 months were as follows: 55, 51, 49, 50, 48, 54, 52, 54, 54, 55, 55, 56, 46, 47, and 48. Assuming that the number of passengers is normally distributed, test the hypothesis that the variance of the monthly passenger traffic is 30, at $\alpha = 0.05$, against the alternative that the variance is different from 30.

13.27. When testing a hypothesis concerning a single variance, H_0: $\sigma^2 = 2$, against the alternative, H_1: $\sigma^2 > 2$, we find that for a sample of 10 observations, $\sum_{i=1}^{10} (X_i - \overline{X})^2 = 40$.

(a) Using a significance level of $\alpha = 0.05$, would you reject the null hypothesis?

(b) If the sample was of size 20 (i.e., $n = 20$) and we still obtained $\sum_{i=1}^{20} (X_i - \overline{X})^2 = 40$, would you change your decision in part a?

(c) Compare and illustrate your answers to parts a and b graphically.

13.28. Use Table P13.14 to test the hypothesis that the variance of the P/E ratio in the drug industry is equal to 10

$$H_0: \quad \sigma^2 = 10$$

against

$$H_1: \quad \sigma^2 \neq 10$$

Use $\alpha = 0.02$.

13.29. "When the hypothesis H_0: $\sigma^2 = \sigma_0^2$ is tested for a given significance level, α, the greater the sample variance, S^2, the greater the chance that H_0 will be rejected." Do you agree with this statement? Give an example to illustrate your answer.

13.30. The annual rate of return on a stock is a normally distributed random variable. A random sample of six observations reveals the following rates of return (in percent): 5, 15, 10, 20, -5, and 0. Use a 5 percent significance level to test the null hypothesis H_0: $\sigma^2 = 30$ against the alternative hypothesis H_1: $\sigma^2 > 30$.

Case Problems

13.1. For the sixth group of mutual funds in Data Set 2, Appendix B, Table B.2, estimate the proportion, p, of annual rates of return that are 10 percent or over.

Now suppose you want to test the hypotheses

$$H_0: \quad p = p_0$$

$$H_1: \quad p < p_0$$

What is the minimum value of p_0 that will lead to rejection of H_0 if the significance level of the test is 5 percent? Explain.

13.2. Estimate the mean rate of return of Eaton & Howard Balanced Fund (fund number 67 in Data Set 2, Appendix B, Table B.2).

(a) Assume that the standard deviation of the rate of return is 20 percent and that the rates of return are normally distributed. Construct a 95 percent confidence interval for the mean.

(b) Repeat part *a*, but this time assume that the standard deviation is unknown. Which of these two intervals is wider? Why?

13.3. Using the data for five funds of your choice in Data Set 2, Appendix B, Table B.2, test the hypothesis that the variance of the rates of return of "Balanced Funds" is 230 (percent squared) against the hypothesis that the variance is smaller. Assume that the rates of return of *all* the funds in this section have the same distribution and that it is normal. Use a 5 percent significance level.

13.4. Suppose you want to estimate the probability that the rate of return on investments in "Flexible Policy Income Funds" (Data Set 2, Appendix B, Table B.2) will be negative in a given year. You assume that the probability distributions of all the rates of return for these funds are the same. You consider two alternative estimators for doing it, one based on one randomly selected fund and the second based on the results of all the funds in this category. Compare the two estimators, assuming in both cases that the data you use are a sample of an infinite population of rates of return—past, present, and future. Can you say which estimator is "better"? Can you construct confidence intervals for the true probability based on each of the estimates? Explain.

APPENDIX 13A:
Type II Errors and the Power Function

The power of a test, denoted by $(1 - \beta)$, is the probability of rejecting H_0 and accepting H_1 when H_1 is in fact correct. The higher the power of the test, the better the test (all other factors held unchanged) since we want a high probability of rejecting H_0 and accepting H_1 when H_1 is correct.

THE POWER OF A ONE-TAILED TEST: AN EXAMPLE

Suppose that the mean weekly wage at a large company is $300. In wage negotiations, the union claims that the workers' wage is below the mean wage of all workers in the same industry, while the firm's management claims that the opposite is true. Assume that the standard deviation is known to be $120. Let us examine the claim of each side in the negotiations, suggest a test, and analyze the power function.

To examine the management position, we test the hypotheses

$$H_0: \quad \mu = \mu_0 = \$300$$

$$H_1: \quad \mu = \mu_1 < \$300$$

where μ is the mean wage of workers in the industry. Thus management, believing that H_1 is correct, claims that the company workers are well off.

To evaluate the workers' claim that the mean industry income is higher than their mean wage, we need to test the following hypotheses:

$$H_0: \quad \mu = \mu_0 = \$300$$

$$H_1: \quad \mu = \mu_1 > \$300$$

Each of these tests is a one-sided composite test since, under H_1, no single value of income is specified for μ_1. The alternative $H_1: \mu > \$300$, for example, means that μ can take any value above $300. For a given significance level, the power of the test is a function—called the **power function**—of the specific value of μ under H_1. Since μ is not specified by a single value, a distinct power is obtained for each value assumed for μ. Thus the power is basically equal to $1 - \beta(\mu_1)$, meaning the value of β is a function of the specific value of μ under H_1.

In order to calculate the power, assume that a sample of 64 observations is taken from the population of all workers in the industry and that we choose the significance level $\alpha = 0.01$. Let us first test the workers' claim. In this case, we have a one-sided test in which the rejection region is located to the right of the null-hypothesis distribution. We reject H_0 if

$$\frac{\overline{X} - 300}{120/\sqrt{64}} > Z_\alpha = 2.326$$

or if we find that the average wage in the sample is

$$\overline{X} > \overline{X}^* = 300 + 2.326 \cdot 120/\sqrt{64} = \$334.89$$

Suppose now that we change the alternative hypothesis to be $H_1: \mu = \$320$. What is the power of the test? The power is given by $P(\text{rejection of } H_0$ given that H_1 is correct), that is,

$$P(\overline{X} > 334.89 \text{ if } H_1 \text{ is correct}) \equiv P_{H_1}(\overline{X} > 334.89)$$

or

$$P_{H_1}\left(\frac{\overline{X} - \mu}{\sigma/\sqrt{n}} > \frac{334.89 - 320}{120/\sqrt{64}}\right) = P\left(Z > \frac{14.89}{15}\right) = P(Z > 0.993) = 0.1604$$

Thus for $H_1: \mu = \$320$, we have a test with a very low power. Note that in the calculation we used $\mu = \$320$, that is, our mean wage under the alternative hypothesis.

Suppose now that H_1: $\mu = \$315$. Through similar calculations we derive the power

$$P_{H_1}\left(\frac{\overline{X} - \mu}{\sigma/\sqrt{n}} > \frac{334.89 - 315}{15}\right) = P(Z > 1.326) = 0.0924$$

Thus the power diminishes even more. For H_1: $\mu = \$300$, the power is equal to the significance level, α, since

$$P_{H_1}\left(\frac{\overline{X} - \mu}{\sigma/\sqrt{n}} > \frac{334.89 - 300}{120/\sqrt{64}}\right) = P(Z > 2.326) = 0.01 = \alpha$$

This is not surprising, because in this case H_0 and H_1 are identical ($\mu_0 = \mu_1 = \$300$), the two distributions overlap, and the probability of rejecting H_0 is simply equal to the established significance level, as can be seen in Figure 13A.1.

If we keep sliding μ_1 to the left, beyond $\mu_0 = \$300$, and still keep the acceptance and rejection regions unchanged, the power will fall below 0.01. This is a technical result only, however, since for a left-hand alternative we would have selected a different critical value (appropriate for a lower-tail test) and the power would have been different.

Graphically, the power of the test is measured by the area under the alternative hypothesis (H_1) curve over the rejection region. Since that area changes with the location of the curve's mean, so does the power of the test. We can see in Figure 13A.1 that as μ_1 approaches μ_0, the area that represents the power decreases. Indeed, the closer μ_1 is to μ_0, the more difficult it becomes to favor μ_1 rather than μ_0 on the basis of a sample mean that is subject to random variations. In other words, when μ_1 and μ_0 are close together, there is a relatively high probability of making a Type II error. So, since $\beta(\mu_1)$ is high, the power, $1 - \beta(\mu_1)$, is relatively low in this case.

We have seen numerically that when μ_1 is in the range from \$300 to \$320, the power of the test is very poor, meaning that the workers have very little chance to prove that their claim is correct even if in fact it is. What can the workers do in such a situation? They are almost sure that the mean weekly pay in the industry is \$320, but they cannot prove it. One way to get out of the trap is to finance a larger sample. On the basis of a sample of 10,000 observations, for example, it can be easily and powerfully determined whether H_0 or H_1 should be favored.

If $n = 10,000$, we can find the power of the test for the hypotheses

$$H_0: \quad \mu = \mu_0 = \$300$$

$$H_1: \quad \mu = \mu_1 = \$320$$

First let us determine the rejection area. We reject the null hypothesis (with $\alpha = 1$ percent as before) if

$$\frac{\overline{X} - \mu_0}{\sigma/\sqrt{n}} = \frac{\overline{X} - 300}{120/\sqrt{10,000}} = \frac{\overline{X} - 300}{1.2} > Z_{0.01} = 2.326$$

TWO-TAILED TEST

The power function of a test behaves differently in the case of a two-tailed test. Recall that H_0 is rejected if $\overline{X}$ is found to be either to the left of the left-hand critical value, $\overline{X}_1^*$, or to the right of the right-hand critical value, $\overline{X}_2^*$ (see Figure 13A.4). What is the probability of rejecting H_0 when H_1 is correct? In a hypothetical situation, when H_0 and H_1 are identical ($\mu_0 = \mu_1$), as in the one-sided test, we find that the power is equal to α. If H_1 is indeed correct, and μ_1 is located to the right of μ_0 (that is, $\mu_1 > \mu_0$), the power of the test is represented by two areas under the H_1 distribution, one to the right of $\overline{X}_2^*$ and one to the left of $\overline{X}_1^*$, as shown in Figure 13A.4. If μ_1 is farther to the right, the area under H_1 to the right of $\overline{X}_2^*$ is greater than before, while the area of the same curve to the left of $\overline{X}_1^*$ is smaller. Because the area to the left of $\overline{X}_1^*$ is usually very small in relation to the area on the right of $\overline{X}_2^*$, it is true that as μ_1 slides toward the right there is an overall gain in power.

Similarly, if μ_1 is located to the left of μ_0 (that is, $\mu_1 < \mu_0$), the power of the test is again represented by two areas, but this time the larger area is located to the left, over the left-hand part of the rejection region. If H_0: $\mu = \mu_0 = \$300$, then if μ_1 is in fact equal to $320, the power is the same as if μ_1 were equal to $280, since in terms of Figure 13A.4, the power in both cases is represented by symmetrical areas. The difference is that if $\mu_1 = \$320$, most of the power is concentrated to the right of $\overline{X}_2^*$, while if $\mu_1 = \$280$, most of it is concentrated to the left of $\overline{X}_1^*$.

The power function, $1 - \beta(\mu_1)$, for the two-tailed test is illustrated in Figure 13A.5. As we explained earlier, it is a symmetrical function around

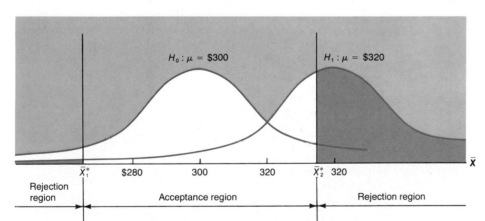

Figure 13A.4

The power of the test when the test is two-tailed and the true distribution mean is greater than its value under H_0

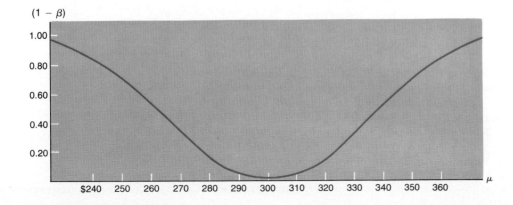

Figure 13A.5

The power function in the case of a two-tailed test when $\alpha = 0.01$

the value μ_0 and it increases as μ_1 shifts to the right or left of μ_0. Obviously, we obtain the probability of committing a Type II error, $\beta(\mu_1)$, by subtracting the power from 1.

As explained in the numerical example, for all tests, whether one-tailed or two-tailed, the power function, $1 - \beta(\mu_1)$, increases as we increase the sample size. Thus, in all cases, for a given significance level, α, we can increase $1 - \beta(\mu_1)$ by increasing n. In each case we should weigh the sampling cost against the cost involved in a Type II error.

APPENDIX PROBLEMS

13A.1. A certain plant runs a machine whose daily output is a random variable, X, and whose distribution is normal with an expected value 600 and a standard deviation of 91: $X \sim N(600, 91)$. A suggestion has been made that the machine be replaced by another whose output is also normally distributed, with a standard deviation of 91 but a higher mean. In order to test whether the mean is indeed higher, the new machine's daily output is checked for 40 days. The 40 days' output provides the sample data for testing whether the new machine has a higher average production rate. Assume $\alpha = 0.05$.

(*a*) What is the rejection region when the alternative hypothesis is that the output of the new machine is higher?

(*b*) What is the rejection region when the alternative hypothesis is that the output of the new machine is different from that of the old machine?

(*c*) What is the power of the test if the alternative hypothesis is $H_1: \mu = 635$?

(*d*) What is the power of the test if the alternative hypothesis is $H_1: \mu = 560$?

13A.2. A common measure for a firm's liquidity is the current ratio—the ratio of current assets (i.e., cash and other assets that can be easily liquidated) to current liabilities (i.e., debts that the firm must pay off within one year's time). Table P13A.2 presents the 1981 current ratio for 12 companies in the aerospace industry.

TABLE P13A.2

Bangor Punta	2.4
Boeing	1.5
Cessna Aircraft	1.6
Fairchild Industries	2.0
Gates Learjet	1.3
General Dynamics	1.6
Grumman	3.5
Lockheed	1.5
McDonnell Douglas	1.2
Northrop	1.2
Rohr Industries	2.4
United Technologies	1.5

Source: *Business Week*, March 1, 1982, p. 53.

(*a*) Assuming that the current ratio is normally distributed with $\sigma = 0.5$, and that the 12 companies are a random sample of an infinite population, test the hypothesis

$$H_0: \quad \mu = 1.6$$

against

$$H_1: \quad \mu = 1.9$$

Use a significance level $\alpha = 0.05$.

(*b*) What is the power of the above test?

(*c*) Assume now that σ is unknown and retest the hypotheses. Compare your results to those of part *a*.

INFERENCES IN COMPARATIVE STUDIES OF TWO POPULATIONS

CHAPTER FOURTEEN OUTLINE

Our study of statistical inferences has so far been confined to one population: Chapter 12 dealt with point and interval estimation and Chapter 13 addressed the topic of hypothesis testing. Frequently, however, statisticians want to compare two or more populations. In this chapter, therefore, we shall deal with inferences (i.e., estimation and hypothesis testing) about two populations; comparisons of more than two populations are left for later chapters. Specifically, we will address the following in this chapter:

1. Difference between two means
   a. Independent samples
   b. Matched samples
2. Difference between two proportions
3. Ratio of two variances

A separate section will be devoted to each of these topics, starting with hypothesis testing and continuing with the construction of confidence intervals.

14.1 Inferences About the Difference Between the Means of Two Populations: Independent Samples

HYPOTHESIS TESTING

The most common example of comparative studies of two populations is a comparison of their means. In many cases we want to determine whether the two means are equal to or different from each other. Denoting the mean of one distribution by μ_1 and the mean of the other by μ_2, we state the null hypothesis as

$$H_0: \quad \mu_1 = \mu_2$$

or

$$H_0: \quad \mu_1 - \mu_2 = 0$$

It is convenient to denote the difference between the means by D, so that $D = \mu_1 - \mu_2$. Using this notation, we can write the null hypothesis as

$$H_0: \quad D = D_0 = 0$$

The alternative hypothesis, H_1, may take any of three familiar forms:

$$H_1: \quad D = D_1 < 0 \quad \text{(meaning } \mu_1 < \mu_2; \text{ lower-tail test)}$$

or

$$H_1: \quad D = D_1 > 0 \quad \text{(meaning } \mu_1 > \mu_2; \text{ upper-tail test)}$$

or

$$H_1: \quad D = D_1 \neq 0 \quad \text{(meaning } \mu_1 \neq \mu_2; \text{ two-tailed test)}$$

We will address ourselves to the third form of H_1, assuming that you are capable of adjusting the relevant equations for the other two forms.

The only difference between tests involving the difference between two means and a test involving only one distribution's mean is the form of the test statistic and its distribution.

Since the sample mean is our point estimate for a distribution's mean, it is only natural for us to estimate the differences $D = \mu_1 - \mu_2$ by using the difference of the means of the samples taken from the two distributions under consideration. When we denote the sample mean of the first and second distributions by $\overline{X}_1$ and $\overline{X}_2$, respectively, our point estimator for $D = \mu_1 - \mu_2$ is $\overline{D} = \overline{X}_1 - \overline{X}_2$. We note that the expected value of $\overline{D} = \overline{X}_1 - \overline{X}_2$ is equal to $D = \mu_1 - \mu_2$:

$$E(\overline{D}) = E(\overline{X}_1 - \overline{X}_2) = E(\overline{X}_1) - E(\overline{X}_2) = \mu_1 - \mu_2 = D \qquad \textbf{(14.1)}$$

Assuming that the observations from the two distributions are independent, we derive the variance of $\overline{D} = \overline{X}_1 - \overline{X}_2$ as follows:[1]

$$V(\overline{D}) = V(\overline{X}_1 - \overline{X}_2) = V(\overline{X}_1) + V(\overline{X}_2) = \frac{\sigma_1^2}{n_1} + \frac{\sigma_2^2}{n_2} \qquad \textbf{(14.2)}$$

Here n_1 and n_2 are the sample sizes taken from the first and second distributions, respectively, and σ_1^2 and σ_2^2 are the variances of the first and second

---

[1] Note that Equation 14.2 holds only if $\overline{X}_1$ and $\overline{X}_2$ are independent of one another. Chapter 7 explains how the variance of a sum or a difference of two random variables is affected by their dependence.

distributions, respectively. The standard error of $\overline{D} = \overline{X}_1 - \overline{X}_2$—that is, $\sigma_{\overline{D}}$—is

$$\sigma_{\overline{D}} = \sigma_{\overline{X}_1 - \overline{X}_2} = \sqrt{\frac{\sigma_1^2}{n_1} + \frac{\sigma_2^2}{n_2}} \qquad (14.3)$$

When $\overline{X}_1$ and $\overline{X}_2$ are normally distributed, the difference, $\overline{D} = \overline{X}_1 - \overline{X}_2$, is also normally distributed. Assuming that H_0 is correct, we get

$$\frac{\overline{D} - D_0}{\sigma_{\overline{D}}} \sim N(0, 1) \qquad (14.4)$$

or

$$Z = \frac{\overline{D} - D_0}{\sigma_{\overline{D}}} \qquad (14.5)$$

which can serve as a test statistic. But if the variances σ_1^2 and σ_2^2 are unknown, then $\sigma_{\overline{D}}$ as given in Equation 14.3 is also unknown, and the test statistic Z from Equation 14.5 cannot be used to test the hypothesis. However, if the distributions of X_1 and X_2 are normal or if the sample sizes are large, we can use the t distribution to test the hypotheses. A more detailed explanation is provided following Example 14.1.

EXAMPLE 14.1

A department-store chain has opened two new stores. After a period of operations, management has decided to test whether the two stores have the same mean daily sales. Suppose the sales are normally distributed and the variances are known to equal 8,000 (dollars squared) for the first store ($\sigma_1^2 = 8,000$) and 10,000 (dollars squared) for the second store ($\sigma_2^2 = 10,000$). Suppose independent random samples of sizes 10 and 14 are taken from the first and second stores, respectively (that is, $n_1 = 10$ and $n_2 = 14$), and these samples produce means of $\overline{X}_1 = \$15,000$ and $\overline{X}_2 = \$14,800$.

With these data we can use the test statistic given in Equation 14.5 to test hypotheses such as the following:

$$H_0: \quad D = 0$$

$$H_1: \quad D \neq 0$$

If we use $\alpha = 0.01$, our acceptance region is the range between $-Z_{0.005}$ and $Z_{0.005}$ (that is, the range from -2.575 to 2.575), and the rejection region is all other values of Z. In our example we find that

$$\sigma_{\overline{D}} = \sqrt{\frac{\sigma_1^2}{n_1} + \frac{\sigma_2^2}{n_2}} = \sqrt{\frac{8,000}{10} + \frac{10,000}{14}} = \sqrt{800 + 714} = 38.9$$

$$Z = \frac{\overline{D} - D_0}{\sigma_{\overline{D}}} = \frac{(15,000 - 14,800) - 0}{38.9} = \frac{200.0}{38.9} = 5.14$$

and the Z value we compute is well within the rejection region. We conclude, then, that the stores do not have the same sales volume. It is worth noting that our test suggests *different* sales volumes for the two stores: since we obtained $\overline{X}_1 > \overline{X}_2$ in the sample, we are led to conclude that the first store has a greater sales volume.

Example 14.1 is largely hypothetical. It is very unlikely that a situation might arise in which the sales variances were known and the means were not; in reality, if the means are unknown, the variances are likely to be unknown as well. We want a statistic that will be useful in this kind of situation. Fortunately, if we can assume that the variances of the two distributions are equal and that the populations are normally distributed, such a statistic is available. We estimate $\sigma_{\overline{D}}$ by using $S_{\overline{D}}$ as follows:

$$S_{\overline{D}} = \sqrt{\left[\frac{(n_1 - 1)S_1^2 + (n_2 - 1)S_2^2}{(n_1 + n_2 - 2)}\right]\left(\frac{n_1 + n_2}{n_1 \cdot n_2}\right)} \tag{14.6}$$

Here S_1^2 and S_2^2 are the estimated variances of the first and second samples, respectively. The test statistic is given by

$$T = \frac{\overline{D} - (\mu_1 - \mu_2)}{S_{\overline{D}}} \sim t^{(n_1 + n_2 - 2)} \tag{14.7}$$

The statistic has a t distribution with $(n_1 + n_2 - 2)$ degrees of freedom.

EXAMPLE 14.2

Nan Rowell, a student of business administration, is deciding which of two processing-by-mail services to use to process her film. She considers two that charge the same price and provide similar quality and selects the one that provides faster service. Her records show the waiting period (in days) between the mailing of the film and the receipt of prints from the two firms:

Waiting period for prints (days)

First mail service	Second mail service
4	5
8	6
10	6
10	4
9	7
8	

Is there a significant difference in the waiting period for the prints between the two companies? Assume a 20 percent significance level.

There is an obvious difference between the sample means of the waiting periods. The difference, however, does not necessarily imply that one service is *significantly* faster than the other, and could very well result from sampling errors only. The hypotheses are

$$H_0: \quad D = \mu_1 - \mu_2 = 0$$

$$H_1: \quad D = \mu_1 - \mu_2 \neq 0$$

Since $n_1 = 6$, $n_2 = 5$, and $\alpha = 0.20$, our critical points are

$$-t_{0.10}^{(6+5-2)} = -t_{0.10}^{(9)} = -1.383$$

and

$$t_{0.10}^{(6+5-2)} = t_{0.10}^{(9)} = 1.383$$

The test statistic is

$$T = \frac{(\overline{X}_1 - \overline{X}_2) - (\mu_1 - \mu_2)}{\sqrt{\left[\dfrac{(n_1 - 1)S_1^2 + (n_2 - 1)S_2^2}{(n_1 + n_2 - 2)}\right]\left(\dfrac{n_1 + n_2}{n_1 \cdot n_2}\right)}} = \frac{\overline{D} - (\mu_1 - \mu_2)}{S_{\overline{D}}}$$

If the value of the test statistic falls within the acceptance region—that is, between -1.383 and 1.383—Nan should accept the null hypothesis; otherwise she should reject it. The calculation of the value of the test statistic in the sample, assuming that H_0 is correct, is presented in Table 14.1 and is equal to 2.32. Since 2.32 is outside the range from -1.383 to 1.383, we conclude that we have 80 percent confidence that the two mean waiting periods are not the same and we reject H_0. Obviously, since $\overline{X}_1 = 8.167 > 5.600 = \overline{X}_2$, the result implies that the faster service is provided by the second mail service.

TABLE 14.1
Calculation of the Test Statistic

i	X_1	X_2	X_1^2	X_2^2
1	4	5	16	25
2	8	6	64	36
3	10	6	100	36
4	10	4	100	16
5	9	7	81	49
6	8	—	64	—
	$\Sigma X_1 = 49$	$\Sigma X_2 = 28$	$\Sigma X_1^2 = 425$	$\Sigma X_2^2 = 162$

Calculation of the test statistic, T

$$\overline{X}_1 = \frac{\Sigma X_1}{n_1} = \frac{49}{6} = 8.167 \qquad S_1^2 = \frac{\Sigma X_1^2 - n_1\overline{X}_1^2}{n_1 - 1} = \frac{425 - 6 \cdot 8.167^2}{5} = \frac{24.8}{5} = 4.96$$

$$\overline{X}_2 = \frac{\Sigma X_2}{n_2} = \frac{28}{5} = 5.600 \qquad S_2^2 = \frac{\Sigma X_2^2 - n_2\overline{X}_2^2}{n_2 - 1} = \frac{162 - 5 \cdot 5.600^2}{4} = \frac{5.2}{4} = 1.3$$

$$T = \frac{(\overline{X}_1 - \overline{X}_2) - (\mu_1 - \mu_2)}{\sqrt{\left[\frac{(n_1 - 1)S_1^2 + (n_2 - 1)S_2^2}{(n_1 + n_2 - 2)}\right]\left(\frac{n_1 + n_2}{n_1 \cdot n_2}\right)}} = \frac{(8.167 - 5.600) - 0}{\sqrt{\left(\frac{5 \cdot 4.96 + 4 \cdot 1.30}{9}\right)\left(\frac{6 + 5}{6 \cdot 5}\right)}}$$

$$= \frac{2.5670}{1.1055} = 2.32$$

Finally, let us note that the null hypothesis does not necessarily have to state that the difference between the means is equal to zero. Any other hypothesized difference between μ_1 and μ_2 can be tested by the procedure established in this section. For example, if we want to test

$$H_0: \quad \mu_1 - \mu_2 = 1$$

$$H_1: \quad \mu_1 - \mu_2 \neq 1$$

the value of the test statistic (see Table 14.1) will be

$$\frac{(8.167 - 5.600) - 1.000}{1.1055} = \frac{1.5670}{1.1055} = 1.417$$

The critical values are still -1.383 and 1.383, and H_0 is rejected. We conclude that we have 80 percent confidence that the difference between the mean waiting periods is different from one day. Again, the sample provides evidence that the second service is faster by more than one day.

CONFIDENCE INTERVALS

The statistic $\overline{D} = \overline{X}_1 - \overline{X}_2$ can be used to construct confidence intervals for the difference between the means, $\mu_1 - \mu_2$. Assuming again that the underlying populations are normally distributed and their variances are equal, the standard error of $\overline{D}$ is given by Equation 14.6 and the confidence interval ranges from $\overline{D} - S_{\overline{D}}t_{\alpha/2}^{(n_1 + n_2 - 2)}$ to $\overline{D} + S_{\overline{D}}t_{\alpha/2}^{(n_1 + n_2 - 2)}$:

$$P(\overline{D} - S_{\overline{D}}t_{\alpha/2}^{(n_1 + n_2 - 2)} \leq \mu_1 - \mu_2 \leq \overline{D} + S_{\overline{D}}t_{\alpha/2}^{(n_1 + n_2 - 2)}) = 1 - \alpha \qquad \textbf{(14.8)}$$

For the data given in Example 14.2, where $\overline{D} = 8.167 - 5.600 = 2.567$, $S_{\overline{D}} = 1.1055$, and $n_1 + n_2 - 2 = 6 + 5 - 2 = 9$, a 95 percent confidence interval ranges from

$$\overline{D} - S_{\overline{D}}t_{0.025}^{(n_1 + n_2 - 2)} = 2.567 - 1.1055 \cdot 2.262 = 0.066$$

to

$$\overline{D} + S_{\overline{D}}t_{0.025}^{(n_1 + n_2 - 2)} = 2.567 + 1.1055 \cdot 2.262 = 5.068$$

The confidence interval constructed above for $\mu_1 - \mu_2$ and the hypothesis test that preceded it are underlined by the assumption that both populations are normal and their variances equal one another. What if these conditions are not met? This depends on the sample size. Nonparametric tests (Chapter 22) are applicable for small and moderate size samples, provided the samples are selected at random. These tests do not assume normality or equality of variances, and they can be directly applied. If the sample size from *each* of the populations is large enough, then the sampling distributions of both $\overline{X}_1$ and $\overline{X}_2$ are approximately normal by the central limit theorem for almost any underlying population distribution. In this case we estimate $S_D^2 = S_{\overline{X}_1}^2 + S_{\overline{X}_2}^2$, where $S_{\overline{X}_1}$ and $S_{\overline{X}_2}$ are simply the standard errors of $\overline{X}_1$ and $\overline{X}_2$, respectively. With this estimator, we can construct confidence intervals and test hypotheses just as we did earlier.

EXAMPLE 14.3

A comparative study of annual income in two industries shows the following results:

$$\overline{X}_1 = \$18{,}800 \qquad S_1 = \sqrt{\frac{\Sigma(X_1 - \overline{X}_1)^2}{n_1 - 1}} = \$3{,}400$$

$$\overline{X}_2 = \$18{,}000 \qquad S_2 = \sqrt{\frac{\Sigma(X_2 - \overline{X}_2)^2}{n_2 - 1}} = \$2{,}900$$

The sample sizes were $n_1 = 230$ and $n_2 = 260$. Suppose we want to construct a 95 percent confidence interval for the difference between the means of annual incomes in the two industries. The sample sizes are large enough, and we can assume that the difference between the sample means is approximately normally distributed. First, we calculate S_D^2:

$$S_D^2 = S_{\overline{X}_1}^2 + S_{\overline{X}_2}^2 = \frac{S_1^2}{n_1} + \frac{S_2^2}{n_2}$$

$$= \frac{3{,}400^2}{230} + \frac{2{,}900^2}{260} = 82{,}607.023$$

and

$$S_{\overline{D}} = \sqrt{82{,}607.023} = 287.414$$

Since $\overline{D} = \overline{X}_1 - \overline{X}_2 = 18{,}800 - 18{,}000 = \$800$ and $Z_{0.025} = 1.96$, the confidence interval ranges from $800 - 287.414 \cdot 1.96 = \$236.67$ to $800 + 287.414 \cdot 1.96 = \$1{,}363.33$. Consequently we have 95 percent confidence that the difference between the means of the annual incomes in the two industries is between \$236.67 and \$1,363.33. Incidentally, since this range does not include the value zero, it is clear that had we tested $H_0: \mu_1 = \mu_2$ against $H_1: \mu_1 \neq \mu_2$ with $\alpha = 0.05$, we would have rejected the null hypothesis.

14.2 Inferences About the Difference Between the Means of Two Populations: Matched Samples

HYPOTHESIS TESTING

Sometimes it is possible to match the observations of one sample with the observations of the other sample, a procedure that typically yields more precise statistical inferences. The procedure is quite simple. For each observation in the first sample, X_{1i}, we obtain the matched value in the second sample, X_{2i}, and calculate the difference $D_i = X_{1i} - X_{2i}$. Then the sample mean values of the D_is is calculated:

$$\overline{D} = \frac{\Sigma D}{n} \tag{14.9}$$

The index i is dropped from D_i for simplicity and n is the number of *pairs* of observations. The standard deviation of D is estimated using the following formula:

$$S_D = \sqrt{\frac{\Sigma(D - \overline{D})^2}{n - 1}} \tag{14.10}$$

The standard error of the estimate $\overline{D}$ is

$$S_{\overline{D}} = \frac{S_D}{\sqrt{n}} \tag{14.11}$$

In short, once the values D_i have been calculated, we treat them as though they were values of a *single* sample and calculate $\overline{D}$, S_D, and $S_{\overline{D}}$ using the standard formulas. The statistic $(\overline{D} - \mu_D)/S_{\overline{D}}$ is used to test the hypothesis about μ_D, where μ_D is the mean value of D under the null hypothesis. If both X_1 and X_2 are normally distributed, then the distribution of D is also normal, and when the standard deviation of D is unknown, the distribution of the test statistic is t with $n - 1$ degrees of freedom:

$$\frac{\overline{D} - \mu_D}{S_{\overline{D}}} \sim t^{(n-1)} \tag{14.12}$$

The use of this statistic for both hypothesis testing and confidence interval estimation is illustrated in the following example.

EXAMPLE 14.4

A firm manufactures tennis balls and seeks to maintain superb quality. The firm employs a relatively large number of inspectors who perform a number of tests on randomly selected balls. Each inspector's productivity is measured by the number of tennis balls given a full inspection during a day. The firm wants to compare the productivity of day-shift inspectors with that of night-shift inspectors. To do so it measures the productivity of each inspector, once on the day shift and once on the night shift. The comparison of these sample data allows us to use the matched samples procedure. The data are given in Table 14.2.

TABLE 14.2
Matched Sample Data of Inspectors'
Productivity
(number of tennis balls inspected per work shift)

	Shift	
Inspector	Day	Night
A	153	157
B	171	167
C	179	175
D	157	157
E	159	153
F	173	163
G	163	155

Since the samples are matched, we can find the difference in productivity between the day and night shift for each worker. Denoting the number of balls inspected on the day shift by X_1 and on the night shift by X_2 and denoting the difference between them by D, we have

$$D = X_1 - X_2$$

A value for D is obtained for each inspector (see Table 14.3). The mean and standard deviation of D, $\overline{D}$, and $S_{\overline{D}}$ are then calculated. From Table 14.3 we get $n = 7$, $\Sigma D = 28$, $\overline{D} = 4$, and $\Sigma(D - \overline{D})^2 = 136$. We then calculate S_D and $S_{\overline{D}}$ as follows:

$$S_D = \sqrt{\frac{\Sigma(D - \overline{D})^2}{n - 1}} = \sqrt{\frac{136}{6}} = 4.761 \text{ balls}$$

$$S_{\overline{D}} = \frac{S_D}{\sqrt{n}} = \frac{4.761}{\sqrt{7}} = 1.799 \text{ balls}$$

To test the hypotheses

$$H_0: \quad \mu_D = 0$$

$$H_1: \quad \mu_D \neq 0$$

TABLE 14.3
A Work Sheet for Calculating the Test Statistic

	Shift				
Inspector	Day X_1	Night X_2	$D = X_1 - X_2$	$D - \overline{D}$	$(D - \overline{D})^2$
A	153	157	−4	−8	64
B	171	167	4	0	0
C	179	175	4	0	0
D	157	157	0	−4	16
E	159	153	6	2	4
F	173	163	10	6	36
G	163	155	8	4	16
Total	1,155	1,127	28	0	136
Mean	$\overline{X}_1 = 165$	$\overline{X}_2 = 161$	$\overline{D} = 4$		

we calculate

$$\frac{\overline{D} - \mu_D}{S_{\overline{D}}} = \frac{4 - 0}{1.799} = 2.223$$

Assuming that X_1 and X_2 are normally distributed, the test statistic has a t distribution with $7 - 1 = 6$ degrees of freedom. And if we assume a 10 percent significance level, our critical value is $t_{0.05}^{(6)} = 1.943$. Since $2.223 > 1.943$, we reject the null hypothesis that the day shift and night shift have the same mean productivity. In fact, Table 14.3 shows that the day-shift sample has a higher mean than the night-shift sample, which leads us to conclude that the day shift's productivity is higher.

Note that the test statistic can also be used to test a null hypothesis other than $\mu_D = 0$. For example, suppose we wanted to test

$$H_0: \quad \mu_D = 2$$

$$H_1: \quad \mu_D > 2$$

We will get

$$\frac{\overline{D} - \mu_D}{S_{\overline{D}}} = \frac{4 - 2}{1.799} = 1.112$$

Comparing the result to $t_{0.10}^{(6)} = 1.440$, we find that $1.112 < 1.440$ and the null hypothesis cannot be rejected.

Comparing the independent samples procedure with the matched samples procedure we find the following:

1. The number of degrees of freedom in the independent samples test is $n_1 + n_2 - 2$, whereas in the matched samples test it is $n - 1$ (presumably $n_1 = n_2 = n$ in matched samples test). With more degrees of freedom, the t distribution is less dispersed and inferences become more reliable. This is an advantage of the independent samples test.

2. The standard error of $\overline{D}$ calculated for matched samples is often considerably smaller than that calculated for independent samples (other things being equal).[2] This gives the matched samples procedure an advantage that often outweighs the disadvantage in the degrees of freedom.

---

[2] For students who have studied Chapter 7, which deals with two random variables, we offer the following explanation. The variance of $\overline{D}$ is given by

$$V(\overline{D}) = V(\overline{X}_1 - \overline{X}_2) = V(\overline{X}_1) + V(\overline{X}_2) - 2COV(\overline{X}_1, \overline{X}_2)$$

When the samples are matched, the covariance term is typically positive, which makes $V(\overline{D})$ smaller than $V(\overline{X}_1) + V(\overline{X}_2)$. But when the samples are independent, the covariance term is zero, which makes $V(\overline{X}_1 - \overline{X}_2) = V(\overline{X}_1) + V(\overline{X}_2)$. Consequently, whenever the covariance term is positive, a matched sample results in a smaller variance compared to independent samples.

Table 14.4 is a work sheet for calculating S_1 and S_2, the standard deviations of X_1 and X_2, respectively, in the tennis balls inspection example, where X_1 and X_2 are considered to be from two independent samples. From the table we determine

$$(n_1 - 1)S_1^2 = \Sigma(X_1 - \bar{X}_1)^2 = 544$$

$$(n_2 - 1)S_2^2 = \Sigma(X_2 - \bar{X}_2)^2 = 368$$

The standard error of $\bar{D}$ in this case is 4.660:

$$S_{\bar{D}} = \sqrt{\left[\frac{(n_1 - 1)S_1^2 + (n_2 - 1)S_2^2}{n_1 + n_2 - 2}\right]\left[\frac{n_1 + n_2}{n_1 n_2}\right]}$$

$$= \sqrt{\left[\frac{544 + 368}{7 + 7 - 2}\right]\left[\frac{7 + 7}{49}\right]} = 4.660$$

TABLE 14.4
A Work Sheet for Calculating S_1 and S_2

| | Shift | | | | | |
| | Day | Night | | | | |
Observation	X_1	X_2	$X_1 - \bar{X}_1$	$(X_1 - \bar{X}_1)^2$	$X_2 - \bar{X}_2$	$(X_2 - \bar{X}_2)^2$
1	153	157	-12	144	-4	16
2	171	167	6	36	6	36
3	179	175	14	196	14	196
4	157	157	-8	64	-4	16
5	159	153	-6	36	-8	64
6	173	163	8	64	2	4
7	163	155	-2	4	-6	36
Total	1,155	1,127	0	544	0	368
Mean	$\bar{X}_1 = 165$	$\bar{X}_2 = 161$				

This value is considerably larger than the value 1.799 obtained earlier when the samples were assumed to be matched. Testing

$$H_0: \quad \mu_D = 0$$

$$H_1: \quad \mu_D \neq 0$$

with $\alpha = 0.10$ and assuming independent rather than matched samples, we use the critical values $\pm t_{0.05}^{(12)} = \pm 1.782$ and calculate

$$\frac{\bar{D} - \mu_D}{S_{\bar{D}}} = \frac{4 - 0}{4.660} = 0.858$$

And since $-1.782 < 0.858 < 1.782$, we do not reject the null hypothesis. Had we not utilized the information that the samples are matched, the standard error of estimate $S_{\bar{D}}$ would have been relatively high compared to the matched samples case, and the resulting value of the test statistic would be lower (0.858 compared to 2.223 in the matched samples case). Consequently, the independent samples test leads to the conclusion that the null hypothesis cannot be rejected. Using the information that allows us to match the samples, we are able to reject the null hypothesis based on the sample data. This result is also intuitively clear. There is a relatively large variance in the productivity among individual inspectors. The variance in the productivity of the inspectors on the day and night shifts is not large compared to the variance across the inspectors. Therefore, when using independent samples, we cannot attribute the differences in the productivity to the shift effect more than to the differences between inspectors. By matching the observations, the effect of a change in shift is better isolated.

CONFIDENCE INTERVALS

The statistic $(\overline{D} - \mu_D)/S_{\overline{D}}$ and its $t^{(n-1)}$ distribution can be used to construct a confidence interval for μ_D $(= \mu_1 - \mu_2)$. The confidence interval ranges from $\overline{D} - S_{\overline{D}}t_{\alpha/2}^{(n-1)}$ to $\overline{D} + S_{\overline{D}}t_{\alpha/2}^{(n-1)}$:

$$P(\overline{D} - S_{\overline{D}}t_{\alpha/2}^{(n-1)} \leq \mu_1 - \mu_2 \leq \overline{D} + S_{\overline{D}}t_{\alpha/2}^{(n-1)}) = 1 - \alpha \qquad \textbf{(14.13)}$$

Thus there is a probability equal to $1 - \alpha$ that the interval (which is the random variable here) will include the difference between the means, μ_D. Going back to the matched samples of productivity of the tennis-ball inspectors, we have $\overline{D} = 4$ and $S_{\overline{D}} = 1.799$. Assuming $\alpha = 0.05$, we use $t_{\alpha/2}^{(n-1)} = t_{0.025}^{(6)} = 2.447$ to construct the confidence interval

$$P(4 - 1.799 \cdot 2.447 \leq \mu_1 - \mu_2 \leq 4 + 1.799 \cdot 2.447) = 0.95$$

or

$$P(-0.402 \leq \mu_1 - \mu_2 \leq 8.402) = 0.95$$

The 95 percent confidence interval for $\mu_1 - \mu_2$ ranges from -0.402 to 8.402, which means there is 95 percent confidence that the mean productivity of the day shift is higher than that of the night shift by between -0.402 and 8.402 balls per shift.

Before continuing our discussion, we should note again that once the differences, D_i, have been calculated for matched samples, the values of D_i are treated as a single sample. If the populations of X_1 and X_2 are not normal, the values of D_i are not likely to be normally distributed. But if the sample size is reasonably large, the central limit theorem applies, allowing us to test hypotheses and provide confidence intervals, assuming that $\overline{D}$ is approximately normally distributed.

14.3 Inferences About the Difference Between Two Proportions

HYPOTHESIS TESTING

We are sometimes interested in testing hypotheses about the difference between proportions. For example, we might want to compare the proportions of credit-card holders in two population strata or the proportions of adult population members owning at least $1,000 worth of common stock in two locations (such as urban versus rural areas). Suppose we hypothesize that the proportions in both populations are equal to each other and to some value p_0:

$$H_0: \quad p_1 = p_2 = p_0$$

$$H_1: \quad p_1 \neq p_2$$

Alternatively, we may define $\Delta p = p_1 - p_2$ and rewrite the hypotheses as follows:

$$H_0: \quad \Delta p = 0$$

$$H_1: \quad \Delta p \neq 0$$

As before, we shall use the sample proportion $\bar{p} = X/n$ as our estimate of the population proportion, p. Since the current problem involves two populations, we will actually obtain two estimates of proportions ($\bar{p}_1 = X_1/n_1$ and $\bar{p}_2 = X_2/n_2$, where the subscripts 1 and 2 denote variables pertaining to the first and second distributions, respectively), one for each population, and denote the difference between the estimated proportions by $\overline{\Delta p}$. The expected value of the sample difference between the proportions is

$$E(\overline{\Delta p}) = E(\bar{p}_1 - \bar{p}_2) = E(\bar{p}_1) - E(\bar{p}_2) = p_1 - p_2 = \Delta p \qquad \textbf{(14.14)}$$

If we assume that the two samples are independent, so that $\bar{p}_1$ and $\bar{p}_2$ are also independent, the variance of the difference between the estimated proportions is equal to the sum of the variances:

$$V(\overline{\Delta p}) = V(\bar{p}_1 - \bar{p}_2) = V(\bar{p}_1) + V(\bar{p}_2) = \frac{p_1 q_1}{n_1} + \frac{p_2 q_2}{n_2}$$

$$\textbf{(14.15)}$$

$$\sigma_{\overline{\Delta p}} = \sqrt{\frac{p_1 q_1}{n_1} + \frac{p_2 q_2}{n_2}}$$

If the null hypothesis is correct, then $p_1 = p_2 = p_0$ (implying that $q_1 = q_2 = q_0$) and

$$\left. \begin{array}{l} E(\overline{\Delta p}) = \Delta p = 0 \\[2em] \sigma_{\overline{\Delta p}} = \sqrt{p_0 q_0 \left(\frac{1}{n_1} + \frac{1}{n_2} \right)} \end{array} \right\} \text{ hold if } H_0 \text{ is correct.} \qquad \textbf{(14.16)}$$

The test statistic we can use to test H_0 against H_1 is

$$P = \frac{\overline{\Delta p} - \Delta p}{\sigma_{\overline{\Delta p}}} = \frac{(\overline{p}_1 - \overline{p}_2) - (p_1 - p_2)}{\sigma_{(\overline{p}_1 - \overline{p}_2)}} \quad \text{(14.17)}$$

where $\sigma_{\overline{\Delta p}}$ is calculated using Equation 14.16.

If the proportion p_0 is not specified under H_0, then we evaluate $\sigma_{\overline{\Delta p}}$ by using $\overline{p}$ instead of p_0, where $\overline{p}$ is the weighted mean of the observed sample proportions:

$$\overline{p} = \frac{n_1\overline{p}_1 + n_2\overline{p}_2}{n_1 + n_2} \quad \text{(14.18)}$$

For example, if we test H_0: $p_1 = p_2$ against H_1: $p_1 \neq p_2$, using $\alpha = 0.05$, and the first sample (with $n_1 = 16$) shows $\overline{p}_1 = 0.75$ and the second (with $n_2 = 20$) shows $\overline{p}_2 = 0.85$, we estimate $\overline{p}$ to be

$$\overline{p} = \frac{16 \cdot 0.75 + 20 \cdot 0.85}{16 + 20} = 0.806$$

The standard error of $\overline{\Delta p}$ is estimated using $\overline{p}$:

$$S_{\overline{\Delta p}} = \sqrt{\overline{p}(1 - \overline{p})\left(\frac{1}{n_1} + \frac{1}{n_2}\right)} \quad \text{(14.19)}$$

Employing Equation 14.19, we calculate

$$S_{\overline{\Delta p}} = \sqrt{(0.806)(1 - 0.806)\left(\frac{1}{16} + \frac{1}{20}\right)} = \sqrt{0.01759} = 0.133$$

Using Equation 14.17 and the estimated value of $\sigma_{\overline{\Delta p}}$, we get

$$P = \frac{\overline{\Delta p} - \Delta p}{S_{\overline{\Delta p}}} = \frac{(0.75 - 0.85) - 0}{0.133} = -0.752$$

Assuming reasonably large samples, the sampling distribution of p is approximately normal. Since $-0.752 < 1.96 = Z_{0.025}$ and $-0.752 > -1.96 = -Z_{0.025}$, we cannot reject the null hypothesis, which asserts that p_1 equals p_2.

CONFIDENCE INTERVALS

Given the estimators $\overline{p}$ (Equation 14.18), $\overline{\Delta p} = \overline{p}_1 - \overline{p}_2$, and $S_{\overline{\Delta p}}$ (Equation 14.19), we can construct a confidence interval for Δp that ranges from $\overline{\Delta p} - S_{\overline{\Delta p}} \cdot Z_{\alpha/2}$ to $\overline{\Delta p} + S_{\overline{\Delta p}} \cdot Z_{\alpha/2}$:

$$P(\overline{\Delta p} - S_{\overline{\Delta p}} \cdot Z_{\alpha/2} \leq \Delta p \leq \overline{\Delta p} + S_{\overline{\Delta p}} \cdot Z_{\alpha/2}) = 1 - \alpha$$

For the example in the last section, where $\overline{\Delta p} = \overline{p}_1 - \overline{p}_2 = 0.75 - 0.85 = -0.10$ and $S_{\overline{\Delta p}} = 0.133$, a 95 percent confidence interval ranges from

$$-0.10 - 0.133 \cdot 1.96 = -0.361 \quad \text{to} \quad -0.10 + 0.133 \cdot 1.96 = 0.161$$

14.4 Inferences About the Ratio of Two Variances

HYPOTHESIS TESTING

In some situations we may be concerned with relationships between the variances of two populations. For example, we may want to compare the variances of the net cash flows of two departments of a given firm or organization or the variances of prospective incomes for business administration graduates in two areas of concentration. A test of this kind would involve the following hypotheses:

$$H_0: \quad \sigma_1^2 = \sigma_2^2$$

$$H_1: \quad \sigma_1^2 > \sigma_2^2$$

If we can assume that the two populations whose variances are being compared are normally distributed and that the two samples are independent, we can use a test statistic whose distribution is F. The statistic is

$$F = \frac{S_1^2/\sigma_1^2}{S_2^2/\sigma_2^2} \tag{14.20}$$

where S_1^2 and S_2^2 are the respective estimates of the variances of the first and second distributions.

The statistic F has $n_1 - 1$ and $n_2 - 1$ degrees of freedom, where n_1 and n_2 are the sizes of samples taken from the first and second populations, respectively.

If the null hypothesis is correct, then σ_1^2 and σ_2^2 may be canceled out in Equation 14.20, in which case F is reduced to S_1^2/S_2^2. Naturally, as the observed ratio of S_1^2 to S_2^2 increases, we become more inclined to believe that H_1, not H_0, is the correct hypothesis. Given a significance level α, we determine the critical value to be $F_\alpha^{(n_1-1, n_2-1)}$. When H_1 suggests the reverse relationship between σ_1^2 and σ_2^2—that is, if H_1 is

$$H_1: \quad \sigma_1^2 < \sigma_2^2$$

we simply reverse the ratio in Equation 14.20 and proceed along the lines described above.

EXAMPLE 14.5

Harvey Advancy is a young, highly motivated business administration student who likes to plan his future in advance. As he is entering his junior year in college, he has to make up his mind about his field of concentration. Two areas appeal to Harvey: accounting and marketing. Since he views both areas as equally interesting, he decides to base his decision on the projected levels of earnings of the two fields. Being a motivated person, Harvey telephones some graduates who currently have jobs in marketing and accounting. His samples reveal the following:

$$n_a = 10 \qquad n_m = 13$$

$$\overline{X}_a = \$14,000 \qquad \overline{X}_m = \$13,700$$

$$S_a = \$2,000 \qquad S_m = \$1,800$$

The subscripts a and m indicate whether the variable pertains to the accounting sample or to the marketing sample. Although Harvey might want to test hypotheses concerning both the mean and the variance of the earnings distributions, we shall concern ourselves only with tests about the variances. Suppose we want to test

$$H_0: \quad \sigma_a^2 = \sigma_m^2$$

against

$$H_1: \quad \sigma_a^2 > \sigma_m^2$$

using $\alpha = 0.01$. Our test statistic is

$$F = \frac{S_a^2/\sigma_a^2}{S_m^2/\sigma_m^2}$$

where F has an F distribution with degrees of freedom $n_a - 1 = 9$ and $n_m - 1 = 12$:

$$F \sim F^{(9,12)}$$

From the F distribution table (Appendix A, Table A.5) we get the critical value $F_{0.01}^{(9,12)} = 4.39$, and the decision rule is to accept H_0 if $F \leq 4.39$ and to reject H_0 if $F > 4.39$.

If H_0 is correct, then F reduces to $F = S_a^2/S_m^2$ and its value in our example is

$$F = \frac{S_a^2}{S_m^2} = \frac{2,000^2}{1,800^2} = \frac{4,000,000}{3,240,000} = 1.235$$

Given this value of F, we do not reject H_0. We do not have enough evidence to justify a conclusion that the variance of income in the area of accounting is greater than in the area of marketing.

If the alternative hypothesis suggests that σ_a^2 is less than σ_m^2—if H_1 had been, for example,

$$H_1: \quad \sigma_a^2 < \sigma_m^2$$

then we would have used the statistic $F = \dfrac{S_m^2/\sigma_m^2}{S_a^2/\sigma_a^2}$, which has an F dis-
tribution with 12 and 9 degrees of freedom and which, under the assumption that H_0 is correct, is reduced to $F = S_m^2/S_a^2$. As we could easily verify, the null hypothesis would not be rejected under this condition either.

CONFIDENCE INTERVALS

Since the ratio $\dfrac{S_1^2/\sigma_1^2}{S_2^2/\sigma_2^2}$ follows the $F^{(n_1-1,\,n_2-1)}$ distribution, we can write

$$P\left(F_{1-\alpha/2}^{(n_1-1,\,n_2-1)} \le \frac{S_1^2/\sigma_1^2}{S_2^2/\sigma_2^2} \le F_{\alpha/2}^{(n_1-1,\,n_2-1)} \right) = 1 - \alpha \qquad \textbf{(14.21)}$$

After multiplying each of the three terms in the parentheses by S_2^2/S_1^2, we obtain

$$P\left(\frac{S_2^2}{S_1^2}\, F_{1-\alpha/2}^{(n_1-1,\,n_2-1)} \le \frac{\sigma_2^2}{\sigma_1^2} \le \frac{S_2^2}{S_1^2}\, F_{\alpha/2}^{(n_1-1,\,n_2-1)} \right) = 1 - \alpha \qquad \textbf{(14.22)}$$

Equation 14.22 provides a confidence interval for the ratio σ_2^2/σ_1^2. Using the data in Example 14.5 where σ_1^2 stands for σ_a^2 and σ_2^2 stands for σ_m^2, and assuming $\alpha = 0.05$, we calculate

$$P\left(\frac{1{,}800^2}{2{,}000^2}\, F_{0.975}^{(9,12)} \le \frac{\sigma_2^2}{\sigma_1^2} \le \frac{1{,}800^2}{2{,}000^2}\, F_{0.025}^{(9,12)} \right) = 0.95$$

The value $F_{0.025}^{(9,12)}$ is given in the F distribution table (Appendix A, Table A.5) as 3.44. To calculate $F_{0.975}^{(9,12)}$, we first find in the table $F_{0.025}^{(12,9)} = 3.87$ and then compute

$$F_{0.975}^{(9,12)} = 1/F_{0.025}^{(12,9)} = 1/3.87 = 0.258$$

Accordingly, the confidence interval ranges from $\dfrac{1{,}800^2}{2{,}000^2} \cdot 0.258 = 0.209$ to $\dfrac{1{,}800^2}{2{,}000^2} \cdot 3.44 = 2.786$. This interval includes the value 1.0, which corresponds to equal variances. This is consistent with our earlier decision not to reject the hypothesis that the variances are equal.

14.5 APPLICATION:
USING THE t TEST FOR MATCHED SAMPLES—
THE BANKING INDUSTRY*

A bank may choose to become a member of the Federal Reserve System (FRS), which, among other things, gives the bank some protection against business failure. But the FRS also imposes constraints on the operations of the bank. For example, a member bank must maintain a minimum ratio of cash reserves to total assets.

In recent years many banks have left the FRS. Their reasons vary, but one reason some banks have left is the high cash reserve requirement. Banks that leave the FRS may reduce their ratio of cash reserves to total assets and use the money to make additional investments or additional loans. In order to examine the effect of leaving the FRS on a bank's financial position, data on 34 banks who left the FRS during the years

* This application is based on R. E. Myers and T. Hoenig, "Relative Operating Performance of Withdrawing 10th Federal Reserve District Member Banks," *Journal of Bank Research*, Autumn 1979, pp. 181–183.

1970–72 were collected. Each of the withdrawing banks was paired with a "control" FRS member bank, which was chosen for its similarity to the withdrawing bank in certain respects. This procedure gave 34 matched pairs of observations to which the t test for matched samples was applied. The samples were used to test several hypotheses, one of which was that leaving the FRS does not indicate a decrease in a bank's cash reserve ratio. Denote

$\overline{X}_w$ The average ratio of cash to total assets of the withdrawing banks

$\overline{X}_c$ The average of the same ratio for the "control" group, namely the 34 banks remaining in the FRS.

$S_{\overline{D}}$ The standard error of $\overline{D} = \overline{X}_w - \overline{X}_c$.

Assuming that the cash reserve ratios are normally distributed, we have

$$\frac{\overline{X}_w - \overline{X}_c}{S_{\overline{D}}} \sim t^{(n-1)}$$

where $n = 34$ pairs.

Table 14.5 shows the value under H_0 of the above t statistic for the ratio of cash to total assets as well as several other ratios of interest. The null hypothesis for each of the ratios is that there is no difference in these ratios between member and nonmember banks. The t value is calculated for the time of withdrawal as well as for one, two, three, and four years following the withdrawal. This allows us to examine changes in the ratios over time.

For example, the t value for the ratio of cash to total assets was 0.36 at the withdrawal date. Since $0.36 < t_{0.05}^{(33)}$, we do not reject the null hypothesis under which no significant difference existed in this ratio between the withdrawing and nonwithdrawing banks at the time of the banks' withdrawal. However, the t values for the years following the withdrawal were as follows:

one year following withdrawal	-2.06
two years following withdrawal	-3.62
three years following withdrawal	-2.25
four years following withdrawal	-3.30

Since all these t values are significant (at $\alpha = 5$ percent) for a one-sided hypothesis ($t_{0.05}^{(33)} \approx 1.692$) we conclude that the withdrawing banks decreased their cash-to-assets ratio following their withdrawal from the FRS, and hence we reject the null hypothesis that asserts that the ratios did not change following withdrawal. Thus, we can conclude that the cash reserve constraint imposed by the FRS was perhaps a major reason for withdrawing from the system. Following their withdrawal from the FRS, the banks tended to change their financial policy, decreasing their cash reserves and increasing their investments and loans. It seems that the cash constraint imposed by the FRS indeed restricts the operation of the banks.

Table 14.5 provides the t-test results for the matched samples for several accounting ratios of interest. There is no evidence that any of the ratios other than cash to total assets follows any significant trend of change following a bank's withdrawal from the FRS.

TABLE 14.5
Average Differences and *t* Values for Selected Balance Sheet Ratios, Withdrawing vs. FRS Member Banks

| Ratio | At withdrawal | | Years after withdrawal | | | | | | | |
| | | | 1 | | 2 | | 3 | | 4 | |
	$\overline{D}$	t	$\overline{D}$	t	$\overline{D}$	t	$\overline{D}$	t	$\overline{D}$	t
Net income measures										
Net income to total assets	−0.17	−1.59	0.01	0.21	0.16	1.23	−0.21	−0.24	−0.06	−0.56
Net income to total operating income	−1.34	−1.60	−2.36	−1.32	−0.98	−0.43	−0.58	−0.40	−1.09	−0.68
Revenue and expense measures										
Total operating income to total assets	−0.12	−0.90	0.21	1.44	0.26	1.54	0.17	1.11	0.16	1.05
Total operating expense to total assets	0.19	1.09	0.27	1.42	0.23	1.06	0.32	1.28	0.17	1.07
Total operating expense to total operating income	5.27	2.79[a]	1.77	0.97	0.69	0.29	2.32	1.04	2.66	1.21
Cash measure										
Cash to total assets	0.28	0.36	−1.54	−2.06[a]	−2.56	−3.62[a]	−1.85	−2.25[a]	−2.52	−3.30[a]

[a]Significant at least at the 5 percent risk level.

Chapter Summary and Review

Test of Two Means: Independent Samples (Standard Deviations Are Known)

Hypotheses	Test statistic	Decision rule
(a) H_0: $\mu_1 \leq \mu_2$ H_1: $\mu_1 > \mu_2$	$Z = \dfrac{(\overline{X}_1 - \overline{X}_2) - (\mu_1 - \mu_2)}{\sqrt{\dfrac{\sigma_1^2}{n_1} + \dfrac{\sigma_2^2}{n_2}}}$	Reject H_0 if test statistic is greater than Z_α.
(b) H_0: $\mu_1 \geq \mu_2$ H_1: $\mu_1 < \mu_2$	Z	Reject H_0 if test statistic is smaller than $-Z_\alpha$.
(c) H_0: $\mu_1 = \mu_2$ H_1: $\mu_1 \neq \mu_2$	Z	Reject H_0 if test statistic is either greater than $Z_{\alpha/2}$ or smaller than $-Z_{\alpha/2}$.

Test of Two Means: Independent Samples (Standard Deviations Are Unknown but Equal to One Another)

Hypotheses	Test statistic	Decision rule
(a) H_0: $\mu_1 \leq \mu_2$ H_1: $\mu_1 > \mu_2$	$T = \dfrac{(\overline{X}_1 - \overline{X}_2) - (\mu_1 - \mu_2)}{\sqrt{\left[\dfrac{(n_1 - 1)S_1^2 + (n_2 - 1)S_2^2}{n_1 + n_2 - 2}\right]\left(\dfrac{n_1 + n_2}{n_1 \cdot n_2}\right)}}$	Reject H_0 if T is greater than $t_\alpha^{(n_1 + n_2 - 2)}$.
(b) H_0: $\mu_1 \geq \mu_2$ H_1: $\mu_1 < \mu_2$	T	Reject H_0 if T is smaller than $-t_\alpha^{(n_1 + n_2 - 2)}$.
(c) H_0: $\mu_1 = \mu_2$ H_1: $\mu_1 \neq \mu_2$	T	Reject H_0 if T is either greater than $t_{\alpha/2}^{(n_1 + n_2 - 2)}$ or smaller than $-t_{\alpha/2}^{(n_1 + n_2 - 2)}$.

Test of Two Means: Matched Samples (Variance of D Is Unknown[a])

Hypotheses	Test statistic	Decision rule
(a) H_0: $\mu_D = \mu_1 - \mu_2 = 0$ H_1: $\mu_D > 0$	$T = \dfrac{\overline{D} - \mu_D}{S_{\overline{D}}}$	Reject H_0 if T is greater than $t_\alpha^{(n-1)}$.
(b) H_0: $\mu_D = \mu_1 - \mu_2 = 0$ H_1: $\mu_D < 0$	T	Reject H_0 if T is smaller than $-t_\alpha^{(n-1)}$.
(c) H_0: $\mu_D = \mu_1 - \mu_2 = 0$ H_1: $\mu_D \neq 0$	T	Reject H_0 if T is greater than $t_{\alpha/2}^{(n-1)}$ or smaller than $-t_{\alpha/2}^{(n-1)}$.

[a]If the variance of D is known, Z replaces the t test.

Test of Two Proportions

Hypotheses	Test statistic	Decision rule
(a) H_0: $p_1 = p_2 = p_0$ H_1: $p_1 > p_2$	$P = \dfrac{\bar{p}_1 - \bar{p}_2}{\sqrt{p_0 q_0 \left(\dfrac{1}{n_1} + \dfrac{1}{n_2}\right)}}$	Reject H_0 if test statistic is greater than Z_α.
(b) H_0: $p_1 = p_2 = p_0$ H_1: $p_1 < p_2$	P	Reject H_0 if test statistic is smaller than $-Z_\alpha$.
(c) H_0: $p_1 = p_2$ H_1: $p_1 \neq p_2$	P	Reject H_0 if test statistic is either greater than $Z_{\alpha/2}$ or smaller than $-Z_{\alpha/2}$.

Explanation: $q_0 = 1 - p_0$ when p_0 is the value given by the null hypothesis; n_1 and n_2 are the numbers of observations in the two samples.

Assumption: The two samples are independent.

Note: If p_0 is not specified under H_0, use $\bar{p} = \dfrac{n_1 \bar{p}_1 + n_2 \bar{p}_2}{n_1 + n_2}$.

Test of Two Variances

Hypotheses	Test statistic	Decision rule
(a) H_0: $\sigma_1^2 = \sigma_2^2$ H_1: $\sigma_1^2 > \sigma_2^2$	$F = \dfrac{S_1^2}{S_2^2}$	Reject H_0 if F is greater than $F_\alpha^{(n_1-1,\, n_2-1)}$.
(b) H_0: $\sigma_1^2 = \sigma_2^2$ H_1: $\sigma_1^2 < \sigma_2^2$	$F = \dfrac{S_2^2}{S_1^2}$	Reject H_0 if F is greater than $F_\alpha^{(n_2-1,\, n_1-1)}$.
(c) H_0: $\sigma_1^2 = \sigma_2^2$ H_1: $\sigma_1^2 \neq \sigma_2^2$	Take $F = \dfrac{S_1^2}{S_2^2}$ if $S_1^2 > S_2^2$ and reject if greater than $F_{\alpha/2}^{(n_1-1,\, n_2-1)}$. Take $F = \dfrac{S_2^2}{S_1^2}$ if $S_1^2 < S_2^2$ and reject if greater than $F_{\alpha/2}^{(n_2-1,\, n_1-1)}$.	

Problems

14.1. "The testing of hypotheses with a sample of an infinite number of observations is characterized by zero probability of Type I and Type II errors." Do you agree with this statement? In your answer distinguish among:

    (a) The testing of hypotheses about one mean

    (b) The testing of hypotheses about two means when one sample is infinite and the other is finite

    (c) The testing of hypotheses about two means when both samples are infinite

14.2. Test the hypothesis that the mean current ratios of the leisure time industry and the instruments industry are equal to one another. The sample data are given in Table P14.2. Use $\alpha = 0.05$ and make the following alternative assumptions:

    (a) The standard deviations of the current ratios are known to be $\sigma = 0.5$ for the instruments industry and $\sigma = 1.0$ for the leisure time industry.

    (b) The standard deviations are unknown, but it is known that they are equal to one another.

TABLE P14.2

The Current Ratio for 18 Companies in the Leisure Time Industry and 11 Companies in the Instrument Industry, 1981[a]

Leisure time		Instruments	
Company	*Ratio*	*Company*	*Ratio*
AMF	1.8	Bausch & Lomb	2.5
American Greetings	1.9	Beckman Instruments	2.8
Bally Mfg.	2.2	Foxboro	2.5
Brunswick	3.0	General Signal	2.4
Columbia Pictures Industries	1.7	Itek	2.4
Disney (Walt) Productions	2.4	Johnson Controls	1.5
Eastman Kodak	2.5	Perkin-Elmer	2.7
Golden Nugget	2.4	Robertshaw Controls	2.2
MCA	2.4	Sybron	2.4
MGM Grand Hotels	0.6	Tektronix	3.1
Mattel	1.4	Western Pacific Industries	4.6
Metro-Goldwyn-Mayer Film	1.3		
Milton Bradley	1.8		
Norlin	2.6		
Outboard Marine	2.8		
Polaroid	3.5		
Twentieth Century-Fox Film	1.4		
Warner Communications	1.4		

[a]The current ratio is the ratio of current assets to current liabilities.
Source: *Business Week*, March 1, 1982, p. 70.

14.3. Use Table P13.14 to test the hypothesis that the mean *P/E* ratio in the container industry is equal to that of the drug industry. Use $\alpha = 0.05$ and a two-tailed test. What assumptions do you need to make to carry out your test?

14.4. A department store conducts a study to test if the monthly mean profit margin (that is, profit as a percentage of sales) is the same in its two branches (denoted by 1 and 2). A random sampling of a few months revealed

$$n_1 = 9 \qquad \overline{X}_1 = 7\%$$

$$n_2 = 16 \qquad \overline{X}_2 = 10\%$$

It is known that the profit margin is normally distributed with $\sigma_1 = 10$ and $\sigma_2 = 12$. Use $\alpha = 0.05$ to test the null hypothesis $H_0: \mu_1 = \mu_2$ against the alternative hypothesis $H_1: \mu_1 \neq \mu_2$.

14.5. The following are measurements of random daily output of two production lines in the same factory (in units):

$$\text{Line 1:} \quad 20, 15, 17, 18, 19$$
$$\text{Line 2:} \quad 10, 8, 9, 15, 24, 19$$

(a) Use a 5 percent level of significance to test the hypothesis that the mean outputs of the two production lines are equal against the alternative that they are not equal.

(b) What assumptions do you need to make for this test?

14.6. The production (in units) of a random sample of five workers in day and night shifts has been recorded as follows:

Worker	Day shift (units)	Night shift (units)
1	6	5
2	4	3
3	8	7
4	6	6
5	4	2

(a) Use a 5 percent significance level and test the null hypothesis H_0: $\mu_1 = \mu_2$ against the alternative hypothesis H_1: $\mu_1 > \mu_2$, where μ_1 stands for the mean production of the day shift and μ_2 is the mean production of the night shift.

(b) What assumptions are needed for this test?

14.7. Two random variables X_1 and X_2 (measured in dollars) are normally distributed. It is known that $\sigma_1 = 10$ and $\sigma_2 = 5$. Two random samples taken from distributions 1 and 2 revealed the following results:

$$\text{Sample 1:} \quad \$5, \$6, \$7, \$8$$
$$\text{Sample 2:} \quad \$4, \$3, \$6, \$9, \$5$$

Construct a 95 percent confidence interval for the difference between the means, $\mu_1 - \mu_2$.

14.8. An examination of the cash balance outstanding on 30-day charge accounts in two branches of a department store yielded the following figures:

$$\text{Sample 1:} \quad n_1 = 100 \quad \overline{X}_1 = \$2,000 \quad S_1 = \$100$$
$$\text{Sample 2:} \quad n_2 = 900 \quad \overline{X}_2 = \$1,500 \quad S_2 = \$200$$

S_1 and S_2 are the sample estimates of the standard deviation in branches 1 and 2, respectively. Establish a 95 percent confidence interval for the difference between the means of the respective distributions.

14.9. The California Citrus Groves Corporation wanted to compare the efficiency of two fertilization treatments for raising yields. It chose 10 trees to undergo Treatment A and 6 trees to undergo Treatment B. The trees' yields (in tens of pounds) were as follows:

$$\text{Treatment } A: \quad 80, 82, 84, 79, 77, 80, 78, 76, 83, 85$$
$$\text{Treatment } B: \quad 80, 78, 74, 82, 79, 80$$

Assume that the weight of the yield is a random variable having a normal distribution, and test whether, on the average, the two fertilization treatments give the same yields. Assume identical variances of the weights under both treatments. Use $\alpha = 0.05$.

14.10. Investor A invested in five stocks that were randomly selected from those traded on the New York Stock Exchange. Investor B invested in five bonds. Assume that the rates of return on stocks and on bonds are normally distributed. Here are recent rates of return on those securities (in percent):

$$\text{Stocks:} \quad 4.0, 3.0, 2.0, 5.0, 6.0$$
$$\text{Bonds:} \quad 2.0, 6.0, 2.0, 2.0, 6.0$$

Assume that the variance of the rate of return on stocks is equal to that on bonds, and test the null hypothesis that the mean rate of return on stocks is equal to the mean rate of return on bonds. Use $\alpha = 0.05$.

14.11. In order to increase efficiency and facilitate performance evaluation, corporations have executive-level managers who are responsible for cost minimization and others who are responsible for profit maximization. A hypothetical study designed to examine variations in opportunity for independent thought among such executives included 46 executives, 23 of each type. They were asked to indicate their feelings concerning their opportunities for independent thought on a seven-point response scale, where 1 indicated "extremely dissatisfied" and 7 "extremely satisfied." Hence, a high score indicated a high degree of satisfaction with respect to the opportunity for independent thought. The sample results are shown in Table P14.11. Test the hypothesis that the mean scores of both types of executive manager are the same. Use $\alpha = 0.05$. Specify the assumptions needed for the test.

TABLE P14.11

Cost managers	Profit managers
5.63	5.28
5.25	6.00
5.79	6.01
5.44	5.79
5.93	5.72
5.31	6.32
5.31	5.28
4.75	5.24
5.54	5.83
5.78	6.18
5.97	5.94
5.42	6.22
5.97	6.26
5.97	6.15
5.75	6.17
5.61	6.20
5.90	6.27
5.89	6.09
5.88	5.89
5.49	4.80
5.17	6.30
4.72	5.02
4.76	5.03

14.12. An investment analyst claims to have mastered the art of forecasting the price changes of gold. The following table gives the actual gold price changes and the changes forecasted by the investment analyst (in percent):

Month	Actual price changes	Forecasted changes
1	7.3	14.9
2	−2.1	−19.7
3	8.5	7.0
4	−1.5	−5.3
5	9.2	1.0
6	6.7	−0.8
7	−4.8	−8.3
8	−0.8	6.7

(a) Apply the t test for matched samples to test the investment analyst's claim. Use a one-tailed test and a 5 percent significance level.

(b) What assumptions do you need to make in order to use this test?

14.13. The milk production of five cows was measured twice: once after they had been fed by a product we shall call Food 1, and once after they had been fed by a product we shall call Food 2. The results (in gallons) are as follows:

Cow	Food 1	Food 2
1	2	2.5
2	3	3.0
3	1	1.5
4	2	2.0
5	3	2.0

Assuming a normal distribution of the milk production and that the standard deviation is the same in both samples, construct a 99 percent confidence interval for the difference in the mean production, where μ_1 is the mean for Food 1 and μ_2 is the mean for Food 2.

14.14. The proportion of defects produced by machine A is p_1 and the proportion of defects produced by machine B is p_2. A sample of $n_1 = 2,000$ units of machine A production and of $n_2 = 3,000$ units of machine B revealed that the number of defects was 10 in machine A and 20 in machine B. Construct a 99 percent confidence interval for the difference between the proportions p_1 and p_2.

14.15. Machine 1 produces 10 defective items in a random sample of 400 units, while machine 2 produces 20 defective items in a sample of 700 units. Test the null hypothesis $H_0: p_1 = p_2$ (where p_1 and p_2 are the proportions of defective items produced by machines 1 and 2, respectively) against the alternative hypothesis $H_1: p_1 \neq p_2$. Use a 1 percent significance level.

14.16. "When the hypothesis of equal variances, $H_0: \sigma_1^2 = \sigma_2^2$, is tested against $H_1: \sigma_1^2 > \sigma_2^2$, H_0 will never be rejected at a significance level of 0.05 if $S_1^2 < S_2^2$." Do you agree? Explain.

14.17. "When the hypothesis of equal variances, $H_0: \sigma_1^2 = \sigma_2^2$, is tested against $H_1: \sigma_1^2 > \sigma_2^2$, if $S_1^2 = 0$ and $S_2^2 > 0$, H_0 will be rejected no matter what the significance level α is, as long as it is greater than zero." Do you agree with this statement? Explain.

14.18. Table P14.18 shows short-term debt as a percentage of total invested capital for firms in various industries. Assume that the ratio is normally distributed and that the populations are infinitely large. Test the null hypothesis that the variance of the ratio in publishing firms is equal to the variance of the ratio in radio and broadcasting companies. Test the null hypothesis against the alternative that the variance in the publishing industry is greater than that in the radio and broadcasting industry. Use $\alpha = 0.05$.

TABLE P14.18

Short-Term Debt as a Percentage of Total Invested Capital, 1978, Various Industries

Publishing

Capital Cities Communications	7.3
Commerce Clearing House	0.0
Dow Jones	2.6
Gannett	0.1
Grolier	4.3
Harcourt Brace Jovanovich	15.9
Knight-Ridder Newspapers	0.8
Macmillan	3.8

(Continued)

TABLE P14.18 (*Continued*)
Short-Term Debt as a Percentage of Total Invested Capital, 1978, Various Industries

Publishing

McGraw-Hill	2.8
Media General	2.1
Meredith	2.8
New York Times	1.1
Playboy Enterprises	12.5
Prentice-Hall	0.0
Time	1.4
Times Mirror	1.1
Washington Post	1.4

Radio and broadcasting

American Broadcasting	0.9
CBS	0.4
Combined Communications	7.8
Cox Broadcasting	4.5
Metromedia	2.9
Outlet	4.6
Storer Broadcasting	5.8
Taft Broadcasting	4.9
Teleprompter	5.0

Railroads

Burlington Northern	2.9
Chessie System	4.9
Chicago & North Western Transportation	8.8
Kansas City Southern Industries	4.1
Missouri Pacific	3.8
Norfolk & Western Railway	3.5
Rio Grande Industries	2.8
St. Louis-San Francisco Railway	3.5
Santa Fe Industries	1.8
Seaboard Coast Line Industries	3.9
Soo Line Railroad	2.8
Southern Pacific	2.5
Southern Railway	3.7
Union Pacific Industries	3.5
Western Pacific Industries	2.6

Real estate and housing

Centex	34.0
Deltona	17.1
Hahn (Ernest W.)	38.2
Kaufman & Broad	29.6
McCulloch Oil	27.1
Shapell Industries	11.7
Tishman Realty & Construction	2.6
U.S. Home	34.6

Source: Data from *Business Week*, October 16, 1978, p. 138.

14.19. Use Table P14.18 to test the hypothesis that the variance of the ratio of short-term debt to total invested capital in the railroad industry is 3 against the alternative that it is greater than 3. Use $\alpha = 0.01$.

14.20. Use Table P14.18 to test the hypothesis that the mean ratio of short-term debt to total invested capital is equal in the real estate and housing industry and in the railroad industry against the alternative that the means differ. Use $\alpha = 0.05$ and assume $\sigma_1 = \sigma_2 = 10$.

14.21. Assume that the monthly rates of return on stocks A and B are normally distributed. Random samples of 5 months for Stock A and 6 months for Stock B yield the following results (in percent):

$$\text{Stock } A: \quad 7, 8, -5, 9, 10$$
$$\text{Stock } B: \quad 6, 7, 0, 4, 9, 15$$

Construct a 95 percent confidence interval for the ratio of the variances σ_1^2/σ_2^2.

14.22. It is claimed that the variance of the weekly income of self-employed lawyers is higher than the variance of the income of lawyers employed by the federal government. Two random samples revealed the following weekly incomes (in $1,000):

$$\text{Self-employed:} \qquad\qquad\qquad\qquad 1, 2, 1.9, 4, 0.5$$
$$\text{Employed by the federal government:} \quad 0.6, 0.7, 0.8, 1.1, 0.4, 0.6$$

Assuming normality, use a 2 percent significance level to test the hypothesis $H_0: \sigma_1^2 = \sigma_2^2$ against the alternative $H_1: \sigma_1^2 > \sigma_2^2$, where σ_1^2 and σ_2^2 are, respectively, the variances of lawyers' incomes in the two sectors.

Case Problems

14.1. A broker wants to know whether the mean rates of return of mutual funds in different categories are equal. Use Data Set 2, Appendix B, Table B.2, to test the hypothesis that the mean rate of return of the funds in the "Balanced Funds" group is equal to the mean rate of return of the funds in the "Flexible Policy Income Funds" group. Treat each of the two categories as representing one population and use $\alpha = 0.05$. What assumptions do you need to make for this test?

14.2. Using Data Set 2, test the hypothesis that the variance of rates of return of funds in the "Common Stock Policy Income Funds" group is the same as that of funds in the "Other Funds" group. Use $\alpha = 0.05$. What assumptions do you need to make for this test?

14.3. The average 30-day *yield* of 72 money market funds is presented in Data Set 3, Appendix B, Table B.3. Divide these funds into two groups: the first should include the funds that have at least a 45 percent investment in U.S. government securities (i.e., treasury and others), and the other should consist of all the other funds. Test the hypothesis that the mean yields of the funds in the two groups are the same. Explain your results.

14.4. Test the hypothesis that the variances of the yield in the two groups of funds in Case Problem 14.3 are the same.

14.5. (a) Assume that the standard deviation of the rates of return of "Sovereign Investors" (fund number 58 in Data Set 2, Appendix B, Table B.2) is 30 percent and that the standard deviation of the rate of return of "Technology Fund" (fund number 59) is 20 percent. Use a 1 percent significance level to test the hypothesis that the mean rates of return of the two funds are equal against the hypothesis that they are unequal.

(b) Repeat part *a*, assuming that the standard deviations of the rates of return of the two funds are unknown but equal.

(c) Repeat part *b* for fund numbers 2 ("Alpha Fund") and 107 ("Delchester Bond Fund"). Discuss your results.

CHI-SQUARE TESTS OF INDEPENDENCE, HOMOGENEITY, AND GOODNESS OF FIT

CHAPTER FIFTEEN OUTLINE

The chi-square distribution of a test statistic was introduced in Chapter 13, where we tested hypotheses about the variance of a distribution. In this chapter we shall deal with three more types of statistical tests involving the chi-square distribution: tests of independence of variables, homogeneity of distributions, and goodness of fit. All of these tests are based on the analysis of frequencies, that is, on the *number* of occurrences of some events. In other words, the tests are based on *count data* and therefore can be applied to quantitative as well as qualitative variables. For example, the tests can be used to find out whether the smoking habits of men and women are different by counting the frequencies of smokers and nonsmokers among men and women in a randomly selected sample.

15.1 Chi-Square Test of Independence

The question of whether two variables are dependent or independent often has significant implications in business. For example, it may be important to find out if the type of community (say, urban versus rural) and the media used for advertising in it (TV, radio, newspapers) are independent in terms of the advertising effectiveness. It is important for a firm's management to know about this type of dependence or independence, since such knowledge can help in the planning of an effective advertising campaign.

Take another example. The Watchdog Company is a wholesaler of burglar and fire-alarm systems for private homes and public buildings. Watchdog operates in 31 states and sells to numerous retailers. Most of Watchdog's sales are made on credit and the company uses a credit-rating service to obtain current information about the financial status of existing and potential customers. The credit-rating service classifies customers as very good,

good, average, or poor. In reviewing their records, Watchdog's accountants suspect that there is little relationship between these classifications and customers' bill-paying behavior. Since the credit information provided to Watchdog is not costless, Watchdog wants to find out whether the information is in fact valuable. One solution is to test the independence of the categories provided by the credit service and the actual credit standing of Watchdog's customers. If a statistical test substantiates the independence of the two variables, the company may very well terminate its use of the credit-rating service.

THE TWO-BY-TWO CONTINGENCY TABLE AND THE TEST OF HYPOTHESES

Table 15.1 is what is known as a **two-by-two (2 × 2) contingency table**, which we will use to explain the test of independence. The following notation will be used in our discussion:

i Index of row categories. Here, i equals either 1 or 2. We will use I as a general notation for the largest value of i, so for Table 15.1, $I = 2$.

j Index of column categories. Here, j equals either 1 or 2. We will use J as a general notation for the largest value of j, so for Table 15.1, $J = 2$.

o_{ij} The observed sample frequency in cell i,j. It is a random variable.

e_{ij} The expected sample frequency in cell i,j.

r_i Sum of cell frequencies in row i. It is a random variable.

c_j Sum of cell frequencies in column j. It is a random variable

n Total number of sample observations: $n = \sum_i r_i = \sum_j c_j$. In any given sample, n is fixed.

The objective of the chi-square test is to determine whether it is likely or unlikely that the two sets of classifications (that is, the row and column classifications) are independent. In fact, we want to test the null hypothesis that the two classification variables are independent, and the alternative hypothesis that the two variables are dependent. In short

H_0: The two variables are independent.

H_1: The two variables are dependent.

In virtually all the hypothesis-testing procedures presented in Chapters 13 and 14, acceptance or rejection of H_0 depends on how the *actually observed* sample value compares with what is *expected to be observed* in the sample under H_0. For example, when we test the hypothesis H_0: $\mu = \mu_0 = 100$ versus

TABLE 15.1
Two-by-Two Contingency Table

i	j		*Total*
	$j = 1$	$j = 2$	
$i = 1$	o_{11}	o_{12}	r_1
$i = 2$	o_{21}	o_{22}	r_2
Total	c_1	c_2	n

$H_1: \mu = \mu_1 \neq 100$, we basically compare the sample mean, $\overline{X}$, to its hypothesized value under H_0. For any given sample size and population standard deviation, it is the deviation of $\overline{X}$ from μ_0 that determines whether H_0 is accepted or rejected: given σ and n, the value of the test statistic $\dfrac{\overline{X} - \mu_0}{\sigma/\sqrt{n}}$ depends only on the deviation, $\overline{X} - \mu_0$. In the test for independence of two variables, we also have to compare the observed sample value to the value expected under H_0. If the deviation between the observed and expected frequencies is significantly large, we reject H_0. Otherwise H_0 is not rejected.

We must now take two steps. First, we determine the expected frequencies in the contingency table that would appear *if H_0 were correct*. These expected frequencies will provide the basis for comparison in the second step. Second, given the expected as well as observed frequencies, we determine whether the deviations of the observed from the expected are small enough to be interpreted as mere sampling variations or large enough to lead us to the conclusion that H_0 should be rejected.

DETERMINING THE EXPECTED FREQUENCIES

Let us now take the first step and determine the expected frequencies. Recall that in our discussion of independent events in Chapter 5 we defined the statistical independence of events A and B as a situation in which the probability of the intersection of the two events is equal to the product of the two probabilities: if A and B are independent, then $P(A \cap B) = P(A)P(B)$.

In terms of our contingency table, each cell may be viewed as an intersection of its respective row and column. Thus, if H_0 is correct—that is, if the row and column classifications are independent—then the probability that an observation will belong to a given cell is the product of the probabilities that it will belong to the respective row and column. The probability that an observation will belong to row i (P_i) can be *estimated* by the following sample proportion:

$$\overline{P}_i = \frac{r_i}{n} \tag{15.1}$$

Similarly, the probability that an observation will belong to column j (P_j) can be *estimated* by this sample proportion:

$$\overline{P}_j = \frac{c_j}{n} \tag{15.2}$$

If H_0 is correct, then the probability that any observation will belong to cell ij (that is, P_{ij}) can be *estimated* in the following way:

$$\overline{P}_{ij} = \overline{P}_i \cdot \overline{P}_j \tag{15.3}$$

or

$$\overline{P}_{ij} = \left(\frac{r_i}{n}\right)\left(\frac{c_j}{n}\right) \tag{15.4}$$

To estimate the expected *frequency* in each cell—that is, e_{ij}—we simply multiply $\overline{P}_{ij}$ by the total number of observations in the sample, n, which yields

$$e_{ij} = \overline{P}_{ij} \cdot n = \left(\frac{r_i}{n}\right)\left(\frac{c_j}{n}\right)n \tag{15.5}$$

This can be more simply represented in the following way:

$$e_{ij} = \frac{r_i c_j}{n} \tag{15.6}$$

THE TEST STATISTIC

The observed and expected frequencies must now be compared throughout the table's cells and a decision rule must be established to allow acceptance or rejection of the null hypothesis. Before doing this, however, we must make sure that the *expected* frequency in each cell is at least five. If this is not the case, categories must be grouped together so that the redefined cells will have at least five expected observations in each. The reason for this is that the test statistic we present below approximates a chi-square distribution. The approximation is not good enough if there are not at least five expected observations in each cell.

The test statistic to be used is the sum over all the table's cells of the expression $(e_{ij} - o_{ij})^2/e_{ij}$. Denoting the test statistic by χ^2 and ignoring indices for simplification, we can write the following equation:

$$\chi^2 = \sum \frac{(e - o)^2}{e} \tag{15.7}$$

If the sample observed frequencies are precisely equal to the expected frequencies in all the table's cells, we have a "perfect fit" and the statistic in Equation 15.7 is equal to zero. The greater the deviations (in either direction) of the observed frequencies, o, from the expected frequencies, e, the greater the value of the test statistic, χ^2. (Thus the test is always an upper-tail test, never lower-tail or two-tailed.) The test statistic approximates a χ^2 distribution, and the larger the sample, the better the approximation.

DEGREES OF FREEDOM OF THE CHI-SQUARE DISTRIBUTION

We have yet to determine the number of **degrees of freedom** of the χ^2 distribution. Given I rows and J columns, there are IJ cells altogether. Suppose the joint probabilities P_{ij} are somehow known and need not be estimated. In this case, the number of degrees of freedom of our test statistic is $IJ - 1$. Why is one degree of freedom lost? Given any sample size, n, it is possible to determine only the frequencies of the number of cells minus one. The frequency of one of the cells can be computed by subtracting the total of the frequencies of all other cells from n. Thus $IJ - 1$ frequencies can be determined independently, but once they are known, the last expected frequency is left with no degree of freedom—it must equal n minus the sum of all the other frequencies.

In most cases, we determine e_{ij} by first estimating the joint probability P_{ij} and then applying Equation 15.5. To estimate P_{ij}, however, we must first estimate the marginal probabilities P_i and P_j. There are I different P_is and J different P_js to estimate, but once $I - 1$ of the P_is have been estimated, the last P_i is, by necessity, the complement of their sum to one. Similarly, once $J - 1$ of the P_js have been estimated, the last P_j is necessarily the complement of their sum to one. As a rule, each estimated parameter absorbs one degree of freedom, so by estimating all the values of P_i and P_j, we "lose" $(I - 1) + (J - 1)$ degrees of freedom. We can now summarize as follows: if the joint probabilities are known on the basis of outside information and need not be estimated, the number of degrees of freedom for the test statistic of a contingency table is equal to $IJ - 1$. If, however, the various P_{ij} values have to be estimated to arrive at the e_{ij} values, as they usually must, then the degrees of freedom are

$$(IJ - 1) - [(I - 1) + (J - 1)] = IJ - 1 - I + 1 - J + 1$$

$$= IJ - I - J + 1 = (I - 1) \cdot (J - 1)$$

This can be clearly stated as follows:

The number of degrees of freedom of χ^2 is	$\begin{cases} IJ - 1 & \text{if all } P_{ij}\text{s are known in advance} \\ (I - 1) \cdot (J - 1) & \text{if all } P_{ij}\text{s are to be estimated} \end{cases}$	(15.8)

This can be stated more generally:

$$\begin{pmatrix} \text{The number of degrees} \\ \text{of freedom of } \chi^2 \end{pmatrix} = IJ - 1 - \begin{pmatrix} \text{the number of parameters} \\ \text{that need to be estimated} \end{pmatrix} \quad (15.9)$$

In a two-by-two contingency table, for example, where $I = J = 2$, the number of degrees of freedom is $IJ - 1 = 2 \cdot 2 - 1 = 3$ if the probabilities P_{ij} are known; the number of degrees of freedom is $(I - 1)(J - 1) = (2 - 1)(2 - 1) = 1$ if they must be estimated.

Now let us proceed with two examples that demonstrate the simplicity of carrying out the test of independence.

EXAMPLE 15.1

A theory in finance known as the **random walk theory** suggests that short-term changes in stock prices follow a random pattern. According to this theory, yesterday's price change can tell us virtually nothing of value about today's price change. Let us denote the *change* in price of a stock in time t—which refers to a given trading day—by ΔP_t and the *change* in price in the next trading day by ΔP_{t+1}. Suppose we observe price changes of 240 stocks that have been randomly selected and obtain the results shown in Table 15.2. To test the hypotheses

TABLE 15.2
Two-by-Two Contingency Table of Observed Daily Stock Price Changes

| Price changes in day $t + 1$ | Price changes in day t | | Total |
	$\Delta P_t > 0$ ($j = 1$)	$\Delta P_t \leq 0$ ($j = 2$)	
$\Delta P_{t+1} > 0$	47	53	100
$\Delta P_{t+1} \leq 0$	63	77	140
Total	110	130	240

H_0: Price changes in day $t + 1$ are independent of changes in day t.
H_1: The two variables are not independent.

we first have to determine the expected frequencies. The estimated joint probabilities are obtained by means of Equation 15.6:

$$e_{11} = \frac{100 \cdot 110}{240} = 45.83$$

$$e_{12} = \frac{100 \cdot 130}{240} = 54.17$$

$$e_{21} = \frac{140 \cdot 110}{240} = 64.17$$

$$e_{22} = \frac{140 \cdot 130}{240} = 75.83$$

Given the observed as well as the expected frequencies, we can go right ahead and compute the test-statistic value. Since the joint probabilities P_{ij} are not given in this example, the number of degrees of freedom of the test statistic is $(I - 1)(J - 1) = (2 - 1)(2 - 1) = 1$. Assuming a 5 percent significance level ($\alpha = 0.05$), the critical value is $\chi^{2(1)}_{0.05} = 3.841$, and so all χ^2 values that are less than 3.841 lead to the acceptance of H_0. Table 15.3, which is a work sheet for computing the test statistic χ^2, shows that in our example we have $\chi^2 = 0.09452 < 3.841$, so we cannot reject the null hypothesis and we view our results as supporting the random walk theory.

TABLE 15.3
Work Sheet for Computation of Test Statistic χ^2

Row and column	e	o	$e - o$	$(e - o)^2$	$\frac{(e - o)^2}{e}$
(1,1)	45.83	47.00	−1.17	1.3689	0.02987
(1,2)	54.17	53.00	1.17	1.3689	0.02527
(2,1)	64.17	63.00	1.17	1.3689	0.02133
(2,2)	75.83	77.00	−1.17	1.3689	0.01805
Total	240.00	240.00	0		$\chi^2 = 0.09452$

EXAMPLE 15.2

Let us modify Example 15.1 and retest a hypothesis concerning the independence of two successive price changes. This time we shall add the assumptions that the stock price is in equilibrium and that the probability of a price increase on the next trading day (day t) is the same as the probability of a price decrease. Also we assume that the probability of a price increase on the following day (day $t + 1$) is equal to the probability of a price decrease, *independent* of the rise or fall of the price on day t.

Suppose we observe the price changes of a stock over 80 trading days and obtain the results shown in Table 15.4. The null hypothesis in this

TABLE 15.4
Two-by-Two Contingency Table of Observed Daily Stock Price Changes

Price changes in day $t + 1$	Price changes in day t		Total
	$\Delta P_t > 0$	$\Delta P_t \leq 0$	
$\Delta P_{t+1} > 0$	18	17	35
$\Delta P_{t+1} \leq 0$	19	26	45
Total	37	43	80

example entails more than the independence of price changes on day t and price changes on day $t + 1$. Under H_0, specific marginal probabilities are assumed. The specific hypotheses to be tested here are

H_0: The directions of price changes on two successive trading days are independent; moreover, $P(\Delta P_t > 0) = P(\Delta P_t \leq 0) = P(\Delta P_{t+1} > 0) = P(\Delta P_{t+1} \leq 0) = \frac{1}{2}$.

H_1: Anything but H_0.

If H_0 is correct, then the joint probabilities P_{ij} are equal to $\frac{1}{4}$, since $P_i = \frac{1}{2}$ and $P_j = \frac{1}{2}$:

$$P_{ij} = P_i \cdot P_j = \frac{1}{4}$$

Substituting this result in Equation 15.5, but using P_{ij} rather than $\overline{P}_{ij}$, we find $e_{ij} = \frac{1}{4} \cdot 80 = 20$. The test statistic is computed in Table 15.5.

TABLE 15.5
Work Sheet for Computation of Test Statistic χ^2

Row and column	e	o	$e - o$	$(e - o)^2$	$\dfrac{(e - o)^2}{e}$
(1,1)	20	18	2	4	0.20
(1,2)	20	17	3	9	0.45
(2,1)	20	19	1	1	0.05
(2,2)	20	26	−6	36	1.80
Total	80	80	0		$\chi^2 = 2.50$

Since the various P_i and P_j values were *assumed* rather than *estimated*, the number of degrees of freedom of the test statistic is $IJ - 1 = 2 \cdot 2 - 1 = 3$. Assuming a significance level $\alpha = 0.05$, we determine the critical point to be $\chi^2_{0.05(3)} = 7.815$. Since $\chi^2 = 2.50$ is *less than* 7.815, our observed statistic falls within the acceptance region and consequently we do not reject H_0. Again, the random walk theory is supported.

EXAMPLE 15.3

Suppose we want to find out whether the amount of money shoppers spend in convenience stores is independent of their sex. A random sample of 548 convenience-store shoppers has revealed the information shown in Table 15.6.

TABLE 15.6
Observed Size of Purchase by Sex

	Size of purchase		
	Under $2	*$2–under $5*	*$5 or more*
Male	40	90	130
Female	66	120	102

To test H_0 the SAS (Statistical Analysis System) package has been used. Figure 15.1 shows a computer printout of the chi-square test of independence; in each of the table cells the data are given in the order listed on the top left of the table. The data are as follows: the observed frequency, the expected frequency, the percent of observed frequency for

Figure 15.1

Reproduction of an SAS computer printout, showing a chi-square test of independence

```
                    TABLE OF SEX BY SIZE OF PURCHASE

        SEX              SIZE OF PURCHASE {DOLLARS}


        FREQUENCY |
        EXPECTED  |
        PERCENT   |
        ROW PCT   |      2 TO
        COL PCT   |UNDER 2 |UNDER 5 |5 OR OVER|  TOTAL
        ----------+--------+--------+---------+
        FEMALE    |    66  |   120  |   102   |   288
                  |  55.7  |  110.4 |  121.9  |
                  |  12.04 |  21.90 |  18.61  |  52.55
                  |  22.92 |  41.67 |  35.42  |
                  |  62.26 |  57.14 |  43.97  |
        ----------+--------+--------+---------+
        MALE      |    40  |    90  |   130   |   260
                  |  50.3  |  99.6  |  110.1  |
                  |  7.30  |  16.42 |  23.72  |  47.45
                  |  15.38 |  34.62 |  50.00  |
                  |  37.74 |  42.86 |  56.03  |
        ----------+--------+--------+---------+
        TOTAL          106     210      232      548
                     19.34   38.32    42.34   100.00


                    STATISTICS FOR 2-WAY TABLES


        CHI-SQUARE            12.645  DF=  2 PROB=0.0018
```

the entire sample, the percent of observed frequency for the row total, and finally, the percent of observed frequency for the column total. Only the observed and expected frequencies are needed for the chi-square test; the rest of the data merely provide extra information. This information can be suppressed by giving the computer an appropriate command, in which case it will not be printed out. The test statistic is $\sum \frac{(e - o)^2}{e}$ and it has a chi-square distribution with $(J - 1)(I - 1) = (3 - 1)(2 - 1) = 2$ degrees of freedom. The printout shows that the value of the test statistic is 12.645, leading to the rejection of the independence hypothesis at all significance levels greater than 0.18 percent (0.0018). If we reject the null hypothesis, we need to determine who is purchasing greater amounts, males or females. This can be learned by using the percent of rows data. We find that small purchases (under $2) are less frequent among males than among females (15.38 percent versus 22.92 percent), whereas large purchases (over $5) are more frequent among men (50.00 percent versus 35.42 percent). Based on the sample results, we conclude that we should accept the hypothesis that males tend to make larger purchases in convenience stores.

15.2 Chi-Square Test of Homogeneity

In Chapter 14 we presented a test of hypothesis concerning two proportions. The chi-square test of homogeneity is, in a way, a generalization of this test. It enables us to compare proportions across two or more populations. The need for such a comparison arises often. Examples are comparing the performance of students in five fields of study in a number of states, comparing the income of employees in different industries when the income is categorized into a number of intervals, and comparing the investment proportions in different investment categories (stocks, bonds, real estate, etc.) between groups of investors. Note the difference between the test of independence and the test of homogeneity. The former challenges the hypothesis that one attribute is independent of another, whereas the latter challenges the hypothesis that different samples come from populations that are equally distributed over a certain attribute. Also, the test of independence involves a single sample taken out of one population, whereas the test of homogeneity involves several independent samples, one from each of two or more possible populations.

The hypotheses for the test of homogeneity are

H_0: $p_{1j} = p_{2j} = p_{3j} = \cdots = p_{Ij}$ for all j ($j = 1, 2, 3, \ldots, J$)
H_1:   Not all the equalities in H_0 hold

where I is the number of populations and J is the number of categories in each population.

The test statistic used for this test is $\sum \frac{(e - o)^2}{e}$, and it is very similar, technically, to the test statistic for testing independence. Let us proceed with an example. The degrees of freedom of the chi-square statistic will be determined first in the framework of the example, then in a more general framework.

EXAMPLE 15.4

Loans of American commercial banks to foreign governments (primarily those of oil-producing countries) have grown in recent years. A series of interviews was conducted with top bank managers to determine their views on the recent trend. The managers were asked to answer some questions concerning the issue, and the interviewer then decided whether the interviewee was generally "in favor of the trend," "against the trend," or "indifferent to the trend." Because of the informal style of the interviews, it is conceivable that the classification process was influenced by the interviewer's perceptions of the interviewees' statements. Four interviewers were involved, each of whom was responsible for 200 interviews. We are interested in finding out if there was any individual bias of interpretation among the interviewers; to do so we will test the homogeneity of classification across the interviewers. The 800 interviews are classified in Table 15.7.

TABLE 15.7
Classification of Opinions, by Interviewer

Inter-viewer	Favor trend $(j = 1)$	Indifferent to trend $(j = 2)$	Against trend $(j = 3)$	Total
A $(i = 1)$	60	60	80	200
B $(i = 2)$	140	10	50	200
C $(i = 3)$	50	130	20	200
D $(i = 4)$	110	60	30	200
Total	360	260	180	800

Specifically, we want to test the null hypothesis that the classification of opinions is homogeneous across the four interviewers against the alternative hypothesis that the classification is not homogeneous. More formally, denoting the proportion of opinion j as classified by interviewer i by p_{ij} so that, for example, the proportion of opinion $j = 2$ as classified by interviewer $i = 3$ is denoted p_{32}, the null hypothesis is as follows:

$$H_0: \quad p_{11} = p_{21} = p_{31} = p_{41} \quad \text{for } j = 1$$

$$p_{12} = p_{22} = p_{32} = p_{42} \quad \text{for } j = 2$$

$$p_{13} = p_{23} = p_{33} = p_{43} \quad \text{for } j = 3$$

The alternative hypothesis includes everything but H_0.

Suppose we want to use $\alpha = 0.01$. Technically, it is a straightforward procedure to find the value of the test statistic, as we shall soon see. Let us first consider the degrees of freedom of the test statistic. Although the joint probability distribution is not known here, we note that each interviewer was *assigned* 200 interviews. Thus we do not need to estimate the various P_i values in this case. Only two values of P_j must be estimated, since, given two such values, the third must complement their total to equal 1.

Since each interviewer was *assigned* a known number of interviews, the total number of independent frequencies in Table 15.7 is 8: 2 per interviewer. Given 2 of the frequencies in the total of 200 per interviewer, the third frequency is easily and not independently determined. Since 2 values of P_j must be estimated at a "cost" of 1 degree of freedom each, the number of degrees of freedom of this test is $8 - 2 = 6$. The critical value is $\chi^2_{0.01(6)} = 16.812$, and the test statistic (Table 15.8) is greater: $218.97 > 16.812$. Therefore we reject H_0 and conclude that the classifications of the interviewers are not homogeneous. It is likely that the interviewers do have personal biases that affect their classifications.

TABLE 15.8
Work Sheet for Computation of Test Statistic χ^2

Row and column	e	o	$e - o$	$(e - o)^2$	$\dfrac{(e - o)^2}{e}$
(1,1)	90	60	30	900	10.00
(1,2)	65	60	5	25	0.38
(1,3)	45	80	−35	1,225	27.22
(2,1)	90	140	−50	2,500	27.78
(2,2)	65	10	55	3,025	46.54
(2,3)	45	50	−5	25	0.56
(3,1)	90	50	40	1,600	17.78
(3,2)	65	130	−65	4,225	65.00
(3,3)	45	20	25	625	13.89
(4,1)	90	110	−20	400	4.44
(4,2)	65	60	5	25	0.38
(4,3)	45	30	15	225	5.00
Total	800	800	0		$\chi^2 = 218.97$

Let us turn now to the determination of the degrees of freedom in a test of homogeneity in general.

DEGREES OF FREEDOM

Just as in the case of a test of independence, there should be at least five expected observations in each cell in order for the chi-square approximation to be reasonably accurate. If this requirement is not met, categories should be grouped together. Assuming the requirement is met, there are $J - 1$ degrees of freedom for each of the I populations: given the population totals, only $J - 1$ cells can be determined independently. In total, there would be $I(J - 1)$ degrees of freedom if no parameter needed to be estimated. Usually, however, H_0 specifies that the various proportions are equal across the populations of interest, but it does not specify the values of those proportions. There are $J - 1$ such proportions to be estimated (the last must be the complement to 1). Thus the number of degrees of freedom is $I(J - 1) - (J - 1) = (I - 1)(J - 1)$. In the previous example we had $(I - 1)(J - 1) = (4 - 1)(3 - 1) = 6$.

15.3 Chi-Square Test of Goodness of Fit

We shall now describe a test that compares an observed probability distribution (either discrete or continuous) with a theoretical, or hypothesized, distribution to determine whether the observed distribution is drawn from the hypothesized distribution. In other words, we are not testing hypotheses concerning a parameter of a given distribution; rather, we are questioning the entire shape of the distribution to see how well it fits that of a hypothesized distribution. In Chapter 14 we presented a test of equality of two proportions where $p_1 = p_2$ under H_0. Here we shall see that an interesting special case of the goodness of fit allows us to test the equality of more than two proportions in a distribution, that is, to test hypotheses such as H_0: $p_1 = p_2 = p_3 = p_4 = \cdots = p_J$.

WHEN DO WE NEED TO CONSIDER GOODNESS OF FIT?

Let us consider some situations in which the form of a distribution may be of interest. Suppose we are using a marketing survey to try to determine which brand of a certain vegetable is most preferred by consumers. Suppose under H_0 we hypothesize that each brand is preferred by an equal proportion of the consumers. In other words, the proportion of consumers preferring a certain brand is equal to the proportion preferring any other brand. If we take a sample of consumers and ask them their preferences, we are bound to find differences. But can we say that these differences are *significant* enough to allow a rejection of the null hypothesis? In other words, we are questioning whether the data fit the hypothesized distribution well; hence the name *goodness of fit*.

Consider another example. When a company places an order for its inventories, a certain amount of time is usually allowed to pass before it expects to receive its order. How early should the order be placed? That depends on the number of items in stock and on the future demand for those items. Future demand is usually unknown, but we may want to estimate its probability distribution in order to make better decisions with regard to the optimal time for ordering new stock. If we have reason to believe (perhaps because of some theoretical considerations) that the probability distribution has the Poisson form, we can test the following hypotheses:

H_0: The probability distribution is of Poisson form.
H_1: The probability distribution is not of Poisson form.

In another situation, we might want to test the hypothesis that a given distribution is normal. Mutual funds, for example, are investment companies that pool funds from many individuals and institutions and invest them in diversified portfolios of bonds and stocks. Whether the distribution of the rates of return on such portfolios is normal or not is important for several reasons. One reason is that a normal distribution is fully specified by only two parameters—the mean and the variance. If indeed a portfolio's rate of return is normally distributed, theoretical as well as practical risk analysis of the returns' distribution can be greatly simplified. In this case we would focus on the mean and the variance and ignore the skewness, kurtosis, and other moments of the distribution. Thus, we might want to test the following hypotheses:

H_0: The probability distribution of the rates of return is normal.

H_1: The probability distribution of the rates of return is not normal.

CARRYING OUT TESTS OF GOODNESS OF FIT

In principle as well as in practice, goodness-of-fit tests are straightforward. We draw a random sample and compare the sample frequency distribution with the frequency we would have expected to see had the null hypothesis been correct. If the fit between the hypothesized frequency under H_0 and the observed sample frequency is good, we favor the null hypothesis, and if it is not good we favor the alternative hypothesis.

The Test Statistic   As usual, we need to develop a test statistic and a decision rule so that our conclusion will not be arbitrary. The test statistic we develop will resemble the one used for the tests of independence and homogeneity:

$$\chi^2 = \sum \frac{(e - o)^2}{e} \tag{15.10}$$

where e and o are the expected and observed frequencies in various intervals or categories of the relevant variable.

Categorizing the Variable   Evidently, then, the variable to be considered must first be classified into categories or intervals. There is no specific rule for this classification; when the variable is continuous, the classification is somewhat arbitrary. We should try to have many intervals, but no interval should include fewer than five *expected* observations. If an interval has fewer than five expected observations, it should be combined with an adjacent interval.

Determining Expected Frequencies   We find the expected frequency in interval j (e_j) by multiplying P_j (the expected proportion of the population in interval j) by n (the sample size):

$$e_j = nP_j \tag{15.11}$$

Degrees of Freedom   The number of degrees of freedom of the test statistic is equal to the number of categories (or intervals) minus one. If, however, the expected frequencies can be derived only after some distribution parameters have been estimated from the sample data, then one degree of freedom per estimated parameter will be lost. For example, if the null hypothesis is

H_0: The density function is normal with parameters $\mu = 100$ and $\sigma = 10$.

then the expected frequencies in the various intervals can be arrived at *without estimating* μ and σ. If, however, the null hypothesis is

H_0: The density function is normal with mean $\mu = 100$.

then the expected frequencies in the various intervals can be computed only after σ has been estimated. By estimating σ we lose one degree of freedom. Finally, if H_0 is

$$H_0: \quad \text{The density function is normal.}$$

we must first estimate both μ and σ and thereby lose two degrees of freedom. Our rule, then, is

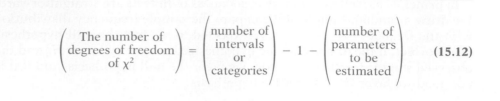

$$\begin{pmatrix} \text{The number of} \\ \text{degrees of freedom} \\ \text{of } \chi^2 \end{pmatrix} = \begin{pmatrix} \text{number of} \\ \text{intervals} \\ \text{or} \\ \text{categories} \end{pmatrix} - 1 - \begin{pmatrix} \text{number of} \\ \text{parameters} \\ \text{to be} \\ \text{estimated} \end{pmatrix} \qquad \textbf{(15.12)}$$

EXAMPLE 15.5

A study on television-watching habits of high school students in 1975 was based on a large number of interviews of students. The sample was large enough to enable us to assume that it gave a close to perfect reflection of the relevant population. The relative frequency distribution of the number of hours spent watching TV per week was found to be as follows:

Hours per week	Relative frequency
Less than 1	0.01
1–3	0.17
4–6	0.30
7–9	0.26
10–13	0.20
More than 13	0.06
	1.00

Last month another sample of 100 high school students yielded the following frequency distribution:

Hours per week	Observed frequency
Less than 1	2
1–3	8
4–6	30
7–9	20
10–13	30
More than 13	10
	100

Let us test the following hypotheses:

H_0: The current distribution of high school students with respect to time spent watching TV is the same as in 1975.

H_1: The current distribution differs from that of 1975.

Our first task is to compute the expected frequencies and the value of the test statistic. If H_0 is indeed correct, the expected relative frequencies will be as in 1975. The expected frequencies are obtained from the 1975 data and the observed frequencies are obtained from the recent data. Following Equation 15.11, we compute the expected frequencies by multiplying P_j by n for the jth category, and then compute the value of the test statistic, as in Table 15.9. Note that the expected frequency in the first category is less than five, and thus we must combine it with the adjacent category. In all further computations, the first two categories are treated as one.

TABLE 15.9
Work Sheet for Computation of Test Statistic χ^2

(1) Category j	(2) Expected relative frequency P_j	(3) = n · (2) Expected frequency e	(4) Observed frequency o	(5) $e - o$	(6) $(e - o)^2$	(7) $\dfrac{(e - o)^2}{e}$
1	0.01	1.00 } 18.00	2.00 } 10.00	8.00	64.00	3.56
2	0.17	17.00	8.00			
3	0.30	30.00	30.00	0.00	0.00	0.00
4	0.26	26.00	20.00	6.00	36.00	1.38
5	0.20	20.00	30.00	−10.00	100.00	5.00
6	0.06	6.00	10.00	−4.00	16.00	2.67
Total	1.00	100.00	100.00	0		χ^2 = 12.61

These two categories are treated as one → { 1, 2 }

The value of the test statistic is 12.61. The number of degrees of freedom is equal to the number of categories minus one: $5 - 1 = 4$. If we assume $\alpha = 0.05$, the critical value is $\chi^2_{0.05(4)} = 9.488$. As the computed value of χ^2 is 12.61, we reject H_0 and conclude that significant evidence exists to indicate that a shift in the distribution has indeed taken place between 1975 and last month.

EXAMPLE 15.6

Truck Rental Service, Inc. (TRS) is a large firm operating nationwide and having many regional offices. Consider one of these offices, located in a large metropolitan area. It is the responsibility of the regional office to replace trucks that have any kind of mechanical or electrical problem that cannot be fixed within a very short time. As a result, the office must maintain a standby truck fleet at all times. How many trucks should be standing by? This depends, of course, on the probability distribution of the number of trucks that must be replaced on any given day. Consider the following hypotheses:

H_0: The probability distribution of the number of replacements per day has the Poisson form.

H_1: The probability distribution does not have the Poisson form.

To test such hypotheses, we need to take a sample of days and record the number of replacements that were needed each day. Suppose a sample of 250 days was taken. The data gathered are presented in Table 15.10.

TABLE 15.10
Frequency Distribution of Truck Replacements

Number of replacements	Frequency of days
0	2
1	8
2	21
3	31
4	44
5	48
6	39
7	22
8	17
9	13
10	5
	250

Using $\alpha = 0.05$, should we accept or reject H_0 on the basis of this sample? As we recall (from Chapter 8), the Poisson distribution is determined by the parameter λ, which in our example is the mean daily number of truck replacements. Since this figure is neither provided nor hypothesized, we must use the sample to estimate it before the expected frequencies can be obtained. The average of daily replacements is equal to the total number of replacements made within the sample period divided by the number of days in the period. In our case, 1,250 replacements took place within 250 days. Note that to calculate the total number of replacements we simply multiply each replacement value by its frequency and add:

$$0 \cdot 2 + 1 \cdot 8 + 2 \cdot 21 + 3 \cdot 31 + \cdots + 10 \cdot 5 = 1,250$$

To get the average daily replacements, we divide the total by the number of days: $1,250/250 = 5$. Using the Poisson equation, $P(X = x) = \dfrac{\lambda^x e^{-\lambda}}{x!}$ where 5 is used for λ, we derive the probabilities for the various numbers of replacements shown in Table 15.11.

TABLE 15.11
Probability Distribution of Truck Replacements

x	$P(x) = \dfrac{5^x e^{-5}}{x!}$
0	0.0067
1	0.0337
2	0.0842
3	0.1404
4	0.1755
5	0.1755
6	0.1462
7	0.1044
8	0.0653
9	0.0363
10	0.0181
11 or more	$1.0 - 0.9863 = 0.0137$
Total	1.0000

Given 250 observations (days), we determine the expected frequencies by multiplying the probability of each category by 250 and then proceed to calculate the test statistic. The calculations are provided in Table 15.12. Note that those categories in which the expected frequency, e, is less than 5 have been grouped together with their adjacent categories.

With 10 categories and one estimated parameter, λ, the number of degrees of freedom of the test statistic is $10 - 1 - 1 = 8$, and the critical value is $\chi^2_{0.05(8)} = 15.507$. Since $\chi^2 = 4.4966 < 15.507$, we do not reject the null hypothesis.

TABLE 15.12ª

Work Sheet for Computing the Test Statistic χ^2

j	P_j	$e = 250 \cdot P_j$	o	$e - o$	$(e - o)^2$	$\dfrac{(e-o)^2}{e}$
0	0.0067	1.675 ⎫ 10.100	2 ⎫ 10	0.100	0.010	0.0010
1	0.0337	8.425 ⎭	8 ⎭			
2	0.0842	21.050	21	0.050	0.002	0.0001
3	0.1404	35.100	31	4.100	16.810	0.4789
4	0.1755	43.875	44	−0.125	0.016	0.0004
5	0.1755	43.875	48	−4.125	17.016	0.3878
6	0.1462	36.550	39	−2.450	6.002	0.1642
7	0.1044	26.100	22	4.100	16.810	0.6441
8	0.0653	16.325	17	;0.675	0.456	0.0279
9	0.0363	9.075	13	;3.925	15.406	1.6976
10	0.0181	4.525 ⎫ 7.950	5 ⎫ 5	2.950	8.702	1.0946
11+	0.0137	3.425 ⎭	0 ⎭			
Total	1.0000	250.000	250	0.000		$\chi^2 = 4.4966$

ªAn additional category (11+) was added so that the expected frequencies as well as the actual frequencies would add up to 250. The probability of this category was calculated by subtracting the sum of all the other categories from 1.

EXAMPLE 15.7

A marketing survey is trying to establish consumer preferences for three different brands of tomatoes. Three hundred people are surveyed (each individual chooses only one brand as "best"). Their preferences are as follows:

	Brand		
A	B	C	Total
85	125	90	300

Suppose we want to test the null hypothesis that the brands are equally desirable to the consumers. If we denote the proportion of consumers preferring brands A, B, and C by p_1, p_2, and p_3, respectively, the null hypothesis is

$$H_0: \quad p_1 = p_2 = p_3$$

The alternative hypothesis, then, is

$$H_1: \quad \text{Not all the proportions are equal.}$$

Under the null hypothesis, the expected proportion of consumers preferring each brand is $\frac{1}{3}$ and the expected frequency is $\frac{1}{3} \cdot 300 = 100$. Given that the expected frequency in each cell is at least 5, we can apply the statistic $\Sigma(e - o)^2/e$, which has a distribution approximately equal to χ^2 with the number of degrees of freedom equal to the number of cells (3) minus 1, namely, 2 in this example.

Since the expected frequency for each brand is 100, the test statistic is equal to

$$\sum \frac{(e - o)^2}{e} = \frac{(100 - 85)^2}{100} + \frac{(100 - 125)^2}{100} + \frac{(100 - 90)^2}{100} = 9.5$$

Using a significance level of 1 percent, we find the critical value to be $\chi^{2(2)}_{0.01} = 9.21$ and we reject the null hypothesis: the brands are not preferred by equal proportions of the consumers. Looking at the data, we can further see that brand B occurs with the highest frequency, which indicates greater preference for this brand.

EXAMPLE 15.8

The management of a large pension fund is interested in studying the probability distribution of monthly rates of return on large, well-diversified portfolios of common stock. In particular, the management is interested in finding out whether such probability distributions can be reasonably assumed to be normal. Intensive data gathering has yielded 90 monthly returns on various large and well-diversified portfolios. These returns (expressed as gross returns per $1,000 invested) had a sample mean $\overline{X} = \$1,010$ and a sample standard deviation $S = \$20$. The data were classified into intervals and had the frequency distribution presented in Table 15.13. Each interval shown in the table includes the lower limit but excludes the upper limit. To determine the expected frequencies, we first standardize the range of gross returns by expressing each nonstandardized range limit X as $Z = (X - \overline{X})/S$. For example, the limit 1,020 is standardized as follows: $(1,020 - 1,010)/20 = 0.5$. Once

TABLE 15.13
Frequency Distribution of Gross Returns

Range[a] (dollars)	Frequency
Less than $970	4
$ 970– 980	4
980– 990	10
990–1,000	13
1,000–1,010	16
1,010–1,020	15
1,020–1,030	13
1,030–1,040	8
1,040–1,050	5
1,050 or more	2

[a]Each closed interval includes the lower limit but excludes the upper limit.

the conversion into standardized ranges has been made, we can determine the relative frequency directly from the normal distribution table (inside the back cover of the book) and then multiply it by 90 (the number of observations) to obtain the frequency in the category. When the expected frequencies are determined and categories with expected frequencies of less than 5 are combined, we continue as usual with the calculation of the test statistic. The calculations are provided in Table 15.14.

TABLE 15.14
Work Sheet for Computing the Test Statistic χ^2

(1) Nonstandardized range X	(2) Standardized range $Z = \dfrac{X - \bar{X}}{S}$	(3) Relative frequency	(4) = (3) · 90 Expected frequency e	(5) o	(6) $e - o$	(7) $(e - o)^2$	(8) $\dfrac{(e - o)^2}{e}$
Less than $970	Less than −2.0	0.023	2.07 ⎫ 6.03	4 ⎫ 8	−1.97	3.881	0.644
$ 970– 980	−2.0 to −1.5	0.044	3.96 ⎭	4 ⎭			
980– 990	−1.5 to −1.0	0.092	8.28	10	−1.72	2.958	0.357
990–1,000	−1.0 to −0.5	0.150	13.50	13	0.50	0.250	0.019
1,000–1,010	−0.5 to 0.0	0.191	17.19	16	1.19	1.416	0.082
1,010–1,020	0.0 to 0.5	0.191	17.19	15	2.19	4.796	0.279
1,020–1,030	0.5 to 1.0	0.150	13.50	13	0.50	0.250	0.019
1,030–1,040	1.0 to 1.5	0.092	8.28	8	0.28	0.078	0.009
1,040–1,050	1.5 to 2.0	0.044	3.96 ⎫ 6.03	5 ⎫ 7	−0.97	0.941	0.156
1,050 or more	2.0 and up	0.023	2.07 ⎭	2 ⎭			
Total		1.000	90.00	90	0.00		$\chi^2 = 1.565$

If μ and σ were known, we would have $8 - 1 = 7$ degrees of freedom. However, since the mean and standard deviation of the returns are calculated on the basis of the sample data, two degrees of freedom have been "used up," and so our χ^2 statistic has $8 - 1 - 2 = 5$ degrees of freedom. The critical value, if $\alpha = 0.05$, is $\chi^2_{0.05(5)} = 11.070$, and as $\chi^2 = 1.565 < 11.070$, we do not reject H_0 and conclude that the returns' distribution is normal. More accurately, we do not have statistical evidence disputing the hypothesis that the distribution is normal.

A CONCLUDING NOTE REGARDING CLASSIFICATION

Tests of goodness of fit to distributions—uniform, exponential, binomial, and so on—follow the same logic and procedure as the tests that have been described in our examples. The difference between one test and another is in the derivation of the expected frequency for which the relevant probability distribution must be used. We would like to note once again that in the case of a continuous distribution, the classification of categories is rather arbitrary, and unless a sufficient number of categories is defined, the test may be meaningless. As an extreme case, suppose we define only two categories in Example 15.8: "less than $1,010" and "1,010 or more." The expected relative frequency will be 50 percent in the first category and 50 percent in the second category.[1] Even if the null hypothesis is accepted in this case, it

---

[1] It is assumed that the mean and standard deviation of the normal distribution are somehow exogenously known. Otherwise there would not be enough degrees of freedom to test such a hypothesis.

would be absolutely wrong to interpret the result as a confirmation of normality. The test would indicate only that normality cannot be rejected on the basis of the test results. But the very same data will lead to the conclusion that we cannot reject a hypothesis that the distribution is uniform if only these two broad categories are used. If the distribution is assumed to be uniform, the expected relative frequency will also be 50 percent in each category and will result in the same value of the test statistic and the same number of degrees of freedom $(2 - 1 = 1)$.[2] Consequently, the decision rule will be the same as for the test of a normal distribution.

We conclude, then, that the categories should be determined in such a way that there will be enough categories to make the expected frequencies resemble the probability distribution hypothesized under H_0, because when other things are held constant,[3] the greater the number of categories, the higher the power of the test (and thus the lower the probability of committing a Type II error).

15.4 APPLICATION:
INFORMATION SOURCES IN RETAIL EMPLOYMENT— CHI-SQUARE TEST OF INDEPENDENCE*

Information about prospective employees constitutes the cornerstone of retail employment decision making. Information gathering includes both a self-report from the potential candidate (the application blank) and reports that by their nature are not self-report, e.g., police reports, polygraph reports, and so on.

The determination to hire or reject an applicant for employment constitutes a crucial decision for the organization. Inappropriate selection judgments contribute to both serious organizational disruptions and expense.

Data from 363 firms have been collected. The data were classified by size of annual sales and by methods used to acquire information regarding job applicants.

Table 15.15 shows the sample frequency of each class of firms that employ a specific information-gathering method. For example, of the 61 sample companies in the category, "less than $1 million worth of assets," 32 employ the personal interview method, 26 use application blanks, 23 use business references, and so on. Many firms use more than one method, so the total of each column is greater than the number of firms in the category. The number of sample firms in each group (N) is given in the table's caption.

The information given in Table 15.15 is presented again in Table 15.16, this time in percentages. It shows, for example, that whereas only 52.5 percent of the sample firms in the group characterized by "less than $1 million worth of assets" use personal interviews, the sample percentage of larger firms using personal interviews is well over 80 percent.

In particular, it seems that business references and testing are more frequently used by firms with larger annual sales volume. Also, police checks are not used heavily by firms with annual sales below $1 million.

* This application is based on C. J. Hollon and M. Gable, "Information Sources in Retail Employment Decision-Making Process," *Journal of Retailing*, Fall 1979, pp. 58–74.

---

[2] It is assumed that the distribution parameters are exogenously known.
[3] In particular, you should remember that a minimum of five *expected* observations should be included in each category.

TABLE 15.15
Information Sources by Annual Sales Volume
(frequency of firms)

Method	Assets (in millions of dollars)				
	Less than 1 (N = 61)	*1–under 10* (N = 135)	*10–under 100* (N = 110)	*100–under 500* (N = 42)	*500 or more* (N = 15)
Personal interview	32	111	104	40	14
Application blank	26	103	102	41	14
Business references	23	89	93	38	14
Personal references	26	89	63	18	10
Credit report	12	50	43	15	4
Police check	1	23	30	11	4
Physical examination	2	7	14	22	5
Testing	0	10	16	4	3
Polygraph	2	2	9	2	2
Assessment center	0	2	4	3	4
Handwriting analysis	0	1	0	0	0

TABLE 15.16
Information Sources by Annual Sales Volume
(percentage reporting usage)

Method	Assets (in millions of dollars)				
	Less than 1 (N = 61)	*1–under 10* (N = 135)	*10–under 100* (N = 110)	*100–under 500* (N = 42)	*500 or more* (N = 15)
Personal interview	52.5	82.2	94.5	95.2	93.3
Application blank	42.6	76.3	92.7	97.6	93.3
Business references	37.7	65.9	84.5	90.5	93.3
Personal references	42.6	65.9	57.3	42.9	66.7
Credit report	19.7	37.0	39.1	35.7	26.7
Police check	1.6	17.0	27.3	26.2	26.7
Physical examination	3.3	5.2	12.7	52.4	33.3
Testing	0.0	7.4	14.5	9.5	20.0
Polygraph	3.3	1.5	8.2	4.8	13.3
Assessment center	0.0	1.5	3.6	7.1	26.7
Handwriting analysis	0.0	0.7	0.0	0.0	0.0

Since the data represent a sample rather than the population, we can apply the chi-square distribution and use the chi-square test of independence to test the following hypotheses regarding each information-gathering method:

H_0: The proportion of retailers using a specific method is independent of the annual sales volume.
H_1: The proportion depends on annual sales volume.

The hypotheses are tested for each information-gathering method separately. A detailed example is given in Table 15.17, a contingency table for the first method, personal interviews. Since 32 of the 61 firms in the group having "less than $1 million worth of assets" use a personal interview, it is clear that $61 - 32 = 29$ firms do not use it. The observed frequencies in the other sales groups were determined in a similar fashion. The total of each column, c_j, and of each row, r_i, is then determined. The expected frequencies are determined by using $e_{ij} = r_i c_j / n$. For example, the expected frequency

TABLE 15.17
The Chi-Square Table

Method	Sales volume (in millions of dollars)					Total
	Less than 1 $(j = 1)$	1–under 10 $(j = 2)$	10–under 100 $(j = 3)$	100–under 500 $(j = 4)$	500 or more $(j = 5)$	
Interview $(i = 1)$	32 (50.6)	111 (111.9)	104 (91.2)	40 (34.8)	14 (12.4)	301
Do not interview $(i = 2)$	29 (10.4)	24 (23.1)	6 (18.8)	2 (7.2)	1 (2.6)	62
Total	61	135	110	42	15	363

for $i = 1$ and $j = 1$ in Table 15.17 is $e_{11} = (301 \cdot 61)/363 = 50.6$. The test statistic is given by $\chi^2 = \Sigma (e - o)^2/e$ and for the data given in Table 15.17 $\chi^2 = 56.38$. The number of degrees of freedom is $(I - 1)(J - 1) = (2 - 1)(5 - 1) = 4$. The value of the test statistic leads to a rejection of the null hypothesis even at significance levels considerably lower than 1 percent.

Table 15.18 summarizes the values of the chi-square test statistic for each of the methods used and its level of significance. It shows that most of the tests lead to the rejection of the null hypothesis at all reasonable significance levels. The conclusion is that retailers of different size use different information-gathering methods. Cost and other considerations may make different methods more effective for companies of different size.

TABLE 15.18
The Test-Statistic Values and Their Significance

Information-gathering method	Value of the chi-square test statistic	Significance[a]
Personal interview	56.38	a
Application blank	72.10	a
Business references	55.60	a
Personal references	13.46	b
Credit report	7.74	d
Police check	19.11	a
Physical examination	71.31	a
Testing	12.51	c
Polygraph	8.82	d
Assessment center	30.88	a
Handwriting analysis	1.50	d

[a]Significance at $\alpha \le 0.001$ is denoted by a. Significance at $\alpha \le 0.010$ is denoted by b. Significance at $\alpha \le 0.050$ is denoted by c. Not significant at $\alpha \le 0.05$ is denoted by d.

Chapter Summary and Review

Test	Degrees of freedom
1. Independence (*I* rows and *J* columns)	$IJ - 1 -$ (number of estimated parameters) If no parameter is hypothesized under H_0, $(I - 1)(J - 1)$
2. Homogeneity	$(I - 1)(J - 1)$ (There are $J - 1$ proportions to estimate)
3. Goodness of fit	$\left(\begin{matrix}\text{Number of}\\\text{intervals}\end{matrix}\right) - 1 - \left(\begin{matrix}\text{Number of estimated}\\\text{parameters}\end{matrix}\right)$

4. The test statistic for all of these tests is $\Sigma\,(e - o)^2/e$ and they are all upper-tail tests.

5. The number of expected observations in each cell or in each interval should not be less than 5. If this requirement is not met, categories or intervals should be grouped together to give at least 5 expected observations.

6. The test of equality of proportions is a special case of the goodness-of-fit test.

Problems

15.1. Explain why the chi-square tests of independence and of goodness of fit are always upper-tail tests.

15.2. "In a chi-square test, whenever the observed frequency is less than 5, categories must be combined before the test can be carried out." Do you agree? Why?

15.3. Is it true that the number of degrees of freedom of the test statistic of a chi-square test of independence is equal to the number of cells in the contingency table minus one? Explain.

15.4. Students who have taken two courses in statistics and economics on a pass–fail basis have the following distribution:

	Statistics		
Economics	*Pass*	*Fail*	*Total*
Pass	583	147	730
Fail	95	29	124
Total	678	176	854

Are passing economics courses and passing statistics courses independent? Show your calculations, and use $\alpha = 0.05$.

15.5. The following table shows the frequency of pass–fail grades by grade and by the relation of the sex of the teacher to that of the student.

Sex of teacher vs. sex of student	Grade		
	Pass	*Fail*	*Total*
Opposite sex	156	8	164
Same sex	284	99	383
Total	440	107	547

Is there any evidence of sex discrimination in the grades? Use a significance level of 5 percent.

15.6. The following table shows the distribution of an insurance company's real estate investments by location and type of investment.

Class	*West*	*South*	*Midwest*	*East*
Offices	10	12	7	9
Industrial	96	26	86	7
Commercial	14	6	7	3
Hotels and motels	0	7	0	6
Apartments	2	1	2	2
Land	1	0	0	0

Source: C. M. Ballard and B. V. Strum, "Pension Funds in Real Estate: New Challenges/Opportunities for Professionals," *Appraisal Journal*, October 1978, pp. 551–569.

Test the hypothesis that the class and geographic location of the property in which the insurance company has invested are independent. Use $\alpha = 0.01$.

15.7. The home ownership of a certain sample is distributed as follows, by income:

Income	Home ownership		
	Yes	*No*	*Total*
$ 0– 4,999	20	347	367
5,000– 9,999	60	124	184
10,000–14,999	272	50	322
15,000 +	498	66	564
Total	850	587	1,437

(a) Explain why home ownership and income are likely to show dependence in a chi-square test applied to the above table.

(b) Test the hypothesis that home ownership and income are independent at a 5 percent significance level.

15.8. There are financial services that rate bonds according to their probability of default (that is, inability to meet interest or repayment of principal). Standard and Poor's is one such service. The service rates bonds as AAA ("triple A") if they are judged to have a negligible risk of default and thus to be of highest quality. AA ("double A") are bonds of high quality but are judged to be not quite so free of default risk as AAA bonds. Bonds rated BBB are of medium quality.

The following table presents the results of a 300-firm sample. Of the 300 firms, 100 had bonds rated AAA, 100 had bonds rated AA, and 100 had bonds rated BBB. The table shows the number of firms that defaulted on their bonds by bond rating.

Bond rating	Number of defaulting firms	Number of firms not defaulting	Total
AAA	5	95	100
AA	5	95	100
BBB	20	80	100
Total	30	270	300

(a) Calculate the expected frequency in each cell, assuming that default and bond rating are independent.

(b) Test the hypothesis that the rating service does not provide valuable information with regard to the chances of default. Formulate the null and alternative hypotheses, and use $\alpha = 0.05$ to test the hypotheses.

15.9. Rework Problem 15.8, assuming that the sample results were as in the following table:

Bond rating	Number of defaulting firms	Number of firms not defaulting	Total
AAA	5	95	100
AA	5	95	100
BBB	80	20	100
Total	90	210	300

15.10. Rework Problem 15.8 once more, this time assuming that the sample showed the following results:

Bond rating	Number of defaulting firms	Number of firms not defaulting	Total
AAA	20	80	100
AA	10	90	100
BBB	0	100	100
Total	30	270	300

Considering the test result, evaluate the bond rating service. Is it worthwhile? (Do not forget to use common sense!)

15.11. The following table shows the observed frequency of a sample of 100 people classified by wealth and habit of drinking Coca-Cola. The people were randomly chosen from the general adult population.

Coca-Cola habit	Rich	Poor	Total
Drinking	25	25	50
Nondrinking	25	25	50
Total	50	50	100

Can you say without carrying out any calculations whether the null hypothesis of independence between the two variables should be accepted or rejected? Explain.

15.12. Consider Problem 15.11 again, this time supposing the sample shows the following result:

Coca-Cola habit	Rich	Poor	Total
Drinking	X	$50 - X$	50
Nondrinking	$50 - X$	X	50
Total	50	50	100

What is the maximum value of X such that $X \leq 25$ and the hypothesis of independence between wealth and Coca-Cola drinking will be rejected at $\alpha = 0.05$?

15.13. A large company employing tens of thousands of employees is considering offering its employees low-cost life insurance rather than a pay raise. A sample of 190 administrators, production workers, and salespeople has shown the following distribution of preference for the plan:

	Preference		
Employees	Pay raise	Life insurance	Indifferent
Administrators	15	20	10
Production workers	18	30	15
Salespeople	25	45	12

Test the hypothesis that the preference for life insurance or pay raise is independent of the job classification; in other words, the preference of the administrators is the same as that of the production workers and the salespeople. Use $\alpha = 0.01$.

15.14. An insurance firm is reexamining its auto insurance premiums. One question currently under consideration is whether young people and old people are involved in more accidents than others. A sample of 400 files has been randomly chosen, including 100 from each of four age groups, and their involvement in accidents has been recorded as follows:

Age group	Was involved in accidents	Was not involved in accidents
Under 26	30	70
26–40	5	95
41–55	10	90
56 +	25	75

Test the null hypothesis, under which involvement in accidents is not dependent on age, against the alternative hypothesis that the involvement in accidents is dependent on age. Do you think the company should set higher auto insurance premiums for young and old drivers?

15.15. A random sample of 98 people were asked about their smoking habits. Their responses are summarized in Table P15.15.

TABLE P15.15

Gender	Nonsmokers	Light smokers	Heavy smokers
Male	24	18	14
Female	28	8	6

Test the hypothesis that a person's smoking habit is independent of gender. Use a significance level of 5 percent.

15.16. It has been hypothesized that stockholders whose marginal tax rate is high prefer stocks that pay low dividends and have a greater growth potential, and stockholders whose marginal tax rate is low prefer stocks that pay high dividends and provide less in capital gains. A random sample of 126 stockholders has shown the following:

Tax rate	Dividend payments	
	High	Low
High	13	51
Low	46	16

(*a*) Test the hypothesis that whether stockholders invest in stocks that pay high or low dividends is independent of their tax rates. Use a 5 percent significance level. Does your result support the hypothesis of independence between the variables, or does it support the other hypothesis raised above? Explain.

(*b*) How would your answer change, if at all, if the contingency table were as follows:

Tax rate	Dividend payment	
	High	Low
High	51	13
Low	16	46

Explain.

15.17. Two schools are preparing for a certain professional test. The test is administered by state authorities and is required for a certain practice license. Sixty students were selected at random from each school to determine whether the percentage of students passing the test is the same in both schools. The results were as follows:

School	Passing	
	Yes	No
A	55	5
B	49	11

Test the hypothesis that the chance of passing the test is the same regardless of which school provides the preparation. Use a level of significance of 5 percent.

15.18. A hypothesis is advanced according to which the absence of workers from their job occurs at a higher rate on rainy days than on nonrainy days.

(*a*) A random sample of 400 days showed the following results:

Weather	Absence	
	Yes	No
Rainy	10	110
Nonrainy	11	269

Use the chi-square test of independence with a 5 percent significance level to infer whether the incidence of absence is higher on rainy days. Show your calculations.

(b) Another sample taken from the same population has shown the following results:

Weather	Absence Yes	Absence No
Rainy	10	110
Nonrainy	12	268

Test the independence of the two variables based on the results of the second sample. Again use a 5 percent significance level. Show your calculations.

(c) In view of the cumulative, albeit insignificant, evidence of the two samples, would you be inclined to accept the hypothesis that the rate of workers' absence increases on rainy days? Can you support your answer by a statistical test? Explain and show your calculations.

15.19. A random sample of 100 unemployed blacks and a random sample of 100 unemployed whites has shown the following frequencies of length of unemployment:

Race	Length of unemployment (in weeks) Up to 5	6–10	11 or more
Blacks	40	40	20
Whites	60	30	10

Using a significance level of 5 percent, can you say that the two populations (of blacks and whites) are homogeneous with respect to their length of unemployment?

15.20. A randomly selected sample of 300 people from New York and another randomly selected sample of 200 people from Iowa have shown the following distribution of annual income:

State	Annual income (thousands of dollars) Under 10	10–under 30	30 or more
New York	60	180	60
Iowa	60	110	30

Are the two populations homogeneous? Use a 1 percent significance level.

15.21. A survey of home heating has been conducted in three areas of the country. In each area a sample of 100 homes was observed. The results were as follows:

Area	Heating method Electricity	Gas	Fireplace	Other
A	50	15	20	15
B	60	30	5	5
C	40	40	10	10

Test the hypothesis that the three areas are homogeneous with respect to the home-heating method. Use a 1 percent significance level.

15.22. The point-of-sale system is a system of payment by which funds are transferred electronically from a customer's bank account to the account of a store where the customer shops. Table P15.22 shows household attitudes toward point-of-sales terminals broken down according to a few demographic characteristics. Assume that the sample includes 5,000 households. Perform the test listed below, noting that the figures in Table P15.22 are percentages and so you need to calculate the frequencies before you can carry out a chi-square test. When determining the frequencies, make sure they add up to 1,000 in each row. If they do not add up to 1,000 because of rounding, adjust the right-hand column frequency so that they will add up to 1,000. Use $\alpha = 0.05$ in all tests.

TABLE P15.22

Demographic characteristics	Dislike very much	Dislike somewhat	Neutral	Like it somewhat	Like very much
Age of head of household					
Under 31 years	23.3%	21.9%	28.8%	21.9%	4.1%
31–40 years	30.4	14.2	29.7	16.9	8.8
41–50 years	33.7	15.3	31.3	15.3	4.3
51–60 years	26.2	18.4	32.6	16.3	6.4
Over 60	36.5	23.5	23.5	11.8	4.7
Education of head of household					
Under 12 years	26.2	14.3	46.4	11.9	1.2
High school graduate	28.4	15.4	30.2	17.3	8.6
Some college	35.2	18.3	28.9	13.4	4.2
College graduate	28.6	21.8	23.3	19.5	6.8
Postcollege	34.9	18.6	23.3	16.3	7.0
Income of total household					
Under $7,000	34.0	12.8	36.2	14.9	2.1
$ 7,000–10,999	32.0	17.3	32.0	9.3	9.3
$11,000–15,999	34.2	18.8	27.5	17.4	2.0
$16,000–20,000	30.2	19.8	26.7	16.4	6.9
Over $20,000	27.5	17.6	30.9	16.7	7.4
Life cycle of household					
Young married, no child	31.6	5.3	47.4	10.5	5.3
Young married, child < 6 years	29.5	19.7	28.7	17.2	4.9
Older married, child > 6 years	30.6	18.1	28.6	18.1	4.4
Older married, no child	33.9	18.8	28.5	11.3	7.5
Sole survivor/single	10.0	20.0	40.0	20.0	10.0
All households	30.0%	18.0%	30.0%	16.0%	6.0%

Source: O. S. Pugh and F. J. Ingram, "EFT and the Public." Reprinted by permission from *The Bankers Magazine*, Vol. 161, No. 2, March–April 1978, pp. 42–51. Copyright © 1978, Warren, Gorham & Lamont Inc., all rights reserved.

(a) Test the hypothesis that the attitude toward use of point-of-sales terminals is homogeneous across the categories of the age of head of household. Assume that the sample includes 1,000 households in each age group.

(b) Test the hypothesis that the attitude is homogeneous across the categories of education of head of household. Assume that the sample includes 1,000 households in each education group.

(c) Test the hypothesis that the attitude is homogeneous across the categories of total household income. Assume that the sample includes 1,000 households in each income group.

(d) Test the hypothesis that the attitude is homogeneous across the categories of household life cycle. Assume that the sample includes 1,000 households in each group.

15.23. Table P15.23, based on a hypothetical survey, shows the number of households that paid all or part of their charge-card bills for the month prior to that in which the survey was made, by demographic characteristics. Each category includes 400 households.

TABLE P15.23

Demographic characteristics	Paid all charges	Paid part of charges
Age of head of household		
Under 31 years	200	200
31–40 years	210	190
41–50 years	240	160
51–60 years	300	100
Over 60	240	160
Education of head of household		
Under 12 years	150	250
High school graduate	180	220
Some college	190	210
College graduate	250	150
Postcollege	300	100

(a) Perform a test of homogeneity across the categories of age of head of household. Use $\alpha = 0.01$.

(b) Perform a test of homogeneity across the categories of education of head of household. Use $\alpha = 0.01$.

15.24. You want to test the null hypothesis that the annual income of workers in a certain industry is distributed as follows: 20 percent earn under $10,000, 30 percent earn $10,000 to under $16,000, 30 percent earn $16,000 to under $22,000, and 20 percent earn $22,000 or more. You take a random sample of the population and you get the following frequencies:

Under $10,000	$10,000–under $16,000	$16,000–under $22,000	$22,000 or more
36	44	60	52

Test the null hypothesis against the alternative hypothesis, namely, that the distribution is different from the probabilities that are specified under the null hypothesis. Use a level of significance of 1 percent.

15.25. A random sample of workers was surveyed to assess their satisfaction with a recently negotiated wage agreement. The sample, which included 60 workers, has shown the following distribution:

Very unhappy	Unhappy	Happy	Very happy
17	20	18	5

Test the hypothesis that the workers are distributed equally among the four satisfaction levels. Use $\alpha = 5$ percent.

15.26. The annual income tax payments of 1,000 randomly selected individuals are distributed as follows:

Interval	Frequency
Less than $1,000	40
$1,000–under $1,500	60
$1,500–under $2,000	170
$2,000–under $2,500	140
$2,500–under $3,000	180
$3,000–under $3,500	210
$3,500–under $4,000	80
$4,000 or more	120

Test the hypothesis that the distribution is normal with a mean of $2,500 and a standard deviation of $1,000. Use $\alpha = 0.05$. DF don't subtract 2 of estimated parameters

15.27. Cash turnover is defined as company sales divided by cash. Table P15.27 presents the cash turnover of 59 firms. Test the hypothesis that the cash turnover is normally distributed with a mean of $\mu = 13.0$ and a standard deviation of $\sigma = 15.0$. When deriving the test statistic, use symmetrical intervals of 7.5 around the mean 13.0. Use $\alpha = 0.01$.

TABLE P15.27

Firm	Cash turnover	Firm	Cash turnover
1	13.9	31	2.0
2	10.9	32	17.1
3	8.9	33	9.7
4	10.0	34	2.6
5	28.9	35	62.0
6	3.6	36	2.0
7	64.1	37	36.6
8	48.9	38	3.2
9	36.2	39	9.1
10	16.2	40	16.0
11	10.8	41	9.2
12	13.4	42	30.3
13	16.7	43	45.6
14	5.1	44	31.5
15	12.2	45	2.7
16	15.2	46	32.5
17	20.2	47	6.5
18	8.5	48	19.1
19	3.8	49	27.3
20	23.2	50	12.6
21	29.9	51	11.8
22	12.8	52	20.7
23	9.3	53	25.7
24	2.9	54	6.1
25	11.5	55	24.9
26	11.8	56	5.5
27	11.7	57	12.1
28	22.7	58	14.9
29	27.4	59	27.5
30	16.3		

15.28. Rework Problem 15.27, this time assuming that while the mean is known to equal 13.0, the standard deviation is unknown.

15.29. Rework Problem 15.27 once more, assuming that both the mean and the standard deviation of the cash turnover are unknown.

15.30. How many degrees of freedom does the test statistic for testing goodness of fit to the normal distribution have when the number of intervals is 12 and the mean and standard deviation are unknown?

15.31. Suppose you test the goodness of fit of sample data to the normal distribution when the mean is known to equal zero. Suppose also that you decide to use two intervals—one for values less than or equal to zero and the other for values greater than zero.

   (a) How many degrees of freedom does the test statistic have?
   (b) Is it a good test? Explain.

15.32. "If $o_i = e_i$ for each class in a goodness-of-fit test, we would not reject the null hypothesis, no matter what shape the distribution assumed under that hypothesis." Do you agree with the statement? Would you necessarily have much confidence that the null hypothesis is indeed correct?

15.33. The price of Zoom Corporation's common stock rose (or stayed unchanged) on 36 days during a sample period of 50 days. It declined on 14 of the 50 days. Use the chi-square goodness-of-fit test to test the null hypothesis that the daily price change is binomially distributed with equal probability of "success" (i.e., price increase or no change) and "failure" (i.e., price decrease). Use $\alpha = 0.01$. Hint: Recall that the expected value of the binomial distribution is np.

15.34. Using the sample data from Problem 15.33, can you test the null hypothesis that the distribution is binomial with $p = \frac{1}{2}$ without using the chi-square goodness-of-fit test? If yes, show your calculations. What is your decision if you use $\alpha = 0.01$?

15.35. Compare the results of Problems 15.33 and 15.34. Which is more accurate?

15.36. The number of tourists at Florida's Disney World was recorded for 90 weeks (excluding such busy seasons as Christmas and Easter). The records show the following distribution:

Number of tourists per week (thousands)	Frequency of weeks
0.00–10.99	0
11.00–13.99	12
14.00–16.99	10
17.00–19.99	15
20.00–22.99	19
23.00–25.99	12
26.00–28.99	14
29.00–31.99	3
32.00–34.99	0
35.00–37.99	4
38.00–40.99	1

(a) Calculate the mean and standard deviation of the sample data.
(b) Test the hypothesis that the distribution is normal. Use $\alpha = 0.05$.

15.37. A carnival roulette wheel is marked 1 through 10. A sample of 100 spins shows the following frequency of numbers:

Number	Frequency
1	7
2	11
3	10
4	10
5	8
6	12
7	11
8	11
9	13
10	7
	100

Test the hypothesis that the roulette wheel is balanced (i.e., that there is an equal probability for each of the numbers 1 through 10).

15.38. Table P15.38 presents the percentage of income increase from March 1981 to March 1982 in the 50 states plus the District of Columbia. In the following tests use $\alpha = 0.05$.

TABLE P15.38

State and region	Percent increase versus year ago	State and region	Percent increase versus year ago
New England		**West north-central**	
Connecticut	6.4	Iowa	5.7
Maine	6.8	Kansas	10.5
Massachusetts	6.1	Minnesota	10.1
New Hampshire	10.9	Missouri	9.1
Rhode Island	7.4	Nebraska	8.7
Vermont	6.8	North Dakota	13.0
Middle Atlantic		South Dakota	8.5
New Jersey	7.6	**West south-central**	
New York	8.2	Arkansas	6.3
Pennsylvania	4.9	Louisiana	10.4
South Atlantic		Oklahoma	8.4
Delaware	8.2	Texas	11.7
Dist. of Columbia	2.5	**Mountain**	
Florida	9.6	Arizona	11.4
Georgia	5.5	Colorado	7.4
Maryland	6.1	Idaho	5.4
North Carolina	5.1	Montana	9.2
South Carolina	5.9	Nevada	6.6
Virginia	7.0	New Mexico	13.7
West Virginia	4.1	Utah	9.2
East north-central		Wyoming	10.0
Illinois	4.2	**Pacific**	
Indiana	3.3	Alaska	11.4
Michigan	3.6	California	11.0
Ohio	4.4	Hawaii	2.5
Wisconsin	6.9	Oregon	5.7
East south-central		Washington	5.1
Alabama	4.7		
Kentucky	5.5		
Mississippi	5.9		
Tennessee	6.3		

Source: Data from *Business Week*, July 26, 1982, p. 82.

(a) Test the hypothesis that the distribution of the percentage increase in income follows a normal distribution with a mean $\mu = 7.35$ percent and a standard deviation $\sigma = 2.69$ percent. In your calculation take the first interval to be $X \le 3$ percent, the second interval as 3 percent $< X \le 4$ percent, the third interval as 4 percent $< X \le 5$ percent, and so on. The last interval is 13 percent $< X$. Be sure to join together intervals with expected values of fewer than five observations.

(b) Would you change your answer if there were no information on the mean and standard deviation, but 7.35 and 2.69 were the sample estimates $\overline{X}$ and S rather than the population parameters μ and σ?

15.39. The period of time from the day a customer is billed to the day the bill is actually paid is referred to as a collection period. A power company's records show that frequencies of collection periods (in days) are as given in Table P15.39.

TABLE P15.39

Collection period (days)	Frequency
0	0
1	0
2	20
3	20
4	40
5	70
6	110
7	100
8	175
9	170
10	165
11	110
12	20
13	0
14	0
	1,000

(a) Test the hypothesis that the collection period is Poisson-distributed with $\lambda = 5.0$. Use $\alpha = 0.05$.

(b) Test the hypothesis that the collection period is Poisson-distributed, but do not assume any value for λ. Rather, estimate λ from Table P15.39. Use $\alpha = 0.05$ again.

15.40. Suppose the vacancies filled for a certain position over a period of 30 years were as shown in Table P15.40.

TABLE P15.40

Year	Number of vacancies filled	Year	Number of vacancies filled
1	2	16	1
2	1	17	2
3	0	18	0
4	1	19	1
5	0	20	0
6	2	21	0
7	1	22	0
8	2	23	0
9	0	24	2
10	2	25	3
11	1	26	0
12	0	27	1
13	0	28	2
14	1	29	1
15	0	30	4

(a) Test the hypothesis that the distribution of vacancies filled in a year is Poisson-distributed with $\lambda = 0.2$. Use a significance level of 5 percent.

(b) Test the hypothesis that the distribution of vacancies filled in a year is Poisson-distributed with the value of λ unspecified. Use a significance level of 5 percent again.

15.41. A sample of 113 drivers showed that 87 of them carry collision insurance and 26 do not. Forty-two of these drivers were involved in car accidents in the last five years, and 71 were not. An SAS computer printout of the chi-square test of independence between being insured and involvement in accidents is shown in Figure P15.41. Discuss the test results.

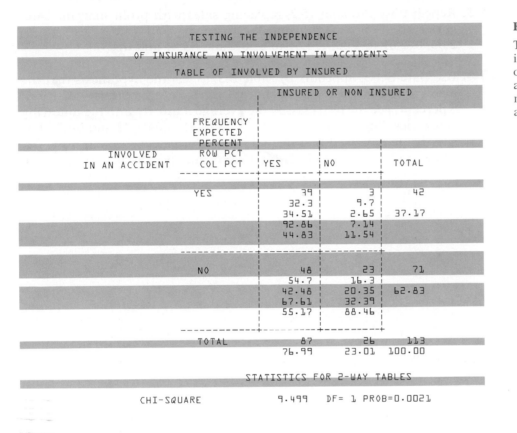

Figure P15.41

Testing the independence of insurance and involvement in accidents

```
              TESTING THE INDEPENDENCE
      OF INSURANCE AND INVOLVEMENT IN ACCIDENTS
          TABLE OF INVOLVED BY INSURED

                              INSURED OR NON INSURED

                   FREQUENCY
                   EXPECTED
                   PERCENT
   INVOLVED        ROW PCT
   IN AN ACCIDENT  COL PCT   YES      NO       TOTAL
                   ----------+--------+--------+
         YES              39        3       42
                        32.3      9.7
                       34.51     2.65     37.17
                       92.86     7.14
                       44.83    11.54
                   ----------+--------+--------+
         NO               48       23       71
                        54.7     16.3
                       42.48    20.35     62.83
                       67.61    32.39
                       55.17    88.46
                   ----------+--------+--------+
         TOTAL           87       26      113
                       76.99    23.01   100.00

              STATISTICS FOR 2-WAY TABLES

   CHI-SQUARE            9.499    DF= 1  PROB=0.0021
```

Case Problems

15.1. The shape and parameters of the distribution of rates of return of mutual funds are important to investors because they define for each investor the expected profitability and the risk associated with it.

(a) Use the data given for the 20 "Flexible Policy Income Funds" in Data Set 2, Appendix B, Table B.2, to test the hypothesis that the rates of return in this category of funds are normally distributed with a mean of 12 percent and a standard deviation of 20 percent. In order to carry out the test, categorize the rates of return into the following categories (in percent): "up to −30," "−30 to under −20," "−20 to under −10," etc., the last category being "40 and up." Use α = 5 percent.

(b) Repeat part a, except this time assume that the mean and standard deviation are unknown and not hypothesized.

15.2. Using Data Set 1, Appendix B, Table B.1, test the hypothesis that profit is independent of sales (use α = 5 percent). For the test, classify sales into the following four categories: "up to 1,672," "1,673 to 2,589," "2,590 to 5,141," and "5,142 and up." Classify profits into the following four categories: "up to 40," "41 to 88," "89 to 197," and "198 and up." Discuss your results.

15.3. Repeat Case Problem 15.2, replacing sales with profit margin. Categorize the profit margin into the following four categories: "up to 2.00," "2.01 to 4.00," "4.01 to 5.50," and "5.51 and up."

15.4. Use Data Set 3, Appendix B, Table B.3, to test the hypothesis that the average 30-day yield is independent of the average maturity. Use α = 5 percent. For the test, classify the average maturity into the following categories: "up to 20," "21 to 27," "28 to 31," and "32 and up." Classify the 30-day yield into the following four categories: "up to 12.7," "12.8 to 13.3," "13.4 to 13.5," and "13.6 and up." Discuss your results.

ANALYSIS OF VARIANCE

CHAPTER SIXTEEN OUTLINE

Key Terms
analysis of variance (ANOVA)
one-way analysis of variance
completely randomized design
randomized block design
mean (average) within the group
grand average
total sum of squares
sum of squares within the groups
unexplained sum of squares
sum of squares between the groups
total sum of squares
mean squared deviations within the groups
mean squared deviations between the groups
two-way analysis of variance
column effect
row effect
interaction effect

16.1 Introduction to Analysis of Variance

So far our discussion of statistical inference has concerned parameters of either one or two populations. In this chapter we shall discuss a technique known as **analysis of variance (ANOVA),** which *allows us to make inferences concerning the means of more than two populations.* This is done by breaking down the variance of the populations into components. These components are then used to construct the sample statistic, hence the term "analysis of variance." Experience shows that analysis of variance is better understood if we consider the general framework first and the detailed equations later. Computer packages with easy-to-use ANOVA programs make the computation of analysis of variance of secondary importance. It is far more important to understand the purpose and approach of ANOVA, which in turn will enable you to set up correct experimental designs and draw correct conclusions from the analysis.[1] We shall describe the computational part of ANOVA primarily to provide deeper insight into the analysis.

THE BASIC APPROACH

We perform analysis of variance when we want to test the hypothesis that the means of several probability distributions are the same against the hypothesis that not all those means are equal to one another. Figure 16.1*a* shows three probability distributions, each with a separate mean. Each of these probability distributions can be thought of as representing a separate population or group. They could, for example, represent the grade distributions of students in three schools or transportation time from City *A* to City *B* by three methods of transportation. A sample is observed from each of these populations, the values of which are drawn below the population density functions and marked ○. The samples' means are shown by solid squares. We want to compare the range of the entire set of observations with that drawn from the individual populations. In Figure 16.1*a*, the range of the entire set of observations (that is, those drawn from all three populations) is far wider than the range of any one sample considered individually, because the means of the populations are widely dispersed.

In Figure 16.1*b* the means of the three populations are closer together. The sample diversity *within* each population remains the same as in 16.1*a*. Here, however, because the population means are closer together, the range of all the observations is narrower than in 16.1*a*.

Finally, Figure 16.1*c* illustrates an extreme case: the three populations are assumed to have the *same* mean, which merges all three densities exactly on top of each other. Here, the diversity of the sample observations in total is therefore of the same magnitude as the diversity of any one of the individual samples.

We can now draw the conclusion that the *reason* the total diversity of the three samples in Figures 16.1*a* and 16.1*b* is greater than the diversity of each separate sample is that the samples are selected from populations with *unequal means*.

From assumed known structured patterns of three populations we have made deductions about the relationships among sample observations drawn from those populations. Reversing our approach, we shall now infer from observed samples the structures of the populations. In Figure 16.2, observations of three samples, each drawn from a different population, are presented in two ways. In Figure 16.2*a* the observations are shown in three separate clusters, leading us to conclude that there is more to this separation than mere chance. Apparently we get three clusters because the means of the three populations are different. In Figure 16.2*b* the observations of all three samples are clustered together, leading us to conclude that we do not have statistical evidence to reject a hypothesis that all three population

---

[1] Experimental design involves the determination of the hypotheses to be tested, the way they are to be tested, and the data that will be used to test the hypotheses.

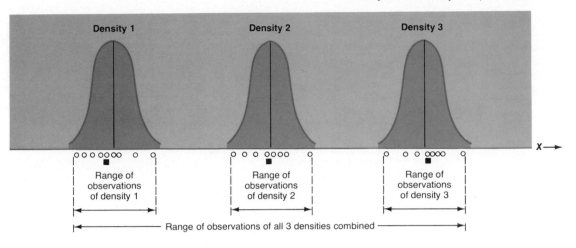

(a) The means of the population are far apart

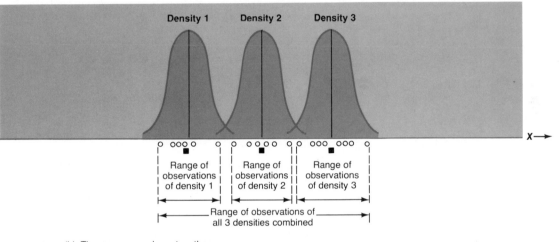

(b) The means are closer together

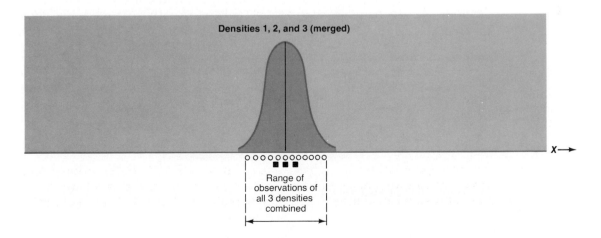

(c) The means are equal to one another

Figure 16.1

Three sets of populations and the relationship among their means

Figure 16.2

Two alternative sample structures leading to different conclusions about the populations from which they are drawn

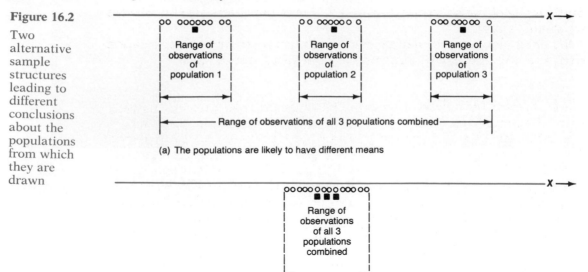

(a) The populations are likely to have different means

(b) The populations are likely to have equal means

means are equal. Formally, we test the null hypothesis

$$H_0: \quad \mu_1 = \mu_2 = \mu_3$$

where μ_1, μ_2, and μ_3 are the means of the three populations, against the alternative:[2]

$$H_1: \quad \text{Not all the } \mu_i \text{ are equal.}$$

Acceptance or rejection of H_0 will depend on the structure of the observations drawn from the three populations. If the structure is like that of Figure 16.2*a*, almost everyone will agree that H_0 should be rejected. If it is like that of Figure 16.2*b*, almost everyone will agree to accept H_0. In real life, of course, the observations are seldom as neatly separated and clustered as in Figure 16.2*a* or as close together as in 16.2*b*. They are usually scattered, like those in Figure 16.3, in which case intuitive conclusions are difficult to reach.

Figure 16.3

A hypothesized relationship among the observations of three samples

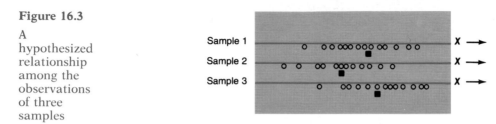

[2] In H_1 the following are included:

$$\mu_1 = \mu_2 \neq \mu_3$$

$$\mu_1 \neq \mu_2 = \mu_3$$

$$\mu_1 \neq \mu_2 \neq \mu_3$$

$$\mu_1 = \mu_3 \neq \mu_2$$

Statistical tools must be used to decide which of the alternative hypotheses we should accept.

We shall now explain the inferential argument (deriving the population structure from the sample structure) using a numerical example.

EXAMPLE 16.1

A cosmetics company is considering four container designs for its new antiperspirant: a metal spray container, a see-through glass spray container, a metal roll-on container, and a see-through glass roll-on container. All containers hold 5 ounces and cost the same to produce. It has been decided that, at least for the time being, only one container design is to be used, and the question, of course, is which of the four is most appealing to consumers. The marketing department decided to set a trial period during which containers of different designs would be sold in randomly selected stores across the country. The results of the trial period are shown in Table 16.1.

Let us first make a few comments about Table 16.1. First, the data are arranged in four groups. (As you recall, our explanation of Figures 16.1 and 16.2 may be extended to include more than three population groups.) Second, analysis of variance can be carried out when the number of observations in the various groups is either equal or unequal. In Table 16.1, not all the groups have the same number of sample observations. Third, the store number is simply a number chosen for convenience. The order in which the observations are listed within each group is arbitrary.

TABLE 16.1
Number of Containers Sold, by Design

Store	Metal spray	Glass spray	Metal roll-on	Glass roll-on
1	95	149	220	362
2	106	153	219	376
3	100	154	217	353
4	98	151	225	350
5	110	145	221	356
6	103	150	218	362
7	—	148	220	348
8	—	150	—	349
Mean	102	150	220	357

Example: The difference between these two figures is due to chance fluctuations.	Example: The difference between these two figures is primarily due to reasons other *than* chance.

One does not have to be an experienced statistician to conclude that the company will be better off selling its antiperspirant in glass roll-on containers. Is it possible that the mean of 357 containers sold in the glass roll-on design is only *by chance* greater than the mean of the sales of the other designs? While the possibility exists, the probability is so remote that it may be considered nil. The diversity of sales across stores *within* any of the four design categories is of far lesser magnitude than the diversity of sales between the four different design groups. Specifically, we attribute the variation in sales of the glass roll-on design among individual stores to chance fluctuations. We also attribute the diversity among sales of individual stores in any of the other three designs to chance fluctuations. But the difference between the 95 metal spray containers sold by the first store (and for that matter any other sales figure taken from the same group) and the 356 glass roll-on containers sold by the fifth store (and for that matter any other sales figure taken from the same group) is primarily attributable to the fact that the glass roll-on design is overwhelmingly preferred by consumers.

The data in Example 16.1 are unusual in that the variations in sales *within* each group are relatively small, while the variations *between* the groups are relatively large. (We set up these hypothetical data in such a way as to make our point as clearly as possible.) When actual rather than hypothetical data are involved, the difference between diversity *within* the groups and diversity *between* the groups is often less clear, and the use of a statistical procedure is required for objective decision making. It is clear, however, that if the variance between the groups is relatively large in comparison to the variances within the groups, we tend to believe that the samples are taken from populations with different means. If the variances within the groups are relatively large, we tend to believe that the difference in the means of the samples merely reflects sampling variations. That is to say, if we repeated the sampling of the various groups many times, the differences between the sample means would tend toward zero. Since we have only one sample from each group, however, statistical tools are needed to interpret the differences.

ALTERNATIVE TYPES OF ANALYSES OF VARIANCE

In this text we shall deal with two types of analyses of variance. The first, known as **one-way analysis of variance**, treats *populations that are classified by one characteristic*. An example is the weight of produce grown with alternative fertilizers. Here the classification is by the type of fertilizer used, and the null hypothesis is that the mean produce weight is the same for all the fertilizers of interest.

When the number of alternative fertilizers is two, we simply use the *t* test for equality of two means. When the number of fertilizers is greater than two, a one-way analysis of variance is used to test the equality of the mean produce weight. It follows that analysis of variance is an extension of the *t* test to more than two populations.

Recall that we have presented two *t* tests for equality of two means: one for two independent samples and the other for two matched samples. Accordingly, there are two sample designs in analysis of variance. The **completely randomized design** *extends the t test of independent samples to J > 2 independent samples*. An example would be a study of the mean level of productivity of production workers on three work shifts. If the sample of each shift consists of randomly selected workers, the design is completely randomized. The **randomized block design** *extends the t test of matched samples to J > 2 matched samples*. An example would be a study of the mean level of productivity of production workers on three work shifts for which we choose a sample of workers to observe during three different shifts. The matching of the observations is obtained by utilizing the very same workers and observing their productivity during different shifts. The workers chosen for the sample are referred to as "blocks," and the randomization is achieved by observing the workers through the work shifts in different orders. For example, if Worker *A* is observed first during shift 1, then during shift 2, and finally during shift 3, Worker *B* might be observed in a different order, say during shifts 3, 1, and 2, in order to randomize the observations. Although the analysis of the randomized block design is quite similar to the analysis of the completely randomized design, only the latter will be presented here.

An extension of the one-way analysis of variance is the **two-way analysis of variance,** which treats populations that are classified by two characteristics. An example is the weight of produce grown with alternative fertilizers and alternative irrigation methods. The type of fertilizer provides one classification scheme and the method of irrigation provides the other scheme. The analysis is flexible and takes the posture that every combination of fertilizer and method of irrigation defines a population whose mean could be different from the mean of the rest of the combinations. With 4 fertilizers and 3 irrigation methods, there are 12 populations of interest, as Table 16.2 shows. We will start our formal treatment with one-way ANOVA and then turn to the presentation of two-way ANOVA.

TABLE 16.2
Populations Classified by Fertilizer and Method of Irrigation

Irrigation method	*Fertilizer*			
	A	*B*	*C*	*D*
X				
Y				
Z				

There are 12 populations, each of which is defined by a combination of fertilizer and irrigation method.

16.2 One-Way Analysis of Variance

Suppose we want to test the hypothesis that the time required to replace old mufflers with new ones in compact cars is the same at three large muffler shops. The time from check-in to check-out is measured at the three shops for a few randomly selected cars. The results (in minutes) are reported in Table 16.3. Naturally, the mean number of minutes spent by the sampled cars in the three shops is unequal. This variation is to be expected, whether the groups' means are equal to one another or not. (That is to say, even if the means were equal, we would expect unequal sample means as a result of sampling errors.) What we want to find out is whether these differences should lead us to conclude that the groups' *means* are unequal. More formally, we want to test

$$H_0: \quad \mu_1 = \mu_2 = \mu_3$$

against

$$H_1: \quad \text{Not all means are equal.}$$

TABLE 16.3
Muffler Replacement Time in Three Muffler Shops
(in minutes)

Observation (i)	Shop (j) 1	Shop (j) 2	Shop (j) 3
1	120	200	160
2	100	160	80
3	174	110	110
4	140	180	100
5	90	100	180
6	90	160	—
7	—	140	—
$\sum_i X_{ij}$	714	1,050	630
n_j	6	7	5
$\bar{X}_{\cdot j}$	$\dfrac{714}{6} = 119$	$\dfrac{1,050}{7} = 150$	$\dfrac{630}{5} = 126$
$\bar{\bar{X}}$	$\dfrac{714 + 1,050 + 630}{6 + 7 + 5} = \dfrac{2,394}{18} = 133$		

BEGINNING THE ANALYSIS: BASIC PROCEDURES

At this point, we must introduce new notation and equations to develop the test statistic and decision rule. Let us briefly consider these new items.

Summing Observations Within Groups   The sample data in Table 16.3 are organized in three columns representing three shops (or groups, in more general terms) and several rows representing the sequential observations in the groups. To facilitate reference to the various sample observations we shall use the notation X_{ij} to denote the ith observation in the jth group. For example, X_{11} is equal to 120, the value of the first observation in Shop 1. Similarly, $X_{21} = 100$, $X_{42} = 180$, and so on. The number of observations in Group j is denoted by n_j. Thus $n_1 = 6$, $n_2 = 7$, and $n_3 = 5$. The sum of all the observations in Group j is given by $\sum_i X_{ij}$, so for $j = 1$ we obtain $\sum_i X_{i1}$, meaning the sum of all the observations within Group 1. Similarly, $\sum_i X_{i2}$ and $\sum_i X_{i3}$ are the sums of all the observations in Groups 2 and 3, respectively. For Table 16.3 we get

$$\sum_i X_{i1} = 714$$

$$\sum_i X_{i2} = 1,050$$

$$\sum_i X_{i3} = 630$$

Finding the Averages Within Groups   To find the **mean (average) value within a given group**, we simply divide the total value of all the observations in the group by the number of observations in that particular group. The group mean is denoted by $\bar{X}_{\cdot j}$, where the dot symbolizes the fact that the average was carried out across the index i. The following formula applies:

AVERAGE WITHIN THE GROUP

$$\bar{X}_{\cdot j} = \frac{\sum\limits_{i} X_{ij}}{n_j} \tag{16.1}$$

For example, if $j = 3$, we get $\sum\limits_{i} X_{i3} = 630$, $n_3 = 5$, and thus $\bar{X}_{\cdot 3} = \frac{630}{5} = 126$.

The Grand Average Here we want to introduce the notations n and $\bar{\bar{X}}$ ("X double bar"). First

$$n = \sum\limits_{j} n_j \tag{16.2}$$

Next

GRAND AVERAGE

$$\bar{\bar{X}} = \frac{\sum\limits_{i}\sum\limits_{j} X_{ij}}{n} \tag{16.3}$$

where $\sum\limits_{i}\sum\limits_{j} X_{ij}$ means summation of all the X_{ij} in all groups. The notation n then stands for the total number of observations in all the available groups.

Since, in our case, $n_1 = 6$, $n_2 = 7$, and $n_3 = 5$, we get

$$n = 6 + 7 + 5 = 18$$

The **grand average**, $\bar{\bar{X}}$, is simply the *mean (average) of all the observations in the sample*. As one can easily verify, the total of all the available observations $\sum\limits_{i}\sum\limits_{j} X_{ij}$ is equal to 2,394, so $\bar{\bar{X}} = \frac{2,394}{18} = 133.$[3]

TOTAL VARIATIONS

Suppose we ignore the grouping of the sample observations and treat them all as observations drawn from the same population. We may then compute the **total sum of squares** by adding up the squared deviations of all of the

[3] Note that

$$\bar{\bar{X}} = \frac{\sum\limits_{i}\sum\limits_{j} X_{ij}}{n} = \frac{\sum\limits_{j}\left(\sum\limits_{i} X_{ij}\right)}{n} = \frac{\sum\limits_{j} n_j \bar{X}_{\cdot j}}{n} = \sum\limits_{j}\left(\frac{n_j}{n}\right)\bar{X}_{\cdot j}$$

where the last term shows that $\bar{\bar{X}}$ is a weighted average of the groups' means.

sample observations from the grand average, $\overline{\overline{X}}$. Denoting the total sum of squares by SS_t, we find

---

TOTAL SUM OF SQUARES

$$SS_t = \sum_i \sum_j (X_{ij} - \overline{\overline{X}})^2 \qquad (16.4)$$

Using the data of Table 16.3, we compute

$$SS_t = (120 - 133)^2 + (100 - 133)^2 + (174 - 133)^2 + \cdots + (180 - 133)^2$$

$$= 23,874$$

Next, as we shall see, the total sum of squares, SS_t, can be separated into two components: the sum of the squares *within* each group and the sum of squares *between* the groups.

WITHIN-GROUP VARIATIONS

To obtain the **sum of squares within the groups**, which we denote by SS_w, we add up the squared deviations of all observations from each group's average:[4]

SUM OF SQUARES WITHIN THE GROUPS

$$SS_w = \sum_j \sum_i (X_{ij} - \overline{X}_{\cdot j})^2 \qquad (16.5)$$

In our example we obtain

for $j = 1$: $(120 - 119)^2 + (100 - 119)^2 + (174 - 119)^2 + (140 - 119)^2$
$+ (90 - 119)^2 + (90 - 119)^2 = 5,510$

for $j = 2$: $(200 - 150)^2 + (160 - 150)^2 + (110 - 150)^2 + (180 - 150)^2$
$+ (100 - 150)^2 + (160 - 150)^2 + (140 - 150)^2 = 7,800$

for $j = 3$: $(160 - 126)^2 + (80 - 126)^2 + (110 - 126)^2 + (100 - 126)^2$
$+ (180 - 126)^2 = 7,120$

and

$$SS_w = 5,510 + 7,800 + 7,120 = 20,430$$

The sum of squares within the groups is sometimes referred to as the **unexplained sum of squares**; since we do not identify any particular cause for this type of variation, we say that it is due to chance.

---

[4] Note that the inside summation sign in Equation 16.5 is for the index i, while the outside summation sign is for the index j. The reason for this is as follows: when there is a double summation we need to sum over the inner index first and over the outer index second. Since we want to obtain the sum of squares within the groups, we need to sum over all the observations in Group 1 before continuing with the second and third groups. This can be achieved if we hold $j = 1$ and sum the squared deviations for the various observations in Group 1, then change j to $j = 2$ and sum the squared deviations for the various observations in Group 2, and so on.

BETWEEN-GROUP VARIATIONS

The **sum of squares between the groups**, SS_b, is a measure that reflects the variability of the sample averages of the groups' means. We add up the squared deviations of each group average ($\overline{X}_{\cdot j}$) from the grand average ($\overline{\overline{X}}$) after it has been multiplied by the number of observations in each group (n_j) to get

---

SUM OF SQUARES BETWEEN THE GROUPS

$$SS_b = \sum_j n_j(\overline{X}_{\cdot j} - \overline{\overline{X}})^2 \tag{16.6}$$

We note that when a squared deviation $(\overline{X}_{\cdot j} - \overline{\overline{X}})^2$ is multiplied by n_j, the group size attains its appropriate weight relative to the sample size, n. In our example we find

$$SS_b = 6 \cdot (119 - 133)^2 + 7 \cdot (150 - 133)^2 + 5 \cdot (126 - 133)^2$$

$$= 6 \cdot 196 + 7 \cdot 289 + 5 \cdot 49$$

$$= 3{,}444$$

Adding up SS_w and SS_b, we compute $20{,}430 + 3{,}444 = 23{,}874$, which is equal to the total sum of squares. Since this result holds in general, we come up with the following formula:

TOTAL SUM OF SQUARES

$$SS_t = SS_w + SS_b \tag{16.7}$$

The **total sum of squares**, SS_t, can be separated into the sum of the squares within the groups, SS_w, and the sum of the squares between the groups, SS_b. In this way, the total variability is separated into its components and analyzed.

MEAN SQUARES WITHIN GROUPS AND BETWEEN GROUPS

As we approach the main purpose of this exercise we must remember that our principal goal in conducting an analysis of variance is to find out whether the primary source of the variance is variations within the groups or between the groups. To that end we analyze SS_t into its components, SS_w and SS_b, and compare the two components. Before we can compare the magnitude of these two components, however, we have to convert them into *mean squared deviations*; thus both SS_w and SS_b must be divided by their respective degrees of freedom.

There are n deviations built into the SS_w formula. Each deviation is measured around its respective group mean. Each group mean is *estimated* by the sample observations and uses up one degree of freedom out of the n independent observations provided by the sample. Denoting the number of groups by J, we conclude that the number of degrees of freedom in SS_w is $n - J$. From this we can derive the following equation:

MEAN SQUARED DEVIATION WITHIN THE GROUPS

$$MS_w = \frac{SS_w}{n - J} \qquad (16.8)$$

Turning now to the SS_b, we realize that there are J group averages and J deviations of the averages around the grand average, $\bar{\bar{X}}$. Since by estimating $\bar{\bar{X}}$ we used up one degree of freedom, the number of degrees of freedom in SS_b is $J - 1$. The following equation can thus be derived:

MEAN SQUARED DEVIATION BETWEEN THE GROUPS

$$MS_b = \frac{SS_b}{J - 1} \qquad (16.9)$$

In our example, where $n = 18$ and $J = 3$, we obtain

$$MS_w = \frac{SS_w}{n - J} = \frac{20,430}{18 - 3} = 1,362$$

and

$$MS_b = \frac{SS_b}{J - 1} = \frac{3,444}{3 - 1} = 1,722$$

THE TEST STATISTIC

Assuming that the sample observations are drawn independently from a normal distribution and that the null hypothesis is correct,[5] it can be shown that the ratio of MS_b to MS_w has an F distribution with $J - 1$ and $n - J$ degrees of freedom.[6]

---

[5] We assume in addition that the variances in the various groups are equal. Thus if H_0 does not hold, the groups differ in their means but are equal in variance.

[6] Assuming that the distributions are normal and that the null hypothesis is correct and recalling our assumption that the variances in the various groups (σ^2) are equal to one another, the quantity SS_b/σ^2 can be shown to have a χ^2 distribution with $J - 1$ degrees of freedom. It follows that

$$\frac{SS_b}{(J - 1)\sigma^2} = \frac{MS_b}{\sigma^2} \sim \frac{\chi^{2(J-1)}}{J - 1}.$$

Similarly it can be shown that the quantity SS_w/σ^2 has a χ^2 distribution with $n - J$ degrees of freedom, so that $\frac{SS_w}{(n - J)\sigma^2} = \frac{MS_w}{\sigma^2} \sim \frac{\chi^{2(n-J)}}{n - J}$. From the definition of the F variable, it follows that

$$\frac{MS_b/\sigma^2}{MS_w/\sigma^2} = \frac{MS_b}{MS_w} \sim F^{(J-1, n-J)}$$

$$\frac{MS_b}{MS_w} \sim F^{(J-1,n-J)} \qquad\qquad (16.10)$$

Thus the ratio in Equation 16.10 serves as a test statistic. A ratio in the neighborhood of 1 indicates that MS_b is about the same magnitude as MS_w. In this case, the null hypothesis, which states that all the groups' means are equal, cannot be rejected. A computed ratio substantially greater than 1, on the other hand, indicates that the mean squared deviation between the groups is large in relation to the mean squared deviation within the groups, and we will tend to reject this null hypothesis.

Given a significance level α, we can easily determine the acceptance and rejection regions and accept or reject H_0 accordingly. Since the numerator of the test statistic is squared, large deviations between the samples' means imply that we obtain a large value for the test statistic. Thus the test is necessarily an upper-tail test; the critical value is given by $F_\alpha^{(J-1,n-J)}$ and the decision rule is

Do not reject H_0 if

$$\frac{MS_b}{MS_w} \leq F_\alpha^{(J-1,n-J)}$$

Reject H_0 if

$$\frac{MS_b}{MS_w} > F_\alpha^{(J-1,n-J)}$$

Returning to our example (Table 16.3) and assuming $\alpha = 0.05$, we find that

$$F_\alpha^{(J-1,n-J)} = F_{0.05}^{(2,15)} = 3.68$$

so that our decision rule is (see Figure 16.4)

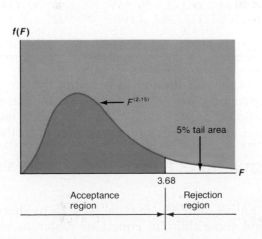

f(F)

$F^{(2,15)}$

5% tail area

3.68

Acceptance region

Rejection region

F

Figure 16.4

Acceptance and rejection regions for a one-way ANOVA

$$\text{Do not reject } H_0 \text{ if } \frac{MS_b}{MS_w} \leq 3.68$$

$$\text{Reject } H_0 \text{ if } \frac{MS_b}{MS_w} > 3.68$$

Substituting the figures derived earlier, we get

$$\frac{MS_b}{MS_w} = \frac{1{,}722}{1{,}362} = 1.264$$

and we cannot reject H_0. It is customary and convenient to summarize the sums of squares, the degrees of freedom, the mean squares, and the test statistic in a table such as Table 16.4. The numerical example is summarized in Table 16.5.

TABLE 16.4
One-Way Analysis of Variance Summary Table

Source of variation	Sum of squares	df	Mean square	F
Between groups	$SS_b = \sum_j n_j(\overline{X}_{.j} - \overline{\overline{X}})^2$	$J - 1$	$MS_b = \dfrac{SS_b}{J - 1}$	
				$\dfrac{MS_b}{MS_w} \sim F^{(J-1, n-J)}$
Within groups	$SS_w = \sum_j \sum_i (X_{ij} - \overline{X}_{.j})^2$	$n - J$	$MS_w = \dfrac{SS_w}{n - J}$	
Total	$SS_t = \sum_i \sum_j (X_{ij} - \overline{\overline{X}})^2$ $= SS_w + SS_b$	$n - 1$		

TABLE 16.5
One-Way Analysis of Variance Summary Table: The Numerical Example

Source of variation	Sum of squares	df	Mean square	F
Between groups	3,444	2	1,722	
				$\dfrac{1{,}722}{1{,}362} = 1.264$
Within groups	20,430	15	1,362	
Total	23,874	17		

Since the value of the test statistic falls within the acceptance region, we conclude that although MS_b is greater than MS_w, the difference may be due to sampling variation. The variance between groups is not large relative to the variance within groups; therefore, we do not reject the null hypothesis.

SHORTCUT EQUATIONS FOR ONE-WAY ANALYSIS OF VARIANCE

The equations for SS_b and SS_w may be written in shortened form. Since some students find these shortcut equations easier to work with, we will present them here. Let us define the quantities A, B, and C as follows:

$$A = \sum_i \sum_j X_{ij}^2 \tag{16.11}$$

$$B = \frac{1}{n}\left(\sum_i \sum_j X_{ij}\right)^2 \tag{16.12}$$

$$C = \sum_j \left(\frac{1}{n_j}\right)\left(\sum_i X_{ij}\right)^2 \tag{16.13}$$

Quantity A is simply the sum of all the *squared* sample observations. Quantity B is the squared value of the sum of all the sample observations, divided by the total sample size. Quantity C is the sum of the squares of the totals of all the groups, each group's total divided by the number of observations in the group. The computations of A, B, and C can be best understood by referring back to the data of Table 16.3:

$$A = 120^2 + 100^2 + 174^2 + \cdots + 180^2 = 342,276$$

$$B = \frac{1}{18}(120 + 100 + 174 + \cdots + 180)^2 = \frac{5,731,236}{18} = 318,402$$

$$C = \frac{1}{6}(120 + 100 + \cdots + 90)^2 + \frac{1}{7}(200 + 160 + \cdots + 140)^2$$

$$+ \frac{1}{5}(160 + 80 + \cdots + 180)^2 = 84,966 + 157,500 + 79,380$$

$$= 321,846$$

It can be shown that

$$SS_b = C - B \tag{16.14}$$

and

$$SS_w = A - C \tag{16.15}$$

In our example

$$SS_b = 321,846 - 318,402 = 3,444$$

$$SS_w = 342,276 - 321,846 = 20,430$$

This is clearly the same sum of squares that we obtained earlier.

Before turning to the next topic, let us look at one more example of one-way analysis of variance.

EXAMPLE 16.2

The Center for Management Development is organizing advanced seminars for the upper and middle management of business firms. The seminars will be held several times every year in three geographical locations, *A*, *B*, and *C*. The Center is interested in knowing whether differences exist between the mean number of applications received in the three locations. The number of applications received for a sample of 31 courses is reported in Table 16.6.

TABLE 16.6
Applications Received in Three Locations

| Observation | Location | | |
	A	B	C
1	200	180	155
2	210	199	200
3	220	223	127
4	202	224	137
5	180	120	200
6	199	250	198
7	177	120	199
8	198	155	210
9	190	230	
10	223	123	
11		120	
12		119	
13		100	

Figure 16.5 presents an SAS (Statistical Analysis System) computer printout showing the analysis-of-variance table. The between-group variation is referred to as the "model" and the within-group variation is referred to as "error." The F ratio is equal to 2.05, a value that bounds a right-hand-side tail equal to 0.1475 on the $F^{(2,28)}$ distribution. Therefore, the null hypothesis of equality of means should not be rejected at significance levels smaller than 14.75 percent. The printout also shows the model's "R-square" (r^2) value, which is equal to 0.127762, or approximately 12.78 percent. This means that the model's sum of squares (6,392.46) is equal to 12.78 percent of the total sum of squares (50,033.94): 6,392.46/50,033.94 = 0.1278. A more thorough explanation of r^2 is provided in the next chapter, which deals with regression analysis.

Figure 16.5

An SAS computer printout reproduction showing one-way analysis of variance

```
                    ANALYSIS OF VARIANCE PROCEDURE

DEPENDENT VARIABLE: SALES

SOURCE           DF   SUM OF SQUARES    MEAN SQUARE   F VALUE  PR > F  R-SQUARE

MODEL             2    6392.45856079  3196.22928040     2.05  0.1475  0.127762

ERROR            28   43641.47692308  1558.62417582

CORRECTED TOTAL  30   50033.93548387
```

16.3 Analysis of Groups

The analysis of variance is not necessarily completed with the acceptance or rejection of the null hypothesis. In many cases we will be interested in obtaining confidence intervals for the means of individual groups or for differences between pairs of means. This type of analysis might be of greater importance when the conclusion of the analysis of variance is that not all the means are equal.

INTERVAL ESTIMATION OF AN INDIVIDUAL MEAN

An assumption we made earlier is that the variances of all the populations (groups) to which we apply the analysis of variance are the same. This assumption is made regardless of whether the null hypothesis is rejected or accepted. Consequently, we can use the entire sample (i.e., the observations of all the groups) to obtain an estimate of the within-group variance. Stated more directly, MS_w, which is an estimator of the within-group variance, serves as an estimator of the variance of any individual group as well as for the entire sample of J groups, regardless of whether or not the groups' means are equal.

When we derived a confidence interval for the mean of a population using the simple t statistic, the $1 - \alpha$ confidence interval was from $\overline{X} - t_{\alpha/2}^{(n-1)}S_{\overline{X}}$ to $\overline{X} + t_{\alpha/2}^{(n-1)}S_{\overline{X}}$, where $S_{\overline{X}} = S/\sqrt{n}$ (assuming an infinite population). To do the same thing for an individual group in an analysis of variance, we proceed as follows:

1. The group mean, μ_j, is estimated by the sample group mean, $\overline{X}_{\cdot j}$.
2. The variance of the group is estimated by MS_w, and the standard deviation is estimated by $\sqrt{MS_w}$.
3. To obtain the estimated variance of $\overline{X}_{\cdot j}$, we divide MS_w by the number of observations in the group: $S_{\overline{X}_{\cdot j}}^2 = MS_w/n_j$. This is analogous to $S_{\overline{X}}^2 = S^2/n$ when calculating the usual confidence interval for the mean of one population and the variance is unknown.
4. Since $S_{\overline{X}_{\cdot j}}^2$ is estimated by MS_w/n_j and since MS_w has $n - J$ degrees of freedom, the t distribution we use is the one that has $n - J$ degrees of freedom.
5. Therefore, a confidence interval for the mean, μ_j, of the jth group is from $\overline{X}_{\cdot j} - t_{\alpha/2}^{(n-J)} \sqrt{\dfrac{MS_w}{n_j}}$ to $\overline{X}_{\cdot j} + t_{\alpha/2}^{(n-J)} \sqrt{\dfrac{MS_w}{n_j}}$, which is analogous to the interval from $\overline{X} - t_{\alpha/2}^{(n-1)} S_{\overline{X}}$ to $\overline{X} + t_{\alpha/2}^{(n-1)} S_{\overline{X}}$ in the simple case of one population.

To summarize:

$$S_{\overline{X}_{\cdot j}}^2 = \frac{MS_w}{n_j} \tag{16.16}$$

and the confidence interval for μ_j is given by

$$\overline{X}_{\cdot j} \pm t_{\alpha/2}^{(n-J)} \cdot S_{\overline{X}_{\cdot j}} \tag{16.17}$$

where

$$S_{\overline{X}_{\cdot j}} = \sqrt{\frac{MS_w}{n_j}} \tag{16.18}$$

For example, the relevant data for constructing a 95 percent confidence interval for the mean of the first group in Table 16.3 are as follows:

$$\overline{X}_{\cdot 1} = 119, n_1 = 6, n = 18, J = 3, \text{ and } MS_w = 1{,}362$$

Next we calculate

$$S^2_{\overline{X}_{\cdot 1}} = \frac{MS_w}{n_1} = \frac{1{,}362}{6} = 227$$

and

$$S_{\overline{X}_{\cdot 1}} = \sqrt{227} = 15.067$$

The value of $t^{(n-J)}_{0.025} = t^{(15)}_{0.025}$ is 2.131, so the 95 percent confidence interval ranges from

$$\overline{X}_{\cdot 1} - t^{(15)}_{0.025} S_{\overline{X}_{\cdot 1}} = 119 - 2.131 \cdot 15.067 = 86.892$$

to

$$\overline{X}_{\cdot 1} + t^{(15)}_{0.025} S_{\overline{X}_{\cdot 1}} = 119 + 2.131 \cdot 15.067 = 151.108$$

We recommend that you construct a 95 percent confidence interval for the mean of Group *A* of Example 16.2.

CONFIDENCE INTERVAL FOR A DIFFERENCE BETWEEN TWO MEANS

A similar procedure can be followed in order to construct a confidence interval for the difference between the means of two groups. The point estimator of the difference is given by the difference between the two sample means: $\overline{X}_{\cdot j'} - \overline{X}_{\cdot j''}$, where j' and j'' are any two groups. The variance of the difference is given by $V(\overline{X}_{\cdot j'} - \overline{X}_{\cdot j''}) = V(\overline{X}_{\cdot j'}) + V(\overline{X}_{\cdot j''})$, since the samples are independent. These variances are estimated by the same statistic as presented earlier when we constructed a confidence interval for one mean:

$$S^2_{\overline{X}_{\cdot j'} - \overline{X}_{\cdot j''}} = \frac{MS_w}{n_{j'}} + \frac{MS_w}{n_{j''}} = MS_w\left(\frac{1}{n_{j'}} + \frac{1}{n_{j''}}\right) \tag{16.19}$$

and here again the variable t has the degrees of freedom of MS_w, namely, $n - J$. In short, the $1 - \alpha$ confidence interval is

$$(\overline{X}_{\cdot j'} - \overline{X}_{\cdot j''}) \pm t^{(n-J)}_{\alpha/2} \sqrt{MS_w\left(\frac{1}{n_{j'}} + \frac{1}{n_{j''}}\right)} \tag{16.20}$$

Using the data given in Table 16.3, let us construct a 95 percent confidence interval for the difference between the means of Groups 1 and 3. The data are as follows:

Group 1	Group 3
$\overline{X}_{\cdot 1} = 119$	$\overline{X}_{\cdot 3} = 126$
$n_1 = 6$	$n_3 = 5$
$n = 18, J = 3, MS_w = 1{,}362, t_{0.025}^{(15)} = 2.131$	

Therefore the confidence interval is from

$$(\overline{X}_{\cdot 1} - \overline{X}_{\cdot 3}) - t_{0.025}^{(15)}\sqrt{MS_w\left(\frac{1}{n_1} + \frac{1}{n_3}\right)} = (119 - 126) - 2.131\sqrt{1{,}362\left(\frac{1}{6} + \frac{1}{5}\right)}$$

$$= -7 - 47.622$$
$$= -54.622$$

to

$$(\overline{X}_{\cdot 1} - \overline{X}_{\cdot 3}) + t_{0.025}^{(15)}\sqrt{MS_w\left(\frac{1}{n_1} + \frac{1}{n_3}\right)} = (119 - 126) + 2.131\sqrt{1{,}362\left(\frac{1}{6} + \frac{1}{5}\right)}$$

$$= -7 + 47.622$$
$$= 40.622$$

Clearly, this interval is much too wide to be meaningful, but this problem could be dealt with in a real situation by increasing the sample size, which in this example is especially small. We recommend that you construct a 95 percent confidence interval for the difference between the means of Groups *A* and *B* of Example 16.2.

MULTIPLE COMPARISONS

Since analysis of variance is carried out on more than two groups, it is clear that we can make more than one pairwise comparison of group means. But the question arises: what level of significance is associated with the *simultaneous* holding of these intervals? If the level of confidence of each of two intervals is $1 - \alpha/2$, the level of confidence we have in the simultaneous holding of *both* intervals is less than $1 - \alpha/2$. But it can be shown that it is *at least* $1 - \alpha$. In general, we can state the following rule:

If each of k confidence intervals is constructed with a confidence level of $1 - \alpha/k$, then we have *at least* a level of confidence of $1 - \alpha$ that all k confidence levels hold simultaneously.

For example, if each of three confidence intervals has a confidence level of 0.98, then we have at least a confidence level of 0.94 that all three intervals hold simultaneously because $k = 3$ and $\alpha = 0.06$ and therefore $1 - \alpha/k = 0.98$ and $1 - \alpha = 0.94$.

16.4 Two-Way Analysis of Variance

One-way analysis of variance is conducted to test the simultaneous equality of means of different probability distributions or groups. The groups are defined by a single classification—location, design, religion, company, and so on. But **two-way analysis of variance**, as its name suggests, is *the analysis of probability distributions or groups defined by dual classification*. In principle, one-way and two-way analyses of variance are similar: the purpose is to find out whether or not the means of all the populations considered are equal to one another.

HOW TWO-WAY ANOVA WORKS: THE FUNDAMENTAL APPROACH

Our explanation of two-way ANOVA will be greatly facilitated by a numerical example. Table 16.7 presents information on the production levels of various crews working on two types of machines. The data measure the results, in units per day, of five days of production by three crews. Thus five observations are given for each combination of machine and crew. The purpose of the two-way analysis of variance is threefold:

1. To determine whether production level varies among the three crews
2. To determine whether production level varies between the two types of machine
3. To determine whether there is an interaction between the type of machine and the crew that uses it, in terms of productivity; that is, we want to determine whether some specific combination of machine and crew results in greater productivity

As in one-way ANOVA, we assign the index i to the table's rows and the index j to its columns, so for Table 16.7 we have $i = 1, 2$ and $j = 1, 2, 3$.

Why would we want to examine differences in productivity? If there is a significant difference in productivity among the crews, it may have implications for wage determination, employee promotion, and so on. If there is a significant difference in the machines' productivity, management may want to use just one type of machine instead of two. Finally, there is a much more delicate question: is it possible that there is an interaction between crews and machines? It may be that Crew *A* produces much more with the first type of machine than with the second type, while the opposite may be true of Crew *B*. If there is evidence to support such a hypothesis, the manager

TABLE 16.7
Production (Units Completed) by Type of Machine and Crew

Type of machine	Crew		
	A ($j = 1$)	*B* ($j = 2$)	*C* ($j = 3$)
Type 1 ($i = 1$)	90 95 80 85 89	75 86 80 83 90	72 88 83 82 78
Type 2 ($i = 2$)	88 85 79 75 78	81 83 74 69 74	69 63 72 80 85

can use it in assigning crews to machines. If such interaction exists, having two types of machine may be the best policy. Thus, a table of data such as Table 16.7 provides the basic input for two-way ANOVA; with the same basic data we can decide whether there is a difference in the average productivity of the two types of machine, whether there is a difference in the average productivity of the crews, and whether there is any interaction between crew and machine.

To pursue our threefold study, we must have at least a few observations in each cell of the dual-classification table. The number of observations in each cell should be the same, and so we shall assume that indeed the same number of observations is available in each. We shall denote the number of columns by J, the number of rows by I, and the number of observations in each cell by K. The index of the observations within the cells is k. Thus

$$i = 1, 2, \ldots, I$$
$$j = 1, 2, \ldots, J$$
$$k = 1, 2, \ldots, K$$

We shall assume that the observations in each cell are drawn from a normal distribution and that the variances of the distributions of all cells are equal.

Each observation in the sample is identifiable by a triple index: *ijk*. Thus X_{ijk} is the value obtained in the sample for the kth observation in the jth column and the ith row. Suppose now that the mean number of units produced is the same for the three crews and two types of machine and that there is no interaction effect on the productivity. In other words, suppose the mean population values in all cells are equal and denote these means by μ. In this case, each observation may be described as

$$X_{ijk} = \mu + Z_{ijk} \tag{16.21}$$

where Z_{ijk} is a random "error" with a normal distribution with mean equals 0 and constant variance[7]. If this is the case, then

$$E(X_{ijk}) = \mu + E(Z_{ijk}) = \mu \tag{16.22}$$

If we hypothetically assume $\mu = 80$ for our production example, the observations' *means* in the various cells are the ones listed in Table 16.8.

TABLE 16.8
Means of Observations in Cells: The Case of Equal Means

Type of machine	Crew			Average of row
	A	B	C	
Type 1	80	80	80	80
Type 2	80	80	80	80
Average of column	80	80	80	80

---

[7] We assume that all the observations are independent random samples drawn from normal distributions with equal variance. When the normality assumption is not plausible, we would use a nonparametric test (see Chapter 22).

The Column Effect   Now suppose, on the other hand, that the three crews have different mean production performances; we still assume that the type of machine has no effect on production. In this situation it is useful to define a parameter, ξ_j (*xi sub j*), for each column, to reflect the difference in mean production performance across the columns, which is called the **column effect**. For example, if $\xi_1 = 5$, $\xi_2 = -8$, and $\xi_3 = 3$, the implication is that the mean number of units produced by Crew *A* is $80 + 5 = 85$ (we still assume that the mean for all the table's cells is 80), that the mean number of units produced by Crew *B* is $80 - 8 = 72$, and that produced by Crew *C* is $80 + 3 = 83$. In this kind of situation we can think of X_{ijk} as the sum of the factors

$$X_{ijk} = \mu + \xi_j + Z_{ijk} \tag{16.23}$$

and

$$E(X_{ijk}) = \mu + \xi_j + E(Z_{ijk}) = \mu + \xi_j \tag{16.24}$$

The cells' means for this case are given in Table 16.9.

TABLE 16.9
Means of Cells When $\xi_1 = 5$, $\xi_2 = -8$, $\xi_3 = 3$: The Column Effect

Type of machine	Crew			Average of row
	A	*B*	*C*	
Type 1	85	72	83	80
Type 2	85	72	83	80
Average of column	$\mu + \xi_1 = 85$	$\mu + \xi_2 = 72$	$\mu + \xi_3 = 83$	$\mu = 80$
	$[\xi_1 = 5]$	$[\xi_2 = -8]$	$[\xi_3 = 3]$	

The Row Effect   Now let us make a different assumption: that the crew has no effect on the mean score but the type of machine does. We can define ψ_i (*psi sub i*) as the **row effect**—a factor that reflects differences between the mean numbers of units produced by the two machines. In this case, the value X_{ijk} can be thought of as

$$X_{ijk} = \mu + \psi_i + Z_{ijk} \tag{16.25}$$

and

$$E(X_{ijk}) = \mu + \psi_i + E(Z_{ijk}) = \mu + \psi_i \tag{16.26}$$

If we assume hypothetically that $\psi_1 = 4$ and $\psi_2 = -4$, the means in the various cells are those listed in Table 16.10.

TABLE 16.10
Means of Cells When $\psi_1 = 4$ and $\psi_2 = -4$: The Row Effect

Type of machine	Crew			Average of row	
	A	*B*	*C*		
Type 1	84	84	84	$\mu + \psi_1 = 84$	$[\psi_1 = 4]$
Type 2	76	76	76	$\mu + \psi_2 = 76$	$[\psi_2 = -4]$
Average of column	80	80	80	$\mu = 80$	

Simultaneous Column and Row Effects So far we have hypothesized a situation in which there is a column effect (ξ_j) with no row effect ($\psi_i = 0$ for all i) and a situation in which there is a row effect (ψ_i) but no column effect ($\xi_j = 0$ for all j). Needless to say, column and row effects may exist simultaneously. To illustrate, let us assume that the previously assumed ξ and ψ values hold simultaneously. Each observation can now be described by

$$X_{ijk} = \mu + \xi_j + \psi_i + Z_{ijk} \tag{16.27}$$

and

$$E(X_{ijk}) = \mu + \xi_j + \psi_i + E(Z_{ijk}) = \mu + \xi_j + \psi_i \tag{16.28}$$

Table 16.11 lists the mean scores in the various cells. It shows, for example, that the mean production by Crew A when it works on the Type 1 machine is 89, which equals the average $\mu = 80$ plus the Crew A effect ($\xi_1 = 5$) plus the Type 1 machine effect ($\psi_1 = 4$): $80 + 5 + 4 = 89$.

TABLE 16.11
Means of Cells When Column and Row Effects Exist Simultaneously

Type of machine	Crew			Average of row	
	A	*B*	*C*		
Type 1	$\mu + \xi_1 + \psi_1 = 89$	$\mu + \xi_2 + \psi_1 = 76$	$\mu + \xi_3 + \psi_1 = 87$	$\mu + \psi_1 = 84$	$[\psi_1 = 4]$
Type 2	$\mu + \xi_1 + \psi_2 = 81$	$\mu + \xi_2 + \psi_2 = 68$	$\mu + \xi_3 + \psi_2 = 79$	$\mu + \psi_2 = 76$	$[\psi_2 = -4]$
Average of column	$\mu + \xi_1 = 85$	$\mu + \xi_2 = 72$	$\mu + \xi_3 = 83$	$\mu = 80$	
	$[\xi_1 = 5]$	$[\xi_2 = -8]$	$[\xi_3 = 3]$		

The Interaction Effect In addition to column and row effects, we may encounter specific interaction effects. For example, it is conceivable that Crew A may get better results on a Type 1 machine than on a Type 2 machine, that Crew B may get better results on a Type 2 machine, and that Crew C may work at the same efficiency on both. Such a specific effect on individual cells is known as the **interaction effect** and is denoted by θ_{ij} (*theta* sub *ij*) for cell *ij*. The interaction effect can be studied only if we have more than one observation in each cell: $K > 1$. Considering column, row, and interaction effects together, we can write

$$X_{ijk} = \mu + \xi_j + \psi_i + \theta_{ij} + Z_{ijk} \tag{16.29}$$

and

$$E(X_{ijk}) = \mu + \xi_j + \psi_i + \theta_{ij} + E(Z_{ijk}) = \mu + \xi_j + \psi_i + \theta_{ij} \tag{16.30}$$

To illustrate, let us assume that $\theta_{11} = 1$, $\theta_{21} = 0$, $\theta_{12} = 2$, $\theta_{22} = -3$, $\theta_{13} = 2$, $\theta_{23} = -2$. The cells' means will now be as listed in Table 16.12.

Note: The mean production of Crew A on the Type 1 machine, 90, equals the average $\mu = 80$ plus the crew effect ($\xi_1 = 5$) plus the Type 1 machine effect ($\psi_1 = 4$) plus the interaction between Crew A and the Type 1 machine ($\theta_{11} = 1$). Thus $90 = 80 + 5 + 4 + 1$.

TABLE 16.12
Means of Cells When Column, Row, and Interaction Effects Exist Simultaneously

Type of machine	Crew			Average of row
	A	*B*	*C*	
Type 1	$\mu + \xi_1 + \psi_1 + \theta_{11} = 90$	$\mu + \xi_2 + \psi_1 + \theta_{12} = 78$	$\mu + \xi_3 + \psi_1 + \theta_{13} = 89$	$\mu + \psi_1 + \dfrac{\theta_{11} + \theta_{12} + \theta_{13}}{3}$ $= 85.67$
Type 2	$\mu + \xi_1 + \psi_2 + \theta_{21} = 81$	$\mu + \xi_2 + \psi_2 + \theta_{22} = 65$	$\mu + \xi_3 + \psi_2 + \theta_{23} = 77$	$\mu + \psi_2 + \dfrac{\theta_{21} + \theta_{22} + \theta_{23}}{3}$ $= 74.33$
Average of column	$\mu + \xi_1 + \dfrac{\theta_{11} + \theta_{21}}{2}$ $= 85.5$	$\mu + \xi_2 + \dfrac{\theta_{12} + \theta_{22}}{2}$ $= 71.5$	$\mu + \xi_3 + \dfrac{\theta_{13} + \theta_{23}}{2}$ $= 83.0$	$\mu = 80$

TESTING HYPOTHESES IN TWO-WAY ANOVA

In performing our two-way ANOVA, we assume that the general relationship given by Equation 16.29 holds and test to see whether the sample data indeed provide substantiating evidence or whether the data lead to the conclusion that all θ_{ij} and/or all ψ_i and/or all ξ_j are equal to zero. To test hypotheses of this kind we need to develop some notation and equations.

Let X_{ijk} denote the specific sample value of the kth observation in the ith row and jth column, and let $\overline{X}_{ij\cdot}$ denote the average value of the k sample observations in the ith row and jth column. Furthermore, let $\overline{X}_{i\cdot\cdot}$ be the average across *all* the observations in the ith row and let $\overline{X}_{\cdot j\cdot}$ be the sample average across *all* the observations in the jth column. Finally, we denote the average of all the sample observations (all rows and all columns) by $\overline{X}_{\cdot\cdot\cdot}$—the sample's grand average.

Disregarding the classification of the data into rows and columns, we can calculate the sum of squared deviations of the sample data around the sample's grand average (this sum of squared deviations we denote by SS_{total}) as follows:

$$SS_{\text{total}} = \sum_{i=1}^{I} \sum_{j=1}^{J} \sum_{k=1}^{K} (X_{ijk} - \overline{X}_{\cdot\cdot\cdot})^2 \qquad (16.31)$$

Just as we separated SS_t into SS_w and SS_b in one-way ANOVA, we separate SS_{total} into its components. In the case of a two-way ANOVA, SS_{total} has four components.

The first component is the sum of squared deviations of the average of the rows around $\overline{X}_{\cdot\cdot\cdot}$, which we call SS_{row}:

$$SS_{\text{row}} = JK \sum_{i=1}^{I} (\overline{X}_{i\cdot\cdot} - \overline{X}_{\cdot\cdot\cdot})^2 \qquad (16.32)$$

Note that we multiply by JK because the averages $\overline{X}_{i\cdot\cdot}$ are obtained over JK observations.

Next we find the sum of squared deviations of the average of the columns around $\overline{X}...$, which we call SS_{column}:

$$SS_{\text{column}} = IK \sum_{j=1}^{J} (\overline{X}_{\cdot j\cdot} - \overline{X}...)^2 \tag{16.33}$$

The sum of squared deviations due to the interaction, which we call $SS_{\text{interaction}}$,[8] can be shown to equal the following:

$$SS_{\text{interaction}} = K \sum_{i=1}^{I} \sum_{j=1}^{J} (\overline{X}_{ij\cdot} - \overline{X}_{i\cdot\cdot} - \overline{X}_{\cdot j\cdot} + \overline{X}...)^2 \tag{16.34}$$

Finally, the unexplained residuals within the cells have the following sum of squares:

$$SS_{\text{residual}} = \sum_{i=1}^{I} \sum_{j=1}^{J} \sum_{k=1}^{K} (X_{ijk} - \overline{X}_{ij\cdot})^2 \tag{16.35}$$

With I rows in the ANOVA table, it can be shown that SS_{row} contains $I - 1$ *independent* squared deviations (i.e., degrees of freedom); with J columns, SS_{column} contains $J - 1$ *independent* squared deviations (that is, degrees of freedom). It can be shown as well that while there are $I \cdot J$ cells, there are only $(I - 1) \cdot (J - 1)$ *independent* squared deviations in $SS_{\text{interaction}}$, and there are $IJ(K - 1)$ *independent* squared deviations (degrees of freedom) in SS_{residual}.

To get the *mean squared deviations* of the rows, the columns, the interaction, and the residuals, we divide the sum of squared deviations by their

---

[8] For any individual observation, the total deviation from the grand average may be broken down into the random deviation from the cell average and "all the rest of the deviations" as follows:

Total deviation = random deviation from the cell mean + "all the rest"
$$X_{ijk} - \overline{X}... = (X_{ijk} - \overline{X}_{ij\cdot}) + (\overline{X}_{ij\cdot} - \overline{X}...)$$

"All the rest" includes row, column, and interaction effects; that is

"All the rest" = row + column + interaction

or

$$\overline{X}_{ij\cdot} - \overline{X}... = (\overline{X}_{i\cdot\cdot} - \overline{X}...) + (\overline{X}_{\cdot j\cdot} - \overline{X}...) + \text{interaction}$$

From this we get

$$\begin{aligned} \text{Interaction} &= (\overline{X}_{ij\cdot} - \overline{X}...) - (\overline{X}_{i\cdot\cdot} - \overline{X}...) - (\overline{X}_{\cdot j\cdot} - \overline{X}...) \\ &= \overline{X}_{ij\cdot} - \overline{X}... - \overline{X}_{i\cdot\cdot} + \overline{X}... - \overline{X}_{\cdot j\cdot} + \overline{X}... \\ &= \overline{X}_{ij\cdot} - \overline{X}_{i\cdot\cdot} - \overline{X}_{\cdot j\cdot} + \overline{X}... \end{aligned}$$

This relationship explains the equation for $SS_{\text{interaction}}$, 16.34.

respective degrees of freedom. Thus

$$MS_{\text{row}} = \frac{SS_{\text{row}}}{I - 1} \tag{16.36}$$

$$MS_{\text{column}} = \frac{SS_{\text{column}}}{J - 1} \tag{16.37}$$

$$MS_{\text{interaction}} = \frac{SS_{\text{interaction}}}{(I - 1)(J - 1)} \tag{16.38}$$

$$MS_{\text{residual}} = \frac{SS_{\text{residual}}}{IJ(K - 1)} \tag{16.39}$$

Note that the degrees of freedom of the four sources of variance add up to $IJK - 1$, which equals the number of degrees of freedom of SS_{total}. The sums of squares, degrees of freedom, and mean squares of the various sources of variance are summarized in Table 16.13.

TABLE 16.13
Two-Way ANOVA Table

Source of variation	Sum of squares	df	Mean square
Between rows	$SS_{\text{row}} = JK \sum\limits_{i=1}^{I} (\overline{X}_{i..} - \overline{X}_{...})^2$	$I - 1$	$MS_{\text{row}} = \dfrac{SS_{\text{row}}}{I - 1}$
Between columns	$SS_{\text{column}} = IK \sum\limits_{j=1}^{J} (\overline{X}_{.j.} - \overline{X}_{...})^2$	$J - 1$	$MS_{\text{column}} = \dfrac{SS_{\text{column}}}{J - 1}$
Interaction	$SS_{\text{interaction}} = K \sum\limits_{i=1}^{I} \sum\limits_{j=1}^{J} (\overline{X}_{ij.} - \overline{X}_{i..} - \overline{X}_{.j.} + \overline{X}_{...})^2$	$(I - 1)(J - 1)$	$MS_{\text{interaction}}$ $= \dfrac{SS_{\text{interaction}}}{(I - 1)(J - 1)}$
Residual error	$SS_{\text{residual}} = \sum\limits_{i=1}^{I} \sum\limits_{j=1}^{J} \sum\limits_{k=1}^{K} (X_{ijk} - \overline{X}_{ij.})^2$	$IJ(K - 1)$	$MS_{\text{residual}} = \dfrac{SS_{\text{residual}}}{IJ(K - 1)}$
Total	$SS_{\text{total}} = \sum\limits_{i=1}^{I} \sum\limits_{j=1}^{J} \sum\limits_{k=1}^{K} (X_{ijk} - \overline{X}_{...})^2$	$IJK - 1$	

SHORTCUT EQUATIONS FOR TWO-WAY ANOVA

Luckily, we can simplify the sum-of-squares equations given in Table 16.13. (Although this "simplification" may seem to be an extra complication, after working out one or two exercises involving two-way ANOVA you will see how useful it can be.) We first define the quantities A, B, C, D, and E as follows:

$$A \equiv \sum_{i=1}^{I} \sum_{j=1}^{J} \sum_{k=1}^{K} X_{ijk}^2 \tag{16.40}$$

$$B \equiv \frac{1}{IJK}\left(\sum_{i=1}^{I}\sum_{j=1}^{J}\sum_{k=1}^{K} X_{ijk}\right)^2 \qquad (16.41)$$

$$C \equiv \frac{1}{JK}\left[\sum_{i=1}^{I}\left(\sum_{j=1}^{J}\sum_{k=1}^{K} X_{ijk}\right)^2\right] \qquad (16.42)$$

$$D \equiv \frac{1}{IK}\left[\sum_{j=1}^{J}\left(\sum_{i=1}^{I}\sum_{k=1}^{K} X_{ijk}\right)^2\right] \qquad (16.43)$$

$$E \equiv \frac{1}{K}\left[\sum_{i=1}^{I}\sum_{j=1}^{J}\left(\sum_{k=1}^{K} X_{ijk}\right)^2\right] \qquad (16.44)$$

Given these quantities, it is possible to derive the following equalities:

$$SS_{\text{total}} = A - B \qquad (16.45)$$

$$SS_{\text{row}} = C - B \qquad (16.46)$$

$$SS_{\text{column}} = D - B \qquad (16.47)$$

$$SS_{\text{interaction}} = B - C - D + E \qquad (16.48)$$

$$SS_{\text{residual}} = A - E \qquad (16.49)$$

Now it becomes obvious that the major computational burden in working out a two-way ANOVA without using a computer is that of calculating the quantities in Equations 16.40 through 16.44. To illustrate, suppose a sample of 30 observations is taken in our study of production performance, as in Table 16.14. Using the figures from Table 16.14, we proceed to compute the

TABLE 16.14
Units of Production Sample, by Crew and Type of Machine

Type of machine	Crew A		Crew B		Crew C		Total
Type 1	90 95 80 85 89	Total = 439	75 86 80 83 90	Total = 414	72 88 83 82 78	Total = 403	1,256
Type 2	88 85 79 75 78	Total = 405	81 83 74 69 74	Total = 381	69 63 72 80 85	Total = 369	1,155
Total	844		795		772		2,411

quantities A, B, C, D, and E:

$$A = 90^2 + 95^2 + 80^2 + 85^2 + 89^2 + 75^2 + \cdots + 85^2 = 195{,}327.00$$

$$B = \frac{1}{2 \cdot 3 \cdot 5} (90 + 95 + 80 + 85 + 89 + 75 + \cdots + 85)^2 = \frac{1}{30} \cdot 2{,}411^2$$

$$= \frac{1}{30} \cdot 5{,}812{,}921 = 193{,}764.03$$

$$C = \frac{1}{3 \cdot 5} (1{,}256^2 + 1{,}155^2) = \frac{1}{15} (1{,}577{,}536 + 1{,}334{,}025)$$

$$= \frac{1}{15} \cdot 2{,}911{,}561 = 194{,}104.06$$

$$D = \frac{1}{2 \cdot 5} (844^2 + 795^2 + 772^2) = \frac{1}{10} (712{,}336 + 632{,}025 + 595{,}984)$$

$$= \frac{1}{10} \cdot 1{,}940{,}345 = 194{,}034.50$$

$$E = \frac{1}{5} \cdot (439^2 + 405^2 + 414^2 + 381^2 + 403^2 + 369^2)$$

$$= \frac{1}{5} (192{,}721 + 164{,}025 + 171{,}396 + 145{,}161 + 162{,}409 + 136{,}161)$$

$$= \frac{1}{5} \cdot 971{,}873 = 194{,}374.60$$

From these results we find

$$SS_{\text{total}} = 195{,}327.00 - 193{,}764.03 = 1{,}562.97$$

$$SS_{\text{row}} = 194{,}104.06 - 193{,}764.03 = 340.03$$

$$SS_{\text{column}} = 194{,}034.50 - 193{,}764.03 = 270.47$$

$$SS_{\text{interaction}} = 193{,}764.03 - 194{,}104.06 - 194{,}034.50 + 194{,}374.60 = 0.07$$

$$SS_{\text{residual}} = 195{,}327.00 - 194{,}374.60 = 952.40$$

Finally we construct the analysis-of-variance table, Table 16.15.

Now that we have prepared the analysis-of-variance table, we are ready to test hypotheses concerning the population's structure.

TABLE 16.15
Analysis-of-Variance Table

Source of variance	Sum of squares	df	Mean square
Between rows	340.03	$2 - 1 = 1$	340.030
Between columns	270.47	$3 - 1 = 2$	135.235
Interaction	0.07	$(2 - 1)(3 - 1) = 2$	0.035
Residual error	952.40	$2 \cdot 3 \cdot (5 - 1) = 24$	39.683
Total	1,562.97	$(2 \cdot 3 \cdot 5) - 1 = 29$	

TESTING HYPOTHESES ABOUT THE INTERACTION EFFECT, THE COLUMN EFFECT, AND THE ROW EFFECT

Earlier we mentioned a threefold purpose for the analysis of variance: to determine the existence (or nonexistence) of the interaction effect, the row effect, and the column effect. We prepared an analysis-of-variance table, which separates the total variability of the data into its components. After the separation, we adjusted each variability component by dividing the sum of squares by the respective degrees of freedom to obtain the mean square deviation of the various sources of variability. After undergoing this process, the sample data are in a form that we can use for statistical inference. We shall determine whether the various effects (interaction, row, and column) in the sample are strong enough to indicate that such effects are likely to exist in the population.

We start by testing the following hypotheses:

$$H_0: \quad \theta_{ij} = 0 \quad \text{for all } i \text{ and } j \text{ combinations}$$

$$H_1: \quad \text{Not all } \theta_{ij} \text{ are zero.}$$

The meaning of H_0 is that no interaction exists between the rows and the columns; H_1 is the hypothesis that at least *some* interaction exists. The statistic used to test the hypotheses is $MS_{\text{interaction}}/MS_{\text{residual}}$, a statistic that has the distribution $F^{[(I-1)(J-1),\ IJ(K-1)]}$. In short

$$\frac{MS_{\text{interaction}}}{MS_{\text{residual}}} \sim F^{[(I-1)(J-1),\ IJ(K-1)]} \tag{16.50}$$

When we test for row effects, the hypotheses are

$$H_0: \quad \psi_i = 0 \quad \text{for all } i = 1, 2, \ldots, I$$

$$H_1: \quad \text{Not all } \psi_i \text{ are zero.}$$

The statistic here is $MS_{\text{row}}/MS_{\text{residual}}$, which has an F distribution with $I - 1$ and $IJ(K - 1)$ degrees of freedom:

$$\frac{MS_{\text{row}}}{MS_{\text{residual}}} \sim F^{[(I-1),\ IJ(K-1)]} \tag{16.51}$$

Acceptance of the null hypothesis means that we conclude that row effects are not likely to exist.

Finally, to test for column effect, we use the hypotheses

$$H_0: \quad \xi_j = 0 \quad \text{for all } j = 1, 2, \ldots, J$$

$$H_1: \quad \text{Not all } \xi_j \text{ are zero.}$$

and the test statistic is $MS_{\text{column}}/MS_{\text{residual}}$, which has an F distribution with

$J - 1$ and $IJ(K - 1)$ degrees of freedom:

$$\frac{MS_{\text{column}}}{MS_{\text{residual}}} \sim F^{[(J-1),\ IJ(K-1)]} \tag{16.52}$$

In all three tests, the rejection region is on the right-hand side of the relevant distribution. For example, if there is a row effect that is significant, we expect a large difference between $\overline{X}_{i\cdot\cdot}$ and $\overline{X}\ldots$, since each row, i, has a different mean. Because the value $JK \sum_i (\overline{X}_{i\cdot\cdot} - \overline{X}\ldots)^2$ is in the numerator of the test statistic, the larger the difference between the averages, the larger the test statistic; hence the rejection region should be on the right-hand side. The specific critical point depends, of course, on the significance level, α.

Let us assume $\alpha = 0.05$ and conduct the three tests using the data in Table 16.14. In testing H_0: $\theta_{ij} = 0$ for all i and j combinations, we get

$$\frac{MS_{\text{interaction}}}{MS_{\text{residual}}} = \frac{0.035}{39.683} = 0.00088$$

The distribution of the test statistic is $F^{[(I-1)(J-1),\ IJ(K-1)]}$, or $F^{[(2-1)(3-1),\ 2\cdot3\cdot(5-1)]}$ $= F^{(2,24)}$. The critical value is $F_{0.05}^{(2,24)} = 3.40$. Since 0.00088 falls in the acceptance region (see Figure 16.6), we decide not to reject H_0; that is, we conclude that there is apparently no interaction effect.

Figure 16.6

Location of the critical value for testing an interaction effect

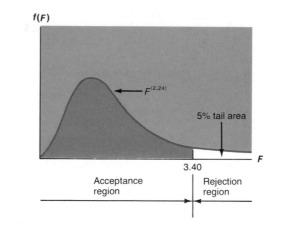

Now let us test

$$H_0: \quad \psi_i = 0 \qquad \text{for all } i = 1, 2, \ldots, I$$

The test statistic is

$$\frac{MS_{\text{row}}}{MS_{\text{residual}}} = \frac{340.030}{39.683} = 8.569$$

The distribution of the test statistic is $F^{[(I-1),\ IJ(K-1)]}$, or $F^{[(2-1),\ 2\cdot3\cdot(5-1)]} = F^{(1,24)}$. The critical value is $F_{0.05}^{(1,24)} = 4.26$, so we obviously reject the null

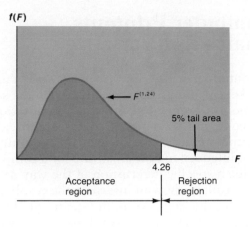

Figure 16.7

Location of the critical value for testing a row effect

hypothesis (see Figure 16.7), concluding that the mean production levels of the two types of machine are unequal.

Next we want to test

$$H_0: \quad \xi_j = 0 \qquad \text{for all } j = 1, 2, \ldots, J$$

The test statistic is

$$\frac{MS_{\text{column}}}{MS_{\text{residual}}} = \frac{135.235}{39.683} = 3.408$$

The distribution of the test statistic is $F^{[(J-1),\ IJ(K-1)]}$, or $F^{[(3-1),2\cdot3\cdot(5-1)]} = F^{(2,24)}$, and the critical value is $F_{0.05}^{(2,24)} = 3.40$ (see Figure 16.6). Since 3.408 is greater than 3.40, we reject the null hypothesis, concluding that the mean production levels of the various crews are *not likely* to be the same.

Thus the production manager knows that not all crews are equally efficient. He may want to establish norms that match the production level set by the best crew. He also knows that a Type 1 machine is significantly better, and he may purchase only this kind of machine in the future. Since there is no interaction between crews and types of machine, however, it does not matter which crew works on which type of machine.

We can also test simultaneously for row, column, and interaction effects by adding the sum of the squares of the three effects and dividing the total by the sum of the degrees of freedom of the three effects. In our example we have $SS_{\text{row}} = 340.03$, $SS_{\text{column}} = 270.47$, and $SS_{\text{interaction}} = 0.07$. The degrees of freedom are 1, 2, and 2, respectively. We find that the sum of the squares is 610.57 (= 340.03 + 270.47 + 0.07) and the degrees of freedom are 5 (= 1 + 2 + 2). The mean square for all three effects combined is $610.57/5 = 122.114$. Dividing 122.114 by the mean square of the residuals (39.683), we get an F value of 3.077 (= 122.114/39.683). The ratio of the two mean squares is thus distributed as F with degrees of freedom $[(I-1) + (J-1) + (I-1)(J-1),\ IJ(K-1)] = [IJ-1,\ IJ(K-1)] = 5, 24$. The critical value is $F_{0.05}^{(5,24)} = 2.62$; since $3.077 > 2.62$, we reject the hypothesis that there is no combined effect of the rows, columns, and interaction.

16.5 Interpreting Computer Printouts of Two-Way Analysis of Variance

Although the computations involved in two-way ANOVA are not too difficult to handle with pocket calculators, particularly when the sample is not large, it is undoubtedly more convenient to omit the computational step and leave the burden to the computer. Computer programs are readily available and can be executed without extensive knowledge of computer programming.

This section is not intended to be a substitute for a computer programming manual or to provide a specific description of the way ANOVA programs are executed. Rather, it explains how to interpret the results.

Figure 16.8 shows results from a computer printout of the two-way ANOVA for the data of Table 16.14.[9] On the left-hand side we have added a sequential number to each line to facilitate reference throughout our explanation.

Figure 16.8

Results from computer printout of a two-way ANOVA

```
 1.  TWO  WAY  EXAMPLE

    (**************A N A L Y S I S   O F   V A R I A N C E***************
    {              PROD
 2. {          BY  CREW
    (              MACHINE
    (****************************************************************************

                                    SUM OF                    MEAN         SIGNIF
 3.  SOURCE  OF  VARIATION          SQUARES     DF      SQUARE      F      OF  F
 4.  MAIN  EFFECTS                  610.496      3     203.499   5.128     0.007
 5.      CREW                       270.463      2     135.231   3.408     0.049
 6.      MACHINE                    340.033      1     340.033   8.569     0.007

 7.  2-WAY  INTERACTIONS             0.067       2       0.033   0.001     0.999
 8.      CREW      MACHINE           0.067       2       0.033   0.001     0.999

 9.  EXPLAINED                      610.562      5     122.112   3.077     0.028

10.  RESIDUAL                       952.402     24      39.683

11.  TOTAL                         1562.964     29      53.895

12.      30  CASES  WERE  PROCESSED.
13.       0  CASES  (   0.0 PCT)  WERE  MISSING.
```

To generate the ANOVA table, 44 computer cards were used—14 program cards and 30 data cards (one per observation). The 14 cards were used to inform the computer about the package to be used, the number and names of the variables involved, the number of observations, and so on. Detailed instructions for setting up these cards are spelled out in a manual for the computer package used—the Statistical Package for Social Sciences (SPSS). Most universities provide assistance to students interested in setting up their computer programs.

Let us interpret the output line by line.

Line 1 A job name provided by the user. We called our job "two-way example."

Line 2 A title indicating that two-way analysis of variance is to follow, with data classified by crew and type of machine.

Line 3 Titles of the various columns.

Line 4 The sum of "main effects" (row and column effects).

---

[9] The computer printout used is that of the Statistical Package for Social Sciences (SPSS), a computer package available in most computer centers.

Line 5   Statistics on the columns: the sum of the squares is 270.463, the degrees of freedom are 2, and the mean square is 270.463/2 = 135.231 (compare these figures with those in Table 16.15: deviations are solely due to rounding). Under the column headed "*F*," the *F* statistic for testing for the existence of column effects is given. Specifically, the *F* value 3.408 is equal to $MS_{column}/MS_{residual}$ = 135.231/39.683. In the next column, headed "Signif. of *F*," we read "0.049." This means that the computed value (that is, 3.408) leaves a right-hand tail equal to 4.9 percent on the $F^{(2,24)}$ distribution. It is thus clear that if we test the hypothesis that there is no column effect (H_0) against the hypothesis that there is a column effect (H_1), the value 0.049 is the maximum α value under which H_0 will not be rejected. For example, if α = 0.050 (that is, greater than 0.049), H_0 will be rejected, while if α = 0.048 or lower, H_0 will be accepted.

Line 6   Similar to line 5, except that here the statistics apply to the rows.

Line 7   The sum of all two-way interactions. Since in our analysis there is only one kind of two-way interaction, line 7 is identical to line 8. When an analysis of variance involving three or more dimensions is studied, the interaction between each pair of variables is listed in line 8. Line 7 shows the sum of all the interactions.

Line 8   Statistics on the interaction effect. The *F* statistic is 0.001, and the existence of interaction should be rejected in all tests of hypotheses when an α value of less than 0.999 is used.

Line 9   The sum of squares here is the total of the sums of squares in lines 5, 6, and 7. Similarly, the degrees of freedom are the sum of the degrees of freedom in those lines. This line provides a sort of simultaneous test for rows, columns, and interaction. In our example the *F* statistic is 3.077 (= 122.112/39.683) and the significance of *F* is 0.028. This means that for all α greater than 2.8 percent we should reject a hypothesis that no effect (either row or column or interaction) exists.

Line 10   The sum of squares, degrees of freedom, and mean square for the residuals.

Line 11   The total sum of squares and the respective degrees of freedom and mean square. The sum of squares and the degrees of freedom in this line are the sums of those in lines 5, 6, 7, and 10.

Line 12   The number of observations in the sample.

Line 13   The number of missing values that the computer has come across.

Let us consider an example in which another computer printout is presented.

EXAMPLE 16.3

In a study on inflation, it is necessary to determine whether price increases of U.S. companies vary according to the size of the company or according to the degree of concentration in the industry in which the company operates. (If there is perfect competition in the industry, concentration is minimal; if there is a monopoly, concentration is at its highest level.) Assume that five levels of concentration and three company sizes are distinguished, and that four observations (four companies) for each combination of size and concentration are available, as summarized in Table 16.16. Note that the numbers in the table are rates of price increases by each company sampled in the past year. The ANOVA

TABLE 16.16
Rates of Price Increases of Sampled Companies,
by Concentration and Size

	Concentration				
Size	1	2	3	4	5
1	3	4	5	9	12
	5	7	7	10	11
	7	7	9	10	9
	4	7	6	7	9
2	12	5	8	10	10
	10	9	8	14	9
	3	7	9	10	11
	5	7	10	11	8
3	5	6	7	11	6
	3	10	11	20	15
	4	9	8	9	9
	2	8	11	8	9

table is given in Figure 16.9. The conclusions from the ANOVA table are as follows (we assume $\alpha = 0.05$ for all tests):

1. The row effect is *not* significant ($0.172 > 0.05$). We do not reject H_0, which claims that the rate of price increase is not a function of the size of the firm.
2. The column effect *is* significant ($0.001 < 0.05$). The rate of price increase varies among the various concentration levels.
3. There is no significant interaction effect.

This example shows that once the *meanings* of the various effects are understood, we can easily use the analysis of variance without having to confront any of the equations presented earlier.

Figure 16.9

Results from computer printout of a two-way ANOVA

```
ADDITIONAL  EXAMPLE
FILE    NONAME
**************A N A L Y S I S   O F   V A R I A N C E**************
              INFLATN
         BY  SIZE
             CONCENT
**************************************************************************
                            SUM OF              MEAN             SIGNIF
SOURCE  OF  VARIATION       SQUARES     DF      SQUARE    F      OF  F
MAIN  EFFECTS               249.467      6      41.578   6.785   0.001
     SIZE                    22.300      2      11.150   1.820   0.172
     CONCENT                227.167      4      56.792   9.268   0.001
2-WAY  INTERACTIONS          54.033      8       6.754   1.102   0.380
     SIZE       CONCENT      54.033      8       6.754   1.102   0.380
EXPLAINED                   303.500     14      21.679   3.538   0.001
RESIDUAL                    275.747     45       6.128
TOTAL                       579.247     59       9.818
     60  CASES  WERE  PROCESSED.
      0  CASES (   0.0  PCT)  WERE  MISSING.
```

A word or two should be said here about the relationship between one-way and two-way analysis of variance. In testing the significance of a possible interaction effect, we must employ a two-way analysis of variance with at least two observations in each cell. In fact, testing the significance of an interaction effect is the main purpose of two-way analysis. We can, however, use two-way ANOVA even when only one observation is available in each cell. In this case it is impossible to test hypotheses regarding interaction effects, but we can test hypotheses concerning column and row effects. A two-way analysis of variance is not a must here, since one-way analysis can be employed twice instead: one analysis can be conducted for row effect and one for column effect. Employing a two-way ANOVA is more economical, however, since it requires a smaller sample size for a given power of the test than that required to perform one-way ANOVA twice.

16.6. APPLICATION:
COMPARING SHOPPERS' COMFORT WITH 10 METHODS OF SHOPLIFTING PREVENTION—ONE-WAY ANOVA*

The problem of shoplifting has grown to immense proportions. It is estimated that it costs the U.S. economy at least $2 billion annually. Retailers looking for the most effective device to prevent shoplifting also want a device that does not offend their shoppers more than other devices do. Therefore, they want to determine the degree to which shoppers feel uncomfortable with various devices that prevent shoplifting. Comparing 10 alternative devices, the retailers' null hypothesis is that shoppers experience no more discomfort with one device than with the alternative devices.

Denoting the percentage of people who feel uncomfortable with the ith device by μ_i, we have the following hypotheses:

$$H_0: \quad \mu_1 = \mu_2 = \cdots = \mu_n$$

$$H_1: \quad \text{Not all the } \mu_i \text{s are equal.}$$

Samples of shoppers were taken in three big shopping centers. Table 16.17 presents the percentage of shoppers who were uncomfortable with the various devices. The table also gives $\sum_{i=1}^{3} X_{ij}$ and $\overline{X}_{\cdot j}$, which are needed to calculate the test statistic in a one-way analysis of variance.

The test statistic is

$$\frac{MS_b}{MS_w} \sim F^{(J-1,\ n-J)}$$

---

* This application is based on H. J. Guffey, Jr., J. R. Harris, and J. F. Laumer, Jr., "Shopper Attitudes Toward Shoplifting and Shoplifting Preventive Devices," *Journal of Retailing*, Fall 1979, pp. 75–89. Some changes have been made to make the application more instructive.

TABLE 16.17
Degree of Shopper Discomfort with 10 Methods of Shoplifting Prevention

Method of shoplifting prevention (j)	Percentage of customers uncomfortable with device at 3 shopping centers ($i = 1, 2, 3$)			$\sum_{i=1}^{3} X_{ij}$	n_j	$\bar{X}_{\cdot j}$
Locked display case	12	17	16	45	3	15
Mirrors	14	10	18	42	3	14
TV cameras	24	12	0	36	3	12
Rings and chains on merchandise	20	15	25	60	3	20
Floor walkers	24	6	15	45	3	15
Uniformed guards	27	13	20	60	3	20
Magnetic detector	18	12	18	48	3	16
Checkers in dressing rooms	35	15	10	60	3	20
Two-way mirrors	29	11	17	57	3	19
Observation tower	23	17	5	45	3	15
Total	226	128	144	498	30	

and we will reject the null hypothesis if $\frac{MS_b}{MS_w} > F_\alpha^{(J-1,\, n-J)}$. We shall calculate MS_b and MS_w.

First let us calculate the quantities A, B, and C for the shortcut formulas $SS_b = C - B$ and $SS_w = A - C$. Noting that $J = 10$ and $n = 30$, we obtain

$$A = \sum_i \sum_j X_{ij}^2 = 9{,}850$$

$$B = \frac{1}{n} \left(\sum_i \sum_j X_{ij} \right)^2 = \frac{1}{30} (498)^2 = 8{,}266.8$$

Since $n_j = 3$ for all j, we have

$$C = \frac{1}{3} \sum_j \left(\sum_i X_{ij} \right)^2 = \frac{1}{3} (25{,}488) = 8{,}496$$

Hence

$$SS_b = C - B = 8{,}496 - 8{,}266.8 = 229.2$$

and

$$MS_b = \frac{SS_b}{J - 1} = \frac{229.2}{10 - 1} = 25.4667$$

Also

$$SS_w = A - C = 9{,}850 - 8{,}496 = 1{,}354$$

and

$$MS_w = \frac{SS_w}{n - J} = \frac{1{,}354}{30 - 10} = 67.7000$$

Thus, the F statistic is given by

$$\frac{MS_b}{MS_w} = \frac{25.4667}{67.7000} = 0.376$$

Looking at the critical F value at the 5 percent significance level, $F_{0.05}^{(9,20)}$, we find that it equals 2.39. Since $0.376 < 2.39$, we cannot reject the null hypothesis, which asserts that all 10 devices give shoppers the same degree of discomfort. Thus, the stores should adopt the device that is least expensive to install and to maintain. Figure 16.10 presents an SPSS computer printout of the analysis-of-variance table from which the calculations can be verified. It shows that the null hypothesis cannot be rejected at any significance level smaller than 93.31 percent. However, differences in group means do exist and an increase in the sample size could very well lead to the conclusion that these differences are statistically significant.

	ANALYSIS OF VARIANCE				
SOURCE	DF	SUM OF SQUARES	MEAN SQUARES	F RATIO	F PROB.
BETWEEN GROUPS	9	229.2000	25.4667	.376	.9331
WITHIN GROUPS	20	1354.0000	67.7000		
TOTAL	29	1583.2000			

Figure 16.10 Reproduction of a computer printout (SPSS) showing analysis of variance results

Chapter Summary and Review

1. One-way ANOVA

	Hypotheses	Statistic	Decision rule

a. H_0: $\mu_1 = \mu_2 = \cdots = \mu_J$

b. H_1: Not all the means are equal.

$\dfrac{MS_b}{MS_w} \sim F^{(J-1,\, n-J)}$ Reject H_0 if $\dfrac{MS_b}{MS_w} > F_\alpha^{(J-1,\, n-J)}$

2. Notation

a. J is the number of groups, n_j is the number of observations in group j, and $n = \sum_j n_j$ is the total number of observations in the sample.

b. $SS_w = \sum_j \sum_i (X_{ij} - \overline{X}_{\cdot j})^2$ and $MS_w = \dfrac{SS_w}{n - J}$

c. $SS_b = \sum_j n_j (\overline{X}_{\cdot j} - \overline{\overline{X}})^2$ and $MS_b = \dfrac{SS_b}{J - 1}$

3. Analysis of groups

a. A confidence interval for one mean:

$$\overline{X}_{\cdot j} \pm t_{\alpha/2}^{(n-J)} \sqrt{\frac{MS_w}{n_j}}$$

b. A confidence interval for the difference between two means:

$$(\overline{X}_{\cdot j'} - \overline{X}_{\cdot j''}) \pm t_{\alpha/2}^{(n-J)} \sqrt{MS_w\left(\frac{1}{n_{j'}} + \frac{1}{n_{j''}}\right)}$$

4. Two-way ANOVA

Hypotheses	Statistic	Decision rule

a. Interaction effect

H_0: $\theta_{ij} = 0$ for all i and j combinations

H_1: Not all θ_{ij} are zero.

$$\frac{MS_{\text{interaction}}}{MS_{\text{residual}}} \sim F^{[(I-1)(J-1),\ IJ(K-1)]}$$

Reject H_0 if $\dfrac{MS_{\text{interaction}}}{MS_{\text{residual}}} > F_{\alpha}^{[(I-1)(J-1),\ IJ(K-1)]}$

b. Row effect

H_0: $\psi_i = 0$ for all $i = 1, 2, \ldots, I$

H_1: Not all ψ_i are zero.

$$\frac{MS_{\text{row}}}{MS_{\text{residual}}} \sim F^{[(I-1),\ IJ(K-1)]}$$

Reject H_0 if $\dfrac{MS_{\text{row}}}{MS_{\text{residual}}} > F_{\alpha}^{[(I-1),\ IJ(K-1)]}$

c. Column effect

H_0: $\xi_j = 0$ for all $j = 1, 2, \ldots, J$

H_1: Not all ξ_j are zero.

$$\frac{MS_{\text{column}}}{MS_{\text{residual}}} \sim F^{[(J-1),\ IJ(K-1)]}$$

Reject H_0 if $\dfrac{MS_{\text{column}}}{MS_{\text{residual}}} > F_{\alpha}^{[(J-1),\ IJ(K-1)]}$

5. Notation

a. I is the number of rows, J is the number of columns, K is the number of observations in each cell, and n is the total number of observations in the sample.

b. $SS_{\text{interaction}} = K \sum\limits_{i=1}^{I} \sum\limits_{j=1}^{J} (\overline{X}_{ij\cdot} - \overline{X}_{i\cdot\cdot} - \overline{X}_{\cdot j\cdot} + \overline{X}_{\cdots})^2$ and $MS_{\text{interaction}} = \dfrac{SS_{\text{interaction}}}{(I-1)(J-1)}$

c. $SS_{\text{row}} = JK \sum\limits_{i=1}^{I} (\overline{X}_{i\cdot\cdot} - \overline{X}_{\cdots})^2$ and $MS_{\text{row}} = \dfrac{SS_{\text{row}}}{I-1}$

d. $SS_{\text{column}} = IK \sum\limits_{j=1}^{J} (\overline{X}_{\cdot j\cdot} - \overline{X}_{\cdots})^2$ and $MS_{\text{column}} = \dfrac{SS_{\text{column}}}{J-1}$

e. $SS_{\text{residual}} = \sum\limits_{i=1}^{I} \sum\limits_{j=1}^{J} \sum\limits_{k=1}^{K} (X_{ijk} - \overline{X}_{ij\cdot})^2$ and $MS_{\text{residual}} = \dfrac{SS_{\text{residual}}}{IJ(K-1)}$

Problems

16.1. Explain the meaning of the sum of squares *within* groups and the sum of squares *between* groups in analysis of variance.

16.2. The following table shows advertising expenditures as a percentage of sales for three firms in the same industry over five years.

Year	Firm A	Firm B	Firm C
1	1.1	1.2	1.3
2	1.1	1.2	1.3
3	1.1	1.2	1.3
4	1.1	1.2	1.3
5	1.1	1.2	1.3

Test the hypothesis that the mean advertising expenditure as a percentage of sales is the same for the three firms. Reach a conclusion without consulting any statistical tables. Are the short-cut equations of ANOVA helpful for this problem? Explain.

16.3. The productivity of three workers, measured by number of units of output per day, is reported in the table below:

Day	Worker A	Worker B	Worker C
1	5	10	20
2	10	10	5
3	15	10	5

Use ANOVA to test the null hypothesis that the productivity of the three workers is equal. Use $\alpha = 0.05$. How would you change your conclusion for a significance level of $\alpha = 0.50$? Reach a decision without using any statistical tables. It is recommended that you do not use the shortcut equations. Can you explain why?

16.4. Is it possible to get a negative MS_b in a sample? A negative MS_w? Explain.

16.5. Suppose the total number of observations in a one-way analysis of variance is $n = 25$. Find the critical value, F_α ($\alpha = 0.05$), for J groups, where J has the following alternative values:

(a) $J = 2$
(b) $J = 3$
(c) $J = 4$
(d) $J = 5$

For a given n, what is the relationship between the critical value, F_α, and the number of groups, J?

16.6. What is the source of the name "analysis of variance"? Use a simple numerical example to demonstrate that

$$SS_t = SS_w + SS_b$$

16.7. Explain the difference between one-way and two-way analysis of variance.

16.8. Explain the meaning of "interaction." Give an example.

16.9. In a two-way analysis of variance with 10 observations per cell, it was found that $\overline{X}_{ij\cdot} = 10$ for all cells. Must the interaction sum of squares, $SS_{interaction}$, equal zero? Explain.

16.10. Suppose we want to test the difference of means of $J = 5$ groups by using one-way ANOVA. Find the critical value of F_α ($\alpha = 0.05$) when the total number of observations is $n = 15, 20, 30$. Explain the relationship between F_α and n.

16.11. Suppose the cost per unit of items produced by four production processes is examined in order to find out whether the mean cost per unit is the same for all four processes. Suppose we carry out the analysis twice: once with the cost expressed in dollars and once with cost expressed in tens of dollars. What is the impact of the units used on SS_t, SS_w, SS_b? Do the units have an impact on the calculated F value? Explain.

16.12. The table below shows the market value of property owned by three individuals in New York and three individuals in Chicago (in thousands of dollars).

New York	Chicago
40	20
50	30
60	40

Test the hypothesis that the average market value of property held by individuals in both cities is the same against the alternative that the mean values are not the same:

$$H_0: \quad \mu_1 = \mu_2$$

$$H_1: \quad \mu_1 \neq \mu_2$$

Test the hypothesis twice: once by using the t distribution and once by using the F distribution ($\alpha = 0.05$). What is the relationship between the results? Is it possible to reach opposite conclusions by the two procedures? Explain.

16.13. In a two-way analysis of variance, the number of rows is $I = 3$, the number of columns is $J = 4$, and the significance level is $\alpha = 0.05$. What is the critical value for testing interaction for the following alternatives of the number of observations per cell, K?

(a) $K = 2$
(b) $K = 3$

16.14. The monthly sales of a given product in three stores in January, February, and March have been recorded and are listed below in thousands of dollars.

Month	Store 1	Store 2	Store 3
January	5	3	1
February	6	10	10
March	7	8	13
Average monthly sales	6	7	8

Suppose the assumptions required for analysis of variance indeed hold, and suppose we tested the null hypothesis (under which the average monthly sales are the same for all 3 stores) and found that it is accepted at a given significance level.

Change the sample data in such a way that the changes will be in the *direction* that will make the null hypothesis more likely to be *rejected*. When making the changes, be sure to keep the average monthly sales of the three stores unchanged. Explain your answer.

16.15. A sample is taken in order to test the hypothesis that five populations have equal means ($J = 5$). The one-way analysis of variance calculations show that $MS_b/MS_w = 3.50$. A second sample from the same population is taken to test the same hypothesis (again, $J = 5$). The second sample shows the same result: $MS_b/MS_w = 3.50$. "It follows that for a given level of significance, if we cannot reject H_0 for the first sample, we cannot reject it for the second sample either." Appraise this statement.

16.16. Four small cars are tested for their fuel efficiency. Table P16.16 shows the miles per gallon achieved in a series of test drives.

TABLE P16.16

| Test | Car | | | |
drive	A	B	C	D
1	30	28	26	28
2	28	30	28	30
3	29	26	25	32
4	40	28	24	30

(a) Perform a one-way analysis of variance to test the hypothesis that all four cars yield the same mean fuel efficiency. Use $\alpha = 0.01$.
(b) Construct a 95 percent confidence interval for the mean miles per gallon of Car B.
(c) Construct a 95 percent confidence interval for the difference between the mean miles per gallon of Cars A and B.

16.17. Table P16.17 shows the production of a worker (in units) who operated four machines on a number of selected days.

TABLE P16.17

| Day | Machine | | | |
	A	B	C	D
1	20	20	40	25
2	25	18	60	35
3	30	20		40
4		25		

(a) Use the level of significance $\alpha = 0.05$ to test whether the differences among the four sample means can be attributed to chance variations.
(b) Construct a 95 percent confidence interval for the difference between the mean production of Machines C and D.

16.18. In a one-way analysis of variance, the number of groups is $J = 4$ and the total number of observations is $n = 20$. Furthermore, the sum of squares between groups is 3,000, and the total sum of squares is 7,000. Determine the value of the sample F statistic.

16.19. A given computation job has been performed by four students on four types of personal computers. The length of time it took to perform the job (measured in minutes) is given in Table P16.19.

TABLE P16.19

Student	Computer			
	A	B	C	D
1	20	18	16	10
2	15	12	9	8
3	25	20	18	10
4	40	35	30	29

(a) Can the difference between the sample means of the four computers be attributed to chance? Use $\alpha = 0.05$ and Figure P16.19, which is a computer printout of the ANOVA table. The four "groups" in the ANOVA table are the four computers (A, B, C, and D).

Figure P16.19

Analysis of variance

ANALYSIS OF VARIANCE					
SOURCE	DF	SUM OF SQUARES	MEAN SQUARES	F RATIO	F PROB.
BETWEEN GROUPS	3	249.1875	83.0625	.861	.4879
WITHIN GROUPS	12	1158.2500	96.5208		
TOTAL	15	1407.4375			

(b) Can the difference between the sample means of the four students be attributed to chance variations? Use $\alpha = 0.05$.

(c) What would you say about this experiment if you knew that the very same students performed the computations on the computers (i.e., each student performed the computations on each one of the computers) and in the same order: on Computer A first and then, in order, on B, C, and D?

16.20. Four new drugs are tested for effectiveness by two hospitals. In each hospital a team of doctors (independent of the team at the other hospital) uses a one-way analysis of variance to test for the equality of the drugs' effectiveness. Suppose the two teams obtain the very same value for the test statistic: $F = MS_b/MS_w$. Nevertheless, and despite the fact that both teams have used the same significance level for their tests, they have reached different conclusions. One team has accepted the hypothesis that the four drugs have the same effectiveness, while the other team has rejected this hypothesis. Is it possible? Why? Explain by means of a numerical example.

16.21. Data on a certain variable can be expressed in dollars or in millions of dollars. Would the unit of measurement make a difference with respect to the accept–reject decision in analysis of variance? Explain.

16.22. U.S. companies publish annual reports in which they provide balance sheets, income statements, and other information for their stockholders. Since the annual report provides a comprehensive summary of a firm's operations and financial position, the firm needs time to prepare it. Therefore, there is a time lag between the end of the year covered by the annual report and the publication date of the report. A sample of the lag (in days) for three firms in the last three years is given below.

Firm	First year	Second year	Third year	Average lag
Bank	10	20	30	20
Computer manufacturer	60	50	40	50
Food chain	80	90	70	80

(a) Apply a one-way ANOVA to test the hypothesis that the mean time lag (in days) of the three firms is equal. Set $\alpha = 0.01$.

(b) Retest the same hypothesis, this time using the following data:

Firm	First year	Second year	Third year	Average lag
Bank	5	20	35	20
Computer manufacturer	100	30	20	50
Food chain	80	40	120	80

(c) Since the average time lag is the same in parts *a* and *b*, how do you account for the difference in the answers obtained?

(d) Draw a chart showing the sample range of the time lag for each of the three firms in parts *a* and *b*. Does the relationship between the ranges help to explain the accept–reject decision as obtained in parts *a* and *b*?

16.23. The Dow Jones Industrial Average is one of the most widely quoted stock market indexes. This index is based on a sample of 30 industrial stocks, the so-called Dow Jones Industrials (DJI), and the average is arrived at by adding up the prices of the 30 stocks and dividing the total by the so-called Dow Jones divisor to obtain an average stock price adjusted for past stock splits and stock dividends.

A similar method is used to calculate the earnings on the Dow Jones Industrial Average: the reported quarterly earnings per share for the 30 DJI stocks are added up and the sum is divided by the DJI divisor. The result reflects average earnings per share adjusted for the cumulative effect of stock splits and stock dividends. The following table gives the quarterly earnings on DJI average for the period 1975–81.

Quarter	1981	1980	1979	1978	1977	1976	1975
1st	31.40	29.66	33.35	22.04	21.91	23.12	16.91
2nd	35.49	30.18	34.55	29.66	27.52	25.85	17.04
3rd	23.26	28.85	33.67	26.40	16.18	23.50	18.37
4th	23.56	33.17	22.89	34.69	23.49	24.25	23.34
Total	113.71	121.86	124.46	112.79	89.10	96.72	75.66

Source: *Barron's*, August 2, 1982. Reprinted by permission of *Barron's*, © Dow Jones & Company, Inc., 1982. All rights reserved.

A glance at the earnings table reveals that second- and fourth-quarter earnings are often higher than first- and third-quarter earnings. This may be due to the effect of seasonal shopping patterns. Use one-way ANOVA to check whether a seasonal pattern is statistically significant.

16.24. Table P16.24 shows yields on short-term financial obligations with various maturities, i.e., 7 days, 1 month, 2 months, 3 months, 6 months, and 1 year, as recorded on 3 days in May 1981, 3 days in June 1981, 3 days in July 1981, and 3 days in August 1981. Regard the yields shown as a small random sample out of a large population of short-term yields that have existed in each of these months.

TABLE P16.24

Month	7 days	1 month	2 months	3 months	6 months	1 year
			Maturity			
May 1981	12.3	13.7	15.0	15.4	15.4	15.2
	17.5	16.3	17.3	17.5	17.1	16.5
	16.7	16.2	16.2	16.1	15.6	15.2
June 1981	16.1	16.2	16.0	15.6	15.4	14.7
	17.7	15.9	15.2	15.0	14.8	14.7
	14.0	14.2	14.4	14.6	14.8	14.6
July 1981	14.1	14.3	14.6	14.9	14.6	14.8
	16.6	14.9	15.2	15.2	15.2	15.1
	13.8	14.7	15.3	15.7	16.3	16.1
August 1981	14.7	14.9	15.2	15.6	16.2	16.2
	16.5	15.6	15.8	16.0	16.9	16.6
	14.5	15.0	15.9	16.1	16.9	16.8

Source: *Wall Street Journal*, various issues.

(a) Test the hypothesis that the mean yields on the short-term financial obligations were the same in the 4 months shown.

(b) Test the hypothesis that the mean yields were the same for the various maturities.

(c) Test the hypothesis that there is an interaction between the maturity and the month.

Use $\alpha = 0.01$ for the above tests.

16.25. In a two-way analysis of variance, there are $I = 5$ rows and $J = 10$ columns. The number of observations in each cell is $K = 5$. The following statistics have been calculated:

$$SS_{\text{total}} = 1,000$$

$$SS_{\text{residual}} = 100$$

$$SS_{\text{row}} = 200$$

$$SS_{\text{column}} = 300$$

Using a level of significance of 1 percent, can you attribute the interaction effect to chance variation only?

16.26. (a) The hourly wage of workers in the auto industry in three countries is under investigation. A sample of data, shown in Table P16.26a, reveals the following wages (all wages are expressed in U.S. dollars):

TABLE P16.26a

Worker	Japan	United States	Germany
		Country	
1	6	8	8
2	7	9	7
3	7	9	8
4	5	10	8
5	6	12	9

Use a significance level of $\alpha = 0.05$ and test whether the differences between the sample means can be attributed to mere chance variations. Interpret your results.

(b) Another sample has been taken to test the same issue raised in part *a*. The second sample reveals the data in Table P16.26*b*, again in U.S. dollars.

TABLE P16.26*b*

Worker	Country		
	Japan	*United States*	*Germany*
1	6	10	9
2	6	9	8
3	5	10	9
4	6	9	8

Again use a significance level of 5 percent to test whether the differences between the sample means can be attributed to mere chance variations.

(c) Combine the data from Tables P16.26*a* and P16.26*b* and again conduct an analysis of variance. What is your conclusion now? Explain and interpret your results.

16.27. (a) A study is being conducted to try to determine the relationship between the display location of Neka detergent and its sales volume. Three different shelves have been tried by a supermarket management: *A*, *B*, and *C*. Table P16.27*a* shows the daily sales of the detergent in a sample of days.

TABLE P16.27*a*
Sales of Neka Detergent by Shelf Display
(units)

Day	Shelf display		
	A	*B*	*C*
1	30	10	9
2	25	9	12
3	28	8	10
4	20	10	10
5	30	12	8
6	40	11	9
7	20	8	11

Use a one-way analysis of variance to test the null hypothesis under which the mean sales of the detergent is the same, regardless of the shelf on which it is displayed, against the alternative hypothesis, which claims that not all the means are equal. Use $\alpha = 0.05$.

(b) The supermarket management uses the same three shelves to examine the effect of shelf display on the sales of a certain hair conditioner. A sample showed the results in Table P16.27*b*.

TABLE P16.27*b*
Hair Conditioner Sales by Shelf Display
(units)

Day	Shelf display		
	A	*B*	*C*
1	20	20	28
2	25	30	27
3	30	25	25
4	20	15	
5		25	

Use $\alpha = 0.05$ to test the hypothesis that the location of the hair conditioner has no effect on the volume of sales.

(c) In light of your answers to parts *a* and *b*, which product would you recommend for display on shelf *A*, the hair conditioner or the Neka detergent? Explain.

16.28. Three test drivers have been assigned to test the fuel efficiency of four small cars. Each driver drove each of the cars three times. The miles per gallon of each of the tests are recorded in Table P16.28.

TABLE P16.28

Car	Driver 1	Driver 2	Driver 3
A	50	25	10
	40	22	12
	42	28	16
B	30	25	30
	35	28	28
	37	31	30
C	35	50	25
	30	45	30
	33	40	30
D	30	25	55
	35	20	60
	35	29	49

(a) Use two-way analysis of variance to test whether there is a difference in the mean mileage per gallon of the four cars, and if there is a difference in the mean mileage per gallon of the three test drivers. Use $\alpha = 0.05$.

(b) Use a significance level of 0.05 to test whether there is an interaction between the test driver and the cars driven. What is your interpretation of the results?

16.29. Table P16.29 represents research and development (R&D) spending as a percentage of sales of a few large U.S. companies in 1980. The data come from three industry groups (paper, tire and rubber, and information processing).

TABLE P16.29

Company	R&D spending as percent of sales	Company	R&D spending as percent of sales
Paper		**Tires, rubber** (*cont.*)	
Bemis	1.8	Firestone Tire & Rubber	1.7
Boise Cascade	0.2	Goodyear Tire & Rubber	2.1
Consolidated Paper	0.7	Uniroyal	1.6
International Paper	0.7		
Lydall	1.9	**Information processing**	
Rexham	1.3	Amdahl	15.8
Union Camp	1.0	Apple Computer	6.2
		Control Data	6.6
Tires, rubber		Digital Equipment	7.9
Amerace	2.5	Honeywell	6.0
Armstrong Rubber	1.5	IBM	5.8
Carlisle	0.4	Prime Computer	7.6

Source: Data from *Business Week*, July 6, 1981, pp. 47, 56, 57.

(a) Calculate the sample average of spending on R&D as a percentage of sales for each industry group.
(b) In view of the fact that the data are only a sample, do you hold the view that the mean percentage spending of the industries is the same? Use a 1 percent significance level in a test that will validate your answer. Use the shortcut equation and present your calculation.
(c) What assumptions do you have to make in order to be able to employ ANOVA?

16.30. A small production department consists of three types of machines and three workers. Only one worker at a time is assigned to each machine. The production manager wants to find out whether significant differences exist in the productivity of the three machines and of the three workers and whether interaction exists between workers and machines. The number of units of production that were produced during sample periods (each one hour long) is given in Table P16.30.

TABLE P16.30

Machine	Worker A	Worker B	Worker C	Average for machine
I	10	10	5	
	15	10	5	10
	20	10	5	
II	5	10	15	
	5	10	15	10
	5	10	15	
III	10	10	10	
	10	10	10	10
	10	10	10	
Average for worker	10	10	10	

(a) Can you say, *without any calculations*, whether there is a difference in mean productivity of the three workers? In mean productivity of the three machines?
(b) Test the significance of the interaction. How can the production manager use the results? Use a significance level of $\alpha = 0.05$.

16.31. Table P16.31 lists the annual rate of return on assets for a sample of seven telephone companies for a recent 10-year period. The telephone industry is regulated: the rates are fixed by government agencies so as to provide an adequate compensation to stockholders. If regulation is effective, the rates of return they earn should be roughly the same.

TABLE P16.31

Year	American Telephone & Telegraph (AT&T)	General Telephone & Utilities	Cincinnati Bell	Mid-Continent Telephone	Mountain State Telephone & Telegraph	Rochester Telephone & Telegraph	United Telecommunication
1	7.8	5.6	7.5	6.8	7.1	6.4	7.3
2	7.9	7.0	7.6	6.7	7.2	6.4	7.8
3	7.8	6.5	7.7	6.5	7.2	6.8	8.0
4	7.5	6.7	7.3	7.5	6.9	6.8	8.2
5	7.6	7.1	6.8	7.4	7.7	7.1	8.7
6	7.5	7.4	7.3	7.4	7.6	7.4	7.4
7	7.5	7.4	7.4	7.9	7.6	7.9	7.4
8	7.7	7.9	7.1	7.8	7.5	8.1	7.5
9	8.0	7.9	7.9	8.3	7.9	8.5	7.6
10	8.0	7.9	8.6	8.5	7.4	7.3	7.7

Source: Derived from the companies' annual reports.

Use one-way analysis of variance to test the null hypothesis that the average profitability (as measured by the rate of return on assets over the sample period) is the same for the seven telephone companies. In your analysis assume $\alpha = 5$ percent level of significance.

Do you think that government regulation is effective?

16.32. In Problem 16.29 you conducted a one-way analysis of variance of R&D spending patterns across three industry groups. In this problem we introduce another classification dimension: total sales. Various indicators of business activity vary with sales (for example, profits on the whole increase as sales increase).

Table P16.32 lists the R&D spending (as a percentage of sales) of a sample of 60 corporations classified by industry and by volume of sales. The sample consists of five industry groups and three sales categories. Each sales category in each industry group is represented by four companies.

TABLE P16.32

Company	R&D spending as percent of sales
Automotive supply	
Sales less than $1 billion	
Champion Spark Plug	1.1
Federal Mogul	0.9
Sheller-Globe	0.7
A. D. Smith	1.8
Sales between $1 billion and $2 billion	
Cummins Engine	3.3
Dana	1.1
Timken	0.8
White Motor	1.0
Sales over $2 billion	
American Motors	1.9
Bendix	1.4
Eaton	1.5
TRW	1.3
Chemicals	
Sales less than $1 billion	
Akzona	2.4
Cabot	2.6
Dexter	3.1
Liquid Air of North America	0.4
Sales between $1 billion and $2 billion	
Diamond Shamrock	1.9
Ethyl	2.2
Hercules	2.2
Olin	1.7
Sales over $2 billion	
Dow Chemical	3.3
Du Pont	3.9
Monsanto	2.9
Union Carbide	2.2
Electrical supply	
Sales less than $1 billion	
Cutler-Hammer	3.3
Globe-Union	1.5
Reliance Electric	3.7
Square D	1.6

TABLE P16.32 (*Continued*)

Company	R&D spending as percent of sales
Sales between $1 billion and $2 billion	
Eltra	1.7
Emerson Electric	2.0
Gould	3.7
McGraw-Edison	0.7
Sales over $2 billion	
General Electric	2.6
North American Philips	1.6
RCA	2.2
Westinghouse Electric	2.2
Food and beverages	
Sales less than $1 billion	
Gerber Products	0.9
Green Giant	0.6
Hershey Foods	0.4
McCormick	0.5
Sales between $1 billion and $2 billion	
Del Monte	0.7
H. J. Heinz	0.5
Kellogg	0.5
Quaker Oats	1.2
Sales over $2 billion	
Coca-Cola	0.3
Carnation	0.4
General Foods	1.0
General Mills	1.0
Machinery	
Sales less than $1 billion	
Black & Decker	1.9
Briggs & Stratton	0.8
Peabody International	0.5
Curtiss-Wright	0.5
Sales between $1 billion and $2 billion	
Allis-Chalmers	3.4
Clark Equipment	1.2
Emhart	2.0
Foster Wheeler	0.6
Sales over $2 billion	
Caterpillar Tractor	3.8
Deere	3.8
Ingersoll-Rand	2.8
FMC	2.4

Source: *Business Week*, July 3, 1978, pp. 61–70.

Conduct a two-way analysis of variance to test the null hypothesis that there are no significant variations in R&D spending patterns across industries and across sales categories. In your analysis of the main effects, check explicitly the interaction component between industry and sales volume. Use $\alpha = 5$ percent and alternatively $\alpha = 1$ percent. Summarize your results verbally.

16.33. Business firms generally use two sources of funds to finance new activities: equity (shareholders' capital, including common stock, accrued earnings, and so on) and debt (in the form of bonds issued to the public, long-term loans from banks and government, and the like). The ratio of debt to total invested capital is known in finance literature as *financial leverage*. A firm's financial leverage is of great importance and is closely watched by bankers, financial analysts, and investors. It is generally assumed that companies in the same industry should have roughly the same financial leverage, and managers will attempt to correct any obvious deviation from the industry mean. Across industries, on the other hand, financial leverage is expected to vary in line with the overall financing needs of each industry.

Table P16.33 lists the 1977 ratio of debt to total invested capital for a sample of 48 companies drawn from four industry groups.

TABLE P16.33

Company	Ratio of debt to total invested capital (percent)	Company	Ratio of debt to total invested capital (percent)
Airlines		**Instruments**	
American Airlines	55.3	Bausch & Lomb	15.8
Braniff International	59.4	Beckman Instruments	17.8
Continental Air Lines	45.5	Bell & Howell	22.4
Delta Air Lines	18.3	Foxboro	11.4
Eastern Air Lines	66.1	General Signal	12.0
National Airlines	23.3	Hewlett-Packard	1.0
Northwest Airlines	11.4	Johnson Controls	18.1
Pan Am	70.7	Perlein-Elmer	19.1
Tiger International	74.5	Sybron	28.4
TWA	65.0	Talley Industries	42.6
UAL	53.0	Technicon	21.4
Western Airlines	43.9	Teletronix	9.9
Food and lodgings		**Office equipmt., computers**	
ARA Services	24.4	Addressograph/Multigraph	26.3
Caesar's World	65.0	Burroughs	8.5
Denny's	40.0	Control Data	22.0
Hilton Hotels	43.7	Data General	25.4
Holiday Inns	36.7	Digital Equipment	10.6
Howard Johnson	4.0	Honeywell	15.3
Hyatt	73.1	IBM	2.0
Marriott	48.3	Memorex	51.5
McDonald's	49.3	NCR	29.5
Ramada Inn	63.8	Pitney-Bowes	33.1
Sambo's Restaurants	63.2	Sperry Rand	21.8
Webb	42.5	Xerox	24.8

Source: Data from *Business Week*, October 16, 1978, pp. 115, 127, 128, 135, 136.

Calculate the average financial leverage for each group and use one-way ANOVA to test whether the group means are equal. Discuss your findings.

Arrange your calculations on detailed worksheets and keep them for the next problem.

Hint: Use the shortcut equations for one-way ANOVA.

16.34. We continue to explore the financial leverage patterns of industry groups. The basic sample information is the same as in Problem 16.33.

(*a*) Use the *t* test to check for equality of mean financial leverage in the following pairs of industry groups:

i. Airlines and food and lodgings.

ii. Instruments and office equipment and computers.

iii. Airlines and instruments.

Use $\alpha = 1$ percent significance level.

Discuss your findings.

(b) Let us treat airlines and food and lodgings as one industry and instruments and office equipment and computers as another industry (can you justify this grouping by use of the findings in part *a*?) Pool the corresponding samples in two groups. Test the two pooled groups for equality of mean financial leverage. Again use $\alpha = 1$ percent significance level in your analysis. Discuss your results.

(c) Compare your findings in part *b* with the results of the one-way ANOVA in Problem 16.33. What results do you find more meaningful? Can you generalize your conclusion?

Case Problems

16.1. (a) Using the rates of return of mutual funds in Data Set 2, Appendix B, Table B.2, test the hypothesis that the mean rates of return in the first three categories of funds (i.e., "Maximum Capital Gains," "Long-Term Growth," and "Growth and Current Income Funds") are equal to one another. Use $\alpha = 5$ percent. Explain the assumptions on which your test is based and draw the conclusions.

(b) Consider the following four groups of funds (Data Set 2):

1. Funds 21–25
2. Funds 26–30
3. Funds 31–35
4. Funds 36–40

Test the hypothesis that the mean rates of return of the four groups are equal using $\alpha = 5$ percent. Explain the assumptions on which your test is based.

16.2. The annual rates of return of mutual funds investment are given in Data Set 2. The data cover a period of 10 years (1971–80) and are organized in eight distinct categories of funds.

Draw a random sample of three funds from each category, and carry out a two-way analysis of variance in which one variable is the category and the other is years. What is the meaning of the interaction in this case? Discuss the results of the analysis.

PART 4

REGRESSION AND CORRELATION (INDUCTION CONTINUED)

Part 3 of this book deals with statistical inference; Part 4 continues the discussion of this topic but focuses on the relationship between two or more variables, using regression analysis, which is one of the analytical tools most frequently used in many areas of business and economics. Chapters 17 and 18 focus on simple regression analysis: the former presents the theory and technique of simple regression and correlation, and the latter presents inference and applications. Chapter 19 extends the analysis to multiple regression, as well as partial and multiple correlation.

Part 4 includes applications and examples in the areas of cost accounting (allocation of indirect costs), finance (measuring security risk), marketing (investment in advertising), and economics (income and consumption). It also includes an application concerning the relationship between return on investments and their risk and an application involving measurement of changes in employee productivity at American Telephone and Telegraph.

SIMPLE LINEAR REGRESSION

Key Terms
simple regression analysis
dependent variable
response variable
independent variable
explanatory variable
multiple regression analysis
disturbance term
statistical relationship
scatter diagram
ordinary least-squares method
normal equations
Gauss-Markov theorem
BLUE: *best linear unbiased estimators*
standard error of estimate
coefficient of determination
coefficient of correlation

17.1 Introduction

We have not yet fully treated the relationship between two or more variables. Regression analysis, which deals with the way one variable tends to change as one or more other variables change, is a way to analyze such a relationship and is perhaps the most frequently used statistical procedure in business and economics; it is so important that we will devote this and the next two chapters to its presentation.

By employing regression analysis, we can find out not only whether a relationship between variables exists, but also the direction and amount of change that can be expected in one variable when other variables change. In addition, it provides the means of assessing the magnitude of the sampling errors of the estimates, or in other words, of making statistical inferences.

HISTORICAL BACKGROUND

Regression analysis takes its name from a study by Sir Francis Galton, published in the *Journal of the Anthropological Institute* in 1885 under the title "Regression Towards Mediocrity in Hereditary Stature." Galton's study dealt with the relationship between the heights of parents and the heights of their children. He found that tall parents tend to have tall children. He also found, however, that at the extremes there is an opposite tendency: children of unusually tall people tend to be shorter than their parents and children of unusually short people tend to be taller than their parents. He concluded that the heights of children of unusually tall and short people tend to *regress* toward the population's mean height. Galton termed the line describing the relationship between the heights of parents and children *the line of regression*.

SIMPLE AND MULTIPLE REGRESSION ANALYSIS

In certain cases we deal with relationships between two variables only; the regression analysis we perform in these cases is called **simple regression analysis.** Here we distinguish between the dependent variable, denoted by Y, and the independent variable, denoted by X. The **dependent variable**, also known as the **response variable**, is usually the *one whose value depends on the value of the other variable*. The **independent variable**, also known as the **explanatory variable**, is the *one whose value normally gives at least a partial explanation of the behavior of the dependent variable*. When regression analysis is applied to the effect of advertising expenditures on sales, for example, "sales" is the dependent variable and "advertising expenditures" is the independent, or explanatory, variable.

In business statistics we often deal with the relationship between a dependent variable (customarily denoted by Y) and a number of independent, or explanatory, variables (customarily denoted by $X_1, X_2, X_3, \ldots, X_K$). This type of regression analysis is called **multiple regression analysis**. For example, the time it takes for a truck to deliver goods from point A to point B is a function of the distance between the two points as well as of a host of other variables—the condition of the roads, the density of traffic, the type of truck driven, and so on. If we use regression analysis to determine the relationship between time and distance only, we perform a simple regression analysis, whereas if we relate the time to other variables as well, we perform a multiple regression analysis. This chapter deals with simple linear regression: we assume that the relationship between the variables is linear. Chapter 18 discusses the statistical inference of the regression, and Chapter 19 extends the analysis to a multiple linear regression.

17.2 Estimated vs. "True" Regression Lines

As a first step let us explain the concept of a statistical linear relationship between two variables. When two variables, X and Y, relate to one another as in Equation 17.1, we say that the relationship is *linear and deterministic*.

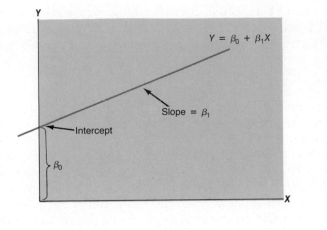

Figure 17.1

Description
of a simple
linear
relationship:
the value of *Y*
is on the line
when the
relationship
is determinis-
tic and
mostly off the
line when it
is statistical

$$Y = \beta_0 + \beta_1 X \tag{17.1}$$

In Equation 17.1, β_0 and β_1 are two parameters (that is, *constants*): β_0 is the value of the Y-intercept and β_1 is the slope of the line (see Figure 17.1). Given a value for the variable X, an accurate corresponding value of Y can be derived. For example, assuming $\beta_0 = 10$ and $\beta_1 = 2$, the value of Y that corresponds to $X = 5$ is $Y = 10 + 2 \cdot 5 = 20$. The relationship in Equation 17.1 is *not* the typical relationship between two variables in the areas of business or economics, where we are more likely to observe a *statistical relationship* like the one expressed by Equation 17.2:

$$Y = \beta_0 + \beta_1 X + u \tag{17.2}$$

Here β_0 and β_1 are two parameters, X is the independent variable, and u, the **disturbance term**, is a *random variable*. The variable Y is the dependent, or response, variable, for its value "depends" on, or "responds" to, the values of the parameters and variables appearing on the right-hand side of Equation 17.2. Since u is a random variable, so is the variable Y, which has u as one of its components. Whereas the variable Y in the deterministic model (Equation 17.1) is not a random variable, the statistical model (Equation 17.2) assumes that it is. The variable X, however, is not assumed to be random in any of these models. A **statistical relationship**, then, is *one in which the dependent variable is not totally determined by the independent variable: it is determined in part by the independent variable and in part by the value of the random disturbance term.*

The regression model of interest to us is the one described in Equation 17.2. And just as we distinguish between a distribution mean (μ) and its sample estimator ($\overline{X}$) and between a distribution standard deviation (σ) and its sample estimator (S), we also distinguish between "real" or "true" regression parameters, β_0 and β_1, and their sample counterparts, b_0 and b_1, which are merely point estimators of β_0 and β_1. (If the true line were known, we would not need to estimate the regression line.)

Generally speaking, the estimates b_0 and b_1 differ from the true regression line's intercept and slope and vary from one sample to another, since they are subject to sampling errors. While there is only one true regression line (which is not observed), many regression lines may be estimated, each with its own value of the intercept b_0 and the slope b_1, as shown in Figure 17.2. This is similar to obtaining different values of a sample mean, $\overline{X}$, from one sample to another, whereas only one true mean, μ, exists in the population.

Figure 17.2

A "true" regression line and three estimated lines

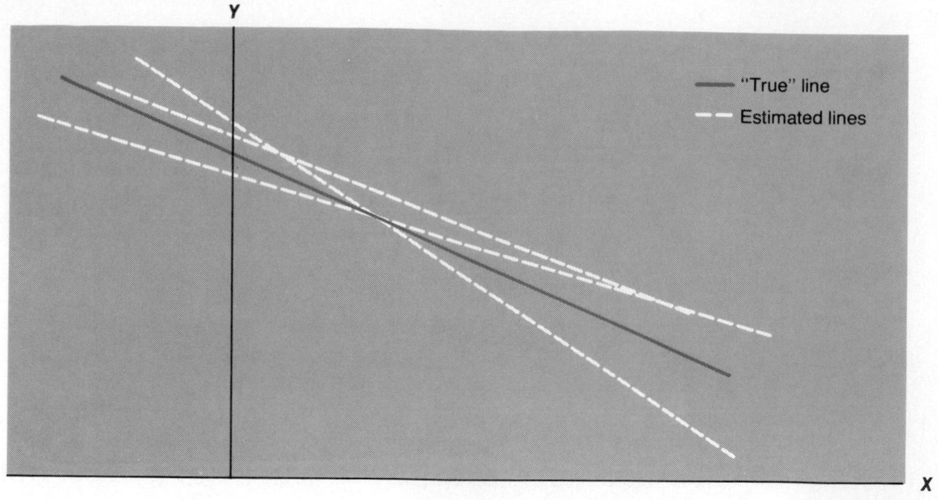

HOW THE VALUE *u* AFFECTS THE VALUE *Y*

To see more clearly why the estimated and true regression lines do not generally coincide, recall that the true regression model is given by

$$Y = \beta_0 + \beta_1 X + u$$

Since *u* is a random variable, a whole probability distribution of *Y* corresponds to any *single* value of *X*. We saw earlier that if $Y = \beta_0 + \beta_1 X$, $\beta_0 = 10$, $\beta_1 = 2$, and $X = 5$, we get a single value of *Y*, namely, $Y = 10 + 2 \cdot 5 = 20$. If, however, $Y = \beta_0 + \beta_1 X + u$ and *u* takes on different values from one observation to the next, so does *Y*. Table 17.1 shows how the value of the dependent variable *Y* varies with *u for a given level of X*.

The consequence of the randomness of *Y* at any value of *X* is shown in Figure 17.3, where a probability distribution of *Y* is drawn for each of the three given levels of *X*. The result is that different samples differ in their *Y* values even for the same values of *X*; consequently, the estimated regression line varies from one sample to the next. Figure 17.3 also shows that the probability distributions of *Y* vary from one value of *X* to the next (in Figure

TABLE 17.1

Alternative Values of *Y* for a Given Value of *X* When the Relationship Is $Y = 10 + 2X + u$ and *u* Is a Random Variable

Observation *i*	Value of independent variable X_i	β_0	β_1	Value of random factor u_i	Value of dependent variable Y_i
1	5	10	2	1.5	21.5
2	5	10	2	0.0	20.0
3	5	10	2	0.2	20.2
4	5	10	2	−1.6	18.4
5	5	10	2	0.9	20.9
6	5	10	2	−2.0	18.0
7	5	10	2	3.0	23.0
8	5	10	2	−1.0	19.0
9	5	10	2	4.0	24.0
10	5	10	2	5.0	25.0

f(Y|X)

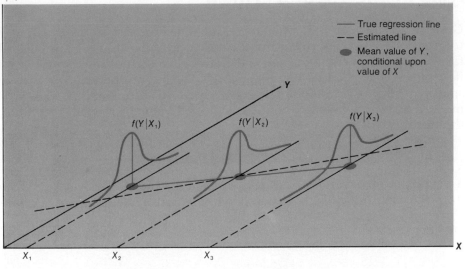

Figure 17.3

The regression
line and the
conditional
probability
distribution,
$f(Y|X_i)$

17.3, the higher the value of X, the higher the mean of Y). In fact, the probability distribution of Y is a conditional probability distribution (conditional, that is, on the respective value of $X:X_i$) and is denoted by $f(Y \mid X_i)$. The following assumptions are made about the conditional distributions $f(Y \mid X_i)$ in the regression analysis:

1. The observations, Y_i, are statistically independent of one another. For example, if for some value X_1 we observed a corresponding value Y_1 below the regression line, it does not imply that the value Y_2 that corresponds to X_2 will also be below the line. Rather, the value Y_2 is independent of the value Y_1 and of the value of any other observation of the dependent variable. In many time series (such as company monthly sales), the values of Y are not independent of one another. The analysis of such time series requires a special technique called time-series analysis. Chapter 20 is devoted to this topic.

2. The variance of the conditional probability distribution, $f(Y \mid X_i)$, which we denote by σ^2, *is the same for all values of X.* Formally we write $V(Y \mid X_i) \equiv V(Y_i) = \sigma^2$, where $V(Y_i)$ should be understood to stand for the variance of Y when X is fixed at the level X_i.

3. The mean of the conditional probability distribution of Y (denoted by μ_i) lies on the true regression line, meaning that

$$Y \mid X_i = \beta_0 + \beta_1 X_i + u_i \equiv \mu_i + u_i$$

and

$$E(Y \mid X_i) \equiv E(Y_i) \equiv \mu_i = \beta_0 + \beta_1 X_i$$

where $E(Y_i)$ stands for the expected value of Y, given that X is fixed at X_i. This assumption can be simply written as $E(u_i) = 0$ for all i. Note the difference between $E(Y)$ and $E(Y_i)$. Whereas $E(Y)$ is the expected value of the entire population of Y, the value $E(Y_i)$ is the same as $E(Y \mid X_i)$ and it is the expected value of those Ys for which X is equal to the specific value X_i.

17.3 Analysis of the Error Term, *u*

Granted, the estimated (sample) regression line differs from the true line due to sampling errors, but this is not the reason why the value of Y is generally found off the regression line and is therefore unknown before observed: even if we knew what the true regression line was, the specific value of Y for any specified value of X would not be known because of the random term u. The model's assumptions imply that the expected value of Y when the value of the variable X is X_i is given by

$$\mu_i = \beta_0 + \beta_1 X_i$$

A particular observation, Y_i, at the explanatory variable's level X_i is drawn from the conditional distribution shown in Figure 17.4, and the deviation of

Figure 17.4

The "true" regression line and the random term *u*

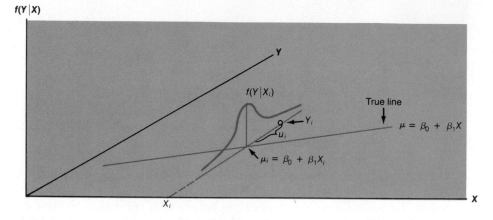

the value Y_i from the line is u_i. When Y_i is above the line, u_i is positive, and when Y_i is below the line, u_i is negative. The deviation u_i is attributable, in principle, to two factors:

1. Errors in measuring the dependent variable. For example, few people can state precisely their consumption expenditures in the past month or year; consequently, a sample of income and consumption is bound to include some degree of measurement error.
2. Even if measurement errors could be avoided, deviations from the line would still exist due to sampling errors. Households of equal income have different consumption levels for a variety of reasons, such as differences in their wealth (assets), their habits, the number of household members, and so on.

THE EXPECTED VALUE AND VARIANCE OF *u*

The above assumptions imply several things about the disturbance term, u. Starting with the model

$$Y = \beta_0 + \beta_1 X + u$$

we can express u as follows:

$$u = Y - (\beta_0 + \beta_1 X) \tag{17.3}$$

At any given level of X, X_i, Equation 17.3 becomes

$$u_i = Y_i - (\beta_0 + \beta_1 X_i) \tag{17.4}$$

and since β_0 and β_1 are constant parameters and X_i is a single value of X—also a constant—we get

$$E(u_i) = E(Y_i) - (\beta_0 + \beta_1 X_i) \tag{17.5}$$

where $E(u_i)$ and $E(Y_i)$ should be interpreted again to represent the expected values of u and Y, respectively, when X is fixed at the level X_i. Recalling that $\beta_0 + \beta_1 X_i = \mu_i$ (see assumption 3), we get the equation

$$E(u_i) = E(Y_i) - \mu_i = \mu_i - \mu_i = 0 \tag{17.6}$$

which is consistent with assumption 3. Taking the variance of Y at a given level of X, X_i, and recalling again that X_i is treated as a constant, we derive the following:

$$V(Y_i) = V(\beta_0 + \beta_1 X_i + u_i) = V(u_i) \tag{17.7}$$

Thus

$$V(Y_i) \equiv \sigma^2 = \sigma_u^2 \equiv V(u_i) \tag{17.8}$$

Note the distinction between $V(Y)$ and $V(Y_i)$. While the former is the variance of the entire population of Y, $V(Y_i)$ is the variance of Y when X is equal to X_i.

As we have seen, the variables Y and u are related to each other. Therefore, the regression assumptions can be written in terms of u rather than Y, as follows:

1. The u_is are independent of one another.
2. $V(u_i) = \sigma_u^2$ and is the same for all levels of X.
3. $E(u_i) = 0$.

Note that at this stage we do not assume a specific probability distribution for Y_i (or u_i). Only in the next chapter when we discuss statistical inference will we introduce the assumption that Y_i and u_i are normally distributed. Many of the derivations in this chapter are not based on the assumption of normality.

17.4 The Relationship Between the Estimated Regression Line and the Distribution of the Error Term, *u*

The true regression model, as we have seen, is given by

$$Y_i = \beta_0 + \beta_1 X_i + u_i \tag{17.9}$$

Given a sample of data, we "fit" an estimated line through them and obtain the following relationship:

$$Y_i = b_0 + b_1 X_i + e_i \tag{17.10}$$

where b_0 and b_1 are the fitted line's intercept and slope, respectively, and e_i is the deviation of the ith observation from the fitted line. This is illustrated in Figure 17.5.

Figure 17.5

The "true" regression line and the estimated regression line

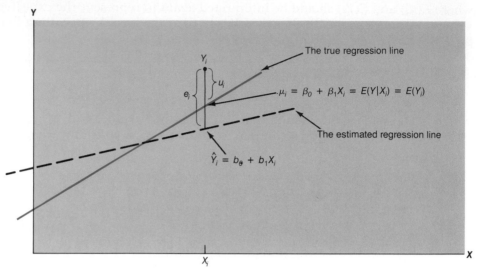

Equations 17.9 and 17.10 differ in two respects, as can be seen in Figure 17.5:

1. Equation 17.9 is formulated in terms of the true but unobserved parameters, β_0 and β_1; Equation 17.10 is formulated in terms of their respective estimators, b_0 and b_1.
2. The deviation u_i in Equation 17.9 is a deviation from the true line, while the deviation e_i in Equation 17.10 is a deviation from the estimated line.

Obviously, when we fit the estimated line through the data we aim to get as close as possible to the true line. But how close we come depends partly on the distribution of the term u. The more condensed the values of u are around their mean, the closer the fitted line will come to the true line (other things being equal, of course). This becomes clear with a glance at Figure 17.6, which shows estimated versus true regression lines under two alternative shapes of the conditional distributions:[1] in Figure 17.6*a* the distributions are relatively condensed and the estimated regression line is relatively close to the true line. In Figure 17.6*b*, which illustrates more dispersed conditional distributions (but leaves all other factors the same), the estimated regression line is subject to greater sampling errors and may not be as close to the true line as in 17.6*a*. In the extreme case, where we assume that the conditional

[1] The conditional distributions in Figure 17.6 are drawn as normal distributions, but this need not necessarily be the case.

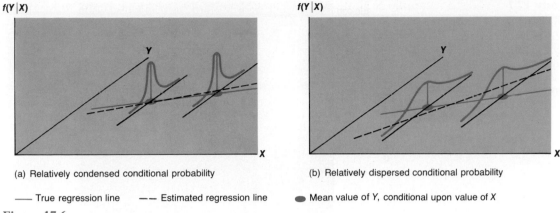

| (a) Relatively condensed conditional probability | (b) Relatively dispersed conditional probability |

—— True regression line   —— Estimated regression line   ● Mean value of Y, conditional upon value of X

Figure 17.6

The true and the estimated regression lines with different dispersions of the conditional probability distribution, $f(Y|X)$

distributions of u_i have no variance (that is, $\sigma_u^2 = 0$), $u_i = 0$, the model is deterministic and is given by $Y_i = \beta_0 + \beta_1 X_i$. In this case all the sample points (X_i, Y_i) lie precisely on the straight line and a sample of size $n = 2$ or greater always yields an estimated line that coincides with the true line. As we shall see later, the dispersion of the conditional distribution of Y is not the only factor that determines the sampling errors in the constants b_0 and b_1. The sample size used in estimating the coefficients and the dispersion of the observed values of X are other important factors.

17.5 Fitting a Regression Line: Preliminary Considerations

In this section we shall consider alternative ways of fitting the estimated regression line to sample data, and show that the so-called ordinary least-squares method is the best.

Let us begin by looking at Figure 17.7, which shows the relationship between annual household income (the independent variable) and household consumption (the dependent variable). We present only households with annual incomes of $10,000, $20,000, and $30,000. For each income level, nine or ten observations are marked (of course many more belong to the population), showing various levels of consumption. The diversity of consumption levels among households of the same income level is due to variations in household size and wealth (assets), wealth and income of relatives, habits, philosophy of life, and so on. For each household, both income and consumption levels are represented by one dot in the diagram. The diagram shows that the higher the income, the higher the *mean* level of consumption of the household. The dependent variable is in fact a random variable, though the independent variable is not. In other words, given a certain level of income, it is impossible to determine the consumption level of a household before that household's consumption has been observed.

The data presented in Figure 17.7 are atypical in the sense that quite a few observations are shown for each of the selected values of the independent variable. The presentation is intended to demonstrate the point that the *Y*

Figure 17.7

Relationship between income (X) and consumption (Y)

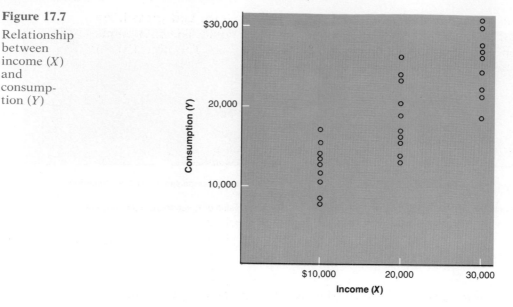

values obtained in a sample for a given value of X differ from one another: they are random. In a more typical case, there will be few observations—often only one—for each of the observed values of the independent variable, X. When these observations are plotted in the (X, Y) plane, a **scatter diagram** is obtained, as in Figure 17.8, the data for which are given in Table 17.2. Note that each observation consists of an income value as well as a consumption value. Ten observations, then, yielded 20 pieces of data. A glance at Figure 17.8 reveals two important facts. First, there appears to be a direct relationship between X and Y: consumption tends to rise as income rises. Second, the observations are scattered and do not lie along a straight line. In order to characterize the relationship between the dependent and independent variables, we wish to draw a straight line through the scattered

Figure 17.8

Scatter diagram based on the data from Table 17.2 and a fitted line $\hat{Y} = b_0 + b_1 x$

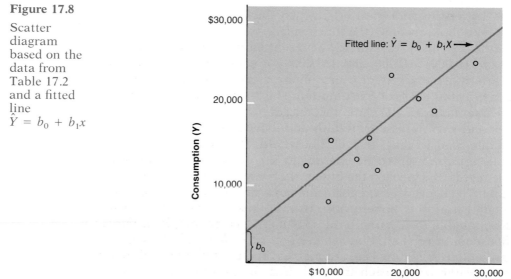

data points in such a way that it will best "fit" the data and provide an estimate for the "true" line relating consumption to income. The data points will, as we have mentioned, deviate from the fitted line. The objective in fitting a line is to minimize any errors involved.

TABLE 17.2
Ten Observations of Household Annual Income and Consumption
(thousands of dollars)

Observation i	Income X_i	Consumption Y_i
1	$10.0	$15.0
2	18.0	23.5
3	28.0	25.0
4	7.0	12.5
5	13.0	13.0
6	16.0	12.0
7	22.0	19.0
8	15.0	16.0
9	20.0	21.0
10	10.0	8.0

THE FITTED-LINE BASIC EQUATION

A straight line relating X to Y in the sample is given by

$$\hat{Y} = b_0 + b_1 X \tag{17.11}$$

where b_0 is the vertical intercept (or Y-intercept), b_1 is the slope of the line, and $\hat{Y}$ is the fitted value of Y (see Figure 17.8). When searching for a line that fits the sample data, we want to find the values b_0 and b_1 that minimize total sampling errors involved.

FITTING THE LINE: METHODS AND CRITERIA

One way of fitting a line through the scattered data is to try a freehand fitting: we simply do our best by approximation. This method is unacceptable, however, because of the large potential errors in determining the line and the resulting inability to quantify the sampling errors. Clearly, we need a quantitative method that will uniquely determine the best line for given sample data. Let us examine some of the possible methods.

One possibility is to find the line that minimizes the sum of *horizontal* deviations of each point from the line (see Figure 17.9). This method is also unacceptable, however, since the horizontal distance between a point and the line simply does not measure any sampling error. As we explained earlier, the dependent variable, Y, is a random variable, while the independent variable is not; therefore, minimizing deviation in X is meaningless. For a given value of X, X_0, the fitted Y value is $\hat{Y}_0 = b_0 + b_1 X_0$. If the sample observation Y_0 is equal to $\hat{Y}_0$, the observation lies on the fitted line, and there is no deviation of the observation from the line. If the observation Y_0 is greater or less than $\hat{Y}_0$, it lies above or below the fitted line, and a positive

Figure 17.9

Horizontal
deviations
from the
fitted line

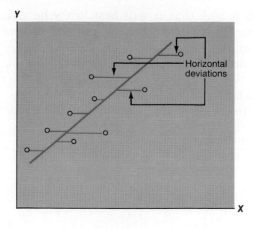

or negative deviation exists. It is the deviation in *Y* that we need to minimize, not that in *X*.

Given that the vertical rather than the horizontal deviations from the fitted line demand our attention, we may want to fit to the data the line that minimizes the sum of all the vertical deviations:

$$\sum_{i=1}^{n} (Y_i - \hat{Y}_i)$$

Here *n* is the sample size, Y_i is the *Y* value of the *i*th observation, and $\hat{Y}_i$ is the corresponding *Y* value on the fitted line. While the minimization of $\sum_{i=1}^{n} (Y_i - \hat{Y}_i)$ may be intuitively a very appealing choice of a criterion for fitting a line through the scattered points, it is perhaps the worst criterion we could choose. If we follow this criterion, we will get a line that does not even come close to the sample points. The reason becomes obvious when we study Figure 17.10. Here two arbitrary lines are presented, one that passes

Figure 17.10

The sum
of the
deviations
from two
arbitrary
(parallel)
lines

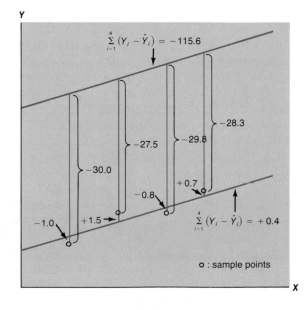

through the sample points and another that passes far above them. The line passing through the points (clearly a better choice for our purpose) gives a sum of deviations of $+0.4$, while the other line, which obviously is far from being the line we are looking for, gives a much *lower* sum of deviations: -115.6. It is clear that the higher the line above the sample points, the lower the quantity $\sum_{i=1}^{n} (Y_i - \hat{Y}_i)$; moreover, the line that minimizes this quantity passes at an infinite distance above the data points. Obviously this criterion is inappropriate.

Instead of minimizing the quantity $\sum_{i=1}^{n} (Y_i - \hat{Y}_i)$ and sending the line off to infinity, we can force the line through the sample points by setting this quantity at zero. In other words, the criterion we want to examine now is the selection of a line that brings the sum of all the deviations to zero: $\sum_{i=1}^{n} (Y_i - \hat{Y}_i) = 0$. This criterion, however, also suffers from a serious drawback. Consider a small sample of five observations, as follows:

Observation	Y	X
1	3	3
2	5	2
3	6	5
4	4	7
5	7	8

The scatter diagram is presented in Figure 17.11. In Figure 17.11*a* the line $\hat{Y} = 3.46155 + 0.30769X$ is drawn and the vertical deviation of each observation from the line is marked. A simple check shows that the sum of the deviations is equal to zero, so the line meets the criterion. Note that the line passes through the point of averages $(\overline{X}, \overline{Y})$. In Figure 17.11*b* the same sample points are shown, but a different line is drawn through the points of averages: $\hat{Y} = 7.5 - 0.5X$. The vertical deviations of the observations from the line are marked here too, and as we can see, they add up to zero again. This

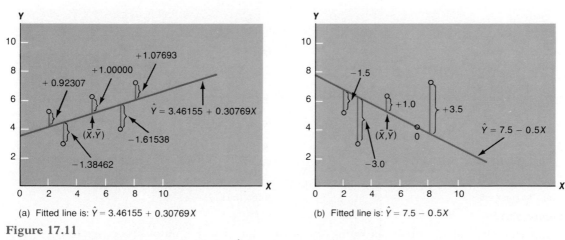

(a) Fitted line is: $\hat{Y} = 3.46155 + 0.30769X$

(b) Fitted line is: $\hat{Y} = 7.5 - 0.5X$

Figure 17.11

Two lines fitted by the criterion $\Sigma(Y_i - \hat{Y}_i) = 0$

line, then, also meets the criterion. In fact, an infinite number of lines can be drawn through the point $(\overline{X}, \overline{Y})$ and all of them meet the criterion. Most of these lines fall far short of characterizing the relationship between X and Y; consequently, this criterion is faulty as well.

Having dismissed the previous criteria for fitting a line as inappropriate, let us see what happens when we bring the magnitude $\sum\limits_{i=1}^{n} |Y_i - \hat{Y}_i|$, the sum of the absolute deviations, to a minimum. This method is significantly better than the others, but it is mathematically complex. It also results in a line whose statistical properties are inferior to those of the line obtained when we bring the sum of squared deviations to a minimum. Therefore, we finally propose the selection of the line that minimizes the sum of squared deviations: $\Sigma(Y_i - \hat{Y})^2$. If you think that minimizing the absolute deviations from the line and minimizing the squared deviations result in the same regression line, let us consider a simple example to show the contrary. Suppose a small sample of three observations provides the following data:

X	Y
2	6
4	14
6	10
$\overline{X} = 4$	$\overline{Y} = 10$

Figure 17.12 shows the scatter diagram with two alternative lines fitted through the data. In Figure 17.12a the line $\hat{Y} = 6 + X$ is drawn through the data and in 17.12b the line $\hat{Y} = 4 + X$ is drawn through the same data. By methods that will be shown later in the chapter, we can definitely say that the line in Figure 17.12a—that is, $\hat{Y} = 6 + X$—brings the sum of the squared deviations from the line to a minimum; no other straight line can be drawn that will bring the sum of squared deviations below the sum obtained by the line $\hat{Y} = 6 + X$. The sum of squared deviations from this line is

$$\Sigma(Y_i - \hat{Y})^2 = (4)^2 + (-2)^2 + (-2)^2 = 16 + 4 + 4 = 24$$

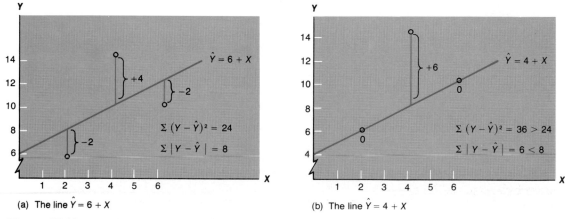

(a) The line $\hat{Y} = 6 + X$ (b) The line $\hat{Y} = 4 + X$

Figure 17.12

Comparing alternative criteria for fitting a regression line: the minimum sum of squared deviations and the minimum sum of absolute deviations

The sum of the absolute deviations is

$$\Sigma |Y_i - \hat{Y}| = |4| + |-2| + |-2| = 4 + 2 + 2 = 8$$

Now consider the line in Figure 17.12*b*: $\hat{Y} = 4 + X$. The sum of the squared deviations, as we could have expected, rises above 24, but at the same time the sum of absolute deviations falls below 8:

$$\Sigma(Y_i - \hat{Y})^2 = (0)^2 + (6)^2 + (0)^2 = 36 > 24$$

and

$$\Sigma |Y_i - \hat{Y}| = |0| + |6| + |0| = 6 < 8$$

This example shows that the two criteria result in two different lines. As we argued earlier, the sum of squared deviations is preferable because it is convenient mathematically and even more so because the resulting regression line has some superior qualities from a statistical standpoint.

Minimizing the sum of squared deviations, $\Sigma(Y_i - \hat{Y})^2$, is called the **ordinary least-squares method.** It is the method used in most regression analyses; we shall devote the rest of this chapter and the next two chapters to its description and its interpretation. The advantages of the method are these:

1. It identifies the vertical (rather than the horizontal) deviation between each point and the line as the relevant deviation magnitude.
2. By squaring each deviation, the criterion overcomes the sign disadvantage of the method that uses the deviation itself.
3. It is much easier to handle mathematically than the method that sums the absolute deviations.
4. There is a theoretical argument in favor of the ordinary least-squares method, known as the Gauss-Markov theorem, which will be discussed in Section 17.7.

17.6 How the Ordinary Least-Squares Method Works

The principle of the ordinary least-squares (OLS) method is as follows: out of all of the possible regression lines that we can draw through the scatter diagram, we choose the one that minimizes the sum of the squared deviations from the line. Figure 17.13 helps to explain this principle. Here a straight line drawn through sample observations in an arbitrary manner is shown. We shall refer to this line as the "arbitrary regression line." From each point representing an observation, we drop or raise a vertical line toward the arbitrary regression line. In this way we obtain for each observation, Y_i, a corresponding point on the arbitrary regression line, which we denote by $\hat{Y}_i$. For each Y_i we now define a deviation, or an "error" term, which we denote by e_i and define as

$$e_i = Y_i - \hat{Y}_i \tag{17.12}$$

Figure 17.13 illustrates the relationship between Y_i and $\hat{Y}_i$ and clearly identifies the "error" term, e_i, for a given observation, which may be positive,

Figure 17.13

An arbitrary
line drawn
through
sample data

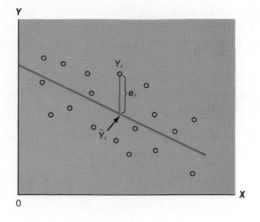

zero, or negative. The OLS method leads us to choose the particular regression line (out of an infinite number of possible lines) that *brings the sum of squared errors to a minimum*. Denoting the parameters of the line by b_0 and b_1, we locate the points $\hat{Y}_i$ on the line by means of the equation

$$\hat{Y}_i = b_0 + b_1 X_i \qquad \textbf{(17.13)}$$

and the *i*th observation, Y_i, deviates from the line by e_i (see Figure 17.13):

$$Y_i = b_0 + b_1 X_i + e_i = \hat{Y}_i + e_i \qquad \textbf{(17.14)}$$

The OLS method leads us to derive the particular b_0 and b_1 that bring the expression Σe_i^2 to a minimum. By Equation 17.14 we get

$$\Sigma e_i^2 = \Sigma(Y_i - \hat{Y}_i)^2 \qquad \textbf{(17.15)}$$

Substituting $\hat{Y}_i = b_0 + b_1 X_i$ in Equation 17.15 yields

$$\Sigma e_i^2 = \Sigma(Y_i - b_0 - b_1 X_i)^2 \qquad \textbf{(17.16)}$$

To bring Σe_i^2 to a minimum by varying b_0 and b_1, we take the partial derivatives of Equation 17.16 with respect to both b_0 and b_1, equate the derivatives to zero, and solve. Following this procedure, we get

$$\frac{\partial \Sigma(Y_i - b_0 - b_1 X_i)^2}{\partial b_0} = \Sigma(2)(Y_i - b_0 - b_1 X_i)(-1) = 0 \qquad \textbf{(17.17)}$$

$$\frac{\partial \Sigma(Y_i - b_0 - b_1 X_i)^2}{\partial b_1} = \Sigma(2)(Y_i - b_0 - b_1 X_i)(-X_i) = 0 \qquad \textbf{(17.18)}$$

From Equations 17.17 and 17.18 we derive Equations 17.19 and 17.20, which are known as the **normal equations:**

$$\Sigma Y_i - n b_0 - b_1 \Sigma X_i = 0 \qquad \textbf{(17.19)}$$

$$\Sigma X_i Y_i - b_0 \Sigma X_i - b_1 \Sigma X_i^2 = 0 \qquad \textbf{(17.20)}$$

Here n stands for the number of observations available. The two unknowns of the normal equations are the constants b_0 and b_1. All the other quantities are sample statistics and are readily available. Solving for b_0 and b_1 we obtain[2]

$$b_1 = \frac{\Sigma X_i Y_i - n\overline{X}\overline{Y}}{\Sigma X_i^2 - n\overline{X}^2} = \frac{\Sigma(X_i - \overline{X})(Y_i - \overline{Y})}{\Sigma(X_i - \overline{X})^2} \qquad (17.21)$$

$$b_0 = \overline{Y} - b_1\overline{X} \qquad (17.22)$$

Given the sample data, we first calculate b_1 from Equation 17.21, then use b_1 along with $\overline{Y}$ and $\overline{X}$ to calculate the value of b_0 by means of Equation 17.22.

USING THE OLS METHOD

Table 17.3 is basically a work sheet for the calculation of the coefficients b_0 and b_1 in our income and consumption example (Table 17.2). Once the sample data have been compiled as shown in Table 17.3, we may proceed

---

[2] After dividing Equation 17.19 by n throughout, we get

$$\frac{\Sigma Y_i}{n} - b_0 - b_1\frac{\Sigma X_i}{n} = 0 \qquad (1)$$

and since $\dfrac{\Sigma Y_i}{n} = \overline{Y}$ and $\dfrac{\Sigma X_i}{n} = \overline{X}$, we may rewrite (1) as follows:

$$b_0 = \overline{Y} - b_1\overline{X} \qquad (2)$$

Substituting (1) in 17.20, we obtain

$$\Sigma X_i Y_i - (\overline{Y} - b_1\overline{X})\Sigma X_i - b_1\Sigma X_i^2 = 0 \qquad (3)$$

or

$$b_1(\overline{X}\Sigma X_i - \Sigma X_i^2) = -\Sigma X_i Y_i + \overline{Y}\Sigma X_i \qquad (4)$$

Since $\Sigma X_i = n\overline{X}$, we get $\overline{X}\Sigma X_i = n\overline{X}^2$ and $\overline{Y}\Sigma X_i = n\overline{X}\overline{Y}$. By substituting these expressions in (4) and multiplying both sides by -1, we obtain

$$b_1(\Sigma X_i^2 - n\overline{X}^2) = \Sigma X_i Y_i - n\overline{X}\overline{Y} \qquad (5)$$

which gives

$$b_1 = \frac{\Sigma X_i Y_i - n\overline{X}\overline{Y}}{\Sigma X_i^2 - n\overline{X}^2} \qquad (6)$$

It is easy to show that the numerator of (6) equals $\Sigma(X_i - \overline{X})(Y_i - \overline{Y})$ and the denominator equals $\Sigma(X_i - \overline{X})^2$, which gives the following formula for b_1:

$$b_1 = \frac{\Sigma(X_i - \overline{X})(Y_i - \overline{Y})}{\Sigma(X_i - \overline{X})^2} \qquad (7)$$

TABLE 17.3
Work Sheet for Calculation of the Coefficients b_0 and b_1

Observation i	Annual income (thousands of dollars) X_i	Annual consumption (thousands of dollars) Y_i	X_i^2	Y_i^2	X_iY_i
1	10.00	15.00	100.00	225.00	150.00
2	18.00	23.50	324.00	552.25	423.00
3	28.00	25.00	784.00	625.00	700.00
4	7.00	12.50	49.00	156.25	87.50
5	13.00	13.00	169.00	169.00	169.00
6	16.00	12.00	256.00	144.00	192.00
7	22.00	19.00	484.00	361.00	418.00
8	15.00	16.00	225.00	256.00	240.00
9	20.00	21.00	400.00	441.00	420.00
10	10.00	8.00	100.00	64.00	80.00
Total	$\Sigma X_i = 159.00$	$\Sigma Y_i = 165.00$	$\Sigma X_i^2 = 2{,}891.00$	$\Sigma Y_i^2 = 2{,}993.50$	$\Sigma X_iY_i = 2{,}879.50$
	$\overline{X} = 15.90$	$\overline{Y} = 16.50$			

directly to calculate the desired coefficients of the estimated regression line. Substituting in Equation 17.21, we get

$$b_1 = \frac{\Sigma X_iY_i - n\overline{X}\overline{Y}}{\Sigma X_i^2 - n\overline{X}^2} = \frac{2{,}879.5 - (10)(15.9)(16.5)}{2{,}891.0 - (10)(15.9)^2} = \frac{256.0}{362.9} = 0.705$$

Using this result, we can also derive the coefficient b_0:

$$b_0 = \overline{Y} - b_1\overline{X} = 16.5 - (0.705)(15.9) = 16.5 - 11.2 = 5.3$$

The sample regression equation is

$$\hat{Y} = 5.3 + 0.705X$$

The interpretation of the regression line is as follows: for each \$1 increase in annual income, we estimate an increase of \$0.705 in average consumption. For households with no income ($X = 0$), we estimate average consumption to be \$5,300. This relationship between X and Y is shown in Figure 17.14.

Figure 17.14

The ordinary least-squares regression line in the income-consumption example

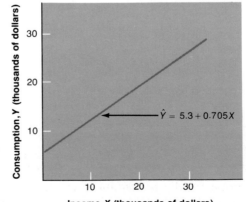

$\hat{Y} = 5.3 + 0.705X$

Consumption, Y (thousands of dollars)

Income, X (thousands of dollars)

17.7 Properties of Ordinary Least-Squares Estimators

Ordinary least-squares estimators have the following important properties:

1. Each is a linear combination of the observations Y_i; thus they are said to be linear estimators.
2. They are unbiased, meaning that the expected values of b_0 and b_1 are equal, respectively, to β_0 and β_1.
3. Among all the unbiased linear estimators, b_0 and b_1 have the lowest variance, a desirable property.

Let us look at these properties in more detail.

OLS ESTIMATORS ARE LINEAR ESTIMATORS

To show the first property, we simply write b_1 as follows:

$$b_1 = \frac{\Sigma(X_i - \overline{X})Y_i}{\Sigma(X_i - \overline{X})^2} - \frac{\Sigma(X_i - \overline{X})\overline{Y}}{\Sigma(X_i - X)^2}$$

Since $\overline{Y}$ is a constant for any given sample, and since $\Sigma(X_i - \overline{X})$ is always equal to zero, we find $\Sigma(X_i - \overline{X})\overline{Y} = \overline{Y}\Sigma(X_i - \overline{X}) = 0$. Denoting $\dfrac{(X_i - \overline{X})}{\Sigma(X_i - \overline{X})^2} = W_i$, we write

$$b_1 = \Sigma W_i Y_i \qquad\qquad \textbf{(17.23)}$$

This demonstrates that the estimator b_1 is a linear combination of the values Y_i and that the W_is are the coefficients of this combination. Since the estimator b_0 is a linear function of b_1, it follows that it is also a linear combination of the observations Y_i.

Later in this chapter we shall consider a procedure for testing hypotheses concerning the estimated parameters b_0 and b_1; this procedure will show the importance of the above property. To test hypotheses concerning b_1, we need to know its distribution. The fact that b_1 is a linear combination of the observations Y_i implies that if the Y_is are normally distributed, so is the estimator b_1. Indeed, we will have to assume that the Y_is are normally distributed in order to test hypotheses concerning b_1.

OLS ESTIMATORS ARE UNBIASED

The unbiasedness of b_0 and b_1 means that

$$E(b_0) = \beta_0 \qquad\qquad \textbf{(17.24)}$$

$$E(b_1) = \beta_1 \qquad\qquad \textbf{(17.25)}$$

While the proof of Equations 17.24 and 17.25 is not overly difficult to follow, it is nevertheless tedious, and we therefore present it in Appendix 17A. The importance of the property of unbiasedness is obvious. If we run many regressions, we expect on the average to hit the true values β_0 and β_1.

THE GAUSS-MARKOV THEOREM

After seeing that b_0 and b_1 are linear unbiased estimators of β_0 and β_1, we turn to the third property, stated in the following well-known theorem:

GAUSS-MARKOV THEOREM

Within the class of linear unbiased estimators of β_0 and β_1, the ordinary least-squares estimators, b_0 and b_1, have the minimum variance.

Although we will not prove this theorem, you should realize that it provides a major justification for use of the ordinary least-squares method of fitting a line to sample data. Obviously, the smaller the variance of the estimator, the better, since the smaller the variance, the higher the chance of fitting the line close to the true line.

The variances of b_0 and b_1 are given by Equation 17.26:

$$V(b_0) \equiv \sigma_{b_0}^2 = \sigma_u^2 \left[\frac{1}{n} + \frac{\overline{X}^2}{\Sigma(X_i - \overline{X})^2} \right] \tag{17.26a}$$

$$V(b_1) \equiv \sigma_{b_1}^2 = \frac{\sigma_u^2}{\Sigma(X_i - \overline{X})^2} \tag{17.26b}$$

(The derivation of $V(b_1)$ is shown in Appendix 17A.) According to the **Gauss-Markov theorem**, there are no linear unbiased estimators of β_0 and β_1 with variances smaller than those given by Equation 17.26. Therefore, the OLS estimators b_0 and b_1 are called **BLUE:** "**best linear unbiased estimators.**"

17.8 The Estimated Standard Deviation of the Dependent Variable, *Y*, and of the Error Term, *e*

In order to analytically assess the sampling errors in our regression analysis, we should first clarify the difference between two important estimators: the estimator of the standard deviation of Y, which we denote by S_Y, and the estimator of the *conditional* standard deviation of Y, given any X value, which we denote by S_e and which is known as the **standard error of estimate.** Obviously, S_Y and S_e are the sample counterparts of the true measures σ_Y and σ_u, respectively, and they are used in statistical inference, as we shall see in the next chapter.

The standard deviation of Y, σ_Y, measures the total variability of the variable Y, regardless of the value of the variable X. Thus, if data are collected relating household consumption (Y) to household income (X), the measure S_Y relates to the diversity of consumption in the total sample, regardless of the differences in income among households in the sample. Obviously, some differences in consumption still exist among households, even after we have accounted for differences in income. This gives rise to the error term u, whose σ_u is estimated by the standard deviation of the sample error terms, e_i, and denoted by S_e. In other words, the standard error of estimate, S_e, measures the degree of scatter of the data about the estimated regression line.

In Figure 17.15, a representative observation (Y_i) deviates from the sample average $(\overline{Y})$ by the amount identified as "total deviation," which equals $Y_i - \overline{Y}$. This "total deviation" is composed of two parts:

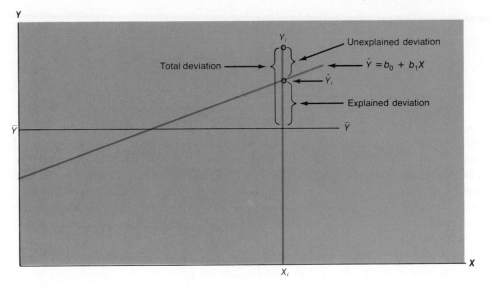

Figure 17.15

Deviation of
an observa-
tion from the
sample
average and
from the
regression
line

1. The deviation $\hat{Y}_i - \overline{Y}$, which is known as the "explained deviation" or "deviation due to the regression."
2. The "unexplained deviation" or "deviation around the regression line," which is given by $Y_i - \hat{Y}_i$.

The relationship between these deviations is as follows:

Total deviation = explained deviation + unexplained deviation

$$Y_i - \overline{Y} = (\hat{Y}_i - \overline{Y}) + (Y_i - \hat{Y}_i) \qquad \text{(17.27)}$$

When the sample data become available, we can use the total deviation to *estimate* the total standard deviation of Y (σ_Y) and the unexplained deviation to *estimate* the standard deviation of Y around the regression line (σ_u). The estimators of σ_Y and σ_u are given by Equations 17.28 and 17.29:[3]

$$S_Y = \sqrt{\frac{\Sigma(Y_i - \overline{Y})^2}{n - 1}} \qquad \text{(17.28)}$$

$$S_e = \sqrt{\frac{\Sigma(Y_i - \hat{Y}_i)^2}{n - 2}} = \sqrt{\frac{\Sigma e_i^2}{n - 2}} \qquad \text{(17.29)}$$

Computational forms of these equations are as follows:

$$S_Y = \sqrt{\frac{\Sigma Y_i^2 - n\overline{Y}^2}{n - 1}} \qquad \text{(17.30)}$$

$$S_e = \sqrt{\frac{\Sigma Y_i^2 - b_0\Sigma Y_i - b_1\Sigma X_i Y_i}{n - 2}} \qquad \text{(17.31)}$$

---

[3] Note that to obtain the deviation $Y_i - \overline{Y}$ we must first estimate $\overline{Y}$, and thereby lose one degree of freedom. To obtain $\hat{Y}_i$ we must first derive the coefficients b_0 and b_1, losing two degrees of freedom. This explains why the sum of squares in S_Y is divided by $n - 1$ and the sum of squares in S_e is divided by $n - 2$.

Another computational formula for S_e is

$$S_e = \sqrt{\frac{\Sigma(Y_i - \overline{Y})^2}{n - 2} - b_1^2 \frac{\Sigma(X_i - \overline{X})^2}{n - 2}}$$ (17.32)

It seems that Equation 17.32 is the simplest way to calculate S_e.[4]

If there are no deviations about the line, $e_i = 0$ for every observation, and hence $S_e = 0$. In this case we have a perfect fit in the sample, and all the variance of Y_i is explained by the relationship between Y_i and X_i. In the consumption and income example, this means that all the variability in consumption (Y_i) is due solely to differences in income (X_i) in the sample observations. In general, the better fit of the regression line to the data, the smaller the ratio of S_e to S_Y.

Since S_e is the estimator of σ_u, we use it for estimating $V(b_0)$ and $V(b_1)$. Substituting S_e for σ_u in 17.26a and 17.26b we get

$$S_{b_0}^2 = S_e^2 \left[\frac{1}{n} + \frac{\overline{X}^2}{\Sigma(X_i - \overline{X})^2} \right]$$ (17.33a)

and

$$S_{b_1}^2 = \frac{S_e^2}{\Sigma(X_i - \overline{X})^2}$$ (17.33b)

COMPUTING THE STATISTICS S_Y AND S_e

Let us compute the statistics S_Y and S_e for the income and consumption example. In Table 17.3 the following magnitudes were computed:

$$\Sigma Y_i = \$165.00$$

$$\Sigma Y_i^2 = 2,993.50$$

$$\Sigma X_i Y_i = 2,879.50$$

$$\overline{Y} = \$16.50$$

$$n = 10$$

On the basis of the sample data we found

$$b_0 = 5.3$$

$$b_1 = 0.705$$

Using these figures, we calculate

$$S_Y = \sqrt{\frac{2,993.5 - (10)(16.5)^2}{10 - 1}} = \sqrt{\frac{271}{9}} = \sqrt{30.11} = 5.49$$

---

[4] With the definitions of b_0 and b_1 and some algebra, it can be shown that Equations 17.31 and 17.32 are equivalent.

and

$$S_e = \sqrt{\frac{2{,}993.5 - (5.3)(165.0) - (0.705)(2{,}879.5)}{10 - 2}} = \sqrt{\frac{88.95}{8}} = \sqrt{11.12} = 3.33$$

Thus, while the total standard deviation of consumption (S_Y) is estimated to equal \$5,490 (that is, 5.49 thousands of dollars), a given portion of it is related to differences in income. When we account for these differences, we find that the remaining unexplained standard deviation of Y is equal to \$3,330.

17.9 The Simple Correlation Coefficient

Consider Figure 17.15 once again. A given observation Y_i is shown, and the distance from the sample mean $\overline{Y}$ is identified as the "total deviation." For the same observation, the distance from the regression line is identified as the "unexplained deviation," and finally the distance from the regression line ($\hat{Y}$) to the average Y value ($\overline{Y}$) is labeled the "explained deviation." This relationship is summarized by Equation 17.27:

Total deviation = explained deviation + unexplained deviation

or

$$Y - \overline{Y} = (\hat{Y} - \overline{Y}) + (Y - \hat{Y})$$

As we could easily verify, this relationship holds for observations below the regression line as well as for those above the line.

THE SAMPLE COEFFICIENT OF DETERMINATION

It can be shown that the sum of squares $\Sigma(Y - \overline{Y})^2$, which is the sum of the squared total deviations across all the sample observations, is equal to the sum of squared explained deviations plus the sum of squared unexplained deviations:

$$\Sigma(Y - \overline{Y})^2 = \Sigma(\hat{Y} - \overline{Y})^2 + \Sigma(Y - \hat{Y})^2 \tag{17.34}$$

With Equation 17.34 we can express the sum of squares of the explained deviations as follows:

$$\Sigma(\hat{Y} - \overline{Y})^2 = \Sigma(Y - \overline{Y})^2 - \Sigma(Y - \hat{Y})^2$$

Noting that $(Y - \hat{Y}) = e$, so that $\Sigma(Y - \hat{Y})^2 = \Sigma e^2$, and dividing all three terms by $\Sigma(Y - \overline{Y})^2$, we get

$$\frac{\Sigma(\hat{Y} - \overline{Y})^2}{\Sigma(Y - \overline{Y})^2} = \frac{\Sigma(Y - \overline{Y})^2}{\Sigma(Y - \overline{Y})^2} - \frac{\Sigma e^2}{\Sigma(Y - \overline{Y})^2} \tag{17.35}$$

or

$$\frac{\Sigma(\hat{Y} - \overline{Y})^2}{\Sigma(Y - \overline{Y})^2} = 1 - \frac{\Sigma e^2}{\Sigma(Y - \overline{Y})^2} \tag{17.36}$$

The term on the left-hand side of Equation 17.36 is a measure of the explained variability of Y in the sample, expressed as a proportion of the total variability of Y. This measure is a sample **coefficient of determination** and is denoted by r^2:

$$r^2 = 1 - \frac{\Sigma e^2}{\Sigma(Y - \overline{Y})^2} \tag{17.37}$$

The coefficient of determination, r^2, measures the fraction of total variability of Y "explained" by the regression. If $r^2 = 0.80$, for example, it means that 80 percent of the total sample variation in Y is explained by the variable X and 20 percent of the sample variation remains unexplained. Thus the coefficient of determination has a straightforward interpretation as a measure of the strength of the relationship between X and Y.

Recall the definition of the standard error of estimate, S_e:

$$S_e = \sqrt{\frac{\Sigma e^2}{n - 2}} \tag{17.38}$$

After squaring and cross-multiplying, we get

$$\Sigma e^2 = S_e^2 \cdot (n - 2) \tag{17.39}$$

Similarly, S_Y is given by

$$S_Y = \sqrt{\frac{\Sigma(Y - \overline{Y})^2}{n - 1}} \tag{17.40}$$

and by squaring and cross-multiplying, we get

$$\Sigma(Y - \overline{Y})^2 = S_Y^2 \cdot (n - 1) \tag{17.41}$$

After dividing Equation 17.39 by $S_Y^2 \cdot (n - 1)$, we have

$$\frac{\Sigma e^2}{\Sigma(Y - \overline{Y})^2} = \frac{S_e^2}{S_Y^2} \cdot \frac{n - 2}{n - 1}$$

and by substituting in Equation 17.37 we obtain the following equation:

$$r^2 = 1 - \frac{S_e^2}{S_Y^2} \cdot \frac{n - 2}{n - 1} \tag{17.42}$$

For the income and consumption example we have calculated $S_Y^2 = 30.11$ and $S_e^2 = 11.12$. And since $n = 10$, r^2 for this example is

$$r^2 = 1 - \frac{11.12}{30.11} \cdot \frac{(10 - 2)}{(10 - 1)} = 0.672$$

About 67.2 percent of the variability of consumption has been explained by differences in income.

When the sample is large, the term $(n - 2)/(n - 1)$ is close to 1, and r^2 may be approximated by the following:

$$r^2 = 1 - \frac{S_e^2}{S_Y^2} \qquad (17.43)$$

THE SAMPLE CORRELATION COEFFICIENT

The coefficient of determination has an intuitive appeal, as we have seen, but when it stands alone it does not tell us the direction of the relationship between the dependent and independent variables. The **coefficient of correlation** is a measure of the *strength* as well as *direction* of the relationship between the variables, as we saw in Chapter 7. The coefficient of correlation is equal to the square root of the coefficient of determination. From Equation 17.42 it follows that the estimated correlation coefficient, r, is given by

$$r = \pm \sqrt{1 - \frac{S_e^2}{S_Y^2} \cdot \frac{n - 2}{n - 1}} \qquad (17.44)$$

The sign of r is the same as the sign of the estimated regression slope: if the slope is positive, r is positive; if it is negative, r is negative. For the income and consumption example we obtain $r = +\sqrt{0.672} = 0.820$. Since the slope of the regression line is positive, the value of r is also positive. A computational formula for r is given by

$$r = \frac{\Sigma(X - \overline{X})(Y - \overline{Y})}{\sqrt{\Sigma(X - \overline{X})^2} \sqrt{\Sigma(Y - \overline{Y})^2}} \qquad (17.45)$$

The equivalence of r in Equations 17.45 and 17.37 (and hence 17.44) is shown in Appendix 17B.

Equation 17.45 may be further simplified to give

$$r = \frac{\Sigma XY - n\overline{X}\overline{Y}}{\sqrt{\Sigma X^2 - n\overline{X}^2} \sqrt{\Sigma Y^2 - n\overline{Y}^2}} \qquad (17.46)$$

THE COEFFICIENT OF DETERMINATION AS A MEASURE OF THE STRENGTH OF THE RELATIONSHIP BETWEEN X AND Y

The correlation coefficient takes on values in the range between -1 and $+1$: $-1 \leq r \leq +1$. It follows that r^2 ranges between 0 and $+1$:

$$0 \leq r^2 \leq 1 \qquad (17.47)$$

Indeed, this is only logical and can be easily verified from Equation 17.43, since r^2 measures the fraction of the total variation explained by the regression, and as such it must range between 0 and 1. The stronger the relationship between the variables X and Y, the closer r^2 is to 1, and conversely, the weaker the relationship, the closer r^2 is to 0.

That r^2 ranges between 0 and 1 can also be seen in another way. Figure 17.16 shows three alternative scatter diagrams. In Figure 17.16*a* all the sample observations lie on the regression line. This is the case when all the e^2s are equal to zero. As a consequence, $\Sigma e^2 = 0$, and from Equation 17.37 it is clear that in this case $r^2 = 1$. In Figure 17.16*c* no relationship seems to exist between the two variables. As a result, the regression line has a zero slope and all the $\hat{Y}_i$ are equal to $\overline{Y}$ (that is, the regression line of Y on X is horizontal and coincides with $\overline{Y}$). In this case the quantity $(\hat{Y} - \overline{Y})$ is equal to zero for all the observations and so $\Sigma(\hat{Y}_i - \overline{Y})^2 = 0$ and the left-hand side of Equation 17.36 is clearly zero, indicating that $r^2 = 0$. Naturally these are the most extreme cases. Figure 17.16*b* shows a scatter diagram for the case in which $r^2 = 0.5$. Here 50 percent of the variation in Y is explained by the regression line. In general, the closer the observations to the regression line (other things held the same), the greater r^2.

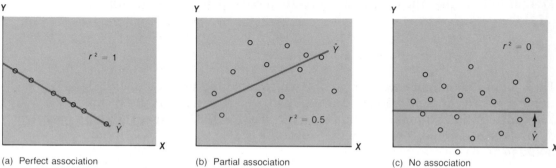

(a) Perfect association   (b) Partial association   (c) No association

Figure 17.16

Alternative scatter diagrams and coefficients of determination

Before concluding the chapter, let us look at an SAS computer printout showing the results of the consumption and income example. The printout is presented in Figure 17.17. The row numbers on the left-hand side have been added for reference. Let us examine the printout line by line.

Line 1:   A statement indicating that consumption is the dependent variable of the regression.

Line 2:   This line provides titles for lines 3 through 5, which give an analysis of variance of the regression. The total variation of the dependent variable is broken down into its sources: the explained variation ("model") and the unexplained variation ("error").

Line 3:   This line analyzes the variation explained by the regression model. Since there is only one explanatory variable in the regression, the number of degrees of freedom is 1. The sum of squares refers to $\Sigma(\hat{Y} - \overline{Y})^2$, which is the explained sum of squared deviations. Since there is only one degree of freedom, the model sum of squares, 180.590, is equal also to the mean square: 180.590/1 = 180.590. The F value shows the significance of the model: the value 15.980 is a value obtained on the F distribution with

Figure 17.17

Reproduction
of an SAS
computer
printout for
the consump-
tion versus
income
example

1. DEP VARIABLE: CONSMP					
2. SOURCE	DF	SUM OF SQUARES	MEAN SQUARE	F VALUE	PROB>F
3. MODEL	1	180.590	180.590	15.980	0.0040
4. ERROR	8	90.410306	11.301288		
5. C TOTAL	9	271.000			
6. ROOT MSE		3.361739	R-SQUARE	0.6664	
7. DEP MEAN		16.500000			

8. VARIABLE	DF	PARAMETER ESTIMATE	STANDARD ERROR	T FOR H0: PARAMETER=0	PROB > |T|
9. INTERCEP	1	5.283687	3.000506	1.761	0.1163
10. INCOME	1	0.705428	0.176470	3.997	0.0040

1 and 8 degrees of freedom (8 being the degrees of freedom of the unexplained variance of Y). The last number in line 3 is 0.0040, which shows that the tail to the right of $F = 15.98$ on the relevant distribution (which is $F^{(1,8)}$) is only 0.0040, or 0.4 percent. This implies that the model provides an explanation for the behavior of the dependent variable that is statistically significant at all significance levels greater than 0.0040. We will elaborate on the significance of a model in the next chapter, which deals with inference.

Line 4: Statistics similar to those given in line 3, except that they are for the unexplained variance of Y (the "error"). With 10 observations in the sample and one explanatory variable, the error has $n - 2 = 8$ degrees of freedom. Note that the F statistic in line 3 is obtained by dividing the model mean square by the error mean square: $180.590/11.301288 = 15.980$.

Line 5: This line shows the total sum of squares: $180.590 + 90.410306 = 271.000$.

Line 6: ROOT MSE refers to the mean square of the error: $\sqrt{11.301288} = 3.361739$. This is the standard error of estimate, S_e, which we measured earlier as 3.33. The difference is solely due to rounding. Line 6 also gives the regression r^2, which again differs from our earlier result because of rounding.

Line 7: This line simply gives the mean value of the dependent variable: 16.50.

Line 8: Titles for the next two lines, where the regression coefficients and their significance are reported.

Line 9: This line shows the statistics of the intercept, the estimator of β_0. The estimator has one degree of freedom, and the point estimate of β_0 is $b_0 = 5.283687$, which, of course, is the same as the rounded value ($b_0 = 5.3$) we obtained earlier through direct calculations. Since b_0 is an estimator, it is a random variable and the printout shows that its standard error is 3.000506. This implies a t value (see next chapter) of $5.283687/3.000506 = 1.761$, which is statistically different from zero for all significance levels greater than 11.63 percent.

Line 10: Same as line 9, except that the statistics are for the slope b_1.

Chapter Summary and Review

1. The true regression model is given by

$$Y_i = \beta_0 + \beta_1 X_i + u_i = \mu_i + u_i$$

2. The sample relationship is given by

$$Y_i = b_0 + b_1 X_i + e_i = \hat{Y}_i + e_i$$

3. Assumptions made in regression analysis are
   a. Y_is are statistically independent
   b. $V(Y \mid X_i) = V(Y_i) = \sigma^2$, constant for all levels of X
   c. $E(Y \mid X_i) = E(Y_i) = \mu_i$

   Alternative formulations of the assumptions are

   a. u_is are statistically independent
   b. $V(u_i) = \sigma_u^2 = \sigma^2$, constant for all levels of X
   c. $E(u_i) = 0$

4. The OLS estimators are BLUE: best linear unbiased estimators; namely, there are no other unbiased estimators with smaller variances.
   a. The slope of the OLS line is

   $$b_1 = \frac{\Sigma XY - n\overline{X}\,\overline{Y}}{\Sigma X^2 - n\overline{X}^2} = \frac{\Sigma(X - \overline{X})(Y - \overline{Y})}{\Sigma(X - \overline{X})^2}$$

   b. The intercept of the OLS line is

   $$b_0 = \overline{Y} - b_1\overline{X}$$

   c. Their expected values are

   $$E(b_0) = \beta_0 \quad \text{and} \quad E(b_1) = \beta_1$$

   Their variances are

   $$V(b_0) = \sigma_u^2 \left[\frac{1}{n} + \frac{\overline{X}^2}{\Sigma(X - \overline{X})^2} \right]$$

   and

   $$V(b_1) = \frac{\sigma_u^2}{\Sigma(X - \overline{X})^2}$$

   And their estimated variances are

   $$S_{b_0}^2 = S_e^2 \left[\frac{1}{n} + \frac{\overline{X}^2}{\Sigma(X - \overline{X})^2} \right] \quad \text{and} \quad S_{b_1}^2 = \frac{S_e^2}{\Sigma(X - \overline{X})^2}$$

5. The standard error of estimate is given by

$$S_e = \sqrt{\frac{\Sigma(Y - \hat{Y})^2}{n - 2}} = \sqrt{\frac{\Sigma e^2}{n - 2}} = \sqrt{\frac{\Sigma Y^2 - b_0 \Sigma Y - b_1 \Sigma XY}{n - 2}}$$

6. The sample coefficient of determination, r^2, is

$$r^2 = \frac{\Sigma(\hat{Y} - \overline{Y})^2}{\Sigma(Y - \overline{Y})^2} = 1 - \frac{\Sigma e^2}{\Sigma(Y - \overline{Y})^2} = 1 - \frac{S_e^2}{S_Y^2} \cdot \frac{n - 2}{n - 1}$$

and for large n the following holds approximately:

$$r^2 = 1 - \frac{S_e^2}{S_Y^2}$$

A computational formula for r is

$$r = \frac{\Sigma(X - \overline{X})(Y - \overline{Y})}{\sqrt{\Sigma(X - \overline{X})^2}\sqrt{\Sigma(Y - \overline{Y})^2}} = \frac{\Sigma XY - n\overline{X}\overline{Y}}{\sqrt{\Sigma X^2 - n\overline{X}^2}\sqrt{\Sigma Y^2 - n\overline{Y}^2}}$$

7. The sample correlation coefficient $r = \pm \sqrt{r^2}$; the sign is determined by the sign of b_1.

8. It is always true that $0 \le r^2 \le 1$ and $-1 \le r \le +1$.

9. The relationship between slope and correlation (see Appendix 17B):

   a. In the sample $b_1 = r \cdot \dfrac{S_Y}{S_X}$

   b. In the population $\beta_1 = \rho \cdot \dfrac{\sigma_Y}{\sigma_X}$

Problems

17.1. "In a simple linear regression model, an increase in the variance of the random term u_i implies an increase in the variance of Y_i." Do you agree? Why?

17.2. "The assumption that $E(u) = 0$ is not a crucial one. Suppose that $E(u) = 4$, for example; then we could define a term $v = u - 4$ and rewrite Equation 17.2 without any essential changes." Do you agree? If you do, demonstrate your answer formally.

17.3. Suppose that in the regression equation

$$Y_i = \beta_0 + \beta_1 X_i + u_i$$

the coefficients are $\beta_0 = 1$ and $\beta_1 = 2$. Suppose also that the probability distribution of u_i is discrete, as follows:

$$u_i = -5 \quad \text{with a probability of } \tfrac{1}{4}$$
$$u_i = \quad 0 \quad \text{with a probability of } \tfrac{1}{2}$$
$$u_i = +5 \quad \text{with a probability of } \tfrac{1}{4}$$

Calculate the expected value and the variance of Y_i for $X_i = 4$. How does the variance of Y_i compare with the variance of u_i?

17.4. The independent variable X explains the behavior of the dependent variable Y. Why is it, then, that for a given level of X, say X_0, we expect to find a given variability of Y_0? Can you explain the reasons for such variability? Give an example.

17.5. Explain the difference between the estimated and the "true" regression lines. Is it possible to get more than one estimated line for one "true" line?

17.6. Is it possible for a "true" regression line to have a positive slope and its estimated line to have a negative slope? Explain.

17.7. It is well known that the ordinary least-squares regression estimators are the best linear unbiased estimators (BLUE).

    (*a*) Explain the properties of BLUE. What is their importance?
    (*b*) Suppose you can sample as many observations as you want from an infinite population with no difficulty. Which is the one property of BLUE that will be most important?

17.8. "If the variance of u, σ_u^2, is equal to zero (that is, $\sigma_u^2 = 0$), the estimated regression line coincides with the true regression line." Prove this statement

    (*a*) Mathematically
    (*b*) By a diagram

17.9. "If in a sample all the error terms are equal to zero (that is, all $e_i = 0$), the implication is that a perfect fit exists between the dependent and the independent variables." Do you agree? Explain.

17.10. Table P17.10 presents data on the education (in number of school years) and weekly income of six randomly selected adults in a sample.

TABLE P17.10

Individual	Weekly income	Education (school years)
1	$200	6
2	300	8
3	350	10
4	400	12
5	600	13
6	700	15

    (*a*) Find the ordinary least-squares line. What do the intercept and the slope of the line indicate?
    (*b*) What is the estimated weekly income of an adult who attended school for 12 years? Compare the estimated income with that of individual number 4 in the sample. Can you account for the deviation? Explain.
    (*c*) Calculate the coefficient of determination for the regression. Is education a "good" explanatory variable of income?

17.11. The sales (Y) and advertising expense (X) of a sample of firms are given in Table P17.11.

TABLE P17.11

Sales (millions of dollars)	Advertising expense (percent of sales)
$150	0.2%
170	0.8
200	1.2
100	0.9
180	1.5
120	0.9
60	0.1
150	0.8
180	0.9
250	2.0

(a) Write the normal equations for this sample.

(b) Find the ordinary least-squares line and explain the meaning of the intercept and the slope.

(c) Calculate the coefficient of correlation and the coefficient of determination. Are the two variables strongly related? Explain.

(d) It is argued that correlation measures the association between variables but does not show a causality relationship. Can you explain this view in relation to the problem at hand?

17.12. Assume that the sample mean of X in the regression $\hat{Y} = b_0 + b_1 X$ is equal to zero: $\overline{X} = 0$. Show that

$$b_0 = \overline{Y}$$

and

$$b_1 = \frac{\Sigma X_i Y_i}{\Sigma X_i^2}$$

17.13. A sample consists of 10 observations: $n = 10$. It is given that $\overline{X} = \overline{Y} = 1$. Show that in the regression $\hat{Y} = b_0 + b_1 X$

$$b_0 = 1 - \frac{\Sigma X_i Y_i - 10}{\Sigma X_i^2 - 10}$$

$$b_1 = \frac{\Sigma X_i Y_i - 10}{\Sigma X_i^2 - 10}$$

17.14. A sample consists of 10 observations. Show that if $\overline{X} = \overline{Y} = 0$, then

$$b_0 = 0$$

and

$$b_1 = \frac{\Sigma X_i Y_i}{\Sigma X_i^2}$$

17.15. Each of three regression lines of the form $\hat{Y} = b_0 + b_1X$ has a slope equal to 2: $b_1 = 2$. Additional information about the regressions is as follows:

Regression A	Regression B	Regression C
$\overline{X} = 1$	$\overline{X} = 2$	$\overline{X} = 0.5$
$\overline{Y} = 0$	$\overline{Y} = 4$	$\overline{Y} = 10.0$

Which of the regressions has the highest intercept, b_0?

17.16. Suppose we run the following regression lines on the same set of data:

$$\hat{Y} = b_0 + b_1X$$

$$\hat{X} = b_0' + b_1'Y$$

Do you agree with the following statements? Prove your answers.

(a) "If $\Sigma(X - \overline{X})^2 = \Sigma(Y - \overline{Y})^2$, then $b_1 = b_1'$."
(b) "If $\overline{X} = \overline{Y}$, then $b_0 = b_0'$."

17.17. The grade point averages (GPA) in high school and in college of 10 randomly selected students are given in Table P17.17.

TABLE P17.17

	GPA	
Student	College	High school
1	3.4	3.1
2	3.8	3.2
3	3.0	4.0
4	3.5	4.2
5	4.8	4.5
6	2.2	2.9
7	3.9	3.1
8	4.6	5.0
9	2.2	2.8
10	4.9	4.9

You want to explain the college GPA by the students' performance in high school.

(a) Draw the scatter diagram.
(b) Find the ordinary least-squares line. What is your interpretation of the intercept and the slope of the line?
(c) Show that $\Sigma e = 0$.
(d) Calculate the standard error of estimate, S_e, and the standard deviation of Y, S_Y.
(e) Does the ratio between S_e and S_Y indicate the strength of the relationship between the variables? Explain.

17.18. The regression line $\hat{Y} = b_0 + b_1X$ was estimated from a sample of 10 observations. Find the value of ΣXY, given the following information:

$$b_0 = 1 \quad \overline{X} = 2$$

$$b_1 = 1 \quad \Sigma X^2 = 100$$

17.19. Net before-tax profit of ABC Corporation is denoted by X. The after-tax profit, Y, is (precisely) equal to $(1 - T)(X)$, so $Y = (1 - T)(X)$, where T is the corporate tax rate. Assume that $T = 0.50$.

   (a) What are the intercept and the slope of the regression line relating Y (dependent) to X (explanatory)?

   (b) What are the intercept and the slope of the regression line relating X (dependent) to Y (explanatory)?

   (c) Draw both regression lines.

   (d) Calculate the correlation coefficient of X and Y.

   (e) Given that Y is precisely equal to $(1 - T)(X)$, are the intercept and slope of the line functions of the specific data collected in a sample? Would you get a different intercept and slope for another company that is subject to the same corporate tax rate?

   (f) Suppose the corporate tax rate is reduced to $T = 0.30$. What are the intercepts and slopes of the regression lines of parts a and b?

17.20. A regression of annual consumption (Y) on annual income (X) of households produces the following estimated equation:

$$\hat{Y} = 3,000 + 0.7X$$

   (a) Suppose *each* of the households in the sample spends exactly \$1,000 annually on entertainment. Denote the spending on entertainment by E. Suppose we ran the regression $\widehat{Y - E} = b_0 + b_1 X$, using the same sample data as before. Can you say what the intercept and slope of this regression line will be?

   (b) Suppose now that *each* of the households in the sample has exactly \$500 in interest income (denoted by I). Suppose we ran the regression $\hat{Y} = b_0 + b_1(X - I)$. Can you say what the regression coefficients will be?

   (c) Find the intercept and slope of the following regression:

$$\widehat{Y - E} = b_0 + b_1(X - I)$$

17.21. Suppose that 40 percent of the consumption of *each* household expenditure in Problem 17.20 is spent on food and that *each* household makes 90 percent of its income from wages. Denote food consumption by F and wage income by W. Recall that the regression of Y on X is given by $\hat{Y} = 3,000 + 0.7X$.

   (a) What are the regression coefficients of $\hat{F} = b_0 + b_1 X$?

   (b) What are the regression coefficients of $\hat{Y} = b_0 + b_1 W$?

   (c) What are the regression coefficients of $\hat{F} = b_0 + b_1 W$?

17.22. Give your own numerical example in which you show that more than one regression equation satisfies the criterion $\Sigma(Y_i - \hat{Y}_i) = 0$ for any one sample. Choose your own data and draw at least two lines that satisfy this criterion.

17.23. The annual savings of individuals at savings banks and the interest rates paid on those savings during four years are as follows:

Year	Savings	Interest rate
1980	\$1,000	9%
1981	800	10
1982	1,200	8
1983	2,000	11

    (*a*) Draw a scatter diagram of savings (dependent) and interest rate (explanatory). Without performing any calculations, draw a regression line through the scattered data points and determine its intercept and slope.

    (*b*) Calculate the OLS regression coefficients and then draw on the same diagram the OLS regression line. Compare the line with the one you drew earlier.

17.24. Using a given randomly selected sample, we can run the regression

$$\hat{Y} = b_0 + b_1 X$$

or, alternatively, use X for the dependent variable and Y for the explanatory variable and run

$$\hat{X} = b_0' + b_1' Y$$

Comment on the following statements:

    (*a*) "If $b_1 = 0$, $b_1' = 0$."
    (*b*) "If b_1 is positive, so is b_1'."
    (*c*) "If b_0 is positive, so is b_0'."

Prove your answers, making use of the equations presented in this chapter.

17.25. The following are three sample points to which a regression line must be fitted:

Y	X
100	70
200	12
600	25

    (*a*) Find the OLS regression equation for the data, and compute the value of $\Sigma(Y - \hat{Y})^2$.
    (*b*) For the line you estimated in part *a*, calculate the magnitude $\Sigma|Y - \hat{Y}|$.
    (*c*) Fit another line through the data points so that the sum of the absolute deviations (that is, $\Sigma|Y - \hat{Y}|$) for the line will be smaller than the value you calculated in part *b*.
    (*d*) Find the sum of squared deviations [that is, $\Sigma(Y - \hat{Y})^2$] from the line you drew in part *c*. What can you conclude from this problem?

17.26. In a study of automobile repair costs, data were collected on cars' ages (in years) and annual repair costs. The data are shown in Table P17.26.

TABLE P17.26

Repair cost	Age
$134	2
56	3
303	5
299	4
0	1
404	2
53	1
0	1
200	3
507	10
360	7
48	1
177	6

(a) Plot the scatter diagram.
(b) Use the OLS method to find the linear relationship between the variables.
(c) Calculate the coefficient of determination and the coefficient of correlation. What does the latter show that the former does not?

17.27. Table P17.27 shows prices (in dollars) and daily demand (in units) for a certain product in 10 states across the country.

TABLE P17.27

Demand (Y) (units)	Price (X)
1,000	$10
1,100	9
700	15
800	15
900	12
950	10
1,000	10
950	11
500	18
1,500	8

(a) Find the ordinary least-squares line when demand (Y) is the dependent variable and price (X) is the independent variable.
(b) In another state, not included in the sample, the price is $X = \$13$. What is the estimated demand for the product in this state?

17.28. The interest on bonds and the time left for their maturity (in years) is as follows:

Interest rate (Y) (percent)	Bond maturity (X) (years)
3	0.25
4	0.50
7	1.00
8	5.00
9	10.00
10	20.00

(a) Find the ordinary least-squares line, $\hat{Y} = b_0 + b_1X$, and explain its meaning.
(b) Calculate the correlation coefficient of X and Y.

17.29. For each pair of variables given below, indicate which is the dependent and which is the independent variable:

(a) Education and personal income.
(b) Density of population (that is, number of inhabitants per square mile) and average rent per room, when measured across various regions around the country.
(c) Number of accidents per 1,000 miles of road and road quality measured numerically by some code.
(d) The number of questionnaires answered and the number of questionnaires distributed.
(e) Time traveled and distance traveled.

17.30. Write the normal equations for the regression $\hat{Y} = b_0 + b_1 X$, using the following sample data:

Y	X
5	10
8	12
14	10

17.31. The ordinary least-squares line was fitted to sample data, which include five observations. The estimated equation is

$$\hat{Y} = -5 + 10X$$

Four of the deviations e_i were as follows:

X_i	0	5	10	15	20
e_i	0	-5	$+5$	4	?

(a) Calculate the value of the fifth deviation.
(b) What are the five Y values in this sample?
(c) Draw the scatter diagram and the regression line on one chart.
(d) Calculate the regression r^2.

17.32. Transaction costs paid on buying or selling stock market securities vary with the type of security, size of transaction, the broker who executes the transaction, and so on. A random sample of transactions yielded the following data on the amount of the transaction and the cost of the transaction as a percentage of the amount:

Cost (Y) (percent)	6	4	2	9	10	5	3	6	3	7	3	8
Amount (X) (thousands of dollars)	8	12	16	3	0.5	10	10	9	7	9	11	7

(a) Estimate the ordinary least-squares line and explain its meaning.
(b) For each value of X, calculate the value $X' = X - \bar{X}$ and for each value of Y calculate the value $Y' = Y - \bar{Y}$, where $\bar{X}$ and $\bar{Y}$ are the sample means. Estimate the regression line of Y' (dependent) on X' (independent). Explain the relationships between the two regression lines.
(c) Calculate the correlation coefficient of X and Y and of X' and Y'. Explain the relationships.

17.33. Suppose you draw a sample and obtain observations such that for each pair $X_i = -Y_i$. Prove that

(a) $\bar{Y} = -\bar{X}$
(b) $b_1 = -1$
(c) $b_0 = 0$
(d) $\Sigma e^2 = 0$

17.34. A random sample of four observations of a dependent variable (Y) and an independent variable (X) yields the following data:

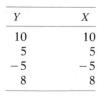

Y	X
10	10
5	5
-5	-5
8	8

(a) Derive the ordinary least-squares line $\hat{Y} = b_0 + b_1 X$.

(b) Calculate the residual e_i for each of the sample observations, and calculate the value Σe^2.

(c) From this problem, can you draw a general conclusion regarding a regression of Y on itself?

17.35. When the coefficient of determination is calculated for Y and X, it is found that

$$\Sigma X^2 = 100 \qquad \Sigma Y^2 = 100$$
$$n\bar{X}^2 = 90 \qquad n\bar{Y}^2 = 90$$

(a) Is it possible that $\Sigma XY = 100$?

(b) What is the maximum value that ΣXY is conceivably equal to, given the above data?

17.36. Calculate r^2 and r for X and Y, once using the data in Table P17.36a and once using the data in Table P17.36b.

TABLE P17.36a			TABLE P17.36b	
X	Y		X	Y
10	5		10	-5
20	10		20	-10
30	15		30	-15

17.37. "If $\Sigma(X_i - \bar{X})(Y_i - \bar{Y}) = \Sigma(X_i - \bar{X})^2$, then the coefficient of determination of X and Y, r^2, equals the slope of the following estimated regression line: $\hat{X} = b_0 + b_1 Y$." Do you agree? Explain.

17.38. "If $\Sigma(X_i - \bar{X})^2 = \Sigma(Y_i - \bar{Y})^2$, then the coefficient of determination of X and Y, r^2, is equal to b_1^2 *and* to c_1^2 where b_1 and c_1 are the slopes of the following regression lines:

$$\hat{Y} = b_0 + b_1 X$$
$$\hat{X} = c_0 + c_1 Y."$$

Evaluate this statement and prove your answer.

17.39. The long-distance telephone bills and the respective number of long-distance calls of a small sample of telephone customers are as follows:

Bill	Number of calls
$25	10
67	15
2	1
30	3

Using the data for the above sample, show numerically that Equations 17.34, 17.36, and 17.37 indeed hold.

17.40. Using the data from Problem 17.39, show numerically the equivalence of Equations 17.45 and 17.37.

17.41. Suppose the coefficient of determination of X and Y is equal to 0.50. What is the correlation coefficient of $X - 10$ and $Y - 20$? What is the correlation coefficient of $\frac{1}{2}X$ and $\frac{3}{4}Y$?

17.42. A firm's personnel department hired employees for a given job primarily on the basis of the results of an aptitude test administered to job applicants. The test grades are 0 through 10 (10 being the best possible grade). The performance of those hired was rated on the same scale by their supervisor a year after they were hired. A sample of the test grades and the supervisor's assigned grades is as follows:

Test grade	Supervisor's grade
5	8
6	8
10	10
2	5
9	7
5	4
7	10
7	6

(a) Draw a scatter diagram showing the test grades on the horizontal axis and the supervisor's grades on the vertical axis.

(b) Can you guess the sign and magnitude of the correlation coefficient before doing any calculations?

(c) Calculate the correlation coefficient.

(d) On the basis of your results, do you think the test is a good indicator of employees' performance on the job? Is it a very good indicator? Explain.

17.43. For the following sample data draw the ordinary least-squares line, using Y as the dependent variable and X as the independent variable:

Y	X
10	5
10	10
10	15
10	20
10	25

Explain your results.

17.44. The following table presents two sets of data related to two cities:

City A		City B	
Y	X	Y	X
2	4	2	4
3	5	2	4
6	7	3	5
8	10	3	5
6	12	6	7
		6	7
		8	10
		8	10
		6	12
		6	12

Y is the dependent variable and X is the independent variable. Calculate the ordinary least-squares line for City A and City B. Draw the scatter diagrams and the regression lines and explain your results.

17.45. Table P17.45 presents the sales and the return on common equity (the net profit as a percentage of the firm's capital that belongs to the common shareholders) of large American textile companies in the first quarter of 1982.

TABLE P17.45

Company	Sales (millions of dollars)	Return on common equity (percent)
Blue Bell	348.5	9.9
Brown Group	347.8	16.4
Burlington Industries	738.1	8.8
Cluett, Peabody	194.8	11.6
Collins & Aikman	148.1	10.0
Cone Mills	155.5	8.9
Dan River	131.4	6.2
Fieldcrest Mills	107.3	6.6
Genesco	167.6	34.8
Hart Schaffner & Marx	230.1	12.1
INTERCO	603.7	12.7
Kellwood	122.4	4.7
Levi Strauss	534.0	15.9
Lowenstein (M.)	137.0	11.1
Manhattan Industries	103.2	17.6
Oxford Industries	95.9	17.6

Source: *Business Week*, May 17, 1982, p. 86.

Find the regression line when sales is the explanatory variable and return on common equity is the dependent variable. In view of the results, does profitability increase with sales? Explain.

17.46. The oil production capacity and estimated actual production of the Organization of Petroleum Exporting Countries (OPEC) for the first quarter of 1979 are shown in Table P17.46.

TABLE P17.46

Country	Estimated sustainable production capacity	Estimated production first quarter 1979
	Millions of barrels per day	
Saudi Arabia	10.7	9.8
Iran	6.5	1.0
Iraq	3.0	3.2
Kuwait	2.9	2.6
Venezuela	2.6	2.3
Libya	2.3	2.1
Nigeria	2.3	2.4
United Arab Emirates	2.3	1.8
Indonesia	1.7	1.6
Algeria	1.3	1.2
Qatar	0.6	0.5
Ecuador	0.2	0.2
Gabon	0.2	0.2

Source: Data from *Business Week*, April 9, 1979, p. 97.

(*a*) Treat capacity as the explanatory variable and draw a scatter diagram of the data.
(*b*). Calculate and draw the regression line through your scatter diagram.

(c) Rework parts *a* and *b*, this time eliminating Iran. Can you tell that Iran was undergoing a political change during the first quarter of 1979 by comparing the two regression lines you have obtained? Explain.

Case Problems

17.1. Data Set 1, Appendix B, Table B.1, provides data on the sales, profit, and profit margin of 100 firms. It is sometimes thought that larger firms have higher profitability (other things being equal), because they enjoy economies of scale both in their operations and in their financing.

> (a) Run the regression of profit (dependent variable) on sales (explanatory variable). What is your interpretation of the regression equation?
>
> (b) Use a computer program to draw the scatter diagram.

17.2. Repeat Case Problem 17.1, this time omitting GM, Ford, and Chrysler. What is the justification for such an omission? Compare the results of Case Problems 17.2 and 17.1.

17.3. Repeat Case Problem 17.2, this time using the profit margin as the dependent variable. Make sure to run this regression after removing the observations of the three automotive firms.

17.4. Repeat Case Problems 17.1 and 17.3 using only the data of the chemicals industry, which consists of firms 50 through 75 in Data Set 1. Do you think that there is reason to eliminate outliers in this case? Explain by analyzing the scatter diagram.

APPENDIX 17A:
Derivation of Some Properties of OLS Estimators

b_0 AND b_1: UNBIASED ESTIMATORS OF β_0 AND β_1

The OLS estimator of β_1, b_1, is given by

$$b_1 = \frac{\Sigma(X_i - \overline{X})(Y_i - \overline{Y})}{\Sigma X_i^2 - n\overline{X}^2} \tag{17A.1}$$

By taking expectations, we get

$$E(b_1) = E\left[\frac{\Sigma(X_i - \overline{X})(Y_i - \overline{Y})}{\Sigma X_i^2 - n\overline{X}^2}\right]$$

$$= E\left[\frac{\Sigma(X_i - \overline{X})Y_i - \Sigma(X_i - \overline{X})\overline{Y}}{\Sigma X_i^2 - n\overline{X}^2}\right] \tag{17A.2}$$

Noting that whereas the variable Y is treated as a random variable, the variable X is *not* treated as a random variable, and noting that $\overline{Y}$ is a constant and $\Sigma(X_i - \overline{X}) = 0$, we may write

$$E(b_1) = E\left[\frac{\Sigma(X_i - \overline{X})Y_i}{\Sigma(X_i - \overline{X})^2}\right] = \frac{[\Sigma(X_i - \overline{X})]E(Y_i)}{\Sigma X_i^2 - n\overline{X}^2}$$

$$= \frac{[\Sigma(X_i - \overline{X})](\beta_0 + \beta_1 X_i)}{\Sigma X_i^2 - n\overline{X}^2} = \frac{\beta_0\Sigma(X_i - \overline{X}) + \beta_1\Sigma(X_i - \overline{X})X_i}{\Sigma X_i^2 - n\overline{X}^2} \quad \textbf{(17A.3)}$$

$$= \beta_1\left[\frac{\Sigma(X_i - \overline{X})X_i}{\Sigma X_i^2 - n\overline{X}^2}\right] = \beta_1\left[\frac{\Sigma X_i^2 - n\overline{X}^2}{\Sigma X_i^2 - n\overline{X}^2}\right] = \beta_1$$

Similarly, $b_0 = \overline{Y} - b_1\overline{X}$. Thus

$$E(b_0) = E(\overline{Y}) - \overline{X}E(b_1) = E(\overline{Y}) - \beta_1\overline{X} \quad \textbf{(17A.4)}$$

But

$$Y_i = \beta_0 + \beta_1 X_i + u_i \quad \text{and} \quad E(Y_i) = \beta_0 + \beta_1 X_i \quad \textbf{(17A.5)}$$

Since $\overline{Y} = \dfrac{\Sigma Y}{n}$, we get

$$E(\overline{Y}) = E\left(\frac{\Sigma Y_i}{n}\right) = \frac{1}{n}(n\beta_0 + \beta_1\Sigma X_i) = \beta_0 + \beta_1\frac{\Sigma X_i}{n} = \beta_0 + \beta_1\overline{X} \quad \textbf{(17A.6)}$$

Substituting this result in $E(b_0)$, we get $E(b_0) = \beta_0 + \beta_1\overline{X} - \beta_1\overline{X} = \beta_0$, which implies that b_0 is an unbiased estimator of β_0. For the variance of b_1 we get

$$V(b_1) = V\left[\frac{\Sigma(X_i - \overline{X})Y_i}{\Sigma X_i^2 - n\overline{X}^2}\right] = \left(\frac{1}{\Sigma X_i^2 - n\overline{X}^2}\right)^2 \cdot V[\Sigma(X_i - \overline{X})Y_i]$$

$$= \left(\frac{1}{\Sigma X_i^2 - n\overline{X}^2}\right)^2 [\Sigma(X_i - \overline{X})^2]V(Y_i) \quad \textbf{(17A.7)}$$

Note, however, that $Y_i = \beta_0 + \beta_1 X_i + u_i$. Hence $V(Y_i) = \sigma_{u_i}^2$, or simply σ_u^2, since by assumption $\sigma_{u_i}^2 = \sigma_u^2$ for all i. Thus

$$V(b_1) = \left[\frac{1}{(\Sigma X_i^2 - n\overline{X}^2)^2}\right](\Sigma X_i^2 - n\overline{X}^2)V(Y_i) = \frac{\sigma_u^2}{\Sigma X_i^2 - n\overline{X}^2} \quad \textbf{(17A.8)}$$

THE VARIANCE OF THE ESTIMATOR $\hat{Y}_i$

The estimator $\hat{Y}_i$ is given by

$$\hat{Y}_i = b_0 + b_1 X_i \quad \textbf{(17A.9)}$$

Since $b_0 = \overline{Y} - b_1\overline{X}$, however, it can be rewritten as

$$\hat{Y}_i = (\overline{Y} - b_1\overline{X}) + b_1 X_i \quad \textbf{(17A.10)}$$

or

$$\hat{Y}_i = \overline{Y} + b_1(X_i - \overline{X}) \tag{17A.11}$$

Since $\overline{Y}$ and b_1 are independent and $X_i - \overline{X}$ is some constant number, we have

$$\sigma^2_{\hat{Y}_i} = \sigma^2_{\overline{Y}} + (X_i - \overline{X})^2\sigma^2_{b_1} \tag{17A.12}$$

But since $\overline{Y} = \dfrac{\Sigma Y_i}{n}$ and all Y_i are independent with a variance of $\sigma^2_{Y_i} = \sigma^2_u$, we have $\sigma^2_{\overline{Y}} = \sigma^2_{Y_i}/n = \sigma^2_u/n$. Having proved before that $\sigma^2_{b_1} = \dfrac{\sigma^2_u}{\Sigma(X_i - \overline{X})^2}$, we finally obtain

$$\sigma^2_{\hat{Y}_i} = \sigma^2_u\left[\frac{1}{n} + \frac{(X_i - \overline{X})^2}{\Sigma(X_i - \overline{X})^2}\right] \tag{17A.13}$$

Note that we can substitute σ_u for σ_{Y_i}, since

$$Y_i = \beta_0 + \beta_1 X_i + u_i \tag{17A.14}$$

and since β_0, β_1, and X_i are constants, $\sigma^2_{Y_i} = \sigma^2_u$.

APPENDIX 17B:
Alternative Formulation of r^2

In this appendix we will reconcile a few alternative formulations of r^2. By definition (see Equations 17.36 and 17.37)

$$r^2 = \frac{\Sigma(\hat{Y}_i - \overline{Y})^2}{\Sigma(Y_i - \overline{Y})^2} \tag{17B.1}$$

This is equivalent to the following equation:

$$r^2 = \frac{[\Sigma(X_i - \overline{X})(Y_i - \overline{Y})]^2}{\Sigma(Y_i - \overline{Y})^2\Sigma(X_i - \overline{X})^2} \tag{17B.2}$$

To see this, recall that $Y_i = b_0 + b_1X_i$, and by definition of the OLS estimators we have

$$b_0 = \overline{Y} - b_1\overline{X} \tag{17B.3}$$

$$b_1 = \frac{\Sigma(Y_i - \overline{Y})(X_i - \overline{X})}{\Sigma(X_i - \overline{X})^2} \tag{17B.4}$$

Substituting for $\hat{Y}_i$ and then for b_0, we can write Equation 17B.1 as

$$r^2 = \frac{\Sigma(b_0 + b_1 X_i - \overline{Y})^2}{\Sigma(Y_i - \overline{Y})^2} = \frac{\Sigma[(\overline{Y} - b_1\overline{X}) + b_1 X_i - \overline{Y}]^2}{\Sigma(Y_i - \overline{Y})^2}$$

$$= \frac{\Sigma[b_1(X_i - \overline{X})]^2}{\Sigma(Y_i - \overline{Y})^2} = b_1^2 \frac{\Sigma(X_i - \overline{X})^2}{\Sigma(Y_i - \overline{Y})^2}$$

(17B.5)

and since $\Sigma(X_i - \overline{X})^2 = S_X^2 \cdot (n - 1)$ and $\Sigma(Y_i - \overline{Y})^2 = S_Y^2 \cdot (n - 1)$, Equation 17B.5 can be written as

$$r^2 = b_1^2 \cdot \frac{S_X^2}{S_Y^2}$$

(17B.6)

Substituting b_1 (Equation 17B.4) in Equation 17B.6, we finally obtain

$$r^2 = \frac{[\Sigma(Y_i - \overline{Y})(X_i - \overline{X})]^2}{[\Sigma(X_i - \overline{X})^2]^2} \cdot \frac{\Sigma(X_i - \overline{X})^2}{\Sigma(Y_i - \overline{Y})^2}$$

which reduces to

$$r^2 = \frac{[\Sigma(Y_i - \overline{Y})(X_i - \overline{X})]^2}{\Sigma(X_i - \overline{X})^2\Sigma(Y_i - \overline{Y})^2}$$

(17B.7)

Thus r is given by the square root of this expression.

SIMPLE LINEAR REGRESSION: INFERENCES AND APPLICATIONS

In Chapter 17 we presented the simple linear regression model and the procedure for estimating its parameters. We have emphasized the difference between the model's true parameters and their estimated values. The OLS estimators b_0 and b_1, like other sample statistics, have their own sampling distributions, and knowing them will enable us to learn about the statistical significance of the estimates we obtain. This chapter extends the discussion of simple linear regression in two directions: we shall discuss the statistical inference involved, and we shall present selected applications to show the importance of regression analysis and the type of studies for which it is suitable.

18.1 Inferences About β_1

To this point, the only assumptions we have made about the distribution of the u_is are that the u_i terms are independent of one another, that their mean is zero, and that their variance is the same for all X values and is denoted by σ_u^2. These assumptions have led us to several important properties of the estimators b_0 and b_1. They are all summarized under the rubric BLUE: "best linear unbiased estimators."

THE SAMPLING DISTRIBUTION OF b_1

The particular sampling distribution of the statistic b_1 depends on the probability distribution of the Y_i terms or, on the probability distribution of the disturbance terms, the u_is. In quite a few cases, the assumption that u

follows the normal distribution is plausible, and if u is indeed normally distributed, the distribution of the estimated slope b_1 is also normal. If the sample is large enough, the distribution of b_1 will be approximately normal (by the central limit theorem) even if u is not normally distributed.[1]

If b_1 is normally distributed, we can standardize it and get

$$Z = \frac{b_1 - \beta_1}{\sigma_{b_1}} \tag{18.1}$$

Since σ_u is unknown and since we know from Equation 17.26b that

$$\sigma_{b_1} = \frac{\sigma_u}{\sqrt{\Sigma(X_i - \overline{X})^2}} = \frac{\sigma_u}{\sqrt{\Sigma X_i^2 - n\overline{X}^2}}$$

it follows that σ_{b_1} is also unknown. When σ_{b_1} is unknown, it is impossible to construct confidence intervals for β_1 or to test hypotheses about it by means of the statistic Z of Equation 18.1. But the sample counterpart of σ_{b_1} is measurable and may be called to the rescue. To obtain the estimator of σ_{b_1}, we use the sample estimate of σ_u, namely, S_e, which yields

$$S_{b_1} = \frac{S_e}{\sqrt{\Sigma X_i^2 - n\overline{X}^2}} \tag{18.2}$$

where S_{b_1} is the estimator of σ_{b_1}.

Assuming the normality of u, we get

$$\frac{b_1 - \beta_1}{S_{b_1}} \sim t^{(n-2)} \tag{18.3}$$

Using this sampling distribution, we can simply construct a confidence interval for β_1. As shown in Figure 18.1, the probability that $(b_1 - \beta_1)/S_{b_1}$ will take on a value in the interval from $-t_{\alpha/2}^{(n-2)}$ to $t_{\alpha/2}^{(n-2)}$ is equal to $1 - \alpha$. This probability can also be expressed by an equation:

$$P\left[-t_{\alpha/2}^{(n-2)} \le \frac{b_1 - \beta_1}{S_{b_1}} \le t_{\alpha/2}^{(n-2)}\right] = 1 - \alpha \tag{18.4}$$

Or finally

$$P[b_1 - S_{b_1} \cdot t_{\alpha/2}^{(n-2)} \le \beta_1 \le b_1 + S_{b_1} \cdot t_{\alpha/2}^{(n-2)}] = 1 - \alpha \tag{18.5}$$

---

[1] In order to use the t distribution, we have to assume that the Y_is are normally distributed. It is insufficient here to invoke the central limit theorem to justify normality of b_1, since the t distribution is a ratio of Z to a square root of a χ^2 variable divided by its degrees of freedom. Even without the assumption of normality, however, the t distribution provides a good approximation if the sample is large.

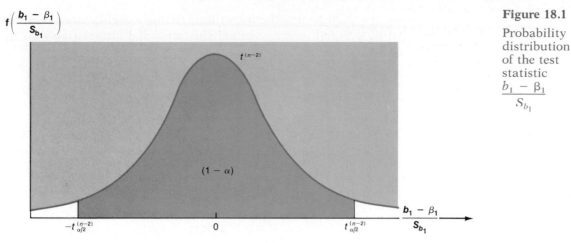

Equation 18.5 provides a confidence interval for β_1. It states that there is a probability of $1 - \alpha$ that the slope β_1 of the true regression line is included in the interval from $b_1 - S_{b_1} \cdot t_{\alpha/2}^{(n-2)}$ to $b_1 + S_{b_1} \cdot t_{\alpha/2}^{(n-2)}$.

TESTING HYPOTHESES ABOUT β_1

With Equation 18.3, it is also possible to test hypotheses about β_1. In testing the null hypothesis

$$H_0: \quad \beta_1 = \beta_1'$$

against

$$H_1: \quad \beta_1 \neq \beta_1'$$

or against a one-sided alternative (H_1: $\beta_1 > \beta_1'$ or $\beta_1 < \beta_1'$) we simply use $(b_1 - \beta_1')/S_{b_1}$ as our test statistic and employ the regular procedure for testing hypotheses of the mean when the standard deviation is unknown.

To illustrate, let us once again consider the income and consumption example of Chapter 17 to construct a 95 percent confidence interval for the slope and then test hypotheses concerning β_1. Given that $S_e = 3.33$, we use Equation 18.2 to estimate the standard error of the slope:

$$S_{b_1} = \frac{S_e}{\sqrt{\Sigma X_i^2 - n\overline{X}^2}} = \frac{3.33}{\sqrt{2{,}891 - (10)(15.9)^2}} = \frac{3.33}{19.05} = 0.1748$$

Recalling that $b_1 = 0.705$ and noticing that $t_{0.025}^{(8)} = 2.306$, we can construct the 95 percent confidence interval for β_1 by using Equation 18.5. Thus

$$b_1 - S_{b_1} \cdot t_{\alpha/2}^{(n-2)} = 0.705 - (0.1748)(2.306) = 0.3019$$

and

$$b_1 + S_{b_1} \cdot t_{\alpha/2}^{(n-2)} = 0.705 + (0.1748)(2.306) = 1.1081$$

Our confidence interval, then, is between 0.3019 and 1.1081.

Now suppose we want to test the hypothesis (using a significance level of 1 percent) that β_1 is equal to zero against the one-sided alternative that β_1 is greater than zero:

$$H_0: \quad \beta_1 = 0$$

$$H_1: \quad \beta_1 > 0$$

With $\dfrac{b_1 - \beta_1'}{S_{b_1}}$ as our test statistic, and the critical value $t_{0.01}^{(8)} = 2.896$, our

decision rule is to reject H_0 if $\dfrac{b_1 - \beta_1'}{S_{b_1}}$ is greater than 2.896 and not to reject

H_0 otherwise. Since $\dfrac{b_1 - \beta_1'}{S_{b_1}} = \dfrac{0.705}{0.1748} = 4.033$, we reject the null hypothesis

and favor the alternative, which implies that consumption indeed tends to rise with income. In Figure 17.17 we presented a computer printout of the

regression that shows a value of 3.997 for $\dfrac{b_1 - \beta_1'}{S_{b_1}}$. The difference, of course,

is due to rounding.

We can also test hypotheses where H_0 does not set β_1 at zero. For example, when testing $H_0: \beta_1 = 0.40$ versus $H_1: \beta_1 > 0.40$, we find

$$\frac{b_1 - \beta_1'}{S_{b_1}} = \frac{0.705 - 0.40}{0.1748} = \frac{0.305}{0.1748} = 1.745$$

Using $\alpha = 0.01$, we cannot reject H_0, since $1.745 < 2.896$. This means that while our point estimate ($b_1 = 0.705$) indicates that for each additional dollar of income, consumption rises by an average of 70.5 cents (or \$0.705), we cannot reject a hypothesis that the increase in consumption is only 40 cents per one dollar additional income. However, the sample size on which this conclusion is based is rather small (10 observations), resulting in a low power. If the sample size were increased, the power would be higher and the conclusion more meaningful.

18.2 Inferences About β_0

In some applications we are interested only in inferences about β_1. Other times we are also interested in inferences about β_0. For example, if we study the effect of advertising (X) on sales (Y), the intercept of the sample regression line is our estimate of the level of sales when there is no advertising at all ($X = 0$). Clearly, we might be interested in knowing the degree of error that is potentially associated with this estimate.

As another example, consider a study of the relationship between risk (X) and rate of return (Y) in stock market investments. The intercept provides an estimate of the riskless rate of return, namely, the rate of return we can expect from a riskless investment. Again we are interested in obtaining not only a point estimate but also a feel for the degree of statistical error to which the estimate is subject.

It can be shown (see Equations 17.24 and 17.26a in Chapter 17) that

$$E(b_0) = \beta_0 \qquad (18.6)$$

and

$$V(b_0) \equiv \sigma_{b_0}^2 = \sigma_u^2 \left[\frac{1}{n} + \frac{\overline{X}^2}{\Sigma(X - \overline{X})^2} \right]$$

The sample estimator of $\sigma_{b_0}^2$ is $S_{b_0}^2$, which is obtained by substituting S_e^2 for σ_u^2:

$$S_{b_0}^2 = S_e^2 \left[\frac{1}{n} + \frac{\overline{X}^2}{\Sigma(X - \overline{X})^2} \right] \qquad (18.7)$$

Assuming that the values Y_i are normally distributed or that the sample is large enough, we can use the following sampling distribution to assess the sampling errors of b_0:

$$\frac{b_0 - \beta_0}{S_{b_0}} \sim t^{(n-2)} \qquad (18.8)$$

Accordingly, the $1 - \alpha$ confidence interval for β_0 ranges from $b_0 - S_{b_0} t_{\alpha/2}^{(n-2)}$ to $b_0 + S_{b_0} t_{\alpha/2}^{(n-2)}$. In the income–consumption example we find

$$b_0 = 5.3$$

$$S_{b_0} = 3.33 \sqrt{\frac{1}{10} + \frac{15.9^2}{362.9}} = 2.972$$

$$t_{0.025}^{(8)} = 2.306$$

so a 95 percent confidence interval for β_0 ranges from $5.3 - 2.972 \cdot 2.306 = -1.55$ to $5.3 + 2.972 \cdot 2.306 = 12.15$. Again, the very wide interval is a direct result of the very small sample size used to illustrate the calculations. In any reasonable case, the sample size would be larger, making the confidence interval markedly narrower than the one we have obtained. Obviously we can use the statistic in Equation 18.8 to test the hypothesis about the value of β_0.

18.3 Confidence Interval for the Mean Response μ_i and Prediction Interval for the Individual Response Y_i

We have emphasized several times that, as a rule, the estimated regression line deviates from the true line. It does so in Figure 18.2, where a true regression line is shown along with a series of estimated lines marked 1, 2, 3, 4, and 5. Let us consider this illustration in more depth.

Figure 18.2

A true
regression
line and five
estimated
lines

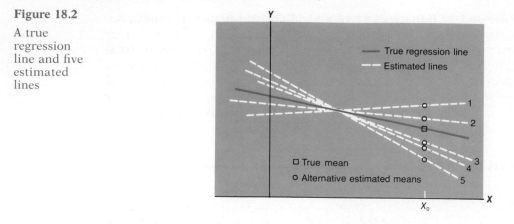

USING $\hat{Y}_i$ AS AN ESTIMATOR OF μ_i

The mean response $\mu_i = \beta_0 + \beta_1 X_i$ is a point on the true line that equals the expected value of Y_i, given that the independent variable, X, takes on the value X_i. The value $\hat{Y}_i$ (which is a point on the estimated line given the same level of the independent variable, X_i) is the estimator of the mean response, μ_i. In other words, to estimate μ_i we use the corresponding value on the estimated regression line, that is, the value $\hat{Y}_i$:

$$\hat{Y}_i = b_0 + b_1 X_i$$

Since b_0 and b_1 are unbiased—that is, $E(b_0) = \beta_0$ and $E(b_1) = \beta_1$—it follows that $\hat{Y}_i$ is an unbiased estimator of the mean response, μ_i:

$$E(\hat{Y}_i) = E(b_0 + b_1 X_i) = E(b_0) + E(b_1) \cdot X_i = \beta_0 + \beta_1 X_i = \mu_i \quad \textbf{(18.9)}$$

DERIVING A CONFIDENCE INTERVAL FOR μ_i

It can be shown (see Appendix 17A) that the variance of $\hat{Y}_i$ is given by Equation 18.10:

$$\sigma_{\hat{Y}_i}^2 = \sigma_u^2 \left[\frac{1}{n} + \frac{(X_i - \overline{X})^2}{\Sigma(X - \overline{X})^2} \right] \quad \textbf{(18.10)}$$

The quantity given within brackets is available from the sample data. If σ_u is known, we can construct a confidence interval around μ_i by using the standard normal distribution. A 95 percent confidence interval is given by

$$\mu_i = \hat{Y}_i \pm Z_{0.025} \cdot \sigma_u \sqrt{\frac{1}{n} + \frac{(X_i - \overline{X})^2}{\Sigma(X - \overline{X})^2}} \quad \textbf{(18.11)}$$

where both limits of the interval are written on the right-hand side: the minus sign applies to the lower limit and the plus sign to the upper limit. If σ_u is unknown, we can substitute its estimator, S_e, switch to the $t^{(n-2)}$ distribution, and construct the interval as follows:

$$\mu_i = \hat{Y}_i \pm t_{0.025}^{(n-2)} \cdot S_e \sqrt{\frac{1}{n} + \frac{(X_i - \overline{X})^2}{\Sigma(X - \overline{X})^2}} \quad \textbf{(18.12)}$$

Holding all other factors unchanged, we obtain the narrowest confidence interval for the mean response, μ_i, at $X_i = \overline{X}$, since the second term under the square root is equal to zero at that point. As X_i is shifted away from $\overline{X}$, to either the left or the right, the value $(X_i - \overline{X})^2$ increases and the confidence interval widens. This causes the confidence interval in Equations 18.11 and 18.12 to vary with the distance of X_i from $\overline{X}$. The closer X_i is to $\overline{X}$, the narrower the confidence interval; the farther X_i is from $\overline{X}$, the wider the confidence interval.

DERIVING A PREDICTION INTERVAL FOR AN INDIVIDUAL RESPONSE, Y_i

Having derived the confidence interval for the mean response, μ_i, when $\hat{Y}_i$ served as its estimator, we shall now derive a prediction interval for an individual response (or observation), Y_i (which deviates from $\hat{Y}_i$ by the random error e_i):

$$Y_i = \hat{Y}_i + e_i \tag{18.13}$$

Consider again the variance of $\hat{Y}_i$ when σ_u is unknown:

$$S_{\hat{Y}_i}^2 = S_e^2\left[\frac{1}{n} + \frac{(X_i - \overline{X})^2}{\Sigma(X - \overline{X})^2}\right]$$

The variance of an individual observation, Y_i, includes the variance of the observation about the regression line, S_e^2, in addition to $S_{\hat{Y}_i}^2$. Because $\hat{Y}_i$ and e_i are independent, $S_{Y_i}^2 = S_{\hat{Y}_i}^2 + S_e^2$. More explicitly, we write

$$S_{Y_i}^2 = S_e^2\left[\frac{1}{n} + \frac{(X_i - \overline{X})^2}{\Sigma(X - \overline{X})^2}\right] + S_e^2$$

or

$$S_{Y_i}^2 = S_e^2\left[\frac{1}{n} + \frac{(X_i - \overline{X})^2}{\Sigma(X - \overline{X})^2} + 1\right] \tag{18.14}$$

Consequently, the 95 percent prediction interval for a single observation is

$$Y_i = \hat{Y}_i \pm t_{0.025}^{(n-2)} \cdot S_e \sqrt{\frac{1}{n} + \frac{(X_i - \overline{X})^2}{\Sigma(X - \overline{X})^2} + 1} \tag{18.15}$$

Of course, if σ_u is known, we can substitute it for S_e in Equation 18.15. In this case we can use $Z_{0.025}$ instead of $t_{0.025}^{(n-2)}$. The result is the following prediction interval:

$$Y_i = \hat{Y}_i \pm Z_{0.025} \cdot \sigma_u \sqrt{\frac{1}{n} + \frac{(X_i - \overline{X})^2}{\Sigma(X - \overline{X})^2} + 1} \tag{18.16}$$

The prediction interval for Y_i is similar to that of μ_i, except that it is wider. Figure 18.3 shows the *confidence bands* for μ_i and Y_i. They are simply bands

Figure 18.3

An estimated regression line and confidence bands for μ_i and Y_i

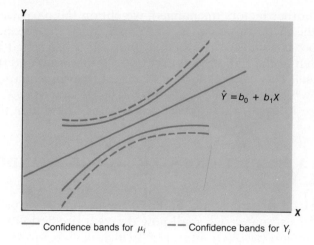

——— Confidence bands for μ_i - - - Confidence bands for Y_i

that show the confidence limits for μ_i and Y_i over all values of X in a given range.

Let us return to our income and consumption example, for which we found that $\overline{X} = 15.9$, $S_e = 3.33$, $\Sigma(X - \overline{X})^2 = 362.9$, $b_0 = 5.3$, $b_1 = 0.705$, and $n = 10$. Suppose we want to construct a 95 percent confidence interval for the mean consumption at an income level of \$25,000. The estimated consumption for \$25,000 income is:

$$\hat{Y}_i = 5.3 + 0.705 \cdot 25 = 22.925$$

Calculating $\sqrt{\dfrac{1}{n} + \dfrac{(X_i - \overline{X})^2}{\Sigma(X - \overline{X})^2}}$, we obtain $\sqrt{\dfrac{1}{10} + \dfrac{(25 - 15.9)^2}{362.9}} = 0.573$, and since $t_{\alpha/2}^{(n-2)} = t_{0.025}^{(8)} = 2.306$, our confidence interval is given by

$$\mu_i = 22.925 \pm 2.306 \cdot 3.33 \cdot 0.573$$

or

$$\mu_i = 22.925 \pm 4.400$$

In other words, the confidence interval ranges from \$18,525 to \$27,325 for the *mean* consumption of households whose income is \$25,000. The 95 percent prediction interval for the consumption of one (yet unknown) household with this level of income is found by calculating

$$\sqrt{\dfrac{1}{n} + \dfrac{(X_i - \overline{X})^2}{\Sigma(X - \overline{X})^2} + 1} = \sqrt{\dfrac{1}{10} + \dfrac{(25 - 15.9)^2}{362.9} + 1} = 1.152$$

Substituting in Equation 18.15, we obtain

$$Y_i = 22.925 \pm 2.306 \cdot 3.33 \cdot 1.152$$

or

$$Y_i = 22.925 \pm 8.846$$

The confidence interval for an individual household is thus considerably wider and ranges from \$14,079 to \$31,771.

EXAMPLE 18.1

We indicated earlier that the variance of b_1, the estimator of β_1, is given by

$$\sigma_{b_1}^2 = \frac{\sigma_u^2}{\Sigma(X_i - \bar{X})^2}$$

When σ_u is unknown, however, the estimated variance of the slope is

$$S_{b_1}^2 = \frac{S_e^2}{\Sigma(X_i - \bar{X})^2}$$

where $S_e^2 = \Sigma e_i^2/(n - 2)$. We remember that e_i is given by the deviation of the observation i from the regression line: $e_i = Y_i - (b_0 + b_1 X_i)$. Recall also that the $1 - \alpha$ confidence interval for μ_i is

$$\mu_i = \hat{Y}_i \pm t_{\alpha/2}^{(n-2)} \cdot S_e \sqrt{\frac{1}{n} + \frac{(X_i - \bar{X})^2}{\Sigma(X - \bar{X})^2}}$$

From the equations above we can see that, given a sample size, n, the accuracy of b_1 depends on S_e as well as on the dispersion of the independent variable, X. The smaller the variability of the error around the regression line, S_e, and the wider the dispersion of the independent-variable values, X_i, about their mean, $\bar{X}$, the more accurate the estimate b_1. Its standard error grows smaller and the confidence interval for β_1 becomes narrower. The impact of S_e on S_{b_1} is intuitively obvious. A small S_e means that the deviations e_i around the regression line are small and the regression line fits the scattered data quite well. Hence, the estimate b_1 is relatively accurate.

The impact of the dispersion of the X_i values on the accuracy of b_1 is harder to see intuitively. Figure 18.4 shows the extreme case, in which there is no dispersion of the X_is whatsoever, and we cannot achieve any accuracy in estimating the slope β_1: the entire sample is taken at a single value of X. The figure shows a number of regression lines fitting through

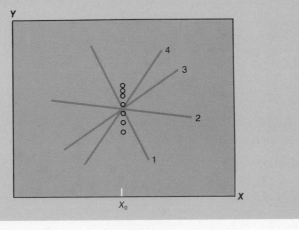

Figure 18.4

Regression lines for a case in which no dispersion occurs in X

the data, none of which can be said to fit the data better than the others.[2] They all yield the same sum of squared deviations, Σe_i^2. The wider the dispersion of the X_is [that is, the greater the quantity $\Sigma(X - \bar{X})^2$], the smaller the standard error of the estimator b_1 and the more accurate the estimate.

We proceed with a numerical illustration showing the impact of S_e on the variability of the estimator b_1 and the confidence interval for β_1.

The Impact of Changes in S_e Tables 18.1 and 18.2 present two sets of data. In each table, five observations of X and Y are given. To demonstrate the impact of a change in S_e alone, *we chose the same X_i values for both tables*. The Y_i values in Table 18.2 have greater variability than those of Table 18.1. We also made sure that the OLS-estimated regression lines in both tables are identical: in both tables $b_0 = 1.2$ and $b_1 = 1.2$, so the estimated line is given by $\hat{Y}_i = 1.2 + 1.2X_i$. Because the variability of Y in Table 18.1 is smaller (and the values X_i are the same), the estimated line in Table 18.1 is more reliable, meaning that we expect it to be closer to the true regression line than the line derived from the Table 18.2 data. This is a direct result of the fact that if b_1 is the same and the X_i values are the same, the value of S_e is smaller the smaller the variability of Y (see Equation 17.32). Consequently, we get narrower confidence intervals for μ_i and Y_i in Table 18.1 than in Table 18.2. Indeed, while the magnitude of $\Sigma(X_i - \bar{X})^2$ is the same in both tables, the

TABLE 18.1
Work Sheet for Calculation of a Regression Line and Its Confidence Interval

X	Y_i	$X_i - \bar{X}$	$(X_i - \bar{X})^2$	$(X_i - \bar{X})Y_i$
0	2	-2	4	-4
1	1	-1	1	-1
2	3	0	0	0
3	7	1	1	7
4	5	2	4	10
$\bar{X} = 2$	$\bar{Y} = 3.60$	$\Sigma(X_i - \bar{X}) = 0$	$\Sigma(X_i - \bar{X})^2 = 10$	$\Sigma(X_i - \bar{X})Y_i = 12$

TABLE 18.1 (Continued)

$\hat{Y}_i = 1.2 + 1.2X_i$	$e_i = Y_i - \hat{Y}_i$	e_i^2	95% confidence interval for the mean response
1.2	0.8	0.64	1.200 ± 4.222
2.4	-1.4	1.96	2.400 ± 2.986
3.6	-0.6	0.36	3.600 ± 2.440
4.8	2.2	4.84	4.800 ± 2.986
6.0	-1.0	1.00	6.000 ± 4.222
		$\Sigma e_i^2 = 8.80$	

[2] Of course, a vertical line passing through the data could be thought to fit the data best. But the *vertical* deviations of the data from such a line are undefined, and the line does not capture the relationship between the variables Y and X.

TABLE 18.2
Work Sheet for Calculation of a Regression Line and Its Confidence Interval

X_i	Y_i	$X_i - \bar{X}$	$(X_i - \bar{X})^2$	$(X_i - \bar{X})Y_i$
0	4	-2	4	-8
1	3	-1	1	-3
2	-3	0	0	0
3	5	1	1	5
4	9	2	4	18
$\bar{X} = 2$	$\bar{Y} = 3.60$	$\Sigma(X_i - \bar{X}) = 0$	$\Sigma(X_i - \bar{X})^2 = 10$	$\Sigma(X_i - \bar{X})Y_i = 12$

TABLE 18.2 (Continued)

$\hat{Y}_i = 1.2 + 1.2X_i$	$e_i = Y_i - \hat{Y}_i$	e_i^2	95% confidence interval for the mean response
1.2	2.8	7.84	1.200 ± 11.096
2.4	0.6	0.36	2.400 ± 7.847
3.6	-6.6	43.56	3.600 ± 6.406
4.8	0.2	0.04	4.800 ± 7.847
6.0	3.0	9.00	6.000 ± 11.096
		$\Sigma e_i^2 = 60.80$	

estimated standard deviation, S_{b_1}, is substantially smaller in Table 18.1 than in 18.2. For the Table 18.1 data we have

$$S_{b_1} = \frac{S_e}{\sqrt{\Sigma(X - \bar{X})^2}} = \frac{\sqrt{\dfrac{\Sigma e_i^2}{n - 2}}}{\sqrt{\Sigma(X - \bar{X})^2}} = \frac{\sqrt{\dfrac{8.80}{3}}}{\sqrt{10}} = 0.542$$

For Table 18.2 data we have

$$S_{b_1} = \frac{\sqrt{\dfrac{60.80}{3}}}{\sqrt{10}} = 1.424$$

Similarly, the 95 percent confidence interval for μ_i, shown in the column to the far right in each table, is given by

$$\mu_i = \hat{Y}_i \pm t_{0.025}^{(3)} \, S_e \sqrt{\frac{1}{n} + \frac{(X_i - \bar{X})^2}{\Sigma(X - \bar{X})^2}}$$

As an example, when $X_i = 0$ in Table 18.1, we get

$$S_e = \sqrt{\frac{\Sigma e_i^2}{n - 2}} = \sqrt{\frac{8.80}{3}} = 1.713$$

and

$$\mu_i = 1.200 \pm 3.182 \cdot 1.713 \cdot \sqrt{\frac{1}{5} + \frac{(0 - 2)^2}{10}} = 1.200 \pm 4.222$$

Figure 18.5

Illustration of
the change in
the regression
line and the
confidence
bands as the
dispersion of
Y increases

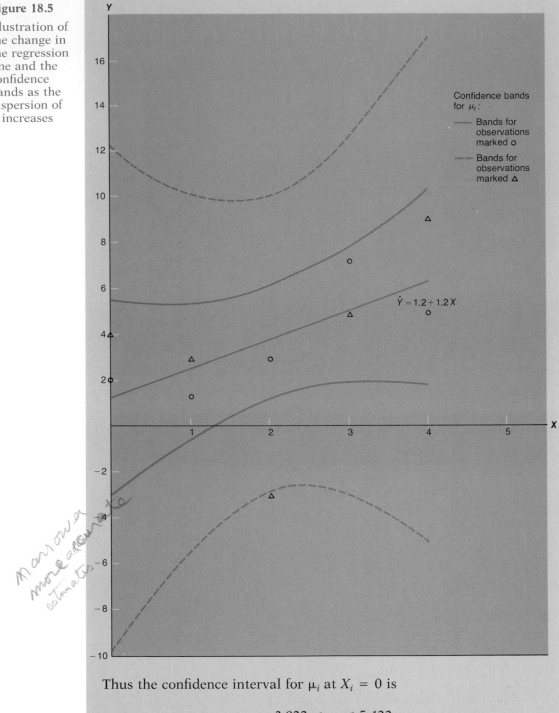

Thus the confidence interval for μ_i at $X_i = 0$ is

$$-3.022 \leq \mu_i \leq 5.422$$

For the same X_i value ($X_i = 0$), we compute in Table 18.2 the following confidence interval:

$$\mu_i = 1.200 \pm 3.182 \cdot 4.502 \cdot \sqrt{\frac{1}{5} + \frac{(0-2)^2}{10}} = 1.200 \pm 11.096$$

or

$$-9.896 \leq \mu_i \leq 12.296$$

This time $S_e = \sqrt{\dfrac{\Sigma e_i^2}{n-2}} = \sqrt{\dfrac{60.80}{3}} = 4.502$, so the interval is substantially wider than the one constructed on the basis of Table 18.1. Note once more that in both tables, $\hat{Y}_i$, $\dfrac{1}{n}$, $t_{\alpha/2}$, and $\dfrac{(X_i - \overline{X})^2}{\Sigma(X - \overline{X})^2}$ are identical, and the difference in the width of the confidence interval is solely attributable to the difference in S_e. A summary of this example is given in Figure 18.5, where the observations of Table 18.1 are indicated by circles and the observations of Table 18.2 are indicated by triangles. It is evident that the circles are closer, overall, to the estimated regression line. The confidence bands for μ_i based on both samples are also displayed in Figure 18.5; we can once again see that the greater dispersion of the observations around the regression line results in a much wider confidence interval.

This example has shown the effect of a change in S_e on the width of the confidence interval for the mean response. It is also possible to make up an example that shows how the confidence intervals get narrower as the dispersion of X becomes greater (see Problem 18.13 at the end of this chapter).

18.4 Inferences About ρ

In Chapter 7, we presented the population correlation coefficient, ρ, and its estimator, r. In Chapter 17 we related r and r^2 to regression analysis, and in this chapter we will learn to draw inferences about ρ. We distinguish between two situations, one in which X is not a random variable but Y is, and one in which both X and Y are random variables.

WHEN X IS NOT A RANDOM VARIABLE

We start by assuming that the dependent variable is a random variable while the independent variable is not. Basically, this is the way we treated the variables X and Y in regression analysis: we assumed that Y relates to X and to a random variable, u; thus Y itself was a random variable, but X was not.

The most relevant question about the correlation coefficient in this case is whether or not it is equal to zero: for if it is, then there is no association between X and Y. We can show that testing H_0: $\rho = 0$ is equivalent to testing H_0: $\beta_1 = 0$, where β_1 is the regression slope coefficient. Denoting

$$S_X^2 = \frac{\Sigma(X - \overline{X})^2}{n-1} \tag{18.17}$$

we have shown (see Appendix 17B) that the regression slope coefficient b_1

and the correlation coefficient r are related in the following way:

$$b_1 = r \cdot \frac{S_Y}{S_X} \tag{18.18}$$

This means that when r equals zero, b_1 also equals zero, and vice versa. The same relationship can be similarly shown to exist for the population

$$\beta_1 = \rho \cdot \frac{\sigma_Y}{\sigma_X} \tag{18.19}$$

Thus testing H_0: $\beta_1 = 0$ is equivalent to testing H_0: $\rho = 0$.

Let us give an example of regression inferences, including inferences based on r^2.

EXAMPLE 18.2

The price of gold (*GOLD*) and the Consumer Price Index in the United States (*CPUS*) by quarters in the period 1970–82 are given in Table 18.3.

TABLE 18.3
Price of Gold (*GOLD*) and the U.S. Consumer Price Index (*CPUS*) for the Period 1970, Q1–1982, Q1

Observation	Quarter	GOLD	CPUS
1	70Q1	35.00	70.7
2	70Q2	35.66	71.8
3	70Q3	35.63	72.6
4	70Q4	37.47	73.6
5	71Q1	38.45	74.1
6	71Q2	39.87	74.9
7	71Q3	49.88	75.7
8	71Q4	42.93	76.1
9	72Q1	47.42	76.7
10	72Q2	55.24	77.4
11	72Q3	66.04	78.0
12	72Q4	63.83	78.7
13	73Q1	74.76	79.8
14	73Q2	104.60	81.6
15	73Q3	109.92	83.4
16	73Q4	100.42	85.4
17	74Q1	149.19	87.7
18	74Q2	163.23	90.2
19	74Q3	149.61	93.0
20	74Q4	175.66	95.7
21	75Q1	178.10	97.4
22	75Q2	167.17	98.9
23	75Q3	156.25	101.1
24	75Q4	140.43	102.7
25	76Q1	130.02	103.7
26	76Q2	125.90	105.0
27	76Q3	110.83	106.6
28	76Q4	129.38	107.8
29	77Q1	140.55	109.7
30	77Q2	144.40	112.1

TABLE 18.3 (Continued)

Observation	Quarter	GOLD	CPUS
31	77Q3	148.05	113.7
32	77Q4	162.17	115.0
33	78Q1	179.87	116.9
34	78Q2	179.35	120.0
35	78Q3	202.37	122.8
36	78Q4	213.83	125.2
37	79Q1	237.84	128.4
38	79Q2	258.59	132.8
39	79Q3	316.84	137.2
40	79Q4	412.91	141.2
41	80Q1	631.40	146.7
42	80Q2	543.98	152.0
43	80Q3	648.02	154.8
44	80Q4	608.06	158.9
45	81Q1	518.64	163.1
46	81Q2	478.86	166.9
47	81Q3	420.99	171.7
48	81Q4	420.41	174.1
49	82Q1	362.84	175.6

Source: International Monetary Fund, *Financial Statistics*, various issues.

There are 49 quarters in this period. Figure 18.6 shows the results of the following regression:

$$\widehat{GOLD} = b_0 + b_1 \, CPUS$$

Let us explain the results.

```
DEP VARIABLE: GOLD

                       SUM OF        MEAN
SOURCE          DF     SQUARES       SQUARE        F VALUE      PROB>F

MODEL           1      1137717       1137717       191.005      0.0001
ERROR           47     279954        5956.478
C TOTAL         48     1417671

      ROOT MSE         77.178221     R-SQUARE      0.8025
      DEP MEAN         202.916


                       PARAMETER     STANDARD      T FOR H0:
VARIABLE        DF     ESTIMATE      ERROR         PARAMETER=0   PROB>|T|

INTERCEP        1      -326.350      39.851366     -8.189        0.0001
CPUS            1      4.839250      0.350151      13.820        0.0001
```

Figure 18.6

Reproduction of an SAS computer printout, showing the results of the regression $\widehat{GOLD} = b_0 + b_1 CPUS$

The top part of the printout shows the analysis of variance of the regression and identifies the source of variance of the dependent variable, namely, the price of gold. The total sum of squares of the dependent variable, $\Sigma(Y - \overline{Y})^2$, is equal to 1,417,671, and out of this, the model explains 1,137,717. Dividing these two numbers we get 1,137,717/1,417,671 = 0.8025, which is the regression's r^2: 80.25 percent of the sum of squares of the price of gold is "explained" by the change in the Consumer Price

Index. However, 279,954/1,417,671 = 0.1975, or 19.75 percent of the variability of gold price, is "unexplained" by *CPUS*.

The regression is very significant: its *F* value is 191.005 and it is significant at all significance levels greater than 0.0001, or 0.01 percent: At all such significance levels we will have to reject a hypothesis claiming that the *CPUS* did not "explain" the behavior of gold prices. The estimated regression equation is

$$\widehat{GOLD} = -326.35 + 4.83925\ CPUS$$

where both $b_0 = -326.35$ and $b_1 = 4.83925$ are very significantly different from zero. The *t* value of b_0 is -8.189 and that of b_1 is 13.820. Both are significantly different from zero at all significance levels greater than 0.0001. Remember that the significance of b_1 implies that the regression's r^2 is also significantly different from zero.

Note the slope of the regression, which equals approximately 4.84. Since it is much greater than 1, it is clear that gold prices have gone up, on average, much faster than consumer prices. Those who invested in gold during the period have obtained capital gains that, on average, have more than protected their investment against the inflation-caused dilution in the real value of their investment. If the relationship between gold prices and *CPUS* were to stay the same in the future, we could expect that, on average, a 1 percent rise in *CPUS* would be accompanied by a 4.84 percent increase in gold prices.

WHEN X AND Y ARE BOTH RANDOM VARIABLES

The second situation that may arise when we are making inferences about ρ is one in which both *X* and *Y* are treated as *random* variables. We shall assume here that the population is infinite. If we can also assume that the *joint* distribution of *X* and *Y* is *bivariate normal*—that is, that for any *X* value the distribution of *Y* is normal and that for any *Y* value the distribution of *X* is normal—then in testing the hypothesis that ρ = 0, we can use a statistic that has a *t* distribution. Specifically, if we test H_0: ρ = 0, then (even for small samples) we can use the test statistic

$$T = r\sqrt{\frac{n-2}{1-r^2}} \tag{18.20}$$

where the statistic *T* has a *t* distribution with $n-2$ degrees of freedom.

Confidence intervals for ρ are presented in Figure 18.7, which shows confidence bands for various sample sizes and various values of *r* at a 95 percent confidence level. Values of the sample correlation coefficient, *r*, are measured along the horizontal axis, and values of the population correlation coefficient, ρ, are measured along the vertical axis. Confidence bands from the lower left to the upper right corner are drawn: a pair of bands for each sample size. For example, suppose the sample size is $n = 15$ and the sample correlation is -0.40. In this case, the two relevant bands are those marked $n = 15$. When a line is drawn straight up from -0.40 on the horizontal axis toward the confidence bands, the line meets the lower band at ρ = -0.75 and the upper band at ρ = $+0.16$. Thus the 95 percent confidence interval for ρ is the interval from -0.75 to $+0.16$. If the sample size is $n = 100$ and

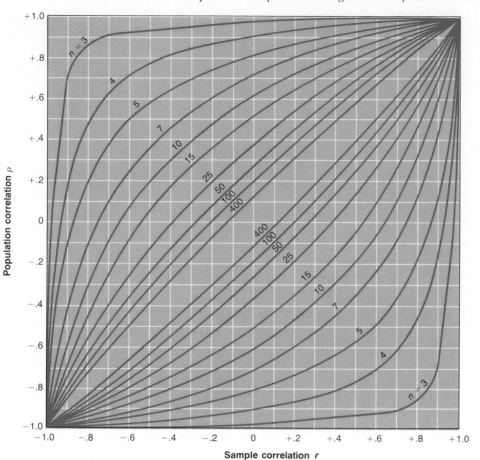

Figure 18.7

95 percent confidence bands for correlation ρ in a bivariate normal population, for various sample sizes *n*

Source: From E. S. Pearson from F. N. David, *Tables of the Ordinates and Probability Integral of the Distribution of the Correlation Coefficient in Small Samples* (Cambridge University Press, 1938). Reproduced with permission of the publisher.

the sample correlation, *r*, is +0.60, the confidence interval is between 0.45 and 0.72. Note that the confidence interval is not symmetrical around *r*.

EXAMPLE 18.3

Many financial institutions—commercial banks, savings and loan associations, mutual savings banks, pension funds, insurance companies, and other so-called "financial intermediaries"—invest tens of billions of dollars in the U.S. capital markets. Economists are interested in studying the behavior of those institutions in the capital markets. As part of a study of this kind, suppose we want to determine the way interest rates in the bond market affect the amount of federal government bonds demanded by corporate and state and local government pension funds. Thus our dependent variable will be the total value of U.S. bonds held by those pension funds. We denote this variable by *GB* (for "government bonds"). Since we are dealing with simple correlation, we shall assume only one explanatory variable: the rate of interest on government bonds, which will be denoted by *IGB*. To avoid unnecessary calculations, we shall assume only 10 observations, each of which represents a three-month average level. The data are given in Table 18.4. A work sheet for calculation of the correlation coefficient is provided in Table 18.5. Using

TABLE 18.4
Government Bonds Held by Pension Funds and
Rate of Interest Paid During Ten Quarters

Quarter	Bonds (GB) (millions of dollars)	Interest (IGB) (percent)
1	$2,030.0	7.1%
2	1,710.0	6.0
3	1,790.0	5.3
4	1,970.0	5.2
5	2,440.0	7.0
6	2,326.0	8.4
7	2,440.0	9.2
8	1,900.0	7.6
9	1,740.0	6.0
10	1,470.0	5.0

TABLE 18.5
Work Sheet for Calculation of Correlation Coefficient

Quarter	GB Y	IGB X	Y^2	X^2	XY
1	2,030	7.1	4,120,900	50.41	14,413.0
2	1,710	6.0	2,924,100	36.00	10,260.0
3	1,790	5.3	3,204,100	28.09	9,487.0
4	1,970	5.2	3,880,900	27.04	10,244.0
5	2,440	7.0	5,953,600	49.00	17,080.0
6	2,326	8.4	5,410,276	70.56	19,538.4
7	2,440	9.2	5,953,600	84.64	22,448.0
8	1,900	7.6	3,610,000	57.76	14,440.0
9	1,740	6.0	3,027,600	36.00	10,440.0
10	1,470	5.0	2,160,900	25.00	7,350.0
Total	19,816	66.8	40,245,976	464.50	135,700.4
Average	1,981.6	6.68			

Equation 17.46, we can find the coefficient of correlation:

$$r = \frac{135,700.4 - (10)(6.68)(1,981.6)}{(\sqrt{464.5 - (10)(6.68)^2})(\sqrt{40,245,976 - (10)(1,981.6)^2})}$$

$$= \frac{3,329.52}{(\sqrt{18.276})(\sqrt{978,591})} = \frac{3,329.52}{(4.275)(989.237)}$$

$$= 0.7873$$

Consequently, $r^2 = 0.7873^2 = 0.6198$, meaning that 61.98 percent of the total variance of *GB* is explained by the interest rate. The positive sign of *r* indicates a direct relationship between *GB* and *IGB* and thus that pension funds tend to increase their purchases of government bonds when the interest on those bonds rises. To test the hypothesis H_0: $\rho = 0$, we can calculate the regression slope coefficient, b_1, and then test the equivalent hypothesis: H_0: $\beta_1 = 0$. If H_0: $\beta_1 = 0$ is accepted, we should also accept H_0: $\rho = 0$, and vice versa. If, however, the independent variable is a *random* variable having a bivariate normal distribution with the dependent variable Y and we want to test H_0: $\rho = 0$ against H_1: $\rho \neq 0$, then we use the test statistic T:

$$T = r \sqrt{\frac{n - 2}{1 - r^2}}$$

In this case we get

$$T = 0.7873 \cdot \sqrt{\frac{10 - 2}{1 - 0.7873^2}} = 3.612$$

Since T has a t distribution with $n - 2 = 8$ degrees of freedom, we must compare the value of 3.612 with the critical value and then make our decision accordingly.

Assuming $\alpha = 0.05$, we get $t_{0.025}^{(8)} = 2.306$. Since $3.612 > 2.306$, we reject H_0 and conclude that ρ is indeed different from zero. Note that a 95 percent confidence interval around $r = 0.7873$, as shown in Figure 18.7, is between 0.30 and 0.95.

18.5 Piecewise Regression Analysis

It is clear that a linear relationship between variables, as common as it may be, is not the only type of relationship that we encounter. We cannot present a comprehensive treatment of nonlinear regression in this book, but the topic is treated briefly in Chapter 20 in the context of time-series analysis. In some cases, though, linear regression can be fitted piecewise to variables with nonlinear relationships. Figure 18.8 shows a scatter diagram of data on annual income and age (up to 65). A careful look at the data reveals that three periods can be identified, each with a distinct income–age relationship pat-

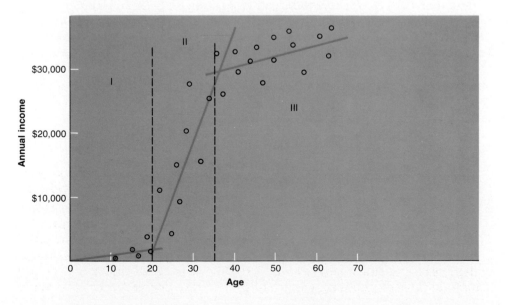

Figure 18.8

Scatter diagram of data relating annual income to age of individuals

tern: there is a period of virtually no income (Zone I), followed by a period of rapid income growth (Zone II), followed by a period of moderate growth in income (Zone III). If a linear regression line is estimated on the basis of observations in the age group 18–35 (Zone II), the estimated line may well approximate the income pattern over this age interval. It is also clear, however, that income prediction based on a Zone II relationship beyond the 18–35 range could lead to substantial errors; thus caution should be taken in the way regression results are interpreted and applied.

An application using piecewise regression analysis is presented in Section 18.9.

18.6 APPLICATION 1:
COST ACCOUNTING—ALLOCATION OF INDIRECT COST

This application presents estimation of regression coefficients and their interpretation. Statistical inference will be covered in the applications that follow.

Firms with more than one production line face some difficulties in measuring the separate production costs of their various products. They must know the separate production costs in order to make decisions about the optimal output of each product. The difficulty is due to the fact that apart from direct costs, there are indirect costs—management salary, rent, and the like—which should be allocated to the various production lines by some sort of accounting technique. Although indirect costs cannot be allocated precisely, there are some key variables (number of workers, number of machines, machine hours, labor hours, and the like) that represent activity level in the various production lines, so indirect costs can be allocated in relation to activity level. (The selected variables by which the firm allocates indirect costs to the various production lines are known in accounting as the *application base*.) It is common to use regression techniques in allocating the indirect costs to the various production lines or departments. The following is an example of the way the indirect-cost allocation can be handled.

Typing Equipment, Inc., is a large manufacturing firm organized in four departments. Department *A* handles all administrative matters, while Departments *B*, *C*, and *D* handle various production processes. Among the costs of Departments *B*, *C*, and *D* is the indirect cost, which includes some items that vary proportionally to direct labor hours (*DLH*). Among these items are electricity, water, and a portion of the maintenance cost. These costs are known as **indirect variable costs**. Among the cost items that *do not* vary directly with *DLH* are depreciation and rent, which are known as **fixed costs**. The total of fixed costs and indirect variable costs makes up the **indirect cost**, which will be denoted by *IC*.

Data of recent months show the following combinations of *IC* (combined for Departments *B*, *C*, and *D*) and *DLH*:

DLH (thousands of hours)	*IC* (thousands of dollars)
100	$200
170	230
150	225
212	270
308	310
345	330
310	325
340	330

Since the *IC* tends to vary directly with *DLH*, we will use *DLH* as the application base.

What is the estimated *IC* for each of the three departments for the next month, if *DLH* will be 40,000 in Department *B*, 150,000 in Department *C*, and 160,000 in Department *D*? We begin by running a regression line, using *IC* as a dependent variable and *DLH* as an explanatory variable. To do this we first develop the work sheet shown in Table 18.6. The regression's estimated parameters follow directly:

$$b_1 = \frac{\Sigma XY - n\overline{X}\overline{Y}}{\Sigma X^2 - n\overline{X}^2} = \frac{572{,}370 - (8)(241.875)(277.50)}{531{,}933 - (8)(241.875)^2}$$

$$= \frac{572{,}370.0 - 536{,}962.5}{531{,}933.0 - 468{,}028.1} = \frac{35{,}407.5}{63{,}904.9} = 0.554$$

$$b_0 = \overline{Y} - b_1\overline{X} = 277.5 - (0.554)(241.875) = 143.50$$

$$r = \frac{\Sigma XY - n\overline{X}\overline{Y}}{\sqrt{\Sigma(X - \overline{X})^2}\,\sqrt{\Sigma(Y - \overline{Y})^2}} = \frac{35{,}407.5}{\sqrt{63{,}905.0}\,\sqrt{19{,}900}} = 0.993$$

and

$$r^2 = 0.993^2 = 0.986$$

The estimated equation is then

$$\widehat{IC} = 143.50 + 0.554DLH$$

TABLE 18.6
Work Sheet for Calculation of Regression Line

Y (IC)	X (DLH)	Y^2	X^2	XY
200	100	40,000	10,000	20,000
230	170	52,900	28,900	39,100
225	150	50,625	22,500	33,750
270	212	72,900	44,944	57,240
310	308	96,100	94,864	95,480
330	345	108,900	119,025	113,850
325	310	105,625	96,100	100,750
330	340	108,900	115,600	112,200
$\Sigma Y = 2{,}220$	$\Sigma X = 1{,}935$	$\Sigma Y^2 = 635{,}950$	$\Sigma X^2 = 531{,}933$	$\Sigma XY = 572{,}370$
$\overline{Y} = 277.50$	$\overline{X} = 241.875$			

Figure 18.9 presents the scatter diagram and estimated line. We can see how the scattered points lie very close to the estimated line, which is the reason why r^2 is so close to 1: 98.6 percent of the variance of the indirect costs is accounted for by differences in *DLH*. Given the estimated line, let us proceed with the cost allocation. Total *DLH* anticipated for the next month is $40 + 150 + 160 = 350$ thousands of hours. Total

Figure 18.9

The estimated regression line relating indirect cost to direct labor hours

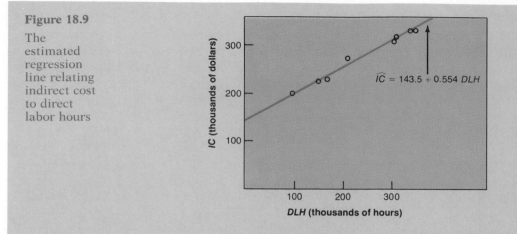

estimated *IC* is

$$\hat{IC} = 143.50 + 0.554 \cdot 350 = 143.50 + 193.90 = 337.40$$

Out of the $337,400 in total indirect costs, a sum of $143,500 is estimated to exist even if *DLH* = 0; thus the $143,500 should be identified as the estimated fixed cost. The balance, $193,900, is the estimated indirect variable cost. The allocation of the fixed cost is proportional to the department's *DLH*. Table 18.7 shows how the *IC* of $337,400 is allocated.

TABLE 18.7

Allocation of Indirect Cost, by Department

(1) *Department*	*(2)* *DLH* *(thousands* *of hours)*	*(3)* *Percent* *DLH/100*	*(4)* *Fixed costs* *($143,500 · col. 3)*	*(5)* *Variable* *indirect cost* *($193,900 · col. 3)*[a]	*(6)* *Total IC* *(col. 4 + col. 5)*
B	40	0.1143	16,400	22,160	38,560
C	150	0.4286	61,500	83,110	144,610
D	160	0.4571	65,600	88,630	154,230
Total	350	1.0000	143,500	193,900	337,400

Note: Figures have been rounded.
[a] Also equal to 0.554 · col.2 · 1,000.

The allocation described in Table 18.7 is the popular allocation procedure in accounting known as the flexible budget.[3] The procedure is useful and important for many reasons. In some cases, for example, the price of a product is determined by the cost of production plus some percentage of profit (this method is known as "cost-plus pricing"). This sort of pricing is common among firms under regulation or working under a special contract. The indirect cost of each product is important in such cases. Suppose the firm in our example needs to decide whether Department *D* should be closed down. Let the revenue of that department be $500,000 per year and its direct cost be $400,000. Should we close the department? Looking at the flexible budget, we see that the total (direct and indirect) cost of the department is

[3] See, for example, Charles T. Horngren, *Cost Accounting: A Managerial Emphasis*, 5th ed. (Englewood Cliffs, N.J.: Prentice-Hall, 1982).

$$\text{Total cost}_D = \$400,000 + \$154,230 = \$554,230$$

Hence the total cost of the department is greater than its revenue, and it seems that it should be closed. A closer look at the figures, however, shows that this is not the case. Out of the $154,230 indirect cost of Department D, $65,600 are fixed costs, which the firm would have to expend even if Department D were to be closed. In the short run, then, only $88,630 indirect variable cost of Department D should be considered. The total cost is thus

$$\text{Total cost}_D = \$400,000 + \$88,630 = \$488,630$$

Closing the department will save $488,630 but will decrease revenues by $500,000. Hence the department should stay open for the short run. In the next chapter we shall discuss multiple regression analysis, in which more than one independent variable is used to explain variations of one dependent variable. The application base of indirect cost allocation often includes more than just one variable, and multiple regression analysis is then used to derive the flexible budget.

18.7 APPLICATION 2:
FINANCE—MEASURING SECURITY RISK

The desirability of any financial investment depends heavily (though not exclusively) on its riskiness. Many stockbrokers, financial consultants, and academicians use a model known as the "beta model" to identify the riskiness of securities. For example, Merrill Lynch, Pierce, Fenner & Smith, the largest brokerage firm in the United States, provides the beta (or β) risk index as a regular service to its customers. The beta coefficient of a security is measured by the simple regression technique. The dependent variable is the rate of return of the security (which will be denoted by Y, or alternatively by SRR), and the independent variable is the rate of return on a portfolio of all the securities traded in the market.[4] This portfolio is known as the "market portfolio," and as its proxy, consultants and brokers usually use the rate of return on some known and readily available market index, such as the Dow-Jones average or Standard & Poor's (S&P) average. The rate of return on such an index serves as our independent variable (we denote the independent variable by X, or alternatively by MRR, for market rate of return). Using past rates of return, we can run the following simple regression:

$$SRR = b_0 + b_1 MRR + e$$

The estimated slope of the regression line, b_1, is used as a risk measure for the particular security whose rates of return are used as the dependent variable. The reason will become clear later. For now, let us illustrate the numerical computations. Suppose data on annual rates of return have been obtained for eight years, as shown in Table 18.8. The broker needs to estimate the regression line and compute S_Y and S_e. To estimate

---

[4] The rate of return is the rate of profit or loss on an investment. If you invest $100 in a stock and realize $125 a year later, your rate of return is 25 percent. If you realize $80, your rate of return is −20 percent.

the regression line, we first develop Table 18.9, which serves as a work sheet, and continue by computing the constants b_0 and b_1:

$$b_1 = \frac{\Sigma XY - n\overline{X}\overline{Y}}{\Sigma X^2 - n\overline{X}^2} = \frac{473 - (8)(2)(2.5)}{284 - (8)(2)^2} = \frac{473 - 40}{284 - 32} = \frac{433}{252} = 1.72$$

$$b_0 = \overline{Y} - b_1\overline{X} = 2.50 - (1.72)(2) = 2.50 - 3.44 = -0.94$$

Given these two estimates, we can write the relationship between *SRR* and *MRR* as follows:

$$\widehat{SRR} = -0.94 + 1.72MRR$$

Here $\widehat{SRR}$ is the estimated *SRR* value. The results should be interpreted to mean that a one-unit change (in this case the unit is 1 percentage point) in the average market rate of return is estimated to be accompanied on the average by 1.72 units of change in the rate of return on the particular stock examined (see Figure 18.10). The slope, 1.72, is the estimated beta coefficient of the particular stock considered; it reflects the sensitivity of the stock's rate of return to changes in the rates of return on the market as a whole. Thus, if the rate of return on the market as a whole goes up 10 percentage points, the stock on hand is estimated to go up 17.2 pecentage points; similarly, a

TABLE 18.8
Rates of Return on the Market Portfolio and on One Stock
(percent)

Independent variable (MRR): average market return X	Dependent variable (SRR): return on stock Y
1.0	2.0
−5.0	−10.0
12.0	18.0
5.0	9.0
7.0	12.0
0.0	−1.0
−6.0	−12.0
2.0	2.0

TABLE 18.9
Work Sheet for Calculation of Regression Estimates

(1) Observation i	(2) MRR X	(3) SRR Y	(4) X^2	(5) Y^2	(6) XY (col. 2 · col. 3)
1	1	2	1	4	2
2	−5	−10	25	100	50
3	12	18	144	324	216
4	5	9	25	81	45
5	7	12	49	144	84
6	0	−1	0	1	0
7	−6	−12	36	144	72
8	2	2	4	4	4
	$\Sigma X = 16$ $\overline{X} = 2$	$\Sigma Y = 20.0$ $\overline{Y} = 2.5$	$\Sigma X^2 = 284$	$\Sigma Y^2 = 802$	$\Sigma XY = 473$

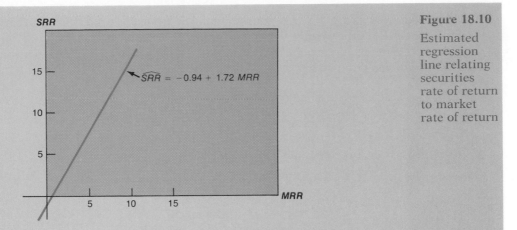

Figure 18.10

Estimated regression line relating securities rate of return to market rate of return

decline of 10 percentage points in the rate of return on the market as a whole is estimated to be associated with a decline of 17.2 percentage points in this stock's rate of return. This is why the slope of this particular regression line is so significant to securities analysts. It is customary to identify all securities with beta coefficients greater than 1.0 as *aggressive* securities, since their rates of return change upward and downward more sharply than the average rates of return of the market. Aggressive securities are considered risky for the same reason. Similarly, securities whose beta coefficients are less than 1.0 are identified as *defensive* securities, since the movement of their rates of return upward and downward is less volatile than the average rate of return of the market as a whole. Accordingly, their rates of return are more stable, and they are considered to be less risky securities. Note that for a zero rate of return on the market, the estimated rate of return on the stock is -0.94 percent.

We continue by computing S_Y and S_e:

$$S_Y = \sqrt{\frac{\Sigma Y^2 - n\bar{Y}^2}{n-1}} = \sqrt{\frac{802 - (8)(2.5)^2}{8-1}} = \sqrt{107.4} = 10.36$$

and

$$S_e = \sqrt{\frac{\Sigma Y^2 - b_0 \Sigma Y - b_1 \Sigma XY}{n-2}} = \sqrt{\frac{802 - (-0.94)(20) - (1.72)(473)}{8-2}}$$

$$= \sqrt{1.21} = 1.10$$

Although the total variability of the rate of return on the stock, as measured by S_Y, is 10.36, a substantial portion of this variability is related to fluctuations in the average rate of return on the market index. When we account for the fluctuations in X, we find that the remaining standard deviation of Y, S_e, is only 1.10. This fact is also expressed by the regression's r^2:

$$r^2 = 1 - \frac{S_e^2}{S_Y^2} \cdot \frac{(n-2)}{(n-1)} = 1 - \frac{1.10^2}{10.36^2} \cdot \frac{(8-2)}{(8-1)} = 0.990$$

Now consider an investor who is interested in buying a given common stock, provided that the stock is not too risky. Specifically, he is willing to buy the stock if its beta coefficient is not greater than 1.50. What advice should we give him if the stock considered is the one for which we just computed $b_1 = 1.72$? One thing we know is that our point estimate ($b_1 = 1.72$) is greater than the investor's maximum acceptable beta coefficient. On the other hand, we know that b_1 is a random variable and that the true parameter could be (and probably is) somewhat different from 1.72. In fact, the standard error of b_1 is estimated to be

$$S_{b_1} = \frac{S_e}{\sqrt{\Sigma X^2 - n\overline{X}^2}} = \frac{1.10}{\sqrt{252}} = \frac{1.10}{15.87} = 0.0693$$

A sound procedure here is to test the hypotheses

$$H_0: \quad \beta_1 \leq 1.50$$

$$H_1: \quad \beta_1 > 1.50$$

For illustration, let us use a 1 percent level of significance. The test statistic is $T = (b_1 - 1.50)/S_{b_1}$ and its distribution is $t^{(n-2)}$. Since $n = 8$, the critical value is $t_{0.01}^{(6)} = 3.143$. Thus, we accept H_0 if $T = (b_1 - 1.50)/S_{b_1}$ is less than or equal to 3.143 and reject H_0 if it is greater than 3.143 (see Figure 18.11). The value of T in this example is

Figure 18.11

Probability distribution of test statistic and acceptance and rejection regions

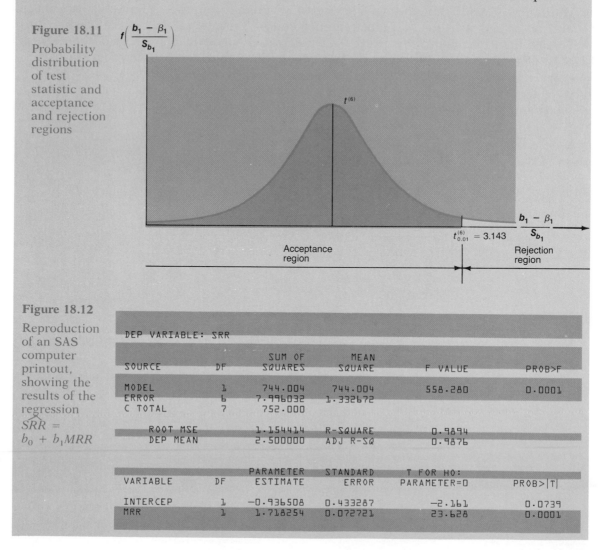

Figure 18.12

Reproduction of an SAS computer printout, showing the results of the regression $\widehat{SRR} = b_0 + b_1 MRR$

DEP VARIABLE: SRR

SOURCE	DF	SUM OF SQUARES	MEAN SQUARE	F VALUE	PROB>F
MODEL	1	744.004	744.004	558.280	0.0001
ERROR	6	7.996032	1.332672		
C TOTAL	7	752.000			

| | ROOT MSE | 1.154414 | R-SQUARE | 0.9894 | |
| | DEP MEAN | 2.500000 | ADJ R-SQ | 0.9876 | |

VARIABLE	DF	PARAMETER ESTIMATE	STANDARD ERROR	T FOR H0: PARAMETER=0	PROB>|T|
INTERCEP	1	−0.936508	0.433287	−2.161	0.0739
MRR	1	1.718254	0.072721	23.628	0.0001

$$T = \frac{b_1 - 1.50}{S_{b_1}} = \frac{1.72 - 1.50}{0.0693} = \frac{0.22}{0.0693} = 3.175$$

and since $T = 3.175$ is greater than 3.143, we reject H_0 and conclude that with a level of significance of 99 percent we should consider β_1 to be greater than 1.50. Our recommendation to the investor, then, is to search for a less risky stock. Figure 18.12 presents a computer printout of the regression $\widehat{SRR} = b_0 + b_1 MRR$ that will allow you to verify some of our calculations. Upon inspection you will also find rounding differences.

18.8 APPLICATION 3:
MARKETING—INVESTMENT IN ADVERTISING

A company's sales of a given product are a function of many factors. Among them we may list variables relating to the general economic conditions in the area in which the product is to be marketed, the effectiveness of competition, and the aggressiveness of the firm marketing the product. Obviously, analyzing the effect on sales of one particular factor while ignoring the simultaneous effects of all other factors leads to misleading results. The simultaneous consideration of many explanatory variables in regression analysis will be presented in the next chapter; for the time being we shall deal with a simplified example in which the effect of advertising on sales is to be estimated and all other factors ignored.

Consider a company whose products are sold nationwide. The marketing network of the company includes 20 regional distribution centers that generate roughly similar revenues each year. A new product is now undergoing market testing by the firm. It has been introduced in 10 regional areas, with different advertising expenditures in each. The advertising expenditures and sales of the product are shown in Table 18.10.

TABLE 18.10
Advertising Expenditures and Sales of New Product, by Region
(thousands of dollars)

Regional area	Advertising expenditures	Sales
1	$20	$160
2	10	120
3	30	220
4	16	120
5	40	235
6	35	225
7	20	160
8	25	200
9	33	220
10	19	120

To determine the effect of advertising expenditures on sales, a simple regression analysis is performed, using sales as the dependent variable (denoted by *SALES*) and advertising expenditure as the independent variable (denoted *AD*). Figure 18.13 is a computer printout showing the regression results. It shows that $b_0 = 61.296$ and $b_1 = 4.706$ (both rounded), so the estimated regression equation is

Figure 18.13

Reproduction of an SAS computer printout, showing the results of the regression $\widehat{SALES} = b_0 + b_1 AD$

DEP VARIABLE: SALES

SOURCE	DF	SUM OF SQUARES	MEAN SQUARE	F VALUE	PROB>F
MODEL	1	17839.723	17839.723	60.211	0.0001
ERROR	8	2370.277	296.285		
C TOTAL	9	20210.000			
ROOT MSE		17.212920	R-SQUARE	0.8827	
DEP MEAN		178.000	ADJ R-SQ	0.8681	

VARIABLE	DF	PARAMETER ESTIMATE	STANDARD ERROR	T FOR H0: PARAMETER=0	PROB > |T|
INTERCEP	1	61.295929	15.994645	3.832	0.0050
AD	1	4.705809	0.606450	7.760	0.0001

$$\widehat{SALES} = 61.296 + 4.706 AD$$

We can use the equation above to predict sales at a given advertising budget. If, for example, $22,000 is to be used for advertising in one of the 20 regional areas, what is the predicted sales level? Substituting 22 for X, we get

$$\widehat{SALES} = 61.296 + (4.706)(22.0) = 164.828$$

or $164,828. What if $80,000 is to be used for advertising in a given regional area? If we again use the estimated equation we get $437,776, since

$$\widehat{SALES} = 61.296 + (4.706)(80.0) = 437.776$$

This prediction is very unreliable, however, and constitutes an improper use of regression analysis. Why? Because in no region has a budget in the neighborhood of $80,000 and its resulting sales been observed. Extrapolation of the estimated regression line to an advertising budget of $80,000 is justified only if we have good reason to believe that the linear relationship we have observed holds true for budgets significantly greater than the ones we have observed. Marketing research studies have indicated the existence of a saturation level—an upper ceiling beyond which sales cannot be made (for a

Figure 18.14

Typical relationship between sales and advertising

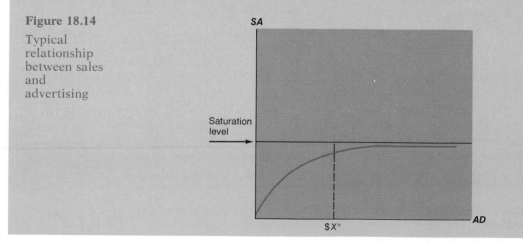

given product price, of course).[5] The relationship between sales and advertising expenditures may thus be described as in Figure 18.14. The figure clearly shows that the global relationship between sales and advertising expenditure is nonlinear but can be approximated by a linear relationship for budgets less than X^* (see Figure 18.14). If $80,000 is beyond the value X^*, our prediction could be greatly in error, as Figure 18.15 shows.

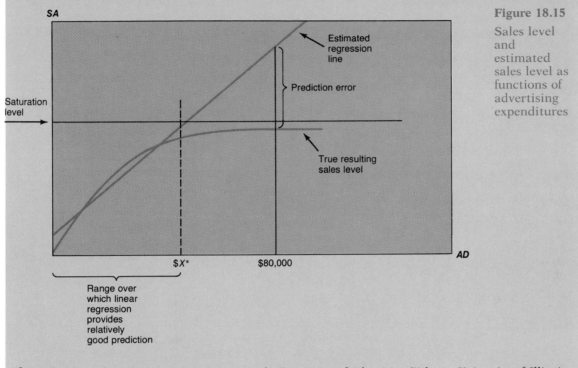

Figure 18.15

Sales level and estimated sales level as functions of advertising expenditures

[5] See, for example, Julian L. Simon, *Issues in the Economics of Advertising* (Urbana: University of Illinois Press, 1970).

18.9 APPLICATION 4:
EMPLOYEE PRODUCTIVITY AT AT&T

In this application we shall analyze trends in American Telephone and Telegraph's employee productivity over time, measured by number of employees per telephone. Using actual data for a recent period of 27 years, we derived regression estimates and confidence intervals that will be presented below by means of computer programs.

As a first step we need to draw the scatter diagram in order to determine by eye which type of regression line seems to be most suitable (linear, nonlinear, or some other type). Table 18.11 presents the data: the number of AT&T employees and the number of AT&T telephones in each of the 27 years. Figure 18.16 is the scatter diagram produced by the computer.[6] The number of employees is measured along the vertical axis and the number of telephones is measured along the horizontal axis. It is evident from the

[6] The computer package used to produce the output for this application is the well-known Statistical Package for Social Sciences (SPSS).

TABLE 18.11
**Employees of AT&T and Telephones in Service in a
Recent Period of 27 Years**

Year	Employees	Telephones (thousands)
1	523,251	34,323
2	551,415	36,387
3	579,513	38,386
4	587,839	40,386
5	578,436	42,215
6	615,895	44,633
7	638,103	47,796
8	640,868	50,879
9	592,130	53,290
10	582,860	56,239
11	580,405	59,391
12	566,648	61,834
13	563,861	64,549
14	571,366	67,247
15	589,667	70,254
16	611,931	73,817
17	650,788	73,817
18	656,313	81,695
19	679,110	85,670
20	735,856	90,293
21	772,980	94,600
22	776,775	98,255
23	777,869	102,623
24	798,934	107,811
25	793,334	112,487
26	770,389	116,212
27	760,040	120,679

Source: Data courtesy of AT&T.

diagram that both the number of employees and the number of telephone lines tended to increase over the period, though not without exception. Running the regression equation

$$Y_t = b_0 + b_1 X_t + e_t$$

(where Y_t is the number of employees, X_t is the number of telephones, and t is the index for the year), we find that the coefficient b_1 is positive, meaning that both variables tend to move in the same direction. The regression equation is given by

$$\hat{Y}_t = 437{,}051.932 + 2.978 X_t$$

Computations show that the estimated standard deviation of the slope b_1 is $S_{b_1} = 0.298$. A test of hypotheses shows that at a level of significance of 1 percent, b_1 is significantly greater than zero, meaning that if the null hypothesis is $H_0: \beta_1 = 0$ and the alternative is $H_1: \beta_1 > 0$, then we reject H_0.

Figure 18.16 shows the confidence bands for the *mean* of $\hat{Y}_i$ (what we referred to as confidence bands for μ_i) as well as prediction bands for individual observations. The inner pair of bands are related to the mean of $\hat{Y}_i$, whereas those on the outside are

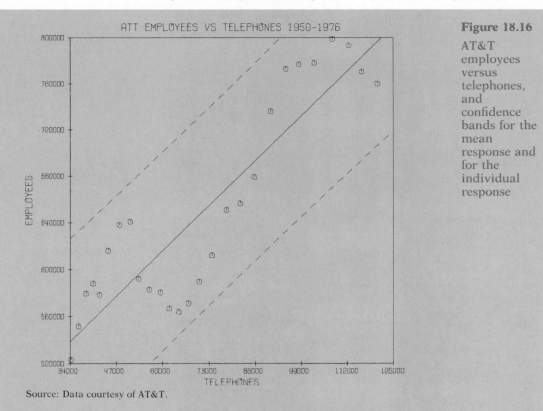

Figure 18.16

AT&T employees versus telephones, and confidence bands for the mean response and for the individual response

Source: Data courtesy of AT&T.

related to individual observations. Although the equations for the confidence interval of the mean and the prediction interval for an individual observation look very much alike, the small difference between them could substantially widen the confidence interval.

Despite the strong relationship between the number of employees and the number of telephones, the regression relating the two variables in the manner presented above cannot directly show whether the productivity of AT&T's employees improved over time. One way to measure productivity is by the number of employees per fixed number of telephones. Figure 18.17 is a scatter diagram for which the number of employees *per 10,000 telephones* was used as the dependent variable, Y, and the number of telephones (in tens of thousands) was the independent variable, X. The diagram shows a marked improvement in productivity: the number of employees per 10,000 telephones dropped from 152 in year 1, when there were 34,323,000 telephones in service, to about 63 in year 27, when 120,679,000 telephones were in service. The regression line relating Y to X yields

$$\hat{Y}_t = 172 - 0.001X_t$$

Note that productivity is estimated to increase with the number of telephones. Thus, for example, if we want to estimate the number of employees per 10,000 telephones when 140 million telephones are in service, on the basis of the above regression, we substitute 140,000 for X (since 140,000 thousands equal 140 million) and get

$$\hat{Y} = 172 - 0.001 \cdot 140,000 = 172 - 140 = 32$$

For 150 million telephones the estimated number of employees is smaller:

$$\hat{Y} = 172 - 0.001 \cdot 150,000 = 172 - 150 = 22$$

Figure 18.17

AT&T employees per 10,000 telephones versus telephones, and confidence bands for the mean response

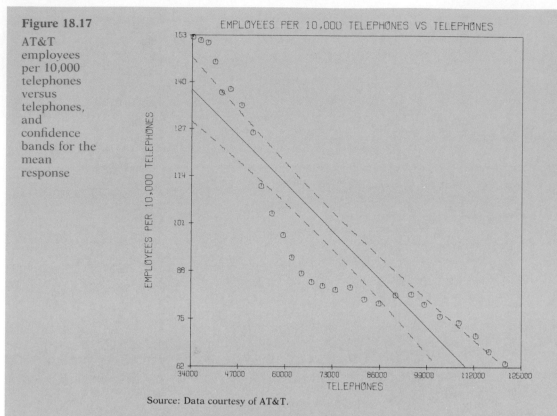

Source: Data courtesy of AT&T.

Looking more closely at Figure 18.17, we realize that the number of employees per 10,000 telephones dropped very sharply in the early years of the period and much more moderately in more recent years. One reason for this change is the move to a new generation of switchboards that took place in the earlier years. These new switchboards increased productivity a great deal. Keeping this in mind, we must realize that two separate regressions, one for the earlier period and one for the later period, are likely to fit the data better and to provide better predictions than one regression line.

Figures 18.17 and 18.18 are reproductions of computer output showing the regression lines as well as the confidence bands for the mean value of $\hat{Y}_i$, once for the entire sample (Figure 18.17) and once for two segments (Figure 18.18)—the first for the period of the first 13 years, and the second for the period of the last 14 years. The first period is the one in which a massive switch to new equipment occurred.

The regression equations for the two separate segments are

$$\hat{Y} = 238.903 - 0.00235X \qquad \text{for the first 13 years}$$

and

$$\hat{Y} = 111.106 - 0.00036X \qquad \text{for the last 14 years}$$

Based on the relationship in the second period, our prediction of the number of employees per 10,000 telephones when 140 million phones are in service is

$$\hat{Y} = 111.106 - 0.00036 \cdot 140{,}000 = 60.7$$

This is very different from our earlier prediction of 32 employees per 10,000 phones, which was based on the regression for the entire period of 27 years.

The two separate regressions fit the data substantially better than the combined one. Even though each of the two segments was based on a smaller number of observations than we used for the entire sample, the 95 percent confidence bands in Figure 18.17 are much narrower than those in Figure 18.18, demonstrating a much better fit. Figure 18.19 shows the prediction bands for a single observation when the entire sample is employed to derive one regression line, and Figure 18.20 shows the prediction bands for a single observation when the sample is broken down into two separate segments. We see here, too, that the prediction bands bound a much wider range when the entire sample is used to derive one regression equation.

Comparing Figures 18.17 and 18.18 with Figures 18.19 and 18.20, we see that the confidence bands in the former pair of diagrams do not cover all the individual observations (in fact, they need not cover them, since they are intended for the mean μ_i rather than for a single observation, Y_i). The confidence bands in the latter pair of figures, which are drawn for individual observation, include all of the observations.

Finally, we should note that a nonlinear regression might fit AT&T's employee productivity trend. But nonlinear regression is beyond the scope of this chapter.

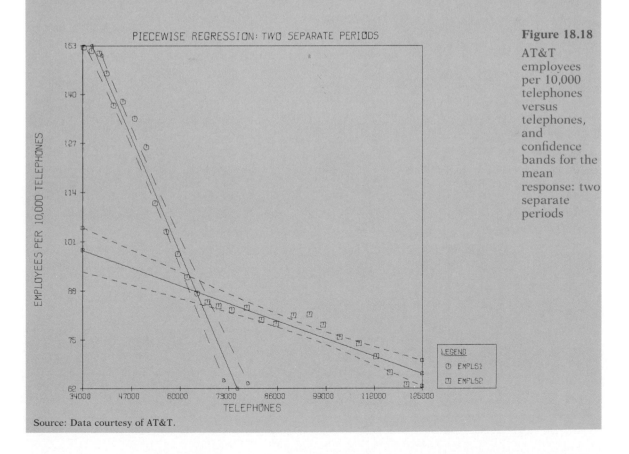

Figure 18.18

AT&T employees per 10,000 telephones versus telephones, and confidence bands for the mean response: two separate periods

Source: Data courtesy of AT&T.

Figure 18.19

Confidence bands for a single observation: the entire 27-year sample

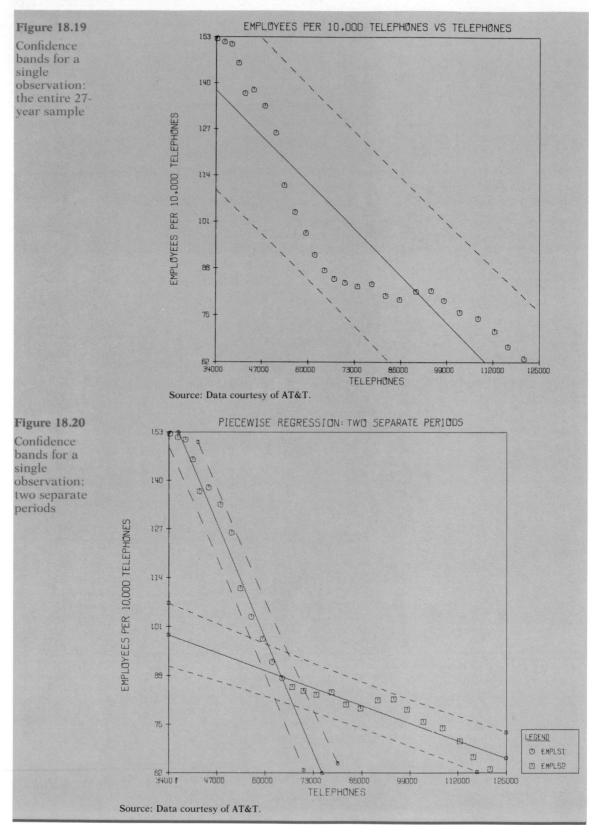

Source: Data courtesy of AT&T.

Figure 18.20

Confidence bands for a single observation: two separate periods

Source: Data courtesy of AT&T.

Chapter Summary and Review

1. If Y_is are normally distributed (or, alternatively, if the sample is large) and σ_u is unknown, then

$$\frac{b_1 - \beta_1}{S_{b_1}} \sim t^{(n-2)}$$

where

$$S_{b_1} = \frac{S_e}{\sqrt{\Sigma X_i^2 - n\overline{X}^2}}$$

and

$$S_e = \sqrt{\frac{\Sigma(Y_i - \hat{Y}_i)^2}{n - 2}} = \sqrt{\frac{\Sigma e_i^2}{n - 2}} = \sqrt{\frac{\Sigma Y_i^2 - b_0\Sigma Y_i - b_1\Sigma X_i Y_i}{n - 2}}$$

2. If Y_is are normally distributed (or, alternatively, if the sample is large) and σ_u is unknown, then

$$\frac{b_0 - \beta_0}{S_{b_0}} \sim t^{(n-2)}$$

where

$$S_{b_0} = S_e \sqrt{\frac{1}{n} + \frac{\overline{X}^2}{\Sigma(X - \overline{X})^2}}$$

3. The $1 - \alpha$ confidence interval for the mean response, μ_i, is given by

$$\mu_i = \hat{Y}_i \pm t_{\alpha/2}^{(n-2)} \cdot S_e \sqrt{\frac{1}{n} + \frac{(X_i - \overline{X})^2}{\Sigma(X - \overline{X})^2}}$$

4. The $1 - \alpha$ prediction interval for an individual observation (response), Y_i, is given by

$$Y_i = \hat{Y}_i \pm t_{\alpha/2}^{(n-2)} \cdot S_e \sqrt{\frac{1}{n} + \frac{(X_i - \overline{X})^2}{\Sigma(X - \overline{X})^2} + 1}$$

5. For inferences about ρ:
   a. If Y is a random variable and X is not, $H_0: \rho = 0$ is equivalent to

$$H_0: \quad \beta_1 = 0$$

In this case use

$$T = \frac{b_1 - \beta_1}{S_{b_1}} \sim t^{(n-2)}$$

b. If X and Y are bivariate normal, use

$$T = r\sqrt{\frac{n-2}{1-r^2}} \sim t^{(n-2)}$$

Problems

18.1. When testing hypotheses with respect to the slope coefficient β_1, we use the statistic $Z = \frac{b_1 - \beta_1}{\sigma_{b_1}}$ if σ_u is known and $T = \frac{b_1 - \beta_1}{S_{b_1}}$ if σ_u is unknown.

(a) Suppose $\sigma_{b_1} = 0.2$, but its value is unknown. Suppose also that the estimated value, S_{b_1}, happens to equal exactly 0.2. Is it possible to reject the null hypothesis H_0: $\beta_1 = \beta_1'$ using the t statistic, given that H_0 would have been accepted had σ_{b_1} been known and had the Z statistic been used with the same significance level? Explain.

(b) Under conditions similar to those of part a, except that S_{b_1} does not necessarily equal 0.2, is it possible that H_0 would be accepted when the statistic Z is used and rejected when t is used?

18.2. Suppose you estimate the slope β_1 by the following term (see Equation 17.23):

$$c_1 = \frac{1}{10} \sum_{i=1}^{n} W_i Y_i$$

where

$$W_i = \frac{X_i - \overline{X}}{(X_i - \overline{X})^2}$$

Would you agree with the assertion that the estimator c_1 has a smaller variance than the BLUE estimator? If so, why don't you use c_1 instead of the BLUE estimator? Explain.

18.3. The amount of earnings per share is a measure of a company's profitability that is obtained by dividing the company's total net earnings by the number of shares outstanding.

Suppose the relationship between the share price and earnings per share across many firms is

$$\hat{Y} = 15 + 10X$$

where Y is price per share and X is earnings per share.

(a) What is the estimated price per share if earnings per share are $4?

(b) If you needed to assess the accuracy of your estimate, how would you go about it? What data would you need?

18.4. Consumer awareness of the existence of new products on the market may be measured by the percentage of customers who have heard about the product a certain length of time (say, six months) after it has been introduced.

A study is supposed to examine the relationship between the amount spent on advertising a new product and consumer awareness of that product. Suppose a sample shows the following data:

Consumer awareness (percent) (Y)	Advertising expenditure (thousands of dollars) (X)
52%	$200
21	180
10	100
90	800
64	610
64	450
56	370
40	190

(handwritten annotations:)

$\hat{y} = b_0 + b_1 X$; $b = \dfrac{\Sigma xy - n\bar{x}\bar{y}}{\Sigma x^2 - n\bar{x}^2}$

$b_0 = \bar{y} - b_1\bar{x}$

$\bar{x} = \dfrac{\Sigma x}{8} = 362.5$

$\bar{y} = \dfrac{\Sigma y}{8} = 49.625$

$\Sigma xy = 183340$

$\Sigma x^2 = 1,470,000$

Est. of b_1

$\dfrac{183340 - (8)(362.5)(49.625)}{(1,470,000)(8)(362.5)^2} = .094$

$b_0 = 49.625 - (.094)(362.5) = 15.4937$

$\hat{y} = 15.4937 + .094X$

$r^2 = 1 - \dfrac{(n-2)S_e^2}{(n-1)S_y^2} = \dfrac{6(141.90)}{7(653.135)} = .8137$

$Se^2 = \dfrac{\Sigma y^2 - b_0 \Sigma y - b_1 \Sigma xy}{n-2} = 24273 - 15.4937(397) - (.094)(183340) = \dfrac{851.3731}{6} = 141.90$

$Se = 11.91$

$S_y^2 = \dfrac{\Sigma y^2 - n\bar{y}^2}{n-1} = \dfrac{24.273 - (8)49.625}{7} = 653125$

(a) Estimate the regression line $\hat{Y} = b_0 + b_1X$.
(b) Would a regression line based on consumer awareness as the independent variable and advertising expenditure as the dependent variable have any meaning? Explain. *calculate r²*
(c) Using a 95 percent confidence level, construct an interval estimate of consumer awareness of a single product, assuming that $700,000 is spent for its promotion. *prediction interval for individual response*
(d) Using a 5 percent significance level, test the hypothesis that advertising expenditure has no impact on consumer awareness.

$\hat{y} = 15.4937 + .094(700) = 81.2937$

$\hat{y} \pm t_{n-2,\alpha/2} \cdot S_{y/x}$

$81.2937 \pm (2.447) \cdot$

18.5. Use the consumption and income example of Table 17.2 in the text to determine the confidence interval for μ_i and for Y_i at the following levels of X_i: 5.0, 15.0, 20.0, 25.0, 35.0. Draw a chart showing the confidence bands for μ_i and Y_i.

18.6. Is it true that for very large samples the 95 percent confidence bands for μ_i at the point $X_i = \bar{X}$ are almost tangent to the estimated regression line? Explain. Would you change your answer for a 99 percent confidence interval?

18.7. Would you change your answer to Problem 18.6 if the confidence bands were for Y_i rather than μ_i? Explain.

GOOD PROBLEM FOR TEST

18.8. The wages (measured in dollars per hour) and the productivity (measured in units produced per day) of a sample of 12 workers in a certain firm are as follows:

Worker	Wage (Y)	Daily production (X)
1	$5	10
2	6	11
3	7	14
4	8	12
5	9	20
6	10	20
7	8	18
8	7	15
9	9	17
10	10	16
11	9	18
12	7	16

(handwritten annotations:)

$H_0: B_1 = 0$

$H_1: B_1 > 0$

TS: $\dfrac{b_1 - B_1}{S_{b_1}} = \dfrac{.094 - 0}{.0148} = 6.12$

$S_{b_1} = \dfrac{Se}{\sqrt{\Sigma x^2 - n\bar{x}^2}} = .0148$

$t^6_{.05} = 1.943$

reject because such a strong $r^2 = .8137$

$S_{y/x}^2 = 141.9\left[\dfrac{1}{8} + \dfrac{(700 + 362.5)^2}{4,470,000 - 8(362.5)} + 1\right]$

$S_{y/x}^2 = 198.24$ $S_{y/x} = 14.08$

CI: 46.98 to 115.88

(a) Calculate the regression coefficients when the wage is taken to be the dependent variable.
(b) What is your interpretation of the slope of the regression line?
(c) Test the hypothesis H_0: $\beta_1 = 0$ against the alternative hypothesis H_1: $\beta_1 \neq 0$. Use a 10 percent level of significance.
(d) Test the hypothesis H_0: $\beta_0 = 0$ against H_1: $\beta_0 \neq 0$ using a significance level of 10 percent.

18.9. Referring back to Problem 18.8, assume that the firm's profit per unit, net of all costs except wages, is $10. Therefore, the contribution of each worker to the firm's daily profit, net of all costs except wages, is $Z = \$10 \cdot$ (daily production of worker, in units).

(a) Run the regression of Y (dependent) on Z (independent) and estimate the regression coefficients. Compare the coefficients to those obtained in Problem 18.8.
(b) Using a significance level of 1 percent, test the hypothesis H_0: $\beta_1 = 0$ against H_1: $\beta_1 \neq 0$.
(c) What is your interpretation of the regression slope? (Hint: recall that Z represents daily profit and the wages are expressed in dollars per hour. Assume that the workday is eight hours.

18.10. The annual maintenance cost (Y) of two model cars by each car's age (X) are as follows:

Age of car (years) X	Maintenance cost, Y	
	Car A	Car B
1	100	60
2	120	70
3	140	80
4	160	90
5	200	100
6	230	110
7	300	140

(a) Run two regressions of the form $\hat{Y} = b_0 + b_1 X$, where Y is the maintenance cost of Car A in the first regression and of Car B in the second regression.
(b) Interpret the regression coefficients.
(c) Test the hypothesis H_0: $\beta_A = 20$ against the alternative H_1: $\beta_A \neq 20$, where β_A is the slope of the "true" line for Car A. Repeat the test for β_B, which is the slope of the line for Car B. Use a 5 percent significance level.
(d) "If the slopes of the two regression lines are identical (i.e., $\beta_A = \beta_B$), the consumer should be indifferent about purchasing one car instead of the other." Assume that all the characteristics of the cars (aside from maintenance costs) are the same and comment on this statement.

18.11. Let Y be annual income (measured in dollars) and X be education (measured in school years). Suppose we find that in the regression $\hat{Y} = b_0 + b_1 X$, $b_0 = \$5,000$ and $b_1 = \$100$.

(a) If we measure X in school years, but measure income (Y) in pounds (£) using an exchange rate of £1 = $2, how would the change affect the coefficients b_0 and b_1?
(b) Suppose we test the null hypothesis H_0: $\beta_1 = \beta_1'$ once using dollars for income and once using pounds. What is the relationship between the value of the statistic computed for the first test (using dollars) and that computed for the second test (using pounds)? Prove your answer.

18.12. Underwriters are large institutional investors who undertake the preparation and marketing of new stocks and bonds. Table P18.12 presents the total volume of securities sold and the number of security issues underwritten in a recent year by the top 25 underwriters.

TABLE P18.12

Underwriters	Volume (Y) (millions of dollars)	Number of issues (X)
Goldman Sachs	$1,967.4	98
Blyth Eastman Dillon	1,211.1	64
First Boston	1,167.5	45
Kidder Peabody	1,138.2	68
Merrill Lynch White Weld	1,125.0	74
E. F. Hutton	1,096.9	51
Smith Barney, Harris Upham	1,014.2	44
Salomon Brothers	1,013.3	45
Bache Halsey Stuart Shields	582.4	31
Paine Webber	549.2	38
Lehman Brothers Kuhn Loeb	425.3	19
Rothschild, Unterberg, Towbin	395.1	38
Alex. Brown & Sons	372.2	14
Wm. R. Hough	357.9	21
Dean Witter Reynolds	345.2	31
Butcher & Singer	318.7	41
Loeb Rhoades Hornblower	312.7	20
John Nuveen	267.7	23
Wertheim	258.8	5
Dain, Kalman & Quail	243.0	20
Matthews & Wright	233.0	15
First Kentucky Securities	223.1	4
Lazard Frères	214.6	10
Piper, Jaffray & Hopwood	193.3	18
Baker Watts	192.0	8

Source: *Institutional Investor*, March 1979.

(a) Estimate the regression equation $\hat{Y} = b_0 + b_1 X$ where Y and X are the volume (in millions of dollars) and number of issues, respectively.

(b) Test the null hypothesis

$$H_0: \quad \beta_1 = 20$$

versus

$$H_1: \quad \beta_1 \neq 20$$

(c) For an underwriter who will underwrite 110 issues, what are your point and interval estimates for volume at the 95 percent confidence level?

(d) Calculate the correlation coefficient for X and Y, and test the hypothesis $H_0: \rho = 0$ against $H_1: \rho \neq 0$. Use $\alpha = 0.05$.

18.13. Tables P18.13*a* and *b* show the data for two samples. The coordinates of Sample 2 are double those of Sample 1. For example, the first observation in Sample 1 is $(-2, -5)$ and in Sample 2 it is $(-4, -10)$, and so on.

TABLE P18.13*a*		TABLE P18.13*b*	
Sample 1		Sample 2	
X	Y	X	Y
−2	−5	−4	−10
−1	+1	−2	+2
0	−2	0	−4
+1	+4	+2	+8
+2	+2	+4	+4

(*a*) Estimate the OLS line for Sample 1.

(*b*) Estimate the OLS line for Sample 2.

(*c*) For each of the following values of X_i provide a 95 percent confidence interval for the mean response: $X_i = -2, 0, +2$. First use the Sample 1 data and then use the Sample 2 data. Explain the reason for the difference.

(*d*) Repeat part *c*, replacing the 95 percent confidence interval for the mean response with a 95 percent prediction interval for the individual response.

18.14. For the data shown in Table P18.13*a* (Problem 18.13), the standard error of estimate is $S_e = 2.652$. This value is obtained from a sample of five observations. Calculate 95 percent confidence intervals for μ_i and Y_i for the values $X = -2, X = 0$, and $X = 2$, assuming that the value $S_e = 2.652$ has been calculated from a sample size n, where n is equal first to 10 and then to 100,000. Compare the interval widths with those obtained in Problem 18.13.

18.15. Some economists hold the view that the inflation rate and the unemployment rate tend to be inversely correlated over time. They claim that monetary expansion may cause inflation but simultaneously it tends to increase the demand for goods and services, an increase that tends to decrease the rate of unemployment. Table P18.15 presents the annual inflation and unemployment rates in the United States in the years 1956–80. Regard the unemployment rate as the dependent variable and the inflation rate as the independent variable.

TABLE P18.15

Year	Unemployment rate	Inflation rate
1956	4.1%	3.1%
1957	4.3	3.4
1958	6.8	1.6
1959	5.5	2.2
1960	5.5	3.1
1961	6.7	1.1
1962	5.5	1.2
1963	5.7	1.2
1964	5.2	1.3
1965	4.5	1.7
1966	3.8	2.9
1967	3.8	2.8
1968	3.6	4.2
1969	3.5	5.4
1970	4.9	5.9
1971	5.9	4.3
1972	5.6	3.3
1973	4.9	6.2
1974	5.6	11.0
1975	8.5	9.1
1976	7.7	5.8
1977	7.0	6.5
1978	6.0	7.6
1979	5.8	11.5
1980	7.1	13.5

Source: *Survey of Current Business*, various issues.

(a) Draw a scatter diagram and calculate the correlation coefficient and the regression coefficients for the period 1956–80. Is the slope coefficient significantly different from zero? Use a 5 percent significance level.

(b) Repeat part a, using the data for the period 1956–67 only.

(c) Repeat part a once again, this time using the data for the period 1968–80 only.

(d) What is the meaning of the slope coefficient of the regression obtained in part b?

(e) Do the data justify breaking the period into two subperiods, or should the analysis of the relationship between the inflation and unemployment rates be done on the data for the whole period, as in part a?

(f) What lesson should we learn from this analysis?

18.16. Maximization of sales or market share is frequently considered to be the goal of the business firm. Many, however, claim that business firms consider profit maximization to be their goal. Some argue that the two goals coincide. Table P18.16 provides data on sales and return on invested capital in the auto industry for the first nine months of 1978.

TABLE P18.16

Company	Sales (millions of dollars)	Return on invested capital (percent)
American Motors	$ 2,026	7.84%
Arvin Industries	352	8.46
Bendix	2,802	10.50
Cummins Engine	1,100	9.75
Dana	1,707	12.04
Eagle-Picher	385	9.87
Eaton	1,949	9.18
Federal Mogul	421	12.40
Ford Motor Co.	31,538	13.41
Freuhauf	1,623	9.85
General Motors	45,477	15.11
International Harvester	5,472	7.94
Questor	313	3.36
Sheller-Globe	459	7.18
Smith (A. O.)	601	9.51
TRW	2,755	10.32
Timken	808	9.93
Total	$99,788	166.65%
Average	5,869.8824	9.8029

Source: Data from *Business Week*, January 8, 1979, p. 34.

(a) Draw a scatter diagram in which returns on invested capital are measured along the vertical axis and sales are measured along the horizontal axis. Can you determine from the diagram whether sales and return on invested capital are closely related?

(b) Calculate the regression coefficient of return on invested capital (dependent) on sales (independent), and test the significance of the slope coefficient.

(c) In light of your results, do you agree that the two goals coincide? If so, to what degree?

18.17. The mean annual rate of return (annual profit in percent) on stocks and bonds as well as the standard deviation of those returns (which is a measure of risk) in 12 European countries for the years 1960–80 are reported in Table P18.17.

(a) Estimate the regression line $Y = b_0 + b_1X$ and explain its meaning.

(b) Using a 5 percent significance level, test the hypothesis that the slope is equal to zero against the alternative that it is positive. Explain your result.

TABLE P18.17

	Measure	
Country	Mean rate of return (Y)	Standard deviation (X)
Austria	10.3	16.9
Belgium	10.1	13.8
Denmark	11.4	24.2
France	8.1	21.4
Germany	10.1	19.9
Italy	5.6	27.2
Netherlands	10.7	17.8
Norway	17.4	49.0
Spain	10.4	19.8
Sweden	9.7	16.7
Switzerland	12.5	22.9
United Kingdom	14.7	33.6

Source: Roger G. Ibbotson, Richard C. Carr, and Anthony W. Robinson, "International Equity and Bond Returns," *Financial Analyst Journal*, July–August 1982.

(c) Using a 5 percent significance level, test the hypothesis that the intercept is equal to zero against the alternative that it is different from zero.

(d) Calculate the correlation coefficient for X and Y.

(e) Using a 5 percent significance level, test the hypothesis that the correlation coefficient is equal to zero. Treat both X and Y as random variables.

18.18. The average rate of return (profit in percent) on stock investments in the United States, Canada, Germany, and France for the period 1970–80 is given in Table P18.18.

TABLE P18.18

	Country			
Year	U.S. (X_1)	Canada (X_2)	Germany (X_3)	France (X_4)
1970	−1.0%	15.8%	−23.8%	−5.1%
1971	18.2	14.1	24.6	1.7
1972	17.7	33.1	18.5	24.8
1973	−18.7	−3.1	−4.4	3.8
1974	−27.8	−26.5	17.2	−22.4
1975	37.5	15.1	30.1	45.1
1976	26.7	9.7	6.6	−20.0
1977	−3.0	−1.4	23.1	5.1
1978	8.5	20.5	27.0	73.2
1979	24.2	52.3	−1.9	28.9
1980	33.2	22.0	−8.2	−1.3

Source: Roger G. Ibbotson, Richard C. Carr, and Anthony W. Robinson, "International Equity and Bond Returns," *Financial Analyst Journal*, July–August 1982.

(a) Calculate the coefficients of the following regression lines:

1. $X_2 = b_0 + b_1 X_1$
2. $X_3 = b_0 + b_1 X_1$
3. $X_4 = b_0 + b_1 X_1$
4. $X_4 = b_0 + b_1 X_3$

(b) For each of the four regressions, test the hypothesis that the slope is equal to zero against the alternative that it is different from zero. Use a 5 percent significance level. What is the meaning of a slope of zero in this example?

(c) Calculate the correlation coefficients for:

    1. X_1 and X_2
    2. X_1 and X_3
    3. X_1 and X_4
    4. X_4 and X_3

(d) Test each of the correlation coefficients to see whether it is significantly different from zero. Use $\alpha = 0.05$. In general, is there a high correlation among the rates of return in these markets?

18.19. The average rates of return on stocks and bonds in the United States in the period 1960–80 are given in Table P18.19.

TABLE P18.19

Year	Stocks	Bonds
1960	0.8%	10.7%
1961	27.5	2.7
1962	−9.3	5.9
1963	21.6	2.3
1964	16.7	4.2
1965	15.3	−0.3
1966	−8.2	1.1
1967	30.5	−4.3
1968	14.9	2.2
1969	−9.9	−4.6
1970	−1.0	14.4
1971	18.2	10.5
1972	17.7	5.8
1973	−18.7	2.3
1974	−27.8	0.2
1975	37.5	12.3
1976	26.7	15.6
1977	−3.0	3.0
1978	8.5	1.2
1979	24.2	2.3
1980	33.2	3.0

Source: Roger G. Ibbotson, Richard C. Carr, and Anthony W. Robinson, "International Equity and Bond Returns," *Financial Analyst Journal*, July–August 1982.

It is traditionally claimed that investors switch their investments from the stock market to the bond market and vice versa. Therefore, it is thought that when the stock market is down, the bond market is up and vice versa. To test this hypothesis, do the following:

(a) Run a regression of the rate of return on bonds (Y) on the rate of return on stocks (X). What is the interpretation of b_0 and b_1 in this regression?

(b) Use a 5 percent significance level to test the hypothesis H_0: $\beta_1 = 0$ against H_1: $\beta_1 < 0$.

(c) Calculate the correlation coefficient for X and Y, and test whether it is significantly different from zero at $\alpha = 0.05$.

(d) Repeat your calculations twice, once for the period 1960–69 and then for the period 1970–80. Are there any differences between the periods?

18.20. In Section 18.7 we introduced beta as a measure of a security's risk and defined aggressive and defensive securities (those with $\beta_1 > 1$ and $\beta_1 < 1$, respectively). Table P18.20 gives the annual rates of return (SRR) (in percent) on three securities—General Motors (GM), International Business Machines (IBM), and American Motors (AMC)—for the period 1970–80. The last column in the table gives proxy data for the market rate of return (MRR) as measured by the annual rates of return of the Fisher stock market index for the same period.

TABLE P18.20

Year	GM	IBM	AMC	Stock market index
1970	22.3	−11.4	−33.3	1.4
1971	4.3	7.5	21.6	15.9
1972	6.5	21.2	17.8	17.8
1973	−37.8	−22.1	7.5	−16.9
1974	−27.6	−30.0	−62.3	−26.8
1975	97.1	37.9	65.4	37.7
1976	47.4	28.3	−27.9	26.3
1977	−11.4	1.8	−6.5	−4.8
1978	−5.4	13.9	31.0	7.4
1979	2.3	−9.5	47.9	21.8
1980	−4.3	11.3	−42.9	32.8

Source: The Center for Research in Security Prices (CRSP), Graduate School of Business. University of Chicago.

(a) Determine the beta estimates of the three securities by regressing each SRR on MRR. On the basis of these point estimates, specify which of the stocks is aggressive and which is defensive.

(b) Test whether each of the above three beta estimates is significantly different from 1. (Use a 5 percent significance level.)

(c) Summarize your results in parts *a* and *b*.

18.21. Paul, Simon, and Joan chose for their term paper in statistics an empirical study of the relationship between stock level and sales volume in food stores. Each selected a sample of nine stores and collected data on monthly stock levels. Paul's and Simon's samples included stores with the same sales figures, whereas the stores in Joan's sample covered a different range of sales; for instance, she managed to obtain data on the stock levels of stores during the annual vacation month, when the monthly sales level was zero. The observation results are summarized in Table P18.21 (in hundreds of thousands of dollars).

TABLE P18.21

Paul's sample Sales	Stocks	Simon's sample Sales	Stocks	Joan's sample Sales	Stocks
1	1.0	1	0.5	0	0.5
1	1.5	1	1.5	0	1.0
1	2.0	1	2.5	0	1.5
2	1.5	2	1.0	2	1.5
2	2.0	2	2.0	2	2.0
2	2.5	2	3.0	2	2.5
3	2.0	3	1.5	4	2.5
3	2.5	3	2.5	4	3.0
3	3.0	3	3.5	4	3.5

(a) Estimate the regression lines of stock level (*Y*) on sales (*X*) for each of the three samples.

(b) Determine the 95 percent confidence band for the mean response of each regression line.

(c) On the same graph draw a scatter diagram of the observations, showing the three regression lines and the confidence intervals.

(d) What factors cause the differences in the confidence intervals of the three regression lines? In your answer concentrate on comparing the confidence intervals of the following pairs: (1) Paul's and Simon's, and (2) Joan's and Simon's.

18.22. Economists argue that the interest rate tends to increase with inflation. The reason is, of course, that *with high inflation* the nominal interest paid should cover some real interest plus compensation for the depreciation of the value of money. Table P18.22 presents the prime interest rate and the annual inflation rate for the years 1968–80. The prime interest rate is the rate banks charge for loans given to their preferred customers.

TABLE P18.22

Year	Prime interest rate	Inflation rate
1968	5.90%	4.20%
1969	7.83	5.37
1970	7.72	5.92
1971	5.11	4.30
1972	4.69	3.30
1973	8.15	6.23
1974	9.87	10.97
1975	6.29	9.14
1976	5.19	5.77
1977	5.59	6.45
1978	8.11	7.60
1979	11.04	11.47
1980	12.78	13.46

Source: *Statistical Abstract of the United States,* 1975; *Survey of Current Business,* various issues; Morgan Guaranty Trust, *World Financial Markets,* various issues.

(a) Draw a scatter diagram for the data, measuring the prime rate along the vertical axis and the inflation rate along the horizontal axis.

(b) Calculate the regression coefficient when the prime rate is taken as the dependent variable and the inflation rate is the independent variable. What is your interpretation of the results?

(c) Test the significance of the regression slope at the 1 percent significance level.

(d) What is your interpretation of the regression slope in this regression?

18.23. A realtor assesses the value of properties in Chicago. A sample of 10 property transactions showed the following prices and assessment values (in thousands of dollars):

Selling price (Y)	Assessed value (X)
$60.5	$55.0
70.5	65.0
85.0	80.0
90.4	85.0
25.3	22.0
120.8	115.0
190.4	170.0
250.1	240.0
60.9	55.0
80.0	75.0

(a) Compute the least-squares regression, using the selling price as the dependent variable and the assessed value as the independent variable.

(b) Use $\alpha = 0.05$ to test the null hypothesis $H_0: \beta_1 = 1$ against the alternative hypothesis $H_1: \beta_1 > 1$. What is your interpretation of the test results?

(c) Suppose the data were obtained in a period of rising real estate prices, and you know that the assessment values were obtained about one year before the actual sale. Would these facts lead you to change your interpretation of the regression results? Explain.

(d) Construct a 95 percent confidence interval for the mean response and a 95 percent prediction interval for an individual observation at $X = \$150$. Explain the meaning of these intervals. Which interval is wider? Why?

18.24. Table P18.24 presents the average daily prices of 30 industrial stocks, 20 transportation stocks, and 20 bonds at the close of each trading day during a recent month.

TABLE P18.24

Day	30 industrials	20 transport companies	20 bonds
1	827.79	219.03	86.67
2	816.96	215.04	86.62
3	823.11	216.84	86.33
6	814.88	215.04	86.44
7	800.07	211.14	86.36
8	807.61	211.53	86.41
9	803.97	210.90	86.34
10	807.09	213.62	86.24
13	792.01	207.64	86.12
14	785.26	205.49	86.26
15	785.60	206.76	86.54
16	794.18	209.49	86.65
17	797.73	210.41	86.91
20	805.61	211.63	86.93
21	804.05	211.04	87.02
22	807.00	212.36	86.96
23	————HOLIDAY————		
24	810.12	214.60	86.98
27	813.84	215.04	86.71
28	804.14	211.87	86.50
29	790.11	208.71	86.44
30	799.03	212.36	86.41

Financial analysts commonly think that all stocks tend to have similar upswings and downswings as a result of some common economy-wide factors (high inflation, high interest rates, and the like) and that no such relationship exists between the prices of stocks and bonds. In order to examine the validity of these views, use Table P18.24 to do the following:

(a) Calculate the value of r for the closing prices of industrial stocks and those of transportation stocks. Show your calculations in detail.

(b) Calculate the value of r for the closing prices of industrial stocks and those of bonds.

(c) Calculate the value of r for the closing prices of transportation stocks and those of bonds.

(d) Test the significance of the correlations you obtained. Use $\alpha = 0.05$.

In view of your results, do you agree with the common view stated above?

Note: Carry all your calculations to four decimal places; otherwise substantial errors may result.

18.25. Table P18.25 shows six data series for the years 1968–80. The first is a series of average weekly earnings in manufacturing, and the second is the nominal prime interest rates (the interest rates banks charge on loans made to their preferred customers). Next, the Consumer Price Index (CPI) is given, followed by the annual inflation rate. The next variable, average earnings in 1967 dollars, is obtained by dividing average weekly earnings in manufacturing by the CPI and then multiplying the result by 100. For example, the average weekly earnings in manufacturing in 1977 was $227.50 and the CPI was 181.50, or 81.50 percent higher than in 1967. Thus the 1977 average weekly earnings figure, expressed in 1967 dollars, is $\frac{\$227.50}{181.50} \cdot 100 =$ $125.34. Finally the real prime interest rate is shown; it is obtained by dividing the nominal rate plus 1 by the inflation rate plus 1, then subtracting 1 from the result. For example, we compute the real rate in 1978 to be $\frac{1 + 0.0811}{1 + 0.076} - 1 = 0.0047$, or 0.47 percent. By expressing the variables in *real* terms, we remove the impact of inflation on those variables.

TABLE P18.25

Year	Nominal average weekly earnings in manufacturing	Nominal prime interest rate	CPI	Inflation rate	Real average weekly earnings in manufacturing	Real prime interest rate
1968	$122.50	5.75%	104.2	4.20%	$117.56	1.49%
1969	129.50	7.61	109.8	5.37	117.94	2.13
1970	133.70	7.31	116.3	5.92	114.96	1.31
1971	142.40	4.85	121.3	4.30	117.39	0.53
1972	154.70	4.47	125.3	3.30	123.46	1.13
1973	165.70	8.08	133.1	6.23	124.49	1.74
1974	176.00	9.89	147.7	10.97	119.16	−0.97
1975	189.50	6.29	161.2	9.14	117.56	−2.61
1976	207.60	5.19	170.5	5.77	121.76	−0.55
1977	227.50	5.59	181.5	6.45	125.34	−0.81
1978	249.27	8.11	195.3	7.60	127.63	0.47
1979	269.34	11.04	217.7	11.47	123.72	−0.39
1980	288.62	12.78	247.0	13.46	116.85	−0.60

Source: *Statistical Abstract of the United States*, 1975; *Survey of Current Business*, various issues; Morgan Guaranty Trust, *World Financial Markets*, various issues.

(*a*) Draw a scatter diagram of the *nominal* average weekly earnings in manufacturing and the *nominal* interest rate. Calculate the correlation coefficient for the two variables. Can you think of an economic explanation for the association between these two variables? Explain.

(*b*) Draw a scatter diagram of the *real* average weekly earnings in manufacturing and the *real* interest rate. Calculate the correlation coefficient for these two variables and test its significance at $\alpha = 0.05$.

(*c*) Compare the results of parts *a* and *b*. How do you explain the difference?

18.26. Table P18.26 presents a classification of loans made by a certain commercial bank by purpose or group of borrowers. The data are given both in dollar amounts and in percentages. Calculate the correlation coefficient for the dollar amount of loans made for each purpose or to each group of borrowers and the percent of total. Test its significance at $\alpha = 0.05$. Is your result surprising? Explain.

TABLE P18.26

Purpose or group of borrowers	Amount (millions of dollars)	Percent of total
Federal and state government	$ 294.8	3.4%
Statutory authorities	110.4	1.3
Agriculture	546.1	6.4
Manufacturing	1,491.0	17.5
Housing	771.9	9.0
Building and construction	543.1	6.4
Real estate	346.1	4.1
Mining and quarrying	98.0	1.2
General commerce	1,801.8	21.1
Business purposes	439.7	5.2
Transport, storage, and communication	122.5	1.4
Hotels, restaurants, and boardinghouses	121.0	1.4
Financial institutions	461.4	5.4
Foreign trade bills	495.8	5.8
All others	890.8	10.4
Total	$8,534.4	100.0%

18.27. Table P18.27 shows the value of the U.S. dollar expressed in terms of other currencies on selected dates.

TABLE P18.27

Country	4/6/82	5/11/82	6/8/82	7/6/82	8/3/82
United States	1.00	1.00	1.00	1.00	1.00
Japan	248.00	232.00	248.00	258.00	258.00
Germany	2.41	2.29	2.41	2.50	2.45
France	6.27	5.96	6.25	6.94	6.81
Switzerland	1.97	1.91	2.05	2.13	2.08

Source: *Wall Street Journal*, various issues.

(a) Calculate the coefficient of correlation between the values of the dollar in terms of the Swiss and German currencies.

(b) Calculate the coefficient of correlation between the values of the dollar in terms of the Japanese and French currencies.

(c) Test the significance of the correlations using $\alpha = 0.01$.

18.28. Suppose you run the following regressions, using two different samples, and obtain $b_1 = c_1 = 1$.

1. $Y = b_0 + b_1 X + e$
2. $Y = c_0 + c_1 X + e$

Also, Σe^2 is the same in both samples. But suppose the X values are different and they are as follows:

$$\text{Sample 1: } 0 \quad 1 \quad 2 \quad 3 \quad 4$$
$$\text{Sample 2: } 0 \quad 4 \quad 6 \quad 8 \quad 20$$

Is it possible to reject the hypothesis that the slope of the first regression is zero and to accept the hypothesis that the slope of the second regression is zero with the same α? Explain.

18.29. An experiment has been conducted in a certain city in order to estimate the relationship between the consumption of milk and its price. The study used the following data:

Price of milk, X (dollars per gallon)	Quantity sold, Y (hundreds of gallons)
$2.00	100
1.90	120
1.70	170
1.60	150
1.30	200
1.00	220
0.80	250
0.50	300
0.40	310
0.30	320
0.20	320
0.10	321
0.08	321
0.05	322
0.01	325

(a) Fit the ordinary least-squares line to the data using Y as the dependent variable.

(b) Calculate the correlation coefficient for X and Y, and test whether it is significantly different from zero. Use $\alpha = 0.05$.

(c) In light of the result in part *a*, it has been recommended to estimate two regression lines, one for prices in the range $0.30–$2.00, and one for the range of prices below $0.30. Carry out the regression analyses and estimate the correlation for these two price ranges separately. Why was there a change in behavior when the prices fell below $0.30 per gallon?

18.30. Consider the following regression line:

$$\hat{Y} = 2 + 6X$$

It is further known that $\Sigma e_i^2 = 100$, and the sample values of X are as follows:

$$X: \quad 0 \quad -2 \quad 4 \quad 6 \quad 8 \quad 10$$

(a) Calculate the 95 percent confidence interval for the mean response, μ_i, at the level $X_i = 10$ and at the level $X_i = 5$.

(b) Calculate the 95 percent prediction interval for the individual observation Y_i at the same levels of X: $X_i = 10$ and $X_i = 5$.

18.31. A sample of sales data from 15 companies for 1981 and 1982 is shown in Figure P18.31*a*.

COMPANY	SALES81	SALES82
1	407	745
2	93813	90294
3	32434	36104
4	122667	120309
5	4821	3020
6	15133	8945
7	321068	366002
8	3223	3580
9	195018	143770
10	350463	343808
11	1063	2535
12	981753	803812
13	6129	6360
14	420194	423822
15	321676	361415

Figure P18.31*a*

1981 and 1982 sales of 15 companies (in thousands of dollars)

Figure P18.31*b* is an SAS computer printout showing the results of the regression $\widehat{SALES}82 = b_0 + b_1SALES81$.

Figure P18.31*b*

Reproduction of an SAS computer printout showing the results of the regression $\widehat{SALES}82 = b_0 + b_1SALES81$

SOURCE	DF	SUM OF SQUARES	MEAN SQUARE	F VALUE	PROB>F
MODEL	1	742573216418	742573216418	496.165	0.0001
ERROR	13	19456146714	1496626670		
C TOTAL	14	762029363133			

	ROOT MSE	38686.259	R-SQUARE	0.9745
	DEP MEAN	180968		

VARIABLE	DF	PARAMETER ESTIMATE	STANDARD ERROR	T FOR H0: PARAMETER=0	PROB>|T|
INTERCEP	1	14759.369	12468.074	1.184	0.2577
SALES81	1	0.868728	0.039001	22.275	0.0001

(*a*) Explain and discuss the results.

(*b*) Had you run similar regressions for many other pairs of consecutive years and found that all the slope coefficients are less than 1, what would it imply about the relative sales of the sample companies? Explain.

18.32. The 1981 net income and tax paid for 10 oil companies are given in Table P18.32.

TABLE P18.32

Company	Net income (billions of dollars)	Tax paid (billions of dollars)
Exxon	$5.57	$2.12
Mobil	2.43	0.94
Standard Oil of Calif.	2.38	1.17
Texaco	2.31	1.12
Standard Oil (Ohio)	1.95	1.44
Standard Oil (Indiana)	1.92	1.66
Shell Oil	1.70	1.21
Atlantic Richfield	1.67	1.39
Gulf Oil	1.23	1.08
Getty Oil	0.86	0.67

Source: *Business Week*, November 22, 1982, p. 24.

Figure P18.32 shows the computer printout of the regression $\widehat{TAX} = b_0 + b_1NET\ INCOME$. Explain and discuss the results.

```
DEP VARIABLE: TAX


               SUM OF      MEAN
SOURCE     DF  SQUARES     SQUARE      F VALUE     PROB>F

MODEL      1   0.853247    0.853247    11.287      0.0099
ERROR      8   0.604753    0.075594
C TOTAL    9   1.458000


  ROOT MSE     0.274944    R-SQUARE    0.5852
  DEP MEAN     1.280000



           PARAMETER   STANDARD   T FOR H0:                VARIABLE
VARIABLE   DF  ESTIMATE   ERROR    PARAMETER=0    PROB>|T|   LABEL

INTERCEP   1   0.752396   0.179503    4.192       0.0030    INTERCEPT
NETINC     1   0.239602   0.071318    3.360       0.0099    NET INCOME
```

Figure P18.32

The results of the regression $TAX = b_0 + b_1 NET\ INCOME$

Case Problems

18.1. Data Set 1, Appendix B, Table B.1, provides data on sales, profit, and profit margin of 100 firms. In line with the explanation given in Case Problem 17.1, where we discussed the fact that the profitability of firms is sometimes related (in part) to their size, carry out the following:

(a) Use the data from firms 50 through 75 (the chemical industry) and run the regression of profit (dependent) on sales (explanatory). If you worked out Case Problem 17.4, you can use its results.

(b) Test the hypothesis that the regression slope is equal to zero. Use a 5 percent significance level. Explain your conclusion.

(c) For sales of $5 and $20 billion determine the 95 percent confidence interval for the mean profit as well as the 95 percent prediction interval.

18.2. Money market funds pool investors' money and invest it in short-term investments. Looking at the average 30-day yield in Data Set 3, Appendix B, Table B.3, which is a measure of the funds' performance in a given period of 30 days, we find differences in performance. In an attempt to reveal the reasons for the differences in their performance, do the following:

(a) Run the regression of yield (dependent variable) against total net assets (explanatory variable), interpret the results of the regression, discuss their statistical significance, and give a 95 percent prediction interval for the yield of a fund with total assets of $5 billion.

(b) Run the regression of yield (dependent variable) against average maturity (explanatory variable), interpret the results of the regression, discuss their statistical significance, and give a 95 percent prediction interval for the yield of a fund with average maturity of 26.0417 days.

(c) For each fund, calculate the percentage of portfolio holdings in U.S. government securities. Then run the regression of yield (dependent) on the percentage holding of U.S. government securities (explanatory). Interpret your results, and explain the significance of the regression slope.

MULTIPLE REGRESSION ANALYSIS

CHAPTER NINETEEN OUTLINE

Key Terms
multiple regression analysis
normal equations
multicollinearity
stepwise regression analysis
dummy variables
indicator variables
multiple correlation
multiple correlation coefficient
partial correlation coefficient

Since real-world situations in business and economics are normally quite complex, accuracy in estimation and prediction of a dependent variable can often be achieved only if more than one explanatory variable is brought into the analysis. For example, the demand for a new cleanser depends on the amount of money spent to promote it, on the price of the new cleanser in relation to the prices of competitive cleansers, on whether it is a powder or a liquid, and, of course, on some measure of quality. Similarly, sales of a given car model depend on its price, the prices of similar models, the price of gasoline, the reputation of the manufacturer, and many other variables. A student's grade on a forthcoming test may be related to his grade-point average, the number of hours devoted to preparation, the number of other tests he will take in the same week, and so on.

In this chapter we deal with regression analysis in which a dependent variable is *linearly* related to a set of K explanatory variables, where K is greater than or equal to 2. This type of regression analysis is known as **multiple regression analysis**. The simplest case of multiple regression is that in which $K = 2$, and we shall deal with this case first.

19.1 Multiple Regression with Two Explanatory Variables

Let a dependent variable Y be a linear function of two explanatory variables, X_1 and X_2, and a random variable u. We can then write the equation

665

$$Y = \beta_0 + \beta_1 X_1 + \beta_2 X_2 + u \qquad (19.1)$$

where β_0, β_1, and β_2 are parameters (constants).

Graphically, Equation 19.1 may be described in a three-dimensional space as illustrated in Figure 19.1, where hypothetical sample observations are presented. Each observation is represented by a point in the space and is determined by the combination of the values Y, X_1, and X_2. The estimated regression equation may be stated as

$$\hat{Y} = b_0 + b_1 X_1 + b_2 X_2 \qquad (19.2)$$

This is an equation of a plane in a three-dimensional space, as depicted in Figure 19.1. It is clear that for each observation, Y, we can identify a sample error term, e; just as we did for simple regression, we drop or raise a vertical line from each point representing an observation (Y) to the regression plane ($\hat{Y}$). This vertical distance is the "error term," e, of the observation (see Figure 19.1):

$$e = Y - \hat{Y} \qquad (19.3)$$

so that Y may be written as follows:

$$Y = b_0 + b_1 X_1 + b_2 X_2 + e$$

The ordinary least-squares principle may now be applied directly. We first substitute the value of $\hat{Y}$ from Equation 19.2 in Equation 19.3 and get

$$e = Y - b_0 - b_1 X_1 - b_2 X_2 \qquad (19.4)$$

Figure 19.1

Scatter diagram of sample points about the regression plane

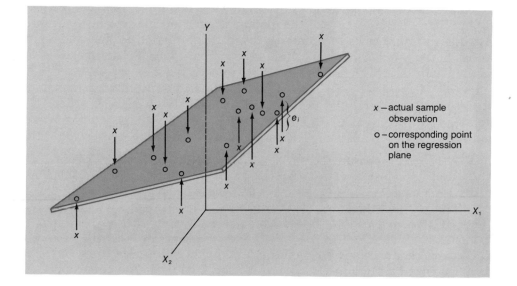

Now we square and sum for all the sample observations and get

$$\Sigma e^2 = \Sigma(Y - b_0 - b_1 X_1 - b_2 X_2)^2 \qquad (19.5)$$

If we take the derivatives of Σe^2 with respect to b_0, b_1, and b_2, equate to zero (to find the minimum of Σe^2), and solve, we obtain the following equations:

$$\Sigma Y = n b_0 + b_1 \Sigma X_1 + b_2 \Sigma X_2$$

$$\Sigma X_1 Y = b_0 \Sigma X_1 + b_1 \Sigma X_1^2 + b_2 \Sigma X_1 X_2 \qquad (19.6)$$

$$\Sigma X_2 Y = b_0 \Sigma X_2 + b_1 \Sigma X_1 X_2 + b_2 \Sigma X_2^2$$

These are the well-known **normal equations**.

Once the sample is observed and the data become available, all the quantities in Equations 19.6 aside from b_0, b_1, and b_2 may be directly computed. This leaves three equations with three unknowns (b_0, b_1, and b_2)—a solvable system of equations.

19.2 Interpretation of the Regression Coefficients

The true regression relationship is given by

$$Y = \beta_0 + \beta_1 X_1 + \beta_2 X_2 + u \qquad (19.7)$$

where β_0, β_1, β_2, and u are unknown coefficients.

Let us examine the meaning of the unknown coefficient β_1. We add 1 to X_1 in Equation 19.7 and write

$$Y' = \beta_0 + \beta_1(X_1 + 1) + \beta_2 X_2 + u$$

or

$$Y' = (\beta_0 + \beta_1 X_1 + \beta_2 X_2 + u) + \beta_1 = Y + \beta_1$$

Similarly, if we subtract 1 from X_1 we get

$$Y'' = \beta_0 + \beta_1(X_1 - 1) + \beta_2 X_2 + u$$

$$= (\beta_0 + \beta_1 X_1 + \beta_2 X_2 + u) - \beta_1$$

$$= Y - \beta_1$$

This shows that Y increases (decreases) by β_1 units for every one-unit increase (decrease) in X_1, when X_2 is held constant. Similarly, it can be easily shown that Y increases (decreases) by β_2 units for every one-unit increase (decrease) in X_2, when X_1 is held constant. When more than two independent variables are used in the regression, the meaning of the coefficient of any one variable is the units of increase (decrease) in Y for each one-unit increase (decrease) in the independent variable, while all the other independent variables remain unchanged.

We interpret the coefficients of the estimated regression line, $\hat{Y} = b_0 + b_1X_1 + b_2X_2$, similarly. The coefficient b_1 is the estimated number of units of change in Y for a one-unit change in X_1 *when the variable X_2 is held unchanged*. The coefficient b_2 is the estimated number of units of change in Y for a one-unit change in X_2 *when the variable X_1 is held unchanged*. The coefficient b_0 is the estimated value of Y when both X_1 and X_2 are equal to zero.

19.3 The Assumptions

As in the case of simple linear regression, here too, in order to conclude that the regression estimators b_0, b_1, and b_2 are best linear unbiased estimators (BLUE) of the true model parameters β_0, β_1, and β_2, we merely have to assume that the random terms u of the various observations are independent of one another, their mean is equal to zero, and their variance, σ_u^2, is the same for all possible values of the independent variables. If we want to determine confidence intervals and test hypotheses concerning a regression coefficient β, we must add the assumption that the random terms u are normally distributed.

Example 19.1 is an illustration of multiple regression analysis with two explanatory variables.

EXAMPLE 19.1

The Omaha Electric Supply Company (OMES) is a power company generating electricity for about a quarter of a million customers. Although OMES has undertaken capital investments in recent years to increase its capacity to generate power, management predictions show that the continually increasing demand will soon exceed the company's capacity. As a result, additional capital investments are now under consideration. John Evan, the financial adviser at OMES, advocates an alternative to additional capital investment. Evan says that the demand for electricity fluctuates during the course of the day at regular intervals; that is, there are peak demand hours and hours of less demand. He argues that if the demand shifts from peak hours to other periods of the day, the existing capacity would be adequate for several more years and capital investment would not be necessary for at least another two years. He further argues that daily demand can be distributed more evenly if the rate is raised for electricity consumed during peak hours and lowered during nonpeak hours. Evan admits, however, that the specific rate that will be appropriate cannot be estimated unless the company undertakes some experimentation. Luckily, management has agreed and has authorized variations in its rates several times within a trial period so that the effect of the rate change on demand can be estimated. Part of the data compiled by OMES during the trial period concerns the following three variables:

1. Average monthly electricity demand per customer *at peak hours*, measured in kilowatt-hours (kwh), denoted interchangeably by *PEAK DEMAND* or Y.
2. Tariff per kwh at peak hours, a variable denoted by *PEAK* or X_1.
3. Tariff per kwh at nonpeak hours, a variable denoted by *NONPEAK* or X_2.

To simplify the example, we assume only nine observations, as given in Table 19.1.

TABLE 19.1
Electricity Demand under Various Tariff Structures

PEAK DEMAND (Y) kwh	PEAK (X_1) cents	NONPEAK (X_2) cents
775	4.0	2.0
820	3.5	2.5
500	6.0	3.0
550	5.0	3.0
660	4.0	2.0
570	5.0	2.5
850	3.0	2.5
810	2.5	2.0
565	6.0	4.0

To estimate the separate effects of *PEAK* and *NONPEAK* on *PEAK DEMAND*, we run a multiple regression analysis. First we develop Table 19.2 as a work sheet and then substitute the numbers in Equations 19.6

TABLE 19.2
Work Sheet for Calculation of Estimated Regression Coefficients

Y (PEAK DEMAND) (kwh)	X_1 (PEAK) (cents)	X_2 (NONPEAK) (cents)	Y^2
775	4.0	2.0	600,625
820	3.5	2.5	672,400
500	6.0	3.0	250,000
550	5.0	3.0	302,500
660	4.0	2.0	435,600
570	5.0	2.5	324,900
850	3.0	2.5	722,500
810	2.5	2.0	656,100
565	6.0	4.0	319,225
$\Sigma Y = 6,100$	$\Sigma X_1 = 39.0$	$\Sigma X_2 = 23.5$	$\Sigma Y^2 = 4,283,850$

TABLE 19.2 (Continued)

X_1^2	X_2^2	$X_1 Y$	$X_2 Y$	$X_1 X_2$
16.00	4.00	3,100	1,550	8.00
12.25	6.25	2,870	2,050	8.75
36.00	9.00	3,000	1,500	18.00
25.00	9.00	2,750	1,650	15.00
16.00	4.00	2,640	1,320	8.00
25.00	6.25	2,850	1,425	12.50
9.00	6.25	2,550	2,125	7.50
6.25	4.00	2,025	1,620	5.00
36.00	16.00	3,390	2,260	24.00
$\Sigma X_1^2 = 181.50$	$\Sigma X_2^2 = 64.75$	$\Sigma X_1 Y = 25,175$	$\Sigma X_2 Y = 15,500$	$\Sigma X_1 X_2 = 106.75$

to get

$$6{,}100 = 9.0b_0 + 39.0b_1 + 23.5b_2 \tag{19.8}$$

$$25{,}175 = 39.0b_0 + 181.50b_1 + 106.75b_2 \tag{19.9}$$

$$15{,}500 = 23.5b_0 + 106.75b_1 + 64.75b_2 \tag{19.10}$$

Dividing Equation 19.8 by 9.0 throughout, Equation 19.9 by 39.0 throughout, and Equation 19.10 by 23.5 throughout yields the following equations:[1]

$$677.77778 = b_0 + 4.3333333b_1 + 2.6111111b_2 \tag{19.11}$$

$$645.51282 = b_0 + 4.6538462b_1 + 2.7371795b_2 \tag{19.12}$$

$$659.57447 = b_0 + 4.5425532b_1 + 2.7553191b_2 \tag{19.13}$$

Subtracting Equation 19.11 from Equation 19.12 yields

$$0.3205128b_1 + 0.1260683b_2 = -32.26496 \tag{19.14}$$

Subtracting Equation 19.13 from Equation 19.12 yields

$$0.1112930b_1 - 0.0181397b_2 = -14.06164 \tag{19.15}$$

Dividing Equation 19.14 by 0.1260683 throughout yields

$$2.5423742b_1 + b_2 = -255.93237 \tag{19.16}$$

And dividing Equation 19.15 by 0.0181397 throughout yields

$$6.1353274b_1 - b_2 = -775.18591 \tag{19.17}$$

Now, adding Equations 19.16 and 19.17 gives us

$$8.6777016b_1 = -1{,}031.1182 \tag{19.18}$$

and

$$b_1 = \frac{-1{,}031.1182}{8.6777016} = -118.82388 \tag{19.19}$$

Substituting this value of b_1 in Equation 19.16 gives

$$-302.09476 + b_2 = -255.93237$$

so that

$$b_2 = 302.09476 - 255.93237 = 46.16239$$

---

[1] Texas Instruments' Business Analyst hand calculator has been used to solve the equations. We present all the decimal places that appear in the calculator's display. We should note that even moderate number rounding can cause significant deviations in the solution.

Substituting the values of b_1 and b_2 in Equation 19.11 yields

$$677.77778 = b_0 - 514.90347 + 120.53512 \qquad \textbf{(19.20)}$$

so that

$$b_0 = 677.77778 + 514.90347 - 120.53512 = 1,072.1461$$

To summarize, the estimated regression coefficients are

$$b_0 = 1,072.1461$$

$$b_1 = -118.8239$$

$$b_2 = 46.1624$$

Given the above coefficients, the estimated (rounded) regression is

$$\widehat{PEAK\ DEMAND} = 1,072.15 - 118.82(PEAK) + 46.16(NONPEAK)$$

where $b_1 = -118.82$ means that for each one-cent increase in price per kwh during peak hours, the demand during peak hours is estimated to be reduced 118.82 kwh per month. Similarly, for a one-cent increase in price per kwh during the nonpeak period, demand in the peak period is estimated to go up 46.16 kwh per month. Technically, we estimate the average monthly demand of electricity to be 1,072.15 kwh if electricity is supplied free of charge ($X_1 = X_2 = 0$). But since none of the sample observations had X_1 and X_2 values in the neighborhood of zero, one must regard the value of b_0 as of technical interest only. The conclusion to be drawn from this regression is that if the company increases the price at peak hours and decreases the price at nonpeak hours, the demand for electricity during peak hours will decrease. It will take a financial analyst to determine the impact of such a decrease on the profitability of OMES, and on its required capital investments. Such impact cannot be estimated without knowing the impact of the rates on *PEAK DEMAND*.

As in simple regression analysis, the standard error of estimate (S_e) in multiple regression is an estimate of the standard deviation of the residuals around the regression plane, and its equation in the case of two explanatory variables is

$$S_e = \sqrt{\frac{\Sigma e^2}{n - 3}} = \sqrt{\frac{\Sigma(Y - \hat{Y})^2}{n - 3}} \qquad \textbf{(19.21)}$$

The denominator under the square root is $n - 3$ because $\hat{Y}$ (which is a prerequisite for computing Σe^2) involves the estimation of β_0, β_1, and β_2, and as usual, one degree of freedom is lost for every parameter that is estimated.

Equation 19.21 is difficult to work with, since it requires the calculation of $\hat{Y}$ for every observation in the sample.

Although an alternative formula for S_e exists and is somewhat easier to handle, it, too, is cumbersome.[2] We shall therefore assume that S_e will not be computed by hand calculations in multiple regression, and defer further discussion to the next section.

19.4 Multiple Regression with Two, Three, or More Explanatory Variables

The generalization of regression analysis from two explanatory variables to more than two is conceptually simple: a dependent variable Y is assumed to be related to K independent variables, $X_1, \ldots, X_K$, in a statistical manner, as follows:

$$Y = \beta_0 + \beta_1 X_1 + \beta_2 X_2 + \cdots + \beta_K X_K + u \tag{19.22}$$

We estimate the relationship by choosing that set of constants $b_0, b_1, \ldots, b_K$ (the estimators of $\beta_0, \beta_1, \ldots, \beta_K$, respectively) which bring the quantity $\Sigma e^2 = \Sigma(Y - \hat{Y})^2$ to a minimum, where $\hat{Y}$ is given by:

$$\hat{Y} = b_0 + b_1 X_1 + \cdots + b_K X_K \tag{19.23}$$

Generally speaking, it is impractical to estimate the constants $b_0, \ldots, b_K$ by hand calculations. If calculation must be done by hand, it is likely to be handled by linear algebra. For the remainder of this chapter we shall assume that a computer is available to do the calculations, and we shall therefore focus on interpretation of the results.

As in the case of two explanatory variables, the constant b_0 is the predicted Y value when X_1 through X_K are all equal to zero. Each of the constants b_1 through b_K is the estimated change in Y as a result of a one-unit change in the respective explanatory variable, *when all the rest are held unchanged*.

We turn now to an example through which we shall discuss the standard deviation of the estimated regression coefficients and the standard error of estimate.

EXAMPLE 19.2

Professional Athletics, a sporting-goods manufacturer, is interested in improving the process it uses to select new salespeople. Instead of using subjective evaluation, the company has decided to use objective criteria. Professional Athletics' management is looking into the relationship between a performance index (*PI*) and the following variables: IQ score

---

[2] Denoting $Y_i^* = Y_i - \bar{Y}_i$, $X_{1i}^* = X_{1i} - \bar{X}_1$, and $X_{2i}^* = X_{2i} - \bar{X}_2$, the equation for S_e is

$$S_e = \sqrt{\frac{\Sigma Y_i^{*2} - b_1 \Sigma Y^* X_1 - b_2 \Sigma Y^* X_2}{n - 3}}$$

(*IQ*); experience (*EXP*), measured in number of years on the job; score on a test related to personality traits (*PER*); and age (*AGE*). Data concerning currently employed salespeople are presented in Table 19.3. Given this sample, we want to estimate the multiple regression coefficients, using *PI* as the dependent variable and *IQ*, *EXP*, *PER*, and *AGE* as the independent variables.

When the data of Table 19.3 are used in the equation

$$\widehat{PI} = b_0 + b_1 IQ + b_2 EXP + b_3 PER + b_4 AGE$$

the following are the resulting estimated coefficients provided by the computer:

$$b_0 = 75.4357$$

$$b_1 = 0.1730$$

$$b_2 = 0.0684$$

$$b_3 = 0.2124$$

$$b_4 = -0.3532$$

TABLE 19.3
Sample Data on Personal Characteristics

i	(PI) Y	(IQ) X_1	(EXP) X_2	(PER) X_3	(AGE) X_4
1	96.8	80.0	9.0	90.3	40.0
2	92.4	100.0	12.0	90.7	40.0
3	104.2	120.0	6.0	110.5	50.0
4	107.8	105.0	1.0	101.0	19.0
5	94.5	118.0	2.0	85.1	40.0
6	96.6	80.0	11.0	103.2	55.0
7	94.7	89.0	22.0	107.9	52.0
8	99.5	93.0	3.0	90.0	39.0
9	97.3	109.0	30.0	85.2	60.0
10	102.8	94.0	9.0	100.3	26.0
11	109.5	114.0	16.0	101.8	36.0
12	109.2	101.0	7.0	88.2	26.0
13	101.1	98.0	18.0	113.3	40.0
14	90.8	82.0	6.0	96.7	42.0
15	104.4	88.0	5.0	109.6	23.0
16	112.6	115.0	4.0	116.8	30.0
17	95.2	107.0	25.0	79.4	43.0
18	107.0	92.0	2.0	119.0	35.0
19	94.3	92.0	11.0	120.6	61.0
20	104.4	87.0	7.0	99.0	27.0
21	106.5	114.0	13.0	117.1	30.0
22	110.1	108.0	12.0	117.5	30.0

The performance index that we predict for a 50-year-old salesman with an IQ of 100.0, 8 years' experience, and a score of 110.0 on the personality trait test is

$$\hat{PI} = 75.4357 + (0.1730)(100.0) + (0.0684)(8)$$
$$+ (0.2124)(110.0) - (0.3532)(50)$$
$$= 75.4357 + 17.3000 + 0.5472$$
$$+ 23.3640 - 17.6600 = 98.9869$$

The computer results are shown in Figure 19.2.[3] To produce these results you do *not* need to be a computer programmer. All you need to do is supply the data, identify the dependent and independent variables, and set up your deck of cards with the help of your university computer center personnel, if necessary.

Figure 19.2

Computer regression printout

```
 1. PROBLEM  TITLE . . . . . . .  PERSONAL  CHARACTERISTICS  REGRESSION
 2. NUMBER  OF  CASES  READ . . . . . . . . . . . . .       22
 3. VARIABLE        MEAN  STANDARD  DEVIATION  ST.DEV/MEAN     MINIMUM       MAXIMUM
 4.   1  Y        101.44091          6.52137       .06429    90.80000     112.60000
 5.   2  X1        99.36364         12.58701       .12668    80.00000     120.00000
 6.   3  X2        10.50000          7.72596       .73581     1.00000      30.00000
 7.   4  X3       101.96364         12.60165       .12359    79.40000     120.60000
 8.   5  X4        38.36364         11.74550       .30616    19.00000      61.00000
 9.   REGRESSION  TITLE . . . . . . .  PERSONAL  CHARACTERISTICS  REGRESSION
10.   DEPENDENT  VARIABLE . . . . . . . . . . . . .       1  Y
11.   TOLERANCE . . . . . . . . . . . . . . . . . . . .0100
12. ALL  DATA  CONSIDERED  AS  A  SINGLE  GROUP
13. MULTIPLE  R          .8448        STD.  ERROR  OF  EST.        3.8781
14. MULTIPLE  R-SQUARE    .7137
15. ANALYSIS  OF  VARIANCE
16.               SUM OF SQUARES    DF    MEAN  SQUARE     F  RATIO   P(TAIL)
17.   REGRESSION      637.415        4      159.354       10.595     .00017
18.   RESIDUAL        255.679       17       15.040
                                         STD. REG
19.   VARIABLE     COEFFICIENT  STD. ERROR    COEFF      T      P(2  TAIL)
20. INTERCEPT        75.436
21.   X1      2       .173        .069        .334     2.516      .022
22.   X2      3       .068        .133        .081      .513      .615
23.   X3      4       .212        .069        .410     3.086      .007
24.   X4      5      -.353        .086       -.636    -4.107      .001
```

The explanation of Figure 19.2, line by line, is as follows:

Line 1 A statement identifying the problem title as "Personal Characteristics Regression."
Line 2 Identifies the sample as one consisting of 22 observations.
Line 3 Titles for the next five lines.
Line 4 Statistics of the variable Y (variable number 1). Its mean and standard deviation are 101.44091 and 6.52137, respectively; the ratio of the standard deviation to the mean is 0.06429; the minimum and maximum sample values of Y are 90.80000 and 112.60000, respectively.
Line 5 Statistics of the variable X_1 (variable number 2).
Line 6 Statistics of the variable X_2 (variable number 3).
Line 7 Statistics of the variable X_3 (variable number 4).
Line 8 Statistics of the variable X_4 (variable number 5).
Line 9 Regression title.

[3] The computer printouts shown in the example were generated using the Biomedical Computer Programs, P series, by Health Sciences Computing Facility, University of California, Los Angeles.

Line 10 Identifies the variable Y as the dependent variable.

Line 11 The tolerance level is 0.0100. An explanatory variable that does not contribute at least 0.0100 to the regression's multiple coefficient of determination (R^2) will not be included in the regression.

Line 12 The statement indicates that all the sample data will be included in the regression. An alternative situation would be the inclusion of the data in parts, creating a piecewise regression analysis.

Line 13 The multiple correlation coefficient (see discussion that follows) is equal to 0.8448, and the standard error of estimate S_e is 3.8781.

Line 14 R^2 is equal to 0.7137. R^2 is the multiple coefficient of determination, and like r^2 in simple regression, it measures the percentage of the variance of Y that is explained by all the explanatory variables in the regression. Specifically, of the total sum of squares $\Sigma(Y - \overline{Y})^2$, the sum of explained deviations $\Sigma(\hat{Y} - \overline{Y})^2$ is 71.37 percent. This also means that $100 - 71.37 = 28.63$ percent of the total sum of squares is not explained by the regression.

Line 15 A title for the next three lines, in which an analysis of variance is presented.

Line 16 Titles for the next two lines.

Line 17 The sum of squares $\Sigma(\hat{Y} - \overline{Y})^2$ is equal to 637.415. The number of degrees of freedom of this sum of squares is 4, and the mean square is $637.415/4 = 159.354$. The F ratio, 10.595, shows that the explanatory variables, as a group, provide a significant explanation of the variable Y. The significance is at all values of α that are greater than 0.00017.

Line 18 The sum of squares of the residuals, $\Sigma(Y - \hat{Y})^2$, is equal to 255.679. It has 17 degrees of freedom and the mean square is $255.679/17 = 15.040$.

Line 19 Titles for the next five lines.

Line 20 The regression intercept is equal to 75.436.

Line 21 The regression coefficient of X_1 (variable number 2) is 0.173, and its standard error is 0.069. The standardized regression coefficient (0.334) was not discussed in this book; it is generally of minor importance. The t value is 2.516 ($0.173/0.069 = 2.516$), where the t distribution here has $n - K - 1 = 22 - 4 - 1 = 17$ degrees of freedom. If we use $\alpha = 0.01$ so that our critical value is $t_{0.01}^{(17)} = 2.567$, a hypothesis such as $H_0: \beta_1 = 0$ cannot be rejected. Here, however, is where we must be very careful in interpreting the regression results. The sample shows that the coefficient b_1 is *different* from zero. It equals 0.173, and so our best inference about β_1 must be that it is positive and equals 0.173. Only if we have some reason to believe that β_1 is in truth equal to zero—perhaps because of a theory or because of some other empirical study from another place or time—will we question our estimate and test a hypothesis such as $H_0: \beta_1 = 0$. Accepting H_0 would merely mean that our sample data do not show strong enough evidence to warrant its rejection.

Line 22 Statistics of the coefficient of X_2.

Line 23 Statistics of the coefficient of X_3.

Line 24 Statistics of the coefficient of X_4.

19.5 Association Between Explanatory Variables: Multicollinearity

One important question concerning the estimated slope coefficients in a multiple regression is their significance. We have seen in Chapter 18 that the statistic $\dfrac{b_1 - \beta_1}{S_{b_1}}$ in a simple regression has a t distribution with $(n - 2)$ degrees of freedom, where n is the number of observations. Similarly, the significance of any estimated slope coefficient b_i, in a multiple regression analysis with K independent variables, is determined by the statistic

$$\frac{b_i - \beta_i}{S_{b_i}} \tag{19.24}$$

which has a t distribution with $(n - K - 1)$ degrees of freedom. Note that in a simple regression analysis, K (i.e., the number of independent variables) is equal to 1, and $n - K - 1$ is equal to $n - 2$, so that it is nothing but a special case of multiple regression analysis. Hand calculation of S_{b_i} is somewhat complex, but virtually all computer multiple regression programs provide the value of S_{b_i} in their standard output. In those outputs we typically also obtain the value of $(b_i - \beta_i)/S_{b_i}$ under the assumption that the null hypothesis is H_0: $\beta_i = 0$. In other words, in addition to b_i, the computer typically provides the values of S_{b_i} and b_i/S_{b_i} (see Figure 19.2).

While we do not present the calculation of S_{b_i} here, we would like to discuss the association between the regression's explanatory variables and its impact on S_{b_i}. Consider the following regression equation with two explanatory variables, X_1 and X_2:

$$\hat{Y} = b_0 + b_1X_1 + b_2X_2$$

The variables X_1 and X_2 may or may not be associated with one another. The higher the association between X_1 and X_2, the higher are the standard errors S_{b_1} and S_{b_2}. As a result, for given estimates b_1 and b_2, the statistics b_1/S_{b_1} and b_2/S_{b_2} are lower as the association between X_1 and X_2 increases. This means also that when between association between the explanatory variables increases, the confidence we have in the estimated slope coefficients decreases, since their values depend more heavily on the particular observations that happen to be in the sample. In fact when the association between X_1 and X_2 is very high, a situation we call **multicollinearity**, we might be better off including only one of the variables in the regression and simply dropping the other. For example, if Y is a firm's total revenues, X_1 is its number of employees, and X_2 is the firm's total expense for wages and salaries, it is likely that X_1 and X_2 are highly associated. Inclusion of both X_1 and X_2 in a regression analysis could increase S_{b_1} and S_{b_2} and decrease the coefficients' t values.

Let us further illustrate this point by describing actual research results.

EXAMPLE 19.3

It is traditional among financial analysts and investors to believe that a positive relationship exists between the rate of return that one can expect to obtain on a stock and the risk associated with the stock: the higher the risk involved, the higher the rate of return the investor can expect to obtain from the investment in the long run. While there is general agreement concerning this principle, there is much less agreement concerning the way risk ought to be measured. Two common measures are the variance of the annual rates of return (σ^2) and the so-called beta coefficient. "Beta" measures the relationship of a stock's rate of return to the average rate of return on the entire stock market (see Section 18.7).

To learn about the relationship between the risk measures and the average rate of return on the stock, a sample of 100 stocks was taken.[4] For each stock, the average annual rate of return over a period of 20 years as well as the two measures of risk, σ^2 and beta, were calculated. We denote the various stocks by i, the average rate of return by *AVERAGE RATE*, the first risk measure (σ^2) by *RISK*1, and the second risk measure ("beta") by *RISK*2. Using the 100 observations, three regressions were studied:

1. $\widehat{AVERAGE\ RATE} = b_0 + b_1(RISK1)$
2. $\widehat{AVERAGE\ RATE} = b_0 + b_1(RISK2)$
3. $\widehat{AVERAGE\ RATE} = b_0 + b_1(RISK1) + b_2(RISK2)$

For the first regression we found that

$$\widehat{AVERAGE\ RATE} = 0.109 + 0.037(RISK1)$$

The value of the statistic $(b_1 - \beta_1)/S_{b_1}$ under the null hypothesis (by which $\beta_1 = 0$) was

$$\frac{b_1 - 0}{S_{b_1}} = \frac{0.037 - 0}{0.00725} = 5.1$$

This statistic has $100 - 2$, or 98, degrees of freedom, and since $t_{0.01}^{(98)} = 2.326$, it is clear that the hypothesis $H_0: \beta_1 = 0$ should be rejected at $\alpha = 0.01$.

For the second regression the following results were obtained:

$$\widehat{AVERAGE\ RATE} = 0.122 + 0.219(RISK2)$$

The value of the statistic $(b_1 - \beta_1)/S_{b_1}$ was

$$\frac{b_1 - 0}{S_{b_1}} = \frac{0.219 - 0}{0.02844} = 7.7$$

so that once again we reject the hypothesis that the slope coefficient is equal to zero.

Finally both risk measures were included as explanatory variables, as in the third regression. The result was as follows:

$$\widehat{AVERAGE\ RATE} = 0.117 + 0.008(RISK1) + 0.197(RISK2)$$

[4] See H. Levy, "Equilibrium in an Imperfect Market: A Constraint on the Number of Securities in the Portfolio," *American Economic Review*, September 1978.

While the value of $(b_1 - 0)/S_{b_1}$ in the first regression was 5.1, its value in the third regression was much lower:

$$\frac{b_1 - 0}{S_{b_1}} = \frac{0.008 - 0}{0.00889} = 0.90$$

By dropping from 5.1 all the way down to 0.9, the coefficient became not significantly different from zero at $\alpha = 0.01$ and even at much higher values of α. The value of the statistic of *RISK2* has also dropped—from 7.7 in the second regression to 5.2 in the third:

$$\frac{b_2 - 0}{S_{b_2}} = \frac{0.197 - 0}{0.03788} = 5.2$$

While this statistic is still significantly different from zero at $\alpha = 0.01$, its value dropped from 7.7 primarily because of the increase in the standard error despite the fact that all three regressions were run on the very same data.

The main reason why the significance in the third regression drops is the association between *RISK1* and *RISK2*. The correlation coefficient between them is $+0.69$.

We should remember that if there is a strong association between explanatory variables—i.e., if there is multicollinearity in the regression—we should carefully examine the significance of the regression coefficients. If they are not significant, we should consider excluding the independent variables which are highly correlated with other independent variables.

19.6 Stepwise Regression Analysis

If we ran the third regression of Example 19.3 without running the first and second regressions, it would have been difficult to fully understand the relationships between the variables, and particularly the extent to which *RISK1* contributes to the regression given that *RISK2* is already included as an explanatory variable. The contribution of an additional explanatory variable to the regression is particularly difficult to assess when the number of explanatory variables is more than two. The **stepwise regression analysis** is a technique designed to alleviate this problem. The technique is accessible to most computer users with no difficulty. The user prepares the data for a multiple regression, which includes a dependent variable Y and all the independent variables considered. Instead of running the multiple regression $Y = b_0 + b_1X_1 + b_2X_2 + \cdots + b_KX_K$, however, the computer will search for the one variable which, if taken alone, gives the best explanation of the dependent variable's variability. In other words, given the sample data, the computer will search for the variable—call it X_1—such that the value of R^2 in the regression

$$\hat{Y} = b_0 + b_1X_1$$

is the highest of all the possible simple regressions. In the next step, the computer will search for a second explanatory variable and choose the one that gives the maximum increase in R^2 compared to the value of R^2 from the first step. Denoting this second explanatory variable by X_2, the computer will run the regression

$$\hat{Y} = b_0 + b_1X_1 + b_2X_2$$

By a similar procedure, the computer will search for an additional variable X_3 and run the regression

$$\hat{Y} = b_0 + b_1X_1 + b_2X_2 + b_3X_3$$

and so on.

The process continues until all the variables are included in the regression or until the contribution of the remaining variables to increasing R^2 is too small to be significant.

EXAMPLE 19.4

The following are recent annual dividends (*DIV*) and net income (*NI*) of Aluminum Company of America as well as the United States inflation rate (*INF*) for each of these years:

Year	DIV (millions of dollars)	NI (millions of dollars)	INF (percent)
1	$38.7	$104.7	4.20%
2	38.7	122.4	5.40
3	38.7	95.5	5.90
4	38.9	52.9	4.30
5	39.3	100.9	3.30
6	43.1	100.3	6.23
7	44.6	174.6	10.97
8	45.2	64.8	9.14
9	47.3	143.8	5.77
10	46.6	195.2	6.48
11	66.3	312.7	9.33

Given these data, we try to explain the dividend level by the level of net income and the inflation rate.

The computer has determined that *NI* is the first explanatory variable to be included in the regression (see Figure 19.3). The regression equation in the first step is

$$\widehat{DIV} = 31.487 + 0.096NI$$

with $S_{b_1} = 0.01794$ and $\dfrac{b_1 - \beta_1}{S_{b_1}} = \dfrac{0.096 - 0}{0.01794} = 5.35$ (see note to Figure

19.3). The inflation rate, *INF*, is the second variable to be included, and the regression in the second step is

$$\widehat{DIV} = 29.524 + 0.0834NI + 0.6460INF$$

```
             S T A T I S T I C A L   A N A L Y S I S   S Y S T E M

                FORWARD SELECTION PROCEDURE FOR DEPENDENT VARIABLE DIV

STEP 1    VARIABLE NI ENTERED    R SQUARE = 0.7617150

                    DF      SUM OF SQUARES      MEAN SQUARE        F       PROB>F

     REGRESSION     1        493.90065904      493.90065904     28.68     0.0005
     ERROR          9        154.96843187       17.21871465
     TOTAL         10        648.86909091

                         B VALUE          STD ERROR           F       PROB>F

     INTERCEPT      31.48733182
     NI              0.09608894         0.01794130          28.68     0.0005


STEP 2    VARIABLE INF ENTERED    R SQUARE = 0.82235579

                    DF      SUM OF SQUARES      MEAN SQUARE        F       PROB>F

     REGRESSION     2        533.60125272      266.80062636     18.52     0.0010
     ERROR          8        115.26783819       14.40847977
     TOTAL         10        648.86909091

                         B VALUE          STD ERROR           F       PROB>F

     INTERCEPT      29.52368829
     NI              0.08335045         0.01811760          21.16     0.0018
     INF             0.64600250         0.38917446           2.76     0.1355
```

Figure 19.3

Note: The t value of the estimated regression coefficients can be found by taking the square root of the respective F value. For example, in step 1, the F value of the variable NI is 28.68, which means that the respective t value is $\sqrt{28.68} = 5.355$. The significance of this value is 0.0005, meaning that only a significance level greater than 0.0005 will lead to a rejection of H_0: $\beta_1 = 0$ against H_1: $\beta_1 \neq 0$.

A part of an SAS computer printout showing a stepwise regression analysis. Step 1: $\widehat{DIV} = b_0 + b_1 NI$; Step 2: $\widehat{DIV} = b_0 + b_1 NI + b_2 INF$

where the standard errors are $S_{b_1} = 0.0181$ and $S_{b_2} = 0.3892$. Consequently

$$T_1 = \frac{b_1 - \beta_1}{S_{b_1}} = \frac{0.0834 - 0}{0.0181} = 4.61$$

and

$$T_2 = \frac{b_2 - \beta_2}{S_{b_2}} = \frac{0.6460 - 0}{0.3892} = 1.66$$

The second explanatory variable increases the regression R^2 from 0.76 to about 0.82. Nevertheless its contribution to the regression is not very significant. The t value of the regression coefficient is 1.66 (F value of $1.66^2 = 2.76$) and with $n - K - 1 = 10 - 2 - 1 = 7$ degrees of freedom, this value is not significant at $\alpha = 0.05$ or any other α less than 0.1355.

19.7 Dummy Variables

All the variables in the regression as presented to this point were quantitative. Quite often there is the need to include qualitative explanatory variables in the analysis. Examples are numerous: sales depend on advertising expenditures (quantitative) and on location (qualitative); income of college graduates depend on their grade-point-average (quantitative), on their major (qualitative), and on region of employment (qualitative). The rent paid for a house depends on its size (quantitative) and on whether it is furnished or not (qualitative). We use **dummy variables** (also called **indicator variables**) to handle qualitative variables in regression analysis. Dummy variables take on the values 0 or 1. Their use in regression analysis is illustrated in the following case study.

CASE STUDY

The Albertson Construction Company (ACC) is investigating the possibility of building houses in a Chicago suburb. The company does not intend to sell the houses but rather to lease them. Obviously, the monthly rent that ACC can charge will be determined by the market demand and supply for such houses. In order to set initial rent levels, ACC took a sample of existing rented houses and determined their rent as a function of the size of the house and some other economic factors. This preliminary study of the market was important since it was supposed to help ACC in making decisions such as whether it should rent furnished houses or unfurnished houses. From ACC's point of view it is worthwhile to rent furnished houses if it gets at least $100 additional rent per month for a furnished house than for an unfurnished house. Similarly, ACC also considered renting houses with private swimming pools. This would have been economically worthwhile for ACC if the rent could be set at least $150 higher for a house with a pool than for a house without a pool.

In order to get a feel for what people would be willing to pay, a random sample of rented houses was taken. ACC first hypothesized that the rent is a function of the house size (measured in square feet) and whether the house is furnished or not. Denoting the variables by *RENT*, *SIZE*, and *FURN*, the regression model would be

$$RENT = \beta_0 + \beta_1\,SIZE + \beta_2\,FURN + u$$

While the variables *RENT* and *SIZE* are quantitative, the variable *FURN* is not. A house is either furnished or unfurnished, and these are qualitative values. The inclusion of *FURN* in the regression is accomplished by defining it as a dummy variable which takes on one of two values: 0 or 1. We then define:

$$FURN = \begin{cases} 0 & \text{if the house is unfurnished} \\ 1 & \text{if the house is furnished} \end{cases}$$

Using this method we in fact convert a qualitative variable into a quantitative one. Note that the choice of which qualitative value is assigned the value 0 and which is assigned the value 1 is arbitrary, but once assigned, the value should be remembered for correct interpretation of the results. Table 19.4 provides the sample data for the regression. Using the SAS regression package, we got the estimated regression coefficients:

$$b_0 = 52.338$$

$$b_1 = 0.257$$

$$b_2 = 21.188$$

TABLE 19.4
Sample Data of House Rents

Observation	RENT (dollars per month)	SIZE (square feet)	FURN
1	$290	1,100	0
2	345	950	1
3	400	1,240	0
4	280	960	0
5	390	1,210	0
6	630	1,830	1
7	620	2,050	1
8	650	2,420	0
9	530	1,710	1
10	660	2,200	0
11	460	1,360	1
12	800	2,500	1
13	640	2,300	0
14	250	1,950	1
15	440	1,420	0
16	360	1,300	0
17	330	1,050	1
18	580	1,700	1

and the estimated regression line is

$$\widehat{RENT} = 52.338 + 0.257\ SIZE + 21.188\ FURN$$

Part of an SAS computer printout of the regression is presented in Figure 19.4. Of a total sum of squares of 444,512.50, about 309,271.12 is explained by the model. The ratio of the explained sum of squares to total sum of squares is approximately 0.6958, which is the regression R^2. The model as a whole is highly significant. This can be seen by the high F value, which equals 17.15, a value that bounds a right-hand tail of less than 0.0001. In other words, the independent variables taken together are very significant in explaining the *RENT* variable.

For each regression coefficient the printout provides an estimate, b_i, standard error of estimate, S_{b_i}, and a t value for testing H_0: $\beta_i = 0$. This t value is given by

$$T = \frac{b_i - 0}{S_{b_i}}$$

Examining each explanatory variable separately, we find that the variable *SIZE* is highly significantly different from zero ($t = 5.76$, which is significant even at a level of 0.0001), but the variable *FURN* is not significantly different from zero at any reasonable significance level. Its t value is only 0.47. Nevertheless *FURN*'s coefficient is 21.19, meaning that we estimate that a furnished house is rented, on average, for $21.19 more than an unfurnished house.

The firm intends to build houses with 2,500 square feet of floor area. The estimated average rent for houses of this size is (the coefficients are rounded):

$$\widehat{RENT} = 52.34 + 0.257 \cdot 2,500 + 21.19 \cdot 0 = \$694.84$$

if the house is unfurnished (*FURN* = 0), and

$$\widehat{RENT} = 52.34 + 0.257 \cdot 2,500 + 21.19 \cdot 1 = \$716.03$$

if the house is furnished (*FURN* = 1).

ACC must charge at least $100 per month more for furnishing a house to cover its costs. However, people renting houses are estimated to be paying only $21.19 more for a furnished house than for an unfurnished house; therefore, ACC should decide to rent unfurnished houses. Note that 716.03 − 694.84 = $21.19, which is the rounded regression coefficient of *FURN*.

Figure 19.5 exhibits the estimated regression lines. The use of a dummy variable has led to two lines with *equal slopes*. This means that when we use the dummy variable technique we implicitly introduce the assumption that the contribution of the incremental size of the house to the rent *is the same* whether the house is furnished or unfurnished. If this assumption is not plausible, two separate regressions should be estimated from two separate samples: one for furnished houses and one for unfurnished houses. The advantage of the dummy variable technique (in the case in which the slopes are hypothesized to be equal to one another) is obvious: sampling errors of the regression coefficients are smaller because a larger sample size is used when all the observations are pooled into one sample.

RENT VS SIZE FURN

GENERAL LINEAR MODELS PROCEDURE

DEP VARIABLE: RENT

SOURCE	DF	SUM OF SQUARES	MEAN SQUARE	F VALUE	PR > F	R-SQUARE
MODEL	2	309271.11556039[a]	154635.55778019	17.15	0.0001	0.695753
ERROR	15	135241.38443961[b]	9016.09229597			STD DEV
CORRECTED TOTAL	17	444512.50000000				94.95310577

PARAMETER	ESTIMATE	T FOR H0: PARAMETER=0	PR>|T|[c]	STD ERROR OF ESTIMATE
INTERCEPT	52.33835845	0.68	0.5073	77.04163711
SIZE	0.25716995	5.76	0.0001	0.04467547
FURN	21.18716653	0.47	0.6446	45.00904700

OBSERVATION	OBSERVED VALUE	PREDICTED VALUE	RESIDUAL
1	290.00000000	335.22530201	-45.22530201
2	345.00000000	317.83742623	27.16257377
3	400.00000000	371.22909482	28.77090518
4	280.00000000	299.22150919	-19.22150919
5	390.00000000	363.51399636	26.48600364
6	630.00000000	544.14598108	85.85301892
7	620.00000000	600.72436979	19.27563021
8	650.00000000	674.68963428	-24.68963428
9	530.00000000	513.28658724	16.71341276
10	660.00000000	618.11224557	41.88775443
11	460.00000000	423.27710519	36.72289481
12	800.00000000	716.45084670	83.54915330
13	640.00000000	643.82924044	-3.82924044
14	250.00000000	575.00737492	-325.00737492
15	440.00000000	417.51968559	22.48031441
16	360.00000000	386.65929175	-26.65929175
17	330.00000000	343.55442110	-13.55442110
18	580.00000000	510.71488775	69.28511225

SUM OF RESIDUALS	0.00000000
SUM OF SQUARED RESIDUALS	135241.38443961

[a] The model sum of squares is $\Sigma(\hat{Y} - \bar{Y})^2$.

[b] The error sum of squares is $\Sigma(Y - \hat{Y})^2$.

[c] This is the probability of obtaining a higher or lower value than T under the appropriate t distribution. In other words, it is the highest value of α (the significance level) under which $H_0: \beta_i = 0$ should be accepted when tested against $H_1: \beta_i \neq 0$. For example, for the variable SIZE this probability is 0.0001. This means that the regression estimate of the variable SIZE is significantly different from zero at all levels of significance greater than 0.0001.

Figure 19.4 Computer regression printout: $\widehat{RENT} = b_0 + b_1 SIZE + b_2 FURN$ (18 observations)

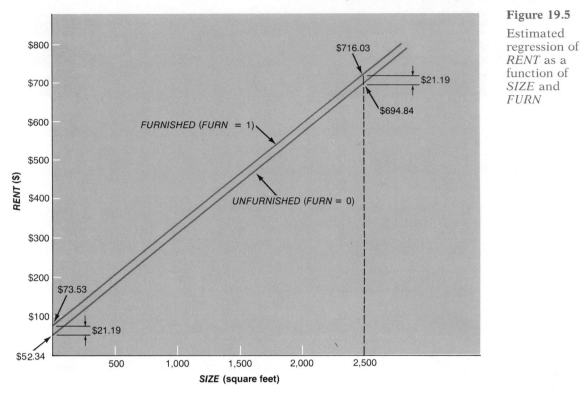

Figure 19.5

Estimated regression of *RENT* as a function of *SIZE* and *FURN*

19.8 Residual Analysis

Examining the residuals of a regression is a very effective way of understanding the significance and adequacy of a regression's results. If a model is properly specified, the correct variables included, and the regression assumptions are holding, then the residuals will be randomly scattered around zero. Only about 5 percent of the residuals will be outside the range $-2S_e$ to $+2S_e$.

However, if they show a nonrandom pattern or if a few observations have an extremely high or extremely low residual value (considerably greater than $+2S_e$ or less than $-2S_e$), the data must be reexamined and corrective measures must be taken. It is difficult to say what these corrective measures must be, since it depends on the reason behind the nonrandomness of the residuals. However, we proceed with one illustration continuing our case study. Figure 19.4 provides for each observation the observed rent value, the predicted value given the estimated regression equation as well as the difference between the two: the residual values.

The last line of Figure 19.4 shows that the sum of squared residuals (Σe^2) is equal to 135,241.38 (rounded). In the top part of the figure we find that the mean square of the residuals (i.e., $\Sigma e^2/(n - K - 1) = 135,241.38/15$) is approximately 9,016.09. When we take the square root of 9,016.09 we get approximately 94.95, which is the value of S_e. This value is shown in Figure 19.4 as *STD DEV* (see top right of the figure).

Figure 19.6 is a reproduction of an **SAS** computer printout showing the residuals of the regression. The range $+2S_e$ to $-2S_e$ is in our case $+2 \cdot 94.95$ = $+189.90$ to -189.90. Examining the residuals in Figure 19.6 we find that 17 out of 18 residuals are within the above range, but one observation lies

Figure 19.6

A computer residual plot (18 observations)

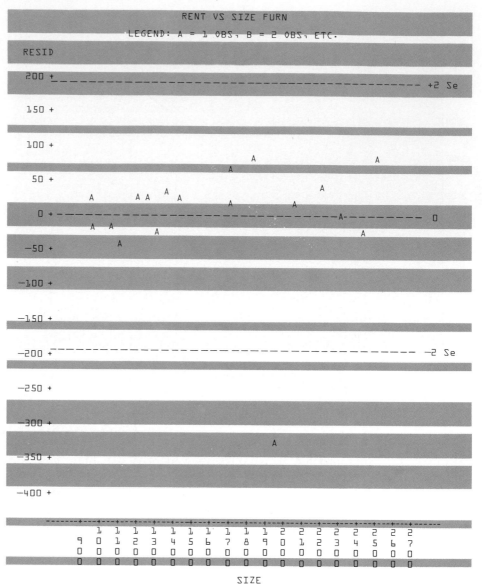

outside it, having an extremely low value. Although 1 outlier observation out of 18 is not a high proportion, the outlier should be checked to determine the reason for the large deviation. Reference to Figure 19.4 shows that the outlier observation is observation number 14, with a residual value of −325.007.

The treatment of outliers usually depends on the reason why the observation is an outlier and the relevance of the outlier to the regression. In our example the predicted rent for observation 14 is about $575, while the actual rent was $250 (see Figure 19.4).

As a first step ACC checked to see if there was an error involved in reporting the rent for house number 14. They found out that there was no error and indeed the rent was $250 per month, but that the house was rented out by the owners to their close relatives at a large discount. Since the rent for house number 14 is subsidized, it clearly does not represent the market rent that ACC can charge. Thus, the regression is rerun with 17 observations after omitting the outlier observation. The results are shown in Figure 19.7, which

```
                         RENT VS SIZE FURN

               GENERAL LINEAR MODE_S PROCEDURE

DEP VARIABLE: RENT

SOURCE        DF    SUM OF SQUARES    MEAN SQUARE    F VALUE    PR > F    R-SQUARE

MODEL          2    373920.58734625   186960.29367312  184.67    0.0001    0.963479

ERROR         14    14173.53030081     1012.39502149              STD DEV

CORRECTED TOTAL 16  388094.11764706                            31.81815553

                         T FOR H0:                      STD ERROR OF
PARAMETER     ESTIMATE   PARAMETER=0      PR>|T|          ESTIMATE

INTERCEPT    17.04498817      0.66        0.5230         26.01709639
SIZE          0.27961803     18.50        0.0001          0.01511054
FURN         60.20787711      3.88        0.0017         15.49857711
```

Figure 19.7

Computer regression printout: $\widehat{RENT} = b_0 + b_1 SIZE + b_2 FURN$ (17 observations)

shows that an outlier observation can influence regression results quite drastically. The regression's R^2 rose to about 0.9635 from a previous value of approximately 0.6958, the regression's F value is 184.67, and both the coefficients of *SIZE* and *FURN* are found to be significantly different from zero at any reasonable significance level: the t value of *SIZE* is 18.50 and that of *FURN* is 3.88. Examining the residuals we find no outliers this time. The value of S_e is approximately 31.82, and all the observations are now in the range $+2S_e$ to $-2S_e$. Note again that a small percentage of observations outside this range is quite normal, but large deviations from this range should be checked. Figure 19.8 presents the residuals of the regression, which seem to be scattered around zero in a random fashion.

The regression coefficients have changed substantially and the equation is now (rounded):

$$\widehat{RENT} = 17.04 + 0.280 \; SIZE + 60.21 \; FURN$$

Thus for houses of 2,500 square feet ACC can charge on average

$$\widehat{RENT} = 17.04 + 0.280 \cdot 2{,}500 + 60.21 \cdot 0 = \$717.04$$

per month if the house is unfurnished and

$$\widehat{RENT} = 17.04 + 0.280 \cdot 2{,}500 + 60.21 \cdot 1 = \$777.25$$

per month if the house is furnished.

After correcting the regression estimates by dropping the outlier observation, we see that ACC can charge \$717.04 per month, but still would rather rent unfurnished houses since furnishing the houses would add an estimated \$60.21 to the monthly rent, which is still below the minimum required by ACC (\$100).

Figure 19.8

A computer residual plot (17 observations)

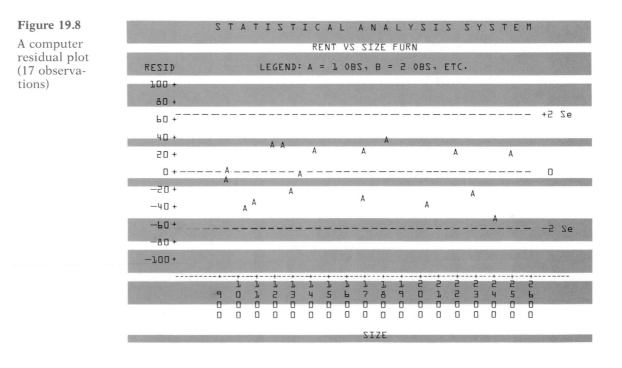

INCLUSION OF MORE THAN ONE DUMMY VARIABLE

Inclusion of a dummy variable as an explanatory variable in a regression allows us to distinguish two qualitative values, such as "the house is furnished" or "the house is not furnished." When more than two qualitative values are relevant, more dummy variables should be included. Extending the ACC case, we now include a dummy variable for the existence of a swimming pool. The regression equation is

$$\widehat{RENT} = b_0 + b_1\ SIZE + b_2\ FURN + b_3\ SWIM$$

where the variables *RENT*, *SIZE*, and *FURN* are defined as before and

$$SWIM = \begin{cases} 0 & \text{if there is no swimming pool} \\ 1 & \text{if there is a swimming pool} \end{cases}$$

The two dummy variables *FURN* and *SWIM* allow for four alternative situations. If both are equal to 0, the house is unfurnished and has no pool; if both are equal to 1, the house is furnished and has a pool; if $FURN = 0$ and $SWIM = 1$, the house is unfurnished but has a pool; and if $FURN = 1$ and $SWIM = 0$, it is furnished but it does not have a swimming pool. Table 19.5 gives the sample data and Figure 19.9 provides a reproduction of SAS computer output for this regression. The R^2 of the regression is now 0.994 and the coefficients of *SIZE*, *FURN*, and *SWIM* are all highly significant. The regression equation (rounded) is

$$\widehat{RENT} = 9.73 + 0.269\ SIZE + 64.83\ FURN + 55.24\ SWIM$$

It is estimated that on the average an additional \$64.83 is paid for a furnished house than for an unfurnished house, and an additional \$55.24 is paid

TABLE 19.5
Sample House-Rent Data

Observation	*RENT* (dollars per month)	*SIZE* (sq. feet)	*FURN*	*SWIM*
1	$290	1,100	0	0
2	345	950	1	0
3	400	1,240	0	1
4	280	960	0	0
5	390	1,210	0	1
6	630	1,830	1	1
7	620	2,050	1	0
8	650	2,420	0	0
9	530	1,710	1	0
10	660	2,200	0	1
11	460	1,360	1	0
12	800	2,500	1	1
13	640	2,300	0	0
14	440	1,420	0	1
15	360	1,300	0	0
16	330	1,050	1	0
17	580	1,700	1	1

RENT VS SIZE, FURN, SWIM

GENERAL LINEAR MODELS PROCEDURE

DEP VARIABLE: RENT

SOURCE	DF	SUM OF SQUARES	MEAN SQUARE	F VALUE	PR > F	R-SQUARE
MODEL	3	385890.03588061	128630.01196020	758.68	0.0001	0.994321
ERROR	13	2204.08176645	169.54475127		STD DEV	
CORRECTED TOTAL	16	388094.11764706		13.02093511		

PARAMETER	ESTIMATE	T FOR H0: PARAMETER=0	PR > |T|	STD ERROR OF ESTIMATE
INTERCEPT	9.72818009	0.91	0.3790	10.68252200
SIZE	0.26865646	42.51	0.0001	0.00631980
FURN	64.82800090	10.18	0.0001	6.36626959
SWIM	55.23936694	8.40	0.0001	6.57436477

Figure 19.9

Computer regression printout: $\widehat{RENT} = b_0 + b_1 SIZE + b_2 FURN + b_3 SWIM$ (17 observations)

for the pleasure of a swimming pool. A house that has a pool and is also furnished is predicted to rent for 64.83 + 55.24 = $120.07 more than a similar unfurnished house that does not have a pool. Thus, ACC decides to rent unfurnished houses without swimming pools since the residents are ready to pay only $55 per month for the privilege of having a swimming pool while ACC would have to charge at least $150 per month for a pool.

19.9 The Multiple Correlation Coefficient

Multiple correlation in multiple regression analysis is the counterpart of simple correlation in simple regression analysis. As we saw earlier, a model of multiple regression such as

$$Y = \beta_0 + \beta_1 X_1 + \beta_2 X_2 + \cdots + \beta_K X_K + u$$

may be estimated to yield

$$\hat{Y} = b_0 + b_1 X_1 + b_2 X_2 + \cdots + b_K X_K$$

The estimated coefficient of determination in multiple regression is denoted by R^2, to distinguish from its counterpart r^2 in simple regression. R^2 is given by the following equation:

$$R^2 = 1 - \frac{\Sigma e^2}{\Sigma(Y - \overline{Y})^2} = 1 - \frac{S_e^2}{S_Y^2} \cdot \frac{n - K - 1}{n - 1} \tag{19.25}$$

This is analogous to the coefficient of determination in simple regression where $K = 1$ and $n - K - 1 = n - 2$. For a large enough sample, R^2 may be approximated by the following:

$$R^2 = 1 - \frac{S_e^2}{S_Y^2} \tag{19.26}$$

The estimated **multiple correlation coefficient** is simply the square root of R^2. Note, though, that in multiple regression, the correlation coefficient is always assigned a positive sign. Therefore we write the following:

$$R = +\sqrt{R^2} \tag{19.27}$$

While the sign of r is determined by the sign of the slope coefficient, b_1, in the simple regression case, the sign of R in the multiple regression case is positive, since different slope coefficients can have different signs.

EXAMPLE 19.5

In Example 18.3 we related the value of U.S. government bonds held by pension funds to the interest rate paid on those bonds. Let us extend this example to a multiple correlation analysis. To avoid undesirable complications, we shall introduce only one more explanatory variable, the interest rate on corporate bonds, which will be denoted by *ICB*. The estimated equation will be

$$\hat{GB} = b_0 + b_1 IGB + b_2 ICB$$

As one can expect, the coefficient b_1 will be positive, since an increase in the interest rate on government bonds (*IGB*) is expected to induce pension funds to buy more bonds (*GB*). On the other hand, when all other factors are held constant, we can expect to find that when the interest rate on corporate bonds (*ICB*) goes up, pension funds find the attractiveness of corporate bonds growing and the demand for government bonds (*GB*) decreasing, and thus we expect to see that b_2 is negative. Suppose the data are as in Table 19.6. Figure 19.10 shows the computer results of the multiple regression

$$\hat{GB} = b_0 + b_1 IGB + b_2 ICB$$

The coefficient of determination, R^2, is equal in this case to 0.9884, meaning that 98.84 percent of the variance of Y is explained by the two explanatory variables *IGB* and *ICB*. According to the computer printout, the variance of *GB* is equal to 108,732 (not shown in Figure 19.10). Using this number and others provided in Figure 19.10, we see that R^2 can also be obtained from Equation 19.25:

$$R^2 = 1 - \frac{S_e^2}{S_Y^2} \cdot \frac{n - K - 1}{n - 1} = 1 - \frac{40.201^2}{108,732.000} \cdot \frac{10 - 2 - 1}{10 - 1}$$
$$= 0.9884$$

TABLE 19.6
Government Bonds Held by Pension Funds and Interest Rate on Government and Corporate Bonds during Ten Quarters

Quarter	GB (millions of dollars)	IGB (percent)	ICB (percent)
1	$2,030.0	7.1%	9.2%
2	1,710.0	6.0	9.2
3	1,790.0	5.3	8.1
4	1,970.0	5.2	7.0
5	2,440.0	7.0	7.5
6	2,326.0	8.4	9.5
7	2,440.0	9.2	10.0
8	1,900.0	7.6	9.9
9	1,740.0	6.0	9.0
10	1,470.0	5.0	9.0

The multiple correlation coefficient is equal to

$$R = +\sqrt{R^2} = +\sqrt{0.9884} = +0.9942$$

The positive sign of R does not mean that the regression slope coefficients are positive. In fact, although the slope coefficient with respect to the first variable is positive, the slope with respect to the second variable is negative.

We shall continue to pursue this example after discussing the partial correlation coefficient.

```
   PROBLEM  TITLE . . . . . .  GOVERNMENT  BOND  HOLDING
NUMBER  OF  CASES  READ . . . . . . . . . . . . .10
VARIABLE           MEAN  STANDARD  DEVIATION  ST.DEV/MEAN     MINIMUM      MAXIMUM
  1  GB         1981.60000       329.74576       .16640   1470.00000   2440.00000
  2  IGB           6.68000         1.42501       .21333      5.00000      9.20000
  3  ICB           8.84000          .99688       .11277      7.00000     10.00000
   REGRESSION  TITLE . . . . . . . . . . . . .  GOVERNMENT  BOND  HOLDING
   DEPENDENT  VARIABLE . . . . . . . . . . .       1  GB
   TOLERANCE . . . . . . . . . . . . . . . .      .0100
ALL  DATA  CONSIDERED  AS  A  SINGLE  GROUP
MULTIPLE  R            .9942          STD.  ERROR  OF  EST.     40.2010
MULTIPLE  R-SQUARE     .9884
ANALYSIS  OF  VARIANCE
                  SUM OF SQUARES    DF     MEAN  SQUARE      F RATIO    P(TAIL)
   REGRESSION       967277.559       2      483638.780      299.259     .00000
   RESIDUAL          11312.841       7        1616.120
                                        STD. REG
   VARIABLE       COEFFICIENT  STD.  ERROR     COEFF       T    P(2 TAIL)
INTERCEPT         2284.446
IGB        2       292.090      11.940        1.262    24.464     0.000
ICB        3      -254.978      17.067        -.771   -14.940     0.000
```

Figure 19.10

Computer printout reproduction showing results of regression of *GB* (denoted *Y*) on *IGB* (denoted X_1) and *ICB* (denoted X_2)

19.10 Partial Correlation

So far, we have introduced simple and multiple correlation. In this section we shall discuss the **partial correlation coefficient**. Consider a dependent variable, Y, with two independent variables, X_1 and X_2, in regression analysis. When the *simple* correlation between Y and X_1 is taken (r_{Y1}), we basically ignore the value of X_2 and calculate a measure pertaining to Y and X_1 only. We leave the variable X_2 "loose" or "uncontrolled." When the *multiple* correlation between Y and X_1 and X_2 is taken ($R_{Y.12}$), we measure the *simultaneous* explanatory power of X_1 and X_2 on the dependent variable Y. Sometimes, however, we want to measure the correlation between Y and X_1 when we *eliminate the effect of X_2 on Y*. No longer do we allow X_2 to vary loosely or in an "uncontrolled" manner. In this case the resulting correlation coefficient is the *partial* correlation coefficient between Y and X_1; it is denoted by $r_{Y1.2}$, where the variable(s) whose subscript follows the dot (in this case X_2) is the one whose impact on Y has been eliminated. The partial determination coefficient between Y and X_1, when there are K independent variables, is $r^2_{Y1.23...K}$. The partial determination coefficient between Y and X_2 is $r^2_{Y2.13...K}$, and so on. We can derive the partial correlation coefficient $r_{Y1.23...K}$ in the following way. First we run the regression of Y (dependent) against all the explanatory variables other than X_1 (namely $X_2, X_3, \ldots, X_K$).

This regression yields the residual values e which are what is left of the Y values after removing the effect of X_2 through X_K. In a similar way, we can remove the effect of X_2 through X_K from the variable X_1, and obtain another set of residuals. The partial correlation $r_{Y1.23...K}$ is equal to the simple correlation between the two residual series.

It can be shown that in the case of two independent variables, the following relationship holds true:

$$r_{Y2.1}^2 = \frac{(1 - r_{Y1}^2) - (1 - R_{Y.12}^2)}{1 - r_{Y1}^2} = 1 - \frac{1 - R_{Y.12}^2}{1 - r_{Y1}^2} \qquad \textbf{(19.28)}$$

Equation 19.28 should be interpreted thus: the ratio $(1 - R_{Y.12}^2)/(1 - r_{Y1}^2)$ is that of the unexplained variance in Y in the multiple regression of Y on X_1 and X_2, to the unexplained variance of Y in the simple regression of Y on X_1 only. Thus $r_{Y2.1}^2$ measures the incremental contribution of X_2 to the proportion of explained variance of Y in the regression of Y on X_1 and X_2 out of the *unexplained* variance of Y in the regression of Y on X_1 alone. A numerical example will clarify this point.

In Example 18.3 we related GB to IGB only. The coefficient of determination was $r_{Y1}^2 = 0.6198$. Thus the proportion of unexplained variance in that regression was

$$1 - r_{Y1}^2 = 1 - 0.6198 = 0.3802$$

In Example 19.5, after inclusion of ICB (which is denoted by X_2), we got

$$R_{Y.12}^2 = 0.9884$$

so that

$$1 - R_{Y.12}^2 = 1 - 0.9884 = 0.0116$$

Out of the total fraction of the unexplained variance from the first regression (0.3802), a total of $0.3802 - 0.0116 = 0.3686$ was explained in the second regression by inclusion of the variable X_2 (or ICB). The partial coefficient of determination between Y and X_2 is

$$r_{Y2.1}^2 = \frac{0.3802 - 0.0116}{0.3802} = \frac{0.3686}{0.3802} = 0.9695$$

The result should be interpreted as follows: after IGB provides its explanation for the variance of GB, the variable ICB can explain 96.95 percent of the *remaining* variance of GB.

Chapter Summary and Review

1. The population relationship is

$$Y = \beta_0 + \beta_1 X_1 + \beta_2 X_2 + \cdots + \beta_K X_K + u$$

2. The sample relationship is

$$Y = b_0 + b_1 X_1 + \cdots + b_K X_K + e$$

3. The normal equations are derived by minimizing

$$\Sigma e^2 = \Sigma(Y - b_0 - b_1 X_1 - b_2 X_2 - \cdots - b_K X_K)^2$$

4. Testing hypotheses concerning β_1: apply the statistic

$$T = \frac{b_i - \beta_i}{S_{b_i}} \sim t^{(n - K - 1)}$$

where S_{b_i} stands for the standard error of b_i, n denotes the number of observations, and K is the number of explanatory variables.

5. High degree of correlation (multicollinearity) between the explanatory variables may cause the statistic T to be insignificant.

6. Stepwise regression: the variables enter the regression step by step according to their contribution to the increase of R^2.

7. Dummy variables (or indicator variables) are assigned only the values 1 or 0.

8. The coefficient of determination is

$$R^2 = 1 - \frac{\Sigma e^2}{\Sigma(Y - \overline{Y})^2} = 1 - \frac{S_e^2}{S_Y^2} \cdot \frac{n - K - 1}{n - 1}$$

9. $0 \le R^2 \le 1$

10. The multiple sample correlation is always positive: $R = +\sqrt{R^2}$ and $0 \le R \le 1$

11. The partial correlation coefficient $r_{Y1.23\ldots K}$ is a simple correlation coefficient between two sets of regression residuals. The first set is from the regression of Y (dependent) on the variables X_2 through X_K, and the second set is from the regression of X_1 (dependent) on X_2 through X_K.

Problems

19.1. The following is an estimated equation of a regression plane:

$$\hat{Y} = 2 + 3X_1 + 2X_2$$

Calculate the value $\sum\limits_{i=1}^{3} e_i^2$ for the following three sample points:

$$Y = 8; \quad X_1 = 1; \quad X_2 = 1$$
$$Y = 10; \quad X_1 = 2; \quad X_2 = 4$$
$$Y = 10; \quad X_1 = 3; \quad X_2 = 4$$

19.2. Suppose we obtain the following estimated regression equation:

$$\hat{Y} = 5 + 2X_1 - 4X_2$$

Is it true that an increase of X_1 by two units is equivalent to a decrease of X_2 by one unit, in terms of the impact on $\hat{Y}$? Explain.

19.3. Using your own numerical example, demonstrate that the coefficient b_i of an independent variable X_i in a multiple regression equation represents the impact of a one-unit increase in X_i when all of the other explanatory variables are held *unchanged*.

19.4. Let Y be annual consumption (in thousands of dollars), X_1 annual income (in thousands of dollars), and X_2 formal education (in number of years of schooling). A study shows the following relationship between the variables:

$$\hat{Y} = 3.000 + 0.500X_1 + 0.125X_2$$

Explain the meaning of each of the three coefficients.

19.5. An insurance company pays its sales representatives a fixed weekly wage (X_1) plus a percentage of net sales made directly by the representative (X_2). The firm, which operates nationwide, is interested in paying the representatives a combination of fixed wage and a percentage of sales that will maximize the sales of insurance policies. Currently the company estimates that the net sales made by a representative are related to his or her income components in the following way:

$$\hat{Y} = 40X_1 + 9X_2$$

where $\hat{Y}$ and X_1 are measured in hundreds of dollars and X_2 is measured in percentage points (e.g., if $X_2 = 1$, the representative's commission is 1 percent of his or her net sales). Currently, $X_1 = 2$ and $X_2 = 1$.

(a) What is the estimated net sales of a representative?
(b) The firm considers adding $100 to the fixed wage component (X_1) or alternatively increasing X_2 from 1 to 1.5. Which of these two alternatives results in a higher estimated average net sales?

19.6. The prices of stocks are related to the average level of earnings per share (EPS) as well as to the variance of EPS. Below is a sample of stock prices, average EPS level in recent years, and standard deviation of the respective EPS.

Price	Average EPS	Standard deviation of EPS
50	6	2
46	5	3
12	1	1
27	6	7
30	3	3
19	5	6

Estimate the coefficients of the regression

$$\hat{Y} = b_0 + b_1X_1 + b_2X_2$$

where Y is the price, X_1 is average EPS, and X_2 is the standard deviation of EPS. Explain the coefficients.

19.7. To test how coupons help advertisers increase sales, a regression analysis was applied to the use of coupons to promote the consumption of processed orange juice. The variables considered were:

1. Total number of coupons redeemed (*CR*)
2. Total coupon drop (the number of coupons issued) (*C*)
3. Coupon value (*V*)
4. Time elapsed since initial coupon drop (*T*)

The reason the relationship of these variables should be studied is that it provides answers to questions that must be addressed during the planning stage of a coupon drop. What, for example, is the size of coupon drop needed to achieve a particular level of consumer redemption? What is the lagged response to an initial coupon drop? How does one plan the budget in view of the anticipated sales activities following a coupon drop?

The data are shown in Table P19.7.

TABLE P19.7

Observation	CR (thousands of coupons)	C (thousands of coupons)	V (cents)	T (months)
1	6,149	40,000	10	5
2	5,566	70,000	15	1
3	7,060	30,000	15	10
4	5,542	50,000	15	1
5	2,171	20,000	10	6
6	4,064	50,000	7	5
7	9,007	40,000	10	12
8	7,569	30,000	20	4
9	5,368	50,000	10	2
10	3,200	60,000	5	3
11	8,863	36,000	20	10
12	1,540	15,000	4	8

(a) Run a simple regression of *CR* (dependent) on *C* (independent). Explain the meaning of the regression equation, and predict the coupon redemption for a 60-million coupon drop.

(b) Run a multiple regression analysis on the computer, using *CR* as the dependent variable and *C*, *V*, and *T* as the independent variables. Write down the regression equation and explain it.

(c) Compare the regression coefficients of the variable *C* in part *a* and in part *b*. What is the importance of including *all* of the relevant variables in a regression analysis?

(d) On the basis of the results of part *b*, what is the best prediction of coupon redemption in an advertising campaign for processed orange juice if each coupon is good for 5 cents and the coupon drop is 65 million coupons? Give your prediction for coupon redemption at the end of each of the first 12 months after the coupon drop. Repeat your calculations for 10-cent and 15-cent coupon values and draw a chart showing three graphs of the predicted coupon redemption (vertical axis) as a function of time (horizontal axis). What is the predicted *value* of the total coupons redeemed after six months for coupons worth 8 cents?

(e) Again on the basis of the multiple regression equation, predict the coupon redemption after six months if each coupon is good for 10 cents. Give your prediction for the following alternative coupon drops (in millions of coupons): 10, 20, 30, 40, 50, 60, and 70.

Draw a chart showing the relationship between coupon redemption and coupon drop six months after the drop for a coupon value of 10 cents.

(f) Do you think the time variable (*T*) is indeed linearly related to *CR*, as we assumed in this problem? Explain.

19.8. The starting salary of graduates of a certain college of business administration depends on the student's grade-point average (GPA) and his or her major. Table P19.8 presents a sample of starting salaries of students who graduated recently.

TABLE P19.8

Salary (dollars per year)	GPA	Major[a]	Salary (dollars per year)	GPA	Major[a]
$18,000	3.1	M	$18,500	3.4	M
20,500	3.3	A	19,500	2.6	O
17,500	2.7	M	18,750	3.8	M
18,500	2.5	F	20,000	2.7	F
21,000	3.9	F	23,000	4.0	O
16,500	2.1	O	19,500	2.8	A
21,000	2.8	F	18,500	2.9	M
17,500	2.9	M	18,500	3.2	F
16,800	2.9	O	17,500	3.0	M
17,000	2.0	A	18,750	3.4	F

[a]A = accounting; F = finance; M = marketing; O = other

(a) Estimate the relationship between salary and GPA (only).
(b) Estimate the relationship between salary and GPA and major where salary is the dependent variable.
(c) Discuss the significance of the variables and the explanatory power of the model.

19.9. A sporting goods firm has four stores, one in each section of a large city. The firm wants to model its sales in the city as a function of the average number of weekly shoppers in the malls in which the stores are located, and the location of the stores. Data were collected for a number of weeks and are given in Table P19.9.

TABLE P19.9

Mall	Number of mall shoppers (thousands)	Sales (thousands of dollars)	Mall	Number of mall shoppers (thousands)	Sales (thousands of dollars)
1	19	16	3	30	15
1	8	9	3	19	9
1	27	21	3	5	5
1	41	35	3	12	8
1	33	32	3	11	5
1	26	19	3	18	11
1	6	7	3	22	19
1	17	11	3	7	3
1	13	8	3	29	15
1	27	20	3	26	13
2	60	58	3	27	15
2	51	49	3	12	6
2	72	80	4	41	55
2	48	45	4	41	40
2	31	37	4	19	25
2	21	16	4	29	32
2	33	31	4	30	36
2	74	66	4	16	16

(a) Estimate the regression of sales as a function of number of mall shoppers and location. *Hint*: You need three dummy variables for the four store locations. Define

$$X_1 = \begin{cases} 1 & \text{if mall location 1} \\ 0 & \text{otherwise} \end{cases}$$

$$X_2 = \begin{cases} 1 & \text{if mall location 2} \\ 0 & \text{otherwise} \end{cases}$$

$$X_3 = \begin{cases} 1 & \text{if mall location 3} \\ 0 & \text{otherwise} \end{cases}$$

(b) Discuss the regression coefficients, their meaning, and their significance. Do the explanatory variables in the regression provide an adequate explanation for sales variability? Explain.

(c) *Optional.* Insert an intentional "error" in the data: change the number of shoppers in the last observation in location 3 from 12 to 120. Run a regression of sales on the number of shoppers (omitting the dummy variables for location). Draw a scatter diagram of the data and the estimated regression line. Explain the effect of the "error." Support your answer by also drawing a scatter diagram of the residuals. Correct the "error," rerun the regression, draw the scatter diagrams of the data and of the residuals, and discuss.

19.10. The management of a department store hypothesizes that the sales of a cosmetic product depend on the store's display. Three different displays are considered: *A*, *B*, and *C*. The management has collected data over a 16-week period. The sample data are shown in Table P19.10.

TABLE P19.10

Sales	Number of store shoppers (in thousands)	Display
$2,150	5.1	B
3,460	5.6	A
3,170	5.5	A
980	4.7	C
1,240	2.4	A
1,100	4.5	C
3,080	5.0	A
950	4.7	C
1,550	2.8	A
760	1.8	B
2,460	5.0	B
3,170	4.5	A
540	3.1	C
1,230	2.6	B
2,110	4.0	A
1,990	4.1	B

(a) Define dummy variables for the product display.

(b) Run a regression explaining sales as a function of number of store shoppers and display. Explain your results.

(c) Run a regression of sales as a function of display only. Explain the results of this regression, comparing the regression coefficients with the average sales for each of the three displays.

(d) Disregard the variable "number of store shoppers" again, and perform a one-way analysis of variance on the sales data according to display. Compare the results of the analysis of variance to the regression results in part *c*.

19.11. Let X_1, X_2, X_3, and X_4 be four dummy variables representing four populations with means μ_1, μ_2, μ_3, and μ_4, respectively. Show that the hypothesis

$$H_0: \quad \mu_1 = \mu_2 = \mu_3 = \mu_4$$

in the analysis of variance is identical to the hypothesis

$$H_0: \quad \beta_1 = \beta_2 = \beta_3 = 0$$

in the regression

$$Y = \beta_0 + \beta_1 X_1 + \beta_2 X_2 + \beta_3 X_3 + u$$

19.12. Using the data in Problem 16.14 (Chapter 16), solve the problem with regression analysis. Denote the sales by Y and define

$$X_1 = \begin{cases} 1 & \text{if the sale was by store 1} \\ 0 & \text{if the sale was not by store 1} \end{cases}$$

$$X_2 = \begin{cases} 1 & \text{if the sale was by store 2} \\ 0 & \text{if the sale was not by store 2} \end{cases}$$

Run the regression $\hat{Y} = b_0 + b_1 X_1 + b_2 X_2$, and compare your results to those obtained by using analysis of variance.

19.13. The hourly wage of industrial employees (Y), the employee experience (X_1), and the employee education (X_2) are presented below.

Hourly wage (in dollars) (Y)	Employee experience (in years) (X_1)	Employee education (years in school) (X_2)
$10	10	10
15	10	12
20	4	16
12	20	8
12	12	12
9	3	10
5	2	8
4	1	8
8	6	4
25	5	20
40	20	15
10	8	9
11	9	12

Figure P19.13 shows the computer printout of the regression $\hat{Y} = b_0 + b_1 X_1 + b_2 X_2$. Interpret the computer printout. In particular, what are the coefficients b_1 and b_2 and what are their meanings? Are they significantly different from zero at $\alpha = 0.05$? What is the regression coefficient of determination and what is the value of the standard error of estimate, S_e? Do the variables X_1 and X_2 when taken together, have statistical significance in this regression? Explain.

19.14. In the multiple regression

$$Y = b_0 + b_1 X_1 + b_2 X_2 + b_3 X_3 + e$$

NUMBER OF CASES READ. 13

VARIABLE	MEAN	STANDARD DEVIATION	COEFFICIENT OF VARIATION	MINIMUM	MAXIMUM
1 WAGE	13.92307	9.68213	0.69540	4.00000	40.00000
2 EXP	8.46153	6.11849	0.72309	1.00000	20.00000
3 EDU	11.07692	4.15254	0.37488	4.00000	20.00000

MULTIPLE R   0.8632   STD. ERROR OF EST.   5.3547
MULTIPLE R-SQUARE   0.7451

ANALYSIS OF VARIANCE

	SUM OF SQUARES	DF	MEAN SQUARE	F RATIO	P(TAIL)
REGRESSION	838.199	2	419.100	14.617	0.00108
RESIDUAL	286.724	10	28.672		

VARIABLE		COEFFICIENT	STD. ERROR	STD. REG COEFF	T	P(2 TAIL)	TOLERANCE
INTERCEPT		-10.02590					
EXP	2	0.73780	0.254	0.466	2.908	0.016	0.991842
EDU	3	1.59846	0.374	0.686	4.277	0.002	0.991842

Figure P19.13
Computer regression printout

it has been found that $S_{b_1} = S_{b_2} = S_{b_3}$ where S_{b_i} is the standard error of the ith coefficient. It has been claimed that "if b_1 is not significantly different from zero (say at $\alpha = 0.05$), then b_2 and b_3 must also be insignificantly different from zero (at the same level of significance $\alpha = 0.05$)." Evaluate this statement.

19.15. In the multiple regression

$$\hat{Y} = b_0 + b_1X_1 + b_2X_2$$

it has been found that $\Sigma e_i^2 = 0$. Which of the following must hold as a result?

(a) $b_1 = b_2 = 0$
(b) $b_1 = b_2 = 1$
(c) $b_0 = 0$
(d) $R^2 = 1$
(e) $b_1 = b_2$ but is not necessarily equal to 1.

Explain your answer.

19.16. The weekly income, Y, as a function of age, X_1 (expressed in years), and number of years on the job, X_2, is given by the following regression equation:

$$\hat{Y} = 200 + 5X_1 + 10X_2$$

(a) According to your prediction, which of the following has a higher expected income: a person who is 40 years of age and 10 years on the job or a person who is 35 years of age and 18 years on the job?
(b) What must the deviations e_i from the regression plane be if the two people mentioned in part a actually earn \$450 per week?

19.17. In Example 19.3, we discussed three regression equations:

$$\widehat{AVERAGE\ RATE} = b_0 + b_1(RISK1)$$

$$\widehat{AVERAGE\ RATE} = b_0 + b_1(RISK2)$$

$$\widehat{AVERAGE\ RATE} = b_0 + b_1(RISK1) + b_2(RISK2)$$

The coefficients of determination of the three regressions were, respectively,

$$r^2 = 0.210$$
$$r^2 = 0.380$$
$$R^2 = 0.381$$

Calculate $r^2_{Y1.2}$ and $r^2_{Y2.1}$. Does *RISK1* contribute an explanatory power to the regression, considering the contribution of *RISK2*? Explain.

19.18. In Example 19.4 we discussed two regression equations:

$$\widehat{DIV} = b_0 + b_1(NI)$$

$$\widehat{DIV} = b_0 + b_1(NI) + b_2(INF)$$

The coefficients of determination of these regressions are, respectively,

$$r^2 = 0.7612$$
$$R^2 = 0.7919$$

The coefficient of determination in the regression

$$\widehat{DIV} = b_0 + b_1(INF)$$

is equal to 0.3584. Calculate $r_{Y1.2}^2$ and $r_{Y2.1}^2$.

19.19. A firm's personnel department uses an aptitude test as a basis for hiring employees. The test grades of a sample of employees, their actual performance (both are measured on a scale from 0 to 10), and their IQs are as follows:

IQ	Test grade	Actual performance
102	5	8
95	6	8
140	10	10
79	2	5
110	9	7
86	5	4
100	7	10
110	7	6

(a) Denoting IQ by X_1, test grade by X_2, and the actual performance by Y, calculate the simple correlations r_{Y1}, r_{Y2}, and r_{12}.
(b) Calculate the multiple correlation coefficient $R_{Y.12}$.
(c) Calculate the partial correlations $r_{Y1.2}$ and $r_{Y2.1}$.
(d) Explain the meaning of each of the coefficients you calculated in parts a, b, and c.

Does the inclusion of IQ as an indicator of employee performance on the job have any merit? Explain.

19.20. In a multiple regression of the form

$$\hat{Y} = b_0 + b_1X_1 + b_2X_2$$

the following sample (of size $n = 100$) figures were obtained:

$$\Sigma Y = \Sigma X_1 = \Sigma X_2 = 100$$

$$\Sigma X_1Y = 200 \quad \Sigma X_2Y = 300$$

$$\Sigma X_1^2 = 150 \quad \Sigma X_2^2 = 200 \quad \text{and} \quad \Sigma X_1X_2 = 200$$

Calculate the regression coefficients, b_0, b_1, and b_2.

19.21. A textile firm investigates the relationship between sales (Y), advertising expense (X_1), and the price of the product (X_2). Y and X_1 are expressed in thousands of dollars, and X_2 is expressed in dollars per unit sold. The regression analysis reveals the following relationship:

$$\hat{Y} = 100 + 2X_1 - 10X_2$$

(a) Interpret the coefficients b_1 and b_2. Explain why this linear relationship must at most be considered valid only over a given range of X_2.
(b) What is the firm's expected sales if advertising is set at $100,000 and the product price is set at $10?
(c) Suppose the production costs (not including advertising expense) are as follows:

Sales (thousands of dollars)	Production costs (thousands of dollars)
$150	50
250	80
350	160
450	260

Assume that the firm has decided to set the price, X_2, at $5 per unit. Which of the following levels of advertising expense would be expected to yield the highest net profit: $50,000, $100,000, $150,000, or $200,000? Explain.

Case Problems

19.1. Money market funds are investment pools that invest in short-term securities such as Treasury bills, commercial paper, bankers acceptances, and so on. The performance (measured in yield) depends on the funds' characteristics and management, as well as on their investment policy, namely, the percentage holding of the various types of securities. To see the reasons for the differences in the performance of the money market funds (see Case Problem 18.2), use Data Set 3, Appendix B, Table B.3, and do the following:

(a) Run the regression of yield (*YIELD*) as a dependent variable against the following explanatory variables: total net assets (*ASSET*), average maturity (*MATUR*), and percentage holding of U.S. Treasury bills (*TBILLS*). Explain your results and discuss their significance. Note that U.S. Treasury bills are low-risk–low-yield securities.

(b) Run the same regression as in part *a*, adding the following explanatory variables: percentage holding in U.S. government securities other than Treasury bills (*OTHERUS*) and percentage holding of certificates of deposit (*CD*).

(c) Run a stepwise regression of the yield on the following explanatory variables: repos (*REPOS*), certificates of deposit (*CD*), commercial paper (*CP*), total net assets (*ASSET*), and U.S. Treasury bills (*TBILLS*). However, instead of including the total net assets as an explanatory variable, use the following dummy variable:

$$D = \begin{cases} 0 & \text{if net asset value is \$100 million or less} \\ 1 & \text{if net asset value is more than \$100 million} \end{cases}$$

Interpret your results. What is the interpretation of the coefficient of the net asset variable (*D*)?

(d) Perform the regression of part *c* using a stepwise procedure. Discuss the importance and contribution of each explanatory variable to the regression.

19.2. Table CP19.2 presents General Motors's production, number of imported cars, per capita gross national product, and gas prices for a recent period of 20 years. Perform a stepwise regression analysis on the data, using GM's production as the dependent variable. Explain your results.

TABLE CP19.2

Year	GM production (number of cars)	Import (number of cars)	GNP per capita (dollars)	Gas prices (dollars)
1	2,726,562	288,741	4,118	0.205
2	3,741,527	387,204	4,289	0.204
3	4,077,300	426,658	4,398	0.201
4	3,956,590	553,189	4,566	0.200
5	4,949,408	590,323	4,782	0.208
6	4,448,634	970,635	5,009	0.216
7	4,117,810	1,190,857	5,089	0.226
8	4,592,077	1,084,350	5,271	0.230
9	4,421,002	1,173,499	5,365	0.239
10	2,979,187	1,331,971	5,293	0.246
11	4,852,949	1,637,785	5,404	0.252
12	4,775,381	1,764,494	5,649	0.244
13	5,252,736	1,975,589	5,921	0.269
14	3,556,953	1,578,678	5,835	0.404
15	3,671,464	1,703,916	5,713	0.455
16	4,891,593	1,735,490	5,963	0.474
17	5,262,192	2,397,574	5,227	0.507
18	5,285,700	2,388,344	6,454	0.531
19	5,092,614	2,801,216	6,588	0.717
20	4,064,546	2,882,495	6,504	0.995

Source: GM production: *Ward's Automotive Yearbook*, various issues; import and GNP per capita: U.S. Department of Commerce, Bureau of Economic Analysis, *Survey of Current Business*, various issues; gas prices: U.S. Department of Energy, *Monthly Review on Petroleum Share*, various issues.

19.3. Referring to Data Set 3, Appendix B, Table B.3, let us denote the yield by Y, total net assets by X_1, average maturity by X_2, percentage holding of U.S. Treasury bills by X_3, and percentage holding of commercial paper by X_4.

(a) Determine the simple correlation between Y and X_4.

(b) Calculate the coefficient of determination of the regression $\hat{Y} = b_0 + b_1X_1 + b_2X_2 + b_3X_3 + b_4X_4$ and explain its meaning.

(c) Calculate the partial coefficient of determination $r^2_{Y4.123}$ and explain its meaning. *Hint*: Run the regression $\hat{Y} = b_0 + b_1X_1 + b_2X_2 + b_3X_3$, and then run $\hat{X}_4 = b_0 + b_1RESID$ where *RESID* is the variable that represents the residuals from the first regression.

PART 5

OTHER SELECTED TOPICS

Part 5 of this book is devoted to selected topics that are not directly discussed earlier in the book. Chapter 20 presents the analysis of time series; Chapter 21 deals with index numbers—a subject that has become increasingly important due to fluctuating inflation rates in recent years; Chapter 22 covers the very important topic of nonparametric statistics; and Chapter 23 is devoted to decision making under uncertainty.

The applications and examples in this part of the book concern production trends, the random walk theory, investment in mutual funds, and other topics.

TIME SERIES ANALYSIS

20

20.1 Introduction

This chapter is devoted to the description and analysis of time-series movements. A **time series** consists of *data concerning the value of a variable over time*, such as monthly sales of a given firm, quarterly inventory levels of an industry, and annual domestic air traffic. Forecasting future values of a time series is of great importance to management and government, as errors in prediction may lead to substandard performance and even insolvency or policy blunders. In order to provide quality forecasts, we must familiarize ourselves with time-series patterns and learn how to apply our knowledge of past patterns to make short-term and long-term time-series forecasts.

At first glance you might think that time-series trends can be studied fully by means of regression analysis. Most time series, however, are subject to time-related movements that violate the basic assumptions of regression analysis. The data points of time series are often *not* scattered around the regression line in a random manner. Rather, they tend to *cluster* above and below the line, contrary to what regression analysis presumes.

For an example, consider the retail sales of women's apparel. The monthly sales data for the period January 1974–July 1980 are shown in Table 20.1

TABLE 20.1

Retail Sales of Women's Apparel, January 1974–July 1980

(millions of dollars)

YEAR	JAN	FEB	MAR	APR	MAY	JUN	JUL	AUG	SEP	OCT	NOV	DEC
1974	744	689	824	917	921	880	879	937	925	997	1008	1519
1975	813	741	943	889	1032	947	932	1071	1040	1124	1126	1716
1976	918	856	971	1083	1049	1047	1051	1064	1132	1208	1212	1791
1977	867	872	1030	1065	1027	989	977	1090	1136	1215	1262	1928
1978	864	846	1158	1101	1133	1114	1104	1257	1316	1321	1397	2140
1979	994	948	1239	1257	1254	1208	1167	1359	1309	1394	1507	2147
1980	1112	1046	1257	1314	1335	1203	1250	*******	*******	*******	*******	*******

Source: Data obtained from U.S. Bureau of the Census.

and in Figure 20.1 (solid line). A clear regularity appears in the data, with sales booming in December of every year, evidently as a result of Christmas shopping. If we want to predict the monthly sales of women's apparel, we can do considerably better than just using a fitted regression line through the data. If we were to use only such a line, we would be neglecting a considerable amount of valuable information. When predicting December sales, for example, we can and should take into consideration the expected positive deviation above the fitted line, a result of the seasonal peak in sales. Similarly, when predicting sales for any other month, we should also take into consideration the nonrandom behavior of the data. For example, January and February sales of each year are markedly below the average for the year, a fact that must be taken into consideration when making predictions of future sales for these months. There are a number of alternative methods by which knowledge of seasonal behavior of time series can be used. Among them are (1) the method of **moving average (MA)**, and (2) the use of **autoregression (AR)**.

Figure 20.1

Retail sales of women's apparel, January 1974–July 1980: a computer-generated chart

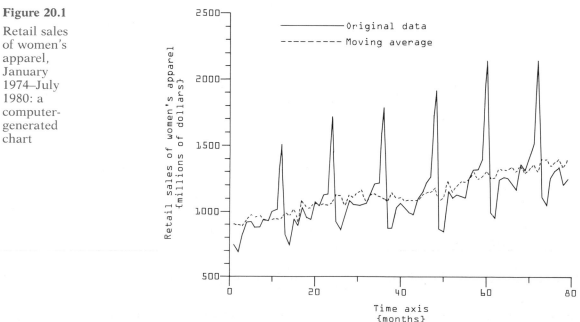

A moving average of a time series replaces time-series data by the mean of a sequence of observations of a time interval that covers the current observation: the observation of any season (month, quarter, and so on) is replaced by the (weighted) mean of the current as well as earlier and later observations. The number of observations covered determines the *term* of the moving average. The result is a relatively smooth series of data such as that described by the broken line in Figure 20.1. By comparing an actual observation in a time series with its corresponding moving average, we get a measure of the deviation that can be used to predict future levels of the time series. By comparing the actual data (solid line) with the moving average (broken line) in Figure 20.1, we can identify the periods in which the actual series regularly appears above or below the moving average, measure the magnitude of the deviation, and use this information for prediction.

Autoregression is another way of dealing with the behavior of time-series data. It focuses on the study of the relationship between one observation and the observations preceding it by k periods (where k is the *lag* of the autoregression). For example, a *first-order* autoregression model with a lag of one period relates Y_t to Y_{t-1}:

$$\hat{Y}_t = b_0 + b_1 Y_{t-1}$$

A first-order model with a lag of k periods takes the form

$$\hat{Y}_t = b_0 + b_1 Y_{t-k}$$

There are autoregressive models of higher orders. The *kth order* autoregression relates Y_t to k previous values of Y. For example, a third-order autoregression takes the form

$$Y_t = b_0 + b_1 Y_{t-1} + b_2 Y_{t-2} + b_3 Y_{t-3}$$

The idea behind the autoregression model is that the level of a variable can be predicted by the level and the trend of the observations in the time series of interest.

The most modern approach to time-series analysis is one that integrates the moving-average and the autoregressive models. It is called ARIMA (autoregressive integrated moving average) model. Box and Jenkins[1] have developed an approach by which ARIMA models can be used. The main stages in setting up a Box-Jenkins forecasting model are:

1. Model identification: Examine the data to see which *term* of moving average and which *order* of autoregression are most appropriate among the ARIMA models.
2. Estimation: Estimate the parameters of the chosen model by least squares.
3. Diagnostic checking: Examine the residuals from the fitted model to determine if the fitted model is adequate.

A detailed description of ARIMA models and the Box-Jenkins procedure is

[1] G. E. Box and G. M. Jenkins, *Time Series Analysis: Forecasting and Control* (San Francisco: Holden-Day, 1976).

beyond the scope of this book. We will confine our analysis to the classical decomposition of time series, which identifies four components in a time series:

1. Secular trend (denoted by T)
2. Seasonal factor (denoted by S)
3. Cyclical factor (denoted by C)
4. Irregular factor (denoted by I)

The **secular trend** is the *long-term pattern* of the data. The **seasonal factor** measures *variations in the activity level of a variable relative to the average annual level of activity;* they are therefore variations of the activity within the course of a year. The **cyclical factor** measures *variations in the level of activity about the long-term trend.* While seasonal variations occur within the course of a year, cyclical movements are those of annual activity levels around the long-term trend. The **irregular factor,** as the name indicates, measures *erratic and irregular activity variations*, specific to the points in time in which they occur; these variations are not explained by the other three components of time series.

The time-series model we present here is known as the **multiplicative model**, since it expresses Y, the variable whose activity level is being studied, as the product of the time-series components. Thus

$$Y = TCSI \qquad (20.1)$$

In Equation 20.1, the value of T is measured in the same units as Y (usually dollars), and the value of each of the other three factors is measured as an index number divided by 100. For example, the average seasonal index is assigned the value 1.00. If in a certain season the seasonal index, S, is equal to 1.10, the activity level in the season is 10 percent above the average, and if S is equal to 0.90, the activity level is 10 percent below the average. The multiplicative model, then, identifies factors associated with each component in such a way that when the components are multiplied, the value of Y is obtained. Let us deal with and explain each of the four components in detail, starting with the secular trend.

20.2 The Secular Trend

The secular trend is denoted by T, and it represents the long-term trend of a dependent variable, Y, whose behavior is being studied. Y usually represents such variables as sales, expenditures, consumption, production, or the like.

TYPES OF SECULAR TRENDS

Although each time series exhibits its own specific trend, such trends may be classified into the several types most frequently observed. These types of trends are depicted in Figure 20.2. In Figure 20.2a, an increasing linear trend is presented. Along this trend line the variable Y grows by an equal absolute

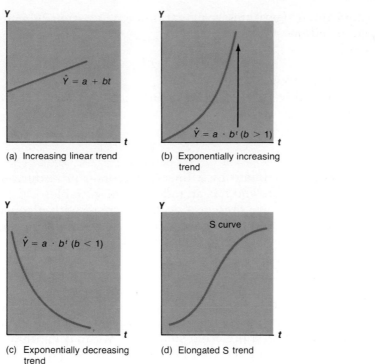

Figure 20.2

Alternative
secular-trend
patterns

amount each period. This relationship between Y and t (time) can be estimated by a simple regression line of Y on t:

$$\hat{Y} = b_0 + b_1 t \qquad \text{(20.2)}$$

Note that a negative value of b_1 should be interpreted as a decreasing linear trend. In Equation 20.2, the value t stands for the year. In Section 20.4 we will work out an example of an estimated trend line. Although a linear growth pattern is not very typical when the activity level Y is observed over a very long time (such as several decades), fitting a linear trend is sometimes useful to approximate the pattern of a shorter period, such as 10 to 20 years.

Figure 20.2b is an example of an exponentially increasing trend. Along this line, the *rate of increase* in Y is constant. Thus, the absolute increase in Y grows as time passes.[2] The estimated relationship between Y and t in this case is

$$\hat{Y} = b_0 \cdot b_1^t \qquad (b > 1) \qquad \text{(20.3)}$$

---

[2] Suppose $b_0 = 1{,}000$ and $b_1 = 1.10$. Let t be arbitrarily equal to 10, 11, and 12 and compute the respective $\hat{Y}$ values:

$$\hat{Y}_{10} = 1{,}000 \cdot 1.10^{10} = 2{,}593.74$$

$$\hat{Y}_{11} = 1{,}000 \cdot 1.10^{11} = 2{,}853.12$$

$$\hat{Y}_{12} = 1{,}000 \cdot 1.10^{12} = 3{,}138.43$$

The *absolute change* between t_{11} and t_{12} is $3{,}138.43 - 2{,}853.12 = 285.31$, and the *absolute change* between t_{10} and t_{11} is $2{,}853.12 - 2{,}593.74 = 259.38$. Thus, the change in the second period is greater when measured in the absolute. In both periods, however, there is a 10 percent increase over the previous period's Y level: $285.31/2{,}853.12 = 259.38/2{,}593.74 = 0.10$ (or 10 percent).

By taking the logarithm, we may transform Equation 20.3 into a linear equation, as follows:

$$\log \hat{Y} = \log b_0 + t \log b_1 \qquad \textbf{(20.4)}$$

and if we denote $\hat{Y}^* = \log \hat{Y}$, $b_0^* = \log b_0$, and $b_1^* = \log b_1$, we may simplify and get

$$\hat{Y}^* = b_0^* + b_1^* t \qquad \textbf{(20.5)}$$

which we can estimate by a linear regression procedure using Y^* as the dependent variable and t as an independent variable.

In Figure 20.2c we present a declining trend with a constant rate of decrease. This function is also exponential, except that the constant b_1 is less than 1:

$$\hat{Y} = b_0 \cdot b_1^t \qquad (b_1 < 1) \qquad \textbf{(20.6)}$$

This kind of trend is typical of the consumption or production of a product or line of products or services with a declining demand—often because of the introduction of a preferred substitute. We may estimate this trend line by linear regression after taking the logarithms of Equation 20.6.

Finally, Figure 20.2d describes the most commonly observed growth curve. Its shape is like an elongated *S* and is indeed often called an *S* curve. In fact, the growth patterns described in Figure 20.2a and 20.2b could sometimes serve as approximations to some segments of the *S* curve. Thus, while linear and exponential curves are often used to project conditions 10 to 15 years in the future, longer-term projections often should use an *S*-curve trend pattern.

SECULAR TRENDS IN ACTUAL ECONOMIC DATA

Let us now examine some examples of secular trends of actual and typical economic time series. First, we present the per capita consumption of cotton and synthetic fibers in the United States from 1948 to 1979. The data are given in Table 20.2 and presented graphically in Figure 20.3.

TABLE 20.2
Per Capita Consumption of Cotton and Synthetic Fibers, United States, 1948–79
(pounds)

Year	Cotton fibers	Synthetic fibers
1948	27.5	7.8
1949	23.3	6.7
1950	29.4	9.5
1951	29.2	9.0
1952	26.5	8.9
1953	26.3	9.0
1954	23.8	8.7
1955	25.3	11.0
1956	25.0	9.7
1957	22.6	9.9
1958	21.3	9.6

TABLE 20.2 (*Continued*)
Per Capita Consumption of Cotton and Synthetic Fibers, United States, 1948–79
(pounds)

Year	Cotton fibers	Synthetic fibers
1959	24.0	11.3
1960	23.3	9.9
1961	21.9	10.7
1962	22.9	12.4
1963	21.8	14.3
1964	22.8	16.2
1965	23.9	18.3
1966	25.1	20.2
1967	23.5	21.4
1968	21.9	26.7
1969	20.9	27.9
1970	19.7	27.8
1971	20.5	33.1
1972	20.0	37.8
1973	18.5	42.1
1974	16.2	36.3
1975	15.1	35.2
1976	17.2	38.1
1977	16.0	41.8
1978	16.2	43.2
1979	15.1	42.7

Source: *Commodity Yearbook,* various issues.

Several important observations can be made concerning per capita fiber consumption. First, the decline of cotton consumption is related to the increase in synthetic fiber consumption. Thus, long-run projections of these two items are likely to be affected by mutual interaction. Second, although the trend of consumption of both types of fiber is nonlinear, a linear trend

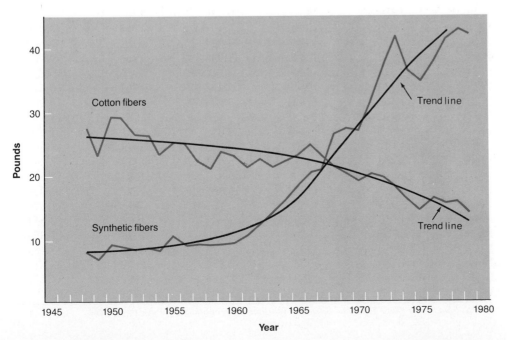

Figure 20.3

Per capita consumption of cotton and synthetic fibers, United States, 1948–79 can provide a fairly good approximation for time intervals within the 1948–79 period, such as the periods 1948–60 and 1968–79. This implies that linear trends can be used for short-term projection if we are careful to avoid using linear trend lines when trend inflection points are approached. Third, it is far easier to fit a trend line to past data than to predict how the trend will continue. The fiber-consumption example clearly shows that long-term projections take more than just plain past statistics. Take synthetic fiber consumption, for example. The only clear indication that we can obtain from past consumption is that the trend is generally upward and follows an exponential pattern. It is basically our knowledge of other economic activity trends that tells us that the growth rate must soon start to slow. Predicting how soon this slowdown will come and how sharp it will be is indeed difficult and requires more knowledge of fiber consumption than that provided by technical trend-line fitting. To narrow our prediction interval we may, for example, decide to try to find out how much of the increase in synthetic fiber consumption came at the expense of a reduction in the consumption of cotton. It may be easier to predict the trend line of per capita cotton consumption, since experience with other fibers that have lost some of their popularity may be studied (wool, for example). Then, given projections of future cotton consumption, it may be easier to predict the derived synthetic fiber consumption trend.

Regardless of the technique used, however, it will always be difficult to predict future events, and the farther into the future we try to predict, the less accurate our predictions are likely to become. To help us to deal with possible errors in prediction, we often conduct a **sensitivity analysis**, in which

TABLE 20.3
Total Newsprint Production, United States and Canada, 1919–80
(thousands of short tons)

Year	Production	Year	Production	Year	Production
1919	2,184	1940	4,783	1961	8,829
1920	2,387	1941	4,786	1962	8,845
1921	2,033	1942	4,407	1963	8,848
1922	2,528	1943	4,024	1964	9,562
1923	2,748	1944	3,985	1965	9,900
1924	2,824	1945	4,316	1966	10,827
1925	3,052	1946	5,277	1967	10,672
1926	3,566	1947	5,646	1968	10,966
1927	3,572	1948	5,850	1969	11,990
1928	3,799	1949	6,076	1970	11,917
1929	4,121	1950	6,293	1971	11,593
1930	3,786	1951	6,641	1972	12,242
1931	3,379	1952	6,834	1973	12,571
1932	2,923	1953	6,805	1974	13,029
1933	2,963	1954	7,195	1975	11,370
1934	3,560	1955	7,743	1976	12,651
1935	3,665	1956	8,186	1977	12,859
1936	4,130	1957	8,222	1978	13,481
1937	4,594	1958	7,853	1979	13,714
1938	3,713	1959	8,358	1980	14,179
1939	4,114	1960	8,777		

Source: *Standard & Poor's Trade and Securities Statistics, Current Statistics,* 1981, pp. 24, 284.

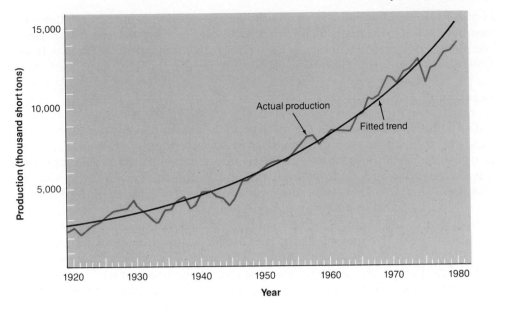

Figure 20.4

Newsprint
production
and fitted
trend line,
United States
and Canada,
1919–80

we change the underlying assumptions of the trend projections. This sensitivity analysis will provide "optimistic," "average," and "pessimistic" projections, which can be translated into relevant quantities of sales, costs, profits, and so on.

Let us consider one more example of an actual time series. Table 20.3 presents newsprint production in the United States and Canada in the period 1919–80. The data are also presented in Figure 20.4.

A glance at the data shows that newsprint production has increased significantly over the years, following an exponentially increasing trend. We note, too, that when a shorter period is considered, such as 1950–80, a linear trend fits the data well. Also notable in Figure 20.4 is the fact that the data points are not randomly scattered around the trend line. Rather, they tend to cluster together above or below the trend line, a fact that indicates that further analysis of the data is required. For example, all the points for the period 1964–74 are above the trend line, whereas all the points for the period 1975–80 are below the line. This fact indicates that the exponential trend line does not in itself capture all of the nonrandom behavior of the data. Furthermore, the secular trend of the data may show what the production of newsprint will be in the coming years *if* future conditions resemble past conditions. Significant changes in prices, taxes, and the competitiveness of substitute products could cause a change in the secular trend. All of these factors demonstrate that long-term projections require a good statistical approach and also knowledge of the specific circumstances of the industry or product involved.

20.3 Seasonal Variations

Analysis of short-term movements and forecasts of time series require the development of a seasonal index, S, to measure seasonal variations. A **seasonal index** is *a measure of the relative activity of a season in comparison with the average annual activity level*. It most commonly takes the form of a quarterly or monthly index. To illustrate, suppose the November seasonal index is 105 for a given activity. This should be interpreted to mean that the November activity level is typically 5 percent above the average for the year. Similarly, if a seasonal index is 88 for a given month, it expresses a level typically 12 percent ($100 - 88 = 12$) below the annual average.

ISOLATING THE *SI* FACTOR

The seasonal component is the most predictable component of a time series in terms of both timing and strength. Yet because the data are also subject to irregular variations, a special statistical technique is required to separate out the seasonal index. Several techniques are used, ranging from simple and somewhat crude methods to sophisticated ones. One commonly used method is the **ratio to moving average**.

Recall that the multiplicative model described in Section 20.1 assumes that $Y = TCSI$. The moving average of a time series averages the irregular and the seasonal indexes across time. Their average is expected to equal 1.0. Therefore, the moving average is a measure of the product of T and C. So, by dividing the original data, Y, by the moving average, we obtain

$$\frac{Y}{\text{Moving average}} = \frac{TCSI}{TC} = SI \qquad \text{(20.7)}$$

and the isolation of the seasonal index itself, S, is accomplished by averaging the factor SI over several years.

Let us now illustrate the isolation of S in detail. Consider Table 20.4, which provides hypothetical sales figures for Seasonal Salad Dressing. Column 2 gives the original quarterly sales figures. Column 3 shows the moving total for four quarters. The first four-quarter total ($1,252) is the total for the first four-quarter sales data (that is, winter, spring, summer, and fall of 1983). To obtain the second four-quarter total ($1,272), we move up and sum the last three quarters of 1983 and the first quarter of 1984. Note that the first four-quarter total, $1,252, is printed in column 3 halfway between the figures for the spring and summer of 1983. The reason is that the midpoint of the year

TABLE 20.4
Isolating the *SI* Factor: Seasonal Salad Dressing Sales

(1) Quarter		*(2)* Sales	*(3)* Four-quarter moving total	*(4)* Eight-quarter moving total	*(5)* Eight-quarter moving average *(col. 4 ÷ 8)*	*(6)* Original data as percentage of moving average *[SI = (col. 2 ÷ col. 5) · 100]*
1983	Winter	$302				
	Spring	350				
			$1,252			
	Summer	280		$2,524	$315.5	88.7%
			1,272			
	Fall	320				
1984	Winter	322				

happens to lie between the *end* of the second and the *beginning* of the third quarter. The second four-quarter total, $1,272, is printed in column 3 half-way between the figures for the summer and fall of 1983. The reason is again that the midpoint of the period lies between the *end* of the summer quarter and the *beginning* of the fall quarter of 1983.

In order to obtain a quarterly average sales volume, we add up the two four-quarter totals and obtain an eight-quarter total. This total appears in column 4 and is positioned exactly *between* the two four-quarter totals. As Table 20.4 shows, the eight-quarter total falls in the summer of 1983.

We now simply divide the eight-quarter total by 8 to get a quarterly moving average that corresponds to the summer of 1983. The quarterly moving average is our measure for the product *TC* for the quarter. Being an average for a period of more than a year, the moving average is expected to "average out" the seasonal and irregular movements within the year considered. Thus, the *SI* factor is now easily isolated. Following Equation 20.7, we divide the original data by the moving average and derive the factor *SI*. In Table 20.4 we compute for the summer quarter of 1983

$$SI = \frac{Y}{TC} = \frac{280.0}{315.5} = 0.887$$

meaning that the sales in the summer of 1983 were 88.7 percent of the average for the period winter 1983 through winter 1984.

ISOLATING THE SEASONAL INDEX

Let us turn to another example, using actual rather than hypothetical data, through which we will show how the isolation of the seasonal index, *S*, from the irregular index, *I*, is accomplished. In Table 20.5 we present the quarterly data of family clothing store sales in the United States in the period 1976–80. Along with the original data, we present the derivation of the ratio to moving average (that is, the *SI* factor), as was just described.

We isolate the seasonal index, *S*, by applying a procedure for averaging out the ratio to moving average (*SI*) over time. In Table 20.6 we organize the ratio to moving average of Table 20.5 by quarters.

TABLE 20.5
Ratio to Moving Average of Family Clothing Store Sales, United States 1976–80
(millions of dollars)

(1) Quarter	(2) Sales	(3) Four-quarter moving total	(4) Eight-quarter moving total	(5) Eight-quarter moving average (col. 4 ÷ 8)	(6) Ratio to moving average [SI = (col. 2 ÷ col. 5) · 100] (percent)
1976 Winter	$1,373				
Spring	1,676				
		$7,224			
Summer	1,714		$14,620	$1,827.50	93.79
		7,396			
Fall	2,461		15,018	1,877.25	131.10
		7,622			*(Continued)*

TABLE 20.5 *(Continued)*
Ratio to Moving Average of Family Clothing Store Sales, United States 1976–80
(millions of dollars)

(1) Quarter	(2) Sales	(3) Four-quarter moving total	(4) Eight-quarter moving total	(5) Eight-quarter moving average (col. 4 ÷ 8)	(6) Ratio to moving average [SI = (col. 2 ÷ col. 5) · 100] (percent)
1977 Winter	1,545		15,465	1,933.12	79.92
		7,843			
Spring	1,902		15,898	1,987.25	95.71
		8,055			
Summer	1,935		16,134	2,016.75	95.95
		8,079			
Fall	2,673		16,144	2,018.00	132.46
		8,065			
1978 Winter	1,569		16,240	2,030.00	77.29
		8,175			
Spring	1,888		16,428	2,053.50	91.94
		8,253			
Summer	2,045		16,611	2,076.38	98.49
		8,358			
Fall	2,751		16,767	2,095.88	131.26
		8,409			
1979 Winter	1,674		16,961	2,120.13	78.96
		8,552			
Spring	1,939		17,217	2,152.13	90.10
		8,665			
Summer	2,188		17,436	2,179.50	100.39
		8,771			
Fall	2,864		17,664	2,208.00	129.71
		8,893			
1980 Winter	1,780		17,803	2,225.38	79.99
		8,910			
Spring	2,061		18,037	2,254.63	91.41
		9,127			
Summer	2,205				
Fall	3,081				

Source: U.S. Department of Commerce, *Survey of Current Business,* various issues.

A glance at Table 20.6 reveals how the seasonal index is calculated. For each season (quarter in our case) we first calculate the modified mean, which is the average of all the values of ratio to moving average for the season, apart from the two extreme values. For example, the modified mean for the fall is the arithmetic average of the two central values for the fall (131.10 and 131.26). The extreme values, 129.71 and 132.46, did not enter the calculation of the average. The reason that the extreme values for each season are left out is that the extremes are likely to be influenced by strong irregular factors that will not be averaged out. Therefore, when the seasonal index is computed, these extreme values are eliminated. Finally, since the sum of the four modified means is not exactly 400, we multiply each modified mean by 400/399.52. This yields the adjusted modified mean. Whereas the average of

TABLE 20.6
Derivation of the Seasonal Index

| | Ratio to moving average | | | | |
Year	Winter	Spring	Summer	Fall	Total
1976			93.79	131.10	
1977	79.92	95.71	95.95	132.46	
1978	77.29	91.94	98.49	131.26	
1979	78.96	90.10	100.39	129.71	
1980	79.99	91.41			
Modified Mean	79.44	91.68	97.22	131.18	399.52
Adjusted Modified Mean	79.53	91.79	97.34	131.34	400.00
= Modified Mean · 400/399.52					

the modified mean does not equal 100, the average of the adjusted modified mean does. Table 20.6 shows that family clothing sales have strong seasonal components. Sales are particularly high in the fall (back to school, Christmas season) and particularly low in the winter.

Once derived, the seasonal index serves two main purposes: to deseasonalize data and to help make short-term forecasts.

DESEASONALIZED DATA

Because activity levels vary from one season to another, we may be interested to know the extent to which a change in a given activity level is attributable to the seasonal factor as opposed to other factors, particularly trend and cyclical movements.

For example, if we look back at Table 20.5, we find that in the fall of 1979 family clothing sales reached $2,864 million, an increase over the $2,188 million in the summer of 1979. To what extent, if any, is the season per se the cause of that increase? To answer that question we refer to the seasonal index. We find that the seasonal index for the summer is 97.34 (see Table 20.6) and the index for the fall is 131.34. The greater volume of clothing sales in the fall compared to the summer quarter is therefore a typical phenomenon. Still, we may want to find out whether all of the increase between the summer and fall quarters of 1979 is accounted for by the seasonal factor, or whether some of it may perhaps indicate some longer-term change. To find out, we deseasonalize the original data by simply dividing each original Y value by the respective seasonal index and then multiply by 100. This is done in Table 20.7, where the deseasonalized data appear in column 4. The deseasonalized data shown in column 5 are obtained by a different method, as explained below.

The deseasonalized data show a *decline* rather than an increase between the summer and fall quarters of 1978. This means that although the original figures show an increase, that increase was *less than* we would have expected to see if only the seasonal factor were affecting the activity level. The decline of the deseasonalized data could (but does not necessarily) indicate a slowdown in the secular trend and/or a downturn of a cyclical movement. One should not jump to conclusions, however, since the deseasonalized data are not free of the irregular factor.

TABLE 20.7
Deseasonalizing the Family Clothing Store Sales Data

(1) Quarter	(2) Family clothing sales (millions of dollars)	(3) Seasonal index	(4) Deseasonalized data [(col. 2 ÷ col. 3) · 100]	(5) Deseasonalized data using the X-11 program
1976 Winter	$1,373	79.53	1,726.39	1,746
Spring	1,676	91.79	1,825.91	1,795
Summer	1,714	97.34	1,760.84	1,783
Fall	2,461	131.34	1,873.76	1,867
1977 Winter	1,545	79.53	1,942.66	1,961
Spring	1,902	91.79	2,072.12	2,041
Summer	1,935	97.34	1,987.88	2,012
Fall	2,673	131.34	2,035.18	2,029
1978 Winter	1,569	79.53	1,972.84	1,985
Spring	1,888	91.79	2,056.87	2,032
Summer	2,045	97.34	2,100.88	2,124
Fall	2,751	131.34	2,094.56	2,088
1979 Winter	1,674	79.53	2,104.87	2,113
Spring	1,939	91.79	2,112.43	2,096
Summer	2,188	97.34	2,247.79	2,153
Fall	2,864	131.34	2,180.60	2,177
1980 Winter	1,780	79.53	2,238.15	2,243
Spring	2,061	91.79	2,245.34	2,232
Summer	2,205	97.34	2,265.26	2,277
Fall	3,081	131.34	2,345.82	2,345

Figure 20.5 is a computer-generated chart presenting both the original and the deseasonalized time series of family clothing store sales for the period 1976–80. It is evident from the figure that the deseasonalized data are smoother and do not have seasonal peaks and troughs; thus they are more reflective of the long-term movement of the time series.

Figure 20.5

Family clothing store sales, actual and deseasonalized, 1976–80

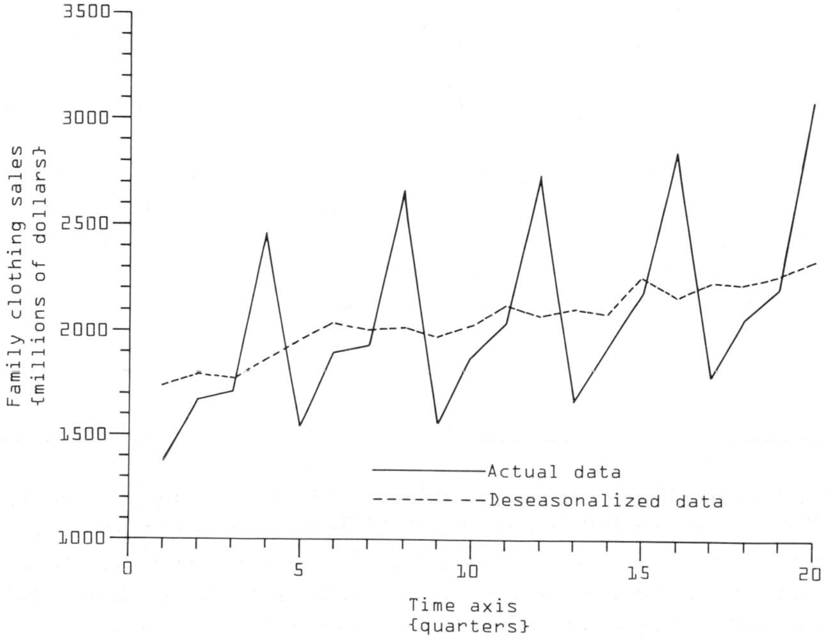

The seasonal index can also be used to provide short-term forecasts of an activity level. After the trend forecast has been adjusted for cyclical movements (see Section 20.4), the forecast data are multiplied by the seasonal index and divided by 100. The result is a forecast that takes the seasonal variations into consideration.

THE X-11 PROGRAM

The explanation of time-series analysis in general and of seasonal adjustment in particular, as presented in this book, follows the classical decomposition of a time series into its components. There are, as we mentioned in the beginning of this chapter, more sophisticated methods of time-series analysis. The Census Bureau's *X*-11 program for seasonal adjustment represents the culmination of a major phase of continuing research in the area of seasonal adjustment. Today, the *X*-11 program is widely used on thousands of economic time series, most of which are decomposed by the multiplicative model. The *X*-11 program is a procedure based on the ratio-to-moving-average method and on removing "extreme" irregulars. However, the program has built-in sophistications that are not presented in this chapter. Among the many options that are available in the *X*-11 program are:

1. A choice of either a multiplicative or additive model. In an additive model the time series is expressed as the sum (rather than product) of the components.
2. An adjustment for trading-day variations so that series such as stock market transactions can be more accurately analyzed.
3. An adjustment for extreme values.
4. Selection of various lengths (weights) of terms for the moving averages.
5. An adjustment of the seasonal index over time. The program does not assume that the seasonal index is the same every year.

In January 1975, Statistics Canada (the bureau of statistics of Canada) introduced a modification of the *X*-11 method, called the *X*-11-ARIMA seasonal adjustment method. It consists of an enlargement of the original time series by one additional year, with forecasts from ARIMA models.

Among the many agencies that use the *X*-11 program are the U.S. Bureau of the Census, the Federal Reserve Board, the U.S. Bureau of Labor Statistics, and Statistics Canada.

In Table 20.7 (column 5) we presented the deseasonalized data of our family clothing store example as obtained by the *X*-11 program. When we compare the *X*-11 adjustment to the adjustments obtained by the classical method (column 4), we find that while the *X*-11 program gives different deseasonalized values, the classical method provides a reasonable approximation.

20.4 Cyclical Variations

The seasonal index does not reflect the extent to which the activity level of the year as a whole varies from the long-term trend. *Those movements of annual economic activity levels about the long-term trend* are known as **cyclical variations**. The forecasting of those cycles is pivotal to short-term and intermediate-term planning of successful business operations.

Figure 20.6

Deseasonal-
ized sales of
general
merchan-
dising stores
and fitted
trend,
1952–80

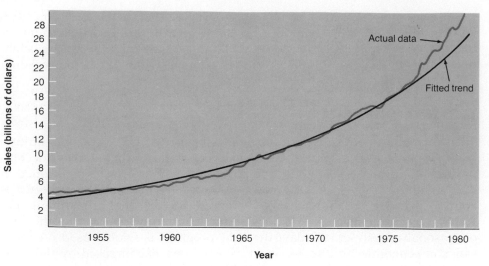

TABLE 20.8
Retail Sales of General Merchandising Stores, Deseasonalized, 1952–80
(billions of dollars)

Year	Winter	Spring	Summer	Fall
1952	$ 4.47	$ 4.59	$ 4.64	$ 4.88
1953	4.68	4.79	4.79	4.73
1954	4.53	4.73	4.72	4.81
1955	4.85	4.99	5.10	4.96
1956	5.06	5.18	5.31	5.17
1957	5.18	5.25	5.52	5.21
1958	5.24	5.32	5.48	5.52
1959	5.69	5.84	5.85	5.95
1960	5.97	5.99	5.95	6.01
1961	6.03	6.13	6.27	6.49
1962	6.58	6.77	6.89	7.03
1963	7.06	7.12	7.31	7.29
1964	7.62	7.89	8.11	8.40
1965	8.56	8.67	8.99	9.33
1966	9.72	9.76	10.04	10.14
1967	9.83	10.11	10.29	10.50
1968	10.79	11.05	11.36	11.47
1969	11.55	11.76	11.98	12.10
1970	12.17	12.22	12.33	12.97
1971	13.17	13.58	13.85	14.09
1972	14.47	14.79	15.37	15.78
1973	16.12	16.47	16.52	16.88
1974	17.29	17.55	17.59	17.30
1975	17.45	18.30	18.60	18.89
1976	19.20	19.13	19.59	20.45
1977	20.61	21.22	22.21	23.82
1978	23.46	24.56	25.03	25.65
1979	25.39	26.19	27.23	28.09
1980	28.42	28.02	28.84	30.28

Source: *Standard & Poor's Trade and Securities Statistics, Current Statistics,* various issues.

In Figure 20.6 we present the deseasonalized quarterly data of retail sales of general merchandising stores in the period 1952–80. The diagram is based on the data of Table 20.8. As you can see, the deseasonalized data, although free of seasonal variations, move in cycles, above and below the long-term trend line.

Unlike seasonal variations, which are predictable with reasonable accuracy with respect to both timing and strength, cyclical fluctuations are troublesome to the forecaster. They are less predictable in their timing, duration, and intensity. Particularly difficult to forecast are turning points (peaks and troughs) and the speed at which a forthcoming upswing or downswing will take place. Failure to predict a business upswing could result in loss of opportunities to make sales, while a failure to predict a business downswing could lead to overinvestment and accumulation of excess inventories, resulting in substantial loss. Continuous failure to make predictions could ultimately lead to business failure.

In studying cyclical fluctuation, we need to learn first how to determine the current state of the activity and then how to go about predicting future cyclical movements. Let us consider these two facets of the study of cyclical movements.

IDENTIFYING THE CURRENT STATE OF THE CYCLE

Technically, the isolation of the cyclical components of a time series is a simple matter. After isolating the trend (T) and the seasonal index (S), we may derive the product, CI, in the following way:

$$\text{Cyclical and irregular components} = \frac{Y}{TS} = \frac{TCSI}{TS} = CI \qquad \textbf{(20.8)}$$

The product, CI, is of course a mixture of a cyclical factor and an irregular movement. In order to separate the cyclical component, C, from the irregular factor, I, we average out a few successive periods. Let us take a close look at the isolation of the cyclical component in the example of general merchandise sales. We note that in order to apply Equation 20.8, we need to know the secular trend line. Figure 20.6 shows an exponential trend line for the data. The trend line is given by

$$\hat{Y} = b_0 \cdot b_1^t$$

and after transforming this equation to logarithmic form we rewrite it as

$$\hat{Y}^* = b_0^* + b_1^* t$$

where $\hat{Y}^* = \log \hat{Y}$, $b_0^* = \log b_0$, and $b_1^* = \log b_1$. Using the quarterly data for the period 1952–80 (Table 20.8), we run a simple regression of Y^* on t and estimate:

$$\hat{Y}^* = 1.308124 + 0.0171940t$$

where $t = 0$ for the first quarter of 1952 and increases by increments of 1 per quarter. On the basis of this trend line, we can isolate the cyclical factor by the process described in Table 20.9.

TABLE 20.9
Isolating the Cyclical Component for General Merchandising Sales, 1976–80

(1) Quarter	(2) t	(3) Deseasonalized data	(4) Trend	(5) CI [(col. 3 ÷ col. 4) · 100]	(6) Weighted three-quarter moving total	(7) C (col. 6 ÷ 4)
1976 Winter	96	$19.20	$19.27	99.64%		
Spring	97	19.13	19.61	97.55	392.94	98.24
Summer	98	19.59	19.95	98.20	394.74	98.69
Fall	99	20.45	20.29	100.79	399.59	99.90
1977 Winter	100	20.61	20.65	99.81	401.46	100.37
Spring	101	21.22	21.00	101.05	405.84	101.46
Summer	102	22.21	21.37	103.93	418.48	104.62
Fall	103	23.82	21.74	109.57	429.13	107.28
1978 Winter	104	23.46	22.12	106.06	430.85	107.71
Spring	105	24.56	22.50	109.16	433.73	108.46
Summer	106	25.03	22.89	109.35	437.99	109.50
Fall	107	25.65	23.29	110.13	436.79	109.20
1979 Winter	108	25.39	23.69	107.18	433.16	108.29
Spring	109	26.19	24.10	108.67	435.57	108.89
Summer	110	27.23	24.52	111.05	443.36	110.84
Fall	111	28.09	24.95	112.59	448.21	112.05
1980 Winter	112	28.42	25.38	111.98	445.07	111.27
Spring	113	28.02	25.82	108.52	438.80	109.70
Summer	114	28.84	26.27	109.78	441.40	110.35
Fall	115	30.28	26.72	113.32		

The table deserves a few comments. First, the trend line was derived from data for the period 1952–80. For brevity, the isolation of the cyclical index is presented only for the period 1976–80. The first quarter of 1976 happens to be the 96th quarter from the winter of 1952. The trend for the first quarter of 1976 is given by

$$\hat{Y} = 3.69923 \cdot 1.017343^{96} = 19.27$$

where 3.69923 is the antilogarithm of 1.308124 and 1.017343 is the antilogarithm of 0.0171940. The trend is determined for the other quarters in a similar way. The deseasonalized data were computed by use of a seasonal index derived from the data for the period 1952–80. Column 6 of Table 20.9 shows the weighted three-quarter moving total. It is the total of the previous quarter's value in column 5, twice the current value of column 5, and the next quarter's value in column 5. For example, the first number in column 6 was computed as follows:

$$392.94 = 99.64 + 2 \cdot 97.55 + 98.20$$

Last, the cyclical component itself is determined by dividing column 6 by 4.

FORECASTING CYCLICAL MOVEMENT: THE USE OF BUSINESS INDICATORS

Experience shows that only by studying the simultaneous behavior of many economic variables can we hope to make high-quality predictions of cyclical movements. Key variables such as the gross national product, personal income, industrial production, retail sales, wholesale prices, stock market prices, and unemployment figures must be considered. In particular, it is desirable to learn the relationships between these variables to establish a network of relevant data that might give early signals of future cyclical trends.

The National Bureau of Economic Research has developed a sophisticated method for such predictions: the use of business indicators. These indicators are used by the U.S. Department of Commerce and are published in *Business Conditions Digest*. Business indicators are time series of economic variables that tend to indicate how the economy is progressing along its cyclical trend; they were developed by careful study of the interrelationships among economic and business time series. The indicators come in three major categories: **leading indicators, roughly coincident indicators**, and **lagging indicators**. The full list of indicators includes 88 variables, of which 36 are leading, 25 are coincident, 11 are lagging, and 16 are unclassified by timing but nevertheless represent important factors of business cycles.[3] In Table 20.10 we present what is known as the *short list* of 26 business indicators: 12 leading, 8 roughly coincident, and 6 lagging.

TABLE 20.10
Cyclical Indicators: Short List of National Bureau of Economic Research

Leading indicators
  Average hourly workweek, production workers, manufacturing
  Average weekly initial claims, state unemployment insurance
  Index of net business formation
  New orders, durable goods industries
  Contracts and orders, plant and equipment
  Index of new building permits, private housing units
  Change in book value, manufacturing and trade inventories
  Index of industrial materials prices
  Index of stock prices, 500 common stocks
  Corporate profits after taxes (quarterly)
  Index: ratio, price to unit labor cost, manufacturing
  Change in consumer installment debt

Roughly coincident indicators
  GNP in current dollars
  GNP in 1958 dollars
  Index of industrial production
  Personal income
  Manufacturing and trade sales
  Sales of retail stores
  Employees on nonagricultural payrolls
  Unemployment rate, total

Lagging indicators
  Unemployment rate, persons unemployed 15 weeks or over
  Business expenditures, new plant and equipment
  Book value, manufacturing and trade inventories
  Index of labor cost per unit of output in manufacturing
  Commercial and industrial loans outstanding in large commercial banks
  Banks rates on short-term business loans

Source: U.S. Department of Commerce.

[3] See Geoffrey H. Moore and Julius Shiskin, *Indicators of Business Expansions and Contractions*, Occasional Paper no. 103 (New York: National Bureau of Economic Research, 1967).

The "quality" of a time series as a business indicator is measured by the following criteria:

1. Economic significance
2. Statistical adequacy
3. Historical conformity to business cycles
4. Consistency during business cycles
5. Smoothness
6. Promptness of publication

These criteria are used to score the indicators on a scale from 0 to 100.

The leading indicators typically reach their peaks and troughs ahead of the coincident and lagging indicators. Similarly, the coincident indicators typically reach their peak and trough levels ahead of the lagging indicators. A typical though simplified set of movements of these indicators in relation to each other is shown in Figure 20.7. Consider the economy at time t_0. Here the leading indicators are starting a downturn while both the coincident and lagging indicators continue their expansion. If we indeed know that the leading indicators precede the others at their peaks and troughs, we predict a downturn of the coincident and lagging indicators soon. The coincident indicators precede the lagging. Thus, when the coincident indicators also turn downward, their movement reinforces our earlier prediction and leads to a conclusion that the lagging indicators will soon turn downward. At time t_1, the coincident and lagging indicators are still on their downward trend, but the leading indicators are turning upward, indicating an upcoming trend in the other indicators as well.

Of course we would like the business indicators to be an early warning system as dependable as the one we have been describing. Unfortunately, this is not exactly the case, for several reasons. First, the indicators vary in their reliability. As we have mentioned, their "quality" is scored on a scale from 0 to 100. A low score for an indicator could mean that the signals it gives may turn out either to come too late or to be false. Second, since there are many indicators in each category (leading, coincident, and lagging), what if some indicators move in the opposite direction from others? Should we interpret such a movement as a signal of expansion or contraction? To deal with this problem, in each category a composite index that reflects the overall direction of the indicators in the category is compiled. Third, the action

Figure 20.7

Typical but simplified relationship among leading, roughly coincident, and lagging indicators

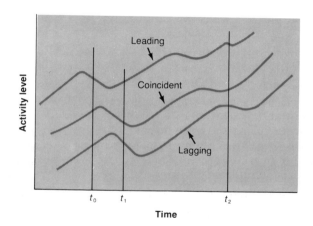

of the indicators is subject not only to cyclical fluctuations but also to irregular movements due to specific circumstances. To illustrate the problem, consider time t_2 in Figure 20.7. At this time the economy is in the midst of an upswing, but a short-term slowdown of leading indicators has occurred for some reason. At time t_2 it is hard to know whether the economy is on the verge of a new slowdown or simply at a temporary disturbance during a longer upswing movement. On such occasions we must sometimes rely on speculation and guesswork as to the direction the economy will go in future months.

Clearly, the study of business indicators contributes a great deal to our competence in predicting future cyclical trends. We must remember, however, that future events will always differ in some way from what we anticipate. Thus, studying the business indicators must be taken as a way to *reduce* rather than *eliminate* uncertainty about the future. The more knowledgeable we become, the more we can reduce uncertainties, but we must accept the fact that some degree of uncertainty is unavoidable.

DIFFUSION INDEX

A **diffusion index** *measures the proportion of the number of components that show increases in a group of statistical series.* When applied to a group of business indicators, it measures the proportion of rising indicators in a given period out of the entire specified group of indicators. For example, if 3 of the 12 leading indicators on the short list are rising in a given month, the diffusion index is 25 (since $\frac{3}{12} = 0.25$). If in the next month 9 indicators are rising, the diffusion index rises to 75 ($\frac{9}{12} = 0.75$). When all 12 indicators fall, the diffusion index is 0, and when all of them rise, the index is 100.

For a diffusion index to be a meaningful measure of economic activity, it should be applied to time series in which the indicators tend to follow the leader: when some indicators reach a turning point and change direction, the others follow. In a case like this, the diffusion index tends to move in one direction—upward or downward—with few disturbances, and in that case it may be indicative of future expansions or contractions. If a series does not exhibit such a relationship, the diffusion index is likely to move in a random fashion, causing confusion rather than measuring diffusion.

The most comprehensive diffusion index is that constructed by the National Bureau of Economic Research; it includes some 400 series, generally in conformity with business-cycle movement.

ECONOMETRIC MODEL BUILDING

The application of statistical analysis, particularly regression analysis, to economic theory is called **econometrics**. One of the most advanced areas of econometrics is what is known as **model building**. An **econometric model** is *a complicated set of regression equations* (up to several hundred of them) *with many dependent and independent variables appearing in the various equations.* The entire economy is basically included in the set of equations. Because the equations are interrelated, they must be solved simultaneously. The result is a short-term forecast—showing directions as well as magnitudes—for the various sectors of the economy. The predictions of some well-known econometric models—the FRB–MIT (Federal Reserve Board–Massachusetts Institute of Technology), the one used at the University of Pennsylvania, the one used at Michigan University, and others—are regularly reported in the *Wall Street Journal* and other financial papers.

Like other methods of forecasting, the econometric model has its strengths and its weakness. It is powerful in the sense that it produces directions as well as magnitudes in its predictions and in addition gives detailed results for a large number of industries. It is also powerful in estimating the effect of one-time changes in some parameters. For example, it could be used to estimate the effect of a proposed tax-law change on tax collection, disposable income, unemployment, production, and so on. Its weakness is that it requires large computer facilities and a lot of input information. Missing data could delay using the model, and this delay could prove to be crucial to the forecaster. In any event, large companies are becoming increasingly interested in such model building.

ANTICIPATORY SURVEYS

Economic activity must be carefully planned, and planning takes time. Business managers are constantly in the process of planning future investment, employment, orders of durable goods, inventory adjustments, construction, and so on in anticipation of future needs. And in turn, a survey of businesses' intentions with respect to such activities can help in the assessment of the status of a cyclical movement in the near future. The results of surveys of business plans, government agency plans, and anticipated consumer spending are published regularly by such well-known publications as *Survey of Current Business* (published by the Department of Commerce), *Business Week*, and *Fortune*.

The major weakness of the surveys is that intentions are not always translated into actions. They serve as useful additions, however, to the methods we described earlier.

Chapter Summary and Review

1. The multiplicative time series model is $Y = TCSI$ where

$$
\begin{aligned}
Y &= \text{the raw data} \\
T &= \text{secular trend} \\
S &= \text{seasonal factor} \\
C &= \text{cyclical factor} \\
I &= \text{irregular factor}
\end{aligned}
$$

2. The trend is estimated by the OLS method
   a. Linear line $\hat{Y} = a + bt$
   b. Exponential: $\hat{Y} = a \cdot b^t$ or $\log \hat{Y} = \log a + t \log b$
3. Isolating the SI factor

$$
\frac{Y}{\text{Moving average}} = \frac{TCSI}{TC} = SI
$$

where the moving average serves as a measure of the value TC.

4. Isolating the seasonal factor, *S*, is done by averaging *SI* across years.

5. Deseasonalized data

$$\frac{Y}{S} = \frac{TCSI}{S} = TCI$$

where *S* is the seasonal factor.

6. Isolating the factor *CI*

$$CI = \frac{Y}{TS} = \frac{TCSI}{TS}$$

Problems

20.1. Why do we need a special technique to study and analyze time series? Why is it not recommended that regular regression techniques be used?

20.2. Identify each of the four components of time series: secular trend, seasonal variations, cyclical variations, and irregular variations.

20.3. What are some common types of secular trends?

20.4. Why do businesspeople need forecasts of the secular trends of sales of their products?

20.5. Why do businesspeople need to forecast the cyclical fluctuations of business?

20.6. "Seasonal fluctuations are not very important for the business executive, since his or her investment decisions are based on long-run business prospects, and for those the executive needs to forecast the secular trend and the cyclical variations, not the seasonal variations." Discuss.

20.7. What are business indicators? Distinguish among leading, roughly coincident, and lagging indicators.

20.8. Explain what a diffusion index is and how it can be used to forecast the cyclical trend.

20.9. The sales of the City Variety Company have been projected to grow 2.5 percent per quarter. The sales level for fall 1983 has been projected to be $1.5 million.

    (*a*) What are the projected sales for each of the four quarters of 1984?
    (*b*) Is the trend line linear in this case? Explain.

20.10. The sales of the Outdoor Furniture Company have been projected to grow $50,000 every quarter. If sales for fall 1983 have been projected to be $2.3 million, what are the projected sales for each of the four quarters in 1984? Does the trend indicate increasing sales at a decreasing rate or increasing sales at an increasing rate? Explain.

20.11. Table P20.11 gives the annual sales values of Firm *A* and Firm *B* for the years 1974–83.

    (*a*) Using the ordinary least-squares method, fit a straight line to both series.
    (*b*) Plot the sales series of Firm *A* and the computed trend values on one diagram. Do the same for Firm *B*.
    (*c*) Does a straight line seem to fit well the sales series of Firm *A*? Does it seem to fit well the sales series of Firm *B*?

TABLE P20.11

Year	Firm A	Firm B
1974	108	87
1975	106	97
1976	120	108
1977	118	114
1978	131	123
1979	133	138
1980	137	153
1981	148	171
1982	139	182
1983	151	198

20.12. Table P20.12 gives a time series of the total book value of manufacturing and trade inventories by quarters for the years 1975–80.

TABLE P20.12

Year	Quarter	Inventories (millions of dollars)	Year	Quarter	Inventories (millions of dollars)
1975	1	$ 811,379	1978	1	$1,028,576
	2	800,856		2	1,070,154
	3	785,352		3	1,087,404
	4	798,499		4	1,133,448
1976	1	804,405	1979	1	1,167,658
	2	836,306		2	1,211,412
	3	869,790		3	1,237,577
	4	900,837		4	1,279,235
1977	1	940,573	1980	1	1,309,776
	2	961,939		2	1,342,852
	3	968,326		3	1,344,001
	4	1,002,102		4	1,375,136

Source: U.S. Department of Commerce, Bureau of Economic Analysis, *Survey of Current Business,* various issues.

(*a*) Derive the seasonal index using the ratio to moving average.
(*b*) Deseasonalize the data.

20.13. The quarterly sales (in thousands of dollars) of Acme stores for the period 1976–83 are shown in Table P20.13.

TABLE P20.13

Quarter	1976	1977	1978	1979	1980	1981	1982	1983
Winter	$100	$110	$115	$116	$118	$115	$116	$120
Spring	120	130	131	132	135	140	141	145
Summer	90	100	98	102	104	105	108	110
Fall	180	200	205	210	215	220	225	240

(*a*) Estimate the sales trend by running the regression $Y = a + bt$.
(*b*) Draw the scatter diagram and the trend line on the same chart.
(*c*) Calculate the statistic $\Sigma e_t / n$.
(*d*) Calculate the statistic $\sum_{t=2}^{n} e_t e_{t-1}$. Given the value of this statistic, do you think a simple

linear regression analysis is appropriate to study and make predictions of Acme's quarterly sales? Explain. Hint: if e_t and e_{t-1} are independent, we expect $\sum_{t=2}^{n} e_t e_{t-1}$ to be close to zero.

20.14. Table P20.14 gives the quarterly consumption of aspirin (in thousands of tablets) for the years 1979–83.

TABLE P20.14

	Quarter			
Year	1	2	3	4
1979	100	80	70	190
1980	110	90	80	200
1981	120	95	90	220
1982	125	90	85	200
1983	120	85	90	180

(a) Draw a line chart of the data and use it to determine if there is a seasonal variation in aspirin consumption.
(b) Calculate the four-quarter moving average and the eight-quarter moving average for the period.
(c) Using your results from part b, isolate the seasonal factor, SI.
(d) Calculate the modified mean of aspirin consumption in each quarter.
(e) Calculate the deseasonalized series.
(f) Plot the original data and the deseasonalized data on the same chart. Discuss and analyze your results.

20.15. Ms. MacIntosh invested $10,000 in 1975. The value of the investment in each of the years 1975–83 was as follows:

Year (t)	Value of investment (Y)
1975	$10,000
1976	11,000
1977	12,120
1978	13,200
1979	14,400
1980	15,300
1981	17,000
1982	19,000
1983	22,000

(a) Calculate the trend by using the linear relationship $\hat{Y} = b_0 + b_1 t$.
(b) Use the following exponential relationship to calculate the trend: $\hat{Y} = b_0 \cdot b_1 t$.
(c) Using these two trend lines, estimate the value of the investment in 1990. Compare and explain your results.
(d) Draw the value of the investment and the two trend lines obtained in parts a and b on the same diagram. Which trend line is more appropriate to this specific set of data? Explain.

20.16. Table P20.16 shows the hypothetical monthly unemployment rate (expressed as a percentage of the work force) for the years 1979–83.

(a) Derive the seasonal index using the ratio to moving average.
(b) Calculate the deseasonalized series of the unemployment rates.

TABLE P20.16

Year	Jan.	Feb.	Mar.	Apr.	May	June	Jul.	Aug.	Sept.	Oct.	Nov.	Dec.
					Month							
1979	9.0%	8.7%	8.7%	9.3%	9.4%	9.4%	9.2%	9.1%	9.0%	8.5%	8.0%	8.1%
1980	9.2	8.8	8.8	9.2	9.5	9.3	9.2	9.2	9.1	8.6	8.0	7.9
1981	9.1	8.8	8.6	9.2	9.4	9.4	9.3	9.3	9.1	8.7	7.9	8.0
1982	9.3	8.8	8.5	9.1	9.3	9.3	9.1	9.2	9.0	8.8	7.9	8.2
1983	9.4	8.9	8.6	9.0	9.4	9.4	9.2	9.1	9.1	8.9	8.0	8.3

20.17. Table P20.17 gives data on United Kingdom imports of crude oil, natural gas liquids, and feedstocks by quarters, 1977–80.

TABLE P20.17

Year	Quarter	U.K. imports of crude oil, natural gas liquids, and feedstocks (thousand metric tons)
1977	1	19,300
	2	18,405
	3	16,372
	4	16,621
1978	1	17,519
	2	16,423
	3	15,978
	4	18,223
1979	1	15,267
	2	14,797
	3	14,945
	4	15,373
1980	1	13,381
	2	12,333
	3	10,100
	4	10,903

Source: Organization for Economic Cooperation and Development, *Quarterly Oil Statistics*, various issues.

(a) Estimate the (linear) trend of the data.
(b) Derive the seasonal index using the ratio to moving average.
(c) Deseasonalize the data.
(d) Using your seasonal index, forecast quarterly imports of the materials in 1981, assuming that the past linear trend will continue and that the cyclical trend will bring a 1 percent decrease per quarter.

20.18. Table P20.18 gives a time series of monthly retail sales of passenger cars in the United States, 1977–80.

(a) Derive the seasonal index using the ratio to moving average.
(b) Deseasonalize the data.

TABLE P20.18

Month	Sales (thousands of cars)			
	1977	*1978*	*1979*	*1980*
1	725	687	784	806
2	811	777	841	812
3	1,084	1,078	1,116	895
4	1,029	1,043	988	743
5	1,054	1,160	1,053	697
6	1,117	1,138	905	702
7	913	930	886	772
8	931	958	916	686
9	829	828	775	672
10	1,014	1,034	899	847
11	881	909	775	698
12	795	769	733	650

Source: U.S. Department of Commerce, Bureau of Economic Analysis, *Survey of Current Business*, various issues.

20.19. A power company had the following demand in the period 1974–83:

Year	Demand (millions of kilowatt-hours)
1974	100
1975	110
1976	120
1977	136
1978	147
1979	160
1980	173
1981	190
1982	206
1983	223

(a) Plot the above time series on a graph.
(b) Estimate the demand trend line, assuming that the trend is linear and using the OLS estimators.
(c) Draw the estimated trend line. Do you think a linear trend line is appropriate for this series? Why?
(d) What is your projection for 1986 sales, using the linear trend?

20.20. For the data of Problem 20.19, assume that the trend line is

$$\hat{Y} = b_0 \cdot b_1^t$$

After taking logarithms on both sides, we get

$$\log \hat{Y} = \log b_0 + t \log b_1$$

(a) Using the last equation, estimate the trend line $\hat{Y} = b_0 \cdot b_1^t$.
(b) What is the projected demand for 1986? Compare your answer here with your answer to part *d* of Problem 20.19. How do you explain the difference?

(c) What is the annual percentage growth in demand implied by your answer to part *a* of this problem?

20.21. Using the data of Problem 20.17 as well as the trend and deseasonalized data of that problem, identify the state of the cycle for each quarter of the years 1977–80.

20.22. The long-term growth of sales of women's boots (in millions of dollars) is estimated by the ordinary least-squares method to yield the following relationship:

$$\hat{Y} = 10 + 0.1t$$

where *Y* is the sales in millions, the intercept 10 represents the sales in January 1983, and *t* stands for the month. The monthly growth is estimated at 0.1 million dollars in sales. Furthermore, from past data we know the following seasonal index in boot sales:

Month:	Jan.	Feb.	Mar.	Apr.	May	June	Jul.	Aug.	Sept.	Oct.	Nov.	Dec.
Seasonal index:	100	50	50	40	40	50	60	70	150	250	260	80

(a) Estimate the total sales for 1986.
(b) Estimate the sales for 1986 for each month.
(c) Estimate the percentage sales change from March 1986 to November 1986, and repeat the calculations using the deseasonalized data. Compare and discuss your results.

20.23. Suppose we find that the deseasonalized data of a given time series are identical to the original time-series data. Then we must conclude that:

(a) There is no change over time in the original data.
(b) The irregular factor is too strong to allow the seasonal factor to be detected.
(c) The seasonal factor is equal to 1.
(d) There is no cyclical factor in this time series.

Which of these statements is correct? Explain your answer.

20.24. The trend in the number of passengers flying from the United States to Europe is estimated by the following parabola:

$$\hat{Y} = 5 + 2X + X^2$$

where *Y* is in ten thousands and *X* stands for quarters (*X* takes the values 1, 2, 3, 4, 5, . . . where 1 is the first quarter of 1980). The seasonal index for the four quarters of each year is as follows:

Quarter:	1	2	3	4
Seasonal index:	50	100	200	50

(a) Use only the trend equation to estimate the number of passengers who fly to Europe for each quarter of the years 1985–86.
(b) Use the seasonal index to estimate the number of passengers who fly to Europe in each of the four quarters of the years 1985–86.
(c) Plot the data obtained in parts *a* and *b* on the same diagram and discuss your results.

Case Problems

20.1. Figure CP20.1 and Table CP20.1*a* show the value of beverage shipments in millions of dollars for the period January 1974–October 1980,
by month. Table CP20.1*b* shows the deseasonalized data as computed
by the *X*-11 program. Use the classical method described in this book
to deseasonalize the series and compare the results to the data shown
in Table CP20.1*b*. Discuss the differences.

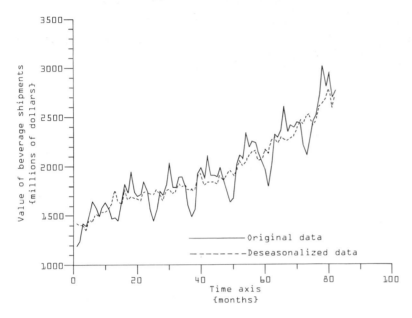

Figure CP20.1

Value of beverage shipments, January 1974–October 1980

TABLE CP20.1*a*

Value of Beverage Shipments for January 1974–October 1980

(millions of dollars)

Year	Jan.	Feb.	Mar.	Apr.	May	June	Jul.	Aug.	Sept.	Oct.	Nov.	Dec.
1974	1,195	1,241	1,421	1,391	1,525	1,646	1,577	1,501	1,593	1,638	1,572	1,476
1975	1,484	1,449	1,638	1,817	1,731	1,947	1,738	1,694	1,718	1,846	1,758	1,575
1976	1,439	1,550	1,750	1,710	1,814	2,036	1,789	1,784	1,894	1,896	1,797	1,610
1977	1,482	1,552	1,932	1,988	1,874	2,115	1,907	1,907	1,895	1,996	1,839	1,744
1978	1,640	1,688	1,982	2,117	2,074	2,349	2,194	2,256	2,243	2,141	2,047	1,979
1979	1,794	2,005	2,323	2,285	2,371	2,611	2,350	2,423	2,394	2,450	2,438	2,215
1980	2,114	2,248	2,448	2,519	2,700	3,025	2,809	2,976	2,692	2,773	—	—

Source: Data obtained from U.S. Bureau of the Census.

TABLE CP20.1*b*

X-11 Deseasonalized Data of the Value of Beverage Shipments for January 1974–October 1980

(millions of dollars)

Year	Jan.	Feb.	Mar.	Apr.	May	June	Jul.	Aug.	Sept.	Oct.	Nov.	Dec.
1974	1,422	1,408	1,406	1,355	1,467	1,433	1,523	1,493	1,539	1,538	1,569	1,620
1975	1,629	1,648	1,620	1,766	1,669	1,696	1,677	1,675	1,658	1,739	1,762	1,728
1976	1,717	1,765	1,726	1,659	1,754	1,772	1,728	1,748	1,828	1,795	1,807	1,767
1977	1,770	1,763	1,906	1,932	1,814	1,841	1,842	1,843	1,826	1,908	1,856	1,915
1978	1,960	1,912	1,952	2,063	2,009	2,045	2,119	2,152	2,165	2,064	2,072	2,174
1979	2,139	2,264	2,294	2,233	2,294	2,278	2,264	2,286	2,310	2,385	2,476	2,432
1980	2,516	2,535	2,419	2,461	2,613	2,644	2,702	2,793	2,601	2,712	—	—

Source: Computed from original series, Table CP20.1*a*.

20.2. Figure CP20.2 and Table CP20.2*a* show the number of men, aged 20 and over, employed in agriculture during January 1974–October 1980. Table CP20.2*b* shows the deseasonalized data as computed by the *X*-11 program. Use the classical method described in this book to deseasonalize the series and compare the results to the data given in Table CP20.2*b*. Discuss the differences.

Figure CP20.2

Agricultural employment of men, aged 20 and over, January 1974–October 1980

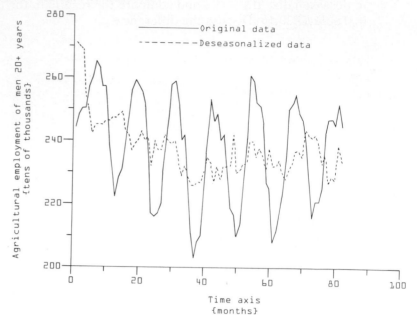

TABLE CP20.2*a*

Agricultural Employment of Men Aged 20 and Over, January 1974–October 1980

(tens of thousands)

Year	Jan.	Feb.	Mar.	Apr.	May	June	Jul.	Aug.	Sept.	Oct.	Nov.	Dec.
1974	2,448	2,483	2,503	2,508	2,571	2,609	2,655	2,634	2,574	2,570	2,415	2,311
1975	2,226	2,282	2,310	2,401	2,499	2,569	2,591	2,579	2,557	2,514	2,362	2,177
1976	2,163	2,174	2,202	2,379	2,468	2,588	2,596	2,531	2,405	2,424	2,248	2,125
1977	2,030	2,081	2,106	2,259	2,423	2,536	2,464	2,492	2,406	2,427	2,283	2,192
1978	2,171	2,105	2,145	2,274	2,393	2,617	2,599	2,525	2,512	2,462	2,277	2,250
1979	2,084	2,117	2,176	2,237	2,342	2,509	2,520	2,554	2,498	2,472	2,403	2,292
1980	2,160	2,213	2,217	2,255	2,422	2,470	2,475	2,455	2,525	2,459	—	—

Source: Data obtained from U.S. Bureau of the Census.

TABLE CP20.2*b*

X-11 Deseasonalized Data on Agricultural Employment of Men Aged 20 and Over, January 1974–October 1980

(tens of thousands)

Year	Jan.	Feb.	Mar.	Apr.	May	June	Jul.	Aug.	Sept.	Oct.	Nov.	Dec.
1974	2,717	2,700	2,698	2,544	2,497	2,421	2,457	2,454	2,457	2,460	2,465	2,473
1975	2,473	2,485	2,493	2,438	2,428	2,379	2,397	2,403	2,439	2,405	2,411	2,325
1976	2,407	2,375	2,377	2,421	2,400	2,390	2,401	2,357	2,291	2,320	2,293	2,262
1977	2,261	2,279	2,275	2,309	2,359	2,337	2,276	2,320	2,289	2,320	2,327	2,325
1978	2,422	2,309	2,316	2,335	2,332	2,409	2,404	2,350	2,387	2,352	2,318	2,380
1979	2,326	2,322	2,349	2,309	2,284	2,310	2,331	2,378	2,370	2,358	2,445	2,420
1980	2,412	2,427	2,391	2,334	2,364	2,275	2,290	2,286	2,391	2,346	—	—

Source: Computed from original series, Table CP20.2*a*.

INDEX NUMBERS

21

Key Terms
index numbers
Consumer Price Index (CPI)
unweighted index
average of price relatives
weighted (arithmetic) average index
Laspeyres price index
Paasche price index
fixed-weights index
quantity indexes
Laspeyres quantity index
Paasche quantity index
value index
deflation
technical shifting
splicing
Standard & Poor's stock price indexes
leading indicators

21.1 The Nature and Meaning of Index Numbers

Index numbers *enable us to easily express the level of an activity or phenomenon in relation to its level at another time or place.* In this chapter we deal primarily with relationships over time. Suppose the price of a certain car was $6,000 in 1983 and the price of the same car in 1984 was $6,300. We may construct an index, *I*, that indicates the *relative level* of the 1984 price compared to the 1983 price. The index is calculated as follows:

$$I = \frac{\text{price 1984}}{\text{price 1983}} \cdot 100 = \frac{\$6,300}{\$6,000} \cdot 100 = 105$$

The index in this example is obtained by dividing the 1984 price by the 1983 price and multiplying the result by 100. The value 105 indicates that the price in 1984 is 5 percent higher *relative to the base-period price*. The base period is 1983, and the 1983 price is assigned the index 100.

Note that the index may be either greater than, equal to, or less than 100. For example, the price of a stock traded on the New York Stock Exchange was $10 on March 1 and $8 on the following April 1. If March 1 is taken as the base, the $10 price is given the index value 100 and the $8 price is given the index value 80:

$$I = \frac{8}{10} \cdot 100 = 80$$

Whenever the index is above 100, the interpretation is that there has been an increase in the measured quantity or activity compared to the base period. Likewise, whenever the index is below 100, a decrease has occurred in the measured quantity or activity.

Business-related indexes may be divided into three general types:

1. Price indexes of the sort discussed above.
2. Quantity indexes, which measure relative economic change in physical units. (An example is the Index of Industrial Production.)
3. Value indexes, which reflect the combined impact of price and quantity changes.

We shall continue now to discuss price indexes alone. They constitute perhaps the most important indexes in business; also, the principal features of index numbers are common to all types of indexes, so that a detailed discussion of one type of index will suffice to clarify the problems involved in constructing, interpreting, and using others as well.

Economists, businesspeople, and financial analysts usually examine indexes over more than just two periods. Here is a hypothetical example based on data on beef prices spanning several years:

Year	Beef price (cents per pound)	Price index
1979	80	100.0
1980	85	106.3
1981	100	125.0
1982	90	112.5
1983	110	137.5
1984	120	150.0

Each year's index indicates the price level of beef relative to the price in the base year, 1979. For example, the index value 137.5 for 1983 is calculated as follows:

$$I_{1983} = \frac{\text{price } 1983}{\text{price } 1979} \cdot 100 = \frac{110}{80} \cdot 100 = 137.5$$

The 1983 price was 37.5 percent higher than the 1979 price. Note that a price index that never falls below 100 does not mean that there are no periods of price decline, and an index that never rises above 100 does not mean that there are no periods of price increase. For example, the index dropped from a high of 125.0 in 1981 to a low of 112.5 in 1982. Although both values are above 100, it is clear that beef prices declined in 1982. Indeed, the price dropped from $1.00 per pound in 1981 to $0.90 in 1982. (Incidentally, the percentage change in the price may be calculated either from the original data or from the index. The percentage change in price between 1981 and 1982 was $90/100 - 1 = 112.5/125 - 1 = -0.1$, or a drop of 10 percent.)

21.2 Choosing the Base Period

One of the most critical points in constructing an index is the choice of the appropriate base period and the time interval to be covered. Since an index is designed to facilitate the analysis of changes in activities over time, great care must be taken to avoid a situation in which misleading conclusions could be drawn because the base period has not been carefully selected. Consider a good whose price decreased steadily from 1964 through 1975 a total of 40 percent, and then increased steadily through 1984 back to its 1964 level. If 1964 is selected as the base year, the index declines from 100 to a low of 60 and then rebounds to 100 in 1984. This price index is illustrated in Figure 21.1a. Looking at the figure, we conclude that the price was the same in 1984 as it was in 1964. This conclusion is based on factual data and is in fact correct. If we choose 1975 as the base year, however (see Figure 21.1b), we conclude that the price has increased in the period 1975–84. This conclusion is also correct, but it may lead to a different interpretation.

The appropriate base period depends on relevant economic factors. For example, if the period following the year 1975 represents a stage of a new economic situation for the specific item under consideration, then 1975 should be preferred as a base period and the years 1964 through 1974 may be regarded as insignificant—perhaps even irrelevant, since that period's economic conditions are no longer pertinent. The disparity between the two indexes in our example demonstrates that the base period must be carefully selected so that the index will reflect relevant variations in activity level.

As another example, suppose the profits of a certain corporation have declined over a given period and then started to increase continuously. Consider a financial analyst who needs to examine the attractiveness of investment in this corporation's stock. By considering the entire period, the analyst may reach the conclusion that the firm's profitability has changed little, if

Figure 21.1

Hypothetical price index pattern

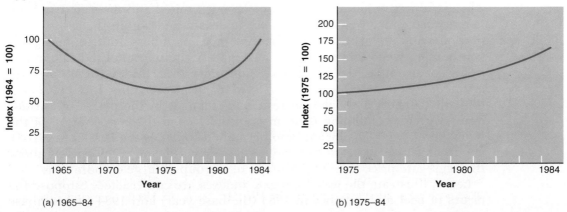

(a) 1965–84   (b) 1975–84

at all, since the current profitability is similar to its level at the beginning of the period. On the other hand, if the trough in profitability led to a replacement of old management by new management, the analyst would be better advised to choose the trough as a base. In this way, the index will show a steady increase in profitability, reflecting the performance of the new management. Profitability growth projections will be more meaningful if the old management's performance is not taken into consideration.

In most real situations, and particularly when the index represents more than one item, it is hard to find a time in which economic conditions turn around in so clear-cut a fashion. The real world is, for better or for worse, a bit more complex. Index-number series normally show some fluctuations over time. As a result, additional factors must be taken into consideration when the base period is selected.

First, the base period should be a "normal" period with regard to the relevant index. Obviously, "normality" is a rather elusive concept, but unless there are clear indications to the contrary, a period of relative price stability should be preferred to a period of strong fluctuations. Most indexes put out by the U.S. government have a three-year period for their base; that is, the average price over the three-year period is given the index 100.

Another consideration in choosing the base period is that it should not be too far in the past. Because of the dynamics of economic development, it is more meaningful to compare current conditions with those of a period from the recent past than with those of a bygone era.

Most indexes, as we shall see in Section 21.3, are designed to measure the relative levels of activity of a *group* of items. Because new products are constantly coming on the market and consumers are continuously shifting their demand from old to new products, and also because old products keep improving in quality, a comparison with a period too far in the past will not be as interesting as a comparison with a period closer to the present. You can easily think of a lot of products that are widely used today that did not even exist a few years ago. To cope with this problem, it is advisable to shift the base period forward every few years. The U.S. government indexes have their base periods shifted forward approximately every decade.

21.3 Aggregative Index: An Index of More Than One Item

The usefulness of indexes of only one item is limited and their contribution is marginal, since we can use the original data and obtain the same information without much extra difficulty. Index numbers contribute significantly more when they reflect the aggregate activity level of more than one item. For example, the well-known **Consumer Price Index (CPI)** *measures price changes of a representative "basket" of items over time.* It is extremely difficult to reach a conclusion regarding changes in the prices of various items without combining them into an index, and the contribution of the index here is very significant. Another famous index is the Dow-Jones (D-J), about which we all hear every day in the news. This index informs us about the aggregate price level of the stocks of a group of large corporations.

Let us illustrate the way aggregate indexes are constructed. Suppose the prices of beef and matches in 1983 (the base year) and 1984 (the nonbase year) were as follows:

	Price (cents)	
Product	1983 (Base year)	1984 (Nonbase year)
Beef (per pound)	110	120
Matches (per box)	5	10

For the sake of simplicity, suppose the consumer buys only beef and matches, and that we want to construct an index of the "consumption basket." The index may be constructed in several ways, each of which leads to a different result.

UNWEIGHTED INDEX NUMBERS

The **unweighted index** is simply the *sum of all the prices in the nonbase period divided by the sum of all the prices in the base period.* In our example this is simply

$$I_{1984} = \frac{120 + 10}{110 + 5} \cdot 100 = \frac{130}{115} \cdot 100 = 113.0$$

In a more general form, the index is obtained by summing the prices in the nonbase period, p_n, and dividing the total by the corresponding sum of all the prices in the base period, p_0:

UNWEIGHTED INDEX

$$I = \frac{\Sigma p_n}{\Sigma p_0} \cdot 100 \tag{21.1}$$

The advantage of this index is its simplicity. It is easy to calculate and easy to understand. The disadvantage is that the index is a function of the units that we choose to use. Suppose that instead of looking at the price of one box of matches, we take the price of a big package containing a dozen small boxes. In this case we get the following numbers:

	Price (cents)	
Product	1983 (Base year)	1984 (Nonbase year)
Beef (per pound)	110	120
Matches (per dozen boxes)	60 (= 12 · 5)	120 (= 12 · 10)

The simple unweighted index based on these prices is

$$I = \frac{120 + 120}{110 + 60} \cdot 100 = \frac{240}{170} \cdot 100 = 141.2$$

compared with the 113.0 that we obtained earlier. Thus, despite its simplicity, the unweighted index is not adequate because its numerical value depends heavily on the units we select for the participating items. Since the units can be chosen arbitrarily, we obtain an arbitrary result. In order to overcome this problem, we can use the average of price relatives, which is discussed next.

THE AVERAGE OF PRICE RELATIVES

The idea behind the **average of price relatives** is to calculate a separate index for each item and then compute the average of all the separate indexes. This technique overcomes the problem of arbitrary choice of units. For the first example above

$$\text{Index for matches} = \frac{10}{5} \cdot 100 = 200$$

$$\text{Index for beef} \quad = \frac{120}{110} \cdot 100 = 109$$

and the average index is (200 + 109)/2 = 154.5.

Now, for the second case, when the price of matches is given per dozen boxes

$$\text{Index for matches} = \frac{120}{60} \cdot 100 = 200$$

$$\text{Index for beef} \quad = \frac{120}{110} \cdot 100 = 109$$

and the arithmetic average of these two separate indexes remains 154.5.

The average of price relatives is also simple to calculate, and it has the advantage of not being vulnerable to disparities in the selected units (pounds, tons, or whatever).

In a more general form, when we have m items in the basket, we use the following formula:

AVERAGE OF PRICE RELATIVES

$$I = \frac{\sum \frac{p_n}{p_0} \cdot 100}{m} \tag{21.2}$$

The summation is over the m items included in the basket, and the ratio $\frac{p_n}{p_0}$ is calculated for each item separately.

As we have seen, this index has the advantage of not being dependent on the selected units. On the other hand, its disadvantage is that the separate price indexes are unweighted. To see why the weights are important, consider the cost-of-living index.

In several countries (Israel, Finland, Brazil), wages are linked to the cost-of-living index. When the index goes up by a certain percentage, employees get a proportionate wage increase. Since the United States experienced double-digit inflation in the mid-1970s, some economists (including the Nobel Prize–winner Milton Friedman) have suggested the establishment of some mode of indexing so that key economic variables (wages, interest rates, and so on) could be linked to the cost-of-living index. Even without a comprehensive indexing system, however, the wages of millions of American workers change with the cost-of-living index. In almost all collective bargaining contracts, both parties watch very carefully for changes in the Consumer Price Index and use them to bolster their arguments in their negotiations.

Suppose that we want to establish an index that will provide an adequate measure for employee compensation. Would you recommend using the average of price relatives?

Using this index in the beef-and-matches example, one would come to the conclusion that prices had increased 54.5 percent between 1983 and 1984, and hence wages should be increased by the same percentage in order to keep up with price increases. Is such an increase in wages indeed justified? The employees would be happy with such a cost-of-living ajdustment, but obviously 54.5 percent will more than compensate for changes in the price level. The reason is that the change in the price of matches, though large in itself, has only a small impact on consumers, since they spend a very small fraction of their income on matches, while a substantially larger proportion is spent on beef. Since the purpose of the cost-of-living adjustment is to keep the wage earner's welfare unchanged despite changes in prices, the wage increase should be based on the weighted average of price changes, the weights being a function of the relative amount of money spent on each item.

WEIGHTED INDEX NUMBERS

Let us continue with the beef-and-matches example, assuming that consumers spend 90 percent of their total expenditure on beef and only 10 percent on matches (recall that we have assumed for simplicity that only these two products are consumed). Now suppose we want to calculate an index that takes into account the weight of each product in the consumption basket. Such an index will reflect the cost of the same basket of goods at the new prices. The price of matches increased 100 percent and hence its index is 200 (see earlier calculations); the index of beef is 109, so the **weighted average index** is

$$I = \frac{200 \cdot 0.1 + 109 \cdot 0.9}{0.1 + 0.9} = \frac{20 + 98}{1} = 118$$

Accordingly, a wage increase of only 18 percent should enable employees to buy the same basket of goods they used to buy before the price increase. Take, for example, an employee who used to spend $200 a week, and bought $180 worth of beef ($200 · 0.9 = $180) and $20 worth of matches ($200 · 0.1 = $20). Assuming the old prices prevail, his earnings are sufficient for 180/1.10 = 163.64 pounds of beef and 20/0.05 = 400 boxes of matches. Suppose now the new prices prevail and the employee gets $236 per week—18 percent over the old earnings. To buy the previous quantities, the employee needs 163.64 · $1.20 = $196.37 for beef and 400 · $0.10 = $40 for matches. He therefore needs a total budget of $196.37 + $40 = $236.37. (The difference between this figure and the $236 obtained when we used the weighted index is only the result of rounding.)

From this example it is obvious that each product included in the basket should have an effect on the index proportional to its importance to consumers. Thus we calculate the weighted average index by the following formula:

WEIGHTED ARITHMETIC AVERAGE INDEX

$$I_w = \frac{\sum\left(\frac{p_n}{p_0} \cdot 100\right)w}{\Sigma w}$$

(21.3)

Here w is the weight of the item in total spending during the base period.

In the specific case in which we have m items all with equal weights—that is, $w = 1/m$—the weighted index reduces to the simple average of price relatives.

Obviously, with weighted averages, the question is what weights to employ. Here we have several options.

Laspeyres Price Index   The **Laspeyres price index**, named after Etienne Laspeyres, who first introduced it in the eighteenth century, uses the quantities consumed in the base period as weights. The following formula applies:

LASPEYRES PRICE INDEX

$$P_L = \frac{\Sigma p_n q_0}{\Sigma p_0 q_0} \cdot 100$$

(21.4)

Here p_n is the price of a given item in the basket in the current period, p_0 is the price of the same item in the base period, and q_0 is the quantity of that item purchased in the base period.

In the cost-of-living example, if the index currently stands at 110, a 10 percent wage increase is required to enable employees to purchase *the same quantities they purchased in the base period* (q_0).

Note that $P_L = I_w$ when we define the weights as $w = p_0 q_0$. To see this, simply replace w in Equation 21.3 by $p_0 q_0$ to obtain

$$I_w = \frac{\sum\left(\frac{p_n}{p_0} \cdot 100\right)p_0 q_0}{\Sigma p_0 q_0} = \frac{\Sigma p_n q_0}{\Sigma p_0 q_0} \cdot 100 = P_L$$

(21.5)

The p_0s that appear in the numerator cancel out.

Paasche Price Index   The **Paasche price index** is also a weighted index, but it uses the current quantities, q_n, as weights, rather than those of the base period, q_0. In the cost-of-living example, the Paasche index indicates what the wage level should be if our objective is to compensate for price increases in such a way that wage earners can buy the *current basket of items* (i.e., a different relative quantity of items) rather than the basket they consumed in the base period. The following formula applies:

PAASCHE PRICE INDEX

$$P_P = \frac{\Sigma p_n q_n}{\Sigma p_0 q_n} \cdot 100 \qquad\qquad (21.6)$$

Note that P_P is obtained from I_w by use of the weights $w = p_0 q_n$. To show this, simply substitute $p_0 q_n$ for w in I_w to obtain

$$I_w = \frac{\Sigma\left(\frac{p_n}{p_0} \cdot 100\right)w}{\Sigma w} = \frac{\Sigma\left(\frac{p_n}{p_0} \cdot 100\right)p_0 q_n}{\Sigma p_0 q_n} = \frac{\Sigma p_n q_n}{\Sigma p_0 q_n} \cdot 100 = P_P \qquad (21.7)$$

Fixed-Weights Price Index   The weighted index numbers are theoretically preferred to the simple unweighted indexes, but they are also more difficult to calculate. The Laspeyres index is used more widely than the Paasche index. It requires information about the weights q_0—about consumer spending on each item in the base period. To determine the weights, then, it is necessary to carry out a survey only once, in the base period. With the Paasche index, one has to determine the quantities q_n every period, which is impractical in most cases, since a separate survey is required every period.

In practice, a modified Laspeyres index is often used; it is known as the **fixed-weights index**, I_F. The quantities, though fixed, do not really stay unchanged forever; they are changed from time to time, as new survey data provide updated information of quantities.

In principle, the fixed-weights index is very similar to the Laspeyres index, since both use quantities for weights. The difference is that in the fixed-weights index the weights are not necessarily representative of the base period, and every now and then they can be changed and updated to reflect current consumer behavior. For example, the Consumer Price Index, published by the Bureau of Labor Statistics, uses weights derived from a consumer survey for the years 1972–73, although the base period is 1967. These fixed weights will remain in use until a new consumer survey is completed and updated weights are obtained.

21.4 Quantity Indexes

In Section 21.3 we explored several types of price indexes in some detail. All of them are designed to measure *value* changes when *quantities are held constant*. **Quantity indexes**, on the other hand, are designed to *measure value changes when prices are held constant*. The purpose of such indexes is to provide a measure of change in physical quantity, such as that of industrial production.

Technically, an unweighted average of relative quantities can be computed by averaging all of the separate $\frac{q_n}{q_0} \cdot 100$ values. This average, however, is meaningless, since the various items are measured in different units. Therefore, we make use of the **Laspeyres and Paasche quantity indexes**, given by Equations 21.8 and 21.9:

LASPEYRES QUANTITY INDEX

$$Q_L = \frac{\Sigma p_0 q_n}{\Sigma p_0 q_0} \cdot 100 \tag{21.8}$$

PAASCHE QUANTITY INDEX

$$Q_P = \frac{\Sigma p_n q_n}{\Sigma p_n q_0} \cdot 100 \tag{21.9}$$

The Laspeyres quantity index measures the change in value that would have occurred as a result of quantity changes had the prices been kept at their *initial* (base-period) level. The Paasche quantity index, in contrast, measures the change in value that would have occurred as a result of quantity changes had the prices been equal to the nonbase period prices in both the base and nonbase periods.

The most widely used quantity index in the United States is the Federal Reserve Board's Index of Industrial Production.

21.5 Value Index

Suppose that the United States currently exports to Japan quantities q_n of various products at unit prices p_n. The respective quantities and prices in the base period are q_0 and p_0. The ratio of $\Sigma p_n q_n$ to $\Sigma p_0 q_0$ represents the change in the value of exports, a change that has two components: changes in export prices and changes in the quantity of exported products. When the ratio is multiplied by 100, it gives an index called a **value index**. It does not measure the separate changes in prices or in quantities; rather, it measures the combined change in the value of our exports—the total amount of dollars we receive from our trade partner. Formally

VALUE INDEX

$$I_V = \frac{\Sigma p_n q_n}{\Sigma p_0 q_0} \cdot 100 \tag{21.10}$$

Let us now look more closely at the Laspeyres and Paasche price and quantity indexes, as well as the value index, using a numerical example.

EXAMPLE 21.1

Suppose a typical consumption basket consists of three products only: beef, bread, and milk. The following were the quantities consumed in the base period, 1983, and in the latest available nonbase year, 1984:

Product	1983 (Base year)	1984 (Nonbase year)
Beef (pounds)	200	210
Bread (loaves)	400	410
Milk (quarts)	200	600

The corresponding prices were (in cents):

Product	1983 (Base year)	1984 (Nonbase year)
Beef (per pound)	200	220
Bread (per loaf)	80	100
Milk (per quart)	60	80

Let us first calculate the Laspeyres and Paasche *price* indexes:

$$P_L = \frac{\Sigma p_n q_0}{\Sigma p_0 q_0} \cdot 100 = \frac{220 \cdot 200 + 100 \cdot 400 + 80 \cdot 200}{200 \cdot 200 + 80 \cdot 400 + 60 \cdot 200} \cdot 100 = \frac{100,000}{84,000} \cdot 100 = 119.0$$

$$P_P = \frac{\Sigma p_n q_n}{\Sigma p_0 q_n} \cdot 100 = \frac{220 \cdot 210 + 100 \cdot 410 + 80 \cdot 600}{200 \cdot 210 + 80 \cdot 410 + 60 \cdot 600} \cdot 100 = \frac{135,000}{110,800} \cdot 100 = 122.0$$

Next, let us calculate the Laspeyres and Paasche *quantity* indexes:

$$Q_L = \frac{\Sigma p_0 q_n}{\Sigma p_0 q_0} \cdot 100 = \frac{200 \cdot 210 + 80 \cdot 410 + 60 \cdot 600}{200 \cdot 200 + 80 \cdot 400 + 60 \cdot 200} \cdot 100 = \frac{110,800}{84,000} \cdot 100 = 131.9$$

$$Q_P = \frac{\Sigma p_n q_n}{\Sigma p_n q_0} \cdot 100 = \frac{200 \cdot 210 + 100 \cdot 410 + 80 \cdot 600}{220 \cdot 200 + 100 \cdot 400 + 80 \cdot 200} \cdot 100 = \frac{135,200}{100,000} \cdot 100 = 135.2$$

Finally, the value index, I_V, is given by

$$I_V = \frac{\Sigma p_n q_n}{\Sigma p_0 q_0} \cdot 100 = \frac{220 \cdot 210 + 100 \cdot 410 + 80 \cdot 600}{200 \cdot 200 + 80 \cdot 400 + 60 \cdot 200} \cdot 100 = \frac{135,200}{84,000} \cdot 100 = 161.0$$

What is the interpretation of these five indexes?

The Laspeyres price index, P_L, indicates how much more the consumer needed to spend in 1984 to purchase the same basket of items as in 1983. Thus it represents the effect of a change in prices on a *given base-period* basket of items. If wages are linked to prices, P_L indicates that a 19 percent increase is in order.

The Paasche price index measures the change in consumer spending resulting from a change in prices on a *given nonbase-period* basket of items. Thus, if a change in consumption patterns has occurred between the base and the current period, the Paasche price index uses the after-the-change quantities. The most notable change in quantities in our example occurs in milk consumption. The Paasche index uses the 1984 quantity, 600 quarts, whereas the Laspeyres index uses the 1983 quantity, 200 quarts. Since the price of milk rose between 1983 and 1984, the Paasche index simply gives more weight to this price increase, so that P_P turns out higher than P_L. (Of course, the index represents the changes in prices of the other two items as well.)

Similarly, the Paasche quantity index turns out higher than the Laspeyres index. Since prices are used here as weights, this is not surprising. Milk prices rose proportionately higher than other prices, so that Paasche gives milk a greater weight than Laspeyres does. Since the rise in consumption was greatest in milk, the Paasche quantity index is higher than the Laspeyres. (Again, it is clear that the index also considers items other than milk.)

The value index, I_V, simply measures the amount in dollars spent in period n relative to the amount in dollars spent in the base period. As we indicated earlier, it answers the following question: how much more (or less) money does the consumer need in a given period (relative to the base period) in order to buy the new basket of items, considering the simultaneous change in prices and quantities?

Note that the product of the Laspeyres price ratio and the Paasche quantity ratio is equal to the product of the Laspeyres quantity ratio and the Paasche price ratio. This product gives the value ratio:

$$\underbrace{\frac{\Sigma p_n q_0}{\Sigma p_0 q_0}}_{\substack{\text{Laspeyres} \\ \text{price} \\ \text{ratio}}} \cdot \underbrace{\frac{\Sigma p_n q_n}{\Sigma p_n q_0}}_{\substack{\text{Paasche} \\ \text{quantity} \\ \text{ratio}}} = \underbrace{\frac{\Sigma p_0 q_n}{\Sigma p_0 q_0}}_{\substack{\text{Laspeyres} \\ \text{quantity} \\ \text{ratio}}} \cdot \underbrace{\frac{\Sigma p_n q_n}{\Sigma p_0 q_n}}_{\substack{\text{Paasche} \\ \text{price} \\ \text{ratio}}} = \underbrace{\frac{\Sigma p_n q_n}{\Sigma p_0 q_0}}_{\substack{\text{Value} \\ \text{ratio}}}$$

In our example

$$1.19 \cdot 1.352 = 1.319 \cdot 1.22 = 1.61$$

21.6 How to Use Index-Number Series

Some methods for using index-number series are presented in this section. We shall discuss *deflation* of value series, *technical shifting* of the base period, and *splicing*.

DEFLATION OF VALUE SERIES BY PRICE INDEXES

A common use of price indexes is the adjustment of value series for changes in the purchasing power of the dollar. This procedure is known as **deflation**, and it results in a restatement of the orginal value series in terms of "constant dollars." The reason such deflation is important is that values stated in "current" or "nominal" figures could change significantly over time or from place to place, solely as a result of inflation. Thus, in order to eliminate the impact of inflation and obtain a picture of the "real" change, not the "nominal" change, we need to deflate the series.

Consider the following hypothetical average annual salary of professors in major American universities in 1970 and 1984:

Year	Average annual salary	Consumer Price Index	"Real" average annual salary
1970	$14,000	100	$14,000
1984	$27,300	210	$13,000

The nominal average salary indeed increased during this period by 95 percent ($27,300/14,000 = 1.95$); but were the professors better off in 1984? The answer, of course, is no. The $27,300 salary in 1984 is not sufficient to buy the same basket of items that $14,000 could buy in 1970. This fact is easily revealed by a comparison of 1970 and 1984 real salaries. To obtain the real salary we deflate the nominal 1984 salary by first dividing the nominal salary by the price index (210) and then multiplying by 100:

$$\frac{27,300}{210} \cdot 100 = \$13,000$$

The following is a more comprehensive example of value-series deflation based on actual data for the United States and West Germany. The example presents a comparison between the gross national product of these two countries over a period of seven years.

EXAMPLE 21.2

The gross national products (GNPs) of the United States and West Germany for the years 1974–80, along with their consumer price indexes, are given in Table 21.1. During this period, the German GNP rose from 986.9 billion to 1,491.9 billion Deutsche marks, so that in 1980 it was 51.2 percent higher than in 1974. During the same period, the U.S. GNP rose from $1,413.3 billion to $2,626.1 billion, or 85.8 percent. The differences between the nominal GNPs are also shown in Figure 21.2a. The question is whether the U.S. standard of living did indeed grow that much more rapidly during the period. To answer the question, we must first switch to real currency figures by deflating each GNP series by its respective CPI. When we do that, a different picture emerges (see Table 21.2).

TABLE 21.1

Gross National Products and Consumer Price Indexes, West Germany and United States, 1974–80

Year	West Germany GNP (billions of Deutsche marks)	West Germany CPI (1975 = 100)	United States GNP (billions of dollars)	United States CPI (1975 = 100)
1974	DM 986.9	94.4	$1,413.3	91.6
1975	1,034.9	100.0	1,549.2	100.0
1976	1,125.0	104.3	1,718.0	105.8
1977	1,200.6	108.1	1,918.0	112.7
1978	1,290.7	111.1	2,156.1	121.2
1979	1,398.2	115.6	2,413.9	134.9
1980	1,491.9	122.0	2,626.1	153.1

Source: International Monetary Fund, *International Financial Statistics*, September 1981.

Figure 21.2

GNPs of the
United States
and West
Germany,
current and
"real"
currencies,
1974–80

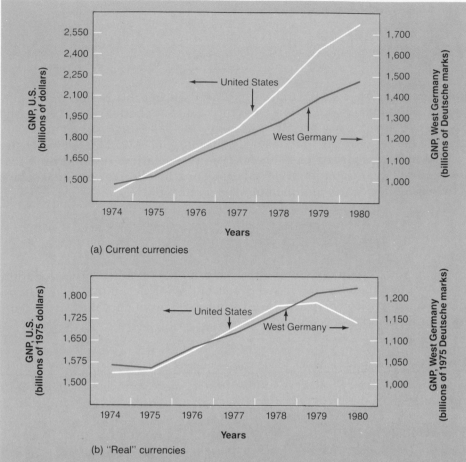

(a) Current currencies

(b) "Real" currencies

Source: International Monetary Fund, *International Financial Statistics*, September 1981.

TABLE 21.2
GNP in Real Terms, West Germany and
United States, 1974–80

Year	West Germany (billions of 1975 Deutsche marks)	United States (billions of 1975 dollars)
1974	DM 1,045.4	$1,542.9
1975	1,034.9	1,549.2
1976	1,078.6	1,623.8
1977	1,110.6	1,701.9
1978	1,161.7	1,779.0
1979	1,209.5	1,789.4
1980	1,222.9	1,715.3

As the numbers as well as Figure 21.2*b* show, the real growth in the
GNP of both countries was substantially more moderate than the nominal growth because of the high inflation rates during the period. Furthermore, the growth in real terms was substantially smaller in the
United States than in West Germany. Note also that while the nominal
GNP in the United States rose by rather substantial amounts in 1980,
real GNP in fact dropped in that year.

SHIFTING THE BASE YEAR

Sometimes it is of interest to compare two indexes either within the same country (such as Standard and Poor's stock index and the Consumer Price Index) or between two countries. Since the indexes may have different base years, they should be adjusted to a common base period so that a meaningful comparison may be made. The procedure, known as **technical shifting**, is quite simple and is best illustrated by a numerical example. Table 21.3 presents two indexes with different base years. In column 1 we have a hypothetical Consumer Price Index whose base year is 1975. Suppose we want to shift the base year to 1980. All we need do is *deflate* the series by the original 1980 index value. If we divide each number in column 1 by 122 and then multiply the result by 100, we will obtain the same index with 1980 as its new base year, as shown in column 2. For example, for 1975 we get $\frac{100}{122} \cdot 100 = 82.0$, for 1976 we get $\frac{110}{122} \cdot 100 = 90.2$, and so on. Note that the percentage change in the index numbers from one year to the next is the same in both columns, and shifting the base year is only a technical adjustment used for presentation purposes.

TABLE 21.3
Hypothetical Consumer Price Indexes Based on 1975 and 1980, Respectively

Year	(1) Consumer Price Index (1975 = 100)	(2) [(col. 1) ÷ 122] · 100 Consumer Price Index (1980 = 100)
1975	100	82.0
1976	110	90.2
1977	112	91.8
1978	114	93.4
1979	118	96.7
1980	122	100.0
1981	130	106.6
1982	135	110.7
1983	140	114.8
1984	150	123.0

To calculate the percentage change in an index from, say, 1983 to 1984, we divide the 1984 price by the 1983 price, subtract 1.0, and multiply the result by 100. Here are the calculations of the percentage change in the index numbers of both columns:

$$\text{Column 1} \qquad\qquad \text{Column 2}$$
$$\left(\frac{150}{140} - 1\right) \cdot 100 = 7.14\% \qquad \left(\frac{123.0}{114.8} - 1\right) \cdot 100 = 7.14\%$$

SPLICING

Occasionally a published index will be discontinued or significantly revised. If a revision occurs, the next index and the old index *do not* measure exactly the same thing, and they therefore must be distinguished. At times, however, we need to use the index over a period that requires data from the old series as well as the new. Despite all the theoretical limitations of using two different indexes as if they were one and the same, this is sometimes the best alternative available. *Combining the two indexes* is known as **splicing**, and it can be done only if the old and the new series have at least one overlapping period, which is normally the case when a revision occurs. Technically, splicing is a very easy procedure; it is illustrated in Table 21.4. For the period 1980–84, the spliced index is identical to the revised index. For the years 1975–79, the spliced index is the same as the old index after it has been deflated by its 1980 level. That is to say, to obtain the spliced index for the 1975–79 period we simply divide the old index figures by 108.7 and then multiply by 100. For 1975, for example, we get $\frac{90.1}{108.7} \cdot 100 = 82.9$, and so on.

TABLE 21.4
Old, Revised, and Spliced Indexes

Year	Old index (1977 = 100)	Revised index (1980 = 100)	Spliced index (1980 = 100)
1975	90.1		82.9
1976	95.0		87.4
1977	100.0		92.0
1978	103.3		95.0
1979	104.6		96.2
1980	108.7	100.0	100.0
1981		110.1	110.1
1982		108.3	108.3
1983		114.2	114.2
1984		121.8	121.8

While the technical work involved in splicing is simple, the index must be used with great caution, since the figures for the "old" years can at best be regarded as rough approximations.

21.7 Some Important U.S. Indexes

THE CONSUMER PRICE INDEX (CPI)

One of the most important indexes compiled by the U.S. government is the Consumer Price Index (CPI). It is a widely accepted measure of inflation, and, as mentioned earlier, is frequently used in wage contract bargaining. The CPI often serves also as a deflator of economic series. It is a major indicator of the general health of the U.S. economy. In some countries major economic variables, such as wages and interest rates, are linked to those countries' Consumer Price Indexes.

The name Consumer Price Index was adopted by the Bureau of Labor Statistics (BLS) and the National Industrial Conference Board during World War I. Initially it measured changes in the retail prices of the goods and services bought by city wage earners and clerical workers. In 1978, a second index, the CPI-U, was also introduced to expand coverage to all urban consumers. A revised version of the old CPI, called the CPI-W, still measures changes in expenditures by city wage earners and clerical workers only. Both indexes are continuous with the old CPI.

The CPI became important at the end of World War I, when data were in demand for use in wage negotiations in shipbuilding cities. Changes in the cost of living were first published in the BLS *Monthly Labor Review* in October 1919, and regular publication began in February 1921. Since 1978, prices of food, fuels, and a few other items have been collected monthly in all cities, and prices of most commodities and services have been collected monthly in the five largest cities, and bimonthly in the remaining cities the index surveys.

Weights used in calculating the index are based on studies of actual expenditures. Quantities and qualities of items in the "market basket" remain essentially the same between consecutive pricing periods, so that the index measures the effect of *price changes alone* on the cost of living. It does not measure changes in the total amount families spend. A study conducted during 1917–19 provided the weights used until 1935. Since then, the index has undergone five major revisions, each of which involved bringing the "market basket" of goods and services up to date, revising the weights, and improving the sample and methodology. The most recent revision, instituted in 1978, adopted 1967 as the reference year (1967 = 100), and introduced new expenditure weights based on a 1972–73 Consumer Expenditure Survey of 216 areas.

The list of items currently priced for the index includes approximately 400 goods and services, which are collected in 85 areas, including cities and suburbs. For some items several different qualities are priced. Characteristics of each item are no longer specified in great detail, but every effort is made to ensure that differences in reported prices are measures of price change only. Researchers attempt to obtain the prices actually paid by consumers, not list prices from which discounts normally are given. All taxes directly associated with the purchase or use of the items are incorporated in the index.

STANDARD & POOR'S (S&P) STOCK PRICE INDEXES

Many indexes measure changes in stock prices. Among them are the Dow-Jones Index, the New York Stock Exchange Index, and the S&P indexes. All are used as indicators for forecasts of changes in the economy, since pessimistic or optimistic attitudes of investors with regard to future corporate earnings are reflected in stock prices.

The **S&P stock price indexes** have been steadily expanding their coverage over the years to supply a dependable measure of the composite price pattern of the majority of stocks. Back in 1923, S&P pioneered with the issuance of a scientifically constructed stock price index organized according to leading industrial groups. At that time, 26 subgroup indexes, based on 233 stock issues, were compiled. Five hundred stocks are now covered, broken down into 88 groups that make up the four main categories: industrials, railroads, utilities, and the 500 composites. There are also four supplementary group series: capital goods companies, consumer goods, high-grade common stocks, and low-priced common stocks. In addition there are 11 group indexes that are not included in the S&P Series of 500 Stocks. These include indexes of bank stocks (New York City and outside New York City), investment companies, property, liability and life insurance companies, trucking companies, and discount stores, and four other groups that were added in 1970 in order to trace the price movement of some of the more recently developed industries: air freight, atomic energy, conglomerates, and multiline insurance companies. Also added in 1970 and included in the Series of 500 Stocks are indexes for forest products, hotels/motels, offshore drilling, real estate, and restaurant operators.

These S&P stock price indexes, which are based on the aggregate market value of the common stocks of all of the companies in the sample, express the observed market value as a percentage of the average market value during the base period. Originally the base period was 1926; it was subsequently shifted to the average of the 1935–39 period, and then finally to the currently used base period, 1941–43, with the average stock value of 1941–43 being set at 10. This base results in a price index level that is more realistic than that of most popular composite stock price measures, in that it is not absurdly distant from the average price level of all stocks listed on the New York Stock Exchange. The group indexes added since 1957 are based on various recent periods.

The 1957 revision of the S&P stock price indexes marked a giant step in another direction. Thanks to electronic computer and input feeders, the four main group indexes are now computed at five-minute intervals. S&P does not publish these frequent readings but does maintain a record of them. Hourly indexes are published in the Daily News section of *S&P Corporation Records*. Daily high, low, and closing indexes are published in the weekly *Outlook* and the monthly *Current Statistics*.

The formula adopted by S&P after much testing is a value index generally defined as a "base-weighted aggregative" expressed in relatives with the average value for the base period (1941–43) equal to 10. This method of computation has two distinct advantages over most index number series: (1) it has the flexibility needed to adjust for arbitrary price changes caused by the issuance of rights, stock dividends, splits, and the like, and (2) the resultant index numbers are accurate and have a relatively high degree of continuity, which is especially important when long-term comparisons are to be made. Certain modifications of the basic formula have been introduced to make it possible to maintain the best possible representation over the years. The character of the stock market is subject to gradual but continuous change, and it is only by periodic checks of coverage that true representation can be maintained.

Each component stock is weighted, so that it will influence the index in proportion to its importance in its respective market. The most suitable weighting factor for this purpose is the number of shares outstanding. The price of any share multiplied by the number of shares outstanding gives the current market value of that particular stock. The market value determines the relative importance of the security.

The base value of a group of stocks is the average of the weekly group values for the period 1941–43. The current group value is expressed as a relative number by dividing it by its base-period value and multiplying the result by 10. In this relative form an index number attains its maximum usefulness for statistical purposes.

The formula for the base-weighted aggregative index is

$$\text{Index} = \frac{\Sigma p_1 q_1}{\Sigma p_0 q_0} \cdot 10$$

where p_1 represents the current market price, p_0 the market price in the base period, q_1 the number of shares currently outstanding, and q_0 the number of shares outstanding in the base period. The denominator of the index is adjusted to reflect new issues of stocks.

Note that instead of choosing a base of 100, S&P chose 10 as the base index number, but this arbitrary choice does not change the conception inherent in the index.

Figure 21.3 gives the CPI and the S&P index for the period 1918–80. Note that while the CPI increased about fivefold during this period, the S&P index increased twelvefold. Roughly, this means that if an investor held one dollar in cash (not invested) since 1918, it would be worth only about 20 cents in 1980. If the investor invested the dollar in 1918 in a portfolio of stocks corresponding to the S&P index, it would be worth $12 in nominal terms or about $2.4 in real terms in 1980 (since CPI increased almost fivefold during this period: $12 \div 5 = 2.4$).

Note that despite the general upward trend, the year-by-year fluctuations in the S&P index are quite large; this implies a substantial risk to investors. For example, between 1972 and mid-1974 the index dropped from about 120 to 80, and hence investors lost about one-third of the 1972 value of their investments. Note also that we shifted the CPI base year so that the two indexes (CPI and S&P) have the same base of 10 in 1941–43.

Among other important indexes, which we shall not discuss in detail, are the Wholesale Price Index, the Industrial Production Index, the Corporate Profits Index, the General Production Index, and the Population Index.

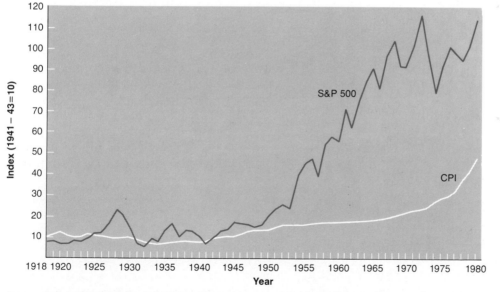

Figure 21.3

Consumer Price Index and Standard & Poor's 500, 1918–80 (1941–43 = 10 for both indexes)

Source: *Standard & Poor's Trade and Securities Statistics, Security Price Index Record* (New York, 1980), p. 4; U.S. Department of Commerce, Bureau of the Census, *Historical Statistics of the United States, Colonial Times to 1970* (Washington, D.C., 1975), pt. 1, Series E 135–166, pp. 210–211; U.S. Department of Commerce, Bureau of Economic Analysis, *Business Conditions Digest*, September 1981, p. 7.

LEADING ECONOMIC INDICATORS

The National Bureau of Economic Research (NBER) established twelve economic indicators, including some important indexes, which attempt to approximate changes in the economy and may thus be used to indicate future business trends or economic cycles. The average of these **leading indicators** is important in policy making. Charts of the twelve leading economic indicators selected by the NBER are regularly published in *Business Conditions Digest*. Some of the indexes included among these indicators are the net business formation (business starts minus failures), new orders by firms, housing permits, inventory accumulation, prices of raw materials, corporate profits, and stock price level (the S&P index).

21.8 International Comparison of Indexes

We often wish to compare one country's activity with another's. International comparison of indexes serves to explain many economic phenomena and helps in the formulation of customs policy, export-import policy, and the like. Obviously, in order to get a meaningful picture one has to shift the indexes of all countries included in the study to a common base year.

Figure 21.4a gives the indexes of total industrial production in the United States, West Germany, and Japan. As we can see, industrial production grew considerably faster in Japan than in the United States and West Germany

Figure 21.4

Indexes of industrial production and consumer prices, United States, Japan, and West Germany, 1965–80 (1970 = 100)

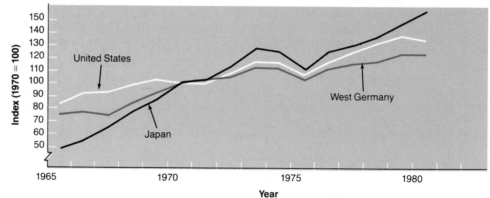

(a) Total industrial production

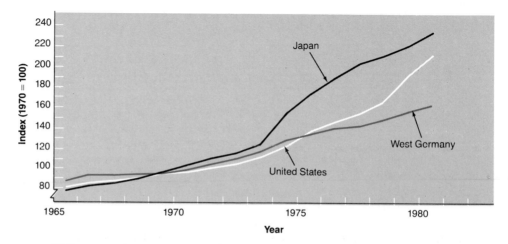

(b) Consumer prices

Source: International Monetary Fund, *International Financial Statistics*, various issues.

during the 1965–80 period. In all three countries, the index declined around 1973, in the wake of the oil crisis that hit the industrial world. Japan, which is totally dependent on imported oil, suffered the most from the crisis. After 1975, however, all three countries overcame the oil crisis and industrial production resumed its growth, returning in 1977 to the level it had reached before the oil crisis.

Figure 21.4*b* compares consumer prices in the same three countries over the same period of time. The figure shows a greater diversity in consumer price behavior in the years following the oil crisis (1973) than in earlier years. Prices in West Germany rose the least during the period. The United States experienced similar price behavior before 1973 but more rapidly increasing prices afterward. Japan was affected the most by the oil crisis: its prices increased significantly faster than those in the other two countries. However, consumer prices also rose more rapidly in Japan before the oil crisis, that is, during the 1965–73 period.

Figure 21.5 compares the indexes of hourly earnings in the same three countries and over the same period of time, 1965–80. While earnings in West Germany increased somewhat faster than in the United States, the most striking fact seen in the figure is that earnings have increased in Japan much more rapidly than in either West Germany or the United States. The higher rate of inflation in Japan (see Figure 21.4*b*) accounts only in part for the steeper increase in wages: the balance represents a genuine increase in real earnings and improvement in the Japanese standard of living. The general trend appears to operate in the direction of a diminishing wage differential among the industrial countries, with the result that traditional cheap-labor countries are losing their advantage.

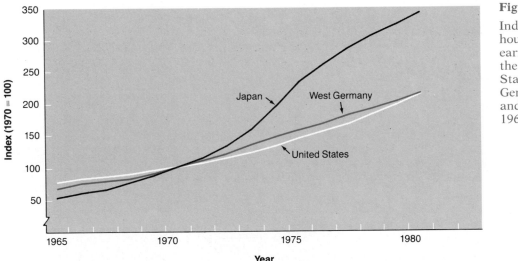

Figure 21.5

Index of hourly earnings in the United States, West Germany, and Japan, 1965–80

Source: International Monetary Fund, *International Financial Statistics*, various issues.

21.9 A Word of Caution

Index numbers can serve only as a proxy for a description of a given phenomenon, and generalizations may be very dangerous. We shall list only some of the major difficulties involved in index numbers.

1. *Choosing the base period.* As we show in Figure 21.1, one can "play around" with the base period and give various impressions of the real trend of the variable. An index based on a given year could lead one to accept the notion that a company's profitability was in good shape, while one based on a different year could suggest the contrary. When we interpret such an index we must always consider the fact that the index measures the firm's profitability only in *relation* to the base period.

2. *Items included in the index.* A change of 10 percent in the Consumer Price Index may be completely irrelevant to a consumer whose consumption pattern is unlike that of the "average consumer." If I consume only bread and milk and the price of these two items has not changed, there is a zero increase in the price level as far as I am concerned. Perhaps somewhat more interesting is the case of the Dow-Jones Industrial Index, which consists of 30 stocks of some of the largest corporations in the United States. In 1939 IBM was removed from the Dow-Jones index and AT&T was substituted. Had IBM remained, the index would have reached 1,017.39 in December 1961 instead of only 734.91.

3. *Quality changes.* Virtually all goods and services in the economy change qualitatively over the years, and sometimes it is hard to reflect this qualitative change in price comparisons between two periods. The more often we conduct a survey to update the weights, the better is the index. Such surveys are conducted only every decade or so, however, since they are quite expensive and complicated.

Chapter Summary and Review

1. Price indexes
   a. Unweighted price index is given by

$$I = \frac{\Sigma p_n}{\Sigma p_0} \cdot 100$$

   b. The average of price relatives index is given by

$$I = \frac{\Sigma \frac{p_n}{p_0} \cdot 100}{m}$$

   (*m* stands for the number of items in the basket.)
   c. The weighted price index is given by

$$I_w = \frac{\Sigma \left(\frac{p_n}{p_0} \cdot 100 \right) w}{\Sigma w}$$

where *w* stands for the weights.

d. Laspeyres price index

$$P_L = \frac{\Sigma p_n q_0}{\Sigma p_0 q_0} \cdot 100$$

and $P_L = I_w$ when we define the weights as $w = p_0 q_0$.

e. Paasche price index

$$P_P = \frac{\Sigma p_n q_n}{\Sigma p_0 q_n} \cdot 100$$

and $P_P = I_w$ when we define the weights as $w = p_0 q_n$.

2. Quantity indexes
   a. Laspeyres quantity index

$$Q_L = \frac{\Sigma p_0 q_n}{\Sigma p_0 q_0} \cdot 100$$

   b. Paasche quantity index

$$Q_P = \frac{\Sigma p_n q_n}{\Sigma p_n q_0} \cdot 100$$

3. Value index

a. $I_V = \dfrac{\Sigma p_n q_n}{\Sigma p_0 q_0} \cdot 100$

b. $I_V = \dfrac{P_L Q_P}{100} = \dfrac{Q_L P_p}{100}$

c. in words: $\begin{pmatrix} \text{Value} \\ \text{ratio} \end{pmatrix} = \begin{pmatrix} \text{Laspeyres} \\ \text{price} \\ \text{ratio} \end{pmatrix} \cdot \begin{pmatrix} \text{Paasche} \\ \text{quantity} \\ \text{ratio} \end{pmatrix}$

$= \begin{pmatrix} \text{Laspeyres} \\ \text{quantity} \\ \text{ratio} \end{pmatrix} \cdot \begin{pmatrix} \text{Paasche} \\ \text{price} \\ \text{ratio} \end{pmatrix}$

Problems

21.1. Why is the selection of a base period important for proper presentation of data by an index? What are the guidelines for choosing a base period?

21.2. What is the disadvantage of an unweighted index?

21.3. The Consumer Price Index (CPI) in a certain country was 100.0 in 1974 and 200.0 in 1984. What was the average annual price increase over the period 1974–84?

21.4. The Consumer Price Index (CPI) in a certain country in 1964, 1974, and 1984 was as follows:

Year	CPI
1964	100.0
1974	100.0
1984	300.0

    (*a*) What was the average annual price increase in the period 1964–74?
    (*b*) What was the average annual price increase in the period 1974–84?
    (*c*) What was the average annual price increase in the period 1964–84?
    (*d*) Was the average annual price increase in the period 1964–84 as calculated in part *c* equal to the average of your answers to parts *a* and *b*? Explain.

21.5. The sales of DAB Corporation in billions of dollars for the years 1974–84 were as follows:

Year	Sales
1974	$5.0
1975	4.5
1976	4.0
1977	3.5
1978	3.0
1979	3.5
1980	4.0
1981	4.5
1982	4.5
1983	4.5
1984	5.0

    (*a*) Construct an index for the dollar value of sales, using 1974 as the base year.
    (*b*) Do you think that 1974 is a good year to serve as a base period? What information do you need in order to select the base period?

21.6. The following are the prices of four products and services bought by consumers during the years 1982, 1983, and 1984:

Product	1982	1983	1984
Bread (cents per loaf)	60.0	65.0	70.0
Transportation (dollars per 10 miles)	1.0	1.5	2.0
Rent (dollars per month)	250.0	260.0	270.0
Recreation (dollars per activity)	8.0	8.0	9.0

Suppose the average consumer spends 35 percent of his or her income on bread, 15 percent on transportation, 30 percent on rent, and 20 percent on recreation.

    (*a*) Compute the unweighted index for the above items, using 1982 as the base.
    (*b*) Compute the average of price relatives on the 1982 base.
    (*c*) Compute the weighted index on the 1982 base.

21.7. The following are the prices of five commodities during the years 1981–84:

Commodity	1981	1982	1983	1984
A	$ 45	$ 45	$ 45	$ 45
B	60	58	57	51
C	100	120	140	160
D	1,000	1,200	1,400	1,800
E	38	43	61	54

    (*a*) Compute the unweighted index for the five commodities, using 1983 as the base.
    (*b*) Compute the average of price relatives on the 1983 base.

21.8. The prices and quantities consumed for commodities *A* and *B* during the years 1974 and 1984 are as follows:

Commodity	Unit price		Quantities consumed	
	1974	*1984*	*1974*	*1984*
A	$1.00	$1.60	30	70
B	2.30	1.80	10	72

(*a*) Compute the 1984 index on the base of 1974 using the average of price relatives.

(*b*) What are the Paasche and Laspeyres price indexes for these data when the base year is 1974?

(*c*) What are the Paasche and Laspeyres quantity indexes for the data when 1974 is the base year?

(*d*) Calculate the value index for the data on the 1974 base.

(*e*) Verify the following relationship using the previous data:

$$\begin{pmatrix} \text{Laspeyres} \\ \text{price} \\ \text{ratio} \end{pmatrix} \cdot \begin{pmatrix} \text{Paasche} \\ \text{quantity} \\ \text{ratio} \end{pmatrix} = \begin{pmatrix} \text{Laspeyres} \\ \text{quantity} \\ \text{ratio} \end{pmatrix} \cdot \begin{pmatrix} \text{Paasche} \\ \text{price} \\ \text{ratio} \end{pmatrix} = \begin{pmatrix} \text{Value} \\ \text{ratio} \end{pmatrix}$$

21.9. Figure P21.9 shows the annual percentage gains in telephones served by the United Telephone System and by the American telephone industry for the years 1966–78.

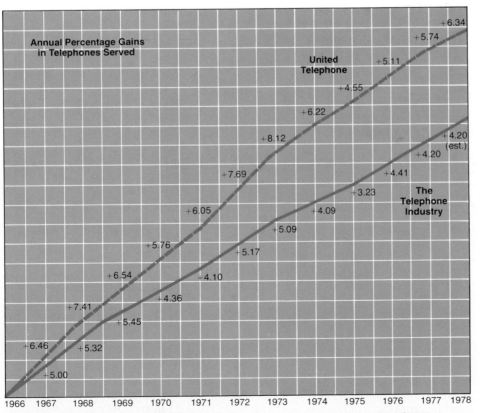

Figure P21.9

Percentage gains in telephones served, by United Telephone and by the telephone industry, 1966–78

Source: Advertisement for United Telecommunications, Inc., in *Institutional Investor*, April 1979.
Reprinted by permission of United Telecom.

(a) From Figure P21.9 construct an index for the number of telephones served by the United Telephone System and by the telephone industry in the United States. Use 1966 as the base year for both indexes.

(b) What is the percentage gain of the United Telephone System and of the telephone industry in the period 1971–78? What is the percentage change in the period 1976–78?

21.10. Canada's index of hourly earnings in the manufacturing field for the years 1973–80 and the Consumer Price Index for those years are shown in Table P21.10. Derive the wage index in real terms (note that 1975 = 100.0).

TABLE P21.10

Year	Wage index	CPI
1973	81.4	76.3
1974	90.3	86.6
1975	100.0	100.0
1976	107.5	113.8
1977	116.1	126.1
1978	126.5	135.2
1979	138.1	147.0
1980	152.1	161.9

Source: International Monetary Fund, *International Financial Statistics*, October 1980 and July 1981.

21.11. The 1974–83 revenues, net earnings, and earnings per share of the hypothetical Metropolitan Psychiatric Centers are shown in Table P21.11. Derive three indexes, one for each of the variables, using 1980 as the base year. Draw the three indexes on one diagram.

TABLE P21.11

Fiscal year ended November 30	Revenues (thousands of dollars)	Net earnings (thousands of dollars)	Earnings per share (dollars)
1974	$ 7,772	$ 987	0.32
1975	11,895	1,360	0.42
1976	15,463	1,514	0.51
1977	16,764	1,800	0.63
1978	20,165	2,136	0.76
1979	27,371	3,352	1.17
1980	32,920	4,881	1.65
1981	40,545	6,370	2.12
1982	59,356	8,429	1.28
1983	90,026	12,703	1.17

21.12. An index of industrial production in Japan for the years 1974–81 is given in Table P21.12.

TABLE P21.12

Year	Index for industrial production (1975 = 100)
1974	112.3
1975	100.0
1976	111.1
1977	115.7
1978	122.9
1979	133.1
1980	142.4
1981	146.8

Source: *Japan Economic Yearbook*, 1981, p. 178.

    (*a*) Calculate the percentage of each year's price increase during the period.
    (*b*) Change the base period of the index from 1975 to 1980.

21.13. The prices and quantities consumed of commodities *A*, *B*, and *C* for the years 1982–84 were as follows:

Commodity	Unit price			Quantities consumed		
	1982	*1983*	*1984*	*1982*	*1983*	*1984*
A	10	12	14	50	52	56
B	8	7	8	3	3	3
C	108	118	132	20	21	24

    (*a*) Compute the price index for the commodities using the average of price relatives, with 1982 as the base year.
    (*b*) What are the Paasche and Laspeyres price indexes for the above data when 1982 is the base year?
    (*c*) What are the Paasche and Laspeyres quantity indexes for the above data when 1982 is the base year?

21.14. A wholesale price index for a given country is based on 1980 prices:

Year	Index
1980	100.0
1981	104.0
1982	111.5
1983	114.7
1984	121.6

The index for earlier years is based on 1975 prices:

Year	Index
1975	100.0
1976	102.1
1977	102.9
1978	103.6
1979	104.7
1980	109.9

    (*a*) Splice the above index series and provide one index series on the base of 1975.
    (*b*) Splice the index series and provide one index series on the base of 1980.
    (*c*) Splice the index series and provide one index series on the base of 1984.

21.15. The annual salary of an employee in a large manufacturing firm for the years 1979–84 was as follows:

Year	Annual salary
1979	$10,000
1980	11,000
1981	12,000
1982	13,000
1983	14,000
1984	15,000

(a) Suppose consumer prices have gone up 2 percent per year during the period. Calculate the employee's "real" salary in each of the years 1979–84.

(b) Rework part *a*, assuming that prices went up 5 percent per year.

(c) Rework part *a* again, assuming that prices went up 10 percent per year.

21.16. The prices shown in the following table are the prices in dollars per pound for four types of wheat as recorded in January 1980 and in January 1984:

Type of wheat	January 1980	January 1984
A	$0.20	$0.30
B	0.18	0.20
C	0.15	0.18
D	0.14	0.20

(a) Construct a simple unweighted index for the wheat prices.

(b) Given that at least 80 percent of the wheat sold in 1980 and in 1984 is of type *A*, what minimum value can the weighted index of prices take?

21.17. It is given that all items to be included in a given price index rise during a given period by 20 percent. "In this specific case all price indexes (unweighted, Laspeyres, Paasche) rise by the same percent." Evaluate this statement.

21.18. The prices (dollars per gallon) and quantities of three types of gas consumed in a certain country are given in Table P21.18.

TABLE P21.18

Type of gas	Prices			Quantities (in millions of gallons)		
	1970	1974	1984	1970	1974	1984
Regular	$0.30	$1.10	$1.09	800	600	900
Premium	0.35	1.25	1.20	1,500	1,200	1,500
Unleaded	0.32	1.18	1.18	500	450	600

(a) Using 1970 as the base year, calculate the Laspeyres price index for 1974 and for 1984.

(b) Now use 1974 as the base year, and calculate the Laspeyres price index for 1984. Compare your answer to that of part *a*.

21.19. Using the data of Table P21.18, construct the Paasche price index for 1974 and 1984, using 1970 as the base year.

21.20. Using the data of Table P21.18, calculate the Laspeyres and Paasche quantity indexes and the value index for the period 1970–74. Explain their relationships.

21.21. The average price per share of stocks listed on two stock exchanges, 1 and 2, and the number of shares traded on each in the period 1980–84 are given in Table P21.21.

TABLE P21.21

	Stock exchange			
	1		2	
Year	Average price	Number of securities (in millions)	Average price	Number of securities (in millions)
1980	$10.0	300	$8.0	35
1981	11.0	320	8.5	36
1982	12.0	355	9.0	38
1983	10.0	381	8.0	40
1984	12.0	402	8.2	41

  (*a*) Construct a simple price index for the stocks listed on stock exchange 1.
  (*b*) Construct a simple price index for the stocks listed on stock exchange 2.
  (*c*) Construct the simple unweighted price index of all stocks for 1984 using 1980 as the base year.
  (*d*) Construct the Laspeyres price index for all stocks, using 1980 as the base year.
  (*e*) Calculate the value index for each year using 1980 as the base year. Interpret your results.

21.22. The following table shows data regarding the average hourly wage of industrial workers and the consumer price index (CPI) in a given country for the years 1980–84.

	Average hourly wage	CPI
1980	$5.50	100
1981	6.50	115
1982	6.50	120
1983	6.80	128
1984	7.00	138

  Construct an index for the average hourly wage and compare it with the CPI. In what years do the workers receive overcompensation for inflation and in what years do they receive undercompensation?

21.23. The following are the annual average prices of gold and silver in dollars per ounce, for seven consecutive years:

Year	1	2	3	4	5	6	7
Gold	650	700	550	600	450	500	550
Silver	25	38	25	18	10	10	12

  (*a*) Find the simple unweighted price index for each of the years, using year 1 as the base year.
  (*b*) Calculate the average of price relatives for each year, using year 1 as the base year.
  (*c*) Assume (hypothetically) that the market value of gold in year 1 was 90 percent of the combined market value of gold and silver. Construct the Laspeyres price index of these two metals, using year 1 as the base year. Compare your results with those of parts *a* and *b*, and discuss your results.

21.24. The following are exchange rates of the British pound against the U.S. dollar (dollar per one British pound) in a recent year.

January	2.11	July	1.79
February	2.01	August	1.80
March	1.98	September	1.65
April	1.80	October	1.60
May	1.75	November	1.58
June	1.78	December	1.58

  (*a*) Calculate an index that reflects the changes in the exchange rate of dollars per one British pound.
  (*b*) Construct an index that shows the exchange rate given in terms of British pound per one dollar.
  (*c*) What is the relationship between the two indexes obtained in parts *a* and *b*?

21.25. Assume that one constructs a price index for 20 different products. Then, "if there is no change in the quantities over time, the Laspeyres and Paasche price indexes are identical." Evaluate this statement.

21.26. In constructing a value index for the exports of a given country, it has been found that quantities of *all* products included in the index rose by 50 percent, and the prices of all those products rose by 20 percent during the period. "It follows that the value index rose by 70 percent." Evaluate this statement.

21.27. Suppose the prices of all products in the market remain unchanged: $p_n = p_0$ for all products. Then, "if the Laspeyres quantity index remains unchanged, the value index must also remain unchanged." Do you agree with this statement? Explain.

21.28. Table P21.28 shows indexes of average hourly earnings and the Consumer Price Index of the United States, West Germany, and Sweden in the years 1976–81.

TABLE P21.28

	Average hourly earnings			CPI		
Year	West Germany	Sweden	U.S.A.	West Germany	Sweden	U.S.A.
1976	106.4	115.2	108.1	104.1	110.3	105.8
1977	113.9	127.3	117.6	108.1	122.9	112.7
1978	120.0	141.5	127.7	111.1	135.1	121.2
1979	126.9	155.0	138.7	115.6	144.9	134.9
1980	135.3	171.2	150.5	122.0	164.7	153.1
1981	142.9	188.7	165.3	129.2	184.7	169.0

Source: International Monetary Fund, *International Financial Statistics*, Yearbook 1980 pp. 189, 395, 433, and July 1982 pp. 176, 388, 426.

(*a*) What was the average annual percentage increase of hourly earnings in each of the three countries?

(*b*) What was the average annual percentage increase of consumer prices in each of the three countries?

(*c*) Derive an index of "real" average hourly earnings for the three countries.

(*d*) What was the average annual percentage increase of "real" hourly earnings in each of the countries?

21.29. Table P21.29 shows the net imports of crude oil, natural gas liquids, and feedstocks in selected countries. For each country derive an index of the imports with 1975 as the base year.

TABLE P21.29

	Imports (thousand metric tons)		
Year	U.S.A.	Japan	U.K.
1974	180,810	237,839	112,815
1975	207,806	223,302	91,360
1976	301,071	228,699	90,466
1977	374,256	236,508	70,698
1978	349,054	230,181	68,143
1979	355,600	239,154	60,382
1980	288,635	216,840	46,717

Source: Organization for Economic Cooperation and Development, *Quarterly Oil Statistics*, 1981.

21.30. Table P21.30 lists annual percentage changes of selected indicators of labor markets in several countries, 1976–80. The percentage changes reflect changes from the previous to the current year. For example, the 13.8 percent change in Canada's hourly earnings in 1976 means that the average hourly earnings in 1976 was 13.8 percent larger than it had been in 1975.

TABLE P21.30

Indicators	1976	1977	1978	1979	1980
Canada					
Hourly earnings	13.8%	10.1%	7.1%	8.7%	10.1%
Employment	1.4	−1.4	1.0	3.0	−1.8
Productivity	5.5	2.2	4.2	4.6	−1.5
United States					
Hourly earnings	8.1	8.8	8.6	8.6	8.5
Employment	3.2	3.9	5.1	5.1	3.6
Productivity	10.7	5.9	5.8	4.2	−3.4
Japan					
Hourly earnings	12.5	9.2	7.1	5.9	6.4
Employment	−2.0	−0.9	−2.3	−0.7	0.6
Productivity	11.1	4.1	6.2	8.3	7.0
Italy					
Hourly earnings	20.9	27.6	16.2	19.3	21.9
Employment	−1.4	1.0	−1.0	0.3	0.6
Productivity	12.4	1.1	2.0	6.6	5.6

Source: International Monetary Fund, *International Financial Statistics*, July 1981.

(*a*) Use 1975 as the base period and derive indexes for hourly earnings, employment, and productivity for 1975–80 in the countries listed.

(*b*) Draw three diagrams, one for each indicator, showing the indexes for the four countries. Summarize the changes verbally.

NONPARAMETRIC METHODS

22

In most of the previous chapters on hypothesis testing, we assumed some knowledge of the distribution of observations (normal distribution, t distribution, and so on) and often made additional assumptions, such as independence of the observations or homogeneity of the population variances.

If one can be sure that the specific assumptions needed for the particular test indeed hold, the parametric tests described in earlier chapters present no difficulties and may be appropriately used. In reality, however, we seldom have complete knowledge of the relevant distributions, and in many studies, particularly those relying on small samples, the assumptions are questionable. The fact that the assumptions regarding the distribution do not exactly hold introduces an error into our inferences. Very rarely is any attention paid to the error caused by the fact that the distribution is not exactly as assumed.

22.1 The Scope of Nonparametric Methods

Suppose that we would like to test the hypothesis, at a significance level of 5 percent, that the average monthly income of a certain population is $1,000 against the alternative hypothesis that the average income is greater than

$1,000. We sample 16 observations and calculate the sample mean, which happens to be $\overline{X} = \$1,200$. For simplicity, assume that the standard deviation in the population is known and is $400. Assuming that the sample is drawn from a normal distribution, we have $\dfrac{\overline{X} - \mu}{\sigma/\sqrt{n}} \sim N(0, 1)$, where μ is the population mean, σ is the standard deviation, and n is the number of observations. If the null hypothesis holds, we should have

$$\frac{\overline{X} - 1,000}{400/\sqrt{16}} = \frac{\overline{X} - 1,000}{100} \sim N(0, 1)$$

Since $\overline{X} = \$1,200$, we get

$$\frac{\overline{X} - 1,000}{100} = \frac{1,200 - 1,000}{100} = 2$$

Should we accept or reject the null hypothesis, by which $\mu = \$1,000$? Since we have a one-tailed test at the 5 percent significance level, we reject H_0 if the statistic $\dfrac{\overline{X} - \mu}{\sigma/\sqrt{n}}$ is greater than 1.645, or if $\overline{X} > \mu + 1.645 \cdot \dfrac{\sigma}{\sqrt{n}} = 1,000 + 1.645 \cdot 100 = 1,164.50$. In our case $\overline{X} = \$1,200$ and hence we reject the null hypothesis (see curve A in Figure 22.1).

Now suppose that the normality assumption does not hold. Indeed, the mean income in the population is $\mu = \$1,000$, but the sampling distribution is not normal and is given by curve B, not by curve A (see Figure 22.1). Since the sampling distribution of the sample mean is given by curve B, we should reject the null hypothesis only if $\overline{X} > \$1,300$: there is a 5 percent probability that $\overline{X} > \$1,300$ with curve B. Thus, the erroneous normality assumption (that is, assuming that the sampling distribution follows the normal curve A rather than curve B) has led us to reject the null hypothesis, H_0: $\mu = \$1,000$. In other words, $\overline{X} = \$1,200$ falls in the rejection region if curve A is the true distribution and in the acceptance region if the true distribution is given by curve B. Hence, by assuming that the distribution is normal when it is not, we calculate the wrong probabilities and reach a wrong decision.

Nonparametric statistical methods of hypothesis testing are available for use in situations in which the underlying distributions are unknown. These methods make no assumptions about the distributions, but they do assume *independent* observations, namely that the sample is random.

As the name "nonparametric" implies, these methods assume nothing about the population parameters. They are "distribution-free" in the sense that they enable us to test a hypothesis and reach conclusions regardless of the shape of the population distribution. To be more specific, the two major assumptions that are made in most statistical tests—homogeneity of variance (of the two or more populations under consideration) and normality can be relaxed when we use nonparametric tests.

The disadvantage of nonparametric tests is that they are less powerful than parametric tests. In other words, for a given significance level (that is, a given probability of committing a Type I error), the probability of committing a Type II error is greater with nonparametric tests than with parametric tests, which implies that the power of the parametric test is greater. In many cases, however, when the number of observations is sufficiently

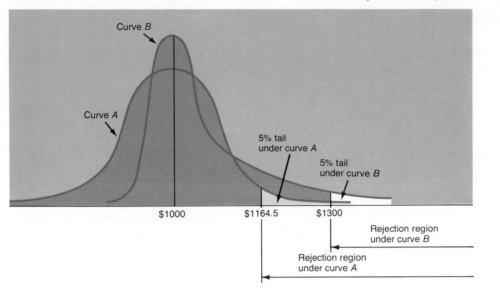

Figure 22.1

Rejection
region under
true distribu-
tion (curve *B*)
and under
assumed
distribution
(curve *A*)

large, the power of the nonparametric test approaches the power of the corresponding parametric test.

There are many nonparametric tests, and many textbooks in statistics devoted solely to this subject. In this chapter we describe what we believe to be the most useful test methods for business and economics. One can classify the various nonparametric tests according to the measurement scale of the data and according to the type of test, that is, its assumptions and its purpose.

Nonparametric tests can be used for the following types of data:

1. *Categories*. This is when qualitative data are coded. For example, Catholic = 0, Protestant = 1, Jewish = 2, Moslem = 3. The order of the codes has no meaning, and alternative codes would do an equally good job; for example, Protestant = 10, Catholic = 9, Jewish = 8, Moslem = 7.
2. *Ranks*. The observations are ordered from lowest to highest (or vice versa) and assigned ranks by their order. For example, suppose three toothpaste brands are ranked by a certain quality. The ranks 1, 2, and 3 indicate an order of quality. But the ranks do not tell us by how much one toothpaste is better than another.
3. *Cardinal scale*. With this type of data one can not only rank the order of the observations but also determine by how much a given observation is greater than another. Income, for example, is measured on a cardinal scale. Given the observations $500, $1,000, and $1,200, we can determine that the second observation is twice as much as the first, the third observation is 20 percent higher than the second, and so on. This is not possible to do with ranked data.

Some of the nonparametric tests deal with one sample and some deal with two or more samples. Some two-sample tests are designed for independent samples, others for dealing with related samples. A description and details of some of these tests are given in this chapter.

22.2 The Binomial Test

The **binomial test** is one that *tests the value of a proportion*. It may be considered a nonparametric test because the probability of a given event can be calculated simply by counting the number of "success" trials and dividing the sum by the total number of trials in the binomial experiment; no distribution parameters are needed. For example, suppose we want to test the hypothesis that there is a probability $p = \frac{1}{2}$ that the price of a certain stock will go up, and a probability $q = \frac{1}{2}$ that it will either go down or stay unchanged. One can collect a sample of 20 daily price changes and count the number of pluses (price increases) and the number of minuses (price decreases or no change), and then see whether the sample results fall in the rejection or acceptance region by simply calculating the probability of the observed event under the null hypothesis ($p = \frac{1}{2}$). Since we have devoted considerable space to the binomial distribution elsewhere (the testing procedure is described in detail in Chapter 13), we shall not extend the discussion of this test here.

Note that though the *test* is indeed nonparametric, the binomial distribution is parametric; its parameters are n and p. In order to calculate a given probability, we must know these parameters. In testing hypotheses, however, the sample size, n, is given, and p is provided by the null hypothesis; hence it is considered a nonparametric test.

22.3 The Chi-Square Test

Under certain conditions having to do with the minimum number of observations in each cell, the **chi-square test** can also be considered a nonparametric test, since nothing is assumed about the distribution of the observations. Goodness-of-fit tests can be carried out by use of the χ^2 distribution. Again, since we covered this distribution in detail in Chapter 15, we shall not repeat it here. We would like to emphasize, however, that some applications of the chi-square test are parametric (e.g., testing value of a variance), whereas others are nonparametric (e.g., testing for goodness of fit). In the first case we have to assume normality, whereas in the second case such an assumption is not necessary.

22.4 Test for Randomness: Runs Test

The one-sample binomial test and the chi-square test use the *frequency* of events in the sample. They ignore the order in which the events are generated. But in certain situations the order of appearance of the events is no less important than the frequency.

WHEN IS THE RUNS TEST APPROPRIATE?

Suppose we observe 10 successive daily price changes of a certain stock and get five plus readings (price up) and five minus readings (price unchanged or down). The binomial test based on this frequency information does not enable us to reject the hypothesis that the number of pluses is equal to the number of minuses; that is, the hypothesis H_0: $p = 0.5$ is not rejected, where p stands for the probability of "price up" on a given day.

Indeed, take $\alpha = 0.1$. In this case the 10 percent two-tailed critical region of the binomial distribution under the null hypothesis for a sample of 10 observations is roughly $n_1 \leq 2$ and $n_1 \geq 8$, where n_1 is the number of plus readings.[1] In other words, there is a 0.90 probability of getting between two and eight plus readings under the null hypothesis H_0: $p = 0.5$. Since the sample gave $n_1 = 5$, the null hypothesis cannot be rejected at this significance level.

The chi-square test (see Chapter 15) gives similar results. Consider the data in Table 22.1. Here the chi-square statistic is zero:

$$\chi^2 = \sum_{i=1}^{2} \frac{(e_i - o_i)^2}{e_i} = 0$$

Obviously, the null hypothesis H_0: $p = 0.5$ cannot be rejected at the $\alpha = 0.1$ level.

TABLE 22.1
Calculation of the Chi-Square Test Statistic for Testing the Hypothesis H_0: $p = 0.5$

Category	Number of pluses	Number of minuses	Total
Observed frequency o_i	5	5	10
Expected frequency e_i	5	5	10
$e_i - o_i$	0	0	0
$\Sigma(e_i - o_i)^2/e_i$	0	0	$\chi^2 = 0$

These two tests, based on the frequency of outcomes, apparently support the hypothesis that there is an equal probability of getting plus or minus. And yet there are several ways we might have obtained five pluses and five minuses from 10 observations. For example, we could have registered samples with the following sequences of pluses and minuses over the 10 days of observations of stock price changes:

1. + + + + + − − − − −
2. − − − − − + + + + +
3. + − + − + − + − + −
4. + + − − + + − − + −
5. + + − + − − + − + −

Each of these samples contains five pluses and five minuses. The frequencies are the same, but the order of appearance of the two events changes. It is hard to imagine that the first two series, in which five successive outcomes of one kind are followed by five successive outcomes of the other kind, do not differ fundamentally from a random sequence of pluses and minuses.

---

[1] The critical values are taken from Appendix A, Table A.1, The Cumulative Binomial Distribution.

Similarly, the third series, with its systematic alternating order of plus and minus, does not look like a random sample generated by a process with equal probabilities of obtaining plus and minus. Most observers will intuitively classify the fifth sample as random, whereas opinions will probably vary with regard to the fourth sample.

In short, the order of the observations in the sample reveals information about the process generating the observations: it indicates whether the process is random or not. The example shows that tests that use the frequency of events while ignoring their order may lose a lot of important information. Thus, when the order of appearance (and not only the proportion of pluses and minuses) is important, the binomial test and the chi-square test are not appropriate.

IDENTIFYING THE RUNS PATTERN

The **runs test** is designed to use the information contained in the *order* of events. A **run** is defined as an *unbroken succession of outcomes of the same kind* in a sample consisting of *outcomes in two categories* (a dichotomous or dichotomizable variable).

Thus the last of our series of stock price ups and downs (sample 5 above) begins with a run of two pluses, followed by a run of one minus, then a run of one plus, a run of two minuses, and so on. The number of events of the same kind in a run is the *length* of the run. Identifying the runs in the above series, we write the corresponding run lengths:

$$+ \ + \ - \ + \ - \ - \ + \ - \ + \ -$$
$$2 \qquad 1 \ \ 1 \quad 2 \qquad 1 \ \ 1 \ \ 1 \ \ 1$$

There is a total of eight runs in this sample: two runs of length 2 and six runs of length 1.

The first series of daily stock price changes has two runs, each of a length of 5 observations:

$$+ \ + \ + \ + \ + \ - \ - \ - \ - \ -$$
$$5 \qquad\qquad\quad 5$$

The third series has 10 runs, each of length 1:

$$+ \ - \ + \ - \ + \ - \ + \ - \ + \ -$$
$$1 \ \ 1 \ \ 1 \ \ 1 \ \ 1 \ \ 1 \ \ 1 \ \ 1 \ \ 1 \ \ 1$$

WHAT THE RUNS PATTERN INDICATES

If the number of runs in a given sample is too small, as in the first two series, a certain grouping of outcomes is indicated: outcomes of the same kind tend to follow one another and the sample is not random. If such bunching actually occurred in stock price changes, it would tend to contradict the hypothesis that plus and minus appear at random, and investors could take advantage of this price change pattern.

At the other extreme, if the number of runs is too large, as in the third series (10 runs in a sample of five pluses and five minuses), a certain type of systematic dependence among the events is indicated: each event is always followed by an event of the opposite type, which also can be used by quick investors in the stock market to their advantage.

If the sample is random, then there is neither a tendency for bunching of identical outcomes nor the opposite type of dependence, in which outcomes of one category are generally followed by outcomes of the other. This, in effect, is the null hypothesis of the runs test, which tests for sample randomness against the alternative of a nonrandom sample.

Note that the symbol we attach to the various outcome categories is not important. In our example, we are dealing with a variable naturally classified into two categories: the increase of the price of a stock and the decrease or lack of change of the price. We may label the category "price up" by "plus" or assign a numerical label, 1. The category "price unchanged or down" may be labeled "minus" or, numerically, 0. We could have reversed the labels, representing plus as 0 and minus as 1, or assigned different numerical labels altogether, such as plus = 15, minus = 107. The price behavior in this setting is adequately described as long as we use two distinct numerical labels for "up" and "unchanged or down."

APPLYING THE RUNS TEST

To apply the runs test, we have to determine the number of runs, r; the number of outcomes in the first category, n_1; and the number of outcomes in the second category, n_2 ($N = n_1 + n_2$ is the sample size). The runs test thus uses both order information (as represented by r) and frequency information (as represented by n_1 and n_2).

The critical values of r for the runs test are usually listed in two tables, one pair for each value of the significance level, α. The two tables correspond to the two tails of the critical region. Tables A.6a and A.6b in Appendix A at the end of the book present, respectively, the lower and the upper tails of the runs distribution for $\alpha = 0.05$ under the null hypothesis of randomness for samples with various combinations of n_1 and n_2. Table A.6a defines, in effect, the number of runs that is "too small" for randomness: the values of r in Table A.6a are so small that the probability of their occurrence under the null hypothesis is $p = \alpha/2 = 0.025$ or less. Table A.6b defines the number of runs that is "too large" for randomness: the values of r in Table A.6b are so large that the probability of their occurrence under the null hypothesis of randomness is $p = \alpha/2 = 0.025$ or less.

In a two-tailed test, if the number of runs, r, corresponding to the observed n_1 and n_2 is less than or equal to the critical value in Table A.6a or greater than or equal to the critical value in Table A.6b, we reject the null hypothesis of randomness at the $\alpha = 0.05$ level of significance. If the direction of deviation from randomness is suspected from the start ("too many" or "too few" runs), a one-tailed test is appropriate and only one of the tables, A.6a or A.6b, should be used. The corresponding one-tailed significance level in this case, of course, is $\alpha = 0.025$.

Note that Tables A.6a and A.6b extend only up to $n_1 = 20$ and $n_2 = 20$. This is the *small-sample case*. For *large samples*, when either n_1 or n_2 is greater than 20, the standard normal approximation applies (see the application below).

Let us now apply the runs test to the five series of daily stock price changes described at the beginning of this section. In each case we shall employ a two-tailed test, and the null hypothesis is that daily price changes over time are random.

Series 1: + + + + + − − − − − In this series we have five pluses and five minuses, so $n_1 = n_2 = 5$. The pluses and minuses form two runs, so $r = 2$.

We enter Table A.6a at the row with $n_1 = 5$ and move to the column with $n_2 = 5$. The critical value in the table is $r_a = 2$. Since $r = 2 \leq r_a$, we reject the null hypothesis at the $\alpha = 0.05$ level. The sample contains too few runs to be random. Thus, the stock price changes are dependent over time, and one can use this information for investment decision making.

Series 2: − − − − − + + + + + Here $n_1 = 5$, $n_2 = 5$, $r = 2$, just as in Series 1. We reject the null hypothesis at the $\alpha = 0.05$ level.

Series 3: + − + − + − + − + − Here $n_1 = 5$, $n_2 = 5$, $r = 10$. Enter Table A.6b at the row with $n_1 = 5$ and move to the column with $n_2 = 5$. The critical value in the table is $r_b = 10$. Since $r = 10 \geq r_b$, we reject the null hypothesis at the $\alpha = 0.05$ level. The sample contains too many runs to be random.

Series 4: + + − − + + − − + − Here $n_1 = 5$, $n_2 = 5$, $r = 6$. From Table A.6a we have $r_a = 2$; from Table A.6b, $r_b = 10$. Thus $r_a < r < r_b$, and the null hypothesis cannot be rejected at the $\alpha = 0.05$ level.

Series 5: + + − + − − + − + − Here $n_1 = 5$, $n_2 = 5$, $r = 8$. Again $r_a < r < r_b$, and the null hypothesis cannot be rejected at the $\alpha = 0.05$ level. The last two series thus appear to be consistent with the hypothesis that stock price changes are random.

In the application that follows we test again for randomness of stock price changes, this time assuming a large series of changes and employing the normal approximation. We illustrate this test by using an approximation.

22.5 APPLICATION:
THE RUNS TEST AND THE RANDOM WALK THEORY

An interesting subject in economics and finance is the analysis of time series of prices. The **random walk theory** asserts that the analysis of past data—in particular past market-price data—cannot be used to forecast future price changes. Thus, those who support the random walk hypothesis imply that the many investors and Wall Street financial analysts who analyze past price data for the purpose of forecasting future prices are wasting their time. In other words, price changes over time are independent of previous price changes.

The random walk theory is not limited to securities prices; it is applied as well to prices of other economic values, such as real estate and commodity prices. Most empirical studies that test the validity of the random walk theory, however, use either commodity prices or stock prices.

In order to test whether past information can be used to forecast future prices and to make decisions, it is natural to apply the runs test for independence over time. For small samples, we simply apply the above procedure and use Tables A.6a and A.6b. In most cases, however, more than 20 daily price changes are available, and we use the normal approximation in order to test the random walk theory. By the random walk model, price increases and decreases have no tendency to bunch together, nor should there be any noticeable tendency toward "reverses." Any given sequence of daily price changes should thus form a random series of plus and minus values.

A year-long series of daily prices of Bendix Corporation stock yielded 242 daily price changes, of which 109 were plus ($n_1 = 109$) and 133 were minus ($n_2 = 133$). The sample contained $r = 80$ runs.

Since both n_1 and n_2 are much greater than 20, Tables A.6*a* and A.6*b* are inapplicable. We are dealing with a large sample and the number of runs is approximately normally distributed, with mean

$$\mu_r = \frac{2n_1 n_2}{n_1 + n_2} + 1 \qquad (22.1)$$

and standard deviation

$$\sigma_r = \sqrt{\frac{2n_1 n_2 (2n_1 n_2 - n_1 - n_2)}{(n_1 + n_2)^2 (n_1 + n_2 - 1)}} \qquad (22.2)$$

Here μ_r and σ_r are the expected number of runs and the standard deviation of the number of runs under the null hypothesis of a random order of appearance (that is, when the random walk theory holds).

The null hypothesis in the case of a large sample may therefore be tested by use of the standard normal variable, Z_r:

$$Z_r = \frac{r - \mu_r}{\sigma_r} \qquad (22.3)$$

In our example, for $n_1 = 109$ and $n_2 = 133$, we get

$$\mu_r = \frac{2 \cdot 109 \cdot 133}{242} + 1 = 120.8$$

$$\sigma_r = \sqrt{\frac{2 \cdot 109 \cdot 133 \cdot (2 \cdot 109 \cdot 133 - 109 - 133)}{(109 + 133)^2 \cdot (109 + 133 - 1)}} = \sqrt{59.06} = 7.7$$

Hence

$$Z_r = \frac{r - \mu_r}{\sigma_r} = \frac{80 - 120.8}{7.7} = -5.30$$

Since Z_r is negative, our sample contains fewer runs than a random sample. To determine whether the difference is significant at the $\alpha = 0.05$ level, we use the table of the standard normal distribution (inside back cover) and define the two-tailed 5 percent critical region:

$$Z \leq -1.96$$

and

$$Z \geq 1.96$$

Since $Z_r = -5.30 < -1.96$, we reject the null hypothesis at the $\alpha = 0.05$ level. Our sample contains too few runs to be random, and the daily price changes show a significant tendency to bunch: an increase in price is likely to lead to further price increases, and a decrease in price will be followed by further price decreases on subsequent days. While under the null hypothesis we have expected approximately 121 runs ($120.8 \approx 121$), we observed only 80, meaning that *bunching has actually occurred*. The deviation of the observed number of runs from those expected to occur, however, could be attributable only to chance variation.

As there is no parametric test for the randomness of a sequence of events, the runs test is unique and therefore particularly important.

22.6 One-Sample Kolmogorov-Smirnov Test for Goodness of Fit

The chi-square goodness-of-fit test measures the goodness of fit between observations classified into k distinct categories and some hypothesized or expected distribution over the same k categories (see Chapter 15). In Chapter 15 we cautioned against low-count categories and advised the pooling of adjacent cells to avoid zero or very low frequencies. This pooling of categories may lead to a certain loss of information, especially when the underlying distribution is continuous, or when it is most appropriate to classify it into numerous narrow categories.

The **Kolmogorov-Smirnov test** avoids this difficulty in that it does not impose a lower limit on the category frequencies. Actually, it does not assume categorized data at all: it is applicable to continuous data, and if classification into distinct categories is done by the user, it is for convenience of calculation only.

The one-sample Kolmogorov-Smirnov test checks for goodness of fit between the observed sample distribution and some given hypothesized or expected distribution. In other words, it tests whether the observed sample data could have come from some hypothesized population distribution.

THE FUNDAMENTAL IDEA OF THE KOLMOGOROV-SMIRNOV TEST

The test is based on the measurement of the "distance" between two *cumulative* relative frequency distributions: the observed sample cumulative relative frequency distribution, which we denote by $O(x)$, and some hypothesized, or expected, cumulative relative distribution, $E(x)$.

The "distance" between the distributions is defined as the absolute value of the difference between the two functions at each point:

$$|E(x) - O(x)|$$

The Kolmogorov-Smirnov statistic, $D(N)$, is defined as follows:

$$D(N) = \text{maximum } |E(x) - O(x)| \qquad \text{(22.4)}$$

That is, $D(N)$ is the *maximum deviation* or the *maximum vertical distance* between the two cumulative relative frequency distributions or between the two cumulative probability distributions over the entire range of the variable. The value of $D(N)$ depends on the sample size, N.

Figure 22.2 shows two hypothetical distributions, $E(x)$ and $O(x)$. In this specific case, the maximum vertical distance, $D(N)$, is obtained for the value x_0, that is, $D(N) = |E(x_0) - O(x_0)|$.

Intuitively, we know that if $D(N)$ is sufficiently small, the hypothesized function $E(x)$ may be treated as a good fit to the observed distribution, $O(x)$ [this, in effect, is the null hypothesis, H_0: $E(x) = O(x)$]. If the maximum deviation, $D(N)$, is large enough, $E(x)$ cannot be accepted as an adequate approximation to the observed $O(x)$, and we reject the null hypothesis.

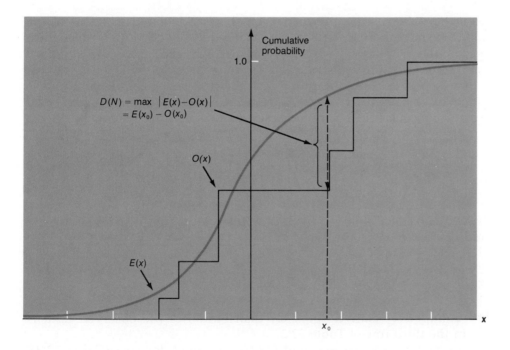

Figure 22.2

Observed, $O(x)$, and hypothesized, $E(x)$, cumulative distribution, and the Kolmogorov-Smirnov statistic $D(N)$

APPLYING THE KOLMOGOROV-SMIRNOV TEST

To illustrate the underlying ideas, let us first apply the Kolmogorov-Smirnov test to a sample of 194 observations classified into three categories. Such categorization is not required for applying the test, but it simplifies the presentation. The sample data are summarized in Table 22.2.

Let us test the null hypothesis that the population distribution is *uniform* over these three categories, that is, that the three categories should contain equal counts. The expected distribution under this null hypothesis is given in Table 22.3.

TABLE 22.2

Observed Frequency, Observed Relative Frequency, and Observed Cumulative Relative Frequency over Three Categories

Category i	1	2	3	Total
Observed frequency: o_i	58	72	64	194
Observed relative frequency: $\dfrac{o_i}{194}$	0.30	0.37	0.33	1.00
Cumulative relative frequency: $O(x)$	0.30	0.67	1.00	

TABLE 22.3

Expected Frequency, Expected Relative Frequency, and Expected Cumulative Relative Frequency Assuming a Uniform Distribution over the Categories

Category i	1	2	3	Total
Expected frequency under null hypothesis: $e_i = 194/3$	64.7	64.7	64.7	194
Expected relative frequency: $e_i/194$	0.333	0.333	0.333	1.00
Cumulative relative frequency: $E(x)$	0.33	0.67	1.00	

Note that whereas the chi-square statistic is calculated in terms of the absolute frequencies o_i and e_i (see Chapter 15), the Kolmogorov-Smirnov test uses cumulative relative frequency distributions that have the standard properties of probability distribution functions: $0 \le E(x) \le 1$, $0 \le O(x) \le 1$.

A first step in deriving the cumulative relative frequency distributions is to calculate the observed *relative frequencies* in each category. The observed relative frequencies in the second row of Table 22.2 are calculated in the usual way:

$$\text{Observed relative frequency in category } i = \frac{o_i}{N} \tag{22.5}$$

The values of the cumulative relative frequency distribution for each category, $O(x)$, are then obtained by adding the relative frequencies up to and including the ith category:

$$O(x) = \text{Total of relative frequencies up to and including} \tag{22.6}$$
$$\text{the relevant category}$$

The cumulative relative frequency distribution of the observed data is given in the third row of Table 22.2.

The same steps can be repeated for the expected data (see Table 22.3). Alternative approaches are possible, of course, based on knowledge of the hypothesized distribution (see Example 22.1).

We now collect the results into a Kolmogorov-Smirnov test table, Table 22.4.

The largest deviation between the observed and the expected cumulative distributions is 0.03:

$$D(N) = \max |E(x) - O(x)| = 0.03$$

To determine whether this is large (poor fit: reject the null hypothesis) or small (good fit: do not reject H_0), we have to consult a table of the sampling

TABLE 22.4
Kolmogorov-Smirnov Test Table

Category i	1	2	3
Observed $O(x)$	0.30	0.67	1.00
Expected $E(x)$	0.33	0.67	1.00
Deviation $|E(x) - O(x)|$	0.03	0.00	0.00

distribution of the Kolmogorov-Smirnov statistic, $D(N)$. We will reject the null hypothesis if the sample value $D(N)$ is greater than the critical value given in the table.

Tables of the critical values of $D(N)$ for various significance levels are usually given in full up to sample size $N = 35$ only (see Appendix A, Table A.7, at the end of the book). For large samples ($N > 35$) the critical values are inversely proportional to $\sqrt{N}$ (see Table A.7). For our specific example, with $N = 194$, we get

Significance level, α:	0.20	0.15	0.10	0.05	0.01
Critical value of $D(N)$: for $N > 35$	$\dfrac{1.07}{\sqrt{N}}$	$\dfrac{1.14}{\sqrt{N}}$	$\dfrac{1.22}{\sqrt{N}}$	$\dfrac{1.36}{\sqrt{N}}$	$\dfrac{1.63}{\sqrt{N}}$
for $N = 194$	0.08	0.08	0.09	0.10	0.12

The last line was obtained by substituting 194 for N in the general expression for the critical value $D(N)$ in the line above it.

If we assume a 10 percent significance level, the maximum $D(N)$ value we can get without rejecting H_0 is 0.09. Since we got a smaller value, 0.03, we do not reject H_0 at the 10 percent significance level.

The values in Table A.7 are critical values for a given significance level, α, and sample size, N. We reject the null hypothesis only if the sample statistic $D(N)$ is larger than these critical values.

Let us consider the application of the Kolmogorov-Smirnov test to another kind of data: instead of categorized data, we shall use a continuous variable.

EXAMPLE 22.1

One of the assertions of the random walk model is that the day-to-day price changes of any given stock are independent. Suppose we calculate a time series of daily stock price changes on any given day (call it ΔP_t) and on the previous day (call it ΔP_{t-1}). A nonzero correlation coefficient between the two time series should enable us to make a quick profit by predicting tomorrow's price change from today's price change. If the correlation coefficient is zero, tomorrow's price change is not correlated with today's price change and information about today's price change cannot in itself lead to profit.

The following correlation coefficients were obtained for 10 separate samples of price changes of Nabisco stock:

Sample	1	2	3	4	5	6	7	8	9	10
Correlation coefficient	0.02	−0.01	0.11	0.08	0.00	−0.02	−0.13	−0.01	0.03	−0.05

Is there any indication in these data that the correlation coefficient of price changes of Nabisco stock is significantly different from zero, or can the deviations from zero be attributed to random sampling errors? To answer this question we need to know the sampling distribution of the correlation coefficient, or we would not be able to determine if the deviations are due to sampling errors. Suppose we want to be more specific and formulate our hypotheses as follows:

H_0: The observed correlation coefficients are drawn from a normal distribution with zero mean and standard deviation 0.1, i.e., $\rho \sim N(0, 0.1)$.

H_1: The observed correlation coefficients come from a different distribution.

Since we are testing a null hypothesis about a specified continuous distribution, the Kolmogorov-Smirnov test is a natural choice. All the sample observations fall inside the range from -0.2 to 0.2. Let us divide this range into eight intervals of 0.05 width. (A finer division can be used if desired, but we have only 10 observations, so eight intervals seems enough.) We rearrange the observations in the specified intervals and determine the interval counts; the results are given in Table 22.5. The table is self-explanatory and the column on the far right gives the cumulative relative frequency distribution of the data, $O(x)$. It remains for us to find the theoretical cumulative distribution $E(x)$ for the values of X corresponding to the right endpoints of the intervals. To accomplish this we have to make a transformation from our variable X, with $\mu = 0$ and $\sigma = 0.1$, to the standard normal variable, Z. Given the relationship $Z = \dfrac{X - \mu}{\sigma}$ and the values for μ and σ we get

$$Z = \frac{X - 0}{0.1} = 10X$$

TABLE 22.5
Relative Frequency and Cumulative Relative Frequency of the Sample Correlation Coefficients

Category	Observations	Frequency	Relative frequency o_i/N	Cumulative relative frequency $O(x)$
$-0.20 < x \le -0.15$	—	0	0.00	0.00
$-0.15 < x \le -0.10$	-0.13	1	0.10	0.10
$-0.10 < x \le -0.05$	-0.05	1	0.10	0.20
$-0.05 < x \le 0.00$	$-0.02, -0.01, -0.01, 0.00$	4	0.40	0.60
$0.00 < x \le 0.05$	$0.02, 0.03$	2	0.20	0.80
$0.05 < x \le 0.10$	0.08	1	0.10	0.90
$0.10 < x \le 0.15$	0.11	1	0.10	1.00
$0.15 < x \le 0.20$	—	0	0.00	1.00
Total		10	1.00	

Applying this transformation formula to the right endpoints of the successive intervals and using the standard normal distribution table for the resulting values of Z, we get the hypothesized cumulative distribution listed in Table 22.6. Note that the normal distribution is unbounded, and hence we include the values $-\infty$ and $+\infty$. The statistic $D(N)$, however, is unchanged.

TABLE 22.6
Calculating Hypothesized Cumulative Probabilities

x	$z = 10x$	$E(x) = P(Z \le z)$
$-\infty$	$-\infty$	0
-0.15	-1.5	0.07
-0.10	-1.0	0.16
-0.05	-0.5	0.31
0.00	0.0	0.50
0.05	0.5	0.69
0.10	1.0	0.84
0.15	1.5	0.93
0.20	2.0	0.98
$+\infty$	$+\infty$	1.00

We now draw the two cumulative distributions (that is, the observed and the hypothesized) in Figure 22.3, and we get the Kolmogorov-Smirnov statistic as illustrated:

$$D(N) = \max |E(x) - O(x)| = 0.30$$

We started with a sample of 10 correlation coefficients, so $N = 10$. Entering the Kolmogorov-Smirnov table (Appendix A, Table A.7) along the appropriate row for $N = 10$, we see that the probability of getting $D(N) = 0.30$ under the null hypothesis is much higher than 20 percent. Alternatively, by fixing $\alpha = 0.05$ (agreeing to tolerate a Type I error of 5 percent), we get a critical value of 0.410, and since $D(N)$ in the sample is lower, only 0.30, we cannot reject the null hypothesis at this significance level.

The results of the Kolmogorov-Smirnov test therefore support the hypothesis that the time series of Nabisco stock price changes have zero correlation, in agreement with the random walk hypothesis.

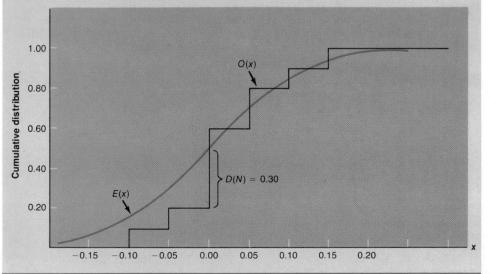

Figure 22.3

Observed, $O(x)$, and hypothesized, $E(x)$, cumulative distributions and the Kolmogorov-Smirnov statistic $D(N)$

Note that the Kolmogorov-Smirnov test may be applied with equal ease to large and small samples (we used it on samples with $N = 194$ and $N = 10$). And, since it uses cumulative frequency distributions and takes into consideration every single measurement, the Kolmogorov-Smirnov test does not run into any difficulties with low-frequency categories—whereas there is no way to apply the chi-square test to the eight data categories in our example without substantially increasing the sample size to achieve sufficient category frequencies or without pooling categories.

We have defined the Kolmogorov-Smirnov statistic as the largest *absolute-value* deviation between the observed and the expected cumulative frequency distributions. By ignoring the signs of the deviations, we have in fact opted for a two-tailed test. The statistic was designed to test for significant deviations *in either direction* from the expected distribution. There are also one-tailed forms of the Kolmogorov-Smirnov test that use a signed statistic: they test whether or not the observed data come from a distribution that lies to the right or to the left of the hypothesized theoretical distribution. We shall not elaborate on the one-tailed Kolmogorov-Smirnov test, however; anyone interested may refer to specialized texts on nonparametric statistics.

22.7 The Sign Test: Two Related Samples

The **sign test** is probably the best known of the nonparametric tests. As its name indicates, the test uses plus and minus signs; pairs of matched observations from two related samples are represented by plus or minus signs, depending on which of the two observations is larger. The test is clearly nonparametric in that we assume nothing about the population from which the two related samples are drawn.

EXAMPLE 22.2

The production department of the Eillon Company has decided to compare the productivity of workers on the day shift with the productivity of workers on the night shift. The productivity (measured in units of output) of one group of workers was recorded for 15 consecutive day shifts and then for 15 consecutive night shifts. Table 22.7 summarizes the observed productivity data.

The sign test is applied to the matched observations in order to determine whether the number of plus signs is significantly greater than the number of minus signs (that is, whether day-shift productivity is significantly greater than night-shift productivity). The one observation with a tie, producing a reading of 0 in the last column, is omitted, and we take $n = 14$ in what follows.

The null hypothesis of the sign test is that the probability of getting plus is equal to the probability of getting minus; that is, the two signs are as if generated by the flipping of a balanced coin. Hence the binomial tables can be used to calculate the probability of getting a given number of plus values in a sample of n observations.

Reference to the table of cumulative binomial probabilities (see Appendix A, Table A.1) shows that there is a probability of 0.212 (about 21 percent) of getting 9 or more plus signs out of 14 trials under the null hypothesis of equal probability of plus and minus signs ($p = \frac{1}{2}$).

TABLE 22.7
Determining the Signs of the Matched Observations

Observations	Day-shift productivity X_D	Night-shift productivity X_N	Direction of difference	Sign
1	84	78	$X_D > X_N$	+
2	85	82	$X_D > X_N$	+
3	69	74	$X_D < X_N$	−
4	75	68	$X_D > X_N$	+
5	87	79	$X_D > X_N$	+
6	73	84	$X_D < X_N$	−
7	92	90	$X_D > X_N$	+
8	70	59	$X_D > X_N$	+
9	74	71	$X_D > X_N$	+
10	79	85	$X_D < X_N$	−
11	70	66	$X_D > X_N$	+
12	65	69	$X_D < X_N$	−
13	79	83	$X_D < X_N$	−
14	89	89	$X_D = X_N$	0
15	80	75	$X_D > X_N$	+

The results in favor of higher productivity on the day shift are thus not significant, since to establish superiority of the productivity of the day shift at the 0.10 level of significance, at least 10 plus signs should have been observed in the last column of Table 22.7 (see Appendix A, Table A.1).

As with the binomial test, for large n one can use the normal approximation to calculate the probabilities of various events.

22.8 The Mann-Whitney Test: Two Independent Samples

Testing whether or not two independent samples come from the same population is usually carried out by the t test. When it is unreasonable to make the assumptions underlying the t test, one can use the **Mann-Whitney test**, which is one of the most powerful nonparametric tests relative to its parametric counterpart, the t test.

Suppose that we have two independent samples of the sizes n_A and n_B. Thus the total number of observations is $N = n_A + n_B$. We arrange all the N observations in ascending order and rank them. To identify the origin of the ranks, we attach the symbol A to each ranked observation from the first sample and B to each rank representing an observation from the second sample. Suppose that $n_A = 4$, $n_B = 6$; consider the following three series of 10 observations each, in which they are ranked from lowest to highest:

1. *AAAABBBBBB*
2. *BBBBBBAAAA*
3. *AABABBBBAB*

In case 1, it is obvious that distribution B is located to the right of distribution A, that is, it has a higher mean. In case 2 it is obvious that the opposite situation prevails. Case 3 is more complicated, and one has to use a statistical test in order to determine whether the distribution of B is located significantly to the right of the distribution of A. The Mann-Whitney test is designed to analyze such a case. We will illustrate how to employ the test by means of an example.

EXAMPLE 22.3

A manager is considering the purchase of one of two competing computer models, which we label A and B. Apart from the other obvious factors (cost and so on), the manager is concerned about the reliability of the computers, measured by the amount of down-time as a percentage of computer capacity (or total use time). Figures about the percentage of monthly down-time out of total usage time, supplied by several installations in which computers A and B operate, are as follows:

Computer A	Computer B
2.54	2.81
2.84	2.14
1.26	2.56
2.12	2.94
	2.64

The null hypothesis is that the percentage down-time is the same for both computers, and the alternative hypothesis is that the percentage of down-time is not the same. As you can see, the number of observations is $n_A = 4$ for computer A and $n_B = 5$ for computer B. The test does not require the constraint $n_A = n_B$, nor does it assume any other matching between the observations in the two samples.

Let us pool the nine observations, arrange them in ascending order, and rank them:

Computer	A	A	B	A	B	B	B	A	B
Ordered observations	1.26	2.12	2.14	2.54	2.56	2.64	2.81	2.84	2.94
Rank	1	2	3	4	5	6	7	8	9

The sum of the ranks of distribution A, which we denote by R_A, is $R_A = 1 + 2 + 4 + 8 = 15$, and similarly the sum of the ranks of distribution B is $R_B = 3 + 5 + 6 + 7 + 9 = 30$.

The statistics T_A and T_B are as follows:

$$T_A = R_A - \frac{n_A(n_A + 1)}{2} = 15 - \frac{4(4 + 1)}{2} = 5 \qquad (22.7)$$

$$T_B = R_B - \frac{n_B(n_B + 1)}{2} = 30 - \frac{5(5 + 1)}{2} = 15 \qquad (22.8)$$

The two statistics T_A and T_B are related by a simple equation: $T_A + T_B = n_A n_B$. Thus if one value is known (T_A, for example), the other can be calculated from this relationship: $T_B = n_A n_B - T_A$. In our case, $n_A = 4$, $n_B = 5$, and $T_A = 5$, so that $T_B = 4 \cdot 5 - 5 = 15$, as we have indeed obtained. Similarly, if T_B is known, we get $T_A = 4 \cdot 5 - 15 = 5$. Because of this relationship between T_A and T_B, Mann-Whitney test tables are normally calculated and published for the smaller of the two statistics (T_A, in our example).

Suppose that we want to test the following null hypothesis at a significance level of $\alpha = 0.10$:

H_0: Both computers have equal down-time characteristics.

H_1: The two computers differ in their down-time characteristics.

This is clearly a two-tailed test. We enter Appendix A, Table A.8, under $n_A = 4$, $n_B = 5$, and for the appropriate value of p, which for the two-tailed test is simply half the significance level, $p = \alpha/2 = 0.05$. The corresponding critical value in the table is 3. Since T_A (the smaller of T_A and T_B) is greater than 3—that is, $T_A = 5 > 3$—we cannot reject the null hypothesis that the two computers have equal down-time characteristics.

ONE-TAILED TEST

Suppose that initially we believe computer A in Example 22.3 to be more reliable than computer B, so we test the following hypotheses:

H_0: Computer A is, at most, as reliable as computer B.

H_1: Computer A is more reliable than computer B.

Note that if A is indeed more reliable (less down-time), we expect to have low R_A and hence low T_A value. Obviously, we have a one-tailed test with $\alpha = 0.10$, as before. We enter Appendix A, Table A.8, for $n_A = 4$, $n_B = 5$, and $p = \alpha = 0.10$ (one-tailed test). The critical value is seen to be 5. Since $T_A = 5 \leq 5$, we reject the one-tailed null hypothesis. Computer A is confirmed to be more reliable at the 10 percent level of significance.

LARGE SAMPLES AND TIES

Let us continue with our example of two computers and conduct a more extensive user survey, sending out questionnaires to a large sample of installations using one of the two computers. Thirty-five questionnaires are completed and returned. For each questionnaire an average score is computed, representing the user's overall evaluation of the computer. The higher the score, the better the computer.

We rank the scores in ascending order from 1 to 35; the results are summarized in Table 22.8. There are several ties in our observations: the score 67 appears twice (in both cases for computer B) and the scores 56 and 106 appear three times each (once for computer A and twice for computer B). Ties are usually assigned the same rank, a rank equal to the average of the consecutive ranks that would have been normally assigned to the tied observations in ascending order. Thus, the three observations producing score

TABLE 22.8
Scores of Two Competing Computers Calculated from User Evaluation Survey

Computer A			Computer B	
Score	*Rank*		*Score*	*Rank*
148	30.0		142	29.0
73	14.0		126	26.0
56	8.0		21	2.0
63	10.0		177	34.0
90	18.0		118	24.0
42	6.0		169	33.0
106	20.0		79	16.0
125	25.0		160	31.0
129	28.0		106	20.0
161	32.0		56	8.0
114	23.0		56	8.0
127	27.0		76	15.0
27	4.0		113	22.0
	$R_A = 245.0$		83	17.0
			64	11.0
			36	5.0
			24	3.0
			106	20.0
			67	12.5
			186	35.0
			67	12.5
			10	1.0
				$R_B = 385.0$

56 are located in positions 7, 8, and 9 in our ranking. All three observations are assigned the same average rank, $(7 + 8 + 9)/3 = 24/3 = 8$. Similarly the two observations with score 67 occupy positions 12 and 13; they are assigned the average rank $(12 + 13)/2 = 25/2 = 12.5$. (Note that this is a general procedure for the ranking of ties in nonparametric tests.) We test the following hypotheses:

H_0: Computer A is, at most, as reliable as computer B.

H_1: Computer A is more reliable than computer B.

A one-tailed test is obviously called for.

In our example we have $n_A = 13$, $n_B = 22$, $R_A = 245$, and $R_B = 385$. When at least one of the sample sizes is greater than 20 (as in our case), we can use the normal approximation for the Mann-Whitney statistic. The expected value and the variance of the Mann-Whitney T where T is either T_A or T_B are given by the following:

$$\mu_T = \frac{n_A n_B}{2} \tag{22.9}$$

$$\sigma_T^2 = \frac{n_A n_B (n_A + n_B + 1)}{12} \tag{22.10}$$

In our case

$$\mu_T = \frac{13 \cdot 22}{2} = 143$$

$$\sigma_T^2 = \frac{13 \cdot 22 \cdot (13 + 22 + 1)}{12} = 858$$

and hence

$$\sigma_T = \sqrt{858} = 29.3$$

Now let us calculate T_A and T_B:

$$T_A = 245 - \frac{13 \cdot 14}{2} = 245 - 91 = 154$$

$$T_B = 385 - \frac{22 \cdot 23}{2} = 385 - 253 = 132$$

Note that if computer A is better than computer B, as H_1 claims, then we expect to have a large value of T_A: recall that

$$T_A = R_A - \frac{n_A(n_A + 1)}{2}$$

and if A is the better computer, it will accumulate higher scores and R_A will be large. This implies, for a given sample size n_A, that T_A is also large. Thus, we can hope to reject the null hypothesis in this one-tailed test for large values of T_A only.

To apply the normal approximation, calculate the standard normal value

$$Z_T = \frac{T_A - \mu_T}{\sigma_T} = \frac{154 - 143}{29.3} = 0.375$$

Since $Z_{0.10} = 1.28$ and $Z_T = 0.375$ falls in the acceptance region, we cannot reject the null hypothesis.

The same conclusion is reached when T_B rather than T_A is used as a test statistic. When T_B is used, the null hypothesis is rejected for low T_B values. Upon calculation we find

$$Z_T = \frac{T_B - \mu_T}{\sigma_T} = \frac{132 - 143}{29.3} = -0.375$$

and the null hypothesis is again not rejected.

The Mann-Whitney test is very powerful. Its power is about 95.5 percent of the power of the t test for large N and approximately 95 percent even for samples of modest size. Thus, one can use the Mann-Whitney instead of the t test with almost no loss of power. The benefit, of course, is that we do not have to adopt the various restrictive assumptions underlying the t test.

22.9 The Kruskal-Wallis Test: Analysis of Variance

The parametric t test is used to test the means of two populations for equality. The means of k populations, where $k > 2$, are tested for equality by the analysis of variance (F distribution). As we have seen, the Mann-Whitney test successfully replaces the t test for two independent samples when no strong evidence is available in favor of the assumptions underlying the t test. By the same argument, when there is no reason to assume normality and homogeneity of variances of the k populations under consideration, the nonparametric **Kruskal-Wallis test** may be used to replace the one-way analysis-of-variance F test.

The Kruskal-Wallis test is in fact a one-way analysis of variance in which ranks are used. It is designed to detect differences among k ($k > 2$) populations, of which k independent samples are drawn and ranked according to a certain property or attribute, and it tests the null hypothesis that all the samples are drawn from the same population against the hypothesis that the k populations vary significantly in the relevant attribute. As we are dealing with a *one-way* analysis of variance and the samples are assumed to be independent, no matching of the sample data is implied and different sample sizes are allowed.

EXAMPLE 22.4

A retail chain has decided to conduct a comparative credit-rating survey of customers at three stores in a metropolitan area: a downtown store, a suburban store in a predominantly young white-collar community, and a store in a shopping center frequented by a mixed cross-section of customers from several nearby communities. The percentage of accounts overdue by more than 30 days in each store is taken as the relevant measure and data have been collected for six months back:

Month	1	2	3	4	5	6
Store 1	5.5	6.2	5.8	4.9	6.0	5.9
Store 2	5.2	4.9	4.5	5.7	6.2	5.0
Store 3	6.8	6.7	5.9	6.1	6.3	5.9

Are there significant differences in the credit ratings of customers in the three stores? Since there is no evidence suggesting homogeneity of variance of the overdue accounts in the three stores and there is no reason to assume a normal distribution of these accounts, we employ a nonparametric test.

To apply the Kruskal-Wallis test, we first rank all the 18 available observations as if they came from a single population and then calculate the rank sums, R_i, for each sample. These ranks are given in Table 22.9. (Note that we treat ties as in the Mann-Whitney test.) The rank sums R_i of the three samples are

$$R_1 = 2.5 + 6 + 8 + 10 + 12 + 14.5 = 53$$

$$R_2 = 1 + 2.5 + 4 + 5 + 7 + 14.5 = 34$$

$$R_3 = 10 + 10 + 13 + 16 + 17 + 18 = 84$$

TABLE 22.9
Credit Rating and Ranks of 18 Observations in Three Stores

Credit-rating measure	Rank	Store
4.5	1	2
4.9	2.5	2
4.9	2.5	1
5.0	4	2
5.2	5	2
5.5	6	1
5.7	7	2
5.8	8	1
5.9	10	1
5.9	10	3
5.9	10	3
6.0	12	1
6.1	13	3
6.2	14.5	2
6.2	14.5	1
6.3	16	3
6.7	17	3
6.8	18	3

Intuitively we know that the smaller the difference among R_1, R_2, and R_3—that is, the more similar the three populations—the smaller the chance that we will reject the null hypothesis of equal distributions.

For the Kruskal-Wallis test we use the **Kruskal-Wallis statistic**, denoted by H, which is given by the following formula:

$$H = \frac{12}{N(N+1)} \left(\sum_{i=1}^{k} \frac{R_i^2}{n_i} \right) - 3(N+1) \qquad (22.11)$$

The null hypothesis is rejected for large values of H, for given n_is and given $N = \Sigma n_i$, the larger the differences among the R_is, the larger is $\sum R_i^2$, and the larger $\sum \frac{R_i^2}{n_i}$. Hence the larger is the value of H.

In our case,

$k = 3$ (three independent samples)

$n_1 = n_2 = n_3 = 6$ (six observations in each sample)

$N = n_1 + n_2 + n_3 = 18$ (a total of 18 observations)

Inserting these values and the three rank sums, we obtain

$$H = \frac{12}{18 \cdot 19} \left(\frac{53^2}{6} + \frac{34^2}{6} + \frac{84^2}{6} \right) - 3 \cdot 19 = 7.45$$

The Kruskal-Wallis statistic, calculated for $k = 3$ samples, is approximately distributed χ^2 with $k - 1 = 2$ degrees of freedom. Using the chi-square table (Appendix A, Table A.4), we see that our result is significant at the $\alpha = 0.05$ significance level, and the null hypothesis is rejected, since the sample statistic H is larger than the critical value $\chi^{2(2)}_{0.05} = 5.991$. Thus there appear to be significant differences in the credit standings of customers in the three stores. (The chi-square distribution provides an adequate approximation in our case because all three samples contain more than five observations.)

Now suppose that, because of technical difficulties, it is possible to cover only five months in Stores 1 and 2 and three months in Store 3.

Thus, $k = 3$, as before, but the other values change:

$$n_1 = 5$$

$$n_2 = 5$$

$$n_3 = 3$$

$$N = n_1 + n_2 + n_3 = 13$$

A new ranking is now needed, based on the samples below:

Month	1	2	3	4	5
Store 1	6.2	5.8	4.9	6.0	5.9
Store 2	5.2	4.5	5.7	6.2	5.0
Store 3	6.8	6.7	6.1		

As in the parametric one-way analysis of variance, the nonparametric test may be carried out with unequal numbers of observations in the samples. The new ranking is given in Table 22.10. The new rank sums are given by

$$R_1 = 2 + 6 + 7 + 8 + 10.5 = 33.5$$

$$R_2 = 1 + 3 + 4 + 5 + 10.5 = 23.5$$

$$R_3 = 9 + 12 + 13 = 34$$

We can now calculate the Kruskal-Wallis statistic for the second set of data:

$$H = \frac{12}{13 \cdot 14} \left(\frac{33.5^2}{5} + \frac{23.5^2}{5} + \frac{34^2}{3} \right) - 3 \cdot 14 = 5.49$$

The chi-square distribution is not a good approximation for H in the small-sample case, especially when none of the samples is larger than five. In the small-sample case, we use a special table for the critical region of the Kruskal-Wallis statistic. Entering Appendix A, Table A.9, at $n_1 = 5$, $n_2 = 5$, $n_3 = 3$, we see that $H \geq 5.49$ is indeed significant at the $\alpha = 0.10$ level.[2] Note that the critical value for $\alpha = 0.10$ is given by

---

[2] The order of the sample sizes makes no difference to the significance of H. Thus, the same critical value applies if, for example, $n_1 = 3$, $n_2 = 5$, and $n_3 = 5$.

4.5451, and since the calculated value of H (5.49) is greater, we reject the null hypothesis.

TABLE 22.10
Credit Rating and Ranking of 13 Observations
in Three Stores

Credit-rating measure	Rank	Store
4.5	1	2
4.9	2	1
5.0	3	2
5.2	4	2
5.7	5	2
5.8	6	1
5.9	7	1
6.0	8	1
6.1	9	3
6.2	10.5	2
6.2	10.5	1
6.7	12	3
6.8	13	3

To sum up the Kruskal-Wallis test, recall that when one of the k samples contains more than five observations ($n_i > 5$ for some i), one can use the chi-square distribution to test the significance of H: if H is greater than $\chi_\alpha^{2(k-1)}$, where α is a significance level chosen in advance, we reject the null hypothesis, which asserts that all the k samples are drawn from the same population.

If all the n_is are less than or equal to 5, we should consult special tables giving the exact distribution of the Kruskal-Wallis statistic in order to reach a decision. In the small-sample case, Table A.9 in Appendix A gives the critical values of H for all relevant combinations of n_1, n_2, and n_3, and for various significance levels. After selecting the significance level α, we enter the table for appropriate combinations of n_1, n_2, and n_3 and obtain the critical value of H. If the observed sample statistic H is greater than the critical value that appears in the table, we reject the null hypothesis. Finally, note that tables for the exact distribution of the Kruskal-Wallis statistic are not readily available for more than three samples ($k \geq 4$), but one may use the approximate chi-square distribution with satisfactory results.

The Kruskal-Wallis test, like the Mann-Whitney test, is very powerful. For large samples its power is about 95 percent of the power of the appropriate parametric test (the F test), and one does not have to make the restrictive assumptions required by the parametric F test.

22.10 Nonparametric Measures of Association

In Chapters 17 through 19 we discussed the correlation coefficient as a parametric measure of association. This correlation coefficient, however, is inapplicable to nominal or to ranked data. Moreover, to test the significance of the parametric correlation coefficient, one has to assume that the sample is drawn from a population characterized by the normal distribution, an assumption totally out of line where nominal or ranked data are concerned.

In this section we discuss nonparametric measures of association between two or more variables. We first introduce two basic rank correlation coefficients, the Spearman rank correlation (which we denote by r_s) and the Kendall rank correlation (which we denote by τ). Finally, we describe the Kendall coefficient of concordance (W), which measures the association among more than two variables.

EXAMPLE 22.5

The buyer of women's fashions for a leading department store ranked the seven identically priced models of summer dresses she saw at a fashion preview according to anticipated sales in the forthcoming season. The model most likely to storm the market in the buyer's opinion was given the highest rank, 1, the candidate for the second-best-selling slot was given the rank 2, and so on. The buyer's ranking served as a basis for the store's purchasing policy for that season, and at the season's end the buyer compared her original ranking with the sales-volume performance of the various models stocked. The buyer's ranking and the actual sales are given in Table 22.11.

TABLE 22.11
Ranking of Previewed Models and Actual Sales for Entire Season

Rank of anticipated acceptance (x)	Actual sales volume (thousands of dollars) (y)
1	$196
2	167
3	152
4	161
5	164
6	121
7	132

The buyer is naturally interested in her record as reflected in her ability to rank correctly the sales of the various models before the season begins. To test the buyer's performance, we need to calculate the extent of association or correlation between the preview ranking (x) and the actual season's sales (y). The standard parametric correlation coefficient is inapplicable to this case (even if we can reasonably assume normality): one of the variables (x) is expressed in the form of ranks, and no numerical values are available for this variable. On the other hand, we can easily rank the observed sales figures, y, converting the numerical values y into ranks. The next step, naturally, is to calculate a *rank* correlation coefficient between the two rankings, x and y, in order to determine the degree of association between the buyer's prediction and the actual sales (both expressed in ranks).

We shall now calculate two standard rank correlation coefficients, using the data of Example 22.5.

SPEARMAN RANK CORRELATION COEFFICIENT

The **Spearman rank correlation coefficient** is given by the following equation:

$$r_s = 1 - \frac{6\Sigma d^2}{N(N^2 - 1)} \qquad (22.12)$$

Here N is the number of pairs of ranks and d is the difference in the ranks of x and y.

Using this formula and the data of Table 22.12, we prepare the work sheet shown in that same table and obtain

$$r_s = 1 - \frac{6 \cdot 10}{7 \cdot 48} = 1 - 0.1786 = 0.8214$$

Note that the values of the Spearman correlation coefficient are bounded by -1 and $+1$. If all the paired observations have the same rank, then all the d values are equal to zero, and hence $r_s = +1$. Similarly, if we have completely opposite rankings, it is possible to show that

$$\frac{6\Sigma d^2}{N(N^2 - 1)} = 2$$

and hence $r_s = 1 - 2 = -1$.

TABLE 22.12
Work Sheet for Calculation of Spearman Correlation Coefficient, r_s

Ranking of anticipated acceptance (x)	Ranking of observed sales (y)	$d = x - y$	d^2
1	1	0	0
2	2	0	0
3	5	-2	4
4	4	0	0
5	3	2	4
6	7	-1	1
7	6	1	1
			$\Sigma d^2 = 10$

No special assumptions are needed in order to test the significance of the sample correlation coefficient r_s. We have the following hypotheses:

H_0: The population correlation is zero.
H_1: The population correlation is greater than zero.

Obviously, this is a one-tailed test. Looking at Table A.10 in Appendix A, we find that for $N = 7$ and significance level of $\alpha = 0.05$, the critical value is

0.714. Since in our sample we obtained $r_s = 0.8214$, we reject the null hypothesis at a 5 percent significance level and conclude that the two variables are indeed positively associated. Note that in a case of suspected negative correlation in the sample, we would carry out a one-tailed test with the alternative hypothesis that r_s is less than zero. The decision rule for negative r_s remains as before, the only difference being that we ignore the sign of the sample r_s when entering Table A.10: if $|r_s|$ is greater than or equal to the critical value in Table A.10, we reject the null hypothesis.

Large Samples If N is larger than 10, one can use the Student t distribution to test r_s for significance: the random variable

$$r_s \sqrt{\frac{N - 2}{1 - r_s^2}}$$

follows a t distribution with $N - 2$ degrees of freedom.

Spearman's rank correlation is very powerful, and it is free of the restrictions imposed by the parametric correlation. The power of the nonparametric measure of association r_s is 91 percent of the power of the parametric coefficient of correlation.

Let us now calculate the Kendall rank correlation coefficient by using the data given in Tables 22.11 and 22.12.

KENDALL RANK CORRELATION COEFFICIENT

The **Kendall rank correlation coefficient** is given by the following equation:

$$\tau = \frac{S}{\frac{1}{2}N(N - 1)} \tag{22.13}$$

Here N is the number of pairs and the statistic S is calculated as follows:

1. Arrange one rank series in an increasing order (see first column in Table 22.12).
2. For each rank in the second column in Table 22.12, count the number of following ranks that are larger.
3. Subtract from this count the number of following ranks that are smaller.
4. Add the differences obtained successively for each rank to get the statistic S.

In our case, the first rank in column 2 of Table 22.12 is 1. It is followed by six ranks, all of which are larger. The first term in S is thus $(6 - 0)$. The second rank in column 2 is 2; it is followed by five larger ranks and no smaller ranks; its contribution to S is thus $(5 - 0)$. The third rank in column 2 is 5; it is followed by two larger ranks (7, 6) and two smaller ranks (4, 3); its contribution to S is thus $(2 \quad 2)$. Similarly, we find

$$S = (6 - 0) + (5 - 0) + (2 - 2) + (2 - 1) + (2 - 0) + (0 - 1) = 13$$

$$\tau = \frac{S}{\frac{1}{2}N(N - 1)} = \frac{13}{\frac{1}{2} \cdot 7 \cdot 6} = 0.6190$$

A glance at Table A.11 in Appendix A shows that the probability of getting $S = 13$ and higher for $N = 7$, under the null hypothesis of no correlation, is

0.035. Thus we reject the null hypothesis at $\alpha = 0.05$ and conclude that there is a positive association between x and y.

Note that for given values of N and S, Table A.11 gives the *probability* of getting this or a larger value of S under the null hypothesis of no correlation. If we select a significance level of $\alpha = 0.05$ and get a probability of less than the chosen α from the table, the null hypothesis is rejected.

The table gives critical values for $N \leq 10$ only. For $N > 10$, we have a normal approximation where

$$\mu_\tau = 0 \tag{22.14}$$

$$\sigma_\tau = \sqrt{\frac{2(2N + 5)}{9N(N - 1)}} \tag{22.15}$$

and the statistic

$$Z_\tau = \frac{\tau - \mu_\tau}{\sigma_\tau} = \frac{\tau}{\sqrt{\frac{2(2N + 5)}{9N(N - 1)}}} \tag{22.16}$$

is distributed according to the standard normal distribution.

KENDALL COEFFICIENT OF CONCORDANCE, *W*

Let us illustrate the use of the **Kendall coefficient of concordance, *W***, by means of a numerical example.

The four members of the Appointments and Promotion Committee in a large corporation were asked to review the files and records of six junior executives and consider the possibility of promoting them to middle-management jobs. The four referees used uniform evaluation sheets and the candidates were ranked by each referee independently in the order of descending total scores. The four independent sets of ranks given by the four committee members on the basis of the respective evaluation sheet scores are shown in Table 22.13. The R_j in the last row of the table is the total score given the jth candidate by all four judges.

Before formulating their recommendations, the committee members asked a statistician to help them determine the consistency of their individual evaluations. The statistician suggested the use of the Kendall coefficient of concordance to determine the correlation among the four rankings:

$$W = \frac{s}{\frac{1}{12}k^2N(N^2 - 1)} \tag{22.17}$$

In this case

    s = sum of squares of the observed deviations of the sums of ranks R_j assigned to each candidate from the mean of R_j:

$$s = \Sigma\left(R_j - \frac{\Sigma R_j}{N}\right)^2$$

    k = number of sets of rankings, that is, number of judges
    N = number of individuals (or objects) ranked

TABLE 22.13
Rankings of Six Candidates by Four Judges

Judge	Candidate					
	a	*b*	*c*	*d*	*e*	*f*
A	1	6	3	2	5	4
B	1	5	6	4	2	3
C	6	3	2	5	4	1
D	2	4	3	1	6	5
R_j	10	18	14	12	17	13

In our case, $k = 4, N = 6$.

The statistic s corresponding to our data is calculated in Table 22.14. Note that the average score is $\Sigma R_j/6 = 84/6 = 14$. The value of W is

$$W = \frac{46}{\frac{1}{12} \cdot 16 \cdot 6 \cdot 35} = \frac{46}{280} = 0.1643$$

Table A.12 in Appendix A shows that for $k = 4$ and $N = 6$, the value $s = 46$ is not significant at the 0.05 level. The four sets of ranks given by the four judges are thus uncorrelated.

Note that in order to determine significance of this measure of association, we look at the table with the desired α value (that is, $\alpha = 0.05$ or $\alpha = 0.01$) and the cell that is applicable to the given values of k and N. In this cell we have the critical value of s. In our example, for $\alpha = 0.05$, $k = 4$, and $N = 6$, we obtain the critical value $s = 143.3$. Since in the sample $s = 46$, which is smaller than the critical value, we cannot reject the null hypothesis of non-association.

The Kendall coefficient of concordance, W, ranges between (and includes) values 0 and 1. If there is perfect agreement among the various rankings—that is, if all judges assign the same rank to each individual—the sum s will be large and W will take the value of 1.0. If, on the other hand, there is complete disagreement in the rankings—that is, each individual is assigned all possible ranks by the judges—then the values of R_j will be either equal to or very nearly equal to each other and to their mean, $\Sigma R_j/N$. In such a case the sum s will vanish and the statistic W will be zero or very nearly zero. Small values of s and W thus do not enable us to reject the null hypothesis of no association, whereas large values of s and W support the existence of significant correlation among the rankings.

TABLE 22.14
Work Sheet for Calculation of Statistic *s*

R_j	$R_j - \dfrac{\Sigma R_j}{6}$	$\left(R_j - \dfrac{\Sigma R_j}{6}\right)^2$
10	−4	16
18	4	16
14	0	0
12	−2	4
17	3	9
13	−1	1
$\Sigma R_j = 84$		$s = 46$

Very seldom will we find complete disagreement among the rankings. A more likely phenomenon occurs when subgroups of rankings are negatively associated among themselves but positively associated within the subgroups. An extreme example of this kind of relationship among the rankings is provided in Table 22.15. Here, the rankings of Judges A and B are perfectly positively correlated, as are the rankings of Judges C and D. However, the rankings of these two subgroups are perfectly negatively correlated, resulting in a zero value of s, since all the R_js are equal to one another and to their mean.

TABLE 22.15
Rankings of Six Candidates by Four Judges

	Candidate					
Judge	a	b	c	d	e	f
A	1	4	2	3	6	5
B	1	4	2	3	6	5
C	6	3	5	4	1	2
D	6	3	5	4	1	2
R_j	14	14	14	14	14	14

Large Samples When $N > 7$, the random variable $\dfrac{s}{\frac{1}{12}kN(N+1)}$ is distributed approximately as χ^2 with $N - 1$ degrees of freedom—that is, for a given significance level, α, we reject the null hypothesis of no association when s is large enough so that the above random variable is greater than $\chi^2_{\alpha(N-1)}$.

Chapter Summary and Review

1. One-sample tests
   a. The binomial test is used to test the value of a proportion.
   b. The chi-square test is used to test goodness of fit.
   c. The runs test is used to test for randomness.
      i. We reject the null hypothesis that asserts randomness if the number of runs is too small ($r \leq r_a$) or too large ($r \geq r_b$) where r_a and r_b serve as critical values and r is the sample number of runs.
      ii. For large n_1 or n_2 we use the normal approximation when n_1 and n_2 denote the number of outcomes in categories 1 and 2, respectively. The test statistic is

$$Z_r = \frac{r - \mu_r}{\sigma_r}$$

where

$$\mu_r = \frac{2n_1 n_2}{n_1 + n_2} + 1$$

and

$$\sigma_r = \sqrt{\frac{2n_1 n_2 (2n_1 n_2 - n_1 - n_2)}{(n_1 + n_2)^2 (n_1 + n_2 - 1)}}$$

d. The Kolmogorov-Smirnov test is used to test goodness of fit.
   i. The null hypothesis is that the random variable belongs to some theoretical distribution whose cumulative distribution is $E(x)$ and observed sample cumulative distribution is $O(x)$. Reject H_0 if $D(N) = \max |E(x) - O(x)|$ is greater than some critical value.

2. Two or more samples
   a. The sign test: testing the differences between two related samples.
      i. For small samples use the binomial distribution.
      ii. For large samples use the normal approximation. According to the normal approximation, the statistic $\dfrac{X - np}{\sqrt{npq}}$ is approximately (standard) normally distributed, where X measures the number of pluses or minuses and n is the total number of pluses and minuses. Under the null hypothesis, $p = \frac{1}{2}$, so that the test statistic is

$$\frac{X - \dfrac{n}{2}}{\sqrt{n/4}}$$

   b. Mann-Whitney test: testing the differences between two independent samples.
      i. For small samples use the Mann-Whitney tables.
      ii. For large samples use the normal approximation. According to the normal approximation, the statistic $\dfrac{T - \mu_T}{\sigma_T}$ is approximately (standard) normally distributed, where T is either T_A or T_B and $\mu_T = \dfrac{n_A n_B}{2}$ and $\sigma_T^2 = \dfrac{n_A n_B (n_A + n_B + 1)}{12}$.

   c. Kruskal-Wallis test: testing the difference in the means of independent groups.
      i. The statistic $H = \dfrac{12}{N(N + 1)} \left(\sum\limits_{i=1}^{k} \dfrac{R_i^2}{n_i} \right) - 3(N + 1) \sim \chi^2$ with $k - 1$ degrees of freedom.

3. Measures of association
   a. Spearman rank correlation coefficient

$$r_s = 1 - \frac{6\Sigma d^2}{N(N^2 - 1)}$$

   b. Kendall rank correlation coefficient

$$\tau = \frac{S}{\frac{1}{2}N(N - 1)}$$

   For large samples use the normal approximation with $\mu_\tau = 0$ and

$$\sigma_\tau = \sqrt{\frac{2(2N + 5)}{9N(N - 1)}}.$$

   c. Kendall coefficient of concordance

$$W = \frac{s}{\frac{1}{12}k^2 N(N^2 - 1)}$$

i. For small N ($N \leq 7$) use Table A.12 in Appendix A.
ii. For large N ($N > 7$) use the following statistic:

$$\frac{s}{\frac{1}{12}kN(N + 1)}$$

which has a chi-square distribution with $N - 1$ degrees of freedom.

Problems

22.1. Explain the difference between parametric and nonparametric methods.

22.2. Give an example in which an assumption with regard to the distribution of the random variable may cause an error in decision making. Illustrate your answer graphically.

22.3. Give an example of two assumptions commonly used in parametric tests.

22.4. In what respect are nonparametric tests inferior to parametric tests?

22.5. Give an example in which the binomial distribution is treated as a nonparametric distribution, and another example in which it is treated as a parametric distribution.

22.6. Give an example of the chi-square distribution in which it is treated as a nonparametric distribution and another in which it is treated as a parametric distribution.

22.7. In his monthly report to the managing director, the production manager indicated that there had been a recent alarming increase in the number of rejects in Department C. He diagnosed the problem as being due to equipment obsolescence and recommended that a new machine be purchased. The cost accountant, summoned by the managing director for a second opinion, checked the previous two weeks' quality-control records and reported that the average number of rejects did not exceed the long-run daily average of 7.5 and she therefore saw no cause for alarm. The production manager countered that the average number of rejects did not mean much and that one should consider the bunching of rejects between successive maintenance sessions. To support his opinion he produced the quality-control records for the previous 10 working days between two successive maintenance sessions (see Table P22.7).

Propose a nonparametric test in order to check whether days with above-average reject counts do indeed bunch together abnormally. Apply the test to the production manager's data. What is your conclusion?

TABLE P22.7

Day after last maintenance	Number of rejects
1	1
2	1
3	1
4	2
5	5
6	12
7	12
8	12
9	14
10	15

22.8. The number of passengers on a 747 jumbo jet in a sample of 10 flights was as follows:

Sample flight	1	2	3	4	5	6	7	8	9	10
Number of passengers	200	210	300	185	250	285	300	320	180	400

(a) Apply the sign test (binomial) to test the null hypothesis that the median number of passengers is 290 against the alternative that it is greater than 290. Use $\alpha = 0.05$.

(b) Apply the sign test to test the null hypothesis that the first quartile of the distribution of the number of passengers (i.e., the 25th percentile) is equal to 190 against the alternative that the first quartile is greater than 190. Use $\alpha = 0.05$.

22.9. The following sequence of M and W shows the order of men (M) and women (W) who enter a bank on a given morning:

$$M \; M \; W \; W \; W \; W \; M \; M \; W \; M \; W \; M$$

Test for randomness at the 0.05 level of significance.

22.10. The following sequence of pluses and minuses are changes in the price of gold over 40 consecutive days. A minus stands for a price drop and a plus stands for no change or price increase:

$$+ \; + \; + \; - \; - \; + \; + \; + \; + \; - \; - \; - \; - \; - \; - \; + \; + \; + \; + \; +$$
$$- \; - \; - \; + \; - \; + \; + \; + \; + \; + \; + \; + \; + \; - \; - \; - \; - \; - \; - \; -$$

Test the randomness of the gold price changes at $\alpha = 0.05$. What is your interpretation of the result?

22.11. Table P22.11 shows a composite monthly stock index for the period 1971–75 as a monthly average of Standard & Poor's stock price indexes (1941–43 = 100). Use a nonparametric method to test whether price increases and price decreases in the stock market, as reflected by this composite index, constitute a random series.

TABLE P22.11

Year	Jan.	Feb.	Mar.	Apr.	May	June	Jul.	Aug.	Sept.	Oct.	Nov.	Dec.	Avg.
1975	72.56	80.10	83.78	84.72	90.10	92.40	92.49	85.71	84.67	88.57	90.07	88.70	86.16
1974	96.11	93.45	97.44	92.46	89.67	89.79	79.31	76.03	68.12	69.44	71.74	67.07	82.55
1973	118.4	114.2	112.4	110.3	107.2	104.8	105.8	103.8	105.6	109.8	102.0	94.78	107.4
1972	103.3	105.2	107.7	108.8	107.7	108.0	107.2	111.0	109.4	109.6	115.1	117.5	109.2
1971	93.49	97.11	99.60	103.0	101.6	99.72	99.00	97.24	99.40	97.29	92.78	99.17	98.29

Source: Standard & Poor's *Trade and Securities Statistics, Security Price Index Record*, 1976 edition, p. 121.

22.12. A roulette wheel is spun over the numbers 1, 2, 3, 4, 5, 6, 7, 8, 9, and 10. If the wheel is balanced, there is an equal probability that it will stop at any of these numbers. A sample of 130 spins reveals the following results:

Number	Frequency
1	10
2	15
3	15
4	20
5	15
6	10
7	10
8	20
9	15
10	0
Total	130

(a) Apply the Kolmogorov-Smirnov statistic to test whether the roulette wheel is balanced. Use $\alpha = 0.05$. If the wheel is imbalanced, the license to operate this casino should be suspended. What is your conclusion?

(b) Employ the chi-square test of goodness of fit to test the hypothesis that the wheel is balanced. Use $\alpha = 0.05$ again and compare the result to the result in part *a*.

22.13. An electronic-instrument assembly plant receives weekly shipments of solid-state components from a semiconductor manufacturer. The components are packed for delivery in boxes of 1,000 units each, and the standard quality-control procedure consists of selecting one box at random and inspecting all the units in it for possible defects. The following table provides a statistical summary of the past inspection records of all weekly shipments received:

Number of defects in inspected box (x)	Relative frequency of occurrence over entire period (f)
0	0.30
1	0.50
2	0.10
3	0.05
4	0.05
5 and over	0.00
	1.00

On the basis of the historical data, the staff statistician estimates that the average number of defects in weekly shipments has a Poisson distribution with $\lambda = 1.05$. The current policy is to accept the entire shipment if the average number of defects per box is less than 1.05; otherwise, the entire shipment is rejected and returned to the component manufacturer. Since the accept/reject decision is based on a sample of one box from each shipment, an entire shipment may be rejected, although the average number of defects per box may be less than 1.05. If this happens, the shipment is erroneously rejected. The firm is prepared to agree to this error (Type I error) as long as its probability is not greater than 10 percent.

(a) Assuming that the distribution is indeed Poisson, as estimated by the statistician, what is the maximum number of defects, x, in the sampled box to justify acceptance of the shipment? For what values of x in the sample should the shipment be returned for Type I error of not larger than 10 percent? (Hint: On the basis of the historical data, $E(X) = V(X) = \lambda = 1.05$, which justifies the statistician's assumption of a Poisson distribution for the average number of defects. Verify this conclusion. Recall that the probability of getting precisely x defects in a Poisson distribution with parameter λ is given by $P(X = x) = \dfrac{e^{-\lambda}\lambda^x}{x!}$. You will need the probabilities $P(X \le x)$ and $P(X > x)$ to solve the problem.)

(b) Suppose now that we are not willing to use the assumption of a Poisson distribution and accept the historical record in the table above as representing the "true" parameter-free distribution of the average number of defects per box in weekly shipments. What is the appropriate accept/reject decision in this case, assuming again a Type I error $\alpha = 10$ percent?

(c) What distribution causes more "acceptable" shipments to be rejected and returned? What is the percentage of returned shipments under the assumption of the Poisson distribution and what is the corresponding percentage under the parameter-free empirical distribution? (Hint: Refer to the table to estimate the percentage of shipments with the appropriate x.)

(d) Assume that the plant receives 100 shipments annually and the true distribution of the average number of defects per box is as given in the table, while the accept/reject decision is based on the Poisson distribution with $\lambda = 1.05$. The handling costs for each returned shipment are $1,000. What is the total *extra* cost incurred by the firm as a result of using the wrong distribution for its accept/reject decisions? (Hint: Calculate the *additional* cost above the cost that the plant is willing to bear in accepting a Type I error of 10 percent with the true distribution.)

(e) What did you learn about the "cost of making an assumption" regarding a distribution and the reason we need nonparametric methods?

22.14. In Chapter 15, Problem 15.38, we considered the percentage increase in personal income in the United States from March 1981 to March 1982 and used the chi-square test to check whether the increases are normally distributed.

Apply the Kolmogorov-Smirnov test to the same data to check the goodness of fit between the distribution of the observed percentage increases in personal income and the normal distribution. (Hint: Use the mean and the standard deviation of the percentage increases as the parameters of the normal distribution.)

What is the technical difference between the application of the chi-square test and the Kolmogorov-Smirnov test?

22.15. In order to decrease the number of accidents at 10 dangerous intersections, the traffic control office has decided to assign a police officer to each of these intersections. The number of accidents in the intersections during a two-week test period was compared to the number of accidents that occurred during a similar period prior to assigning the police officers. The results are given in Table P22.15.

TABLE P22.15

| Intersection | Number of accidents | |
	Before	After
1	10	9
2	11	10
3	12	14
4	8	12
5	6	4
6	10	8
7	9	7
8	15	14
9	20	15
10	30	20

Use the sign test for related samples to test the null hypothesis that the presence of police officers does not reduce the number of accidents. Use $\alpha = 0.05$. What is your conclusion from this experiment?

22.16. The number of employees absent from the production departments of General Cars and General Trucks in a sample of 12 winter days was as follows:

General Cars: 20 30 15 17 19 18 19 10 12 18 20 20
General Trucks: 30 28 20 20 22 16 16 11 14 22 25 18

Use the sign test for related samples at the level $\alpha = 0.05$ to test the null hypothesis that the mean number of absences is the same in the two departments against the alternative hypothesis that the mean number of absences is different.

22.17. Diversification of investment is a basic strategy intended to protect portfolios from extreme losses that could result from exposure to risk. By spreading the investment among various assets, we stabilize our return on investment—provided, of course, that we have not inadvertently invested in assets whose values increase or decrease all at the same time. For diversification to work as intended, some assets must depreciate in value, while others must appreciate.

The latest fashion in portfolio management is international diversification—that is, spreading investment dollars among stocks of various countries, on the assumption that the stock markets in those countries do not rise or fall simultaneously. The last column in Table P22.17 shows the weekly changes in the stock market indexes of 10 industrial countries during the week ending December 22, 1978. The changes are expressed in index points for each country, and the figures are thus not comparable numerically.

TABLE P22.17

	High	Low	Close	Week's change
Australia	566.79	441.19	537.97	− 1.96
Austria	2,277.00	2,243.00	2,277.00	+ 12.00
Belgium	119.37	96.10	107.87	− 0.68
Canada	1,322.65	996.88	1,298.27	+ 14.42
France	127.35	78.10	121.64	+ 0.90
Italy	4,883.00	3,086.00	3,991.00	− 27.00
Japan	5,968.26	4,867.91	5,884.29	−146.07
Netherlands	100.20	85.90	89.80	− 1.00
Switzerland	323.70	279.00	N.A.	
United Kingdom	535.50	433.40	479.30	− 1.70
West Germany	863.80	759.40	819.60	− 1.60

Source: *Barron's*, December 25, 1978.

Use the sign test to test the hypothesis that the fluctuations among the 10 stock indexes in the sample have equal probabilities. Can you justify the use of the sign test in this case? What other test could you suggest for this purpose?

22.18. Mutual funds provide the individual investor with a convenient medium for diversification. A mutual fund spreads its investment among numerous securities, so individuals who purchase shares in a mutual fund in fact invest in a highly diversified portfolio, something that they could hardly have achieved on their own with limited funds. Mutual funds tailor their diversification strategies to different investor groups. There are capital-growth funds, current-income funds, equity funds, bond funds, and so on. Table P22.18 lists the average annual total return for various categories of mutual funds for the period 1971–77. (The annual total return roughly represents the percentage of profit on invested dollars.)

TABLE P22.18

	Average total returns (percent)						
Fund strategy	1977	1976	1975	1974	1973	1972	1971
Maximum capital gain	7.3	27.5	37.9	− 27.6	− 29.4	12.7	28.3
Long-term growth	− 0.4	22.4	32.0	− 27.0	− 22.7	13.6	20.7
Growth and current income	− 3.2	24.2	32.4	− 21.6	− 15.8	12.6	15.7
Balanced	− 0.9	23.5	26.6	− 17.2	− 12.0	11.4	13.9
Income funds:							
Common stock policy	− 0.4	30.3	33.6	− 14.8	− 11.2	10.7	12.8

Source: Reprinted by permission from the *Wiesenberger Investment Companies Service*, 1978 Edition, Copyright © 1978, Warren, Gorham & Lamont Inc., 210 South Street, Boston, Mass. All rights reserved.

(*a*) Use a nonparametric test to check whether there are any significant differences among the total returns that various fund strategies promise to the individual investor.

(*b*) What parametric test can be used for the same purpose? Why use a nonparametric test?

22.19. Three researchers used questionnaires to investigate some job-satisfaction variables of male and female salespersons in the pharmaceutical industry. Historically, selling pharmaceuticals is a male-dominated occupation. Since earlier research had shown that women in traditionally male fields were less satisfied with their jobs than men who held the same types of jobs, the researchers tested the hypothesis:

H_1: Female pharmaceutical salespersons will be less satisfied with their jobs than males

as an alternative to the null hypothesis

H_0: Female and male pharmaceutical salespersons will display the same job-satisfaction characteristics

Table P22.19 gives the ranking (on a three-point scale of low, medium, and high) assigned by 160 male and 29 female salespersons to several job-satisfaction variables.

TABLE P22.19

Variable	Sex	Distribution[a]			Chi-square[b]
		Low	Med.	High	
Satisfaction					
Pay	M	29%	38%	33%	0.797
	F	28	31	41	NS
Promotion	M	18	48	34	2.37
	F	28	38	35	NS
Supervision	M	21	18	62	6.36
	F	28	35	38	S
Work	M	18	70	13	6.95
	F	21	55	24	S
Coworkers	M	27	37	36	18.43
	F	48	45	7	S**
Self-confidence					
Working with people	M	14	37	49	3.91
	F	14	45	41	NS
Product knowledge	M	9	72	19	7.07
	F	14	86	0	S
Calling on a specialist	M	10	67	23	32.08
	F	14	86	0	S**
Sales ability	M	12	67	21	11.94
	F	7	93	0	S*
Job security	M	13	59	29	8.35
	F	21	65	14	S
Salary	M	33	33	33	5.36
	F	48	37	15	NS

[a] Totals may not equal 100% due to rounding.
[b] S   = significant with probability less than or equal to 0.05.
  S*   = probability less than or equal to 0.01.
  S** = probability less than or equal to 0.001.
  NS = not significant.
Source: J. E. Swann, C. M. Futrell, and J. T. Todd, "Same Job—Different Views: Women and Men in Industrial Sales," *Journal of Marketing,* 42 (January 1978): 95; published by the American Marketing Association.

Use the Mann-Whitney test to test the null hypothesis for the two variables "Pay" and "Co-workers" at the $\alpha = 5$ percent significance level. What are your conclusions from these two tests? (Hint: Convert the percentages in the table to absolute number of respondents and allow for ties in your combined ranking.)

22.20. Two types of batteries are compared. The first, produced by Firm *A*, costs $0.50 per battery. The second, produced by Firm *B*, costs $0.75 per battery. The lifetimes of 10 batteries of the first manufacturer (Firm *A*) and 6 batteries of the second (Firm *B*) have been determined, and they are as follows (in hours):

Firm *A*: 12.0, 13.2, 14.5, 14.4, 5.6, 10.1, 10.2, 11.0, 11.1, 9.4
Firm *B*: 12.1, 9.5, 10.1, 9.8, 5.5, 10.0

(*a*) Apply the Mann-Whitney statistic to test the null hypothesis under which the mean lifetime of the two types of batteries is the same against the alternative hypothesis that asserts that the more expensive battery has a longer lifetime. Use α = 0.05.
(*b*) Do you consider the batteries of one of the firms to be a better bargain compared to the batteries of the other firm? Explain.

22.21. Individuals often invest for the long run, so long-term returns are what really count. Investment decisions, however, are often made on impulse or on the basis of last week's performance. Table P22.21 gives the performance averages for eight categories of mutual funds employing different investment strategies. The figures include the *annual* performance for the year ending December 21, 1978 (long-term performance) and the *weekly* change for the week ending the same day (short-term results).

TABLE P22.21

Number and type of fund	Percent change, year to 12/21/78	Percent change, week ended 12/21/78
54 Capital appreciation	+11.23	−2.01
176 Growth	+10.34	−1.51
87 Growth and income	+ 5.90	−1.46
22 Balanced	+ 3.26	−1.19
102 Income	+ 2.08	−0.91
3 Insurance	+ 9.23	−2.00
15 Specialty	+ 8.10	−0.10
10 Option	+ 1.57	−1.44

Source: *Barron's*, December 25, 1978.

Suggest a nonparametric method to check whether investment decisions based on last week's figures will on the whole pick up the best performers on an annual basis.

22.22. In Problem 22.17 we investigated the conditions for international diversification. Now let us see if mutual funds that spread their investments over various countries manage to achieve significantly better results than the more traditional funds, which restrict their investment to U.S. assets.

Table P22.22 gives the 1977 total returns (with all distributions reinvested) of five mutual funds specializing in international issues versus the average 1977 total returns of various categories of mutual funds investing in U.S. securities.

(*a*) Use a nonparametric test that will enable you to check whether the international funds did better in 1977 than mutual funds investing in U.S. securities only.
(*b*) Some will argue that Canadian Fund cannot properly be classified as an internationally diversified mutual fund. Exclude this fund from the sample and repeat the same test as in part *a*. Are the results any different? If so, can you explain why?
(*c*) What is the parametric counterpart of this test? Apply it to the same data.
(*d*) Discuss the results obtained by the two tests. Which is the more appropriate in our case?

TABLE P22.22

Fund	Total return (percent)
Internationally diversified funds	
Canadian Fund	−1.1
International Investors	32.9
Research Capital Fund	32.2
Scudder International Fund	−0.4
Templeton Growth Fund	20.3
Funds investing in U.S. securities only	
Maximum capital gains	7.3
Long-term growth	−0.4
Growth and current income	−3.2
Balanced	−0.9
Income funds: common stock policy	−0.4
Income funds: flexible policy	3.2
Income funds: senior securities policy	4.9
Insurance and bank stocks	5.7
Public utility stock	7.7
Tax-exempt bonds	6.8

Source: Reprinted by permission from the *Wiesenberger Investment Companies Service*, 1978 Edition, Copyright © 1978, Warren, Gorham & Lamont Inc., 210 South Street, Boston, Mass. All rights reserved.

22.23. Table P22.23 shows the after-tax return on average invested capital (in percent) for a sample of 21 computer companies in the first nine months of 1978 and the corresponding period in 1977.

TABLE P22.23

Company	1978	1977
Amdahl	27.11%	24.15%
Burroughs	8.10	7.84
Control Data	6.36	5.77
Data General	14.63	14.08
Datapoint	15.19	11.93
Digital Equipment	10.39	11.01
General Automation	10.08	2.29
Harris	12.45	11.50
Hewlett-Packard	13.14	12.53
Honeywell	8.98	7.53
IBM	15.96	14.87
Itel	6.94	6.77
Lanier Business Products	18.42	20.50
NCR	8.23	6.29
National Semi-Conductor	14.80	8.89
Perkin-Elmer	11.92	10.21
Prime Computer	17.23	13.80
Sperry Rand	9.76	8.57
Texas Instruments	12.88	12.20
Wang Laboratories	12.49	10.88
Xerox	12.26	11.14

Source: Data from *Business Week*, January 8, 1979, p. 42.

(*a*) Calculate the Kendall rank correlation coefficient between the 1978 and 1977 returns. Is the result significant at the α = 5 percent level? How do you interpret the results?

(*b*) Calculate the Spearman rank correlation coefficient and the ordinary parametric correlation coefficient. Test these coefficients for significance.

(*c*) Compare the three coefficients. Which would you recommend for our problem?

22.24. The advertising expense as percentage of monthly sales in three department stores during five months was as follows:

	Month				
Store	*1*	*2*	*3*	*4*	*5*
1	2.5	2.8	2.3	2.1	2.4
2	1.8	1.9	2.0	2.0	2.2
3	0.1	0.2	0.1	0.2	0.2

Apply the Kruskal-Wallis statistic to test the null hypothesis under which the mean percentage of sales spent on advertising in the three department stores is the same against the alternative hypothesis that the stores differ in their percentage spending on advertising. Use $\alpha = 0.01$.

22.25. The inflation and unemployment rates in six Western countries in 1984 were as follows:

Country	*Inflation*	*Unemployment*
1	10.1%	2.1%
2	8.5	6.1
3	12.0	4.1
4	0.2	12.0
5	22.1	2.0
6	55.1	0.1

(*a*) Calculate the Spearman (r_s) and Kendall (τ) rank correlation coefficients.

(*b*) Test the null hypothesis that the Spearman rank correlation is equal to zero against the alternative hypothesis that it differs from zero. Use $\alpha = 0.10$.

(*c*) Repeat part *b* for the Kendall rank correlation. What is the interpretation of the test results?

22.26. The diving of five swimmers in the Olympic Games was ranked by three judges. The ranks are as follows:

	Swimmer				
Judge	*1*	*2*	*3*	*4*	*5*
A	2	1	3	4	5
B	1	2	3	4	5
C	2	1	4	3	5

(*a*) Calculate the Kendall coefficient of concordance, *W*.

(*b*) Use $\alpha = 0.05$ to test the hypothesis that the coefficient is zero against the alternative that the coefficient is positive. What is your conclusion? Is there an agreement among the three judges?

22.27. One of the intriguing questions in investment analysis is to what extent the top performers of last year will come out on top this year. Wiesenberger Investment Company Service, the foremost authority on mutual funds in the United States, invariably adds a cautionary sentence to all historical statistical analyses that it publishes: "The results shown should under no circumstances be construed as an indication of future performance." The individual investor, however, is often tempted to decide on the basis of last year's results.

Consider the five categories of mutual funds in Problem 22.18 and focus your attention on the average total returns for the four years 1974–77. Is there consistency in the performance of the various funds over the years? Discuss the implications of your findings. Is the Wiesenberger warning justified?

22.28. Suppose we ordered the income of males (*M*) and females (*F*). The following lists show ordered income by earner in five samples. Count the number of runs in each sample.

(a) *M M M M M F F F*
(b) *F F F F F M M M*
(c) *M M M M M M M F*
(d) *M F M F M F M F*
(e) *F M F M F M F M*

22.29. The stock price of GSB on eleven successive days in 1980 was as follows:

$$\$20, \$20\tfrac{1}{4}, \$20\tfrac{3}{4}, \$21, \$21\tfrac{1}{2}, \$22, \$21, \$21, \$21, \$19, \$18$$

Test the hypothesis that the daily price changes are random.

22.30. Repeat the test of Problem 22.29 with the following two alternative price series:

(a) $\$20, \$19, \$20, \$18, \$18\tfrac{1}{2}, \$18\tfrac{1}{4}, \$18\tfrac{1}{2}, \$18, \$19, \$18\tfrac{1}{2}, \$19$
(b) $\$20, \$21, \$18, \$19, \$20, \$19, \$20, \$21, \$16, \$15, \$13$

22.31. Suppose in the runs test we obtain $n_1 = 50$ (price up) and $n_2 = 50$ (price down). It is also given that the number of runs, *r*, is 51. The null hypothesis is that all of the observations were drawn at random from a given population. Would you accept or reject the null hypothesis? Draw your conclusion without the help of any statistical tables.

22.32. Draw a theoretical cumulative distribution of your choice on a chart. On the same chart draw a hypothetical cumulative distribution of empirical data (this will be a step function). Indicate the Kolmogorov-Smirnov *D* statistic on your chart.

22.33. The average productivity of high school graduates and high school dropouts on a given production line is to be tested. Suppose a statistical test is needed to decide the equality or inequality of productivity. If the assumption of equal variances cannot be made and the sample is small, what test would you choose for this purpose? Explain your choice.

22.34. When the value of the Mann-Whitney statistic is calculated, the following values are computed:

$$T_A = 10$$

$$T_B = 50$$

$$n_A = 12$$

Find the value of n_B.

22.35. The monthly incomes of men and women in a sample of nine observations are as follows:

$$\begin{array}{ccccccccc} F & F & M & F & M & M & M & F & M \end{array}$$
$$\$600, \$650, \$700, \$700, \$750, \$800, \$850, \$900, \$1,000$$

Test the hypothesis that the income of men is equal to that of women, where H_1 is the hypothesis that the two groups have different averages.

22.36. Using the Kruskal-Wallis test with three groups where $n_1 = n_2 = n_3 = 3$, we found that $R_1 = R_2 = R_3$. What is the value of the statistic H? Use Equation 22.11. Would you reject the null hypothesis?

22.37. Suppose the monthly incomes of two samples (X and Y) are as follows:

X	Y
$1,000	$1,000
1,500	1,500
2,000	4,000

Write down the ranks of the observations for each of the samples. Do we lose information by switching from numerical data to ranks? Is it meaningful to calculate the mean and variance of ranks? Explain your answer.

22.38. One of the issues investigated by Leo Bogart in his article "Is All This Advertising Necessary?" in the *Journal of Advertising Research* for October 1978 is the following: is there a significant correlation between the amount of national advertising behind product brands in a given year and the amount of slogan identification by consumers in the next year? The data, taken from a series of national surveys conducted between September 1976 and February 1977, are presented in Table P22.38.

Calculate the Spearman and Kendall rank correlations and determine if they are significantly different from zero at $\alpha = 0.05$ significance level.

TABLE P22.38

Brand	1976 Advertising expenditure	Percent of consumers identifying slogan in early 1977
Charmin	$ 7,289,000	82%
Alka-Seltzer	11,730,000	79
Chiffon	1,166,000	58
Morton's (Salt)	1,016,000	57
Contact	8,952,000	55
Hertz	5,511,000	47
Ragú	5,357,000	45
Meow Mix	6,296,000	41
McDonald's	81,831,000	38
Dynamo	5,010,000	37
Aim	12,087,000	33
Schlitz	16,244,000	23
Coca-Cola	46,768,000	16

Source: R. H. Bruskin Associates, *Bruskin Report,* May 1977.

Case Problems

22.1. Use the rate of return data in Data Set 2, Appendix B, Table B.2, to test the hypothesis that positive returns ($+$) and nonpositive returns ($-$) of Phoenix-Chase Growth Fund Series (fund number 19) constitute a random series. Use a significance level of 5 percent.

22.2. Suppose the rates of return of the first 10 funds in Data Set 2, Appendix B, Table B.2, are drawn from the same distribution. Test the hypothesis that the distribution is normal with a mean of 10 percent and a standard deviation of 20 percent. Use the Kolmogorov-Smirnov test. Before you carry out the test, classify the rates of return into the following categories: "over (-60) to (-40)," "over (-40) to (-20)," "over (-20) to 0," "over 0 to 20," "over 20 to 40," "over 40 to 60," and "over 60 to 80." Use a 5 percent significance level.

22.3. (*a*) Use the Mann-Whitney statistic to test the hypothesis that the rate of return of the Explorer Fund (Data Set 2, fund number 8) has the same distribution as the Hartwell Growth Fund (fund number 12). Use a significance level of 10 percent.

(*b*) Repeat part *a*, this time comparing the distributions of the rate of return of the Explorer Fund and the Canadian Fund (fund number 115 in Data Set 2).

22.4. (*a*) Apply the Kruskal-Wallis statistic to test the hypothesis that the rates of return on funds numbered 1, 5, 10, and 15 in Data Set 2 are drawn from the same populations. Use a 5 percent significance level.

(*b*) Repeat part *a* for funds numbered 1, 20, 80, 100, and 125. Discuss your results.

DECISION MAKING UNDER UNCERTAINTY

23

Businesspeople and other individuals are often faced by the need to select one of several alternative activities. In a world of uncertainty, making a prudent choice is at times a complex matter. At the core of the problem is the obvious difficulty of anticipating the consequences of each activity. Quantitative approaches are available to deal with these situations. In some of these approaches, the various possible outcomes are evaluated without the use of probabilistic methods. Other approaches employ probability assessments derived either objectively or subjectively by the individual (or group of individuals) making the choice. In this chapter, we shall describe some of these methods.

23.1 The Payoff Matrix

Let us assume that a businessman faced by an investment decision has to choose among three possible activities. In his assessment of the future, he envisions three possible states of the economy: inflation, recession, and stagflation. (Stagflation, incidentally, is a relatively new phenomenon that began with the oil crisis of 1974. While under normal circumstances inflation is associated with an active economy, stagflation is a situation in which stagnation and inflation prevail simultaneously.)

We shall use A_1, A_2, and A_3 to denote the three activities among which our investor must choose:

A_1 An investment project in the construction industry
A_2 An investment project in the cigarette-manufacturing industry
A_3 A project in the bakery-products industry

The three possible states of the economy, which are frequently dubbed "states of nature," are denoted by S_1, S_2, and S_3:

S_1 Inflation
S_2 Stagflation
S_3 Recession

To consider all these possibilities, the businessman sets up a **payoff matrix**, which is simply *a table that lists the anticipated profit from each investment* (in millions of dollars, say) *under the various possible states of nature.* Table 23.1 illustrates such a payoff matrix.

TABLE 23.1
Payoff Matrix

		State of nature		
	Activity	S_1 *Inflation*	S_2 *Stagflation*	S_3 *Recession*
A_1	Construction	500	300	10
A_2	Cigarettes	40	150	100
A_3	Bakery products	80	60	70

Note that the consumption of bread, hence the profit from investment A_3, does not change much with the various states of nature: bread is a basic consumption good, which people don't give up easily. The construction industry, however, is highly vulnerable to economic conditions. People do not usually buy new or bigger houses in a recession. On the other hand, cigarettes sell better in bad times than in good: feeling nervous about job security, people may seek relief in increased smoking.

Given this payoff matrix, which project ("activity") would you recommend for the investor? Several possible decision rules are available.

23.2 Decisions Based on Extreme Values

Some decision rules are nonprobabilistic and are based on only one value per activity in the payoff matrix. Other decision criteria consider the entire distribution of payoffs. We shall start with the nonprobabilistic decision rules.

THE MAXIMAX CRITERION

Some individuals are born optimists. Whatever activity they choose, optimists expect the state of nature that is most favorable for that activity to prevail. Thus, if they invest in A_1, they expect inflation and a profit of 500. If they invest in A_2, they expect stagflation and a profit of 150. If they choose A_3, they again expect inflation and a profit of 80. From each activity, they expect to get the maximum value of the appropriate row in the payoff matrix. Consequently, optimists naturally choose the activity with the largest of these maximum values. Their decision rule is correspondingly called **maximax**: *the maximum value of the rows' maxima*. In our specific example, we have

$$\max A_1 = 500$$

$$\max A_2 = 150$$

$$\max A_3 = 80$$

The maximum of these maxima is 500, and if our investor follows the maximax rule, he will choose to invest in construction (A_1).

THE MAXIMIN CRITERION

The **maximin criterion** is a decision rule for born pessimists. Whatever activity they choose, pessimists expect nature to work against them. If they are going to drop a buttered slice of bread, they believe that the buttered side will always hit the floor, no matter which side they decide to butter. Therefore, when choosing among activities, they consider the minimum value of each activity and choose the one corresponding to the maximum of all the minima. In our specific example

$$\min A_1 = 10$$

$$\min A_2 = 40$$

$$\min A_3 = 60$$

Pessimists now naturally pick the activity with the largest anticipated minimum payoff as the best of bad choices: the maximum of the anticipated minima is 60, and under the maximin criterion investors will choose to invest in bakery products (A_3).

THE MINIMAX CRITERION

When the profit figures in a payoff table are replaced with costs (that is, money outlays required to achieve a given goal), the **minimax criterion**—*the minimum of all maxima*—naturally replaces the maximin criterion. For example, suppose that three possible activities may be undertaken to achieve a given volume of sales—specifically, three advertising methods, which we denote by A_1, A_2, and A_3. Table 23.2 describes the corresponding cost matrix.

TABLE 23.2
Cost Matrix

		State of nature		
	Activity	S_1 Inflation	S_2 Stagflation	S_3 Recession
A_1	Advertise on TV	10	20	35
A_2	Advertise in newspapers	60	40	50
A_3	Advertise by mail	20	30	25

The born pessimist always expects the worse, so whatever the promotion campaign, he or she expects the costs to reach the maximum figure. The maximum cost under each activity is given by

$$\max A_1 = 35$$
$$\max A_2 = 60$$
$$\max A_3 = 30$$

The minimum of all these maximum costs is 30; therefore the minimax criterion leads the investor to choose activity A_3, which ensures the lowest possible exposure in terms of maximum outlay.

Thus, the minimax criterion is conceptually related to the maximin criterion. The minimax is used when dealing with costs or outlays of cash, while the maximin is used when the payoff matrix represents profit or incoming cash flow.

THE MINIMIN CRITERION (WALD CRITERION)

An optimistic investor who applies the maximax criterion to a payoff matrix will use the **minimin criterion** when faced with a cost matrix. In Table 23.2 the anticipated minimum costs for each activity are

$$\min A_1 = 10$$
$$\min A_2 = 40$$
$$\min A_3 = 20$$

Thus the minimum of all minima is 10, and activity A_1 is chosen. This decision maker is an optimist in the sense that whatever activity he chooses, he expects nature to act in his favor: for each activity he considers the lowest possible cost.

THE MINIMAX REGRET CRITERION

Leonard Savage suggests the **minimax regret criterion,** which advises us to calculate the maximum possible regret for each activity and then to choose the activity that minimizes the maximum regret.[1] Suppose that the investor selected activity A_i and state of nature S_j actually occurred. If activity A_i

---

[1] Leonard J. Savage, "The Theory of Statistical Decision," *Journal of the American Statistical Association,* 46 (1951): 55–67.

gives the maximum profit (or minimum cost) in the given state of nature, there is no regret: the investor chose wisely. If, however, some activity other than A_i (A_k, say) promises the maximum profit in this state of nature, the investor can be said not to have chosen wisely; his or her regret is measured by the difference between the maximum profit in state of nature S_j (which the investor would have attained had he or she chosen A_k) and the profit actually made by having chosen A_i.

To illustrate the minimax regret criterion, we turn again to the payoff matrix in Table 23.1. Suppose we choose A_1 and inflation occurs. Then the regret of choosing A_1 is clearly zero: it gives the maximum possible outcome in the column corresponding to inflation. If we had chosen A_2, the regret would have been the difference between the maximum payoff attainable under inflation (500) and the payoff obtained with A_2 (40). So for A_2 we get Regret = 500 − 40 = 460, which is indeed the opportunity loss caused by choosing A_2 rather than the best activity under inflation, A_1. Similarly, if we had chosen A_3, the regret would have been 420: 500 − 80 = 420. Under stagflation we subtract the corresponding payoff from the column maximum of 300 and under recession we deduct the payoffs from the highest payoff attainable under this state of nature, which is 100. The resulting **regret table** is shown in Table 23.3.

TABLE 23.3
Regret Table

| | State of nature | | |
| | S_1
Inflation | S_2
Stagflation | S_3
Recession |
Activity			
A_1 Construction	0	0	90
A_2 Cigarettes	460	150	0
A_3 Bakery products	420	240	30

The maximum regret (or opportunity loss) for each activity is given by

$$\max A_1 = 90$$

$$\max A_2 = 460$$

$$\max A_3 = 420$$

Now we choose the minimum of these three values, 90. Activity A_1, the construction industry, should be selected by the minimax regret criterion.

23.3 The Drawbacks of the Various Rules

THE DRAWBACKS OF THE MAXIMAX AND MAXIMIN RULES

Suppose that regardless of the particular activity chosen by our investor, he becomes entitled to a government grant of $100 if and only if inflation occurs. The grant is for a fixed amount, independent of the action taken by the businessman. Should it affect his decision? Obviously, a reasonable decision rule should be independent of a *fixed* grant that is given regardless of the activity chosen. So let us see if the decisions arrived at by the previous criteria would change as a result of the grant.

TABLE 23.4
Payoff Matrix with Inflation Grant

| | State of nature | | |
Activity	S_1 Inflation	S_2 Stagflation	S_3 Recession
A_1 Construction	600	300	10
A_2 Cigarettes	140	150	100
A_3 Bakery products	180	60	70

The minimax regret criterion is not affected by the grant: a fixed amount has been added to all the payoffs under inflation, and it simply cancels out when each payoff is subtracted from the column maximum. We thus get exactly the same regret matrix as before, and the activity selected according to this decision rule is the same as it was without the grant. As for the other criteria, Table 23.4 presents the payoff matrix (Table 23.1) after the inflation grant has been added.

The decisions are *not* unaffected by the inflation grant. For example, the maximin rule now gives

$$\min A_1 = 10$$

$$\min A_2 = 100$$

$$\min A_3 = 60$$

and the maximin is 100. Hence A_2 is chosen, whereas before the introduction of the fixed grant, A_3 was selected by the maximin rule. By the same argument, one can show (by adding some fixed amount to the other columns) that none of the other rules—no matter if we deal with income or cost—except the minimax regret criterion is unaffected by changes by a constant amount in a given state of nature.

A KEY DRAWBACK OF THE MINIMAX REGRET RULE

The best-known drawback of the minimax regret rule is that it is not "independent of the irrelevant alternatives."[2] Let us demonstrate this drawback by a numerical example. We use the same payoff matrix as before, adding a fourth activity, A_4 (say, acquiring corporations after they have gone bankrupt). This activity yields a high profit only in a recession, when many corporations may be expected to go bankrupt. Thus, we have the payoff matrix in Table 23.5.

Using the maximin criterion, we choose activity A_3, as we had done without the opportunity of investing in A_4. With the minimax regret criterion, however, the addition of activity A_4 changes our decision. Let us first construct the regret table (Table 23.6).

Recall that the regret table is obtained by subtraction of the payoffs in each column from the maximum payoff in the corresponding column. Applying the minimax regret rule to Table 23.6, we select A_3 (bakery products), while without activity A_4 we selected A_1 (construction), as discussed before.

Why is action A_4 called an "irrelevant alternative"? The answer is simply

[2] See Robert D. Luce and Howard Raiffa, *Games and Decisions* (New York: Wiley, 1957), pp. 27, 127.

TABLE 23.5
Payoff Matrix with Irrelevant Alternative

		State of nature		
	Activity	S_1 Inflation	S_2 Stagflation	S_3 Recession
A_1	Construction	500	300	10
A_2	Cigarettes	40	150	100
A_3	Bakery products	80	60	70
A_4	Acquisitions	0	100	500

TABLE 23.6
Regret Table with Irrelevant Alternative

		State of nature		
	Activity	S_1 Inflation	S_2 Stagflation	S_3 Recession
A_1	Construction	0	0	490
A_2	Cigarettes	460	150	400
A_3	Bakery products	420	240	430
A_4	Acquisitions	500	200	0

that A_4 is selected neither by the maximin rule nor by the minimax regret rule. Obviously, if A_4 had been sufficiently attractive to be selected, it would and should have had an impact on our decision. But how is it that a poor investment that is appropriately *not* selected should bring about a change in chosen activities? The unattractive alternative, A_4, is clearly irrelevant and should not affect our decision. The fact that it *does* change the decision obtained by the minimax regret criterion—whereas it does not change the decision obtained by the maximin rule—highlights the most serious relative deficiency of the minimax regret criterion.

THE EFFECT OF THE EXTREME VALUES

Finally, another deficiency common to all decision rules mentioned so far in this chapter is that they rely completely on one extreme value in each row. In other words, if a number in the table is not the extreme in its row, its specific value is not taken into account. If we go back to our original payoff table (Table 23.1) and use the maximax criterion, we select activity A_1. If we change the payoff strongly *against* A_1 and strongly *in favor* of A_2 and A_3, however, the alteration still may have no impact on the decision reached under the maximax rule. For example, let us introduce the changes as in Table 23.7. Still the maximax is 500 and A_1 is selected. Thus, dramatic changes in the payoff matrix had no impact on our decision.

TABLE 23.7
Revised Payoff Matrix

		State of nature		
	Activity	S_1 Inflation	S_2 Stagflation	S_3 Recession
A_1	Construction	500	0	0
A_2	Cigarettes	499	490	490
A_3	Bakery products	499	490	493

All the rules discussed so far rely on one extreme value per activity and therefore suffer from the same serious drawback. Below we suggest additional decision rules that take into account all the possible outcomes as well as the probabilities (objective or subjective) of their occurrence.

23.4 The Maximum Expected Return Rule

Rather than concentrating on one extreme value per activity, we now suggest looking at all the outcomes and their corresponding probabilities—and *then* selecting the option with the highest expected value.

In some cases objective probabilities are available for the various states of nature. (For example, we can calculate the expected value of a lottery prize, since the probability of each event is well defined.) The probabilities of other investments may be subjective, since they are a function of the investor's experience and judgment. In still other cases, when the probabilities are unknown and we do not wish to venture a guess, equal probabilities may be assigned to each state of nature.

Applying equal probabilities to the three states of nature in our original payoff matrix (Table 23.1) yields the following:

$$E(A_1) = 500 \cdot \tfrac{1}{3} + 300 \cdot \tfrac{1}{3} + 10 \cdot \tfrac{1}{3} = 270.0$$

$$E(A_2) = 40 \cdot \tfrac{1}{3} + 150 \cdot \tfrac{1}{3} + 100 \cdot \tfrac{1}{3} = 96.7$$

$$E(A_3) = 80 \cdot \tfrac{1}{3} + 60 \cdot \tfrac{1}{3} + 70 \cdot \tfrac{1}{3} \quad = 70.0$$

and activity A_1, with the highest expected payoff, is chosen. Note that our decision will be different if the revised payoff matrix (Table 23.7) is used. In this case we will get

$$E(A_1) = 500 \cdot \tfrac{1}{3} + 0 \cdot \tfrac{1}{3} + 0 \cdot \tfrac{1}{3} \quad = 166.7$$

$$E(A_2) = 499 \cdot \tfrac{1}{3} + 490 \cdot \tfrac{1}{3} + 490 \cdot \tfrac{1}{3} = 493.0$$

$$E(A_3) = 499 \cdot \tfrac{1}{3} + 490 \cdot \tfrac{1}{3} + 493 \cdot \tfrac{1}{3} = 494.0$$

Now our selection is A_3.

The rule we have used here, the **maximum expected return rule**, is based on the expected value of the outcomes. This rule overcomes the drawback of relying on a single extreme value, but it still is not wholly satisfactory. Most businesspeople and individual investors indicate by their revealed preferences that they are not satisfied with this rule. In other words, their everyday behavior is not consistent with it. Consider a numerical example. Suppose that by a flip of a coin you can either gain or lose $10,000. Heads, you pay $10,000; tails, you win $10,000. Are you willing to participate in it? Most surveys and experiments of this kind show that people are wary of such a game; they are not indifferent to its dangers. Although the expected outcome is zero, most people will not accept the challenge and will decline to play this "fair game." And yet the maximum expected return rule indicates that one should be indifferent to the dangers of such a game since the expected profit from it is exactly zero.

The reason we are reluctant to enter such a game is that if we lose $10,000, the hurt is much greater than the corresponding benefit we enjoy if we win $10,000. The words "hurt" and "enjoy" imply that we actually consider the **utility** derived from money rather than the amount of money as such.

This leads us to the next rule, the expected utility rule. But before we go into this in more detail, let us further demonstrate the fallacy of the maximum expected return rule by the well-known St. Petersburg paradox. This paradox is of historical interest: it occupied the minds of the best mathematicians of the eighteenth century and indeed paved the way for the concept of utility and the expected utility rule, which is now acknowledged by most academicians.

THE ST. PETERSBURG PARADOX

The classic problem known as the St. Petersburg paradox was first formulated by the Swiss mathematician Nicolas Bernoulli:[3] Peter tosses a coin and continues to do so until it lands "heads" when it comes to ground. He agrees to give Paul $1 if he gets heads on the very first throw, $2 if he gets it on the second, $4 if on the third, $8 if on the fourth, and so on, so that with each additional throw the number of dollars he must pay is doubled. Suppose we seek to determine the value of Paul's expectation.

In general, if heads first appears on the nth toss, the player is awarded a prize equal to 2^{n-1}. The size of the prize is uncertain, and depends on the results of each experiment, but when the coin lands heads for the first time, the game is over, so that only one prize is awarded per game. Naturally, the player would like heads to appear only after a long series of tails, since this would increase his prize. Note that the number of games played is a geometric random variable with the probability of "success" equal to $\frac{1}{2}$ (see Chapter 8).

What would be a fair price for Paul to pay for the opportunity to play such a game? If heads comes up on the first toss, the prize is $1; the probability of this outcome is $\frac{1}{2}$ since there is an equal probability of obtaining heads and tails when an unbiased coin is tossed. What is the probability of winning $2 on the second toss? The probability of getting tails on the first toss is $\frac{1}{2}$, and since the two tosses are independent events, the probability of getting heads on the second toss is also $\frac{1}{2}$. The joint probability of the event *TH* (that is, tails followed by heads) is given by the product of the two probabilities: $\frac{1}{2} \cdot \frac{1}{2} = \frac{1}{4}$.[4] Theoretically, the game can continue a long time before the coin lands heads for the first time, but the probability of the game's lasting for a great number of tosses is, of course, very small.

The maximum expected return rule suggests that the game's expected value constitutes the maximum price for Paul to pay for this fair gamble. To facilitate the calculation of the expected value, we have set out the possible results of the coin tossing and their probabilities in Table 23.8. If we

---

[3] The first published analysis of the problem was written by Daniel Bernoulli (a younger cousin) during his stay in St. Petersburg as a visiting scholar (1725–33), hence the name "St. Petersburg paradox." The problem as formulated by Nicolas Bernoulli is quoted by Daniel Bernoulli in "Specimen Theoriae Novae de Mensura Sortis," *Papers of the Imperial Academy of Sciences in Petersburg,* 5 (1738). An English translation, "Exposition of a New Theory on the Measurement of Risk," appears in *Econometrica,* 22, no. 1 (January 1954): 23–36.

[4] Since the outcome of each toss is independent of the outcomes of the other tosses, $P(H \cap T) = P(H) \cdot P(T) = \frac{1}{2} \cdot \frac{1}{2} = \frac{1}{4}$. See Chapter 5.

TABLE 23.8
St. Petersburg Game

Toss on which heads first appears	Result[a]	Probability of result	Prize
1	H	$\frac{1}{2}$	1
2	TH	$\frac{1}{4}$	2
3	TTH	$\frac{1}{8}$	4
4	TTTH	$\frac{1}{16}$	8
.	.	.	.
.	.	.	.
.	.	.	.
n	$\overbrace{TT \cdots TH}^{(n-1)\text{ times}}$	$\frac{1}{2^n}$	2^{n-1}

[a]H = heads; T = tails.

denote the possible prize by X, the expected income of the St. Petersburg game can be calculated as follows:

$$E(X) = \tfrac{1}{2} \cdot 1 + \tfrac{1}{4} \cdot 2 + \tfrac{1}{8} \cdot 4 + \tfrac{1}{16} \cdot 8 + \cdots = \tfrac{1}{2} + \tfrac{1}{2} + \tfrac{1}{2} + \tfrac{1}{2} + \cdots = \infty$$

Since there is no theoretical limit to the number of tosses, the mathematical expectation of the game is infinite; that is, invoking the maximum expected return rule, Paul should be prepared to pay any sum, however large, for the opportunity to play the game!

Now assume that you are offered the opportunity to play such a game. How much would you pay for the opportunity? An experiment conducted with a group of students revealed that most were prepared to pay only $2 or $3 for a chance to play. A few were willing to pay as much as $8, but no one offered more than that. This contradiction between the amount that most people are willing to pay for an opportunity to play the game and its infinite mathematical expectation constitutes the so-called St. Petersburg paradox.

Special interest attaches to the solutions proposed independently by the mathematician Daniel Bernoulli and by his contemporary Gabriel Cramer, who sought to resolve the problem by rejecting the maximum expected return rule and substituting expected utility in its place. Their efforts constitute an important intellectual milestone leading to the modern theory of choice under conditions of uncertainty.

23.5 The Concept of Utility and the Maximum Expected Utility Rule

The St. Petersburg paradox, as well as common sense, indicates that each dollar has a certain utility and that in decision making one should consider the utility derived from each activity and apply the **maximum expected utility rule** rather than the maximum expected return rule. As we shall see, the expected utility rule resolves Peter's problems, and in addition it clarifies many problems that businesspeople are faced with every day.

Consider an individual who must choose between the two alternative investment projects outlined in Table 23.9. Note that the two projects under

TABLE 23.9
Alternative Investments

Investment A		Investment B	
Net income	Probability	Net income	Probability
$100	$\frac{1}{2}$	$ 0	$\frac{1}{2}$
300	$\frac{1}{2}$	400	$\frac{1}{2}$
Expected income $200		$200	

consideration have the same expected income, $200. A glance at the two investments suffices to show that the uncertainty involved in investment *B* is greater than that of investment *A*. We shall show below that despite the equal expected returns, investment *A* is indeed preferred to investment *B*. The intuitive explanation for the preference of investment *A* can be clarified if we examine the difference in the monetary outcomes of two proposals. Suppose that the investor who tentatively chooses investment *A* considers shifting from *A* to *B*. What changes are induced by such a shift? The differences between the two projects can be summarized as follows: if the lower outcome occurs, the investor will realize $100 less on investment *B* than on investment *A*, while if the higher outcome occurs, investment *B* yields $100 more. Thus, if the investor changes his mind and shifts from *A* to *B*, he has a 50 percent chance of gaining $100 but he also has a 50 percent chance of losing $100. Is it worthwhile to shift from investment *A* to investment *B*?

In general, most investors *will not* switch from *A* to *B*, since the subjective satisfaction (or utility gain) that they derive from the additional $100 is less than the dissatisfaction (or utility loss) that they face if they lose $100. To help to clarify this argument, consider an individual who uses the monetary return to buy consumer goods. Most individuals reveal **diminishing marginal utility**, which means that *the satisfaction (utility gain) from consumption diminishes as consumption increases.* That is to say, the consumer initially satisfies her more essential needs, and hence the utility that she derives from spending, say, the first $100 is relatively large. Once she has satisfied her more basic needs, we expect that the additional utility she derives from spending a second increment of $100 will be lower, and so on for each additional increment of income.

The concept of diminishing marginal utility is illustrated in Table 23.10. As we can see, total utility increases as income rises, so that the higher the income, the larger the satisfaction derived from it. The marginal (that is, incremental) utility is diminishing, however; the utility of the first $100 increment is 10 "utiles," the additional utility derived from the second $100 increment is 8 utiles, and the next two $100 increments add 7 and 5 utiles,

TABLE 23.10
The Utility Function

Income	Utility (utiles)	Marginal utility (utiles)
$ 0	0	
100	10	10
200	18	8
300	25	7
400	30	5

TABLE 23.11
Expected Utility Calculations

	Investment A			Investment B	
Probability	Income	Utility	Probability	Income	Utility
$\frac{1}{2}$	$100	10	$\frac{1}{2}$	$ 0	0
$\frac{1}{2}$	300	25	$\frac{1}{2}$	400	30
Expected net income	$200			$200	
Expected utility[a]	17.5			15	

[a]The expected utilities of investments *A* and *B* are given by $10 \cdot \frac{1}{2} + 25 \cdot \frac{1}{2} = 17.5$ and $0 \cdot \frac{1}{2} + 30 \cdot \frac{1}{2} = 15$, respectively.

respectively. In Table 23.11 we present the expected utility calculations for investments *A* and *B*. The data of Table 23.11 indicate that while investments *A* and *B* are characterized by the same expected income, they differ with respect to expected utility. The expected utility derived from investment *A* is 17.5 utiles, compared to investment *B*'s expected utility of only 15 utiles. Thus, whereas the expected return rule cannot discriminate between investments *A* and *B*, the expected utility rule indicates a clear preference for investment *A*, which, as we have already noted, is considerably less uncertain with regard to possible future income. Moreover, the ranking of investment *A* over *B* holds for all utility functions, as long as the utility function has the property of diminishing marginal utility. This statement can be proved by an examination of individuals' attitudes toward risk.

Indeed, John von Neumann and Oskar Morgenstern have shown that when we have uncertain future income induced by a given activity, every rational investor should select his or her activity according to the expected utility rule rather than the expected return rule.[5] The mathematical proof of this claim and the way it solves the St. Petersburg paradox can be found in many books in finance and economics.[6] Here, we will take a look at the various ways individuals approach risk in their everyday dealings.

ALTERNATIVE ATTITUDES TOWARD UNCERTAINTY

In general, an investment or an activity that generates an uncertain income is said to be risky. The more uncertain the outcome, the riskier the investment. Thus, we use the words *"uncertainty"* and *"risk"* interchangeably.

It is convenient for the purposes of our analysis to distinguish among three classes of investors: those who dislike risk, whom we shall call "risk averters"; those who prefer more risky to less risky investments, whom we shall call "risk lovers"; and those who disregard risk altogether, whom we shall call "risk neutral." As the bulk of the theoretical and empirical evidence supports the view that the typical investor is a risk averter, we shall concentrate on that broad class of individuals.

[5] John von Neumann and Oskar Morgenstern, *Theory of Games and Economic Behavior*, rev. ed. (Princeton, N.J.: Princeton University Press, 1953). A more popular version is given in Luce and Raiffa, *Games and Decisions.*
[6] See, e.g., Haim Levy and Marshall Sarnat, *Investment and Portfolio Analysis* (New York: Wiley, 1972).

Suppose an individual is offered the opportunity of investing $100 in the following project:

Income	Probability
$ 90	$\frac{1}{2}$
110	$\frac{1}{2}$

The expected income of such an investment is $90 \cdot \frac{1}{2} + 110 \cdot \frac{1}{2} = 100$. Thus, the expected value equals the initial investment. In other words, the expected monetary profit from the investment is zero. Can an individual be expected to invest in such a project? Since we have rejected the expected return rule and have tentatively replaced it with the expected utility rule, our answer depends on the individual's attitude toward risk: that is, on the degree to which he or she likes or dislikes to trade a safe prospect (the initial $100 investment) for an uncertain one (the income generated by the investment).

The preferences of risk averters are characterized by diminishing marginal utility, as in Table 23.10: the utility increases with income, but at an ever-diminishing rate. It follows that every risk averter prefers a perfectly certain investment to an uncertain one that has the same expected return. A risk averter will not invest in this project because in terms of utility, the possible loss of $10 more than offsets the possible gain of $10.

This conclusion can be confirmed by a graphic device. Figure 23.1 sets out the same investment problem: the investment of $100 in a project with equal probabilities of returning $90 and of returning $110. The possible dollar values of income are measured along the horizontal axis, and utility is measured along the vertical axis in utiles. The concave form of the individual's utility function expresses the risk averter's characteristic of diminishing marginal utility.

Now remember that the individual's attention is ultimately focused on his or her level of utility. Money is important only insofar as it gives rise to utility. The individual who wants to decide whether or not to pay $100 for the investment approaches this problem in the following manner. The $90 income, if it occurs, will give rise to U_1 utiles. If $110 turns up, the utility

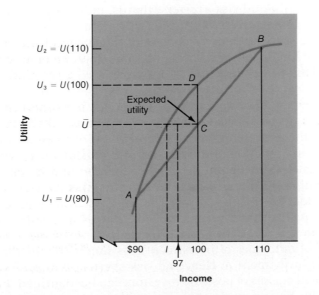

Figure 23.1

A utility function over income and expected utility

will be U_2 utiles. On the average, then, the investor can expect $\overline{U} = U_1 \cdot \frac{1}{2}$ + $U_2 \cdot \frac{1}{2}$ utiles, which is the expected utility of the investment. For a risk averter, whose utility function is concave like the one in Figure 23.1, the utility of $100 (denoted by U_3) is greater than $\overline{U}$. Since the individual focuses on utility rather than on income per se, he or she will decide not to pay $100 for the uncertain income. Why should an individual give up U_3 utiles only to get back a lesser (expected) number of utiles, $\overline{U}$? The investor will obviously be better off keeping the $100 and refraining from investment. Graphically, the expected utility, $\overline{U}$, may be easily located when only two possible uncertain outcomes are involved. Raising a perpendicular line from the expected monetary value on the horizontal axis ($100 in our example), we find at its intersection with the line segment connecting points A and B in Figure 23.1 the point C, whose height measured from the horizontal axis is equal to $\overline{U}$.

Now let us assume that the same individual is offered the same investment project but at a lower initial investment, say $97. The expected income remains $100, so the project has a positive expected net income ($100 − $97 = $3). Will the risk-averse individual invest in the project? Despite the lower price, Figure 23.1 clearly shows that the investor will not be willing to invest in this project because the utility of a perfectly certain sum of $97 still exceeds the expected utility of the risky project ($\overline{U}$). How far must the initial investment fall before our risk-averse investor will be willing to accept the project? Again the answer can be readily inferred from Figure 23.1. The maximum investment that the investor will be willing to make is represented by point I on the horizontal axis. At this point the utility of the initial investment, $U(I)$, is just equal to the expected utility of the risky investment. The distance between 100 and I measures the **risk premium** required to induce the risk-averse individual to invest in the project. At investments lower than I (points to the left of I on the horizontal axis) the project is attractive to our individual, since it represents a gain in expected utility. Conversely, at investments above I, as we have already seen, the risky project represents a loss of expected utility for the risk-averse investor.

Having explained the basic properties of risk-aversion concepts, let us make a graphic analysis of the original example in Table 23.9. Recall that we have asserted that all risk averters (that is, individuals characterized by diminishing marginal utility of money) will prefer investment A to investment B because of the greater dispersion of the latter for an equal expected income. Figure 23.2 displays the data of Table 23.9. Since we are assuming risk aversion, the utility function is drawn as a concave curve rising from the origin. The expected utility of project A is then $U(100) \cdot \frac{1}{2} + U(300) \cdot \frac{1}{2}$ = $10 \cdot \frac{1}{2} + 25 \cdot \frac{1}{2} = 17.5$. This value corresponds to point A of Figure 23.2, the intersection of the vertical line rising from point 200 on the horizontal axis (which is the expected monetary return) and the appropriate line segment on the utility function. Similarly, point B indicates the expected utility from investment B. Since point A is higher than point B, it follows that the risk averter will prefer investment A to investment B.

The reason for this result can also be inferred from Figure 23.2. Other things being equal, risk averters do not like a wide dispersion of outcomes. From the graph it is clear that both projects have the same expected profit, but the range of outcomes of investment B is much greater than the range of outcomes of investment A. Hence all risk averters will prefer A over B.

Two additional classes of possible investors can be identified. First we have risk lovers, who have a preference rather than an aversion to risk. Such

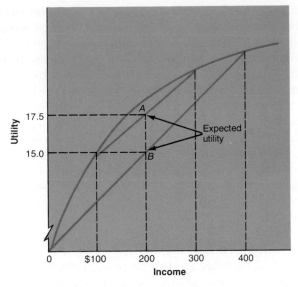

Figure 23.2

Expected utility of investments *A* and *B* in Table 23.9

individuals are characterized by convex utility functions, which implies that the marginal utility of each additional dollar increases. Upon reflection we see that this is not a very realistic assumption.

Then we have those investors who are risk-neutral, that is, neither risk averters nor risk lovers. Such individuals have linear utility functions and display constant marginal utility of money. Risk neutrality constitutes a middle ground between risk lovers and risk averters. Risk-neutral individuals choose their investments solely according to their respective expected incomes, and they completely ignore the dispersion of the various returns.

Figure 23.3 illustrates the utility functions of a risk lover and a risk-neutral person side by side.

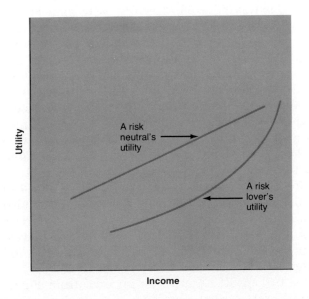

Figure 23.3

Utility functions of a risk lover and a risk-neutral person

UNITS OF MEASUREMENT AND THE UTILITY SCALE

Consider the Fahrenheit temperature scale. Suppose the high temperature on Monday was 50°F and on Tuesday it was 68°F. Between Monday and

Tuesday the temperature rose 18 degrees, so that Tuesday's temperature was 36 percent higher than Monday's (18/50 = 0.36). Can we say that it was 36 percent warmer on Tuesday than on Monday? A statement like this will surely be incorrect. To see why, let us switch to a different temperature scale: the Celsius scale. Subtract 32 from a Fahrenheit temperature and then multiply by $\frac{5}{9}$ to get the corresponding Celsius temperature. Using this transformation, we get $(50 - 32) \cdot \frac{5}{9} = 10°C$ and $(68 - 32) \cdot \frac{5}{9} = 20°C$. Comparing Monday's and Tuesday's temperatures by the Celsius scale, we get quite a different picture. Monday's temperature was 10°C and Tuesday's was *twice* as warm: 20°C. So, when we use the metric scale, it appears that between Monday and Tuesday the temperature rose by 100 percent. We note, then, that both scales indicate that Tuesday's temperature was higher than Monday's, but neither can uniquely measure *how much* warmer it was on Tuesday than on Monday. Should we then conclude that temperature is only some sort of ranking system? Or perhaps that temperatures entail more information than simple ranks? The answer to the last question is positive: a temperature scale does indeed entail more information than simple ranks. To see this point, let us consider a scale of ranks. Suppose there are three different paint qualities: A (best), B (medium), and C (worst). If A and C were mixed together in equal quantities, the mixture would be of lesser quality than A but of better quality than C. Call the quality of the mixture D. Is D a better-quality paint than B, or is it equivalent or perhaps worse than B? Since the paint qualities are measured only by ranks, it is impossible to answer these questions. We do not have enough information to compare the qualities of D and B. To see that temperature scales do entail more information than simple ranks, suppose Wednesday's high temperature was 59°F (or 15°C). Was the average of Monday's and Tuesday's temperatures higher or lower than Wednesday's temperature? Here we can give a definitive answer. Using the Fahrenheit scale, we find that the average temperature of Monday and Tuesday was $(50 + 68)/2 = 59°F$, which is just equal to Wednesday's temperature. The same answer is obtained when we use the Celsius scale: Wednesday's temperature was 15 degrees, which is exactly the average of Monday's and Tuesday's temperatures: $(10 + 20)/2 = 15°C$.

This example shows that even though a temperature scale does not uniquely reflect changes in the level of heat, it still is definitely superior to ranks because of its ability to compare separate temperatures and their combinations. A utility scale reflects one's level of satisfaction in the same way a temperature scale reflects the level of heat. It can be subjected (like a temperature scale) to a positive linear transformation. This means: if $U(X)$ is an individual's utility function for income, X, then $U^*(X) = a + b \cdot U(X)$ is an analogous utility function of the same individual, where a and b are constants and $b > 0$. For example, if $U(100) = 5$, one can switch to a comparable utility function $U^*(X) = 1{,}000 + 100 \cdot U(X)$, such that $U^*(100) = 1{,}000 + 100 \cdot U(100) = 1{,}000 + 100 \cdot 5 = 1{,}500$, without altering the underlying utility. Ranking uncertain investments according to $U(X)$ or $U^*(X)$ will always lead to the same investment decisions.

23.6 The Mean-Variance Rule

Although the expected utility rule is normatively the best criterion available, sometimes it is very hard to implement. We frequently do not know the investor's utility function; furthermore, we often face a conflict-of-interest situation, as in the case of a manager who must act on behalf of many stockholders, each of whom has a different utility function from that of the others. Thus, despite its sound theoretical foundations, the expected utility rule is often replaced by the mean-variance rule, which provides a more practical decision criterion.

According to the **mean-variance rule**, *the expected return (mean) measures an investment's profitability, while the variance (or dispersion) of returns measures its risks*. Consider the following four projects, with the means and variances specified:

Investment project	Mean	Variance
A	$10	100
B	9	80
C	8	90
D	7	95

A pairwise comparison of the investment projects shows that project *B* dominates projects *C* and *D*, since *B* has a higher profit and a lower risk than both *C* and *D*. There is no clear-cut decision with regard to project *A*, however, since $E(A) > E(B)$ but $V(A) > V(B)$. Here the investor, apart from and in addition to statistical tools, needs to use judgment when considering the trade-off between profit and risk. Some investors will find it worthwhile to undertake the higher risk in return for the higher expected return. Others will not wish to undertake project *A*. They will prefer the lower variance even at the expense of some expected return.

23.7 Bayesian Decision Making: Prior and Posterior Probabilities

The more sophisticated decision-making methods—the maximum expected return rule, the maximum expected utility rule, the mean-variance rule, and others that have not been mentioned—are probabilistic in nature. Obviously, the methods can be only as good as the data they use. Generally, when additional information becomes available, a better decision is reached.

In this section, we discuss the way additional information can be incorporated into the decision-making process to revise the probabilities used in the probabilistic decision-making methods. The initial probabilities are referred to as **prior probabilities**, and the revised probabilities are called **posterior probabilities.** Probabilities may be revised by the collection of data or by the acquisition of relevant information in some other way. The way additional information is used to revise probabilities is illustrated by Example 23.1.

EXAMPLE 23.1

A company is considering the production of a luxury product on which it expects to make a $100 net profit per unit sold. The initial information available to the company is that 5 percent of American consumers will buy the product, most of them wealthier than the national average.

Specifically, it is estimated that 26 percent of those with $30,000 or more in annual income will buy the product, while only 1 percent of those with lower annual incomes will buy it. Sixteen percent of American consumers have annual incomes of $30,000 or more, and 84 percent have annual incomes of less than $30,000. The company is considering the construction of a manufacturing plant at an investment of $4 million and is planning to market the product in an area with a population of a million consumers. It will not make the investment unless $4 million or more is expected to be realized in net profit in the first year of operation.

The expected annual profit, not considering the $4 million investment, is

$$0.05 \cdot 1,000,000 \cdot \$100 = \$5,000,000$$

where 0.05 represents the percentage of consumers who are expected to buy the product, 1 million is the number of potential consumers, and $100 is the profit per item sold. Since the $5 million is more than the minimum required by the firm ($4 million), the firm should decide to make the investment.

Before committing itself to a $4 million investment, however, the company may wish to find out the number of wealthier consumers (income of $30,000 or more) among the million potential consumers. Additional information is collected and reveals that only 10 percent of the potential consumers have annual incomes of $30,000 or more, compared to 16 percent in the U.S. population as a whole. With this additional information, the company's decision changes. The number of consumers expected to buy the product is equal to the sum of 26 percent of 100,000 "wealthy" consumers and 1 percent of the remaining 900,000. And since the profit per item is $100, we can expect the following annual profit:

$$(0.26 \cdot 100,000 + 0.01 \cdot 900,000) \cdot 100$$
$$= (26,000 + 9,000) \cdot 100 = \$3,500,000$$

Since this amount will not cover the initial investment in the first year, the firm decides not to undertake the project.

Note that 5 percent of the U.S. population is expected to buy the product. So if we choose one person at random, the probability that he or she will be a buyer is 0.05. Denote the following events concerning a consumer chosen at random:

A_1 Annual income is $30,000 or more.
A_2 Annual income is less than $30,000.
B He or she is a buyer of the product.

It is given that in the total population we have

$$P(B \mid A_1) = 0.26$$
$$P(B \mid A_2) = 0.01$$

so that we can confirm the probability of B by calculating (see Chapter 5)

$$P(B) = P(B \mid A_1) \cdot P(A_1) + P(B \mid A_2) \cdot P(A_2)$$

$$= 0.26 \cdot 0.16 + 0.01 \cdot 0.84$$

$$= 0.05$$

Events A_1, A_2, and B are illustrated by a Venn diagram in Figure 23.4. Note that the part of event B in A_1 accounts for 26 percent of A_1 while its part in A_2 accounts for only 1 percent of A_2. On the whole, event B (shown in the light color) occupies 5 percent of the combined areas of A_1 and A_2.

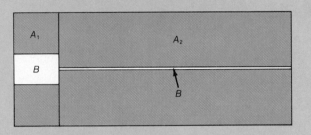

Figure 23.4

Venn diagram: U.S. consumers, by income and by willingness to buy a specific luxury product

The million potential consumers of the product, in the area where the firm plans to market the product, have an income distribution that is *different* from the overall U.S. distribution. Specifically, the percentage of wealthy people in that location is smaller. This means that the relevant diagram should show a smaller A_1 area than that in Figure 23.4. The area, of course, must be proportional to the percentage of wealthy people in the million potential consumers. The correct proportions are 10 percent for A_1 and 90 percent for A_2, which are shown in Figure 23.5. Comparing Figure 23.5 with Figure 23.4, we see that the relevant per-

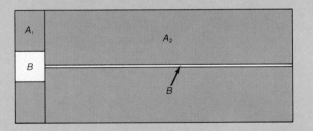

Figure 23.5

Venn diagram: consumers in one specific geographic location, by income and by willing-ness to buy the product

centage of B in the total area is smaller. Indeed, the calculations show that

$$P(B) = P(B \mid A_1) \cdot P(A_1) + P(B \mid A_2) \cdot P(A_2)$$

$$= 0.26 \cdot 0.10 + 0.01 \cdot 0.90$$

$$= 0.035$$

meaning that we can expect only 3.5 percent of the potential customers actually to buy the product. The expected profit, then, is

$$0.035 \cdot 1,000,000 \cdot \$100 = \$3,500,000$$

as obtained earlier.

This process of decision making, *the revising of probabilities by means of Bayes' formula*, is called **Bayesian decision making**. One can also calculate additional relevant probabilities with Bayes' theorem. For example, if a person is selected at random among the potential customers, what is the probability that the person's income is \$30,000 or more? The probability is given by the percentage of people we called "wealthy" in the population: $P(A_1) = 0.10$, or 10 percent.

Suppose, however, we know that the individual is a buyer of the product. Then we calculate the probability this way:

$$P(A_1 \mid B) = \frac{P(A_1 \cap B)}{P(B)} = \frac{P(B \mid A_1) \cdot P(A_1)}{P(B \mid A_1) \cdot P(A_1) + P(B \mid A_2) \cdot P(A_2)}$$

$$= \frac{0.26 \cdot 0.10}{0.26 \cdot 0.10 + 0.01 \cdot 0.90} = \frac{0.026}{0.035}$$

$$= 0.743$$

The additional information (that is, that the individual chosen is a buyer of the product) has raised the probability from 10 percent all the way up to 74.3 percent. This can also be described diagrammatically. Of the million potential customers, 35,000 (3.5 percent) buy the product. The individual chosen must then be one of the 35,000 buyers. There are 100,000 consumers with \$30,000 or more in annual income, and 26,000 of them (26 percent) are buyers. Among the rest of the 900,000 consumers in the population, 1 percent are buyers, or 9,000 consumers. This means (see Figure 23.6) that the 35,000 buyers consist of 26,000 wealthy customers and 9,000 nonwealthy customers. The 26,000 wealthy ones indeed are 74.3 percent of the buyers: 26,000/35,000 = 0.743.

Figure 23.6

Venn diagram: potential purchasers of the product, grouped according to income

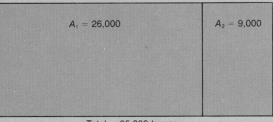

Total = 35,000 buyers

The probabilities used before the new information about the wealth of the potential customers was collected are called "prior probabilities," while the revised (conditional) probabilities calculated on the basis of the additional information are called "posterior probabilities."

In what follows we illustrate two aspects of the Bayesian approach: (1) how sample information may be used in order to get a "better fix" on a parameter, namely how the prior distribution and sample information are combined to obtain a posterior distribution, and (2) how the prior and posterior distributions can be used, after specifying an objective function, to make decisions under uncertainty. In particular, it highlights how the use of sample information may lead to an alternative decision to the one that would be reached without it.

Consider a company who developed a new product and has to decide whether or not to introduce this product in a certain market area. The demand, that is, the proportion of the population that will buy the product at the fixed selling price of $5, is uncertain; but the manager estimates a prior probability distribution of the proportion, p. This distribution is shown in Table 23.12. Other data relevant to the decision are the following:

1. If the company enters the market, it will incur set-up costs of $19,000.
2. The profit per unit sold (disregarding the set-up cost) is $1.
3. The total population in the market area is 100,000.

To get a "better" estimate of the true value of the parameter p, the manager takes a random sample of five people ($n = 5$) and determines the number of people indicating they would buy the product. (As a practical matter, a sample size of only five people would not provide reliable statistical evidence. However, there are also cost considerations involved in picking the optimal sample size. We will not consider these issues here.)

Suppose that only one person answers yes ("I will buy the product"), ($X = 1$). Under the appropriate assumptions, the probability distribution of observing x answers of yes in a sample of five, given a value of p, is given by the binomial distribution

$$P(X = x \mid n, p_0) = \binom{n}{x}(p_0)^x(1 - p_0)^{n-x}$$

where

x stands for the number of successes (yes responses) observed
n stands for the sample size
p_0 indicates that the probability is derived assuming that the true value of the random variable p is equal to p_0

Consider the sample result $X = 1$. If in truth the proportion is $p = 0.10$, then the likelihood of obtaining $X = 1$ in a sample of five observations is given by

$$P(X = 1 \mid n = 5, p = 0.10) = \binom{5}{1}(0.10)^1(0.90)^4 = 0.32805$$

The probability of obtaining $X = 1$ if the true proportion is $p = 0.20$ is given by

$$P(X = 1 \mid n = 5, p = 0.20) = \binom{5}{1}(0.20)^1(0.80)^4 = 0.40960$$

TABLE 23.12
Prior Probability Distribution of the Proportion of the Population, p, Likely to Buy the Product

Value of p	Probability
0.10	0.50
0.20	0.25
0.30	0.15
0.50	0.10
	1.00

In a similar fashion we can derive the likelihood of the sample result (X = 1) for each of the alternative values that p can take on. These probabilities are shown in column 3 of Table 23.13.

The prior probability of p = 0.10 is equal to 0.50 (see Table 23.12). Given the sample result X = 1, we may ask, "What is the conditional probability that p = 0.10 *given* that the sample shows X = 1?" This probability is the posterior probability of p = 0.10, and we can expect it to differ (in general) from the prior probability of 0.50. The posterior probability can be calculated by using Bayes' theorem:

$$P(p = 0.10 \mid X = 1) = \frac{P(X = 1 \mid n = 5, p = 0.10)P(p = 0.10)}{\sum_i P(X = 1 \mid n = 5, p = p_i)P(p = p_i)}$$

$$= \frac{0.32805 \cdot 0.50}{0.3360}$$

$$= 0.4881$$

where $P(X = 1 \mid n = 5, p = p_i)$ is the probability of obtaining the sample results assuming that the true value of p is p_i (which can be 0.10, 0.20, 0.30, or 0.50). This probability is called the likelihood (of the sample result), as we saw. The probability $P(p = p_i)$ is simply the prior probability of p_i. For example, $P(p = 0.10)$ = 0.50. The denominator of the above formula is equal to 0.3360 (see Table 23.13). The value 0.3360 is the sum of the weighted likelihoods (shown in column 4) where the prior probabilities (column 2) serve as weights. Table 23.13 gives the posterior probabilities for all the possible values of p.

At this point, it is instructive to compare the expected net profit (π), based on the prior and the posterior distributions.

Expected net profit based on the prior distribution:

$$\pi_0 = [0.50 \cdot 0.10 \cdot 100,000 \cdot \$1 + 0.25 \cdot 0.20 \cdot 100,000 \cdot \$1$$
$$+ 0.15 \cdot 0.30 \cdot 100,000 \cdot \$1 + 0.10 \cdot 0.50 \cdot 100,000 \cdot \$1] - \$19,000$$
$$= \$19,500 - \$19,000$$
$$= \$500$$

TABLE 23.13
The Posterior Distribution for n = 5, X = 1

(1) p	(2) Prior probability	(3) Likelihood[a]	(4) (col. 2 × col. 3)	(5) Posterior probability
0.10	0.50	0.32805	0.1640	0.4881
0.20	0.25	0.40960	0.1024	0.3047
0.30	0.15	0.36015	0.0540	0.1607
0.50	0.10	0.15625	0.0156	0.0465
Total	1.00	1.25405	0.3360	1.0000

[a]The likelihood is calculated as follows:

$$P(X = 1 \mid n = 5, p = p_i) = \binom{5}{1}(p_i)^1(1 - p_i)^4$$

For example, for p = 0.10 we get:

$$P(X = 1 \mid n = 5, p = 0.10) = \binom{5}{1}(0.10)^1(1 - 0.10)^4 = 0.32805$$

Expected net profit based on the posterior distribution:

$$
\begin{aligned}
\pi_1 &= [0.4881 \cdot 0.10 \cdot 100{,}000 \cdot \$1 + 0.3047 \cdot 0.20 \cdot 100{,}000 \cdot \$1 \\
&\quad + 0.1607 \cdot 0.30 \cdot 100{,}000 \cdot \$1 + 0.0465 \cdot 0.50 \cdot 100{,}000 \cdot \$1] \\
&\quad - \$19{,}000 \\
&= \$18{,}121 - \$19{,}000 \\
&= -\$879
\end{aligned}
$$

π_1 is less than π_0 because the sample suggests a lower probability for high values of p. Furthermore, π turns from positive to negative when posterior rather than prior probabilities are used.

Suppose the manager now takes another sample of $n = 5$ and finds that four people respond yes, that is, $X = 4$. The manager is in a position to revise previously obtained posterior probabilities. The calculations are presented in Table 23.14. Note that the entries in column 2 of Table 23.14 are identical to the entries in column 5 of Table 23.13.

The expected net profit based on the second posterior distribution is as follows:

$$
\begin{aligned}
\pi_2 &= [0.0157 \cdot 0.10 \cdot 100{,}000 \cdot \$1 + 0.1394 \cdot 0.20 \cdot 100{,}000 \cdot \$1 \\
&\quad + 0.3256 \cdot 0.30 \cdot 100{,}000 \cdot \$1 + 0.5193 \cdot 0.50 \cdot 100{,}000 \cdot \$1] \\
&\quad - \$19{,}000 \\
&= \$38{,}678 - \$19{,}000 \\
&= \$19{,}678
\end{aligned}
$$

The evidence from the second sample indicates that the value of p is likely to be higher than what is indicated by the first sample. Hence we get $\pi_2 > \pi_0 > \pi_1$.

An important feature of the Bayesian approach is that when independent samples are taken, the same posterior distribution is obtained if we calculate the posteriors successively or calculate the posterior after all the samples are taken. To see this, suppose we had taken a sample of 10 people and observed that 5 of them responded yes; thus $n = 10$ and $X = 5$, which is the same as obtaining the results of the two samples all at once (Table 23.15).

TABLE 23.14
Posterior Distribution Based on the Second Sample, $n = 5$, $X = 4$

(1) p	(2) Prior probability[a]	(3) Likelihood[b]	(4) (col. 2 × col. 3)	(5) Posterior probability
0.10	0.4881	0.00045	0.0002196	0.0157
0.20	0.3047	0.00640	0.0019501	0.1394
0.30	0.1607	0.02835	0.0045558	0.3256
0.50	0.0465	0.15625	0.0072656	0.5193
Total	1.0000	0.19145	0.0139911	1.0000

[a]Values are from Table 23.13.
[b]The likelihood is calculated as follows:

$$
P(X = 4 \mid n = 5, p = p_i) = \binom{5}{4}(p_i)^4(1 - p_i)^1
$$

For example, for $p = 0.10$ we get

$$
P(X = 4 \mid n = 5, p = 0.10) = \binom{5}{4}(0.10)^4(0.9)^1 = 0.00045
$$

TABLE 23.15

Posterior Probabilities Calculated on the Basis of a Single Sample, $n = 10$, $X = 5$

(1) p	(2) Prior probability	(3) Likelihood[a]	(4) (col. 2 × col. 3)	(5) Posterior probability
0.10	0.50	0.00149	0.000745	0.0157
0.20	0.25	0.02642	0.006605	0.1394
0.30	0.15	0.10292	0.015438	0.3257
0.50	0.10	0.24609	0.024609	0.5192
Total	1.00	0.37692	0.047397	1.0000

[a]The calculations are similar to those of Tables 23.13 and 23.14; column 3 entries are now given by

$$P(X = 5 \mid n = 10, p = p_i) = \binom{10}{5}(p_i)^5(1 - p_i)^5$$

For example, with $p_i = 0.10$, we get

$$P(X = 5 \mid n = 10, p = 0.10) = \binom{10}{5}(0.10)^5(0.90)^5 = 0.00149$$

The differences between column 5 of Table 23.15 and column 5 of Table 23.14 are due solely to rounding errors.

23.8 Decision Trees

The decision flow diagram, or **decision tree**, facilitates decision making when uncertainty prevails, especially when the problem involves a sequence of decisions.[7] In a sequential decision problem, in which the actions taken at one stage depend on actions taken earlier, the evaluation of alternatives can become very complicated. In such cases, the decision-tree technique facilitates project evaluation by enabling the firm to write down all the possible future decisions, as well as their monetary outcomes, in a systematic manner.

Perhaps the best way to explain the decision tree is to demonstrate its use through a specific example.

EXAMPLE 23.2

Suppose that an oil company owns drilling rights in the North Sea and that the company initially must decide whether or not to make a seismic test that will indicate the chances of finding oil in this area. Hence, undertaking the test, which is a costly venture, or proceeding without it is the first in our sequence of decisions (see Figure 23.7). In stage 2, the firm again faces two alternatives: either to sell its drilling rights to another company or to drill with the hope of finding oil. As one can see in Figure 23.7, these two simple alternatives yield radically different

[7] Readers who wish to pursue this subject further may consult John F. Magee, "Decision Trees for Decision Making," *Harvard Business Review*, July–August 1964, and "How to Use Decision Trees in Capital Investment," *Harvard Business Review*, September–October 1964; or Howard Raiffa, *Decision Analysis: Introductory Lectures on Choices Under Uncertainty* (Reading, Mass.: Addison-Wesley, 1968).

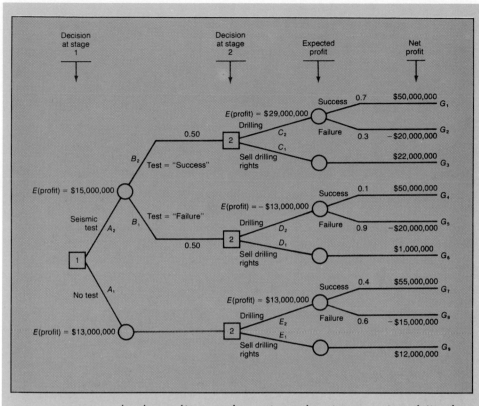

Figure 23.7

Decision tree: decisions concerning seismic testing, drilling for oil, and selling drilling rights in a specific geographic area

monetary rewards, depending on the action taken in stage 1 and (in the event that the firm decides to make the test) on the test's success or failure. Hence, the first stage is characterized in Figure 23.7 by two branches of possible action, denoted by A_1 and A_2. If the firm decides to make the seismic test (that is, to follow branch A_2) it will, in the second stage, again be confronted by two possible decisions (branches B_1 and B_2). Thus, each successive decision in the sequence has its own branches to represent further decisions: hence the name "decision tree."

If the firm decides not to carry out the seismic test, it can sell the drilling rights for $12 million (see branch G_9); alternatively, the company can drill for oil without making the seismic test. In the latter event, the monetary outcome depends solely on whether or not oil is actually found. Suppose that the oil company estimates the probability of finding oil at 0.4 and the probability of finding a dry hole at 0.6. If we assume that the drilling cost is $15 million, there is a probability of 0.6 of losing this sum (see branch G_8). On the other hand, there is a probability of 0.4 of striking oil, in which case the firm will earn a profit (after deducting the drilling and other costs) of $55 million (see branch G_7). The expected profit, should the firm decide to drill *without* a seismic test, is $13 million, since E(profit) $= 0.4 \cdot \$55,000,000 + 0.6 \cdot (-\$15,000,000)$ $= \$13,000,000$.

Let us turn now to the monetary consequences of following branch A_2: we now assume that the firm decides to make the seismic test in the first stage. We further assume that this seismic test costs $5 million and that there exists a probability of 0.5 that the test will yield good results (denoted as "success" in Figure 23.7) and a probability of 0.5 that it will fail. The decision at stage 2 obviously will depend on the test results. Should the company decide to sell the drilling rights after the seismic test fails, it will realize a lower price than it could have obtained without the seismic test. Clearly the poor results of the test (which we assume are public knowledge) will lower the market value of the drilling rights. Let us assume that if the test fails, the firm can sell its concession for $6 million, which will net the firm only $1 million because we have assumed that the seismic test costs $5 million (see branch G_6). On the other hand, the firm might still decide to drill despite the failure of the seismic test. As a result of the failure of the test, however, the company revises its estimates of the probability of finding oil (this is Bayesian decision making; see Section 23.7). The probability of hitting oil is now estimated to be only 0.1 (as compared with 0.4 without the additional information provided by the seismic test). Should the firm fail to find oil, the loss will be $20 million—the assumed drilling cost of $15 million plus the $5 million cost of the seismic test (see branch G_5). Should the firm strike oil, the net profit will be $50 million, which reflects a profit of $55 million from the net oil revenues minus the cost of the seismic test (see branch G_4). The expected profit should the firm decide to drill even if the seismic test fails turns into a loss of $13 million: E(profit) = $0.10 \cdot \$50,000,000 + 0.90 \cdot -\$20,000,000 = -\$13,000,000$.

The probability of a successful seismic test is described by branch B_2. Clearly a successful test will increase the value of the drilling rights, say to $27 million, and since the company spent $5 million on the seismic test, its net income from selling the rights would be $22 million (see branch G_3). Obviously, a successful seismic test also increases the probability of finding oil, so we assume that the firm now estimates this probability at 0.7 (branch G_1). Thus the expected profit, should the firm decide to drill following a successful seismic test, is $29 million: E(profit) = $0.70 \cdot \$50,000,000 + 0.30 \cdot -\$20,000,000 = \$29,000,000$.

Now that we have obtained the monetary outcomes from all the possible branches of Figure 23.7, which decision sequence is optimal? Clearly, the decision depends on the utility that the firm attributes to each possible outcome. But in order to see the use of the decision-tree technique, let us assume for simplicity that the firm reaches its decision according to the criterion of maximum expected profit. Following this rule, we calculate the expected profit for each branch of Figure 23.7, and the course of action represented by the branch with the highest expected profit will be chosen. This is not as simple as it might seem, however. First we must examine the profit of stage 2 in order to choose the optimal course of action (branch) for stage 2; only then can we "fold back" the tree and choose the optimal decision for stage 1.

Our first step is to compare the expected profit of the branches in stage 2. Assuming that the firm makes the seismic test, the expected profit of branch C_2 ($29 million) is higher than the profit from selling the contract, branch C_1; hence the course of action denoted by branch C_1 can be discarded and should be ignored in our further calculations. Similarly, branch D_1 results in a higher expected profit ($1 million) than does branch D_2, so D_2 can also be discarded. If, on the other hand, the firm decides not to make the seismic test, branch E_2 has a higher expected profit ($13 million) than E_1, and therefore the latter can be discarded.

Having first made these eliminations in the second-stage decisions, we can then evaluate the first-stage decision as follows. The expected profit of the seismic test becomes 0.50 · $29,000,000 + 0.50 · $1,000,000 = $15,000,000.

The expected profit in the case of no seismic test is $13,000,000, as explained earlier. Note that this calculation of stage 1 exploits the previous screening of the alternatives of stage 2. If the test is successful, branch C_2 is chosen, so the expected profit of that alternative is $29 million. If the test is unsuccessful, the best path to follow is branch D_1, which results in a profit of $1 million. Similarly, if we fold back the other branches, the maximum expected profit when the seismic test is *not* made is the $13 million that results from the option of drilling without the test.

Examining our results, we find that the optimal decision at the first stage under the maximum expected return rule is to make the seismic test. If successful, the firm will go ahead at stage 2 with the decision to drill for oil; should the test prove unsuccessful, the optimal second-stage decision will be to sell the drilling rights. In terms of Figure 23.7, the optimal path follows branches A_2, B_2, and C_2 if the test is a success and branch A_2 followed by B_1 and D_1 should it fail. Note that in both cases we start with branch A_2, the decision to make the seismic test; the *next decision in the sequence is taken only after the results of the test have been obtained.*

In summary, the decision-tree technique permits us to transport ourselves in conceptual time to the extremities of the tree, where expectations are calculated in terms of the alternative outcomes and their probabilities of occurrence. We then work our way back by folding back, so to speak, the branches of the tree, choosing only those paths that yield the maximum expected profit at each decision junction.

Recall that we selected the best sequence of decisions according to the maximum expected profit rule. The same technique can be employed when the objective is to maximize expected utility: for every monetary outcome, simply substitute the corresponding utility. Moreover, one can calculate the mean and the variance of each branch of the tree and use the mean-variance rule. No matter what decision rule is used, decision trees are useful when a sequence of decisions must be faced.

Chapter Summary and Review

1. Decision making based on extreme values
   a. Maximax criterion: decision rule of the optimist (minimin criterion used with a cost rather than an income matrix)
   b. Maximin criterion: decision rule of the pessimist (minimax criterion used with a cost rather than an income matrix)
   c. Minimax regret criterion

   Drawbacks: All rules rely on extreme values and ignore intermediate outcomes. Rules *a* and *b* are affected by adding a constant number to all results in a given state. Rule *c* is affected by the "irrelevant" alternative.

2. Rules that rely on all outcomes
   a. Maximum expected return criterion: $E(X)$
   b. Maximum expected utility criterion: $E[U(X)]$
   c. The mean-variance criterion: $E(X)$, $V(X)$

3. Other approaches to decision making under uncertainty
   a. Bayesian decision making: revising the decision on the basis of sample information
   b. Decision tree: appropriate when a sequence of decisions across time is involved

Problems

23.1. An entrepreneur is considering investing in one of the following three business lines: auto manufacturing, oil refining, or frozen-food processing. Her expected profit in each line as a function of future oil prices is given in the following payoff matrix:

	State of nature		
Activity	S_1 Price of oil is up	S_2 Price of oil is down	S_3 Price of oil is unchanged
A_1 Auto manufacturing	100	500	300
A_2 Oil refining	400	200	250
A_3 Frozen-food processing	290	310	300

(*a*) What is the maximin strategy?
(*b*) What is the maximax strategy?
(*c*) If the entrepreneur decides to invest in the auto industry, is she a pessimist or an optimist? Explain.

23.2. Give an example of a payoff matrix in which you apply the minimin criterion.

23.3. Use the payoff table of Problem 23.1 to establish the regret table.

(*a*) Explain the notion of "regret."
(*b*) Which strategy would you choose according to the minimax regret criterion?

23.4. Reconsider Problem 23.1. Suppose that if the entrepreneur faces another oil crisis and oil prices go up, the government will give her a grant of $200, no matter what activity she has selected.

(*a*) Do you think that such a grant, given regardless of the activity selected, should change her decision?
(*b*) Reconstruct the payoff table of Problem 23.1 to include the effect of the $200 grant and find the selected strategy according to the maximax, maximin, and minimax regret rules.
(*c*) Compare your results with those you obtained in Problem 23.1. Which rules are independent of the grant of a constant amount of dollars in a given state of nature?

23.5. Repeat Problem 23.1 but add another alternative: investing directly in stocks of oil firms. Thus we have the following payoff table:

	State of nature		
Activity	S_1 *Price of oil is up*	S_2 *Price of oil is down*	S_3 *Price of oil is unchanged*
A_1 Auto manufacturing	100	500	300
A_2 Oil refining	400	200	250
A_3 Frozen-food processing	290	310	300
A_4 Purchase of oil stocks	600	150	400

(a) Which activity would you choose by the maximax rule? Which would you choose by the maximin rule? Which by the minimax regret criterion? Compare your results with those of Problem 23.1.

(b) According to the minimax regret criterion, purchase of oil stocks constitutes the "irrelevant alternative." Explain this concept.

23.6. Referring to the payoff matrix of Problem 23.1, assume that the entrepreneur makes decisions according to the expected profit criterion.

(a) What activity will she choose if she believes that the following probabilities characterize the three states of nature: $P(S_1) = \frac{1}{3}$, $P(S_2) = \frac{1}{3}$, $P(S_3) = \frac{1}{3}$?

(b) What activity will she choose if it is given that $P(S_1) = 0.1$, $P(S_2) = 0.8$, $P(S_3) = 0.1$?

(c) In what respect does the maximum expected profit rule differ from the other rules (maximax, minimax, minimax regret)?

23.7. A businessman considers investing in a project in one of the following three areas: auto industry, food industry, or oil industry. The income of each investment is a function of two states of nature: state 1, under which the OPEC (oil) cartel is expected to break and oil prices are expected to drop sharply; and state 2, under which the existence of the OPEC cartel is expected to continue. The net income from the three projects in the two states of nature is as follows:

	State of nature	
Investment	*1*	*2*
A_1 Auto industry	200	100
A_2 Food industry	150	140
A_3 Oil industry	80	300

(a) Which investment would you consider best if you used the maximax criterion?

(b) Which investment would you consider best if you used the maximin criterion?

(c) Which investment would you choose by the expected return rule, knowing that the probability of state 1 is 0.2 and that of state 2 is 0.8?

23.8. An investor considers purchasing a share of one of four mutual funds. The performance of the funds (given in annual rates of return) is a function of the market condition and is as follows:

	Fund			
Market condition	*1*	*2*	*3*	*4*
"Bullish" (strong market)	30%	12%	15%	7%
"Bearish" (weak market)	−20%	10%	12%	7%

(a) Which fund would be selected by an optimistic investor? Which by a pessimistic investor?

(*b*) How would you change your answer to part *a* if the investor had to choose from funds 2, 3, and 4?

23.9. Which is the best fund in Problem 23.8 by the minimax regret criterion?

23.10. An investor faces the following two investment options (both cost the same):

Option A		Option B	
Return	*Probability*	*Return*	*Probability*
−10%	$\frac{1}{2}$	−20%	$\frac{1}{2}$
+30%	$\frac{1}{2}$	+40%	$\frac{1}{2}$

If the investor prefers option *B* over option *A*, is the individual a risk lover or a risk averter? Explain.

23.11. The utility function of Ms. MacIntosh is given by

$$U(W) = W - 0.05\ W^2$$

where *W* is measured in dollars.

(*a*) Calculate the utility of the values $W = 0, 5, 15, 20$, and 100, and sketch the graph of Ms. MacIntosh's utility function over the range $0 to $100.

(*b*) Ms. MacIntosh has to choose between a sure income of $40 and a game that offers a 50 percent chance of winning $0 and a 50 percent chance of winning $100. Which option will she choose?

(*c*) Assume now that Ms. MacIntosh considers a game that promises $0 with probability of $\frac{1}{2}$, or W^* with probability of $\frac{1}{2}$. What is the value W^* if she is indifferent between the game and winning a sure amount of $10?

23.12. Mr. Smith owns a house and faces the following probabilities: 0.01 that fire will strike sometime during the next year and reduce the value of his house to $W_1 = \$10,000$, and a probability of 0.99 that a fire will not strike and the value of his house will be $W_2 = \$100,000$. Mr. Smith's utility function is $U(W) = \sqrt{W}$.

(*a*) Is Mr. Smith a risk lover or a risk averter? Explain.
(*b*) Calculate the risk premium of Mr. Smith.
(*c*) Repeat parts *a* and *b*, making the alternative assumption that Mr. Smith's utility function is given by $U(W) = \log_{10}(W)$.

23.13. A textile firm considers buying one of two machines: machine *A* or machine *B*. Machine *A* is bigger and is also more efficient in production of large quantities. A demand for large quantities will exist only if the economy is good.

Machine *A* costs $1 million and machine *B* costs $500,000. The income from machine *A* will be $0.7 million in the case of a weak economy and $3 million in the case of a strong economy. The income from machine *B* will be $0.6 million in the case of a weak economy and $1 million in the case of a strong economy.

(*a*) Draw the decision tree for this problem.
(*b*) Which of the machines would you buy if the probability for a weak economy was 0.2 and for a strong economy was 0.8?
(*c*) Repeat part *b* assuming that the probability for a weak economy was 0.9 and for a strong economy was 0.1. Compare and discuss your results.

23.14. The Internal Revenue Service has found that the percentage of dishonest income reporting increases with income. Table P23.14 presents data on the distribution of tax returns by income and by the percentage of dishonest reporting.

TABLE P23.14

Income (in thousands of dollars)	Percentage of tax returns in this category	Percentage of dishonest reporting
Under 5	15%	0.1%
5–under 10	20	1.5
10–under 20	15	2.5
20 or over	50	4.0

(*a*) One tax return is sampled at random. What is the probability that its income is $20,000 or over?

(*b*) A tax return has been found to contain dishonest information. What is the probability that it is from the income group $20,000 or over?

23.15. (*a*) Describe the St. Petersburg game. How much would you be willing to pay in order to participate in such a game? What is the expected value of the prize?

(*b*) Suppose that we change the St. Petersburg game as follows: if heads appears in one of the first 10 tosses (inclusive), you get $1,000, but if it first appears on the eleventh toss or later, you get 2^{n-1}, as in the original game. How much would you be willing to pay to participate in such a game? What is the expected value?

23.16. Suppose you have to choose one of the following two options:

Option A		Option B	
Probability	Profit	Probability	Profit
$\frac{1}{2}$	90	$\frac{1}{2}$	80
$\frac{1}{2}$	110	$\frac{1}{2}$	120

(*a*) Which option would you choose according to the expected profit rule?

(*b*) Which option would you choose according to the expected utility rule, knowing that the marginal utility of money diminishes? Illustrate your answer graphically.

23.17. Define "risk averter," "risk lover," and "risk neutral."

23.18. Suppose there is a 50 percent chance that ABC stock will sell at $300 next week and a 50 percent chance that it will sell at $400. A risk averter is willing to pay a maximum of $320 for this stock. What is the risk premium? Show graphically at least three points on his utility function. (Draw two as you wish, but the third point must be determined by the data of this problem.)

23.19. Suppose that an individual's utility function is given by $U(x) = \sqrt{x}$. The individual has to select between the following two options:

Option A		Option B	
Probability	Net profit	Probability	Net profit
$\frac{1}{3}$	0	$\frac{3}{4}$	0
$\frac{1}{3}$	100	$\frac{1}{4}$	1,600
$\frac{1}{3}$	900		

(a) Which option has a higher expected profit?
(b) Which option would you select when $U(x) = \sqrt{x}$? Is the individual a risk averter or risk lover?
(c) Which option would you choose if your utility function is given by $U^*(x) = 10 + 2\sqrt{x}$?
(d) Compare and explain your answers to parts *b* and *c*.

23.20. Which of the two options in Problem 23.19 would you select as better if you used the mean-variance rule?

23.21. Suppose the means and variances of the profits of six investment options are as follows:

Option	Mean	Variance
A	5	14
B	7	10
C	8	8
D	9	3
E	10	12
F	4	8

Which of the options would you certainly reject if you used the mean-variance rule?

23.22. Explain the concept of Bayesian decision making.

23.23. International Car, Inc., is considering investing $10 million in an African country in order to manufacture cars for the local market. Financial analysis has shown that International Car will make a net profit of $500 per car sold. The company will invest only if it estimates that all of the $100 million can be recovered in the first year (if 20,000 cars will be sold).

The population of the African country consists of 1 million families, 2 percent of whom are considered "rich" and 98 percent "poor." It is estimated that 90 percent of the rich and only 1 percent of the poor will buy cars from International Car.

(a) Should the firm invest in the country?
(b) Suppose there is a 10 percent chance of a revolution in the country (political risk). International Car will continue to operate, but 80 percent of the rich will leave the country. With this additional information, should International Car invest?

23.24. XYZ company has just received an order for 1,000 widgets. The production process has not been inspected in a while, and hence the proportion of defectives that are produced, θ, is uncertain. However, from experience the manager is able to estimate a prior probability distribution for θ (see Table P23.24). There are two corrective actions available: (1) Have the service company make a routine overhaul; this ensures that θ will be no higher than 0.10, that is, if the true θ was 0.15 or greater, then it is brought down to 0.10; if the true θ was 0.10 or less, the overhaul has no effect. This costs $25. (2) Have the service company make a thorough check and replace all worn-out parts. This ensures that θ will be 0.05. This costs $100.

First, the manager takes a sample of 10 items ($n = 10$) to study the state of the processes. He observes five defectives ($r = 5$). On the basis of this sample, he obtains a revised or posterior distribution for θ.

Now the manager must choose one of the following actions:

A_1 Leave the process as it is
A_2 Have the service company make a routine overhaul
A_3 Have the service company make a major overhaul

He will choose the action that maximizes expected net profit. Other relevant data: net profit per item is $0.50; the cost of replacing defective items is $2.00 per item.

What action should he choose?

TABLE P23.24
Prior Probability Distribution of θ, the Proportion of Defectives

θ_i	$P(\theta = \theta_i)$
0.05	0.60
0.10	0.30
0.15	0.08
0.25	0.02
	1.00

APPENDIX A
STATISTICAL TABLES

TABLE A.1
The Cumulative Binomial Distribution

n	x						p				
		0.05	0.10	0.15	0.20	0.25	0.30	0.35	0.40	0.45	0.50
2	0	0.9025	0.8100	0.7225	0.6400	0.5625	0.4900	0.4225	0.3600	0.3025	0.2500
	1	0.9975	0.9900	0.9775	0.9600	0.9375	0.9100	0.8775	0.8400	0.7975	0.7500
	2	1.0000	1.0000	1.0000	1.0000	1.0000	1.0000	1.0000	1.0000	1.0000	1.0000
3	0	0.8574	0.7290	0.6141	0.5120	0.4219	0.3430	0.2746	0.2160	0.1664	0.1250
	1	0.9928	0.9720	0.9392	0.8960	0.8438	0.7840	0.7183	0.6480	0.5748	0.5000
	2	0.9999	0.9990	0.9966	0.9920	0.9844	0.9730	0.9571	0.9360	0.9089	0.8750
	3	1.0000	1.0000	1.0000	1.0000	1.0000	1.0000	1.0000	1.0000	1.0000	1.0000
4	0	0.8145	0.6561	0.5220	0.4096	0.3164	0.2401	0.1785	0.1296	0.0915	0.0625
	1	0.9860	0.9477	0.8905	0.8192	0.7383	0.6517	0.5630	0.4752	0.3910	0.3125
	2	0.9995	0.9963	0.9880	0.9728	0.9492	0.9163	0.8735	0.8208	0.7585	0.6875
	3	1.0000	0.9999	0.9995	0.9984	0.9961	0.9919	0.9850	0.9744	0.9590	0.9375
	4	1.0000	1.0000	1.0000	1.0000	1.0000	1.0000	1.0000	1.0000	1.0000	1.0000
5	0	0.7738	0.5905	0.4437	0.3277	0.2373	0.1681	0.1160	0.0778	0.0503	0.0313
	1	0.9774	0.9185	0.8352	0.7373	0.6328	0.5282	0.4284	0.3370	0.2562	0.1875
	2	0.9988	0.9914	0.9734	0.9421	0.8965	0.8369	0.7648	0.6826	0.5931	0.5000
	3	1.0000	0.9995	0.9978	0.9933	0.9844	0.9692	0.9460	0.9130	0.8688	0.8125
	4	1.0000	1.0000	0.9999	0.9997	0.9990	0.9976	0.9947	0.9898	0.9815	0.9688
	5	1.0000	1.0000	1.0000	1.0000	1.0000	1.0000	1.0000	1.0000	1.0000	1.0000
6	0	0.7351	0.5314	0.3771	0.2621	0.1780	0.1176	0.0754	0.0467	0.0277	0.0156
	1	0.9672	0.8857	0.7765	0.6554	0.5339	0.4202	0.3191	0.2333	0.1636	0.1094
	2	0.9978	0.9842	0.9527	0.9011	0.8306	0.7443	0.6471	0.5443	0.4415	0.3437
	3	0.9999	0.9987	0.9941	0.9830	0.9624	0.9295	0.8826	0.8208	0.7447	0.6563
	4	1.0000	0.9999	0.9996	0.9984	0.9954	0.9891	0.9777	0.9590	0.9308	0.8906
	5	1.0000	1.0000	1.0000	0.9999	0.9998	0.9993	0.9982	0.9959	0.9917	0.9844
	6	1.0000	1.0000	1.0000	1.0000	1.0000	1.0000	1.0000	1.0000	1.0000	1.0000

ii

TABLE A.1
The Cumulative Binomial Distribution (Continued)

n	x	p 0.05	0.10	0.15	0.20	0.25	0.30	0.35	0.40	0.45	0.50
7	0	0.6983	0.4783	0.3206	0.2097	0.1335	0.0824	0.0490	0.0280	0.0152	0.0078
	1	0.9556	0.8503	0.7166	0.5767	0.4449	0.3294	0.2338	0.1586	0.1024	0.0625
	2	0.9962	0.9743	0.9262	0.8520	0.7564	0.6471	0.5323	0.4199	0.3164	0.2266
	3	0.9998	0.9973	0.9879	0.9667	0.9294	0.8740	0.8002	0.7102	0.6083	0.5000
	4	1.0000	0.9998	0.9988	0.9953	0.9871	0.9712	0.9444	0.9037	0.8471	0.7734
	5	1.0000	1.0000	0.9999	0.9996	0.9987	0.9962	0.9910	0.9812	0.9643	0.9375
	6	1.0000	1.0000	1.0000	1.0000	0.9999	0.9998	0.9994	0.9984	0.9963	0.9922
	7	1.0000	1.0000	1.0000	1.0000	1.0000	1.0000	1.0000	1.0000	1.0000	1.0000
8	0	0.6634	0.4305	0.2725	0.1678	0.1001	0.0576	0.0319	0.0168	0.0084	0.0039
	1	0.9428	0.8131	0.6572	0.5033	0.3671	0.2553	0.1691	0.1064	0.0632	0.0352
	2	0.9942	0.9619	0.8948	0.7969	0.6785	0.5518	0.4278	0.3154	0.2201	0.1445
	3	0.9996	0.9950	0.9786	0.9437	0.8862	0.8059	0.7064	0.5941	0.4770	0.3633
	4	1.0000	0.9996	0.9971	0.9896	0.9727	0.9420	0.8939	0.8263	0.7396	0.6367
	5	1.0000	1.0000	0.9998	0.9988	0.9958	0.9887	0.9747	0.9502	0.9115	0.8555
	6	1.0000	1.0000	1.0000	0.9999	0.9996	0.9987	0.9964	0.9915	0.9819	0.9648
	7	1.0000	1.0000	1.0000	1.0000	1.0000	0.9999	0.9998	0.9993	0.9983	0.9961
	8	1.0000	1.0000	1.0000	1.0000	1.0000	1.0000	1.0000	1.0000	1.0000	1.0000
9	0	0.6302	0.3874	0.2316	0.1342	0.0751	0.0404	0.0207	0.0101	0.0046	0.0020
	1	0.9288	0.7748	0.5995	0.4362	0.3003	0.1960	0.1211	0.0705	0.0385	0.0195
	2	0.9916	0.9470	0.8591	0.7382	0.6007	0.4628	0.3373	0.2318	0.1495	0.0898
	3	0.9994	0.9917	0.9661	0.9144	0.8343	0.7297	0.6089	0.4826	0.3614	0.2539
	4	1.0000	0.9991	0.9944	0.9804	0.9511	0.9012	0.8283	0.7334	0.6214	0.5000
	5	1.0000	0.9999	0.9994	0.9969	0.9900	0.9747	0.9464	0.9006	0.8342	0.7461
	6	1.0000	1.0000	1.0000	0.9997	0.9987	0.9957	0.9888	0.9750	0.9502	0.9102
	7	1.0000	1.0000	1.0000	1.0000	0.9999	0.9996	0.9986	0.9962	0.9909	0.9805
	8	1.0000	1.0000	1.0000	1.0000	1.0000	1.0000	0.9999	0.9997	0.9992	0.9980
	9	1.0000	1.0000	1.0000	1.0000	1.0000	1.0000	1.0000	1.0000	1.0000	1.0000

TABLE A.1
The Cumulative Binomial Distribution (Continued)

n	x	p 0.05	0.10	0.15	0.20	0.25	0.30	0.35	0.40	0.45	0.50
10	0	0.5987	0.3487	0.1969	0.1074	0.0563	0.0282	0.0135	0.0060	0.0025	0.0010
	1	0.9139	0.7361	0.5443	0.3758	0.2440	0.1493	0.0860	0.0464	0.0233	0.0107
	2	0.9885	0.9298	0.8202	0.6778	0.5256	0.3828	0.2616	0.1673	0.0996	0.0547
	3	0.9990	0.9872	0.9500	0.8791	0.7759	0.6496	0.5138	0.3823	0.2660	0.1719
	4	0.9999	0.9984	0.9901	0.9672	0.9219	0.8497	0.7515	0.6331	0.5044	0.3770
	5	1.0000	0.9999	0.9986	0.9936	0.9803	0.9527	0.9051	0.8338	0.7384	0.6230
	6	1.0000	1.0000	0.9999	0.9991	0.9965	0.9894	0.9740	0.9452	0.8980	0.8281
	7	1.0000	1.0000	1.0000	0.9999	0.9996	0.9984	0.9952	0.9877	0.9726	0.9453
	8	1.0000	1.0000	1.0000	1.0000	1.0000	0.9999	0.9995	0.9983	0.9955	0.9893
	9	1.0000	1.0000	1.0000	1.0000	1.0000	1.0000	1.0000	0.9999	0.9997	0.9990
	10	1.0000	1.0000	1.0000	1.0000	1.0000	1.0000	1.0000	1.0000	1.0000	1.0000
11	0	0.5688	0.3138	0.1673	0.0859	0.0422	0.0198	0.0088	0.0036	0.0014	0.0005
	1	0.8981	0.6974	0.4922	0.3221	0.1971	0.1130	0.0606	0.0302	0.0139	0.0059
	2	0.9848	0.9104	0.7788	0.6174	0.4552	0.3127	0.2001	0.1189	0.0652	0.0327
	3	0.9984	0.9815	0.9306	0.8389	0.7133	0.5696	0.4256	0.2963	0.1911	0.1133
	4	0.9999	0.9972	0.9841	0.9496	0.8854	0.7897	0.6683	0.5328	0.3971	0.2744
	5	1.0000	0.9997	0.9973	0.9883	0.9657	0.9218	0.8513	0.7535	0.6331	0.5000
	6	1.0000	1.0000	0.9997	0.9980	0.9924	0.9784	0.9499	0.9006	0.8262	0.7256
	7	1.0000	1.0000	1.0000	0.9998	0.9988	0.9957	0.9878	0.9707	0.9390	0.8867
	8	1.0000	1.0000	1.0000	1.0000	0.9999	0.9994	0.9980	0.9941	0.9852	0.9673
	9	1.0000	1.0000	1.0000	1.0000	1.0000	1.0000	0.9998	0.9993	0.9978	0.9941
	10	1.0000	1.0000	1.0000	1.0000	1.0000	1.0000	1.0000	1.0000	0.9998	0.9995
	11	1.0000	1.0000	1.0000	1.0000	1.0000	1.0000	1.0000	1.0000	1.0000	1.0000
12	0	0.5404	0.2824	0.1422	0.0687	0.0317	0.0138	0.0057	0.0022	0.0008	0.0002
	1	0.8816	0.6590	0.4435	0.2749	0.1584	0.0850	0.0424	0.0196	0.0083	0.0032
	2	0.9804	0.8891	0.7358	0.5583	0.3907	0.2528	0.1513	0.0834	0.0421	0.0193
	3	0.9978	0.9744	0.9078	0.7946	0.6488	0.4925	0.3467	0.2253	0.1345	0.0730
	4	0.9998	0.9957	0.9761	0.9274	0.8424	0.7237	0.5833	0.4382	0.3044	0.1938

n	x						p				
		0.05	0.10	0.15	0.20	0.25	0.30	0.35	0.40	0.45	0.50
	5	1.0000	0.9995	0.9954	0.9806	0.9456	0.8822	0.7873	0.6652	0.5269	0.3872
	6	1.0000	0.9999	0.9993	0.9961	0.9857	0.9614	0.9154	0.8418	0.7393	0.6128
	7	1.0000	1.0000	0.9999	0.9994	0.9972	0.9905	0.9745	0.9427	0.8883	0.8062
	8	1.0000	1.0000	1.0000	0.9999	0.9996	0.9983	0.9944	0.9847	0.9644	0.9270
	9	1.0000	1.0000	1.0000	1.0000	1.0000	0.9998	0.9992	0.9972	0.9921	0.9807
	10	1.0000	1.0000	1.0000	1.0000	1.0000	1.0000	0.9999	0.9997	0.9989	0.9968
	11	1.0000	1.0000	1.0000	1.0000	1.0000	1.0000	1.0000	1.0000	0.9999	0.9998
	12	1.0000	1.0000	1.0000	1.0000	1.0000	1.0000	1.0000	1.0000	1.0000	1.0000
13	0	0.5133	0.2542	0.1209	0.0550	0.0238	0.0097	0.0037	0.0013	0.0004	0.0001
	1	0.8646	0.6213	0.3983	0.2336	0.1267	0.0637	0.0296	0.0126	0.0049	0.0017
	2	0.9755	0.8661	0.6920	0.5017	0.3326	0.2025	0.1132	0.0579	0.0269	0.0112
	3	0.9969	0.9658	0.8820	0.7473	0.5843	0.4206	0.2783	0.1686	0.0929	0.0461
	4	0.9997	0.9935	0.9658	0.9009	0.7940	0.6543	0.5005	0.3530	0.2279	0.1334
	5	1.0000	0.9991	0.9925	0.9700	0.9198	0.8346	0.7159	0.5744	0.4268	0.2905
	6	1.0000	0.9999	0.9987	0.9930	0.9757	0.9376	0.8705	0.7712	0.6437	0.5000
	7	1.0000	1.0000	0.9998	0.9988	0.9944	0.9818	0.9538	0.9023	0.8212	0.7095
	8	1.0000	1.0000	1.0000	0.9998	0.9990	0.9960	0.9874	0.9679	0.9302	0.8666
	9	1.0000	1.0000	1.0000	1.0000	0.9999	0.9993	0.9975	0.9922	0.9797	0.9539
	10	1.0000	1.0000	1.0000	1.0000	1.0000	0.9999	0.9997	0.9987	0.9959	0.9888
	11	1.0000	1.0000	1.0000	1.0000	1.0000	1.0000	1.0000	0.9999	0.9995	0.9983
	12	1.0000	1.0000	1.0000	1.0000	1.0000	1.0000	1.0000	1.0000	1.0000	0.9999
	13	1.0000	1.0000	1.0000	1.0000	1.0000	1.0000	1.0000	1.0000	1.0000	1.0000
14	0	0.4877	0.2288	0.1028	0.0440	0.0178	0.0068	0.0024	0.0008	0.0002	0.0001
	1	0.8470	0.5846	0.3567	0.1979	0.1010	0.0475	0.0205	0.0081	0.0029	0.0009
	2	0.9699	0.8416	0.6479	0.4481	0.2811	0.1608	0.0839	0.0398	0.0170	0.0065
	3	0.9958	0.9559	0.8535	0.6982	0.5213	0.3552	0.2205	0.1243	0.0632	0.0287
	4	0.9996	0.9908	0.9533	0.8702	0.7415	0.5842	0.4227	0.2793	0.1672	0.0898
	5	1.0000	0.9985	0.9885	0.9561	0.8883	0.7805	0.6405	0.4859	0.3373	0.2120

TABLE A.1
The Cumulative Binomial Distribution (Continued)

n	x	0.05	0.10	0.15	0.20	0.25	0.30	0.35	0.40	0.45	0.50
	6	1.0000	0.9998	0.9978	0.9884	0.9617	0.9067	0.8164	0.6925	0.5461	0.3953
	7	1.0000	1.0000	0.9997	0.9976	0.9897	0.9685	0.9247	0.8499	0.7414	0.6047
	8	1.0000	1.0000	1.0000	0.9996	0.9978	0.9917	0.9757	0.9417	0.8811	0.7880
	9	1.0000	1.0000	1.0000	1.0000	0.9997	0.9983	0.9940	0.9825	0.9574	0.9102
	10	1.0000	1.0000	1.0000	1.0000	1.0000	0.9998	0.9989	0.9961	0.9886	0.9713
	11	1.0000	1.0000	1.0000	1.0000	1.0000	1.0000	0.9999	0.9994	0.9978	0.9935
	12	1.0000	1.0000	1.0000	1.0000	1.0000	1.0000	1.0000	0.9999	0.9997	0.9991
	13	1.0000	1.0000	1.0000	1.0000	1.0000	1.0000	1.0000	1.0000	1.0000	0.9999
	14	1.0000	1.0000	1.0000	1.0000	1.0000	1.0000	1.0000	1.0000	1.0000	1.0000
15	0	0.4633	0.2059	0.0874	0.0352	0.0134	0.0047	0.0016	0.0005	0.0001	0.0000
	1	0.8290	0.5490	0.3186	0.1671	0.0802	0.0353	0.0142	0.0052	0.0017	0.0005
	2	0.9638	0.8159	0.6042	0.3980	0.2361	0.1268	0.0617	0.0271	0.0107	0.0037
	3	0.9945	0.9444	0.8227	0.6482	0.4613	0.2969	0.1727	0.0905	0.0424	0.0176
	4	0.9994	0.9873	0.9383	0.8358	0.6865	0.5155	0.3519	0.2173	0.1204	0.0592
	5	0.9999	0.9978	0.9832	0.9389	0.8516	0.7216	0.5643	0.4032	0.2608	0.1509
	6	1.0000	0.9997	0.9964	0.9819	0.9434	0.8689	0.7548	0.6098	0.4522	0.3036
	7	1.0000	1.0000	0.9994	0.9958	0.9827	0.9500	0.8868	0.7869	0.6535	0.5000
	8	1.0000	1.0000	0.9999	0.9992	0.9958	0.9848	0.9578	0.9050	0.8182	0.6964
	9	1.0000	1.0000	1.0000	0.9999	0.9992	0.9963	0.9876	0.9662	0.9231	0.8491
	10	1.0000	1.0000	1.0000	1.0000	0.9999	0.9993	0.9972	0.9907	0.9745	0.9408
	11	1.0000	1.0000	1.0000	1.0000	1.0000	0.9999	0.9995	0.9981	0.9937	0.9824
	12	1.0000	1.0000	1.0000	1.0000	1.0000	1.0000	0.9999	0.9997	0.9989	0.9963
	13	1.0000	1.0000	1.0000	1.0000	1.0000	1.0000	1.0000	1.0000	0.9999	0.9995
	14	1.0000	1.0000	1.0000	1.0000	1.0000	1.0000	1.0000	1.0000	1.0000	1.0000
	15	1.0000	1.0000	1.0000	1.0000	1.0000	1.0000	1.0000	1.0000	1.0000	1.0000
20	0	0.3585	0.1216	0.0388	0.0115	0.0032	0.0008	0.0002	0.0000	0.0000	0.0000
	1	0.7358	0.3917	0.1756	0.0692	0.0243	0.0076	0.0021	0.0005	0.0001	0.0000
	2	0.9245	0.6769	0.4049	0.2061	0.0913	0.0355	0.0121	0.0036	0.0009	0.0002

TABLE A.1
The Cumulative Binomial Distribution (Continued)

n	x	p									
		0.05	0.10	0.15	0.20	0.25	0.30	0.35	0.40	0.45	0.50
	3	0.9841	0.8670	0.6477	0.4114	0.2252	0.1071	0.0444	0.0160	0.0049	0.0013
	4	0.9974	0.9568	0.8298	0.6296	0.4148	0.2375	0.1182	0.0510	0.0189	0.0059
	5	0.9997	0.9887	0.9327	0.8042	0.6172	0.4164	0.2454	0.1256	0.0553	0.0207
	6	1.0000	0.9976	0.9781	0.9133	0.7858	0.6080	0.4166	0.2500	0.1299	0.0577
	7	1.0000	0.9996	0.9941	0.9679	0.8982	0.7723	0.6010	0.4159	0.2520	0.1316
	8	1.0000	0.9999	0.9987	0.9900	0.9591	0.8867	0.7624	0.5956	0.4143	0.2517
	9	1.0000	1.0000	0.9998	0.9974	0.9861	0.9520	0.8782	0.7553	0.5914	0.4119
	10	1.0000	1.0000	1.0000	0.9994	0.9961	0.9829	0.9468	0.8725	0.7507	0.5881
	11	1.0000	1.0000	1.0000	0.9999	0.9991	0.9949	0.9804	0.9435	0.8692	0.7483
	12	1.0000	1.0000	1.0000	1.0000	0.9998	0.9987	0.9940	0.9790	0.9420	0.8684
	13	1.0000	1.0000	1.0000	1.0000	1.0000	0.9997	0.9985	0.9935	0.9786	0.9423
	14	1.0000	1.0000	1.0000	1.0000	1.0000	1.0000	0.9997	0.9984	0.9936	0.9793
	15	1.0000	1.0000	1.0000	1.0000	1.0000	1.0000	1.0000	0.9997	0.9985	0.9941
	16	1.0000	1.0000	1.0000	1.0000	1.0000	1.0000	1.0000	1.0000	0.9997	0.9987
	17	1.0000	1.0000	1.0000	1.0000	1.0000	1.0000	1.0000	1.0000	1.0000	0.9998
	18	1.0000	1.0000	1.0000	1.0000	1.0000	1.0000	1.0000	1.0000	1.0000	1.0000
	19	1.0000	1.0000	1.0000	1.0000	1.0000	1.0000	1.0000	1.0000	1.0000	1.0000
	20	1.0000	1.0000	1.0000	1.0000	1.0000	1.0000	1.0000	1.0000	1.0000	1.0000

TABLE A.2
The Cumulative Poisson Distribution

x	$\lambda = 0.1$	$\lambda = 0.2$	$\lambda = 0.3$	$\lambda = 0.4$	$\lambda = 0.5$
0	0.90484	0.81873	0.74082	0.67032	0.60653
1	0.99532	0.98248	0.96306	0.93845	0.90980
2	0.99985	0.99885	0.99640	0.99207	0.98561
3	1.00000	0.99994	0.99973	0.99922	0.99825
4		1.00000	0.99998	0.99994	0.99983
5			1.00000	1.00000	0.99999
6					1.00000

x	$\lambda = 0.6$	$\lambda = 0.7$	$\lambda = 0.8$	$\lambda = 0.9$	$\lambda = 1.0$
0	0.54881	0.49658	0.44933	0.40657	0.36788
1	0.87810	0.84419	0.80879	0.77248	0.73576
2	0.97688	0.96586	0.95258	0.93714	0.91970
3	0.99664	0.99425	0.99092	0.98654	0.98101
4	0.99961	0.99921	0.99859	0.99766	0.99634
5	0.99996	0.99991	0.99982	0.99966	0.99941
6	1.00000	0.99999	0.99998	0.99996	0.99992
7		1.00000	1.00000	1.00000	0.99999
8					1.00000

x	$\lambda = 2$	$\lambda = 3$	$\lambda = 4$	$\lambda = 5$	$\lambda = 6$
0	0.13534	0.04979	0.01832	0.00674	0.00248
1	0.40601	0.19915	0.09158	0.04043	0.01735
2	0.67668	0.42319	0.23810	0.12465	0.06197
3	0.85712	0.64723	0.43347	0.26503	0.15120
4	0.94735	0.81526	0.62884	0.44049	0.28506
5	0.98344	0.91608	0.78513	0.61596	0.44568
6	0.99547	0.96649	0.88933	0.76218	0.60630
7	0.99890	0.98810	0.94887	0.86663	0.74398
8	0.99976	0.99620	0.97864	0.93191	0.84724
9	0.99995	0.99890	0.99187	0.96817	0.91608
10	0.99999	0.99971	0.99716	0.98630	0.95738
11	1.00000	0.99993	0.99908	0.99455	0.97991
12		0.99998	0.99973	0.99798	0.99117
13		1.00000	0.99992	0.99930	0.99637
14			0.99998	0.99977	0.99860
15			1.00000	0.99993	0.99949
16				0.99998	0.99982
17				1.00000	0.99994
18					0.99998
19					1.00000

Source: E. C. Molina, *Poisson's Binomial Exponential Limit*, 1942. Reprinted by permission of Bell Laboratories.

TABLE A.2
The Cumulative Poisson Distribution (Continued)

x	$\lambda = 7$	$\lambda = 8$	$\lambda = 9$	$\lambda = 10$
0	0.00091	0.00033	0.00012	0.00004
1	0.00730	0.00302	0.00123	0.00050
2	0.02964	0.01375	0.00623	0.00277
3	0.08176	0.04238	0.02123	0.01034
4	0.17299	0.09963	0.05496	0.02925
5	0.30071	0.19124	0.11569	0.06709
6	0.44971	0.31337	0.20678	0.13014
7	0.59871	0.45296	0.32390	0.22022
8	0.72909	0.59255	0.45565	0.33282
9	0.83050	0.71662	0.58741	0.45793
10	0.90148	0.81589	0.70599	0.58304
11	0.94665	0.88808	0.80301	0.69678
12	0.97300	0.93620	0.87577	0.79156
13	0.98719	0.96582	0.92615	0.86446
14	0.99428	0.98274	0.95853	0.91654
15	0.99759	0.99177	0.97796	0.95126
16	0.99904	0.99628	0.98889	0.97296
17	0.99964	0.99841	0.99468	0.98572
18	0.99987	0.99935	0.99757	0.99281
19	0.99996	0.99975	0.99894	0.99655
20	0.99999	0.99991	0.99956	0.99841
21	1.00000	0.99997	0.99982	0.99930
22		0.99999	0.99993	0.99970
23		1.00000	0.99998	0.99988
24			0.99999	0.99995
25			1.00000	0.99998
26				0.99999
27				1.00000

TABLE A.3
Exponential Functions

x	e^x	e^{-x}	x	e^x	e^{-x}
0.00	1.000	1.000	3.00	20.086	0.050
0.10	1.105	0.905	3.10	22.198	0.045
0.20	1.221	0.819	3.20	24.533	0.041
0.30	1.350	0.741	3.30	27.113	0.037
0.40	1.492	0.670	3.40	29.964	0.033
0.50	1.649	0.607	3.50	33.115	0.030
0.60	1.822	0.549	3.60	36.598	0.027
0.70	2.014	0.497	3.70	40.447	0.025
0.80	2.226	0.449	3.80	44.701	0.022
0.90	2.460	0.407	3.90	49.402	0.020
1.00	2.718	0.368	4.00	54.598	0.018
1.10	3.004	0.333	4.10	60.340	0.017
1.20	3.320	0.301	4.20	66.686	0.015
1.30	3.669	0.273	4.30	73.700	0.014
1.40	4.055	0.247	4.40	81.451	0.012
1.50	4.482	0.223	4.50	90.017	0.011
1.60	4.953	0.202	4.60	99.484	0.010
1.70	5.474	0.183	4.70	109.947	0.009
1.80	6.050	0.165	4.80	121.510	0.008
1.90	6.686	0.150	4.90	134.290	0.007
2.00	7.389	0.135	5.00	148.413	0.007
2.10	8.166	0.122	5.10	164.022	0.006
2.20	9.025	0.111	5.20	181.272	0.006
2.30	9.974	0.100	5.30	200.337	0.005
2.40	11.023	0.091	5.40	221.406	0.005
2.50	12.182	0.082	5.50	244.692	0.004
2.60	13.464	0.074	5.60	270.426	0.004
2.70	14.880	0.067	5.70	298.867	0.003
2.80	16.445	0.061	5.80	330.300	0.003
2.90	18.174	0.055	5.90	365.037	0.003
3.00	20.086	0.050	6.00	403.429	0.002

TABLE A.4
The Chi-Square Distribution

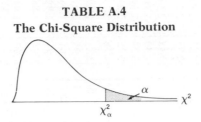

The following table provides the values of χ_α^2 that correspond to a given right-tail area α and a specified number of degrees of freedom.

df	Right-tail area, α							
	0.99	0.975	0.95	0.90	0.10	0.05	0.025	0.01
1	0.00016	0.00098	0.0039	0.016	2.706	3.841	5.024	6.635
2	0.02001	0.05064	0.103	0.211	4.605	5.991	7.378	9.210
3	0.115	0.216	0.352	0.584	6.251	7.815	9.348	11.345
4	0.297	0.484	0.711	1.064	7.779	9.488	11.143	13.277
5	0.554	0.831	1.145	1.610	9.236	11.070	12.832	15.086
6	0.872	1.237	1.635	2.204	10.645	12.592	14.449	16.812
7	1.239	1.690	2.167	2.833	12.017	14.067	16.013	18.475
8	1.646	2.180	2.733	3.490	13.362	15.507	17.535	20.090
9	2.088	2.700	3.325	4.168	14.684	16.919	19.023	21.666
10	2.558	3.247	3.940	4.865	15.987	18.307	20.483	23.209
11	3.053	3.816	4.575	5.578	17.275	19.675	21.920	24.725
12	3.571	4.404	5.226	6.304	18.549	21.026	23.337	26.217
13	4.107	5.009	5.892	7.042	19.812	22.362	24.736	27.688
14	4.660	5.629	6.571	7.790	21.064	23.685	26.119	29.141
15	5.229	6.262	7.261	8.547	22.307	24.996	27.488	30.578
16	5.812	6.908	7.962	9.312	23.542	26.296	28.845	32.000
17	6.408	7.564	8.672	10.085	24.769	27.587	30.191	33.409
18	7.015	8.231	9.390	10.865	25.989	28.869	31.527	34.805
19	7.633	8.907	10.117	11.651	27.204	30.144	32.852	36.191
20	8.260	9.591	10.851	12.443	28.412	31.410	34.170	37.566
21	8.897	10.283	11.591	13.240	29.615	32.671	35.479	38.932
22	9.542	10.982	12.338	14.041	30.813	33.924	36.781	40.289
23	10.196	11.689	13.091	14.848	32.007	35.172	38.076	41.638
24	10.856	12.401	13.848	15.659	33.196	36.415	39.364	42.980
25	11.524	13.120	14.611	16.473	34.382	37.652	40.646	44.314
26	12.198	13.844	15.379	17.292	35.563	38.885	41.923	45.642
27	12.879	14.573	16.151	18.114	36.741	40.113	43.194	46.963
28	13.565	15.308	16.928	18.939	37.916	41.337	44.461	48.278
29	14.256	16.047	17.708	19.768	39.087	42.557	45.722	49.588
30	14.953	16.791	18.493	20.599	40.256	43.773	46.979	50.892

Source: Table 4, in Ronald A. Fisher and Frank Yates, *Statistical Tables for Biological, Agricultural and Medical Research* (London: Longman Group Ltd., previously published by Oliver & Boyd, Edinburgh). Reprinted by permission of the authors and publishers.

TABLE A.5
The F Distribution

TABLE A.5a
Upper 5% Points (0.95 Fractiles)

$J-1 \rightarrow$

$N-J \rightarrow$

n_1 / n_2	1	2	3	4	5	6	7	8	9	10	12	15	20	24	30	40	60	120	∞
1	161.4	199.5	215.7	224.6	230.2	234.0	236.8	238.9	240.5	241.9	243.9	245.9	248.0	249.1	250.1	251.1	252.2	253.3	254.3
2	18.51	19.00	19.16	19.25	19.30	19.33	19.35	19.37	19.38	19.40	19.41	19.43	19.45	19.45	19.46	19.47	19.48	19.49	19.50
3	10.13	9.55	9.28	9.12	9.01	8.94	8.89	8.85	8.81	8.79	8.74	8.70	8.66	8.64	8.62	8.59	8.57	8.55	8.53
4	7.71	6.94	6.59	6.39	6.26	6.16	6.09	6.04	6.00	5.96	5.91	5.86	5.80	5.77	5.75	5.72	5.69	5.66	5.63
5	6.61	5.79	5.41	5.19	5.05	4.95	4.88	4.82	4.77	4.74	4.68	4.62	4.56	4.53	4.50	4.46	4.43	4.40	4.36
6	5.99	5.14	4.76	4.53	4.39	4.28	4.21	4.15	4.10	4.06	4.00	3.94	3.87	3.84	3.81	3.77	3.74	3.70	3.67
7	5.59	4.74	4.35	4.12	3.97	3.87	3.79	3.73	3.68	3.64	3.57	3.51	3.44	3.41	3.38	3.34	3.30	3.27	3.23
8	5.32	4.46	4.07	3.84	3.69	3.58	3.50	3.44	3.39	3.35	3.28	3.22	3.15	3.12	3.08	3.04	3.01	2.97	2.93
9	5.12	4.26	3.86	3.63	3.48	3.37	3.29	3.23	3.18	3.14	3.07	3.01	2.94	2.90	2.86	2.83	2.79	2.75	2.71
10	4.96	4.10	3.71	3.48	3.33	3.22	3.14	3.07	3.02	2.98	2.91	2.85	2.77	2.74	2.70	2.66	2.62	2.58	2.54
11	4.84	3.98	3.59	3.36	3.20	3.09	3.01	2.95	2.90	2.85	2.79	2.72	2.65	2.61	2.57	2.53	2.49	2.45	2.40
12	4.75	3.89	3.49	3.26	3.11	3.00	2.91	2.85	2.80	2.75	2.69	2.62	2.54	2.51	2.47	2.43	2.38	2.34	2.30
13	4.67	3.81	3.41	3.18	3.03	2.92	2.83	2.77	2.71	2.67	2.60	2.53	2.46	2.42	2.38	2.34	2.30	2.25	2.21
14	4.60	3.74	3.34	3.11	2.96	2.85	2.76	2.70	2.65	2.60	2.53	2.46	2.39	2.35	2.31	2.27	2.22	2.18	2.13
15	4.54	3.68	3.29	3.06	2.90	2.79	2.71	2.64	2.59	2.54	2.48	2.40	2.33	2.29	2.25	2.20	2.16	2.11	2.07
16	4.49	3.63	3.24	3.01	2.85	2.74	2.66	2.59	2.54	2.49	2.42	2.35	2.28	2.24	2.19	2.15	2.11	2.06	2.01
17	4.45	3.59	3.20	2.96	2.81	2.70	2.61	2.55	2.49	2.45	2.38	2.31	2.23	2.19	2.15	2.10	2.06	2.01	1.96
18	4.41	3.55	3.16	2.93	2.77	2.66	2.58	2.51	2.46	2.41	2.34	2.27	2.19	2.15	2.11	2.06	2.02	1.97	1.92
19	4.38	3.52	3.13	2.90	2.74	2.63	2.54	2.48	2.42	2.38	2.31	2.23	2.16	2.11	2.07	2.03	1.98	1.93	1.88
20	4.35	3.49	3.10	2.87	2.71	2.60	2.51	2.45	2.39	2.35	2.28	2.20	2.12	2.08	2.04	1.99	1.95	1.90	1.84
21	4.32	3.47	3.07	2.84	2.68	2.57	2.49	2.42	2.37	2.32	2.25	2.18	2.10	2.05	2.01	1.96	1.92	1.87	1.81
22	4.30	3.44	3.05	2.82	2.66	2.55	2.46	2.40	2.34	2.30	2.23	2.15	2.07	2.03	1.98	1.94	1.89	1.84	1.78
23	4.28	3.42	3.03	2.80	2.64	2.53	2.44	2.37	2.32	2.27	2.20	2.13	2.05	2.01	1.96	1.91	1.86	1.81	1.76
24	4.26	3.40	3.01	2.78	2.62	2.51	2.42	2.36	2.30	2.25	2.18	2.11	2.03	1.98	1.94	1.89	1.84	1.79	1.73
25	4.24	3.39	2.99	2.76	2.60	2.49	2.40	2.34	2.28	2.24	2.16	2.09	2.01	1.96	1.92	1.87	1.82	1.77	1.71
26	4.23	3.37	2.98	2.74	2.59	2.47	2.39	2.32	2.27	2.22	2.15	2.07	1.99	1.95	1.90	1.85	1.80	1.75	1.69
27	4.21	3.35	2.96	2.73	2.57	2.46	2.37	2.31	2.25	2.20	2.13	2.06	1.97	1.93	1.88	1.84	1.79	1.73	1.67
28	4.20	3.34	2.95	2.71	2.56	2.45	2.36	2.29	2.24	2.19	2.12	2.04	1.96	1.91	1.87	1.82	1.77	1.71	1.65
29	4.18	3.33	2.93	2.70	2.55	2.43	2.35	2.28	2.22	2.18	2.10	2.03	1.94	1.90	1.85	1.81	1.75	1.70	1.64
30	4.17	3.32	2.92	2.69	2.53	2.42	2.33	2.27	2.21	2.16	2.09	2.01	1.93	1.89	1.84	1.79	1.74	1.68	1.62
40	4.08	3.23	2.84	2.61	2.45	2.34	2.25	2.18	2.12	2.08	2.00	1.92	1.84	1.79	1.74	1.69	1.64	1.58	1.51
60	4.00	3.15	2.76	2.53	2.37	2.25	2.17	2.10	2.04	1.99	1.92	1.84	1.75	1.70	1.65	1.59	1.53	1.47	1.39
120	3.92	3.07	2.68	2.45	2.29	2.17	2.09	2.02	1.96	1.91	1.83	1.75	1.66	1.61	1.55	1.50	1.43	1.35	1.25
∞	3.84	3.00	2.60	2.37	2.21	2.10	2.01	1.94	1.88	1.83	1.75	1.67	1.57	1.52	1.46	1.39	1.32	1.22	1.00

Illustration: The value that bounds a 5% right-tail area under the $F_{(5,6)}$ distribution is 4.39.

TABLE A.5
The F Distribution (Continued)

TABLE A.5b
Upper 2.5% Points (0.975 Fractiles)

n_2 \ n_1	1	2	3	4	5	6	7	8	9	10	12	15	20	24	30	40	60	120	∞
1	647.8	799.5	864.2	899.6	921.8	937.1	948.2	956.7	963.3	968.6	976.7	984.9	993.1	997.2	1001	1006	1010	1014	1018
2	38.51	39.00	39.17	39.25	39.30	39.33	39.36	39.37	39.39	39.40	39.41	39.43	39.45	39.46	39.46	39.47	39.48	39.49	39.50
3	17.44	16.04	15.44	15.10	14.88	14.73	14.62	14.54	14.47	14.42	14.34	14.25	14.17	14.12	14.08	14.04	13.99	13.95	13.90
4	12.22	10.65	9.98	9.60	9.36	9.20	9.07	8.98	8.90	8.84	8.75	8.66	8.56	8.51	8.46	8.41	8.36	8.31	8.26
5	10.01	8.43	7.76	7.39	7.15	6.98	6.85	6.76	6.68	6.62	6.52	6.43	6.33	6.28	6.23	6.18	6.12	6.07	6.02
6	8.81	7.26	6.60	6.23	5.99	5.82	5.70	5.60	5.52	5.46	5.37	5.27	5.17	5.12	5.07	5.01	4.96	4.90	4.85
7	8.07	6.54	5.89	5.52	5.29	5.12	4.99	4.90	4.82	4.76	4.67	4.57	4.47	4.42	4.36	4.31	4.25	4.20	4.14
8	7.57	6.06	5.42	5.05	4.82	4.65	4.53	4.43	4.36	4.30	4.20	4.10	4.00	3.95	3.89	3.84	3.78	3.73	3.67
9	7.21	5.71	5.08	4.72	4.48	4.32	4.20	4.10	4.03	3.96	3.87	3.77	3.67	3.61	3.56	3.51	3.45	3.39	3.33
10	6.94	5.46	4.83	4.47	4.24	4.07	3.95	3.85	3.78	3.72	3.62	3.52	3.42	3.37	3.31	3.26	3.20	3.14	3.08
11	6.72	5.26	4.63	4.28	4.04	3.88	3.76	3.66	3.59	3.53	3.43	3.33	3.23	3.17	3.12	3.06	3.00	2.94	2.88
12	6.55	5.10	4.47	4.12	3.89	3.73	3.61	3.51	3.44	3.37	3.28	3.18	3.07	3.02	2.96	2.91	2.85	2.79	2.72
13	6.41	4.97	4.35	4.00	3.77	3.60	3.48	3.39	3.31	3.25	3.15	3.05	2.95	2.89	2.84	2.78	2.72	2.66	2.60
14	6.30	4.86	4.24	3.89	3.66	3.50	3.38	3.29	3.21	3.15	3.05	2.95	2.84	2.79	2.73	2.67	2.61	2.55	2.49
15	6.20	4.77	4.15	3.80	3.58	3.41	3.29	3.20	3.12	3.06	2.96	2.86	2.76	2.70	2.64	2.59	2.52	2.46	2.40
16	6.12	4.69	4.08	3.73	3.50	3.34	3.22	3.12	3.05	2.99	2.89	2.79	2.68	2.63	2.57	2.51	2.45	2.38	2.32
17	6.04	4.62	4.01	3.66	3.44	3.28	3.16	3.06	2.98	2.92	2.82	2.72	2.62	2.56	2.50	2.44	2.38	2.32	2.25
18	5.98	4.56	3.95	3.61	3.38	3.22	3.10	3.01	2.93	2.87	2.77	2.67	2.56	2.50	2.44	2.38	2.32	2.26	2.19
19	5.92	4.51	3.90	3.56	3.33	3.17	3.05	2.96	2.88	2.82	2.72	2.62	2.51	2.45	2.39	2.33	2.27	2.20	2.13
20	5.87	4.46	3.86	3.51	3.29	3.13	3.01	2.91	2.84	2.77	2.68	2.57	2.46	2.41	2.35	2.29	2.22	2.16	2.09
21	5.83	4.42	3.82	3.48	3.25	3.09	2.97	2.87	2.80	2.73	2.64	2.53	2.42	2.37	2.31	2.25	2.18	2.11	2.04
22	5.79	4.38	3.78	3.44	3.22	3.05	2.93	2.84	2.76	2.70	2.60	2.50	2.39	2.33	2.27	2.21	2.14	2.08	2.00
23	5.75	4.35	3.75	3.41	3.18	3.02	2.90	2.81	2.73	2.67	2.57	2.47	2.36	2.30	2.24	2.18	2.11	2.04	1.97
24	5.72	4.32	3.72	3.38	3.15	2.99	2.87	2.78	2.70	2.64	2.54	2.44	2.33	2.27	2.21	2.15	2.08	2.01	1.94
25	5.69	4.29	3.69	3.35	3.13	2.97	2.85	2.75	2.68	2.61	2.51	2.41	2.30	2.24	2.18	2.12	2.05	1.98	1.91
26	5.66	4.27	3.67	3.33	3.10	2.94	2.82	2.73	2.65	2.59	2.49	2.39	2.28	2.22	2.16	2.09	2.03	1.95	1.88
27	5.63	4.24	3.65	3.31	3.08	2.92	2.80	2.71	2.63	2.57	2.47	2.36	2.25	2.19	2.13	2.07	2.00	1.93	1.85
28	5.61	4.22	3.63	3.29	3.06	2.90	2.78	2.69	2.61	2.55	2.45	2.34	2.23	2.17	2.11	2.05	1.98	1.91	1.83
29	5.59	4.20	3.61	3.27	3.04	2.88	2.76	2.67	2.59	2.53	2.43	2.32	2.21	2.15	2.09	2.03	1.96	1.89	1.81
30	5.57	4.18	3.59	3.25	3.03	2.87	2.75	2.65	2.57	2.51	2.41	2.31	2.20	2.14	2.07	2.01	1.94	1.87	1.79
40	5.42	4.05	3.46	3.13	2.90	2.74	2.62	2.53	2.45	2.39	2.29	2.18	2.07	2.01	1.94	1.88	1.80	1.72	1.64
60	5.29	3.93	3.34	3.01	2.79	2.63	2.51	2.41	2.33	2.27	2.17	2.06	1.94	1.88	1.82	1.74	1.67	1.58	1.48
120	5.15	3.80	3.23	2.89	2.67	2.52	2.39	2.30	2.22	2.16	2.05	1.94	1.82	1.76	1.69	1.61	1.53	1.43	1.31
∞	5.02	3.69	3.12	2.79	2.57	2.41	2.29	2.19	2.11	2.05	1.94	1.83	1.71	1.64	1.57	1.48	1.39	1.27	1.00

Illustration: The value that bounds a 2.5% right-tail area under the $F_{(5,6)}$ distribution is 5.99.

TABLE A.5
The F Distribution (Continued)

TABLE A.5c
Upper 1% Points (0.99 Fractiles)

n_2 \ n_1	1	2	3	4	5	6	7	8	9	10	12	15	20	24	30	40	60	120	∞
1	4052	4999.5	5403	5625	5764	5859	5928	5981	6022	6056	6106	6157	6209	6235	6261	6287	6313	6339	6366
2	98.50	99.00	99.17	99.25	99.30	99.33	99.36	99.37	99.39	99.40	99.42	99.43	99.45	99.46	99.47	99.47	99.48	99.49	99.50
3	34.12	30.82	29.46	28.71	28.24	27.91	27.67	27.49	27.35	27.23	27.05	26.87	26.69	26.60	26.50	26.41	26.32	26.22	26.13
4	21.20	18.00	16.69	15.98	15.52	15.21	14.98	14.80	14.66	14.55	14.37	14.20	14.02	13.93	13.84	13.75	13.65	13.56	13.46
5	16.26	13.27	12.06	11.39	10.97	10.67	10.46	10.29	10.16	10.05	9.89	9.72	9.55	9.47	9.38	9.29	9.20	9.11	9.02
6	13.75	10.92	9.78	9.15	8.75	8.47	8.26	8.10	7.98	7.87	7.72	7.56	7.40	7.31	7.23	7.14	7.06	6.97	6.88
7	12.25	9.55	8.45	7.85	7.46	7.19	6.99	6.84	6.72	6.62	6.47	6.31	6.16	6.07	5.99	5.91	5.82	5.74	5.65
8	11.26	8.65	7.59	7.01	6.63	6.37	6.18	6.03	5.91	5.81	5.67	5.52	5.36	5.28	5.20	5.12	5.03	4.95	4.86
9	10.56	8.02	6.99	6.42	6.06	5.80	5.61	5.47	5.35	5.26	5.11	4.96	4.81	4.73	4.65	4.57	4.48	4.40	4.31
10	10.04	7.56	6.55	5.99	5.64	5.39	5.20	5.06	4.94	4.85	4.71	4.56	4.41	4.33	4.25	4.17	4.08	4.00	3.91
11	9.65	7.21	6.22	5.67	5.32	5.07	4.89	4.74	4.63	4.54	4.40	4.25	4.10	4.02	3.94	3.86	3.78	3.69	3.60
12	9.33	6.93	5.95	5.41	5.06	4.82	4.64	4.50	4.39	4.30	4.16	4.01	3.86	3.78	3.70	3.62	3.54	3.45	3.36
13	9.07	6.70	5.74	5.21	4.86	4.62	4.44	4.30	4.19	4.10	3.96	3.82	3.66	3.59	3.51	3.43	3.34	3.25	3.17
14	8.86	6.51	5.56	5.04	4.69	4.46	4.28	4.14	4.03	3.94	3.80	3.66	3.51	3.43	3.35	3.27	3.18	3.09	3.00
15	8.68	6.36	5.42	4.89	4.56	4.32	4.14	4.00	3.89	3.80	3.67	3.52	3.37	3.29	3.21	3.13	3.05	2.96	2.87
16	8.53	6.23	5.29	4.77	4.44	4.20	4.03	3.89	3.78	3.69	3.55	3.41	3.26	3.18	3.10	3.02	2.93	2.84	2.75
17	8.40	6.11	5.18	4.67	4.34	4.10	3.93	3.79	3.68	3.59	3.46	3.31	3.16	3.08	3.00	2.92	2.83	2.75	2.65
18	8.29	6.01	5.09	4.58	4.25	4.01	3.84	3.71	3.60	3.51	3.37	3.23	3.08	3.00	2.92	2.84	2.75	2.66	2.57
19	8.18	5.93	5.01	4.50	4.17	3.94	3.77	3.63	3.52	3.43	3.30	3.15	3.00	2.92	2.84	2.76	2.67	2.58	2.49
20	8.10	5.85	4.94	4.43	4.10	3.87	3.70	3.56	3.46	3.37	3.23	3.09	2.94	2.86	2.78	2.69	2.61	2.52	2.42
21	8.02	5.78	4.87	4.37	4.04	3.81	3.64	3.51	3.40	3.31	3.17	3.03	2.88	2.80	2.72	2.64	2.55	2.46	2.36
22	7.95	5.72	4.82	4.31	3.99	3.76	3.59	3.45	3.35	3.26	3.12	2.98	2.83	2.75	2.67	2.58	2.50	2.40	2.31
23	7.88	5.66	4.76	4.26	3.94	3.71	3.54	3.41	3.30	3.21	3.07	2.93	2.78	2.70	2.62	2.54	2.45	2.35	2.26
24	7.82	5.61	4.72	4.22	3.90	3.67	3.50	3.36	3.26	3.17	3.03	2.89	2.74	2.66	2.58	2.49	2.40	2.31	2.21
25	7.77	5.57	4.68	4.18	3.85	3.63	3.46	3.32	3.22	3.13	2.99	2.85	2.70	2.62	2.54	2.45	2.36	2.27	2.17
26	7.72	5.53	4.64	4.14	3.82	3.59	3.42	3.29	3.18	3.09	2.96	2.81	2.66	2.58	2.50	2.42	2.33	2.23	2.13
27	7.68	5.49	4.60	4.11	3.78	3.56	3.39	3.26	3.15	3.06	2.93	2.78	2.63	2.55	2.47	2.38	2.29	2.20	2.10
28	7.64	5.45	4.57	4.07	3.75	3.53	3.36	3.23	3.12	3.03	2.90	2.75	2.60	2.52	2.44	2.35	2.26	2.17	2.06
29	7.60	5.42	4.54	4.04	3.73	3.50	3.33	3.20	3.09	3.00	2.87	2.73	2.57	2.49	2.41	2.33	2.23	2.14	2.03
30	7.56	5.39	4.51	4.02	3.70	3.47	3.30	3.17	3.07	2.98	2.84	2.70	2.55	2.47	2.39	2.30	2.21	2.11	2.01
40	7.31	5.18	4.31	3.83	3.51	3.29	3.12	2.99	2.89	2.80	2.66	2.52	2.37	2.29	2.20	2.11	2.02	1.92	1.80
60	7.08	4.98	4.13	3.65	3.34	3.12	2.95	2.82	2.72	2.63	2.50	2.35	2.20	2.12	2.03	1.94	1.84	1.73	1.60
120	6.85	4.79	3.95	3.48	3.17	2.96	2.79	2.66	2.56	2.47	2.34	2.19	2.03	1.95	1.86	1.76	1.66	1.53	1.38
∞	6.63	4.61	3.78	3.32	3.02	2.80	2.64	2.51	2.41	2.32	2.18	2.04	1.88	1.79	1.70	1.59	1.47	1.32	1.00

Illustration: The value that bounds a 1% right-tail area under the $F^{(5,6)}$ distribution is 8.75.

Source: Table 18, in E. S. Pearson and H. O. Hartley, *Biometrika Tables for Statisticians,* Vol. I, published for the Biometrika Trustees at the University Press, Cambridge. Reprinted by permission of the Biometrika Trustees.

TABLE A.6
Critical Values of *r* in the Runs Test

Given in the bodies of Table A.6a and Table A.6b are various critical values of *r* for various values of n_1 and n_2. For the one-sample runs test, any value of *r* which is equal to or smaller than that shown in Table A.6a or equal to or larger than that shown in Table A.6b is significant at the A.6b .05 level.

TABLE A.6a

n_1 \ n_2	2	3	4	5	6	7	8	9	10	11	12	13	14	15	16	17	18	19	20
2											2	2	2	2	2	2	2	2	2
3					2	2	2	2	2	2	2	2	2	3	3	3	3	3	3
4				2	2	2	3	3	3	3	3	3	3	3	4	4	4	4	4
5			2	2	3	3	3	3	3	4	4	4	4	4	4	4	5	5	5
6		2	2	3	3	3	3	4	4	4	4	5	5	5	5	5	5	6	6
7		2	2	3	3	3	4	4	5	5	5	5	5	6	6	6	6	6	6
8		2	3	3	3	4	4	5	5	5	6	6	6	6	6	7	7	7	7
9		2	3	3	4	4	5	5	5	6	6	6	7	7	7	7	8	8	8
10		2	3	3	4	5	5	5	6	6	7	7	7	7	8	8	8	8	9
11		2	3	4	4	5	5	6	6	7	7	7	8	8	8	9	9	9	9
12	2	2	3	4	4	5	6	6	7	7	7	8	8	8	9	9	9	10	10
13	2	2	3	4	5	5	6	6	7	7	8	8	9	9	9	10	10	10	10
14	2	2	3	4	5	5	6	7	7	8	8	9	9	9	10	10	10	11	11
15	2	3	3	4	5	6	6	7	7	8	8	9	9	10	10	11	11	11	12
16	2	3	4	4	5	6	6	7	8	8	9	9	10	10	11	11	11	12	12
17	2	3	4	4	5	6	7	7	8	9	9	10	10	11	11	11	12	12	13
18	2	3	4	5	5	6	7	8	8	9	9	10	10	11	11	12	12	13	13
19	2	3	4	5	6	6	7	8	8	9	10	10	11	11	12	12	13	13	13
20	2	3	4	5	6	6	7	8	9	9	10	10	11	12	12	13	13	13	14

TABLE A.6
Critical Values of *r* in the Runs Test (Continued)

TABLE A.6b

n_1＼n_2	2	3	4	5	6	7	8	9	10	11	12	13	14	15	16	17	18	19	20
2																			
3																			
4				9	9														
5			9	10	10	11	11												
6			9	10	11	12	12	13	13	13	13								
7				11	12	13	13	14	14	14	14	15	15	15					
8				11	12	13	14	14	15	15	16	16	16	16	17	17	17	17	17
9					13	14	14	15	16	16	16	17	17	18	18	18	18	18	18
10					13	14	15	16	16	17	17	18	18	18	19	19	19	20	20
11					13	14	15	16	17	17	18	19	19	19	20	20	20	21	21
12					13	14	16	16	17	18	19	19	20	20	21	21	21	22	22
13						15	16	17	18	19	19	20	20	21	21	22	22	23	23
14						15	16	17	18	19	20	20	21	22	22	23	23	23	24
15						15	16	18	18	19	20	21	22	22	23	23	24	24	25
16							17	18	19	20	21	21	22	23	23	24	25	25	25
17							17	18	19	20	21	22	23	23	24	25	25	26	26
18							17	18	19	20	21	22	23	24	25	25	26	26	27
19							17	18	20	21	22	23	23	24	25	26	26	27	27
20							17	18	20	21	22	23	24	25	25	26	27	27	28

Source: Adapted from Frieda S. Swed and C. Eisenhart, "Tables for testing randomness of grouping in a sequence of alternatives," *Ann. Math. Statist.*, 1943, *14*, 83–86. Reprinted with the kind permission of the authors and publisher.

TABLE A.7
Critical Values of $D(N)$ in the Kolmogorov-Smirnov
One-Sample Test

Sample size (N)	Level of significance for $D(N)=\text{maximum}\,\lvert E(x)\text{-}O(x)\rvert$				
	0.20	0.15	0.10	0.05	0.01
1	0.900	0.925	0.950	0.975	0.995
2	0.684	0.726	0.776	0.842	0.929
3	0.565	0.597	0.642	0.708	0.828
4	0.494	0.525	0.564	0.624	0.733
5	0.446	0.474	0.510	0.565	0.669
6	0.410	0.436	0.470	0.521	0.618
7	0.381	0.405	0.438	0.486	0.577
8	0.358	0.381	0.411	0.457	0.543
9	0.339	0.360	0.388	0.432	0.514
10	0.322	0.342	0.368	0.410	0.490
11	0.307	0.326	0.352	0.391	0.468
12	0.295	0.313	0.338	0.375	0.450
13	0.284	0.302	0.325	0.361	0.433
14	0.274	0.292	0.314	0.349	0.418
15	0.266	0.283	0.304	0.338	0.404
16	0.258	0.274	0.295	0.328	0.392
17	0.250	0.266	0.286	0.318	0.381
18	0.244	0.259	0.278	0.309	0.371
19	0.237	0.252	0.272	0.301	0.363
20	0.231	0.246	0.264	0.294	0.356
25	0.210	0.220	0.240	0.270	0.320
30	0.190	0.200	0.220	0.240	0.290
35	0.180	0.190	0.210	0.230	0.270
Over 35	$\dfrac{1.07}{\sqrt{N}}$	$\dfrac{1.14}{\sqrt{N}}$	$\dfrac{1.22}{\sqrt{N}}$	$\dfrac{1.36}{\sqrt{N}}$	$\dfrac{1.63}{\sqrt{N}}$

Source: Adapted from F. J. Massey, Jr., "The Kolmogorov-Smirnov test for goodness of fit," *Amer. Statist. Ass.*, 1951, *46*, 70. Reprinted with the kind permission of the author and publisher.

TABLE A.8
Quantiles of the Mann-Whitney Test Statistic

n_A	p	$n_B=2$	3	4	5	6	7	8	9	10	11	12	13	14	15	16	17	18	19	20
2	0.001																			
	0.005																		1	1
	0.01												1	1	1	1	1	1	2	2
	0.025							1	1	1	1	2	2	2	2	2	3	3	3	3
	0.05				1	1	1	2	2	2	2	3	3	4	4	4	4	5	5	5
	0.10		1	1	2	2	2	3	3	4	4	5	5	6	6	6	7	7	8	8
3	0.001																1	1	1	1
	0.005								1	1	1	2	2	2	3	3	3	3	4	4
	0.01						1	1	2	2	2	3	3	3	4	4	5	5	5	6
	0.025				1	2	2	3	3	4	4	5	5	6	6	7	7	8	8	9
	0.05		1	1	2	3	3	4	5	5	6	6	7	8	8	9	10	10	11	12
	0.10	1	2	2	3	4	5	6	6	7	8	9	10	11	11	12	13	14	15	16
4	0.001									1	1	1	2	2	2	3	3	4	4	4
	0.005					1	1	2	2	3	3	4	4	5	6	6	7	7	8	9
	0.01				1	2	2	3	4	4	5	6	6	7	8	8	9	10	10	11
	0.025			1	2	3	4	5	5	6	7	8	9	10	11	12	12	13	14	15
	0.05		1	2	3	4	5	6	7	8	9	10	11	12	13	15	16	17	18	19
	0.10	1	2	4	5	6	7	8	10	11	12	13	14	16	17	18	19	21	22	23

Note: The entries in this table are the quantiles t_p of the Mann-Whitney test statistic T_A, for selected values of p. Note that $P(T_A < t_p) \leq p$. Upper quantiles may be found from the equation

$$t_{1-p} = n_A n_B - t_p$$

Critical regions correspond to values less than (or greater than) but not including the appropriate quantile.

Source: Adapted from Table 1, in L. R. Verdooren "Extended tables of critical values for Wilcoxon's test statistic," *Biometrika, 50,* 177–86. Reprinted by permission of the Biometrika Trustees.

TABLE A.8
Quantiles of the Mann-Whitney Test Statistic (Continued)

n_A	p	$n_B=2$	3	4	5	6	7	8	9	10	11	12	13	14	15	16	17	18	19	20
5	0.001							1	2	2	3	3	4	4	5	6	6	7	8	8
	0.005				1	2	2	3	4	5	6	7	8	8	9	10	11	12	13	14
	0.01			1	2	3	4	5	6	7	8	9	10	11	12	13	14	15	16	17
	0.025		1	2	3	4	6	7	8	9	10	12	13	14	15	16	18	19	20	21
	0.05	1	2	3	5	6	7	9	10	12	13	14	16	17	19	20	21	23	24	26
	0.10	2	3	5	6	8	9	11	13	14	16	18	19	21	23	24	26	28	29	31
6	0.001							2	3	4	5	5	6	7	8	9	10	11	12	13
	0.005				2	3	4	5	6	7	8	10	11	12	13	14	16	17	18	19
	0.01			1	3	4	5	7	8	9	10	12	13	14	16	17	19	20	21	23
	0.025		2	2	4	6	7	9	11	12	14	15	17	18	20	22	23	25	26	28
	0.05	1	3	4	6	8	9	11	13	15	17	18	20	22	24	26	27	29	31	33
	0.10	2	4	6	8	10	12	14	16	18	20	22	24	26	28	30	32	35	37	39
7	0.001						2	3	4	6	7	8	9	10	11	12	14	15	16	17
	0.005				2	4	5	7	8	10	11	13	14	16	17	19	20	22	23	25
	0.01			2	4	5	7	8	10	12	13	15	17	18	20	22	24	25	27	29
	0.025		2	4	6	7	9	11	13	15	17	19	21	23	25	27	29	31	33	35
	0.05	1	3	5	7	9	12	14	16	18	20	22	25	27	29	31	34	36	38	40
	0.10	3	5	7	9	12	14	17	19	22	24	27	29	32	34	37	39	42	44	47
8	0.001				1	2	3	5	6	7	9	10	12	13	15	16	18	19	21	22
	0.005			1	3	5	7	8	10	12	14	16	18	19	21	23	25	27	29	31
	0.01		1	3	5	7	8	10	12	14	16	18	21	23	25	27	29	31	33	35
	0.025		3	5	7	9	11	14	16	18	20	23	25	27	30	32	35	37	39	42
	0.05	1	4	6	9	11	14	16	19	21	24	27	29	32	34	37	40	42	45	48
	0.10	3	6	8	11	14	17	20	23	25	28	31	34	37	40	43	46	49	52	55

TABLE A.8
Quantiles of the Mann-Whitney Test Statistic (Continued)

n_A	p	$n_B=2$	3	4	5	6	7	8	9	10	11	12	13	14	15	16	17	18	19	20
9	0.001				2	3	4	6	8	9	11	13	15	16	18	20	22	24	26	27
	0.005		1	2	4	6	8	10	12	14	17	19	21	23	25	28	30	32	34	37
	0.01		2	4	6	8	10	12	15	17	19	22	24	27	29	32	34	37	39	41
	0.025	1	3	5	8	11	13	16	18	21	24	27	29	32	35	38	40	43	46	49
	0.05	2	5	7	10	13	16	19	22	25	28	31	34	37	40	43	46	49	52	55
	0.10	3	6	10	13	16	19	23	26	29	32	36	39	42	46	49	53	56	59	63
10	0.001			1	2	4	6	7	9	11	13	15	18	20	22	24	26	28	30	33
	0.005		1	3	5	7	10	12	14	17	19	22	25	27	30	32	35	38	40	43
	0.01		2	4	7	9	12	14	17	20	23	25	28	31	34	37	39	42	45	48
	0.025	1	4	6	9	12	15	18	21	24	27	30	34	37	40	43	46	49	53	56
	0.05	2	5	8	12	15	18	21	25	28	32	35	38	42	45	49	52	56	59	63
	0.10	4	7	11	14	18	22	25	29	33	37	40	44	48	52	55	59	63	67	71
11	0.001			1	3	5	7	9	11	13	16	18	21	23	25	28	30	33	35	38
	0.005		1	3	6	8	11	14	17	19	22	25	28	31	34	37	40	43	46	49
	0.01		2	5	8	10	13	16	19	23	26	29	32	35	38	42	45	48	51	54
	0.025	1	4	7	10	14	17	20	24	27	31	34	38	41	45	48	52	56	59	63
	0.05	2	6	9	13	17	20	24	28	32	35	39	43	47	51	55	58	62	66	70
	0.10	4	8	12	16	20	24	28	32	37	41	45	49	53	58	62	66	70	74	79
12	0.001			1	3	5	8	10	13	15	18	21	24	26	29	32	35	38	41	43
	0.005		2	4	7	10	13	16	19	22	25	28	32	35	38	42	45	48	52	55
	0.01		3	6	9	12	15	18	22	25	29	32	36	39	43	47	50	54	57	61
	0.025	2	5	8	12	15	19	23	27	30	34	38	42	46	50	54	58	62	66	70
	0.05	3	6	10	14	18	22	27	31	35	39	43	48	52	56	61	65	69	73	78
	0.10	5	9	13	18	22	27	31	36	40	45	50	54	59	64	68	73	78	82	87

TABLE A.8
Quantiles of the Mann-Whitney Test Statistic (Continued)

n_A	p	$n_B=2$	3	4	5	6	7	8	9	10	11	12	13	14	15	16	17	18	19	20
13	0.001			2	4	6	9	12	15	18	21	24	27	30	33	36	39	43	46	49
	0.005		2	4	8	11	14	18	21	25	28	32	35	39	43	46	50	54	58	61
	0.01	1	3	6	10	13	17	21	24	28	32	36	40	44	48	52	56	60	64	68
	0.025	2	5	9	13	17	21	25	29	34	38	42	46	51	55	60	64	68	73	77
	0.05	3	7	11	16	20	25	29	34	38	43	48	52	57	62	66	71	76	81	85
	0.10	5	10	14	19	24	29	34	39	44	49	54	59	64	69	75	80	85	90	95
14	0.001			2	4	7	10	13	16	20	23	26	30	33	37	40	44	47	51	55
	0.005		2	5	8	12	16	19	23	27	31	35	39	43	47	51	55	59	64	68
	0.01	1	3	7	11	14	18	23	27	31	35	39	44	48	52	57	61	66	70	74
	0.025	2	6	10	14	18	23	27	32	37	41	46	51	56	60	65	70	75	79	84
	0.05	4	8	12	17	22	27	32	37	42	47	52	57	62	67	72	78	83	88	93
	0.10	5	11	16	21	26	32	37	42	48	53	59	64	70	75	81	86	92	98	103
15	0.001			2	5	8	11	15	18	22	25	29	33	37	41	44	48	52	56	60
	0.005		3	6	9	13	17	21	25	30	34	38	43	47	52	56	61	65	70	74
	0.01	1	4	8	12	16	20	25	29	34	38	43	48	52	57	62	67	71	76	81
	0.025	2	6	11	15	20	25	30	35	40	45	50	55	60	65	71	76	81	86	91
	0.05	4	8	13	19	24	29	34	40	45	51	56	62	67	73	78	84	89	95	101
	0.10	6	11	17	23	28	34	40	46	52	58	64	69	75	81	87	93	99	105	111
16	0.001			3	6	9	12	16	20	24	28	32	36	40	44	49	53	57	61	66
	0.005		3	6	10	14	19	23	28	32	37	42	46	51	56	61	66	71	75	80
	0.01	1	4	8	13	17	22	27	32	37	42	47	52	57	62	67	72	77	83	88
	0.025	2	7	12	16	22	27	32	38	43	48	54	60	65	71	76	82	87	93	99
	0.05	4	9	15	20	26	31	37	43	49	55	61	66	72	78	84	90	96	102	108
	0.10	6	12	18	24	30	37	43	49	55	62	68	75	81	87	94	100	107	113	120

TABLE A.8
Quantiles of the Mann-Whitney Test Statistic (Continued)

n_A	p	$n_B=2$	3	4	5	6	7	8	9	10	11	12	13	14	15	16	17	18	19	20
17	0.001		1	3	6	10	14	18	22	26	30	35	39	44	48	53	58	62	67	71
	0.005		3	7	11	16	20	25	30	35	40	45	50	55	61	66	71	76	82	87
	0.01	1	5	9	14	19	24	29	34	39	45	50	56	61	67	72	78	83	89	94
	0.025	3	7	12	18	23	29	35	40	46	52	58	64	70	76	82	88	94	100	106
	0.05	4	10	16	21	27	34	40	46	52	58	65	71	78	84	90	97	103	110	116
	0.10	7	13	19	26	32	39	46	53	59	66	73	80	86	93	100	107	114	121	128
18	0.001		1	4	7	11	15	19	24	28	33	38	43	47	52	57	62	67	72	77
	0.005		3	7	12	17	22	27	32	38	43	48	54	59	65	71	76	82	88	93
	0.01	1	5	10	15	20	25	31	37	42	48	54	60	66	71	77	83	89	95	101
	0.025	3	8	13	19	25	31	37	43	49	56	62	68	75	81	87	94	100	107	113
	0.05	5	10	17	23	29	36	42	49	56	62	69	76	83	89	96	103	110	117	124
	0.10	7	14	21	28	35	42	49	56	63	70	78	85	92	99	107	114	121	129	136
19	0.001		1	4	8	12	16	21	26	30	35	41	46	51	56	61	67	72	78	83
	0.005		4	8	13	18	23	29	34	40	46	52	58	64	70	75	82	88	94	100
	0.01	2	5	10	16	21	27	33	39	45	51	57	64	70	76	83	89	95	102	108
	0.025	3	8	14	20	26	33	39	46	53	59	66	73	79	86	93	100	107	114	120
	0.05	5	11	18	24	31	38	45	52	59	66	73	81	88	95	102	110	117	124	131
	0.10	8	15	22	29	37	44	52	59	67	74	82	90	98	105	113	121	129	136	144
20	0.001		1	4	8	13	17	22	27	33	38	43	49	55	60	66	71	77	83	89
	0.005		4	9	14	19	25	31	37	43	49	55	61	68	74	80	87	93	100	106
	0.01	2	6	11	17	23	29	35	41	48	54	61	68	74	81	88	94	101	108	115
	0.025	3	9	15	21	28	35	42	49	56	63	70	77	84	91	99	106	113	120	128
	0.05	5	12	19	26	33	40	48	55	63	70	78	85	93	101	108	116	124	131	139
	0.10	8	16	23	31	39	47	55	63	71	79	87	95	103	111	120	128	136	144	152

TABLE A.9
Critical Values of the Kruskal-Wallis Test Statistic for Three
Samples and Small Sample Sizes[a]

n_1	n_2	n_3	Critical Value	α	n_1	n_2	n_3	Critical Value	α
2	1	1	2.7000	0.500	4	2	2	6.0000	0.014
2	2	1	3.6000	0.200				5.3333	0.033
2	2	2	4.5714	0.067				5.1250	0.052
			3.7143	0.200				4.4583	0.100
								4.1667	0.105
3	1	1	3.2000	0.300					
3	2	1	4.2857	0.100	4	3	1	5.8333	0.021
			3.8571	0.133				5.2083	0.050
								5.0000	0.057
3	2	2	5.3572	0.029				4.0556	0.093
			4.7143	0.048				3.8889	0.129
			4.5000	0.067					
			4.4643	0.105					
					4	3	2	6.4444	0.008
3	3	1	5.1429	0.043				6.3000	0.011
			4.5714	0.100				5.4444	0.046
			4.0000	0.129				5.4000	0.051
								4.5111	0.098
3	3	2	6.2500	0.011				4.4444	0.102
			5.3611	0.032					
			5.1389	0.061					
			4.5556	0.100	4	3	3	6.7455	0.010
			4.2500	0.121				6.7091	0.013
								5.7909	0.046
3	3	3	7.2000	0.004				5.7273	0.050
			6.4889	0.001					
			5.6889	0.029				4.7091	0.092
			5.6000	0.050				4.7000	0.101
			5.0667	0.086					
			4.6222	0.100					
					4	4	1	6.6667	0.010
4	1	1	3.5714	0.200				6.1667	0.022
								4.9667	0.048
4	2	1	4.8214	0.057				4.8667	0.054
			4.5000	0.076				4.1667	0.082
			4.0179	0.114				4.0667	0.102

[a]The null hypothesis may be rejected at the level α if the Kruskal-Wallis test statistic (H), given by Equation (22.11), is *equal to or greater than* the critical value given in the table.

Source: W. H. Kruskal and W. A. Wallis, "Use of ranks in one-criterion variance analysis," *J. Amer. Statist. Ass.*, 1952, 583–621. Reprinted by permission.

TABLE A.9
Critical Values of the Kruskal-Wallis Test Statistic (Continued)

Sample sizes n_1	n_2	n_3	Critical Value	α	Sample sizes n_1	n_2	n_3	Critical Value	α
4	4	2	7.0364	0.006	5	3	2	6.9091	0.009
			6.8727	0.011				6.8281	0.010
			5.4545	0.046				5.2509	0.049
			5.2364	0.052				5.1055	0.052
			4.5545	0.098				4.6509	0.091
			4.4455	0.103				4.4121	0.101
4	4	3	7.1439	0.010	5	3	3	7.0788	0.009
			7.1364	0.011				6.9818	0.011
			5.5985	0.049				5.6485	0.049
			5.5758	0.051				5.5152	0.051
			4.5455	0.099				4.5333	0.097
			4.4773	0.102				4.4121	0.109
4	4	4	7.6538	0.008	5	4	1	6.9545	0.008
			7.5385	0.011				6.8400	0.011
			5.6923	0.049				4.9855	0.044
			5.6538	0.054				4.8600	0.056
			4.6539	0.097				3.9873	0.098
			4.5001	0.104				3.9600	0.102
5	1	1	3.8571	0.143	5	4	2	7.2045	0.009
								7.1182	0.010
5	2	1	5.2500	0.036				5.2727	0.049
			5.0000	0.048				5.2682	0.050
			4.4500	0.071				4.5409	0.098
			4.2000	0.095				4.5182	0.101
			4.0500	0.119					
					5	4	3	7.4449	0.010
5	2	2	6.5333	0.005				7.3949	0.011
			6.1333	0.013				5.6564	0.049
			5.1600	0.034				5.6308	0.050
			5.0400	0.056				4.5487	0.099
			4.3733	0.090				4.5231	0.103
			4.2933	0.112					
					5	4	4	7.7604	0.009
5	3	1	6.4000	0.012				7.7440	0.011
			4.9600	0.048				5.6571	0.049
			4.8711	0.052				5.6176	0.050
			4.0178	0.095				4.6187	0.100
			3.8400	0.123				4.5527	0.102

TABLE A.9
Critical Values of the Kruskal-Wallis Test Statistic (Continued)

n_1	n_2	n_3	Critical Value	α	n_1	n_2	n_3	Critical Value	α
5	5	1	7.3091	0.009				5.6264	0.051
			6.8364	0.011				4.5451	0.100
			5.1273	0.046				4.5363	0.102
			4.9091	0.053					
			4.1091	0.086	5	5	4	7.8229	0.010
			4.0364	0.105				7.7914	0.010
								5.6657	0.049
5	5	2	7.3385	0.010				5.6429	0.050
			7.2692	0.010				4.5229	0.100
			5.3385	0.047				4.5200	0.101
			5.2462	0.051					
			4.6231	0.097	5	5	5	8.0000	0.009
			4.5077	0.100				7.9800	0.010
								5.7800	0.049
5	5	3	7.5780	0.010				5.6600	0.051
			7.5429	0.010				4.5600	0.100
			5.7055	0.046				4.5000	0.102

Sample sizes header spans n_1, n_2, n_3.

TABLE A.10
Critical Values of r_s, the Spearman Rank
Correlation Coefficient

N	Significance level (one-tailed test)	
	0.05	0.01
4	1.000	
5	0.900	1.000
6	0.829	0.943
7	0.714	0.893
8	0.643	0.833
9	0.600	0.783
10	0.564	0.746
12	0.506	0.712
14	0.456	0.645
16	0.425	0.601
18	0.399	0.564
20	0.377	0.534
22	0.359	0.508
24	0.343	0.485
26	0.329	0.465
28	0.317	0.448
30	0.306	0.432

Source: Adapted from E. G. Olds, "Distributions of sums of squares of rank differences for small numbers of individuals," *Ann. Math. Statist.*, 1938, 9, 133–48, and E. G. Olds, "The 5% significance levels for sums of squares of rank differences and a correlation," *Ann. Math. Statist.*, 1949, 20, 117–18. Reprinted with the kind permission of the author and the publisher.

TABLE A.11
Probabilities Associated with Values as Large as Observed Values of *S* in
the Kendall Rank Correlation Coefficient

S	Values of N				S	Values of N		
	4	5	8	9		6	7	10
0	0.625	0.592	0.548	0.540	1	0.500	0.500	0.500
2	0.375	0.408	0.452	0.460	3	0.360	0.386	0.431
4	0.167	0.242	0.360	0.381	5	0.235	0.281	0.364
6	0.042	0.117	0.274	0.306	7	0.136	0.191	0.300
8		0.042	0.199	0.238	9	0.068	0.119	0.242
10		0.0083	0.138	0.179	11	0.028	0.068	0.190
12			0.089	0.130	13	0.0083	0.035	0.146
14			0.054	0.090	15	0.0014	0.015	0.108
16			0.031	0.060	17		0.0054	0.078
18			0.016	0.038	19		0.0014	0.054
20			0.0071	0.022	21		0.00020	0.036
22			0.0028	0.012	23			0.023
24			0.00087	0.0063	25			0.014
26			0.00019	0.0029	27			0.0083
28			0.000025	0.0012	29			0.0046
30				0.00043	31			0.0023
32				0.00012	33			0.0011
34				0.000025	35			0.00047
36				0.0000028	37			0.00018
					39			0.000058
					41			0.000015
					43			0.0000028
					45			0.00000028

Source: Reproduced by permission of the publishers, Charles Griffin & Company Ltd of London and High Wycombe, from *Kendall Rank Correlation Methods*, 4th Edition, 1970.

TABLE A.12
Critical Values of *s* in the Kendall Coefficient
of Concordance

k	N					Additional values for *N* = 3	
	3[a]	4	5	6	7	k	s
Values at the 0.05 level of significance							
3			64.4	103.9	157.3	9	54.0
4		49.5	88.4	143.3	217.0	12	71.9
5		62.6	112.3	182.4	276.2	14	83.8
6		75.7	136.1	221.4	335.2	16	95.8
8	48.1	101.7	183.7	299.0	453.1	18	107.7
10	60.0	127.8	231.2	376.7	571.0		
15	89.8	192.9	349.8	570.5	864.9		
20	119.7	258.0	468.5	764.4	1,158.7		
Values at the 0.01 level of significance							
3			75.6	122.8	185.6	9	75.9
4		61.4	109.3	176.2	265.0	12	103.5
5		80.5	142.8	229.4	343.8	14	121.9
6		99.5	176.1	282.4	422.6	16	140.2
8	66.8	137.4	242.7	388.3	579.9	18	158.6
10	85.1	175.3	309.1	494.0	737.0		
15	131.0	269.8	475.2	758.2	1,129.5		
20	177.0	364.2	641.2	1,022.2	1,521.9		

[a]Notice that additional critical values of *s* for *N* = 3 are given in the righthand column of this table.

Source: Adapted from M. Friedman, "A comparison of alternative tests of significance for the problem of *m* rankings," *Ann. Math. Statist.*, 1940, *11*, 86–92. Reprinted with the kind permission of the author and the publisher.

TABLE A.13
Random Numbers

02210	74243	72156	86376	69839	91080	37535	07012	17386	46293
96728	48767	00659	77549	03130	95774	40313	92411	70850	44301
09347	32715	57093	49490	20602	09302	96276	73874	14263	66795
08369	63862	54640	09896	88634	55245	28734	42887	53430	52905
39198	23832	72291	35735	73716	76410	67487	80109	35775	18835
27517	77887	47527	73649	76648	15453	20051	93733	80556	85564
75894	02212	41179	79483	56216	59854	02573	89249	50159	08301
38732	29814	89966	41027	06644	03397	82327	12035	06243	41735
69089	73579	00778	45042	39753	79361	28555	73078	56023	93661
71322	83386	95924	62434	99576	28139	27519	00634	11028	59363
19436	69841	93368	01286	04894	69708	75215	91160	92473	62784
06943	64103	84630	18357	10967	88088	07670	48683	23625	91100
96480	46486	73089	07658	49353	77539	41441	65997	06452	42767
22834	65593	38437	66538	07659	34608	98775	16628	51715	47443
18280	49162	67958	22213	92601	68027	87750	73747	69741	67218
86858	86385	62461	39740	61211	62569	88819	57291	06872	86891
20696	54652	79155	04441	98457	56789	89349	12494	33318	25034
12435	87413	24931	48804	05945	08935	37608	57732	54573	34534
78539	47935	43256	15621	66918	51576	49223	43651	56406	58072
21718	40457	09787	17893	67062	49095	64374	84405	23296	07372
16389	80510	31943	96249	97519	61140	17983	45660	74613	75757
63564	87931	62171	69143	82181	72119	65148	47538	65944	36005
60030	51368	89023	08953	90004	28047	40819	20013	75056	82044
94723	94240	75435	91942	64760	28545	25929	11173	28824	60996
69060	47103	41664	38553	93845	71406	64455	41890	91262	12081
86377	39492	97052	60613	99650	39880	95068	41834	67114	33314
41409	61129	68406	51897	35459	32674	52673	34473	29725	23900
51580	87925	29266	96769	54724	69920	35490	70276	78565	51406
38851	82946	85521	20889	57527	44663	12738	61955	19594	47465
29052	13998	60023	53341	77246	43957	78541	20639	93202	39033
89479	24323	88751	73896	04635	50245	77744	68829	75176	80904
99511	81431	30488	37456	38377	20137	28708	78518	75239	67727
78982	29056	22678	87064	44214	63635	82765	56803	41565	73119
02134	32773	21664	62559	32833	21459	04239	68938	85726	52696
50215	85477	97707	56964	58647	48288	80057	33252	41490	37177
87845	74168	91902	03603	88765	22486	96302	62944	26560	61642
28612	38947	86320	55946	78706	88253	41330	29765	30885	34312
53669	43320	14396	08996	61910	96995	98331	24550	94780	64766
79126	04359	51516	82367	68060	20441	02314	10347	78756	91921
19780	66527	14682	01846	16437	94512	56646	01763	38258	26188
50304	21365	43427	55781	93654	23541	46636	55448	75462	41242
30793	01083	91859	28910	09228	17324	24492	96458	61677	89438
55964	53233	46783	52704	25225	86813	85405	56395	69515	02967
19068	71398	37498	94902	30562	25000	37438	87132	48347	93391
87731	26637	86905	94200	20554	11984	80614	04038	63803	93344

TABLE A.13
Random Numbers (Continued)

71793	03160	10321	54010	79451	21889	83892	18853	95584	16330
75222	16866	38308	30866	32536	39491	67263	60664	03883	56778
31779	85828	36522	95914	33315	75617	08635	19862	96042	32491
21825	73967	22276	13141	83174	95191	57217	99081	82967	77038
21974	37688	65858	31540	44461	29592	15205	62601	25050	73788
30679	07478	31260	92243	72299	83894	16565	68166	04425	72455
12057	32739	74572	29590	31116	65504	49521	25839	61778	09283
49197	75858	39575	67322	77392	17250	62529	07425	44282	86373
17798	96641	57174	14233	62462	34177	05400	12305	87732	03152
08184	10032	03657	75273	47047	92326	06969	85250	86280	62931
61438	77490	55384	52609	76613	26302	84824	15265	82488	44817
35995	93175	20506	96954	34675	47957	86829	59910	21576	43855
05191	13337	04191	57676	45843	31528	35752	10758	80283	02621
99230	68531	33239	28707	89404	82288	48410	43558	63155	99415
34407	88683	15066	01045	08176	52150	76824	95907	70640	99505

APPENDIX B
DATA SETS

Data Set 1

The data provided in this set includes the 1981 sales, profit, and profit margin of 100 firms. The sales and profit data are measured in millions of dollars, and the profit margin is given in percent. The profit margin simply measures the percent of profit out of sales.

TABLE B.1
Sales, Profit, and Profit Margin of 100 Companies

		Sales	*Profit*	*Profit margin*
1	UNITED TECHNOLOGIES	13668.	458.	3.35
2	BOEING	10073.	473.	4.70
3	MCDONNELL DOUGLAS	7385.	177.	2.40
4	ROCKWELL INTERNATIONAL	7269.	292.	4.02
5	LOCKHEED	5176.	155.	2.99
6	GENERAL DYNAMICS	5063.	124.	2.45
7	NORTHROP	1991.	48.	2.41
8	GRUMMAN	1949.	21.	1.08
9	FAIRCHILD INDUSTRIES	1339.	64.	4.78
10	CESSNA AIRCRAFT	1060.	61.	5.75
11	TRANSWORLD	5266.	42.	0.80
12	UAL	5141.	-71.	-1.38
13	AMERICAN AIRLINES	4109.	17.	0.41
14	PAN AMERICAN WORLD AIRWAYS	3797.	-260.	-6.85
15	EASTERN AIRLINES	3727.	-66.	-1.77
16	DELTA AIRLINES	3533.	147.	4.16
17	NORTHWEST AIRLINES	1854.	11.	0.59
18	REPUBLIC AIRLINES	1448.	-46.	-3.18
19	BRANIFF INTERNATIONAL	1189.	-161.	-13.54
20	USAIR	1111.	51.	4.59
21	CONTINENTAL AIR LINES	1091.	-60.	-5.50
22	SINGER	2834.	38.	1.34
23	WHIRLPOOL	2437.	135.	5.54
24	WHITE CONSOLIDATED INDUST.	2173.	62.	2.85
25	SUNBEAM	1519.	48.	3.16
26	ZENITH RADIO	1275.	16.	1.25
27	GENERAL MOTORS	62699.	333.	0.53
28	FORD MOTOR	38247.	-1060.	-2.77
29	CHRYSLER	10822.	-476.	-4.40
30	INTERNATIONAL HARVESTER	7018.	-636.	-9.06
31	BENDIX	4425.	205.	4.63
32	EATON	3165.	82.	2.59
33	DANA	2751.	116.	4.22
34	AMERICAN MOTORS	2589.	-137.	-5.29
35	CUMMINS ENGINE	1963.	115.	5.86
36	PACCAR	1785.	85.	4.76
37	PEPSICO	7027.	334.	4.75
38	COCA-COLA	5889.	482.	8.18
39	ANHEUSER-BUSCH	3847.	217.	5.64
40	HEUBLEIN	2050.	88.	4.29
41	COORS	930.	52.	5.59
42	OWENS-ILLINOIS	4071.	154.	3.78
43	OWENS-CORNING FIBERGLAS	2405.	50.	2.08
44	MANVILLE	2221.	60.	2.70
45	JIM WALTER	2041.	19.	0.93
46	EVANS PRODUCTS	1537.	15.	0.98

TABLE B.1
Sales, Profit, and Profit Margin of 100 Companies (Continued)

		Sales	*Profit*	*Profit margin*
47	SHERWIN-WILLIAMS	1537.	31.	2.02
48	U.S. GYPSUM	1522.	74.	4.86
49	LONE STAR INDUSTRIES	986.	56.	5.68
50	NATIONAL GYPSUM	981.	32.	3.26
51	DU PONT	22810.	1081.	4.74
52	DOW CHEMICAL	11873.	564.	4.75
53	UNION CARBIDE	10168.	649.	6.38
54	MONSANTO	6948.	445.	6.40
55	GRACE\W.R.	6586.	361.	5.48
56	ALLIED	6407.	348.	5.43
57	CELANESE	3752.	144.	3.84
58	AMERICAN CYANAMID	3649.	197.	5.40
59	DIAMOND SHAMROCK	3376.	230.	6.81
60	HERCULES	2718.	137.	5.04
61	NATIONAL DISTILLERS + CHEMIC	2032.	137.	6.74
62	KOPPERS	2019.	52.	2.58
63	OLIN	2001.	93.	4.65
64	INTL. MINERALS + CHEMICAL	1985.	154.	7.76
65	SCM	1938.	57.	2.94
66	ETHYL	1777.	91.	5.12
67	ROHM + HAAS	1885.	93.	4.93
68	STAUFFER CHEMICAL	1726.	150.	8.69
69	AIR PRODUCTS + CHEMICAL	1570.	126.	8.03
70	WITCO CHEMICAL	1305.	39.	2.99
71	AKZONA	1194.	12.	1.01
72	PENNWALT	1060.	37.	3.49
73	MORTON-NORWICH PRODUCTS	958.	53.	5.53
74	REICHOLD CHEMICALS	950.	17.	1.79
75	LUBRIZOL	899.	92.	10.23
76	INTERNATIONAL TEL. + TEL.	23197.	695.	3.00
77	TENNECO	15462.	813.	5.26
78	LTV	7511.	405.	5.39
79	CITY INVESTING	5797.	120.	2.07
80	SIGNAL	5488.	214.	3.90
81	TRW	5338.	229.	4.29
82	LITTON INDUSTRIES	4943.	312.	6.31
83	LOEWS	4776.	268.	5.61
84	IC INDUSTRIES	4195.	134.	3.19
85	TEXTRON	3328.	146.	4.39
86	MARTIN MARIETTA	3294.	200.	6.07
87	TELEDYNE	3238.	412.	12.72
88	NORTHWEST INDUSTRIES	3122.	279.	8.94
89	KIDDE	2849.	99.	3.47
90	ALCO STANDARD	2530.	58.	2.29
91	BALDWIN-UNITED	2492.	86.	3.45
92	AVCO	2326.	70.	3.01
93	IU INTERNATIONAL	2323.	63.	2.71
94	COLT INDUSTRIES	2243.	110.	4.90
95	WHITTAKER	1672.	69.	4.13
96	LEAR SIEGLER	1531.	76.	4.96
97	U.S.INDUSTRIES	1041.	43.	4.13
98	FUQUA INDUSTRIES	707.	-16.	-2.26
99	CONTINENTAL GROUP	5194.	242.	4.66
100	AMERICAN CAN	4836.	77.	1.59

Data Set 2

The data provided in this set are annual rates of return on stock of mutual funds for the years 1971–80. The rates of return measure the performance (profitability) of the mutual funds. For example, the rate of return of fund number 1 (Afuture Fund) in 1971 was 67.5 percent. This implies that $100 invested at the beginning of 1971 in this fund had grown to be worth $167.50 at the end of the year.

Mutual funds have diverse investment strategies. Some concentrate in growth stocks seeking maximum capital gains; some select securities that provide high current income (cash dividends); some concentrate their portfolio in senior securities (mainly safe bonds); and so on. The funds in this set are listed in groups according to their investment strategies.

TABLE B.2

A 10-Year Record of Annual Rates of Return of 125 Mutual Funds, 1971–80

	1971	1972	1973	1974	1975	1976	1977	1978	1979	1980	1-20 MAXIMUM CAPITAL GAIN
1 AFUTURE FUND	67.5	19.2	-35.2	-42.0	63.7	19.3	3.6	20.0	40.3	37.5	
2 ALPHA FUND	28.5	27.5	-32.0	-28.2	22.5	22.8	-4.2	10.5	24.0	18.0	
3 AMERICAN GENERAL COMSTOCK	12.4	-1.3	-16.9	-17.2	64.5	34.2	13.9	13.7	47.7	32.7	
4 COLUMBIA GROWTH FUND	36.8	5.9	-25.6	-22.5	42.5	31.1	-0.4	8.1	40.6	39.9	
5 DREYFUS LEVERAGE FUND	28.8	12.6	-15.5	-26.3	25.9	25.2	7.5	10.8	41.2	36.6	
6 EATON + HOWARD SPECIAL FUND	28.9	3.8	-32.3	-40.8	27.3	19.3	13.0	7.4	45.9	34.6	
7 EVERGREEN FUND	32.0	10.1	-26.2	-21.4	60.1	48.8	25.4	38.0	46.3	48.1	
8 EXPLORER FUND	24.8	21.1	-25.8	-35.4	22.8	16.8	28.1	20.6	33.8	55.4	
9 FIDUCIARY GROWTH ASSOCIAT	33.0	23.9	-39.7	-40.4	59.5	24.9	3.7	-2.3	86.1	55.7	
10 44 WALL STREET FUND	71.8	-5.4	-46.8	-52.2	184.1	46.5	16.5	32.9	73.6	36.4	
11 FRANKLIN DYNATECH SERIES	25.6	16.0	-35.4	-33.8	32.1	22.0	4.5	13.3	34.1	37.4	
12 HARTWELL GROWTH FUND	37.7	-9.5	-34.7	-24.7	45.8	26.9	16.8	18.9	40.6	70.0	
13 IVEST FUND	21.5	11.8	-32.3	-33.4	30.7	14.5	1.2	16.2	18.1	33.6	
14 KEYSTONE S-4\LOWER PRICED	35.2	13.0	-40.5	-44.0	36.8	32.5	8.8	19.9	47.1	60.9	
15 MATHERS FUND	19.8	16.1	-37.2	-30.6	57.1	44.4	14.2	15.1	46.6	40.3	
16 OPPENHEIMER A.I.M. FUND	32.8	12.5	-22.0	-33.1	29.3	19.7	-0.2	13.4	50.5	62.0	
17 PACE FUND	43.6	18.0	-42.5	-15.4	34.2	27.8	28.6	23.5	45.4	44.9	
18 PARTNERS FUND	13.6	-8.4	-26.5	3.3	18.1	31.2	7.0	16.3	42.9	34.1	
19 PHOENIX-CHASE GROWTH FUND	28.8	-5.6	-31.4	-36.6	36.4	10.6	-6.0	8.0	24.7	30.3	
20 SECURITY ULTRA FUND	49.5	19.2	-41.7	-26.4	48.4	54.9	3.0	23.7	58.9	72.3	

	Fund	21–40 LONG-TERM GROWTH; INCOME SECONDARY / 41–60 GROWTH + CURRENT INCOME FUNDS									
21	AMCAP FUND	18.9	13.3	-33.4	-28.5	52.1	30.4	16.4	22.4	51.9	27.9
22	ANCHOR GROWTH FUND	19.7	8.5	-32.7	-27.2	31.2	17.8	-6.9	9.0	22.1	19.1
23	ARMSTRONG ASSOCIATES	12.5	13.2	-33.7	-31.6	53.2	44.4	-0.7	29.2	25.3	44.8
24	BEACON GROWTH FUND	15.4	4.5	-32.5	-18.1	23.3	11.6	-3.2	2.0	16.7	31.5
25	BOSTON COMPANY CAPITAL APP	26.5	25.1	-21.2	-31.6	31.9	16.9	-5.2	8.4	20.1	28.1
26	CHARTER FUND	36.5	36.9	-13.5	-27.1	32.7	41.8	5.2	32.3	44.0	33.7
27	COLONIAL GROWTH SHARES	20.9	11.6	-21.6	-29.6	21.6	14.3	-10.2	5.8	38.6	41.4
28	COUNTRY CAPITAL GROWTH	26.9	11.6	-20.1	-23.5	27.0	14.8	2.7	2.6	20.0	30.7
29	ENERGY FUND	8.8	11.5	-6.9	-18.6	33.4	32.9	-4.6	5.6	49.7	41.0
30	FRANKLIN GROWTH SERIES	23.2	20.0	-16.8	-30.6	24.1	11.3	-8.1	15.6	8.6	14.8
31	FRANKLIN OPTION FUND	17.9	21.4	-33.0	-26.6	41.6	22.0	19.8	10.2	27.1	40.1
32	GROWTH FUND OF AMERICA	17.0	-20.5	-26.3	-21.9	35.6	18.2	-13.6	26.7	45.8	39.8
33	JOHN HANCOCK GROWTH FUND	13.5	15.0	-23.9	-34.9	26.3	12.5	5.8	15.8	34.0	58.3
34	INVESTORS RESEARCH FUND	24.1	20.7	-14.4	-12.8	22.8	11.7	-7.3	14.2	18.3	73.7
35	IVY FUND	17.9	14.2	-24.2	-33.0	30.0	18.2	2.4	4.9	30.9	34.7
36	KEMPER GROWTH FUND	20.2	6.3	-18.6	-27.7	42.1	29.0	-7.1	17.8	40.8	44.1
37	LEXINGTON RESEARCH FUND	13.1	13.2	-22.5	-25.2	44.0	26.0	-6.3	7.0	31.9	22.8
38	MAGNACAP FUND	32.2	10.0	-43.2	-27.7	33.6	28.2	2.1	6.0	27.5	12.3
39	NEWTON GROWTH FUND	27.7	20.2	-37.5	-25.4	16.2	19.4	40.0	8.4	25.0	45.3
40	SIGMA VENTURE SHARES	30.1	21.1	-45.2	-36.5	88.1	24.5	-6.9	21.4	34.7	41.1
41	AFFILIATED FUND	8.6	12.1	-5.8	-16.0	39.4	34.3	1.9	3.2	28.9	24.1
42	AMERICAN MUTUAL FUND	13.7	11.2	-10.7	-15.9	35.1	34.2	-5.9	12.3	21.5	25.3
43	COLONIAL FUND	12.8	10.3	-8.1	-19.9	23.0	16.4	-4.4	5.7	17.7	24.3
44	COMPOSITE FUND	10.7	4.6	-26.6	-10.8	29.6	17.1	-3.1	5.6	30.4	26.4
45	DELAWARE FUND	16.4	7.6	-25.3	-16.2	36.5	34.1	-8.4	2.3	23.9	25.9
46	DIVIDEND SHARES	12.6	15.9	-14.3	-21.8	35.3	22.3	-6.1	4.7	11.9	23.2
47	DODGE + COX STOCK FUND	15.6	-12.5	-12.5	-24.6	38.9	22.2	-7.1	9.6	20.8	33.2
48	EATON + HOWARD STOCK FUND	13.7	14.8	-17.9	-33.7	21.3	15.8	3.6	6.4	17.3	24.8
49	FINANCIAL INDUSTRIAL FUND	14.1	20.2	-11.9	-23.6	34.5	30.1	-5.8	7.6	38.2	27.8
50	FUNDAMENTAL INVESTORS	17.6	7.6	-21.7	-22.5	36.5	19.6	-2.9	6.3	15.3	21.3
51	GENERAL SECURITIES	-1.0	-4.2	-30.0	-16.1	61.8	35.9	-7.9	15.2	14.3	23.9
52	INVESTMENT TRUST OF BOSTON	7.9	11.8	-10.9	-19.4	34.0	21.3	-7.3	11.2	18.0	43.9
53	INVESTORS STOCK FUND	17.1	15.5	-17.9	-27.4	35.1	23.8	-7.7	4.9	20.5	26.4
54	MANN(HORACE) FUND	21.1	18.4	-10.9	-25.0	22.7	12.6	-1.7	4.0	25.1	36.3
55	NATIONAL INDUSTRIES FUND	18.0	9.5	-22.5	-27.0	36.2	29.9	-3.9	8.0	29.9	35.8
56	NATIONAL STOCK FUND	9.0	8.1	-16.2	-14.3	38.8	33.6	-2.8	4.9	25.4	32.5
57	NEL EQUITY FUND	17.9	7.3	-0.9	-29.5	29.3	29.5	-4.9	8.9	25.4	20.5
58	SOVEREIGN INVESTORS	12.6	9.6	-13.8	-20.8	38.1	28.7	-1.6	3.6	23.4	20.2
59	TECHNOLOGY FUND	15.6	9.4	-17.1	-22.2	37.1	25.6	-4.0	22.4	32.7	49.8
60	WASHINGTON MUTUAL FUND	12.1	8.7	-9.0	-17.3	44.7	31.2		7.9	14.4	24.0

TABLE B.2

A 10-Year Record of Annual Rates of Return of 125 Mutual Funds, 1971–80 (Continued)

	1971	1972	1973	1974	1975	1976	1977	1978	1979	1980	
61 AMERICAN BALANCED FUNDS	12.5	10.6	-13.1	-15.5	25.0	26.0	0.7	6.2	7.6	14.3	61–79 BALANCED FUNDS
62 AXE-HOUGHTON FUND B	17.7	8.4	-7.0	-8.4	21.8	29.0	1.7	4.2	10.0	22.2	
63 BOSTON FOUNDATION FUND	13.4	9.0	-15.8	-20.3	26.5	22.6	1.9	1.5	14.0	14.4	
64 COMPOSITE BOND + STOCK	12.3	8.3	-9.0	-10.4	28.4	24.5	-0.9	1.8	20.1	17.3	
65 CONVERTIBLE YIELD SECURITY	13.1	11.2	-11.1	-13.8	24.5	22.4	-1.0	3.9	16.2	34.6	
66 DODGE + COX BALANCED FUND	10.9	11.4	-9.7	19.3	29.4	25.3	-3.3	6.1	13.5	21.7	
67 EATON + HOWARD BALANCED FUND	11.4	14.7	-4.5	-20.1	20.7	19.7	-5.7	4.4	11.4	26.0	
68 JOHN HANCOCK BALANCED FUND	9.2	12.7	-17.3	-13.9	30.8	28.0	-2.1	1.3	6.7	17.4	
69 INVESTORS MUTUAL	14.5	13.6	-13.9	-17.7	24.5	22.2	-1.5	3.1	11.3	18.7	
70 LOOMIS-SAYLES MUTUAL FUND	16.7	10.9	-7.5	-24.9	25.6	15.9	-4.0	4.9	13.7	15.0	
71 MASSACHUSETTS FUND	17.1	15.8	-8.6	-18.1	20.1	21.5	-0.8	7.1	15.0	24.9	
72 NATIONWIDE SECURITIES	12.8	11.1	-9.3	-14.2	30.5	25.4	-2.9	1.4	9.9	13.1	
73 PUTNAM(GEORGE) FUND	18.1	20.1	-10.9	-23.6	26.1	24.1	-3.5	5.7	15.5	17.0	
74 SENTINEL BALANCED FUND	11.3	8.3	-5.0	-7.3	22.0	23.9	1.4	-1.7	14.1	11.3	
75 SIGMA TRUST SHARES	13.2	13.0	-19.0	-8.6	26.7	29.7	5.6	5.5	9.5	15.6	
76 STATE FARM BALANCED FUND	9.4	9.7	-16.5	-13.9	27.2	24.5	3.5	9.8	26.6	18.6	
77 STEIN ROE + FARNHAM BALNCED	22.1	18.7	-14.7	-26.5	28.5	14.9	-5.7	6.7	17.1	26.6	
78 UNITED CONTINENTAL INCOME	16.9	6.3	-17.0	-20.6	27.1	25.6	1.6	1.3	11.9	20.8	
79 WELLINGTON FUND	8.9	11.0	-11.8	-17.7	25.2	23.4	-4.3	5.3	13.5	22.5	
80 AMERICAN NATIONAL INCOME	14.4	7.9	-12.2	-4.2	33.5	34.8	7.2	8.3	25.0	18.8	80–84 COMMON STOCK POLICY INCOME FUNDS
81 BLC INCOME FUND	13.5	13.5	-17.5	-14.9	50.0	35.6	-1.3	3.9	14.5	24.6	
82 DIVERSIFIED FUND ST.BD.+MTG.	9.6	10.2	-14.2	-22.1	39.7	30.1	-0.2	3.0	18.3	27.5	
83 SAFECO INCOME FUND	13.6	15.0	-15.3	-15.7	38.2	34.9	2.4	1.8	21.4	22.2	
84 TRANSAMERICA INCOME FUND	17.0	9.0	-5.1	-5.0	17.5	20.7	-0.5	3.5	4.5	5.2	

	Fund												85–104 FLEXIBLE POLICY INCOME FUNDS	105–114 SENIOR SECURITIES POLICY	115–125 OTHER FUNDS
85	AXE-HOUGHTON INCOME FUND	16.4	7.1	-15.8	-4.0	17.9	22.3	4.9	0.6	1.9	7.8
86	BABSON INCOME TRUST	7.0	9.0	-3.0	1.8	9.0	11.7	2.9	0.6	2.4	2.9
87	CG INCOME FUND	9.8	6.9	-9.1	-7.0	21.6	18.5	5.9	0.7	-0.8	3.2
88	COLONIAL INCOME FUND	15.9	9.4	0.2	-9.7	15.2	19.4	6.7	1.4	-1.1	0.4
89	DECATUR INCOME FUND	16.9	6.4	-14.3	-11.7	34.3	37.6	2.6	2.6	25.8	24.5
90	FIDELITY PURITAN FUND	13.3	11.1	-7.2	-12.2	32.3	30.8	0.7	4.5	14.8	20.3
91	FIRST INVESTORS NAT'L RES.	8.1	12.7	-21.5	-22.5	26.4	31.2	0.5	0.8	5.1	11.6
92	FRANKLIN INCOME SERIES	19.3	3.7	-4.8	-13.0	24.9	21.9	8.0	7.6	27.8	19.0
93	LIBERTY FUND	23.6	7.4	-28.3	-29.0	29.5	26.1	-5.7	2.1	11.7	-0.8
94	LORD ABBETT INCOME FUND	11.7	13.0	-15.1	-12.2	34.1	32.6	2.3	0.4	3.0	2.8
95	MASS. INCOME DEVELOPMENT	11.9	6.9	-11.7	-11.9	28.3	28.0	1.4	0.3	10.7	19.0
96	MIF NATIONWIDE FUND	10.2	9.7	-6.7	-20.3	38.6	26.7	-9.1	0.8	9.8	17.9
97	NATIONAL DIVIDEND FUND	15.3	5.4	-16.0	-13.5	28.7	39.7	3.9	4.7	24.1	31.7
98	NATIONAL INCOME FUND	17.4	6.9	-13.1	-10.9	27.0	36.3	5.1	5.2	13.8	16.4
99	NEWTON INCOME FUND	11.2	16.0	-11.9	-27.2	28.3	24.3	-5.2	0.3	-1.2	3.5
100	NORTHEAST INVESTORS TRUST	14.9	9.5	0.0	-7.7	17.7	22.0	6.6	-0.8	-1.1	-0.1
101	PUTNAM INCOME FUND	13.8	10.6	-2.4	-7.5	17.2	20.6	5.5	-0.3	-1.9	-0.2
102	STEADMAN ASSOCIATED FUND	15.7	7.4	-12.3	-13.2	20.1	23.7	4.6	-1.4	8.8	9.5
103	VALUE LINE INCOME FUND	13.5	9.1	-15.5	-16.1	41.7	34.5	1.8	11.1	27.6	26.8
104	WISCONSIN INCOME FUND	14.2	8.4	-20.4	-26.1	34.2	22.8	-5.0	-2.3	-2.8	-2.7
105	ALPHA INCOME FUND	12.3	15.0	-15.2	-17.8	15.7	17.1	5.7	2.3	-3.9	-2.3
106	AMERICAN GEN'L HIGH YIELD	20.4	4.9	-6.7	-11.5	25.2	27.2	2.9	9.0	24.3	33.5
107	DELCHESTER BOND FUND	12.3	7.6	0.7	-8.2	16.2	22.6	6.1	2.2	1.7	0.7
108	INVESTORS SELECTIVE FUND	13.9	8.6	2.1	-2.9	14.4	20.9	2.8	2.2	-0.2	1.1
109	KEYSTONE B-1\INV. BOND	11.2	7.8	3.6	-1.1	10.6	15.9	4.2	1.7	3.6	1.9
110	KEYSTONE B-2\MEDIUM GRAD	18.0	9.7	-1.0	-7.5	19.3	22.6	7.2	2.0	5.8	6.4
111	KEYSTONE B-4\DISCOUNT	21.5	11.9	-7.3	-8.2	25.1	26.9	7.6	4.5	1.9	8.6
112	NATIONAL BOND FUND	14.0	6.8	-4.6	-10.9	18.7	23.2	6.7	-0.8	1.5	-1.4
113	SECURITY BOND FUND	3.0	4.9	5.1	6.5	16.0	18.3	7.6	1.9	1.2	0.3
114	UNITED BOND FUND	13.9	8.5	0.3	-8.7	13.9	22.0	4.0	0.5	-3.5	-0.8
115	CANADIAN FUND	10.2	24.4	-1.7	-21.7	10.7	4.2	-1.2	12.9	30.7	20.5
116	INTERNATIONAL INVESTORS	-3.7	60.3	91.9	11.0	-24.1	-28.5	32.8	9.5	176.7	64.6
117	PUTNAM INTERNATIONAL EQUI	33.7	21.4	-25.7	-20.8	35.1	24.0	-1.0	22.8	19.6	25.5
118	SCUDDER INTERNATIONAL FUND	6.0	30.0	-8.9	-23.5	29.4	6.1	-0.4	21.3	19.3	26.9
119	TEMPLETON GROWTH FUND	21.8	68.6	-9.9	-12.1	37.6	46.6	20.5	19.2	26.8	25.9
120	TRANSATLANTIC FUND	17.9	28.4	-3.2	-12.2	32.4	1.5	5.8	25.6	15.5	49.2
121	AMERICAN INSURANCE + IND	45.7	44.8	-25.4	-20.7	18.1	34.1	5.1	8.2	23.3	15.1
122	CENTURY SHARES TRUST	30.8	20.2	-13.4	-32.1	14.0	36.4	-2.3	9.6	21.3	6.0
123	LIFE INSURANCE INVESTORS	29.2	33.6	-26.3	-32.7	10.4	43.1	14.2	14.6	28.8	2.4
124	FRANKLIN UTILITIES SERIES	-2.7	6.7	-30.0	-22.0	41.0	28.9	7.7	-0.4	-0.9	5.6
125	NATIONAL AVIATION + TECH.	29.3	0.7	-38.0	-18.3	50.4	34.8	3.9	34.0	18.8	29.1

Source: Selective data reprinted by permission from Wiesenberger Investment Companies Service, 1981 Edition. Copyright 1981, Warren, Gorham & Lamont, Inc. 210 South Street, Boston, Mass. All rights reserved.

Data Set 3

This set provides data on 72 money market funds in July 1982. For each fund, the following data is given:

1. The value of total assets, in millions of dollars
2. Average 30-day yield. The yield is annualized, and it measures the percentage profit the fund would have realized on its assets if the rate of profit of July 1982 had continued for a whole year.
3. Average maturity. The money market funds invest in a variety of short-term investments whose average maturity in days is given.
4. The percent of the assets invested in each of six types of securities. For example, the first fund (Alliance Capital Reserve) has invested 7 percent of its assets in Treasury bills (T-bills), 3 percent in repurchase agreements (repos.), 28 percent in certificates of deposit (CD), 23 percent in Bankers Acceptances (Bankers accept), and 39 percent in commercial papers (CP), a total of 100 percent.

TABLE B.3

Total Assets, Average 30-Day Yield, Average Maturity, and Portfolio Composition of 72 Money Market Funds, July 1982

	Net assets (millions)	Yield	Average maturity (days)	T-bill	Other U.S.	Repos.	CD	Bankers accept	CP
1 ALLIANCE CAPITAL RESERVE	1505	13.3	25	7	0	3	28	23	39
2 ALPHA CASH MGMT.-GOVT. SEC.	5	12.2	82	0	90	10	0	0	0
3 AMERICAN GENERAL RESERVE FUND	414	13.3	23	0	0	0	0	1	99
4 AMERICAN NATIONAL MM FUND	12	13.9	58	0	0	0	28	0	72
5 ASTA GOVT. SECURITIES MM	28	12.2	32	14	49	37	0	0	0
6 BABSON MONEY MARKET FUND	86	13.5	33	0	0	1	10	33	56
7 BOSTON COMPANY CASH MGMT.	279	13.7	26	0	0	0	37	2	28
8 CAPITAL CASH MANAGEMENT TRUST	156	13.5	25	0	0	0	26	41	33
9 CAPITAL PRESERVATION FUND II	1118	12.6	3	0	0	100	0	0	0
10 CASH EQUIVALENT FUND	4094	14.1	36	0	0	0	15	0	57
11 CASH RESERVE MANAGEMENT TRUST	7200	13.5	29	8	0	2	6	2	65
12 COLONIAL MONEY MARKET TRUST	14	13.3	26	0	0	7	8	4	81
13 COMPOSITE CASH MANAGEMENT CO.	352	13.3	30	0	0	1	30	12	55
14 CURRENT INTEREST	1552	13.3	35	8	0	0	14	18	60
15 DAILY INCOME FUND	787	13.3	33	0	9	6	41	27	16

No.	Fund							Days	Yield	Assets
16	DBL CASH FUND-MM. PORT.	41	13	27	0	0	1	31	13.7	989
17	DOLLAR RESERVES	18	34	12	16	0	0	22	13.5	113
18	DREYFUS MM-GOVT. SEC. SERIES	0	0	0	51	0	49	29	12.7	662
19	DREYFUS MM-MM SERIES	14	7	12	0	0	0	25	13.8	2438
20	E.G.T. MONEY MARKET TRUST	34	5	21	0	4	0	29	13.3	153
21	FAHNE STOCK DAILY INCOME FUND	19	29	42	6	0	0	34	13.4	158
22	FEDERATED MASTER TRUST	92	0	0	2	0	0	29	13.6	3816
23	FIDELITY DAILY INCOME TRUST	0	29	43	0	61	8	35	13.6	3710
24	FIDELITY MM TR.-U.S. GOVT.	0	0	0	31	55	0	28	12.7	692
25	FIDELITY U.S. GOVT. RESERVES	0	0	0	45	3	0	24	12.1	304
26	FINANCIAL PLANNERS FED. SEC.	0	0	0	97	3	0	1	12.4	16
27	FIRST VARIABLE RATE FUND	0	0	0	78	12	10	20	13.0	1403
28	FRANKLIN FEDERAL MONEY FUND	0	0	0	100	0	0	3	12.7	155
29	FUND FOR GOVT. INVESTORS	0	0	0	21	11	68	20	12.6	1312
30	GRANDISON CASH RESERVES TRUST	51	27	22	66	7	27	28	13.3	720
31	HILLIARD LYONS CASH MANAGEMENT	63	13	15	2	0	1	22	12.3	208
32	INA CASH FUND	53	11	34	0	7	11	30	13.7	749
33	INSTL. LIQ. ASSETS--PRIME	41	1	40	2	0	11	30	13.8	2824
34	INTERCAPITAL LIQUID ASSETS FUND	0	0	0	0	0	0	40	13.6	9423
35	KEMPER GOVT. MONEY MARKET	49	19	21	89	0	0	13	12.3	103
36	LEGG MASON CASH RESERVE	0	0	0	0	5	0	32	13.4	338
37	LEHMAN GOVERNMENT FUND, INC.	8	12	24	100	0	0	1	12.4	161
38	LIQUID CAPITAL INCOME TRUST	36	21	41	3	0	19	20	13.4	2117
39	LIQUID GREEN TRUST	28	2	28	2	0	0	25	13.3	135
40	LUTHERAN BROTHERHOOD MM FUND	0	24	26	28	11	0	33	13.4	703
41	MCDONALD MONEY MARKET FUND	37	6	56	26	6	0	28	12.9	206
42	MERRILL LYNCH INSTNL. FUND	0	0	0	56	0	0	20	13.6	1168
43	MIDWEST INC. TST.--SHORT TERM	1	17	63	0	0	21	12	12.4	271
44	MONEY FUND OF U.S. TREAS. SEC.	38	2	41	18	0	0	4	12.7	5
45	MONEY MARKET TRUST	21	63	8	100	4	19	31	13.7	2861
46	MONEY MART ASSETS	46	6	37	0	0	0	28	13.7	3976
47	MUTUAL OF OMAHA CASH RESERVES	51	32	10	4	0	0	16	12.6	24
48	NATIONAL LIQUID RESERVES	70	30	0	0	15	0	30	13.6	1932
49	NEWTON MONEY MARKET	52	14	9	7	0	0	31	13.3	9
50	OFFERMAN MONEY MARKET FUND	47	1	27	0	0	0	22	13.0	13
51	OPPENHEIMER MONEY MARKET FUND	58	0	8	1	11	6	30	13.6	1639
52	PAINE WEBBER CASH FUND	0	6	0	0	6	0	33	13.5	6411
53	PLIMONEY FUND	37	0	39	100	0	0	27	13.8	67
54	PRINCIPAL PROTECTION G. INV. FUND	0	9	0	18	0	0	1	11.7	5
55	QUAKER CASH RESERVES	30	27	36	85	0	0	29	13.1	4
56	RESERVE FUND--GOVT. PORTFOLIO	0	0	0	1	15	19	5	12.6	361
57	SCUDDER CASH INVESTMENT TRUST	30	14	36	0	0	0	33	13.2	1296
58	SECURITIES GROUP MONEY FUND	100	0	0	0	0	0	15	13.3	27

TABLE B.3

Total Assets, Average 30-Day Yield, Average Maturity, and Portfolio Composition of 72 Money Market Funds, July 1982

	Net assets (millions)	Yield	Average maturity (days)	T-bill	Other U.S.	Repos.	CD	Bankers accept	CP
59 SELECTED MONEY MARKET FUND--GEN.	70	13.2	29	0	0	0	21	35	44
60 SENTINEL CASH MANAGEMENT FUND	26	13.1	32	0	4	21	10	35	30
61 SHEARSON DAILY DIVIDEND	5826	13.7	24	0	0	0	41	15	0
62 SHORT TERM INCOME FUND	278	13.4	32	0	0	14	32	41	13
63 SIGMA GOVT. SECURITIES FUND	4	11.9	6	25	69	6	0	0	0
64 STEIN ROE CASH RESERVES	914	13.5	30	0	0	0	40	26	20
65 TEMPORARY INVEST. FUND	4136	13.7	33	9	0	0	30	14	47
66 TRANSAMERICA CASH RESERVES	354	13.7	25	3	0	15	11	9	40
67 TRUST FOR S/T FED. SEC.	1225	12.8	22	20	48	32	0	0	0
68 TRUST FOR S/T U.S. GOVT. SEC.	5793	12.7	35	20	36	44	0	0	0
69 TUCKER ANTHONY CASH MGMT. FUND	360	13.2	30	0	0	0	5	60	35
70 USAA MONEY MARKET	158	13.3	25	0	11	0	16	28	45
71 VANGUARD MM TRUST-FEDERAL	494	12.7	28	6	63	31	0	0	0
72 WEBSTER CASH RESERVES	1383	13.6	29	1	0	7	37	16	31

Source: Selective data reprinted by permission from Wiesenberger Investment Companies Service, 1981 Edition. Copyright 1981, Warren, Gorham & Lamont, Inc. 210 South Street, Boston, Mass. All rights reserved.

APPENDIX C

Answers to Selected
Odd-Numbered Problems

Chapter 4

4.3	Median = $91,428.6
4.11	a. 28.6 b. 29.5 c. μ_3 = 199.4375, Coefficient of skewness = 0.4530
4.13	a. $\overline{X}$ = 16, S = 6.66 b. 72.22%, 94.44%
4.17	$10,748.0
4.19	a. $6.4 million b. σ^2 = 25.44, σ = 5.0438 c. 0.788
	d. $0.8 million e. $8.3 million f. $6.0 million
4.21	a. $\overline{X}$ = 13.21, S = 0.2598 b. 0.0111 c. 13 and 13.3
4.23	a. 40 (thousand dollars) b. 30.53 c. 587.5 d. 0.60596
	e. μ_3 = 11,937.5
4.25	a. Food: $\overline{X}$ = 7.5, Oil: $\overline{X}$ = 9.58 b. Food: S^2 = 21.186, Oil: S^2 = 31.60
4.27	μ_w = 8.14%
4.31	$\overline{X}_{Aaa}$ = 11.265, $\overline{X}_{Aa}$ = 11.84, $\overline{X}_A$ = 12.36
4.33	μ = 0.535, σ^2 = 0.332
4.35	The coefficient of variation of the electric bills is greater (0.2).
4.37	a. 69.13%
4.39	a. 3,085.5 b. 2,715 c. 1,143.21
4.41	a. 0.65625 b. S^2 = 9.88, S = 3.14
	c. Median = −1.50, Mode = −2.5 and −0.5
4.43	a. 0.3348, 0.3530, 0.4009 b. 0.3975 c. 0.0137

Appendix 4A

4A.1	a. 90.54 b. 302.76 c. 45.4

Appendix 4B

4B.1	μ_w = 6%
4B.7	a. Year 1: 3.2%, Year 2: 2.8%, Year 3: 4.6%, Year 4: 4.7%
	b. The geometric mean is 3.8%.

Chapter 5

5.7	0
5.9	c. 0.7, 0.8
5.15	b. 0.75, c. 0.625
5.17	a. 0.01 b. 0.18 c. 0.81
5.19	0.0001049, 0.0060466
5.21	a. 0.4 b. 0.24 c. 0.76 d. 0.4 e. 0.24 f. 0.76
5.23	0.3
5.25	a. 0.08 b. 0.22
5.29	a. 0.06, 0.17, 0.5625
5.31	a. $\dfrac{89}{252}$

5.33   c. 0.4, 0.01, 0.46, 0.67   d. 0, $\frac{1}{17}$, $\frac{2}{15}$, 0, 0, 0, 0, 0.37

5.35   0.54

5.37   a. 0.4656   b. 0.2045

5.39 $\frac{1}{3}$

5.41   0.4628

5.45   a. \$12,900   b. \$18,210   c. \$28,760

5.47   a. 792   b. $\frac{7}{22}$ c. $\frac{1}{132}$

5.49   a. 9,600   b. 91,390

5.51   440

5.53   a. $6.40240 \cdot 10^{15}$ b. $3.2012 \cdot 10^{15}$

5.55   a. $2.6336 \cdot 10^{13}$ b. $5.0039 \cdot 10^{13}$

5.57   a. 1,404,000   b. 14,040,000

Appendix 5A

5A.3 $\frac{2}{3}$

Chapter 6

6.5   a. 0.25, 0.85, 0.6, 0.6

6.9   c. $V(X_1) = 125$, $V(X_2) = 175$, $V(X_3) = 225$

6.15   c. $\frac{1}{6}$

6.17 $V(X) = 100$, $SD(X) = 10$

6.21 $-331.08\ DM$

6.23   a. 0.84, 0.63, 0.49, 0.69   b. $E(X) = 2.56$, $SD(X) = 1.7568$

6.25   0.9375, 0.9844

6.29   a. $\frac{1}{6}, \frac{7}{30}, \frac{26}{30}, 0$ b. $\frac{1}{3}$

6.31   a. $-1.82574, -0.91287, 0, 0.91287, 1.82574$

6.33   a. $E(X) = 30,000$, $V(X) = 50,000,000$ b. $E(Y) = 30$, $V(Y) = 50$
       c. $E(\pi) = 0$, $V(\pi) = 12,500,000$

6.35 $E(Y) = \$100.4$, $V(Y) = 2,847.84$

Appendix 6A

6A.3 $E(X) = 20$, $V(X) = 33.33$, $SD(X) = 5.7735$, $\mu_3 = 0$

6A.7   b. 1   c. 0.805   d. 291.166   e. 1,055.693

Chapter 7

7.5   b. 0.2, 0.6, 0

7.7 $COV(X_1, X_2) = 133$, $COV(Y_1, Y_2) = -134.8$, $\rho(X_1, X_2) = 0.87$, $\rho(Y_1, Y_2)$
       $-\ -0.93$

7.9 -0.5

7.11 $COV(D, W) = -5,356$, $\rho(D, W) = -0.1807$

7.13 $COV(X, Y) = 0.0439$, $\rho(X, Y) = 0.07687$

7.15   a. $E(X) = 2.06$, $E(Y) = 3.78$, $E(X+Y) = 5.84$
       b. $SD(X) = 3.84$, $SD(Y) = 5.41$
       c. $COV(X, Y) = 5.2532$, $\rho(X, Y) = 0.253$ d. 7.3847

7.19   b. 0, $\frac{2}{3}$

7.21 0.715
7.23 a. 15,000, 9,531   b. 15,000, 15,000   c. 15,000, 18,952
7.25 $P_1 = 0.764, P_2 = 0.236$
7.27 a. $E(X_1) = E(X_2) = 22.1$ b. $SD(X_1) = SD(X_2) = 1.92$
      d. $E(Z) = 176.8, SD(Z) = 10.87$
7.31 d. $E(X) = 104,200, SD(X) = 11,315.476$
      f. $E(Z) = -400, V(Z) = 74,040,000$
7.33 a. $\bar{X} = -4.19, \bar{Y} = 4.14, S_X = 25.85, S_Y = 22.17$ b. 0.687

Chapter 8

8.3   a. 0.07776, 0.25920, 0.34560, 0.23040, 0.07680, 0.01024
8.5   a. $11 \cdot 10^{-9}$ b. 0.000037   c. 0.4044
8.7   a. 0.216   b. 0.3456   c. 0.042
8.9   a. 0.0000041   b. 0.0268
8.11 0.8226, 0.0169
8.13 a. 0.729   b. 0.59049   c. 2,236.96   d. 763.04
8.15 $E(X) = 1.8, V(X) = 1.62$
8.17 a. 0.13184   b. 0.058399   c. At least 14 questions
8.19 0.4511, 0.7218, 0.5414, 0.2707
8.21 a. 0.5665   b. 0.0733   c. 9.6555   d. 0.000335
8.23 0.5654
8.25 a. 0.9048   b. 0.00015   c. 0.0951
8.27 0.98304, 0.986
8.33 a. $\dfrac{1}{9,880}$ b. $\dfrac{56}{9,880}$ c. $\dfrac{1,920}{9,880}$
8.35 0.547
8.39 a. 0.0186   b. 0.2284   c. 0.7535

Chapter 9

9.1   a. 0.3085   b. 0.9893   c. 0.9332   d. 0.0165   e. 0.1357
      f. 0.0062   g. 0.9999
9.3   a. 0.1587   b. 0.2266   c. 0.8944   d. 0.3976   e. 0.0228
      f. 0.1517   g. 0.2426
9.5   a. 70   b. 63.28   c. 80.24
9.7   4,684
9.9   a. 0.0228   b. 0.3085   c. 0.5
9.11 a. 30.85%   b. 40.13%
9.13 92.90
9.15 a. 0.1587   b. 0.5328
9.17 $P(X_1 < 5) = 0.3821, P(X_2 < 5) = 0.4129$
9.19 $P(X > 14.6) = 0.1991, P(Y > 14.6) = 0.1875$
9.21 0.9177
9.23 0.8502
9.25 a. 0.8664, 0.9544, 0.9974, 1   b. 0.555, 0.75, 0.88, 0.9375   c. 0.68, 0.95, 1

Chapter 10

10.1   a. 0.393   b. 0.3296   c. 0.4493
10.3   0.383
10.7   a. 0.6171, 0.7631, 0.056
10.9   0.231
10.11 a. 0.9997   b. 0.9999999   c. 0.000005998   d. 0.000006

Chapter 11

11.5 1
11.7 $13.3 \cdot 10^{-9}$
11.9 0.6, 0.3
11.15 100
11.19 0.6826, 0.9924, 0.9973, 0.9992

Chapter 12

12.1 a. $\hat{\mu} = 2.4$, $\hat{\sigma} = 3.78$ b. 1.69, 1.647
12.5 a. 0.9999366   b. From 100.715 to 103.285
12.7 From 153.218 to 186.782
12.9 0.1359
12.11 0.9772
12.13 2,171
12.15 From -153.6 to 1193.6
12.17 From 54.738 to 75.548
12.19 a. From 0 to 0.106   b. 1,825
12.21 a. 0.03   b. From 0 to 0.061   c. 0.0968   d. 0   e. 7,300
12.25 a. 28   b. From 26.76 to 29.24   c. 0.673   d. 40
12.27 a. $567   b. 0.9128
12.29 a. 30.19%   b. From 10.59% to 49.79%   c. From 1.03% to 59.35%
12.33 a. 5.77   b. From 2.729 to 19.23

Chapter 13

13.7 The null hypothesis is rejected at all values of α.
13.9 Critical value = 10.8225
13.11 Critical value = 4,917.75
13.13 Test statistic = -2.397
13.15 Critical value = 1654.4
13.19 Test statistic = 0.878
13.21 a. $\beta = 0.67$, Power = 0.33
        b. $\beta = 0$, Power = 1
13.23 a. Critical value = 0.41775   b. 0.9948
13.25 Critical values: 0.37, 0.43
13.27 a. Test statistic = 20
        b. Test statistic = 20

Appendix 13A

13A.1 a. Rejection region is $\overline{X} > 623.67$ b. Critical values: 571.80, 628.20
        c. 0.7852   d. 0.8708
13A.2 a. The critical value is 1.837 and the test statistic is 1.808. The null
        hypothesis is not rejected.   b. 0.6668   c. The critical value is 1.948
        and the test statistic is 1.808. The null hypothesis is not rejected.

Chapter 14

14.3 Test statistic = -7.29
14.5 a. Critical values: -6.73, 6.73
14.7 Critical values: -9.63, 11.83
14.9 Test statistic = 1.0395
14.11 Test statistic = -2.275
14.13 Critical values: -1.26, 1.26
14.15 Critical values: -0.0262, 0.0262
14.19 Test statistic = 12.096
14.21 Critical values: 0.200, 13.853

Chapter 15

15.5   Test statistic = 32.0920
15.7   Test statistic = 775.41
15.9   Test statistic = 178.56
15.13   Test statistic = 2.70359
15.15   Test statistic = 5.454
15.17   Test statistic = 2.596
15.19   Test statistic = 8.762
15.21   Test statistic = 30.170
15.23   a. Test statistic = 63.07
         b. Test statistic = 172.92
15.25   Test statistic = 9.198
15.27   Test statistic = 16.5156
15.29   Test statistic = 9.438
15.31   a. 1
15.33   Test statistic = 9.68
15.37   Test statistic = 3.8
15.39   a. Test statistic = 3,540.77
         b. Test statistic = 197.67

Chapter 16

16.5   a. 4.28   b. 3.44   c. 3.07   d. 2.87
16.13   a. 3.00   b. 2.51
16.17   b. Interval limits: 1.94, 31.4
16.23   Test statistic = 0.68
16.25   Test statistic = 22.22
16.29   a. 1.0857, 1.6333, 7.9857   b. Test statistic = 21.50
16.31   Test statistic = 1.74
16.33   Test statistic = 10.93

Chapter 17

17.3 $E(Y|X=4) = 9, V(Y) = 12.5$
17.11   b. $\hat{Y} = 85.8764 + 75.40166X$ c. $r = 0.785, r^2 = 0.6163$
17.15   a. $b_o = -2$ b. $b_o = 0$ c. $b_o = 9$
17.17   b. $\hat{Y} = 0.263 + 0.893X$ d. $S_e = 0.653, S_Y = 0.976$
17.19   a. $\hat{Y} = 0.5X$ b. $\hat{X} = 2Y$ d. 1   f. $\hat{Y} = 0.7X, \hat{X} = 1.42857Y$
17.21   a. $\hat{F} = 1,200 + 0.28X$ b. $\hat{Y} = 3,000 + \dfrac{7}{9}W$ c. $\hat{F} = 1,200 + \dfrac{28}{90}W$
17.23   b. $\hat{Y} = -840 + 220X$
17.25   a. $\hat{Y} = 448.3137 - 4.15794X, \Sigma(Y-\hat{Y})^2 = 108,001.10$ b. 511.34
17.27   a. $\hat{Y} = 1,812.11 - 73.91X$ b. 851.28
17.31   a. -4 b. $-5, 40, 100, 149, 191$ d. $r^2 = 0.9967$
17.35   b. 100
17.41   0.707, 0.707
17.43 $\hat{Y} = 10$
17.45 $\hat{Y} = 13.09783 - 0.00112X$

Chapter 18

18.3   a. 55
18.9   a. $\hat{Y} = 2.04204 + 0.0377Z$
18.13   a. $\hat{Y} = 1.7X$ b. $\hat{Y} = 1.7X$
18.15   a. $\hat{Y} = 4.8506 + 0.1354X$
         b. $\hat{Y} = 6.8127 - 0.795X$
         c. $\hat{Y} = 4.469 + 0.1909X$
18.17   a. $\hat{Y} = 5.90121 + 0.21252X$ c. Test statistic = 3.223   d. 0.6809
         e. Test statistic = 2.94

18.19   1960–1980: a. $\hat{Y} = 7.30965 + 0.68395X$ c. $r = 0.2083$, Test statistic
$= 0.928$
1960–1969: a. $\hat{Y} = 11.24889 - 0.63261X$ c. $r = 0.1863$, Test statistic
$= 0.536$
1970–1980: $\hat{Y} = 0.08813 + 1.62225X$ c. $r = 0.4373$, Test statistic
$= 1.45$
18.21   a. $\hat{Y} = 1 + 0.5X$
18.23   a. $\hat{Y} = 2.18901 + 1.05199X$ b. Test statistic $= 2.59$
d. Critical values: 156.23, 163.75; Critical values: 150.306, 169.668
18.25   a. $r = 0.61$ b. $r = -0.0091$
18.27   a. 0.9321   b. 0.9306, Test statistic $= 4.457, 4.4039$
18.29   a. $\hat{Y} = 339.32703 - 112.30394X$ b. $r = 0.989$, Test statistic $= 24.107$
c. $\hat{Y} = 356.45575 - 123.87466X$, $r = 0.9912$, $\hat{Y} = 323.80469 - 22.78143X$,
$r = 0.8433$

Chapter 19

19.5   a. \$8,900
19.17 $r^2_{Y1.2} = 0.0016$, $r^2_{Y2.1} = 0.216$
19.19   a. 0.6534, 0.6064, 0.8857   b. 0.65617,   c. $r_{Y1.2} = 0.3152$, $r_{Y2.1} = 0.0781$

Chapter 21

21.3   7.2%
21.9   b. 1971–1978: 29.4%, 52.9%; 1976–1978: 4.4%, 12.4%
21.13   a. 105.6, 120.7   b. Paasche: 111.1, 125.2; Laspeyres: 111.1, 125.3
c. Paasche: 104.8, 118.2; Laspeyres: 104.8, 118.3   d. 116.4, 148.1
e. 116.4, 148.1
21.19   361.69, 353.49

Chapter 22

22.7   Runs test: $r = 2$
22.9   Runs test: $r = 7$
22.11   Runs test: $Z_r = -0.61$
22.13   a. Maximum number of defects that justify acceptance: 1.
22.15   The null hypothesis is not rejected.
22.17   The null hypothesis is not rejected at 10% significance level.
22.19 $Z_T = 0.570$, $Z_T = -3.00$
22.21 $r_s = -0.67$
22.23   a. $Z_\tau = 4.7711$ b. $T_s = 8.5498$, $T_r = 8.874$
22.25   a. $r_s = -0.9428$, $\tau = -0.8666$
22.27 $S = 64.50$
22.29 $r = 2$
22.31 $Z_r = 0$
22.35 $T_F = 4.5$
22.39 $r_s = -0.489$, $t_r = -1.859$, $Z_\tau = -1.586$

Chapter 23

23.1   a. A_3 b. A_1
23.3   b. A_3
23.5   Maximax: A_4, Maximin: A_1, Minimax regret: A_2
23.7   a. A_3 b. A_2 c. A_3
23.9   Fund 3
23.11   c. 21.26
23.13   b. A c. B
23.19   a. B b. A c. A
23.21 A, B, C, F
23.23   a. Yes   b. Yes

INDEX OF NAMES

INDEX OF SUBJECTS

ABOUT THE AUTHORS

Moshe Ben-Horim received his education in statistics, and B.A. and M.A. degrees in economics, from the Hebrew University of Jerusalem. He received his Ph.D. from the Graduate School of Business Administration at New York University.

Professor Ben-Horim is the director of the Center for Management Development at the Hebrew University of Jerusalem. He has held research positions in statistics and finance at the National Bureau of Economic Research in New York, the Israeli Institute of Financial Research, the Hebrew University of Jerusalem, and a number of other institutions. He has also taught statistics, decision-making, and finance at New York University, the University of Florida, McGill University, the Hebrew University, and Montclair State College.

The author of a number of articles in professional journals, Professor Ben-Horim has served as a consultant to public utilities and government agencies in the United States and elsewhere.

Haim Levy received B.A. and M.A. degrees in statistics and economics, and his Ph.D., from the Hebrew University of Jerusalem. He has taught statistics, finance, and decision-making at the Hebrew University, the University of Illinois, the University of California at Berkeley, the University of Florida, and the Wharton School at the University of Pennsylvania.

Professor Levy has written more than one hundred articles and books. His articles have appeared in leading journals, including the *American Economic Review, Management Science, Econometrica*, the *Review of Economics and Statistics*, the *Journal of Finance*, and the *Journal of Financial and Quantitative Analysis*. He is also the editor of the journal *Research in Finance*.

He has served as a consultant to numerous firms in the United States and Israel. His consulting work has focused mainly on the application of statistical tools and quantitative methods to economic and business problems faced by firms and governments.

Table of Areas for Standard Normal Probability Distribution

Mean

Z	0.00	0.01	0.02	0.03	0.04	0.05	0.06	0.07	0.08	0.09
0.0	0.0000	0.0040	0.0080	0.0120	0.0160	0.0199	0.0239	0.0279	0.0319	0.0359
0.1	0.0398	0.0438	0.0478	0.0517	0.0557	0.0596	0.0636	0.0675	0.0714	0.0753
0.2	0.0793	0.0832	0.0871	0.0910	0.0948	0.0987	0.1026	0.1064	0.1103	0.1141
0.3	0.1179	0.1217	0.1255	0.1293	0.1331	0.1368	0.1406	0.1443	0.1480	0.1517
0.4	0.1554	0.1591	0.1628	0.1664	0.1700	0.1736	0.1772	0.1808	0.1844	0.1879
0.5	0.1915	0.1950	0.1985	0.2019	0.2054	0.2088	0.2123	0.2157	0.2190	0.2224
0.6	0.2257	0.2291	0.2324	0.2357	0.2389	0.2422	0.2454	0.2486	0.2518	0.2549
0.7	0.2580	0.2612	0.2642	0.2673	0.2704	0.2734	0.2764	0.2794	0.2823	0.2852
0.8	0.2881	0.2910	0.2939	0.2967	0.2995	0.3023	0.3051	0.3078	0.3106	0.3133
0.9	0.3159	0.3186	0.3212	0.3238	0.3264	0.3289	0.3315	0.3340	0.3365	0.3389
1.0	0.3413	0.3438	0.3461	0.3485	0.3508	0.3531	0.3554	0.3577	0.3599	0.3621
1.1	0.3643	0.3665	0.3686	0.3708	0.3729	0.3749	0.3770	0.3790	0.3810	0.3830
1.2	0.3849	0.3869	0.3888	0.3907	0.3925	0.3944	0.3962	0.3980	0.3997	0.4015
1.3	0.4032	0.4049	0.4066	0.4082	0.4099	0.4115	0.4131	0.4147	0.4162	0.4177
1.4	0.4192	0.4207	0.4222	0.4236	0.4251	0.4265	0.4279	0.4292	0.4306	0.4319
1.5	0.4332	0.4345	0.4357	0.4370	0.4382	0.4394	0.4406	0.4418	0.4429	0.4441
1.6	0.4452	0.4463	0.4474	0.4484	0.4495	0.4505	0.4515	0.4525	0.4535	0.4545
1.7	0.4554	0.4564	0.4573	0.4582	0.4591	0.4599	0.4608	0.4616	0.4625	0.4633
1.8	0.4641	0.4649	0.4656	0.4664	0.4671	0.4678	0.4686	0.4693	0.4699	0.4706
1.9	0.4713	0.4719	0.4726	0.4732	0.4738	0.4744	0.4750	0.4756	0.4761	0.4767
2.0	0.4772	0.4778	0.4783	0.4788	0.4793	0.4798	0.4803	0.4808	0.4812	0.4817
2.1	0.4821	0.4826	0.4830	0.4834	0.4838	0.4842	0.4846	0.4850	0.4854	0.4857
2.2	0.4861	0.4864	0.4868	0.4871	0.4875	0.4878	0.4881	0.4884	0.4887	0.4890
2.3	0.4893	0.4896	0.4898	0.4901	0.4904	0.4906	0.4909	0.4911	0.4913	0.4916
2.4	0.4918	0.4920	0.4922	0.4925	0.4927	0.4929	0.4931	0.4932	0.4934	0.4936
2.5	0.4938	0.4940	0.4941	0.4943	0.4945	0.4946	0.4948	0.4949	0.4951	0.4952
2.6	0.4953	0.4955	0.4956	0.4957	0.4959	0.4960	0.4961	0.4962	0.4963	0.4964
2.7	0.4965	0.4966	0.4967	0.4968	0.4969	0.4970	0.4971	0.4972	0.4973	0.4974
2.8	0.4974	0.4975	0.4976	0.4977	0.4977	0.4978	0.4979	0.4979	0.4980	0.4981
2.9	0.4981	0.4982	0.4982	0.4983	0.4984	0.4984	0.4985	0.4985	0.4986	0.4986
3.0	0.49865	0.4987	0.4987	0.4988	0.4988	0.4989	0.4989	0.4989	0.4990	0.4990
4.0	0.4999683									

Illustration: For $Z = 1.93$, shaded area is 0.4732 out of total area of 1.

Source: John Neter, William Wasserman, and George A. Whitmore, *Fundamental Statistics for Business and Economics*, 4th ed. Copyright © 1973 by Allyn and Bacon, Inc., Boston. Reprinted by permission.